ADMINISTRATIVE LAW
Cases and Materials

ADMINISTRATIVE LAW
Cases and Materials

Second Edition

Daniel J. Gifford
Robins, Kaplan, Miller & Ciresi Professor of Law
University of Minnesota Law School

978-1-4224-7687-1 (Hardbound)

Library of Congress Cataloging-in-Publication Data

Gifford, Daniel J., 1932-
Administrative law : cases and materials / Daniel J. Gifford. -- 2nd ed.
p. cm.
Includes index.
978-1-4224-7687-1 (Hardbound)
1. Administrative law--United States--Cases. 2. Judicial review of administrative acts--United States--Cases.
I. Title.
KF5402.G54 2010
342.73'06--dc22

2010000373

NOTE TO USERS

To ensure that you are using the latest materials available in this area, please be sure to periodically check the LexisNexis Law School web site for downloadable updates and supplements at www.lexisnexis.com/lawschool.

Editorial Offices
121 Chanlon Rd., New Providence, NJ 07974 (908) 464-6800
201 Mission St., San Francisco, CA 94105-1831 (415) 908-3200
www.lexisnexis.com

MATTHEW♦BENDER

Table of Contents

Table of Contents

Table of Contents

Chapter 1

ADMINISTRATIVE REGULATION: AN INTRODUCTION

A. WHAT ADMINISTRATIVE LAW IS ABOUT

The field that has come to be known as administrative law deals with the work of government officials and agencies. For the most part, the material in this book focuses upon the role of courts in reviewing the work of these officials and agencies.

Although the Congress bears the responsibility for legislating and the President and the executive branch bear the responsibility for administering and enforcing legislation, it is apparent upon reflection that Congress is institutionally incapable of providing in legislation itself a detailed answer for every issue that may arise under it. The same is true for state legislatures. When a legislature enacts a statute limiting the rates (i.e., prices) which a public utility may charge, it does not ordinarily set out the maximum in dollar figures or by formula. Recognizing that such rates properly are influenced by a variety of economic factors which are constantly changing, legislatures generally require that rates be set at a "reasonable" level and delegate to an agency (generally a public service commission) the role of determining what rates are, and are not, "reasonable" within the meaning of the statute. When Congress set out to regulate the issuance of radio (and later television) licenses, it required that such licenses be issued under a standard of furthering the public interest, convenience and necessity; and it left the actual application of that standard to the Federal Communications Commission.

When an affected person objects to an agency decision, that person often has a right to challenge the agency action in court. There are various grounds for challenging such an action. The agency may have acted beyond its authority or its action may lack rational support or, in the case of agency actions required to be taken on a record, the agency's action may lack the requisite record support. Most, but not all, action by federal agencies has been governed by the federal Administrative Procedure Act, since its enactment in 1946. Most states have their own state administrative procedure acts which similarly govern the actions of their agencies. In this course, you will study the legal issues which are raised by court review of administrative action.

During the early history of the United States there was less need (than at present) for courts to review the actions of officials administering the laws, because the laws were few in number and did not often deal with complex subject matters. In the state court systems, judicial review of actions by officials sometimes employed the so-called "prerogative writs" which the English courts had employed. The most important of these were certiorari, mandamus, prohibition, quo warranto, and habeas corpus. The federal courts could not routinely employ these writs, however, because outside of the District of Columbia the federal courts were courts of limited jurisdiction, possessing only that jurisdiction which Congress affirmatively conferred upon them. For that reason the powers to issue the prerogative writs to which the state courts succeeded after the Revolution were not deemed to have been passed on to the federal courts. In the District of Columbia, however, the situation was different. Because the District was composed of portions of Maryland and Virginia, the federal court sitting in the District of Columbia was deemed to have inherited the powers of the courts of those states which, in turn, had inherited the powers of the English courts.

B. A SHORT OVERVIEW OF THE HISTORY OF ADMINISTRATIVE REGULATION

The first modern administrative agency was the Interstate Commerce Commission (the "ICC"), established by the Interstate Commerce Act in 1887 to ensure that railroad rates were reasonable and not discriminatory. When Congress, in 1914, decided to enact new antitrust provisions to complement the Sherman Act, it established the Federal Trade Commission (the "FTC") to administer the Federal Trade Commission Act. Section 5 of that Act forbade "unfair methods of competition" and the Commission was given the task of determining what business practices fell within (and without) the scope of that prohibition. Like the ICC, the FTC was composed of members who held office for a term of years.

It was in the 1930s, however, with the advent of President Franklin Roosevelt's "New Deal" that a great expansion in the number of regulatory agencies occurred. Roosevelt took office in March 1933 at the height of the Great Depression and was searching for methods to restore the nation's economic health. In its early period, the New Deal followed a philosophy of cartelizing U.S. industry on the general ground that production (and hence employment) could best be stimulated when prices could be driven up to a level above costs. Pursuant to this basic approach, the National Industrial Recovery Act (the "NIRA") authorized the establishment of so-called "codes of fair competition" for the various U.S. industries. These codes, it was contemplated, would be drafted by the business firms in each industry and would be subject to Presidential approval. When the NIRA was struck down by the U.S. Supreme Court as unconstitutional because it provided for the delegation by Congress of its basic lawmaking powers, the New Deal switched its primary emphasis to regulatory laws-laws which were designed to reduce market malfunctions or to foster the provision of transportation services. The National Labor Relations Board (the "NLRB") was established to protect workers in organizing into labor unions and through those unions to bargain collectively with their employers. The Securities and Exchange Commission (the "SEC") was established to oversee the operations of the securities markets. The ICC was given power to regulate motor carriers; and the Civil Aeronautics Board (the "CAB") was given power to regulate air transportation.

During World War II the federal government, in an effort to prevent inflation, controlled prices of most commodities, rents, and wages through the Office of Price Administration (the "OPA"). This effort at government control was probably the most extensive exercise in centralized control ever undertaken in this country. Price control was temporarily reinstituted during the Korean War.

Following the end of World War II in 1945, several events took place which had significance for administrative law. First, the federal Administrative Procedure Act was enacted in 1946, providing a procedural framework for most federal regulation. Second, in 1948, Congress enacted the Taft-Hartley Act, which modified the National Labor Relations Act, inter alia, by separating the General Counsel (who has charge of enforcement) from the National Labor Relations Board. Third, the Commissioners on Uniform State Laws promulgated the first of several versions of a "model" state administrative procedure act in 1946. (Successive versions were promulgated in 1961 and in 1981.) Later in the post-war period, Congress turned the nuclear technology which the Government had developed during the war over to private industry. At that time, Congress established the Atomic Energy Commission (now the Nuclear Regulatory Agency) to oversee that industry.

During the late 1940s and early 1950s and coincident with the beginnings of the so-called "cold war" with the Soviet Union, various administrative tribunals were established to oversee programs dealing with the loyalty of federal employees and with access of persons to classified data. Conflicts between individuals who sought to keep their jobs or their access to classified information and government tribunals produced an important caselaw dealing with issues of procedural fairness.

In the period from the mid 1960s through the mid 1970s, Congress enacted a substantial number of regulatory statutes. During that period, it enacted, inter alia, the Consumer Product Safety Act of 1972; the Occupational Safety and Health Act of 1970; the Coal Mine Health and Safety Act of 1969; the National Traffic and Motor Vehicle Safety Act, the Clean Air Act of 1970, the Clean Water Act of 1972, and substantially amended the regulatory provisions of other statutes: Federal Trade Commission improvements Act of 1975; the Securities Act Amendments of 1975.

In the late 1970s and continuing into the 1980s, Congress began the era of deregulation. Beginning with the airline industry, Congress removed economic regulatory controls from most of the transportation industries. Today, in 2010, we are in a period in which there is a widespread call for regulation of the financial industry.

C.   CRITIQUES OF THE ADMINISTRATIVE PROCESS AND REFORMS

In the years immediately preceding this country's entry into World War IL there arose significant criticism of the work of the New Deal agencies from the bar and from members of Congress. Many of these critics charged that the various regulatory agencies often decided cases with careless procedures and with inadequate evidence. As a result of this criticism, President Roosevelt established the Attorney General's Committee to Study Administrative Procedure. That Committee produced an exhaustive study of the work of most of the federal agencies, and completed its work with its summary and recommendations in a Final Report submitted in January, 1941. Although the War imposed a halt to administrative procedural reform for its duration, in 1946 the Congress enacted the Administrative Procedure Act, an Act which drew on both the majority and the minority views of the Attorney General's Committee's Final Report. That Act establishes procedures for several of the most common forms of administrative action.

At the same time that the federal government was studying the question of administrative reform, a similar study directed at state agencies was being carried on in New York State under the chairmanship of Robert Benjamin. The conclusion of that study embodied in the so-called "Benjamin Report" — took New York down a different road than the one taken by the federal government in 1946. The Benjamin Report concluded that the various administrative agencies were just so different from one another and dealt with such a wide variety of subjects that a comprehensive code of administrative procedure would be undesirable. New York then followed the recommendations of that report until the 1970s. In 1975, after several unsuccessful attempts, the New York legislature passed and Governor Carey signed into law a State Administrative Procedure Act.

In the 1950s, academic critics began to develop theories about the "life cycle" of administrative agencies. According to Bernstein, one of such critics, agencies usually start out with a strong sense of purpose, since the circumstances which gave rise to the creation of the agency are still quite fresh. After a time, however, the situations with which the agency must deal depart substantially from those which gave rise to the agency's creation. The agency lacks criteria for dealing with these newer problems confronting it; and the history of its enabling act furnishes it no guidance. The agency then begins to founder, uncertain about what course to take. It is at this stage, moreover, that the problem of "capture" becomes most serious.

In order to regulate an industry effectively, an agency needs information about that industry. The best source for information about an industry is obviously the industry itself. The combination of the agency's need for information with the industry itself being the best source of the needed information has been asserted to engender an undesirable dependence of regulatory agencies upon the industries which they are charged with regulating. Moreover, these industries want to tell the agency or agencies regulating them about industry problems and the agencies ought to learn about those problems. The difficulty is that an agency may, in the process, develop an industry point of view. This is, in essence, the problem of "capture".

The problem of "capture" had become widely discussed by the 1960s. Moreover, Ralph Nader, a prominent consumer activist, had brought that problem to the attention of a wide public in a series of books published under his auspices. Academics, such as Mancur Olson, Theodore Lowi, and George Stigler were developing theories generally known as "public choice". Public choice focuses upon the power of concentrated interests to influence legislators and other government officials, often prevailing over larger but more diffused sectors of the public possessing conflicting interests. Capture and public choice theories contributed to the way in which the regulatory statutes of the 1965–1975 period were drafted. Earlier regulatory statutes entrusted to regulatory authorities to administer had been written in broad language. The Federal Trade Commission Act, for example, had charged that Commission with enforcing the Act's ban on "unfair methods of competition." The statutory prohibition was intentionally phrased broadly in order to permit the Commission scope to work out the meaning of the prohibition over the course of time. The Federal Communications Commission is charged with issuing radio and television licenses under a statutory standard of furthering the "public interest, convenience and necessity". Such broadly drawn standards now were thought to facilitate "capture". In order to prevent the regulating agencies from being co-opted by the industries under their supervision, the newer statutes have employed more precisely drawn provisions, limiting the administering agency's discretion to alter the meaning of the prohibition.

D. REGULATION AND DEREGULATION

1. *Market failure.*

Much regulation has been justified upon a theory of market failure. Under this theory, regulation is needed because the normal operations of the marketplace have failed to protect the public from actual or potential abuses of power by business firms. Thus, for example, utilities are widely regulated on the theory that certain services can be effectively provided only by a single firm which is, by definition, a monopoly supplier. The suppliers of local telephone, electricity, natural gas, and water services are familiar examples. Regulatory supervision over the rates of such utilities has been seen as necessary to protect the public from monopoly power. In that context, regulation is a substitute for the constraints which a competitive marketplace places upon business firms.

Radio and television regulation is justified on a market theory rationale: without regulation, the dynamics of the marketplace would encourage more stations to broadcast in population centers than the radio frequency spectrum could tolerate without interference. Regulation of the securities industry is concerned largely with ensuring that investors have access to relevant information. This kind of regulation has been seen as assisting the financial market to function more effectively, since, in theory, markets operate optimally when the participants have access to relevant information. The Federal Trade Commission's charge to eliminate unfair methods of competition has also been explained as helping the markets to operate more effectively: When all competing firms play by the same rules—and those rules are fair ones—then the competitive process encourages socially beneficial results: better quality and lower prices over the long run.

Regulation of working conditions under the Occupational Safety and Health Act and other statutes also proceeds upon the premise that the market does not operate effectively to produce safe working conditions. Because business firms could not always be counted upon to minimize safety hazards on their own, government must impose safety standards. Similarly, environmental regulation under the Clean Air Act and other statutes is necessary because the market would not discourage air and other pollution. Pollution is an "externality" in the market calculations of business firms. That is, the pollution of the air which results from some forms of industrial production is a social cost borne by the public; but that cost never shows up on the books of the producing firms. Therefore, they take no action to hold down those costs, as they do for other costs which they pay for out-of-pocket. Since the market does not work in this case, regulation is required.

2. *Transportation regulation.*

Federal regulation over transportation had begun with the enactment of the Interstate Commerce Act in 1887 and the establishment of the Interstate Commerce Commission. This assertion of federal supervision over railroad rates followed years in which the states had attempted to control railroad rates within their boundaries. This popular demand for rate regulation arose from widely held beliefs that the railroads were exploiting monopoly positions and discriminating in their rate structures between long and short distance shippers. In addition, it was believed that rate regulation was necessary, because the railroad industry was capital intensive. And in capital intensive industries where competition does exist-competition may force prices to below-cost levels, since in such industries marginal cost is likely to be below average total cost. At such low prices (and negative return on investment) further investment would be discouraged. Regulation was needed, it was believed, to protect shippers against monopoly rates where the railroads possessed monopolies and, conversely, was needed to protect the railroads against themselves where they were competing.

Airline regulation began in 1938 with the enactment of the Civil Aeronautics Act. That Act was seen largely as a means by which the government could encourage the development of a fledgling aviation industry. Again, many of the same concerns about the need for the government to protect the industry from excessive or cutthroat competition underlay this regulation. Motor transport became federally regulated in 1935 largely because a freely operating motor carrier industry would have threatened government regulation of railroad rates, but also in order to prevent the excessive or cutthroat competition which was seen as a threat to the other transportation industries.

3. *Governmental oversight and information.*

It has become commonplace to assert that because a regulatory agency focuses its attention upon a particular industry or upon a narrow area of behavior, the agency tends to be more knowledgeable about those matters than are reviewing courts whose caseload spans the whole arena of human conduct. This, together with the agency's staff, account for so-called agency "expertise" in its area of regulation. That particular difference in perspective suggests that agencies may be more expert than courts on technical issues, but that courts-because of their broader perspective- are better able to make judgments about the extent and scope of a regulatory scheme and where it fits within the wider framework of the law.

During the New Deal period James Landis, a contemporary administrative law theorist, saw the government contribution to regulation as going beyond the mere expertise. Indeed, Landis saw government control ultimately extending to a stage in which "the economic well-being of an industry" becomes the chief goal of regulation. Underlying such an approach is the belief that government can make decisions which are superior to those which individual business firms can make.

By at least 1960, however, the theoretical underpinnings of the superiority of government over private decision-making had been substantially eroded. The capture and administrative life-cycle theories had been widely disseminated.

Professors March and Simon had, in 1958, published a brilliant summary of developments in organization theory. March and Simon had pointed out that information is a scarce commodity, a point implicit in the capture theory. As a result, decision-makers cannot collect all relevant information; rather, they must act in a state of partial ignorance and uncertainty. Decision-makers therefore tend to "satisfice" (produce satisfactory results) rather than to optimize. Charles Lindblom followed up in 1959 by setting forth his "muddling through" theory of administration. Because administrators lack much information about the potential consequences of their actions, they tend to utilize the best source of information available: what has just happened. If past administration has not caused dire consequences, they know that they can avoid disaster by avoiding drastic departures from what they have done in the past. Regulatory changes, according to Lindblom, thus tend to proceed only incrementally. Changes that produce undesired results can be withdrawn; changes that advance regulatory goals slightly can be followed by further small changes.

Finally, public attention recently has been drawn to the political element inherent in governmental decision-making. Proposals have been made for "industrial policy," in which government decision-makers would select particular industries for special forms of government support. Even if government decision-makers were able to identify the potential for long-term success before normal market mechanisms routed capital to those industries, the problem of politically skewed decision-making has so far remained unresolved. Would not government decision-makers be responsive to the large numbers of unemployed workers (who are also voters) in declining industries rather than to the potential of small industries with only a promise of future growth? And therefore would not government decision-makers be likely to neglect the so-called sunshine industries in favor of subsidizing sunset industries? The answers to these questions will be critical to the future of economic regulation. The basic question which must be answered for any form of economic regulation is whether regulation will produce results which are better—on some socially acceptable criterion of worth—than the results which the market would produce by itself. That is a test which is difficult, but not impossible, to meet.

4.   *Deregulation.*

By the late 1970s it was becoming increasingly apparent that airline regulation was working perversely. The Civil Aeronautics Board controlled airline rates and routes, encouraging competition in "service" — which meant primarily number of flights. The result was that carriers operated more flights than could be filled. Yet they could not encourage passengers by cutting rates. Indeed, these excess flights reduced the passenger load of each flight, thereby increasing the cost allocated to each passenger. The system increased the costs of per passenger carriage and imposed the rates which would cover these passenger costs. The alternative of removing regulation would, it was believed, encourage the carriers to compete on price in an effort to fill flights. Moreover, because airplanes are easily transferable from location to location, existing carriers would allocate their equipment to those routes in accordance with demand and new carriers would enter the market to serve routes where demand was unsatisfied. Flights thus would be scheduled on those runs where, with market responsive rates, they could be filled. The result would be flights responding to passenger demand, ticket prices geared to filling flights and reduced per passenger costs. Airline deregulation began in the late 1970s; and it produced the anticipated results: lower per passenger costs; lower fares; and allocation of flights to routes in accordance with demand. It remains to be seen whether the airline industry will transform itself from the highly competitive industry which it was in the immediate period following the end of regulation into a less responsive industry as a result of a series of mergers. The danger is that a more concentrated and oligopolistic industry will undo the work produced in the post-regulation competitive era.

Under motor carrier regulation, truck rates were set to ensure that a carrier covered its costs even though a truck returned empty. Again, regulation operated to engender inefficient operation of a transportation industry. The argument for removing motor carriers from regulation was apparent. Moreover, truck transportation, once removed from government rate control, would provide competition for the railroads, helping to ensure that the latter would not exploit market power. Railroads and motor carriers followed the airline industry down the path of deregulation.

A final point on transportation regulation and deregulation. One of the premises of transport regulation was that the industries were composed of common carriers which had an obligation to serve even a small demand. Trains ran and airplanes flew on routes which produced losses for the carriers; those losses were made up from profits on the more profitable routes. Under a regime of deregulation, the profitable routes no longer subsidize the unprofitable routes. The emphasis is no longer on a carrier's obligation to serve even an unremunerative market. The new focus is on the allocation of resources in a way that produces the maximum consumer benefit. Passengers on the well travelled New York to Chicago routes no longer subsidize the fares of those who travel to more outlying locations. The prevailing view is that the maximum social benefit occurs without that subsidy.

It will be observed that the arguments in favor of deregulation of the transportation industries are not applicable generally to all regulation. Deregulation has worked in the transportation industries because it produces socially more beneficial results than were produced under regulation.

5. *Public choice.*

During the last decade government decision-making has come under increasing attack from critics who contend that elected officials act not to further the overall social good, but to achieve their own re-election. This usually means capitulating to interest groups pressures and, in all events, to avoid offending interest groups which can adversely affect the chances for re-election. In this view, legislation is effectively the result of a "deal" worked out between contending interest groups. Moreover, in order to avoid giving offence to powerful interest groups, legislative officials tend to avoid making hard policy choices and to legislate in generalities, delegating to administrators the task of making sense out of intentionally vague or ambiguous statutory terms. Because legislators act ambiguously, they can avoid responsibility by blaming the administrators when one group of constituents complain about the action of a regulatory agency, and simultaneously the same legislators can take credit for the identical action when a different constituent group approves of it. For excellent discussions of public choice theory, *see* D. Farber & P. Frickey, *Law and Public Choice (1991)* and Aranson, Gellhorn & Robinson, *A Theory of Delegation,* 68 Cornell L. Rev. *1 (1982).*

E. THE ORGANIZATIONAL STRUCTURE OF ADMINISTRATIVE AGENCIES AND THEIR PLACE IN GOVERNMENT

Because legislation cannot be so detailed as to provide a ready answer for every issue which might arise, the result is that administering officials and the courts are forced to supply the answers to many questions to which legislation does not respond or does not respond clearly.

When the first modern regulatory agency, the ICC, was established, it was given many attributes of a court, because its mandates (to ensure reasonable rates and to prevent discrimination in rates) could not be applied without reference to the facts upon which the railroad established its rates. The ICC was expected to impartially discover the facts and to make its decision on those facts. Later the FTC, in *1914,* and the New Deal agencies in the *1930s* were also given judicial attributes for similar reasons.

It was widely recognized that these agencies did more than discover the facts. They also interpreted the statute which they were applying in the process of deciding particular cases. Indeed, many agencies developed a substantial caselaw in which, over a series of cases, they developed elaborate policies from broad statutory commands. For example, the FCC construed its statutory charge to issue radio licenses in the public interest to mean that it should encourage local programming by limiting the amount of time which a local station could allocate to network programming.

The structure of many modern regulatory agencies is based upon the ICC and FTC models. To institute a proceeding, the FTC issues a complaint, charging a respondent with having committed an "unfair method of competition" and demanding that the respondent "cease and desist" from that behavior. The decision to issue the complaint may be made by one of the units of the Commission's staff, such as its bureau of competition. The Commission itself (i.e., the five Commissioners), however, approve the issuance of the complaint or at least the guidelines under which the complaint is issued. If the respondent contests the charge, a trial is held before an Administrative Law judge (formerly a "trial examiner" or a "hearing officer"). The ALJ's decision is then subject to review by the Commission itself. Review by the Commission is the traditional way in which the Commission controls policy. Since each Commission decision is in part an interpretation of how its statutory mandate should be applied and constitutes a precedent for future reference, the Commissioners traditionally have exercised their control over policy by sitting in review over the decisions of particular cases.

Since the mid *1960s,* many regulatory agencies have emphasized rulemaking as a way of carrying out their regulatory responsibilities. The FTC began to emphasize rulemaking when, in *1966*, it proposed a rule requiring warnings of health risks on cigarette packages. Congress took over this issue from the FTC by legislation which specifically mandated such warnings, but the FTC continued its rulemaking activities by issuing rules on a wide variety of matters. Subsequently, the courts upheld the FTC's rulemaking powers under its original enabling statute and later the Congress amended the Federal Trade Commission Act to explicitly give the Commission rulemaking power and to establish procedures for its exercise.

Some agencies, including some relatively new regulatory agencies, are organized in a way that compels them to control policy by rule. The Occupational Safety and Health Act, for example, is administered by the Occupational Safety and Health Administration, under the supervision of an Administrator, who is an official within the Department of Labor. The Administrator issues rules ("standards") governing workplace safety and brings citations against business firms which the Administrator deems to be in violation. A monetary penalty is generally imposed upon a violator. A respondent who contests such a charge is entitled to a hearing before an Administrative Law Judge, but review is had not before the charging agency (as in FTC proceedings, for example) but before an independent agency, the Occupational Safety and Health Review Commission. Since the Administrator has no opportunity to shape policy at stage of administrative review, the Administrator must set forth its policies in rules beforehand.

It will be observed that policy-making in the process of deciding cases is a technique which best fits an agency which handles a small volume of cases, the disposition of each of which raises important policy issues. When caseloads become very large, it becomes impractical for an agency head to control policy by sitting as the final reviewing tribunal. In the latter circumstances, agency heads cannot possibly sit on each case nor are policies effectively communicated to hearing tribunals through case opinions. When case decisions number in hundreds each month, they are too numerous to play an effective role as precedents. Agencies handling extremely large caseloads, such as many benefit agencies, must therefore as a practical matter control the policies through which their programs are administered by rules or generalized directives.

Chapter 2

JUDICIAL REVIEW OF AGENCY ACTION: AN INITIAL LOOK

A. PRELIMINARY CONSIDERATION OF THE POLICIES AND LANGUAGE OF JUDICIAL REVIEW.

Let's look at two contemporary cases involving judicial review of agency action. Notice the language that the Court employs in both cases about judicial review and how the Court describes the role of the courts in relation to the agencies. First, lets try our hand at identifying some policies that the opinions indicate govern judicial review. Lawyers skilled in the complexities of judicial review are masters of the language that the courts employ and understand how the meanings of key terms have developed over the years. Then we will turn our attention to the major standards governing judicial review: the substantial evidence standard and the arbitrary-and-capricious standard, and the origins and development of those standards into their current form.

IMMIGRATION AND NATURALIZATION SERVICE v. VENTURA
537 U.S. 12 (2002)

Per Curiam.

Federal statutes authorize the Attorney General, in his discretion, to grant asylum to an alien who demonstrates "persecution or a well-founded fear of persecution . . . on account of . . . [a] political opinion," and they require the Attorney General to withhold deportation where the alien's "life or freedom would be threatened" for that reason. Immigration and Nationality Act, §§ 101(a)(42)(A), 208(a), 243(h), 66 Stat. 166, as amended, 8 U.S.C. §§ 1101(a)(42), 1158(a), 1253(h)(1) (1994 ed. and Supp. V). The Board of Immigration Appeals (BIA) determined that respondent Fredy Orlando Ventura failed to qualify for this statutory protection because any persecution that he faced when he left Guatemala in 1993 was not "*on account of*" a "*political opinion.*" The Court of Appeals for the Ninth Circuit reversed the BIA's holding. 264 F.3d 1150 (2001) (emphasis added).

The Court of Appeals then went on to consider an alternative argument that the Government had made before the Immigration Judge, namely, that Orlando Ventura failed to qualify for protection regardless of past persecution because conditions in Guatemala had improved to the point where no realistic threat of persecution currently existed. Both sides pointed out to the Ninth Circuit that the Immigration Judge had held that conditions had indeed changed to that point but that the BIA itself had not considered this alternative claim. And both sides asked that the Ninth Circuit remand the case to the BIA so that it might do so. . . .

The Court of Appeals, however, did not remand the case. Instead, it evaluated the Government's claim itself. And it decided the matter in Orlando Ventura's favor, holding that the evidence in the record failed to show sufficient change. . . . The Government, seeking certiorari here, argues that the Court of Appeals exceeded its legal authority when it decided the "changed circumstances" matter on its own. We agree with the Government that the Court of Appeals should have remanded the case to the BIA. And we summarily reverse its decision not to do so.

I

We shall describe the basic proceedings so far. In 1993 Orlando Ventura, a citizen of Guatemala, entered the United States illegally. In 1995 the Attorney General began deportation proceedings. And in 1998 an Immigration Judge considered Orlando Ventura's application for asylum and withholding of deportation, an application based upon a fear and threat of persecution "on account of" a "political opinion." 8 U.S.C. §§ 1101(a)(42)(A), 1253(h) (1994 ed. and Supp. V). Orlando Ventura testified that he had received threats of death or harm unless he joined the guerrilla army, that his family members had close ties to the Guatemalan military, and that, in his view, the guerrillas consequently believed he held inimical political opinions.

The Immigration Judge denied relief. She recognized that Orlando Ventura subjectively believed that the guerrillas' interest in him was politically based. And she credited testimony showing (a) that Orlando Ventura's family had many connections to the military, (b) that he was very close to one cousin, an army lieutenant who had served for almost 12 years, (c) that in 1987 his uncle, a local military commissioner responsible for recruiting, was attacked by people with machetes, and (d) that in 1988 his cousin (a soldier) and the cousin's brother (a civilian) were both shot at and the soldier-cousin killed. Nonetheless, Orlando Ventura had failed objectively "to demonstrate that the guerillas' interest" in him was "on account of his political opinion.". . . . The Immigration Judge added that "conditions" in Guatemala had changed significantly. Even "if the guerillas" once had had a politically based "interest" in Orlando Ventura, the evidence failed to show that the guerrillas would "continue to have motivation and inclination to persecute him in the future." *Ibid.*

The BIA, considering the matter *de novo*, "agree[d]" with the Immigration Judge that Orlando Ventura "did not meet his burden of establishing that he faces persecution 'on account of' a qualifying ground. . . ." The BIA added that it "need not address" the question of "changed country conditions."

The Court of Appeals, reviewing the BIA's decision, decided that this evidence "*compel[led]*" it to reject the BIA's conclusion. 264 F.3d, at 1154 (emphasis added); see *INS v. Elias-Zacarias*, 502 U.S. 478, 481, n. 1 (1992) ("To reverse the BIA finding we must find that the evidence not only *supports* that conclusion, but *compels* it . . ." (emphasis in original)). It recognized that the BIA had not decided the "changed circumstances" question and that "generally" a court should remand to permit that consideration. 264 F.3d, at 1157. Cf. *Castillo v. INS*, 951 F.2d 1117,

1120–1121 (C.A.9 1991) (specifying that the court of appeals must review the decision of the BIA, not the underlying decision of the immigration judge). But the Court of Appeals added that it need "not remand . . . when it is clear that we would be compelled to reverse the BIA's decision if the BIA decided the matter against the applicant." . . . And it held that the record evidence, namely, a 1997 State Department report about Guatemala, "clearly demonstrates that the presumption of a well-founded fear of future persecution was not rebutted." . . . Hence, it concluded, "remand . . . is inappropriate." . . .

The Government challenges the decision not to remand. And it says the matter is important. The "error," it says, is a "recurring error [that] puts the Ninth Circuit in conflict with other courts of appeals, which generally respect the BIA's role as fact-finder by remanding to the BIA in similar situations." . . . After examining the record, we find that well-established principles of administrative law did require the Court of Appeals to remand the "changed circumstances" question to the BIA.

II

No one disputes the basic legal principles that govern remand. Within broad limits the law entrusts the agency to make the basic asylum eligibility decision here in question. *E.g.*, 8 U.S.C. § 1158(a); 8 U.S.C. § 1253(h)(1) (1994 ed.); *Elias-Zacarias, supra*, at 481; *INS v. Aguirre-Aguirre*, 526 U.S. 415 (1999). See also 8 CFR § 3.1 (2002). In such circumstances a "judicial judgment cannot be made to do service for an administrative judgment." *SEC v. Chenery Corp.*, 318 U.S. 80, 88 (1943). Nor can an "appellate court . . . intrude upon the domain which Congress has exclusively entrusted to an administrative agency." . . . A court of appeals "is not generally empowered to conduct a *de novo* inquiry into the matter being reviewed and to reach its own conclusions based on such an inquiry." *Florida Power & Light Co. v. Lorion*, 470 U.S. 729, 744 (1985). Rather, "the proper course, except in rare circumstances, is to remand to the agency for additional investigation or explanation." . . . Cf. *SEC v. Chenery Corp.*, 332 U.S. 194, 196 (1947) (describing the reasons for remand).

Generally speaking, a court of appeals should remand a case to an agency for decision of a matter that statutes place primarily in agency hands. This principle has obvious importance in the immigration context. The BIA has not yet considered the "changed circumstances" issue. And every consideration that classically supports the law's ordinary remand requirement does so here. The agency can bring its expertise to bear upon the matter; it can evaluate the evidence; it can make an initial determination; and, in doing so, it can, through informed discussion and analysis, help a court later determine whether its decision exceeds the leeway that the law provides.

These basic considerations indicate that the Court of Appeals committed clear error here. It seriously disregarded the agency's legally-mandated role. Instead, it independently created potentially far-reaching legal precedent about the significance of political change in Guatemala, a highly complex and sensitive matter. And it did so without giving the BIA the opportunity to address the matter in the first instance in light of its own expertise.

The Court of Appeals rested its conclusion upon its belief that the basic record evidence on the matter — the 1997 State Department report about Guatemala — compelled a finding of insufficiently changed circumstances. But that foundation is legally inadequate for two reasons. First, the State Department report is, at most, ambiguous about the matter. The bulk of the report makes clear that considerable change has occurred. The report says, for example, that in December 1996 the Guatemalan Government and the guerrillas signed a peace agreement, that in March 1996 there was a cease fire, that the guerrillas then disbanded as a fighting force, that "the guerrillas renounced the use of force to achieve political goals," and that "there was [a] marked improvement in the overall human rights situation." Bureau of Democracy, Human Rights and Labor, U.S. Dept. of State, Guatemala-Profile of Asylum Claims & Country Conditions 2–4 (June 1997).

As the Court of Appeals stressed, two parts of the report can be read to the contrary. They say that (1) even "after the March cease-fire, guerrillas continued to employ death threats" and (2) "the level of crime and violence now seems to be higher than in the recent past." *Id.*, at 3–4. Yet the report itself qualifies these statements. As to the second, the report (as the Court of Appeals noted) says: "*Although* the level of crime and violence now seems to be higher than in the recent past, *the underlying motivation in most asylum cases now appears to stem from common crime and/or personal vengeance,*" i.e., not politics. *Id.*, at 4 (emphasis added). And the report (in sections to which the Court of Appeals did not refer) adds that in the context of claims based on political opinion, in "our experience, only party leaders or high-profile activists generally would be vulnerable to such harassment and usually only in their home communities." *Id.*, at 8. This latter phrase "only in their home communities" is particularly important in light of the fact that an individual who can relocate safely within his home country ordinarily cannot qualify for asylum here. See 8 CFR § 208.13(b)(1)(i) (2002).

Second, remand could lead to the presentation of further evidence of current circumstances in Guatemala — evidence that may well prove enlightening given the five years that have elapsed since the report was written. See §§ 3.1, 3.2 (permitting the BIA to reopen the record and to remand to the Immigration Judge as appropriate).

III

We conclude that the Court of Appeals should have applied the ordinary "remand" rule. We grant the Government's petition for certiorari. We reverse the judgment of the Court of Appeals for the Ninth Circuit insofar as it denies remand to the agency. And we remand the case for further proceedings consistent with this opinion.

So ordered.

DICKINSON v. ZURKO
527 U.S. 150 (1999)

JUSTICE BREYER delivered the opinion of the Court.

The Administrative Procedure Act (APA) sets forth standards governing judicial review of findings of fact made by federal administrative agencies. 5 U.S.C. § 706. We must decide whether § 706 applies when the Federal Circuit reviews findings of fact made by the Patent and Trademark Office (PTO). We conclude that it does apply, and the Federal Circuit must use the framework set forth in that section.

I

Section 706, originally enacted in 1946, sets forth standards that govern the "Scope" of court "review" of, *e.g.*, agency factfinding (what we shall call court/agency review). It says that a

"reviewing court shall — . . . .

"(2) hold unlawful and set aside agency . . . findings . . . found to be —

"(A) arbitrary, capricious, [or] an abuse of discretion, or . . .

. . . . .

"(E) unsupported by substantial evidence in a case subject to sections 556 and 557 of this title or otherwise reviewed on the record of an agency hearing provided by statute; . . .

. . . . .

"In making the foregoing determinations, the court shall review the whole record or those parts of it cited by a party. . . ."

Federal Rule of Civil Procedure 52(a) sets forth standards that govern appellate court review of findings of fact made by a district court judge (what we shall call court/court review). It says that the appellate court shall set aside those findings only if they are "clearly erroneous." Traditionally, this court/court standard of review has been considered somewhat stricter (*i.e.*, allowing somewhat closer judicial review) than the APA's court/agency standards. 2 K. Davis & R. Pierce, Administrative Law Treatise § 11.2, p. 174 (3d ed.1994) (hereinafter Davis & Pierce).

The Court of Appeals for the Federal Circuit believes that it should apply the "clearly erroneous" standard when it reviews findings of fact made by the PTO. *In re Zurko*, 142 F.3d 1447, 1459 (C.A.Fed.1998) (case below). The Commissioner of Patents, the PTO's head, believes to the contrary that ordinary APA court/agency standards apply. . . .

The case before us tests these two competing legal views. Respondents applied for a patent upon a method for increasing computer security. The PTO patent examiner concluded that respondents' method was obvious in light of prior art, and so it denied the application. See 35 U.S.C. § 103 (1994 ed., Supp. III). The PTO's review board (the Board of Patent Appeals and Interferences) upheld the examiner's decision. Respondents sought review in the Federal Circuit, where a panel treated the question of what the prior art teaches as one of fact, and agreed with respondents that the PTO's factual finding was "clearly erroneous." *In re Zurko*, 111 F.3d 887, 889, and n. 2 (1997).

The Federal Circuit, hoping definitively to resolve the review-standard controversy, then heard the matter en banc. After examining relevant precedents, the en banc court concluded that its use of the stricter court/court standard was legally proper. The Solicitor General, representing the Commissioner of Patents, sought certiorari. We granted the writ in order to decide whether the Federal Circuit's review of PTO factfinding must take place within the framework set forth in the APA.

* * * *

III

The Federal Circuit also advanced several policy reasons which in its view militate against use of APA standards of review. First, it says that both bench and bar have now become used to the Circuit's application of a "clearly erroneous" standard that implies somewhat stricter court/court review. It says that change may prove needlessly disruptive. . . . Supporting *amici* add that it is better that the matter remain " 'settled than that it be settled right.' " . . .

This Court has described the APA court/agency "substantial evidence" standard as requiring a court to ask whether a "reasonable mind might accept" a particular evidentiary record as "adequate to support a conclusion." *Consolidated Edison*, 305 U.S., at 229. It has described the court/court "clearly erroneous" standard in terms of whether a reviewing judge has a "definite and firm conviction" that an error has been committed. *United States v. United States Gypsum Co.*, 333 U.S. 364, 395 (1948). And it has suggested that the former is somewhat less strict than the latter. *Universal Camera*, 340 U.S., at 477, 488 (analogizing "substantial evidence" test to review of jury findings and stating that appellate courts must respect agency expertise). At the same time the Court has stressed the importance of not simply rubber-stamping agency factfinding. . . . The APA requires meaningful review; and its enactment meant stricter judicial review of agency factfinding than Congress believed some courts had previously conducted. . . .

The upshot in terms of judicial review is some practical difference in outcome depending upon which standard is used. The court/agency standard, as we have said, is somewhat less strict than the court/court standard. But the difference is a subtle one — so fine that (apart from the present case) we have failed to uncover a single instance in which a reviewing court conceded that use of one standard rather than the other would in fact have produced a different outcome. Cf. *International Brotherhood of Electrical Workers v. NLRB*, 448 F.2d 1127, 1142 (C.A.D.C.1971) (Leventhal, J., dissenting) (wrongly believing — and correcting himself — that he had found the "case dreamed of by law school professors" where the agency's findings, though "clearly erroneous," were "nevertheless" supported by "substantial evidence").

The difficulty of finding such a case may in part reflect the basic similarity of the reviewing task, which requires judges to apply logic and experience to an evidentiary record, whether that record was made in a court or by an agency. It may in part reflect the difficulty of attempting to capture in a form of words intangible factors such as judicial confidence in the fairness of the factfinding process. *Universal Camera, supra,* at 489; Jaffe, Judicial Review: "Substantial Evidence on the Whole Record," 64 Harv. L.Rev. 1233, 1245 (1951). It may in part reflect the comparatively greater importance of case-specific factors, such as a finding's dependence upon agency expertise or the presence of internal agency review, which factors will often prove more influential in respect to outcome than will the applicable standard of review.

These features of review underline the importance of the fact that, when a Federal Circuit judge reviews PTO factfinding, he or she often will examine that finding through the lens of patent-related experience — and properly so, for the Federal Circuit is a specialized court. That comparative expertise, by enabling the Circuit better to understand the basis for the PTO's finding of fact, may play a more important role in assuring proper review than would a theoretically somewhat stricter standard.

Moreover, if the Circuit means to suggest that a change of standard could somehow immunize the PTO's fact-related "reasoning" from review, we disagree. A reviewing court reviews an agency's reasoning to determine whether it is "arbitrary" or "capricious," or, if bound up with a record-based factual conclusion, to determine whether it is supported by "substantial evidence." *E.g., SEC v. Chenery Corp.,* 318 U.S. 80, 89–93 (1943).

Second, the Circuit and its supporting *amici* believe that a change to APA review standards will create an anomaly. An applicant denied a patent can seek review either directly in the Federal Circuit, see 35 U.S.C. § 141, or indirectly by first obtaining direct review in federal district court, see § 145. The first path will now bring about Federal Circuit court/agency review; the second path might well lead to Federal Circuit court/court review, for the Circuit now reviews federal district court factfinding using a "clearly erroneous" standard . . . The result, the Circuit claims, is that the outcome may turn upon which path a disappointed applicant takes; and it fears that those applicants will often take the more complicated, time-consuming indirect path in order to obtain stricter judicial review of the PTO's determination.

We are not convinced, however, that the presence of the two paths creates a significant anomaly. The second path permits the disappointed applicant to present to the court evidence that the applicant did not present to the PTO. . . . The presence of such new or different evidence makes a factfinder of the district judge. And nonexpert judicial factfinding calls for the court/court standard of review. We concede that an anomaly might exist insofar as the district judge does no more than review PTO factfinding, but nothing in this opinion prevents the Federal Circuit from adjusting related review standards where necessary. . . .

Finally, the Circuit reasons that its stricter court/court review will produce better agency factfinding. It says that the standard encourages the creation of "administrative records that more fully describe the metes and bounds of the patent grant" and "help avoid situations where board factfinding on matters such as anticipation or the factual inquiries underlying obviousness become virtually unreviewable." 142 F.3d, at 1458. Neither the Circuit nor its supporting *amici*, however, have explained convincingly why direct review of the PTO's patent denials demands a stricter fact-related review standard than is applicable to other agencies. Congress has set forth the appropriate standard in the APA. For the reasons stated, we have not found circumstances that justify an exception.

For these reasons, the judgment of the Federal Circuit is reversed. We remand the case for further proceedings consistent with this opinion.

So ordered.

Questions and Comments

Did you get a sense of substantial-evidence review from these cases? What was wrong with the Ninth Circuit itself determining that the Orlando Ventura faced "persecution or a well-founded fear of persecution . . . on account of . . . [a] political opinion" in Guatemala? Do you remember the evidence on which the court acted? Did the court give a reason for not remanding the case to the INS? Why did the Supreme Court reverse? Were the Court's reasons for reversing convincing?

The *Dickinson* case involved an appeal to the Federal Circuit from a decision of the Board of Patent Appeals upholding a patent examiner's denial of a patent application. Should judicial review of the Board of Patent Appeals be governed by the same standard as that governing the denial of an application for political asylum? Why are not these decisions so different as to require different standards for judicial review? What review standard should govern a court's review of the decisions of the Board of Patent Appeals? Do you remember the arguments in behalf of that standard? What did the Supreme Court think of the policy arguments advanced in favor of the standard used by the Federal Circuit? How similar are the "clearly erroneous" standard and the "substantial evidence" standard in application? If these standards often reach similar results, what difference does it make which standard is used? Is the fact that all patent appeals are routed to the Federal Circuit relevant to the issues in this case?

B.   JUDICIAL REVIEW OF AGENCY ORDERS ISSUED IN TRIAL-TYPE HEARINGS

The *Universal Camera* Cases

One of the most important facets of judicial review of agency action concerns judicial review of agency orders issued as a result of a trial-type hearing. The *Universal Camera* cases are the foundation upon which much of the modern law governing such judicial review is based. When these cases reached the courts, both the federal Administrative Procedure Act and the Taft-Hartley Act were relatively new. The Administrative Procedure Act (which was designed to regulate agency procedures and judicial review of agency actions) had been enacted in 1946 after substantial study of these matters in the years prior to the entry of the United States into World War II. The Taft-Hartley Act, passed over President Truman's veto in 1947, was an amendment to the National Labor Relations Act (Wagner Act) which had been enacted during the early New Deal period in 1935. Both Acts contained provisions dealing with judicial review and it is the construction and application of those provisions which was the subject of the *Universal Camera* cases.

National Labor Relations Board v. Universal Camera Corp., 179 F.2d 749 (2d Cir. 1950). The Labor Board had ordered the Universal Camera Corp. to reinstate with back pay a supervisory employee named Chairman. If Chairman was discharged because in a prior Board hearing on representation, he had given testimony adverse to his employer, then Chairman's discharge (under the law in effect when he was discharged) was illegal. If, however, he was discharged because of insubordination, then his discharge was lawful. The issue on judicial review was whether there was adequate evidence in the record to support the Board's determination. An extract from the opinion of the Court of Appeals for the Second Circuit follows:

> The substance of the evidence was as follows. On November 30, 1943, Chairman and Kende testified at the hearing upon representation, after which Kende told Chairman that he had "perjured" himself; and on the stand in the proceeding at bar Kende testified that Chairman "was either ignorant of the true facts regarding the organization within the company . . . or . . . he was deliberately lying, not in one instance, but in many instances, all afternoon"; and "that there was definite doubt regarding his suitability for a supervisory position of that nature." The examiner believed the testimony of Chairman that two other employees, Goldson and Politzer, had cautioned him that the respondent would take it against him, if he testified for the "maintenance employees"; and Kende swore that he told another employee, Weintraub-the personnel manager that he thought that Chairman was a Communist. After Politzer reported to him on December second or third that this was a mistake, Kende told him to keep an eye on Chairman. From all this it is apparent that at the beginning of December Kende was hostile to Chairman; but he took no steps at that time to discharge him.

> Nothing much happened until the very end of that month, when Chairman and Weintraub got into a quarrel, about disciplining a workman, named Kollisch. Chairman swore that Weintraub demanded that he discharge Kollisch for loafing; and Weintraub swore that he only demanded that Chairman put Kollisch to work. In any event high words followed; Chairman told Weintraub that he was drunk; Weintraub brought up a plant guard to put Chairman out of the premises, and the quarrel remained hot, until one, Zicarelli, a union steward, succeeded in getting the two men to patch up an apparent truce. Two days later Weintraub saw Politzer and told him that he had heard that Politzer was looking into Chairman's statement that Weintraub was drunk, and on this account Weintraub asked Politzer to

discharge Chairman. Politzer testified that he answered that Chairman was going to resign soon anyway, and this the examiner believed. He did not, however, believe Politzer's further testimony that Chairman had in fact told Politzer that he was going to resign; he thought that Politzer either was mistaken in so supposing, or that he had made up the story in order to quiet Weintraub. Probably his reason for not believing this part of Politzer's testimony was that he accepted Chairman's testimony that ten days later Politzer intimated to Chairman that it would be well for him to resign, and Chairman refused. Whatever the reason, Weintraub did not, after his talk with Politzer, press the matter until January 24, 1944, when, learning that Chairman was still in the factory, he went again to Politzer and asked him why this was. When Politzer told him that Chairman had changed his mind, Weintraub insisted that he must resign anyway, and, upon Politzer's refusal to discharge him, they together went to Kende. Weintraub repeated his insistence that Chairman must go, giving as the reason that his accusation of drunkenness had undermined Weintraub's authority. Kende took Weintraub's view and Politzer wrote out an order of dismissal. No one testified that at this interview, or any time after December first, any of the three mentioned Chairman's testimony at the representation hearing.

As we have said, the examiner was not satisfied that the Board had proved that Chairman's testimony at the representation proceeding had been an actuating cause of his discharge; but, not only did the majority of the Board reverse his ruling as to that, but they also overruled his finding that Politzer had told Weintraub on January first that Chairman was going to resign. They then found that Kende and Weintraub had agreed to bring about Chairman's discharge, at some undefined time after December first, because of Chairman's testimony; and that Weintraub's complaint on January 24 was a cover for affecting that purpose. Whether these findings were justified is the first, and indeed the only important, question of fact. . . .

. . . We cannot agree that our review has been "broadened" [by the Taft-Hartley Act]; we hold that no more was done than to make definite what was already implied. Just what that review was is another and much more difficult matter-particularly, when it comes to deciding how to treat a reversal by the Board of a finding of one of its own examiners. Obviously no printed record preserves all the evidence, on which any judicial officer bases his findings; and it is principally on that account that upon an appeal from the judgment of a district court, a court of appeals will hesitate to reverse. Its position must be: "No matter what you saw of the witnesses and what else you heard than these written words, we are satisfied from them alone that you were clearly wrong. Nothing which could have happened that is not recorded, could have justified your conclusion in the face of what is before us." . . . On the one hand we are not to assume that the Board must accept the finding [of the examiner], unless what is preserved in the record makes it "clearly erroneous." That would assimilate examiners to masters, and, if that had been intended, we should expect a plainer statement. . . . on the other hand. . . . [certain] decisions we have cited certainly do mean that, when the Board reverses a finding, it shall count in the court's review of the Board's substituted finding . . . On the whole we find ourselves unable to apply so impalpable a standard without bringing greater perplexity into a subject already too perplexing. . . . We hold that, although the Board would be wrong in totally disregarding his findings, it is practically impossible for a court, upon review of those findings to consider the Board's reversal as a factor in the court's own decision. This we say, because we cannot find any middle ground between doing that and treating such a reversal as error, whenever it would be such, if done by a judge to a master in equity.

. . . One ground why the evidence failed to convince the examiner of any agreement between Kende and Weintraub to discharge Chairman, was that he thought it quite as likely that the quarrel between Weintraub and Chairman at the end of December still rankled in Weintraub's mind, and induced him to insist upon Chairman's discharge on January 24, 1944. It became important in this view to explain why Weintraub waited for over three weeks; and this the examiner did explain because he believed that Politzer had told Weintraub that Chairman was going to resign. When the majority of the Board refused to accept this finding, they concluded that, since this left Weintraub's delay unexplained, his motive was to be related back to the quarrel of Kende and Chairman on November 30. We should feel obliged in our turn to reverse the reversal of this finding, if we were dealing with the finding of a judge who had reversed the finding of a master, because the reasons given do not seem to us enough to overbear the evidence which the record did not preserve and which may have convinced the examiner. . . .

There remains the question whether, with this explanation of Weintraub's delay missing, there was "substantial evidence" that the cause of Chairman's discharge was his testimony; and on that the Board had the affirmative; so that it is not enough that Kende and Weintraub might have agreed to find a means of getting rid of Chairman, or that Kende unassisted might have been awaiting an opportunity. . . . When Weintraub went to Politzer on January 24, 1944, with his complaint at Chairman's continued presence in the factory, and when the two went to Kende because Politzer would not discharge Chairman, if Weintraub was acting in accordance with an agreement between Kende and himself, he was concealing the facts from Politzer. So too was Kende at the ensuing interview; indeed, we must assume that the two had arranged beforehand to keep Politzer in the dark, else Weintraub could scarcely have relied upon Kende to play his part. This appears to us to be constructed substantially out of whole cloth, so improbable is it that they should have gone to such devious means to deceive Politzer. On the other hand, although it is possible that Kende had been waiting for a proper occasion, independently of Weintraub, and that he seized upon Weintraub's complaint, being secretly actuated by his old grievance, we do not read the majority's decision as distinctly indicating that they meant so to find. But, if they did, unless we assume that Weintraub's complaint was trumpeted up ad hoc, to deceive Politzer, it becomes the merest guess that Kende did not find it alone a sufficient reason for his action, and reverted to his concealed spite.

Nevertheless, in spite of all this we shall direct the Board's order to be enforced. If by special verdict a jury had made either the express finding of the majority that there was an agreement between Kende and Weintraub, or the alternate finding, if there be one, that Kende without Weintraub's concurrence used Weintraub's complaint as an excuse, we should not reverse the verdict; and we must understand our function in cases of this kind to be the same. Such a verdict would be within the bounds of rational entertainment. When all is said, Kende had been greatly outraged at Chairman's testimony; he then did propose to get him out of the factory; he still thought at the hearings that he was unfit to remain; and he had told Weintraub to keep watch on him. We cannot say that, with all these circumstances before him, no reasonable person could have concluded that Chairman's testimony was one of the causes of his discharge, little as it would have convinced us, were we free to pass upon the evidence in the first instance.

UNIVERSAL CAMERA CORP. v. NATIONAL LABOR RELATIONS BOARD
340 U.S. 474 (1951)

Mr. Justice Frankfurter delivered the opinion of the Court.

The essential issue raised by this case . . . is the effect of the Administrative Procedure Act and the legislation colloquially known as the Taft-Hartley Act on the duty of Courts of Appeals when called upon to review orders of the National Labor Relations Board.

The Court of Appeals for the Second Circuit granted enforcement of an order directing, in the main, that petitioner reinstate with back pay an employee found to have been discharged because he gave testimony under the Wagner Act and cease and desist from discriminating against any employee who files charges or gives testimony under that Act. The court below, Judge Swan dissenting, decreed full enforcement of the order. . . . Because the views of that court regarding the effect of the new legislation on the relation between the Board and the Courts of Appeals in the enforcement of the Board's orders conflicted with those of the Court of Appeals for the Sixth Circuit, we brought both cases here. . . .

I.

Want of certainty in judicial review of Labor Board decisions partly reflects the intractability of any formula to furnish definiteness of content for all the impalpable factors involved in judicial review. But in part doubts as to the nature of the reviewing power and uncertainties in its application derive from history, and to that extent an elucidation of this history may clear them away.

The Wagner Act provided: "The findings of the Board as to the facts, if supported by evidence, shall be conclusive." . . . This Court read "evidence" to mean "substantial evidence and we said that "[s]ubstantial evidence is more than a mere scintilla. It means such relevant evidence as a reasonable mind might accept as adequate to support a conclusion. Accordingly, it "must do more than create a suspicion of the existence of the fact to be established. . . . it must be enough to justify, if the trial were to a jury, a refusal to direct a verdict when the conclusion sought to be drawn from it is one of fact for the jury." . . .

The very smoothness of the "substantial evidence" formula as the standard for reviewing the evidentiary validity of the Board's findings established its currency. But the inevitably variant applications of the standard to conflicting evidence soon brought contrariety of views and in due course bred criticism. Even though the whole record may have been canvassed in order to determine whether the evidentiary foundation of a determination by the Board was "substantial," the phrasing of this Court's process of review readily lent itself to the notion that it was enough that the evidence supporting the Board's result was "substantial" when considered by itself. It is fair to say that by imperceptible steps regard for the fact-finding function of the Board led to the assumption that the requirements of the Wagner Act were met when the reviewing court could find in the record evidence which, when viewed in isolation, substantiated the Board's findings. . . . This is not to say that every member of this Court was consciously guided by this view or that the Court ever explicitly avowed this practice as doctrine. What matters is that the belief justifiably arose that the Court had so construed the obligation to review.

[The Court then discussed the history of the substantial evidence standard. It recounted widespread criticism of the manner in which the courts had been reviewing actions of the Labor Board in the pre-World War II period. Criticism of the Labor Board's operations had resulted in passage of the Walter-Logan bill in 1940, a bill which was vetoed by President Roosevelt. Roosevelt, however, then appointed the Attorney General's Committee on Administrative Procedure to make recommendations for reform. That Committee issued its final report in January 1941. Although the majority of the Committee endorsed the continuing use of the "substantial evidence" standard for judicial review, three dissenters recommend that Congress enact principles of review providing that judicial review could extend to "findings, inferences, or conclusions of fact unsupported, upon the whole record, by substantial evidence."]

So far as the history of this movement for enlarged review reveals, the phrase "upon the whole record" makes its first appearance in this recommendation of the minority of the Attorney General's Committee. This evidence of the close relationship between the phrase and the criticism out of which it arose is important, for the substance of this formula for judicial review found its way into the statute books when Congress with unquestioning-we might even say uncritical-unanimity enacted the Administrative Procedure Act.

One is tempted to say "uncritical" because the legislative history of that Act hardly speaks with that clarity of purpose which Congress supposedly furnishes courts in order to enable them to enforce its true will. On the one hand, the sponsors of the legislation indicated that they were reaffirming the prevailing "substantial evidence" test. But with equal clarity they expressed disapproval of the manner in which the courts were applying their own standard. The committee reports of both houses refer to the practice of agencies to rely upon "suspicion, surmise, implications, or plainly incredible evidence," and indicate that courts are to exact higher standards "in the exercise of their independent judgment" and on consideration of "the whole record."

[The Court then recounted a similar dissatisfaction with the federal courts' application of the "substantial evidence" standard reflected in the legislative history of the Taft-Hartley Act.]

It is fair to say that in all this Congress expressed a mood. And it expressed its mood not merely by oratory but by legislation. As legislation that mood must be respected, even though it can only serve as a standard for judgment and not as a body of rigid rules assuring sameness of application. Enforcement of such broad standards implies subtlety of mind and solidity of judgment. But it is not for us to question that Congress may assume such qualities in the federal judiciary.

From the legislative story we have summarized, two concrete conclusions do emerge. One is the identity of aim of the Administrative Procedure Act and the Taft-Hartley Act regarding the proof with which the Labor Board must support a decision. The other is that now Congress has left no room for doubt as to the kind of scrutiny which a Court of Appeals must give the record before the Board to satisfy itself that the Board's order rests on adequate proof.

Whether or not it was ever permissible for courts to determine the substantiality of evidence supporting a Labor Board decision merely on the basis of evidence which in and of itself justified it, without taking into account contradictory evidence or evidence from which conflicting inferences could be drawn, the new legislation definitively precludes such a theory of review and bars its practice. The substantiality of evidence must take into account whatever in the record fairly detracts from its weight. This is clearly the significance of the requirement in both statutes that courts consider the whole record. . . .

To be sure, the requirement for canvassing "the whole record" in order to ascertain substantiality does not furnish a calculus of value by which a reviewing court can assess the evidence. Nor was it intended to negative the function of the Labor Board as one of those agencies presumably equipped or informed by experience to deal with a specialized field of knowledge, whose findings within that field carry the authority of an expertness which courts do not possess and therefore must respect. Nor does it mean that even as to matters not requiring expertise a court may displace the Board's choice between two fairly conflicting views, even though the court would justifiably have made a different choice had the matter been before it *de novo*. Congress has merely made it clear that a reviewing court is not barred from setting aside a Board decision when it cannot conscientiously find that the evidence supporting that decision is substantial, when viewed in the light that the record in its entirety furnishes, including the body of evidence opposed to the Board's view.

There remains, then, the question whether enactment of these two statutes has altered the scope of review other than to require that substantiality be determined in the light of all that the record relevantly presents. . . . Retention of the familiar "substantial evidence" terminology indicates that no drastic reversal of attitude was intended.

. . . . The legislative history of these Acts demonstrates a purpose to impose on courts a responsibility which has not always been recognized. . . . To find the change so elusive that it cannot be precisely defined does not mean that it may be ignored.

We conclude, therefore, that the Administrative Procedure Act and the Taft-Hartley Act direct that courts must now assume more responsibility for the reasonableness and fairness of Labor Board decisions than some courts have shown in the past. Reviewing courts must be influenced by a feeling that they are not to abdicate the conventional judicial function. Congress has imposed on them responsibility for assuring that the Board keeps within reasonable grounds. That responsibility is not less real because it is limited to enforcing the requirement that evidence appear substantial when viewed, on the record as a whole, by courts invested with the authority and enjoying the prestige of the Courts of Appeals. The Board's findings are entitled to respect; but they must nonetheless be set aside when the record before a Court of Appeals clearly precludes the Board's decision from being justified by a fair estimate of the worth of the testimony of witnesses or its informed judgment on matters within its special competence or both.

Our power to review the correctness of application of the present standard ought seldom to be called into action. . . . This Court will intervene only in what ought to be the rare instance when the standard appears to have been misapprehended or grossly misapplied.

II.

Our disagreement with the view of the court below that the scope of review of Labor Board decisions is unaltered by recent legislation does not of itself . . . require reversal of its decision. The court may have applied a standard of review which satisfies the present Congressional requirement.

The decision of the Court of Appeals is assailed on two grounds. It is said (1) that the court erred in holding that it was barred from taking into account the report of the examiner on questions of fact insofar as that report was rejected by the Board, and (2) that the Board's order was not supported by substantial evidence on the record considered as a whole, even apart from the validity of the court's refusal to consider the rejected portions of the examiner's report.

The latter contention is easily met. . . . [I]t is clear from the court's opinion . . . that it in fact did consider the "record as a whole," and did not deem itself merely the judicial echo of the Board's conclusion. . . .

The first contention, however, raises serious questions to which we now turn.

III.

The Court of Appeals deemed itself bound by the Board's rejection of the examiner's findings because the court considered these findings not "as unassailable as a master's." . . . They are not. Section 10(c) of the Labor Management Relations Act provides that "If upon the preponderance of the testimony taken the Board shall be of the opinion that any person named in the complaint has engaged in or is engaging in any such unfair labor practice, then the Board shall state its findings of fact . . .." The responsibility for decision thus placed on the Board is wholly inconsistent with the notion that it has power to reverse an examiner's findings only when they are "clearly erroneous." Such a limitation would make so drastic a departure from prior administrative practice that explicitness would be required.

The Court of Appeals concluded from this premise "that, although the Board would be wrong in totally disregarding his findings, it is practically impossible for a court, upon review of those findings which the Board itself substitutes, to consider the Board's reversal as a factor in the court's own decision. This we say, because we cannot find any middle ground between doing that and treating such a reversal as error, whenever it would be such, if done by a judge to a master in equity." . . . Much as we respect the logical acumen of the Chief Judge of the Court of Appeals, we do not find ourselves pinioned between the horns of his dilemma.

We are aware that to give the examiner's findings less finality than a master's and yet entitle them to consideration in striking the account, is to introduce another and an unruly factor into the judgmatical process of review. But we ought not to fashion an exclusionary rule merely to reduce the number of imponderables to be considered by reviewing courts.

. . . . Surely an examiner's report is as much a part of the record as the complaint or the testimony. According to the Administrative Procedure Act, "All decisions (including initial, recommended, or tentative decisions) shall become a part of the record. . . ." § 8(b) . . .

It is therefore difficult to escape the conclusion that the plain language of the statutes directs a reviewing court to determine the substantiality of evidence on the record including the examiner's report. The conclusion is confirmed by indications in the legislative history that enhancement of the status and function of the trial examiner was one of the important purposes of the movement for administrative reform.

This aim was set forth by the Attorney General's Committee on Administrative Procedure:

> "In general, the relationship upon appeal between the hearing commissioner and the agency ought to a considerable extent to be that of trial court to appellate court. Conclusions, interpretations, law, and policy should, of course, be open to full review. On the other hand, on matters which the hearing commissioner, having heard the evidence and seen the witnesses, is best qualified to decide, the agency should be reluctant to disturb his findings unless error is clearly shown."

. . . . [The Administrative Procedure Act] permits agencies to use examiners to record testimony but not to evaluate it, and contains the rather obscure provision that an agency which reviews an examiner's report has "all the powers which it would have in making the initial decision."

But this refusal to make mandatory the recommendations of the Attorney General's Committee should not be construed as a repudiation of them. Nothing in the statutes suggests that the Labor Board should not be influenced by the examiner's opportunity to observe the witnesses he hears and sees and the Board does not. . . .

We do not require that the examiner's findings be given more weight than in reason and in the light of judicial experience they deserve. The "substantial evidence" standard is not modified in any way when the Board and its examiner disagree. We intend only to recognize that evidence supporting a conclusion may be less substantial when an impartial, experienced examiner who has observed the witnesses and lived with the case has drawn conclusions different from the Board's than when he has reached the same conclusion. The findings of the examiner are to be considered along with the consistency and inherent probability of testimony. The significance of his report, of course, depends largely on the importance of credibility in the particular case. To give it this significance does not seem to us materially more difficult than to heed the other factors which in sum determine whether evidence is "substantial."

We therefore remand the cause to the Court of Appeals. On reconsideration of the record it should accord the findings of the trial examiner the relevance that they reasonably command in answering the comprehensive question whether the evidence supporting the Board's order is substantial. . . .

Judgment vacated and cause remanded.

Questions and Comments

1.   Under the Wagner Act, what was the standard for judicial review of orders of the National Labor Relations Board? How was that standard construed by the courts? Was that standard changed by the Administrative Procedure Act? by the Taft-Hartley Act?

2.   What does the term "substantial evidence" mean? Where did that phrase originate? What is the standard by which courts determine whether a plaintiff has enough evidence to get to a jury in a civil case? Is that the standard by which a court rules on a motion by the defendant for summary judgment? When a phrase like "substantial evidence" is carried over from private civil litigation to describe a standard by which courts review agency orders, is not the meaning of the phrase transformed? Explain.

3.   Where did the "on the record as a whole" part of the substantial-evidence standard originate? Where do you find that standard in the Administrative Procedure Act? What is the "mood" (referred to by Justice Frankfurter) which Congress expressed in the Administrative Procedure Act and in the Taft-Hartley Act? To what extent is it possible for the Supreme Court to enforce this "mood" on the courts of appeals?

4.   Can you locate the provision in the Administrative Procedure Act that says the examiner's report is part of the record? Did the Court treat the examiner's

report as "evidence"? Explain.

5. How much weight must the Board give to the examiner's report? Does the examiner possess any advantages over the Board in deciding a case? What are those advantages? To what extent is it an advantage that the examiner has seen and heard the witnesses? that the examiner has "lived with the case"? that the examiner is "experienced"? Does not the Board also live with the case? Is the Board not experienced? What is the meaning of the phrase in section 557 of the Administrative Procedure Act that "on appeal from or review of the initial decision, the agency has all the powers which it would have in making the initial decision"?

6. At the end of Part I of the Court's opinion, Justice Frankfurter stated: "Our power to review the correctness of application of the present standard ought seldom to be called into action. . . . This Court will intervene only in what ought to be the rare instance when the standard appears to have been misapprehended or grossly misapplied."

Does Justice Frankfurter's quoted statement mean that the courts of appeals in fact will rarely be reversed? In what type of case would you expect the Supreme Court would review and reverse a court of appeals decision which had reviewed an agency order under the substantial evidence standard?

7. Does the structure of the court system dictate that the Supreme Court can review only a small number of the decisions of the courts of appeals? What standard should the Supreme Court employ in deciding whether or not to review a decision of a court of appeals?

8. How do the structures of the various regulatory systems affect the standards employed by the courts to review the decisions of administrative agencies? Would it be practical for the courts of appeals to provide de novo review for all agency decisions? Why or why not? Would such review be constitutional? Explain. If the courts of appeals in fact did provide de novo review for all agency decisions, the courts would in fact be redoing the work of the agencies, would they not? In such a case, what would be the rationale for the existence of those agencies?

9. Does the substantial-evidence review standard reflect the limited supervisory role which the courts of appeals possess over the various regulatory agencies? Explain.

10. The preceding questions reflect a general facet of any hierarchical organizational structure that the higher levels will not redo the work of the lower levels. Does such a structure not imply that the higher levels will only grant review sufficient to ensure that the basic direction of the work performed at lower levels is consistent with organizational goals? Explain.

NATIONAL LABOR RELATIONS BOARD v. UNIVERSAL CAMERA CORP.
190 F.2d 429 (2d Cir. 1951)

L. HAND, CIRCUIT JUDGE.

. . . . The Supreme Court vacated our order and remanded the cause to us for reconsideration in two particulars. The first was that, although the amendment of the old act was in terms limited to adding that courts of appeal should scrutinize the whole record on reviewing findings of the Board, its implications were more extended. The second was that in considering whether the Board's findings were adequately supported by the evidence we were not altogether to disregard the findings of its examiner. As to the first, the Court agreed that in the case at bar we had based our review upon the whole record, but it held that the amendment . . . was intended to prescribe an attitude in courts of appeal less complaisant towards the Board's findings than had been proper before; not only were they to look to the record as a whole, but they were to be less ready to yield their personal judgment on the facts; at least less ready than many at times had been. Presumably that does not extend to those issues on which the Board's specialized experience equips it with major premises inaccessible to judges, but as to matters of common knowledge we are to use a somewhat stiffer standard. Just where the Board's specialized experience ends it may no doubt be hard to say; but we are to find the boundary and beyond it to deem ourselves as competent as the Board to pass upon issues of fact. We hold that all the issues at bar are beyond the boundary and for that reason we cannot accept the Board's argument that we are not in as good a position as itself to decide what witnesses were more likely to be telling the truth in this labor dispute.

Upon the second issue we had said that we could find no practicable measure between giving the findings of an examiner the immunity which a court must give to those of a master, and saying that, although the Board should no doubt treat them as having some evidentiary value, it was impossible for us to measure what that ought to be; and that therefore we would decide the appeal, as though there had been no findings. Although this went too far, again it is plain that the weight which we should insist that the Board should give them must be left at large; except that we must count them for something, and particularly when . . . they were based on that part of the evidence which the printed words do not preserve. Often that is the most telling part, for on the issue of veracity the bearing and delivery of a witness will usually be the dominating factors, when the words alone leave any rational choice. Perhaps as good a way as any to state the change effected by the amendment is to say that an examiner's findings on veracity must not be overruled without a very substantial preponderance in the testimony as recorded.

Order reversed; complaint to be dismissed.

FRANK, CIRCUIT JUDGE (concurring).

Recognizing, as only a singularly stupid man would not, Judge Hand's superior wisdom, intelligence and learning, I seldom disagree with him, and then with serious misgivings. In this instance, I have overcome my misgivings because I think that his modesty has moved him to interpret too sweepingly the Supreme Court's criticism of our earlier opinion written by him. I read the Supreme Court's opinion as saying that we had obeyed the new statute with but one exception: We had wholly disregarded the examiner's finding which the Board rejected.

I think, then, that we must thus conclude: (1) Except that we did not consider the examiner's findings which differed from the Board's, we had not in this case disobeyed the new statute; (2) that statute does not put us, vis a vis the Board, in the same position we occupy with respect to a trial court; (3) even as to matters not within the area of the Board's so-called "expertise," we may not try Board cases *de novo*.

Concerning our error in disregarding the examiner's findings, Judge Hand, as I understand him, interprets as follows the Supreme Court's ruling: The Board may never reject an examiner's finding if it rests on his evaluation of the credibility of oral testimony unless (1) that rejection results from the Board's rational use of the Board's specialized knowledge or (2) the examiner has been absurdly naive in believing a witness. This, I think, is somewhat more restrictive of the Board's powers than the Supreme Court suggested, for it said: "The responsibility for decision thus placed on the Board is wholly inconsistent with the notion that it has power to reverse an examiner's findings only when they are 'clearly erroneous'."

I would also, by way of caution, add this qualification (to which, judging from his opinions elsewhere, I gather Judge Hand will not demur): An examiner's finding binds the Board only to the extent that it is a "testimonial inference," or "primary inference," *i.e.*, an inference that a fact to which a witness orally testified is an actual fact because that witness so testified and because observation of the witness induces a belief in that testimony. The Board, however, is not bound by the examiner's "secondary inferences," or "derivative inferences," *i.e.*, facts to which no witness orally testified but which the examiner inferred from facts orally testified by witnesses whom the examiner believed. The Board may reach its own "secondary inferences," and we must abide by them unless they are irrational; in that way, the Board differs from a trial judge (in a juryless case) who hears and sees the witnesses, for, although we are usually bound by his "testimonial inferences," we need not accept his "secondary inferences" even if rational, but, where other rational "secondary inferences" are possible, we may substitute our own. Since that is true, it is also true that we must not interfere when the Board adopts either (1) its examiner's "testimonial inferences" and they are not absurd, or (2) his rational "secondary inferences."

Except as noted above, I concur.

Questions and Comments

1.   Judge Hand had compared the relation between a hearing examiner and the agency with the relation between a trial judge and a master, and concluded that the two relationships were different. He thought that the agency should be freer to reverse the examiner's findings than a judge is to reverse a master's findings. At the time, a trial judge reviewed a master's findings under a "clearly erroneous" standard. That is the same standard under which an appellate court reviews the findings of a trial court sitting without a jury. See Federal Rule of Civil Procedure (FRCP) 52(a)(6). The standard by which a judge reviews a master's findings was changed in 2003. FRCP 63(f)(3) now requires the judge to review a master's findings de novo, unless the parties stipulate otherwise.

2.   Is the relationship between an agency and a reviewing court similar to the relationship between a court sitting without a jury and an appellate court? Between a jury and the judge? Between a jury and an appellate court? What review standard(s) govern these relationships? How do these relationships differ? Explain.

3.   In his concurring opinion on remand, Judge Frank distinguished between matters of primary or testimonial inference and matters of secondary or derivative inference. Is that distinction helpful in responding to the questions in paragraphs 1 and 2 above? Why does Judge Frank believe that a court would be usurping an agency's function were the court to reject a rational secondary inference of an agency? Is Judge Frank suggesting that the task of drawing secondary inferences has been delegated by Congress to the agency? Is this delegated function independent of any "experience" or "expertise" which the agency may have developed in handling any other cases? Explain.

4.   What was Judge Frank's reason for suggesting that the agency was free to reject even a rational secondary inference by an examiner? Have you implicitly answered this question in your answers to the questions in paragraph 3 above?

5.   What were Judge Frank's criteria for determining when inferences were "rational" and when they were not? Do the criteria for determining the rationality of testimonial inferences differ from the criteria for determining the rationality of derivative inferences?

6.   Is the rationality of a derivative inference determined with reference to the purposes and goals of the statute which the agency is administering? Are courts the decisional bodies which make the ultimate determinations about the purposes and goals underlying a statute? Does not an agency often possess a wide scope for choosing means for furthering statutory goals? When an agency draws secondary inferences, is it performing a task through which the statutory goals are furthered? Do the courts retain a role of ensuring that the agency's secondary inferences are compatible with the goals of the underlying statute? Is this role compatible with the court's supervisory place in the regulatory structure? *See* Questions and Comments, paras. 8–10, following the opinion of the Supreme Court in *Universal Camera Corp. v. National Labor Relations Board, supra.*

7.   Does Judge Frank's analysis describe the difference in the "clearly erroneous" standard by which courts of appeals review the findings of fact of a trial judge sitting without a jury and the "substantial evidence" standard by which courts of

appeals review the decisions of agencies? Does his analysis imply that the difference is solely because a court of appeals is free to supply derivative inferences in the former case but not in the latter? In *Anderson v. City of Bessemer City*, 470 U.S. 564 (1985) the Supreme Court clarified the relation of an appellate court to a trial court sitting without a jury when the former is reviewing the factual findings of the latter under the "clearly erroneous" review standard of FRCP 52(a). The Court's discussion in that case may carry implications for the application by courts of appeals of the narrower substantial-evidence review standard which normally governs their review of agency orders. Extracts from the Court's opinion are set forth below:

> Although the meaning of the phrase "clearly erroneous" is not immediately apparent, certain general principles governing the exercise of the appellate court's power to overturn findings of a district court may be derived from our cases. The foremost of these principles . . . is that "a finding is 'clearly erroneous' when although there is evidence to support it, the reviewing court on the entire evidence is left with the definite and firm conviction that a mistake has been committed." . . . This standard plainly does not entitle a reviewing court to reverse the finding of the trier of fact simply because it is convinced that it would have decided the case differently. The reviewing court oversteps the bounds of its duty under Rule 52 if it undertakes to duplicate the role of the lower court. . . . If the district court's account of the evidence is plausible in light of the record viewed in its entirety, the court of appeals may not reverse it even though convinced that had it been sitting as the trier of fact, it would have weighed the evidence differently. . . .

> This is so even when the district court's findings do not rest on credibility determinations, but are based instead on physical or documentary evidence or inferences from other facts. . . .

> The rationale for deference to the original finder of fact is not limited to the superiority of the trial judge's position to make determinations of credibility. The trial judge's major role is the determination of fact, and with experience in fulfilling that role comes expertise. Duplication of the trial judge's efforts in the court of appeals would very likely contribute only negligibly to the accuracy of fact determinations at a huge cost in diversion of judicial resources. . . .

8.   Does the extract from the Court's opinion in *Anderson v. City of Bessemer City* carry ramifications for review by courts of appeals of agency decisions? Since the substantial-evidence review standard is less intrusive than the clearly erroneous standard, do the Court's remarks in *Anderson v. City of Bessemer City* apply *a fortiori* to courts of appeals reviewing agency determinations under a substantial-evidence standard? Must, therefore, a court of appeals generally accept an agency's derivative inference even outside of the agency's scope of expertise? Was this not also Judge Frank's conclusion in his concurring opinion in *Universal Camera* on remand?

9.   *Anderson v. City of Bessemer City, supra,* also dealt with the review by a court of appeals of a trial judge's findings on an issue involving the judge's belief in

the credibility of witnesses:

> When findings are based on determinations regarding the credibility of witnesses, Rule 52(a) demands even greater deference to the trial court's findings; for only the trial judge can be aware of the variations in demeanor and tone of voice that bear so heavily on the listener's understanding of and belief in what is said. . . . This is not to suggest that the trial judge may insulate his findings from review by denominating them credibility determinations, for factors other than demeanor and inflection go into the decision whether or not to believe a witness. Documents or objective evidence may contradict the witness' story; or the story itself may be so internally inconsistent or implausible on its face that a reasonable fact-finder would not credit it. Where such factors are present, the court of appeals may well find clear error even in a finding purportedly based on a credibility determination. . . . But when a trial judge's finding is based on his decision to credit the testimony of one of two or more witnesses, each of whom has told a coherent and facially plausible story that is not contradicted by extrinsic evidence, that finding, if not internally inconsistent, can virtually never be clear error.

10.   If the standard set forth in the last extract from *Anderson v. City of Bessemer City* were applied to the review by the court of appeals of the decision of the Labor Board in the *Universal Camera* case, would the court uphold the decision of the Board? of the examiner? Why or why not? Did the Labor Board's decision turn on its belief or disbelief in the credibility of witnesses? Did the Labor Board see and hear the witnesses testifying? Did the examiner?

11.   Must the examiner always be upheld on credibility determinations? Why or why not? Does the fact that agencies like the Labor Board may engage in more intrusive review of decisions below than permitted by the clearly-erroneous rule (applied in *Bessemer City, supra*) mean that the extract in paragraph 9 above has less relevance to agency review of credibility determinations made by hearing examiners (or their successors, Administrative Law Judges)?

Note: Agency Adjudication (Part 1)

Did the Act Occur?

In an agency adjudication, the agency generally must decide how a statute applies to a private party; often this involves determining whether a private party did or did not perform an act prohibited by statute. Thus, for example, the Federal Trade Commission has been required to decide whether a respondent has engaged in "unfair methods of competition" or "unfair or deceptive acts or practices" or has engaged in price discrimination which "may have lessened competition or tend to create a monopoly"; the Interstate Commerce Commission formerly had to decide whether a carrier had charged rates which were or were not "reasonable"; the Federal Communications Commission has had to decide whether the issuance of a new radio or television broadcast license would serve the "public convenience, interest, or necessity."

When we consider carefully the type of decision which an agency has to make in such cases, we confront a definitional problem. How, in each of the examples involving the FCC and the ICC , is the "act" in question to be defined? In the examples, the prohibited act is phrased in "conclusory" language. That is to say, the commission of an "unfair or deceptive act or practice" is made unlawful by statute-but the statute does not tell us precisely what an unfair or deceptive practice is. The statute is couched in abstract terms. Our awareness of the abstract nature of many statutes suggests to us that the process of determining whether an unfair or deceptive act or practice has occurred involves not merely a "factual" inquiry as to what has happened or may happen: not merely what were the physical occurrences giving rise to the allegation that an unfair or deceptive act or practice had occurred. But it also involves the application (and sometimes the formulation) of a judgment criterion or standard applied to the facts as they are discovered. This criterion must be used to evaluate the physical facts as found for their significance under the statute.

Let us first try this with a typical accident case with which we are all familiar. Here the decision about liability is made, not by an administrative agency, but by a jury. Nevertheless, the decisional process is analytically similar. Witnesses testify — sometimes in a contradictory manner. As a result of the testimony, let us say, the jury concludes (in the jury room) that the defendant drove an automobile at night with only one working headlight. Let us also assume that the jury has found that the defendant's automobile collided with the plaintiff's. The jury still has to determine whether the defendant's driving at night with one headlight was or was not "negligent" in the particular case. And if it was negligent, the jury must decide whether the negligence was the "proximate cause" of the accident. Let us further suppose that the defendant's reason for driving at night was the imminent need of his ailing wife for a prescription available only at a distant drugstore. But the defendant could have taken a taxi. What would a reasonably prudent person have done? That is the jury's criterion for judgment on the question of negligence. If the defendant is found to have been "negligent", did the negligence "proximately cause" the accident? The defendant's automobile did have one light working. Why was that not enough to warn the plaintiff? Here the jury has to evaluate the physical occurrences which it found existed. Its common experience is its guide — its criterion for passing judgment.

Restating this example for clarity: the jury first must determine the physical occurrences. Did the defendant drive with a malfunctioning headlight? Did the cars of the plaintiff and defendant collide? After it determines the physical events, the jury must apply judgment criteria to those physical events to arrive at a decision as to whether the defendant was "negligent" and as to whether that "negligence" (if found) "proximately caused" the plaintiff's injuries. In tabular form, the jury's functions might appear:

Physical or Near-physical events	Judgments to be made after Answering 1st column questions	Judgment criteria
1. Did the defendant drive with only one head light?	1. Was the defendant's driving under the circumstances determined in the answers to questions 1 and 2 in the first column "negligent"?	1. Prudent person standard based on common experience.
2. If so, why did the defendant drive with only one working headlight?	2. If so, was that negligence the "proximate cause" of the accident?	
3. Did the cars of plaintiff and defendant collide?		

Now let us consider the analogous decision-making of a government agency. Consider, for example, a large toy retailer chain. If such a retailer conditions its purchases from its suppliers on the suppliers not selling identical products to its competing toy outlets, is that retailer committing a prohibited "unfair method of competition"? Does it make a difference if the suppliers condition their refusal to sell to rival toy outlets on their own rival suppliers doing the same? Does it matter if the large retailer persuades each supplier to engage in this behaviour by assuring it that its rivals are also declining to sell to the rival retail outlets? Here the physical-or near physical-events are the retailer conditioning its purchases on its suppliers not selling identical products to competing retail outlets; that the suppliers are conditioning their refusal to sell to rival outlets on their own rival suppliers doing the same; and that the large retailer is persuading each supplier to engage in this behavior by assuring it that its rivals are also declining to sell to the rival retail outlets. If there is any dispute about these events, the agency must resolve the dispute. But even after the agency resolves that dispute about what happened, the agency must still resolve a dispute about how to evaluate the events that the agency decided did happen: The agency must make an evaluative judgment as to whether the physical-or near physical events found are or are not "unfair methods of competition". And in order to make that evaluative judgment, the agency must formulate some criterion for judgment — just as the jury has the reasonably prudent person criterion to determine negligence and its everyday experience as the criterion for proximate causation. In tabular form, the agency decisional process appears:

Physical or near physical events	Judgment to be made after answering 1st column questions.	Judgment criterion
1. Did the respondent toy retailer condition its purchases on its suppliers not selling to competing retailers? 2. Did the suppliers condition their refusal to sell to rival toy outlets on their own rival suppliers doing the same? 3. Did the respondent retailer persuade each supplier to engage in this behavior by assuring it that its rivals were are also declining to sell to the rival retail outlets?	1. If the behaviors described in column 1 occurred, did the respondent commit an "unfair method of competition"/	?

Here the judgment criterion to be used in determining the applicability of the words of conclusion (i.e., "unfair methods of competition") is not so obvious as the judgment criteria to be used in determining the applicability of the words of conclusion in the preceding example (i.e., "negligence", "proximate cause"). In the preceding example, common experience furnished the judgment criteria. But common experience will not provide an answer to whether a certain type of condition attached to a purchase is or is not an "unfair method of competition".

The essential point of this analysis, of course, is to recognize the need for an agency to develop judgment criteria to answer questions about the applicability of statutory "words of conclusion" to physical or near physical events. Once we have recognized the need for an agency to use a judgment criterion and to create that criterion, we are in a position to inquire what that criterion is. In some cases that criterion may be quite fully formulated. Consider, for example, the judgment criterion used by the National Labor Relations Board in the *Curtin Matheson Scientific, Inc.* case, *infra*, where the Board determined that the employer had committed an unfair labor practice by failing to bargain with the union because, contrary to the employer's contentions, the employer did not possess "a reasonable good faith doubt as to the majority status of the union". In *Curtin Matheson* — as the case brings out — the judgment criterion employed by the Board to determine that question was a complex one consisting of presumptions and rules about their use.

The Board had formulated a judgment criterion which said, in effect, that after a union is once certified, (1) the Board will presume that the union commands support from a majority of the workers unless the employer overcomes that presumption by evidence of a good faith doubt; but (2) the Board will not accept evidence that the original majority of union supporters has been replaced by substitutes hired during a strike as indicative by itself that the union no longer commands majority support. This rather complex judgment criterion was described in the case. Observe that judgment criterion in *Curtin Matheson* is quite precise and once we discover it, we know how the agency will decide other cases involving replacement workers. Sometimes, however, agencies are not so forthright about revealing their judgment criteria as was the NLRB and we are left to infer those criteria from limited data at our disposal.

Note, however, that although we have determined the content of the judgment criterion used by the Labor Board (a presumption and rules about inferences to be drawn from evidence about replacements), we have not yet focused upon the question of how the Board arrived at this judgment criterion. The Board might have arrived at its complex judgment criterion as a result of its experience in labor relations. It might have learned from experience that substitute workers often sympathize with the union and accept jobs replacing strikers only reluctantly and out of economic necessity. It might have learned from its experience that the substitute workers support the union as the workers' representative because they hope to benefit from the union's representation during the post-strike period. Or, the Board might have adopted its judgment criterion solely as a matter of choosing the policy which will best further the goals of the National Labor Relations Act. Or, the Board may have adopted the judgment criterion from a combination of its experience with its judgments about policy.

Consider the judgment criterion employed by the Board in the *Stow Manufacturing* Co. case *infra*. Was the Board's judgment criterion fully formulated? Was it formulated in a manner which would be applicable to many cases? What factors from the Board's "experience" would have been influential in the formulation of the Board's judgment criterion? Was Judge Hand correct when he asserted that the Board had "an access to valid general propositions which make sequences causal that are not causal to untutored minds"? Why are not the Board's "valid general propositions" known outside the Board? Or are they? Does Judge Hand mean that the Board has been entrusted with authority to formulate "valid general propositions" and that those propositions are judgment criteria or are the premises upon which the Board may formulate judgment criteria? If so, then the Board was doing the same thing in *Stow* as it did in *Curtin*, was it not? The question remains as to what factors from the Board's "experience" were drawn upon in the formulation of the judgment criteria employed by the Board in the *Stow* case. In referring to the Board's access to general propositions, Judge Hand may have been saying that he himself either did not know those factors or did not agree with the Board's judgment criteria which were developed from them.

In reading the following cases, try to discover:

1) The judgment criterion used by the agency in each case to determine the applicability (or inapplicability) of the relevant words of conclusion to the facts before it.

2) The factors which gave rise to that judgment criterion.

3) Consider in each case whether those factors always arose from the agency's "experience."

NLRB v. CURTIN MATHESON SCIENTIFIC, INC.
494 U.S. 775 (1990)

JUSTICE MARSHALL delivered the opinion of the Court.

This case presents the question whether the National Labor Relations Board, in evaluating an employer's claim that it had a reasonable basis for doubting a union's majority support, must presume that striker replacements oppose the union. We hold that the Board acted within its discretion in refusing to adopt a presumption of replacement opposition to the union and therefore reverse the judgment of the Court of Appeals.

I

Upon certification by the NLRB as the exclusive bargaining agent for a unit of employees, a union enjoys an irrebuttable presumption of majority support for one year. . . . During that time, an employer's refusal to bargain with the union is per se an unfair labor practice under §§ 8(a)(1) and 8(a)(5) of the National Labor Relations Act. . . . After the first year, the presumption continues but is rebuttable. . . . Under the Board's longstanding approach, an employer may rebut that presumption by showing that, at the time of the refusal to bargain, either (1) the union did not in fact enjoy majority support, or (2) the employer had a "good faith" doubt, founded on a sufficient objective basis, of the union's majority support. . . . The question presented in this case is whether the Board must, in determining whether an employer has presented sufficient objective evidence of a good-faith doubt, presume that striker replacements oppose the union.

The Board has long presumed that new employees hired in nonstrike circumstances support the incumbent union in the same proportion as the employees they replace. . . . The Board's approach to evaluating the union sentiments of employees hired to replace strikers, however, has not been so consistent. Initially, the Board appeared to assume that replacements did not support the union. . . . [Later] the Board reversed course completely, stating that striker replacements, like new employees generally, are presumed to support the union in the same ratio as the strikers they replaced. . . .

In 1987, after several Courts of Appeals rejected the Board's approach, the Board determined that no universal generalizations could be made about replacements' union sentiments that would justify a presumption either of support for or of opposition to the union. Station *KKHI*, 284 N.L.R.B. 1339 (1987). On the one hand, the Board found that the prounion presumption lacked empirical foundation because "incumbent unions and strikers sometimes have shown hostility toward the permanent replacements" and "replacements are typically aware of the union's primary concern for the striker's welfare, rather than that of the replacements." . . . On the other hand, the Board found that an antiunion presumption was "equally unsupportable" factually. . . . The Board observed that a striker replacement "may be forced to work for financial reasons, or may disapprove of the strike in question but still desire union representation and would support other union initiatives." . . . Moreover, the Board found as a matter of policy that adoption of an antiunion presumption would "substantially impair the 'employees' right to strike by adding to the risk of replacement the risk of loss of the bargaining representative as soon as replacements equal in number to the strikers are willing to cross the picket line." . . . Accordingly, the Board held that it would not apply any presumption regarding striker replacements' union sentiments, but would determine their views on a case-by-case basis.

We now turn to the Board's application of its Station KKHI no-presumption approach in this case. Respondent Curtin Matheson Scientific, Inc., buys and sells laboratory instruments and supplies. In 1970, the Board certified Teamsters Local 968, General Drivers, Warehousemen and Helpers as the collective-bargaining agent for respondent's production and maintenance employees. On May 21, 1979, the most recent bargaining agreement between respondent and the Union expired. Respondent made its final offer for a new agreement on May 25, but the Union rejected that offer. Respondent then locked out the 27 bargaining-unit employees. On June 12, respondent renewed its May 25 offer, but the Union again rejected it. The Union then commenced an economic strike. The record contains no evidence of any strike-related violence or threats of violence.

Five employees immediately crossed the picket line and reported for work. On June 25, while the strike was still in effect, respondent hired 29 permanent replacement employees to replace the 22 strikers. The Union ended its strike on July 16, offering to accept unconditionally respondent's May 25 contract offer. On July 20, respondent informed the Union that the May 25 offer was no longer available. In addition, respondent withdrew recognition from the Union and refused to bargain further, stating that it doubted that the Union was supported by a majority of the employees in the unit. Respondent subsequently refused to provide the Union with information it had requested concerning the total number of bargaining-unit employees on the payroll, and the job classification and seniority of each employee. As of July 20, the bargaining unit consisted of 19 strikers, 25 permanent replacements, and the 5 employees who had crossed the picket line at the strike's inception.

On July 30, the Union filed an unfair labor practice charge with the Board. Following an investigation, the General Counsel issued a complaint, alleging that respondent's withdrawal of recognition, refusal to execute a contract embodying the terms of the May 25 offer, and failure to provide the requested information violated §§ 8(a)(1) and 8(a)(5) of the NLRA . . . In its defense to the charge, respondent claimed that it had a reasonably based, good-faith doubt of the Union's majority status. The Administrative Law judge agreed with respondent and dismissed the complaint. The Board, however, reversed, holding that respondent lacked sufficient objective basis to doubt the Union's majority support. . . .

First, the Board noted that the crossover of 5 of the original 27 employees did not in itself support an inference that the 5 had repudiated the Union, because their failure to join the strike may have "indicate[d] their economic concerns rather than a lack of support for the union." . . . Second, the Board found that the resignation from their jobs of two of the original bargaining-unit employees, including the chief shop steward, after the commencement of the strike did not indicate opposition to the Union, but merely served to reduce the size of the bargaining unit as of the date of respondent's withdrawal of recognition. . . . Third, the Board discounted statements made by six employees to a representative of respondent during the strike. Although some of these statements may have indicated rejection of the Union as the bargaining representative, the Board noted, others "appear[ed] ambiguous at best." . . . Moreover, the Board stated, "[e]ven attributing to them the meaning most favorable to the Respondent, it would merely signify that 6 employees of a total bargaining unit of approximately 50 did not desire to keep the Union as the collective-bargaining representative

Finally, regarding respondent's hiring of striker replacements, the Board stated that, in accordance with the Station *KKHI* approach, it would "not use any presumptions with respect to [the replacements'] union sentiments," but would instead "take a case-by-case approach [and] require additional evidence of a lack of union support on the replacements' part in evaluating the significance of this factor in the employer's showing of good-faith doubt

The Board noted that respondent's only evidence of the replacements' attitudes toward the Union was its employee relations director's account of a conversation with one of the replacements. The replacement employee reportedly told her that he had worked in union and nonunion workplaces and did not see any need for a union as long as the company treated him well; in addition, he said that he did not think the Union in this case represented the employees. . . . The Board did not determine whether this statement indicated the replacement employee's repudiation of the Union, but found that the statement was, in any event, an insufficient basis for "inferring the union sentiments of the replacement employees as a group." . . .

The Board therefore concluded that "the evidence [was] insufficient to rebut the presumption of the Union's continuing majority status.". . . Accordingly, the Board held that respondent had violated §§ 8(a)(1) and 8(a)(5) by withdrawing recognition from the Union, failing to furnish the requested information, and refusing to execute a contract embodying the terms respondent had offered on May 25, 1979. The Board ordered respondent to bargain with the Union on request, provide the requisite information, execute an agreement, and make the bargaining-unit employees whole for whatever losses they had suffered from respondent's failure to execute a contract.

The Court of Appeals, in a divided opinion, refused to enforce the Board's order, holding that respondent was justified in doubting the Union's majority support. . . .

III

A

This Court has emphasized often that the NLRB has the primary responsibility for developing and applying national labor policy. . . . This Court therefore has accorded Board rules considerable deference. . . . We will uphold a Board rule as long as it is rational and consistent with the Act. . . . even if we would have formulated a different rule had we sat on the Board. . . . Furthermore, a Board rule is entitled to deference even if it represents a departure from the Board's prior policy.

B

Before assessing the Board's justification for rejecting the antiunion presumption, we will make clear precisely how that presumption would differ in operation from the Board's current approach. . . . [T]he starting point for the Board's analysis is the basic presumption that the union is supported by a majority of bargaining-unit employees. The employer bears the burden of rebutting that presumption, after the certification year, either by showing that the union in fact lacks majority support or by demonstrating a sufficient objective basis for doubting the union's majority status. Respondent here urges that in evaluating an employer's claim of a good-faith doubt, the Board must adopt a second, subsidiary presumption — that replacement employees oppose the union. Under this approach, if a majority of employees in the bargaining unit were striker replacements, the employer would not need to offer any objective evidence of the employees' union sentiments to rebut the presumption of the union's continuing majority status. The presumption of the replacements' opposition to the union would, in effect, override the presumption of continuing majority status. In contrast, under its no-presumption approach the Board "take[s] into account the particular circumstances surrounding each strike and the hiring of replacements, while retaining the long-standing requirement that the employer must come forth with some objective evidence to substantiate his doubt of continuing majority status." . . .

C

We find the Board's no-presumption approach rational as an empirical matter. Presumptions normally arise when proof of one fact renders the existence of another fact "so probable that it is sensible and timesaving to assume the truth of [the inferred] fact . . . until the adversary disproves it." . . . Although replacements often may not favor the incumbent union, the Board reasonably concluded, in light of its long experience in addressing these issues, that replacements may in some circumstances desire union representation despite their willingness to cross the picket line. Economic concerns, for instance, may force a replacement employee to work for a struck employer even though he otherwise supports the union and wants the benefits of union representation. . . . In addition, a replacement, like a nonstriker or a strike crossover, may disagree with the purpose or strategy of the particular strike and refuse to support that strike, while still wanting that union's representation at the bargaining table.

In sum, the Board recognized that the circumstances surrounding each strike and replacements' reasons for crossing a picket line vary greatly. Even if replacements often do not support the union, then, it was not irrational for the Board to conclude that the probability of replacement opposition to the union is insufficient to justify an antiunion presumption.

D

The Board's refusal to adopt an antiunion presumption is also consistent with the Act's "overriding policy" of achieving " 'industrial peace.' " . . . In *Fall River*, the Court held that the presumption of continuing majority support for a union "further[s] this policy by promot[ing] stability in collective-bargaining relationships, without impairing the free choice of employees.' " . . . The Court reasoned that this presumption "enable[s] a union to concentrate on obtaining and fairly administering a collective-bargaining agreement without worrying that, unless it produces immediate results, it will lose majority support." . . . In addition, this presumption "remove[s] any temptation on the part of the employer to avoid good-faith bargaining in the hope that, by delaying, it will undermine the union's support among the employees." . . .

The Board's approach to determining the union views of strike replacements is directed at this same goal because it limits employers' ability to oust a union without adducing any evidence of the employees' union sentiments and encourages negotiated solutions to strikes. It was reasonable for the Board to conclude that the antiunion presumption, in contrast, could allow an employer to eliminate the union merely by hiring a sufficient number of replacement employees. That rule thus might encourage the employer to avoid good-faith bargaining over a strike settlement, and instead to use the strike as a means of removing the union altogether. . . .

Furthermore, it was reasonable for the Board to decide that the antiunion presumption might chill employees' exercise of their statutory right to engage in "concerted activities," including the right to strike. . . . The Board's no-presumption approach is rationally directed at protecting the bargaining process and preserving employees' right to engage in concerted activity. We therefore find, in light of the considerable deference we accord Board rules, . . . that the Board's approach is consistent with the Act.

IV

We hold that the Board's refusal to adopt a presumption that striker replacements oppose the union is rational and consistent with the Act. We therefore reverse the judgment of the Court of Appeals and remand for further proceedings consistent with this opinion.

It is so ordered.

Justice Scalia, with whom Justice O'Connor and Justice Kennedy join, dissenting.

The Court makes heavy weather out of what is, under well-established principles of administrative law, a straightforward case. The National Labor Relations Board (NLRB or Board) has established as one of the central factual determinations to be made in § 8(a)(5) unfair-labor-practice adjudications, whether the employer had a reasonable, good-faith doubt concerning the majority status of the union at the time it requested to bargain. The Board held in the present case that such a doubt was not established by a record showing that at the time of the union's request a majority of the bargaining unit were strike replacements, and containing no affirmative evidence that any of those replacements supported the union. The question presented is whether that factual finding is supported by substantial evidence. Since the principal employment-related interest of strike replacements (to retain their jobs) is almost invariably opposed to the principal interest of the striking union (to replace them with its striking members) it seems to me impossible to conclude on this record that the employer did not have a reasonable, good-faith doubt regarding the union's majority status. The Board's factual finding being unsupported by substantial evidence, it cannot stand. I therefore dissent from the judgment reversing the Fifth Circuit's refusal to enforce the Board's order.

III

The Court never directly addresses the question whether there was substantial evidence to support the Board's conclusion that respondent had not established a reasonable good-faith doubt of the union's majority status. Indeed, it asserts that that question is not even at issue, since "[t]he question on which we granted the Board's petition for certiorari is whether, in *assessing* whether a particular employer possessed a good-faith-doubt, the Board must adopt a general presumption of replacement opposition to the union." . . . The mistake here is to treat as equivalent elements of decisionmaking, the presumption that strike replacements do support the union, and the evidentiary inference that strike replacements do not support the union. They are not different applications of the same device, and it does not display a commitment to be governed only by the "real facts" to reject both the one and the other. The former was applied "as a matter of law," . . . and not as the product of inference, which is "[a] process of reasoning by which a fact or proposition sought to be established is deduced as a logical consequence from other facts, or a state of facts, already proved or admitted." Black's Law Dictionary 700 (5th ed. 1979). One can refer to the product of an inference as a presumption. . . . But that sort of presumption, which the text writers used to call "presumption of fact," see 9 J. Wigmore, Evidence § 2491, p. 304 (J. Chadbourn rev. ed. 1981), is quite different from the . . . "presumption of law" insofar as concerns both agency power and judicial review, as I shall proceed to explain.

It is the proper business of the Board, as of most agencies, to deal in both presumptions (i.e., presumptions of law) and inferences (presumptions of fact). The former it may create and apply *in the teeth of the* facts, as means of implementing authorized law or policy in the course of adjudication. An example is the virtually irrebuttable presumption of majority support for the union during the year following the union's certification by the Board. . . . The latter, however—inferences (or presumptions of fact) — are not creatures of the Board but its masters, representing the dictates of reason and logic that must be applied in making adjudicatory factual determinations. Whenever an agency's action is reversed in court for lack of "substantial evidence," the reason is that the agency has ignored inferences that reasonably must be drawn, or has drawn inferences that reasonably cannot be. As I have discussed above, that is what happened here.

Of course the Board may choose to implement authorized law or policy in adjudication by forbidding a rational inference, just as it may do so by requiring a nonrational one (which is what a presumption of law is). And perhaps it could lawfully have reached the outcome it did here in that fashion — saying that even though it must reasonably be inferred that an employer has good-faith doubt of majority status when more than half of the bargaining unit are strike replacements whose job rights have not been resolved, we will not permit that inference to be made. (This would produce an effect close to a rule of law eliminating the good-faith doubt defense except for cases in which the employer can demonstrate, by employee statements, lack of support for the union.) But that is not what the agency did here. It relied on the reasoning of Station KKHI, which rested upon the conclusion that, as a matter of logic and reasoning, "the hiring of permanent replacements who cross a picket line, in itself, does not support an inference that the replacements repudiate the union as collective-bargaining representative." . . . That is simply false. It is bad fact-finding, and must be reversed under the "substantial evidence" test.

Questions and Comments

1.   Do you agree with Justice Marshall that the issue was the lawfulness of the Board's refusal to accept a presumption "that striker replacements oppose the union"? Or do you agree with Justice Scalia that the issue should be stated in terms of whether the Board's decision was based upon substantial evidence?

2.   How many presumptions were involved in *Curtin Matheson?* Were these presumptions of law or presumptions of fact?

3.   Is a presumption of fact really an inference?

4.   Was Justice Scalia correct in his contention that the Labor Board and the Court majority were confusing presumptions of fact with presumptions of law?

5.   Was the Labor Board employing a presumption (of law) as a means of furthering labor policy? How do you think that Judges Hand and Frank would have decided *Curtin Matheson?* Would they have phrased the opinion in terms of presumptions or in terms of the application of the substantial evidence standard?

6.   Why did not Justice Scalia vote to uphold the Board on the ground that the Board's decision was the result of applying the Board's policy to the facts? Would Justice Scalia deny that the Board — and not the Court — is charged by Congress with developing labor policy under the National Labor Relations Act?

7.   Suppose the Labor Board had adopted as a rule the requirement that the presumption of majority support for the union cannot be rebutted by evidence that the majority of workers are replacements. Do you think that Justice Scalia would vote to uphold such a rule? Could you describe such a rule as a "presumption of law"? If the Board had forthrightly adopted such a rule, would Justice Scalia be as quick to condemn it as he was to condemn the Board's actual decision?

8.   Does Justice Scalia believe that the Board's result could only have been reached on policy grounds? Was Justice Scalia's rejection of the Board's position based upon his view that the Board was not honest in describing the policy basis for

its result? In *SEC v. Chenery Corp.*, 318 U.S. 80 (1943), *infra*, Chapter 6, the Court held that when reviewing an action of an agency, the court must base its review on the rationale used by the agency to justify its action. Could Justice Scalia have drawn support for his position in *Curtin* from *Chenery?*

9.   The Labor Board has far more experience with labor matters than any court, including the Supreme Court. Might the Labor Board be better able to generalize about the probabilities that replacement workers support (or do not support) the union than a court? Could not the Board incorporate such probabilities into presumptions of fact? The ability to draw such inferences is one of the advantages which a specialized agency like the Labor Board possesses. Courts sometimes refer to that ability as "expertise".

10.   Does Justice Marshall rely at all on the Board's expertise? How do you think Justice Scalia would reply to the contention that he [Justice Scalia] fails to accord adequate respect to the Board's expertise?

The *Stow* Case: A Predecessor of *Curtin?*

NLRB v. Stow Mfg. Co., **217 F.2d 900 (2d Cir. 1954)**, *cert denied*, *348 U.S. 964 (1955).* A majority of the respondent's employees had signed cards authorizing the Machinists Union to represent them. Both the respondent and the union petitioned the Board to hold an election. Despite a prohibition on such activities, the respondent held various meetings with its employees prior to the election at which it discussed working conditions. The union lost the election. The Board ordered the employer nonetheless to bargain with the union on the ground that it was the employer's pre-election activities which caused the union to lose the election. On review, the Second Circuit upheld the Board's determination on causation: "The Board is the tribunal to determine the effect of what was done upon the minds of the employees who were present at those meetings. . . . The immunity of the Board's conclusions from judicial review on such occasions is a consequence of its putative specialized experience in the field of labor relations: an experience that is thought to enable it to appraise causes and consequences that escape the perception of those less widely acquainted with those relations. Thus, we accept the conclusions of a specialized tribunal, made upon evidence that would not prove them to an ordinary, or 'lay' court, so to say. This involves imputing to the specialized tribunal an access to valid general propositions which make sequences causal that are not causal to untutored minds."

Questions and Comments

1.   Did Judge Hand really believe that the Labor Board can perceive causes and consequences that others cannot see? That it has access to "valid general propositions" to which others have no access? Or did he use this phraseology as a means of saying that the Board's decisions — within a wide range — were immune from judicial correction? Do you think his choice of words reflected his disagreement with the Board's conclusions?

2.   The unique insight into causes and consequences which Hand attributed to the Labor Board was said to rest upon the Board's "specialized experience". Would

Judge Hand have granted the same deference to the conclusions of the Board on an issue which the Board decided for the first time (and on which, therefore, the Board possessed no experience)?

3.   In *Stow* the union which once had a majority lost an election after the employer had engaged in unfair labor practices (i.e., the employer's pre-election meetings and discussions of working conditions with its employees). Would the Labor Board have been justified in adopting a general approach to all such cases which attributed a causal connection between the unfair labor practice and the loss of the election? Would such an approach discourage unfair labor practices? Would such a general approach therefore further the goals of the National Labor Relations Act? Would such an approach therefore be justified under the Act? Would the fact (if true) that it was difficult to prove a causal connection in any individual case provide further support for such a general approach?

4.   Is Judge Hand's exotic language in *Stow* merely saying that the Board will be upheld on policy grounds? That the Board's attribution of a causal connection between the unfair labor practice and the union's loss of the election is a rational way of furthering the goals of the Labor Act? Could the attribution of such a causal connection be cast in terms of a presumption? If so, would the presumption be one of fact or law?

5.   How do you think that Justice Scalia would have decided the *Stow* case?

Must an Agency be Forthright about the Standards of Proof it Employs?

Justice Scalia was concerned in *Curtis Matheson Scientific* that the Labor Board was not being forthright about its use of presumptions. Had the agency adopted a presumption that the employer could not rebut? Or had it imposed a higher level of proof for rebuttal than preponderance-of-the-evidence (the normal standard of proof in a trial proceeding)? Was the Board forthright in *Stow*? Was the Board imposing a presumption for policy reasons that causation would always be found between an employer's unlawful pre-election activities and the union's later loss of an election? These issues came to a head in the case below.

In ***Allentown Mack Sales & Service, Inc. v. NLRB*, 522 U.S. 359 (1998)**, an employer informed union representatives that it doubted that the union enjoyed majority support among its employees and arranged for a poll of the employees to determine their support or lack of support of the union. In an unfair labor practice proceeding, the Board ruled that the employer failed to establish its good faith doubt. On judicial review, the Supreme Court considered the obligation of the Board to be forthright about the proof required of an employer seeking to establish its good faith doubt. After reviewing the evidence, the Court continued as follows:

> . . . . Giving fair weight to Allentown's circumstantial evidence, we think it quite impossible for a rational factfinder to avoid the conclusion that Allentown had reasonable, good-faith grounds to doubt — to be uncertain about — the union's retention of majority support.

IV

That conclusion would make this a fairly straightforward administrative-law case, except for the contention that the Board's factfinding here was not an aberration. Allentown asserts that, although "the Board continues to cite the words of the good faith doubt branch of its withdrawal of recognition standard," a systematic review of the Board's decisions will reveal that "it has in practice eliminated the good faith doubt branch in favor of a strict head count." . . . The Board denies (not too persuasively) that it has insisted upon a strict head count, but does defend its factfinding in this case by saying that it has regularly rejected similarly persuasive demonstrations of reasonable good-faith doubt in prior decisions. The Court of Appeals in fact accepted that defense, relying on those earlier, similar decisions to conclude that the Board's findings were supported by substantial evidence here. . . . That the current decision may conform to a long pattern is also suggested by academic commentary. One scholar, after conducting "[a] thorough review of the withdrawal of recognition case law," concluded that

"circumstantial evidence, no matter how abundant, is rarely, if ever, enough to satisfy the good-faith doubt test. In practice, the Board deems the test satisfied only if the employer has proven that a majority of the bargaining unit has expressly repudiated the union. Such direct evidence, however, is nearly impossible to gather lawfully. Thus, the Board's good-faith doubt standard, although ostensibly a highly fact-dependent totality-of-the-circumstances test, approaches a per se rule in application. . . ." Flynn, The Costs and Benefits of "Hiding the Ball": NLRB Policymaking and the Failure of Judicial Review," 75 B.U.L.Rev. 387, 394–395 (1995) (footnotes omitted).

See also Weeks, The Union's Mid-Contract Loss of Majority Support: A Waivering Presumption, 20 Wake Forest L.Rev. 883, 889 (1984). Members of this Court have observed the same phenomenon. See *NLRB v. Curtin Matheson Scientific, Inc.*, 494 U.S. 775, 797 (1990) (REHNQUIST, C.J., concurring) ("[S]ome recent decisions suggest that [the Board] now requires an employer to show that individual employees have 'expressed desires' to repudiate the incumbent union in order to establish a reasonable doubt of the union's majority status"); Id., at 799 (Blackmun, J., dissenting) ("[T]he Board appears to require that good-faith doubt be established by express avowals of individual employees").

It is certainly conceivable that an adjudicating agency might consistently require a particular substantive standard to be established by a quantity or character of evidence so far beyond what reason and logic would require as to make it apparent that the announced standard is not really the effective one. And it is conceivable that in certain categories of cases an adjudicating agency which purports to be applying a preponderance standard of proof might so consistently demand in fact more than a preponderance, that all should be on notice from its case law that the genuine burden of proof is more than a preponderance. The question arises, then, whether, if that should be the situation that obtains here, we ought to measure the evidentiary support for the Board's decision against the standards consistently applied rather than the standards recited. As a theoretical matter (and leaving aside the question of legal authority), the Board could certainly have raised the bar for employer polling or withdrawal of recognition by imposing a more stringent requirement than the reasonable-doubt test, or by adopting a formal requirement that employers establish their reasonable doubt by more than a preponderance of the evidence. Would it make any difference if the Board achieved precisely the same result by formally leaving in place the reasonable-doubt and preponderance standards, but consistently applying them as though they meant something other than what they say? We think it would.

The Administrative Procedure Act, which governs the proceedings of administrative agencies and related judicial review, establishes a scheme of "reasoned decisionmaking." *Motor Vehicle Mfrs. Assn. of United States, Inc. v. State Farm Mut. Automobile Ins. Co.*, 463 U.S. 29, 52 (1983). Not only must an agency's decreed result be within the scope of its lawful authority, but the process by which it reaches that result must be logical and rational. Courts enforce this principle with regularity when they set aside agency regulations which, though well within the agencies' scope of authority, are not supported by the reasons that the agencies adduce. See *SEC v. Chenery Corp.*, 318 U.S. 80 (1943); *SEC v. Chenery Corp.*, 332 U.S. 194. The National Labor Relations Board, uniquely among major federal administrative agencies, has chosen to promulgate virtually all the legal rules in its field through adjudication rather than rulemaking. See, e.g., *NLRB v. Bell Aerospace Co.*, 416 U.S. 267, 294–295 (1974). (To our knowledge, only one regulation has ever been adopted by the Board, dealing with the appropriate size of bargaining units in the health care industry. See 29 C.F.R. § 103.30 (1997)). But adjudication is subject to the requirement of reasoned decisionmaking as well. It is hard to imagine a more violent breach of that requirement than applying a rule of primary conduct or a standard of proof which is in fact different from the rule or standard formally announced. And the consistent repetition of that breach can hardly mend it.

Reasoned decisionmaking, in which the rule announced is the rule applied, promotes sound results, and unreasoned decisionmaking the opposite. The evil of a decision that applies a standard other than the one it enunciates spreads in both directions, preventing both consistent application of the law by subordinate agency personnel (notably administrative law judges), and effective review of the law by the courts. These consequences are well exemplified by a recent withdrawal-of-recognition case in which the Board explicitly reaffirmed its adherence to the preponderance-of-the-evidence standard. One of the Board's ALJ's, interpreting the agency's prior cases as many others have, had concluded that the Board in fact required " 'clear, cogent, and convincing' " evidence that the union no longer commanded a majority. *Laidlaw Waste Systems, Inc.*, 307 N.L.R.B. 1211 (1992). On review the Board rejected that standard, insisting that "in order to rebut the presumption of an incumbent union's majority status, an employer must show by a preponderance of the evidence . . . objective factors sufficient to support a reasonable and good-faith doubt of the union's majority." Ibid. So far, so good. The Board then went on to add, however, that "[t]his is not to say that the terms 'clear, cogent, and convincing' have no significance at all in withdrawal of recognition cases." Ibid. It then proceeded to make the waters impenetrably muddy with the following:

> "It is fair to say that the Board will not find that an employer has supported its defense by a preponderance of the evidence if the employee statements and conduct relied on are not clear and cogent rejections of the union as a bargaining agent, i.e., are simply not convincing manifestations, taken as a whole, of a loss of majority support. The opposite of "clear, cogent, and convincing" evidence in this regard might be fairly described as "speculative, conjectural, and vague" — evidence that plainly does not meet the preponderance-of-the-evidence burden of proof." Id., at 1211–1212.

Each sentence of this explanation is nonsense, and the two sentences together are not even compatibly nonsensical. "Preponderance of the evidence" and "clear and convincing evidence" describe well known, contrasting standards of proof. To say, as the first sentence does, that a preponderance standard demands "clear and convincing manifestations, taken as a whole" is to convert that standard into a higher one; and to say, as the second sentence does, that whatever is not "speculative, conjectural or vague" meets the "clear, cogent, and convincing" standard is to reconvert that standard into a lower one. And the offsetting errors do not produce rationality but compounded confusion. If the Board's application of the preponderance standard is indeed accurately described by this passage, it is hard for the ALJ to know what to do with the next case.

A case like *Laidlaw*, or a series of cases that exemplify in practice its divorcing of the rule announced from the rule applied, also frustrates judicial review. If revision of the Board's standard of proof can be achieved thus subtly and obliquely, it becomes a much more complicated enterprise for a court of appeals to determine whether substantial evidence supports the conclusion that the required standard has or has not been met. It also becomes difficult for this Court to know, when certiorari is sought, whether the case involves the generally applicable issue of the Board's adoption of an unusually high standard of proof, or rather just the issue of an allegedly mistaken evidentiary judgment in the particular case. An agency should not be able to impede judicial review, and indeed even political oversight, by disguising its policymaking as factfinding.

Because reasoned decisionmaking demands it, and because the systemic consequences of any other approach are unacceptable, the Board must be required to apply in fact the clearly understood legal standards that it enunciates in principle, such as good-faith reasonable doubt and preponderance of the evidence. Reviewing courts are entitled to take those standards to mean what they say, and to conduct substantial-evidence review on that basis. Even the most consistent and hence predictable Board departure from proper application of those standards will not alter the legal rule by which the agency's factfinding is to be judged.

That principle is not, as JUSTICE BREYER'S dissent suggests, inconsistent with our decisions according "substantial deference to an agency's interpretation of its own regulations." *Thomas Jefferson Univ. v. Shalala*, 512 U.S. 504, 512 (1994). Substantive review of an agency's interpretation of its regulations is governed only by that general provision of the Administrative Procedure Act which requires courts to set aside agency action that is "arbitrary, capricious, an abuse of discretion, or otherwise not in accordance with law," 5 U.S.C. § 706(2)(A). It falls well within this text to give the agency the benefit of the doubt as to the meaning of its regulation. On-the-record agency factfinding, however, is also governed by a provision which requires the agency action to be set aside if it is "unsupported by substantial evidence," § 706(2)(E) — which is the very specific requirement at issue here. See also 29 U.S.C. § 160(e) ("The findings of the Board with respect to questions of fact if supported by substantial evidence on the record considered as a whole shall be conclusive"). The "substantial evidence" test itself already gives the agency the benefit of the doubt, since it requires not the degree of evidence which satisfies the court that the requisite fact exists, but merely the degree that could satisfy a reasonable factfinder. See *Columbian Enameling & Stamping Co.*, 306 U.S., at 300. This is an objective test, and there is no room within it for deference to an agency's eccentric view of what a reasonable factfinder ought to demand. We do not, moreover (we could not possibly), search to find revisions of the agency's rules — revisions of the requisite fact that the adjudication is supposed to determine — hidden in the agency's factual findings. In the regime envisioned by the dissent — a regime in which inadequate factual findings become simply a revision of the standard that the Board's (adjudicatorily adopted) rules set forth, thereby converting those findings into rule-interpretations to which judges must defer — the "substantial evidence" factual review provision of the APA becomes a nullity.

The Board can, of course, forthrightly and explicitly adopt counterfactual evidentiary presumptions (which are in effect substantive rules of law) as a way of furthering particular legal or policy goals — for example, the Board's irrebuttable presumption of majority support for the union during the year following certification, see, e.g., *Station KKHI*, 284 N.L.R.B. 1339, 1340 (1987), enf'd, 891 F.2d 230 (C.A.9 1989). The Board might also be justified in forthrightly and explicitly adopting a rule of evidence that categorically excludes certain testimony on policy grounds, without reference to its inherent probative value. (Such clearly announced rules of law or of evidentiary exclusion would of course be subject to judicial review for their reasonableness and their compatibility with the Act.) That is not the sort of Board action at issue here, however, but rather the Board's allegedly systematic undervaluation of certain evidence, or allegedly systematic exaggeration of what the evidence must prove. See, e.g., Westbrook Bowl,

293 N.L.R.B. 1000, 1001, n. 11 (1989) ("The Board has stated that 'testimony concerning conversations directly with the employees involved . . . is much more reliable than testimony concerning merely a few employees ostensibly conveying the sentiments of their fellows' "), quoting *Sofco, Inc.*, 268 N.L.R.B. 159, 160, n. 10 (1983). When the Board purports to be engaged in simple factfinding, unconstrained by substantive presumptions or evidentiary rules of exclusion, it is not free to prescribe what inferences from the evidence it will accept and reject, but must draw all those inferences that the evidence fairly demands. "Substantial evidence" review exists precisely to ensure that the Board achieves minimal compliance with this obligation, which is the foundation of all honest and legitimate adjudication.

For the foregoing reasons, we need not determine whether the Board has consistently rejected or discounted probative evidence so as to cause "good faith reasonable doubt" or "preponderance of the evidence" to mean something more than what the terms connote. The line of precedents relied on by the ALJ and the Court of Appeals could not render irrelevant to the Board's decision, and hence to our review, any evidence that tends to establish the existence of a good-faith reasonable doubt. It was therefore error, for example, for the ALJ to discount Ron Mohr's opinion about lack of union support because of "the Board's historical treatment of unverified assertions by an employee about another employee's sentiments." And it was error for the Court of Appeals to rely upon the fact that "[t]he Board has consistently questioned the reliability of reports by one employee of the antipathy of other employees toward their union." 83 F.3d, at 1488, citing *Westbrook Bowl, supra*, at 1001, n. 11; *Sofco, Inc., supra*, at, 160, n. 10. Assuming that those assessments of the Board's prior behavior are true, they nonetheless provide no justification for the Board's factual inferences here. Of course the Board is entitled to be skeptical about the employer's claimed reliance on second-hand reports when the reporter has little basis for knowledge, or has some incentive to mislead. But that is a matter of logic and sound inference from all the circumstances, not an arbitrary rule of disregard to be extracted from prior Board decisions.

The same is true of the Board precedents holding that "an employee's statements of dissatisfaction with the quality of union representation may not be treated as opposition to union representation," and that "an employer may not rely on an employee's anti-union sentiments, expressed during a job interview in which the employer has indicated that there will be no union." 83 F.3d, at 1488, citing *Destileria Serralles, Inc.*, 289 N.L.R.B. 51 (1988), enf'd, 882 F.2d 19 (C.A.1 1989), and *Middleboro Fire Apparatus, Inc.*, 234 N.L.R.B. 888, 894, enf'd, 590 F.2d 4 (C.A.1 1978). It is of course true that such statements are not clear evidence of an employee's opinion about the union — and if the Board's substantive standard required clear proof of employee disaffection, it might be proper to ignore such statements altogether. But that is not the standard, and, depending on the circumstances, the statements can unquestionably be probative to some degree of the employer's good-faith reasonable doubt.

* * *

We conclude that the Board's "reasonable doubt" test for employer polls is facially rational and consistent with the Act. But the Board's factual finding that Allentown Mack Sales lacked such a doubt is not supported by substantial evidence on the record as a whole. The judgment of the Court of Appeals for the D.C. Circuit is therefore reversed, and the case is remanded with instructions to deny enforcement.

It is so ordered.

Note: Agency Adjudication (Part II)

Did the Act Occur?

1.   In Part I of this Note *supra*, we discovered the "judgment criteria" which an agency often must use in determining whether statutory words of conclusion are or are not applicable to specific sets of physical or near-physical facts. Let us backtrack for a moment to inquire how the determination of physical or near-physical facts can best be made. Here the *Universal Camera* cases are helpful. Although the larger issue in *Universal Camera* was the commission of an "unfair labor practice", the narrow and more precise issue was whether employee Chairman had been discharged for his anti-employer testimony at a prior Board hearing or whether, on the contrary, he had been discharged for insubordination. The issue was thus one of the employer's "motive" for the discharge. And it appears that the motivation could be determined from the testimony of witnesses. And belief or disbelief in the testimony of the several witnesses was crucial to the decision of the issue of motivation. Read carefully those parts of the opinion of the Court of Appeals on remand which discuss the relevance of the examiner's having seen and heard the witnesses testifying. Compare the analogous part of Justice Frankfurter's opinion. Was Justice Frankfurter saying the same thing as Judge Hand? Did Justice Frankfurter focus only upon the examiner's having seen and heard the witnesses or did he also consider relevant that an extensive amount of time on a case was spent by an examiner and/or that the examiner possessed substantial experience? Try to clarify in your own mind the attitudes which Justice Frankfurter would have towards the resolution of a question of conflicting testimony. Who, in the justice's view, would be best qualified to resolve such an issue? Ask yourself the same thing about Judge Hand (the author of the Second Circuit's majority opinions) and Judge Frank (concurring in the Second Circuit's decision on remand).

Let us now reconsider our terminology. We have referred to the problem of determining the existence or non-existence of physical or near-physical facts. We have seen the relevance of *Universal Camera* in deciding questions which turn on the belief or disbelief in witnesses testifying. And since the existence or non-existence of physical or near-physical facts is often determined from the testimony of witnesses, *Universal Camera* is highly relevant to our consideration of how the existence or non-existence of those facts can best be determined.

The issue in *Universal Camera*, however, was one of "motive". "Motive" certainly is not a "physical" fact. Is it a "near-physical" fact? The difficulty in answering the latter question suggests that our terminology is faulty. More precisely, our focus is in the wrong place. Instead of classifying issues by the type of substantive dispute (such as the existence or non-existence of physical or near-physical facts), perhaps we should focus upon the *method of* decision. *Universal Camera* told us some things about those issues which can best be decided from the testimony of witnesses. Let us take advantage of the *Universal Camera* analyses and change our perspective from one which asks questions about the substance of the issues in dispute to a perspective which asks: What types of issues can best be decided from the testimony of witnesses? For those issues — the ones that turn on the belief or disbelief in the testimony of witnesses (testifying as to matters which they have seen or heard), the *Universal Camera* analyses about the importance of demeanor evidence and of the access of the decision-maker to that evidence will be important. For issues turning upon witness credibility, the hearing officer (or Administrative Law judge ["ALJ"], as that person is called today) has an advantage over everyone else. *Universal Camera* shows that an agency cannot easily overturn an ALJ's decision on credibility issues.

On noncredibility issues, however, the agency can operate with greater freedom. When an agency accepts an ALJ's determinations of physical fact but overturns the ALJ's decision on policy grounds, then — as Judge Frank makes clear in his concurring opinion on remand in *Universal Camera* — the agency is in the strongest possible position.

2.   *The Davis* terminology. Professor Kenneth Culp Davis has attempted to describe the type of issue for which an evidentiary hearing is necessary. That type of issue he calls an issue of "adjudicative fact". An extract from Davis' discussion of "adjudicative facts" appears in Chapter 3 in Questions and Comments, para. 6 following the *Bi-Metallic* opinion. Familiarize yourself with it. Most "adjudicative facts" would probably be decided upon the basis of witnesses' testimony, and so the *Universal Camera* analyses would often be applicable to decisions of "adjudicative facts". Can you think of instances when the *Universal Camera* analyses would not be applicable to issues of adjudicative fact? Consider an issue about the net income of a business firm which would be determined from its financial records. Would the issue as to the firm's net income be one of adjudicative fact? Would it turn on the decision-maker's belief or disbelief of witnesses testifying?

3.   What approach ought to be followed in allocating various types of decision-making between courts and agencies? Judge Hand's attribution of importance to the observation of witnesses testifying — of opportunity to observe their demeanor suggests his view as to who ought to resolve issues turning on disputed testimony. Consider also Judge Frank's views on these matters. Is his a more precise formulation of Judge Hand's view? Study Judge Frank's allocation of decision-making between courts and agencies. Especially note his distinction between testimonial (or primary) inferences on one hand and secondary (or derivative) inferences on the other. Judge Frank would find that the examiner generally could best decide issues of testimonial inference. Why? Would Judge Hand agree with him? Would Justice Frankfurter? Suppose the testimony was all in the form of

written affidavits? Or written answers to interrogatories? To what extent would Judge Frank's analysis hold? Explain.

Judge Frank said that an appellate court is usually bound by the testimonial inferences of a trial judge. Why? Suppose the trial judge made his testimonial inferences from written affidavits or from written answers to interrogatories. Would an appellate court still be bound, in Judge Frank's view, to the trial court's testimonial inferences? Under *City of Bessemer*, the appellate court would be bound, would it not?

Why would the Board have greater freedom to reach secondary inferences different from the examiner than to reach testimonial inferences different from the examiner? Why would a reviewing court be more strongly bound by the Board's secondary inferences than it would by a trial court's secondary inferences?

4. Further comments on terminology: The resolution of matters that Judge Frank called "primary inferences" are commonly called "evidentiary facts."

Although Judge Frank used the terms "primary inference" and "testimonial inference" interchangeably, primary inferences can be drawn from nontestimonial evidence as well as from testimonial evidence. Therefore, the ALJ does not have an advantage in deciding all matters of primary inference or all evidentiary facts: The ALJ has no advantage in deciding such questions when the relevant evidence is nontestimonial. The resolution of matters that Judge Frank calls "secondary inferences" involves the finding of "ultimate facts."

B. Questions of "fact" and questions of "law"

It is hornbook law that courts decide questions of law and juries decide questions of fact. When courts review agency orders, it also has been hornbook law (until the *Chevron* case infra, part C) that courts decide questions of law and review agencies' determinations of fact under the substantial evidence standard. In the last section, we examined the substantial evidence review standard and gave some attention to how courts treat agency determinations of policy under that standard. In the present chapter, we will try to distinguish those questions which are ultimately decided by the courts (and which, accordingly, are often called questions of law) from other, superficially similar, questions which are ultimately decided by agencies (and which, accordingly, have often been called questions of fact).

The Classic Deference Cases of the 1940s

Gray v. Powell, 314 U.S. 402 (1941). The Bituminous Coal Act of 1937 was a piece of New Deal legislation designed to aid the recovery of the coal industry from the devastating impact of the Great Depression. The principal means employed by the Act to stimulate that recovery was the establishment of minimum prices for coal.

Section 4 of the Act (the "code") authorized the coal producers to organize themselves under the Act (or in the statutory terms to become "code members"). The producers, so organized, were authorized to establish some twenty district boards which could propose minimum prices for code members, proposals which the Bituminous Coal Commission could approve, modify or disapprove. The Commission was also given power to set the maximum price of coal for code members. The sale, delivery or offer for sale of coal by code members at prices below the minimum or above the maximum prescribed by the Commission was prohibited by the Act. The Act imposed a 19-1/2 % tax on the sale of coal, but exempted from this tax those producers who were code members. It thus created a strong incentive on producers to become code members.

Seaboard Air Line Railway, a large consumer of coal, wished to assure itself of its requirements of coal at a cost below the minimum price specified by the Bituminous Coal Commission:

> The first step was a lease of coal lands by Seaboard from the landowners which granted to Seaboard the right to mine coal for fourteen months, with the privilege of yearly renewals. . . . A per-ton royalty, as rent, was reserved to the landowners with an annual minimum of $16,200 payable quarterly. . . .

> The second step in this arrangement was for the landowner lessors of the lease just described to lease simultaneously to a contractor selected by Seaboard the mining equipment on the demised premises, consisting of buildings, tipples, machinery and other appurtenances necessary or convenient for extracting the coal. . . .

> The final step was an operating contract between the contractor, Daniel H. Pritchard, . . . and Seaboard for the extraction of the coal by the contractor or supplier and delivery of it to Seaboard for consumption. This contract also was made simultaneously with the coal lease. It contained a provision requiring the contractor to obtain a lease of the mining equipment. . . . For a flat per-ton cost on a sliding scale dependent upon volume, the supplier agreed to mine the coal. His compensation was subject to variation by fluctuations in costs beyond his control, such as taxes, wages, machinery and explosives. . . . The supplier was called an independent contractor in the document. This he was, at least in the sense that he managed the mining in his own way without a right of direction in Seaboard. He agreed that the coal supplied would be clean, i.e., free of non-combustible matter, and would pass inspection of Seaboard for compliance with its specifications. The supplier paid and assumed all obligations to the landowner except the royalty, including taxes. He carried employer's liability and casualty insurance, and agreed to bear the cost of all repairs, additions or betterments, ... Seaboard, in an extension agreement, obtained the privilege of termination on sixty days' notice, if the supplier defaulted by not lowering his contract price to meet the market price of similar coal.

> The landowner, the contractor and Seaboard, by this series of coordinated and synchronized contracts caused the entire output of the mine to be delivered to Seaboard for its consumption, at a fixed price, subject to variations for factors beyond the supplier-contractor's control.

Seaboard did not want these transactions in coal subjected to the provisions of the Bituminous Coal Act. That Act, in section 4-11(l) exempted "coal consumed by the producer." In section 4-A the Act provided that any producer could petition the

Bituminous Coal Commission for a ruling that it was exempt from the Act and provided (in section 6(b)) for judicial review of a Commission denial of an exemption. Accordingly, Seaboard sought a ruling from the Director of the Bituminous Coal Division of the Department of the Interior, the successor to the Bituminous Coal Commission, that it was exempt under section 4-11(l) as a producer-consumer. The Director ruled against Seaboard; Seaboard was successful on review by the court of appeals; and then lost before the Supreme Court. An extract from the Court's opinion follows:

> In a matter left specifically by Congress to the determination of an administrative body, as the question of exemption was here by §§ 4-1 and 4-A, the function of review placed upon the courts by § 6(b) is fully performed when they determine that there has been a fair hearing, with notice and opportunity to present the circumstances and arguments to the decisive body, and an application of the statute in a just and reasoned manner.

> Such a determination as is here involved belongs to the usual administrative routine. Congress, which could have legislated specifically as to the individual exemptions from the code, found it more efficient to delegate that function to those whose experience in a particular field gave promise of a better informed, more equitable, adjustment of the conflicting interests of price stabilization upon the one hand and producer consumption upon the other. By thus committing the execution of its policies to the specialized personnel of the Bituminous Coal Division, the Congress followed a familiar practice. . . .

> Where, as here, a determination has been left to an administrative body, this delegation will be respected and the administrative conclusion left untouched. Certainly, a finding on Congressional reference that an admittedly constitutional act is applicable to a particular situation does not require such further scrutiny. Although we have here no dispute as to the evidentiary facts, that does not permit a court to substitute its judgment for that of the Director. It is not the province of a court to absorb the administrative functions to such an extent that the executive or legislative agencies become mere fact-finding bodies deprived of the advantages of prompt and definite action. . . . [T]here must be left to [the Bituminous Coal Division], the determination of "producer." The separation of production and consumption is complete when a buyer obtains supplies from a seller totally free from buyer connection. Their identity is undoubted when the consumer extracts coal from its own land with its own employees. Between the two extremes are the innumerable variations that bring the arrangements closer to one pole or the other of the range between exception and inclusion. To determine upon which side of the median line the particular instance falls calls for the expert, experienced judgment of those familiar with the industry. Unless we can say that a set of circumstances deemed by the Commission to bring them within the concept "producer" is so unrelated to the tasks entrusted by Congress to the Commission as in effect to deny a sensible exercise of judgment, it is the Court's duty to leave the Commission's judgment undisturbed.

Questions and Comments

1.   *Gray v. Powell* is the classic case according ultimate authority to an administering agency to apply statutory terms to specific sets of facts. In applying these terms, the agency necessarily gave them meaning. In *Gray v. Powell* the agency construed a statutory term and resolved what previously had been an ambiguity in its application.

2.   In *Gray v. Powell* did the Court indicate the boundaries of the agency's authority to construe the statutory term "producer-consumer"? Would the agency have been upheld in *Gray v. Powell* had it decided that the railroad was a producer-consumer? On what facts would such a determination not be upheld?

3.   Did the Court allocate to the agency authority to make the ultimate decision in the middle ranges of a continuum of factual situations? On one end of the continuum a firm would unambiguously be a producer-consumer, would it not? And on the other end of the continuum the firm would unambiguously be a purchaser on the market, would it not? Was not the Court saying that the poles of the continuum marked the limits of the agency's authority?

4.   Whose task was it to determine the poles of the continuum? The court's? On the basis of what factors would such a determination be made?

5.   How could the Congress allocate less authority to the administering agency and more to the reviewing court? Could the Congress employ statutory terms which were less broad and carried more antecedently determined meaning? Could the Congress have limited the authority of the Bituminous Coal Division under the statute involved in the instant case by comprehensively defining "producer-consumer" in the statute?

6.   When the agency determined that the railroad was not a producer-consumer, was it engaged in the process of drawing a secondary inference? Can its actions be described in the analysis set forth by Judge Frank in his concurring opinion in the Universal Camera case on remand?

7.   Judge Frank had said that an agency's derivative inferences must be respected by a reviewing court if they are "rational." Did the Supreme Court take the same position here? Where did the court suggest where the boundaries of the "rational" lie? Was the Court's use of the factual continuum bounded by poles in which the meaning of the statutory term was unambiguous a way of portraying the boundaries of rational decision-making?

NATIONAL LABOR RELATIONS BOARD v. HEARST PUBLICATIONS, INC.
322 U.S. 111 (1944)

Mr. Justice Rutledge delivered the opinion of the court.

These cases arise from the refusal of respondents, publishers of four Los Angeles daily newspapers, to bargain collectively with a union representing newsboys who distribute their papers on the streets of that city. Respondents' contention that they were not required to bargain because the newsboys are not their "employees" within the meaning of that term in the National Labor Relations Act . . . presents the important question which we granted certiorari to resolve.

[The Board had found respondents to have violated §§ 8(l) and 8(5) of the Act and had ordered them to bargain collectively with the union. The Court of Appeals reversed on the ground that the newsboys were not "employees" under the Act.]

The findings of the Board disclose that the Los Angeles Times and the Los Angeles Examiner, published daily and Sunday, are morning papers. Each publishes several editions which are distributed on the streets during the evening before their dateline, between about 6:00 or 6:30 p.m. and 1:00 a.m., and other editions distributed during the following morning until about 10:00 o'clock. The Los Angeles Evening Herald and Express, published everyday but Sunday, is an evening paper, which has six editions on the presses between 9:00 a.m. and 5:30 p.m. The News, also published every day but Sunday, is a twenty-four hour paper with ten editions.

The newsboys work under varying terms and conditions. They may be "bootjackers," selling to the general public at places other than established corners, or they may sell at fixed "spots." They may sell only casually or part-time, or full-time; and they may be employed regularly and continuously or only temporarily. The units which the Board determined to be appropriate are composed of those who sell full-time at established spots. Those vendors, misnamed boys, are generally mature men, dependent upon the proceeds of their sales for their sustenance, and frequently supporters of families. Working thus as news vendors on a regular basis, often for a number of years, they form a stable group with relatively little turnover, in contrast to schoolboys and others who sell as bootjackers, temporary and casual distributors.

Over-all circulation and distribution of the papers are under the general supervision of circulation managers. But for purposes of street distribution each paper has divided metropolitan Los Angeles into geographic districts. Each district is under the direct and close supervision of a district manager. His function in the mechanics of distribution is to supply the newsboys in his district with papers which he obtains from the publisher and to turn over to the publisher the receipts which he collects from their sales, either directly or with the assistance of "checkmen" or "main spot" boys. The latter, stationed at the important corners or "spots" in the district, are newsboys who, among other things, receive delivery of the papers, redistribute them to other newsboys stationed at less important corners, and collect receipts from their sales. For that service, which occupies a minor portion of their working day, the checkmen receive a small salary from the publisher. The bulk of their day, however, they spend in hawking papers at their "spots" like other full-time newsboys. . . .

The newsboys' compensation consists in the difference between the prices at which they sell the papers and the prices they pay for them. The former are fixed by the publishers and the latter are fixed either by the publishers or, in the case of the News, by the district manager. In practice the newsboys receive their papers on credit. They pay for those sold either sometime during or after the close of their selling day, returning for credit all unsold papers. Lost or otherwise unreturned papers, however, must be paid for as though sold. Not only is the "profit" per paper thus effectively fixed by the publisher, but substantial control of the newsboys' total "take home" can be effected through the ability to designate their sales areas and the power to determine the number of papers allocated to each. . . .

In addition to effectively fixing the compensation, respondents in a variety of ways prescribe, if not the minutiae of daily activities, at least the broad terms and conditions of work. This is accomplished largely through the supervisory efforts of the district managers, who serve as the nexus between the publishers and the newsboys. The district managers assign "spots" or corners to which the newsboys are expected to confine their selling activities. Transfers from one "spot" to another may be ordered by the district manager for reasons of discipline or efficiency or other cause. Transportation to the spots from the newspaper building is offered by each of the respondents. Hours of work on the spots are determined not simply by the impersonal pressures of the market, but to a real extent by explicit instructions from the district managers. Adherence to the prescribed hours is observed closely by the district managers or other supervisory agents of the publishers. Sanctions, varying in severity from reprimand to dismissal, are visited on the tardy and the delinquent. By similar supervisory controls minimum standards of diligence and good conduct while at work are sought to be enforced. . . . [D]istrict managers' instructions in what the publishers apparently regard as helpful sales technique are expected to be followed. . . . In this pattern of employment the Board found that the newsboys are an integral part of the publishers' distribution system and circulation organization. And the record discloses that the newsboys and checkmen feel they are employees of the papers; and respondents' supervisory employees, if not respondents themselves, regard them as such.

. . . [R]espondents urge that . . . [the newsboys] cannot be considered their employees. They base this conclusion on the argument that by common-law standards the extent of their control and direction of the newsboys' working activities creates no more than an "independent contractor" relationship. . . .

I

The principal question is whether the newsboys are "employees." Because Congress did not explicitly define the term, respondents say its meaning must be determined by reference to common-law standards. . . .

The argument assumes that there is some simple, uniform and easily applicable test which the courts have used, in dealing with . . . problems [unrelated to the Wagner Act], to determine whether persons doing work for others fall in one class or the other. Unfortunately this is not true. Only by a long and tortuous history was the simple formulation worked out which has been stated most frequently as "the test" for deciding whether one who hires another is responsible in tort for his wrongdoing. But this formula has been by no means exclusively controlling in the solution of other problems. And its simplicity has been illusory because it is more largely simplicity of formulation than of application. Few problems in the law have given greater variety of application and conflict in results than the cases arising in the borderland between what is clearly an employer-employee relationship and what is clearly one of independent, entrepreneurial dealing. This is true within the limited field of determining vicarious liability in tort. It becomes more so when the field is expanded to include all of the possible applications of the distinction.

. . . It is enough to point out that, with reference to an identical problem, results may be contrary over a very considerable region of doubt in applying the distinction, depending upon the state or jurisdiction where the determination is made, and that within a single jurisdiction a person who, for instance, is held to be an "independent contractor" for the purpose of imposing vicarious liability in tort may be an "employee" for the purposes of particular legislation, such as unemployment compensation. . . .

Mere reference to these possible variations as characterizing the application of the Wagner Act in the treatment of persons identically situated in the facts surrounding their employment and in the influences tending to disrupt it, would be enough to require pause before accepting a thesis which would introduce them into its administration. . . .

Two possible consequences could follow. One would be to refer the decision of who are employees to local state law. The alternative would be to make it turn on a sort of pervading general essence distilled from state law. . . . Both the terms and the purposes of the statute, as well as the legislative history, show that Congress had in mind no such patchwork plan for securing freedom of employees' organization and of collective bargaining. The Wagner Act is federal legislation, administered by a national agency, intended to solve a national problem on a national scale. . . . Nothing in the statute's background, history, terms or purposes indicates its scope is to be limited by such varying local conceptions, either statutory or judicial, or that it is to be administered in accordance with whatever different standards the respective states may see fit to adopt for the disposition of unrelated, local problems. . . .

Whether, given the intended national uniformity, the term "employee" includes such workers as these newsboys must be answered primarily from the history, terms and purposes of the legislation. . . . Congress had in mind a wider field that the narrow technical legal relation of "master and servant," as the common law had worked this out in all its variations, and at the same time a narrower one than the entire area of rendering service to others. The question comes down therefore to how much was included of the intermediate region between what is clearly and unequivocally "employment," by any appropriate test, and what is as clearly entrepreneurial enterprise and not employment.

The Act . . . was designed to avert the "substantial obstructions to the free flow of commerce" which result from "strikes and other forms of industrial strife or unrest" by eliminating the causes of that unrest. It is premised on explicit findings that strikes and industrial strife themselves result in large measure from the refusal of employers to bargain collectively and the inability of individual workers to bargain successfully for improvements in their "wages, hours or other working conditions" with employers who are "organized in the corporate or other forms of ownership association.

The mischief at which the Act is aimed and the remedies it offers are not confined exclusively to "employees" within the traditional legal distinctions separating them from "independent contractors." Myriad forms of service relationship, with infinite and subtle variations in the terms of employment, blanket the nation's economy. Some are within this Act, others beyond its coverage. Large numbers will fall clearly on one side or on the other, by whatever test may be applied. But intermediate there will be many, the incidents of whose employment partake in part of the one group, in part of the other, in varying proportions of weight. And consequently the legal pendulum, for purposes of applying the statute, may swing one way or the other, depending upon the weight of this balance and its relation to the special purpose at hand.

It is not necessary in this case to make a completely definitive limitation around the term "employee." That task has been assigned primarily to the agency created by Congress to administer the Act. Determination of "where all the conditions of the relation require protection" involves inquiries for the Board charged with this duty. Everyday experience in the administration of the statute gives it familiarity with the circumstances and backgrounds of employment relationships in various industries, with the abilities and needs of the workers for self-organization and collective action, and with the adaptability of collective bargaining for the peaceful settlement of their disputes with their employers. The experience thus acquired must be brought frequently to bear on the question who is an employee under the Act. Resolving that question, like determining whether unfair labor practices have been committed, "belongs to the usual administrative routine" of the Board. . . .

In making that body's determination as to the facts in these matters conclusive, if supported by evidence, Congress entrusted to it primarily the decision whether the evidence establishes the material facts. Hence in reviewing the Board's ultimate conclusions, it is not the court's function to substitute its own inferences of fact for the Board's when the latter have support in the record. . . . Undoubtedly questions of statutory interpretation, especially when arising in the first instance in judicial proceedings, are for the courts to resolve, giving appropriate weight to the judgment of those whose special duty is to administer the questioned statute. . . . But where the question is one of specific application of a broad statutory term in a proceeding in which the agency administering the statute must determine it initially, the reviewing court's function is limited. Like the commissioner's determination under the Longshoremens' & Harbor Workers' Act, that a man is not a "member of a crew" . . . or that he was injured "in the course of employment" . . . and the Federal Communications Commission's determination that one company is under the "control" of another . . . the Board's determination that specified persons are "employees" under this Act is to be accepted if it has "warrant in the record" and a reasonable basis in law.

. . . Stating that "the primary consideration in the determination of the applicability of the statutory definition is whether effectuation of the declared policy and purposes of the Act comprehend securing to the individual the rights guaranteed and protection afforded by the Act," the Board concluded that the newsboys are employees. The record sustains the Board's findings and there is ample basis in the law for its conclusion.

Questions and Comments

1.   Did the Court follow the same approach to the allocation of authority to apply a statutory term in *Hearst* as it did in *Gray v. Powell?* Did the Court suggest any boundaries to the Labor Board's authority to apply the term "employee"? Did Congress define that term in the statute? Did it define it in such a way as to maximize the authority of the Board to apply it? Explain.

2.   Was the Board's determination that the newsboys were "employees" within the meaning of the National Labor Relations Act the determination of a question of fact? Would such a determination be reviewable by a court under the "substantial evidence" standard? Can you analyze the process by which such review would take place?

3.   What, if any, significance attaches to the elaborate detail in which the Court described the working conditions of the newsboys and their economic relations with the publishers?

4.   Did the Court decide any question of law in *Hearst?* What were those questions? What factors did the Court rely upon to decide those questions? Would the materials needed to decide those questions be found in the record of the testimony and exhibits in the case before the Labor Board? Or would the materials needed to decide those questions be found in a law library?

5.   Did the Court decide any questions in *Hearst* which have significance for the decision of other cases? What were those questions? Did the Board decide any such questions? Explain.

6.   When Congress enacted the Taft-Hartley Act, it expressly disapproved of the Court's ruling in *Hearst* that independent contractors could be "employees" protected by the National Labor Relations Act. *See* 29 U.S.C. § 152(3) (1982). *See also* H.R. Rep. No. 245, 80th Cong., 1st Sess., 18 (1947). Was the question of whether the Act automatically excluded independent contractors a question of law? Did Congress agree with the Court that question was one of law and disagree only over how that question of law should have been decided? Does the Congressional overruling of the Court's decision in *Hearst* on the issue of the Act's protection of independent contractors show that the issue was one of law? Explain. Is it generally practical for Congress to overrule a regulatory agency on an issue of fact? Explain.

7.   Are the phrases "questions of law" and "questions of fact" words of conclusion? Explain.

Unemployment Compensation Commission v. Aragon, 329 U.S. 143 (1946) is the third of the classic deference cases. In that case the substantive issue was whether employees of certain canning factories in Alaska were entitled to workers' compensation benefits under an Alaska unemployment compensation statute. That statute denied benefits for an eight week period to workers who were unemployed due to a labor dispute.

The claimants contended that because the companies and the union had failed to reach an agreement by the beginning of the canning season — a time when the companies had asserted an agreement had to be reached if they were to conduct operations at all — their unemployment thereafter was no longer due to a labor dispute in active progress. Hence, according to the claimants, they were entitled to unemployment benefits.

The Alaska Unemployment Compensation Commission rejected that view and ruled that a labor dispute was in active progress for the entire eight week disqualification period. On review, the U.S. Supreme Court ruled that the record showed that one company (the Alaska Salmon Company) would not have operated during the canning season for independent reasons. There was no labor dispute in active progress involving that company. With respect to all of the other companies, however, the Court ruled that the determination of the Alaska Commission that a labor dispute was in active progress was a reasonable one and had to be respected. Citing *Hearst*, the Court ruled: "To sustain the Commission's application of this statutory term, we need not find that its construction is the only reasonable one, or even that it is the result we would have reached had the question arisen in the first instance in judicial proceedings."

PACKARD MOTOR CAR CO. v. NATIONAL LABOR RELATIONS BOARD
330 U.S. 485 (1947)

MR. JUSTICE JACKSON delivered the opinion of the Court.

The question presented by this case is whether foremen are entitled as a class to the rights of self-organization, collective bargaining, and other concerted activities as assured to employees generally by the National Labor Relations Act. The case grows out of conditions in the automotive industry, and so far as they are important to the legal issues here the facts are simple.

The Packard Motor Car Company employs about 32,000 rank-and-file workmen. Since 1937 they have been represented by the United Automobile Workers of America affiliated with the Congress of Industrial Organizations. These employees are supervised by approximately 1,100 employees of foreman rank, consisting of about 125 "general foremen," 643 "foremen," 273 "assistant foremen," and 65 "special assignment men." Each general foreman is in charge of one or more departments, and under him in authority are foremen and their assistant foremen. Special assignment men are described as "troubleshooters."

The function of these foremen in general is typical of the duties of foremen in mass-production industry generally. Foremen carry the responsibility for maintaining quantity and quality of production, subject, of course, to the overall control and supervision of the management. . . .

The foremen as a group are highly paid and, unlike the workmen, are paid for justifiable absence and for holidays, are not docked in pay when tardy, receive longer paid vacations, and are given severance pay upon release by the Company.

These foremen determined to organize as a unit of the Foremen's Association of America, an unaffiliated organization which represents supervisory employees exclusively. Following the usual procedure, after the Board had decided that "all general foremen, foremen, assistant foremen, and special assignment men employed by the Company at its plants in Detroit, Michigan, constitute a unit appropriate for the purpose of collective bargaining within the meaning of § 9(b) of the Act," the Foremen's Association was certified as the bargaining representative. The Company asserted that foremen were not "employees" entitled to the advantages of the Labor Act, and refused to bargain with the union. [The Board ordered the Company to bargain, the Court of Appeals decreed the enforcement of the Board's order, and the Supreme Court granted certiorari.]

The issue of law as to the power of the National Labor Relations Board under the National Labor Relations Act is simple and our only function is to determine whether the order of the Board is authorized by the statute.

The privileges and benefits of the Act are conferred upon employees, and § 2(3) of the Act, so far as relevant, provides "The term 'employee' shall include any employee. . . . ". . . The point that these foremen are employees both in the most technical sense at common law as well as in common acceptance of the term, is too obvious to be labored. The Company, however, turns to the Act's definition of employer, which it contends reads foremen out of the employee class and into the class of employers. Section 2(2) reads: "The term 'employer' includes any person acting in the interest of an employer, directly or indirectly. . . ." The context of the Act, we think, leaves no room for a construction of this section to deny the organizational privilege to employees because they act in the interest of an employer. Every employee, from the very fact of employment in the master's business, is required to act in his interest. . . .

The purpose of § 2(2) seems obviously to render employers responsible in labor practices for acts of any persons performed in their interests. . . .

Even those who act for the employer in some matters, including the service of standing between management and manual labor, still have interests of their own as employees. Though the foreman is the faithful representative of the employer in maintaining a production schedule, his interest properly may be adverse to that of the employer when it comes to fixing his own wages, hours, seniority rights or working conditions. . . . [W]e see no basis in this Act whatever for holding that foremen are forbidden the protection of the Act when they take collective action to protect their collective interests.

The company's argument is really addressed to the undesirability of permitting foremen to organize. It wants selfless representatives of its interest. It fears that if foremen combine to bargain advantages for themselves, they will sometimes be governed by interests of their own or of their fellow foremen, rather than by the company's interest. There is nothing new in this argument. It is rooted in the misconception that because the employer has the right to wholehearted loyalty in the performance of the contract of employment, the employee does not have the right to protect his independent and adverse interest in the terms of the contract itself and the conditions of work. But the effect of the National Labor Relations Act is otherwise, and it is for Congress, not for us, to create exceptions or qualifications at odds with its plain terms.

There is no more reason to conclude that the law prohibits foremen as a class from constituting an appropriate bargaining unit than there is for concluding that they are not within the Act at all. Section 9(b) of the Act confers upon the Board a broad discretion to determine appropriate units. . . . Our power of review also is circumscribed by the provision that findings of the Board as to the facts, if supported by evidence, shall be conclusive. . . .

We are invited to make a lengthy examination of views expressed in Congress while this and later legislation was pending to show that exclusion of foremen was intended. There is, however, no ambiguity in this Act to be clarified by resort to legislative history, either of the Act itself or of subsequent legislative proposals which failed to become law.

Counsel also would persuade us to make a contrary interpretation by citing a long record of inaction, vacillation and division of the National Labor Relations Board in applying this Act to foremen. . . . Whatever special questions there are in determining the appropriate bargaining unit for foremen are for the Board, and the history of the issue in the Board shows the difficulty of the problem committed to its discretion. We are not at liberty to be governed by those policy considerations in deciding the naked question of law whether the Board is now, in this case, acting within the terms of the statute.

It is also urged upon us most seriously that unionization of foremen is from many points bad industrial policy, that it puts the union foreman in the position of serving two masters, divides his loyalty and makes generally for bad relations between management and labor. However we might appraise the force of these arguments as a policy matter, we are not authorized to base decision of a question of law upon them. They concern the wisdom of the legislation; they cannot alter the meaning of otherwise plain provisions.

The judgment of enforcement is
Affirmed.

Questions and Comments

1. What were the legal questions which the Court decided in the *Packard* case? Were these questions about the extent of the Labor Board's authority? Did the resolution of any of these questions require the Court to construe the statutory term "employee"? Explain.

2. Can you identify the parts of the opinion which deal with the Board's choice of an appropriate bargaining unit as distinguished from those parts of the opinion which deal with the authority of the Board over foremen?

3. Did the Court say that various considerations of policy affecting the appropriate bargaining unit for foremen are for the Board to determine? Did the Court also say that policy considerations were irrelevant to the questions before the Court? How could the Court know that the term "employee" included foremen if the Court could not weigh policy matters?

4. What factors did the Court rely upon to decide whether foremen were "employees" under the Act? Would the materials needed to decide that question be found in the record of the testimony and exhibits in the case before the Labor

Board? Or would the materials needed to decide that question be found in a law library?

5.   Was *Packard* an important precedent? Explain. Did the Court's decision in *Packard* provide direction or guidance to the Board as to how it should act in other cases? to the courts of appeals?

6.   What, if any, significance attaches to the concise manner in which the Court described the duties and working conditions of the foremen? Is it significant that the working conditions of the newsboys and their economic relations with the publishers were described in substantially greater detail in the *Hearst* case?

7.   When Congress enacted the Taft-Hartley Act, it expressly disapproved of the Court's ruling in *Packard* that foremen were protected by the National Labor Relations Act. *See* 29 U.S.C. § 152(3) (1982); S. Rep. No. 105, 80th Cong., 1st Sess., pp. 3–5 (1947); H.R. Rep. No. 245, 80th Cong., lst Sess., pp. 13–17 (1947). Does that mean that the question of whether foremen were employees was not a question of law? Perhaps the Congress felt that the Court had been procedurally correct in treating the issue as a question of law but substantively incorrect in deciding that the statutory term embraced foremen.

8.   Explain why the determination of whether foremen were employees was a question of law in *Packard* but the determination of whether newsboys were employees was a question of fact in *Hearst*. Consider whether you agree with the following proposition: The question of whether newsboys were employees was a question of fact in *Hearst* but the question of whether independent contractors were entirely excluded from the scope of the term employees was a question of law. Explain your position.

9.   Can you identify the factors which influenced the Court to treat the application of the statutory term "employee" as a question of fact for the Board in *Hearst* and as a question of law in *Packard?* the generality of the decision to other cases? the relative independence of the decision from facts peculiar to one factual setting? the extent to which the decision identifies the basic parameters of the governing statute as distinguished from applying it to particular sets of facts? the extent to which the decision provides overall direction to the administering agency or to the courts? the extent to which the decision is dependent upon traditional methods of statutory interpretation, such as reading the various statutory provisions in juxtaposition or having recourse to legislative history? Observe that Congress will rarely have an ascertainable intent about the details of a regulatory scheme, but may manifest a relatively clear intent about its main outlines. The main outlines, therefore, are more easily ascertained through the traditional methods of statutory construction by the courts.

C.   JUDICIAL DEFERENCE TO AGENCY INTERPRETATIONS

To what extent must a court defer to an agency's construction of a statute which the agency is administering? And to what extent does the court have a responsibility for imposing its own construction of the governing statute on the agency? These questions cannot be answered by simplistically allotting the decisions of questions of "law" to the courts while giving free rein to agencies on other questions. We know, for example, that the determination of what is — and is not — a question of law is itself a complex determination. And, as the following materials demonstrate, the determination of questions that are openly acknowledged to be matters of statutory construction is not always a matter for judicial determination.

Does the judicial obligation outlined in *Gray v. Powell, supra*, and *NLRB v. Hearst Publications, Inc., supra*, to accept agency determinations of ultimate fact carry over to require judicial deference to agency legal interpretations made in less fact-specific circumstances than in those cases? To what extent is Judge Frank's analysis — contained in his concurring opinion on remand in *Universal Camera* — helpful in answering this question? Consider the extent to which the material below provides the basis for an approach. Consider especially Judge Breyer's analysis in *Mayburg and* Justice Scalia's comments in *Cardoza Fonesca*.

CHEVRON, U.S.A., INC. v. NATURAL RESOURCES DEFENSE COUNCIL, INC.
467 U.S. 837 (1984)

JUSTICE STEVENS delivered the opinion of the Court.

In the Clean Air Act Amendments of 1977 . . . Congress enacted certain requirements applicable to States that had not achieved the national air quality standards established by the Environmental Protection Agency (EPA) pursuant to earlier legislation. The amended Clean Air Act required these "nonattainment" States to establish a permit program regulating "new or modified major stationary sources" of air pollution. Generally, a permit may not be issued for a new or modified major stationary source unless several stringent conditions are met. The EPA regulation promulgated to implement this permit requirement allows a State to adopt a plantwide definition of the term "stationary source." Under this definition, an existing plant that contains several pollution-emitting devices may install or modify one piece of equipment without meeting the permit conditions if the alteration will not increase the total emissions from the plant. The question presented by this case is whether EPA's decision to allow States to treat all of the pollution-emitting devices within the same industrial grouping as though they were encased within a single "bubble" is based on a reasonable construction of the statutory term "stationary source."

[When the regulations were challenged before the Court of Appeals for the District of Columbia, that court set them aside. The court observed that the Clean Air Act "does not explicitly define what Congress envisioned as a 'stationary source', to which the permit program . . . should apply, and further stated that the precise issue was not 'squarely addressed in the legislative history.' " Based on two of its own earlier decisions concerning the applicability of the bubble concept to certain Clean Air Act programs, however, the court ruled that the bubble concept was mandatory in programs designed to maintain existing air quality, but that it was inappropriate in programs designed to improve air quality. Since the court believed that the permit program was designed to improve air quality, the regulations were ruled invalid.]

The basic legal error of the Court of Appeals was to adopt a static judicial definition of the term stationary source when it had decided that Congress itself had not commanded that definition. . . .

II

When a court reviews an agency's construction of the statute which it administers, it is confronted with two questions. First, always, is the question whether Congress has directly spoken to the precise question at issue. If the intent of Congress is clear, that is the end of the matter; for the court, as well as the agency, must give effect to the unambiguously expressed intent of Congress. If, however, the court determines Congress had not directly addressed the precise question at issue, the court does not simply impose its own construction on the statute, as would be necessary in the absence of an administrative interpretation. Rather, if the statute is silent or ambiguous with respect to the specific issue, the question for the court is whether the agency's answer is based on a permissible construction of the statute.

"The power of an administrative agency to administer a congressionally created . . . program necessarily requires the formulation of policy and the making of rules to fill any gap left, implicitly or explicitly, by Congress." *Morton v. Ruiz.* . . . If Congress has explicitly left a gap for the agency to fill, there is an express delegation of authority to the agency to elucidate a specific provision of the statute by regulation. Such legislative regulations are given controlling weight unless they are arbitrary, capricious, or manifestly contrary to the statute. Sometimes the legislative delegation to an agency on a particular question is implicit rather than explicit. In such a case, a court may not substitute its own construction of a statutory provision for a reasonable interpretation made by the administrator of an agency.

. . . . [I]t is clear that the Court of Appeals misconceived the nature of its role in reviewing the regulations at issue. Once it determined, after its own examination of the legislation, that Congress did not actually have an intent regarding the applicability of the bubble concept to the permit program, the question before it was not whether in its view the concept is "inappropriate" in the general context of a program designed to improve air quality, but whether the Administrator's view that it is appropriate in the context of this particular program is a reasonable one. Based on . . . [an] examination of the legislation and its history . . . we agree with the Court of Appeals that Congress did not have a specific intention on the applicability of the bubble concept in these cases, and conclude that the EPA's use of that concept here is a reasonable policy choice for the agency to make.

. . . . [The legislative history of the Act] plainly identifies the policy concerns that motivated the enactment; the plantwide definition is fully consistent with one of those concerns — the allowance of reasonable economic growth — and, whether or not we believe it most effectively implements the other, we must recognize that the EPA has advanced a reasonable explanation for its conclusion that the regulations serve the environmental objectives as well. . . . Indeed, its reasoning is supported by the public record developed in the rulemaking process, as well as by certain private studies.

Our review of the EPA's varying interpretations of the word "source" — both before and after the 1977 Amendments — convince us that the agency primarily responsible for administering this important legislation has consistently interpreted it flexibly — not in a sterile textual vacuum, but in the context of implementing policy decisions in a technical and complex arena. The fact that the agency has from time to time changed its interpretation of the term source does not, as respondents argue, lead us to conclude that no deference should be accorded the agency's interpretation of the statute. An initial agency interpretation is not instantly carved in stone. On the contrary, the agency, to engage in informed rulemaking, must consider varying interpretations and the wisdom of its policy on a continuing basis. Moreover, the fact that the agency has adopted different definitions in different contexts adds force to the argument that the definition itself is flexible, particularly since Congress has never indicated any disapproval of a flexible reading of the statute.

In these cases, the Administrator's interpretation represents a reasonable accommodation of manifestly competing interests and is entitled to deference: the regulatory scheme is technical and complex, the agency considered the matter in a detailed and reasoned fashion, and the decision involves reconciling conflicting policies. Congress intended to accommodate both interests, but did not do so itself on the level of specificity presented by these cases. Perhaps that body consciously desired the Administrator to strike the balance at this level, thinking that those with great expertise and charged with responsibility for administering the provision would be in a better position to do so; perhaps it simply did not consider the question at this level; and perhaps Congress was unable to forge a coalition on either side of the question, and those on each side decided to take their chances with the scheme devised by the agency. For judicial purposes, it matters not which of these things occurred.

Judges are not experts in the field, and are not part of either political branch of the Government. Courts must, in some cases, reconcile competing political interests, but not on the basis of the judges' personal policy preferences. In contrast, an agency to which Congress has delegated policy-making responsibilities may, within the limits of that delegation, properly rely upon the incumbent administration's views of wise policy to inform its judgments. While agencies are not directly accountable to the people, the Chief Executive is, and it is entirely appropriate for this political branch of the Government to make such policy choices — resolving the competing interests which Congress itself either inadvertently did not resolve, or intentionally left to be resolved by the agency charged with the administration of the statute in light of everyday realities.

When a challenge to an agency construction of a statutory provision, fairly conceptualized, really centers on the wisdom of the agency's policy, rather than whether it is a reasonable choice within a gap left open by Congress, the challenge must fail. In such a case, federal judges—who have no constituency have a duty to respect legitimate policy choices made by those who do. . . .

We hold that the EPA's definition of the term "source" is a permissible construction of the statute which seeks to accommodate progress in reducing air pollution with economic growth. . . .

The judgment of the Court of Appeals is reversed.

It is so ordered.

Notes and Related Material: the Pre-Chevron law

1)   Agency policy reversals have not always been treated so tolerantly. *See, e.g., Motor Vehicle Mfgrs. Ass'n v. State Farm Mutual Auto. Ins. Co.*, 463 U.S. 29 (1983), *infra* Chapter 8.

2)   Consider *Skidmore v. Swift & Co.*, 323 U.S. 134 (1944), where the Court had earlier articulated the deference which courts owed administrative interpretations. That case involved the application of the Fair Labor Standards Act, an act which was enforceable in court in an action brought by workers themselves against their employer or by the Act's Administrator. In *Skidmore*, employees had brought an action against their employer to collect overtime pay which was due them if their time in general fire duties (where they were free to engage in their own activities so long as they were ready to answer a fire alarm) counted as "time worked" for purposes of the Fair Labor Standards Act. Although the Administrator had not previously considered the precise question involved, he had considered analogous questions and had set forth his views of the application of the Act under different circumstances in an interpretative bulletin and in informal rulings. When the case reached the Supreme Court, that Court indicated that that although the Administrator's rulings were not binding on the courts, they were a relevant source of information and experience:

> We consider that the rulings, interpretations and opinions of the Administrator under this Act, while not controlling upon the courts by reason of their authority, do constitute a body of experience and informed judgment to which courts and litigants may properly resort for guidance. The weight of such a judgment in a particular case will depend upon the thoroughness evident in its consideration, the validity of its reasoning, its consistence with earlier and later pronouncements, and all those factors which give it power to persuade, if lacking power to control.

3)   The following cases are illustrative of the Court's response to agency interpretations in the immediate pre-*Chevron* period.

Bureau of Alcohol, Tobacco and Firearms v. Federal Labor Relations Authority, 464 U.S. 89 (1983). Title VII of the Civil Service Reform Act of 1978 requires federal agencies to grant "official time" to employees representing their union in collective bargaining with the agencies, thereby allowing employee negotiators to be paid as if they were at work. Relying upon that provision of the Act, the Federal Labor Relations Authority (FLRA) issued an "Interpretation and Guidance" requiring federal agencies to pay salaries, travel expenses and per diem allowances to union representatives engaged in collective bargaining with federal agencies. In a case in which the authority of the FLRA to require federal agencies to pay travel expenses and per diem allowances was challenged, the Supreme Court rejected the FLRA's construction of the statute:

> . . . the 'deference owed to an expert tribunal cannot be allowed to slip into a judicial inertia which results in the unauthorized assumption by an agency of major policy decisions properly made by Congress.' . . . Accordingly, while reviewing courts should uphold reasonable and defensible constructions of an agency's enabling Act. . . . they must not 'rubber-stamp . . . administrative decisions that they deem inconsistent with a statutory mandate or that frustrate the congressional policy underlying a statute.'

The Court then examined the Civil Service Reform Act and its legislative history and concluded that although Congress intended to permit employee negotiators to be paid, Congress did not so provide in the Act; that the provisions of the Act suggest that unions would ordinarily pay their own expenses, including the travel expenses of their negotiators; and that the legislative history of the Act showed that Congress did not intend to depart from the basic pattern which had guided collective-bargaining during the pre-Act period under a series of executive orders under which agencies were not obliged to pay travel expenses or per diem allowances to union negotiators.

Aluminum Co. of America v. Central Lincoln Peoples' Utility Dist., **467 U.S. 380 (1984).** Under the Bonneville Project Act of 1937 (Project Act), the Bonneville Power Administration (BPA) markets low-cost hydroelectric power generated by a series of dams along the Columbia River. Under § 4(a) of that Act, public bodies and cooperatives were given preference over other customers. Because the amount of power generated depends upon streamflow, the BPA cannot accurately predict the amount of power that it can generate. The BPA therefore has sold two types of power. Firm power is energy that BPA expects to produce under predictable streamflow conditions; and nonfirm power is energy in excess of firm power and is provided only when such excess exists. Originally all power was sold on a "firm" basis, but as demand increased over the years the BPA began marketing nonfirm power as well. In the 1970s when demand for power had expanded beyond the amount generated by the Columbia River dams, the BPA inserted interruptability provisions in power contracts entered into with nonpreference industrial customers. Under those provisions 25% of the power supplied to those customers was interruptible; this provision made the top quartile of the power supplied to industrial users subject to the preference provisions of the Act and enabled preference utilities to interrupt it whenever they wanted nonfirm power.

In 1980 the Congress enacted the Pacific Northwest Electric Power Planning and Conservation Act (Regional Act) which provided in part that the BPA should offer long-term contracts to its industrial customers providing the same amount of power to each customer as that customer was entitled under contracts executed in 1975. Section 5(d)(1)(A) of the Regional Act provided that sales to industrial users under the new contracts were to "provide a portion of the Administrator's reserves for firm power loads within the region." Acting under this provision, the BPA offered industrial users contracts that allowed interruption only to protect BPA's firm loads and not to make sales of nonfirm energy.

Respondents (preference customers) contended that by failing to make the contracts with industrial users interruptible for sales of nonfirm power to preference users, the BPA was ignoring the preference provisions of the Project Act. Reciting an obligation of reviewing courts to defer to the statutory interpretations of an administering agency, the Court rejected the respondents' contentions:

> Under established administrative law principles, it is clear that the Administrator's interpretation of the Regional Act is to be given great weight. 'We have often noted that the interpretation of an agency charged with the administration of a statute is entitled to substantial deference To uphold [the agency's interpretation] "we need not find that [its] construction is the only reasonable one, or even that it is the result we would have reached had the question arisen in the first instance in judicial proceedings We need only conclude that it is a reasonable interpretation of the relevant provisions.' . . . American *Paper Institute, Inc. v. American Electric Power Service* Corp. . . . quoting *Unemployment Compensation Comm'n v. Aragon.* . . .

> These principles of deference have particular force in the context of this case. The subject under regulation is technical and complex. BPA has longstanding expertise in the area, and was intimately involved in the drafting and consideration of the statute by Congress. Following enactment of the statute, the agency immediately interpreted the statute in the manner now under challenge. Thus, BPA's interpretation represents "a contemporaneous construction of a statute by the men charged with the responsibility of setting its machinery in motion, of making the parts work efficiently and smoothly while they are yet untried and new.", . . .

> Giving the Administrator's interpretation the deference that it is due, we are convinced that his interpretation is a fully reasonable one. . . .

The Court then went on to demonstrate that the Respondents' contentions were inconsistent with various provisions of the Regional Act.

Note: The Political Responsibility Analysis *of Chevron.*

In *Chevron*, Justice Stevens grounded the judicial obligation to defer to a "permissible" agency construction of a statute on the ground that the agency would be reflecting the policy views of the incumbent administration. It was more appropriate, Justice Stevens ruled, for policy choices to be made by the President — who is responsible to the electorate at the polls — than for courts — which are not politically responsible-to make those policy choices.

Justice Stevens' concern that policy be made by officials who are responsible to the electorate reflects a view different from that of the so-called "progressives" whose ideology had been widely followed in the earlier part of the twentieth century. Under the progressive ideology, politicians were removed as much as possible from the work of day-to-day governance which the progressives believed was best performed by a professional administrator. The city manager form of municipal government embodies such an approach: The elected members of the city council appoint a nonpolitical manager who does the actual work of administration.

The Federal Trade Commission (FTC) is an example at the federal level: The Commission is charged, inter alia, with enforcing the Federal Trade Commission Act's prohibition of "unfair methods of competition," a phrase whose meaning the statute intentionally left to the Commission to work out over time in administering the Act. Although the Commission thus was given a significant policy-making role, it was designed to be independent from politics and politicians. The Commissioners are appointed by the President and confirmed by the Senate to hold office for a term of years; the terms are staggered; and the President is prohibited from appointing more than a specified number of Commissioners from the same political party. The Commission is thus intended to be independent and nonpartisan. It exemplifies the progressive model of governmental administration by nonpolitical experts and technicians. Many of the agencies created during the New Deal period followed the "progressive" design of the FTC model.

Because of the way the terms of agency members are staggered, it often happens that a new President is unable to obtain a working majority on many of the independent agencies until he has been in office for many months. Early in his administration the independent agencies may still be carrying out the policies of the former administration. Had the EPA been a multi-headed independent agency, it might have been resisting the bubble concept during the early years of the Reagan administration. How, therefore, should a court react to a policy position maintained by an independent agency which is at variance with the policies of the incumbent administration? Justice Stevens' rationale for deferring to the politically responsible instrumentality would not so easily apply, would it? Yet the new President ultimately will achieve control over all of the independent agencies. Ultimately judicial deference to agency policy positions will bring the position of the courts into line with the policy positions of the incumbent administration. A refusal to accept the policies of the independent agencies would require the courts to make the policy choices. And judicial policy choices would be permanent, since there is no available rationale for courts sua sponte to change their views on statutory interpretation when administrations change.

Questions and Comments

1.   To what extent does the *Chevron* case assert a different judicial attitude towards agency statutory construction than was manifested in earlier cases such as *Gray v. Powell, NLRB v. Hearst Publications, Inc.* and *Packard Motor Car Co. v. NLRB?* Has the Court required a greater degree of judicial deference in *Chevron* than it did in these other cases? Explain.

2.   Does *Chevron's* significance rest on the fact that the issue before the Court was the validity of an agency regulation? *Chevron* differs from *Gray v. Powell* and *NLRB v. Hearst Publications, Inc.* because it is not fact specific. Because the EPA had approved the incorporation of the bubble concept into the statutory term "stationary source" in a regulation, the Court's deference to the agency interpretation could not be explained as an instance of a court upholding an agency factual determination, could it? The required judicial deference thus had to be explained as

deference on an issue of law. Does *Chevron* modify *Packard?*

3. What did Justice Stevens mean in *Chevron* when he referred to a "gap" left in the statute by Congress for the agency to fill? When would Justice Stevens find an express delegation of authority by Congress to the agency? an implicit delegation?

4. Is the Court's citation to *Unemployment Compensation Commn v. Aragon* in the *Aluminum Co.* case misplaced? Why or why not? Does the *Aluminum Co.* case involve a particular application of a broad statutory term? Does *Chevron?* Does *Bureau of Alcohol, Tobacco & Firearms v. FELA?*

5. Why did the Court defer to the agency's statutory construction in *Chevron* and *Aluminum Co.* but reject it in *Bureau of Alcohol, Tobacco & Firearms?* Can you determine when a court is likely to defer to an agency's construction of a governing statute and when it is likely to reject it? What factors did the Court refer to in the *Aluminum Co.* case as a basis for its deference to the agency's construction? Are those factors still relevant?

6. What inquiries is the Court making in these cases? Does it examine the structure of the statute? its legislative history? Will the Court defer to the agency when those inquiries indicate a clear (to the Court) congressional intent? What is the relevance (if any) of the complexity of the statute? of its technical nature? Why did the Court mention these factors in the *Aluminum Co.* case?

7. Explain how, under *Chevron*, the factors which the Court referred to in *Aluminum Co.* would justify the Court's deference to the BPA's interpretation. If *Chevron* requires judicial deference whenever the Congressional intent is not "clear", then would not the agency's construction of the statute have to be followed regardless of whether the agency had expertise, was intimately involved in the statute's drafting, and regardless of how the agency construed the statute immediately after its enactment?

8. In **Rust v. Sullivan, 500 U.S. 173 (1991),** the Court relied upon *Chevron* to uphold regulations of the Department of Health and Human Services prohibiting the recipients of federal funds under Title X of the Public Health Service Act from engaging in activities that "encourage, promote or advocate abortion as a method of family planning," and forbids recipients from referring a pregnant woman to an abortion provider, even upon specific request. The relevant statutory language provided that "[n]one of the funds appropriated under this subchapter shall be used in programs where abortion is a method of family planning." The Court read this language as not speaking directly to the issues of counseling, referral, advocacy, or program integrity and further held that the statutory ambiguity was not resolved by the legislative history. The Court then ruled that the Secretary's construction of the statute, embodied in the regulations, was a plausible one to which the courts, under *Chevron*, must defer. Although the Secretary had reversed an earlier interpretation which had permitted "nondirective counseling," the Court held that the Secretary "amply justified his change of interpretation with a 'reasoned analysis.' "

9. *Chevron and Legislative History.* The proper role of legislative history in applying the *Chevron* analysis has received continual judicial attention. In *Chevron*

itself, after determining that the statutory text did not answer the question in issue, the Court resorted to legislative history in an attempt to ascertain Congressional intent. Only after finding legislative history unhelpful, did the Court refer to the agency interpretation. But could legislative history be used in other ways? Use of legislative history in a supplemental way to confirm an independent determination that the statute is ambiguous seems unproblematic. Would it be proper to resort to legislative history in order to establish an ambiguity which does not appear in an otherwise apparently clear statutory text? This issue, of course, can arise in a variety of contexts. See, e.g., *Connecticut Nat'l Bank v. Germain*, 503 U.S. 249, 252–55 (1992). In the context of agency regulation, however, a determination that Congressional intent is ambiguous carries consequences about institutional competence, for if the Congressional intent is ambiguous, then the authority to interpret switches from the courts to the administering agency. But extra-textual authority probably cannot be used to establish an ambiguity when the text is otherwise unambiguous. See *K Mart Corp. v. Cartier, Inc.*, 486 U.S. 281, 293 n.4 (1988) ("the purported gloss any party gives to the statute, or any reference to legislative history, is in the first instance irrelevant.") (plurality opinion). Adverting to this question in *Alex v. City of Chicago*, 29 F.3d 1235, 1239 (7th Cir.), *cert. denied*, 513 U.S. 1057 (1994), the Seventh Circuit took a similar view, stating: that "when statutory meaning is clear with respect to the issue at bar judicial inquiry normally should end without heed to the embellishments of secondary materials like legislative history, regulations or administrative rulings." Accord, *Ball, Ball & Brosamer, Inc. v. Reich*, 24 F.3d 1447, 1452 (D.C. Cir. 1994); *Arkansas AFL-CIO v. FCC*, 11 F.3d 1430, 1440 (8th Cir. 1993); *Mississippi Poultry Ass'n v. Madigan*, 9 F.3d 1113, 1115 (5th Cir. 1993). On rehearing en banc in the latter case the Fifth Circuit conceded that the prohibition on making recourse to legislative history when the statutory text is unambiguous is a sound rule but not an absolute one. *Mississippi Poultry Ass'n v. Madigan*, 31 F.3d 293, 305 (5th Cir 1994) (en banc).

Early Scholarly Commentary on *Chevron*

Compare the following comments on *Chevron*:

For several reasons . . . a general rule of judicial deference to all agency interpretations of law would be unsound. Under the constitutional system, it is ordinarily for courts to say what the law is, and the case for deference to agency interpretations of law must therefore depend in the first instance on the law in the form of congressional instruction. If Congress has told courts to defer to agency interpretations, courts should do so. But many of the recent regulatory statutes were born out of legislative distrust for agency discretion; these statutes hardly call for deference to agency interpretations. . . . [T]hey represent an effort to limit administrative authority through clear legislative specifications. A rule of deference in the face of ambiguity would be inconsistent with an appreciation, endorsed by Congress, of the considerable risks posed by administrative discretion. An ambiguity is not a delegation of law-interpreting power. *Chevron* elides the two.

C.R. Sunstein, After the Rights Revolution: Reconceiving the Regulatory State 142–143 (1990).

Justice Stevens reasoned that because there was no clear congressional intent with respect to the application of the term *stationary source* to the bubble concept, the agency had discretion to adopt the flexible definition rather than insist that each point source comply with pollution limits. But the inquiry into whether Congress had an intention (or even 'purpose') relevant to the bubble proposal is obviously an inquiry into where the bounds are on the continuum of conceivable agency constructions of the statutory term, just as the Court in *Hearst Publications v. NLRB* had to explore the limits on NLRB discretion in applying the term *employee.* In *Chevron*, as in *Hearst* forty years earlier, the Court's framework was to ask whether this definitional question was fairly answerable using the tools of judges and lawyers, or was it instead more suitable for the tools of agency officials charged with exercising policy discretion and staffed with bureaucratic resources to make specialized factual determinations. The statutory interpretation form of choice only recapitulates the law-fact-policy distinction. . . . . .

C.F. EDLEY, JR., ADMINISTRATIVE LAW: RETHINKING JUDICIAL CONTROL OF BUREAUCRACY 99–100 (1990).

Immediate Post-Chevron Judicial Responses

***Mayburg v. Secretary of Health & Human Services*, 740 F.2d 100 (1st Cir. 1984).** Under HHS' interpretation of the Medicare Act, an elderly woman living in a nursing home in order to receive custodial rather than medical care would be denied medical benefits. In general, the Act provides in-patient hospital coverage for each 90-day "spell of illness" and requires a 60-day period under which a person is not an inpatient of a hospital or skilled nursing facility before the next covered "spell of illness" occurs. HHS interpreted the Act as preventing anyone living in a skilled nursing facility, even if for nonmedical reasons, from meeting the condition of a 60-day inteveral between spells of illness. Writing for the First Circuit, then Judge Breyer refused to accept this interpretation, despite the Court's then-recent ruling in *Chevron*.

> The Secretary . . . argues that this court should simply defer to HHS's interpretation of the statute. She points to a line of Supreme Court cases that, she argues, compel such deference. . . . A different line of Supreme Court cases, however, cautions us that "deference" is not complete; sometimes a different, and more independent judicial attitude is appropria-te. . . . Moreover, the Administrative Procedure Act states that "the reviewing court," not the agency, "shall decide all relevant questions of law." 5 U.S.C. § 706.

> In order to apply correctly what Judge Friendly has described as conflicting authority . . . we must ask *why* courts should ever defer, or give special weight, to an agency's interpretation of a statute's meaning. And, here there are at least two types of answers, neither of which supports more than a modicum of special attention here.

> First, one might argue that specialized agencies, at least sometimes, know better than the courts what Congress actually intended the words of the statute to mean. Thus, in *Skidmore v. Swift & Co.*, 323 U.S. 134, 65 S. Ct. 161, 89 L.Ed. 124 (1944), the Supreme Court wrote

We consider that the rulings, interpretations and opinions of the Administrator under this [Fair Labor Standards] Act, while not controlling upon the courts by reason of their authority, do constitute a body of experience and informed judgment to which courts and litigants may properly resort for guidance. The weight of such a judgment in a particular case will depend upon the thoroughness evident in its consideration, the validity of its reasoning, its consistency with earlier and later pronouncements, and all those factors which give it power to persuade, if lacking power to control.

. . . The fact that a question is closely related to an agency's area of expertise may give an agency greater "power to persuade." Its interpretation may also carry more persuasive power if made near the time the statute was enacted when congressional debates and interest group positions were fresh in the administrators' minds. . . . An interpretation that has proved to be administratively workable because it is consistent and longstanding is typically more persuasive . . . as is an interpretation that has stood throughout subsequent reenactment of the statute. . . . All these factors help to convince a court that the agency is familiar with the context, implications, history and consequent meaning of the statute. But, still, under *Skidmore* the agency ultimately must depend upon the *persuasive power* of its argument. The simple fact that the agency *has* a position, in and of itself, is of only marginal significance.

Second, a court might give special weight to an agency's interpretation of a statute because Congress intended it to do just that in respect to the statute in question. In *Social Security Board v. Nierotko*, 327 U.S. 358, 66 S.Ct. 637, 90 L.Ed 718 (1946), for example, the Court noted that an agency, "when it interprets a statute" may act "as a delegate to the legislative power." And the Court added that "such interpretive power may be included in the agencies' administrative functions." . . . If Congress expressly delegates a law-declaring function to the agency, of course, courts must respect that delegation. . . . But, if Congress is silent, courts may still infer from the particular statutory circumstances an implicit congressional instruction about the degree of respect or deference they owe the agency on a question of law. *See Chevron v. National Resources Defense Council, Inc.*, __ U.S. __, 104 S.Ct. 2778, 2781–82, 81 L.Ed.2d 694 (U.S. 1984). They might do so by asking what a sensible legislator would have expected given the statutory circumstances. The less important the question of law, the more interstitial its character, the more closely related to the everyday administration of the statute and to the agency's (rather than the court's) administrative or substantive expertise, the less likely it is that Congress (would have) "wished" or "expected" the courts to remain indifferent to the agency's views. . . . Conversely, the larger the question, the more its answer is likely to clarify or stabilize a broad area of law, the more likely Congress intended the courts to decide the question themselves. *Compare NLRB v. Hearst Publications, Inc.*, 322 U.S. 111 (1944) with *Packard Motor Car Co. v. NLRB*, 330 U.S. 485 (1947).

In this instance, the "spell of illness" provision is central to the statutory scheme. The interpretative skills called for seem primarily judicial, not administrative, in nature. The "administrative" implications seem trifling, or non-existent. And, nothing else suggests any specific congressional intent to place the power to construe this statutory term primarily in the agency's hands. Thus, the arguments for completely deferring to the agency's interpretation of the statute are not strong here.

In sum, we have paid particular attention to HHS's arguments; we have taken note of its experience administering the statute and of its administrative needs; we have reached our decision with all those factors in mind. Having done so, we nonetheless believe . . . that the agency's interpretation is incorrect.

Immigration and Naturalization Service v. Cardoza-Fonesca, 480 U.S. 421 (1987). Respondent, a 38-year old Nicaraguan citizen against whom the INS had commenced deportation proceedings, conceded that she was in the United States illegally but sought withholding of deportation pursuant to § 243(h) of the Immigration and Nationality Act and asylum as a refugee pursuant to § 208(a) of that Act. Under § 208(a), a person is entitled to refugee status by showing a "well founded fear of persecution" whereas under § 243(h) a person is entitled to withholding of deportation to a particular nation only if that person proves that it is more likely than not that he or she will be subject to persecution upon deportation.

The INS argued that the § 208(a) refugee provision should be construed as embodying the same objective standard as § 243(h). The Court rejected that position, holding that § 208(a) was broader than § 243(h), making refugee status available to those who possess a reasonable fear of persecution, even though actual persecution is not the most probable result of deportation. Concurring in the result, Justice Scalia criticized Justice Stevens' majority opinion as confusing on the issue of the deference owed to an agency interpretation:

> . . . The Court's discussion is flatly inconsistent with this well established interpretation [of *Chevron*]. The Court first implies that courts may substitute their interpretation of a statute for that of an agency whenever, '[e]mploying traditional tools of statutory construction,' they are able to reach a conclusion as to the proper interpretation of the statute. . . . But this would make deference a doctrine of desperation, authorizing courts to defer only if they would otherwise be unable to construe the enactment at issue. This is not an interpretation but an evisceration of *Chevron.*

> The Court also implies that courts may substitute their interpretation of a statute for that of an agency whenever they face "a pure question of statutory construction for the courts to decide," . . . rather than a "question of interpretation [in which] the agency is required to apply [a legal standard] to a particular set of facts,". . . . No support is adduced for this proposition, which is contradicted by the case the Court purports to be interpreting, since in *Chevron* the Court deferred to the Environmental Protection Agency's abstract interpretation of the phrase "stationary source."

Questions and Comments

1.   In *Mayburg*, Judge Breyer is using the deference cases of the 1940s (*Hearst*, *Packard*) as a guide to *Chevron* deference. Is he correct in doing so? What are the differences between deference in *Hearst* and deference in *Chevron*? Does it matter that *Hearst* dealt with the application of the agency's enabling statute to a specific factual setting whereas *Chevron* dealt with statutory interpretation as applied to a host of settings?

2.   Is this issue part of what was troubling Justice Scalia in *Cardoza-Fonesca*? Is it fair to conclude that Justice Scalia believes that the Court should have reversed Judge Breyer's decision in *Mayburg*?

3.   What else in *Cardoza-Fonesca* troubles Justice Scalia? Why does he object to a court using traditional tools of statutory construction? Would not Justice Scalia use those tools himself? Perhaps his position is that a court may use traditional tools of statutory construction to determine whether congressional intent is clear. If that intent is not clear, deference to the agency's interpretation is required, even if a court could arrive at a probable interpretation using the traditional tools of statutory construction.

4.   Note that Justice Stevens (who wrote the Court's opinion in *Chevron*) also authored the opinion in *Cardoza-Fonesca*. Does his opinion in *Cardoza-Fonesca* indicate that he believes that he wrote too strongly in *Chevron*?

The Current Chevron Landscape

1) Limiting Chevron's Scope:

Christensen v. Harris County, 529 U.S. 576 (2000). The Fair Labor Standards that governs the payment of wages and overtime compensation applies not only to private employers but also to states and their political subdivisions. Under that Act employees may be compensated for overtime by cash compensation or by compensatory time or "comp time," which entitles them to take time off work with full pay. If the employees do not use their accumulated compensatory time, the employer is obligated to pay cash compensation under certain circumstances.

As its employees accumulated compensatory time, Harris County became concerned that it lacked the resources to pay monetary compensation to employees who worked substantial amounts of overtime. As a result, the county began looking for a way to reduce accumulated compensatory time. It wrote to the United States Department of Labor's Wage and Hour Division, asking "whether the Sheriff may schedule non-exempt employees to use or take compensatory time." The Acting Administrator of the Division replied:

> "[I]t is our position that a public employer may schedule its nonexempt employees to use their accrued FLSA compensatory time as directed if the prior agreement specifically provides such a provision.

"Absent such an agreement, it is our position that neither the statute nor the regulations permit an employer to require an employee to use accrued compensatory time."

Harris County nonetheless adopted a policy requiring its employees to schedule time off in order to reduce the amount of accrued compensatory time.

Ruling that the opinion letter was not entitled to *Chevron*-type deference, the Court, through Justice Thomas, had this to say:

In an attempt to avoid the conclusion that the FLSA does not prohibit compelled use of compensatory time, petitioners and the United States contend that we should defer to the Department of Labor's opinion letter, which takes the position that an employer may compel the use of compensatory time only if the employee has agreed in advance to such a practice. Specifically, they argue that the agency opinion letter is entitled to deference under our decision in *Chevron U.S.A. Inc. v. Natural Resources Defense Council, Inc.*, 467 U.S. 837 (1984). In *Chevron*, we held that a court must give effect to an agency's regulation containing a reasonable interpretation of an ambiguous statute. *Id.*, at 842–844.

Here, however, we confront an interpretation contained in an opinion letter, not one arrived at after, for example, a formal adjudication or notice-and-comment rulemaking. Interpretations such as those in opinion letters — like interpretations contained in policy statements, agency manuals, and enforcement guidelines, all of which lack the force of law — do not warrant *Chevron*-style deference. See, *e.g.*, *Reno v. Koray*, 515 U.S. 50, 61 (1995) (internal agency guideline, which is not "subject to the rigors of the Administrative Procedur[e] Act, including public notice and comment," entitled only to "some deference" (internal quotation marks omitted)); *EEOC v. Arabian American Oil Co.*, 499 U.S. 244, 256–258 (1991) (interpretative guidelines do not receive *Chevron* deference); *Martin v. Occupational Safety and Health Review Comm'n*, 499 U.S. 144, 157 (1991) (interpretative rules and enforcement guidelines are "not entitled to the same deference as norms that derive from the exercise of the Secretary's delegated lawmaking powers"). See generally 1 K. Davis & R. Pierce, Administrative Law Treatise § 3.5 (3d ed.1994). Instead, interpretations contained in formats such as opinion letters are "entitled to respect" under our decision in *Skidmore v. Swift & Co.*, 323 U.S. 134, 140 (1944), but only to the extent that those interpretations have the "power to persuade," *ibid.* See *Arabian American Oil Co., supra*, at 256–258. As explained above, we find unpersuasive the agency's interpretation of the statute at issue in this case.

Of course, the framework of deference set forth in *Chevron* does apply to an agency interpretation contained in a regulation. But in this case the Department of Labor's regulation does not address the issue of compelled compensatory time. The regulation provides only that "[t]he agreement or understanding [between the employer and employee] *may* include other provisions governing the preservation, use, or cashing out of compensatory time so long as these provisions are consistent with [§ 207(*o*)]." 29 CFR

§ 553.23(a)(2) (1999) (emphasis added). Nothing in the regulation even arguably requires that an employer's compelled use policy *must* be included in an agreement. The text of the regulation itself indicates that its command is permissive, not mandatory.

Seeking to overcome the regulation's obvious meaning, the United States asserts that the agency's opinion letter interpreting the regulation should be given deference under our decision in *Auer v. Robbins*, 519 U.S. 452 (1997). In *Auer*, we held that an agency's interpretation of its own regulation is entitled to deference. *Id.*, at 461. See also *Bowles v. Seminole Rock & Sand Co.*, 325 U.S. 410 (1945). But *Auer* deference is warranted only when the language of the regulation is ambiguous. The regulation in this case, however, is not ambiguous — it is plainly permissive. To defer to the agency's position would be to permit the agency, under the guise of interpreting a regulation, to create *de facto* a new regulation. Because the regulation is not ambiguous on the issue of compelled compensatory time, *Auer* deference is unwarranted.

UNITED STATES v. MEAD CORPORATION
533 U.S. 218 (2001)

JUSTICE SOUTER delivered the opinion of the Court.

The question is whether a tariff classification ruling by the United States Customs Service deserves judicial deference. The Federal Circuit rejected Customs's invocation of *Chevron U.S.A. Inc. v. Natural Resources Defense Council, Inc.*, 467 U.S. 837 (1984), in support of such a ruling, to which it gave no deference. We agree that a tariff classification has no claim to judicial deference under *Chevron*, there being no indication that Congress intended such a ruling to carry the force of law, but we hold that under *Skidmore v. Swift & Co.*, 323 U.S. 134, 65 S.Ct. 161, 89 L.Ed. 124 (1944), the ruling is eligible to claim respect according to its persuasiveness.

I

A

Imports are taxed under the Harmonized Tariff Schedule of the United States (HTSUS), 19 U.S.C. § 1202. Title 19 U.S.C. § 1500(b) provides that Customs "shall, under rules and regulations prescribed by the Secretary [of the Treasury] . . . fix the final classification and rate of duty applicable to . . . merchandise" under the HTSUS. Section 1502(a) provides that "[t]he Secretary of the Treasury shall establish and promulgate such rules and regulations not inconsistent with the law . . . and may disseminate such information as may be necessary to secure a just, impartial, and uniform appraisement of imported merchandise and the classification and assessment of duties thereon at the various ports of entry." The Secretary provides for tariff rulings before the entry of goods by regulations authorizing "ruling letters" setting tariff classifications for particular imports. 19

CFR § 177.8 (2000). Under those regulations, a ruling letter "represents the official position of the Customs Service with respect to the particular transaction or issue described therein and is binding on all Customs Service personnel" until modified or revoked.

The Respondent Mead Corporation imports "day planners," three-ring binders with pages having room for notes of daily schedules and phone numbers and addresses, together with a calendar and suchlike. The tariff schedule on point falls under the HTSUS heading for "[r]egisters, account books, notebooks, order books, receipt books, letter pads, memorandum pads, diaries and similar articles," HTSUS subheading 4820.10, which comprises two subcategories. Items in the first, "[d]iaries, notebooks and address books, bound; memorandum pads, letter pads and similar articles," were subject to a tariff of 4.0% at the time in controversy. Objects in the second, covering "[o]ther" items, were free of duty. HTSUS subheading. Between 1989 and 1993, Customs repeatedly treated day planners under the "other" HTSUS subheading. In January 1993, however, Customs changed its position, and issued a Headquarters ruling letter classifying Mead's day planners as "Diaries . . . , bound" subject to the 4% tariff. Mead's protest of the change in classification were rejected by Customs. Mead sought relief before the U.S. Court of International Trade, but that Court granted summary judgment to the Government. On appeal, the U.S. Court for the Federal Circuit reversed, holding that Customs classifications rulings were not entitled to *Chevron* deference.]

We granted certiorari . . . in order to consider the limits of Chevron deference owed to administrative practice in applying a statute. We hold that administrative implementation of a particular statutory provision qualifies for Chevron deference when it appears that Congress delegated authority to the agency generally to make rules carrying the force of law, and that the agency interpretation claiming deference was promulgated in the exercise of that authority. Delegation of such authority may be shown in a variety of ways, as by an agency's power to engage in adjudication or notice-and-comment rulemaking, or by some other indication of a comparable congressional intent. The Customs ruling at issue here fails to qualify, although the possibility that it deserves some deference under *Skidmore* leads us to vacate and remand.

II

A

When Congress has "explicitly left a gap for an agency to fill, there is an express delegation of authority to the agency to elucidate a specific provision of the statute by regulation," *Chevron*, 467 U.S., at 843–844, and any ensuing regulation is binding in the courts unless procedurally defective, arbitrary or capricious in substance, or manifestly contrary to the statute. . . . But whether or not they enjoy any express delegation of authority on a particular question, agencies charged with applying a statute necessarily make all sorts of interpretive choices, and while not all of those choices bind judges to follow them, they certainly may influence courts facing questions the agencies have already answered. "[T]he well-reasoned views of the agencies implementing a statute 'constitute a body of experience and informed judgment to which courts and litigants may properly resort for guidance,'" *Bragdon v. Abbott*, 524 U.S. 624, 642 (1998) (quoting *Skidmore*, 323 U.S., at 139–140), and "[w]e have long recognized that considerable weight should be accorded to an executive department's construction of a statutory scheme it is entrusted to administer. . . ." *Chevron, supra*, at 844. . . . The fair measure of deference to an agency administering its own statute has been understood to vary with circumstances, and courts have looked to the degree of the agency's care, its consistency, formality, and relative expertness, and to the persuasiveness of the agency's position, see *Skidmore, supra*, at 139–140. The approach has produced a spectrum of judicial responses, from great respect at one end, see, *e.g., Aluminum Co. of America v. Central Lincoln Peoples' Util. Dist.*, 467 U.S. 380, 389–390 (1984) (" 'substantial deference' " to administrative construction), to near indifference at the other, see, *e.g., Bowen v. Georgetown Univ. Hospital*, 488 U.S. 204, 212–213 (1988) (interpretation advanced for the first time in a litigation brief). Justice Jackson summed things up in *Skidmore v. Swift & Co.*:

> "The weight [accorded to an administrative] judgment in a particular case will depend upon the thoroughness evident in its consideration, the validity of its reasoning, its consistency with earlier and later pronouncements, and all those factors which give it power to persuade, if lacking power to control." 323 U.S., at 140.

Since 1984, we have identified a category of interpretive choices distinguished by an additional reason for judicial deference. This Court in *Chevron* recognized that Congress not only engages in express delegation of specific interpretive authority, but that "[s]ometimes the legislative delegation to an agency on a particular question is implicit." . . . Congress, that is, may not have expressly delegated authority or responsibility to implement a particular provision or fill a particular gap. Yet it can still be apparent from the agency's generally conferred authority and other statutory circumstances that Congress would expect the agency to be able to speak with the force of law when it addresses ambiguity in the statute or fills a space in the enacted law, even one about which "Congress did not actually have an intent" as to a particular result. . . . When circumstances implying such an expectation exist, a reviewing court has no business rejecting an agency's exercise of its generally conferred authority to resolve a particular statutory ambiguity simply because the agency's chosen resolution seems unwise, . . . but is obliged to accept the agency's position if Congress has not previously spoken to the point at issue and the agency's interpretation is reasonable. . . .

We have recognized a very good indicator of delegation meriting *Chevron* treatment in express congressional authorizations to engage in the process of rulemaking or adjudication that produces regulations or rulings for which deference is claimed. See, *e.g., EEOC v. Arabian American Oil Co.*, 499 U.S. 244, 257 (1991) (no *Chevron* deference to agency guideline where congressional delegation did not include the power to " 'promulgate rules or regulations' " (quoting *General Elec. Co. v. Gilbert*, 429 U.S. 125, 141) (1976)); see also *Christensen v. Harris County*, 529 U.S. 576, 596–597 (2000) (BREYER, J., dissenting) (where it is in doubt that Congress actually intended to delegate particular interpretive authority to an agency, *Chevron* is "inapplicable"). It is fair to assume generally that Congress contemplates administrative action with the effect of law when it provides for a relatively formal administrative procedure tending to foster the fairness and deliberation that should underlie a pronouncement of such force. . . . Thus, the overwhelming number of our cases applying *Chevron* deference have reviewed the fruits of notice-and-comment rulemaking or formal adjudication. That said, and as significant as notice-and-comment is in pointing to *Chevron* authority, the want of that procedure here does not decide the case, for we have sometimes found reasons for *Chevron* deference even when no such administrative formality was required and none was afforded, see, *e.g.*, *NationsBank of N.C., N.A. v. Variable Annuity Life Ins. Co.*, 513 U.S. 251, 256–257, 263 (1995). The fact that the tariff classification here was not a product of such formal process does not alone, therefore, bar the application of *Chevron*.

There are, nonetheless, ample reasons to deny *Chevron* deference here. The authorization for classification rulings, and Customs's practice in making them, present a case far removed not only from notice-and-comment process, but from any other circumstances reasonably suggesting that Congress ever thought of classification rulings as deserving the deference claimed for them here.

B

No matter which angle we choose for viewing the Customs ruling letter in this case, it fails to qualify under *Chevron*. On the face of the statute, to begin with, the terms of the congressional delegation give no indication that Congress meant to delegate authority to Customs to issue classification rulings with the force of law. We are not, of course, here making any global statement about Customs's authority, for it is true that the general rulemaking power conferred on Customs . . . authorizes some regulation with the force of law, or "legal norms". . . . It is true as well that Congress had classification rulings in mind when it explicitly authorized, in a parenthetical, the issuance of "regulations establishing procedures for the issuance of binding rulings prior to the entry of the merchandise concerned," 19 U.S.C. § 1502(a). The reference to binding classifications does not, however, bespeak the legislative type of activity that would naturally bind more than the parties to the ruling, once the goods classified are admitted into this country. And though the statute's direction to disseminate "information" necessary to "secure" uniformity, 19 U.S.C. § 1502(a), seems to assume that a ruling may be precedent in later transactions, precedential value alone does not add up to *Chevron* entitlement; interpretive rules may sometimes function as precedents, see Strauss, *The Rulemaking Continuum*, 41 Duke L.J. 1463, 1472–1473 (1992), and they enjoy no *Chevron* status as a class. In any event, any precedential claim of a classification ruling is counterbalanced by the provision for independent review of Customs classifications by the CIT, see 28 U.S.C. §§ 2638–2640; the scheme for CIT review includes a provision that treats classification rulings on par with the Secretary's rulings on "valuation, rate of duty, marking, restricted merchandise, entry requirements, drawbacks, vessel repairs, or similar matters," § 1581(h); see § 2639(b). It is hard to imagine a congressional understanding more at odds with the *Chevron* regime.

It is difficult, in fact, to see in the agency practice itself any indication that

Customs ever set out with a lawmaking pretense in mind when it undertook to make classifications like these. Customs does not generally engage in notice-and-comment practice when issuing them, and their treatment by the agency makes it clear that a letter's binding character as a ruling stops short of third parties; Customs has regarded a classification as conclusive only as between itself and the importer to whom it was issued, 19 CFR § 177.9(c) (2000), and even then only until Customs has given advance notice of intended change, §§ 177.9(a), (c). Other importers are in fact warned against assuming any right of detrimental reliance. § 177.9(c).

Indeed, to claim that classifications have legal force is to ignore the reality that 46 different Customs offices issue 10,000 to 15,000 of them each year. . . . Any suggestion that rulings intended to have the force of law are being churned out at a rate of 10,000 a year at an agency's 46 scattered offices is simply self-refuting. Although the circumstances are less startling here, with a Headquarters letter in issue, none of the relevant statutes recognizes this category of rulings as separate or different from others; there is thus no indication that a more potent delegation might have been understood as going to Headquarters even when Headquarters provides developed reasoning, as it did in this instance.

Nor do the amendments to the statute made effective after this case arose disturb our conclusion. The new law requires Customs to provide notice-and-comment procedures only when modifying or revoking a prior classification ruling or modifying the treatment accorded to substantially identical transactions, 19 U.S.C. § 1625(c); and under its regulations, Customs sees itself obliged to provide notice-and-comment procedures only when "changing a practice" so as to produce a tariff increase, or in the imposition of a restriction or prohibition, or when Customs Headquarters determines that "the matter is of sufficient importance to involve the interests of domestic industry," 19 CFR §§ 177.10(c)(1)(2) (2000). The statutory changes reveal no new congressional objective of treating classification decisions generally as rulemaking with force of law, nor do they suggest any intent to create a *Chevron* patchwork of classification rulings, some with force of law, some without.

In sum, classification rulings are best treated like "interpretations contained in policy statements, agency manuals, and enforcement guidelines." *Christensen*, 529 U.S., at 587. They are beyond the *Chevron* pale.

C

To agree with the Court of Appeals that Customs ruling letters do not fall within *Chevron* is not, however, to place them outside the pale of any deference whatever. *Chevron* did nothing to eliminate *Skidmore*'s holding that an agency's interpretation may merit some deference whatever its form, given the "specialized experience and broader investigations and information" available to the agency, . . . and given the value of uniformity in its administrative and judicial understandings of what a national law requires. . . .

There is room at least to raise a *Skidmore* claim here, where the regulatory scheme is highly detailed, and Customs can bring the benefit of specialized experience to bear on the subtle questions in this case: whether the daily planner with room for brief daily entries falls under "diaries," when diaries are grouped with "notebooks and address books, bound; memorandum pads, letter pads and similar articles," HTSUS subheading 4820.10.20; and whether a planner with a ring binding should qualify as "bound," when a binding may be typified by a book, but also may have "reinforcements or fittings of metal, plastics, etc.," Harmonized Commodity Description and Coding System Explanatory Notes to Heading 4820, p. 687. . . . A classification ruling in this situation may therefore at least seek a respect proportional to its "power to persuade," *Skidmore, supra,* at 140. . . . Such a ruling may surely claim the merit of its writer's thoroughness, logic and expertness, its fit with prior interpretations, and any other sources of weight.

D

Underlying the position we take here, like the position expressed by Justice SCALIA in dissent, is a choice about the best way to deal with an inescapable feature of the body of congressional legislation authorizing administrative action. That feature is the great variety of ways in which the laws invest the Government's administrative arms with discretion, and with procedures for exercising it, in giving meaning to Acts of Congress. Implementation of a statute may occur in formal adjudication or the choice to defend against judicial challenge; it may occur in a central board or office or in dozens of enforcement agencies dotted across the country; its institutional lawmaking may be confined to the resolution of minute detail or extend to legislative rulemaking on matters intentionally left by Congress to be worked out at the agency level.

Although we all accept the position that the Judiciary should defer to at least some of this multifarious administrative action, we have to decide how to take account of the great range of its variety. If the primary objective is to simplify the judicial process of giving or withholding deference, then the diversity of statutes authorizing discretionary administrative action must be declared irrelevant or minimized. If, on the other hand, it is simply implausible that Congress intended such a broad range of statutory authority to produce only two varieties of administrative action, demanding either Chevron deference or none at all, then the breadth of the spectrum of possible agency action must be taken into account. Justice SCALIA's first priority over the years has been to limit and simplify. The Court's choice has been to tailor deference to variety. This acceptance of the range of statutory variation has led the Court to recognize more than one variety of judicial deference, just as the Court has recognized a variety of indicators that Congress would expect *Chevron* deference.

Our respective choices are repeated today. Justice SCALIA would pose the question of deference as an either-or choice. On his view that *Chevron* rendered *Skidmore* anachronistic, when courts owe any deference it is *Chevron* deference that they owe . . . Whether courts do owe deference in a given case turns, for him, on whether the agency action (if reasonable) is "authoritative." . . . The character of the authoritative derives, in turn, not from breadth of delegation or the agency's procedure in implementing it, but is defined as the "official" position of an agency, . . . and may ultimately be a function of administrative persistence alone. . . .

The Court, on the other hand, said nothing in *Chevron* to eliminate *Skidmore*'s recognition of various justifications for deference depending on statutory circumstances and agency action; *Chevron* was simply a case recognizing that even without express authority to fill a specific statutory gap, circumstances pointing to implicit congressional delegation present a particularly insistent call for deference. Indeed, in holding here that *Chevron* left *Skidmore* intact and applicable where statutory circumstances indicate no intent to delegate general authority to make rules with force of law, or where such authority was not invoked, we hold nothing more than we said last Term in response to the particular statutory circumstances in *Christensen*, to which Justice SCALIA then took exception, . . . just as he does again today.

We think, in sum, that Justice SCALIA's efforts to simplify ultimately run afoul of Congress's indications that different statutes present different reasons for considering respect for the exercise of administrative authority or deference to it. Without being at odds with congressional intent much of the time, we believe that judicial responses to administrative action must continue to differentiate between *Chevron* and *Skidmore*, and that continued recognition of *Skidmore* is necessary for just the reasons Justice Jackson gave when that case was decided.

* * *

Since the *Skidmore* assessment called for here ought to be made in the first instance by the Court of Appeals for the Federal Circuit or the Court of International Trade, we go no further than to vacate the judgment and remand the case for further proceedings consistent with this opinion.

It is so ordered.

JUSTICE SCALIA, dissenting.

Today's opinion makes an avulsive change in judicial review of federal administrative action. Whereas previously a reasonable agency application of an ambiguous statutory provision had to be sustained so long as it represented the agency's authoritative interpretation, henceforth such an application can be set aside unless "it appears that Congress delegated authority to the agency generally to make rules carrying the force of law," as by giving an agency "power to engage in adjudication or notice-and-comment rulemaking, or . . . some other [procedure] indicat[ing] comparable congressional intent," and "the agency interpretation claiming deference was promulgated in the exercise of that authority." . . . What was previously a general presumption of authority in agencies to resolve ambiguity in the statutes they have been authorized to enforce has been changed to a presumption of no such authority, which must be overcome by affirmative legislative intent to the contrary. And whereas previously, when agency authority to resolve ambiguity did not exist the court was free to give the statute what it considered the best interpretation, henceforth the court must supposedly give the agency view some indeterminate amount of so-called *Skidmore* deference. We will be sorting out the consequences of the *Mead* doctrine, which has today replaced the *Chevron* doctrine, for years to come. I would adhere to our established jurisprudence, defer to the reasonable interpretation the Customs Service has given to the statute it is charged with enforcing, and reverse the judgment of the Court of Appeals.

. . . .

The principal effect will be protracted confusion. As noted above, the one test for *Chevron* deference that the Court enunciates is wonderfully imprecise: whether "Congress delegated authority to the agency generally to make rules carrying the force of law, . . . as by . . . adjudication[,] notice-and-comment rulemaking, or . . . some other [procedure] indicat[ing] comparable congressional intent." But even this description does not do justice to the utter flabbiness of the Court's criterion, since, in order to maintain the fiction that the new test is really just the old one, applied consistently throughout our case law, the Court must make a virtually open-ended exception to its already imprecise guidance: In the present case, it tells us, the absence of notice-and-comment rulemaking (and "[who knows?] [of] some other [procedure] indicat[ing] comparable congressional intent") is not enough to decide the question of *Chevron* deference, "for we have sometimes found reasons for *Chevron* deference even when no such administrative formality was required and none was afforded." . . . . The opinion then goes on to consider a grab bag of other factors — including the factor that used to be the sole criterion for *Chevron* deference: whether the interpretation represented the *authoritative* position of the agency. . . . It is hard to know what the lower courts are to make of today's guidance.

(2)

Another practical effect of today's opinion will be an artificially induced increase in informal rulemaking. Buy stock in the GPO. Since informal rulemaking and formal adjudication are the only more-or-less safe harbors from the storm that the Court has unleashed; and since formal adjudication is not an option but must be mandated by statute or constitutional command; informal rulemaking — which the Court was once careful to make voluntary unless required by statute, see *Bell Aerospace*, *supra*, and *Chenery*, *supra* — will now become a virtual necessity. As I have described, the Court's safe harbor requires not merely that the agency have been given rulemaking authority, but also that the agency have *employed* rulemaking as the means of resolving the statutory ambiguity. . . .

(3)

Worst of all, the majority's approach will lead to the ossification of large portions of our statutory law. Where *Chevron* applies, statutory ambiguities remain ambiguities subject to the agency's ongoing clarification. They create a space, so to speak, for the exercise of continuing agency discretion. As *Chevron* itself held, the Environmental Protection Agency can interpret "stationary source" to mean a single smokestack, can later replace that interpretation with the "bubble concept" embracing an entire plant, and if that proves undesirable can return again to the original interpretation. . . . For the indeterminately large number of statutes taken out of *Chevron* by today's decision, however, ambiguity (and hence flexibility) will cease with the first judicial resolution. *Skidmore* deference gives the agency's current position some vague and uncertain amount of respect, but it does not, like *Chevron, leave* the matter within the control of the Executive Branch for the future. Once the court has spoken, it becomes *unlawful* for the agency to take a contradictory position; the statute now *says* what the court has prescribed. . . . It will be bad enough when this ossification occurs as a result of judicial determination (under today's new principles) that there is no affirmative indication of congressional intent to "delegate"; but it will be positively bizarre when it occurs simply because of an agency's failure to act by rulemaking (rather than informal adjudication) before the issue is presented to the courts.

*   *   *   *

***Barnhart v. Walton*, 535 U.S. 212 (2002)** involved a construction of a regulation by the Social Security Administration interpreting the provisions governing disability benefits. Speaking through Justice Breyer, the Court ruled that the agency's construction was "permissible," that it reflected the agency's "own longstanding interpretation," and that the Court "normally accord[s] particular deference to an agency interpretation of 'longstanding' duration. In addition, Congressional reenactment of the provisions in question showed that Congress "intended the Agency's interpretation or at least understood the interpretation to be statutorily permissible." Justice Breyer continued:

> . . . the Agency's interpretation is one of long standing. . . . And the fact that the Agency previously reached its interpretation through means less formal than "notice and comment" rulemaking, see 5 U.S.C. § 553, does not automatically deprive that interpretation of the judicial deference otherwise its due. Cf. *Chevron*, 467 U.S., at 843 (stating, without delineation of means, that the " 'power of an administrative agency to administer a congressionally created . . . program necessarily requires the formulation of policy' " (quoting *Morton v. Ruiz*, 415 U.S. 199, 231 (1974)). If this Court's opinion in *Christensen v. Harris County*, 529 U.S. 576 (2000), suggested an absolute rule to the contrary, our later opinion in *United States v. Mead Corp.*, 533 U.S. 218 (2001), denied the suggestion. *Id.*, at 230–231 ("[T]he want of" notice and comment "does not decide the case"). Indeed, *Mead* pointed to instances in which the Court has applied *Chevron* deference to agency interpretations that did not emerge out of notice-and-comment rulemaking. 533 U.S., at 230–231 (citing *NationsBank of N. C., N.A. v. Variable Annuity Life Ins. Co.*, 513 U.S. 251, 256–257 (1995)). It indicated that whether a court should give such deference depends in significant part upon the interpretive method used and the nature of the question at issue. 533 U.S., at 229–231. And it discussed at length why *Chevron* did not require deference in the circumstances there present — a discussion that would have been superfluous had the presence or absence of notice-and-comment rulemaking been dispositive. 533 U.S., at 231–234.

In this case, the interstitial nature of the legal question, the related expertise of the Agency, the importance of the question to administration of the statute, the complexity of that administration, and the careful consideration the Agency has given the question over a long period of time all indicate that *Chevron* provides the appropriate legal lens through which to view the legality of the Agency interpretation here at issue. See *United States v. Mead Corp., supra;* cf. also 1 K. Davis & R. Pierce, Administrative Law Treatise §§ 1.7, 3.3 (3d ed.1994).

For these reasons, we find the Agency's interpretation lawful.

NATIONAL CABLE & TELECOMMUNICATIONS ASSOCIATION v. BRAND X INTERNET SERVICES
545 U.S. 967 (2005)

JUSTICE THOMAS delivered the opinion of the Court.

Title II of the Communications Act of 1934, 48 Stat.1064, as amended, 47 U.S.C. § 151 *et seq.*, subjects all providers of "telecommunications servic[e]" to mandatory common-carrier regulation,§ 153(44). In the order under review, the Federal Communications Commission concluded that cable companies that sell broadband Internet service do not provide "telecommunications service[e]" as the Communications Act defines that term, and hence are exempt from mandatory common-carrier regulation under Title II. We must decide whether that conclusion is a lawful construction of the Communications Act under *Chevron U.S.A. Inc.* v. *Natural Resources Defense Council, Inc.*,467 U.S.837 (1984), and the Administrative Procedure Act,5 U.S.C.§ 555 *et seq.* We hold that it is.

* * * *

In September 2000, the Commission initiated a rule-making proceeding to, among other things, apply these classifications to cable companies that offer broadband Internet service directly to consumers. In March 2002, that rulemaking culminated in the *Declaratory Ruling* under review in these cases. In the *Declaratory Ruling*, the Commission concluded that broadband Internet service provided by cable companies is an "information service" but not a "telecommunications service" under the Act, and therefore not subject to mandatory Title II common-carrier regulation. . . .

* * * *

III

We first consider whether we should apply *Chevron*'s framework to the Commission's interpretation of the term "telecommunications service." We conclude that we should. We also conclude that the Court of Appeals should have done the same, instead of following the contrary construction it adopted in *Portland*.

A

In *Chevron*, this Court held that ambiguities in statutes within an agency's jurisdiction to administer are delegations of authority to the agency to fill the statutory gap in reasonable fashion. Filling these gaps, the Court explained, involves difficult policy choices that agencies are better equipped to make than courts. 467 U.S., at 865–866. If a statute is ambiguous, and if the implementing agency's construction is reasonable, *Chevron* requires a federal court to accept the agency's construction of the statute, even if the agency's reading differs from what the court believes is the best statutory interpretation. *Id.*, at 843–844, and n.11.

The *Chevron* framework governs our review of the Commission's construction. Congress has delegated to the Commission the authority to "execute and enforce" the Communications Act,§ 151, and to "prescribe such rules and regulations as may be necessary in the public interest to carry out the provisions" of the Act, § 201(b); *AT&T Corp.* v. *Iowa Utilities Bd.*, 525 U.S. 366, 377–378 (1999). These provisions give the Commission the authority to promulgate binding legal rules; the Commission issued the order under review in the exercise of that authority; and no one questions that the order is within the Commission's jurisdiction. See *Household Credit Services, Inc.* v. *Pfennig*, 541 U.S. 232, 238–239 (2004); *United States* v. *Mead Corp.*, 533 U.S. 218, 231–234 (2001); *Christensen* v. *Harris County*, 529 U.S. 576, 586–588 (2000). Hence, as we have in the past, we apply the *Chevron* framework to the Commission's interpretation of the Communications Act. See *National Cable & Telecommunications Assn., Inc.* v. *Gulf Power Co.*, 534 U.S.327, 333–339 (2002); *Verizon*, 535 U.S., at 501–502. Some of the respondents dispute this conclusion, on the ground that the Commission's interpretation is inconsistent with its past practice. We reject this argument. Agency inconsistency is not a basis for declining to analyze the agency's interpretation under the *Chevron* framework. Unexplained inconsistency is, at most, a reason for holding an interpretation to be an arbitrary and capricious change from agency practice under the Administrative Procedure Act. See *Motor Vehicle Mfrs. Assn. of United States, Inc. v. State Farm Mut. Automobile Ins. Co.*, 463 U.S. 29, 46–57 (1983). For if the agency adequately explains the reasons for a reversal of policy, "change is not invalidating, since the whole point of *Chevron* is to leave the discretion provided by the ambiguities of a statute with the implementing agency." *Smiley v. Citibank (South Dakota), N.A.*, 517 U.S. 735, 742 (1996); see also *Rust v. Sullivan*, 500 U.S. 173, 186–187 (1991); *Barnhart v. Walton*, 535 U.S.212, 226 (2002)(SCALIA, J., concurring in part and concurring in judgment). "An initial agency interpretation is not instantly carved in stone. On the contrary, the agency . . . must consider varying interpretations and the wisdom of its policy on a continuing basis," *Chevron, supra*, at 863–864, for example, in response to changed factual circumstances, or a change in administrations, see *State Farm, supra*, at 59 (REHNQUIST, J., concurring in part and dissenting in part). That is no doubt why in *Chevron* itself, this Court deferred to an agency interpretation that was a recent reversal of agency policy. See 467 U.S., at 857–858. We therefore have no difficulty concluding that *Chevron* applies.

B

The Court of Appeals declined to apply *Chevron* because it thought the Commission's interpretation of the Communications Act foreclosed by the conflicting construction of the Act it [i.e., the court] had adopted in [its own prior decision in] *Portland, supra.* See 345 F.3d, at 1127 –1132. It based that holding on the assumption that *Portland*'s construction overrode the Commission's, regardless of whether *Portland* had held the statute to be unambiguous. 345 F.3d, at 1131. That reasoning was incorrect.

A court's prior judicial construction of a statute trumps an agency construction otherwise entitled to *Chevron* deference only if the prior court decision holds that its construction follows from the unambiguous terms of the statute and thus leaves no room for agency discretion. This principle follows from *Chevron* itself. *Chevron* established a "presumption that Congress, when it left ambiguity in a statute meant for implementation by an agency, understood that the ambiguity would be resolved, first and foremost, by the agency, and desired the agency (rather than the courts) to possess whatever degree of discretion the ambiguity allows." *Smiley, supra,* at 740–741. Yet allowing a judicial precedent to foreclose an agency from interpreting an ambiguous statute, as the Court of Appeals assumed it could, would allow a court's interpretation to override an agency's. *Chevron*'s premise is that it is for agencies, not courts, to fill statutory gaps. See 467 U.S., at 843–844, and n.11. The better rule is to hold judicial interpretations contained in precedents to the same demanding *Chevron* step one standard that applies if the court is reviewing the agency's construction on a blank slate: Only a judicial precedent holding that the statute unambiguously forecloses the agency's interpretation, and therefore contains no gap for the agency to fill, displaces a conflicting agency construction.

A contrary rule would produce anomalous results. It would mean that whether an agency's interpretation of an ambiguous statute is entitled to *Chevron* deference would turn on the order in which the interpretations issue: If the court's construction came first, its construction would prevail, whereas if the agency's came first, the agency's construction would command *Chevron* deference. Yet whether Congress has delegated to an agency the authority to interpret a statute does not depend on the order in which the judicial and administrative constructions occur. The Court of Appeals' rule, moreover, would "lead to the ossification of large portions of our statutory law," *Mead, supra,* at 247 (SCALIA, J., dissenting), by precluding agencies from revising unwise judicial constructions of ambiguous statutes. Neither *Chevron* nor the doctrine of *stare decisis* requires these haphazard results.

The dissent answers that allowing an agency to override what a court believes to be the best interpretation of a statute makes "judicial decisions subject to reversal by Executive officers." *Post,* at 13 (opinion of SCALIA, J.). It does not. Since *Chevron* teaches that a court's opinion as to the best reading of an ambiguous statute an agency is charged with administering is not authoritative, the agency's decision to construe that statute differently from a court does not say that the court's holding was legally wrong. Instead, the agency may, consistent with the court's holding, choose a different construction, since the agency remains the authoritative interpreter (within the limits of reason) of such statutes. In all other respects, the court's prior ruling remains binding law (for example, as to agency interpretations to which *Chevron* is inapplicable). The precedent has not been "reversed" by the agency, any more than a federal court's interpretation of a State's law can be said to have been "reversed" by a state court that adopts a conflicting (yet authoritative) interpretation of state law.

The Court of Appeals derived a contrary rule from a mistaken reading of this Court's decisions. It read *Neal* v. *United States*, 516 U.S.284 (1996), to establish that a prior judicial construction of a statute categorically controls an agency's contrary construction. 345 F.3d, at 1131–1132; see also *post*, at 12, n.11 (SCALIA, J., dissenting). *Neal* established no such proposition. *Neal* declined to defer to a construction adopted by the United States Sentencing Commission that conflicted with one the Court previously had adopted in *Chapman* v. *United States*, 500 U.S. 453 (1991). *Neal, supra*, at 290–295. *Chapman*, however, had held the relevant statute to be unambiguous. See 500 U.S., at 463 (declining to apply the rule of lenity given the statute's clear language). Thus, *Neal* established only that a precedent holding a statute to be unambiguous forecloses a contrary agency construction. That limited holding accorded with this Court's prior decisions, which had held that a court's interpretation of a statute trumps an agency's under the doctrine of *stare decisis* only if the prior court holding "determined a statute's *clear* meaning." *Maislin Industries, U.S., Inc.* v. *Primary Steel, Inc.*, 497 U.S. 116,131 (1990) (emphasis added); see also *Lechmere, Inc.* v. *NLRB*, 502 U.S. 527, 536–537 (1992). Those decisions allow a court's prior interpretation of a statute to override an agency's interpretation only if the relevant court decision held the statute unambiguous.

Against this background, the Court of Appeals erred in refusing to apply *Chevron* to the Commission's interpretation of the definition of "telecommunications service," 47 U.S.C. § 153(46). Its prior decision in *Portland* held only that the *best* reading of § 153(46) was that cable modem service was a "telecommunications service," not that it was the *only permissible* reading of the statute. See 216 F.3d, at 877–880. Nothing in *Portland* held that the Communications Act unambiguously required treating cable Internet providers as telecommunications carriers. Instead, the court noted that it was "not presented with a case involving potential deference to an administrative agency's statutory construction pursuant to the *Chevron* doctrine," *id.*, at 876; and the court invoked no other rule of construction (such as the rule of lenity) requiring it to conclude that the statute was unambiguous to reach its judgment. Before a judicial construction of a statute, whether contained in a precedent or not, may trump an agency's, the court must hold that the statute unambiguously requires the court's construction. *Portland* did not do so.

* * * *

IV

We next address whether the Commission's construction of the definition of "telecommunications service," 47 U.S.C. § 153(46), is a permissible reading of the Communications Act under the *Chevron* framework. *Chevron* established a familiar two-step procedure for evaluating whether an agency's interpretation of a statute is lawful. At the first step, we ask whether the statute's plain terms "directly addres[s] the precise question at issue." 467 U.S., at 843. If the statute is ambiguous on the point, we defer at step two to the agency's interpretation so long as the construction is "a reasonable policy choice for the agency to make." *Id.*, at 845. The Commission's interpretation is permissible at both steps.

Questions and comments

1.   In *Mead*, Justice Scalia expressed his concern over what he saw as a loss of agency flexibility to institute changes of policy. Does the Court's ruling in *Brand X* help to mitigate some of Justice Scalia's concerns over its ruling in *Mead*?

2.   Consider the Court's discussion of *Neal v. United States*, a case relied upon by the court below. Was the court below correct to conclude that a prior judicial decision would freeze agency policy? Prior to the Supreme Court's *Brand X* decision, would the bar generally have believed that judicial review of an agency interpretive rule would impose such a freeze? Or not? Would the *Chevron* decision have undermined such a belief?

3.   *Brand X* has now reaffirmed agency control over policy. Do you think that the *Brand X* result was always implicit in *Chevron*?

4.   How do you assess the argument that *Brand X* has given agencies the power to agencies to reverse judicial determinations?

Note: Judicial deference to an agency's interpretation of its regulations.

In *Christensen*, Justice Thomas referred to **Auer v. Robbins**, 519 U.S. 452 (1997) and **Bowles v. Seminole Rock & Sand Co.**, 325 U.S. 410 (1945) as commanding judicial deference to an agency's interpretation of its own regulations. According to those cases, an agency's interpretation of its own regulations is controlling unless "plainly erroneous or inconsistent with the regulation." One reason for this broad deference given by Justice Thomas is that the agency can freely amend its regulations, so it would make little sense to limit the agency's power to interpret them. Moreover, the Court apparently accords deference to agency interpretations of their own regulations, even when those interpretations lack the formality that would assure them *Chevron* deference. *Coeur Alaska, Inc. v. Southeast Alaska Conservation Council*, 129 S.Ct. 2458 (2009).

Could an agency obtain judicial deference for its policy positions where they would not qualify for *Chevron* deference by casting them as interpretations of its regulations, rather than interpretations of the underlying statute? In his dissent in *Mead*, Justice Scalia raised that possibility. There he was concerned about the limits that the majority had placed on *Chevron*-based deference. Since *Mead* predated *Brand X*, Justice Scalia was concerned that agencies would lose their flexibility to alter their interpretations once the relevant statutory provision had been construed by a court. He then described a procedure in which agencies would effectively pre-empt judicial interpretations by first issuing vacuous interpretive rules and then seeking deference, under *Auer*, for their interpretations of these rules:

> Agencies will now have high incentive to rush out barebones, ambiguous rules construing statutory ambiguities, which they can then in turn further clarify through informal rulings entitled to judicial respect.

The Court has twice rejected such attempts, however. That issue came up in *Christensen*, where the Department of Labor argued that its position (under the Fair Labor Standards Act denying employers the right to compel their employees to use compensatory time rather than to demand payment in cash) should be upheld under *Auer* as a reasonable interpretation of its own regulations, but Justice Thomas' opinion for the Court refused *Auer* deference in such a situation:

> Seeking to overcome the regulation's obvious meaning, the United States asserts that the agency's opinion letter interpreting the regulation should be given deference under our decision in *Auer v. Robbins*, 519 U.S. 452 (1997). In *Auer*, we held that an agency's interpretation of its own regulation is entitled to deference. *Id.*, at 461. See also *Bowles v. Seminole Rock & Sand Co.*, 325 U.S. 410 (1945). But *Auer* deference is warranted only when the language of the regulation is ambiguous. The regulation in this case, however, is not ambiguous — it is plainly permissive. To defer to the agency's position would be to permit the agency, under the guise of interpreting a regulation, to create *de facto* a new regulation.

The issue again arose in *Gonzales v. Oregon*, 546 U.S. 243 (2006). In *Gonzales*, the Attorney General had issued an "Interpretive Rule" that would have substantially interfered with physician-assisted suicides authorized by Oregon's Death with Dignity Act. This Interpretive Rule interpreted a prior Justice Department regulation issued under the Controlled Substances Act. The earlier regulation provided, inter alia, that "A prescription for a controlled substance to be effective must be issued for a legitimate medical purpose by an individual practitioner acting in the usual course of his professional practice." The Interpretive Rule, construing that language, took the position that: "[A]ssisting suicide is not a 'legitimate medical purpose' within the meaning of 21 CFR 1306.04 (2001), and that prescribing, dispensing, or administering federally controlled substances to assist suicide violates the Controlled Substances Act." In the case, the Government contended that the Attorney General's interpretation of his prior regulation was owed deference under *Auer*. Writing for the majority, Justice Kennedy rejected that position:

> In *Auer*, the underlying regulations gave specificity to a statutory scheme the Secretary was charged with enforcing and reflected the considerable experience and expertise the Department of Labor had acquired over time with respect to the complexities of the Fair Labor Standards Act. Here, on the other hand, the underlying regulation does little more than restate the terms of the statute itself. The language the Interpretive Rule addresses comes from Congress, not the Attorney General, and the near equivalence

of the statute and regulation belies the Government's argument for *Auer* deference. . . .

Simply put, the existence of a parroting regulation does not change the fact that the question here is not the meaning of the regulation but the meaning of the statute. An agency does not acquire special authority to interpret its own words when, instead of using its expertise and experience to formulate a regulation, it has elected merely to paraphrase the statutory language.

Do you see a conflict between *Auer* and *Chevron*? *Auer* requires the courts to defer to an agency's interpretation of its own regulations. But a court will not follow such an interpretation if the regulation being interpreted conflicts with the court's understanding of unambiguous congressional intent. In that case, the issue is resolved at under *Chevron* (step one) and we need not deal with *Auer*. Conversely, if the regulation being interpreted is based upon a reasonable interpretation of the statute (and *Chevron* applies), then judicial deference to the agency's interpretation of its regulation is governed by *Auer*. Suppose, however, that *Chevron* is inapplicable because the agency's policy is formulated informally, say, in an opinion letter. This is where a possible conflict lies. If the court is not persuaded (under *Skidmore*) to accept the agency's interpretation of the statute, then it will not accept an agency's interpretation of its regulation that is based upon the judicially rejected interpretation.

Interpretative Rules and Legislative Rules Compared

When an agency issues a rule pursuant to a grant of rulemaking power conferred upon it by Congress, the agency is said to issue a "legislative" rule. When an agency (traditionally apart from any rulemaking authority conferred upon it by Congress), embodies its interpretation of the statute which it is administering in the form of a rule, the agency is said to issue an "interpretative" rule. Interpretative rules differ from legislative rules in several respects: First, an agency is normally required to employ the public participation procedures contained in § 553 of the APA when it issues a legislative rule. However, when an agency issues an interpretative rule, it is exempt from those procedures. 5 U.S.C. § 553(b)(A). This difference in the procedural requirements for the two types of rulemaking may create an incentive for some agencies to employ interpretative, rather than legislative, rulemaking in situations where the agencies have a choice. (You will see one federal agency consistently and successfully avoiding the § 553 rulemaking procedures in the *Wyman-Gordon* and *Bell Aerospace* cases, *infra* Chapter 6.) Courts have had a notoriously difficult time in determining whether an agency rule is legislative — and thus subject to notice-and-comment procedures under § 553 — or an interpretative rule (or policy statement) and thus not subject to those procedures. Consider the following case in which the court explains its approach to distinguishing legislative rules from interpretative rules:

DISMAS CHARITIES, INC. v. U.S. DEPARTMENT OF JUSTICE
401 F.3d 666 (6th Cir. 2005)

ROGERS, CIRCUIT JUDGE.

. . . .

[Dismas Charities, Inc. is a nonprofit corporation that owns and operates eighteen community correction centers (or "CCCs") in seven states. Under the prior policy of the Bureau of Prisons (BOP), federal offenders could be housed in CCCs. Under the Bureau's new policy, that would no longer be the case. Dismas brought suit to challenge the Bureau's new policy. In particular, the new policy was embodied in two memoranda, one by a Deputy Attorney General instructing the BOP to transfer offenders out of CCCs and the other by the Director of the Bureau of Prisons notifying federal judges that the BOP would no longer place offenders in CCCs. Dismas claimed that two memoranda issued to implement the new policy were "rules" that were issued without notice and comment procedure and therefore void. The court rejected that contention in the part of its opinion set forth below.]

The rulemaking requirements of § 553 of the APA do not apply to "interpretative rules." § 553(a).[1] Both the Thompson and Sawyer memoranda, assuming that either may be categorized as a "rule,"[2] clearly fall in the category of interpretative rule. The Attorney General's Manual on the Administrative Procedure Act, persuasive authority on the meaning of the APA, describes an interpretive rule as one "issued by an agency to advise the public of the agency's construction of the statutes and rules which it administers.". The difference between legislative and interpretative rules "has to do in part with the authority — law-making versus law-interpreting — under which the rule is promulgated." . . . "For purposes of the APA, substantive rules are rules that create law," while in contrast "[i]nterpretive rules merely clarify or explain existing law or regulations and go to what the administrative officer thinks the statute or regulation means.". . . . "[R]ules are legislative when the agency is exercising delegated power to make law through rules, and rules are interpretative when the agency is not exercising such delegated power in issuing them.".

The distinction reflects the primary purpose of Congress in imposing notice and

---

[1] We assume, but need not decide, that the BOP policy is not exempt under the provision of § 553 exempting "general statements of policy." *See generally* Syncor International Corp. v. Shalala, 127 F.3d 90, 94–95 (D.C. Cir. 1997). (distinguishing "general statements of policy" from "interpretative rules" for § 553 purposes).

[2] For purposes of § 553 analysis, we focus on the December 16, 2002 memorandum by Deputy Attorney General Larry Thompson and on the December 20, 2002 memorandum issued by Federal Bureau of Prison Director Kathleen Hawk Sawyer. There is no general requirement that agency policies require notice and comment. . . . Instead, the requirement applies to *rules*. In this case, the only thing that can possibly be identified as a BOP rule is the Thompson memo or the Sawyer memo. See 5 U.S.C. § 551(4) (" 'rule' means the whole or a part of an agency *statement* . . ." (emphasis added)). We assume without deciding that the Thompson memo or the Sawyer memo is a "rule" for APA purposes.

comment requirements for rulemaking — to get public input so as to get the wisest rules. That purpose is not served when the agency's inquiry or determination is not "what is the wisest rule," but "what is the rule." The interpretative rule exception reflects the idea that public input will not help an agency make the legal determination of what the law already is. The D.C. Circuit, for instance, in applying the interpretative rule exception, has "generally sought to distinguish cases in which an agency is merely explicating Congress' desires from those cases in which the agency is adding substantive content of its own." *American Hosp. Ass'n v. Bowen*, 834 F.2d 1037, 1045 (D.C. Cor. 1987). *Cf. Sentara-Hampton Gen. Hosp. v. Sullivan*, 980 F.2d 749, 759 (D.C. Cir. 1992). ("the 'interpretative rule' exception was designed to provide agencies with a degree of flexibility where 'substantive rights are not at stake' ").

It follows that the Thompson and Sawyer memoranda, assuming that either is a rule otherwise subject to the notice and comment requirements of the APA, are paradigm examples of interpretative rules. . . . The memoranda each state that the statutory interpretation by the [Office of Legal Counsel or OLC"] will henceforth be implemented. The Thompson memorandum in its operative language relies specifically and directly on the unlawfulness of its previous practice as determined by the OLC.[3] Even more clearly, the Sawyer memorandum does not make any kind of policy analysis or determine what is the better, or more effective, or less burdensome, rule. Instead, the BOP changed its procedure because the "OLC . . . determined that the [BOP's] practice of using CCCs as a substitute for imprisonment contravenes well-established caselaw, and is inconsistent with U.S.S.G. § 5C1.1." Memorandum of BOP Director Kathleen Hawk Sawyer, December 20, 2002, at 1. Clearly, the memo simply determines what the law is, and does so by reliance upon a legal interpretation by the OLC. Notice and comment rulemaking procedures are simply not designed as a means for agencies to improve their legal analysis. And it is the agency's legal analysis that Dismas challenges.[4]

We recognize that some district courts have found that the BOP policy required notice and comment. Some of these cases rely on the idea that a rule is legislative rather than interpretative if it is "binding" or "nondiscretionary," and that the BOP policy, since binding, is not interpretative. . . . The argument mistakes the extent to which a reviewing *court* is bound by a regulation with the extent to which an

---

[3] The memorandum does add a policy consideration in favor of the change in policy-the risk of inappropriately favorable treatment of white collar criminals under the previous interpretation-but the operative determination to change BOP practice is clearly based on the statutory interpretation made by the OLC.

[4] In Gordon v. Shalala, 55 F.3d 101 (2d Cir. 1995), the Second Circuit came to a similar conclusion in a case involving a determination by the Secretary of Health and Human Services to acquiesce in a Second Circuit opinion:

> plaintiff claims that the *Ruppert* Acquiescence Ruling had to have been publicly promulgated pursuant to the Administrative Procedure Act (the "APA") in order to be effective. This argument is frivolous. The general rule on acquiescence rulings is that although they "do not have the force and effect of law," they constitute Social Security Administration interpretations of its own regulations and the statute which it administers. . . . The *Ruppert* Acquiescence Ruling was interpretive, not substantive. It did not create rights or impose obligations. It merely interpreted this Court's mandate in *Ruppert* to the effect that imputed income must provide the SSI recipient with an "actual economic benefit." It was not subject to the notice and comment requirements of the APA.

agency is bound. It is true that an interpretative rule is not binding upon a court, whereas a properly authorized legislative rule is so binding. But using that distinction, the BOP policy is interpretative, because the BOP's interpretation is not binding on reviewing courts, which may of course disagree with the government's statutory interpretation (as many have already done, *see Goldings*, 383 F.3d at 28–29, *Elwood*, 386 F.3d at 847). An interpretative regulation is binding on an *agency*, on the other hand, not by virtue of the promulgation of the regulation (as in the case of a legislative regulation), but by virtue of the binding nature of the interpreted statute. Such a binding nature cannot render a rule legislative, else every interpretative rule would become legislative.

Nor does the BOP memorandum lose its interpretative nature because of its substantial impact, as implied by the district court in *Iacaboni v. United States*, 251 F.Supp.2d 1015, 1040 (D. Mass. 2003). The policies underlying the notice and comment requirement, and the apparent reasons for the exception for interpretative rules, are unrelated to the substantial impact of a rule. A pure statutory interpretation can have an enormous impact, yet be based entirely on statutory analysis for which public input would be of minimal value. Our court has accordingly rejected substantial impact as a basis for determining the applicability of the interpretative rule exception. *See Friedrich v. Sec. of Health and Humas Servs.*, 894 F.2d 829, 836 (6th Cir. 1990) (stating that "[t]he extent of the impact is not an indicative factor" in characterizing the nature of a rule); *Sanders*, 946 F.2d at 1189 (noting that "the substantive impact test . . . has been disfavored recently by [the Sixth Circuit] and other courts"). *See also Alcaraz v. Block*, 746 F.2d 593, 613 (9th Cir. 1984) (rejecting the argument that "for the purposes of imposing notice and comment requirements on the agency for a particular rule, we look to the 'substantial impact' of the rule").

Finally, the rule is not legislative simply because it departs from the BOP's prior interpretation of § 3621, as implied in cases such as *Howard v. Ashcroft*, 248 F.Supp.2d 518, 536 (M.D. La. 2003) and *McDonald*, 2003 U.S. Dist. LEXIS 14035, at *18–19. As the Second Circuit has explained clearly,

> an interpretive rule changing an agency's interpretation of a statute is not magically transformed into a legislative rule. If the rule is an interpretation of a statute rather than an extra-statutory imposition of rights, duties or obligations, it remains interpretive even if the rule embodies the Secretary's changed interpretation of the statute.

White v. Shalala, 7 F.3d 296, 304 (2d Cir. 1993) (citations omitted). Other circuits agree that "a new position does not necessarily make a rule legislative rather than interpretive." *Metropolitan School Dist. v. Davila*, 969 F.2d 485, 490 (7th Cir. 1992) (citing as authority *State of Michigan v. Thomas*, 805 F.2d 176, 182–84 (6th Cir. 1986); *Alcaraz*, 746 at 613–14; and *American Postal Workers Union v. United States Postal Service*, 707 F.2d 548, 559–60 (D.C. Cir. 1983). This court accordingly has held that certain provisions of the Medicare Provider Reimbursement Manual were interpretative and therefore not subject to notice and comment despite the plaintiff's argument in that case that the provisions had changed: "We also find unpersuasive St. Francis's argument regarding the Secretary's 'inconsistent' interpretation of its regulations. As this Court has stated, '[a]dministrative agencies are not bound by their own prior construction of a statute. . . .' " *St. Francis Health Care Ctr v. Shalala*, 205 F.3d 937, 947–48 n.11 (quoting *Crounse Corp. v. ICC*, 781 F.2d 1176, 1186 (6th Cir. 1986).

It is true that once an agency gives a *regulation* an interpretation, notice and comment will often be required before the interpretation of that regulation can be changed. *See Shell Offshore Inc. v. Babbitt*, 238 F.3d 622, 629 (5th Cir. 2001); *Alaska Prof'l Hunters Ass'n v. Fed. Aviation Adm'n*, 177 F.3d 1030, 1033–34 (D.C. Cir. 1999). This is because once an agency has promulgated its own regulation, a change in the interpretation of that regulation is likely to reflect the agency's reassessment of wise policy rather than a reassessment of what the agency itself originally meant. The determination of wise policy—unlike legal interpretation—is the kind of determination for which notice and comment procedures are particularly appropriate. However, when an agency is changing its interpretation of a *statute*, it is much more likely that the agency is not trying to determine what is the wiser rule, but rather what *is* the rule. Thus, in *Alaska Hunters*, the D.C. Circuit explained that "an agency has less leeway in its choice of the method of changing its interpretation of its regulations than in altering its construction of the statute" because " '[r]ule making,' as defined in the APA, includes not only the agency's process of formulating a rule, but also the agency's process of modifying a rule." 177 F.3d at 1034. Agencies in contrast cannot modify a statute, and *statutory* interpretation can therefore more easily be distinguished from legislative rulemaking. This is particularly so where, as here, the agency's change in interpretation resulted from an opinion by the OLC concluding that the agency's interpretation of the statute was unlawful.

We take no position on the merits of Dismas's legal challenge to the BOP policy. We hold only that, under the interpretative rule exception, a rule that embodies a pure legal determination of what the applicable law already is does not require notice and comment under APA § 553(b). Because Dismas's claim based on § 553 of the APA fails as a matter of law, the district court properly dismissed that aspect of Dismas's case as well.

For the foregoing reasons, we AFFIRM the judgment of the district court.

Interpretative Rules and Legislative Rules Compared, continued

Second. The distinction between interpretative and legislative rules has been important to the way questions of judicial review were discussed. If Congress delegates to an agency the power to adopt a rule which has statutory force, then the courts must accord the same respect to the legislative rule as they do to the statute. But if an agency issues a rule which merely sets forth its own interpretation of the governing statute, then it has been easier in the past for courts to reject the agency's interpretation (as in *Mayburg v. Secretary of Health & Human Services, supra)* and replace it with their own. After all, it is the traditional function of the courts to interpret statutes. *Chevron*, however, altered that landscape. *Chevron* raises a presumption that Congress delegated to agencies the responsibility of construing ambiguous statutes. Under *Chevron* courts defer to the agency's interpretations whether contained in a legislative or in an interpretive rule.

A further difficulty, however, is that a statutory grant of power to an agency to issue legislative rules is itself subject to interpretation; and a court may, by the process of interpreting the statute, conclude that the scope for agency to issue legislative rules is narrower than the agency has thought. But, as cases like *Chevron* suggest, Congress often implicitly confers upon an agency the ultimate authority to make (at least some) interpretations of the governing statute. While the courts will always be the final authorities on the basic goals and design of the underlying statute, the administering agency may very well be given the last word on many nterpretive issues.

Related Matters

Agencies not only interpret statutes; they sometimes interpret their own rules or regulations. Should a court defer more to an agency's interpretation of its own regulation than to an agency's interpretation of the statute which it is administering? See discussion above.

Agency interpretations are not always in the form of rules. An agency interpretation can be announced in the process of an agency's decision of a particular case, as in *Chenery, Wyman-Gordon* and other cases which you will read in chapter 6. But an agency's interpretation of a statute can also be announced in a press release or in an after-dinner speech. Even though such interpretations may be important ones, the very informality of the way in which they are announced or the tentative or imprecise way in which the interpretations are phrased may impede efforts to have the courts review them. These matters are taken up in chapter 10, infra.

Deference in the Split-Enforcement
(or Split-Administrative) Model

The organizational structure in which administration and enforcement occurs may have an impact upon the matter of judicial deference to agency policies. In most regulatory agencies, the agency head sits as a final reviewing authority over the decisions below. In the most typical case, an administrative law judge (ALJ) presides over adjudications and the decision of the ALJ is subject to review by an intermediate review board and thence to review by the agency head, or it is subject to direct review by the agency head. This reserved power of review by the agency head (which is not always exercised in every case) is the method by which the agency head controls agency policy.

When a court reviews a decision of such a regulatory agency,[5] it is often required to defer to the agency's derivative inferences and interpretations, as we have seen. Especially since the late 1960s, Congress has not always structured regulatory agencies in the traditional way. In the Occupational Safety and Health Act, for

---

[5] In the traditionally-structured regulatory agency, an enforcement action takes place entirely within the agency organization and the agency head sits as the final reviewing tribunal. In the case of the Federal Trade Commission, for example, an enforcement action begins when the Commission's Bureau of Competition recommends the issuance of a complaint against a respondent. If the Commissioners concur in the Bureau's recommendation, a complaint is issued in the name of the Commission. A trial proceeding takes place before an ALJ. The ALJ's decision is then subject to review by the "Commission", i.e., the five Commissioners heading the agency. Further review is in the courts. When a court reviews a decision of the Commission, therefore, it is reviewing the derivative inferences and interpretations of the Commission, the head of the agency administering the statute being enforced.

example, Congress entrusted administration primarily to the Secretary of Labor, but established an independent tribunal — whose members were appointed by the President and confirmed by the Senate — to review decisions by ALJs in adjudications under the Act. Administration of the Federal Mine Safety and Health Act takes place under a similar administrative structure.

Most benefit programs involve adjudication by bodies which are independent, in fact if not in form, from the agency primarily in charge of administration. Thus, for example, under the disability program of the Social Security Administration a dissatisfied claimant first must seek review of a rejection by requesting reconsideration. Ultimately, if the claimant is unsuccessful, he or she is entitled to a hearing before a federal ALJ. The ALJ's decisions may be reviewed by the Appeals Council of the Social Security Administration and further review is in the federal courts. The ALJs are formally independent of SSA control and the Appeals Council is independent in fact.

When a court reviews a decision of such an independent adjudicating tribunal, it is often not clear whether the court should defer to the adjudicating tribunal or to the interpretations of the administering and enforcing agency, or, indeed, whether the court should defer to any administrative body at all.

In the case below, the courts wrestled with the issue of where deference is due under the Occupational Safety and Health Act. Under that Act the OSHA Administrator is an official within the Department of Labor. The Administrator issues rules (called standards) governing workplace conditions. When the Administrator believes an employer to have violated a standard, the Administrator issues a citation to the employer, requiring the employer to correct the defect and pay a civil penalty. The employer is entitled to contest the citation in a hearing before an ALJ. Review is then before the Occupational Safety and Health Review Commission (OSHRC), an agency which is structurally independent from the Administrator. OSHRC decisions are reviewable in court. In the case below, the Administrator had issued a standard which he interpreted differently from OSHRC. Whose interpretation should the courts accept?

MARTIN v. OCCUPATIONAL SAFETY AND HEALTH REVIEW COMMISSION
499 U.S. 144 (1991)

JUSTICE MARSHALL delivered the opinion of the Court.

In this case, we consider the question to whom should a reviewing court defer when the Secretary of Labor and the Occupational Safety and Health Review Commission furnish reasonable but conflicting interpretations of an ambiguous regulation promulgated by the Secretary under the Occupational Safety and Health Act of 1970. . . . The Court of Appeals concluded that it should defer to the Commissions interpretation under such circumstances. We reverse.

I

A

The Occupational Safety and Health Act of 1970 (OSH Act or Act) establishes a comprehensive regulatory scheme designed "to assure so far as possible . . . safe and healthful working conditions" for "every working man and woman in the Nation." . . . To achieve this objective, the Act assigns distinct regulatory tasks to two independent administrative actors: the Secretary of Labor (Secretary); and the Occupational Safety and Health Review Commission (Commission), a three-member board appointed by the President with the advice and consent of the Senate. . . .

The Act charges the Secretary with responsibility for setting and enforcing workplace health and safety standards. . . . The Secretary establishes these standards through the exercise of rulemaking powers. . . . If the Secretary (or the Secretary's designate) determines upon investigation that an employer is failing to comply with such a standard, the Secretary is authorized to issue a citation and to assess the employer a monetary penalty. . . .

The Commission is assigned to "carr[y] out adjudicatory functions" under the Act. . . . If an employer wishes to contest a citation, the Commission must afford the employer an evidentiary hearing and "thereafter issue an order, based on findings of fact, affirming, modifying, or vacating the Secretary's citation or proposed penalty." . . . Initial decisions are made by an administrative law judge (ALJ), whose ruling becomes the order of the Commission unless the Commission grants discretionary review. . . . Both the employer and the Secretary have the right to seek review of an adverse Commission order in the court of appeals, which must treat as "conclusive" Commission findings of fact that are "supported by substantial evidence." . . .

B

This case arises from the Secretary's effort to enforce compliance with OSH Act standards relating to coke-oven emissions. Promulgated pursuant to the Secretary's rulemaking powers, these standards establish maximum permissible emissions levels and require the use of employee respirators in certain circumstances. See 29 CFR § 1910.1029 (1990). An investigation by one of the Secretary's compliance officers revealed that respondent CF & I Steel Corporation (CF & I) had equipped 28 of its employees with respirators that failed an "atmospheric test" designed to determine whether a respirator provides a sufficiently tight fit to protect its wearer from carcinogenic emissions. As a result of being equipped with these loose-fitting respirators, some employees were exposed to coke-oven emissions exceeding the regulatory limit. Based on these findings, the compliance officer issued a citation to CF & I and assessed it a $10,000 penalty for violating 29 CFR § 1910.1029(g)(3) (1990), which requires an employer to "institute a respiratory protection program in accordance with [29 CFR] § 1910-134." CF & I contested the citation.

The ALJ sided with the Secretary, but the full Commission subsequently granted review and vacated the citation. See CF & 1, 12 OSHC 2067 (1986). In the Commission's view, the "respiratory protection program" referred to in § 1910.1029(g)(3) expressly requires only that an employer train employees in the proper use of respirators;[2] the obligation to assure proper fit of an individual employee's respirator, the Commission noted, was expressly stated in another regulation, namely, § 1910.1029 (g)(4)(i).[3] . . . Reasoning, inter alia, that the Secretary's interpretation of § 1910.1029(g)(3) would render § 1910.1029(g)(4) superfluous, the Commission concluded that the facts alleged in the citation and found by the ALJ did not establish a violation of § 1910.1029(g)(3). . . . Because § 1910.1029(g)(3) was the only asserted basis for liability, the Commission vacated the citation. . . .

The Secretary petitioned for review in the Court of Appeals for the Tenth Circuit, which affirmed the Commission's order. . . . The court concluded that the relevant regulations were ambiguous as to the employer's obligation to assure proper fit of an employee's respirator. The court thus framed the issue before it as whose reasonable interpretation of the regulations, the Secretary's or the Commission's, merited the court's deference. . . . The court held that the Commission's interpretation was entitled to deference under such circumstances, reasoning that Congress had intended to delegate to the Commission "the normal complement of adjudicative powers possessed by traditional administrative agencies" and that "[s]uch an adjudicative function necessarily encompasses the power to 'declare' the law. The court therefore deferred to the Commission's interpretation without assessing the reasonableness of the Secretary's competing view. . . .

The Secretary thereafter petitioned this Court for a writ of certiorari. We granted the petition in order to resolve a conflict among the Circuits on the question whether a reviewing court should defer to the Secretary or to the Commission when these actors furnish reasonable but conflicting interpretations of an ambiguous regulation under the OSH Act. . . .

II

It is well established "that an agency's construction of its own regulations is entitled to substantial deference." . . . In situations in which "the meaning of [regulatory] language is not free from doubt," the reviewing court should give effect to the agency's interpretation so long as it is "reasonable," . . . that is, so long as the interpretation "sensibly conforms to the purpose and wording of the

---

[2] "For safe use of any respirator, it is essential that the user be properly instructed in its selection, use, and maintenance. Both supervisors and workers shall be so instructed by competent persons. Training shall provide the men an opportunity to handle the respirator, have it fitted properly, test its face-piece-to-face seal, wear it in normal air for a long familiarity period, and, finally, to wear it in a test atmosphere." 29 CFR § 1910-134(e)(5) (1990).

[3] This regulation states in pertinent part: "Respirator usage. (i) The employer shall assure that the respirator issued to the employee exhibits minimum facepiece leakage and that the respirator is fitted properly." 29 CFR § 1910.1029(g)(4) (1990). According to the Commission, the compliance officer who issued the citation "acknowledged that [§ 1910.1029(g)(4)(i)] applied," and "that he might have cited the wrong standard." CF & 1, 12 OSHC 2067, 2078 (1986).

regulations," . . . Because applying an agency's regulation to complex or changing circumstances calls upon the agency's unique expertise and policymaking prerogatives, we presume that the power authoritatively to interpret its own regulations is a component of the agency's delegated lawmaking powers. . . . The question before us in this case is to which administrative actor — the Secretary or the Commission — did Congress delegate this "interpretive" lawmaking power under the OSH Act.[5]

which entity has interpretable lawmaking power?

To put this question in perspective, it is necessary to take account of the unusual regulatory structure established by the Act. Under most regulatory schemes, rulemaking, enforcement, and adjudicative powers are combined in a single administrative authority. . . . Under the OSH Act, however, Congress separated enforcement and rulemaking powers from adjudicative powers, assigning these respective functions to two independent administrative authorities. The purpose of this "split enforcement" structure was to achieve a greater separation of functions than exists within the traditional "unitary" agency, which under the Administrative Procedure Act (APA) generally must divide enforcement and adjudication between separate personnel, see 5 U.S.C. § 554(d). See generally Johnson, The Split-Enforcement Model: Some Conclusions from the OSHA and MSHA Experiences, 39 Admin.L.Rev. 315, 317–319 (1987).

Although the Act does not expressly address the issue, we now infer from the structure and history of the statute. . . . that the power to render authoritative interpretations of OSH Act regulations is a "necessary adjunct" of the Secretary's powers to promulgate and to enforce national health and safety standards. The Secretary enjoys readily identifiable structural advantages over the Commission in rendering authoritative interpretations of OSH Act regulations. Because the Secretary promulgates these standards, the Secretary is in a better position than is the Commission to reconstruct the purpose of the regulations in question. Moreover, by virtue of the Secretary's statutory role as enforcer, the Secretary comes into contact with a much greater number of regulatory problems than does the Commission, which encounters only those regulatory episodes resulting in contested citations. Cf. Note, Employee Participation in Occupational Safety and Health Review Commission Proceedings, 85 Colum.L.Rev. 1317, 1331 and n. 90 (1985) (reporting small percentage of OSH Act citations contested between 1979 and 1985). Consequently, the Secretary is more likely to develop the expertise relevant to assessing the effect of a particular regulatory interpretation. Because historical familiarity and policymaking expertise account in the first instance for the presumption that Congress delegates interpretive lawmaking power to the agency rather than to the reviewing court. . . . we presume here that Congress intended to invest interpretive power in the administrative actor in the best position to develop these attributes.

a interpretive power ↓ rulemaking + enforcement

The legislative history of the OSH Act supports this conclusion. The version of the Act originally passed by the House of Representatives vested adjudicatory power in the Commission and rulemaking power in an independent standards board, leaving the Secretary with only enforcement power. . . . The Senate

---

[5] The parties do not challenge the Court of Appeals' conclusion that the regulations at issue in this case are ambiguous. We assume that this conclusion is correct for purposes of our analysis.

version dispensed with the standards board and established the division of responsibilities that survives in the enacted legislation. The Senate Committee Report explained that combining legislative and enforcement powers in the Secretary would result in "a sounder program" because it would make a single administrative actor responsible both for "formulat[ing] rules . . . and for seeing that they are workable and effective in their day-to-day application," and would allow Congress to hold a single administrative actor politically "accountable for the overall implementation of that program." S.Rep. No. 91-1282, p. 8 (1970), U.S. Code Cong. & Admin.News 1970, pp. 5175, 5184, 5185, reprinted in Legislative History 148. Because dividing the power to promulgate and enforce OSH Act standards from the power to make law by interpreting them would make two administrative actors ultimately responsible for implementing the Act's policy objectives, we conclude that Congress did not expect the Commission to possess authoritative interpretive powers.

For the same reason, we reject the Court of Appeals' inference that Congress intended "to endow the Commission with the normal complement of adjudicative powers possessed by traditional administrative agencies." . . . Within traditional agencies — that is, agencies possessing a unitary structure — adjudication operates as an appropriate mechanism not only for factfinding, but also for the exercise of delegated lawmaking powers, including lawmaking by interpretation. See *NLRB v. Bell Aerospace Co.*, 416 U.S. 267 (1974); *SEC v. Chenery Corp.*, 332 U.S. 194, 201–203 (1947). But in these cases, we concluded that agency adjudication is a generally permissible mode of law and policymaking only because the unitary agencies in question also had been delegated the power to make law and policy through rulemaking. See *Bell Aerospace, supra,* 416 U.S., at 292–294; *Chenery Corp., supra,* 332 U.S., at 202–203. See generally Shapiro, The Choice of Rulemaking or Adjudication in the Development of Administrative Policy, 78 Harv.L.Rev. 921 (1965). Insofar as Congress did not invest the Commission with the power to make law or policy by other means, we cannot infer that Congress expected the Commission to use its adjudicatory power to play a policymaking role. Moreover, when a traditional, unitary agency uses adjudication to engage in lawmaking by regulatory interpretation, it necessarily interprets regulations that it has promulgated. This, too, cannot be said of the Commission's power to adjudicate.

Consequently, we think the more plausible inference is that Congress intended to delegate to the Commission the type of nonpolicymaking adjudicatory powers typically exercised by a court in the agency-review context. Under this conception of adjudication, the Commission is authorized to review the Secretary's interpretations only for consistency with the regulatory language and for reasonableness. In addition, of course, Congress expressly charged the Commission with making authoritative findings of fact and with applying the Secretary's standards to those facts in making a decision. . . . The Commission need be viewed as possessing no more power than this in order to perform its statutory role as "neutral arbiter." . . .

CF & I draws a different conclusion from the history and structure of the Act. Congress, CF & I notes, established the Commission in response to concerns that combining rulemaking, enforcement, and adjudicatory power in the Secretary would leave employers unprotected from regulatory bias. Construing the Act to separate enforcement and interpretive powers is consistent with this purpose, CF & I argues, because it protects regulated employers from biased prosecutorial interpretations of the Secretary's regulations. Indeed, interpretations furnished in the course of administrative penalty actions, according to CF & 1, are mere "litigating positions," undeserving of judicial deference under our precedents. See, e. g., *Bowen v. Georgetown University Hospital*, 488 U.S. 204, 212 (1988).

Although we find these concerns to be important, we think that they are overstated. It is clear that Congress adopted the split-enforcement structure in the OSH Act in order to achieve a greater separation of functions than exists in a conventional unitary agency. See S.Rep. No. 91-1282, supra, at 56, U.S. Code Cong. & Admin.News 1970, p. 5220, reprinted in Legislative History 195 (individual views of Sen. Javits) (noting that adjudication by independent panel goes beyond division of functions under the APA but defending split-enforcement structure as "more closely [in] accor[d] with traditional notions of due process"). But the conclusion that the Act should therefore be understood to separate enforcement powers from authoritative interpretive powers begs the question just how much Congress intended to depart from the unitary model. Sponsors of the Commission purported to be responding to the traditional objection that an agency head's participation in or supervision of agency investigations results in biased review of the decisions of the hearing officer, notwithstanding internal separations within the agency. . . . Vesting authoritative factfinding and ALJ-review powers in the Commission, an administrative body wholly independent of the administrative enforcer, dispels this concern.

We harbor no doubt that Congress also intended to protect regulated parties from biased interpretations of the Secretary's regulations. But this objective is achieved when the Commission and ultimately the court of appeals review the Secretary's interpretation to assure that it is consistent with the regulatory language and is otherwise *reasonable*. Giving the Commission the power to substitute its reasonable interpretations for the Secretary's might slightly increase regulated parties' protection from overzealous interpretations. But it would also clearly frustrate Congress' intent to make a single administrative actor "accountable for the overall implementation" of the Act's policy objectives by combining legislative and enforcement powers in the Secretary. . . .

We are likewise unpersuaded by the contention that the Secretary's regulatory interpretations will necessarily appear in forms undeserving of judicial deference. Our decisions indicate that agency "litigating positions" are not entitled to deference when they are merely appellate counsel's "post hoc rationalizations" for agency action, advanced for the first time in the reviewing court. See *Bowen v. Georgetown University Hospital, supra*, at 212; *Burlington Truck Lines, Inc. v. United States*, 371 U.S. 156, 168 (1962). Because statutory and regulatory interpretations furnished in this setting occur after agency proceedings have terminated, they do not constitute an exercise of the agency's delegated lawmaking powers. The Secretary's interpretation of OSH Act regulations in an administrative adjudication, however, is agency action, not a post hoc rationalization of it. Moreover, when embodied in a citation, the Secretary's interpretation assumes a form expressly provided for by Congress. . . . Under these circumstances, the

Secretary's litigating position before the Commission is as much an exercise of delegated lawmaking powers as is the Secretary's promulgation of a workplace health and safety standard.

In addition, the Secretary regularly employs less formal means of interpreting regulations prior to issuing a citation. These include the promulgation of interpretive rules. . . . and the publication of agency enforcement guidelines, see United States Department of Labor, OSHA Field Operations Manual (3d ed. 1989). See generally S. Bokat & H. Thompson, Occupational Safety and Health Law 658–660 (1988). Although not entitled to the same deference as norms that derive from the exercise of the Secretary's delegated lawmaking powers, these informal interpretations are still entitled to some weight on judicial review. See *Batterton v. Francis*, 432 U.S. 416, 425–426, and n. 9 (1977); *Skidmore v. Swift & Co.*, 323 U.S. 134, 140 (1944); *Whirlpool, supra*, 445 U.S., at 11. A reviewing court may certainly consult them to determine whether the Secretary has consistently applied the interpretation embodied in the citation, a factor bearing on the reasonableness of the Secretary's position. . . .

III

We emphasize the narrowness of our holding. We deal in this case only with the division of powers between the Secretary and the Commission under the OSH Act. We conclude from the available indicia of legislative intent that Congress did not intend to sever the power authoritatively to interpret OSH Act regulations from the Secretary's power to promulgate and enforce them. Subject only to constitutional limits, Congress is free, of course, to divide these powers as it chooses, and we take no position on the division of enforcement and interpretive powers within other regulatory schemes that conform to the split-enforcement structure. Nor should anything we say today be understood to bear on whether particular divisions of enforcement and adjudicative power within a unitary agency comport with § 554(d) of the APA.

In addition, although we hold that a reviewing court may not prefer the reasonable interpretations of the Commission to the reasonable interpretations of the Secretary, we emphasize that the reviewing court should defer to the Secretary only if the Secretary's interpretation is reasonable. The Secretary's interpretation of an ambiguous regulation is subject to the same standard of substantive review as any other exercise of delegated lawmaking power. See 5 U.S.C. § 706(2)(A). . . . As we have indicated, the Secretary's interpretation is not undeserving of deference merely because the Secretary advances it for the first time in an administrative adjudication. But as the Secretary's counsel conceded in oral argument, Tr. of Oral Arg. 18–19, 20–21, the decision to use a citation as the initial means for announcing a particular interpretation may bear on the adequacy of notice to regulated parties, see *Bell Aerospace*, 416 U.S., at 295; *Bowen v. Georgetown University Hospital*, 488 U.S., at 220, (SCALIA, J., concurring), the quality of the Secretary's elaboration of pertinent policy considerations, see *Motor Vehicle Mfrs. Assn. of United States, Inc. v. State Farm Mut. Automobile Ins. Co.*, 463 U.S. 29, 43 (1983), and other factors relevant to the reasonableness of the Secretary's exercise of delegated lawmaking powers.

The judgment of the Court of Appeals is reversed, and the case is remanded for further proceedings consistent with this opinion.

It is so ordered.

Questions and Comments

1.   Do you agree with the result? The court below reached an opposite result. Could you construct an argument to support the position of the court below?

2.   Why should the court defer to the Secretary and not the Commission? Are you convinced that the Secretary's policy responsibility would be undermined by a decision in favor of the Commission? The Secretary can ultimately prevail on the issue by issuing an amended regulation, can he not?

3.   Does *Chevron* support the Secretary's position? Do *Hearst, Gray* and *Aragon? Auer* had not yet been decided at the time that *Martin* was decided. In retrospect, do you think that Auer adds strength to the Court's decision in *Martin*?

4.   Is the result of this case that the Secretary need not embody his interpretations in actual regulations in order to bind the courts (and, by extension, the Commission)? Is this a good result?

As we will see, issuing regulations imposes significant transactions costs upon the Secretary. Is it fair to say that this decision decreases the costs of administering the Occupational Safety and Health Act? The Split-Enforcement Model is the subject of further attention in Chapter 5, below.

REICH v. OCCUPATIONAL SAFETY AND HEALTH REVIEW COMMISSION
998 F.2d 134 (3d Cir. 1993)

WEIS, CIRCUIT JUDGE.

In this proceeding seeking review of an order by the Occupational Safety and Health Review Commission, we . . . reject the Secretary of Labor's contention that the Commission lacks authority to reduce an other-than-serious violation to one of a de minimis level. We therefore will dismiss the cross-petition and deny review of the Secretary's petition.

After Erie Coke Company refused to include a provision in a collective bargaining agreement requiring payment for 'employees' protective gloves, the United Steelworkers filed a complaint with the Occupational Safety and Health Administration. The union alleged that the company's policy required its employees to pay for the flame resistant gloves needed for work at the coke oven batteries. After investigating the complaint, the Secretary issued a citation directing that the practice be abated, but did not seek assessment of a penalty.

Following a hearing, an ALJ found that the company had violated 29 C.F.R. § 1910.1029(h)(1)(ii) which states that an employer "shall provide and assure the use of appropriate protective clothing . . . such as . . . [f]lame resistant gloves."

The ALJ affirmed the citation and the Occupational Safety and Health Review Commission granted discretionary review.

. . . .

Concluding that Erie had failed to comply with the terms of the regulation, the Commission determined, nevertheless, that the violation should be characterized as de minimis rather than other-than-serious. The Commission, finding that Erie's employees had not suffered any safety impairment because they had paid for the gloves, determined the infraction to be de minimis.

II.

We come then to the sole remaining issue in this appeal — the Secretary's contention that the Commission was barred from reducing the offense from other-than-serious to de minimis. The difference between the two levels is that an other-than-serious designation requires abatement of the violation and a de minimis classification does not.

. . . .

In determining the appropriate classification of Erie's violation, the Commission noted that 29 U.S.C. § 658(a) refers to "de minimis" violations as those that "have no direct or immediate relationship to safety or health." The Commission found that the Secretary had not introduced any evidence to show that Erie's employees had suffered any direct impairment of safety or health as a result of having had to pay for the gloves. The facts in the record did not establish that "employees were wearing torn or otherwise ineffective gloves beyond their useful life in order to save money, thereby exposing their hands to possible burns and coke oven emissions." On those uncontroverted facts, the Commission found the violation was de minimis.

Over the years, the courts and the Commission have read the Act as classifying violations into three categories: serious, non-serious, and de minimis. . . . Apparently, until the advent of the case at hand, the Secretary acquiesced in that classification. Now, however, despite that twenty-year history, he views the de minimis status as merely a preliminary charging decision over which the Commission has no authority.

The Secretary contends that by lowering the offense to a de minimis level and, thus, not requiring abatement, the Commission usurped his authority to enforce the applicable standard. . . .

The precise issue of the Commission's authority to characterize an offense as de minimis was decided by the Court of Appeals for the First Circuit in *Donovan v. Daniel Construction Co.*, 692 F.2d 818 (1st Cir.1982). After reviewing the functions of the Commission, the Court held that "[t]here is no doubt (and it is agreed) that the Act gives the Commission authority, in appropriate cases, to reduce violations to the de minimis category." . . . The Court went on to say that "the Commission could properly decide that de minimis treatment of an OSHA violation is acceptable if there is a very attenuated relationship between the existence of the violation and the health and safety of the employees." . . .

In *Martin*, the Supreme Court referred to the Commission's role as a "neutral arbiter" and said "Congress expressly charged the Commission with making authoritative findings of fact and with applying the Secretary's standards to those facts in making a decision." . . . That is what occurred in this case. The Commission made a specific finding of fact that the safety of Erie's employees was not jeopardized by the company's failure to pay for protective gloves. We conclude that the Commission's finding is supported by substantial evidence.

The Commission has the statutory authority to affirm, modify, or vacate the Secretary's citation, or to direct other appropriate relief. Its action in reducing the violation to de minimis status clearly falls within that grant of power. The reduction of the offense level is analogous to the power of a court to reduce a criminal offense to a lesser level than the one charged in an indictment. That traditional procedure has not been considered to be a usurpation of prosecutorial discretion, but rather a necessary prerogative of the court. Moreover, the Secretary does not challenge the Commission's authority to reduce a serious violation to non-serious status. Thus, it appears that it is not the Commission that is seeking to enhance its authority, but the Secretary who is attempting to enlarge his power at the expense of the "neutral arbiter."

We need not elaborate on *Daniel*. . . . Here, we are content to rely on the well-reasoned opinion and holding of the Court of Appeals for the First Circuit.

. . . .

Accordingly, the Secretary's petition for review will be denied and Erie's petition for cross-review will be dismissed.

Becker, Circuit Judge, concurring and dissenting.

I share the majority's concern about the Secretary's change in legal position on this issue after having conceded, for almost twenty years, that the Commission had the authority to reclassify violations as de minimis. Nevertheless, it is clear that an agency may, in appropriate circumstances, alter its previous interpretation of a statute. . . .

If the Secretary decides to issue a citation rather than a de minimis notice, he must, perforce, have concluded that the health and safety considerations at issue warrant the enforcement of the regulation. In reclassifying a violation as de minimis, the Commission invades and overrides these prosecutorial and policymaking functions, which are reserved to the Secretary under the structure of the Act. . . .

In sum, by reclassifying a citation as de minimis, the Commission eviscerates the Secretary's ability to force an employer to comply with validly issued regulations and thereby effectively substitutes its judgment for the Secretary's as to the need to enforce that standard.

For the reasons discussed above, I respectfully dissent.

Questions and Comments

1.   Why do you think that the Secretary changed his position over the authority of the Commission to classify violations as de minimis? Do you think that the Supreme Court's opinion in *Martin* persuaded the Secretary to take the new position?

2.   Is there a difference between determining that a violation is de minimis on the particular facts and therefore unenforceable and determining that a regulation (here an occupational safety and health standard) is never enforceable? The court here decided that the Commission has the authority to make the former determination. Has the Commission the authority to make the latter kind of determination? Making the latter kind of determination would pose a greater threat to the enforcement authority of the Secretary, would it not?

3.   The alternative model of administration also comes up in *Director, Office of Workers' Compensation Programs v. Newport News Shipbuilding & Dry Dock Co.*, 514 U.S. 122 (1995), *infra* and *Thunder Basin Coal co. v. Reich*, 510 U.S. 200 (1994), *infra*.

D.   JUDICIAL REVIEW OF INFORMAL ACTION

1.   *The background of judicial review of informal agency action and the traditional approach of the courts.*

The material in section A above dealt with judicial review of agency orders which had been entered after the conclusion of an administrative proceeding taking the form of a trial-type hearing, i.e., a hearing modeled upon a judicial trial. Such a hearing produces, like its judicial analogue, a record of testimony and exhibits. When a court reviews an agency order issued in such a proceeding, the court can easily apply the substantial-evidence review standard because the court has before it the record of the proceeding before the agency, a record which resembles the record of any case tried before a court.

When an agency acts outside of a formal proceeding, it is more difficult for a court to review the agency's action. Since there is no proceeding, there is no record produced by such a proceeding. In the absence of such a record, the court cannot inquire as to whether the record contains substantial evidence in support of the agency's action.

The traditional way in which a person challenged an agency action taking place outside of any formal proceeding was to bring a lawsuit against the agency for an injunction (or, in later years, for a declaratory judgment). Since there was no record produced by an administrative proceeding, the factual basis for challenging the agency's action had to be established at trial in court.

The agency's action was presumed lawful, and the plaintiff bore the burden of proving it otherwise. The plaintiff, therefore, generally had to establish by proof that there was no rational basis for the agency's action under the governing statute; alternatively, the plaintiff had to establish that agency was acting without authority.

As will be seen from the materials on judicial review of agency rulemaking, the burden cast upon a plaintiff to establish an agency's lack of authority to issue a rule was an extremely heavy one. Since rules were issued upon the basis of facts in general, e.g., that pilots over age 60 were more susceptible to heart attacks than pilots under age 60, the plaintiff had to disprove facts which were general rather than facts which were concrete and particular.

When a plaintiff challenged an agency's application of a statute or a rule to a set of particular facts involving the plaintiff and the lawfulness of the agency's action turned upon what those facts were, the plaintiff's burden was sometimes easier to carry since particularized concrete facts are usually established on the basis of witnesses' testimony about matters which they have seen or heard.

Earlier in this chapter, we observed that when Congress enacted the Administrative Procedure Act, it incorporated in that Act the substantial-evidence standard governing judicial review of agency action in formal proceedings. 5 U.S.C. § 706(2)(E). It also incorporated in other clauses of § 706 the review standards governing judicial review of informal agency action.

2.   *The enactment of Hobbs Act and its assumptions.*

In 1950 Congress enacted the Hobbs Act which provided for review in the courts of appeals of "final orders" of the Federal Communications Commission, certain final orders of the Secretary of Agriculture, the Federal Maritime Commission or the Maritime Administration, all final orders of the Atomic Energy Commission and all rules, regulations or final orders of the Interstate Commerce Commission. The Hobbs Act is presently codified in Chapter 158 of 28 U.S.C. For an informative discussion of the Hobbs Act, see Carl Auerbach, *Informal Rule Making: A Proposed Relationship Between Administrative Procedures and judicial Review,* 72 N.WU.L. Rev. 15, 26–28 (1977). The Act provided that the agency should file with the court "the record on review" (as provided by 28 U.S.C. § 2112). At the time the Hobbs Act was enacted, it was understood that the "record" to be filed was a record prepared in a trial-type hearing before the agency governed by §§ 556 and 557 of the Administrative Procedure Act. See Auerbach, *supra.* If there was no such record (because there had been no trial-type hearing before the agency), or the record was incomplete and there were material unresolved factual issues, the Act established the procedure for creating the record necessary to the resolution of those issues. It provided as follows:

28 U.S.C. § 2347. Petition to review; proceedings

(a) Unless determined on a motion to dismiss, petitions to review orders reviewable under this chapter are heard in the court of appeals on the record of the pleadings, evidence adduced and proceedings before the agency, when the agency has held a hearing whether or not required to do so by law.

(b) When the agency has not held a hearing before taking the action of which review is sought by the petition, the court of appeals shall determine whether a hearing is required by law. After that determination, the court shall

(1) remand the proceedings to the agency to hold a hearing, when a hearing is required by law;

(2) pass on the issues presented, when a hearing is not required by law and it appears from the pleadings and affidavits filed by the parties that no genuine issue of material fact is presented; or

(3) transfer the proceedings to a district court for the district in which the petitioner resides or has its principal office for a hearing and determination as if the proceedings were originally initiated in the district court, when a hearing is not required by law and a genuine issue of material fact is presented. The procedure in these cases in the district court is governed by the Federal Rules of Civil Procedure.

(c) If a party to a proceeding to review applies to the court of appeals in which the proceeding is pending for leave to adduce additional evidence and shows to the satisfaction of the court that

(1) the additional evidence is material; and

(2) there were reasonable grounds for filing to adduce the evidence before the agency; the court may order the additional evidence and any counterevidence the opposite party desires to offer to be taken by the agency. The agency may modify its findings of fact, or make new findings, by reason of the additional evidence so taken, and may modify or set aside its order, and shall file in the court the additional or new findings, and the modified order or the order setting aside the original order.

The purpose of the Hobbs Act was to provide for review in the courts of appeals of agency orders which previously had been reviewable in an action before a three judge panel of a federal district court, a pattern for review which had been established by the Urgent Deficiencies Act of 1913 for review of orders of the Interstate Commerce Commission.

It will be observed that when an agency had not held a hearing which was required by law, the court was required to remand the case to the agency for such a hearing. If an agency had not held a hearing and no hearing was required by law, but there was a genuine issue of material fact, the court of appeals was required to remand the case to the district court for resolution of the factual issue. Thus the record on judicial review of an agency order (issued without an agency hearing and where none was required) would be prepared in a hearing before a federal district court. In its provisions for review of an agency order issued without an agency hearing where none was required by law, the Hobbs Act replicated the traditional practice of resolving factual disputes in court upon a record prepared there.

In short, when people wished to challenge an agency order which adversely affected them and that order was not issued on the basis of a trial-type agency hearing, the plaintiffs would have to challenge the factual assumptions of the order in court. They would prevail if they could show that, on the facts which they established in court, the agency order could not be justified as a rational means of implementing the statute.

The materials in the following section and elsewhere in this book show how, since 1971, a drastic revision has taken place in the way informal agency action, including informal rulemaking, has been reviewed in court. The leading authority for the new method of review is *Citizens to Preserve Overton Park, Inc. v. Volpe*, 401 U.S. 402 (1971). As will be seen later, the new approach has utilized a revisionist history of the Hobbs Act. See *Florida Power & Light Co. v. United States Nuclear Regulatory Commission*, 470 U.S. 729 (1985).

3.   Overton Park *and its progeny.*

CITIZENS TO PRESERVE OVERTON PARK, INC. v. VOLPE, SECRETARY OF TRANSPORTATION
401 U.S. 402 (1971)

Opinion of the Court by MR. JUSTICE MARSHALL, announced by MR. JUSTICE STEWART

The growing public concern about the quality of our natural environment has prompted Congress in recent years to enact legislation designed to curb the accelerating destruction of our country's natural beauty. We are concerned in this case with § 4(f) of the Department of Transportation Act of 1966, as amended, and § 18(a) of the Federal-Aid Highway Act of 1968. . . . These statutes prohibit the Secretary of Transportation from authorizing the use of federal funds to finance the construction of highways through public parks if a "feasible and prudent" alternative route exists. If no such route is available, the statutes allow him to approve construction through parks only if there has been "all possible planning to minimize harm" to the park.

Petitioners, private citizens as well as local and national conservation organizations, contend that the Secretary has violated these statutes by authorizing the expenditure of federal funds for the construction of a six-lane interstate highway through a public park in Memphis, Tennessee. Their claim was rejected by the District Court, which granted the Secretary's motion for summary judgment, and the Court of Appeals for the Sixth Circuit affirmed. . . .

Section 4(f) of the Department of Transportation Act and § 138 of the Federal-Aid Highway Act are clear and specific directives. Both . . . provide that the Secretary "shall not approve any program or project" that requires the use of any public parkland "unless (1) there is no feasible and prudent alternative to the use of such land, and (2) such program includes all possible planning to minimize harm to such park This language is a plain and explicit bar to the use of federal funds for construction of highways through parks — only the most unusual situations are exempted.

Despite the clarity of the statutory language, respondents argue that the Secretary has wide discretion. They recognize that the requirement that there be no "feasible" alternative route admits of little administrative discretion. For this exemption to apply the Secretary must find that as a matter of sound engineering it would not be feasible to build the highway along any other route. Respondents argue, however, that the requirement that there be no other "prudent" route requires the Secretary to engage in a wide-ranging balancing of competing interests. They contend that the Secretary should weigh the detriment resulting from the destruction of parkland against the cost of other routes, safety considerations, and other factors, and determine on the basis of the importance that he attaches to these other factors whether, on balance, alternative feasible routes would be "prudent."

But no such wide-ranging endeavor was intended. It is obvious that in most cases considerations of cost, directness of route, and community disruption will indicate that parkland should be used for highway construction whenever possible. . . . [T]here will always be a smaller outlay from the public purse when parkland is used since the public already owns the land and there will be no need to pay for right-of-way. And since people do not live or work in parks, if a highway is built on parkland no one will have to leave his home or give up his business. Such factors are common to substantially all highway construction. Thus, if Congress intended these factors to be on an equal footing with preservation of parkland there would have been no need for the statutes.

    . . . . The few green havens that are public parks were not to be lost unless there were truly unusual factors present in a particular case or the cost or community disruption resulting from alternative routes reached extraordinary magnitudes. . . .

    . . . . Certainly the Secretary's decision is entitled to a presumption of regularity. . . . But that presumption is not to shield his action from a thorough, probing, in-depth review.

The court is first required to decide whether the Secretary acted within the scope of his authority. . . . This determination naturally begins with a delineation of the scope of the Secretary's authority and discretion. . . . As has been shown, Congress has specified only a small range of choices that the Secretary can make. Also involved in this initial inquiry is a determination of whether on the facts the Secretary's decision can reasonably be said to be within that range. The reviewing court must consider whether the Secretary properly construed his authority to approve the use of parkland as limited to situations where there are no feasible alternative routes or where feasible alternative routes involve uniquely difficult problems. And the reviewing court must be able to find that the Secretary could have reasonably believed that in this case there are no feasible alternatives or that alternatives do involve unique problems.

Scrutiny of the facts does not end, however, with the determination that the Secretary has acted within the scope of his statutory authority. Section 706(2)(A) requires a finding that the actual choice made was not "arbitrary, capricious, an abuse of discretion, or otherwise not in accordance with law." 5 U.S.C. § 706(2)(A) (1964 ed., Supp. V). To make this finding the court must consider whether the decision was based on a consideration of the relevant factors and whether there has been a clear error of judgment. . . . Although this inquiry into the facts is to be searching and careful, the ultimate standard of review is a narrow one. The court is not empowered to substitute its judgment for that of the agency.

The final inquiry is whether the Secretary's action followed the necessary procedural requirements. Here the only procedural error alleged is the failure of the Secretary to make formal findings and state his reason for allowing the highway to be built through the park.

Undoubtedly, review of the Secretary's action is hampered by his failure to make such findings, but the absence of formal findings does not necessarily require that the case be remanded to the Secretary. . . . [The Court ruled that the Secretary was not required to have made formal findings.] Moreover, there is an administrative record that allows the full, prompt review of the Secretary's action that is sought without additional delay which would result from having a remand to the Secretary.

That administrative record is not, however, before us. The lower courts based their review on the litigation affidavits that were presented. These affidavits were merely *"post hoc"* rationalizations . . . which have traditionally been found to be an inadequate basis for review. . . . And they clearly do not constitute the "whole record" compiled by the agency: the basis for review required by § 706 of the Administrative Procedure Act. . . .

Thus it is necessary to remand this case to the District Court for plenary review of the Secretary's decision. That review is to be based on the full administrative record that was before the Secretary at the time he made his decision. But since the bare record may not disclose the factors that were considered or the Secretary's construction of the evidence it may be necessary for the District Court to require some explanation in order to determine if the Secretary acted within the scope of his authority and if the Secretary's action was justifiable under the applicable standard.

The court may require the administrative officials who participated in the decision to give testimony explaining their action. Of course, such inquiry into the mental processes of administrative decision-makers is usually to be avoided. *United States v. Morgan*, 313 U.S. 409, 422 (1941). And where there are administrative findings that were made at the same time as the decision, as was the case in *Morgan*, there must be a strong showing of bad faith or improper behavior before such inquiry may be made. But here there are no such formal findings and it may be that the only way there can be effective judicial review is by examining the decision-makers themselves. . . .

The District Court is not, however, required to make such an inquiry. It may be that the Secretary can prepare formal findings . . . that will provide an adequate explanation for his action. Such an explanation will, to some extent, be a "post hoc rationalization" and thus must be viewed critically. If the District Court decides that additional explanation is necessary, that court should consider which method will prove the most expeditious so that full review may be had as soon as possible.

Reversed and remanded.

Note on the Ramifications of *Overton Park*

First — The procedure:

1.   The approach of the Court to judicial review of the Secretary's action was a dramatic departure from tradition because the Court here required that review take place on the "administrative record" that was before the Secretary at the time he acted. The Court thus acted on the assumption that there was a "record" before the Secretary which could be used as the basis for judicial review.

2.   There was no record analogous to the record of a formal administrative proceeding, however. Indeed, there was no "record" at all. The case was remanded so that the district court could review the Secretary's actions on the "administrative record." But the district court could not easily summon such a record. The administrative record had to be created by the trial court through the introduction of testimony and documentary evidence. The resulting procedure thus resembled the traditional one: the record for the review of the Secretary's action was created in litigation before a federal district court (as opposed to a record generated in administrative proceedings).

3.   *Overton Park* has ramifications for other cases, however, especially those in which a plaintiff challenges the validity of an agency rule issued after notice-and-comment proceedings under § 553 of the Administrative Procedure Act. In such cases there is an "administrative record", even though it is not the type of record produced by a trial-type hearing. Under the procedure mandated by *Overton Park*, the agency rule would be reviewed on the record of the informal rulemaking proceeding, a drastic departure from the traditional way in which rules had been previously reviewed by courts.

Second — The standard of review:

4.   Did the Court set forth criteria for determining whether the Secretary acted within the scope of his statutory authority? What were those criteria? How would a court apply them in a case like *Overton Park?* Explain.

5.   Did the Court set forth criteria for determining whether the Secretary's decision was "arbitrary, capricious, an abuse of discretion, or otherwise not in accordance with law"? What were those criteria? How do they differ from the criteria used to determine whether the Secretary acted within his statutory authority?

6.   If the court believed that the Secretary made a "clear error of judgment", the court would set aside the Secretary's decision on the ground of arbitrariness, would it not? This "clear error of judgment" standard is less intrusive than the linguistically related "clearly erroneous" standard, is it not? How do you know that? Explain.

7.   How do you think the "arbitrariness" standard differs from the "substantial evidence" standard? Are the standards different because the record for review is created differently? Is there an arbitrariness standard built into the substantial evidence standard? See Judge Frank's concurring opinion in the Second Circuit's

Universal Camera opinion on remand, *supra*

8. Were the "relevant factors" upon which the Secretary had to base his decision clear to you? How does one determine what factors are relevant and what factors are irrelevant? Suppose that the Secretary's decision was influenced by pressures exerted upon him by members of Congress. Would his decision in that case be influenced by irrelevant factors and therefore be "arbitrary" under the *Overton Park* standard? *See D.C. Federation of Civic Associations v. Volpe*, 459 F.2d 1231 (D.C. Cir. 1972), *cert. denied*, 405 U.S. 1030 (1972).

9. Further variations on the *Overton Park* theme will be found in Chapter 7 *infra*.

4. *Procedures governing informal agency action.*

a) Informal rulemaking is governed by § 553 of the APA. *See* chapter 6 *infra*.

b) Informal adjudication is governed by § 555 of the APA. *See Pension Benefit Guarantee Corp. v. LTV Corp.*, 496 U.S. 633 (1990), chapter 4 *infra*.

Note: Judicial Review in the State Courts

Many attempts to reform state administrative law have been undertaken since the immediate pre-World War II period. In 1942 Robert Benjamin conducted an extensive study of New York State administrative procedures. Benjamin concluded that the procedures and tasks of the numerous agencies were so diverse that a generally-applicable administrative procedure act was not desirable.

In 1946 the Commissioners on Uniform State Laws promulgated a "model" state administrative procedure act. The commissioners promulgated revised model acts in 1961 and again in 1981. Most of the administrative procedure legislation in the states is copied in significant part from one or another version of the model acts.

The 1946, 1961 and 1981 model acts contain procedures for rulemaking and for trial-type proceedings. These acts provide for judicial review, *inter alia*, of trial-type proceedings, which the 1946 and 1961 acts refer to as "contested cases" and which the 1981 act refers to as "adjudicative proceedings". The 1946 and 1981 acts provide that an agency decision may be vacated if not supported by substantial evidence on the whole record. 1946 Model Act § 12(7)(e); 1981 Model Act § 5-116(c)(7). The 1961 Model Act authorizes the reviewing court to reverse or modify an agency decision when it is "clearly erroneous in view of the reliable, probative, and substantial evidence on the whole record." 1961 Model Act § 15(g)(5). How, if at all, would you expect this latter standard to differ from the substantial evidence standard as it was applied in *Universal Camera?*

The 1946 and 1961 model acts also contain provisions governing judicial review of rules. 1946 Model Act § 6; 1961 Model Act § 7. The 1981 model act explicitly extends judicial review to agency action which is neither an order resulting from an adjudicative proceeding nor a rule. 1981 Model Act § 1-102(2), § 5-102.

Chapter 3

CONSTITUTIONAL RIGHTS TO HEARINGS UNDER THE DUE PROCESS CLAUSES OF THE FIFTH AND FOURTEENTH AMENDMENTS

A. THE CONSTITUTIONAL PARAMETERS

Londoner v. Denver, **210 U.S. 373 (1908).** The plaintiffs were landowners suing to be relieved from an assessment to pay the cost of paving a street upon which their lands abutted. They had been assessed pursuant to provisions of the Denver city charter which provided that the board of public works (upon the petition of a majority of the owners of the frontage to be assessed) could recommend to the city council that a street be paved. The council then decided whether the work should be undertaken. After the work was completed, the charter provided for notice by publication to the owners of the property to be assessed, specifying the entire cost and the amount recommended by the board to be apportioned to each lot. Complaints or objections could be made in writing to the city council within thirty days from the notice. The council (acting as a board of equalization) then decided whether to accept the board's assessment recommendations or to modify them. In holding that this procedure was constitutionally deficient, the Court explained:

In the assessment, apportionment and collection of taxes upon property within their jurisdiction the Constitution of the United States imposes few restrictions upon the States. In the enforcement of such restrictions as the Constitution does impose this court has regarded substance and not form. But where the legislature of a State, instead of fixing the tax itself, commits to some subordinate body the duty of determining whether, in what amount, and upon whom it shall be levied, and of making its assessment and apportionment, due process of law requires that at some stage of the proceedings before the tax becomes irrevocably fixed, the taxpayer shall have an opportunity to be heard, of which he must have notice, either personal, by publication, or by a law fixing the time and place of the hearing. . . . It must be remembered that the law of Colorado denies the landowner the right to object in the courts to the assessment, upon the ground that the objections are cognizable only by the board of equalization.

If it is enough that, under such circumstances, an opportunity is given to submit in writing all objections to and complaints of the tax to the board, then there was a hearing afforded in the case at bar. But we think that something more than that, even in proceedings for taxation, is required by due process of law. Many requirements essential in strictly judicial proceedings may be dispensed with in proceedings of this nature. But even here a hearing in its very essence demands that he who is entitled to it shall have the right to support his allegations by argument however brief, and, if need be, by proof, however informal. . . . It is apparent that such a hearing was denied to the plaintiffs in error. The denial was by the city council, which, while acting as a board of equalization, represents the State. . . .

BI-METALLIC INVESTMENT CO. v. STATE BOARD OF EQUALIZATION OF COLORADO
239 U.S. 441 (1915)

MR. JUSTICE HOLMES delivered the opinion of the court.

This is a suit to enjoin the State Board of Equalization and the Colorado Tax Commission from putting in force, and the defendant Pitcher as assessor of Denver from obeying, an order of the boards increasing the valuation of all taxable property in Denver forty per cent. The order was sustained and the suit directed to be dismissed by the Supreme Court of the State. . . . The plaintiff is the owner of real estate in Denver and brings the case here on the ground that it was given no opportunity to be heard and that therefore its property will be taken without due process of law, contrary to the Fourteenth Amendment of the Constitution of the United States. . . .

For the purposes of decision we assume that the constitutional question is presented in the baldest way — that neither the plaintiff nor the assessor of Denver . . . nor any representative of the city and county, was given an opportunity to be heard, other than such as they may have had by reason of the fact that the time of meeting of the boards is fixed by law. On this assumption it is obvious that injustice may be suffered if some property in the county already has been valued at its full worth. But if certain property has been valued at a rate different from that generally prevailing in the county the owner has had his opportunity to protest and appeal as usual in our system of taxation . . . so that it must be assumed that the property owners in the county all stand alike. The question then is whether all individuals have a constitutional right to be heard before a matter can be decided in which all are equally concerned, — here, for instance, before a superior board decides that the local taxing officers have adopted a system of undervaluation throughout a county. . . .

Where a rule of conduct applies to more than a few people it is impracticable that every one should have a direct voice in its adoption. The Constitution does not require all public acts to be done in town meeting or an assembly of the whole. General statutes within the state power are passed that affect the person or property of individuals, sometimes to the point of ruin, without giving them a chance to be heard. Their rights are protected in the only way that they can be in a complex society, by their power, immediate or remote, over those who make the rule. If the result in this case had been reached as it might have been by the State's doubling the rate of taxation, no one would suggest that the Fourteenth Amendment was violated unless every person affected had been allowed an opportunity to raise his voice against it before the body entrusted by the state constitution with the power. . . . There must be a limit to individual argument in such matters if government is to go on. In *Londoner v. Denver,* 210 U.S. 373, 385, a local board had to determine "whether, in what amount, and upon whom" a tax for paving a street should be levied for special benefits. A relatively small number of persons was concerned, who were exceptionally affected, in each case upon individual grounds, and it was held that they had a right to a hearing. But that decision is far from reaching a general determination dealing only with the principle upon which all the assessments in a county had been laid.

Judgment affirmed.

Questions and Comments

1. In *Londoner* the Court said that before a tax becomes irrevocably fixed, the taxpayer has a right to a hearing. How does the *Bi-Metallic* opinion contribute to your understanding of this language? What are the attributes of the hearing required under *Londoner?*

2. How did the *Bi-Metallic* opinion distinguish *Londoner?* Was the factual setting different in the two cases? Were the claims different?

3. Do you agree with the decision in the *Bi-Metallic* case? If the Bi-Metallic Investment Company had been granted a hearing, how do you think that Company would have constructed its case for submission at the hearing before the state board of equalization? What arguments would it make? What evidence would it submit?

4. If the Bi-Metallic Investment Company had been successful in its contention that it was entitled to a hearing, would other property owners in Denver also have a right to hearings in connection with the proposed 40% increase in their assessments? What arguments would each of these other property owners make at their hearings? What evidence would they submit? Would the board of equalization have to sit through thousands of hearings, all addressing exactly the same issue? and in which each property owner made the same arguments and presented the same evidence? What purpose would such duplicative hearings serve?

5. The distinction which Justice Holmes employed is not concerned solely with numbers, is it? Can you not think of examples in which many people would be entitled to hearings under the *Londoner* ruling? What was the significance of Holmes' reference to *Londoner* as involving persons uniquely affected? Was he referring to the type of issue involved in *Londoner?* Was he doing more than that? How did the type of issue involved in *Londoner* differ from the type of issue involved in *Bi-Metallic?* Would the method of proof employed by litigants contesting those issues differ? How?

6. Professor Kenneth Culp Davis has coined the terms "adjudicative facts" and "legislative facts." According to Davis: "Adjudicative facts are the facts about the parties and their activities, businesses, and properties. Adjudicative facts usually answer the questions of who did what, where, when, how, why, with what motive or intent; adjudicative facts are roughly the kind of facts that go to a jury in a jury case. Legislative facts do not usually concern the immediate parties but are general facts which help the tribunal decide questions of law and policy and discretion." K. Davis, *Administrative Law Treatise*§ 7.02 (1958). See also K. Davis, *Administrative Law Treatise § 12*.3 (2d ed. 1979). Is Davis' distinction helpful in distinguishing the holdings of *Londoner* and *Bi-Metallic?*

7. Is the proof of an "adjudicative fact" different from the proof of a "legislative fact"? Explain. Is an evidentiary hearing more suitable for proof of an "adjudicative fact" than for a "legislative fact"? Why?

8. But it is not merely that the type of issue in the two cases differed. Nor that the methods for proof differed in the two cases. The Court's ruling in *Londoner* also identified the parties who may raise those issues, did it not? It is only the landowners uniquely affected who can contest those unique effects on them, is it not? Unassessed neighbors who object to the paving or to the manner in which it was performed have no right to be heard on the assessment issues, do they? *Londoner*, therefore, is indicative of more than the type of issue or the method of its proof.

9. Are the parties who are entitled to a hearing under *Londoner* those who are likely to know most about the issues? to have the motivation to learn about them? to have the motivation to present the best case to the deciding tribunal? Would those parties be likely to make a similarly unique contribution to the decision of "legislative facts"? Explain.

10. Could it be argued that underlying the decisions in *Londoner* and *Bi-Metallic* is a principle that persons should be heard who have the most to contribute to the decisional process? that the principle embraced by those decisions is one of furthering the accuracy of the decisional process? Why or why not?

11. Justice Holmes noted that no representative of the city or county had been given an opportunity to be heard before the state board of equalization. Should the board have heard such representatives? What kind of case would you expect city or county representatives to have made, if they had been given the opportunity? Would those cases have been substantially different from the one which the Bi-Metallic Investment Company would have made, had it been given the opportunity? Would Holmes' objections to the impracticality of granting thousands of hearings apply to allowing a hearing by a representative of all of the affected property owners? Yet he did rule that the board had no obligation to hear such a representative, did he not? Such a ruling effectively precludes other arguments for group representation, as through the administrative equivalent of a class action, does it not? Is it relevant that class actions were unknown at the time of the *Bi-Metallic* decision?

12. If the Bi-Metallic Investment Company believed that the state board of equalization had acted unlawfully in raising assessments, could the Company get a hearing on this question in the courts? Explain.

13. Could Denver deny hearings before the city council to landowners faced with an assessment for an improvement if Colorado permitted landowners the right to object in the courts to the assessment? Explain.

14. Justice Holmes said that "if the state constitution had declared that Denver had been undervalued . . . and had decreed that for the current year the valuation should be forty per cent higher" no objection could be made that the affected people had not been afforded a hearing. Does it then follow that the state board of equalization could do the same thing without a hearing? Did the Court in *Londoner* suggest that the legislature could do some things without providing a hearing that a subordinate body could not do? Does it not follow a fortiori that the state

constitution can do things that a subordinate body cannot do? Did Holmes deal with that part of the *Londoner* opinion which suggests that subordinate bodies are under a greater obligation to provide hearings?

B.   NOTE: PROCEDURAL DUE PROCESS DEVELOPMENTS OF THE 1950s AND EARLY 1960s

Attempts by the federal government in the 1950s to counter perceived threats to national security from within gave rise to numerous lawsuits, several of which contributed significantly to the case law governing the application of the due process clauses. In many of these cases, the Supreme Court reached its decision by examining the authority of the governmental institution to perform the challenged action. In this way, the Court was often able to avoid casting its rulings in constitutional terms.

In 1951 the Court decided *Joint Anti-Fascist Refugee Committee v. McGrath*, 341 U.S. 123 (1951). An Executive Order required the Attorney General to furnish an official list of organizations deemed subversive to the Loyalty Review Board which, in turn, was to disseminate information from the list to all government departments and agencies for use as evidence in evaluating the loyalty of their employees. Without providing any opportunity to meet and disprove information on which he acted, the Attorney General had included the several plaintiff organizations on his list. The result, it was claimed, would be to impair the plaintiffs' ability to raise funds through the solicitation of voluntary contributions. Claiming that the designations were false, the plaintiffs sued to enjoin the Attorney General from including them on his list of subversive organizations. An overconfident Government made a tactical blunder: The Government demurred to the complaint, thus conceding for the purpose of demur the truthfulness of the plaintiffs' allegations. Thus when the case reached the Supreme Court, the Government had put itself in the position of asserting a right to label legitimate and nonsubversive organizations as subversive ones: ". . . we conclude that, if *the allegations of the complaints are taken as true* (as they must be on the motions to dismiss), the Executive Order does not authorize the Attorney General to furnish the Loyalty Review Board with a list containing such a designation as he gave to each of these organizations without other justification. Under such circumstances his own admissions render his designations patently arbitrary because they are contrary to the alleged and uncontroverted facts constituting the record before us." (emphasis in the original). Deciding the case in this way, the plurality did not reach constitutional problems inherent in the way in which the Attorney General had reached his challenged decisions. Concurring, Justice Frankfurter reached the constitutional issues, concluding that the due process clause of the Fifth Amendment applied to the circumstances before him and that the procedures which it mandated had not been met, because "the right to be heard before being condemned to suffer grievous loss of any kind . . . is a principle basic to our society."

On the same day that the Court decided *Joint Anti-Fascist Refugee Committee v. McGrath*, it affirmed by an equally divided Court the decision of the U.S. Court of Appeals for the District of Columbia in *Bailey v. Richardson*, 341 U.S. 918 (1951), *affirmed by an equally divided Court*, 182 F.2d 46 (D.C. Cir. 1950). In the *Bailey* case, a government employee in the classified civil service was discharged on the basis that "reasonable grounds exist for belief that [she] . . . is disloyal to the Government of the United States." The determination that such reasonable grounds existed was made without giving Miss Bailey a chance to confront the witnesses against her or to cross-examine them. When Miss Bailey challenged the procedure in court, her claim was rejected on the grounds, *inter alia*, that the due process clause of the Fifth Amendment was inapplicable because no life, liberty or property interest of hers was affected: "It has been held repeatedly and consistently that Government employ is not 'property' and that in this particular it is not a contract. We are unable to perceive how it could be held to be 'liberty'. Certainly it is not 'life'. . . . [I]t is said that . . . she has been stigmatized and her chances of making a living seriously impaired. . . . [T]hat even if executive authority had power to dismiss Miss Bailey without a judicial hearing, they had no power to hurt her while doing so . . . But if no constitutional right of the individual is being impinged and officials are acting within the scope of official authority, the fact that the individual concerned is injured in the process neither invalidates the official act nor gives the individual a right to redress. . . ."

Greene v. McElroy, 360 U.S. 474 (1959). Greene was an aeronautical engineer employed by a private manufacturer which produced goods for the armed services. Greene was discharged when the Government revoked his security clearance and he thereby lost access to classified information which he needed to perform his job. After his discharge, Greene was unable to secure employment as an aeronautical engineer and for all practical purposes that field of endeavor was then closed to him. Claiming that the revocation of his security clearance was unlawful, Greene brought suit to set it aside.

The revocation of Greene's security clearance was the culmination of several proceedings conducted by several agencies of the Defense Department from 1951 to 1953. The type of hearings which these agencies afforded him is shown by a statement which the Chairman of the Eastern Industrial Personnel Security Board (EIPSB) made to Greene:

> The transcript to be made of this hearing will not include all material in the file of the case, in that, it will not include reports of investigation conducted by the Federal Bureau of Investigation or other investigative agencies which are confidential. Neither will it contain information concerning the identity of confidential informants or information which will reveal the source of confidential evidence. The transcript will contain only the Statement of Reasons, your answer thereto and the testimony actually taken at this hearing.

As in the *Joint Anti-Fascist Refugee Committee* case, the Court decided the case on the issue of the authority of the agency involved (here the Defense Department) to take the challenged action. An excerpt from the Court's opinion follows:

> Petitioner contends that the action of the Department of Defense in barring him from access to classified information on the basis of statements of confidential informants made to investigators was not authorized by Congress or the President and has denied him "liberty" and "property" without "due process of law" in contravention of the Fifth Amendment. The

alleged property is petitioner's employment; the alleged liberty is petitioner's freedom to practice his chosen profession. . . . Although the right to hold specific private employment and to follow a chosen profession free from unreasonable governmental interference comes within the "liberty" and "property" concepts of the Fifth Amendment. . . . respondents contend that the admitted interferences which have occurred are indirect by-products of necessary governmental action to protect the integrity of secret information and hence are not unreasonable and do not constitute deprivations within the meaning of the Amendment. . . .

The issue, as we see it, is whether the Department of Defense has been authorized to create an industrial security clearance program under which affected persons may lose their jobs and may be restrained in following their chosen professions on the basis of fact determinations concerning their fitness for clearance made in proceedings in which they are denied the traditional procedural safeguards of confrontation and cross-examination.

Certain principles have remained relatively immutable in our jurisprudence. One of these is that where government action seriously injures an individual, and the reasonableness of the action depends on fact findings, the evidence used to prove the Government's case must be disclosed to the individual so that he has an opportunity to show that it is untrue. While this is important in the case of documentary evidence, it is even more important where the evidence consists of the testimony of individuals whose memory might be faulty or who, in fact, might be perjurers or persons motivated by malice, vindictiveness, intolerance, prejudice, or jealously. We have formalized these protections in the requirements of confrontation and cross-examination. They have ancient roots. They find expression in the Sixth Amendment which provides that in all criminal cases the accused shall enjoy the right "to be confronted with the witnesses against him." This Court has been zealous to protect these rights from erosion. It has spoken out not only in criminal cases . . . but also in all types of cases where administrative and regulatory actions were under scrutiny. . . .

The Court then examined two Executive Orders limiting access to classified information and concluded that neither purported to authorize the establishment of a security clearance program which denied affected persons the right to confront and to cross-examine witnesses against him. The Court also concluded that no statute purported to authorize such a program. It continued:

. . . . Before we are asked to judge whether, in the context of security clearance cases, a person may be deprived of the right to follow his chosen profession without full hearings where accusers may be confronted, it must be made clear that the President or Congress, within their respective constitutional powers, specifically has decided and warranted and has authorized their use. . . . We decide only that in the absence of explicit authorization from either the President or Congress the respondents were not empowered to deprive petitioner of his job in a proceeding in which he was not afforded the safeguards of confrontation and cross-examination.

In a subsequent case, *Cafeteria & Restaurant Workers Union v. McElroy*, 367 U.S. 886 (1961) the Court faced both the authority issues and the constitutional issues. In that case the Court upheld the right of the Commandant of the Naval Gun Factory, summarily and without a hearing, to bar a worker (Rachel Brawner) for a privately operated cafeteria located on the Gun Factory grounds from entering those grounds on the basis that she had failed to meet the security requirements of the installation. The Court concluded that Commandants of military and naval bases traditionally have possessed almost unfettered power to exclude; and that the Commandant's action did not seriously impair Ms. Brawner's other employment opportunities:

> [M]ost assuredly . . . [it did not affect her] right to follow a chosen trade or profession. . . . Rachel Brawner remained entirely free to obtain employment as a short-order cook or to get any other job, either with M & M [the operator of the cafeteria at the Gun Factory] or with any other employer. . . . [T]his is not a case where government action has operated to bestow a badge of disloyalty or infamy, with an attendant foreclosure from other employment opportunity. . . . As pointed out by Judge Prettyman . . . "Nobody has said that Brawner is disloyal or is suspected of the slightest shadow of intentional wrongdoing. . . ." For all that appears, the Security Officer and the Superintendent may have simply thought that Rachel Brawner was garrulous, or careless with her identification badge.

Questions and Comments

1. Is it better for the Court to avoid the decision of constitutional issues by basing its decision on questions of authority or to meet the constitutional issues directly? What are the considerations which must be weighed in answering this question?

2. Is it easier for counsel to persuade the courts to invalidate governmental action when argument is cast in terms of unauthorized action or in constitutional terms? Explain. Should counsel raising a constitutional claim always consider the advisability of also raising an issue of agency authority?

3. Do you think that Justice Frankfurter would apply the due process clause whenever governmental action imposed "grievous loss" upon a person? Would he not have to discover an adversely affected life, liberty or property interest before that clause became applicable? Did the Court in *Greene* address the question of whether Greene possessed an affected liberty or property interest?

4. Although the Court in *Greene* decided on the basis of the lack of the Defense Department's authority to establish the challenged security-clearance procedures, it also articulated its views as to what the due process clause would probably require, did it not? Would you expect that this articulation would have an effect upon the approach of the lower courts? upon the Supreme Court's own future decisions? upon the future action of Congress and the Executive?

5. What developments do you see in the judicial understanding of "liberty" as used in the due process clause during the 1950s? Was the Court in *Greene* repudiating the approach of the District of Columbia Circuit taken eight years

earlier in *Bailey v. Richardson?* Did the *Cafeteria Workers* case help to confirm that newer understanding of liberty? Explain.

C.   THE *GOLDBERG v. KELLY* PARADIGM

Extract from Reich, *The New Property,* 73 Yale LJ. 733, 785–786 (1964):

. . . [T]he growth of government power based on the dispensing of wealth must be kept within bounds. Second, there must be a zone of privacy for each individual beyond which neither government nor private power can push — a hiding place from the all-pervasive system of regulation and control. Finally, it must be recognized that we are becoming a society based upon relationship and status — status deriving primarily from source of livelihood. Status is so closely linked to personality that destruction of one may well destroy the other. Status must therefore be surrounded with the kinds of safeguards once reserved for personality.

Eventually those forms of largess which are closely linked to status must be deemed to be held as of right. Like property, such largess could be governed by a system of regulation plus civil or criminal sanctions, rather than a system based upon denial, suspension and revocation. As things now stand, violations lead to forfeitures — outright confiscation of wealth and status. But there is surely no need for these drastic results. Confiscation, if used at all, should be the ultimate, not the most common and convenient penalty. The presumption should be that the professional man will keep his license, and the welfare recipient his pension. These interests should be "vested." If revocation is necessary, not by reason of the fault of the individual holder, but by reason of overriding demands of public policy, perhaps payment of just compensation would be appropriate. The individual should not bear the entire loss for a remedy primarily to benefit the community.

The concept of right is most urgently needed with respect to benefits like unemployment compensation, public assistance, and old age insurance. These benefits are based upon a recognition that misfortune and deprivation are often caused by forces far beyond the control of the individual, such as technological change, variations in demand for goods, depressions, or wars. The aim of these benefits is to preserve the self-sufficiency of the individual, to rehabilitate him where necessary, and to allow him to be a valuable member of a family and a community; in theory they represent part of the individual's rightful share in the commonwealth. Only by making such benefits into rights can the welfare state achieve its goal of providing a secure minimum basis for individual well-being and dignity in a society where each man cannot be wholly the master of his own destiny. . . .

GOLDBERG, COMMISSIONER OF SOCIAL SERVICES OF THE CITY OF NEW YORK v. KELLY
397 U.S. 254 (1970)

MR. JUSTICE BRENNAN delivered the opinion of the Court.

The question for decision is whether a State that terminates public assistance payments to a particular recipient without affording him the opportunity for an evidentiary hearing prior to termination denies the recipient procedural due process in violation of the Due Process Clause of the Fourteenth Amendment. This action was brought in the District Court for the Southern District of New York by residents of New York City receiving financial aid under the federally assisted program of Aid to Families with Dependent Children (AFDC) or under New York State's general Home Relief program. Their complaint alleged that the New York State and New York City officials administering these programs terminated, or were about to terminate, such aid without prior notice and hearing, thereby denying them due process of law. . . .

[Under the governing New York State regulations] local officials proposing to discontinue or suspend a recipient's financial aid [must] do so according to a procedure that conforms to either subdivision (a) or subdivision (b) of § 351.26 of the regulations. . . . The City of New York elected to promulgate a local procedure according to subdivision (b). That subdivision, so far as here pertinent, provides that the local procedure must include the filing of notice to the recipient of the reasons for a proposed discontinuance or suspension at least seven days prior to its effective date, with notice also that upon request the recipient may have the proposal reviewed by a local welfare official holding a position superior to that of the supervisor who approved the proposed discontinuance or suspension, and, further, that the recipient may submit, for purposes of review, a written statement to demonstrate why his grant should not be discontinued or suspended. The decision by the reviewing official whether to discontinue or suspend aid must be made expeditiously, with written notice of the decision to the recipient. The section further expressly provides that "[a]ssistance shall not be discontinued or suspended prior to the date such notice of decision is sent to the recipient and his representative, if any, or prior to the proposed effective date of discontinuance or suspension, whichever occurs later."

Pursuant to subdivision (b), the New York City Department of Social Services promulgated Procedure No. 68-18. A caseworker who has doubts about the recipient's continued eligibility must first discuss them with the recipient. If the caseworker concludes that the recipient is no longer eligible, he recommends termination of aid to a unit supervisor. If the latter concurs, he sends the recipient a letter stating the reasons for proposing to terminate aid and notifying him that within seven days he may request that a higher official review the record, and may support the request with a written statement prepared personally or with the aid of an attorney or other person. If the reviewing official affirms the determination of ineligibility, aid is stopped immediately and the recipient is informed by letter of the reasons for the action. Appellees' challenge to this procedure emphasizes the absence of any provisions for the personal appearance of the recipient before the reviewing official, for oral presentation of evidence, and for confrontation and cross-examination of adverse witnesses. However, the letter does inform the recipient that he may request a post-termination "fair-hearing." This is a proceeding before an independent state hearing officer at which the recipient may appear personally, offer oral evidence, confront and cross-examine the witnesses against him, and have a record made of the hearing. If the recipient prevails at the "fair hearing" he is paid all funds erroneously withheld. . . . A recipient whose aid is not restored by a "fair hearing" decision may have judicial review. . . .

I

The constitutional issue to be decided, therefore, is the narrow one whether the Due Process Clause requires that the recipient be afforded an evidentiary hearing *before* the termination of benefits. . . .

Appellant does not contend that procedural due process is not applicable to the termination of welfare benefits. Such benefits are a matter of statutory entitlement for persons qualified to receive them. . . . The constitutional challenge cannot be answered by an argument that public assistance benefits are "a 'privilege' and not a 'right.' ". . . . The extent to which procedural due process must be afforded the recipient is influenced by the extent to which he may be "condemned to suffer grievous loss," *Joint Anti-Fascist Refugee Committee v. McGrath*, 341 U.S. 123, 168 (1951) (Frankfurter, J., concurring), and depends upon whether the recipient's interest in avoiding that loss outweighs the governmental interest in summary adjudication. . . .

It is true, of course, that some governmental benefits may be administratively terminated without affording the recipient a pre-termination evidentiary hearing. But we agree with the District Court that when welfare is discontinued, only a pre-termination evidentiary hearing provides the recipient with procedural due process. . . . For qualified recipients, welfare provides the means to obtain essential food, clothing, housing, and medical care. . . . Thus the crucial factor in this context — a factor not present in the case of the blacklisted government contractor, the discharged government employee, the taxpayer denied a tax exemption, or virtually anyone else whose governmental entitlements are ended — is that termination of aid pending resolution of a controversy over eligibility may deprive an *eligible* recipient of the very means by which to live while he waits. . . . His need to concentrate upon finding the means for daily subsistence, in turn, adversely affects his ability to seek redress from the welfare bureaucracy.

Moreover, important governmental interests are promoted by affording recipients a pre-termination evidentiary hearing. From its founding the Nation's basic commitment has been to foster the dignity and well-being of all persons within its borders. We have come to recognize that forces not within the control of the poor contribute to their poverty. . . . Welfare, by meeting the basic demands of subsistence, can help bring within the reach of the poor the same opportunities that are available to others to participate meaningfully in the life of the community. At the same time, welfare guards against the societal malaise that may flow from a widespread sense of unjustified frustration and insecurity. . . . The same governmental interests that counsel the provision of welfare, counsel as well its uninterrupted provision to those eligible to receive it; pre-termination evidentiary hearings are indispensable to that end.

Appellant does not challenge the force of these considerations but argues that they are outweighed by countervailing governmental interests in conserving fiscal and administrative resources. These interests, the argument goes, justify the delay of any evidentiary hearing until after discontinuance of the grants. Summary adjudication protects the public fisc by stopping payments promptly upon discovery of reason to believe that a recipient is no longer eligible. Since most terminations are accepted without challenge, summary adjudication also conserves both the fisc and administrative time and energy by reducing the number of evidentiary hearings actually held.

. . . [T]hese governmental interests are not overriding in the welfare context. . . . Much of the drain on fiscal and administrative resources can be reduced by developing procedures for prompt pre-termination hearings and by skilful use of personnel and facilities. . . . . Thus, the interest of the eligible recipient in uninterrupted receipt of public assistance, coupled with the State's interest that his payments not be erroneously terminated, clearly outweigh the State's competing concern to prevent any increase in its fiscal and administrative burdens. . . .

[T]he pre-termination hearing need not take the form of a judicial or quasi-judicial trial. We bear in mind that the statutory "fair hearing" will provide the recipient with a full administrative review. Accordingly, the pre-termination hearing has one function only: to produce an initial determination of the validity of the welfare department's grounds for discontinuance of payments in order to protect a recipient against an erroneous termination of his benefits. . . . Thus, a complete record and a comprehensive opinion, which would serve primarily to facilitate judicial review and to guide future decisions, need not be provided at the pre-termination stage. . . . We wish to add that we, no less than the dissenters, recognize the importance of not imposing upon the States or the Federal Government in this developing field of law any procedural requirements beyond those demanded by rudimentary due process.

. . . . In the present contest these [due process] principles require that a recipient have timely and adequate notice detailing the reasons for a proposed termination, and an effective opportunity to defend by confronting any adverse witnesses and by presenting his own arguments and evidence orally. . . .

The opportunity to be heard must be tailored to the capacities and circumstances of those who are to be heard. It is not enough that a welfare recipient may present his position to the decision maker in writing or second-hand through his caseworker. Written submissions are an unrealistic option for most recipients, who lack the educational attainment necessary to write effectively and who cannot obtain professional assistance. Moreover, written submissions do not afford the flexibility of oral presentations; they do not permit the recipient to mold his argument to the issues the decision maker appears to regard as important. Particularly where credibility and veracity are at issue, as they must be in many termination proceedings, written submissions are a wholly unsatisfactory basis for decision. The second-hand presentation to the decision-maker by the caseworker has its own deficiencies; since the caseworker usually gathers the facts upon which the charge of ineligibility rests, the presentation of the recipient's side of the controversy cannot safely be left to him. Therefore a recipient must be allowed to state his position orally. . . .

In almost every setting where important decisions turn on questions of fact, due process requires an opportunity to confront and cross-examine adverse witnesses. . . . We do not say that counsel must be provided at the pre-termination hearing, but only that the recipient must be allowed to retain an attorney if he so desires. Counsel can help delineate the issues, present the factual contentions in an orderly manner, conduct cross-examination, and generally safeguard the interests of the recipient. . . .

Finally, the decisionmaker's conclusion as to a recipient's eligibility must rest solely on the legal rules and evidence adduced at the hearing. . . . To demonstrate compliance with this elementary requirement, the decision maker should state the reasons for his determination and indicate the evidence he relied on. . . . And, of course, an impartial decision maker is essential. . . . [P]rior involvement in some aspects of a case will not necessarily bar a welfare official from acting as a decision maker. He should not, however, have participated in making the determination under review.

Affirmed.

Questions and Comments

1.   What criterion did the Court use to determine that the due process clause was applicable to the termination of welfare benefits? Did the use of this criterion involve a balancing of various factors? Explain.

2.   What did the Court say about the distinction between a "right" and a "privilege"? Did the Court say that welfare benefits are "rights"? What turned on the distinction between rights and privileges in the past? On what basis did the Court conclude that welfare benefits are not privileges?

3.   The Court cited the article by Reich quoted above with approval. Did the *Goldberg* opinion generally adopt the outlook and approach which had been advocated by Professor Reich?

4.   Did the state contend that the due process clause did not apply to the termination of welfare benefits?

5.   What criteria did the Court employ to determine that welfare recipients were entitled to an evidentiary hearing prior to the termination of benefits? Did the use of these criteria involve a balancing of various factors? Explain.

6.   What was the significance of the Court's reference to Justice Frankfurter's concurring opinion in *Joint Anti-Fascist Refugee Committee v. McGrath?* Is the termination of welfare benefits a "grievous loss"? If so, what follows from that conclusion?

7.   What specific procedures were required for the pre-termination hearing? In the view of the Court what was the function of the pre-termination hearing? How

did those functions differ from those of the post-termination hearing that New York already provided? If a state provided all of the procedures which the Court required for a pre-termination hearing, what additional procedures would it have to provide in a post-termination hearing? Explain. Would you expect that after the *Goldberg* decision, New York would collapse the pre-termination and the post-termination decision-making process into one evidentiary hearing held prior to termination? Why?

8.   Exactly what was at stake in *Goldberg?* Both sides agreed that welfare recipients were entitled to an evidentiary hearing to decide the termination-of-benefits issue, did they not? *Goldberg* thus was concerned only with the procedures necessary to protect the recipients' interests during the time from termination to the later decision in the post-termination hearing. The substantiality of the injury which the affected persons may suffer from an erroneous initial decision until a final decision is made after a full evidentiary hearing may vary with the circumstances. Dean Carl Auerbach has called this injury an "interim harm".

9.   In order to determine the kind of procedures necessary to protect the welfare recipients against deprivation during this interim period, what factors did the Court weigh? What factors would the Court weigh to determine the procedures necessary to a decision to terminate welfare benefits permanently? Would the factors weighed or the balance reached be different? Explain.

10.   Note that *Goldberg* is premised upon the welfare recipients possessing an entitlement. To the extent that welfare reforms have changed, or might change, recipients' entitlements into discretionary benefits, recipients' hearing rights then would be affected.

BOARD OF REGENTS OF STATE COLLEGES v. ROTH
408 U.S. 564 (1972)

MR. JUSTICE STEWART delivered the opinion of the Court.

In 1968 the respondent, David Roth, was hired for his first teaching job as assistant professor of political science at Wisconsin State University-Oshkosh. He was hired for a fixed term of one academic year. The notice of his faculty appointment specified that his employment would begin on September 1, 1968, and would end on June 30, 1969. The respondent completed that term. But he was informed that he would not be rehired for the next academic year.

The procedural protection afforded a Wisconsin State University teacher before he is separated from the University corresponds to his job security. . . . Rules promulgated by the Board of Regents provide that a nontenured teacher "dismissed" before the end of the year may have some opportunity for review of the "dismissal." But the Rules provide no real protection of a nontenured teacher who simply is not re-employed for the next year. He must be informed by February 1 "concerning retention or non-retention for the ensuing year." But "no reason for non-retention need be given. No review or appeal is provided in such case."

In conformance with these Rules, the President of Wisconsin State University-Oshkosh informed the respondent before February 1, 1969, that he would not be rehired for the 1969-1970 academic year. He gave the respondent no reason for the decision and no opportunity to challenge it at any sort of hearing.

The respondent then brought this action in Federal District Court alleging that the decision not to rehire him for the next year infringed his Fourteenth Amendment rights. He attacked the decision both in substance and procedure. First, he alleged that the true reason for the decision was to punish him for certain statements critical of the University administration, and that it therefore violated his right to freedom of speech. Second, he alleged that the failure of University officials to give him notice of any reason for nonretention and an opportunity for a hearing violated his right to procedural due process of law.

The District Court granted summary judgment for the respondent on the procedural issue, ordering the University officials to provide him with reasons and a hearing. . . . The Court of Appeals, with one judge dissenting, affirmed this partial summary judgment. . . . We granted certiorari. . . . The only question presented to us at this stage in the case is whether the respondent had a constitutional right to a statement of reasons and a hearing on the University's decision not to rehire him for another year. We hold that he did not.

I

The requirements of procedural due process apply only to the deprivation of interests encompassed by the Fourteenth Amendment's protection of liberty and property. When protected interests are implicated, the right to some kind of prior hearing is paramount. . . .

The District Court decided that procedural due process guarantees apply in this case by assessing and balancing the weights of the particular interests involved. It concluded that the respondent's interest in re-employment at Wisconsin State University-Oshkosh outweighed the University's interest in denying him reemployment summarily. . . . Undeniably, the respondent's re-employment prospects were of major concern to him — concern that we surely cannot say was insignificant. And a weighing process has long been a part of any determination of the form of hearing required in particular situations by procedural due process. But, to determine whether due process requirements apply in the first place, we must look not to the "weight" but to the nature of the interests at stake. . . . We must look to see if the interest is within the Fourteenth Amendment's protection of liberty and property.

"Liberty" and "property" are broad and majestic terms. They are among the "[g]reat [constitutional] concepts . . . purposely left to gather meaning from experience. . . . [T]hey relate to the whole domain of social and economic fact, and the statesmen who founded this Nation knew too well that only a stagnant society remains unchanged For that reason, the Court has fully and finally rejected the wooden distinction between "rights" and "privileges" that once seemed to govern the applicability of procedural due process rights. The Court has also made clear that the property interests protected by procedural due process extend well beyond actual ownership of real estate, chattels, or money. By the same token, the Court has required due process protections for deprivations of liberty beyond the sort of formal constraints imposed by the criminal process.

"While this Court has not attempted to define with exactness the liberty . . . guaranteed [by the Fourteenth Amendment], the term. . . . denotes not merely freedom from bodily restraint but also the right of the individual to contract, to engage in any of the common occupations of life, to acquire useful knowledge, to marry, establish a home and bring up children, to worship God according to the dictates of his own conscience, and generally to enjoy those privileges long recognized . . . as essential to the orderly pursuit of happiness by free men." . . .

The State, in declining to rehire the respondent, did not make any charge against him that might seriously damage his standing and associations in his community. It did not base the nonrenewal of his contract on a charge, for example, that he had been guilty of dishonesty, or immorality. . . .

Similarly, there is no suggestion that the State, in declining to re-employ the respondent, imposed on him a stigma or other disability that foreclosed his freedom to take advantage of other employment opportunities. . . .

To be sure, the respondent has alleged that the nonrenewal of his contract was based on his exercise of his right to freedom of speech. But this allegation is not now before us. The District Court stayed proceedings on this issue, and the respondent has yet to prove that the decision not to rehire him was, in fact, based on his free speech activities.

Hence, on the record before us, all that clearly appears is that the respondent was not rehired for one year at one university. It stretches the concept too far to suggest that a person is deprived of "liberty" when he simply is not rehired in one job but remains as free as before to seek another. . . .

III

The Fourteenth Amendment's procedural protection of property is a safeguard of the security of interests that a person has already acquired in specific benefits. Those interests — property interests — may take many forms. . . .

Certain attributes of "property" interests protected by procedural due process emerge from these [prior] decisions. To have a property interest in a benefit, a person clearly must have more than an abstract need or desire for it. He must have more than a unilateral expectation of it. He must, instead, have a legitimate claim of entitlement to it. It is a purpose of the ancient institution of property to protect those claims upon which people rely in their daily lives, reliance that must not be arbitrarily undermined. It is a purpose of the constitutional right to a hearing to provide an opportunity for a person to vindicate those claims.

Property interests, of course, are not created by the Constitution. Rather, they are created and their dimensions are defined by existing rules or understandings that stem from an independent source such as state law—rules or understandings that secure certain benefits and that support claims of entitlement to those benefits. Thus, the welfare recipients in *Goldberg v. Kelly* . . . had a claim of entitlement to welfare payments that was grounded in the statute defining eligibility for them. . . .

Just as the welfare recipient's "property" interest in welfare payments was created and defined by statutory terms, so the respondent's "property" interest in employment at Wisconsin State University-Oshkosh was created and defined by the terms of his appointment. Those terms secured his interest in employment up to June 30, 1969. But the important fact in this case is that they specifically provided that the respondent's employment was to terminate on June 30. They did not provide for contract renewal absent "sufficient cause." Indeed, they made no provision for renewal whatsoever.

Thus, the terms of the respondent's appointment secured absolutely no interest in re-employment for the next year. They supported absolutely no possible claim of entitlement to re-employment. Nor, significantly, was there any state statute or University rule or policy that secured his interest in re-employment or that created any legitimate claim to it. In these circumstances, the respondent surely had an abstract concern in being rehired, but he did not have a property interest sufficient to require the University authorities to give him a hearing when they declined to renew his contract of employment.

IV

We must conclude that the summary judgment for the respondent should not have been granted, since the respondent has not shown that he was deprived of liberty or property protected by the Fourteenth Amendment. The judgment of the Court of Appeals, accordingly, is reversed and the case is remanded for further proceedings consistent with this opinion.

It is so ordered.

Perry v. Sinderman, 408 U.S. 593 (1972). From 1959 to 1969 respondent Sinderman was employed as a teacher in the Texas state college system under a series of one-year contracts. In 1965 he became a professor of Government and Social Science at Odessa Junior College. During the 1968–1969 academic year, controversy arose between the respondent and the college administration. The respondent was elected president of the Texas Junior College Teachers Association. In this capacity he left his teaching duties on several occasions to testify before committees of the Texas Legislature and publicly disagreed with the policies of the college's Board of Regents. In May 1969 his then current one-year employment contract terminated and the Board of Regents voted not to offer him a new contract for the next academic year. The Regents issued a press release setting forth allegations of the respondent's insubordination. But they provided him no official statement of the reasons for the nonrenewal of his contract. And they allowed him no opportunity for a hearing to challenge the basis of the nonrenewal.

Respondent brought suit in federal court, alleging that the decision not to rehire him was based on his public criticism of the college administration and thus infringed his right to freedom of speech. He also alleged that their failure to provide him an opportunity for a hearing violated the Fourteenth Amendment's guarantee of procedural due process. The district court entered summary judgment against respondent and in favor of petitioners — members of the Board of Regents and the president of the college. The Court of Appeals then reversed and the Supreme Court granted certiorari. On the free-speech issue, the Court had this to say:

> The first question presented is whether the respondent's lack of a contractual or tenure right to re-employment, taken alone, defeats his claim that the nonrenewal of his contract violated the First and Fourteenth Amendments. We hold that it does not.

> For at least a quarter-century, this Court has made clear that even though a person has no "right" to a valuable governmental benefit and even though the government may deny him the benefit for any number of reasons, there are some reasons upon which the government may not rely. It may not deny a benefit to a person on a basis that infringes his constitutionally protected interests — especially his interest in freedom of speech. For if the government could deny a benefit to a person because of his constitutionally protected speech or associations, his exercise of those freedoms would in effect be penalized and inhibited. . . .

> In this case, of course, the respondent has yet to show that the decision not to renew his contract was, in fact, made in retaliation for his exercise of the constitutional right of free speech. . . . But we agree with the Court of Appeals that there is a genuine dispute as to "whether the college refused to renew the teaching contract on an impermissible basis — as a reprisal for the exercise of constitutionally protected rights." . . .

> For this reason we hold that the grant of summary judgment against the respondent, without full exploration of this issue, was improper.

On his procedural due process claim, Sinderman was more successful than was Roth:

> . . . [T]he respondent's allegations — which we must construe most favorably to the respondent at this stage of the litigation — do raise a genuine issue as to his interest in continued employment at Odessa Junior College. He alleged that this interest, though not secured by a formal contractual tenure provision, was secured by a no less binding understanding fostered by the college administration. In particular, the respondent alleged that the college had a *de facto* tenure program, and that he had tenure under that program. He claimed that he and others legitimately relied upon an unusual provision that had been in the college's official Faculty Guide for many years:

> "Teacher Tenure: Odessa College has no tenure system. The Administration of the College wishes the faculty member to feel that he has permanent tenure as long as his teaching services are satisfactory and as long as he displays a cooperative attitude toward his co-workers and his superiors, and as long as he is happy in his work."

Moreover, the respondent claimed legitimate reliance upon guidelines promulgated by the Coordinating Board of the Texas College and University System that provided that a person, like himself, who had been employed as a teacher in the state college and university system for seven years or more has some form of job tenure. . . .

We have made clear in *Roth* . . . that "property" interests subject to procedural due process protection are not limited by a few rigid, technical forms. Rather, "property" denotes a broad range of interests that are secured by "existing rules or understandings." . . . A person's interest in a benefit is a "property" interest for due process purposes if there are such rules or mutually explicit understandings that support his claim of entitlement to the benefit and that he may invoke at a hearing.

A written contract with an explicit tenure provision clearly is evidence of a formal understanding that supports a teacher's claim of entitlement to continued employment unless sufficient "cause" is shown. Yet absence of such an explicit contractual provision may not always foreclose the possibility that a teacher has a "property" interest in reemployment. For example, the law of contracts in most, if not all, jurisdictions long has employed a process by which agreements, though not formalized in writing, may be "implied." . . .

In this case, the respondent has alleged the existence of rules and understandings, promulgated and fostered by state officials, that may justify his legitimate claim of entitlement to continued employment absent "sufficient cause." We disagree with the Court of Appeals insofar as it held that a mere subjective "expectancy" is protected by procedural due process, but we agree that the respondent must be given an opportunity to prove the legitimacy of his claim of entitlement in light of "the policies and practices of the institution." . . . Proof of such a property interest would not, of course, entitle him to reinstatement. But such proof would obligate college officials to grant a hearing at his request, where he could be informed of the grounds for his nonretention and challenge their sufficiency.

Therefore, while we do not wholly agree with the opinion of the Court of Appeals, its judgment remanding this case to the District Court is *Affirmed.*

Questions and Comments

1.   Has the Court been successful in abandoning the old distinction between rights and privileges as a basis for application of the due process clause? How would it have been determined, in the past, whether a claimant possessed a "right" or merely a "privilege"? Was one of the functions of the right-privilege distinction to determine when the due process clause applied and when it did not? Unless the due process clause applies to every governmental decision, there must be some basis for determining when it applies and when it does not apply. How did the Court decide whether the due process clause applied in the *Roth* and *Sinderman* cases? Did it

apply a different approach than it applied in *Goldberg?* Explain.

2.   In *Roth* the Court again cited Professor Reich's articles with approval. Did the Court embrace Reich's recommendations in its decisions in these cases? What are the pros and cons of Reich's recommendations? Does Reich provide workable recommendations for drawing the boundaries between what should be protectable as "property" and what should not? Explain.

3.   Has the Court merely replaced the right-privilege distinction with new boundary concepts determining when the due process clause applies and when it does not? The boundary concepts applied in *Roth* and *Sinderman* are property and liberty. These concepts must have underlain the right-privilege distinction, because the due process clause extends in terms only to deprivations of life, liberty and property. How, then, did the Court in *Roth, Sinderman* and in *Goldberg* see that it was taking a new approach?

4.   Is the "property" concept which the Court applied in *Roth* an improvement over the older approach or not? Why or why not? Is it more rigid that the older approach? Was Frankfurter saying in *Joint Anti-Fascist Refugee Committee* that anytime the government inflicts a "grievous loss" upon someone, it has interfered with that person's "rights"? Was he therefore suggesting that the due process clause applies or does not apply depending upon a balancing process involving, *inter alia*, the degree of loss inflicted upon the affected person? Did the Court ever embrace such a view? Did it act as if it had embraced such a view?

5.   Did the Court articulate its definition of "property" in *Roth* as a means of limiting the impact of *Goldberg?* Or of limiting the involvement of the courts in routine decision-making of educational and other public institutions? Will the Court's definition of "property" produce a limiting effect? Will some claimants suffering grievous losses lack recourse under the due process clause as a result of the *Roth* decision? Will some claimants suffering relatively trivial injuries be entitled to due process protections under *Roth?* Is this a result of the rigidity of the property definition which the Court adopted in *Roth?*

6.   Can you define the meaning which the Court gave to "liberty" in *Roth?* Where did this meaning come from? Was the Court equating defamation with a deprivation of liberty? Explain.

7.   Both Roth and Sinderman alleged that they were terminated because of activity protected by the First and Fourteenth Amendments, did they not? Were these claims one of substantive—as opposed to procedural—due process? Explain. If either Roth or Sinderman proved that his contract was not renewed because of his exercise of rights of free-speech, would he have stated a claim for relief? In what tribunal would the validity of these free-speech claims be determined? Who would bare the burden of proof? In the *Roth* case the court of appeals had held that an opportunity for a hearing and a statement of reasons were required "as a *prophylactic* against non-retention decisions improperly motivated by exercise of protected rights." This claim was rejected by the Court. *See* 408 U.S. at 575 n.14. *See also* 408 U.S. at 599 n.5.

Note: The Decisional Process Re-examined

In *Morrissey v. Brewer*, 408 U.S. 471 (1972) and *Gagnon v. Scarpelli*, 411 U.S. 778 (1973), the Court applied much of the *Goldberg* procedure to parole and probation revocation decisions. In these cases, however, the Court noted that revocation decisions involved more than mere determinations of whether the parolee or probationer committed a prohibited act. They also involved a second (or evaluative) level of decision-making: If the violation occurred, what should be done about it? Should the parolee or probationer be placed in confinement or should some other measure be taken? The arguments — at this second and evaluative stage — might sometimes become quite complex and beyond the capacity of the parolee or probationer to make. In *Gagnon v. Scarpelli*, the Court indicated that counsel should be provided *inter alia* in those cases where the arguments to be made would be difficult or complex to develop:

> . . . . Presumptively, it may be said that counsel should be provided in cases where, after being informed of his right to request counsel, the probationer or parolee makes such a request, based on a timely and colorable claim (i) that he has not committed the alleged violation of the conditions upon which he is at liberty; or (ii) that, even if the violation is a matter of public record or is uncontested, there are substantial reasons which justified or mitigated the violation and make revocation inappropriate, and that the reasons are complex or otherwise difficult to develop or present.

Although the factfinder is required to supply a written statement as to the evidence relied upon and the reasons for the revocation, the Court has later indicated that the factfinder is not required to provide "an express statement . . . that alternatives to incarceration were considered and rejected." *Black, Director, Missouri Dep't of Corrections & Human Resources v. Romano*, 471 U.S. 606, 612 (1985).

D. *GOLDBERG* RECONSIDERED: THE DEVELOPING BOUNDARIES OF THE NEW APPROACH

Excerpt from Henry J. Friendly, *Some Kind of Hearing*, 123 U. Pa. L. Rev. 1267 (1975):

Good sense would suggest that there must be some floor below which no hearing of any sort is required. . . . [P]rocedural requirements entail the expenditure of limited resources, [and] . . . at some point the benefit to individuals from an additional safeguard is substantially outweighed by the cost of providing such protection, and . . . the expense of protecting those likely to be found undeserving will probably come out of the pockets of the deserving. This is particularly true in an area such as public housing where the number of qualified applicants greatly exceeds the available space, so that, from an overall standpoint, the erroneous rejection or even the eviction of one family may mean only that an equally deserving one will benefit. . . .

It is unfortunate that, five years after *Goldberg*, we have so little empirical knowledge how it has worked in its own field, let alone in others where its principles have been applied. For one thing, one would wish to know whether the procedural safeguards that *Goldberg* required have really been applied, and, if not, whether the failure has been due to bureaucratic obduracy or to basic impracticability. One would wish also to know the costs, both of administrative expenses that would not otherwise have been incurred and of continuation of unjustified payments, in relation to the benefits of injustices prevented. This is not to suggest that benefits can be precisely quantified in dollar terms or that *some* excess of the costs would call for reconsideration of the required procedures. As Mr. Justice Brennan has rightly said, administrative fairness usually does entail "some additional administrative burdens and expense." But if the excess of costs over estimated benefits were, say, four-fold, with the concomitant likelihood that, in the Chief Justice's words, "new layers of procedural protection may become an intolerable drain on the very funds earmarked for food, clothing, and other living essentials," one would at least wish to examine whether it would not be possible to devise some less cumbersome but nevertheless fair procedures.

Goss v. Lopez, 419 U.S. 565 (1975). Students suspended from an Ohio high school for up to 10 days challenged the procedures under which they were suspended. The Court ruled that the suspensions affected "property" interests because under Ohio law the students "plainly had legitimate claims of entitlement to a public education". The Court also ruled that the disciplinary actions affected "liberty" interests because the suspensions were based on charges of misconduct, and hence were likely to affect the students' reputations adversely. Because the Court recognized a need to maintain institutional discipline, it did not require:

> "even truncated trial-type procedures [which] might well overwhelm administrative facilities in many places and, by diverting resources, cost more than it would save in educational effectiveness. On the other hand, requiring effective notice and informal hearing permitting the student to give his version of the events will provide a meaningful hedge against erroneous action. At least the disciplinarian will be alerted to the existence of disputes about facts and arguments about cause and effect. . . .

> Requiring that there be at least an informal give-and-take between student and disciplinarian, preferably prior to the suspension, will add little to the factfinding function where the disciplinarian himself has witnessed the conduct forming the basis for the charge. But things are not always as they seem to be, and the student will at least have the opportunity to characterize his conduct and put it in what he deems the proper context."

Questions and Comments

1. Was *Goss* the kind of trivial case which Judge Friendly would have considered as meriting no hearing of any sort? What was actually at stake in *Goss*? Should the due process clause extend to cases like *Goss*? Why or why not? Was the extension of the due process clause to the *Goss* situation compelled by the property definition which the Court adopted in *Roth?* by the liberty definition which it adopted in *Roth?*

2. Do you believe that the Court's decision in *Goss* creates a major potential for interference with school administration? Explain. Was the *Goss* decision a way of avoiding the impact of *Roth's* rigid property definition?

3. Is a hearing required before a student is kept after school for tardiness, chewing gum in class, or other misbehavior? Explain.

4. Would the liberty interests of the students have been adequately protected by a post-suspension hearing?

MATHEWS, SECRETARY OF HEALTH, EDUCATION, AND WELFARE v. ELDRIDGE
424 U.S. 319 (1976)

Mr. Justice Powell delivered the opinion of the Court.

The issue in this case is whether the Due Process Clause of the Fifth Amendment requires that prior to the termination of Social Security disability benefit payments the recipient be afforded an opportunity for an evidentiary hearing.

Cash benefits are provided to workers during periods in which they are completely disabled under the disability insurance benefits program created by the 1956 amendments to Title II of the Social Security Act. . . . Respondent Eldridge was first awarded benefits in June 1968. In March 1972, he received a questionnaire from the state agency charged with monitoring his medical condition. Eldridge completed the questionnaire, indicating that his condition had not improved and identifying the medical sources including physicians, from whom he had received treatment recently. The state agency then obtained reports from his physician and a psychiatric consultant. After considering these reports and other information in his file the agency informed Eldridge by letter that it had made a tentative determination that his disability had ceased in May 1972. The letter included a statement of reasons for the proposed termination of benefits, and advised Eldridge that he might request reasonable time in which to obtain and submit additional information pertaining to his condition.

In his written response, Eldridge disputed one characterization of his medical condition and indicated that the agency already had enough evidence to establish his disability. The state agency then made its final determination that he had ceased to be disabled in May 1972. This determination was accepted by the Social Security Administration (SSA), which notified Eldridge in July that his benefits would terminate after that month. The notification also advised him of his right to seek reconsideration by the state agency of this initial determination within six months.

Instead of requesting reconsideration Eldridge commenced this action challenging the constitutional validity of the administrative procedures established by the Secretary of Health, Education, and Welfare for assessing whether there exists a continuing disability. He sought an immediate reinstatement of benefits pending a hearing on the issue of his disability. . . .

The District court concluded that the administrative procedures pursuant to which the Secretary had terminated Eldridge's benefits abridged his right to procedural due process. . . . Relying entirely upon the District court's opinion, the Court of Appeals for the Fourth Circuit affirmed the injunction barring termination of Eldridge's benefits prior to an evidentiary hearing . . .

We reverse.

A

This Court consistently has held that some form of hearing is required before an individual is finally deprived of a property interest. . . .

In recent years this Court has had occasion to consider the extent to which due process requires an evidentiary hearing prior to the deprivation of some type of property interest even if such a hearing is provided thereafter. In only one case, *Goldberg v. Kelly* . . . has the Court held that a hearing closely approximating a judicial trial is necessary. In other cases requiring some type of pretermination hearing as a matter of constitutional right the Court has spoken sparingly about the requisite procedures.

B

The disability insurance program is administered jointly by state and federal agencies. State agencies make the initial determination whether a disability exists, when it began, and when it ceased. 42 U.S.C. § 421(a). The standards applied and the procedures followed are prescribed by the Secretary, see § 421(b), who has delegated his responsibilities and powers under the Act to the SSA. See 40 Fed. Reg. 4473. In order to establish initial and continued entitlement to disability benefits a worker must demonstrate that he is unable "to engage in any substantial gainful activity by reason of any medically determinable physical or mental impairment which can be expected to result in death or which has lasted or can be expected to last for a continuous period of not less than 12 months.. 42 U.S.C. § 423(d) (1)(A).

To satisfy this test the worker bears a continuing burden of showing, by means of "medically acceptable clinical and laboratory diagnostic techniques," § 423 (d)(3), that he has a physical or mental impairment of such severity that "he is not only unable to do his previous work but, cannot, considering his age, education, and work experience, engage in any other kind of substantial gainful work which exists in the national economy, regardless of whether such work exists in the immediate area in which he lives, or whether a specific job vacancy exists for him, or whether he would be hired if he applied for work." § 423 (d)(2)(A).

The principal reasons for benefits terminations are that the worker is no longer disabled or has returned to work. As Eldridge's benefits were terminated because he was determined to be no longer disabled, we consider only the sufficiency of the procedures involved in such cases.

The continuing-eligibility investigation is made by a state agency acting through a "team" consisting of a physician and a nonmedical person trained in disability evaluation. The agency periodically communicates with the disabled worker, usually by mail — in which case he is sent a detailed questionnaire — or by telephone, and requests information concerning his present condition, including current medical restrictions and sources of treatment, and any additional information that he considers relevant to his continued entitlement to benefits. . . .

Information regarding the recipient's current condition is also obtained from his sources of medical treatment. . . . If there is a conflict between the information provided by the beneficiary and that obtained from medical sources such as his physician, or between two sources of treatment, the agency may arrange for an examination by an independent consulting physician. . . . Whenever the agency's tentative assessment of the beneficiary's condition differs from his own assessment, the beneficiary is informed that benefits may be terminated, provided a summary of the evidence upon which the proposed determination to terminate is based, and afforded an opportunity to review the medical reports and other evidence in his case file. He also may respond in writing and submit additional evidence. . . .

The state agency then makes its final determination, which is reviewed by an examiner in the SSA Bureau of Disability Insurance. . . . If, as is usually the case, the SSA accepts the agency determination it notifies the recipient in writing, informing him of the reasons for the decision, and of his right to seek *de novo* reconsideration by the state agency. . . . Upon acceptance by the SSA, benefits are terminated effective two months after the month in which medical recovery is found to have occurred. 42 U.S.C. § 423(a) (1970 ed., Supp. 111).

If the recipient seeks reconsideration by the state agency and the determination is adverse, the SSA reviews the reconsideration determination and notifies the recipient of the decision. He then has a right to an evidentiary hearing before an SSA administrative law judge. . . . The hearing is nonadversary, and the SSA is not represented by counsel. As at all prior and subsequent stages of the administrative process, however, the claimant may be represented by counsel or other spokesmen. . . . if this hearing results in an adverse decision, the claimant is entitled to request discretionary review by the SSA Appeals Council . . . and finally may obtain judicial review.

Should it be determined at any point after termination of benefits, that the claimant's disability extended beyond the date of cessation initially established, the worker is entitled to retroactive payments. . . . If, on the other hand, a beneficiary receives any payments to which he is later determined not to be entitled, the statute authorizes the Secretary to attempt to recoup these funds in specified circumstances. 42 U.S.C. § 404.

C

Despite the elaborate character of the administrative procedures provided by the Secretary, the courts below held them to be constitutionally inadequate, concluding that due process requires an evidentiary hearing prior to termination. . . . [W]e think this was error.

Since a recipient whose benefits are terminated is awarded full retroactive relief if he ultimately prevails, his sole interest is in the uninterrupted receipt of this source of income pending final administrative decision on his claim. . . .

Only in *Goldberg* has the Court held that due process requires an evidentiary hearing prior to a temporary deprivation. It was emphasized there that welfare assistance is given to persons on the very margin of subsistence. . . . Eligibility for disability benefits, in contrast, is not based upon financial need. . . .

As we recognized [in another case] . . . "the possible length of wrongful deprivation of . . . benefits [also] is an important factor in assessing the impact of official action on the private interests." The Secretary concedes that the delay between a request for a hearing before an administrative law judge and a decision on the claim is currently between 10 and 11 months. Since a terminated recipient must first obtain a reconsideration decision as a prerequisite to invoking his right to an evidentiary hearing, the delay between the actual cutoff of benefits and final decision after a hearing exceeds one year.

In view of the torpidity of this administrative review process . . . and the typically modest resources of the family unit of the physically disabled worker, the hardship imposed upon the erroneously terminated disability recipient may be significant. Still, the disabled worker's need is likely to be less than that of a welfare recipient. In addition to the possibility of access to private resources, other forms of government assistance will become available where the termination of disability benefits places a worker or his family below the subsistence level. . . . in view of these potential sources of temporary income, there is less reason here than in *Goldberg* to depart from the ordinary principle, established by our decisions, that something less than an evidentiary hearing is sufficient prior to adverse administrative action.

D

An additional factor to be considered here is the fairness and reliability of the existing pre-termination procedures, and the probable value, if any of additional procedural safeguards. Central to the evaluation of any administrative process is the nature of the relevant inquiry. . . . In order to remain eligible for benefits the disabled worker must demonstrate by means of "medically acceptable clinical and laboratory diagnostic techniques," 42 U.S.C. § 423(d)(3), that he is unable "to engage in any substantial gainful activity by reason of any *medically determinable* physical or mental impairment. § 423(d)(1)(a) (emphasis supplied).

In short, a medical assessment of the worker's physical or mental condition is required. This is a more sharply focused and easily documented decision than the typical determination of welfare entitlement. In the latter case, a wide variety of information may be deemed relevant, and issues of witness credibility and veracity often are critical to the decisionmaking process. *Goldberg* noted that in such circumstances "written submissions are a wholly unsatisfactory basis for decision." . . .

By contrast, the decision whether to discontinue disability benefits will turn, in most cases, upon "routine, standard, and unbiased medical reports by physician specialists" . . . concerning   a   subject   whom   they   have   personally examined. . . . To be sure, credibility and veracity may be a factor in the ultimate disability assessment in some cases. But procedural due process rules are shaped by the risk of error inherent in the truthfinding process as applied to the generality of cases, not the rare exceptions. The potential value of an evidentiary hearing, or even oral presentation to the decisionmaker, is substantially less in this context than in *Goldberg.*

The detailed questionnaire which the state agency periodically sends the recipient identifies with particularity the information relevant to the entitlement decision, and the recipient is invited to obtain assistance from the local SSA office in completing the questionnaire. More important, the information critical to the entitlement decision usually is derived from medical sources, such as the treating physician. Such sources are likely to be able to communicate more effectively through written documents than are welfare recipients or the lay witnesses supporting their cause. The conclusions of physicians often are supported by X-rays and the results of clinical or laboratory tests, information typically more amenable to written than to oral presentation.

A further safeguard against mistake is the policy of allowing the disability recipient's representative full access to all information relied upon by the state agency. In addition, prior to the cutoff of benefits the agency informs the recipient of its tentative assessment, the reasons therefor, and provides a summary of the evidence that it considers most relevant. Opportunity is then afforded the recipient to submit additional evidence or arguments, enabling him to challenge directly the accuracy of information in his file as well as the correctness of the agency's tentative conclusions. These procedures . . . enable the recipient to "mold" his argument to respond to the precise issues which the decisionmaker regards as crucial.

[The Court ruled that reversal rate statistics, while relevant, were not controlling. Because the recipient may always submit new evidence which may result in additional medical examinations, administrative review often takes place on a file different from the one upon which the decision appealed from was based. Thus an administrative reversal of a prior decision is not necessarily evidence that the prior decision was erroneous.]

E

Financial cost alone is not a controlling weight in determining whether due process requires a particular procedural safeguard prior to some administrative action. But the Government's interest, and hence that of the public, in conserving scarce fiscal and administrative resources, is a factor that must be weighed. At some point the benefit of an additional safeguard to the individual affected by the administrative action and to society in terms of increased assurance that the action is just, may be outweighed by the cost. Significantly, the cost of protecting those whom the preliminary administrative process has identified as likely to be found undeserving may in the end come out of the pockets of the deserving since resources available for any particular program of social welfare are not unlimited. . . .

But more is implicated . . . than *ad hoc* weighing of fiscal and administrative burdens against the interests of a particular category of claimants. The ultimate balance involves a determination as to when, under our constitutional system, judicial-type procedures must be imposed upon administrative action to assure fairness. . . . The judicial model of an evidentiary hearing is neither a required, nor even the most effective, method of decisionmaking in all circumstances. The essence of due process is the requirement that "a person in jeopardy of serious loss [be given] notice of the case against him and opportunity to meet it." . . . In assessing what process is due in this case, substantial weight must be given to the good-faith judgments of the individuals charged by Congress with the administration of social welfare programs that the procedures they have provided assure fair consideration of the entitlement claims of individuals. . . . This is especially so where, as here, the prescribed procedures not only provide the claimant with an effective process for asserting his claim prior to any administrative action, but also assure a right to an evidentiary hearing, as well as to subsequent judicial review, before the denial of his claim becomes final. . . .

We conclude that an evidentiary hearing is not required prior to the termination of disability benefits and that the present administrative procedures *fully* comport with due process.

The judgment of the Court of Appeals is
Reversed.

Questions and Comments

1.   Did the parties in *Mathews* dispute whether the due process clause applies to the termination of disability benefits? What was the precise issue in *Mathews?* Did this case involve the procedures necessary to protect the social security disability recipients against an erroneous termination for the interim period between the termination and a post-termination hearing? Why was not this case resolved in the same way that *Goldberg* was resolved?

2.   Is *Goldberg* unique in requiring an evidentiary hearing prior to the termination of benefits? What were the special features of *Goldberg* that were missing from *Mathews?* Did the Court indicate that the welfare-recipient situation was unique even at the time that *Goldberg* was decided?

3.   The Court in *Mathews* did not say that no pre-termination procedure was required before disability benefits were terminated, did it? What kind of criteria measure the adequacy of the pre-termination procedure?

4.   Were the factors that the Court balanced in *Mathews* different from the factors which the Court balanced in *Goldberg?* What new factor(s) entered the *Mathews* balance? If the adequacy of pre-termination decisional procedures applicable to welfare administration were to be tested under the *Mathews* criteria, would the Court reach the same result which it reached in *Goldberg?* Explain. Were the pre-termination procedures in *Mathews* more likely to be accurate than the ones involved in *Goldberg?* Explain.

5.   Consider the marginal cost-benefit approach which the Court took to the question of the need to provide additional procedures. How did the Court measure the accuracy of existing procedures? Would reversal rate figures be useful in evaluating the accuracy of existing procedures? Explain. How did the Court determine the potential for increased accuracy of additional procedures? How would you (as counsel) shape your case to show that additional procedures would be justified on a marginal cost-benefit approach? How would the courts determine the cost of additional procedures? When the Court speaks of additional procedures does it mean procedures more like judicial (or trial-type) procedures?

6.   Judge Friendly, *supra*, had suggested that the harm resulting from an erroneous decision evicting tenants from public housing would be offset by the availability of the premises to equally deserving new tenants. Does *Mathews* indicate that the Court would be receptive to such a contention?

Walters v. National Association of Radiation Survivors, 473 U.S. 305 (1985). 38 U.S.C. § 3404(c) limits to $10 the fee that may be paid an attorney or agent who represents a veteran seeking benefits for service-connected death or disability. The District Court held such limitation unconstitutional on the ground that it effectively prevents claimants from being competently represented in a veterans' benefit proceeding, but the Supreme Court reversed. Part of the Court's treatment of the *Mathews* V. *Eldridge* decision is excerpted below:

Passing the problems with quantifying the likelihood of an erroneous deprivation, however, under *Mathews* we must also ask what value the proposed additional procedure may have in reducing such error. In this case we are fortunate to have statistics that bear directly on this question. . . .

Ultimate Success Rates Before the Board of Veterans Appeals by Mode of Representation

American Legion	16.2%
American Red Cross	16.8%
Disabled American Veterans	16.6%
Veterans of Foreign Wars	16.7%
Other non-attorney	15.8%
No representation	15.2%
Attorney/Agent	18.3%

Reliable evidence before the District Court showed that claimants represented by lawyers have a slightly better success rate before the BVA than do claimants represented by service representatives, and both have a slightly better success rate than claimants who were not represented at all. Evidence also showed that there may be complex issues of causation in comparatively few out of the hundreds of thousands of cases before the VA, but there is no adequate showing of the effect the availability of lawyers would have on the proper disposition of these cases. Neither the difference in success rate nor the existence of complexity in some cases is sufficient to warrant a conclusion that the right to retain and compensate an attorney in

VA cases is a necessary element of procedural fairness under the Fifth Amendment.

Questions and Comments

Did the claimants in *Walters* adequately present their case? Had the Court previously indicated a sensitivity to the need for representation in complex cases? In those earlier cases, had the Court implicitly said that representation was necessary because it would be likely to improve the accuracy of the administering agency's decisional process? Where had the Court so stated? Should the plaintiffs in *Walters* have have drawn from *Gagnon v. Scarpelli, supra,* in shaping their contentions? If the Court had previously indicated that legitimate claims to be represented by counsel existed in cases involving complex factual or legal arguments, would it not have been wise for the plaintiffs in *Walters* to have focused upon the need for counsel in complex cases and to have provided the Court with analyses of those cases?

Londoner and *Bi-Metallic* Updated

Atkins v. Parker, 472 U.S. 115 (1985). Prior to 1981, federal law provided that 20 percent of a household's earned income should be deducted, or disregarded, in computing eligibility for food-stamp benefits. In 1981 Congress amended the Food Stamp Act to reduce this deduction from 20 to 18 percent. In December 1981, the Massachusetts Department of Public Welfare sent out the following notice, in English and Spanish versions, to food-stamp recipients:

> * * * IMPORTANT NOTICE-READ CAREFULLY
>
> RECENT CHANGES IN THE FOOD STAMP PROGRAM HAVE BEEN MADE IN ACCORDANCE WITH 1981 FEDERAL LAW. UNDER THIS LAW, THE EARNED INCOME DEDUCTION FOR FOOD STAMP BENEFITS HAS BEEN LOWERED FROM 20 TO 18 PERCENT. THIS REDUCTION MEANS THAT A HIGHER PORTION OF YOUR HOUSEHOLD'S EARNED INCOME WILL BE COUNTED IN DE-TERMINING YOUR ELIGIBILITY AND BENEFIT AMOUNT FOR FOOD STAMPS. AS A RESULT OF THIS FEDERAL CHANGE, YOUR BENEFITS WILL EITHER BE REDUCED IF YOU REMAIN ELI-GIBLE OR YOUR BENEFITS WILL BE TERMINATED. (FOOD STAMP MANUAL CITATION 106 CMR:364.400).
>
> YOUR RIGHT TO A FAIR HEARING:
>
> YOU HAVE THE RIGHT TO REQUEST A FAIR HEARING IF YOU DISAGREE WITH THIS ACTION. IF YOU ARE REQUESTING A HEARING, YOUR FOOD STAMP BENEFITS WILL BE REIN-STATED . . . IF YOU HAVE QUESTIONS CONCERNING THE COR-RECTNESS OF YOUR BENEFITS COMPUTATION OR THE FAIR HEARING PROCESS, CONTACT YOUR LOCAL WELFARE OFFICE. YOU MAY FILE AN APPEAL AT ANY TIME IF YOU FEEL THAT YOU

ARE NOT RECEIVING THE CORRECT AMOUNT OF FOOD STAMPS.

An excerpt from the Court's opinion follows:

. . . . [T]he District Court concluded that the December notice was defective because it did not advise each household of the precise change in its benefits, or with the information necessary to enable the recipient to calculate the correct change; because it did not tell recipients whether their benefits were being reduced or terminated; and because the reading level and format of the notice made it difficult to comprehend. Based on the premise that the statutorily mandated reduction or termination of benefits was a deprivation of property subject to the full protection of the Fourteenth Amendment, the Court held that the Due Process Clause had been violated.

The record in this case indicates that members of petitioners' class had their benefits reduced or terminated for either or both of two reasons: (1) because Congress reduced the earned-income disregard from 20 percent to 18 percent; or (2) because inadvertent errors were made in calculating benefits. These inadvertent errors, however, did not necessarily result from the statutory change, but rather may have been attributable to a variety of factors that can occur in the administration of any large welfare program.[1] . . . The procedural component of the Due Process Clause does not "impose a constitutional limitation on the power of Congress to make substantive changes in the law of entitlement to public benefits." . . .

The participants in the food-stamp program had no greater right to advance notice of the legislative change — in this case, the decision to change the earned-income disregard level-than did any other voters. . . .

As a matter of constitutional law there can be no doubt concerning the sufficiency of the notice describing the effect of the amendment in general terms. Surely Congress can presume that such a notice relative to a matter as important as a change in a household's food-stamp allotment would prompt an appropriate inquiry if it is not fully understood. The entire structure of our democratic government rests on the premise that the individual citizen is capable of informing himself about the particular policies that affect his destiny. To contend that this notice was constitutionally insufficient is to reject that premise.

The judgment of the Court of Appeals is reversed.

It is so ordered.

In his dissent in *Atkins*, Justice Brennan asserted that "it is a novel and ill-considered suggestion to 'put . . . to one side' unintended but foreseeable administrative errors that concededly had adverse effects on valid property

---

[1] By hypothesis, an inadvertent error is one that the Department did not anticipate; for that reason, the Department could not give notice of a reduction that was simply the consequence of an unintended mistake.

interests. Such errors are at the *heart* of due process analysis. If the Constitution provides no protection against the visiting of such errors on statutory entitlement claimants, then the development of this Court's 'new property' jurisprudence over the past 15 years represents a somewhat hollow victory. The fact that errors inevitably occur in the administration of any bureaucracy requires the conclusion that when the State administers a property entitlement program, it has a constitutional obligation to provide *some* type of notice to recipients before it implements adverse changes in the entitlement level, for the very reason that 'inadvertent' erroneous reductions or terminations of benefits — that is, deprivations of property — are otherwise effected without any due process of law."

O'Bannon v. Town Court Nursing Center, 447 U.S. 773 (1980). In this case, Town Court, which had been certified as a "skilled nursing facility," was notified by the Department of Health, Education, and Welfare that it no longer met the governing standards for skilled nursing facilities. HEW also notified Town Court that its Medicare and Medicaid provider agreement would not be renewed, since its continued qualification as a skilled nursing facility was a condition of the provider agreements. Both Town Court and the patients challenged the HEW procedures which provided only a post termination evidentiary hearing on the decertification to Town Court. The Third Circuit, sitting *en banc*, ruled that the procedures were adequate for the nursing home, but that the patients were entitled to an evidentiary hearing on the issue of whether Town Court's Medicare and Medicaid provider agreements should be renewed.

The Supreme Court reversed on the ground that the patients had no property interest in a continued residence in Town Court. The patients had a right to receive benefits for care, and they had a right to remain — free from government interference — in a home that continued to be qualified. They had no right to care in a facility that entitled them to a hearing before the government could decertify that facility. The Court also ruled that no liberty interest of the patients would be adversely affected by the home's decertification, even if the patients' health were adversely affected by the necessity to transfer to another institution, because those effects were "indirect" results of the government's action against the nursing home.

Justice Blackmun, concurring, thought that the patients had failed to establish that the decertification adversely affected their liberty interests because they could not show that transfer trauma was a substantial danger. Blackmun, however, thought that the patients did possess an affected property interest in remaining in the home, because under the governing statute they could not be forced to move from a qualified home and Town Court could not be decertified unless the government established its noncompliance with program participation requirements. These factors together, Blackmun thought, created a legitimate expectation by the patients that they could not be forced by the government to transfer to another facility, even as a result of government action directed against the nursing home. Nonetheless, Blackmun felt that despite the property interest which he found in the patients, they were not entitled to an evidentiary hearing on Town Court's decertification: "That the asserted deprivation of property extends in a nondiscriminatory fashion to some 180 patients also figures in my calculus." After quoting from *Bi-Metallic*, he continued: "When governmental action affects more than a few individuals, concerns beyond economy, efficiency and expedition tip the balance against finding that due process attaches. We may expect that as the sweep of governmental action broadens, so too does the power of the affected group to protect its interests outside rigid constitutionally imposed procedures."

Questions and Comments

1.   Did *Atkins* properly apply *Bi-Metallic?* Were the recipients in *Atkins* complaining about the procedures used by Congress to adopt the new policy of a lower earned-income "disregard"? Were they complaining about the procedures used to implement that policy? Did they claim a constitutional right to receive notice of the action of the state administrators of the food-stamp program? On what theory did they claim a right to receive notice? Could you set forth their claim in terms that met the standards of *Londoner?* Better than the plaintiffs did in the case? Explain.

2.   Why do you think that Court in *Atkins* refused to find the notice defective? Could you have predicted in advance that the Court would have ruled as it did? What would be the ramifications of a ruling in favor of the plaintiffs? Would those ramifications have extended beyond the food-stamp program? Explain.

3.   Do you agree with Justice Blackmun that the nursing home patients had a property interest in receiving benefits for care in the Town Court facility? Why did Blackmun bother to write a lengthy concurrence to establish that the patients possessed a property right in remaining at the nursing facility if he also concluded (as he did) that the property right did not confer upon them a right to a pre-decertification hearing on the compliance of Town Court with the program requirements? Was Blackmun laying the groundwork for a later assault upon the rigidity of the *Roth* approach to procedural due process analysis?

4.   After arguing for a broad concept of property, Blackmun then drew upon *BiMetallic* as support for the conclusion that the patients had no right to an evidentiary hearing on Town Court's decertification. Blackmun suggested, however, that the patients' rights were adequately represented by Town Court as it defended itself in decertification proceedings. Does Blackmun's overall approach suggest that he wants to expand hearing rights but only under careful judicial supervision? Does his use of the *Bi-Metallic* case as a precedent suggest that he wants to limit hearing rights to the party who is uniquely affected by the government action? How does this approach differ from the Court's limitation of hearing rights to those "directly" affected?

E. THE REMEDY AS DEFINING THE RIGHT

ARNETT, DIRECTOR, OFFICE OF ECONOMIC OPPORTUNITY v. KENNEDY
416 U.S. 134 (1974)

MR. JUSTICE REHNQUIST announced the judgment of the Court in an opinion in which The Chief Justice and MR. JUSTICE STEWART join.

Prior to the events leading to his discharge, appellee Wayne Kennedy was a nonprobationary federal employee in the competitive Civil Service. He was a field representative in the Chicago Regional Office of the Office of Economic Opportunity (OEO). In March 1972, he was removed from the federal service pursuant to the provisions of the Lloyd-LaFollette Act . . . after Wendall Verduin, the Regional Director of the OEO, upheld written administrative charges made in the form of a "Notification of Proposed Adverse Action" against appellee. The charges listed five events occurring in November and December 1971; the most serious of the charges was that appellee "without any proof whatsoever and in reckless disregard of the actual facts" known to him or reasonably discoverable by him had publicly stated that Verduin and his administrative assistant had attempted to bribe a representative of a community action organization with which OEO had dealings. The alleged bribe consisted of an offer of a $100, 000 grant of OEO funds if the representative would sign a statement against appellee and another OEO employee.

Appellee was advised of his right under regulations promulgated by the Civil Service Commission and the OEO to reply to the charges orally and in writing, and to submit affidavits to Verduin. He was also advised that the material on which the notice was based was available for inspection in the Regional Office, and that a copy of the material was attached to the notice of proposed adverse action.

Appellee did not respond to the substance of the charges against him, but instead asserted that the charges were unlawful because he had a right to a trial-type hearing before an impartial hearing officer before he could be removed from his employment, and because statements made by him were protected by the First Amendment to the United States Constitution. . . .

Appellee then instituted this suit in the United States District Court for the Northern District of Illinois on behalf of himself and others similarly situated, seeking both injunctive and declaratory relief. . . . The court held that the discharge procedures authorized by the [Lloyd-La Follette] Act and attendant Civil Service Commission and OEO regulations denied appellee due process of law because they failed to provide for a trial-type hearing before an impartial agency official prior to removal; the court also held the Act and implementing regulations unconstitutionally vague because they failed to furnish sufficiently precise guidelines as to what kind of speech may be made the basis of a removal action. The court ordered that appellee be reinstated in his former position with backpay, and that he be accorded a hearing prior to removal in any future removal proceedings. . . .

I

The statutory provisions which the District Court held invalid are found in 5 U.S.C. § 7501. Subsection (a) of that section provides that "[a]n individual in the competitive service may be removed or suspended without pay only for such cause as will promote the efficiency of the service."

Subsection (b) establishes the administrative procedures by which an employee's rights under subsection (a) are to be determined, providing:

"(b) An individual in the competitive service whose removal or suspension without pay is sought is entitled to reasons in writing and to

"(1) notice of the action sought and of any charges preferred against him;

"(2) a copy of the charges;

"(3) a reasonable time for filing a written answer to the charges, with affidavits; and

"(4) a written decision on the answer at the earliest practicable date.

"Examination of witnesses, trial, or hearing is not required but may be provided in the discretion of the individual directing the removal or suspension without pay. . . ."

The codification of the Lloyd-La Follette Act is now supplemented by the regulations of the Civil Service Commission, and, with respect to the OEO, by the regulations and instructions of that agency. . . . The regulations of the Commission and the OEO, in nearly identical language, require that employees "avoid any action . . . which might result in, or create the appearance of . . . [a]ffecting adversely the confidence of the public in the integrity of [OEO and] the Government," and that employees not "engage in criminal, infamous, dishonest, immoral, or notoriously disgraceful or other conduct prejudicial to the Government-." . . . The Commission's regulations provide, inter alia, that . . . the employee shall have an opportunity to appear before the official vested with authority to make the removal decision in order to answer the charges against him, that the employee must receive notice of an adverse decision on or before its effective date, and that the employee may appeal from an adverse decision. This appeal may be either to a reviewing authority within the employing agency, or directly to the Commission, and the employee is entitled to an evidentiary trial-type hearing at the appeal stage of the proceeding. The only trial-type hearing available within the OEO is, by virtue of its regulations and practice, typically held after actual removal; but if the employee is reinstated on appeal, he receives full backpay, less any amounts earned by him through other employment during that period.

The Lloyd-La Follette Act was enacted as one section of the Post Office Department appropriation bill for the fiscal year 1913. . . . That Act, as now codified, 5 U.S.C. § 7501, together with the administrative regulations issued by the Civil Service Commission and the OEO, provided the statutory and administrative framework which the Government contends controlled the proceedings against appellee. The District Court, in its ruling on appellee's procedural contentions, in effect held that the Fifth Amendment . . . prohibited Congress, in the Lloyd-La

Follette Act, from granting protection against removal without cause and at the same time—indeed, in the same sentence specifying that the determination of cause should be without the full panoply of rights which attend a trial-type adversary hearing. We do not believe that the Constitution so limits Congress in the manner in which benefits may be extended to federal employees.

In Board of *Regents v. Roth*, we said:

"Property interests, of course, are not created by the Constitution. Rather, they are created and their dimensions are defined by existing rules or understandings that stem from an independent source such as state laws — rules or understandings that secure certain benefits and that support claims of entitlement to those benefits." 408 U.S., at 577.

Here appellee did have a statutory expectancy that he not be removed other than for "such cause as will promote the efficiency of [the] service." But the very section of the statute which granted him that right, a right which had previously existed only by virtue of administrative regulation, expressly provided also for the procedure by which "cause" was to be determined, and expressly omitted the procedural guarantees which appellee insists are mandated by the Constitution. Only by bifurcating the very sentence of the Act of Congress which conferred upon appellee the right not to be removed save for cause could it be said that he had an expectancy of that substantive right without the procedural limitations which Congress attached to it. . . . Where the focus of the legislation was thus strongly on the procedural mechanism for enforcing the substantive right which was simultaneously conferred, we decline to conclude that the substantive right may be viewed wholly apart from the procedure provided for its enforcement. The employee's statutorily defined right is not a guarantee against removal without cause in the abstract, but such a guarantee as enforced by the procedures which Congress has designated for the determination of cause.

. . . . Here the property interest which appellee had in his employment was itself conditioned by the procedural limitations which had accompanied the grant of that interest. . . .

Appellee also contends . . . that because of the nature of the charges on which his dismissal was based, he was in effect accused of dishonesty, and that therefore a hearing was required before he could be deprived of this element of his "liberty" protected by the Fifth Amendment against deprivation without due process- . . . . The liberty here implicated by appellants' action is not the elemental freedom from external restraint such as was involved in *Morrissey v. Brewer*, 408 U.S. 471 (1972), but is instead a subspecies of the right of the individual "to enjoy those privileges long recognized . . . as essential to the orderly pursuit of happiness by free men." . . . But that liberty is not offended by dismissal from employment itself, but instead by dismissal based upon an unsupported charge which could wrongfully injure the reputation of an employee. Since the purpose of the hearing in such a case is to provide the person "an opportunity to clear his name," a hearing afforded by administrative appeal procedures after the actual dismissal is a sufficient compliance with the requirements of the Due Process Clause. . . .

[The Court also held that the Lloyd-La Follette Act is not impermissibly vague or overbroad in its regulation of the speech of federal employees and therefore unconstitutional on its face.]

Accordingly, we reverse the decision of the District Court on both grounds on which it granted summary judgment and remand for further proceedings not inconsistent with this opinion.

Reversed and remanded.

MR. JUSTICE POWELL, with whom MR. JUSTICE BLACKMUN joins, concurring in part and concurring in the result in part.

The plurality opinion evidently reasons that the nature of appellee's interest in continued federal employment is necessarily defined and limited by the statutory procedures for discharge and that the constitutional guarantee of procedural due process accords to appellee no procedural protections against arbitrary or erroneous discharge other than those expressly provided in the statute. The plurality would thus conclude that the statute governing federal employment determines not only the nature of appellee's property interest, but also the extent of the procedural protections to which he may lay claim. It seems to me that this approach is incompatible with the principles laid down in *Roth* and *Sindermann.* Indeed, it would lead directly to the conclusion that whatever the nature of an individual's statutorily created property interest, deprivation of that interest could be accomplished without notice or a hearing at any time. This view misconceives the origin of the right to procedural due process. That right is conferred, not by legislative grace, but by constitutional guarantee. While the legislature may elect not to confer a property interest in federal employment, it may not constitutionally authorize the deprivation of such an interest, once conferred, without appropriate procedural safeguards. . . .

Note: The Subsequent History of the Arnett Plurality Analysis

The property-interest analysis employed by Justice Rehnquist in his *Arnett* plurality opinion was approved by Chief Justice Burger and Justice Stewart; but it was rejected by a majority of the Court: Justices Powell, Blackmun, White, Marshall, Douglas and Brennan all indicated their rejection of the plurality position that a property interest can be defined by the procedure statutorily provided for its divestment. The Court's later ruling in *Goss v. Lopez*, 419 U.S. 565 (1975) that public high school students had an entitlement to public schooling under Ohio law which prevented their disciplinary suspension without a rudimentary hearing was inconsistent with the *Arnett* plurality opinion's view that the statute conferring the entitlement could limit its extent by providing the procedures for taking it away. However, Justice Powell's dissenting opinion in *Goss v. Lopez* contains some language reminiscent of that of *Arnett* plurality. (". . . the very legislation which 'defines' the 'dimension' of the student's entitlement, while providing a right to education generally, does not establish this right free of discipline imposed in accord with Ohio law.") The majority opinion in *Bishop v. Wood*, 426 U.S. 341 (1976) took the view that a discharged police chief had no right to a hearing prior to his dismissal because the ordinance defining his position conditioned his "removal on compliance with certain specified procedures" which did not include a hearing. Although the majority indicated that the ex-police chief's position was different from the OEO worker in *Arnett* because the police chief had possessed no property interest in his former position, the majority's analysis appeared close to that of the *Arnett* plurality. In 1980 Justice Blackmun, concurring in *O'Bannon v. Town Court Nursing Center*, 447 U.S. 773 (1980), took the view that although nursing home residents possessed a "property" interest in remaining in their home, that interest did not necessarily entitle them to a hearing before the home was decertified; Blackmun then went on to say that "a majority of the Justices of this Court are already on record as concluding that the term "property" sometimes incorporates limiting characterizations of statutorily bestowed interests," citing the *Arnett* plurality opinion and the *Goss v. Lopez* dissent. 477 U.S. at 795. As the following opinion points out, however, Court majorities took positions inconsistent with the *Arnett* plurality in *Vitek v. Jones*, 445 U.S. 480, 491 (1980) and in *Logan v. Zimmerman Brush Co.*, 455 U.S. 422, 432 (1982).

CLEVELAND BOARD OF EDUCATION v. LOUDERMILL
470 U.S. 532 (1985)

JUSTICE WHITE delivered the opinion of the Court.

In 1979 the Cleveland Board of Education . . . hired respondent James Loudermill as a security guard. On his job application, Loudermill stated that he had never been convicted of a felony. Eleven months later, as part of a routine examination of his employment records, the Board discovered that in fact Loudermill had been convicted of grand larceny in 1968. By letter dated November 3, 1980, the Board's Business Manager informed Loudermill that he had been dismissed because of his dishonesty in filling out the employment application. Loudermill was not afforded an opportunity to respond to the charge of dishonesty or to challenge his dismissal. On November 13, the Board adopted a resolution officially approving the discharge.

Under Ohio law, Loudermill was a "classified civil servant." Ohio Rev. Code Ann. § 124.11 (1984). Such employees can be terminated only for cause, and may obtain administrative review if discharged. § 124–34 (1984). Pursuant to this provision, Loudermill filed an appeal with the Cleveland Civil Service Commission on November 12. The Commission appointed a referee, who held a hearing on January 29, 1981. Loudermill argued that he had thought that his 1968 larceny conviction was for a misdemeanor rather than a felony. The referee recommended reinstatement. On July 20, 1981, the full Commission heard argument and orally announced that it would uphold the dismissal. . . .

Although the Commission's decision was subject to judicial review in the state courts, Loudermill instead brought the present suit in the Federal District Court for the Northern District of Ohio. The complaint alleged that § 124–34 was unconstitutional on its face because it did not provide the employee an opportunity to respond to the charges against him prior to his removal. . . .

Before a responsive pleading was filed, the District Court dismissed for failure to state a claim on which relief could be granted. . . . it held that because the very statute that created the property right in continued employment also specified the procedures for discharge, and because those procedures were followed, Loudermill was, by definition, afforded all the process due. The post-termination hearing also adequately protected Loudermill's liberty interests. . . .

The other case before us arises on similar facts and followed a similar course. Respondent Richard Donnelly was a bus mechanic for the Parma Board of Education. In August 1977, Donnelly was fired because he had failed an eye examination. He was offered a chance to retake the exam but did not do so. Like Loudermill, Donnelly appealed to the Civil Service Commission. After a year of wrangling about the timeliness of his appeal, the Commission heard his case. It ordered Donnelly reinstated, though without backpay. In a complaint essentially identical to Loudermill's, Donnelly challenged the constitutionality of the dismissal procedures. The district Court dismissed for failure to state a claim. . . . and the cases were consolidated for appeal. A divided panel of the Court of Appeals for the Sixth Circuit reversed in part and remanded. . . . It disagreed with the District Court's original rationale. Instead, it concluded that the compelling private interest in retaining employment, combined with the value of presenting evidence prior to dismissal, outweighed the added administrative burden of a pretermination hearing. . . . With regard to the alleged deprivation of liberty, and Loudermill's 9-month wait for an administrative decision, the court affirmed the District Court, finding no constitutional violation. . . .

II

. . . [The] argument, which was accepted by the District Court, has its genesis in the plurality opinion in *Arnett v. Kennedy*. . . . The plurality reasoned that where the legislation conferring the substantive right also sets out the procedural mechanism for enforcing that right, the two cannot be separated. . . .

This view garnered three votes in *Arnett*, but was specifically rejected by the other six Justices. . . . Since then, this theory has at times seemed to gather some additional support. See *Bishop v. Wood*, 426 U.S. 341, 355–361 (1976) (White, J., dissenting); *Goss v. Lopez*, 419 U.S. at 586–587 (Powell, J., joined by Burger, CJ., and Blackmun and Rehnquist, JJ., dissenting). More recently, however, the Court has clearly rejected it. In *Vitek v. Jones*, 445 U.S. 480, 491 (1980), we pointed out that "minimum [procedural] requirements [are] a matter of federal law, they are not diminished by the fact that the State may have specified its own procedures that it may deem adequate for determining the preconditions to adverse official action." This conclusion was reiterated in *Logan v. Zimmerman Brush Co.*, 455 U.S. 422, 432 (1982), where we reversed the lower court's holding that because the entitlement arose from a state statute, the legislature had the prerogative to define the procedures to be followed to protect that entitlement.

In the light of these holdings, it is settled that the "bitter with the sweet" approach misconceives the constitutional guarantee. If a clearer holding is needed, we provide it today. The point is straightforward: the Due Process Clause provides that certain substantive rights — life, liberty, and property — cannot be deprived except pursuant to constitutionally adequate procedures. The categories of substance and procedure are distinct. Were the rule otherwise, the Clause would be reduced to a mere tautology. . . .

In short, once it is determined that the Due Process Clause applies, "the question remains what process is due." *Morrissey v. Brewer*, 408 U.S. 471, 481 (1972). The answer to that question is not to be found in the Ohio statute.

III

An essential principle of due process is that a deprivation of life, liberty, or property "be preceded by notice and opportunity for hearing appropriate to the nature of the case." . . . We have described the "root requirement" of the Due Process Clause as being "that an individual be given an opportunity for a hearing *before* he is deprived of any significant property interest." . . . This principle requires "some kind of a hearing" prior to the discharge of an employee who has a constitutionally protected property interest in his employment. . . .

The need for some form of pretermination hearing . . . is evident from a balancing of the competing interests at stake. These are the private interests in retaining employment, the governmental interest in the expeditious removal of unsatisfactory employees and the avoidance of administrative burdens, and the risk of an erroneous termination. See *Mathews v. Eldridge*, 424 U.S. 319, 335 (1976).

. . . . [S]ome opportunity for the employee to present his side of the case is recurringly of obvious value in reaching an accurate decision. . . . Even where the facts are clear, the appropriateness or necessity of the discharge may not be; in such cases, the only meaningful opportunity to invoke the discretion of the decisionmaker is likely to be before the termination takes effect. See *Goss v. Lopez*, 419 U.S. at 583–584; *Gagnon v. Scarpelli*, 411 U.S. 778. 784–786 (1973).

. . . . As we shall explain, affording the employee an opportunity to respond prior to termination would impose neither a significant administrative burden nor intolerable delays. Furthermore, the employer shares the employee's interest in avoiding disruption and erroneous decisions; and until the matter is settled, the employer would continue to receive the benefit of the employee's labors. . . . A governmental employer also has an interest in keeping citizens usefully employed rather than taking the possibly erroneous and counter-productive step of forcing its employees onto the welfare roles. Finally, in those situations where the employer perceives a significant hazard in keeping the employee on the job, it can avoid the problem by suspending with pay.

IV

The foregoing considerations indicate that the pretermination "hearing," though necessary, need not be elaborate. . . . In general, "something less" than a full evidentiary hearing is sufficient prior to adverse administrative action. *Mathews v. Eldridge*, 424 U.S. at 343. . . . Here, the pretermination hearing need not definitively resolve the propriety of the discharge. It should be an initial check against mistaken decisions — essentially a determination of whether there are reasonable grounds to believe that the charges against the employee are true and support the proposed action. . . .

The essential requirements of due process, and all that respondents seek or the Court of Appeals required, are notice and an opportunity to respond. The opportunity to present reasons, either in person or in writing, why proposed action should not be taken is a fundamental due process requirement. . . . The tenured public employee is entitled to oral or written notice of the charges against him, an explanation of the employer's evidence, and an opportunity to present his side of the story. . . . To require more than this prior to termination would intrude to an unwarranted extent on the government's interest in quickly removing an unsatisfactory employee.

V

. . . . In his cross-petition Loudermill asserts, as a separate constitutional violation, that his administrative proceedings took too long. . . . At some point, a delay in the post-termination hearing would become a constitutional violation. . . . In the present case, however, the complaint. . . . reveals nothing about the delay except that it stemmed in part from the thoroughness of the procedures. . . . The chronology of the proceedings set out in the complaint, coupled with the assertion that nine months is too long to wait, does not state a claim of a constitutional deprivation.

VI

We conclude that all the process that is due is provided by a pretermination opportunity to respond, coupled with post-termination administrative procedures as provided by the Ohio statute. Because respondents allege in their complaints that they had no chance to respond, the District Court erred in dismissing for failure to state a claim. The judgment of the Court of Appeals is affirmed, and the case is remanded for further proceedings consistent with this opinion.

So ordered.

Questions and Comments

1.   Do you find Rehnquist's "bitter with the sweet" analysis convincing? Is it true that such an approach would automatically legitimate whatever process the state provided? Would that approach eliminate the due process clauses of the Fifth and Fourteenth Amendments as guarantors of appropriate procedures?

2.   Do you find satisfactory the *Loudermill* view that the adequacy of procedures is a matter of federal law? To what authority must a lawyer look to determine the adequacy of state-provided procedures? If procedures vary in each circumstance, is their adequacy ever ascertainable other than through litigation? How?

3.   *Is Loudermill* consistent with *Roth?* If property interests are created and limited by state law, how can federal law govern the procedures for divesting them? Are not all property interests defined by the procedures for enforcing and divesting

them? Are not property interests really bundles of procedural rights? Does the viability of *Loudermill* depend upon the viability of a distinction between substance and procedure? Is such a distinction viable?

4.   Does *Loudermill* mean that the states will be reluctant to create job security in government employment because the federal courts may impose more elaborate procedures for the protection of such employment than the state is willing to provide? Does *Loudermill* force the states to choose between federally defined procedures or providing no job security at all? Do the states face similar choices with benefit programs?

5.   In *Bishop v. Wood*, 426 U.S. 341, 345 (1976), *supra*, the Court upheld a lower court's construction of a city ordinance "as granting no right to continued employment but merely conditioning an employee's removal on compliance with certain specified procedures" such as written notice of discharge. The Court stated that the lower court's ruling that the employee " 'held his position at the will and pleasure of the city' necessarily establishes that he had no property interest." Does this mean that the employee had no right to the specified procedures when he was terminated? Could he have been terminated without those procedures? Did he have a limited property interest in the procedures? Can the Court always avoid the logic in the *Arnett* plurality analysis?

6.   The Surface Transportation Assistance Act of 1982 protects employees in the commercial motor transportation industry from being discharged in retaliation for refusing to operate a motor vehicle that does not comply with state and federal safety regulations or for filing complaints alleging noncompliance. A driver, one Hufstetler, was discharged by his employer for allegedly disabling several lights on his assigned truck in order to obtain extra pay while waiting for repairs. Hufstetler claimed that he was discharged in retaliation for having previously complained of safety violations. The Secretary of Labor (through the Occupational Safety and Health Administration) investigated and agreed with Hufstetler. May the Secretary of Labor order the employer to reinstate Hufstetler forthwith or is some kind of a hearing required? If so, what is the constitutionally protected interest of the employer upon which its right to a hearing is based? *See Brock v. Roadway Express, Inc.*, 481 U.S. 252 (1987).

F.   LIBERTY

PAUL, CHIEF OF POLICE, LOUISVILLE v. DAVIS
424 U.S. 693 (1976)

Mr. Justice Rehnquist delivered the opinion of the Court.

We granted certiorari . . . in this case to consider whether respondent's charge that petitioners' defamation of him, standing alone and apart from any other governmental action with respect to him, stated a claim for relief under 42 U.S.C. § 1983 and the Fourteenth Amendment. For the reasons hereinafter stated, we conclude that it does not.

Petitioner Paul is the Chief of Police of the Louisville, Ky., Division of Police, while petitioner McDaniel occupies the same position in the Jefferson County, Ky., Division of Police. In late 1972 they agreed to combine their efforts for the purpose of alerting local area merchants to possible shoplifters who might be operating during the Christmas season. In early December petitioners distributed to approximately 800 merchants in the Louisville metropolitan area a "flyer," which began as follows:

"TO: BUSINESS MEN IN THE METROPOLITAN AREA

"The Chiefs of The Jefferson County and City of Louisville Police Departments, in an effort to keep their officers advised on shoplifting activity, have approved the attached alphabetically arranged flyer of subjects known to be active in this criminal field.

. . . This flyer is being distributed to you, the business man, so that you may inform your security personnel to watch for these subjects. These persons have been arrested during 1971 and 1972 or have been active in various criminal fields in high density shopping areas.

"Only the photograph and name of the subject is shown on this flyer, if additional information is desired, please forward a request in writing. . . .

The flyer consisted of five pages of "mug shot" photos, arranged alphabetically. Each page was headed:

"NOVEMBER 1972
CITY OF LOUISVILLE
JEFFERSON COUNTY
POLICE DEPARTMENTS
ACTIVE SHOPLIFTERS"

In approximately the center of page 2 there appeared photos and the name of the respondent, Edward Charles Davis III.

Respondent appeared on the flyer because on June 14, 1971, he had been arrested in Louisville on a charge of shoplifting. He had been arraigned on this charge in September 1971, and, upon his plea of not guilty, the charge had been "filed away with leave [to reinstate]," a disposition which left the charge outstanding. Thus, at the time petitioners caused the flyer to be prepared and circulated respondent had been charged with shoplifting but his guilt or innocence of that offense had never been resolved. Shortly after circulation of the flyer the charge against respondent was finally dismissed by a judge of the Louisville Police Court.

At the time the flyer was circulated respondent was employed as a photographer by the Louisville Courier-Journal and Times. The flyer, and respondent's inclusion therein, soon came to the attention of respondent's supervisor, the executive director of photography for the two newspapers. This individual called respondent in to hear his version of the events leading to his appearing in the flyer. Following this discussion, the supervisor informed respondent that although he would not be fired, he "had best not find himself in a similar situation" in the future.

Respondent thereupon brought this § 1983 action in the District Court for the Western District of Kentucky, seeking redress for the alleged violation of rights guaranteed to him by the Constitution of the United States. . . . The District Court [ruled] . . . that "[t]he facts alleged in this case do not establish that plaintiff has been deprived of any right secured to him by the Constitution of the United States."

Respondent appealed to the Court of Appeals for the Sixth Circuit. . . . The Court of Appeals concluded that respondent had set forth a § 1983 claim "in that he has alleged facts that constitute a denial of due process of law." . . . In its view our decision in *Wisconsin v. Constantineau*, 400 U.S. 433 (1971), mandated reversal of the District Court.

I

Respondent's due process claim is grounded upon his assertion that the flyer, and in particular the phrase "Active Shoplifters" appearing at the head of the page upon which his name and photograph appear, impermissibly deprived him of some "liberty" protected by the Fourteenth Amendment. His complaint asserted that the "active shoplifter" designation would inhibit him from entering business establishments for fear of being suspected of shoplifting and possibly apprehended, and would seriously impair his future employment opportunities. Accepting that such consequences may flow from the flyer in question, respondent's complaint would appear to state a classical claim for defamation actionable in the courts of virtually every state. . . .

Respondent brought his action, however, not in the state courts of Kentucky, but in a United States District Court for that State. He asserted not a claim for defamation under the laws of Kentucky, but a claim that he had been deprived of rights secured to him by the Fourteenth Amendment. . . . Concededly if the same allegations had been made about respondent by a private individual, he would have nothing more than a claim for defamation under state law. But, he contends, since petitioners are respectively an official of city and of county government, his action is thereby transmuted into one for deprivation by the State of rights secured under the Fourteenth Amendment.

If respondent's view is to prevail, a person arrested by law enforcement officers who announce that they believe such person to be responsible for a particular crime in order to calm the fears of an aroused populace, presumably obtains a claim against such officers under § 1983. And since it is surely far more clear from the language of the Fourteenth Amendment that "life" is protected against state injury, it would be difficult to see why the survivors of an innocent bystander mistakenly shot by a policeman or negligently killed by a sheriff driving a government vehicle, would not have claims equally cognizable under § 1983.

It is hard to perceive any logical stopping place to such a line of reasoning. Respondent's construction would seem almost necessarily to result in every legally cognizable injury which may have been inflicted by a state official acting under "color of law" establishing a violation of the Fourteenth Amendment. We think it would come as a great surprise to those who drafted and shepherded the adoption of that Amendment to learn that it worked such a result, and a study of our decisions convinces us they do not support the construction urged by respondent.

II

The result reached by the Court of Appeals . . . must be bottomed on one of two premises. The first is that the Due Process Clause . . . and § 1983 make actionable many wrongs inflicted by government employees which had heretofore been thought to give rise only to state-law tort claims. The second premise is that the infliction by state officials of a "stigma" to one's reputation is somehow different in kind from the infliction by the same official of harm or injury to other interests protected by state law, so that an injury to reputation is actionable under § 1983 and the Fourteenth Amendment even if other such harms are not. We examine each of these premises in turn.

A

The first premise would be contrary to pronouncements in our cases on more than one occasion. . . . [In *Monroe v. Pape*, 365 U.S. 167 (1961)] the Court was careful to point out that the complaint stated a cause of action under the Fourteenth Amendment because it alleged an unreasonable search and seizure violative of the guarantee "contained in the Fourth Amendment [and] made applicable to the States by reason of the Due Process Clause of the Fourteenth Amendment.". . . . Respondent, however, has pointed to no specific constitutional guarantee safeguarding the interest he asserts has been invaded. Rather, he apparently believes that the Fourteenth Amendment's Due Process Clause should *ex proprio vigore* extend to him a right to be free of injury whenever the State may be characterized as the tortfeasor. But such a reading would make of the Fourteenth Amendment a font of tort law to be superimposed upon whatever systems may already be administered by the States. We have noted the "constitutional shoals" that confront any attempt to derive from congressional civil rights statutes a body of general federal tort law. . . . *a fortiori*, the procedural guarantees of the Due Process Clause cannot be the source for such law.

B

The second premise upon which the result reached by the Court of Appeals could be rested — that the infliction by state officials of a "stigma" to one's reputation is somehow different in kind from infliction by a state official of harm to other interests protected by state law — is equally untenable. . . . While we have in a number of our prior cases pointed out the frequently drastic effect of the "stigma" which may result from defamation by government in a variety of contexts, this line of cases does not establish the proposition that reputation alone, apart from some more tangible interests such as employment, is either "liberty" or "property" by itself sufficient to invoke the procedural protection of the Due Process Clause. . . . While not uniform in their treatment of the subject, we think that the weight of our decisions establishes no constitutional doctrine converting every defamation by a public official into a deprivation of liberty within the meaning of the Due Process Clause of the Fifth or Fourteenth Amendment.

. . . . [In *Wisconsin v. Constantineau*] the Court held that a Wisconsin statute authorizing the practice of "posting" was unconstitutional because it failed to provide procedural safeguards of notice and opportunity to be heard, prior to an individual's being "posted." Under the statute "posting" consisted of forbidding in writing the sale or delivery of alcoholic beverages to certain persons who were determined to have become hazards to themselves, to their family, or to the community by reason of their "excessive drinking." The statute also made it a misdemeanor to sell or give liquor to any person so posted. . . .

There is undoubtedly language in *Constantineau*, which is sufficiently ambiguous to justify the reliance upon it by the Court of Appeals:

> "Yet certainly where the state attaches 'a badge of infamy' to the citizen, due process comes into play. . . . '[T]he right to be heard before being condemned to suffer grievous loss of any kind, even though it may not involve the stigma and hardships of a criminal conviction, is a principle basic to our society.' *Anti-Fascist Committee v. McGrath*, 341 U.S. 123, 168 (Frankfurter, J., concurring).

> "Where a person's good name, reputation, honor, or integrity is at stake *because of what the government is doing to him*, notice and an opportunity to be heard are essential." Id., at 437 (emphasis supplied).

The last paragraph of the quotation could be taken to mean that if a government official defames a person, without more, the procedural requirements of the Due Process Clause . . . are brought into play. . . .

We think that the italicized language in the last sentence quoted, "because of what the government is doing to him," referred to the fact that the governmental action taken in that case deprived the individual of a right previously held under state law — the right to purchase or obtain liquor in common with the rest of the citizenry. "Posting," therefore significantly altered her status as a matter of state law, and it was that alteration of legal status which, combined with the injury resulting from the defamation, justified the invocation of procedural safeguards. The "stigma" resulting from the defamatory character of the posting was doubtless an important factor in evaluating the extent of the harm worked by that act, but we do not think that such defamation, standing alone, deprived Constantineau of any "liberty" protected by the procedural guarantees of the Fourteenth Amendment.

. . . While *Roth* recognized that governmental action defaming an individual in the course of declining to rehire him could entitle the person to notice and an opportunity to be heard as to the defamation, its language is quite inconsistent with any notion that a defamation perpetrated by a government official but unconnected with any refusal to rehire would be actionable under the Fourteenth Amendment:

> "The state, *in declining to rehire the respondent*, did not make any charge against him that might seriously damage his standing and associations in his community. . . .

> "Similarly, there is no suggestion that the State, *in declining to reemploy the respondent*, imposed on him a stigma or other disability that

foreclosed his freedom to take advantage of other employment opportunities (emphasis supplied).

Thus it was not thought sufficient to establish a claim under § 1983 and the Fourteenth Amendment that there simply be defamation by a state official; the defamation had to occur in the course of the termination of employment. Certainly there is no suggestion in *Roth* to indicate that a hearing would be required each time the State in its capacity as employer might be considered responsible for a statement defaming an employee who continues to be an employee.

In each of . . . [certain prior] cases, as a result of the state action complained of, a right or status previously recognized by state law was distinctly altered or extinguished. It was this alteration, officially removing the interest from the recognition and protection previously afforded by the State, which we found sufficient to invoke the procedural guarantees contained in the Due Process Clause of the Fourteenth Amendment. But the interest in reputation alone which respondent seeks to vindicate in this action in federal court is quite different from the "liberty" or "property" recognized in those decisions. Kentucky law does not extend to respondent any legal guarantee of present enjoyment of reputation which has been altered as a result of petitioners' actions. Rather his interest in reputation is simply one of a number which the State may protect against injury by virtue of its tort law, providing a forum for vindication of those interests by means of damages actions. . . .

Respondent . . . cannot assert denial of any right vouchsafed to him by the State and thereby protected under the Fourteenth Amendment. That being the case, petitioners' defamatory publications, however seriously they may have harmed respondent's reputation, did not deprive him of any "liberty" or "property" interests protected by the Due Process Clause.

[The Court also held that respondent's complaint did not state a claim for invasion of a constitutionally protected right to privacy.]

None of the respondent's theories of recovery were based upon rights secured to him by the Fourteenth Amendment. Petitioners therefore were not liable to him under § 1983. The judgment of the Court of Appeals holding otherwise is *Reversed*.

INGRAHAM v. WRIGHT
430 U.S. 651 (1977)

Mr. Justice Powell delivered the opinion of the Court.

This case presents questions concerning the use of corporal punishment in public schools: First, whether the paddling of students as a means of maintaining school discipline constitutes cruel and unusual punishment in violation of the Eighth Amendment; and, second, to the extent that paddling is constitutionally permissible, whether the Due Process Clause of the Fourteenth Amendment requires prior notice and an opportunity to be heard.

I

Petitioners James Ingraham and Roosevelt Andrews filed the complaint in this case on January 7, 1971, in the United States District Court for the Southern District of Florida. At the time both were enrolled in the Charles R. Drew Junior High School in Dade County, Florida. . . . [The petitioners complained that their subjection to paddling constituted cruel and unusual punishment in violation of the Eighth Amendment and that their subjection to this punishment without a prior hearing violated the procedural protections contained in the due process clause of the Fourteenth Amendment. The District Court dismissed the complaint after the presentation of petitioners' case. Although a panel of the Court of Appeals voted to reverse, the *en banc* Court of Appeals affirmed the District Court's dismissal of the action. In affirming the dismissal, the Supreme Court first ruled that paddling did not constitute cruel and unusual punishment.]

IV

. . . . [W]e find that corporal punishment in public schools implicates a constitutionally protected liberty interest, but we hold that the traditional common-law remedies are fully adequate to afford due process.

B

"[T]he question remains what process is due." *Morrissey v. Brewer*. . . . Were it not for the common-law privilege permitting teachers to inflict reasonable corporal punishment on children in their care, and the availability of the traditional remedies for abuse, the case for requiring advance procedural safeguards would be strong indeed. . . .

1

Because it is rooted in history, the child's liberty interest in avoiding corporal punishment while in the care of public school authorities is subject to historical limitations. Under the common law, an invasion of personal security gave rise to a right to recover damages in a subsequent judicial proceeding. 3 W Blackstone, Commentaries *120–121. But the right of recovery was qualified by the concept of justification. Thus, there could be no recovery against a teacher who gave only "moderate correction" to a child. Id., at *120. To the extent that the force used was reasonable in light of its purpose, it was not wrongful, but rather "justifiable or lawful." *Ibid.*

The concept that reasonable corporal punishment in school is justifiable continues to be recognized in the laws of most States. . . . It represents "the balance struck by this country between the child's interest in personal security and the traditional view that some limited corporal punishment may be necessary in the course of a child's education. Under that longstanding accommodation of interests, there can be no deprivation of substantive rights as long as disciplinary corporal punishment is within the limits of the common-law privilege.

2

Florida has continued to recognize, and indeed has strengthened by statute, the common-law right of a child not to be subjected to excessive corporal punishment in school. Under Florida law the teacher and principal of the school decide in the first instance whether corporal punishment is reasonably necessary under the circumstances in order to discipline a child who has misbehaved. But they must exercise prudence and restraint. For Florida has preserved the traditional judicial proceedings for determining whether the punishment was justified. If the punishment inflicted is later found to have been excessive — not reasonably believed at the time to be necessary for the child's discipline or training — the school authorities inflicting it may be held liable in damages to the child and, if malice is shown, they may be subject to criminal penalties.

. . . . [B]ecause paddlings are usually inflicted in response to conduct directly observed by teachers in their presence, the risk that a child will be paddled without cause is typically insignificant. . . . Teachers and school authorities are unlikely to inflict corporal punishment unnecessarily or excessively when a possible consequence of doing so is the institution of civil or criminal proceedings against them.

3

But even if the need for advance procedural safeguards were clear, the question would remain whether the incremental benefit could justify the cost. . . . Given the impracticability of formulating a rule of procedural due process that varies with the severity of the particular imposition, the prior hearing petitioners seek would have to precede any paddling, however moderate or trivial.

Such a universal constitutional requirement would significantly burden the use of corporal punishment as a disciplinary measure. Hearings — even informal hearings — require time, personnel, and a diversion of attention from normal school pursuits. School authorities may well choose to abandon corporal punishment rather than incur the burdens of complying with the procedural requirements. Teachers, properly concerned with maintaining authority in the classroom, may well prefer to rely on other disciplinary measures — which they may view as less effective — rather than confront the possible disruption that prior notice and a hearing may entail. . . .

Elimination or curtailment of corporal punishment would be welcomed by many as a societal advance. But when such a policy choice may result from this Court's determination of an asserted right to due process, rather than from the normal processes of community debate and legislative action, the societal costs cannot be dismissed as insubstantial. . . .

"At some point the benefit of an additional safeguard to the individual affected . . . and to society in terms of increased assurance that the action is just, may be outweighed by the cost. *Mathews v. Eldridge*, 424 U.S. at 348. We think that point has been reached in this case. In view of the low incidence of abuse, the openness of our schools, and the common-law safeguards that already exist, the risk of error that may result in violation of a schoolchild's substantive rights can only be regarded as minimal. Imposing additional administrative safeguards as a constitutional requirement might reduce that risk marginally, but would also entail a significant intrusion into an area of primary educational responsibility. We conclude that the Due Process Clause does not require notice and a hearing prior to the imposition of corporal punishment in the public schools, as that practice is authorized and limited by the common law.

Affirmed.

Mr. Justice Stevens, dissenting.

When only an invasion of a property interest is involved, there is a greater likelihood that a damages award will make a person completely whole than when an invasion of the individual's interest in freedom from bodily restraint and punishment has occurred. In the property context, therefore, frequently a postdeprivation state remedy may be all the process that the Fourteenth Amendment requires. It may also be true — although I do not express an opinion on the point — that an adequate state remedy for defamation may satisfy the due process requirement when a State has impaired an individual's interest in his reputation. On that hypothesis, the Court's analysis today gives rise to the thought that *Paul v. Davis*, 424 U.S. 693, may have been correctly decided on an incorrect rationale. Perhaps the Court will one day agree with Mr. Justice Brennan's appraisal of the importance of the constitutional interest at stake in *id.*, at 720–723, 734 (dissenting opinion), and nevertheless conclude that an adequate state remedy may prevent every state-inflicted injury to a person's reputation from violating 42 U.S.C. § 1983.

Questions and Comments

1.   Did Justice Rehnquist, in *Paul v. Davis*, insist that defamation by a state official impaired a liberty interest only when it was accompanied by a change of status? Did he mean that defamation impairs a liberty interest only when the plaintiff is simultaneously deprived of a property interest?

2.   Such a position is not consistent with the opinion in *Roth*, is it? Because Roth's contract expired by its terms, he had no property interest at the time that the University of Wisconsin at Oshkosh declined to renew his contract. Yet Justice Rehnquist, in his *Paul v. Davis* opinion, conceded that Roth would have had a § 1983 claim if he had been defamed at the time that the University of Wisconsin at Oshkosh declined to renew his contract, did he not?

3.   The change of status which must accompany the defamation giving rise to a § 1983 claim therefore need not be one which gives rise to an impairment of a property interest. Indeed, the change of status can be one, like Roth's change of status, which occurs without any affirmative state action.

4.   Justice Rehnquist, in his discussion of *Monroe v. Pape*, 365 U.S. 167 (1961), indicates that the specific constitutional guarantees of protection against government intrusion may give rise to § 1983 actions. Is this source of § 1983 claims different from § 1983 claims grounded upon invasions of "property" and "liberty" claims under the *Roth/Sinderman* line of cases? Is it correct to say that specific

constitutional guarantees give rise to property and liberty interests?

5.   In *Ingraham v. Wright* the Court had to recognize the existence of a "liberty" interest, because the case dealt with an invasion of bodily integrity. There would have to be a hearing at which a person could seek vindication, would there not? Where would that hearing take place?

6.   Is the hearing in state court — which occurs in the tort action against the disciplinarian — mandated by the United States Constitution? Why? If so, Florida could not abolish the right to sue the disciplinarian, could it?

7.   Did *Ingraham v. Wright* accurately apply the *Mathews v. Eldridge* approach to determine the need for additional pre-deprivation procedures? Is it correct to describe that analysis as a marginal cost-benefit analysis?

8.   Do you agree with the revisionist analysis of *Paul v. Davis* set forth in Justice Stevens' concurring opinion in *Ingraham v. Wright?* If a post deprivation hearing is adequate for defamation, then the state-court action for defamation would have provided the necessary hearing, even if the majority had not redefined the scope of the affected "liberty" interest. Can you think of other circumstances in which a state-court action in tort would fulfill a "hearing" requirement mandated by the due process clause?

Note: Due Process and the Administration of Educational Institutions

In recent decades the administration of educational institutions has come under repeated contact with the due process clause of the Fourteenth Amendment. Although the Court has tried to be sensitive to the conflicting values involved in these cases and has, in general, tried to avoid undue interference in the administration of educational institutions, the caselaw which it has produced is not entirely consistent.

1.   *Discipline.*

In **Goss v. Lopez, 419 U.S. 565 (1975)** the Court held that students were entitled to a rudimentary hearing before they could be suspended for periods of up to 10 days. The Court grounded its ruling on the provisions of the Ohio statutes which, the Court held, created a property interest in attending school; and upon the disciplinary nature of the suspensions which the Court held adversely affected the students' reputations and therefore their liberty interests. In *Ingraham v. Wright, supra,* the Court held that the administration of corporal punishment required no pre-deprivation hearing.

2.   *Academic decision-making.*

In ***Board of Curators of Univ. of Missouri v. Horowitz***, **435 U.S. 78 (1978)** the respondent was dismissed from medical school of a state university because of her poor ratings in clinical work. The evaluation process was apparently a careful and deliberate one: Her poor clinical work was noted during the previous academic year and she was advanced into her final year on a probationary status. Her faculty advisor rated her clinical skills as unsatisfactory and the Council of Evaluation, after review of her case, recommended that absent "radical improvement," respondent be dropped from the school. She was permitted to spend a substantial portion of time with seven practicing physicians, only two of whom recommended that respondent be allowed to graduate on schedule. The Council, again reviewing respondent's performance, noted that she was rated as "low-satisfactory" on surgery rotation. It recommended that she not be allowed to re-enroll, barring receipt of reports of radical improvement. When a negative report on her emergency rotation was thereafter received, the Council reaffirmed its recommendation that respondent be dropped from the school. The Coordinating Committee and the Dean approved the recommendation. The respondent appealed in writing to the University's Provost for Health Sciences who sustained the school's actions.

Respondent challenged her dismissal in a § 1983 action, claiming that she had been deprived of a "liberty" interest without due process of law in violation of the Fourteenth Amendment. Justice Rehnquist's opinion for the Court hinted that no liberty interest of the respondent's could be adversely affected when she was merely dismissed by the university without publicizing allegations harmful to her reputation. Rehnquist avoided deciding that question, however, by holding that even if a liberty or property interest of hers was affected, the respondent had received all the process that was due her. Observing that all that *Goss v. Lopez* required in a disciplinary context was an "informal give-and-take", the Court indicated that because the decision of which respondent complained was an academic evaluation, it did not require a "formal hearing at which respondent could defend her academic ability and performance." In its opinion, the Court indicated that "there are distinct differences between decisions to suspend or dismiss a student for disciplinary purposes and similar actions taken for academic reasons which may call for hearings in connection with the former but not the latter." Discussing academic decision-making, the Court stated:

> Academic evaluations of a student . . . bear little resemblance to the judicial and administrative factfinding proceedings to which we have traditionally attached a full-hearing requirement. . . . The decision to dismiss respondent . . . rested on the academic judgment of school officials that she did not have the necessary clinical ability to perform adequately as a medical doctor and was making insufficient progress toward that goal. Such a judgment is by its nature more subjective and evaluative than the typical factual questions presented in the average disciplinary decision. Like the decision of an individual professor as to the proper grade for a student in his course, the determination whether to dismiss a student for academic reasons requires an expert evaluation of cumulative information and is not readily adapted to the procedural tools of judicial or administrative decisionmaking.

After denying her procedural due process claim, the Court ruled that respondent had made no showing that she had been evaluated more stringently than other students because of her sex, religion and physical appearance. It therefore did not decide whether "the courts can review under . . . a standard [of arbitrariness or capriciousness] an academic decision of a public educational institution," but it noted that "courts are particularly ill-equipped to evaluate academic performance." In *Regents of Univ. of Michigan v. Ewing*, 474 U.S. 214 (1985), the Court again expressed reluctance to engage in substantive due process review of academic decisionmaking, indicating that courts may not override an academic judgment "unless it is such a substantial departure from accepted academic norms as to demonstrate that the person or committee responsible did not actually exercise professional judgment."

Due Process and the Administration of Prisons and Parole

Procedural due process for convicted offenders was first recognized in *Wollf v. McDonnell*, 418 U.S. 539 (1974). The evolution of procedural due process in this context is traced in the case below:

SANDIN v. CONNER
515 U. S. 472 (1995)

CHIEF JUSTICE REHNQUIST delivered the opinion of the Court.

[Conner was convicted of various crimes including murder, kidnapping, robbery, and burglary, for which he was serving an indeterminate sentence of 30 years to life in a Hawaii prison. When he was subjected to a strip search by a prison officer, Conner directed "angry and foul language" at the officer. Eleven days thereafter he received a notice charging him with disciplinary infractions. The notice charged Conner with "high misconduct" for using physical interference to impair a correctional function and "low moderate misconduct" for using abusive or obscene language and for harassing employees.]

Conner appeared before an adjustment committee on August 28, 1987. The committee refused Conner's request to present witnesses at the hearing, stating that "[w]itnesses were unavailable due to move [sic] to the medium facility and being short staffed on the modules." At the conclusion of proceedings, the committee determined that Conner was guilty of the alleged misconduct. It sentenced him to 30 days' disciplinary segregation in the Special Holding Unit[2] for the physical obstruction charge, and four hours segregation for each of the other two charges to be served concurrent with the 30 days. Conner's segregation began August 31, 1987, and ended September 29, 1987.

Conner sought administrative review within 14 days of receiving the committee's decision. Nine months later, the deputy administrator found the high misconduct charge unsupported and expunged Conner's disciplinary record with respect to that charge. But before the deputy administrator decided the appeal, Conner had

---

[2]   The Special Holding Unit (SHU) houses inmates placed in disciplinary segregation, § 17-201-19(c), administrative segregation, § 17- 201-22, and protective custody, § 17-201-23. Single-person cells comprise the SHU and conditions are substantially similar for each of the three classifications of inmates housed there. Compare Exh. 60, 1 App. 142- 155, with Exh. 61, 1 App. 156-168. With the exception of one extra phone call and one extra visiting privilege, inmates segregated for administrative reasons receive the same privilege revocations as those segregated for disciplinary reasons.

brought this suit against the adjustment committee chair and other prison officials in the United States District Court for the District of Hawaii based on Rev. Stat. § 1979, 42 U.S.C. § 1983. His amended complaint prayed for injunctive relief, declaratory relief, and damages for, among other things, a deprivation of procedural due process in connection with the disciplinary hearing. The District Court granted summary judgment in favor of the prison officials.

The Court of Appeals for the Ninth Circuit reversed the judgment. It concluded that Conner had a liberty interest in remaining free from disciplinary segregation and that there was a disputed question of fact with respect to whether Conner received all of the process due under this Court's pronouncement in *Wolff v. McDonnell*, 418 U.S. 539 (1974). [The Court of Appeals based its conclusion on a prison regulation that instructs the committee to find guilt when a charge of misconduct is supported by substantial evidence; that therefore the committee's duty to find guilt or innocence was nondiscretionary. On this reasoning, the court concluded that the state of Hawaii had created a liberty interest] and therefore held that respondent was entitled to call witnesses by virtue of our opinion in *Wolff, supra*. We granted the State's petition for certiorari, 513 U.S. 921 (1994), and now reverse.

II

Our due process analysis begins with *Wolff*. There, Nebraska inmates challenged the decision of prison officials to revoke good time credits without adequate procedures. Inmates earned good time credits under a state statute that bestowed mandatory sentence reductions for good behavior, revocable only for "'flagrant or serious misconduct,'" We held that the Due Process Clause itself does not create a liberty interest in credit for good behavior, but that the statutory provision created a liberty interest in a "shortened prison sentence" which resulted from good time credits, credits which were revocable only if the prisoner was guilty of serious misconduct. The Court characterized this liberty interest as one of "real substance" and articulated minimum procedures necessary to reach a "mutual accommodation between institutional needs and objectives and the provisions of the Constitution," Much of *Wolff* 's contribution to the landscape of prisoners' due process derived not from its description of liberty interests, but rather from its intricate balancing of prison management concerns with prisoners' liberty in determining the amount of process due. Its short discussion of the definition of a liberty interest, *Wolff, supra*, led to a more thorough treatment of the issue in *Meachum v. Fano*, 427 U.S. 215 (1976).

Inmates in *Meachum* sought injunctive relief, declaratory relief, and damages by reason of transfers from a Massachusetts medium security prison to a maximum security facility with substantially less favorable conditions. The transfers were ordered in the aftermath of arson incidents for which the transferred inmates were thought to be responsible, and did not entail a loss of good time credits or any period of disciplinary confinement. The Court began with the proposition that the Due Process Clause does not protect every change in the conditions of confinement having a substantial adverse impact on the prisoner. It then held that the Due Process Clause did not itself create a liberty interest in prisoners to be free from intrastate prison transfers. It reasoned that transfer to a maximum security facility, albeit one with more burdensome conditions, was "within the normal limits or range of custody which the conviction has authorized the State to impose." See also *Montanye v. Haymes*, 427 U.S. 236 (1976). The Court distinguished *Wolff* by noting that there the protected liberty interest in good time credit had been created by state law; here no comparable Massachusetts law stripped officials of the discretion to transfer prisoners to alternative facilities "for whatever reason or for no reason at all." *Meachum, supra*, at 228.[4]

Shortly after *Meachum*, the Court embarked on a different approach to defining state-created liberty interests. Because dictum in *Meachum* distinguished *Wolff* by focusing on whether state action was mandatory or discretionary, the Court in later cases laid ever greater emphasis on this somewhat mechanical dichotomy. *Greenholtz v. Inmates of Neb. Penal and Correctional Complex*, 442 U.S. 1 (1979), foreshadowed the methodology that would come to full fruition in *Hewitt v. Helms*, 459 U.S. 460 (1983). The *Greenholtz* inmates alleged that they had been unconstitutionally denied parole. Their claim centered on a state statute that set the date for discretionary parole at the time the minimum term of imprisonment less good time credits expired. The statute ordered release of a prisoner at that time, unless one of four specific conditions were shown. The Court apparently accepted the inmates' argument that the word "shall" in the statute created a legitimate expectation of release absent the requisite finding that one of the justifications for deferral existed, since the Court concluded that some measure of constitutional protection was due. Nevertheless, the State ultimately prevailed because the minimal process it had awarded the prisoners was deemed sufficient under the Fourteenth Amendment.

The Court made explicit in *Hewitt* what was implicit in *Greenholtz*. In evaluating the claims of inmates who had been confined to administrative segregation, it first rejected the inmates' claim of a right to remain in the general population as protected by the Due Process Clause on the authority of *Meachum, Montanye*, and *Vitek*. The Due Process Clause standing alone confers no liberty interest in freedom from state action taken "'within the sentence imposed.'" It then concluded that the transfer to less amenable quarters for nonpunitive reasons was "ordinarily contemplated by a prison sentence." Examination of the possibility that the State had created a liberty interest by virtue of its prison regulations followed. Instead of looking to whether the State created an interest of "real substance" comparable to the good time credit scheme of *Wolff*, the Court asked whether the State had gone beyond issuing mere procedural guidelines and had used "language of an unmistakably mandatory character" such that the incursion on liberty would not occur "absent specified substantive predicates." Finding such mandatory directives

---

[4] Later cases, such as *Vitek v. Jones*, 445 U.S. 480 (1980), found that the Due Process Clause itself confers a liberty interest in certain situations. In *Vitek*, a prisoner was to be transferred involuntarily to a state mental hospital for treatment of a mental disease or defect; the Court held that his right to be free from such transfer was a liberty interest irrespective of state regulation; it was "qualitatively different" from the punishment characteristically suffered by a person convicted of crime, and had "stigmatizing consequences." *Washington v. Harper*, 494 U.S. 210, 221-222, (1990), likewise concluded that, independent of any state regulation, an inmate had a liberty interest in being protected from the involuntary administration of psychotropic drugs.

in the regulations before it, the Court decided that the State had created a protected liberty interest. It nevertheless, held, as it had in *Greenholtz*, that the full panoply of procedures conferred in *Wolff* were unnecessary to safeguard the inmates' interest and, if imposed, would undermine the prison's management objectives.

As this methodology took hold, no longer did inmates need to rely on a showing that they had suffered a '"grievous loss"' of liberty retained even after sentenced to terms of imprisonment. For the Court had ceased to examine the "nature" of the interest with respect to interests allegedly created by the State. In a series of cases since *Hewitt*, the Court has wrestled with the language of intricate, often rather routine prison guidelines to determine whether mandatory language and substantive predicates created an enforceable expectation that the State would produce a particular outcome with respect to the prisoner's conditions of confinement.

****

I

By shifting the focus of the liberty interest inquiry to one based on the language of a particular regulation, and not the nature of the deprivation, the Court encouraged prisoners to comb regulations in search of mandatory language on which to base entitlements to various state-conferred privileges. Courts have, in response, and not altogether illogically, drawn negative inferences from mandatory language in the text of prison regulations. The Court of Appeals' approach in this case is typical: It inferred from the mandatory directive that a finding of guilt "shall" be imposed under certain conditions the conclusion that the absence of such conditions prevents a finding of guilt.

Such a conclusion may be entirely sensible in the ordinary task of construing a statute defining rights and remedies available to the general public. It is a good deal less sensible in the case of a prison regulation primarily designed to guide correctional officials in the administration of a prison. Not only are such regulations not designed to confer rights on inmates, but the result of the negative implication jurisprudence is not to require the prison officials to follow the negative implication drawn from the regulation, but is instead to attach procedural protections that may be of quite a different nature. Here, for example, the Court of Appeals did not hold that a finding of guilt could *not* be made in the *absence* of substantial evidence. Instead, it held that the "liberty interest" created by the regulation entitled the inmate to the procedural protections set forth in *Wolff*.

Hewitt has produced at least two undesirable effects. First, it creates disincentives for States to codify prison management procedures in the interest of uniform treatment. Prison administrators need be concerned with the safety of the staff and inmate population. Ensuring that welfare often leads prison administrators to curb the discretion of staff on the front line who daily encounter prisoners hostile to the authoritarian structure of the prison environment. Such guidelines are not set forth solely to benefit the prisoner. They also aspire to instruct subordinate employees how to exercise discretion vested by the State in the warden, and to confine the authority of prison personnel in order to avoid widely different treatment of similar incidents. The approach embraced by *Hewitt* discourages this desirable development: States may avoid creation of "liberty" interests by having scarcely any regulations, or by conferring standardless discretion on correctional personnel.

Second, the *Hewitt* approach has led to the involvement of federal courts in the day-to-day management of prisons, often squandering judicial resources with little offsetting benefit to anyone. In so doing, it has run counter to the view expressed in several of our cases that federal courts ought to afford appropriate deference and flexibility to state officials trying to manage a volatile environment. . . .

In light of the above discussion, we believe that the search for a negative implication from mandatory language in prisoner regulations has strayed from the real concerns undergirding the liberty protected by the Due Process Clause. The time has come to return to the due process principles we believe were correctly established and applied in *Wolff and Meachum.*[5] Following *Wolff,* we recognize that States may under certain circumstances create liberty interests which are protected by the Due Process Clause. See also *Board of Pardons v. Allen,* 482 U.S. 369 (1987). But these interests will be generally limited to freedom from restraint which, while not exceeding the sentence in such an unexpected manner as to give rise to protection by the Due Process Clause of its own force, see, *e.g., Vitek,* 445 U.S., at 493 (transfer to mental hospital), and *Washington,* 494 U.S., at 221-222 (involuntary administration of psychotropic drugs), nonetheless imposes atypical and significant hardship on the inmate in relation to the ordinary incidents of prison life.

Conner asserts, incorrectly, that any state action taken for a punitive reason encroaches upon a liberty interest under the Due Process Clause even in the absence of any state regulation. Neither *Bell v. Wolfish,* 441 U.S. 520 (1979), nor *Ingraham v. Wright,* 430 U.S. 651 (1977), requires such a rule. *Bell* dealt with the interests of pretrial detainees and not convicted prisoners. . . . The Court in *Bell* correctly noted that a detainee "may not be punished prior to an adjudication of guilt in accordance with due process of law." The Court expressed concern that a State would attempt to punish a detainee for the crime for which he was indicted via preconviction holding conditions. Such a course would improperly extend the legitimate reasons for which such persons are detained—to ensure their presence at trial.[6]

The same distinction applies to *Ingraham,* which addressed the rights of

---

[5] Such abandonment of *Hewitt's* methodology does not technically require us to overrule any holding of this Court. The Court in *Olim v. Wakinekona,* 461 U.S. 238 (1983), and *Kentucky Dept. of Corrections v. Thompson,* 490 U.S. 454 (1989), concluded no liberty interest was at stake. Although it did locate a liberty interest in *Hewitt,* it concluded that due process required no additional procedural guarantees for the inmate. As such, its answer to the anterior question of whether the inmate possessed a liberty interest at all was unnecessary to the disposition of the case. Our decision today only abandons an approach that in practice is difficult to administer and which produces anomalous results.

[6] Similar concerns drove the conclusion in *Kennedy v. Mendoza-Martinez,* 372 U.S. 144 (1963), holding that free citizens must receive procedural protections prior to revocation of citizenship for draft evasion. Without discussing "liberty interests," the Court recognized that deprivation of the "most precious right" of citizenship necessitated process by way of jury trial under the Fifth and Sixth Amendments. *Id.,* at 159. As in *Bell,* the Court feared the Government would enforce the criminal law

schoolchildren to remain free from arbitrary corporal punishment. The Court noted that the Due Process Clause historically encompassed the notion that the State could not "physically punish an individual except in accordance with due process of law" and so found schoolchildren sheltered. Although children sent to public school are lawfully confined to the classroom, arbitrary corporal punishment represents an invasion of personal security to which their parents do not consent when entrusting the educational mission to the State.

The punishment of incarcerated prisoners, on the other hand, serves different aims than those found invalid in *Bell* and *Ingraham*. The process does not impose retribution in lieu of a valid conviction, nor does it maintain physical control over free citizens forced by law to subject themselves to state control over the educational mission. It effectuates prison management and prisoner rehabilitative goals. Admittedly, prisoners do not shed all constitutional rights at the prison gate, *Wolff*, 418 U.S., at 555, but "'[l]awful incarceration brings about the necessary withdrawal or limitation of many privileges and rights, a retraction justified by the considerations underlying our penal system.'" Discipline by prison officials in response to a wide range of misconduct falls within the expected perimeters of the sentence imposed by a court of law.

This case, though concededly punitive, does not present a dramatic departure from the basic conditions of Conner's indeterminate sentence. Although Conner points to dicta in cases implying that solitary confinement automatically triggers due process protection, *Wolff, supra*, at 571, n. 19, . . . this Court has not had the opportunity to address in an argued case the question whether disciplinary confinement of inmates itself implicates constitutional liberty interests. We hold that Conner's discipline in segregated confinement did not present the type of atypical, significant deprivation in which a State might conceivably create a liberty interest. The record shows that, at the time of Conner's punishment, disciplinary segregation, with insignificant exceptions, mirrored those conditions imposed upon inmates in administrative segregation and protective custody.[7] We note also that the State expunged Conner's disciplinary record with respect to the "high misconduct" charge nine months after Conner served time in segregation. Thus, Conner's confinement did not exceed similar, but totally discretionary, confinement in either duration or degree of restriction. Indeed, the conditions at Halawa involve significant amounts of "lockdown time" even for inmates in the general population.[8] Based on a comparison between inmates inside and outside disciplinary segregation, the State's actions in placing him there for 30 days did not work a major disruption in his environment.[9]

---

punishing draft evasion through the back door of denaturalization without prosecution for said crimes. 372 U.S., at 186.

[7] Hawaii has repealed the regulations describing the structure of inmate privileges in the SHU when confined in administrative segregation, but it retains inmate classification category "Maximum Custody I" in which inmate privileges are comparably limited.

[8] General population inmates are confined to cells for anywhere between 12 and 16 hours a day, depending on their classification.

[9] The State notes, ironically, that Conner requested that he be placed in protective custody after he had been released from disciplinary segregation. Conner's own expectations have at times reflected a personal preference for the quietude of the SHU. Although we do not think a prisoner's subjective

***

We hold, therefore, that neither the Hawaii prison regulation in question, nor the Due Process Clause itself, afforded Conner a protected liberty interest that would entitle him to the procedural protections set forth in *Wolff*. The regime to which he was subjected as a result of the misconduct hearing was within the range of confinement to be normally expected for one serving an indeterminate term of 30 years to life.[11]

The judgment of the Court of Appeals is accordingly

Reversed.

Questions and Comments

1. After *Sandin,* is a prisoner who is placed in solitary confinement as punishment for violation of prison regulations entitled to a hearing or to other procedures in which he has the opportunity to show his innocence? Does your answer depend upon how long the inmate is held in solitary confinement? Did *Sandin* overrule *Wolff*?

2. If solitary confinement does not trigger the due process clause, what would? Does *Sandin* give unreviewable discretion to prison officials to treat inmates anyway they please?

3. Does the Court's reference to "grievous loss" suggest the wisdom of Justice Frankfurter's formulation of procedural due process rights in *Joint-AntiFascist Refugee Committee v. McGrath*? Is the Court attempting to codify "grievous loss" in its new standard of "atypical and significant hardship" in relation to the ordinary incidents to prison life.

4. What is the Court's rationale for ruling that mandatory regulations do not create liberty interests in inmates? Do you agree with the Court that inmates procedural due process rights discouraged states from adopting mandatory regulations governing the conduct of correctional personnel? Do mandatory regulations benefit inmates, even if they create no liberty interests in them?

Wilkinson v. Austin
545 U.S. 209 (2005)

CHIEF JUSTICE REHNQUIST delivered the opinion of the Court.

This case involves a challenge by inmates to the procedures employed in assigning them to a "supermax" prison (the Ohio State Penitentiary (or "OSP").

---

expectation is dispositive of the liberty interest analysis, it does provide some evidence that the conditions suffered were expected within the contour of the actual sentence imposed.

[11] Prisoners such as Conner, of course, retain other protection from arbitrary state action even within the expected conditions of confinement. They may invoke the First and Eighth Amendments and the Equal Protection Clause of the Fourteenth Amendment where appropriate, and may draw upon internal prison grievance procedures and state judicial review where available.

Supermax facilities are maximum-security prisons with highly restrictive conditions, designed to segregate the most dangerous prisoners from the general prison population.

Under the governing Ohio procedure a classification review occurs either upon entry into the prison system or during the term of incarceration. The review process begins when a prison official prepares a three-page form detailing matters such as the inmate's recent violence, escape attempts, gang affiliation, underlying offense, and other pertinent details. A three-member Classification Committee reviews the proposed classification and holds a hearing. The inmate is notified 48 hours in advance with a summary of the conduct or offense triggering the review, and has access to the three-page form. The inmate, however, is not permitted to call witnesses at the hearing. If the Committee recommends OSP placement, it documents its decision in a Classification Committee Report setting forth the nature of the threat the inmate presents and the committee's reasons for the recommendation and a summary of any information presented at the hearing. This Report is then forwarded to the warden. If the warden agrees with the recommendation, he provides his reasons and forwards the report to the Bureau of Classification. A copy of the Report is then served upon the inmate, who has 15 days to file objections. At the end of that period, the Bureau reviews the Report and makes a final determination.

Consider this excerpt from Justice Kennedy's opinion for the Court:

The *Sandin* standard requires us to determine if assignment to OSP "imposes atypical and significant hardship on the inmate in relation to the ordinary incidents of prison life.". . .
In *Sandin*'s wake the Courts of Appeals have not reached consistent conclusions for identifying the baseline from which to measure what is atypical and significant in any particular prison system. . . . This divergence indicates the difficulty of locating the appropriate baseline, an issue that was not explored in the briefs. We need not resolve the issue here, however, for we are satisfied that assignment to OSP imposes an atypical and significant hardship under any plausible baseline. . .

Applying the three factors set forth in *Mathews* [the private interest affected, the risk of an erroneous deprivation, and the probable value, if any, of additional or substitute procedural safeguards], we find Ohio's New Policy provides a sufficient level of process.

Questions and Comments

In *Meachem v. Fano*, the Court ruled that the transfer of prisoners from a medium security prison to a maximum security facility with substantially less favourable conditions did not trigger procedural due process rights in the prisoners. How did the transfers involved in *Wilkerson* differ from those in *Meachem*? Is the "atypical and significant hardship" standard administrable?

G.   NOTE: THE DUE PROCESS CLAUSE AND REMEDIES FOR NEGLIGENCE AND INTENTIONAL TORTS

In *Paul v. Davis, supra*, Justice Rehnquist expressed his concern that the Fourteenth Amendment not be turned into "a font of tort law to be superimposed upon whatever systems may already be administered by the states." The Court soon discovered, however, that this concern was not easily effectuated. Six years after its 1976 decision in Paul v. Davis, the Court stumbled into *Parratt v. Taylor*, 451 U.S. 527 (1981) where it began an ill-conceived venture into the use of the Fourteenth Amendment as a device for the creation of tort law. Indeed, it was Justice Rehnquist himself who wrote the Parratt opinion.

In *Parratt v. Taylor*, an inmate of a Nebraska prison sued the Warden and Hobby Manager of the prison under § 1983 for the negligent loss of a $23.50 hobby kit by prison employees. In an opinion by Justice Rehnquist, the Court held that the prison employees had acted under color of state law, that the hobby kit fell within the definition of property and that the alleged loss, even though negligently caused, amounted to a deprivation but that the availability of state tort remedies provided the "process" required by the Fourteenth Amendment.

Shortly after its decision in *Parratt*, the Court decided *Logan v. Zimmerman Brush Co.*, 455 U.S. 422 (1982). In Logan, the Illinois Supreme Court had ruled that the failure of the Illinois Fair Employment Practices Commission to schedule a fact-finding conference within 120 days as required by statute divested an allegedly unlawfully discharged employee of his rights under the Illinois Fair Employment Practices Act (FEPA). The U.S. Supreme Court (through Justice Blackmun) ruled that the employee's remedies under that act were "property" within the meaning of the due process clause which could not be divested in that way, and that the state Commission was therefore required to hear his case. The Court rejected the contention that under *Parratt* the loss of the employee's remedies under the Illinois FEPA did not constitute a due process violation because of the availability to the employee of an action in tort against the state (because of the Commission's negligence) under the Illinois Court of Claims Act:

> This argument misses *Parratt*'s point. In *Parratt*, the Court emphasized that it was dealing with "a tortious loss of . . . property as a result of a random and unauthorized act by a state employee . . . not a result of some established state procedure. Here, in contrast, it is the state system itself that destroys a complainant's property interest, by operation of law, whenever the Commission fails to convene a timely conference whether the Commission's action is taken through negligence, maliciousness, or otherwise. . . . Unlike the complainant in *Parratt*, Logan is challenging not the Commission's error, but the "established state procedure" that destroys his entitlement without according him proper safeguards.

In *Hudson v. Palmer*, 468 U.S. 517 (1984) an inmate of a Virginia correctional institution brought a § 1983 suit charging that an officer at the institution intentionally destroyed a pillowcase during a search of his cell for contraband. The Supreme Court, in an opinion by Chief Justice Burger, ruled that unauthorized intentional destruction of an inmate's property by state employees does not violate the Due Process clause when adequate state post-deprivation remedies are available. The Court distinguished *Logan v. Zimmerman Brush Co., supra*, on the ground that the deprivation there took place "pursuant to an established state procedure" whereas in *Hudson v. Palmer* the deprivation, although intentional, was unauthorized. Since it was unauthorized, it was impracticable to provide other than post-deprivation process.

In early 1986, however, the Court decided two cases, *Daniels v. Williams*, 474 U.S. 327 (1986) and *Davidson v. Cannon*, 474 U.S. 344 (1986), which were designed to restructure the Court's approach to tort law. In *Daniels v. Williams*, the petitioner, a prisoner in the city jail of Richmond, Virginia, brought a § 1983 action to recover damages for back and ankle injuries allegedly sustained when he fell on a prison stairway as a result of slipping on a pillow negligently left on the stairs by a correctional deputy stationed at the jail. Because the deputy claimed that he was entitled to the defense of sovereign immunity in a state tort suit, the petitioner asserted that he was without an adequate state remedy and therefore was deprived of his "liberty" interest in freedom from bodily injury without due process of law. In an opinion by Justice Rehnquist, the Court overruled *Parratt* "to the extent that it states that mere lack of due care by a state official may 'deprive' an individual of life, liberty or property under the Fourteenth Amendment." To follow *Parratt* would "trivialize" the principle of due process of law which is concerned with "abuse" of power and "the large concerns of the governors and the governed."

In *Davidson v. Cannon* the petitioner, an inmate of the New Jersey State Prison sent a note to Cannon, the Assistant Superintendent of the prison reporting that another prisoner (McMillian) had threatened him. Cannon forwarded the note to a corrections sergeant who attended to other matters and forgot about the note. Neither Cannon nor the sergeant worked for the next two days, so the officers on duty were unaware of the threat. During this period the petitioner was attacked by McMillian who used a fork as a weapon to inflict injuries upon him. The Court, following *Daniels v. Williams*, ruled that although the prison authorities had been negligent in failing to take steps to protect the petitioner, that negligence did not constitute a deprivation in violation of the due process clause of the Fourteenth Amendment. Justice Brennan dissented in *Davidson* on the ground that the state's conduct amounted to "recklessness" or "deliberate indifference." Justice Blackmun, in a dissent in which Justice Marshall joined, expressed the view that by incarcerating the petitioner the state assumed the responsibility of exercising care in protecting him and that its negligent failure to do so was arbitrary action and an abuse of state power. Moreover, the state did not provide any post-deprivation remedy.

A more recent decision, *Zinermon v. Burch*, 494 U.S. 113 (1990), shows that negligence of state authorities can indeed give rise to a constitutional deprivation, and if the circumstances in which the negligence occurs is foreseeable, even the post-deprivation remedies required by *Parratt* will be insufficient. In this case, respondent Burch sued eleven physicians, administrators and staff of Florida State Hospital under § 1983 for admitting him as a "voluntary" mental patient when he was incompetent to give his informed consent to admission. Burch claimed that by so doing he was deprived of his liberty without due process. The defendants unsuccessfully asserted a *Parratt* defense: They claimed that "the State could not possibly have provided predeprivation process to prevent the kind of 'random, unauthorized' wrongful deprivation of liberty Burch alleges, so the postdeprivation remedies provided by Florida's statutory and common law necessarily are all the process Burch was due." In rejecting that defence, the Court (through Justice Blackmun) held that — contrary to the contentions of the defendants — it is foreseeable that some prospective patients will be incapable of giving informed consent to admission. In such circumstances, therefore, the state has a duty to take steps to ensure that such persons are not admitted on their own consent.

Burch, according to the allegations of his complaint, was deprived of a substantial liberty interest without either valid consent or an involuntary placement hearing, by the very state officials charged with the power to deprive mental patients of their liberty and the duty to implement procedural safeguards. Such a deprivation is foreseeable, due to the nature of mental illness, and will occur, if at all, at a predictable point in the admission process. Unlike *Parratt* and *Hudson*, this case does not represent the special instance of the *Mathews* due process analysis where post deprivation process is all that is due because no predeprivation safeguards would be of use in preventing the kind of deprivation alleged.

In so ruling, *Zinermon is* reaffirming the broad approach of *Mathews* which requires a pre-deprivation decisional process to be tested for accuracy. Because the pre-deprivation decisional process was susceptible to a high risk of error, the process itself was in need of reformation.

Justice Kennedy's concurring opinion in *Albright v. Oliver*, 510 U.S. 266 (1994) provides a later application of the issue involved in *Parratt*. A warrant was issued for the arrest of Albright for selling a substance which looked like an illegal drug. Upon learning of the warrant, Albright surrendered and was released on bail. Oliver (the detective to whom Albright surrendered) testified at the preliminary hearing that Albright sold the look-alike substance to another person, and the court found probable cause to bind him over for trial. Later the prosecution was dismissed on the ground that the charge did not state an offense under the law of Illinois, where the events occurred. Albright then brought a section 1983 action against Oliver, alleging that Oliver deprived him of substantive due process under the Fourteenth Amendment. In Albright's view, substantive due process conferred on him a right to be free from prosecution without probable cause. Justice Rehnquist, writing for a plurality, ruled that Albright could not state such a claim in substantive due process, because such claims do not lie where the Constitutional text provides an explicit source of protection. Under that analysis, Albright's claim should have been asserted as a Fourth Amendment claim, the Fourth Amendment applying to the states through the Fourteenth Amendment.

Justice Kennedy, concurring in the result, thought that Albright should seek his remedy in state court: "The common-sense teaching of *Parratt* is that some questions of property, contract, and tort law are best resolved by state legal systems without resort to the federal courts, even when a state actor is the alleged wrongdoer." 510 U.S. at 284. "As *Parratt's* precedential force must be acknowledged, I think it disposes of this case. Illinois provides a tort remedy for malicious prosecution. . . . Given the state remedy and the holding of *Parratt*, there is neither need nor legitimacy in invoking § 1983 in this case." *Id.*, at 285.

Chapter 4

THE BACKGROUND AND GENESIS OF THE ADMINISTRATIVE PROCEDURE ACT

A. THE *MORGAN* CASES AND RELATED MATTERS

MORGAN v. UNITED STATES
298 U.S. 468 (1936)

Mr. Justice Hughes delivered the opinion of the Court.

These are fifty suits, consolidated for the purpose of trial, to restrain the enforcement of an order of the Secretary of Agriculture, fixing maximum rates to be charged by market agencies for buying and selling livestock at the Kansas City Stock Yards. Packers and Stockyards Act, 1921. . . .

The proceeding was instituted by an order of the Secretary of Agriculture in April, 1930, directing an inquiry into the reasonableness of existing rates. Testimony was taken and an order prescribing rates followed in May, 1932. An application for rehearing, in view of changed economic conditions, was granted in July, 1932. After the taking of voluminous testimony, which was concluded in November, 1932, the order in question was made on June 14, 1933. Rehearing was refused on July 6, 1933.

Plaintiffs then brought these suits attacking the order, so far as it prescribed maximum charges for selling livestock, as illegal and arbitrary and as depriving plaintiffs of their property without due process of law in violation of the Fifth Amendment of the Constitution. The District Court of three judges entered decrees sustaining the order and dismissing the bills of complaint. . . . Plaintiffs bring this direct appeal. . . .

On the merits, plaintiffs assert that the ultimate basis for the reduction in commission rates is the Secretary's opinion that there are too many market agencies, too many salesmen, and too much competition in the business; that the Secretary has departed entirely from the evidence as to the actual cost of employing salesmen in selling cattle at these yards and has made an allowance for salaries which is based on pure speculation and is wholly inadequate to meet the cost of the service; that he has substituted in place of his accountants' figures as to actual expenditures, with respect to the item entitled "Business Getting and Maintaining Expense," a hypothetical allowance greatly less than actual cost; and that the Secretary has thus made findings without evidence and an order, essentially arbitrary, which prescribes unreasonable rates. . . .

Before reaching these questions we meet at the threshold of the controversy plaintiffs' additional contention that they have not been accorded the hearing which the statute requires. They rightly assert that the granting of that hearing is a prerequisite to the making of a valid order. The statute provides . . .

"Sec. 310. Whenever after full hearing upon a complaint made . . . or after full hearing under an order for investigation and hearing made by the Secretary on his own initiative, . . . the Secretary is of the opinion that any rate, charge, regulation, or practice of a stockyard owner or market agency, for or in connection with the furnishing of stockyard services, is or will be unjust, unreasonable, or discriminatory, the Secretary

(a) May determine and prescribe what will be the just and reasonable rate or charge, or rates or charges, to be thereafter observed in such case, or the maximum or minimum, or maximum and minimum, to be charged, and what regulation or practice is or will be just, reasonable, and non-discriminatory to be thereafter followed. . . ."

The allegations as to the failure to give a proper hearing . . . in substance are:. . . . That at the conclusion of the taking of the testimony before an examiner, a request was made that the examiner prepare a tentative report, which should be subject to oral argument and exceptions, so that a hearing might be had before the Secretary without undue inconvenience to him, but that the request was denied and no tentative report was exhibited to plaintiffs and no oral argument upon the issues presented by the order of inquiry and the evidence was at any time had before the Secretary. That the Secretary, without warrant of law, delegated to Acting Secretaries the determination of issues with respect to the reasonableness of the rates involved. That when the oral arguments were presented after the original hearing, and after the rehearing, the Secretary was neither sick, absent, nor otherwise disabled, but was at his office in the Department of Agriculture and the appointment of any other person as Acting Secretary was illegal. That the Secretary at the time he signed the order in question had not personally heard or read any of the evidence presented at any hearing in connection with the proceeding and had not heard or considered oral arguments relating thereto or briefs submitted on behalf of the plaintiffs, but that the sole information of the Secretary with respect to the proceeding was derived from consultation with employees in the Department of Agriculture out of the presence of the plaintiffs or any of their representatives.

On motion of the Government, the District Court struck out all the allegations in Paragraph IV of the bill of complaint and the plaintiffs were thus denied opportunity to require an answer to these allegations or to prove the facts alleged.

Certain facts appear of record. The testimony was taken before an examiner. At its conclusion, counsel for respondents stated "that he would continue to demand that the Secretary hear personally the argument of the evidence in behalf of the individual respondents, or at least have some definite course of procedure adopted whereby the examiner, or some one else, should formulate a report on the evidence so that the respondents could have the character of hearing and right to present their side of the issues in this case, which they believe the law entitles them to." The Government does not suggest that this request was granted and plaintiffs say that it was denied. Oral argument upon the evidence was had before the Acting Secretary of Agriculture. Subsequently, brief was filed on plaintiffs' behalf. Thereafter, reciting "careful consideration of the entire record in this proceeding," findings of fact and conclusions, and an order prescribing rates, were signed by the Secretary of Agriculture.

. . . . [I]n determining whether in conducting an administrative proceeding of this sort the Secretary has complied with the statutory prerequisites, the recitals of his procedure cannot be regarded as conclusive. Otherwise the statutory conditions could be set at naught by mere assertion. If upon the facts alleged, the "full hearing" required by the statute was not given, plaintiffs were entitled to prove the facts and have the Secretary's order set aside. Nor is it necessary to go beyond the terms of the statute in order to consider the constitutional requirement of due process as to notice and hearing. For the statute itself demands a full hearing and the order is void if such a hearing was denied. . . .

Second. — The outstanding allegation, which the District Court struck out, is that the Secretary made the rate order without having heard or read any of the evidence, and without having heard the oral arguments or having read or considered the briefs which the plaintiffs submitted. The only information which the Secretary had as to the proceeding was what he derived from consultation with employees of the Department.

The other allegations of the stricken paragraph do not go to the root of the matter. Thus, it cannot be said that the failure to hear the respondents separately was an abuse of discretion. Again, while it would have been good practice to have the examiner prepare a report and submit it to the Secretary and the parties, and to permit exceptions and arguments addressed to the points thus presented, — a practice found to be of great value in proceedings before the Interstate Commerce Commission — we cannot say that that particular type of procedure was essential to the validity of the hearing. The statute does not require it and what the statute does require relates to substance and not form.

Nor should the fundamental question be confused with one of mere delegation of authority. The Government urges that the Acting Secretary who heard the oral argument was in fact the Assistant Secretary of Agriculture whose duties are prescribed by the Act of February 9, 1889 . . . providing for his appointment and authorizing him to perform such duties in the conduct of the business of the Department of Agriculture as may be assigned to him by the Secretary. If the Secretary had assigned to the Assistant Secretary the duty of holding the hearing, and the Assistant Secretary accordingly had received the evidence taken by the examiner, had heard argument thereon and had then found the essential facts and made the order upon his findings, we should have had simply the question of delegation. But while the Assistant Secretary heard argument he did not make the decision. The Secretary who, according to the allegation, had neither heard nor read evidence or argument, undertook to make the findings and fix the rates. The Assistant Secretary, who had heard, assumed no responsibility for the findings or order, and the Secretary, who had not heard, did assume that responsibility.

Third. — What is the essential quality of the proceeding under review, and what is the nature of the hearing which the statute prescribes?

The proceeding is not one of ordinary administration, conformable to the standards governing duties of a purely executive character. It is a proceeding looking to legislative action in the fixing of rates of market agencies. And, while the order is legislative and gives to the proceeding its distinctive character . . . it is a proceeding which by virtue of the authority conferred has special attributes. The Secretary, as the agent of Congress in making the rates, must make them in accordance with the standards and under the limitations which Congress has prescribed. Congress has required the Secretary to determine, as a condition of his action, that the existing rates are or will be "unjust, unreasonable, or discriminatory." If and when he so finds, he may "determine and prescribe" what shall be the just and reasonable rate, or the maximum or minimum rate, thereafter to be charged. That duty is widely different from ordinary executive action. It is a duty which carries with it fundamental procedural requirements. There must be a full hearing. There must be evidence adequate to support pertinent and necessary findings of fact. Nothing can be treated as evidence which is not introduced as such. . . . Facts and circumstances which ought to be considered must not be excluded. Facts and circumstances must not be considered which should not legally influence the conclusion. Findings based on the evidence must embrace the basic facts which are needed to sustain the order. . . .

A proceeding of this sort requiring the taking and weighing of evidence, determinations of fact based upon the consideration of the evidence, and the making of an order supported by such findings, has a quality resembling that of a judicial proceeding. Hence it is frequently described as a proceeding of a *quasi-judicial* character. The requirement of a "full hearing" has obvious reference to the tradition of judicial proceedings in which evidence is received and weighed by the trier of the facts. The "hearing" is designed to afford the safeguard that the one who decides shall be bound in good conscience to consider the evidence, to be guided by that alone, and to reach his conclusion uninfluenced by extraneous considerations which in other fields might have play in determining purely executive action. The "hearing" is the hearing of evidence and argument. If the one who determines the facts which underlie the order has not considered evidence or argument, it is manifest that the hearing has not been given.

There is thus no basis for the contention that the authority conferred by § 310 of the Packers and Stockyards Act is given to the Department of Agriculture, as a department in the administrative sense, so that one official may examine evidence, and another official who has not considered the evidence may make the findings and order. In such a view, it would be possible, for example, for one official to hear the evidence and argument and arrive at certain conclusions of fact, and another official who had not heard or considered either evidence or argument to overrule those conclusions and for reasons of policy to announce entirely different ones. It is no answer to say that the question for the court is whether the evidence supports the findings and the findings support the order. For the weight ascribed by law to the findings — their conclusiveness when made within the sphere of the authority conferred — rests upon the assumption that the officer who makes the findings has addressed himself to the evidence and upon that evidence has conscientiously reached the conclusions which he deems it to justify. That duty cannot be performed by one who has not considered evidence or argument. It is not an impersonal obligation. It is a duty akin to that of a judge. The one who decides must hear.

This necessary rule does not preclude practicable administrative procedure in obtaining the aid of assistants in the department. Assistants may prosecute inquiries. Evidence may be taken by an examiner. Evidence thus taken may be sifted and analyzed by competent subordinates. Argument may be oral or written. The requirements are not technical. But there must be a hearing in a substantial sense. And to give the substance of a hearing, which is for the purpose of making determinations upon evidence, the officer who makes the determinations must consider and appraise the evidence which justifies them. That duty undoubtedly may be an onerous one, but the performance of it in a substantial manner is inseparable from the exercise of the important authority conferred.

Our conclusion is that the District Court erred in striking out the allegations . . . of the bill of complaint with respect to the Secretary's actions. The defendants should be required to answer these allegations and the question whether plaintiffs had a proper hearing should be determined.

Reversed.

Questions and Comments

1.   The plaintiffs were "marketing agencies", firms performing a function similar to brokering at the Kansas City stockyards. Under the governing Packers and Stockyards Act, they were entitled to a "full hearing" before the Secretary of Agriculture ordered their rates reduced. They had an extensive hearing before a hearing officer as this and the next case make clear. Why did not this hearing fulfill the statutory requirements for a full hearing?

2.   The plaintiffs are not claiming that just because the hearing officer did not issue the rate order, they were not given a full hearing, are they? The plaintiffs, therefore, accept, do they not, the legitimacy of the hearing being presided over by an official who himself does not decide?

3.   Who presided at oral argument after the conclusion of the proceeding before the hearing officer? Who issued the rate order? Are the plaintiffs complaining because the official who presided at oral argument was the Assistant Secretary of Agriculture while the official who issued the rate order was the Secretary? Were the plaintiffs complaining because they believed that the Secretary of Agriculture was not adequately informed about the case?

4.   Did the proceeding before the hearing officer help to inform either the Acting Secretary or the Secretary about the case? If neither official was present at the proceeding before the hearing officer, how could that proceeding educate either official about the case? Explain.

5.   Did the proceeding before the hearing officer provide a background for oral argument before the Acting Secretary? Would the arguments of the marketing agencies and the government help the Acting Secretary to find those parts of the record of the proceeding before the hearing officer which were most relevant to a final disposition of the case? Would the Acting Secretary be adequately informed

about the case as a result of the procedure used (i.e., trial before a hearing officer, followed by oral and written argument to the Acting Secretary)?

6.   The Court said that it would have been "good practice" for the hearing officer (i.e., the examiner) to have prepared a report and that such a procedure was found of "great value" in proceedings before the Interstate Commerce Commission. Why would the examiner's preparation of a report have been of value? of value to whom? Why did the Court not require the preparation of such a report if it would have substantially aided the decisional process?

7.   If the procedure actually used was adequate to inform the Acting Secretary about the case, why could not he (i.e., the Acting Secretary) issue the rate order in the name of the Secretary? Was this done? not done? How do you know? Would the Court have upheld a rate order issued by the Acting Secretary in the name of the Secretary? Did the Court advert to that issue?

8.   The Court ruled that the "one who decides must hear." The Court further stated that the Secretary's obligation was not an impersonal one. Did the Court mean that the Secretary had to preside at oral argument? to read the briefs? Is it practicable for the Secretary of Agriculture personally to preside at oral argument and to read the briefs in every rate hearing where an order is ultimately issued in his name? Was the Court therefore implying that the Secretary would have to delegate the task of issuing rate orders to those of his subordinates who had the time to preside at oral arguments and to ponder the briefs submitted in connection with those arguments? To what extent could the Secretary be aided by assistants? Could a judicious use of assistants within the Department help the Secretary both to be informed about the case and to economize on his time for use on other tasks? If the Secretary could receive help from assistants, why could not the Secretary be aided on the case by the Assistant Secretary who had the benefit of oral argument? Had the Secretary been so aided, would he then have been deemed properly to have "heard" the case? and therefore have been entitled to "decide" it?

MORGAN v. UNITED STATES
304 U.S. 1 (1938)

Mr. Justice Hughes delivered the opinion of the Court.

The case comes here for the second time. . . .

After the remand, the bills were amended and interrogatories were directed to the Secretary which he answered. The [District] Court received the evidence which had been introduced at its previous hearing, together with additional testimony bearing upon the nature of the hearing accorded by the Secretary. This evidence embraced the testimony of the Secretary and of several of his assistants. The District Court rendered an opinion . . . holding that the hearing before the Secretary was adequate and, on the merits, that his order was lawful. . . .

In the record now before us the controlling facts stand out clearly. The original administrative proceeding was begun on April 7, 1930, when the Secretary of Agriculture issued an order of inquiry and notice of hearing with respect to the reasonableness of the charges of appellants for stockyard services at Kansas City. The taking of evidence before an examiner of the Department was begun on December 3, 1930, and continued until February 10, 1931. The Government and appellants were represented by counsel and voluminous testimony and exhibits were introduced. In March, 1931, oral argument was had before the Acting Secretary of Agriculture and appellants submitted a brief. On May 18, 1932, the Secretary issued his findings and an order prescribing maximum rates. In view of changed economic conditions, the Secretary vacated that order and granted a rehearing. That was begun on October 6, 1932 and the taking of evidence received at the first hearing was re-submitted and this was supplemented by additional testimony and exhibits. On March 24, 1933, oral argument was had before Rexford G. Tugwell as Acting Secretary.

It appears that there were about 10,000 pages of transcript of oral evidence and over 10,000 pages of statistical exhibits. The oral argument was general and sketchy. Appellants submitted the brief which they had presented after the first administrative hearing and a supplemental brief dealing with the evidence introduced upon the rehearing. No brief was at any time supplied by the Government. Apart from what was said on its behalf in the oral argument, the Government formulated no issues and furnished no statement or summary of its contentions and no proposed findings. Appellants' request that the examiner prepare a tentative report, to be submitted as a basis for exceptions and argument, was refused.

Findings were prepared in the Bureau of Animal Industry, Department of Agriculture, whose representatives conducted the proceedings for the Government, and were submitted to the Secretary, who signed them, with a few changes in the rates, when his order was made on June 14, 1933. These findings, 180 in number, were elaborate. They dealt with the practices and facilities at the Kansas City livestock market, the character of appellants' business and services, their rates and the volume of their transactions, their gross revenues, their methods in getting and maintaining business, their joint activities, the economic changes since the year 1929, the principles which governed the determination of reasonable commission rates, the classification of cost items, the reasonable unit costs plus a reasonable amount of profits to be covered into reasonable commission rates, the reasonable amounts to be included for salesmanship, yarding salaries and expenses, office salaries and expenses, business getting and maintaining expenses, administrative and general expenses, insurance, interest on capital, and profits, together with summary and the establishment of the rate structure. Upon the basis of the reasonable costs as thus determined, the Secretary found that appellants' schedules of rates were unreasonable and unjustly discriminatory and fixed the maximum schedules of the just and reasonable rates thereafter to be charged.

No opportunity was afforded to appellants for the examination of the findings thus prepared in the Bureau of Animal Industry until they were served with the order. Appellants sought a rehearing by the Secretary but their application was denied on July 6, 1933, and these suits followed.

The part taken by the Secretary himself in the departmental proceedings is shown by his full and candid testimony. The evidence had been received before he took office. He did not hear the oral argument. The bulky record was placed upon his desk and he dipped into it from time to time to get its drift. He decided that probably the essence of the evidence was contained in appellants' briefs. These, together with the transcript of the oral argument, he took home with him and read. He had several conferences with the Solicitor of the Department and with the officials in the Bureau of Animal Industry and discussed the proposed findings. He testified that he considered the evidence before signing the order. The substance of his action is stated in his answer to the question whether the order represented his independent conclusion, as follows:

"My answer to the question would be that very definitely was my independent conclusion as based on the findings of the men in the Bureau of Animal Industry. I would say, I will try to put it as accurately as possible, that it represented my own independent reactions to the findings of the men in the Bureau of Animal Industry."

Save for certain rate alterations, he "accepted the findings."

In the light of this testimony there is no occasion to discuss the extent to which the Secretary examined the evidence, and we agree with the Government's contention that it was not the function of the court to probe the mental processes of the Secretary in reaching his conclusions if he gave the hearing which the law required. The Secretary read the summary presented by appellants' briefs and he conferred with his subordinates who had sifted and analyzed the evidence. We assume that the Secretary sufficiently understood its purport. But a "full hearing" — a fair and open hearing requires more than that. The right to a hearing embraces not only the right to know the claims of the opposing party and to meet them. The right to submit argument implies that opportunity; otherwise the right may be but a barren one. Those who are brought into contest with the Government in a quasi-judicial proceeding aimed at the control of their activities are entitled to be fairly advised of what the Government proposes and to be heard upon its proposals before it issues its final command.

No such reasonable opportunity was accorded appellants. The administrative proceeding was initiated by a notice of inquiry into the reasonableness of appellants' rates. No specific complaint was formulated and, in a proceeding thus begun by the Secretary on his own initiative, none was required. Thus, in the absence of any definite complaint, and in a sweeping investigation, thousands of pages of testimony were taken by the examiner and numerous complicated exhibits were introduced bearing upon all phases of the broad subject of the conduct of the market agencies. In the absence of any report by the examiner or any findings proposed by the Government, and thus without any concrete statement of the Government's claims, the parties approached the oral argument.

Nor did the oral argument reveal these claims in any appropriate manner. The discussion by counsel for the Government was "very general," as he said, in order not to take up "too much time." It dealt with generalities both as to principles and procedure. Counsel for appellants then discussed the evidence from his standpoint. The Government's counsel closed briefly, with a few additional and general observations. The oral argument was of the sort which might serve as a preface to a discussion of definite points in a brief, but the Government did not submit a brief.

And the appellants had no further information of the Government's concrete claims until they were served with the Secretary's order.

Congress, in requiring a "full hearing," had regard to judicial standards, — not in any technical sense but with respect to those fundamental requirements of fairness which are of the essence of due process in a proceeding of a judicial nature. If in an equity cause, a special master or the trial judge permitted the plaintiff's attorney to formulate the findings upon the evidence, conferred ex parte with the plaintiff's attorney regarding them, and then adopted his proposals without affording an opportunity to his opponent to know their contents and present objections, there would be no hesitation in setting aside the report or decree as having been made without a fair hearing. The requirements of fairness are not exhausted in the taking or consideration of evidence but extend to the concluding parts of the procedure as well as to the beginning and intermediate steps.

The answer that the proceeding before the Secretary was not of an adversary character, as it was not upon complaint but was initiated as a general inquiry, is futile. It has regard to the mere form of the proceeding and ignores realities. In all substantial respects, the Government acting through the Bureau of Animal Industry was prosecuting the proceeding against the owners of the market agencies. The proceeding had all the essential elements of contested litigation, with the Government and its counsel on the one side and the appellants and their counsel on the other. . . .

The Government adverts to an observation in our former opinion that, while it was good practice — which we approved — to have the examiner, receiving the evidence in such a case, prepare a report as a basis for exceptions and argument, we could not say that that particular type of procedure was essential to the validity of the proceeding. That is true. . . . Conceivably, the Secretary, in a case the narrow limits of which made such a procedure practicable, might himself hear the evidence and the contentions of both parties and make his findings upon the spot. Again, the evidence being in, the Secretary might receive the proposed findings of both parties, each being notified of the proposals of the other, hear argument thereon and make his own findings. But what would not be essential to the adequacy of the hearing if the Secretary himself makes the findings is not a criterion for a case in which the Secretary accepts and makes as his own the findings which have been prepared by the active prosecutors for the Government, after an *ex parte* discussion with them and without according any reasonable opportunity to the respondents in the proceedings to know the claims thus presented and to contest them. That is more than an irregularity in practice; it is a vital defect.

As the hearing was fatally defective, the order of the Secretary was invalid. In this view, we express no opinion upon the merits. The decree of the District Court is *Reversed.*

Questions and Comments

1. Do you have a better understanding of the Secretary's method of deciding the case after having read the Supreme Court's second *Morgan* opinion? Was the Secretary in fact informed about the issues in the case? The Court here was not concerned that the Secretary was issuing an order in a case which he knew nothing about, was it?

2. How did the Secretary learn about the issues in the case? From the officials in the Bureau of Animal Industry? What employees in the Department of Agriculture knew more about the case than the employees in the Bureau of Animal Industry? Is it accurate to say that the Secretary learned about the issues in the case from those people within his Department who were most informed about them?

3. The Court referred to the conferences between the Secretary and the officials of the Bureau of Animal Industry as analogous to an *ex parte* conference by the trial judge with the plaintiff's attorney. Later the Court referred to those officials as "the active prosecutors for the Government." Was the Court's concern that the information supplied to the Secretary by the officials in the Bureau of Animal Industry may have been skewed or warped by their adversary roles?

4. The Secretary of Agriculture has (and had) many responsibilities. The determination of the rates for marketing agencies in the Kansas City stockyards was a minor one, to which the Secretary could not practically devote substantial time. Yet the record contained over 10,000 pages of transcript and over 10,000 pages of statistical exhibits. Clearly the Secretary could not actually read 20,000 pages of evidence and still perform his other Departmental responsibilities.

5. It was also evident that the argument before the Acting Secretary was probably not of much help even to the Acting Secretary in understanding the case. The Government did not submit a brief and its oral argument was sketchy. Then how did the Government think that it could get its case to the Secretary? The Government was obviously relying on some method of educating the Secretary other than the formal proceedings, was it not?

6. It was unnecessary for the Government to set forth its arguments precisely in a brief or in oral argument, because the officials who were preparing the Government's case conferred directly with the Secretary outside of the formal proceedings.

7. Why did the Court bring up again the fact that the examiner had not prepared a report? Was the Court here adverting to the fact that the formal procedures were incapable of adequately informing the Secretary about the case?

8. If the examiner had prepared a report, that report could have been the basis upon which the contending sides could have focused their briefs and oral arguments to the Secretary, could it not? Without such a report, each side is left with 20,000 pages of evidence to discuss in its brief. With such a report, each side can focus its brief on the parts of the report with which it disagrees. The report thus could serve as a mechanism for focusing and narrowing the issues for argument before the Secretary.

9.   Without a report expressing the examiner's conclusions on the evidence submitted, the formal procedures just could not work adequately to inform the Secretary about the issues involved in the rate case. With such a report, the formal procedures could have educated the Secretary about the relevant issues; and they could have done so without imposing unreasonable time demands upon him.

Note

The *Morgan* cases bring to our attention a number of problematic features of administrative regulation. First, the decisions in those cases were made as a result of ex parte consultation between the ultimate decision-maker and officials or employees of the department which he headed. To the extent that the final decision-maker relied upon *ex parte* communications with these other officials, the private parties had no opportunity to challenge or explain away the input of those officials and the decisional process was taken out of the adversary mode in which it was formally cast.

Second, the *ex parte* communications came from officials who had been cast in an adversary role. Although these officials were probably extremely well informed about the issues in the case, their adversary role may have distorted their capacity for independent judgment. When they communicated with the Secretary, therefore, they may have provided information and views on the case that was skewed in favor of their own litigating position. And the private parties had no opportunity to challenge or explain away any such distortions.

Third, as the questions following the case bring out, a problem in complex cases like the *Morgan* ones is how the final decision-maker can be adequately informed about the issues through procedures which provide for meaningful participation by the affected parties. The formally established procedures in the *Morgan* cases did not operate to educate the decision-maker about the issues. That is why the Secretary felt that he had to learn about those issues from consultations with the officials in the Bureau of Animal Industry.

Fourth, the *Morgan* cases begin to raise issues which are broader than the facts of those cases themselves. Because of the way the officials of the Department (including the Secretary) freely consulted among themselves about a pending case, an observer might be tempted to perceive the rate dispute as between the private parties and the Department as such. Yet viewed in such a way the Department becomes both a "prosecutor" or advocate and a judge or adjudicator. And the combination, at least in one person, of the functions of prosecutor and judge has long been viewed as improper. Can the combination of prosecutor and judge in one Department — headed by a single individual — be a proper one? Can private parties expect to be treated fairly by such a department? Are special safeguards needed to ensure fairness by such a department?

These are all classic questions of administrative law. They were addressed in a forthright and thorough way in the Final Report of the Attorney General's Committee to Study Administrative Procedure, an extract from which appears below.

Excerpt from Final Report of Attorney General's Committee on Administrative Procedure, Separation of the Adjudicating Function From Other Administrative Activities (S. Doc. No. 8, 77th Cong., lst Sess. 1941):

Two characteristic tasks of a prosecutor are those of investigation and advocacy. It is clear that when a controversy reaches the stage of hearing and formal adjudication the persons who did the actual work of investigating and building up the case should play no part in the decision. This is because the investigators, if allowed to participate, would be likely to interpolate facts and information discovered by them ex parte and not adduced at the hearing, where the testimony is sworn and subject to cross-examination and rebuttal. In addition, an investigator's function may in part be that of a detective, whose purpose is to ferret out and establish a case. Of course, this may produce a state of mind incompatible with the objective impartiality which must be brought to bear in the process of deciding. For this same reason, the advocate — the agency's attorney who upheld a definite position adverse to the private parties at the hearing — cannot be permitted to participate after the hearing in the making of the decision. A man who has buried himself in one side of an issue is disabled from bringing to its decision that dispassionate judgment which Anglo-American tradition demands of officials who decide questions. Clearly the advocate's view ought to be presented publicly and not privately to those who decide.

These types of commingling of functions of investigation or advocacy with the function of deciding are thus plainly undesirable. But they are also avoidable and should be avoided by appropriate internal division of labor. For the disqualifications produced by investigation or advocacy are personal psychological ones which result from engaging in those types of activity; and the problem is simply one of isolating those who engage in the activity. Creation of independent hearing commissioners insulated from all phases of a case other than hearing and deciding will, the Committee believes, go far toward solving this problem at the level of the initial hearing provided the proper safeguards are established to assure the insulation. A similar result can be achieved at the level of final decision on review by the agency heads by permitting the views of the investigators and advocates to be presented only in open hearing where they can be known and met by those who may be adversely affected by them.

A distinctive function, which may be regarded as one of prosecution, is that of making preliminary decisions to issue a complaint or to proceed to formal hearing in cases which later the agency heads will decide. Before a complaint is issued — if an agency has power to initiate proceedings on its own motion or on charges filed by a private person — or before an application raising doubtful questions is set down for formal hearing, a determination must be made that the action is proper. The Committee has heretofore recommended, on grounds of administrative efficiency, that authority to make such preliminary determinations should be delegated as far as possible to appropriate officers. Where this is done, no question can arise that the ultimate deciding officers have been biased through having made, ex parte, a preliminary determination in a case which they have later to decide. Yet such delegation, of course, cannot be complete; novel and difficult questions must from time to time be presented to the heads of the agency. The question must be faced, therefore, whether the making of such a preliminary determination in itself works unfairness in the final decision. Assuming that the agency heads simply pass on the sufficiency of material developed and presented to them by others, the Committee is satisfied that no such unfairness results. What is done is wholly comparable to what a court does in the first stage of a show cause proceeding, or in the issuance of a writ of certiorari. No decision on the merits is made; the court, or the agency, merely concludes that the situation warrants further examination in formal proceedings. The ultimate judgment of the agency heads need be no more influenced by the preliminary authorization to proceed than is the ultimate judgment of a court by the issuance of a temporary restraining order pending a formal hearing for a permanent injunction.

Questions and Comments

1.   Examine § 554(d) of the APA. Can you identify the ways in which the *Morgan* cases influenced its provisions?

2.   Examine § 556 of the APA. Can you identify the ways in which its drafters were influenced by the *Morgan* cases?

3.   Although the *Morgan* cases influenced the structure of § 554(d), the provisions of § 554(d) do not apply to rate cases like the *Morgan* cases. Proceedings for future ratemaking fall within the definition of rulemaking and hence not within the adjudication provisions of § 554. *See §§* 551(4), (5). Proceedings governing past rates do not fall within the definition of rulemaking and hence involve adjudication; but they are exempted from the provisions of § 554(d). *See §§* 551(4), (5), (6), (7) and § 554(d)(B).

4.   The reasons why the APA is structured in these ways is considered below.

OHIO BELL TELEPHONE CO. v. PUBLIC UTILITIES COMMISSION OF OHIO
301 U.S. 292 (1937)

Mr. Justice Cardozo delivered the opinion of the Court.

[In consolidated rate proceedings concerning the Ohio Bell Telephone Company's rates for several years, thousands of pages of testimony and many exhibits were received in evidence. As part of the process of determining just and reasonable rates, the Commission made a determination as to the value of the Company's property. The proceedings which had been underway since 1924 lasted into 1934.1

. . . On January 16, 1934, the Commission made its findings and order setting forth what purports to be a final valuation. The intrastate property as of June 30,

1925, was valued at $93,707,488; the total property, interstate and intrastate, at $96,422,276.

The Commission did not confine itself however, to a valuation of the property as of the date certain. It undertook also to fix a valuation for each of the years 1926 to 1933 inclusive. For this purpose it took judicial notice of price trends during those years, modifying the value which it had found as of the date certain by the percentage of decline or rise applicable to the years thereafter. The first warning that it would do this came in 1934 with the filing of its report. "The trend of land values was ascertained," according to the findings, "from examination of the tax value in communities where the company had its largest real estate holdings." "For building trends resort was had to price indices of the Engineering News Record, a recognized magazine in the field of engineering construction." "Labor trends were developed from the same sources." Reference was made also to the findings of a federal court in Illinois . . . as to the price levels upon sales of apparatus and equipment by Western Electric, an affiliated corporation. The findings were not in evidence, though much of the testimony and exhibits on which they rested had been received by stipulation for certain limited purposes, and mainly to discover whether the prices paid to the affiliate were swollen beyond reason. . . . The Commission consulted these findings as indicative of market trends and leaned upon them heavily. By resort to these and cognate sources, the value at the beginning of 1926 was fixed at 98.73% of the value at the date certain; the 1927 value at 95.7%; the 1928 value at 95%; the 1929 value at 96.3%; the 1930 value at 92.2%; the 1931 value at 86.6%; the 1932 value at 76.8%; the 1933 value at 79.1%. Upon that basis the company was found to have been in receipt of excess earnings of $13,289,172, distributed as follows: for 1925, $1,822,647; for 1926, $2,041,483; for 1927, $1,986,610; for 1928, $1,925,301; for 1929, $1,463,347; for 1930, $1,481,689; for 1931, $1,659,760; for 1932, $908,335; for 1933, nothing. The excess was arrived at by figuring a return of 7% upon the value as a reasonable rate for the years 1925 to 1929 inclusive; 6.5% for the years 1930 and 1931; and 5.5% for the years 1932 and 1933. . . . [The Commission prescribed] a refund of the full amount of the excess for the years in which excess earnings were found to have been realized. . . .

The company protested and moved for a rehearing. In its protest it stated that the trend percentages accepted in the findings as marking a decline in values did not come from any official sources which the Commission had the right to notice judicially; that they had not been introduced into evidence; that the company had not been given an opportunity to explain or rebut them; and that their use by the Commission had denied a fair hearing in contravention of the requirements of the Fourteenth Amendment. . . . By order dated March 1, 1934, the protests were overruled. . . .

First: The fundamentals of a trial were denied to the appellant when rates previously collected were ordered to be refunded upon the strength of evidential facts not spread upon the record.

The Commission had given notice that the value of the property would be fixed as of a date certain. Evidence directed to the value at that time had been laid before the triers of the facts in thousands of printed pages. To make the picture more complete, evidence had been given as to the value at cost of additions and retirements. Without warning or even the hint of warning that the case would be considered or determined upon any other basis than the evidence submitted, the Commission cut down the values for the years after the date certain upon the strength of information secretly collected and never yet disclosed. The company protested. It asked disclosure of the documents indicative of price trends, and an opportunity to examine them, to analyze them, to explain and to rebut them. The response was a curt refusal. Upon the strength of these unknown documents refunds have been ordered for sums mounting into millions, the Commission reporting its conclusion, but not the underlying proofs. The putative debtor does not know the proofs today. This is not the fair hearing essential to due process. It is condemnation without trial.

An attempt was made by the Commission and again by the state court to uphold this decision without evidence as an instance of judicial notice. Indeed, decisions of this court were cited . . . as giving rise to the new doctrine that the values of land and labor and buildings and equipment, with all their yearly fluctuations, no longer call for evidence. Our opinions have been much misread if they have been thought to point that way. Courts take judicial notice of matters of common knowledge. . . . They take judicial notice that there has been a depression, and that a decline of market values is one of its concomitants. . . . How great the decline has been for this industry or that, for one material or another, in this year or the next, can be known only to the experts, who may even differ among themselves. . . . Moreover, notice, even when taken, has no other effect than to relieve one of the parties to a controversy of the burden of resorting to the usual forms of evidence. Wigmore, Evidence § 2567; 1 Greenleaf, Evidence, 16th ed., p. 18. "It does not mean that the opponent is prevented from disputing the matter by evidence if he believes it disputable.". . . .

What was done by the Commission is subject, however, to an objection even deeper. . . . There has been more than an expansion of the concept of notoriety beyond reasonable limits. From the standpoint of due process — the protection of the individual against arbitrary action — a deeper vice is this, that even now we do not know the particular or evidential facts of which the Commission took judicial notice and on which it rested its conclusion. Not only are the facts unknown; there is no way to find them out. When price lists or trade journals or even government reports are put in evidence upon a trial, the party against whom they are offered may see the evidence or hear it and parry its effect. Even if they are copied in the findings without preliminary proof, there is at least an opportunity in connection with a judicial review of the decision to challenge the deductions made from them. The opportunity is excluded here. The Commission, withholding from the record the evidential facts that it has gathered here and there, contents itself with saying that in gathering them it went to journals and tax lists, as if a judge were to tell us, "I looked at the statistics in the Library of Congress, and they teach me thus and so." This will never do if hearings and appeals are to be more than empty forms.

. . . . [H]ow was it possible for the appellate court to review the law and the facts and intelligently decide that the findings of the Commission were supported by the evidence when the evidence was unknown and unknowable?. . . . What the Supreme Court of Ohio did was to take the word of the Commission as to the outcome of a secret investigation, and let it go at that. . . .

The decree is reversed and the cause remanded for further proceedings not inconsistent with this opinion.

Reversed.

Questions and Comments

1.   How do you think that the Commission arrived at the formulas for transforming the 1925 valuation into valuations for the years 1926 through 1933? Did the Commission members themselves develop the formulas? Is it not likely that the Commissioners were probably political appointees lacking the sophisticated mathematical abilities to perform that task? If so, then the Commissioners must have relied on their staff to perform the function of transforming the 1925 value into values for the other years.

2.   If the Commissioners did rely upon their staff to perform this complex task, it is likely that the staff members charged with this responsibility put their conclusions into written form, together with explanatory material, and transmitted it to the Commissioners. Then they may have discussed this written report and its contents with the Commissioners.

3.   To what extent would the interaction between the Commissioners and members of their staff described in paragraph 2 above resemble the interaction between the Secretary and the officials in the Bureau of Animal Industry dealt with by the Court in the *Morgan* cases? How would it differ?

4.   Do the answers to the questions in paragraph 3 depend upon the charge which the Ohio Commissioners gave to their staff? Would it make a difference whether the staff was charged to try to arrive at the lowest possible valuations for the Ohio Bell Company's assets or whether it was charged to determine the valuations which were, in the view of the staff, the most accurate ones? Would the former charge produce a different input into their report from the latter one? Would the former charge also tend to engender an adversary mentality in the staff members which might grow stronger as they applied themselves to their task?

5.   Even if the charge to the staff members was to make an objective determination about the value of the Company's assets, should their report have been included in the record of the administrative proceeding? Is that what the Supreme Court in effect said in its opinion in the *Ohio Bell* case?

6.   If the staff members who prepared the valuation report in the *Ohio Bell* case had been given a charge to evaluate the assets in an objective way, how did their task differ from that of a law clerk? Law clerks are told to assess the state of the law or of the evidence objectively, and then to report their conclusions to the judge, are they not? Yet parties do not see the memoranda or reports of law clerks. Should the parties see them?

7.   Consider whether the following extract from some remarks of Carl Kaysen affects your answers to the above questions. Kaysen who was then an economics professor was appointed a clerk for Judge Wysanski to assist him in the decision of an antitrust case.

"Notice" and "Legislative Facts" in Other Contexts

Issues involving "notice" taken by decision-makers and "legislative facts" come before the courts periodically. Consider the following:

In *City of Erie v. PAP's A.M.*," 529 U.S. 277 (2000), the Court upheld a city ordinance banning nude dancing, partially relying upon the "legislative facts" determined by the city council. In so doing, the Court analogized the legislative facts found by the city council to the legislative facts that an administrative agency might determine as a matter of official notice. "The city council members, familiar with commercial downtown Erie, are the individuals who would likely have had firsthand knowledge of what took place at and around nude dancing establishments in Erie, and can make particularized, expert judgments about the resulting harmful secondary effects. Analogizing to the administrative agency context, it is well established that, as long as a party has an opportunity to respond, an administrative agency may take official notice of such 'legislative facts' within its special knowledge, and is not confined to the evidence in the record in reaching its expert judgment. See *FCC v. National Citizens Comm. for Broadcasting*, 436 U.S. 775 (1978); *Republic Aviation Corp. v. NLRB*, 324 U.S. 793 (1945); 2 K. Davis & R. Pierce, Administrative Law Treatise § 10.6 (3d ed.1994)."

In *Heckler v. Campbell*, 461 U.S. 458 (1983) infra, the Social Security Administration employed notice-and-comment rulemaking to determine the availability of employment opportunities for various categories of individuals suffering from differing types of physical impairments. The results were embodied in guidelines published in the Code of Federal Regulations. Under the disability program, persons were entitled to receive payments if they suffered impairments that prevented them from gainful employment. In individual hearings a disability claimant was entitled to offer evidence to establish his or her physical or mental impairment. The Administration, however, relied upon the guidelines to determine whether employment was available for a person with the claimant's impairments. In these hearings, the claimant was not permitted to offer evidence to rebut the conclusions of the guidelines.

AN ECONOMIST AS THE JUDGE'S LAW CLERK IN SHERMAN ACT CASES[*]
Professor Carl Kaysen
Cambridge Massachusetts

I am here this morning in a double capacity: first, so to speak, as an exhibit, and second, as a speaker. As an exhibit, I perhaps may best be described as an unprecedented precedent without a consequence, as will be apparent from what both Mr. Webster and I have to say. As a speaker, I will try to do three things: to tell you briefly what I did in U.S. v. *United Shoe Machinery Company* when I served as law clerk to Judge Charles E. Wyzanski, Jr. of the District Court of Massachusetts, to give my own views on whether this particular arrangement was one which ought to be repeated, and to say something more broadly about the role of economists in the administration of the Antitrust Laws. . . .

---

[*] 2 A.B.A. Antitrust Section 43 (1958).

In considering the question of whether the experiment Judge Wyzanski made when he enlisted my help as an economic law clerk is one which other judges would do well to repeat, I feel I should begin by saying that I myself have no doubts as to the wisdom and justice of this device in the particular instance. I say this not from foolish arrogance nor any desire to praise myself in public, but rather to emphasize that I have no doubt as to the ability of Judge Wyzanski to make just such use of whatever was valid in the assistance I gave him as was desirable, and his equal ability to reject whatever may have been irrelevant or inappropriate from the point of view of his judicial task. Nonetheless, I feel that there are strong reasons to doubt that the experiment can be transformed into a routine with any success, or that it should be so transformed. To take the second problem first, I think there are two serious questions of fairness which this arrangement poses: One is a question of fairness to the parties. My report was not offered to the parties for comment before the final disposition of the case. It was a strictly private document seen only by the judge. In general, it may be argued that everything that goes forward influencing the Court's decision, outside what is in the mind of the judge himself, should be spread on the record. The second issue of fairness is a broader and perhaps more important one. Even if it is assumed that every judge is as well able to interpret what an economic expert tells him in private, use what is lawful, and reject what is not, as Judge Wyzanski clearly was and that therefore the parties are in no way prejudiced by this procedure, it may be argued that the adversary process is changed in an undesirable way. Ideally, the judge functions as an expert only in law; in other areas he is a layman, one unusually gifted in the art of receiving instruction from those temporary experts, counsel for the contending parties, on the substantive, non-legal facts before him. So instructed, he decides between the contending views presented to him. To inject into this process an expert in a particular class of facts and to allow him private access to the judge, protected from the scrutiny of examination by the parties, undermines to some extent the adversary character of the proceeding. The more weight the expert has in the outcome, the more it can be argued that an *ex parte* process is being substituted, for the traditional adversary proceedings. The arguments above, to be sure, are legal or jurisprudential in character, not economic, and I am not an expert in these matters. But they carry enough weight in my mind to make me dubious as to the desirability of incorporating the economist as a law clerk as a standard feature of the regular antitrust trial.

Questions and Comments

1. Why did Professor Kaysen think that Judge Wysanski's experiment should not be repeated? Did his reservations about economists as law clerks extend to all law clerks? How did Professor Kaysen's functions as a clerk differ from the normal functions of any law clerk?

2. Do your answers to the questions in the preceding paragraph help you to define the proper scope to be accorded to the *Ohio Bell* case?

Note

1.   In connection with the *Ohio Bell* case, consider § 556(e) of the APA. It contains a provision making the "transcript of testimony and exhibits, together with all papers and requests filed in the proceeding" the "exclusive record" for decision. It also provides that "[w]hen an agency decision rests on official notice of a material fact not appearing in the evidence in the record, a party is entitled, on timely request, to an opportunity to show the contrary."

2.   Section 556(e), of course, would not apply to a proceeding of a state agency like that of the Ohio Commission involved in the *Ohio Bell* case. If a federal regulatory agency today wanted to act in the manner of the Ohio Commission, would its actions be circumscribed by § 556(e)? Would the staff report have to be placed in the record? Would § 556(e) provide the utility with a right to rebut the material contained in the report?

3.   Do your answers to the questions in paragraph 2 above depend upon whether the material in the report is properly characterizable as "factual" matter? Should they so depend?

When considering the responses of the drafters of the APA to the problems identified in the *Morgan* cases and in *Ohio Bell*, consider a case like the New Jersey case extracted below. In what ways does *Mazza v. Cavicchia* differ from the cases considered above, and therefore, raise issues different from those cases?

***Mazza v. Cavicchia*, 15 N.J. 498, 105 A.2d 545 (1954).** The appellant operated the Traveler's Hotel & Restaurant and held a retail consumption liquor license. Agents of the New Jersey Division of Alcoholic Beverage Control filed a complaint with the Director of the Division charging that Mazza had violated a rule of the Division in that he had allowed lewdness and immoral activity on the premises and that in violation of another such rule, Mazza had permitted the sale of contraceptives on the premises. By notice Mazza was required to show cause why his license should not be revoked or suspended.

A hearing was held before a "hearer" of the Division. An inspector and two investigators of the Division were the only witnesses for the State. At the conclusion of the hearing the hearer advised the parties that the matter would be submitted to the Director for determination and that all parties would be advised of the result. Subsequently the hearer forwarded the record of the hearing to the Director together with a report of his findings and conclusions, but a copy thereof was not furnished to Mazza. The Director found Mazza guilty of the charges and ordered his license suspended for 180 days.

On appeal, Mazza contended that the failure to supply him with the hearer's report was reversible error. Agreeing with Mazza's contention, the New Jersey Supreme Court first concluded that the report was used by the Director in deciding: "It is argued . . . [by] the respondent Director that his determination was made 'upon the basis of his own independent findings and not by a subordinate.' This, however, is not saying that the hearer's report was not used by him in the process of deciding the case. . . . What possible purpose could the consistent submission of such reports for 21 years have served, but to furnish the Director a key to the facts and the law of each case?" The court then ruled that failure to supply Mazza a copy of the report was error: "The principle of the exclusiveness of the record necessarily bars the use of the hearer's report (which it is conceded in the instant case was submitted to the respondent Director with the record without disclosure thereof to the appellant) as an aid in the administrative decision process unless it is made part of the record. As the noted Benjamin Report on Administrative Adjudication in New York puts it, 'whatever actually plays a part in the decision should be known to the parties, and subject to being controverted'. . . . The individual litigant is entitled to be apprised of the materials upon which the agency is acting. He has a right not only to refute but, what in a case like this is usually more important, to supplement, explain, and give different perspective to the hearer's view of the case."

Questions and Comments

1.   Was the New Jersey court concerned that the Director was deciding a case without being adequately informed about it? Was the court concerned that the hearer's report was distorted by an adversary bias?

2.   Was the New Jersey court concerned that the hearer's report might contain an erroneous evaluation of the case? and that the hearer's errors could have been corrected by Mazza if he had the opportunity to read it? Did the court explain the procedure by which Mazza would correct the errors in the report that he discovered? Does the court's opinion assume that Mazza has a right to be heard before the Director, in addition to being heard by the hearer?

3.   What kind of errors would Mazza be likely to find in the report? What kinds of issues were litigated at the hearing? Were they not factual issues? Did Mazza allow prostitutes on the premises, etc.? How would those issues be decided by the hearer? On the basis of his assessment of the credibility of witnesses testifying as to matters that they had seen or heard? Would the "errors" which Mazza would be likely to discover, therefore, be decisions on the credibility of witnesses with which Mazza disagrees?

4.   How would the Director be likely to dispose of arguments by Mazza that the determinations of the hearer on matters of witness credibility were erroneous? If the Director reversed the hearer on an issue of witness credibility, how would a court deal with that reversal on review? In answering these questions, consider the *Universal Camera* cases and accompanying notes, *supra*, chapter 2.

Note: The Basic Structure of the APA

1.   The APA establishes procedures for three basic types of proceedings: informal rulemaking governed by § 553, formal rulemaking governed by §§ 556 and 557; and formal adjudication governed by §§ 554, 556 and 557. The residue is informal adjudication, which is discussed in paragraph 9 below.

2.   The APA definitions (§ 551) are crucial in determining the procedure applicable to a given proceeding. The definitions do not necessarily correspond with colloquial usage of the terms "adjudication" and "rule making."

Note that the APA definition of "rule" in § 551(4) controls the definitions of rulemaking in § 551 (5), order in § 551(6) and adjudication in § 551(7). The rule definition in § 551(4) is complex: it embraces matters of "particular" as well as of "general" applicability. It also has three parts to it: it embraces agency statements designed to implement, interpret or prescribe law or policy for the future; it embraces an agency's organizational and procedural requirements; and the final part of the rule definition explicitly brings within its coverage various agency actions of an economic regulatory nature.

3.   If a proceeding fits the definition of rule making, it may be governed by section 553. Section 553 provides a general requirement for notice-and-comment procedures for all rulemaking, unless one of the exceptions applies. The most important exceptions are in clauses (A) and (B) of § 553(b). Clause (A) exempts "interpretative rules, general statements of policy, or rules of agency organization, procedure, or practice," and clause (B) exempts rules for which the agency finds notice and public procedure thereon to be "impracticable, unnecessary, or contrary to the public interest."

The last sentence of § 553(c) is very important. When the "rules are required by statute to be made on the record after opportunity for an agency hearing," then the more trial-like procedures of §§ 556 and 557 are substituted for the comment procedures imposed by § 553(c). Rulemaking under §§ 556 and 557 is generally referred to as formal rulemaking.

4.   If a proceeding does not fit the definition of rule making, then it is an "adjudication". When an adjudication "is required by statute to be determined on the record after opportunity for an agency hearing," it is (unless an exception applies) governed by § 554. Under § 554(c)(2), §§ 556 and 557 govern such an adjudication. Section 554(d) adds additional procedures to those imposed by §§ 556 and 557. This kind of adjudication is generally referred to as formal adjudication.

5.   Evidentiary or trial-type hearings are governed by §§ 556 and 557. Section 556 contains various provisions applicable to such proceedings, including (in § 556(e)) an exclusiveness-of-the-record provision and an official notice provision. Section 557 contains provisions designed to narrow and to focus the issues through recommended, initial, or tentative decisions and arguments upon those decisions.

6.   As Justice Rehnquist pointed out in *Florida East Coast Ay, infra,* chapter 6, § 556(d) provides that an agency can adopt procedures for the submission of all or part of the evidence in certain proceedings governed by §§ 556 and 557 in written form so long as "a party will not be prejudiced thereby."

7.   You will note that while the APA could be described as establishing procedures for two types of rulemaking and one type of adjudication, that description would be misleading insofar as it did not take into account the very idiosyncratic definitions of rule and rulemaking employed by the APA.

8.   A description of the APA that pointed out that it provides procedures for two types of trial-type proceedings and one type of comment proceeding would be a more accurate one, at least as of the date of the APA's enactment. That is, two of the three types of procedures set forth in the APA concern proceedings governed by §§ 556 and 557. Formal rulemaking is governed by §§ 556 and 557 and formal

adjudication differs from formal rulemaking largely because formal adjudication is also governed by § 554. (Informal rulemaking is governed primarily by § 553.)

9. The APA does not deal explicitly with informal adjudication: adjudication which is not required by statute to be determined on the record after opportunity for agency hearing. Section 555, however, contains general procedural requirements applicable to all proceedings. Informal adjudication, therefore, is governed by § 555. *Pension Benefit Guaranty Corp. v. LTV Corp.*, 496 U.S. 633 (1990). Should the proceeding involve a particularized impairment of a "liberty" or "property" interest, then the procedures mandated by the due process clause, of course, would also apply. *See* Chapter 3, above.

Note: The Underlying Assumptions of the APA Design

1. The drafters of the APA assumed that — in addition to informal rulemaking, largely governed by § 553 — there were primarily two types of administrative proceedings: (i) those in which a person or firm was accused of a breach of a rule or other form of wrongdoing. In those proceedings the issues would tend to be simple ones, often turning upon the belief or disbelief in the truth of witnesses testifying as to matters which they had seen or heard. (ii) The other type of administrative proceeding was one which involved economic, engineering or other complexities and in which no one was accused of wrongdoing. *Mazza* and *Universal Camera* are examples of accusatory proceedings; and the *Morgan* cases and Ohio *Bell* are examples of technical-complex proceedings.

2. When the APA was adopted, it was assumed that rate-making proceedings would normally involve trial-type (or evidentiary) hearings. The substantive statute establishing the rate requirements and the administering agency would almost invariably contain language stating that rates could be set after hearing. The APA was designed to key into such substantive statutes.

3. Ratemaking for the future was defined as rulemaking. *See* §§ 551(4),(5). The proceeding would initially, therefore, be routed to § 553. The requirement of the substantive statute that rates be made after hearing would trigger the last sentence of § 553(c), and route the proceeding into §§ 556 and 557.

4. An accusatory proceeding, such as a license revocation proceeding, was defined as adjudication. *See* §§ 551(6),(7),(8), and (9). Such a proceeding is governed by §§ 554, 556 and 557.

5. The difference in the hearing procedures governing ratemaking or other technical-complex proceedings and the procedures governing adjudications is largely (although not entirely) the application of the provisions of § 554(d) to the latter but not to the former. The reason is that in technical-complex proceedings, the need of the decision-makers for staff advice is greater and the need to conform to a purely judicial model of decision-making is less than in the often more simple accusatory proceedings. You will observe, however, that the ways in which the provisions of § 554(d) affect the administrative law judge and the agency members are significantly different.

B. PREJUDGMENT AND BIAS

When the Final Report of the Attorney General's Committee addressed questions of fairness arising from the combination of the functions of advocacy and deciding in the regulatory agencies, the authors identified two ways in which the combination of functions within an agency might adversely affect the quality and fairness of the decisional process. [*See* above.] First, developing or presenting a case against a respondent might engender in an individual a one-sided perspective—a so-called adversary mentality. A person who had developed such a mentality could not be trusted to judge a case dispassionately. Moreover, communications or recommendations from such a person to the decision-maker could be distorted by his adversary perspective. Secondly, an individual who investigated a case would be a problematic judge of the same case because his investigative activities would have given him access to information which had not been tested by the adversary process and hence was not fully trustworthy.

In the next section, we will see how the concerns expressed in the Attorney General's Committee have influenced the structure of the federal Administrative Procedure Act. In the present section we will examine the notions of prejudgment and bias. We will observe that a person may develop a biased outlook for reasons other than his (or her) assignment to an adversary role. We will attempt to identify various types of prejudgment and various types of bias; and we will attempt to evaluate their significance.

Withrow v. Larkin, **421 U.S. 35 (1975).** In this case the Court refused to condemn under the due process clause of the fourteenth amendment a Wisconsin procedure under which a medical Examining Board (composed of practicing physicians) held an investigative hearing to determine probable cause of unprofessional conduct, and then ruled on those charges at a contested hearing. In the investigative hearing the attorney representing the physician under investigation was permitted to be present throughout and was provided the opportunity to explain any of the testimony presented to the Board. In the contested hearing, the accused physician was present, represented by counsel, and entitled to confront adverse witnesses, to cross-examine them, and to present his own witnesses. At the conclusion of the contested hearing, the Board could suspend the physician's license temporarily; or could refer the case to the district attorney for the institution of license revocation proceedings in court or for the institution of criminal proceedings.

In that case the Court stated:

> The contention that the combination of investigative and adjudicative functions necessarily creates an unconstitutional risk of bias in administrative adjudication has a. . . . difficult burden of persuasion to carry. It must overcome a presumption of honesty and integrity in those serving as adjudicators; and it must convince that, under a realistic appraisal of psychological tendencies and human weakness, conferring investigative and adjudicative powers on the same individuals poses such a risk of actual bias or prejudgment that the practice must be forbidden if the guarantee of due process is to be adequately implemented. . . . That the combination of investigative and adjudicative functions does not, without more, consti-

tute a due process violation, does not, of course, preclude a court from determining from the special facts before it that the risk of unfairness is intolerably high. Findings of that kind made by judges with special insights into local realities are entitled to respect, but injunctions resting on such factors should be accompanied by at least the minimum findings required by [Federal] Rules [of Civil Procedure] 52(a) and 65(d).

In *Withrow v. Larkin* the same individuals who held the investigative hearing were the individuals who presided at the contested hearing and who thereafter decided whether to suspend the respondent's license. They could not easily erase from their minds information which they received at the investigative hearing, even when that same information was not presented at the contested hearing. In context, the Court did not think this was a major problem. Why? Whether the individuals who conducted the investigative hearing would also develop an adversary bias as a result of their roles in the investigation, the Court also viewed as less than problematic. In the view of the Court, the likelihood that the decision-makers would develop such a disabling bias would vary with the factual setting: the existence of such a bias in the decision-makers ought to be a matter of proof and should not be presumed solely from the fact that investigative and decision-making responsibilities are combined in the same persons. Was the Court casting doubt upon the validity of the analyses of the authors of the Final Report of the Attorney General's Committee? Or was it merely leaving to the legislatures the primary task of resolving when and in what circumstances individuals entrusted with decisional responsibilities could also be trusted with responsibilities for developing the case against a respondent? If the latter, when, if ever, would the combining of judicial and nonjudicial responsibilities in the same person become a matter of judicial concern?

***Gibson v. Berryhill*, 411 U.S. 564 (1973).** In 1965 the laws of Alabama relating to the practice of optometry were amended to delete the provisions which had expressly permitted a business firm or corporation to maintain a department in which "eyes are examined or glasses fitted," provided that such department was in the charge of a licensed optometrist. The Alabama Optometric Association, a professional organization whose membership was limited to independent practitioners of optometry not employed by others, filed charges before the Alabama Board of Optometry against certain licensed optometrists who were salaried employees of Lee Optical Co. The gravamen of these charges was that the named optometrists, by accepting employment from Lee Optical, a corporation, had engaged in "unprofessional conduct" within the meaning of § 206 of the Alabama optometry statute. The Board held these proceedings in abeyance while it brought its own suit in state court state court against Lee Optical and 13 optometrists employed by it, seeking to enjoin the company from engaging in the "unlawful practice of optometry" and to enjoin the 13 individuals from aiding and abetting the company in its illegal activities. The state trial court enjoined Lee Optical from practicing optometry without a license and from employing licensed optometrists, a decision which was ultimately reversed by the Alabama Supreme Court. After the trial court entered its injunction against Lee Optical, the Board reactivated its proceedings against the individual optometrists. In a separate suit by the latter, a federal court halted the Board's proceedings on the ground that, because of bias, the Board could not conduct a fair and impartial hearing in conformity with due process of law. An excerpt from the U.S. Supreme Court opinion affirming the lower federal court's injunction follows:

> The District Court thought the Board to be impermissibly biased for two reasons. First, the Board had filed a complaint in state court alleging that appellees had aided and abetted Lee Optical Co. in the unlawful practice of optometry and also that they had engaged in other forms of "unprofessional conduct" which, if provided, would justify revocation of their licenses. These charges were substantially similar to those pending against appellees before the Board and concerning which the Board had noticed hearings following its successful prosecution of Lee Optical in the state trial court.

> Secondly, the District Court determined that the aim of the Board was to revoke the licenses of all optometrists in the State who were employed by business corporations such as Lee Optical, and that these optometrists accounted for nearly half of all the optometrists practicing in Alabama. Because the Board of optometry was composed solely of optometrists in private practice for their own account, the District Court concluded that success in the Board's efforts would possibly redound to the personal benefit of members of the Board, sufficiently so that in the opinion of the District Court the Board was constitutionally disqualified from hearing the charges filed against the appellees.

> The District Court apparently considered either source of possible bias — prejudgment of the facts or personal interest — sufficient to disqualify the members of the Board. Arguably, the District Court was right on both scores, but we need reach, and we affirm, only the latter ground of possible personal interest.

> It is sufficiently clear from our cases that those with substantial pecuniary interest in legal proceedings should not adjudicate these disputes. . . . The District Court . . . concluded that the pecuniary interest of the members of the Board of Optometry had sufficient substance to disqualify them, given the context in which this case arose. As remote as we are from the local realities underlying this case and it being very likely that the District Court has a firmer grasp of the facts and of their significance to the issues presented, we have no good reason on this record to overturn its decision and we affirm it.

FTC v. Cement Institute, 333 U.S. 683 (1948). In a proceeding which it instituted against a trade association of cement producers and its members, the FTC ruled, inter alia, that the concerted use of multiple-basing-point pricing by members of the association was an unfair method of competition under § 5 of the Federal Trade Commission Act (FTCA). In upholding the FTC's ruling, the Court also rejected a contention of one of the respondents (Marquette Cement Mfg. Co.) that the parties failed to receive a fair hearing because the FTC had prejudged the case:

Marquette introduced numerous exhibits intended to support its charges. In the main these exhibits were copies of the Commission's reports made to Congress or to the President, as required by § 6 of the Trade Commission Act. . . . These reports, as well as the testimony given by members of the Commission before congressional committees, make it clear that long before the filing of this complaint the members of the Commission at that time, or at least some of them, were of the opinion that the operation of the multiple basing point system as they had studied it was the equivalent of a price fixing restraint of trade in violation of the Sherman Act. We therefore decide this contention . . . on the assumption that such an opinion had been formed by the entire membership of the Commission as a result of its prior official investigations. But we also agree with . . . [the] holding [of the court below] that this belief did not disqualify the Commission.

In the first place, the fact that the Commission had entertained such views as the result of its prior *ex parte* investigations did not necessarily mean that the minds of its members were irrevocably closed on the subject of the respondents' basing point practices. Here, in contrast to the Commission's investigations, members of the cement industry were legally authorized participants in the hearings. They produced evidence — volumes of it. They were free to point out to the Commission by testimony, by cross-examination of witnesses, and by arguments, conditions of the trade practices under attack which they thought kept these practices within the range of legally permissible business activities.

Moreover, Marquette's position, if sustained, would to a large extent defeat the congressional purposes which prompted passage of the Trade Commission Act. Had the entire membership of the Commission disqualified in the proceedings against these respondents, this complaint could not have been acted upon by the Commission or by any other government agency. Congress had provided for no such contingency. It has not directed that the Commission disqualify itself under any circumstances, has not provided for substitute commissioners should any of its members disqualify, and has not authorized any other government agency to hold hearings, make findings, and issue cease and desist orders in proceedings against unfair trade practices. Yet if Marquette is right, the Commission, by making studies and filing reports in obedience to congressional command, completely immunized the practices investigated, even though they are "unfair," from any cease and desist order by the Commission or any other governmental agency.

There is no warrant in the Act for reaching a conclusion which would thus frustrate its purposes. If the Commission's opinions expressed in congressionally required reports would bar its members from acting in unfair trade proceedings, it would appear that opinions expressed in the first basing point unfair trade proceeding would similarly disqualify them from ever passing on another. . . . Thus experience acquired from their work as commissioners would be a handicap instead of an advantage. Such was not the intendment of Congress. For Congress acted on a committee report stating: 'It is manifestly desirable that the terms of the commissioners shall be long enough to give them an opportunity to acquire the expertness in dealing with these special questions concerning industry that comes from experience.' Report of Committee on Interstate Commerce, No. 597, June 13, 1914, 63d Cong., 2d Sess. 10-11.

Marquette also seems to argue that it was a denial of due process for the Commission to act in these proceedings after having expressed the view that industry-wide use of the basing point system was illegal . . . [*Tumey v. Ohio*, 273 U.S. 510 (1927)] provides no support for the contention. In that case Tumey had been convicted of a criminal offence, fined, and committed to jail by a judge who had a direct, personal, substantial, pecuniary interest in reaching his conclusion to convict. . . .

Neither the *Tumey* decision nor any other decision of this Court would require us to hold that it would be a violation of procedural due process for a judge to sit in a case after he had expressed an opinion as to whether certain types of conduct were prohibited by law. In fact, judges frequently try the same case more than once and decide identical issues each time, although these issues involve questions both of law and fact. . . .

Cinderella Career & Finishing Schools, Inc. v. FTC, 425 F.2d 583 (D.C. Cir. 1970). Cinderella Career & Finishing School was found by the FTC to have engaged in false, misleading and deceptive representations and advertising, after the hearing officer had dismissed the case against it. While the appeal from the examiner's decision was pending before the Commission, Commission Chairman Dixon included the following remarks in a speech before a newspaper association in which he discussed the role which newspapers could play in protecting the public from deceptive advertising:

> What about carrying ads that offer college educations in five week-s. . . . or becoming an airline's hostess by attending a charm school?. . . . Granted that newspapers are not in the advertising policing business, their advertising managers are savvy enough to smell deception when the odor is strong enough.

The court ruled that Dixon should have disqualified himself from participating in the decision:

> We indicated . . . that "there is in fact and law authority in the Commission, acting in the public interest, to alert the public to suspected violations of the law by factual press releases whenever the Commission shall have reason to believe that a respondent is engaged in activities made unlawful by the Act. . . ." This does not give individual Commissioners license to prejudge cases or to make speeches which give the appearance that the case has been prejudged. Conduct such as this may have the effect of entrenching a Commissioner in a position which he has publicly stated, making it difficult, if not impossible, for him to reach a different conclusion in the event he deems it necessary to do so after consideration of the record. There is a marked difference between the issuance of a press release which states that the Commission has filed a complaint because it has "reason to believe" that there have been violations, and statements by

a Commissioner after an appeal has been filed which give the appearance that he has already prejudged the case and that the ultimate determination of the merits will move in predestined grooves. . . . The test for disqualification has been succinctly stated as being whether "a disinterested observer may conclude that [the agency] has in some measure adjudged the facts as well as the law of a particular case in advance of hearing it. . . ."

Questions and Comments

1.   The facts in *Cement Institute* show that the Commission had submitted reports to Congress stating that the concerted use of a multiple-basing system of pricing was equivalent to a price-fixing agreement in violation of the Sherman Act. Had not the Commission, therefore, prejudged the issue of the lawfulness of multiple-basing point pricing? If various Commissioners had testified before Congressional Committees that multiple-basing point pricing was equivalent to an illegal price-fixing agreement, had they not shown that they had already made up their minds as to the lawfulness of the respondents' behavior?

2.   Was the Court in *Cement Institute* saying that it was legitimate for the Commissioners to have made up their minds about the lawfulness of the multiple-basing point method of pricing and then sit as adjudicators in a case where that issue would be in dispute? Were the respondents in the *Cement Institute* case tried before an unbiased tribunal? Explain.

3.   How does the prejudgment issue in *Cement Institute* differ from the issues involved in *Withrow v. Larkin* and from the issue underlying the decision in *Gibson v. Berryhill?* Were there prejudgment issues in the latter cases?

4.   How did the prejudgment issue in *Cinderella Career & Finishing Schools* differ from the issue involved in *Cement Institute?* Were the issues in dispute in *Cement Institute* issues of evidentiary fact? ultimate fact? policy? law? Is Professor Davis' dichotomy between issues of adjudicative fact and issues of legislative fact helpful in understanding *Cement Institute?* Was there a dispute about what happened? about the legal significance of what happened?

C.   MORE ON THE STRUCTURE OF THE FEDERAL ADMINISTRATIVE PROCEDURE ACT

Take a close look at the APA:

1. Read § 554(d) carefully. Had the drafters of § 554(d) read the *Morgan* cases? What provisions in § 554(d) evidence familiarity with issues raised in the *Morgan* cases? Had the drafters of that section read the Final Report? Explain.

2. Would § 554(d) apply to a case like the *Morgan* cases? Why not? An answer to this question requires reference to the basic structure of the APA.

3. The APA is structured upon a carefully worded set of definitions contained in § 551. A good way to begin is to look at the definition of "adjudication" in § 551(7). You will observe that "adjudication" in § 551(7) is defined in terms of "order" which is defined in § 551(6). Section 551(6) defines "order" largely in terms of what is not

"rule making". "Rule making", in turn, is defined in § 551(5) in terms of "rule". An elaborate definition of "rule" is contained in § 551(4). It thus turns out that the "rule" definition in 551(4) largely controls the meaning assigned to "rule making", "order", and "adjudication".

The latter part of § 551(4)'s definition of "rule" includes within that term "the approval or prescription for the future of rates" or "valuations", thus bringing within that definition a large part of the *Morgan* proceedings. Insofar as the Morgan proceedings involved ratemaking for the future, they would thus be classified as rulemaking proceedings under the APA and would escape § 554(d) which applies only to "adjudications".

Indeed, even those parts of the *Morgan* proceedings that were concerned with the reasonableness of past rates and therefore did not fall within § 551(4)'s definition of "rule" would not be governed by § 554(d). Do you see why? Those parts of the *Morgan* proceedings would be defined as "adjudication" [since § 551(7)- through the provisions of §§ 551(6), (5) and (4)-defines "adjudication" in terms of what is not rulemaking]. But proceedings evaluating the reasonableness of past rates would be exempt from § 554 by virtue of clause (B) in § 544(d). The rationale for this result is explained in the note below.

Note: A more detailed note on the APA structure[1]

1. An overall view of the APA's provisions governing administrative proceedings. The APA contains numerous provisions dealing with procedures at the agency level, judicial review, access to information, administrative law judges and other matters. in this section of the material, our focus is upon the basic structure of the APA provisions governing procedures in administrative proceedings.

In large measure the APA is structured to govern three types of administrative proceedings: First, in § 553, it imposes a minimum set of procedures on the issuance of all legislative rules. That section requires that before such rules are issued, the agency provide notice of its intent to issue rules and then accept comment on its proposals from interested persons. This imposition of a generally-applicable notice-and-comment procedure for the issuance of all legislative rules was one of the major innovations of the APA.

Second. In addition to notice-and-comment procedures governing most rulemaking, the APA also establishes procedures for rulemaking which is made on the record after opportunity for an agency hearing. This is so-called formal rulemaking: rulemaking which is on the record and whose procedures resemble in greater or lesser degree those of a judicial trial. Formal rulemaking is governed by §§ 556 and 557. (As pointed out below, the labels can be confusing, because some formal rulemaking proceedings look very much like adjudication in that they are concerned

---

[1] The matters discussed in this note are more extensively treated in Daniel J. Gifford, *Report on Administrative Law to the Tennessee Law Revision Commission*, 20 Vand. L. Rev. 777, 851–858 (1967); Louis Jaffe, *Basic Issues: An Analysis in Symposium-Hoover Commission and Task Force Reports on Legal Services and Procedures*, 30 N.Y.U. L. Rev. 1273, 1281 (1955).

with an individual respondent and are not designed to produce a generally applicable rule.)

Third. The APA provides a set of procedures governing formal adjudication: adjudication which is required to be on the record after opportunity for an agency hearing. The APA does not specifically deal with what might be called informal adjudication: adjudication for which no hearing is required.

2.   The design of the APA provisions governing trial type proceedings. The APA provides structures for two types of trial type proceedings. As developed below, the Act provides a basic set of procedures for trial-type proceedings in §§ 556 and 557. But the Act is drafted on the premise that trial proceedings fall into one of two types: (i) those which tend to be technical and complex but are nonaccusatory; and (ii) those which tend to be accusatory and in which the issues tend to involve the relatively simple question of whether the respondent violated a statute, agency rule or condition of its license. It is structured in such a way as to exempt the former, but not the latter, from the provisions of § 554(d).

In the first (technical/complex) type of proceeding, the drafters thought that the strict provisions of § 554(d) designed to isolate the decision-makers from parts of the agency staff would be unwise. The more technical and complex the issues are, the greater need does a decision-maker have to consult with staff experts on the evaluation of data in the record. The decision-maker may, for example, need the assistance of engineers, accountants, scientists, technicians, etc. in order to understand and to evaluate the material before him. Moreover, because the respondent is not being accused of any wrongdoing, consultation by the decision-makers with experts on the agency staff does not appear unfair.

By contrast, when a respondent is accused of wrongdoing and may be punished for that wrongdoing (as, for example, by a suspension or revocation of its license), the drafters believed that more elaborate procedural safeguards more closely resembling those of a judicial trial would be appropriate. Moreover, because the drafters believed that in such an accusatory proceeding the issues would tend to the relatively simple ones of whether the accused did or did not violate a standard of conduct, the decision-makers would not need to consult with engineering, accounting, scientific or other experts. Thus such consultation was thought both objectionable from a fairness standpoint and unnecessary from a standpoint of practical administration.

A principal mechanism for applying procedural constraints to technical/complex proceedings which are more lenient than those applied to accusatory proceedings is the "rule" definition in § 551(4). Observe that this definition really has three parts. Except for the awkward "or particular" phrase, the first part of § 551(4) describes the common understanding of a rule: ". . . the whole or a part of an agency statement of general . . . applicability and future effect designed to implement, interpret, or prescribe law or policy. . . . "The next part of § 551(4) brings procedural and organizational matters within the "rule" definition: ". . . describing the organization, procedure, or practice requirements of an agency. . . ." It is principally the final part of § 551(4) which helps to allocate technical and complex proceedings away from § 554(d) and to allocate accusatory proceedings towards § 554(d). This final part of § 551(4) is phrased in substantive terms: in essence, it brings prospective ratemaking and other prospective economic regulatory proceedings within the "rule" definition.

3.   The APA terminology. Verbally, the APA divides proceedings into "adjudications" and "rulemaking" proceedings, and classifies "rulemaking" proceedings into two types: so-called informal rulemaking which is governed by the notice-and-comment procedures set forth in § 553; and formal rulemaking which is governed by the procedures set forth in §§ 556 and 557. The APA sets forth procedures governing formal adjudication in § 554, 556 and 557. You will observe that § 556 contains provisions governing the conduct of a trial-like hearing and § 557 contains provisions governing the contents of decisions (such as findings and conclusions) and appeals or review within the agency structure. And you will also observe that since both formal rulemaking and formal adjudication are governed by §§ 556 and 557, they are really two types of trial-type proceedings governed by the APA. Indeed, putting aside the APA's labels, that Act sets forth procedures for three basic types of proceedings: two types of trial proceedings (those governed by §§ 556, 557, and 554 and those governed only by §§ 556 and 557) and one type of comment proceeding (governed by § 553).

Through its rule definition, the Act initially allocates proceedings either to § 553 (the provision governing rulemaking) or to § 554 (the provision governing adjudication). In most cases, the governing law (apart from the APA) will require that when an agency acts against a particular individual, that individual is entitled to a hearing at which he (or she) can assert a defense. Such proceedings will generally fall under the APA definition of adjudication. The drafters accordingly believed that these proceedings would be routed to § 554, and thence also to §§ 556 and 557. At the time the APA was enacted, formal rulemaking was a novelty which was largely associated with the Food & Drug Act. The APA provided procedures for such rulemaking, however. Those rules would meet the definition of rule in § 551(4), and thence be routed to § 553. The hearing requirement in the Food & Drug Act was thought to trigger the last sentence of § 553(c) and thence route the proceedings to §§ 556 and 557.

4.   Ratemaking under the APA's provisions. Traditionally, it had been generally understood that ratemaking proceedings had to involve evidentiary hearings. Almost all of the statutes governing ratemaking authorized the administering agency to set rates after a "hearing". The last sentence in § 553(c) which routes a proceeding out of § 553 and into §§ 556 and 557 was thought to be triggered by these hearing requirements of the substantive ratemaking statutes. Thus the APA is structured to route ratemaking to §§ 556 and 557 by a complex process involving several steps: Future ratemaking is defined as a rule under § 551(4); a proceeding to set future rates is therefore initially routed to the rulemaking section, § 553; but because the substantive statute establishing rate control in an agency almost invariably required a "hearing" prior to the rate decision, that hearing requirement was thought to trigger the provision in the last sentence of § 553(c) which routed the proceeding out of § 553 and to §§ 556 and 557.

A proceeding assessing the reasonableness of past rates is defined as an "adjudication". Do you see why? It results from the definition of "rule" in § 551(4). Although it is governed by § 554, the stringent procedural constraints of § 554(d) are made inapplicable to it by clause (B) in § 554(d). Again, the basic plan of exempting ratemaking and other technical/complex proceedings from the § 554(d) constraints is followed.

5. Licensing decisions. The APA definitions make licensing proceedings adjudications and thus subject to §§ 554, 556 and 557 when they are required to be made on the record after opportunity for an agency hearing. But § 554(d)(A) exempts initial licensing proceedings from § 554(d). This fits the basic plan of the APA as described above. Initial licensing was thought by the drafters to be nonacccusatory and as often involving technical issues. But license revocation and suspension proceedings were usually accusatory and focused upon the simple and nontechnical issues of whether the licensee had violated a rule of the licensing authority. Indeed, in this respect license renewal proceedings were thought to resemble revocation and suspension proceedings rather than initial licensing proceedings, because existing licenses generally were renewed unless the licensee had violated a rule or condition of its license.

Note: The vocabulary of the APA and its implications Issues of fact and other issues

Both formal rulemaking and formal adjudication are subject to § 556(e) which contains an exclusiveness of the record provision and a provision governing official notice. Read § 556(e) carefully. Are these provisions concerned primarily with "factual" issues which are proved by "evidence" in the record? If the agency consults extra-record authority in the law library, has it gone outside of the record in violation of § 556(e)? Explain. May an administrative law judge or an agency member consult a staff expert on the evaluation of evidence in the record, consistent with the terms of § 556(e)?

Observe that § 554(d) limits consultation by an administrative law judge on a "fact" in issue. May an administrative law judge consult a member of the agency staff on a question of law? on a question of policy? on the evaluation of a matter of evidentiary fact? Explain. Why are agency members exempted from the provisions of § 554(d) by its clause (C)? May an agency member deciding a case of formal adjudication consult with a person who had performed an investigative or prosecuting function in that case? on any type of issue? Why not?

Note: Procedural approaches to ratemaking in the various states

1. *Uniform Commissioners' Model State Administrative Procedure Act (1981).* What are the procedural constraints governing a ratemaking proceeding under the Model Act? See § 4-215 (exclusiveness of the evidence provision); § 4-212(f) (official notice); § 4-213 (ex parte communications)[see especially § 4-213(b)]; § 4-214 (separation of functions).

2. *New York State: State Administrative Procedure Act.* How does New York deal with ratemaking? See § 307(2). See also § 306 (exclusiveness of the evidence;

official notice). Do you see parallels in the New York Act to the federal APA?[2]

3. *Minnesota: Administrative Procedure Act.* Minn. Stat. § 14.60(2) (exclusiveness of the record); § 14.60(4) (official notice).

4. As the above questions implicitly suggest, state legislation has often ignored the need of the adjudicating officials for staff assistance in complex cases. Few states follow the lead of the federal APA which was designed to provide two types of trial proceedings, one for the more accusatory cases and one for the more technical and complex cases. New York, however, is an exception. New York has followed the lead of the federal APA by defining prospective ratemaking as rulemaking, thereby taking ratemaking proceedings out of the provisions governing adjudicatory proceedings. See N.Y State APA § 102(a)(ii). Moreover, just as the federal APA makes § 554(d) inapplicable to proceedings governing past rates (i.e., reparations proceedings), the New York Act makes its analogue to § 554 inapplicable to proceedings governing past rates as well. N.Y State APA § 307(2).

5. Consultation between decision-making officials and staff are regulated in most state administrative procedure legislation (1) through provisions governing official notice; (2) provisions making the record the exclusive basis for decision; (3) provisions prohibiting ex parte consultations. See 1946 Model Act § 9(2) (exclusiveness of the record); § 9(4) (judicial notice); 1961 Model Act § 9(e)(2), (3) (including in the record all evidence received or considered and all matters officially noticed); § 10(4) (official notice provisions). The 1961 Act also specifically includes "staff memoranda or data" in the category of official notice. See 1961 Model Act § 9(e)(7) and § 10(4). The 1961 Act also included a provision specifically prohibiting certain ex parte consultations. 1961 Act § 13.

Almost all of these provisions in the 1946 and 1961 model acts are drafted on the assumption that communications fall into two categories: fact and law. Since the scope of the factual blends into the scope of the legal (as a moment's reflection upon the meaning of an "ultimate" — as opposed to an "evidentiary" — fact demonstrates), the boundaries of these provisions are not always clear.

The 1981 Model Act is markedly more sophisticated than its predecessors. It incorporates provisions governing official notice [§ 4-212] and ex parte communications [§ 4-213]. In addition, it has a provision dealing with separation of functions. 1981 Model Act § 4-214. These provisions of the 1981 act are not subject to the criticisms expressed above directed at its predecessors.

---

[2] *See* Daniel J. Gifford, *The New York Administrative Procedure Act: Some Reflections Upon its Structure and Legislative History,* 26 BUFFALO L. REV. 589 (1977).

D. PROCEDURES NOT MODELED UPON EITHER A TRIAL OR RULEMAKING; LIMITATIONS (AND LIMITS) OF THE APA

1. *Section 555 and "informal adjudication."*

When a proceeding is defined as rulemaking (whether or not after opportunity for a hearing on the record) or as adjudication after opportunity for a hearing on the record, the APA provides carefully crafted sets of procedures. When a proceeding meets the APA definition of "adjudication" but is not required by statute to be held on the record after opportunity for an agency hearing, the adjudication provisions of § 554, by their terms, do not apply. Does the APA have anything at all to say about such proceedings?

An adjudication which is not governed by § 554 is commonly referred to as "informal adjudication." Unless a proceeding is specifically exempted from the APA, § 555 would govern informal adjudication (as it governs other types of APA proceedings). Section 555 contains a limited set of procedural provisions, dealing, *inter alia* with rights to counsel, appearances, transcripts, subpoenas, and the supplying by the agency of reasons for denials of applications. Section 555 has been cited by the Supreme Court as stating not only the minimum procedures but as the maximum procedures which a court can require of an agency in informal adjudication.

Pension Benefit Guaranty Corp. v. LTV Corp., 496 U.S. 633 (1990). This case involved the Pension Benefit Guaranty Corporation (PBGC) which administers a mandatory Government insurance program that protects private-sector workers participating in pension plans covered by Title IV of the Employee Retirement Income Security Act of 1974 (ERISA).

After certain pension plans of one of its subsidiaries had been terminated by PBGC to protect the insurance program from the risk of large losses which loomed as a result of LTV's apparent inability to continue to fund the plans, LTV renegotiated new pension agreements with the Steelworkers union. PBGC objected to the new agreements as attempts to cause PBGC to subsidize LTV's ongoing pension program in a way not contemplated by the Act. Because of PBGC's objections to the new agreements and because PBGC determined that the financial factors on which it had relied in terminating the plans had changed, PBGC issued a Notice of Restoration of the terminated plans under § 4047 of ERISA, which authorizes the PBGC to undo a termination "in any . . . case in which [it] determines such action to be appropriate and consistent with its duties under [Title IV].

By restoring the pension plans, the PBGC reimposed financial responsibility for those plans on LTV. In issuing its Notice of Restoration, the PBGC was acting in a way that the APA defines as adjudication. Because no statute requires that Notices of Restoration be determined on the record after opportunity for an agency hearing, the PBGC's action was not governed by 554, 556 or 557 of the APA. Rather, it was "informal" adjudication and subject only to the provisions of § 555. LTV's objections to the procedures to which it was subjected were eventually considered by the Supreme Court. In the following excerpt, the Court considers those objections:

Finally, we consider the Court of Appeals' ruling that the agency procedures were inadequate in this particular case. Relying upon a passage in *Bowman Transportation, Inc. v. Arkansas-Best Freight System, Inc.*, 419 U.S. 281, 288, n. 4 (1974), the court held that the PBGC's decision was arbitrary and capricious because the "PBGC neither apprised LTV of the material on which it was to base its decision, gave LTV an adequate opportunity to offer contrary evidence, proceeded in accordance with ascertainable standards. . . . nor provided [LTV] a statement showing its reasoning in applying those standards." 875 F.2d, at 1021. The court suggested that on remand the agency was required to do each of these things.

The PBGC argues that this holding conflicts with *Vermont Yankee Nuclear Power Corp. v. Natural Resources Defense Council, Inc.*, 435 U.S. 519 (1978), where, the PBGC contends, this Court made clear that when the Due Process Clause is not implicated and an agency's governing statute contains no specific procedural mandates, the Administrative Procedure Act establishes the maximum procedural requirements a reviewing court may impose on agencies. Although *Vermont Yankee* concerned additional procedures imposed by the Court of Appeals for the District of Columbia Circuit on the Atomic Energy Commission when the agency was engaging in informal rulemaking, the PBGC argues that the informal adjudication process by which the restoration decision was made should be governed by the same principles.

Respondents counter by arguing that courts, under some circumstances, do require agencies to undertake additional procedures. As support for this proposition, they rely on *Citizens to Preserve Overton Park, Inc. v. Volpe*, 401 U.S. 402 (1971). In *Overton Park*, the Court concluded that the Secretary of Transportation's "post hoc rationalizations" regarding a decision to authorize the construction of a highway did not provide "an [a]dequate basis for [judicial] review" for purposes of § 706 of the APA. *Id.*, at 419. Accordingly, the Court directed the District Court on remand to consider evidence that shed light on the Secretary's reasoning at the time he made the decision. Of particular relevance for present purposes, the Court in *Overton Park* intimated that one recourse for the District Court might be a remand to the agency for a fuller explanation of the agency's reasoning at the time of the agency action. See *id.*, at 420-421. Subsequent cases have made clear that remanding to the agency in fact is the preferred course. See *Florida Power & Light Co. v. Lorion*, 470 U.S. 729, 744 (1985) ("[I]f the reviewing court simply cannot evaluate the challenged agency action on the basis of the record before it, the proper course, except in rare circumstances, is to remand to the agency for additional investigation or explanation"). Respondents contend that the instant case is controlled by *Overton Park* rather than *Vermont Yankee*, and that the Court of Appeals' ruling was thus correct.

We believe that respondents' argument is wide of the mark. We begin by noting that although one initially might feel that there is some tension between *Vermont Yankee* and *Overton Park*, the two cases are not necessarily inconsistent. *Vermont Yankee* stands for the general proposition that courts are not free to impose upon agencies specific procedural requirements that have no basis in the APA. See 435 U.S., at 524. At most, *Overton Park* suggests that § 706(2)(A) of the APA, which directs a court to ensure that an agency action is not arbitrary and capricious or otherwise contrary to law, imposes a general "procedural" requirement of sorts by mandating that an agency take whatever steps it needs to provide an explanation that will enable the court to evaluate the agency's rationale at the time of decision.

Here, unlike in *Overton Park*, the Court of Appeals did not suggest that the administrative record was inadequate to enable the court to fulfill its duties under § 706. Rather, to support its ruling, the court focused on "fundamental fairness" to LTV. 875 F.2d, at 1020–1021. With the possible exception of the absence of "ascertainable standards" — by which we are not exactly sure what the Court of Appeals meant — the procedural inadequacies cited by the court all relate to LTV's role in the PBGC's decision-making process. But the court did not point to any provision in ERISA or the APA which gives LTV the procedural rights the court identified. Thus, the court's holding runs afoul of *Vermont Yankee* and finds no support in *Overton Park*.

Nor is *Arkansas-Best*, the case on which the Court of Appeals relied, to the contrary. The statement relied upon (which was dictum) said: "A party is entitled, of course, to know the issues on which decision will turn and to be apprised of the factual material on which the agency relies for decision so that he may rebut it." 419 U.S., at 288, n. 4. That statement was entirely correct in the context of *Arkansas-Best*, which involved a formal adjudication by the Interstate Commerce Commission pursuant to the trial-type procedures set forth in §§ 5, 7 and 8 of the APA, 5 U.S.C. §§ 554, 556–557, which include requirements that parties be given notice of "the matters of fact and law asserted," § 554(b)(3), an opportunity for "the submission and consideration of facts [and] arguments," § 554(c)(1), and an opportunity to submit "proposed findings and conclusions" or "exceptions," § 557(c)(1), (2). See 5 U.S.C. § 554(a). . . . The determination in this case, however, was lawfully made by informal adjudication, the minimal requirements for which are set forth in § 555 of the APA, and do not include such elements. A failure to provide them where the Due Process Clause itself does not require them (which has not been asserted here) is therefore not unlawful.

Questions and Comments

Does *Pension Benefit Guaranty Corp. v. LTV Corp.* suggest that the Court is becoming less persuaded that the determinant of constitutional fairness is a trial model of procedure? What kind of procedural guarantees can be drawn from § 555?

2. *Inquisitorial Procedures.*

In a number of statutes, the Congress has authorized the use of hearings in which the hearing officer is required to ferret out and evaluate all of the available evidence, not only that favoring the individual appearing before the officer, but the evidence against the individual as well. In such cases, the hearing officers are part prosecutor, part defense counsel and part judge. Can such a combination of functions in one person ever be compatible with the APA? Can it be compatible with basic concepts of fairness?

In *Wong Yang Sung v. McGrath*, 339 U.S. 33 (1950), the Supreme Court ruled unlawful — as inconsistent with the APA — the practice of the Immigration and Naturalization Service under which a single "presiding inspector" performed the functions in a deportation case of eliciting the evidence, including the evidence against an individual and of evaluating it:

> This hearing, which followed the uniform practice of the Immigration Service, was before an immigrant inspector, who, for purposes of the hearing, is called the "presiding inspector." Except with consent of the alien, the presiding inspector may not be the one who investigated the case . . . But the inspector's duties include investigation of like cases; and while he is today hearing cases investigated by a colleague, tomorrow his investigation of a case may be heard before the inspector whose case he passes on today. An "examining inspector" may be designated to conduct the prosecution . . . but none was in this case; and, in any event, the examining inspector also has the same mixed prosecutive and hearing functions. The presiding inspector, when no examining inspector is present, is required to "conduct the interrogation of the alien and the witnesses in behalf of the Government and shall cross-examine the alien's witnesses and present such evidence as is necessary to support the charges in the warrant of arrest." . . . It may even become his duty to lodge an additional charge against the alien and proceed to hear his own accusation in like manner . . . . Then, as soon as practicable, he is to prepare a summary of the evidence, proposed findings of fact, conclusions of law, and a proposed order. A copy is furnished the alien or his counsel, who may file exceptions and brief . . . whereupon the whole is forwarded to the Commissioner.

> The Administrative Procedure Act did not go so far as to require a complete separation of investigating and prosecuting functions from adjudicating functions. But that the safeguards it did set up were intended to ameliorate the evils from the commingling of functions as exemplified here is beyond doubt. And this commingling, if objectionable anywhere, would seem to be particularly so in the deportation proceeding, where we frequently meet with a voteless class of litigants who not only lack the influence of citizens, but who are strangers to the laws and customs in which they find themselves involved and who often do not even understand the tongue in which they are accused. Nothing in the nature of the parties or proceedings suggests that we should strain to exempt deportation proceedings from reforms in administrative procedure applicable generally to federal agencies.

339 U.S. at 45–46.

Congress may have believed that exclusion and deportation proceedings were not within the scope of the APA, because of the provision in 556(a) now exempting proceedings "by or before boards or other employees specially provided for by or designated under statute." In any event, Congress responded to this decision by legislation exempting exclusion and deportation decisions from the APA in the Supplemental Appropriations Act of 1951. Subsequently, in the Immigration and Nationality Act of 1952, Congress provided a substitute procedure for exclusion and deportation. Although the separation of functions provisions of the APA are omitted, many other provisions of the APA have analogues in the 1952 Act. In *Marcello v. Bonds* 349 U.S. 302, 311 (1955), the Court held that the mere fact that the special inquiry officer conducting a deportation hearing was subject to the supervision and control of officials in the Immigration Service charged with investigative and prosecuting functions did not so strip "the hearing of fairness and impartiality as to make the procedure violative of due process."

Benefit agencies commonly employ procedures in which the hearing officer performs the tasks of developing both the claimant's case and the case against the claimant and then of rendering a decision. In *Richardson v. Perales*, 402 U.S. 389 (1971), the Supreme Court upheld this procedure in the administration of the Social Security disability insurance program:

> We need not decide whether the APA has general application to social security disability claims, for the social security administrative procedure does not vary from that prescribed by the APA. . . .
>
> Neither are we persuaded by the advocate-judge-multiple-hat suggestion. It assumes too much and would bring down too many procedures designed, and working well, for a governmental structure of great and growing complexity. The social security hearing examiner, furthermore, does not act as counsel. He acts as an examiner charged with developing the facts. The 44.2% reversal rate for all federal disability hearings in cases where the state agency does not grant benefits . . . attests to the fairness of the system and refutes the implication of impropriety.

402 U.S. at 409–410.

Inquisitorial procedures continue to be employed in Social Security disability proceedings. A description of such proceedings can be found in *Mathews v. Eldridge, supra*. Similarly, the administration of veterans' benefits has traditionally been viewed as a proceeding in which the presiding officers bear both the responsibility for case development and the responsibility for decision.

Questions and Comments

1. In *Richardson v. Perales*, the Court indicated its belief in the overall fairness of the inquisitorial procedures used by the Social Security Administration. Do you agree with the Court that a presiding officer who is responsible for the full development of all sides of the case can decide that case fairly?

2. If you can accept the Court's view that the procedure in *Richardson v. Perales* was fair, can you also agree with the Court's earlier expressed view that the procedure in *Wong Yang Sung v. McGrath* was unfair? Why was the procedure in *Marcello v. Bonds* not considered unfair? How do you think it was better (if at all) than the procedure in *Wong Yang Sung?* From what you know, do you think that the procedures in *Richardson v. Perales* were more or less fair than those in *Wong Yang Sung?* If the procedure in *Wong Yang Sung* violated the APA, then would not the procedure in *Richardson v. Perales* also violate the APA? Is it essential to the operation of the Social Security disability program to exclude it from governance by the APA? In *Richardson v. Perales, supra*, the Supreme Court refused to decide whether the APA governs social security disability proceedings.

3. Back in 1940, the Attorney General's Committee on Administrative Procedure expressed the view that hearings held in administering veterans' benefit programs were "investigatory" rather than the sole basis upon which a decision was reached: Those hearings were said to be "merely incidental to an ex parte investigatory process; decisions rest upon the whole investigation, rather than merely upon that portion of it embraced by the hearing."

This view of the hearing process avoids the difficulties encountered in evaluating the fairness of inquisitorial procedures, because in 1940 there was no pretense that the decision on a claim for veterans' benefits was made solely on the hearing record. If a hearing were not the sole basis for a decision, then the expectations of a claimant about what fairness requires would be significantly different from his or her expectations under a regime in which the hearing creates a record which is the sole basis for decision, would they not? The limited role for benefit hearings described by the Attorney General's Committee, however, is at odds with the entitlement approach underlying *Goldberg v. Kelly [supra]*, Chapter 31.

Perales, however, makes clear the Court's view that it is possible to construct an efficient and fair procedure for administering benefit programs which makes use of an inquisitorial-type hearing. Indeed, the use of an inquisitorial hearing format may be the most practical method for administering mass-benefit programs.

Chapter 5

AN ALTERNATIVE MODEL OF ADMINISTRATION: INDEPENDENT ADJUDICATION

A. THE TRADITIONAL AGENCY MODEL

The traditional regulatory agencies are designed to permit the agency head to sit as the final administrative tribunal to hear disputes. Disputes in the first instance are tried before an administrative law judge with review by the agency head. The agency head possesses the final power of review to ensure that the agency head retains full power over agency policy. The assumption underlying this organizational structure is that significant amounts of policy are formulated in adjudications.

The majority of the Final Report of the Attorney General's Committee believed that significant policy was made in adjudications. That was why they insisted upon the agency head possessing the power of final review. They also believed that fairness to litigants primarily involved a disinterested determination of evidentiary facts. Accordingly, they recommended that hearings be conducted by hearing officers who possessed a status and independence (from agency control) which would generate confidence in the fairness of their decisions. Policy determinations, however, would be made by the agency head which would review the decisions of the hearing officers.

The APA was drafted to fit this model of decision-making. Hearing officers — now administrative law judges — were made free of agency control by taking decisions about their promotion and salary away from the agency for whom they worked. Their independence was further strengthened by according them tenure in office. Their status was to be raised by providing them with more generous compensation. Subsequently, their status has been further raised by changing their title to administrative law judge.

Following the recommendations of the Final Report's majority, the APA contemplates that ALJ decisions will be — or may be — reviewed by the agency head. Indeed, the APA literally gives the agency exceedingly broad powers on review:

> On appeal from or review of the initial decision, the agency has all the powers which it would have in making the initial decision except as it may limit the issues on notice or by rule.

5 U.S.C. § 557(b).

You know from the *Universal Camera* cases and related materials studied in Chapter 2, however, that while this language ensures that the agency head has full control over policy, the agency head nevertheless may not easily be able to overturn the credibility determinations of an administrative law judge.

B. AN ALTERNATIVE MODEL

Some regulatory and benefit programs are administered through a different agency structure. Under the Occupational Safety and Health Act, for example, the Secretary of Labor is charged with reducing workplace hazards. The Secretary, acting through the Occupational Safety and Health Administration, issues rules (called occupational safety and health standards), which are binding upon employers. These rules are issued as a result of notice-and-comment proceedings. Workplaces are subject to inspection by OSHA inspectors for compliance with these rules.

When OSHA determines that an employer has violated a safety and health standard, the employer is cited for a violation and ordered to pay a fine. Should the employer wish to contest the asserted violation, the employer is entitled to a hearing before an administrative law judge, with review by an independent tribunal, the Occupational Safety and Health Review Commission (OSHRC). The members of OSHRC are appointed by the President to the Commission for a term of years and confirmed by the Senate. They are not subject to the Secretary of Labor or anyone else in the Department of Labor.

The legislative history of the Occupational Safety and Health Act shows that this organizational structure was chosen in order to achieve both the fact and the appearance of fairness. Reflection will reveal as well, however, that in implementing the Occupational Safety and Health Act there is no need for policy to be made in adjudications. There is, therefore, no need for the traditional agency structure whose rationale is based upon a perceived need for policy to be made in adjudications.

Rather than making policy case-by-case in adjudications, effective implementation of the Occupational Safety and Health Act requires that the administering agency issue widely applicable rules which specify in advance the conduct which is to be required of employers. These rules must spell out the required conduct in sufficient detail to enable employers to obey them.

Since policy must be incorporated in rules, the Secretary of Labor controls policy under the Act without the need to sit as an adjudicator. The independent OSHRC is able to hear appeals from the ALJ without interfering with the Secretary's control over policy. Should the Secretary disagree with an interpretation which OSHRC places upon an occupational safety and health standard, the Secretary is free to amend the rule in issue to incorporate his own approach.

Excerpt from Verkuil, *The Purposes and Limits of Independent Agencies*, 1988 Duke LJ. 257, 268:

> The idea of an independent agency tailored to the adjudicatory function and linked to an executive agency that exercises policyrnaking and prosecution responsibilities need not be invented; it exists already in at least two statutes administered by the Department of Labor, an executive department. The Department's Occupational Safety and Health Administration (OSHA) has responsibility for setting and enforcing health and safety standards. Challenges to OSHA's standard enforcement are adjudicated before a three-member independent agency, the Occupational Safety

and Health Review Commission (OSHRC). A similar arrangement exists for mine safety and health, where the Mine Safety and Health Administration (MSHA) sets and enforces safety and health standards and the independent, five-member Federal Mine Safety and Health Review Commission (FMSHRC) adjudicates them.

These innovative arrangements are the product of political compromise that overcame an attempt to give all three functions (rulemaking, prosecution and adjudication) directly to the Secretary of Labor (or his/her designate). Senator Javits is given credit for working the compromise that brought an independent agency into an executive department to satisfy what he labeled "traditional notions of due process." The Senator undoubtedly used this phrase for its rhetorical value, since due process dictates have long been satisfied by a commingling of functions. But this coordinated independent/ executive agency arrangement enhances the appearance if not the reality of fairness. . . .

C. THE BENEFIT AGENCIES

The largest benefit program is the Social Security Administration's disability insurance program. The disability program is a federal one, but is partially administered by the states. A person making a disability claim is required to make the claim at an agency of the state in which he or she resides. If the claim is denied, the claimant may ask that it be reconsidered. If it is still denied, the claimant may seek an adjudication of the claim before a federal administrative law judge. Decisions of federal ALJs may be appealed to the SSA's Appeals Council. Further review is in the courts.

Although the Secretary of Health and Human Services administers the entire program, the Secretary has established the Appeals Council to act on the Secretary's behalf on appeals. In form, the Appeals Council is not therefore independent from the Secretary. In practice, however, the Appeals Council does not perform an effective policy-implementing role, because in context such a role is not practical. The volume of cases adjudicated before ALJs and the Appeals Council is so large that the Secretary's control over policy cannot be exercised through attention to results in individual cases. (In fiscal 1986 ALJs disposed of 220,313 cases and the 20-member Appeals Council disposed of 52,000 review level cases, a number which had risen to 79,500 in fiscal 1988. Koch & Kaplow, *The Fourth Bite at the Apple: A Study of the Operation and Utility of the Social Security Administration's Appeals Council*, 17 Fla. St. U.L. Rev. 199, 223 n. 136, 242 n.233 (1990).) In fiscal 1999, the ALJ caseload was 455,192, rising to 491,404 in fiscal 2000 and to 525,383 in fiscal 2002. Frank S. Bloch, Jeffrey S. Lubbers & Paul R. Verkuil, *Developing a Full and Fair Evidentiary Record in a Nonadversary Setting: Two Proposals for Improving Social Security Disability Adjudications*, 25 Cardozo L. Rev. 1, 5 (2003). Rather, the Secretary must control policy through the issuance of rules or other directives (Social Security Rulings).

Thus the administration of the disability program seems to fit the model of independent adjudication. Adjudication takes place before independent ALJs and appeals are to an Appeals Council which is practically, if not formally, independent of the Secretary. This practical independence is a result of the extremely large volume of cases decided by the Appeals Council: the large volume effectively precludes the Secretary from using the Appeals Council as a vehicle for formulating and controlling agency policy.

D. POLICY COORDINATION AND THE PROBLEM OF DEFERENCE

MARTIN v. OCCUPATIONAL SAFETY AND HEALTH REVIEW COMMISSION
499 U.S. 157 (1991)

REICH V. OCCUPATIONAL SAFETY AND HEALTH REVIEW COMMISION
998 F.2d 134 (3d Cir. 1993)

[*See* Chapter 2, supra]

E. ATTEMPTS BY THE SOCIAL SECURITY ADMINISTRATION TO REDUCE THE LEVEL OF INCONSISTENT DECISION-MAKING BY ALJs

BARRY v. HECKLER
620 F. Supp. 779 (N.D. Cal. 1985)

ORRICK, DISTRICT JUDGE.

The issue framed by the cross-motions for summary judgment in this supplementary security income ("SSI") case brought by plaintiff, an unemployed carpenter, against defendant Margaret Heckler, Secretary of Health and Human Services ("Secretary"), is whether plaintiff was assured due process in the manner in which his application for SSI benefits was reviewed. The Court holds that he was not, and that review program following the so-called Bellmon Amendment (hereafter the "Bellmon Review Program") impermissibly infringed his due process rights. For the reasons hereafter set forth, the Court grants the plaintiff's motion for summary judgment and denies the defendant's cross-motion.

A

The Bellmon Review Program was installed by the Secretary to implement Congress' mandate to "[review], on his own motion, decisions rendered by administrative law judges." Pub.L.No. 96-265, § 304(g), 94 Stat. 441, 456 (1980) (The Bellmon Amendment). Congress intended, in passing the Amendment, to improve the quality of decision-making, to redress the high rate at which ALJ's were reversing decision made at state levels, and to redress perceived imbalances between the reversal rates of the various ALJs. . . .

In implementing the program, the Secretary authorized the Office of Hearings and Appeals to target specific ALJs who had high rates of allowing disability benefits (Memorandum from the Associate Director of the Social Security Administration, Louis B. Hayes, Sept. 24, 1982; Exhibit "B" to Plaintiff's Memorandum In Support). Initially, an ALJ would be targeted for review if he or she had a 66-2/3% or higher allowance rate. By April, 1983, the program was supplemented to allow targeting based on the rate at which the Appeals Council reversed the ALJ. Under both criteria, only ALJs with a high allowance rate formed the pool from which targeted ALJs were selected for review.

When an ALJ was selected for review, all of the judge's decisions were subject to Council scrutiny. The judges were also eligible for a mandatory "counseling" program, which included feedback sessions. The sessions were designed to "educate" the ALJs and work on "decisional weaknesses." Although never implemented, the counseling program was described in the memorandum circulated to the ALJs. Finally, the ALJs were advised that if, after further review, their performance did not improve, "other steps" would be considered. (See, Memorandum of the Associate Director, supra).[1]

B

Plaintiff was employed as a carpenter from 1958 until January, 1981, when he suffered a heart attack. He returned to work after July, 1981 but suffered chest pains and back pains that prevented him from performing sustained activity throughout the work day. He stopped working on December 28, 1981, and has not been gainfully employed since January, 1982.

Plaintiff brought a claim for disability payments under 42 U.S.C. § 423(a)(1)(D). The Administrative Law judge ("AlJ") granted the plaintiff disability benefits, and determined that the plaintiff had the residual capacity to perform "sedentary work" as defined by 20 C.F.R. § 404.1567. The Appeals Council, on its own motion, chose to review the ALJ's decision. On December 6, 1983, the Appeals Council reversed the ALJ and concluded that the plaintiff was not entitled to disability benefits. Specifically, the Council found that the plaintiff had the "maximum sustained capacity for a full range of medium work activities." (Tr., pp. 1213).

The Secretary . . . argues that even if the program violated due process principles in general, the plaintiff here was not in any way injured by the program and therefore lacks standing. Specifically, the Secretary asserts that: (1) the ALJ was the only adjudicator affected by the program and here he held in favor of the plaintiff, and (2) due process analysis is irrelevant given that the Council's decision was supported by substantial evidence.

Addressing the first argument, although it is true that the ALJ reached a decision in plaintiff's favor, plaintiff was certainly harmed by the targeting

---

[1] The individual ALJ portion of the Bellmon review program was eliminated by the Office of Hearings and Appeals of the Social Security Administration on June 22, 1984. However, plaintiff's case was heard prior to the program's demise by an ALJ who was subject to the program.

program. Had the program not been in effect, the Council would not have automatically reviewed the favorable decision of the ALJ, thereby decreasing the likelihood that benefits would ultimately be denied.

As to the second argument, due process rights can be violated even if the Appeals Council had sufficient evidence for its decision. . . .

The plaintiff claims that the Bellmon review program deprived him of his Fifth Amendment rights by creating incentives for high-allowance ALJs to reduce their rate of allowances. By keeping their rates down, it is argued, the ALJs can avoid scrutiny of all their decisions, avoid feedback sessions, and avoid the threat of "other steps" taken if "no improvement" is made. Additionally, the plaintiff argues that the Appeals Council, by targeting only high-allowance judges, had a hidden agenda to "blue-pencil" or "second-guess" the ALJs.

The Due Process Clause of the Fifth Amendment requires that the plaintiff receive a "trial before an unbiased judge." This due process rule is applicable to administrative as well as judicial proceedings. *Gibson v. Berryhill*, 411 U.S. 564, *Hummel v. Heckler, supra*, 736 F. 2d at 93. In fact, the requirement of impartiality is applied even more strictly to administrative adjudicators because of the absence of procedural safeguards normally available in a judicial proceeding. . . .

The Secretary's application of the Bellmon Amendment put pressure on selected ALJs to reduce their percentage of benefit allowances, thereby denying claimants of their right to an impartial ALJ. This pressure was applied primarily by way of memoranda from the Office of Hearings and Appeals informing ALJs that: (1) all of their decisions would be scrutinized by the Appeals Council, (2) they would be eligible for special peer counseling, and (3) they would be subject to "other steps" if necessary. Such pressure was recognized in *Association of Administrative Law Judges v. Heckler, supra*, as having adverse consequences on ALJ decision-making:

> . . . the evidence as a whole, persuasively demonstrated that [the Secretary] retained an unjustifiable preoccupation with allowance rates, to the extent that ALJs could reasonably feel pressure, in close cases, and in particular . . . that pressure may have intruded upon the factfinding process and may have influenced some outcomes. 594 F. Supp. at 1142.

In addition to depriving a claimant of the right to an impartial ALJ, application of the Bellmon review program impermissibly affected the Appeals Council. Common sense indicates that targeting certain ALJs with the objective of limiting allowance rates is a method by which the Appeals Council reviewed "liberal" ALJs with an eye toward reversal. Application of the Bellmon Amendment is the way to deprived [sic] claimants of their due process rights to an impartial tribunal.

Therefore, IT IS HEREBY ORDERED, that the plaintiff's motion for summary judgment is granted and the defendant Secretary's motion for summary judgment is denied. The determination of the Secretary is reversed and remanded.

Excerpt from Richard J. Pierce, Jr., *Political Control Versus Impermissible Bias in Agency Decisionmaking: Lessons from* Chevron *and* Mistretta, 57 U. Chi. L. Rev. 481, 507–515 (1990):

B. *Improving Consistency*

Like promptness, consistency in adjudication is a due process value: we want our legal system to produce like results in like cases. If all individuals in a large class are judged by the same standard, the risk that the government will unfairly single out some individuals for harsh treatment decreases.

ALJs reverse benefit denials at an average rate of 50 percent. Reversal rates vary widely among ALJs, however, with about 10 percent of ALJs reversing 75 percent of the benefit denials appealed to them and about 10 percent reversing only 25 percent. Independent researchers investigating the ALJ decisionmaking process have reached startling conclusions. First, "It1he inconsistency of the disability decision process is patent." Second, "the outcome of cases depends more on who decides the case than on what the facts are." Third, the reversal rates of individual ALJs correlate strongly with their personal philosophies. Fourth, statistical analysis of ALJ decisionmaking demonstrates that "the most error-prone judges are those whose reversal rate deviates most from the mean."

With the blessing (indeed prodding) of Congress, the SSA addressed the problem of ALJ inconsistency, and thereby took steps directed at improving SSA process, by ordering its Appeals Council to review on its own motion large numbers of ALJ decisions. Most of the decisions selected for review had been made by ALJs with aberrationally high rates of reversal of benefit denials. The Appeals Council initially reviewed 100 percent of the decisions of ALJs with reversal rates higher than 74 percent. . . .

Reducing the variation in ALJ reversal rates inevitably enhances consistency. Given the large number of cases decided by each ALJ and the random assignment of cases to ALJs, the wide variation in reversal rates suggests that ALJs are using much different decisional standards. According to elementary statistical analysis, if all ALJs applied the same decisional standard, over 95 percent of ALJs would have a reversal rate between 45 and 55 percent; over 99 percent would have a reversal rate between 40 and 60 percent. Moreover, the reversal rate of an individual ALJ would vary randomly around the mean reversal rate from period to period. Thus, the probability that an individual ALJ's reversal rate would fall outside the 40 to 60 percent range in two consecutive years is less than one-tenth of one percent. Forcing ALJs to have reversal rates within a certain range likely induces them to use similar decisional standards.

Moreover, reducing the variation in ALJ reversal rates does more than further the due process value of consistency; consistency is itself an excellent proxy for accuracy, another primary goal of the Due Process Clause.

To understand why consistency is a good measure, and perhaps the only measure, of accuracy in this context, consider the nature of typical disability cases. A majority of the cases that reach the ALJ level involve allegations of chronic pain. The second largest category involves allegations of neuroses-usually anxiety or depression. Neither pain nor neurosis can be measured objectively. . . .

The courts, moreover, have rejected efforts by Congress, the SSA, and ALJs to objectify the process of measuring pain and neurosis, thereby making even more difficult the assurance of accuracy in disability reviews. Until the 1960s, the SSA had applied a strict but relatively clear standard to evaluate the degree of an applicant's pain. The standard had first been enunciated in a 1937 Learned Hand opinion, in which Hand had written:

A man may have to endure discomfort or pain and not be totally disabled; much of the best work of life goes on under such disabilities- . . . . The only work available to the insured must do more than hurt, it must substantially aggravate his malady.[2]

In the '60s, however, despite indications of approval from Congress, the courts unanimously rejected this strict standard. The ALJs and courts were forced to resort to subjective evaluations of pain and neuroses, and the disability thresholds were inevitably lowered.

The courts have also frustrated the achievement of accuracy in SSA disability evaluations by forcing the SSA and its ALJs to give weight to unreliable evidence at the expense of reliable evidence. According to the "treating physician rule" — a judicially created exception to the deferential substantial evidence test — the SSA and its ALJs must give greater weight to the opinions of applicants' treating physicians than to the opinions of consulting physicians. The exception is premised on the courts' belief that treating physicians' opinions are more reliable than consulting physicians' opinions — a belief that the courts are alone in holding. Congress, the SSA, ALJs, and independent investigators agree that "as a matter of both bias and degree of qualification the consulting physician is likely to be much the better information source."

Thus, in the context of chronic pain and neuroses — the typical disability cases that reach the ALJ level — the courts have stymied efforts to improve and objectify a highly subjective decisionmaking process. What exists instead is a subjective process in which ALJs are required to make yes-or-no decisions on disability when the applicant's ability to work and the severity of the underlying illness could fall anywhere along a vast spectrum. The ALJ can hope to do little more than draw a line on the

---

[2] Theberge v United States, 87 F2d 697, 698 (2d Cir 1937). Judge Hand's interpretation of disabling pain antedated the Social Security disability program, but the SSA adopted his standard and applied it for over twenty years before the courts struck it down. Mashaw, Social Security Hearings at 142-46 (cited in note 86).

Congress revisited the issue of disabling pain through a statutory amendment enacted in 1984. A finding of pain-induced disability must be predicated on medical signs and findings, established by medically acceptable clinical or laboratory diagnostic techniques, which show the existence of a medical impairment that results from anatomical, physiological, or psychological abnormalities which could reasonably be expected to produce the pain or other symptoms alleged and which, when considered with all evidence required to be furnished . . . would lead to a conclusion that the individual is under a disability.

Social Security Disability Benefits Reform Act of 1984, Pub L No 98-480, 98 Stat 1799 (1984), codified at 42 USC § 423(d)(5) (1982 & Supp 1989). It is hard to see how this longwinded amendment advances the goals of accuracy and consistency.

disability spectrum and use her judgment to determine on which side of the line individual cases fall.

Accuracy in an objective sense obviously is not a realistic goal in this context. Accuracy in a relative sense is attainable only by forcing ALJs to locate the yes-no line on the same point along the disability spectrum. The comparative advantage of using ALJs lies in their ability to place pain cases on a spectrum; for example, from one to ten, with "one" meaning slight pain and "ten" meaning extreme pain. The disadvantage of using ALJs is that different ALJs draw the line separating tolerable pain from disabling pain at different points on the spectrum; for example, some ALJs will find level two pain disabling while others will find level nine pain tolerable. Consistency, and hence "accuracy," is attainable only by forcing each ALJ to maintain a reversal rate that lies within a relatively narrow range; for example, 40 to 60 percent. This constrains ALJs by making them draw the line between tolerable pain and disabling pain at about the same point on the relative pain spectrum.

It follows that the SSA should go further than it has to date to control the variation in ALJ reversal rates. Forcing ALJs to adopt consistent reversal rates does not jeopardize due process values. Rather, it significantly furthers consistency and accuracy, two important due process values. An ALJ should thus be removed for cause if her reversal rate falls outside the presumptive boundaries unless she can support the highly improbable proposition that her aberrational reversal rate is attributable to differences between her mix of assigned cases and the total mix of cases.

C. Changing the Mean Reversal Rate

. . . . The SSA may also have changed the mean, however, whether or not it intended to do so. . . . All judges who have reviewed the SSA's control systems have balked at a change in the mean, referring to such an effect pejoratively as an introduction of impermissible systemic bias.

A change in the mean reversal rate is potentially defensible on either of two grounds. A modest unintended change in the mean might be defended simply as a tolerable price to pay for enhanced consistency and accuracy. . . .

The SSA may, however, have intended to change the mean, its protestations notwithstanding. To explore this possibility, it is easy enough to hypothesize a control system that would unambiguously indicate an intent to change the mean. Suppose that the SSA established a mandatory range of ALJ reversal rates of 30 to 50 percent. With an *ex ante* mean reversal rate of 50 percent, the inescapable inference would be that the SSA intended to change the mean as well as the variance. Yet, it is my contention that even this intuitively unpalatable method of controlling the behavior of adjudicatory decisionmakers should be upheld in the context of ALJ disability decisionmaking.

A mandatory change in the mean reversal rate would not single out individuals for adverse treatment, the only context in which due process values trump political process values. Rather, a mandatory change in the mean would represent a change in policy with respect to the threshold of pain or neurosis required to justify permanent public support. It would be a modest step toward a return to the [formerly objective] standard announced by Learned Hand. Politically unaccountable ALJs and federal judges were the authors of the gradual policy shift to lower the pain and neurosis threshold over the last three decades. Surely, the politically accountable branches have the power to reverse or amend that judicial policy decision.

Once a change in the threshold for receiving benefits is recognized as a policy issue, the legitimacy of such a change should be evaluated with reference to the political rather than judicial process. The question whether the SSA can change the mean is answered by applying the two-step test announced in *Chevron.* Step one: Did Congress "directly [speak] to the precise question at issue?" While the Bellmon Amendment was motivated in part by fiscal concerns and in part by the high rate at which ALJs were reversing benefit denial decisions, Congress did not specifically mandate a change in the mean reversal rate. Thus, Congress did not directly speak to the policy question at issue, and we move to step two: Is the agency's resolution of the policy issue "permissible?"

Whatever "permissible" means in this context, it should not authorize administrative law judges to substitute their policy views for those of agency officials accountable to the executive. The definition of "permissible" should have a statutory and a procedural dimension, which may be realized by asking the following two questions. First, is the agency's resolution of the policy dispute within the range of resolutions that Congress left open? Here, the answer to this question is an easy yes. Although Congress did not *mandate* a reduction in mean ALJ reversal rates, it clearly did not intend to *preclude* SSA from pursuing that goal. Second, did the agency follow congressionally prescribed procedures in reaching its policy decision? The Ninth Circuit held the Bellmon Review Program invalid on the ground that the SSA should have used notice and comment rulemaking in deciding whether to adopt the program. This is a close question, but the Ninth Circuit may have answered it correctly. At the least, notice and comment rulemaking would have provided a higher degree of confidence that the SSA's decision to lower the mean reversal rate was consistent with Congress's views on this important policy issue. Thus, the only potential flaw in the Bellmon Review Program lay in the SSA's failure to use notice and comment rulemaking in deciding whether to adopt it.

F. COMPARING THE ATTRIBUTES OF THE TRADITIONAL AGENCY STRUCTURE WITH THE ALTERNATIVE INVOLVING INDEPENDENT ADJUDICATION

From Daniel J. Gifford, *Adjudication in Independent Tribunals: The Role of an Alternative Agency Structure,* 66 NOTRE DAME L. REV. 965, 994–999 (1991):

. . . . [T]he traditional structure assumes that in some significant number of adjudications, policy application to the particular respondents is salient. Otherwise policy could be formulated by rule. Even the review-board modification is premised upon this assumption. . . .

The usefulness of the traditional structure thus depends both upon the nature and size of the agency's caseload and its operational goals. When the agency needs to shape conduct on a mass scale or to administer a mass benefit program, the traditional model, even with the review-board or limited-review modifications, begins to lose its organizational advantages. It is also ill-adapted to regulatory or administrative tasks involving adjudication of a very large number of cases.

First, the mere size of the agency's caseload may render ineffective the use of adjudication as a policy formulating device. When the caseload becomes very large, then the disposition of a single case does not raise a salient matter of policy. At that point, the agency head no longer needs to possess reviewing authority over particular cases, which the traditional agency structure provides. This is surely true of the administration of welfare or the social security disability program.

Second, when an agency bears the responsibility for imposing behavioral standards upon large numbers of subjects, that task calls for (1) more precise standards than adjudication can provide and (2) standards articulated in advance—a task for which rulemaking is best adapted. Moreover, without the further power to impose rules backed by penalties, the agency cannot hope to effectively regulate the conduct of large numbers of subjects. Only penalties, not cease-and-desist orders, provide incentives for nonparties to observe agency policies. Again, therefore, the ability of the traditional regulatory structure to confer ultimate adjudicatory authority upon the agency head becomes useless in these circumstances. Thus, even when an agency is not burdened with a huge caseload, if all or most of its policy decisions are generic ones, then its task can be performed effectively through rulemaking.[3] To the extent that policyrnaking is generic, therefore, the traditional agency structure loses its rationale, regardless of the size of the adjudicative caseload.

Thus, in regulation concerned with workplace safety or with the environment[4] for example, regulation involves the use of generic rules and

---

[3] Generic policyrnaking through rulemaking is appropriate when the full range of applicable factual contexts can be identified in advance. By contrast, adjudication as a method of formulating policy is useful for limiting the scope of policy pronouncements to stated factual contexts. When factual configurations may vary in unpredictable ways, formulating policy and expanding its scope cautiously and incrementally through a series of adjudications has the advantage of limiting policy applications to factual contexts that are fully understood at the time of application. When an agency must impose behavioral standards upon a wide range of conduct immediately, however, it is denied the luxury of proceeding incrementally through a series of fact-intensive adjudicatory pronouncements.

[4] In its administration of the Clean Air Act, the Environmental Protection Agency (EPA) possesses elements of both a traditional agency structure and an alternative structure. This structure may reflect a congressional belief that while most policy issues are generic ones, some issues of application are

small or moderate adjudicatory caseloads. This is because the mandated goals involve widespread and immediate compliance with precise behavioral standards. In such contexts, adjudication should be limited, so far as possible, to factual disputes over whether respondents have complied with outstanding rules. Ideally, most policy issues would be resolved in rule-making; adjudications would be factually (rather than policy) focused and they would be relatively few in number.

In the benefit agencies, the efficient disposition of a large volume of benefit claims demands the use of relatively precise standards, whose applications do not raise significant policy issues. Welfare administration had generally been moving in that direction since at least the 1960s. Moreover, the judicialization of benefit procedure required under *Goldberg v. Kelly* was compatible with the transformation of welfare programs from an approach involving individualized approvals of grants for special purposes into an approach involving general purpose grants. The result was less individualization in administration and a greater use of more precise and broadly applicable standards — the paradigm case for rulemaking.

In a mass-justice agency, adjudication is unsuited for use as a vehicle for announcing or formulating policy. The cases come too fast and in too great a volume for decisionmakers to look to other cases as guides; sorting out, distinguishing or following large volumes of cases whose holdings are necessarily circumscribed by their unique factual configurations is impractical.[5] Thus, in a mass-justice agency, the agency head does not rely on adjudication to control policy and, accordingly, does not sit as a final adjudicator. Moreover, the removal of the agency head from control of adjudication is fully consistent with the agency head's policy responsibility because no individual case is programmatically salient. The agency head is not concerned with the disposition of any one case, but with the policies applied to large classes of cases.

---

nonetheless regulatorally salient. The EPA issues national ambient air quality standards (NAAQS) which the states are to implement through the issuance and enforcement of EPA-approved state implementation plans (SIPs). Under this scheme, the EPA would set standards, but enforcement would be left primarily to the states. For violations of state enforcement plans, however, the EPA retains enforcement authority which it exercises by issuing orders enforceable in the courts or by bringing civil actions for penalties. 42 U.S.C. § 7413(a)(b) (1988). See, e.g., General Motors Corp. v. United States, 110 S.Ct. 2528, 2530 (1990). Persons charged with violations of stationary-source emission limitations who challenge notice of noncompliance are entitled to be heard in an on-the-record proceeding. 42 U.S.C. § 7420(b)(5) (1988). The structure of this regulatory scheme, which is designed to employ state enforcement, assumes that major policy matters will be disposed of in the issuance of the NAAQS and the approval of the state SIPs. The EPA (but not necessarily the state) enforcement employs the traditional administrative structure to deal with the significant, albeit lesser, policy matters arising in cases where stationary source operators challenge notices of noncompliance. See 40 C.F.R. § 66.95 (1989).

[5] Adjudicative decisions can be used, however, as a data base from which the policy making authorities can later draw to issue directives on how to dispose of selected issues raised in some of the cases. Thus the Social Security Administration uses cases to issue Social Security Rulings. In a similar vein, the Internal Revenue Service issues Revenue Rulings which are those of its private rulings raising the most important policy issues. See Caplin, *Taxpayer Rulings Policy of the Internal Revenue Service: A Statement of Principles*, 20 INST. ON FED. TAX'N 1 (1962); Gifford, *supra* note 88, at 258.

These differing regulatory approaches are the necessary result of the underlying differences in the regulatory or administrative tasks assigned to the agencies. The approaches correspond, respectively, to the differing structural capacities of the traditional regulatory agency on the one hand, and of an agency which deals with a high-volume caseload or regulates large numbers of subjects on the other. Indeed, the ideal design of agency organization could be represented on a chart which relates the kinds of policy applications to their appropriate decisional structure.

	Traditional structure	agency with review board	mass-justice agency
Regulatory salience of applying policy to particular respondents	X	X	
		X	X

The traditional structure, for reasons already stated, is best suited to administer a regulatory program in which a small number of cases will be adjudicated and each case is regulatory salient. As the caseload increases in volume, the disposition of some particular cases may remain salient, but the individual dispositions of many cases will not raise significant issues of regulatory or administrative policy. For such a caseload, the traditional structure augmented by an intermediate review board is a good response. This structure allows the agency head to sit as final adjudicator for those cases raising significant policy issues, but allocates to the review board the disposition of routine cases. For agencies with extremely large caseloads, typically no individual disposition decisions are salient in themselves. Important issues of policy are resolved in generic rulemaking proceedings which produce standards governing behavior or the disposition of future cases. This type of caseload, accordingly, tends to be centered on the resolution of factual disputes rather than policy issues.[6] For this type of caseload, adjudication of cases by a separate or quasi-separate administrative organ is the best response. Indeed, in the case of large-scale benefit or other programs, the volume of adjudication may be so large as to render ineffective attempts to control policy through the administrative appellate review process.

---

[6] Even in this regulatory context, some agencies do respond to large numbers of requests for advice, the answers to which may involve the resolution of issues of policy. These responses, though, typically do not involve the participation of the agency head, except indirectly in the form of general supervision over a staff of lower-level employees charged with dealing with routine responses. The Internal Revenue Service, for example, responds to large numbers of requests for advance rulings on the tax consequences of proposed transactions. It is able to perform this task by delegating the responsibility for routine responses to lower echelon officials. It then selects a small number of the most important rulings for higher-level review and publication as Revenue Rulings in the Internal Revenue Bulletin. In this way, the agency as an institution is able to resolve numerous fact-specific issues of policy without imposing heavy commitments upon the time of the agency head.

Other agencies, like OSHA, do not conform to the traditional model, even though the number of adjudications arising under their regulatory statutes would not necessarily preclude it. For such agencies, the traditional structure has no appealing advantage. These agencies, which are charged with implementing behavioral changes on a wide scale, announce the required conduct norms through precisely drafted rules. Controversial policy issues are addressed in rulemaking, so that subsequent enforcement disputes involve primarily factual and lesser policy issues. Because major policy issues are resolved in rulemaking, and the dispositions of particular factual disputes are not in themselves regulatorily salient, there is little reason for the policymaking organ to adjudicate, even though the adjudicatory caseload would not itself preclude it. In this context, the traditional structure loses its appeal.

Chapter 6

THE CHOICE OF ACTION BY RULE OR BY AD HOC ADJUDICATION OR OTHER MEANS

A. AGENCY DISCRETION: THE BASIC FACTORS

The *Chenery* Cases

SEC v. Chenery Corp., 318 U. S. 80 (1943). Under the Public Utility Holding Company Act, Congress had imposed a limit to the number of holding companies which could participate in a chain of ownership of a public utility company. Corporate structures including more than the permitted number of holding companies were required to be brought into compliance with the Act's requirements by reorganization. Reorganizations were supervised by the Securities and Exchange Commission in order to ensure that the terms of the reorganization were "fair and equitable" and not "detrimental to the interests of investors."

When companies were reorganized under the Act, existing securities of one company were converted into securities of another company into which the first company was absorbed. Part of the process of reorganization involved placing a value on the assets of such a company as a means for determining the extent to which outstanding securities of various classes would participate in the reorganization by being transformed into securities of a surviving company. Naturally, if the assets of a company were insufficient to cover all of the claims against them, the stock with the least priority would be wiped out.

The respondents were officers, directors and controlling stockholders of Federal Water Service Corporation ("Federal"), a public utility holding company owning securities of subsidiary water, gas, electric, and other companies in several states and one foreign country. The respondents controlled Federal through their control of its parent, Utility Operators Company, which owned all of Federal's Class B common stock. Federal's management had filed three earlier plans which had provided for the participation by Class B stockholders in the equity of the proposed reorganized company, a feature to which the Commission objected.

A fourth plan of reorganization was accepted by the Commission. This plan proposed a merger of Federal, Utility Operators Company, and Federal Water and Gas Corporation, a wholly-owned inactive subsidiary of Federal. This plan contained no provision for participation by the Class B stock. Instead, that class of stock was to be surrendered for cancellation, and the preferred and Class A common stock of Federal were to be converted into common stock of the new corporation. Except for 5.3 per cent of the new common stock allocated to the holders of Federal's Class A stock, substantially all of the equity of the reorganized company was to be given to Federal's preferred stockholders. The Commission, however, conditioned its approval of the fourth plan on the nonparticipation of those shares of preferred stock which had been purchased by the respondents during the period in which successive reorganization plans proposed by Federal's management were before the Commission. That stock was to be surrendered at cost plus 4 per cent interest, under the plan approved by the Commission.

An extract from the Court's opinion follows:

> During the period from November 8, 1937, to June 30, 1940, while the successive reorganization plans were before the Commission, the respondents purchased a total of 12,407 shares of Federal's preferred stock. (The total number of outstanding shares of Federal's preferred stock was 159,269.) These purchases were made on the over-the-counter market through brokers at prices lower than the book value of the common stock of the new corporation into which the preferred stock would have been converted under the proposed plan. If this feature of the plan had been approved by the Commission, the respondents through their holdings of Federal's preferred stock would have acquired more than 10 per cent of the common stock of the new corporation. The respondents frankly admitted that their purpose in buying the preferred stock was to protect their interests in the company.

> In ascertaining whether the terms of issuance of the new common stock were "fair and equitable" or "detrimental to the interests of investors" within § 7 of the Act, the Commission found that it could not approve the proposed plan so long as the preferred stock acquired by the respondents would be permitted to share on a parity with other preferred stock. The Commission did not find fraud or lack of disclosure, but it concluded that the respondents, as Federal's managers, were fiduciaries and hence under a "duty of fair dealing" not to trade in the securities of the corporation while plans for its reorganization were before the Commission. . . .

> We completely agree with the Commission that officers and directors who manage a holding company in process of reorganization . . . occupy positions of trust. . . . But to say that a man is a fiduciary only begins analysis; it gives direction to further inquiry. To whom is he a fiduciary? What obligations does he owe as a fiduciary? In what respect has he failed to discharge these obligations? And what are the consequences of his deviation from duty?

> The Commission did not find that the respondents as managers of Federal acted covertly or traded on inside knowledge, or that their position as reorganization managers enabled them to purchase the preferred stock at prices lower than they would otherwise have had to pay, or that their acquisition of the stock in any way prejudiced the interests of the corporation or its stockholders. To be sure, the new stock into which the respondents' preferred stock would be converted under the plan of reorganization would have a book value — which may or may not represent market value — considerably greater than the prices paid for the preferred stock. But that would equally be true of purchasers of preferred stock made by other investors. The respondents, the Commission tells us, acquired

their stock as the outside world did, and upon no better terms. The Commission dealt with this as a specific case, and not as the application of a general rule formulating rules of conduct for reorganization managers. Consequently, it is a vital consideration that the Commission conceded that the respondents did not acquire their stock through any favoring circumstances. In its own words, "honesty, full disclosure, and purchase at a fair price" characterized the transactions. The Commission did not suggest that, as a result of their purchases of preferred stock, the respondents would be unjustly enriched. On the contrary, the question before the Commission was whether the respondents, simply because they were reorganization managers, should be denied the benefits to be received by the 6,000 other preferred stockholders. Some technical rule of law must have moved the Commission to single out the respondents and deny their preferred stock the right to participate equally in the reorganization. To ascertain the precise basis of its determination, we must look to the Commission's opinion.

In reaching [its] . . . result the Commission stated that it was merely applying "the broad equitable principles enunciated in [certain judicial decisions]" . . . Since the decision of the Commission was explicitly based upon the applicability of principles of equity announced by the courts, its validity must likewise be judged on that basis. The grounds upon which an administrative order must be judged are those upon which the record discloses that its action was based.

In confining our review to a judgment upon the validity of the grounds upon which the Commission itself based its action, we do not disturb the settled rule that, in reviewing the decision of a lower court, it must be affirmed if the result is correct "although the lower court relied upon a wrong ground or gave a wrong reason.

The reason for this rule is obvious. It would be wasteful to send a case back to a lower court to reinstate a decision which it had already made but which the appellate court concluded should properly be based on another ground within the power of the appellate court to formulate. But it is also familiar appellate procedure that where the correctness of the lower court's decision depends upon a determination of fact which only a jury could make but which has not been made, the appellate court cannot take the place of the jury. Like considerations govern review of administrative orders. If an order is valid only as a determination of policy or judgment which the agency alone is authorized to make and which it has not made, a judicial judgment cannot be made to do service for an administrative judgment. For purposes of affirming no less than reversing its orders, an appellate court cannot intrude upon the domain which Congress has exclusively entrusted to an administrative agency.

. . . . Since the Commission professed to decide the case before it according to settled judicial doctrines, its action must be judged by the standards which the Commission itself invoked. And judged by those standards, i.e., those which would be enforced by a court of equity, we must conclude that the Commission was in error in deeming its actions controlled by established judicial principles.

In determining whether to approve the plan of reorganization proposed by Federal's management, the Commission could inquire, under § 7(d)(6) and (e) of the Act, whether the proposal was "detrimental to the public interest or the interest of investors or consumers," and, under § 11(e), whether it was "fair and equitable." That these provisions were meant to confer upon the Commission broad powers for the protection of the public plainly appears from the reports of the Congressional committees in charge of the legislation. . . .

But the difficulty remains that the considerations urged here in support of the Commission's order were not those upon which its action was based. The Commission did not rely upon "its special administrative competence"; it formulated no judgment upon the requirements of the "public interest or the interest of investors or consumers" in the situation before it. . . . Had the commission, acting upon its experience and peculiar competence, promulgated a general rule of which its order here was a particular application, the problem for our consideration would be very different. Whether and to what extent directors or officers should be prohibited from buying or selling stock of the corporation during its reorganization, presents problems of policy for the judgment of Congress or of the body to which it has delegated power to deal with the matter. Abuse of corporate position, influence, and access to information may raise questions so subtle that the law can deal with them effectively only by prohibitions not concerned with the fairness of a particular transaction. But before transactions otherwise legal can be outlawed or denied their usual business consequences, they must fall under the ban of some standards of conduct prescribed by an agency of government authorized to prescribe such standards — either the courts or Congress or an agency to which Congress has delegated its authority. Congress itself did not proscribe the respondents' purchases of preferred stock in Federal. Established judicial doctrines do not condemn these transactions. Nor has the Commission, acting under the rule-making powers delegated to it by § 11(e), promulgated new general standards of conduct. . . . The Commission's determination can stand, therefore, only if it found that the specific transactions under scrutiny showed misuse by the respondents of their position as reorganization managers, in that as such managers they took advantage of the corporation or the other stockholders or the investing public. The record is utterly barren of any such showing. Indeed, such a claim against the respondents was explicitly disavowed by the Commission.

The cause should therefore be remanded to the Court of Appeals with directions to remand to the Commission for such further proceedings, not inconsistent with this opinion, as may be appropriate.

So ordered.

Questions and Comments

1.	Did Justice Frankfurter explain why a court must review an agency's action on the rationale provided by the agency? Does his explanation resemble Judge Frank's analysis of the relation between courts and agencies contained in his concurring opinion on remand in *Universal Camera?* Judge Frank, you will remember, suggested that an appellate court could revise the derivative inferences of a trial court sitting without a jury but could not revise the derivative inferences of an agency. He reached that result because he believed that Congress had entrusted the agency with a policy formulation role which a court would invade if it failed to respect the agency's derivative inferences. In *Chenery*, Justice Frankfurter was also concerned about the integrity of the agency's policy formulating role. For a court to uphold an agency's action upon a rationale different from the rationale supplied by the agency would involve the court in policymaking which was entrusted by Congress to the agency. The court can decide whether the agency's rationale is lawful, but it cannot supply a new rationale to take the place of an agency rationale which the court has determined to be defective.

2.	What was the SEC's objection to the participation of the Chenery group in the reorganized company? How would the SEC's goal be furthered by excluding the Chenery group from participating?

3.	The SEC was not saying that members of the Chenery group acted unethically by purchasing stock during the reorganization period, was it? Justice Frankfurter in *Chenery I* states that the SEC had not found any wrongdoing on the part of the Chenery or his group. Was the SEC nonetheless convinced that Chenery was acting improperly by buying stock at prices which were below its book value? Did Frankfurter deal with this aspect of the stock purchase? How? How were the purchases made? In private transactions or on the public market? Was the preferred stock available to others at the same prices? Were those prices set by public trading? Did others buy the stock at those prices? Did Chenery have any advantage over others trading in the preferred stock? Is your answer affected by learning that the reorganization plans were public documents, available for inspection by interested persons?

4.	Was anyone injured by anything that Chenery did? By his purchase of stock during the reorganization period? Were other preferred stockholders injured? Were the preferred stockholders who sold their shares to Chenery injured? How? Were the preferred stockholders who did not sell their shares to Chenery injured by his purchase of shares from others? How?

5.	By the time the reorganization was approved, the shares of preferred stock previously purchased by Chenery had appreciated in value. Who was benefited by the SEC's requirement that Chenery sell his shares back to the Company at cost plus 4% interest?

6.	In barring Chenery from participating in the reorganization, was the SEC trying to compensate persons whom Chenery had injured? Or was the SEC attempting to punish Chenery for acting improperly? Or was the SEC attempting to establish a new standard of conduct forbidding trading in the stock of a reorganizing company by its officers and directors?

7. If the SEC was trying to create a new standard of conduct for officers and directors, why did it not apply the standard prospectively only? What did it gain from surprising Chenery with a standard which was created only after he had purchased his stock?

8. If the SEC was trying to create a new standard, why did it refuse to issue a general rule forbidding trading by officers and directors during the periods when their companies were being reorganized?

9. Consider Justice Frankfurter's statement that:

Abuse of corporate position, influence, and access to information may raise questions so subtle that the law can deal with them effectively only by prohibitions not concerned with the fairness of a particular transaction.

Was Frankfurter suggesting in this passage that the problem that the SEC was concerned about was properly dealt with by general rules? Explain. Under that approach, would Chenery have been required to divest his stock?

10. Consider Justice Frankfurter's further statement that:

. . . [B]efore transactions otherwise legal can be outlawed or denied their usual business consequences, they must fall under the ban of some standards of conduct prescribed by an agency of government authorized to prescribe such standards — either the courts or Congress or an agency to which Congress has delegated its authority.

Was Justice Frankfurter in this passage saying that the SEC could not formulate a new standard of conduct relating to officer-and-director stock purchases during reorganization periods and apply that standard retroactively to purchases that had already occurred? How would Frankfurter respond to the contention that courts create new standards of conduct and apply those new standards to evaluate behavior which had been performed previously?

The Commission's decision on remand: *In the Matter of Federal Water Service Corp.*, 18 S.E.C. 231 (1945). The Commission reconsidered the case and reached the same result which it had reached initially. This time the Commission drew upon its regulatory "experience":

> It has been our experience under the Act that the normal influence of a holding company management pervades the entire system down to the lowest tier of operating companies. . . . [T]he personal integrity of these particular intevenors is not a question at issue in this case. For obvious reasons we do not conceive it our function to try to guess whether a reorganization manager, faced with a choice of conducting the reorganization for the accomplishment of his own objectives or for the benefit of security holders generally, is the kind of man who would be likely to take one course and not another. What we say is that when reorganization managers have undertaken a program of acquiring their company's securities for their own account, in contemplation of or during the reorganization proceedings under their charge, they have placed themselves in a position where they are peculiarly susceptible to temptation to conduct the reorganization for personal gain rather than the public good; the program

of making advantageous purchases of stock could have had an important influence-even though subconsciously-upon great numbers of business decisions all along the way. . . . The problem before us is, therefore, one of temptations combined with powers of accomplishment. Since the achieving of personal gain through the use of fiduciary power is unfair, we believe the incentive to misuse such power must be removed so that the potentialities of harm to investors and the public will to that extent be eliminated. . . . Now that we have had the question sharply focused in this and other cases before us, and have had an extensive period in which to consider the problems involved, we may well decide that a general rule, with adequately flexible provisions, would be both practicable and desirable; but we do not see how the promulgation of such a rule now or later would affect our duty to act by order in this case in deciding whether this plan is fair and equitable and meets the other standards of the Act. We therefore reserve for further consideration the question whether or not a rule should be adopted. . . .

SEC v. Chenery Corp., 332 U. S. 194 (1947). After the court's first decision in the *Chenery* litigation, the case was remanded to the Commission. The Commission reconsidered its decision and reached the same result, this time based upon the potential power of officers and directors for abusing their trust. The case then made its way back to the Supreme Court, which this time upheld the Commission's action. An excerpt from Justice Murphy's opinion for the Court follows:

When the case was first here, we emphasized a simple but fundamental rule of administrative law. That rule is to the effect that a reviewing court, in dealing with a determination or judgment which an administrative agency alone is authorized to make, must judge the propriety of such actions solely by the grounds invoked by the agency.

If those grounds are inadequate or improper, the court is powerless to affirm the administrative action by substituting what it considers to be a more adequate or proper basis. To do so would propel the court into the domain which Congress has set aside exclusively for the administrative agency.

We also emphasized in our prior decision an important corollary of the foregoing rule. If the administrative action is to be tested by the basis upon which it purports to rest, that basis must be set forth with such clarity as to be understandable. It will not do for a court to be compelled to guess at the theory underlying the agency's action; nor can a court be expected to chisel that which must be precise from what the agency has left vague and indecisive. . . .

The latest order of the Commission definitely avoids the fatal error of relying on judicial precedents which do not sustain it. This time, after a thorough reexamination of the problem in the light of the purposes and standards of the Holding Company Act, the Commission has concluded that the proposed transaction is inconsistent with the standards of §§ 7 and 11 of the Act. It has drawn heavily upon its accumulated experience in dealing with utility reorganizations. And it has expressed its reasons with a clarity and thoroughness that admit of no doubt as to the underlying basis of its order.

The argument is pressed upon us, however, that the Commission was foreclosed from taking such a step following our prior decision. It is said that, in the absence of findings of conscious wrongdoing on the part of Federal's management, the Commission could not determine by an order in this particular case that it was inconsistent with the statutory standards to permit Federal's management to realize a profit through the reorganization purchases. All that it could do was to enter an order allowing an amendment to the plan so that the proposed transaction could be consummated. Under this view, the Commission would be free only to promulgate a general rule outlawing such profits in future utility reorganizations; but such a rule would have to be prospective in nature and have no retroactive effect upon the instant situation.

We reject this contention, for it grows out of a misapprehension of our prior decision and of the Commissions statutory duties. . . .

The absence of a general rule or regulation governing management trading during reorganization did not affect the Commission's duties in relation to the particular proposal before it. The Commission was asked to grant or deny effectiveness to a proposed amendment to Federal's reorganization plan whereby the management would be accorded parity treatment on its holdings. It could do that only in the form of an order, entered after a due consideration of the particular facts in light of the relevant and proper standards. That was true regardless of whether those standards previously had been spelled out in a general rule or regulation. Indeed, if the Commission rightly felt that the proposed amendment was inconsistent with those standards, an order giving effect to the amendment merely because there was no general rule or regulation covering the matter would be unjustified.

It is true that our prior decision explicitly recognized the possibility that the Commission might have promulgated a general rule dealing with this problem under its statutory rule-making powers, in which case the issue for our consideration would have been entirely different from that which did confront us. . . . But we did not mean to imply thereby that the failure of the Commission to anticipate this problem and to promulgate a general rule withdrew all power from that agency to perform its statutory duty in this case. To hold that the Commission had no alternative in this proceeding but to approve the proposed transaction, while formulating any general rules it might desire for use in future cases of this nature, would be to stultify the administrative process. That we refuse to do.

Since the Commission, unlike a court, does have the ability to make new law prospectively through the exercise of its rule-making powers, it has less reason to rely upon *ad hoc* adjudication to formulate new standards of conduct within the framework of the Holding Company Act. The function of filling in the interstices of the Act should be performed, as much as possible, through this quasi-legislative promulgation of rules to be applied in the future. But any rigid requirement to that effect would make the administrative process inflexible and incapable of dealing with many of the specialized problems which arise. . . . Not every principle essential to the effective administration of a statute can or should be cast immediately into the mold of a general rule. Some principles must await their own development, while others must be adjusted to meet particular, unforeseeable situations. In performing its important functions in these respects, therefore, an administrative agency must be equipped to act either by general rule or by individual order. . . . [P]roblems may arise in a case which the administrative agency could not reasonably foresee, problems which must be solved despite the absence of a relevant general rule. Or the agency may not have had sufficient experience with a particular problem to warrant rigidifying its tentative judgment into a hard and fast rule. Or the problem may be so specialized and varying in nature as to be impossible of capture within the boundaries of a general rule. In those situations, the agency must retain power to deal with the problems on a case-to-case basis if the administrative process is to be effective. There is thus a very definite place of the case-by-case evolution of statutory standards. And the choice made between proceeding by general rule or by individual, *ad hoc* litigation is one that lies primarily in the informed discretion of the administrative agency. . . .

Hence we refuse to say that the Commission, which had not previously been confronted with the problem of management trading during reorganization, was forbidden from utilizing this particular proceeding for announcing and applying a new standard of conduct. . . . That such action might have a retroactive effect was not necessarily fatal to its validity. Every case of first impression has a retroactive effect, whether the new principle is announced by a court or by an administrative agency. But such retroactivity must be balanced against the mischief of producing a result which is contrary to a statutory design or to legal and equitable principles. If that mischief is greater than the ill effect of the retroactive application of a new standard, it is not the type of retroactivity which is condemned by law. See *Addison v. Holy Hill Co.*, 322 U. S. 607, 620.

Questions and Comments

1. Did Justices Murphy and Frankfurter agree that a court must evaluate the lawfulness of an agency's action on the rationale provided by the agency? Did they both agree that the rationale originally provided by the SEC was inadequate to uphold the SEC's action? Compare Justice Scalia's statement in *Allentown Mack Sales & Service v. NLRB*, 522 U.S. 359 (1998) that "the process by which [an agency] reaches [its] result must be logical and rational. Courts enforce this principle with regularity when they set aside agency regulations which, though well within the agencies' scope of authority, are not supported by the reasons that the agencies adduce." In the second *Chenery* case, Justice Murphy apparently believed that the rationale provided by the SEC on remand was an adequate basis upon which to uphold that action. What was that rationale? Is it adequate in your mind as a basis for upholding that agency's action? Why or why not?

2. Did the SEC try to justify its action on the basis of its expertise in intracorporate relationships? Explain. Could the SEC have used this expertise to justify a rule banning stock trading by corporate officers and directors during reorganization periods? Could it have used this expertise to ban Chenery from participating in this particular reorganization? Explain the difference.

3. Consider the passage from Frankfurter's opinion in *Chenery I* quoted in paragraph 9 of the Questions and Comments following that case. Does that help in answering questions about how the SEC could have employed its expertise over intracorporate relations?

4. How does the approach taken in Justice Murphy's opinion for the Court in the second *Chenery* case differ from that taken by Justice Frankfurter in the first *Chenery* case? Did Frankfurter contemplate that the SEC would draw upon its expertise in intracorporate structure on remand? In what way could the SEC have drawn upon that expertise consistent with the approach taken by Frankfurter? Did Justice Murphy accord any different scope for the SEC's expertise than did Frankfurter? Explain.

5. How would the administrative process be stultified if the SEC was required to act by general rule?

6. What was the extent of the retroactive impact of the SEC's action in *Chenery?* What was Frankfurter's approach to such retroactivity? Consider the passage from Frankfurter's opinion in *Chenery I* quoted in paragraph 10 of the Questions and Comments following that case. What was Murphy's approach to agency action with a retroactive impact? Did Murphy place any limitations on such action? Did he provide a balancing test? What factors were to be balanced? If you applied Murphy's balancing test to the facts of *Chenery*, at what result would you arrive? Explain. If the mischief to be eliminated was trading by corporate officers and directors during reorganization periods, what would be the precise benefit of forcing Chenery to give up the appreciated value of stock acquired prior to the formulation of any prohibition on such trading? Explain.

7. Does it make sense to analyze the SEC's action as punishment of Chenery for trading during the reorganization period? Why or why not? If analyzed as punishment, does the SEC's action appear as irrational? Explain. If analyzed as an attempt to deter future trading in like circumstances, why did the SEC direct its action against a past trader? Is there any rationale under which the SEC's action can be evaluated as rational means of furthering a statutory goal? Explain.

8. When an agency's change of position has the potential for injuring those who have relied upon prior agency positions, courts may find procedural ways of preventing those results. *See, e.g., NLRB v. E & B Brewing Co.*, 276 F.2d 594 (6th Cir. 1960), *cert. denied*, 366 U.S. 908 (1961). The Labor Board had initially ruled that a provision requiring an employer to hire exclusively from a union hiring hall did not in itself violate the National Labor Relations Act. The respondent company and the union representing its employees had included such a provision in their collective-bargaining contract. When the union insisted upon compliance with that provision, the company discharged an employee who had been hired in violation of that provision. The Board then changed its position about union-hiring-hall provisions in

collective-bargaining contracts, ruled them illegal unless they contained certain safeguards, and ordered the respondent company to reinstate with back pay the discharged employee.

The court refused to say that the Board could not reverse its position on the lawfulness of union-hiring-hall provisions in collective bargaining contracts. It overturned the Board's order, however, on the ground that the new policy had not been properly adopted. The Board had not adopted its new policy in either of the ways contemplated by the APA: It had not acted by rulemaking, since it had made no attempt to employ the rulemaking provisions of § 553 of the APA. It had not properly adopted its new policy in an adjudication, because in an adjudication the agency is required under § 554(b)(3) to give the parties notice of the "matters of fact and law asserted", and it had failed to give notice to the respondent that it was contemplating a change of policy. *See also NLRB v. APW Products Co.*, 316 F.2d 899 (2d Cir. 1963). For general background on the NLRB's approach to the hiring-hall problem at this time, see HENRY J. FRIENDLY, THE FEDERAL ADMINISTRATIVE AGENCIES: THE NEED FOR BETTER DEFINITION OF STANDARDS 46–52 (1962).

9. In the *Chenery* cases an agency adopted a new policy and applied it retroactively to a completed transaction. A different but analogous case arises when a government official or agent provides advice which an agency later repudiates. Although persons or organizations which have relied on that advice may incur a hardship, they will often find that no relief is available. If the official or agent was not authorized to provide that advice, or if the advice was erroneous at the time it was given, the advisee's defense against the implementation of the agency policy is one of estoppel. In *Heckler v. Community Health Services of Crawford County, Inc.*, 467 U.S. 51 (1984) the Court refused to say that estoppel is never available against the government, but ruled that the Government was entitled to reimbursement from an overpaid Medicare provider despite the latter's reliance upon advice from an insurance intermediary that the excess payments (now spent) were proper. The case is summarized below.

10. In *Lyng v. Payne*, 476 U.S. 926 (1986) and in *Heckler v. Community Health Services of Crawford County, Inc.*, 467 U.S. 51 (1984), the Court considered contentions that the Government should be estopped or otherwise adversely affected by prior advice given by it or on its behalf.

In both cases the Government prevailed against estoppel or estoppel-like claims. In the *Community Health Services* case, Community, a provider of medical services, had been advised by Travelers Insurance Company (Travelers), a Medicare fiscal intermediary, that it was entitled to double reimbursement of certain employment costs (under both the Medicare program and the Comprehensive Employment and Training Act [CETA]). Because it had followed Travelers' advice in applying for double reimbursement, Community argued that the Government could not seek reimbursement. In ruling against Community, the Court rejected an estoppel defense. Observing that

> [w]hen the Government is unable to enforce the law because the conduct of its agents has given rise to an estoppel, the interest of the citizenry as a whole in obedience to the rule of law is undermined. . . . [The] Government may not be estopped on the same terms as any other litigant.

The Court, however, refused to say that the Government could never be estopped under any circumstances. In the case before it, the Court ruled that the respondent had not made out the traditional elements of estoppel. It suffered no legally cognizable detriment:

> Respondent did receive an immediate benefit as a result of the double reimbursement. Its detriment is the inability to retain money that it should never have received in the first place.

Nor did respondent reasonably rely on the advice from Travelers:

> As a participant in the Medicare program, respondent had a duty to familiarize itself with the legal requirements for cost reimbursement. Since it also had elected to receive reimbursement through Travelers, it also was acquainted with the nature and limitations on the role of a fiscal intermediary.

The Court also added the following comments:

> The fact that Travelers' advice was erroneous is, in itself, insufficient to raise an estoppel, as is the fact that the Secretary had not anticipated this problem and made a clear resolution available to respondent, There is simply no requirement that the Government anticipate every problem that may arise in the administration of a complex program such as Medicare; neither can it be expected to ensure that every bit of informal advice given by its agents in the course of such a program will be sufficiently reliable to justify expenditure of sums of money as substantial as those spent by respondent.

In *Lyng v. Payne*, 476 U.S. 926 (1986), respondents contended that in notifying farmers of a loan program, the Secretary of Agriculture had failed to comply with the rules of the Farmers Home Administration (FmHa). Because of the allegedly inadequate notice, the court below had ordered the loan program reopened beyond the date at which it officially terminated. The Court first ruled that the respondents had not made out a case of equitable estoppel:

> We acknowledge that the practical effect of the injunction requiring the reopening of the loan program is to estop the FmHa from relying on the validly promulgated regulatory deadline as a basis for refusing to process further loan applications. And we readily agree that, had the respondents sought relief on an equitable estoppel theory, they could not prevail [since the respondents had not demonstrated detrimental reliance].

The Court then continued as follows:

> As the Court of Appeals correctly observed, however, respondents' inability to satisfy the stringent requirements of common-law estoppel does not independently decide the case. Indeed, beginning with their initial complaint and throughout the course of the litigation, respondents have never sought to rely on estoppel as a basis for recovery. Their theory instead, and the theory on which the lower courts granted the injunction, is that the Administrative Procedure Act, 5 U.S.C. § 551 *et seq.* (APA), authorizes this kind of relief to remedy the FmHa's alleged failure to comply with its duly promulgated notice regulations. It may well be that some of the same

concerns that limit the application of equitable estoppel against the Government bear on the appropriateness of awarding other remedies that have a close substantive resemblance to an estoppel. We reject, however, petitioner's suggestion that any remedy that can be analogized to an equitable estoppel is necessarily invalid, regardless of the source of the cause of action, unless the plaintiff succeeds in proving all the elements of common-law estoppel. . . . Indeed, any other rule has the potential for divesting the courts of the remedial authority specifically envisioned by Congress under the APA. If, for example, a farmer had filed a loan application prior to the expiration of the loan deadline and a court determined that the denial of the application after the deadline's expiration was "arbitrary, capricious [and] not in accordance with law," 5 U.S.C. § 706(2)(A), the appropriate remedy under the APA would be to direct that the application be granted or reconsidered. Although this would, in a sense, estop the Government from applying the deadline, we have never suggested that the applicant would be under an obligation to satisfy the requirements of proving an equitable estoppel to obtain the relief specifically available under the APA.

The Court ruled, however, that the Secretary had complied with FmHa rules in giving notice of the loan program and therefore there was no basis for relief.

11.   If the *Community Health Services* case had been decided earlier, would it have been cited by the Court in either or both of the *Chenery* cases? For what proposition(s)?

12.   When an agency reverses itself on a significant policy matter, it may face a variety of challenges. In *Chevron*, the Court ruled that at least some statutory interpretations may vary with the political views of the incumbent administration and that the courts must respect agency statutory interpretations, including those which have changed for political reasons. In *Motor Vehicle Mfgrs. Ass'n v. State Farm Mutual Auto Ins. Co.*, the Court required that such a change of policy must be adequately explained and when the rationale for the new policy is factually based, that rationale must have adequate support in a rulemaking record. Sometimes a change in agency policy is challenged because the agency failed to employ the rulemaking procedures of the APA to accomplish them. In the *Wyman-Gordon* case below, the Court wrestled with such a contention.

NATIONAL LABOR RELATIONS BOARD v. WYMAN-GORDON CO.
394 U.S. 759 (1969)

[In connection with an election in which two unions were vying to represent the production and maintenance workers of the Wyman-Gordon Company, the Board ordered the Company to furnish a list of the names and addresses of its employees who could vote in the election, so that the unions could use the list for election purposes. The Company refused; and both unions lost the election. The Board ordered a new election and this time issued a subpoena ordering the Company to provide either the list or its personnel and payroll records. The district court enforced the subpoena, but the Court of Appeals for the First Circuit reversed. The court thought that the order was invalid because it was based upon a rule laid down in an earlier decision by the Board, *Excelsior Underwear Inc.*, 156 N. L. R. B. 1236

(1966), and the *Excelsior* rule had not been promulgated in accordance with the requirements that the Administrative Procedure Act prescribes for rulemaking.

In *Excelsior Underwear* the Board "invited certain interested parties" to file briefs and to participate in oral argument on the issue whether the Board should require the employer to furnish lists of employees to labor unions prior to an election. Various employer groups and trade unions did so, as *amici curiae*. The Board then announced its decision in *Excelsior*. It purported to establish the general rule that such a list must be provided, but it declined to apply its new rule to the companies involved in the *Excelsior* case. Instead, it held that the rule would apply "only in those elections that are directed, or consented to, subsequent to 30 days from the date of [the *Excelsior*] Decision.]

MR. JUSTICE FORTAS announced the judgment of the Court and delivered an opinion in which The Chief Justice, MR. JUSTICE STEWART, and MR. JUSTICE WHITE join.

. . . . The Administrative Procedure Act contains specific provisions governing agency rule making, which it defines as "an agency statement of general or particular applicability and future effect". . . . The Act requires, among other things, publication in the Federal Register of notice of proposed rule making and of hearing; opportunity to be heard; a statement in the rule of its basis and purposes; and publication in the Federal Register of the rule as adopted. . . . The Board asks us to hold that it has discretion to promulgate new rules in adjudicatory proceedings, without complying with the requirements of the Administrative Procedure Act.

. . . . There is no warrant in law for the Board to replace the statutory scheme with a rule-making procedure of its own invention. Apart from the fact that the device fashioned by the Board does not comply with statutory command, it obviously falls short of the substance of the requirements of the Administrative Procedure Act. The "rule" created in *Excelsior* was not published in the Federal Register, which is the statutory and accepted means of giving notice of a rule as adopted; only selected organizations were given notice of the "hearing," whereas notice in the Federal Register would have been general in character; under the Administrative Procedure Act, the terms or substance of the rule would have to be stated in the notice of hearing, and all interested parties would have an opportunity to participate in the rule making.

The Solicitor General does not deny that the Board ignored the rule-making provisions of the Administrative Procedure Act. But he appears to argue that *Excelsior's* command is a valid substantive regulation, binding upon this respondent as such, because the Board promulgated it in the *Excelsior* proceeding, in which the requirements for valid adjudication had been met. This argument misses the point. There is no question that, in an adjudicatory hearing, the Board could validly decide the issue whether the employer must furnish a list of employees to the union. But that is not what the Board did in *Excelsior*. The Board did not even apply the rule it made to the parties in the adjudicatory proceeding, the only entities that could properly be subject to the order in that case. . . .

Adjudicated cases may and do, of course, serve as vehicles for the formulation of agency policies, which are applied and announced therein. . . . They generally provide a guide to action that the agency may be expected to take in future cases. Subject to the qualified rule of *stare decisis* in the administrative process, they may serve as precedents. But this is far from saying, as the Solicitor General suggests, that commands, decisions, or policies announced in adjudication are "rules" in the sense that they must, without more, be obeyed by the affected public.

In the present case, however, the respondent itself was specifically directed by the Board to submit a list of the names and addresses of its employees for use by the unions in connection with the election. This direction, which was part of the order directing that an election be held, is unquestionably valid. . . . Absent this direction by the Board, the respondent was under no compulsion to furnish the list because no statute and no validly adopted rule required it to do so.

Because the Board in an adjudicatory proceeding directed the respondent itself to furnish the list, the decision of the Court of Appeals for the First Circuit must be reversed.

MR. JUSTICE BLACK, with whom MR. JUSTICE BRENNAN and MR. JUSTICE MARSHALL join, concurring in the result.

. . . . I cannot subscribe to the criticism in [the plurality] . . . opinion of the procedure followed by the Board in . . . the *Excelsior* case. . . . Although the [plurality] opinion is apparently intended to rebuke the Board and encourage it to follow the plurality's conception of proper administrative practice, the result instead is to free the Board from all judicial control whatsoever regarding compliance with procedures specifically required by applicable federal statutes such as the National Labor Relations Act . . . and the Administrative Procedure Act. . . . Apparently, under the prevailing opinion, courts must enforce any requirement announced in a purported "adjudication' even if it clearly was not adopted as an incident to the decision of a case before the agency, and must enforce "rules" adopted in a purported "rule making" even if the agency materially violated the specific requirements that Congress has directed for such proceedings in the Administrative Procedure Act. I for one would not give judicial sanction to any such illegal agency action.

In the present case, however, I am convinced that the *Excelsior* practice was adopted by the Board as a legitimate incident to the adjudication of a specific case before it, and for that reason I would hold that the Board properly followed the procedures applicable to "adjudication" rather than "rule making. . . . The Board's opinion should not be regarded as any less an appropriate part of the adjudicatory process merely because the reason it gave for rejecting the unions' position was not that the Board disagreed with them as to the merits of the disclosure procedure but rather . . . that . . . the Board did not feel that it should upset the Excelsior Company's justified reliance on previous refusals to compel disclosure by setting aside this particular election.

MR. JUSTICE DOUGLAS, dissenting.

I would hold the agencies governed by the rule-making procedure strictly to its requirements and not allow them to play fast and loose as the National Labor Relations Board apparently likes to do.

MR. JUSTICE HARLAN, dissenting.

The language of the Administrative Procedure Act does not support the Government's claim that an agency is "adjudicating" when it announces a rule which it refuses to apply in the dispute before it. The Act makes it clear that an agency "adjudicates" only when its procedures result in the "formulation of an *order.*" 5 U.S.C. § 551(7). (Emphasis supplied.) An "order" is defined to include "the whole or a part of a final disposition . . . of an agency in a matter *other than rule* making 5 U.S.C. § 551(6). (Emphasis supplied.) This definition makes it apparent that an agency is not adjudicating when it is making a rule, which the Act defines as "an agency statement of general or particular applicability and future effect. . . ." 5 U.S.C. § 551(4). (Emphasis supplied.) Since the Labor Board's *Excelsior rule* was to be effective only 30 days after its promulgation, it clearly falls within the rule-making requirements of the Act.

Nor can I agree that the natural interpretation of the statute should be rejected because it requires the agency to choose between giving its rules immediate effect or initiating a separate rule-making proceeding. An agency chooses to apply a rule prospectively only because it represents such a departure from pre-existing understandings that it would be unfair to impose the rule upon the parties in pending matters. But it is precisely in these situations, in which established patterns of conduct are revolutionized, that rule-making procedures perform the vital functions that my Brother Douglas describes so well in a dissenting opinion with which I basically agree.

Given the fact that the Labor Board has promulgated a rule in violation of the governing statute, I believe that there is no alternative but to affirm the judgment of the Court of Appeals in this case. . . .

Since the major reason the Board has given in support of its order is invalid, *Chenery* requires remand. . . . Since the *Excelsior* rule was invalidly promulgated, it is clear that, at a minimum, the Board is obliged on remand to recanvass all of the competing considerations before it may properly announce its decision in this case. We cannot know what the outcome of such a reappraisal will be. Surely, it cannot be stated with any degree of certainty that the Board will adopt precisely the same solution as the one which was embraced in *Excelsior.* The plurality simply usurps the function of the National Labor Relations Board when it says otherwise.

I would affirm the judgment of the Court of Appeals.

Questions and Comments

1. Is the objection to the Board's choice of announcing policy through adjudication in *Wyman-Gordon* a different objection from the objection of Justice Frankfurter in *Chenery I* ? What is the objection here? Why was the Board's failure to use informal rulemaking procedures deemed objectionable by a majority of the Justices? Was the Board's failure to use informal rulemaking procedures more than a technical defect in its action? Did the Justices believe that objective of the Congress to facilitate public participation in rulemaking through the notice-and-comment procedures of § 553 were being frustrated by the Board's action? Who are the beneficiaries of the public-participation procedures of § 553? Those who submit comments? The agency? How would an agency benefit from those procedures? Do those procedures ensure that agency action will be based upon more information than the agency otherwise might possess? Who besides the agency itself is likely to be most knowledgeable about the problem at which a new rule is directed?

2. Were the public participation goals of § 553 actually frustrated by the manner in which the Board proceeded? What was the subject of the "rule" adopted in the *Excelsior* case? How many different viewpoints would you anticipate about such a rule? Would you expect that there might be a "management" viewpoint on such a matter as the disclosure of names and addresses of workers for use by a union in electioneering? Would there be a "labor" viewpoint? Is this the kind of matter that there would likely be different viewpoints between craft unions and industrial unions? In addition to "management" and "labor" viewpoints, what other viewpoints might there be on such a matter?

3. If the Board had invited both labor and management to express their views and offer any relevant information on the disclosure proposal in the *Excelsior* case, what viewpoint failed to be represented in the proceedings conducted by the Board? Do most rules governing labor-management relations have merely two viewpoints?

4. Does your answer to the last question provide an insight as to why the Labor Board has chronically failed to use § 553 rulemaking procedures? Was a rule involving labor relations a good vehicle for the Court to insist that the public-participation procedures be used by regulatory agencies?

5. Justice Fortas said that the Board acted improperly in promulgating its policy in *Excelsior* but nonetheless its new policy could be enforced by order in the *Wyman-Gordon* case. Was Justice Fortas' position that the Board acted improperly but that there was no remedy for the Board's improper action? How does that view differ from that of Justice Black? From those of Justices Douglas and Harlan?

6. According to Justice Black is the agency's choice to use rulemaking or adjudication in the formulation of new policy one which must be left entirely to the agency's discretion? Explain.

7. Do you agree with Harlan that Fortas' opinion is inconsistent with the precedent of the *Chenery* cases? Explain.

8. If the SEC had allowed members of the Chenery group to participate in the reorganization but announced that henceforth no officers or directors who had purchased stock during the period in which their company was undergoing a

reorganization would be allowed to participate in that reorganization with stock so purchased, would Frankfurter have approved of that action? Would Harlan? Would Black?

9. Why did the Labor Board not order the Excelsior Company to disclose the names and addresses of its employees for use by the union in electioneering? Justice Black referred to the Excelsior Company's "justified reliance on previous refusals to compel disclosure." Did Chenery possess a reliance interest? Was the Excelsior Company's reliance interest the same or different from the kind of reliance interest possessed by Chenery?

10. Was Black suggesting that there might have been a retroactivity problem had the Board applied its new rule to the Excelsior Company? Was he correct? Or incorrect? How would the application of the disclosure rule to Excelsior differ from the application of this rule to the Wyman-Gordon company? Does your answer to the last question reveal *Excelsior* to be an essentially different kind of case from *Chenery?*

11. How did Harlan attempt to tie together the retroactivity problem underlying the *Chenery* cases and the public-participation concerns underlying the *Wyman-Gordon* case?

12. Does *Wyman-Gordon* show that the courts are powerless to insist that agencies use rulemaking procedures to formulate and to announce new policies?

***NLRB v. Bell Aerospace Co.,* 416 U. S. 267 (1974).** Bell Aerospace Co. ("Bell") refused to bargain with a union of that company's buyers. The Second Circuit Court of Appeals refused enforcement of a Board order compelling Bell to bargain with the union. Although the Board was not precluded from holding that buyers, or some types of buyers, were not "managerial employees," the court thought that, in view of a long line of Board cases holding the contrary, the Board could not accomplish this change of position by adjudication. Rather, the Board should conduct a rulemaking proceeding. On review by the U. S. Supreme Court, this part of the lower court's decision was reversed:

> The views expressed in *Chenery II* and *Wyman-Gordon* make plain that the Board is not precluded from announcing new principles in an adjudicative proceeding and that the choice between rulemaking and adjudication lies in the first instance within the Board's discretion. Although there may be situations where the Board's reliance on adjudication would amount to an abuse of discretion or a violation of the Act, nothing in the present case would justify such a conclusion. . . . Moreover, duties of buyers vary widely depending on the company or industry. It is doubtful whether any generalized standard could be framed which would have more than marginal utility. The Board thus has reason to proceed with caution, developing its standards in a case-by-case manner with attention to the specific character of the buyers' authority and duties in each company. . . .

The Labor Board continues to prefer making policy by adjudication. Recall *NLRB v. Curtin Matheson Scientific, Inc.,* 494 U.S. 775 (1990), chapter 2 *supra.* In that case Justice Scalia criticized the Board for disguising its policy-making as fact-finding in order to escape the obligation to employ notice-and-comment procedures:

> Despite the fact that the NLRB has explicit rulemaking authority. . . . it has chosen — unlike any other major agency of the federal government-to make almost all its policy through adjudication. It is entitled to do that, see *NLRB v. Bell Aerospace Co.*, 416 U. S. 267, 294-295, (1974), but it is not entitled to disguise policy-making as fact-finding, and thereby to escape the legal and political limitations to which policy-making is subject. Thus, when the Board purports to find no good-faith doubt because the facts do not establish it, the question for review is whether there is substantial evidence to support that determination. Here there is not, and the Board's order should not be enforced.

> What the Court has permitted the Board to accomplish in this case recalls Chief Justice Hughes' description of the unscrupulous administrator's prayer: "Let me find the facts for the people of my country, and I care little who lays down the general principles."

By accusing the Board of disguising policy-making as fact-finding, has Justice Scalia implicitly invoked *Chenery I* as an aid in overturning the Board's decision? Under *Chenery I* the Court is required to evaluate the agency's decision on the fact-finding rationale used by the agency, is it not? Does that reasoning support Justice Scalia's use of the substantial evidence standard in *Curtin?* What standard did the majority employ? See chapter 2 supra.

In **Weight Watchers International, Inc. v. Federal Trade Commission, 47 F.3d 990 (9th Cir. 1995)**, plaintiff Weight Watchers claimed that the FTC violated statutory rulemaking procedures by altering the existing legal guidelines regulating the weight loss industry on an adjudicatory case-by-case basis. The court avoided ruling on Weight Watchers' claim on the ground that it was not "ripe" for review. Only after the FTC issued a final order against Weight Watchers would the latter's complaint be sufficiently ripe to permit judicial review to go forward. The court did permit judicial review, however, of the FTC's denial of a petition for rulemaking by Weight Watchers. [An edited version of this case appears in chapter 10,*infra*.]

Section 553's Exceptions for Agency Interpretations and Procedural Rules

Section 553(b)(A) and (B) create exceptions to that section's public-participation requirements. Section 553(b)(B) provides that the notice-and-comment procedures do not apply "when the agency for good cause finds . . . that notice and public procedure thereon are impracticable, unnecessary, or contrary to the public interest." Section 553(b)(A), however, creates a broad exception for "interpretative rules, general statements of policy, or rules of agency organization, procedure or practice." An agency therefore can avoid the mandates of § 553's notice-and-comment procedure whenever it can incorporate its policies in an "interpretative rule", can it not? How do "interpretative" rules differ from "legislative" rules? Can you always tell the difference? The rule involved in the *Chevron* case *[supra*, chapter 2]* incorporating the so-called "bubble" concept into the Clean Air Act appears to have been issued as a legislative rule after notice-and-comment procedures, but it nonetheless involved an interpretation of the statute. Could the NLRB have adopted the policy incorporated in the *Excelsior* opinion as an "interpretative" rule and thereby avoided all claims that it was evading § 553? If § 553's notice-and-comment proceedings can be so easily avoided, why did the Court not uphold the Board in *Wyman-Gordon* on the simple ground that the "rule" under challenge was "interpretative"? Consider the extent that the cases below help us to decide whether a rule is interpretative (and therefore exempt from the notice-and-comment requirements of § 553) or legislative (and therefore not exempt).

SPLANE v. WEST
216 F.3d 1058 (Fed.Cir. 2000)

CLEVENGER, CIRCUIT JUDGE.

Petitioners, Edward T. Splane and the Paralyzed Veterans of America, seek review of a precedential opinion issued by the Department of Veterans Affairs ("DVA") general counsel on October 2, 1998 ("VAOPGCPREC 14-98"). . . . .[Splane, a veteran, was seeking benefits under a statute [38 U.S.C. § 1112(a) (1994)] that provided:

> in the case of any veteran who served for ninety days or more during a period of war . . . multiple sclerosis developing a 10 percent degree of disability or more within seven years from the date of separation from such service . . . shall be considered to have been incurred in or aggravated by such service, notwithstanding there is no record of evidence of such disease during the period of service.

In a proceeding before the Board of Veterans Affairs Splane sought to show that he had developed an MS-related disability of at least 10 percent within 7 years of being discharged from the service. His claim was initially denied on the ground that although MS was present to a compensable degree within the 7-year presumptive period following discharge, Splane was not entitled to the statutory presumption of incurrence or aggravation because his condition predated his entry into the service and was not aggravated thereby. Although he appealed this decision to the Court of Appeals for Veterans Claims, that court (on joint motion of the parties) remanded his case to the Board of Veterans Affairs for further evidentiary development.

[While his case was still before the Veterans' Administration,] the DVA general counsel issued precedential opinion VAOPGCPREC 14-98, dated October 2, 1998, a synopsis of which was published in the Federal Register on October 22, 1998. *See* 63 Fed.Reg. 56,705 (Oct. 22, 1998). The opinion concluded that 38 U.S.C. § 1112(a) does not establish a presumption of aggravation for a chronic disease that existed before entry into the service. It further concluded that a document in a veteran's file could be temporarily removed for the purpose of obtaining an "untainted" IME opinion. Finally, it concluded that the requirement of 38 U.S.C. § 7109(c), that the Board "furnish the claimant with a copy of [an IME] opinion when it is received by the Board," is satisfied if a copy of the opinion is delivered to the claimant's authorized representative.

* * * *

II

Petitioners challenge the procedural correctness of the general counsel's opinion, as well as its substance. Procedurally, Petitioners argue that VAOPGCPREC 14-98 is a "legislative rule," subject to the notice and comment rulemaking requirements of 5 U.S.C. § 553 (1994), rather than an interpretative rule that is exempt from notice and comment rulemaking procedures. Petitioners also argue that the DVA failed to comply with 5 U.S.C. § 552(a)(1) by not publishing the entire text of VAOPGCPREC 14-98 in the Federal Register.[1] . . .

A

Petitioners first argue that VAOPGCPREC 14-98 is procedurally defective because it was not issued in accordance with APA notice and comment rulemaking procedures. *See* 5 U.S.C. § 553 (1994). This argument is based on the assumption that VAOPGCPREC 14-98 is a "legislative" rule rather than an "interpretive" rule. The distinction is important because the APA exempts from notice and comment rulemaking any "interpretative rules, general statements of policy, or rules of agency organization, procedure, or practice." 5 U.S.C. § 553(b)(3)(A) (1994).

We have explained the distinction between substantive (*i.e.*, legislative) rules and interpretive rules as follows:

> "[S]ubstantive rules" [are] those that effect a change in existing law or policy or which affect individual rights and obligations. 'Interpretive rules,' on the other hand, clarify or explain existing law or regulation and are exempt from notice and comment under section 553(b)(3)(A). . . . "[A]n interpretive statement simply indicates an agency's reading of a statute or a rule. It does not intend to create new rights or duties, but only reminds affected parties of existing duties."

Paralyzed Veterans of America v. West, 138 F.3d 1434, 1436 (Fed.Cir.1998) (quoting *Orengo Caraballo v. Reich*, 11 F.3d 186, 195 (D.C.Cir.1993)) (other citations omitted). With this guidance in mind, we must decide whether VAOPGCPREC 14-98 is essentially legislative or interpretive in nature. We conclude that the opinion is essentially interpretive because it represents the agency's reading of statutes and rules rather than an attempt to make new law or modify existing law.

Each section of the opinion begins with the text of the relevant statute, *e.g.*, 38 U.S.C. § 1112(a), and the DVA's corresponding regulation, *e.g.*, 38 C.F.R. §§ 3.307(a), (c). The opinion then proceeds to interpret the meaning of the statute with respect to the specific question presented, invoking the traditional rules of statutory

---

[1] Petitioners also argue that the Agency violated its own regulation regarding notification of parties when an opinion is being sought. We cannot reach this issue, however, because it falls outside our jurisdiction under 38 U.S.C. § 502. Specifically, the Agency's alleged failure to personally notify Splane or his attorney of the requested opinion is not "[a]n action of the Secretary to which section 552(a)(1) or 553 of title 5 (or both)" refers. Instead, the alleged violation concerns 38 C.F.R. §§ 20.901, 20.903, which do not warrant "direct review" under § 502.

[handwritten margin note: statutory interpretation, no policy analysis]

interpretation, including textual and contextual analysis and a study of the legislative history. Notably, the opinion does not engage in the type of "policy analysis" one would expect in the rulemaking context, such as weighing the pro's and con's of one course of action versus another. Finally, the opinion makes clear, throughout its text, that the agency is engaging in statutory interpretation, rather than "gap filling" or an exercise of its rulemaking power. *See, e.g.*, VAOPGCPREC 14-98 at 3 ("we conclude that the regulation represents a proper *interpretation* of section 1112(a)" (emphasis added)). The D.C. Circuit has recognized that "an agency's characterization of its own action, while not decisive, is a factor [to] consider. . . ." *American Hosp. Ass'n v. Bowen*, 834 F. 2d 1037, 1047 (D.C.Cir.1987).

[handwritten margin note: precedential nature?]

Petitioners argue, however, that VAOPGCPREC 14-98 must be deemed legislative in nature because it was intended to have the "force and effect of law." They point to 38 U.S.C. § 7104(c), which states that "[t]he Board shall be bound in its decisions by the . . . precedent opinions of the chief legal officer of the Department." According to Petitioners, this is a critical factor in determining whether a rule is legislative or interpretive, citing *Virginia Department of Education v. Riley*, 86 F.3d 1337, 1347 (4th Cir.), *vacated en banc*, 106 F. 3d 559 (4th Cir.1997) and *Chief Probation Officers v. Shalala*, 118 F.3d 1327, 1333 (9th Cir.1997). Both *Riley* and *Chief Probation Officers* cite *Shalala v. Guernsey Memorial Hospital*, 514 U.S. 87, 115 S.Ct. 1232, 131 L.Ed.2d 106 (1995), for the proposition that interpretive rules do not have the force and effect of law.

Guernsey involved a challenge to the validity of a Medicare reimbursement guideline, adopted without notice and comment procedures. The Supreme Court held that the agency's rule was not invalid for lack of notice and comment because it was "a prototypical example of an interpretive rule issued by an agency to advise the public of the agency's construction of the statutes and rules which it administers." 514 U.S. at 99, 115 S.Ct. 1232 (citing *Chrysler Corp. v. Brown*, 441 U.S. 281, 302, n. 31, 99 S.Ct. 1705, 60 L.Ed.2d 208 (1979)) (internal quotations omitted). As an aside, the Court noted that "[i]nterpretive rules do not require notice and comment, although . . . they also do not have the force and effect of law and are not accorded that weight in the adjudicatory process." *Id.*

[handwritten margin note: binding on agency tribunal]

According to Petitioners, because VAOPGCPREC 14-98 is binding on the Board by statute, it necessarily has the "force and effect of law," which, under the corollary logic of *Guernsey*, means that it cannot be an interpretive rule. In other words, Petitioners assert that any agency rule that is binding on an *agency tribunal* has the "force and effect of law," and must therefore be deemed legislative in nature. We disagree.

The Supreme Court's statement in *Guernsey* must be read in context. In particular, we note that the interpretive rule at issue in *Guernsey* (affecting the agency's reimbursement of Medicare costs to hospitals) was certainly binding on agency officials insofar as any directive by an agency head must be followed by agency employees. *See Metropolitan Sch. Dist. v. Davila*, 969 F.2d 485, 493 (7th Cir.1992) ("All rules which interpret the underlying statute must be binding because they set forth what the agency believes is congressional intent."). In *Chrysler*, which was relied upon in *Guernsey*, the Court faced the task of interpreting a statute that contained a special exception for activities "authorized by law." The question before the Court was whether a certain agency regulation had the necessary "force and effect of law" to trigger the statutory exception. The *Chrysler* court stated:

> It has been established in a variety of contexts that properly promulgated, substantive agency regulations have the "force and effect of law." This doctrine is so well established that agency regulations implementing federal statutes have been held to preempt state law under the Supremacy Clause.

441 U.S. at 295-96, 99 S.Ct. 1705.

It is clear from *Chrysler* and *Guernsey* that the Court's reference to a regulation having the "force and effect of law" is to the binding effect of that regulation on tribunals *outside* the agency, not on the agency itself. *See also Animal Legal Defense Fund v. Quigg*, 932 F.2d 920, 929-30 (Fed.Cir.1991) ("A limitation of [agency] discretion, by itself, does not make an agency action 'substantive.' ") In the present case, because Petitioners do not suggest that VAOPGCPREC 14-98 has any binding effect whatsoever outside the agency, on the CAVC, or on this court, their reliance on *Guernsey* is misplaced.

We conclude that VAOPGCPREC 14-98 is an interpretive rule and therefore not subject to the notice and comment procedures of the APA.

Shalala v. Guernsey Memorial Hospital, 514 U.S. 87 (1995). [A hospital refinanced its debt obligations, saving $12 million in debt servicing costs. The refinancing, however, produced an "advance refunding" or "defeasance" loss on its books of $672,581, for which the hospital sought reimbursement under the Medicare Act.] The Court upheld a determination by the Secretary of Health and Human Services (HHS) to deny reimbursement to a health care provider for a bookkeeping loss that did not reflect an actual expenditure for patient services. In making her determination, the Secretary applied a provision [§ 233] of the HHS Medicare Provider Reimbursement Manual. In rejecting a claim by the provider that § 233 should have been promulgated using the notice-and-comment provisions of the APA, the Court said:

> PPM § 233 is a prototypical example of an interpretative rule 'issued by an agency to advise the public of the agency's construction of the statutes and rules which it administers.' " Interpretative rules do not require notice and comment, although, as the Secretary recognizes, they also do not have the force and effect of law and are not accorded that weight in the adjudicatory process.
>
> We can agree that APA rulemaking would still be required if PRM § 233 adopted a new position inconsistent with any of the Secretary's existing regulations. . . . [H]er regulations do not require reimbursement according to [generally accepted accounting principles or] GAAP. PRM § 233 does not . . . "effect[t] a substantive change in the regulations."
>
> . . . . Because the Secretary's regulations do not bind her to make Medicare reimbursements in accordance with GAAP, her determination in PRM § 233 to depart from GAAP by requiring bond defeasance losses to be

amortized does not amount to a substantive change to the regulations. It is a valid interpretative rule, and it was reasonable for the Secretary to follow that policy here to deny respondent's claim for full reimbursement of its defeasance loss in 1985.

PUBLIC CITIZEN v. DEPARTMENT OF STATE
276 F.3d 634 (D.C.Cir. 2001)

TATEL, CIRCUIT JUDGE:

[Public Citizen, a non-profit public interest organization requested from the Department of State records describing its "current system for managing word processing files . . . and electronic mail messages," and the "disposition schedule[s] submitted to the National Archives concerning the transfer or disposal" of these materials."]

When the State Department responds to Freedom of Information Act requests, it generally declines to search for documents produced after the date of the requester's letter. Challenging this "date-of-request cut-off" policy, appellant claims that the Department promulgated it without notice and opportunity to comment as required by the Administrative Procedure Act, and that, in any event, the policy is unreasonable both generally and as applied to appellant's particular request because it forces FOIA requesters to file multiple requests. . . .

II

We begin with Public Citizen's claim that the Department unlawfully promulgated the cut-off policy without the notice and opportunity to comment required by the APA. The Department responds that its cut-off policy is procedural and thus covered by the APA's exemption from notice and comment for "rules of agency organization, procedure, or practice," 5 U.S.C. § 553(b)(3)(A). According to Public Citizen, the cut-off policy cannot be considered procedural because it "substantially . . . affects rights" by "needlessly multipl[ying] the number of FOIA requests that must be submitted to obtain access to records." Appellant's Opening Br. at 33-34. We have, however, characterized agency rules as procedural even where their effects were far harsher than the Department's date-of-request cut-off policy. For example, in *Ranger v. FCC*, we found an agency rule establishing a cut-off date for the filing of radio license applications to be procedural even though the failure to observe the rule cost appellants a radio broadcast license. 294 F.2d 240, 243-44 (D.C.Cir.1961).

As we recognized in *American Hospital Ass'n v. Bowen*, "[o]ver time, our circuit in applying the § 553 exemption for procedural rules has gradually shifted focus from asking whether a given procedure has a 'substantial impact' on parties to . . . inquiring more broadly whether the agency action . . . encodes a substantive value judgment." 834 F.2d 1037, 1047 (D.C.Cir.1987) (citation omitted). This "gradual move," we noted, "reflects a candid recognition that even unambiguously procedural measures affect parties to some degree." *Id.* More recently, in *JEM Broadcasting Co. v. FCC*, we found that FCC "hard look rules," which required the dismissal of flawed license applications without leave to amend, were procedural despite their sometimes harsh effects. 22 F.3d 320, 327-28 (D.C.Cir.1994). In doing so, we rejected the argument that the rules encoded substantive value judgments because they valued applications without errors over those with minor errors. *Id.* Clarifying the *American Hospital* standard, we held that in referring to "value judgments" in that case, we had not intended to include "judgment[s] about what mechanics and processes are most efficient" because to do so would "threaten[ ] to swallow the procedural exception to notice and comment, for agency housekeeping rules often embody [such] judgment[s]." *Id.* at 328.

Because the Department's cut-off policy applies to all FOIA requests, making no distinction between requests on the basis of subject matter, it clearly encodes no "substantive value judgment," *Am. Hosp.*, 834 F.2d at 1047. To be sure, the policy does represent a "judgment" that a date-of-request cut-off promotes the efficient processing of FOIA requests, but a "judgment about procedural efficiency . . . cannot convert a procedural rule into a substantive one." *James v. Hurson Assocs., Inc. v. Glickman*, 229 F.3d 277, 282 (D.C.Cir.2000) (internal quotation marks and citation omitted). Consequently, we agree with the district court that the Department's cut-off policy represents a prototypical procedural rule properly promulgated without notice and comment.

[On the other issues, the court ruled in favor of Public Citizen on some issues and against it on others, remanding the case to the lower court for a final determination consistent with these rulings.]

Questions and Comments

In *Public Citizen* the court said that a rule might have a substantial impact without losing its procedural character. Do you nonetheless see how a showing of substantial impact might persuade the court that the rule does not fall within the procedural exception? When the impact is designed to fall on one class of persons and not on another, does it thereby embody a "substantive value judgment? Can you construct a similar argument for dealing with the interpretative exception? Can a rule that changes rights and/or remedies be an "interpretative" rule? Can an interpretative rule do more than "remind" a person of her or her obligations? Can it create new obligations that did not exist under the pre-existing set of rules? Does an interpretative rule carry the force of law? The courts have employed all of these phrases in attempting to distinguish legislative from interpretative rules. Do you find any of these formulations helpful? Does the courts' lack of clarity suggest that the courts themselves find the distinction a difficult one? Can you nonetheless use these formulations creatively? Can you improve on them?

BOWEN v. GEORGETOWN UNIVERSITY HOSPITAL
488 U.S. 204 (1988)

[Under the Medicare program, health care providers, such as hospitals, are reimbursed by the Government for expenses incurred in providing benefits to Medicare beneficiaries. The Secretary of Health and Human Services is authorized to promulgate regulations setting limits on reimbursable costs. On June 30, 1981, the Secretary issued a cost-limit schedule that changed the method for calculating the "wage index", a factor used to reflect the salary levels for hospital employees in different geographical areas. Under the prior rule, the wage index for an area was calculated by using the average salary levels for all hospitals in the area; the 1981 rule excluded from the computation wages paid by Federal Government hospitals. Various hospitals in the District of Columbia challenged the 1981 schedule; and on April 29, 1983, the district court struck down the 1981 rule on the ground that the Secretary had failed to provide prior notice and an opportunity for public comment as required under the APA. On November 26, 1984, the Secretary — after providing the requisite notice and opportunity for comment — reissued the 1981 schedule to apply to Medicare reimbursement for a 15-month period commencing July 1, 1981. (The 15-month period to which the revised schedule applied was the period from the date of the original rule to the date when Congress amended the Medicare Act to require significantly different cost-reimbursement procedures.)

Respondents, seven hospitals, who had benefited from the invalidation of the 1981 schedule, were required under the new rule to return over $2 million in reimbursement payments. They then brought this suit, claiming that the retroactive nature of the 1984 rule made it invalid under both the APA and the Medicare Act. The district court granted summary judgment for the respondent hospitals and the court of appeals affirmed.]

JUSTICE KENNEDY delivered the opinion of the Court.

It is axiomatic that an administrative agency's power to promulgate legislative regulations is limited to the authority delegated by Congress. In determining the validity of the Secretary's retroactive cost-limit rule, the threshold question is whether the Medicare Act authorized retroactive rulemaking.

Retroactivity is not favored in the law. Thus, congressional enactments and administrative rules will not be construed to have retroactive effect unless their language requires this result. . . . By the same principle, a statutory grant of legislative rulemaking authority will not, as a general matter, be understood to encompass the power to promulgate retroactive rules unless that power is conveyed by Congress in express terms. . . .

The authority to promulgate cost reimbursement regulations is set forth in § 1395x(v)(1)(A). That subparagraph also provides that:

> "Such regulations shall . . . (ii) provide for the making of suitable retroactive corrective adjustments where, for a provider of services for any fiscal period, the aggregate reimbursement produced by the methods of determining costs proves to be either inadequate or excessive." *Ibid.*

This provision on its face permits some form of retroactive action. We cannot accept the Secretary's argument, however, that it provides authority for the retroactive promulgation of cost-limit rules. To the contrary, we agree with the Court of Appeals that clause (ii) directs the Secretary to establish a procedure for making case-by-case adjustments to reimbursement payments where the regulations prescribing computation methods do not reach the correct result in individual cases. The structure and language of the statute require the conclusion that the retroactivity provision applies only to case-by-case adjudication, not to rulemaking.

Section 1395x(v)(1)(A), of which clause (ii) is a part, directs the Secretary to promulgate regulations (including cost-limit rules) establishing the methods to be used in determining reasonable costs for "institutions" and "providers" that participate in the Medicare program. Clause (i) of § 1395x(v)(1)(A) requires these cost-method regulations to take into account both direct and indirect costs incurred by "providers." Clause (ii) mandates that the cost method regulations include a mechanism for making retroactive corrective adjustments. These adjustments are required when, for "a *provider*," the "aggregate reimbursement produced by the methods of determining costs" is too low or too high. By its terms, then, clause (ii) contemplates a mechanism for adjusting the reimbursement received by a provider, while the remainder of § 1395x(v)(1)(A) speaks exclusively in the plural. The distinction suggests that clause (ii), rather than permitting modifications to the cost-method rules in their general formulation, is intended to authorize case-by-case inquiry into the accuracy of reimbursement determinations for individual providers. Indeed, it is difficult to see how a corrective adjustment could be made to the aggregate reimbursement paid "a provider" without performing an individual examination of the provider's expenditures in retrospect.

Our conclusion is buttressed by the statute's use of the term "adjustments." Clause (ii) states that the cost-method regulations shall "provide for the making of . . . adjustments." In order to derive from this language the authority to promulgate cost-limit rules, the "adjustments" that the cost-method regulations must "provide for the making of" would themselves be additional cost-method regulations. Had Congress intended the Secretary to promulgate regulations providing for the issuance of further amendatory regulations, we think this intent would have been made explicit.

It is also significant that clause (ii) speaks in terms of adjusting the aggregate reimbursement amount computed by one of the methods of determining costs. As the Secretary concedes, the cost-limit rules are one of the methods of determining costs, and the retroactive 1984 rule was therefore an attempt to change one of those methods. Yet nothing in clause (ii) suggests that it permits changes in the *methods* used to compute costs; rather it expressly contemplates corrective adjustments to the aggregate amounts of reimbursement produced pursuant to those methods. We cannot find in the language of clause (ii) an independent grant of authority to promulgate regulations establishing the methods of determining costs.

The Secretary nonetheless suggests that, whatever the limits on his power to promulgate retroactive regulations in the normal course of events, judicial invalidation of a prospective rule is a unique occurrence that creates a heightened need, and thus a justification, for retroactive curative rulemaking. The Secretary warns that congressional intent and important administrative goals may be frustrated unless an invalidated rule can be cured of its defect and made applicable to past time periods. The argument is further advanced that the countervailing reliance interests are less compelling than in the usual case of retroactive rulemaking, because the original, invalidated rule provided at least some notice to the individuals and entities subject to its provisions.

Whatever weight the Secretary's contentions might have in other contexts, they need not be addressed here. . . . Our interpretation of the Medicare Act compels the conclusion that the Secretary has no authority to promulgate retroactive cost-limit rules.

The 1984 reinstatement of the 1981 cost-limit rule is invalid. The judgment of the Court of Appeals is *Affirmed.*

JUSTICE SCALIA, concurring.

. . . . I write separately because I find it incomplete to discuss general principles of administrative law without reference to the basic structural legislation which is the embodiment of those principles, The Administrative Procedure Act (APA). . . . I agree with the District of Columbia Circuit that the APA independently confirms the judgment we have reached. The first part of the APA's definition of "rule" states that a rule

> "means the whole or any part of an agency statement of general or particular applicability and *future effect* designed to implement, interpret, or prescribe law or policy or describing the organization, procedure, or practice requirements of an agency. . . .

5 U.S.C. § 551(4) (emphasis added)

The only plausible reading of the italicized phrase is that rules have legal consequences only for the future. It could not possibly mean that merely some of their legal consequences must be for the future, though they may also have legal consequences for the past, since that description would not enable rules to be distinguished from "orders", see 5 U.S.C. § 551(6), and would thus destroy the entire dichotomy upon which the most significant portions of the APA are based. (Adjudication — the process for formulating orders, see § 551(7) — has future as well as past consequences, since the principles announced in an adjudication cannot be departed from in future adjudications without reason. . . .

Nor could "future effect" in this definition mean merely *"taking effect* in the future," that is, having a future effective date even though, once effective, altering the law applied in the past. That reading, urged by the Government, produces a definition of "rule" that is meaningless, since obviously all agency statements have "future effect" in the sense that they do not take effect until after they are made. (One might argue, I suppose, that "future effect" excludes agency statements that take effect immediately, as opposed to one second after promulgation. Apart from the facial silliness of making the central distinction between rulemaking and adjudication hang upon such a thread, it is incompatible with § 553(d), which makes clear that, if certain requirements are complied with, a rule can be effective immediately.) Thus this reading, like the other one, causes § 551(4) to fail in its central objective, which is to distinguish rules from orders. All orders have "future effect" in the sense that they are not effective until promulgated.

In short, there is really no alternative except the obvious meaning, that a rule is a statement that has legal consequences only for the future. If the first part of the definition left any doubt of this, however, it is surely eliminated by the second part. . . . After the portion set forth above, the definition continues that a rule "includes the approval or prescription for *the future* of rates, wages, corporate or financial structures or reorganizations thereof, price, facilities, appliances, services or allowances therefor or of valuations, costs, or accounting, or practices bearing on any of the foregoing." 5 U.S.C. § 551(4).

It seems to me clear that the phrase "for the future" — which even more obviously refers to future operation rather than a future effective date — is not meant to add a requirement to those contained in the earlier part of the definition, but rather to repeat, in a more particularized context, the prior requirement "of future effect." . . .

[Justice Scalia then drew support for this interpretation of the APA rule definition from the 1947 Attorney General's Manual on the Administrative Procedure Act (AG's Manual), a document issued by the Office of the Assistant Solicitor General that had advised Congress in the latter stages of enacting the APA. Justice Scalia than referred to the House Report on the APA] That Report states that "[t]he phrase 'future effect' does not preclude agencies from considering and, so far as legally authorized, dealing with past transactions in prescribing rules for the future." . . . The Treasury Department might prescribe, for example, that for purposes of assessing future income tax liability, income from certain trusts that has previously been considered nontaxable will be taxable whether those trusts were established before or after the effective date of the regulation. That is not retroactivity in the sense at issue here, i.e., in the sense of altering *past* legal consequences of past actions. Rather, it is what have been characterized as "secondary" retroactivity. . . . A rule with exclusively future effect (taxation of future trust income) can unquestionably *affect* past transactions (rendering the previously established trusts less desirable in the future), but it does not for that reason cease to be a rule under the APA. Thus, with respect to the present matter, there is no question that the Secretary could have applied her new wage-index formulas to respondents in the future, even though respondents may have been operating under long-term labor and supply contracts negotiated in reliance upon the preexisting rule. But when the Secretary prescribed such a formula for costs reimbursable while the prior rule was in effect, she changed the law retroactively, a function not performable by rule under the APA.

A rule that has unreasonable secondary retroactivity — for example, altering future regulation in a manner that makes worthless substantial past investment incurred in reliance upon the prior rule — may for that reason be "arbitrary or capricious," see 5 U.S.C. § 706, and thus invalid. In reference to such situations, there are to be found in many cases statements to the effect that "[w]here a rule has retroactive effects, it may nonetheless be sustained in spite of such retroactivity if it is reasonable. It is erroneous, however, to extend this "reasonableness" inquiry to purported rules that not merely affect past transactions but change what was the law in the past. Quite simply, a rule is an agency statement "of future effect," not "of future effect and/or reasonable past effect!

This case cannot be disposed of, as the Government suggests, by simply noting that retroactive rulemaking is similar to retroactive legislation, and that the latter has long been upheld against constitutional attack where reasonable. . . . The issue here is not constitutionality, but rather whether there is any good reason to doubt that the APA means what it says. For purposes of resolving that question, it does not at all follow that, since Congress itself possesses the power retroactively to change its laws, it must have meant agencies to possess the power retroactively to change their regulations. Retroactive legislation has always been looked upon with disfavor . . . and even its constitutionality has been conditioned upon a rationality requirement beyond that applied to other legislation. . . . It is entirely unsurprising, therefore, that even though Congress wields such a power itself, it has been unwilling to confer it upon the agencies. . . .

. . . . [Retroactive rules] are . . . not a device indispensable to efficient government. It is important to note that the retroactivity limitation applies only to rulemaking. Thus, where legal consequences hinge upon the interpretation of statutory requirements, and where no preexisting interpretive rule construing those requirements is in effect, nothing prevents the agency from acting retroactively through adjudication. . . . Moreover, if and when an agency believes that the extraordinary step of retroactive rulemaking is crucial, all it need do is persuade Congress of that fact to obtain the necessary ad hoc authorization. It may even be that implicit authorization of particular retroactive rulemaking can be found in existing legislation. If, for example, a statute prescribes a deadline by which particular rules must be in effect, and if the agency misses that deadline, the statute may be interpreted to authorize a reasonable retroactive rule despite the limitation of the APA. . . .

. . . . The Government contends that the evils generally associated with retroactivity do not apply to reasonable "curative" rulemaking-that is, the correction of a mistake in an earlier rulemaking proceeding. Because the invalidated 1981 wage-index rule furnished respondents with "ample notice" of the standard that would be applied, the government asserts that it is not unfair to apply the identical 1984 rule retroactively. I shall assume that the invalidated rule provided ample notice, though that is not at all clear. It makes no difference. The issue is not whether retroactive rulemaking is fair; it undoubtedly may be, just as may prospective adjudication. The issue is whether it is a permissible form of agency action under the particular structure established by the APA. . . .

For these reasons in addition to those stated by the Court, I agree that the judgment of the District of Columbia Circuit must be affirmed.

Questions and Comments

1. Does Justice Kennedy's opinion for the Court say anything about how the Court will treat retroactive rulemaking, apart from the Medicare Act? What does he say explicitly? What inferences can you draw from his approach to interpreting the Medicare Act? What does Justice Kennedy say, if anything, about the propriety of "curative" retroactive rulemaking? Why did he not have to address the Government's arguments on "curative" rulemaking in the case before him?

2. The Government had cited the Supreme Court's 1947 decision in *SEC v. Chenery Corp.*, 332 U. S. 194 (1947) as support for its retroactive action. In response, Justice Scalia stated that *Chenery* was irrelevant: first, because *Chenery*

was not decided under the APA; and second, because *Chenery* involved adjudication rather than rulemaking:

. . . [T]he utterly crucial distinction is that *Chenery* involved that form of administrative action where retroactivity is not only permissible but standard. Adjudication *deals* with what the law was; rulemaking deals with what the law will be. That is why we said in *Chenery:*

> Since the Commission, unlike a court, *does have the ability to make new law prospectively through the exercise of its rule-making powers*, it has less reason to rely upon ad hoc adjudication to formulate new standards of conduct. . . . The function of filling in the interstices of the Act should be performed, as much as possible, *through this quasi-legislative promulgation of rules to be applied in the future. 332* U. S., at 202 (emphasis added).
>
> And just as suggested that rulemaking was prospective, the opinions in *NLRB v. Wyman-Gordon Co.*, 394 U. S. 759 (1969), suggested the obverse: that adjudication could *not* be purely prospective, since otherwise it would constitute rulemaking. . . . Side by side these two cases, *Chenery* and *Wyman-Gordon*, set forth quite nicely the "dichotomy between rulemaking and adjudication" upon which "the entire [APA] is based. . . ."

3.   Does Justice Scalia's interpretation of the APA unduly limit the options available to agencies? Can you think of situations in which administrative regulation would break down because an agency was unable to issue a retroactive rule?

4.   May an agency, in Justice Scalia's view, issue a retroactive "interpretative" rule?

5.   Do you understand Justice Scalia's distinction between primary and secondary retroactivity?

6.   Justice Scalia says that in unusual cases an agency can ask Congress for ad hoc authorization to issue a retroactive rule. What is the objection to this suggestion? If legislation is required to give the agency power to remedy a situation, Congress can as easily remedy the situation directly by enacting substantive legislation, can it not? The purpose of agencies is to regulate where (because of changing circumstances or the need for constant supervision or otherwise) it is impractical for legislatures to do more than provide general directions, is it not?

7.   Justice Scalia suggests that in certain cases authority for the issuance of retroactive rules may be found in the substantive statute which the agency is enforcing, despite the fact that the APA does not contemplate the issuance of retroactive rules. (His example was an agency which has failed to promulgate a rule by the time specified in the governing statute; the subsequently issued rule, Justice Scalia suggests, may be made to apply retroactively to the date which Congress had required the rule to be in place.) But does not an agency's rulemaking power always come from the substantive statute?

The SEC's rulemaking power — referred to but not exercised in *Chenery* — predated the APA. Is it permissible to read the APA as restricting a prior grant of rulemaking power? Conversely, why could not post-APA grants of rulemaking power be construed to override APA limitations on rulemaking?

8. How do Justices Kennedy and Scalia differ on the subject of retroactive rules? Did Kennedy really leave the question of retroactive rules under statutes other than the Medicare Act open, as his opinion superficially suggests? Does Justice Kennedy require an explicit grant of power to issue retroactive rules? When would he not require such an explicit grant? If the substantive statute explicitly granted an agency power to issue retroactive rules, Justice Scalia would accept that grant as overriding the APA, would he not?

MORTON v. RUIZ
415 U. S. 199 (1974)

[The respondents, Ramon Ruiz and his wife, Anita, are Papago Indians and U.S. citizens. In 1940 they left the Papago Reservation in Arizona to seek employment 15 miles away at the Phelps-Dodge copper mines at Ajo. The Ruizes have lived in Ajo continuously since 1940. Apart from Mr. Ruiz' employment with Phelps-Dodge, they have not been assimilated into the dominant culture, and they have maintained a close tie with the nearby reservation. In 1967 when the mine was closed by a prolonged strike, Mr. Ruiz applied for general assistance benefits from the Bureau of Indian Affairs (BIA). He was immediately notified by letter that he was ineligible for general assistance because of the provision (in effect since 1952) in 66 Indian Affairs Manual 3.1.4 (1965) that eligibility is limited to Indians living "on reservations" and in jurisdictions under the BIA in Alaska and Oklahoma. Appeals within the agency were unsuccessful. The sole ground for the denial of general assistance benefits was that the Ruizes resided outside the boundaries of the Papago Reservation.

The respondents brought suit against the Secretary of the Interior, claiming entitlement under the Snyder Act. 25 U. S. C. § 13. The district court granted summary judgment for the Secretary, but the court of appeals reversed.

After examining the Snyder Act and the congressional legislation appropriating funds under it, the Court concluded that Congress intended to appropriate funds "to cover welfare services at least to those Indians residing 'on or near' the reservation." The Court then ruled that even though Congress intended to provide welfare services for Indians on or near reservations, the Secretary could properly create reasonable classifications and eligibility requirements in order to allocate the limited funds available to him for this purpose. An excerpt from Justice Blackmun's opinion for the Court follows:]

. . . . Thus, if there were only enough funds appropriated to provide meaningfully for 10,000 needy Indian beneficiaries and the entire class of eligible beneficiaries numbered 20,000, it would be incumbent upon the BIA to develop an eligibility standard to deal with this problem, and the standard, if rational and proper, might leave some of the class otherwise encompassed by the appropriation without benefits. But in such a case the agency must, at a minimum, let the standard be generally known so as to assure that it is being applied consistently and so as to avoid both the reality and the appearance of arbitrary denial of benefits to potential beneficiaries.

. . . . No matter how rational or consistent with congressional intent a particular decision might be, the determination of eligibility cannot be made on an ad hoc basis by the dispenser of funds.

The Administrative Procedure Act was adopted to provide, *inter* alia, that administrative policies affecting individual rights and obligations be promulgated pursuant to certain stated procedures so as to avoid the inherently arbitrary nature of unpublished *ad hoc* determinations. . . . That Act states in pertinent part:

> "Each Agency shall separately state and currently publish in the Federal Register for the guidance of the public (D) substantive rules of general applicability adopted as authorized by law, and statements of general policy or interpretations of general applicability formulated and adopted by the agency."

The sanction added in 1967 by Pub.L. 90-23, 81 Stat. 54, provides:

> "Except to the extent that a person has actual and timely notice of the terms thereof, a person may not in any manner be required to resort to, or be adversely affected by, a matter required to be published in the Federal Register and no so published." *Ibid.*

In the instant case the BIA itself has recognized the necessity of formally publishing its substantive policies and has placed itself under the structure of the APA procedures. The 1968 introduction to the Manual reads:

> *"Code of Federal Regulations:* Directives which relate to the public, including Indians, are published in the Federal Register and codified in 25 Code of Federal Regulations (25 CFR). These directives inform the public of privileges and benefits available; eligibility qualifications, requirements and procedures; and of appeal rights and procedures. They are published in accordance with rules and regulations issued by the Director of the Federal Register and the Administrative Procedure Act as amended. . . .

> *"Bureau* of, *Indian* Affairs *Manual:* Policies, procedures, and instructions which do not relate to the public but are required to govern the operations of the Bureau are published in the Bureau of Indian Affairs Manual." 0 BIAM 1.2

Unlike numerous other programs authorized by the Snyder Act and funded by the annual appropriations, the BIA has chosen not to publish its eligibility requirements for general assistance in the Federal Register or in the CFR. This continues to the present time. The only official manifestation of this alleged policy of restricting general assistance to those directly on the reservations is the material in the Manual which is, by BIA's own admission, solely an internal-operations brochure intended to cover policies that "do not relate to the public." Indeed, at oral argument the Government conceded that for this to be a "real legislative rule," itself endowed with the force of law, it should be published in the Federal Register. . . .

Where the rights of individuals are affected, it is incumbent upon agencies to follow their own procedures. This is so even where the internal procedures are possibly more rigorous than otherwise would be required. . . . The BIA, by its Manual, has declared that all directives that "inform the public of privileges and benefits available" and of "eligibility requirements" are among those to be published. The requirement that, in order to receive general assistance, an Indian must reside directly "on" a reservation is clearly an important substantive policy that fits within this class of directives. Before the BIA may extinguish the entitlement of these otherwise eligible beneficiaries, it must comply, at a minimum, with its own internal procedures.

The Secretary has presented no reason why the requirements of the Administrative Procedure Act could not or should not have been met. Cf. *SEC v. Chenery Corp.*, 332 U.S. 194, 202 (1947). The BIA itself has not attempted to defend its rule as a valid exercise of its "legislative power," but rather depends on the argument that Congress itself has not appropriated funds for Indians not directly on the reservations. The conscious choice of the Secretary not to treat this extremely significant eligibility requirement, affecting rights of needy Indians, as a legislative-type rule, renders it ineffective so far as extinguishing rights of those otherwise within the class of beneficiaries contemplated by Congress is concerned.

Questions and Comments

1. *Is Ruiz* an attempt by the Court to force agencies generally to act through rules? or do the facts of *Ruiz* impose severe limits upon its applicability as a precedent?

2. What provisions of the Administrative Procedure Act did the Court use as a basis for its decision? Were the provisions of § 552(a)(1)(D) controlling in the *Ruiz* case? The Court also referred to the sanctions set forth in Pub. L. 90-23 and included in § 552(a). Was Mr. Ruiz required "adversely affected" by "a matter required to be published in the Federal Register and not so published"? Was this the basis for the Court's ruling?

3. Did Mr. Ruiz receive "actual and timely notice" of the BIA policy disqualifying him for general assistance benefits when he applied for them? He received "actual" notice of the policy at that time, did he not? When would notice of such a policy be "timely"? Why would such notice not be timely when provided at the time of application for benefits? Did Mr. Ruiz have any reliance interest which was adversely affected because of failure of the BIA to provide pre-application notice of its disqualification policy? Is the sanction set forth in Pub. L. 90-23 and § 552(a) generally useful in compelling agencies to act by rule?

4. Could the Court in *Wyman-Gordon* have used § 552(a) as a basis for compelling the Labor Board to act by rule? Can *Ruiz* and § 552(a) be used as a means for compelling agencies to comply with the § 553 notice-and-comment procedures? Can you describe how this could be done?

5. Was the "rule" promulgated in the *Excelsior* case published in the Federal Register? If not, would that omission have been a violation of § 552(a)(1)? How would § 552(a)(2) apply to the "rule" promulgated in *Excelsior?* What matters fall within the scope of § 552(a)(2)(B)? What kinds of matters fall within § 552(a)(2)(B) and outside of § 552(a)(1)(D)?

6. Assume the "rule" promulgated in *Excelsior* should have been published in the Federal Register under § 552(a)(1)(D) but was not so published. If this omission had been brought to Justice Fortas' attention, would he have changed his ruling that the Wyman-Gordon company was required to comply with the Labor Board's order to disclose the names and addresses of its employees? Would he have ruled that the order addressed to Wyman-Gordon was "actual and timely notice" of the Board's policy? Would he have ruled that the Board's order was not "actual and timely notice" of a pre-existing policy, but was "actual and timely notice" of the policy embodied in the particular order addressed to Wyman-Gordon? How did the Court avoid the ramifications of such an analysis in *Ruiz?*

7. Did *Ruiz* hold that determinations of eligibility for benefits have to be made by rule? Is this holding independent from the opinion's discussion of § 552(a)(1)(D)? Is this holding a precedent for all welfare eligibility determinations? What is the authority for such a ruling? If this ruling is independent from § 552(a)(1)(D), is it based upon a construction of the Snyder Act? the appropriations acts which implement the Snyder Act? the Fifth Amendment? Is *Ruiz* a precedent for holding that state welfare agencies must determine eligibility by rule?

8. What was the significance for the *Ruiz* decision that the BIA had "placed itself under the structure of the APA"? Would not the APA apply to the BIA by its own force? Is § 553(a)(2) relevant to your answer? Does § 552 apply regardless of the applicability of § 553? Why did the Court emphasize the need for agencies to follow their own procedures? Was this part of the Court's opinion a recognition that the APA by itself would not have been controlling? Explain.

9. *Ruiz* was decided on February 20, 1974. On the following April 23, the Court decided *NLRB v. Bell Aerospace* Co., *supra*. Does the *Bell Aerospace* decision indicate that the significance of *Ruiz* as a vehicle for compelling agency action by rule is sharply limited? Explain.

Note: Rulemaking Procedure Under State Administrative Procedure Statutes

1. The 1946 model act established a notice-and-comment procedure not unlike that of the federal APA. See 1946 Model Act § 2(3). The 1961 and 1981 model acts similarly established notice-and-comment procedures. The latter acts also required the agency to hold an oral hearing upon the request of 25 or more persons. 1961 Model Act § 3; 1981 Model Act § 3-104.

2. Minnesota has established elaborate rulemaking procedures. See Minn. Stat. §§ 14.05-14-365. Why do you think that Minnesota has adopted such cumbersome procedures? Does Minn. Stat. § 14.10 require a notice-and-comment procedure even before the official institution of rulemaking? What kind of a burden is placed upon an agency by the requirement of a statement of need and responsibleness? See Minn. Stat. §§ 14.131; 14.23.

B. THE USE OF INFORMAL RULEMAKING BY AGENCIES TO AVOID OR SHORTEN TRIAL-TYPE PROCEEDINGS

Heckler v. Campbell, 461 U.S. 458 (1983).[2] Under the Social Security Act disability benefits are provided to persons who are unable "to engage in any substantial gainful activity by reason of any medically determinable physical or mental impairment." The Act specified that a person must "not only [be] unable to do his previous work but [must be unable], considering his age, education, and work experience, [to] engage in any other kind of substantial gainful work which exists in the national economy, regardless of whether such work exists in the immediate area in which he lives, or whether a specific job vacancy exists for him, or whether he would be hired if the claimant applied for work."

Prior to 1978, the Secretary relied upon vocational experts to establish the existence of suitable jobs in the national economy. After a claimant's limitations and abilities had been determined at a hearing, a vocational expert ordinarily would testify whether work existed that the claimant could perform.

In 1978 the Secretary promulgated medical-vocational guidelines. These guidelines relieve the Secretary of the need to rely on vocational experts to establish the types and numbers of jobs that exist in the national economy. The guidelines consist of a matrix of the four factors identified by Congress—physical ability, age, education, and work experience—and set forth rules that identify whether jobs requiring specific combinations of these factors exist in significant numbers in the national economy. Where a claimant's qualifications correspond to the job requirements identified by a rule, the guidelines direct a conclusion as to whether work exists that the claimant could perform. If such work exists, the claimant is not considered disabled.

In a case brought by a former hotel maid suffering from a back condition and hypertension, an Administrative Law judge determined that the claimant retained the physical capacity to do light work; and that a significant number of jobs existed that a person of the claimant's abilities could perform. An excerpt from the opinion of the Supreme Court upholding the medical-vocational guidelines were upheld follows:

> We do not think that the Secretary's reliance on medical-vocational guidelines is inconsistent with the Social Security Act. It is true that the statutory scheme contemplates that disability hearings will be individualized determinations based on evidence adduced at a hearing. . . . But this does not bar the Secretary from relying on rulemaking to resolve certain classes of issues. . . .

> The Secretary's decision to rely on medical-vocational guidelines is consistent with *Texaco* and *Storer*. . . [I]n determining whether a claimant can perform less strenuous work, the Secretary must make two determinations. She must assess each claimant's individual abilities and then determine whether jobs exist that a person having the claimant's qualifi-

---

[2] The phrasing of the summary draws heavily from the Court's opinion.

cations could perform. The first inquiry involves a determination of historic facts, and the regulations properly require the Secretary to make these findings on the basis of evidence adduced at a hearing. We note that the regulations afford claimants ample opportunity both to present evidence relating to their own abilities and to offer evidence that the guidelines do not apply to them. The second inquiry requires the Secretary to determine an issue that is not unique to each claimant — the types and numbers of jobs that exist in the national economy. This type of general factual issue may be resolved as fairly through rulemaking as by introducing the testimony of vocational experts at each disability hearing. . . .

The [lower] court's reference to notice and an opportunity to respond appears to be based on a principle of administrative law—that when an agency takes official or administrative notice of facts, a litigant must be given an adequate opportunity to respond. See 5 U.S.C. § 556(e). . .

This principle is inapplicable, however, when the agency has promulgated valid regulations. Its purpose is to provide a procedural safeguard: to ensure the accuracy of the facts of which an agency takes notice. But when the accuracy of those facts already has been tested fairly during rulemaking, the rulemaking proceeding itself provides sufficient procedural protection.

***Lopez v. Davis*, 531 U.S. 230 (2001).** Congress has provided in 18 U.S.C. § 3621(e)(2)(B) that the Bureau of Prisons may reduce by up to one year the prison term of an inmate convicted of a nonviolent felony, if the prisoner successfully completes a substance abuse program. In 1997 the Bureau promulgated a regulation that excludes from early release eligibility offenders who possessed a firearm in connection with their offenses. This regulation relies upon "the discretion allotted to the Director of the Bureau of Prisons in granting a sentence reduction to exclude [enumerated categories of] inmates," rather than by attempting to define the statutory term "prisoner convicted of a nonviolent offense" or the cognate term "crimes of violence." Upholding the regulation, the Court considered Lopez's contention that the agency could not make categorical exclusions but was required to make case-by-case assessments:

> We also reject Lopez's argument, echoed in part by the dissent . . . that the agency must not make categorical exclusions, but may rely only on case-by-case assessments. "[E]ven if a statutory scheme requires individualized determinations," which this scheme does not, "the decisionmaker has the authority to rely on rulemaking to resolve certain issues of general applicability unless Congress clearly expresses an intent to withhold that authority." *American Hospital Assn. v. NLRB*, 499 U.S. 606, 612 (1991); accord, *Heckler v. Campbell*, 461 U.S. 458, 467 (1983). The approach pressed by *Lopez* — case-by-case decisionmaking in thousands of cases each year, . . . — could invite favoritism, disunity, and inconsistency. The Bureau is not required continually to revisit "issues that may be established fairly and efficiently in a single rulemaking proceeding." *Heckler*, 461 U.S., at 467.

The technique of deciding a generic issue in advance through rule-making originated in *United States v. Storer Broadcasting Co.*, 351 U.S. 192 (1956). Under the Communications Act, licenses for radio and television broadcasting are issued by the Federal Communications Commission (FCC) under a standard of serving the "public convenience, interest, or necessity." 47 U. S. C. § 307 (1982). Section 309 of the Communications Act then provided that the FCC could not deny a license application without affording the applicant a hearing. 48 Stat. § 309 (1934). The FCC, after notice-and-comment proceedings under the provision now embodied in 5 U.S.C. § 553, issued rules limiting the number of licenses which would be issued to any one party. Storer owned interests, inter alia, in 5 television stations, the limit under the rules; on the day the rules were adopted, a pending application of Storer for a license to operate an additional television station at Miami was dismissed on the basis of the rules.

Storer contended that the rules unlawfully deprived license applicants of their right under § 309 of the Communications Act to a hearing before their applications were denied. Storer's contention was upheld by the District of Columbia Court of Appeals but was rejected by the Supreme Court:

> [Storer] urges that an application cannot be rejected under 47 U. S. C. § 309 without a "full hearing" to applicant. We agree that a "full hearing" under § 309 means that every party shall have the right to present his case or defense by oral or documentary evidence, to submit rebuttal evidence, and to conduct such cross-examination as may be required for a full and true disclosure of the facts. . . .

> We do not read the hearing requirement, however, as withdrawing from the power of the Commission the rule-making authority necessary for the orderly conduct of its business. As conceded by Storer, "Section 309(b) does not require the Commission to hold a hearing before denying a license to operate a station in ways contrary to those that the Congress has determined are in the public interest." . . .

> We read the Act and Regulations as providing a "full hearing" for applicants who have reached the existing limit of stations, upon their presentation of applications . . . that set out adequate reasons why the Rules should be waived or amended. The Act, considered as a whole, requires no more. We agree with the contentions of the Commission that a full hearing, such as is required by § 309(b) . . . would not be necessary on all such applications. . . . [I]t is necessary for the accompanying papers to set forth reasons, sufficient if true, to justify a change or waiver of the Rules. We do not think Congress intended the Commission to waste time on applications that do not state a valid basis for a hearing.

The *Storer* case was followed in *Federal Power Commission v. Texaco, Inc.*, 377 U.S. 33 (1964) where the Federal Power Commission rejected an application for a pipeline construction certificate without providing a statutorily-required hearing on the ground that the certificate application showed noncompliance with FPC rules:

> We think . . . that the present case is governed by the principle of *United States v. Storer Broadcasting Co.*, . . . and that the statutory requirement

for a hearing under § 7 [of the Natural Gas Act] does not preclude the Commission from particularizing statutory standards through the rulemaking process and barring at the threshold those who neither measure up to them nor show reasons why in the public interest the rule should be waived.

***Baltimore Gas & Electric Co. v. NRDF*, 462 U. S. 87 (1983).** Section 102(2)(C) of the National Environmental Policy Act (NEPA) requires federal agencies to consider the environmental impact of any major federal action. As part of generic rulemaking proceedings to evaluate the environmental effects of the nuclear fuel cycle for nuclear power plants, the Nuclear Regulatory Commission decided that licensing boards should assume, for purposes of NEPA, that the permanent storage of certain nuclear wastes would have no significant environmental impact and thus should not affect the decision whether to license a particular nuclear plant. In upholding the Commission's decision to remove the issue of the environmental effects of waste storage from individual plant licensing proceedings, the Supreme Court (through Justice O'Connor) stated:

> Here, the agency has chosen to evaluate generically the environmental impact of the fuel cycle and inform individual licensing boards, through the Table S-3 rule, of its evaluation. The generic method chosen by the agency is clearly an appropriate method of conducting the "hard look" required by NEPA. . . . The environmental effects of much of the fuel cycle are not plant specific, for any plant, regardless of its particular attributes, will create additional wastes that must be stored in a common long-term repository. Administrative efficiency and consistency of decision are both furthered by a generic determination of these effects without needless repetition of the litigation in individual proceedings, which are subject to review by the Commission in any event.

***American Hospital Association v. NLRB*, 499 U.S. 606 (1991).** Section 9(b) of the National Labor Relations Act requires the Board to decide "in each case" whether, in order to achieve the goals of the Act, "the unit appropriate for collective bargaining shall be the employer unit, craft unit, plant unit, or subdivision thereof." The NLRB promulgated a rule providing that only eight units in acute care hospitals are appropriate for bargaining: physicians, registered nurses, other professional employees, medical technicians, skilled maintenance workers, clerical workers, guards, and other nonprofessional employees. Exceptions are provided for extraordinary circumstances, cases in which nonconforming units already exist, and cases in which labor organizations seek to combine two or more of the eight specified units. In upholding the rule against the contention that § 9(b) required the Board to proceed on a case-by-case approach, the Court stated:

> The requirement that the Board exercise its discretion in every disputed case cannot fairly or logically be read to command the Board to exercise standardless discretion in each case. As a noted scholar on administrative law has observed: "[T]he mandate to decide 'in each case' does not prevent the Board from supplanting the original discretionary chaos with some degree of order, and the principal instruments for regularizing the system of deciding 'in each case' are classifications, rules, principles, and precedents.

Sensible men could not refuse to use such instruments and a sensible Congress would not expect them to." K. Davis, Administrative Law Text 145 (3d ed. 1972). This reading of the "in each case" requirement comports with our past interpretations of similar provisions in other regulatory statutes. See *United States v. Storer Broadcasting Co.*, 351 U. S. 192, 205 (1956); *FPC v. Texaco, Inc.*, 377 U. S. 33, 41 (1964); *Heckler v. Campbell*, 461 U. S. 458, 467 (1983). These decisions confirm that, even if a statutory scheme requires individualized determinations, the decisionmaker has the authority to rely on rulemaking to resolve certain issues of general applicability unless Congress clearly expresses an intent to withhold that authority.

Questions and Comments

1.   What was the rationale employed by the Court in *Storer* to deny that company a hearing on its application for an additional license? Would you describe the rationale as a procedural one or as a substantive one? What is the meaning of the Court's statement that for a full hearing an applicant in the position of Storer must set forth in the papers accompanying its application "reasons, sufficient if true, to justify a change or waiver of the Rules"? Was the Court suggesting that it was establishing a rebuttable presumption? Why or why not? Explain.

2.   How, if at all, did the Court's language in *Heckler v. Campbell* upholding the medical-vocational guidelines differ from the language which it had employed in *Storer* and *Texaco*? Were the medical-vocational guidelines rebuttable? Were the rules in *Storer* rebuttable? in *Texaco*? Explain. Did the private parties have the same right to prove in a hearing that the rules were inapplicable to their situations under both *Heckler v. Campbell* and *Storer*?

3.   Does the Court's opinion in *Heckler v. Campbell* significantly erode that aspect of the doctrine of official notice which allows a litigant to rebut a noticed fact? Does the Court's ruling now mean that a fact established in rulemaking is irrebuttable? Does it matter whether the party challenging the noticed fact took part in the rulemaking proceeding? Or had an opportunity to take part in the rulemaking proceeding? Do the facts established in a rulemaking proceeding have to be generic ones? Explain.

4.   Do you agree with Justice O'Connor that treatment of generic questions in rulemaking enhances both administrative efficiency and consistency? Is the *Storer* line of cases the logical result of *Bimetallic Investment Co. v. State Bd. of Equalization* [*supra*, chapter 3]?

5.   The NLRB rule involved in *American Hospital Association* provided an exception for "extraordinary circumstances". This is similar to the *Storer* rule which provided for waivers in unusual cases. Too many exceptions or waivers, however, tend to destroy the advantages of a rule. In the court below, Judge Posner discussed [899 F.2d 651, 659-660] the advantages and disadvantages of rules and the question of how many exceptions to make:

> The lumping together of all acute-care hospitals into one category for purposes of prescribing proper bargaining units does of course overlook a great deal of relevant diversity. What the hospital industry refuses to

acknowledge is that this is the very nature of rules. A rule makes one or a few of a mass of particulars legally decisive, ignoring the rest. The result is a gain in certainty, predictability, celerity, and economy, and a loss in individualized justice. Often the tradeoff is worthwhile; at least the prevalence of rules in our legal system so suggests. . . .

The decision how complex to make a rule—that is, how many exceptions to recognize—is judgmental, like the decision whether to make rules by formal rulemaking or by the common law method of case-by-case adjudication. . . . The decision how much discretion to eliminate from the decisional process is itself a discretionary judgment, entitled to broad judicial deference. . . . It is not for us to fine-tune the regulatory process by telling the Labor Board that its rule should make slightly more distinctions than it does, or slightly fewer. . . .

C. THE EXPANDING USE OF INFORMAL RULEMAKING

UNITED STATES v. FLORIDA EAST COAST RAILWAY
410 U.S. 224 (1973)

MR. JUSTICE REHNQUIST delivered the opinion of the Court.

Appellees, two railroad companies, brought this action in the District Court for the Middle District of Florida to set aside the incentive per them rates established by appellant interstate Commerce Commission in a rulemaking proceeding. . . . The District Court held that the language of § 1(14)(a) of the Interstate Commerce Act . . . required the Commission in a proceeding such as this to act in accordance with the Administrative Procedure Act, 5 U.S.C. § 556(d), and that the Commission's determination to receive submissions from the appellees only in written form was a violation of that section because the appellees were "prejudiced" by that determination within the meaning of that section.

. . . . We here decide that the Commission's proceeding was governed only by § 553 of that [Administrative Procedure] Act, and that appellees received the "hearing" required by § 1(14)(a) of the Interstate Commerce Act. We, therefore, reverse the judgment of the District Court and remand the case to that court for further consideration of appellees' other contentions that were raised there, but which we do not decide.

[Because of a chronic freight-car shortage, Congress in 1966 amended § 1(14)(a) of the Interstate Commerce Act to enlarge the Commission's authority to prescribe per them charges for the use by one railroad of freight cars owned by another. In that year the Commission commenced an investigation into whether it should increase per them charges. In December 1967 the Commission initiated rulemaking proceedings. In 1969 the slow pace of Commission action was criticized by members of a Senate subcommittee. In December 1969 the Commission issued an interim report announcing a tentative decision to adopt incentive per them charges on standard boxcars, payable by any railroad using a standard boxcar owned by another railroad. The Commission concluded that the 1966 amendment permitted it to impose a charge creating an "incentive" for the using railroad to return the car to its owner, in addition to a charge reflecting a fair return on investment.] It did so by means of a proposed schedule that established such [incentive] charges on an across-the-board basis for all common carriers by railroads subject to the Interstate Commerce Act. Embodied in the report was a proposed rule adopting the Commission's tentative conclusions and a notice to the railroads to file statements of position within 60 days, couched in the following language:

> "That verified statements of facts, briefs, and statements of position respecting the tentative conclusions reached in the said interim report, the rules and regulations proposed in the appendix to this order, and any other pertinent matter, are hereby invited to be submitted pursuant to the filing schedule set forth below by an interested person whether or not such person is already a party to this proceeding.
>
> . . . .
>
> "That any party requesting oral hearing shall set forth with specificity the need therefor and the evidence to be adduced. . . ."

Both appellee railroads filed statements objecting to the Commission's proposal and requesting an oral hearing, as did numerous other railroads. In April 1970, the Commission, without having held further "hearings, issued a supplemental report making some modifications in the tentative conclusions earlier reached, but overruling in toto the requests of appellees.

The District Court held that in so doing the Commission violated § 556(d) of the Administrative Procedure Act, and it was on this basis that it set aside the order of the Commission.

II. APPLICABILITY OF ADMINISTRATIVE PROCEDURE ACT

Both of the district courts that reviewed this order of the Commission concluded that its proceedings were governed by the stricter requirements of §§ 556 and 557 of the Administrative Procedure Act, rather than by the provisions of § 553 alone. The conclusion of the District Court for the Middle District of Florida, which we here review, was based on the assumption that the language in § 1(14)(a) of the Interstate Commerce Act requiring rulemaking under that section to be done "after hearing" was the equivalent of a statutory requirement that the rule "be made on the record after opportunity for an agency hearing." Such an assumption is inconsistent with our decision in [*United States v. Allegheny-Ludlum Steel Corp.*, 406 U.S. 742 (1972), a case decided the preceding term.] . . .

The District Court for the Eastern District of New York reached the same conclusion by a somewhat different line of reasoning. That court felt that because § 1(14)(a) of the Interstate Commerce Act had required a "hearing," and because that section was originally enacted in 1917, Congress was probably thinking in terms of a "hearing" such as that described in the opinion of this Court in the roughly contemporaneous case of *ICC v. Louisville & Nashville R. Co.*, 227 U.S. 88, 93 (1913). The ingredients of the "hearing" were there said to be that "[all] parties must be fully apprised of the evidence submitted, or to be considered, and must be given opportunity to cross-examine witnesses, to inspect documents and to offer evidence in explanation of rebuttal." Combining this view of congressional understanding of the term "hearing" with comments by the Chairman of the Commission at the time of the adoption of the 1966 legislation regarding the necessity for "hearings," that court concluded that Congress had, in effect, required that these proceedings be "on the record after opportunity for an agency hearing" within the meaning of § 553 (c) of the Administrative Procedure Act.

Insofar as this conclusion is grounded on the belief that the language "after hearing" of § 1(14)(a), without more, would trigger the applicability of §§ 556 and 557, it, too, is contrary to our decision in *Allegheny-Ludlum, supra.* The District Court observed that it was "rather hard to believe that the last sentence of § 553(c) was directed only to the few legislative spots where the words 'on the record' or their equivalent had found their way into the statute book." . . . This is, however, the language which Congress used, and since there are statutes on the books that do use these very words, see, e.g., the Fulbright Amendment to the Walsh-Healey Act, 41 U.S.C. § 43a, and 21 U.S.C. § 371(e)(3), the regulations provision of the Food and Drug Act, adherence to that language cannot be said to render the provision nugatory or ineffectual. We recognized in *Allegheny-Ludlum* that the actual words "on the record" and "after . . . hearing" used in § 553 were not words of art, and that other statutory language having the same meaning could trigger the provisions of §§ 556 and 557 in rulemaking proceedings. But we adhere to our conclusion, expressed in that case, that the phrase "after hearing" in § 1(14)(a) of the Interstate Commerce Act does not have such an effect.

III. "HEARING" REQUIREMENT OF § 1(14)(a) OF THE INTERSTATE COMMERCE ACT

Inextricably intertwined with the hearing requirement of the Administrative Procedure Act in this case is the meaning to be given to the language "after hearing" in § 1(14)(a) of the Interstate Commerce Act. Appellees . . . contend that the Commission procedure here fell short of that mandated by the "hearing" requirement of § 1(14)(a), even though it may have satisfied § 553 of the Administrative Procedure Act. . . . Thus, even though the Commission was not required to comply with §§ 556 and 557 of that Act, it was required to accord the "hearing" specified in § 1(14)(a) of the Interstate Commerce Act. . . .

The term "hearing" in its legal context undoubtedly has a host of meanings. Its meaning undoubtedly will vary, depending on whether it is used in the context of a rulemaking-type proceeding or in the context of a proceeding devoted to the adjudication of particular disputed facts. It is by no means apparent what the drafters of the Esch Car Service Act of 1917 . . . which became the first part of § 1(14)(a) of the Interstate Commerce Act meant by the term. Such an intent would surely be an ephemeral one if, indeed, Congress in 1917 had in mind anything more specific than the language it actually used, for none of the parties refer to any legislative history that would shed light on the intended meaning of the words "after hearing." What is apparent, though, is that the term was used in granting authority to the Commission to make rules and regulations of a prospective nature.

Under these circumstances, confronted with a grant of substantive authority made after the Administrative Procedure Act was enacted, we think that reference to that Act, in which Congress devoted itself exclusively to questions such as the nature and scope of hearings, is a satisfactory basis for determining what is meant by the term "hearing" used in another statute. Turning to that Act, we are convinced that the term "hearing" as used therein does not necessarily embrace either the right to present evidence orally and to cross-examine opposing witnesses, or the right to present oral argument to the agency's decisionmaker.

Section 553 excepts from its requirements rulemaking devoted to "interpretative rules, general statements of policy, or rules of agency organization, procedure, or practice," and rulemaking "when the agency for good cause finds . . . that notice and public procedure thereon are impracticable, unnecessary, or contrary to the public interest." This exception does not apply, however, "when notice or hearing is required by statute"; in those cases, even though interpretative rulemaking be involved, the requirements of § 553 apply. But since these requirements themselves do not mandate any oral presentation. . . . it cannot be doubted that a statute that requires a "hearing" prior to rulemaking may in some circumstances be satisfied by procedures that meet only the standards of § 553. . . .

Similarly, even where the statute requires that the rulemaking procedure take place "on the record after opportunity for an agency hearing," thus triggering the applicability of § 556, subsection (d) provides that the agency may proceed by the submission of all or part of the evidence in written form if a party will not be "prejudiced thereby." Again, the Act makes it plain that a specific statutory mandate that the proceedings take place on the record after hearing may be satisfied in some circumstances by evidentiary submission in written form only.

We think this treatment of the term "hearing" in the Administrative Procedure Act affords a sufficient basis for concluding that the requirement of a "hearing" contained in § 1(14)(a), in a situation where the Commission was acting under the 1966 statutory rulemaking authority that Congress had conferred upon it, did not by its own force require the Commission either to hear oral testimony, to permit cross-examination of Commission witnesses, or to hear oral argument. . . .

The basic distinction between rulemaking and adjudication is illustrated by this Court's treatment of two related cases under the Due Process Clause of the Fourteenth Amendment. In *Londoner v. Denver* . . . the Court held that due process had not been accorded a landowner who objected to the amount assessed against his land as its share of the benefit resulting from the paving of a street. Local procedure had accorded him the right to file a written complaint and objection, but not to be heard orally. This Court held that due process of law required that he "have the right to support his allegations by argument however brief, and, if need be, by proof, however informal." . . . But in the later case of *Bi-Metallic Investment Co. v. State Board of Equalization* . . . the Court held that no hearing at all was constitutionally required prior to a decision by state tax officers in Colorado to increase the valuation of all taxable property in Denver by a substantial percentage. The Court distinguished *Londoner* by stating that there a small number of persons "were exceptionally affected, in each case upon individual grounds."

Later decisions have continued to observe the distinction adverted to in *Bi-Metallic Investment Co., supra.* . . . While the line dividing them may not always be a bright one, these decisions present a recognized distinction in administrative law between proceedings for the purpose of promulgating policy-type rules or standards, on the one hand, and proceedings designed to adjudicate disputed facts in particular cases on the other.

Here, the incentive payments . . . adopted in [the Commission's] . . . final order, were applicable across the board to all of the common carriers by railroad subject to the Interstate Commerce Act. No effort was made to single out any particular railroad for special consideration based on its own peculiar circumstances. Indeed, one of the objections of appellee Florida East Coast was that it and other terminating carriers should have been treated differently from the generality of railroads. But the fact that the order may in its effects have been thought more disadvantageous by some railroads than by others does not change its generalized nature. . . .

The Commission's procedure satisfied both the provisions of § 1(14)(a) of the Interstate Commerce Act and of the Administrative Procedure Act, and were not inconsistent with prior decisions of this Court. We, therefore, reverse the judgment of the District Court, and remand the case so that it may consider those contentions of the parties that are not disposed of by this opinion.

It is so ordered.

Extract From Henry J. Friendly, *Some Kind of Hearing*, 123 U. Pa. L. Rev. 1267 (1975)

If the case stood only for the proposition that the provision of the APA requiring trial-type procedures when rules, in the ordinary sense of that term, "are required by statute to be made on the record after opportunity for an agency hearing" should be limited to the few statutes that used these words or something very much like them, the decision would be of relatively little moment. Indeed. . . . I would took with special favor on a development that prevented a spread of the infection of full trial-type hearings to the sort of rulemaking that is predominantly a determination of policy.

However, the sweep of the *Florida East Coast* decision goes far beyond that. The opinion seems to say that "hearing" provisions in regulatory statutes, which had long been regarded as requiring trial-type hearings, have been modified by the Administrative Procedure Act so that nothing more than notice and written comment is required if the action falls within the APA's expansive definition of rulemaking, and implicitly, of course, that this comports with due process. The definition of rulemaking is exceedingly broad, about the only limitation being that a rule can have only future effect. Although the *Florida East Coast* opinion noted that the incentive payments "were applicable across the board to all of the common carriers by railroad subject to the Interstate Commerce Act," the APA definition of "rule" refers to a "statement of general *or particular* applicability," and one can hardly believe Mr. Justice Rehnquist's decision would have been different if the Commission had used its power to exempt certain railroads from payment of incentive per them charges.

The *Florida East Coast* decision thus signals a large expansion of what can be done by notice and comment rulemaking and a corresponding retraction of the area where a trial-type hearing is required in the regulatory field. A clear example would be the division of joint rates, a subject closely akin to charges for car hire. In *The New England Divisions Case* [261 U.S. 184 (1923)] Justice Brandeis took great pains to justify the Commission's action, pursuant to section 15(6) of the Interstate Commerce Act, in fixing divisions on a regional basis to assist the New England lines in the face of an argument by other roads that the Commission was obliged to consider divisions among carriers on an individual basis. Characterizing the proceeding as "adjudication," he described the lengthy hearings and extensive evidence received by the Commission in satisfaction of the "full hearing" requirement of the statute. If the Commission today were to think it desirable to increase divisions for the beleaguered roads in the Northeast, *Florida East Coast* seems to say that notice and comment rulemaking might suffice.

Still more important is ratemaking, the approval or prescription of which is specifically incorporated in the APA definition of a rule. Why would not the order of the Secretary of Agriculture fixing future rates for fifty stockyard agencies in Kansas City, which was before the Court in *Morgan II* [*supra* Chapter 41, now constitute rulemaking subject only to notice and comment procedures unless it matters that the pertinent statute spoke of a "full hearing" rather than simply a hearing? The *Florida East Coast* majority, although unwilling to commit itself, evidently thinks it might be. Indeed, why would not a future rate order like that in *ICC v. Louisville & Nashville R.R.*, which was held to have required a trial-type hearing, now constitute rulemaking which can be effectuated by mere notice and comment, since a rule is nonetheless a rule despite its "particular applicability"? Although the *Florida East Coast* majority sought to distinguish the *Louisville & Nashville* situation by calling it adjudication rather than rulemaking, the distinction did not carry much conviction to the dissenters, nor does it to me.

Hard-pressed agencies will not be slow to draw such lessons from the *Florida East Coast* decision. I am not saying that, from a policy standpoint, this development is bad; I am saying that it is quite as revolutionary in the sense of retracting what had been thought to be procedural rights as *Goldberg* [supra Chapter 3] was in advancing them. . . .

The Court is going to have to engage in more hard thinking about the location of what Justice Rehnquist conceded to be the not very bright line "between proceedings for the purpose of promulgating policy-type rules or standards, on the one hand, and proceedings designed to adjudicate disputed facts in particular cases on the other." The line becomes especially difficult to draw in ratemaking. The process in fixing a future rate for a single power company or for a particular rail movement is much more like the process in determining the reasonableness of past rates than the process in setting nationwide safety standards or in prescribing rules for solicitation of proxies. Much more than that, since even in rulemaking that is predominantly of the policy type, there may be subsidiary issues on which notice-and-comment procedures will not always assure fair agency decisionmaking and permit meaningful judicial review, it may be doubted that they will inevitably fill the statutory or constitutional bill.

Questions and Comments

1.   In *Florida East Coast* the Commission adopted a set of per them charges that applied across the board to all railroads, did it not? Is it surprising that the Court permitted an agency to adopt such a measure after conducting notice-and-comment proceedings which complied with § 553? What caused the controversy in *Florida East Coast* was the statutory requirement (in § 1(14)(a) of the Interstate Commerce Act) that a "hearing" be held prior to agency action, was it not?

2.   Does not *Florida East Coast* hold merely that the term "hearing" may sometimes encompass notice-and-comment procedures? Does it hold that the term "hearing" may encompass notice-and-comment procedures when the object of the hearing *is* the promulgation of a rule of general application and the issues to be explored at the hearing are matters of legislative fact? Why would such a holding be viewed as surprising?

3.   Judge Friendly mentioned ratemaking as an area in which *Florida East Coast* would have major significance. Is that because ratemaking had traditionally been carried out through the use of evidentiary hearings? Will *Florida East Coast* affect the procedures used in those ratemaking cases which are concerned with the rates of a single utility? Would *Florida East Coast* be likely to affect the procedure employed by an agency such as the former Federal Power Commission which set generally-applicable rates for many similarly situated producers? What federal agencies are doing this today?

4.   In what fields of regulation does *Florida East Coast* have significance outside of ratemaking? Would it have significance for environmental regulation? Explain.

Chapter 7

JUDICIAL REVIEW OF AGENCY RULES AND RULEMAKING: AN INTRODUCTION

A. AGENCY RULEMAKING IN THE PRE-ADMINISTRATIVE PROCEDURE ACT PERIOD

Rulemaking procedure in general. Prior to the enactment of the federal Administrative Procedure Act in 1946, no statutory code of procedures governed agency rulemaking. Most agencies were legally free to promulgate rules without consulting any outside interests. In practice, however, agencies frequently consulted with affected interests before issuing rules. Such consultations were often essential means for the agencies to inform themselves about aspects of the operation of the rules which they would ultimately promulgate. Agency consultations with affected interests sometimes took the form of oral and written exchanges. Sometimes they took the form of specially summoned conferences. Sometimes they took place through advisory committees, i.e., committees whose membership included representatives from affected interest groups. Sometimes agencies would hold public hearings in which interested and affected persons or groups could set forth their views about a proposed rule orally or in writing, submitting such factual information, analyses, policy or legal arguments as they wished.

Formal rulemaking. In this period a number of statutes had specifically required an agency "hearing" prior to agency action. Such a requirement was common in statutes which empowered an agency to establish or to approve rates. Such hearings were usually modeled upon a trial in court. In 1941, the Attorney General's Committee described such hearings as follows:

> Rate fixing for public utilities has been attended by a high degree of procedural formality; and the same kind of procedure has been employed under the Packers and Stockyards Act as respects both stockyard companies and "market agencies," or commission merchants. In these instances, however, the number of enterprises having their rates fixed in a single proceeding is quite limited, with the consequence that rate fixing has come to be thought of as adjudication rather than as rulemaking.

By the late 1930s, however, the Congress had enacted a few statutes which imposed a trial model of decision-making upon the rulemaking[1] activities of a few agencies. The skepticism of the Attorney General's Committee about this type of procedure is evident in the following excerpt:

---

[1] The term "rulemaking" is used here in its broad sense: the activity which produces a rule governing the lawfulness or legal effects of a class of behavior.

Recent statutes containing these [trial-type procedural] requirements go far in prescribing procedures previously encountered only in connection with adjudication. They require findings of fact to support the administrative regulations and either require in terms that these findings be based exclusively upon evidence in the record of the hearing or authorize the courts, in statutory review proceedings, to set aside the regulations because an essential finding lacks substantial evidence in the record to support it. The agencies subject to these requirements are thus compelled to bring forth the entire bases of their rule-making determinations at oral hearings and to record in writing the stages by which they arrive at their conclusions.

The application of the procedures of a judicial trial to administrative rule making is limited, however, by the distinctive characteristics of rule-making proceedings. The issues are normally complex and numerous; the parties may be diverse and not alignable into classes; the outcome will involve a judgment concerning the consequences of rules to be prescribed for the future and a discretion in devising measures to effectuate the policies of the statute. These factors differentiate these proceedings from the normal judicial trial in which adversary hearings are traditionally employed and accordingly limit the possibility of defining issues in advance, of addressing evidence to them, of permitting systematic cross-examination, and of stating the findings and conclusions fully. The problem is evident, for example, in the case of a set of regulations which in thousands of paragraphs lays down rules for ship construction or one which governs as discretionary a matter as the nature of the disclosures to be made in a registration statement for new issues of securities.

No general statement of the types of rule making in which adversary hearings should be used seems possible. Provision for their use must necessarily be left to specific regulatory laws and to administrative rules of practice. It is too early to attempt to pass final judgment upon the wisdom of the provisions for adversary hearings contained in the Bituminous Coal Act, the Fair Labor Standards Act, and the Food, Drug, and Cosmetic Act just cited. The earliest of these dates only from 1937. Not only are the results of so brief an experience difficult to measure, but improvements in administrative detail are probable.

Thus far the resulting procedure has been cumbersome and expensive. The record and exhibits lying back of the recent bituminous-coal price order totaled over 50,000 pages; the trial examiner's report embraced approximately 2,800 pages in addition to exhibits, and the Director's report consisted of 545 single-spaced legal-size pages, exclusive of indices, annexes, and price appendices. Wage-order records under the Fair Labor Standards Act run from 600 to 10,000 pages each. The hearing process under the Food, Drug, and Cosmetic Act has required from 5 to 11 months for completion. The bituminous-coal price order was issued more than two years after the present phase of the procedure leading to it was begun.

B. AGENCY RULEMAKING UNDER THE ADMINISTRATIVE PROCEDURE ACT

In 1946, Congress enacted the Administrative Procedure Act. That Act, in what in now codified in 5 U.S.C. § 553, imposed a generally applicable notice-and-comment procedure upon agency rulemaking. That general requirement, however, is subject to certain exceptions: This requirement does not apply to interpretative rules, general statements of policy, rules of agency organization, procedure, or practice, and is subject to an exception for good cause. (These notice-and-comment procedures are often referred to in the cases and the relevant literature as "informal" rulemaking procedures.)

The APA also contains provisions governing "formal" rulemaking, i.e., rulemaking modeled in substantial part upon courtroom trials. Section 553 provides that when the substantive statute empowering an agency to issue a rule requires that those rules are "to be made on the record after opportunity for an agency hearing," the proceeding is to be governed by sections 556 and 557 of the APA. Sections 556 and 557 set forth in detail a set of procedures modeled upon a judicial trial.

C. JUDICIAL REVIEW OF AGENCY RULEMAKING

1.   *The traditional approach to judicial review of rules.*

Except for review of so-called "formal" rulemaking, the courts generally reviewed agency rules in collateral proceedings, such as injunction, declaratory judgment, or enforcement proceedings. Hence, in the judicial review of those rules (as in the judicial review of statutes for their constitutionality) any factual challenge to the rules had to be developed in the court proceedings. In such judicial review proceedings, the courts traditionally reviewed rules under a rationality or arbitrariness standard. In so doing they presumed the rationality (and, hence, non-arbitrariness) of the rule and cast the burden of proving otherwise on the person objecting to it. They generally took this approach whether the attack was upon the constitutionality of the rule or upon the rational relation of the rule in question to the underlying statute authorizing the agency to issue the rule.

The enactment of the APA in 1946 did not change this basic approach. The contemporaneous understanding of the effect of the APA was as follows: Although under the APA agencies were required generally to employ notice-and-comment procedures in rulemaking, the use of these procedures by agencies did not affect the approach of the courts to judicial review. Since informal or notice-and-comment rulemaking was not modeled upon a judicial trial (as was formal rulemaking), rules were not issued upon the basis of an administrative "record". Accordingly, any factual development necessary to an objector's case against a rule had to be made out in court in the manner described above.

Questions and Comments

How would courts review rules for rationality or arbitrariness? What standards would they employ? What procedural steps would be required of a plaintiff seeking such review? What would such a plaintiff have to show to have a rule invalidated? What kinds of evidence would such a plaintiff use?

Pacific States Box & Basket Co. v. White, 296 U.S. 176 (1935). Plaintiff was a manufacturer of containers for raspberries and strawberries. It brought suit under the Fourteenth Amendment to enjoin the Oregon Director of Agriculture and the Chief of the Oregon Division of Plant Industry from enforcing a regulation setting standards for raspberry and strawberry containers which were incompatible with the type of containers manufactured by the Plaintiff. On review of the lower court's dismissal of the suit, the Supreme Court affirmed. Speaking through Justice Brandeis, that Court stated:

> The order here in question deals with a subject clearly within the scope of the police power. . . . When such legislative action "is called into question, if any state of facts reasonably can be conceived that would sustain it, there is a presumption of the existence of that state of facts, and one who assails the classification must carry the burden of showing by a resort to common knowledge or other matters which may be judicially noticed, or to other legitimate proof, that the action is arbitrary." . . . It is urged that this rebuttable presumption of the existence of a state of facts sufficient to justify the exertion of the police power attaches only to acts of legislature; and that where the regulation is the act of an administrative body, no such presumption exists, so that the burden of proving the justifying facts is upon him who seeks to sustain the validity of the regulation. The contention is without support in authority or reason, and rests upon misconception. Every exertion of the police power, either by the legislature or by an administrative body, is an exercise of delegated power. Where it is by statute, the legislature has acted under power delegated to it through the Constitution. Where the regulation is by an order of an administrative body, that body acts under a delegation from the legislature. The question of law may, of course, always be raised whether the legislature had power to delegate the authority exercised. . . . But where the regulation is within the scope of authority legally delegated, the presumption of the existence of facts justifying its specific exercise attaches alike to statutes, to municipal ordinances, and to orders of municipal bodies. . . . Here there is added reason for applying the presumption of validity; for the regulation now challenged was adopted after notice and public hearing as the statute required. . . .

Questions and Comments

1. Was the Court in the *Pacific States* case concerned with a constitutional challenge to a state regulation? If not, how did the case get to the U.S. Supreme Court? What were the grounds on which the plaintiff challenged the regulation? What standard of judicial review did the U.S. Supreme Court apply in its ruling?

What is the relation, if any, between the review standards applied by the Court in this case and the standards that the Court would have applied in reviewing a state regulatory statute for its constitutionality? What is the relation, if any, between the review standards applied by the Court in this case and the standards that would have been applied by the lower courts to review a regulation under a rationality or arbitrariness standard?

2.   Under the procedure employed in *Pacific States*, what steps must be taken by a person who wishes to have the rule invalidated by a court? Under the review standard employed in *Pacific States*, what matters must a plaintiff establish to have the rule invalidated? What kinds of evidence must such a plaintiff present to the court? Who bears the burden of persuasion? What must a plaintiff do to satisfy that burden? Is that burden easily satisfied? Explain.

3.   **City of Chicago, Ill. v. FPC, 458 F.2d 731 (D.C. Cir. 1971), cert. denied, 405 U.S. 1074 (1972).** In order to stimulate the search for new natural gas deposits in a circumstance of declining reserves, the FPC directed that natural gas produced by pipeline companies from post- 1969 leases be valued at the rate applicable to independent producers. In upholding this rule against a challenge, the court made the following remarks:

> . . . review would be a relatively futile exercise in formalism if no inquiry were permissible into the existence or nonexistence of the condition which the Commission advances as the predicate for its regulatory action. A regulation perfectly reasonable and appropriate in the face of a given problem may be highly capricious if that problem does not exist. . . . [A]lthough the process leading to the promulgation of a rule frequently resembles the legislative process and although a rule frequently has an impact similar to that of a statute, rule-making is not fully equivalent to the action of the legislature. Clearly, rule-making is the action of a body subordinate to the legislature. That the same deference accorded "findings" of the legislature is not to be given the findings of the Commission is implicit in the law governing legislative delegation of authority. Were "findings" of the Commission in a rule-making proceeding automatically exempt from judicial review, the law governing delegation would also become little more than formalistic mutterings, for it makes little sense to require that the legislature articulate intelligible standards to govern agency action if realistic inquiry into whether those standards are being followed were foreclosed. Thirdly, the Commission has broad discretion to seek a given objective either through ad hoc adjudicatory proceedings or through rule-making. To argue that, if the latter route is followed, judicial inquiry into the factual basis for the agency's action is impermissible, is to say that in large measure the agency itself has the discretion to determine whether its action will be subject to meaningful review.

4.   Is the approach of the court to judicial review of an agency's rule in the *City of Chicago* case different from the Supreme Court's approach in *Pacific States Box & Basket, supra*? Did the Court in *Pacific States* hold that inquiry into the factual predicate for an agency's rule was impermissible? Or that the factual predicate was presumptively true? Was that presumption rebuttable? How could it be rebutted?

5. Did the Court in *Pacific States* give the same deference to a rule of an administrative agency that it would give to a statute passed by a legislature? Did the court in *City of Chicago* reject that approach? Would the *Pacific States* approach have prevented judicial inquiry into the factual premises of an agency promulgated rule? Under *Pacific States*, would not a court inquire into the factual premises of a statute which was challenged under the due process clause? Did the court in *City of Chicago* confuse the issue when it spoke about the permissibility or impermissibility of judicial inquiry into the factual premises of an agency rule? Should the court have stated the issue in terms of the extent of the deference which a reviewing court is required to accord to an agency's factual premise?

6. Where did the court in *City of Chicago* contribute an element of clarity that was missing from the *Pacific States* opinion? How is judicial review of an agency rule necessarily different from judicial review of a statute? Does the delegation issue make that review different in kind? Does the delegation issue affect the standards for rationality review? Explain. How did *Pacific States* deal with the delegation issue? Is the delegation issue different when a federal court reviews a rule of a federal agency (as in *City of Chicago*) from when the Supreme Court reviews a rule of a state agency (as in *Pacific States*)?

2.   *Judicial review of notice-and-comment rulemaking after the enactment of the APA and prior to the developments of the 1960s and 1970s.*

The procedural practice followed by courts in reviewing rules promulgated under the notice-and-comment provisions of the APA, as it had evolved by 1960, is illustrated in ***Air Line Pilots Association, International v. Quesada*, 276 F.2d 892 (2d Cir. 1960).** In that case thirty-five individual pilots, their union and the its president brought suit in district court for a judgment declaring invalid and enjoining a regulation of the Administrator of the Federal Aviation Agency (FAA) prohibiting persons over 60 years of age from piloting commercial aircraft. In affirming the district court's denial of a preliminary injunction, the court of appeals observed that it could reverse the Administrator only if he "had no reasonable basis for his exercise of judgment." The court then recited several of the findings which the Administrator had made after the notice-and-comment proceedings and in support of the regulation: The number of commercial pilots over sixty years of age had been increasing rapidly; that older pilots because of their seniority often fly the newest, largest, and fastest planes; that medical studies show that sudden incapacitation due to heart attacks or strokes become more frequent as men approach age sixty and that it is impossible accurately to predict which individuals will be affected; that a number of foreign air carriers had mandatory retirement ages of sixty or less; and that numerous aviation safety experts advocated establishing a maximum age of sixty or younger. The court then concluded that it was "not the business of courts to substitute their untutored judgment for the expert knowledge of those who are given authority to implement the general directives of Congress. . . . We can only ask whether the regulation is reasonable in relation to the standards prescribed in the statute and the facts before the Administrator. Of that there can be no doubt in this case."

In the *Quesada* case the Federal Aviation administrator had provided a rationale for his rule setting a maximum age for air carrier pilots. This fact in itself made the plaintiff's case less burdensome than the plaintiff's case was stated to be under *Pacific States Box & Basket Co.*, did it not? What role did the comment proceeding play in *Quesada?* Note that the court accepted the Administrator's findings on the comment record as the factual predicate for the Administrator's regulation. Could the plaintiff have forced the Administrator to relitigate some or all of those facts in court? Or was the plaintiff bound by the findings made after the notice and comment proceedings? [Consider *Heckler v. Campbell, supra,* Chapter 6] If the plaintiff challenged the Administrator's finding about increasing exposure to heart attacks and strokes of persons approaching age 60, would the issue be whether there is in fact increasing exposure to such ailments or whether the medical studies which had been available to the FAA show such increasing exposure? Could the plaintiff introduce a new study which had not been available to the Administrator purporting to negate this increasing exposure and to rebut earlier studies? Could the Administrator introduce a new study in the court proceedings justifying his earlier-issued regulation?

We know that in *Quesada* the notice-and-comment proceedings played a role in judicial review, because it is the Administrator's findings after conclusion of the comment period which form the factual predicate for the regulation. Review of agency regulations is taking place in district court, apparently upon a record which may be open to development in the district court proceedings.

3.   *Judicial review of formal rulemaking.*

Judicial review of formal rulemaking was modeled upon judicial review of administrative proceedings involving named parties. It was based upon the record of the administrative proceeding and usually employed a "substantial evidence" standard for review. As a relatively novel method for review of widely-applicable rules, the Attorney General's Committee in 1941 expressed its doubts about that method in its Final Report:

> Some of the recent statutes conferring rule-making power . . . provide for a much more detailed judicial review of certain administrative regulations. . . . They require that the regulations in question be based upon findings of fact; that these, in turn, be based upon evidence made of record at a hearing; and that a reviewing court set aside a regulation not only for failure of the findings to support it, but also for failure of a finding to be based upon substantial evidence in the record. Review by the courts is had in statutory proceedings which may be instituted within a prescribed time by parties aggrieved by regulations and which result in a certification of the administrative record to the court. A judgment adverse to a regulation results in setting it aside.

> In these review proceedings a court is required not merely to pass upon the presence of a rational relationship between a regulation and the governing statute, but to judge the fundamental soundness of the details of the administrative reasoning process. The regulation does not speak for itself, with a limited amount of evidence or argument to aid in judging it;

the entire administrative record must be examined.

The full significance of this novel type of judicial review becomes apparent only when the characteristics of the problems to be resolved in regulations are considered. A leading characteristic is the discretion required for their solution. In an ordinary trial the question is whether the facts bring the case within a rule or principle of law or not. The issues can be framed as issues of fact, and findings based upon evidence can be made. The issues are always of limited scope, relating to the particular circumstances or transactions, and the evidence bearing upon them can be incorporated into a record.

The situation is different in rule making or other discretionary determinations which involve, in effect, the formulation of new policies. For example, whether railroad, air lines, or steamship companies shall be required to install expensive safety devices; what shall be the nature of the elaborate accounting systems prescribed for communications companies or other utilities; what shall be the standards of identity and quality for foods; what shall be the definition of improper practices by trust officers of national banks — these and a thousand other determinations which must be made in administrative regulations involve important choices of policy. Such choices must be made in the light of facts; but the chief issues are not factual. They relate either to the proper balancing of objectives — safety of transportation as against minimizing the expenditures of transportation companies; conformity to the idea of consumers as against freedom for manufacturers to follow practices of their own choosing; and the like — or to a choice of methods to achieve given objectives, such as the best way to produce an adequate record of the financial affairs of certain corporations or the most workable procedure for judging the fitness of applicants for certain types of licenses.

Questions and Comments

1. Does the Committee believe that judicial review of formal rulemaking involves issues different from those present in appellate judicial review of an ordinary trial? Would judicial review of formal rulemaking resemble judicial review of administrative proceedings involving named parties, such as judicial review of a license revocation proceeding? Why or why not? How does judicial review of formal rulemaking differ from judicial review over informal rulemaking?

2. What does the Committee mean when it says that judicial review of formal rulemaking is "a much more detailed judicial review" than the courts have practiced in the past? In what does this "detail" consist? Explain.

3. Is the Committee assuming that "detailed" judicial review is appropriate when the agency is required to use formal procedures in adopting a rule? Is "detailed" judicial review always implied by formal rulemaking procedures? Does a statutory provision for "detailed" judicial review imply that the agency is required to employ formal rulemaking procedures?

D.   THE COMPLEX HISTORY OF JUDICIAL REVIEW OF INFORMAL RULEMAKING

The Final Report of the Attorney General's Committee on Administrative Procedure, published in 1941, set forth the common contemporary understanding of the way in which agency rules were subjected to judicial review. This understanding was the same as that reflected in *Pacific States Box & Basket Co. v. White, supra.*

Several subsequent events contributed to an evolving change in the way that courts approached the judicial review of agency rules. First, in the *Chenery* cases *(supra,* Chapter 6) the Supreme Court had ruled that courts would be usurping agency roles if they were to supply a rationale for agency action which was different from that supplied by the agencies themselves. Although the *Chenery* cases did not involve the judicial review of agency rules, the implications of the *Chenery* cases were clear: When an agency supplied a rationale for its action in any kind of proceeding, the courts must review the agency action on the agency-supplied rationale.

Second, the Administrative Procedure Act, which was enacted in 1946, contained in § 553, its provision governing informal rulemaking, the following requirement:

> After consideration of the relevant matter presented, the agency shall incorporate in the rules adopted a concise general statement of their basis and purpose.

5 U.S.C. § 553(c) (1982). Although a contemporaneous explanation of this provision by the U.S. Attorney General indicated that the provision was primarily concerned with informing the press and the lay public generally about what was happening in government, the provision did have the effect of requiring agencies to provide a rationale for their rulemaking. In combination with the requirements of the *Chenery* cases, the required basis-and-purpose statement meant that agencies were required to provide a rationale for their rulemaking and that judicial review of that rulemaking would be based upon an agency-provided rationale.

Third, beginning in the 1960s, the Congress enacted a number of statutes which called for agency rulemaking using notice-and-comment procedures; judicial review of that rulemaking on the record of the administrative proceeding; and the use of a "substantial evidence" standard by the courts in performing their review.

Fourth, the Supreme Court's 1971 decision in *Citizens to Preserve Overton Park, Inc. v. Volpe* [*supra,* Chapter 2] called for review on the administrative record of a decision of the Secretary of Transportation approving the expenditure of federal funds for the construction of a highway through a park. That case carried implications for informal rulemaking. If informal action of this type was to be reviewed on the administrative record, then there was no obvious reason why the notice-and-comment record should not be used as the basis for judicial review of all informal rulemaking, including informal rulemaking under the statutes of the pre-1960s era. Such review would drastically depart from the traditional understanding of judicial review of administrative rules, as described in the Final Report of the Attorney General's Committee on Administrative Procedure and as exemplified by *Pacific States Box & Basket Co. v. White* [*supra*] and (to a lesser extent) by

Airline Pilots Ass'n v. Quesada [supra].

These several events began to interact in ways that provoked turmoil in the way the courts approached the review of rulemaking. In your reading of the cases and other material below, try to distinguish the factors in the court decisions which are likely to have continuing significance from those that are not.

Automotive Parts & Accessories Assn v. Boyd, 407 F.2d 330 (D.C. Cir. 1968) illustrates some of these changes in judicial review of rules and rulemaking that were taking place in the late 1960s and 1970s. A rule issued by the Secretary of Transportation under the National Traffic and Motor Vehicle Safety Act of 1968 requiring that all new passenger cars manufactured for sale in the United States must be factory-equipped with front seat head restraints meeting specific federal standards. The rule was challenged by a manufacturer of automobile accessories (including head restraints) and two trade associations representing persons engaged in the auto accessory business whose markets would be foreclosed if head restraints were required to be factory installed. The challengers complained that the informal rulemaking procedures followed by the Secretary were inadequate:

> . . . [P]etitioners refer to the judicial review provisions of the Safety Act, and argue that they make manifest a Congressional intent that the "rules are required by statute to be made on the record after opportunity for an agency hearing," APA § 4(b)[§ 553(b)], and therefore are to be the product of formal rulemaking. This is said to be implicit in (1) the requirement that, where review is sought of an order establishing a standard, there shall be filed in court "the record of the proceedings on which the Secretary based his order," (2) the jurisdiction given the court to review safety standards "in accordance with" Section 10 of the APA, and (3) the provision made for remand by the court, at the request of a petitioner for the taking of additional evidence. Petitioners argue that all these aspects of the judicial review contemplated and authorized by the Safety Act are instinct with the idea of a record compiled in formal evidentiary hearings, from which record the agency makes findings and conclusions required to be supported, in the familiar adjudicatory sense, by substantial evidence in the record. Otherwise, so it is said, the judicial review provisions would be meaningless.

> We are not persuaded. . . . As to petitioners' first contention, there is a record compiled in a Section 4 [§ 553] proceeding, and available for filing in Court. It consists of submissions made in response to the invitations issued for written comments. And, as to the third, a court could, at the instance of a petitioner dissatisfied with the state of such a record, remand it to the agency for the receipt of further expressions of views and related information. Thus, there is nothing in these two provisions from the Safety Act's judicial review section which renders them completely inapt in relation to judicial scrutiny of the product of a Section 4 [§ 553] proceeding; and Congress can, accordingly, be rationally taken as having fashioned them with such a proceeding in view.

> Petitioners press closely upon us the reference in the judicial review provisions of the Safety Act to Section 10 of the Administrative Procedure Act. They point to paragraph (e) . . . which . . . is generally concerned

with the scope of the review by a court of agency action, and in particular, to subparagraph (b) (5) [§ 706(2)(E)] which directs that the court shall set aside agency action "unsupported by substantial evidence in a case subject to [Sections 7 and 8 of the APA] or otherwise reviewed on the record of an agency hearing provided by statute." We think that this language of Section 10, although not free from ambiguity, suggests that this "substantial evidence" standard for judicial review is addressed to the review of formal hearings, either under Sections 7 and 8 or other special statutory provision. Since we have found that a formal hearing is not required by the Safety Act, Subsection (b) (5) by its own terms appears to have no application to this case. . . . This is not to say, however, that Congress has given no guidance as to the proper standards for judicial review of informal proceedings. . . . The other standards set out in that section [10(e)], all of which would apply to informal rulemaking, allow an appellate court to apply 10(c) quite apart from subsection (B) (5).

In any event, although the judicial review provisions of the Safety Act and the APA contain some terms which are normally associated with formal evidentiary hearings, we refuse to infer that Congress, in this unnecessarily oblique way, intended to require the procedures of formal rule making for the issuance of safety standards. . . .

We think also that the statement in the text of the promulgation of the Standard, when considered in the light of the reasons stated by the Administrator's denial of rehearing, is "a concise general statement" which passes muster under Section 4 of the APA. However, on the occasion of this first challenge to the implementation of the new statute it is appropriate for us to remind the Administrator of the ever present possibility of judicial review, and to caution against an overly literal reading of the statutory terms "concise" and "general." These adjectives must be accommodated to the realities of judicial scrutiny, which do not contemplate that the court itself will, by a laborious examination of the record, formulate in the first instance the significant issues faced by the agency and articulate the rationale of their resolution . . . We . . . expect that, if the judicial review which Congress has thought it important to provide is to be meaningful, the "concise general statement of . . . basis and purpose" mandated by Section 4 will enable us to see what major issues of policy were ventilated by the informal proceedings and why the agency reacted to them as it did.

Questions and Comments

1. Was the court correct in rejecting the petitioners' contention that the statute contemplated formal rulemaking? Explain. The statute contemplated a procedure different from that involved in the *Quesada* case *supra*, did it not?

2. Did the court review the agency rule in the same way that it would have reviewed formal adjudication of the type involved in *Universal Camera?* [*supra*, Chapter 2] Explain. Did the court review the agency rule on the "record" of the agency proceeding? Did it employ a "substantial evidence" standard of review? If not, what standard did the court employ? Is there a difference between judicial review under a "substantial evidence" standard and judicial review under an arbitrariness standard? If so, how would you describe that difference? Does the availability of an administrative record affect the standard for review which a court will employ? Explain.

3. Was the basis and purpose statement required by § 553 of the APA originally intended as an aid to judicial review? Does it necessarily provide that basis? Could a reviewing court uphold a rule under a rationale different from the one contained in the basis and purpose statement? Explain. *See* the *Chenery* cases [*supra*, Chapter 6].

4. Was the court using the basis and purpose statement as an aid to identifying the issues? as a means of imposing a conceptual order upon a proceeding involving vast amounts of evidence and numerous potential issues? Would this use of the basis and purpose statement be necessary if the court had not been required to conduct judicial review on the "record" of the proceeding?

More on the Basis and Purpose Statement

Another influential case of that era was ***Portland Cement Ass'n v. Ruckelsbaus, 486 F.2d 375 (D.C. Cir. 1973).*** In that case the court read the provisions of section 533, including the basis-and-purpose statement as establishing the framework for a dialogue between a regulatory agency and the regulated parties. In the court's understanding, the agency was required, in its basis-and-purpose statement or otherwise, to respond to important input from the parties in such a way as to communicate to the reviewing court that it had considered those matters and, if it rejected that input, that it was justified in doing so

In that case, cement manufacturers attacked EPA-promulgated stationary source standards restricting the amounts of particulate matter that was permitted to be emitted from new or modified cement plants. Under the governing provisions of the Clean Air Act, the Administrator of the EPA had to determine that the achievability of the emission limitations embodied in the standards had been "adequately demonstrated." This determination was based in part upon tests that the EPA had conducted. When the standards were proposed they were accompanied by a "Background" document that disclosed some information about the tests, but did not identify the location or the methodology used in the one successful test upon which the EPA was relying. In an expanded statement of reasons issued subsequent to the promulgation of the final standards, the EPA referred to a second set of tests, but again, only a summary of the test results were disclosed. Only a month later were the details of the two sets of tests disclosed by the EPA. Consider the following excerpt from the opinion in that case:

> We find a critical defect in the decision-making process in arriving at the standard under review in the initial inability of petitioners to obtain — in timely fashion — the test results and procedures used on existing plants which formed a partial basis for the emission control level adopted, and in the subsequent seeming refusal of the agency to respond to what seem to be legitimate problems with the methodology of these tests.

After Intervenor Northwestern States Portland Cement Company received the detailed test information in mid-April, 1972, it submitted the test data, for analysis of reliability and accuracy, to Ralph H. Striker, an engineer experienced in the design of emission control systems for portland cement plants. He concluded that the first series of tests run at the Dragon Cement Company were "grossly erroneous" due to inaccurate sampling techniques to measure particulate matter. Northwestern States then moved this Court to remand the record to EPA so that the agency might consider the additional comments on the tests. This motion was granted. . . .

In this case, EPA made no written submission as to the additional comments made by petitioners. . . . All that EPA did was to comply with the mandate that the analysis of Mr. Striker be added to the certified record. It may be that EPA considers Mr. Striker's analysis invalid — but we have no way of knowing this. As the record stands, all we have is Mr. Striker's repudiation of the test data without response. The purpose of our prior remand cannot be realized unless we hear EPA's response to his comments, and the record must be remanded again, for that purpose.

We are not establishing any broad principle that EPA must respond to every comment made by manufacturers on the validity of its standards or the methodology and scientific basis for their formulation. In the case of the Striker presentation, however, our prior remand reflects this court's view of the significance, or at least potential significance, of this presentation. If this were a private lawsuit, we might reverse the order under appeal for failure of its proponent to meet the burden of refutation or explanation. Since this is a matter involving the public interest, in which the court and agency are in a kind of partnership relationship for the purpose of effectuating the legislative mandate, we remand. . . . Manufacturers' comments must be significant enough to step over a threshold requirement of materiality before any lack of agency response or consideration becomes of concern. The comment cannot merely state that a particular mistake was made in a sampling operation; it must show why the mistake was of possible significance in the results of the tests. . . .

In order that rule-making proceedings to determine standards be conducted in orderly fashion, information should generally be disclosed as to the basis of a proposed rule at the time of issuance. If this is not feasible, as in case of statutory time constraints [which in this case required the EPA to issue the final standards within 90 days of the proposed regulation], information that is material to the subject at hand should be disclosed as it becomes available, and comments received, even though subsequent to issuance of the rule — with court authorization where necessary.

The concept of § 553 as imposing a procedural dialogue was further articulated, inter alia, in **Northside Sanitary Landfill, Inc. v. Thomas, 849 F.2d 1516 (D.C. Cir. 1988)**, where the court focused upon the obligation of the regulated private party to identify the issues precisely. In that case the owner of a hazardous waste, objecting to the action of the Environmental Protection Agency placing its site on the

National Priorities List for cleanup action, complained that the agency had failed to respond it its objections to the agency action:

> It is certainly incumbent upon the EPA under 5 U.S.C. § 553(c) to "respond [ ] in a reasoned manner to significant comments received." *United States Satellite Broadcasting Co., Inc. v. FCC*, 740 F.2d 1177, 1188 (D.C.Cir.1984) . . . But the "dialogue" between administrative agencies and the public "is a two-way street." *Home Box Office*, 567 F.2d at 35. Just as "the opportunity to comment is meaningless unless the agency responds to significant points raised by the public," id. at 35–36 (footnote omitted), so too is the agency's opportunity to *respond* to those comments meaningless unless the interested party clearly states its position. *See Wisconsin Electric Power Co. v. Costle*, 715 F.2d 323, 326 (7th Cir.1983) ("the rules of administrative law apply across the board, to agencies and interested parties alike").

> We hold that when Northside submitted its comments to the EPA, Northside should have been specific as to why and how it thought the 420 pages of documents were relevant to the scoring of the Northside site. We are not suggesting that Northside should have commented in great detail on every study, but we do conclude that Northside could and should have done far more than it did do to alert the EPA to its positions, which would have then required and allowed the EPA fully to consider Northside's version of the facts, and to act upon them appropriately.[2] We therefore conclude that the EPA's failure to respond to the specific issues which Northside asserts were presented by its comments was neither arbitrary nor capricious. *See Home Box Office*, 567 F.2d at 35–36 n. 58. We agree with the EPA that Northside never presented its objections to the agency in a way which could reasonably have permitted the agency to examine those contentions.

Questions and Comments

1. Were the courts in *Portland Cement* and *Northside Sanitary Landfill* imposing procedural requirements upon the agency that are not in the APA? As we will see below, the Supreme Court ruled in *Vermont Yankee* that courts may not impose procedural requirements upon agencies that are not mandated by the APA. Although *Portland Cement* was decided before *Vermont Yankee*, *Northside Sanitary Landfill* was decided ten years after that decision. Did the court in *Portland Cement* derive the EPA's duty to comment upon the Striker analysis from the APA? From the agency's obligation to issue a statement of a rule's basis and purpose? Was it implied as incident to the court's duty to review the agency's action for rationality

---

[2] At the very least, Northside itself could have pointed out those facts which it believed that the EPA had overlooked in the EPA's response to Northside's comments. Specifically, when Northside received the EPA's response to its comments, it was on notice that the EPA had not interpreted those comments as Northside evidently expected the agency would. At that point, pursuant to 5 U.S.C. § 553(e) . . . , Northside was free to petition the EPA to reconsider its position concerning those comments in the light of the specific objections which Northside now raises before this court. *See Wisconsin Electric*, 715 F.2d at 327–28. However, Northside did not take advantage of that opportunity.

or arbitrariness? Did the court have inherent power to order the agency to respond?

2.　Do the decisions in *Portland Cement* and *Northside Sanitary Landfill* provide a basis for a construction of § 553 under which the agency and interested parties have a continuing obligation to comment upon the last significant submissions of the other side? How long would such a dialogue last? Would the submissions necessarily all be in the form of writings? Would testimony and cross-examination ever be necessary? Who would decide such questions?

Some Limits on Judicial Power over Agencies

NATURAL RESOURCES DEFENSE COUNCIL, INC. v. UNITED STATES NUCLEAR REGULATORY COMMISSION
547 F.2d 633 (D.C. Cir. 1976)

BAZELON, CHIEF JUDGE:

The problems posed in both these cases relate to the manner and extent to which information concerning the environmental effects of radioactive wastes must be considered on the public record in decisions to license nuclear reactors.

Appeal number 74-1586 involves a rulemaking proceeding which the [Nuclear Regulatory] Commission instituted . . . with specific reference to the *Vermont Yankee* decision. The purpose of the rulemaking was to consider whether environmental effects of all stages of the uranium fuel cycle should be included in the cost-benefit analysis for licensing individual reactors. . . . The Commission concluded the environmental effects of the fuel cycle, including waste disposal, were "relatively insignificant," but that it was preferable to take them into account. Therefore, a rule was promulgated requiring a series of specified numerical values (set out as Table S-3 accompanying the rule) be factored into the cost-benefit analysis for an individual reactor. . . .

The notice of proposed rulemaking . . . suggested . . . that a series of specified numerical values (set out as Table S-3 in the notice) be factored into the cost-benefit analysis for individual reactors. These values were intended to represent the incremental contribution of a hypothetical 1000 MWe model light water reactor to the total environmental effect of the uranium fuel cycle. While expressed as numerical values in Table S-3, a fair summary of the conclusions incorporated into the rule is that the environmental effects of the fuel cycle are "insignificant." The notice further stated that the "supporting data for this summary table" is contained in a staff document entitled the "Environmental Survey of the Nuclear Fuel Cycle" which was simultaneously made public.

An "informal rulemaking hearing" of the "legislative-type" was scheduled to receive comments in the form of "oral or written statements."

The primary argument advanced by the public interest intervenors is that the decision to preclude "discovery or cross-examination" denied them a meaningful opportunity to participate in the proceedings as guaranteed by due process. They do not question the Commission's authority to proceed by informal rulemaking, as opposed to adjudication. They rely instead on the line of cases indicating that in particular circumstances procedures in excess of the bare minima prescribed by the Administrative Procedure Act, 5 U.S.C. § 553, may be required.

The Government concedes that "basic considerations of fairness may under exceptional circumstances" require additional procedures in "legislative-type proceedings," but contends that the procedures here were more than adequate. Thus, we are called upon to decide whether the procedures provided by the agency were sufficient to ventilate the issues.

. . . . [S]upport for a rule limiting consideration of environmental issues to the numbers in Table S-3 must be found in one of three places: the Environmental Survey, the back-up documentation to which it refers, and the oral and written testimony offered at the hearing. It is to these sources we must look for a thorough ventilation of the underlying issues.

. . . .

The only discussion of high-level waste disposal techniques was supplied by a 20-page statement by Dr. Frank K. Pittman, Director of the AEC's[3] Division of Waste Management and Transportation. This statement, delivered during the oral hearings, was then incorporated, often verbatim, into the revised version of the Environmental Survey published after the comment period. . . .

Dr. Pittman concludes with the judgments that:

> . . . (1) the program being followed by the industry under AEC regulation and by the AEC offers assurance that the commercial high-level waste will be managed safely from its initial production; (2) the surface storage method, to be used by the AEC, is good for as long as adequate human surveillance and maintenance effort is continued; (3) the probability that work currently under way will demonstrate the use of bedded salt as a safe, acceptable, ultimate disposal method within the next ten to fifteen years is very high; (4) should bedded salt not prove to be acceptable other acceptable geologic disposal concepts offer reasonable probability of reaching a point of acceptability within two or three decades; and (5) the waste in initial storage will be easily retrievable for either near- or far-term disposal methods when they are developed.

. . . There is no discussion of how "adequate human surveillance and maintenance" can be assured for the periods involved, nor what the long-term costs of such a commitment are, nor of the dangers if surveillance is not maintained. Nor is any explanation offered for Dr. Pittman's optimism regarding bedded salt as a disposal method, since the problems which have surfaced and delayed that program are not mentioned. Nor does the statement anywhere describe what "other acceptable geologic disposal concepts" are under consideration.

In substantial part, the materials uncritically relied on by the Commission in promulgating this rule consist of extremely vague assurances by agency personnel

---

[3] [The Atomic Energy Commission (AEC) was the predecessor of the Nuclear Regulatory Commission (NRC).]

that problems as yet unsolved will be solved. That is an insufficient record to sustain a rule limiting consideration of the environmental effects of nuclear waste disposal to the numerical values in Table S-3. To the extent that uncertainties necessarily underlie predictions of this importance on the frontiers of science and technology, there is a concomitant necessity to confront and explore fully the depth and consequences of such uncertainties. Not only were the generalities relied on in this case not subject to rigorous probing in any form — but when apparently substantial criticisms were brought to the Commission's attention, it simply ignored them, or brushed them aside without answer. Without a thorough exploration of the problems involved in waste disposal, including past mistakes, and a forthright assessment of the uncertainties and differences in expert opinion, this type of agency action cannot pass muster as reasoned decisionmaking.

Many procedural devices for creating a genuine dialogue on these issues were available to the agency — including informal conferences between intervenors and staff, document discovery, interrogatories, technical advisory committees composed of outside experts with differing perspectives, limited cross-examination, funding independent research by intervenors, detailed annotation of technical reports, surveys of existing literature, memoranda explaining methodology. We do not presume to intrude on the agency's province by dictating to it which, if any of these devices it must adopt to flesh out the record. It may be that no combination of the procedures mentioned above will prove adequate, and the agency will be required to develop new procedures to accomplish the innovative task of implementing NEPA through rulemaking. On the other hand, the procedures the agency adopted in this case, if administered in a more sensitive, deliberate manner might suffice. Whatever techniques the Commission adopts, before it promulgates a rule limiting further consideration of waste disposal and reprocessing issues, it must in one way or another generate a record in which the factual issues are fully developed.

. . . .

The Commission's action in cutting off consideration of waste disposal and reprocessing issues in licensing proceedings based on the cursory development of the facts which occurred in this proceeding was capricious and arbitrary. The portions of the rule pertaining to these matters are set aside and remanded.

Questions and Comments

1.   What was Judge Bazelon's principal objection to the NRC's rule? Did the rule have an adequate basis in the record? What standard of review was the court employing?

2.   Did the court order the agency to undertake further procedures to ventilate the issues? What was the source of the court's authority to order further procedures?

3.   The most explicit articulation of the position that a reviewing court possesses authority to impose procedures on agencies beyond those found in the APA occurred in *Mobil Oil Corp. v. Federal Power Commission*, **483 F.2d 1238 (D.C.Cir. 1973)**. In that case the D.C. Circuit had taken the position that section 553 set forth the minimum procedural requirements for rulemaking, that sections 556

and 557 set forth the maximum requirements and that the court could order procedures that fit anywhere in the range between these two poles. Would you say that the approach of the court here in reviewing the agency procedures was similar to the approach of the court in the *Mobil* case, *supra?* Or was it more like the approach in *Portland Cement?* Explain.

VERMONT YANKEE NUCLEAR POWER CORP. v. NATURAL RESOURCES DEFENSE COUNCIL, INC.
435 U.S. 519 (1978)

Mr. Justice Rehnquist delivered the opinion of the Court.

. . . . Vermont Yankee argues that the court invalidated the rule because of the inadequacy of the procedures employed in the proceedings. . . . Respondents, on the other hand, labeling petitioner's view of the decision a "straw man," argue to this Court that the court merely held that the record was inadequate to enable the reviewing court to determine whether the agency had fulfilled its statutory obligation. . . . But we unfortunately have not found the parties' characterization of the opinion to be entirely reliable; it appears here . . . that "in this Court the parties changed positions as nimbly as if dancing a quadrille."

After a thorough examination of the opinion itself, we conclude that while the matter is not entirely free from doubt, the majority of the Court of Appeals struck down the rule because of the perceived inadequacies of the procedures employed in the rulemaking proceedings. The court first determined the intervenors' primary argument to be "that the decision to preclude 'discovery or cross-examination' denied them a meaningful opportunity to participate in the proceedings as guaranteed by due process". . . . The court then went on to frame the issue for decision thus:

> Thus, we are called upon to decide whether the procedures provided by the agency were sufficient to ventilate the issues. . . .

The court conceded that absent extraordinary circumstances it is improper for a reviewing court to prescribe the procedural format an agency must follow, but it likewise clearly thought it entirely appropriate to "scrutinize the record as a whole to insure that genuine opportunities to participate in a meaningful way were provided. . . ." The court also refrained from actually ordering the agency to follow any specific procedures. . . . but there is little doubt in our minds that the ineluctable mandate of the court's decision is that the procedures afforded during the hearings were inadequate. This conclusion is particularly buttressed by the fact that after the court examined the record, particularly the testimony of Dr. Pittman, and declared it insufficient, the court proceeded to discuss at some length the necessity for further procedural devices or a more "sensitive" application of those devices employed during the proceedings. . . . The exploration of the record and the statement regarding its insufficiency might initially lead one to conclude that the court was only examining the sufficiency of the evidence, but the remaining portions of the opinion dispel any doubt that this was certainly not the sole or even the principal basis of the decision. Accordingly, we feel compelled to address the opinion on its own terms, and we conclude that it was wrong.

In prior opinions we have intimated that even in a rule-making proceeding when an agency is making a " 'quasi-judicial' " determination by which a very small number of persons are " 'exceptionally affected, in each case upon individual grounds,' " in some circumstances additional procedures may be required in order to afford the aggrieved individuals due process. *United States v. Florida East Coast R. Co.* . . . quoting from *Bi-Metallic Investment Co. v. State Board of Equalization.* . . . It might also be true, although we do not think the issue is presented in this case and accordingly do not decide it, that a totally unjustified departure from well-settled agency procedures of long standing might require judicial correction.

But this much is absolutely clear. Absent constitutional constraints or extremely compelling circumstances the "administrative agencies 'should be free to fashion their own rules of procedure and to pursue methods of inquiry capable of permitting them to discharge their multitudinous duties.' " . . .

Respondent NRDC argues that § 4 of the Administrative Procedure Act, 5 U.S.C. § 553 (1976 ed.), merely establishes lower procedural bounds and that a court may routinely require more than the minimum when an agency's proposed rule addresses complex or technical factual issues or "Issues of Great Public Import.". . . . We have, however, previously shown that our decisions reject this view. . . . We also think the legislative history . . . does not bear out its contention. . . . [The legislative history of the APA] leaves little doubt that Congress intended that the discretion of the *agencies* and not that of the courts be exercised in determining when extra procedural devices should be employed.

There are compelling reasons for construing § 4 in this manner. In the first place, if courts continually review agency proceedings to determine whether the agency employed procedures which were, in the court's opinion, perfectly tailored to reach what the court perceives to be the "best" or "correct" result, judicial review would be totally unpredictable. And the agencies, operating under this vague injunction to employ the "best" procedures and facing the threat of reversal if they did not, would undoubtedly adopt full adjudicatory procedures in every instance. Not only would this totally disrupt the statutory scheme, through which Congress enacted "a formula upon which opposing social and political forces have come to rest," . . . but all the inherent advantages of informal rulemaking would be totally lost.

Secondly, it is obvious that the court in these cases reviewed the agency's choice of procedures on the basis of the record actually produced at the hearing . . . and not on the basis of the information available to the agency when it made the decision to structure the proceedings in a certain way. This sort of Monday morning quarterbacking not only encourages but almost compels the agency to conduct all rulemaking proceedings with the full panoply of procedural devices normally associated only with adjudicatory hearings.

Finally, and perhaps most importantly, this sort of review fundamentally misconceives the nature of the standard for judicial review of an agency rule. The court below uncritically assumed that additional procedures will automatically result in a more adequate record because it will give interested parties more of an opportunity to participate in and contribute to the proceedings. But informal rulemaking need not be based solely on the transcript of a hearing held before an agency. Indeed, the agency need not even hold a formal hearing. See 5 U.S.C. § 553(c) (1976 ed.). Thus, the adequacy of the "record" in this type of proceeding is not correlated directly to the type of procedural devices employed, but rather turns on whether the agency has followed the statutory mandate of the Administrative Procedure Act or other relevant statutes. If the agency is compelled to support the rule which it ultimately adopts with the type of record produced only after a full adjudicatory hearing, it simply will have no choice but to conduct a full adjudicatory hearing prior to promulgating every rule. In sum, this sort of unwarranted judicial examination of perceived procedural shortcomings of a rulemaking proceeding can do nothing but seriously interfere with that process prescribed by Congress.

In short, nothing in the APA, NEPA, the circumstances of this case, the nature of the issues being considered, past agency practice, or the statutory mandate under which the Commission operates permitted the court to review and overturn the rulemaking proceeding on the basis of the procedural devices employed (or not employed) by the Commission so long as the Commission employed at least the statutory *minima*, a matter about which there is no doubt in this case.

There remains, of course, the question of whether the challenged rule finds sufficient justification in the administrative proceedings that it should be upheld by the reviewing court. Judge Tamm, concurring in the result reached by the majority of the Court of Appeals, thought that it did not. There are also intimations in the majority opinion which suggest that the judges who joined it likewise may have thought the administrative proceedings an insufficient basis upon which to predicate the rule in question. We accordingly remand so that the Court of Appeals may review the rule as the Administrative Procedure Act provides. We have made it abundantly clear before that when there is a contemporaneous explanation of the agency decision, the validity of that action must "stand or fall on the propriety of that finding, judged, of course, by the appropriate standard of review. If that finding is not sustainable on the administrative record made, then the Comptroller's decision must be vacated and the matter remanded to him for further consideration." *Camp v. Pitts.* . . . See also *SEC v. Chenery Corp. [supra]*, Chapter 61 . . . The court should engage in this kind of review and not stray beyond the judicial province to explore the procedural format or to impose upon the agency its own notion of which procedures are "best" or most likely to further some vague, undefined public good.

Questions and Comments

1. After the decision in *Vermont Yankee*, is the *Mobil* case still good law? To what extent is the precedent value of *Portland Cement* affected by the *Vermont Yankee* decision?

2. Did Justice Rehnquist say that the lower court had to affirm the agency's rule? That it had to accept Dr. Pittman's testimony as a sufficient basis for the rule? Under the approach to judicial review adopted in *Vermont Yankee*, what should Judge Bazelon do on remand if he feels that the Dr. Pittman's testimony does not provide an adequate support for the NRC rule?

3. Is there a meaningful distinction between a court holding that the administrative record is inadequate to support the agency's action and a court holding that the agency should have employed different procedures? Could Judge Bazelon's opinion be construed as embodying either or both of those holdings? Assess the significance of the *Vermont Yankee* decision in the light of your answers to these questions.

4. Was Justice Rehnquist correct that the lower court's approach to judicial review would disrupt the statutory scheme for rulemaking embodied in the APA? Explain. Was he correct that the lower court's approach to judicial review would engender pressure upon agencies to employ trial-type procedures in most cases? Did the relevant lower court decisions with which you are familiar establish workable criteria for the selection of rulemaking procedures? Could agencies employ these criteria with confidence that their selection of rulemaking procedures would be respected on judicial review?

5. In another part of Justice Rehnquist's *Vermont Yankee* opinion, he ruled that the court of appeals had ruled improperly in a licensing proceeding involving the construction by Consumers Power Co. of two nuclear reactors in Michigan. The court of appeals had held that the Licensing Board should have returned the ACRS report in that proceeding for further elaboration in terms understandable to a layman of a reference in that report to certain other problems "identified by the Regulatory Staff and the ACRS and cited in previous ACRS reports." In overturning this part of the court of appeals decision, Rehnquist had this to say:

> . . . . The Commission very well might be able to remand a report for further clarification, but there is nothing to support a court's ordering the Commission to take that step or to support a court's requiring the ACRS to give a short explanation, understandable to a layman, of each generic safety concern.
>
> All this leads us to make one further observation of some relevance to this case. To say that the Court of Appeals' final reason for remanding is insubstantial at best is a gross understatement. Consumers Power first applied in 1969 for a construction permit — not even an operating license, just a construction permit. The proposed plant underwent an incredibly extensive review. The reports filed and reviewed literally fill books. The proceedings took years, and the actual hearings themselves over two weeks. To then nullify that effort seven years later because one report refers to other problems, which problems admittedly have been discussed at length in other reports available to the public, borders on the Kafkaesque. Nuclear energy may some day be a cheap, safe source of power or it may not. But Congress has made a choice to at least try nuclear energy, establishing a reasonable review process in which courts are to play only a limited role. The fundamental policy questions appropriately resolved in Congress and in the state legislatures are *not* subject to re-examination in the federal courts under the guise of judicial review of agency action. Time may prove wrong the decision to develop nuclear energy, but it is Congress or the States within their appropriate agencies which must eventually make that judgment. . . . Administrative decisions should be set aside . . . only

for substantial procedural or substantive reasons as mandated by statute. . . . not simply because the court is unhappy with the result reached. . . .

6. Did the extract from Rehnquist's opinion quoted in the last paragraph provide an insight into his perception of the broader context of the *Vermont Yankee* decision? Was Rehnquist concerned that the courts were undermining Congressional goals by being overzealous in ensuring that agency procedures fully "ventilated" the underlying issues? Should not those issues be ventilated? Where does Justice Rehnquist think they should be ventilated?

7. Was Rehnquist saying that, in mandating agency procedures, the courts had usurped a political role that belonged to the Congress? In the part of his opinion quoted in paragraph 5 above, was he saying that, under the guise of judicial review, the court of appeals had interfered with Congress' determination to develop nuclear energy?

8. To what extent are public participation procedures open to abuse? Does Rehnquist think that those procedures have been abused? That they have been employed solely for purposes of delaying the operation of nuclear plants or of increasing the costs of obtaining an operating license? Is his criticism of the court of appeals also a criticism of the procedural design of the licensing proceedings? Of the underlying statutory scheme? Of its modification by court decisions reading new or more elaborate procedures into it? Explain.

Reno v. Flores, 507 U.S. 292, 300–301 (1993) involved a challenge to a regulation of the Immigration and Naturalization Service. The INS permits adult aliens detained on suspicion of being deportable to be released pending deportation hearings. Under a regulation relating to juveniles, however, the INS will release a juvenile only to a parent or legal guardian. In this case a class of detained alien juveniles challenged the validity of the regulation. In an opinion for the Court upholding the regulation, Justice Scalia, began his analysis as follows:

> First, this is a facial challenge to INS regulation 242.24. . . . We have before us no findings of fact, indeed no record, concerning the INS's interpretation of the regulation or the history of enforcement. We have only the regulation itself and the statement of basis and purpose that accompanied its promulgation. To prevail in such a facial challenge, respondents 'must establish that no set of circumstances exists under which the [regulation] would be valid' *United States v. Salerno*, 481 U.S. 739, 745 (1987). That is true as to both the constitutional challenge, see *Schall v. Martin*, 467 U.S. 253, 268, n.18 (1984), and the statutory challenge, see *NCIR*, [*INS v. National Center for Immigrants' Rights*, 502 U.S. 183 (1991)] 502 U.S. at 188.

His opinion goes on to hold that the rationale for the regulation contained in the basis and purpose statement was reasonable and therefore that the regulation did not exceed the scope of the Attorney General's discretion to continue custody over arrested aliens. (The basis and purpose statement justified the regulation on two propositions: (1) that "concern for the welfare of the juvenile will not permit release to just any adult" and (2) that "the Service has neither the expertise nor the resources to conduct home studies for placement of each juvenile."

Questions and Comments

1.   Note the initial language of Scalia's opinion is cast in the rhetoric of *Pacific States Box & Basket Co. v. White*. Then observe that on the nonconstitutional challenge, he focuses upon whether the challenging class has disproved the rationale contained in the basis and purpose statement.

2.   Why do you think that Justice Scalia did not require that judicial review proceed upon the administrative record? Could not the Court have remanded for the creation of a record (as in *Overton*)? Could the explanation lie in the way that the issue was framed? How does a facial challenge to a regulation differ from a challenge to a regulation as arbitrary as applied? Is it relevant that the case here was brought under the general federal question jurisdictional statute rather than under a statutory provision providing for judicial review of rulemaking? If the regulation in question were viewed as an interpretative rule, would Justice Scalia's language be easier to accept? Why or why not? Justice Scalia is not restructuring judicial review of rulemaking back to model of the pre-*Overton Park* period, is he?

E.   *A VERMONT YANKEE* ANALOGUE: PROCEDURES IN INFORMAL ADJUDICATION

In *Pension Benefit Guaranty Corp. v. LTV Corp.*, 496 U.S. 633 (1990), the lower courts set aside a decision of the Pension Benefit Guaranty Corp. (PBGC) on the grounds that its procedures were unfair. The Supreme Court reversed on the ground that the proceedings of the PBGC were "informal adjudication" governed by § 555 of the APA and, relying on *Vermont Yankee*, the Court held that (except where the due process clause requires otherwise) the courts could not require any more procedural protections from the PBGC than is provided in § 555. *See* Chapter 4 *supra*.

F.   OTHER JUDICIAL INVOLVEMENTS IN ADMINISTRATION

In addition to special problems raised by the appellate courts' venture of the 1970s into imposing so-called "hybrid" procedures on informal rulemaking proceedings which came to an abrupt halt with the Supreme Court's *Vermont Yankee* decision, the courts are continually asked to impose procedural requirements on agencies. In the cases below, consider the extent to which the courts overstepped their role as reviewing bodies and became involved in the tasks of administration. In which cases would you have been able to predict the Court's ruling in advance? Explain.

In *Heckler v. Day*, 467 U.S. 104 (1984) plaintiffs had brought a class action contending that delays in the administration of the social security disability program violated their statutory rights. The Supreme Court vacated a lower-court injunction requiring the Secretary of Health and Human Services to provide reconsideration determinations within 90 days of requests and requiring ALJs to provide hearings within 90 days of requests. The Court agreed with the Secretary that the legislative history of the Act and its amendments showed "that Congress repeatedly has been made aware of the long delays associated with resolution of disputed disability claims and repeatedly has considered and expressly rejected suggestions that mandatory deadlines be imposed to cure that problem. . . . that Congress expressly has balanced the need for timely disability determinations against the need to ensure quality decisions in the face of heavy and escalating workloads and limited agency resources." The Court concluded that "[i]n light of the unmistakable intention of Congress, it would be an unwarranted judicial intrusion into this pervasively regulated area for federal courts to issue injunctions imposing deadlines with respect to future disability claims."

Strycker's Bay Neighborhood Council, Inc. v. Karlen, 444 U.S. 223 (1980). In 1962 the New York City Planning Commission, acting in conjunction with the U.S. Dept. of Housing and Urban Development (HUD), began formulating a plan for the renewal of 20 square blocks known as the West Side Urban Renewal Area. The plan originally called for a mix of 70% middle-income housing and 30% low income housing and designated the site at issue as the location for a middle-income project. Because of a increasing need for low-income housing, the Commission amended the plan in 1969 to redesignate the site as the future location of a high-rise building containing 160 units of low-income housing. HUD approved this amendment in December 1972. Trinity Episcopal School Corp. (Trinity) which had built a combination school and middle-income housing development nearby sued to enjoin the construction of low-income housing on the site in issue. The District Court denied relief. The Court of Appeals, however, held that although HUD was not required to prepare a full-scale environmental impact statement under § 102(2)(C) of the National Environmental Policy Act (NEPA), HUD was required to "study, develop, and describe appropriate alternatives to recommended courses of action in any proposal which involves unresolved conflicts concerning alternative uses of available resources." 42 U.S.C. § 4332(2)(E). The Court required HUD to explain "how within the framework of the Plan its objective of economic integration can best be achieved with a minimum of adverse environmental impact." HUD prepared a report which recognized problems associated with the impact on social fabric and community structure but concluded that they were not so serious as to render the use of the site for low-income housing unacceptable. HUD accepted a Commission study which found no acceptable alternative locations for the project and that any relocation of units would force a two-year delay. According to HUD, "[m]easured against the environmental costs associated with a two-year delay, the benefits seem insufficient to justify a mandated substitution of sites." The District Court again entered judgment in favor of the defendants; and the Second Circuit vacated and again remanded. On review, the U.S. Supreme Court, reversed: "Concentrating on HUD's finding that development of an alternative location would entail an unacceptable delay, the appellate court held that such delay could not be 'an overriding factor' in HUD's decision to proceed with the development. . . . According to the court, when HUD considers such projects, 'environmental factors, such as crowding low-income housing into a concentrated area, should be given determinative weight.' . . . As we stressed in [*Vermont Yankee Nuclear Power Corp. v. NRDC*] . . . NEPA was designed to 'insure a fully informed and well-considered decision,' but not necessarily 'a decision the judges of the Court of Appeals or of this Court would have reached had they been members of the decisionmaking unit of the agency.' . . . Vermont *Yankee* cuts sharply against the Court of Appeals' conclusion that an agency, in selecting a course of action, must elevate environmental concerns over other appropriate considerations. On the contrary, once an agency has made a decision subject to NEPA's procedural requirements, the only role for a court is to insure that the agency has considered the environmental consequences; it cannot " 'interject itself within the area of discretion of the executive as to the choice of the action to be taken. " '. . . In the present case there is no doubt that HUD considered the environmental consequences of its decision to redesignate the proposed site for low-income housing. NEPA requires no more. . . .'"

Questions and Comments

1. When the Second Circuit ordered HUD to give environmental factors "determinative weight," was the court making a procedural or substantive ruling? If the latter, then was not the *Vermont Yankee* decision an irrelevant precedent? Why was the Second Circuit's decision not a ruling about the substantive importance of environmental legislation vis-à-vis other relevant legislation? Was the court trying to affect the substantive decision of HUD by imposing procedural tasks upon it?

2. Did the Supreme Court view *Strycker's Bay* as another case (like *Vermont Yankee)* in which the administrative process was being made unworkable by endless judicial demands for increasingly refined decision-making? How can a lower court determine when further remands to an administrative body will be perceived by the Supreme Court as unwarranted judicial interference with administration?

3. Can you visualize circumstances in which injunctions like the ones issued in *Heckler v. Day* would be proper? *Is Heckler v. Day* explainable solely by the legislative history of the disability act and its amendments? Ought courts normally to issue injunctions requiring agencies to meet timetables on their cases? What responsibilities do courts take upon themselves when they do issue such injunctions? Why might courts not be equipped to carry out those responsibilities?

4. Some of the standing cases raise, in acute form, the issue of the extent to which courts may properly intrude into matters of administration. *See, e.g., Allen v. Wright*, 468 U.S. 737 (1984), infra, Chapter 10.

Chapter 8

THE "HARD LOOK" DOCTRINE AND JUDICIAL REVIEW OF AGENCY REASONING

A. THE "HARD LOOK" DOCTRINE

MOTOR VEHICLE MANUFACTURERS ASS'N v. STATE FARM MUTUAL AUTOMOBILE INSURANCE CO.
463 U.S. 29 (1983)

[Under the National Traffic and Motor Vehicle Safety Act of 1966, the Secretary of Transportation is required to issue motor vehicle safety standards. Safety standards providing for protection of occupants of automobiles has proved difficult and controversial.

Shortly after the enactment of the Act, the Department of Transportation issued a safety standard requiring the installation of safety belts in all automobiles. Many people, however, failed to use them. In 1972, therefore, the Department issued a safety standard which would have required all vehicles manufactured after August 1975 to be equipped with passive restraints, i.e., safety devices which work automatically and which do not depend upon any action by the vehicle's occupants. Vehicles manufactured between August 1973 and August 1975 were to be equipped either with passive restraints or lap and shoulder belts coupled with an ignition interlock that would prevent the vehicle from starting if the belts were not connected.

Most automobile manufactures chose to equip their 1974 model cars with ignition interlock systems rather than with passive restraints. Ignition interlocks proved highly unpopular and Congress amended the Act to prohibit safety standards requiring or permitting ignition interlocks.

In June 1976 — during the last months of the Ford Administration — Secretary of Transportation William T. Coleman, Jr., initiated new rulemaking proceedings, culminating in his extending the optional alternatives indefinitely and suspended the passive restraint requirement. Believing that there would be widespread public resistance to passive restraint systems, Coleman proposed a demonstration project involving up to 500,000 cars installed with passive restraints, in order to smooth the way for public acceptance of passive restraints at a later date.

President Carter's Secretary of Transportation, Brock Adams decided the demonstration project was unnecessary. He issued a new mandatory passive restraint regulation, mandating the phasing in of passive restraints beginning with large cars in model year 1982 and extending to all cars by model year 1984. Under the Brock standard, manufacturers could choose either airbags or passive belts.

When the Reagan Administration took office, Secretary of Transportation Andrew Lewis reopened the rulemaking due to changed economic circumstances and, in particular, the difficulties of the automobile industry. After receiving written comments and holding public hearings, NHTSA issued a final rule that rescinded the passive restraint requirement.]

JUSTICE WHITE delivered the opinion of the Court.

Petitioner Motor Vehicle Manufacturers Association (MVMA) . . . [contends] that the rescission of an agency rule should be judged by the same standard a court would use to judge an agency's refusal to promulgate a rule in the first place — a standard petitioner believes considerably narrower that the traditional arbitrary-and-capricious test. We reject this view. . . . [T]he revocation of an extant regulation is substantially different than a failure to act. Revocation constitutes a reversal of the agency's former views as to the proper course. A "settled course of behavior embodies the agency's informed judgment that, by pursuing that course, it will carry out the policies committed to it by Congress. There is, then, at least a presumption that those policies will be carried out best if the settled rule is adhered to." . . . Accordingly, an agency changing its course by rescinding a rule is obligated to supply a reasoned analysis for the change beyond that which may be required when an agency does not act in the first instance.

V

The ultimate question before us is whether NHTSA's rescission of the passive restraint requirement of Standard 208 was arbitrary and capricious. We conclude . . . that it was. . . .

A

The first and most obvious reason for finding the rescission arbitrary and capricious is that NHTSA apparently gave no consideration whatever to modifying the Standard to require that airbag technology be utilized. Standard 208 sought to achieve automobile crash protection by requiring automobile manufacturers to install either of two passive restraint devices: airbags or automatic seatbelts. There was no suggestion in the long rulemaking process that led to Standard 208 that if only one of these options were feasible, no passive restraint standard should be promulgated. Indeed, the agency's original proposed Standard contemplated the installation of inflatable restraints in all cars. Automatic belts were added as a means of complying with the Standard because they were believed to be as effective as airbags in achieving the goal of occupant crash protection. . . . At that time, the passive belt approved by the agency could not be detached. Only later, at a manufacturer's behest, did the agency approve of the detachability feature — and only after assurances that the feature would not compromise the safety benefits of the restraint. Although it was then foreseen that 60% of the new cars would contain airbags and 40 % would have automatic seatbelts, the ratio between the two was not significant as long as the passive belt would also assure greater passenger safety.

The agency has now determined that the detachable automatic belts will not attain anticipated safety benefits because so many individuals will detach the mechanism. Even if this conclusion were acceptable in its entirety. . . . standing alone it would not justify any more than an amendment of Standard 208 to disallow compliance by means of the one technology which will not provide effective passenger protection. It does not cast doubt on the need for a passive restraint standard or upon the efficacy of airbag technology. . . . Given the effectiveness ascribed to airbag technology by the agency, the mandate of the Act to achieve traffic safety would suggest that the logical response to the faults of detachable seat belts would be to require the installation of airbags. At the very least this alternative way of achieving the objectives of the Act should have been addressed and adequate reasons given for its abandonment. But the agency . . . did not even consider the possibility in its 1981 rulemaking. Not one sentence of its rulemaking statement discussed the airbags-only option. . . . We have frequently reiterated that an agency must cogently explain why it has exercised its discretion in a given manner . . . and we reaffirm this principle again today.

. . . . We do not require today any specific procedures which NHTSA must follow. Nor do we broadly require an agency to consider all policy alternatives in reaching decision. It is true that rulemaking "cannot be found wanting simply because the agency failed to include every alternative device and thought conceivable by the mind of man . . . regardless of how uncommon or unknown that alternative may have been. But the airbag is more than a policy alternative to the passive restraint Standard; it is a technological alternative within the ambit of the existing Standard. We hold only that given the judgment made in 1977 that airbags are an effective and cost-beneficial lifesaving technology, the mandatory passive restraint rule may not be abandoned without any consideration whatsoever of an airbags-only requirement.

B

Although the issue is closer, we also find that the agency was too quick to dismiss the safety benefits of automatic seatbelts. NHTSA's critical finding was that, in the light of the industry's plans to install readily detachable passive belts, it could not reliably predict "even a 5 percentage point increase as the minimum level of expected usage increase." . . . The Court of Appeals rejected this finding because there is "not one iota" of evidence that Modified Standard 208 will fail to increase nationwide seatbelt use by at least 13 percentage points, the level of increased usage necessary for the Standard to justify its cost. Given the lack of probative evidence, the court held that "only a well justified refusal to seek more evidence could render rescission non-arbitrary." . . .

Petitioners object to this conclusion. In their view, "substantial uncertainty" that a regulation will accomplish its intended purpose is sufficient reason, without more, to rescind a regulation. We agree with petitioners that just as an agency reasonably may decline to issue a safety standard if it is uncertain about its efficacy, an agency may also revoke a standard on the basis of serious uncertainties if supported by the record and reasonably explained. Rescission of the passive restraint requirement would not be arbitrary and capricious simply because there was no evidence in direct support of the agency's conclusion. It is not infrequent that the available data do not settle a regulatory issue, and the agency must then exercise its judgment in moving from the facts and probabilities on the record to a policy conclusion. Recognizing that policymaking in a complex society must account for uncertainty, however, does not imply that it is sufficient for an agency to merely recite the terms "substantial uncertainty" as a justification for its actions. As previously noted, the agency must explain the evidence which is available, and must offer a "rational connection between the facts found and the choice made." . . . Generally, one aspect of that explanation would be a justification for rescinding the regulation before engaging in a search for further evidence.

In these cases, the agency's explanation for rescission of the passive restraint requirement is not sufficient to enable us to conclude that the rescission was the product of reasoned decisionmaking. To reach this conclusion, we do not upset the agency's view of the facts, but we do appreciate the limitations of this record in supporting the agency's decision. We start with the accepted ground that if used, seatbelts unquestionably would save many thousands of lives and would prevent tens of thousands of crippling injuries. . . . [T]he safety benefits of wearing seatbelts are not in doubt, and it is not challenged that were those benefits to accrue, the monetary costs of implementing the Standard would be easily justified.

[Surveys of drivers of automobiles equipped with passive belts showed more than a doubling of the usage rate experienced with manual belts. The agency maintained in its rulemaking statement that doubling of seatbelt usage could not be extrapolated to an across the board mandatory standard because the passive seatbelts were guarded by an ignition interlock.] We believe that it is within the agency's discretion to pass upon the generalizability of these field studies. This is precisely the type of issue which rests within the expertise of NHTSA, and upon which a reviewing court must be most hesitant to intrude.

But accepting the agency's view of the field tests on passive restraints indicates only that there is no reliable real-world experience that usage rates will substantially increase. To be sure, NHTSA opines that "it cannot reliably predict even a 5 percentage point increase as the minimum level of expected increased usage." But this and other statements that passive belts will not yield substantial increases in seat belt usage apparently take no account of the critical difference between detachable automatic belts and current manual belts. A detached passive belt does require an affirmative act to reconnect it, but — unlike a manual seat belt — the passive belt, once reattached, will continue to function automatically unless again disconnected. Thus, inertia-a factor which the agency's own studies have found significant in explaining the current low usage rates for seat belts — works in favor of, not against use of the protective devices. Since 20% to 50% of motorists currently wear seat belts on some occasions, there would seem to be grounds to believe that seatbelt use by occasional users will be substantially increased by the detachable passive belts. Whether this is in fact the case is a matter for the agency to decide, but it must bring its expertise to bear on the question.

The agency is correct to look at the costs as well as the benefits of Standard 208. The agency's conclusion that the incremental costs of the requirements were no longer reasonable was predicated on its prediction that the safety benefits of the regulation might be minimal. . . . When the agency reexamines its findings as to the likely increase in seatbelt usage, it must also reconsider its judgment of the reasonableness of the monetary and other costs associated with the Standard. . . .

The agency also failed to articulate a basis for not requiring nondetachable belts under Standard 208. It is argued that the concern of the agency with the easy detachability of the currently favored design would be readily solved by a continuous passive belt, which allows the occupant to "spool out" the belt and create the necessary slack for easy extrication from the vehicle. . . .

By failing to analyze the continuous seatbelts option in its own right, the agency has failed to offer the rational connection between facts and judgment required to pass muster under the arbitrary-and-capricious standard. . . . NHTSA was satisfied [in 1978] that this [continuous passive] belt design assured easy extricability: "[t]he agency does not believe that the use of [such] release mechanisms will cause serious occupant egress problems While the agency is entitled to change its view on the acceptability of continuous passive belts, it is obligated to explain its reasons for doing so.

VI

An agency's view of what is in the public interest may change, either with or without a change in circumstances. But an agency changing its course must supply a reasoned analysis. . . . We do not accept all of the reasoning of the Court of Appeals but we do conclude that the agency has failed to supply the requisite "reasoned analysis" in this case. Accordingly, we vacate the judgment of the Court of Appeals and remand the cases to that court with directions to remand the matter to the NHTSA for further consideration consistent with this opinion.

So ordered.

Comments

The Court in *State Farm* applied what has become known as the "hard look" doctrine, a doctrine which has often been associated with *Greater Boston Television Corp. v. FCC*, 444 F.2d 841 (D.C. Cir. 1970). In the latter case, the court reviewed a decision of the FCC under which the license of a Boston television station was awarded to a competing applicant. In that case Judge Leventhal described the reviewing court's role in the following way:

> Its supervisory function calls on the Court to intervene not merely in case of procedural inadequacies, or bypassing of the mandate in the legislative charter, but more broadly if the court becomes aware, especially from a combination of danger signals, that the agency has not really taken a "hard took" at the salient problems, and has not genuinely engaged in reasoned decision-making. . . . If satisfied that the agency has taken a hard took at the issues with the use of reasons and standards, the court will uphold its findings, though of less than ideal clarity, if the agency's path may reasonably be discerned, though of course the court must not be left to guess as to the agency's findings or reasons.

As in *State Farm*, the agency involved in Greater *Boston had* been changing course. In the past the agency had generally favored existing licensees against competing applicants when their licenses came up for renewal. But in *Greater Boston* a hearing examiner who had decided for the existing applicant in accord with that policy was reversed. In an opinion on rehearing, the Commission explained various circumstances (principally involving *Greater Boston's* prior behavior and its operation under a series of temporary authorizations) that, in the Commission's view, distinguished the *Greater Boston* case from "the conventional applicant for renewal of a broadcast license." In his opinion affirming the Commission's decision, Judge Leventhal adverted expressly to the role of a reviewing court where an agency's policies are in flux or changing:

> Judicial vigilance to enforce the Rule of Law in the administrative process is particularly called upon where, as here, the area under consideration is one wherein the Commission's policies are in flux. An agency's view of what is in the public interest may change, either with or without a change in circumstances. But an agency changing its course must supply a reasoned analysis indicating that prior policies and standards are being deliberately changed, not casually ignored, and if an agency glosses over or swerves from prior precedents without discussion it may cross the line from the tolerably terse to the intolerably mute.

The "hard look" doctrine — as evidenced in *Greater Boston* and in *State Farm* — requires that the agency supply a reasoned basis for its action. In *Chevron* (as in *State Farm* and *Greater Boston*) the agency had abandoned a prior policy position and adopted a new one. But did the Court apply a "hard look" at the agency's change of position in *Chevron* [*supra*, Chapter 2]? *Chevron* is nonetheless consistent with *Greater Boston* and *State Farm*, is it not? Explain.

Although *State Farm* has been widely understood as subjecting an agency's decision to change course to especially stringent review, the Court has recently disavowed such an interpretation. In *FCC v. Fox Telev. Stations, Inc.*, 129 S.Ct. 1800, 1810 (2009) the Court upheld a ruling by the FCC adopting a more stringent approach to the broadcasting of indecent language than it had taken in the past. The majority, however, refused to impose a heightened standard of review to agency rulings which change course. An excerpt from Justice Scalia's majority opinion follows:

> In overturning the Commission's judgment, the Court of Appeals here relied in part on Circuit precedent requiring a more substantial explanation for agency action that changes prior policy. The Second Circuit has interpreted the Administrative Procedure Act and our opinion in *State Farm* as requiring agencies to make clear " 'why the original reasons for adopting the [displaced] rule or policy are no longer dispositive' as well as " 'why the new rule effectuates the statute as well as or better than the old rule' ". . . . The Court of Appeals for the District of Columbia Circuit as similarly indicated that a court's standard of review is "heightened somewhat" when an agency reverses course. . . .

> We find no basis in the Administrative Procedure Act or in our opinions for a requirement that all agency change be subjected to more searching

review. The Act mentions no such heightened standard. And our opinion in *State Farm* neither held nor implied that every agency action representing a policy change must be justified by reasons more substantial than those required to adopt a policy in the first instance. That case, which involved the rescission of a prior regulation, said only that such action requires "a reasoned analysis for the change beyond that which may be required when an agency *does not act* in the first instance." . . . Treating failures to act and rescissions of prior action differently for purposes of the standard of review makes good sense, and has basis in the text of the statute, which likewise treats the two separately. It instructs a reviewing court to "compel agency action unlawfully withheld or unreasonably delayed," 5 U.S.C. § 706(1), and to "hold unlawful and set aside agency action, findings, and conclusions found to be [among other things] . . . arbitrary [or] capricious," § 706(2)(A). The statute makes no distinction, however, between initial agency action and subsequent agency action undoing or revising that action.

Justice Breyer, joined by Justices Stevens, Souter and Ginsburg, dissented, arguing that:

> the Federal Communications Commission failed adequately to explain why it changed its indecency policy from a policy permitting a single "fleeting use" of an expletive, to a policy that made no such exception. Its explanation fails to discuss two critical factors, at least one of which directly underlay its original policy decision. Its explanation instead discussed several factors well known to it the first time around, which by themselves provide no significant justification for a change of policy. Consequently, the FCC decision is "arbitrary, capricious, an abuse of discretion."

In a separate concurring opinion, Justice Kennedy underscored:

> Certain background principles for the conclusion that an agency's decision to change course may be arbitrary and capricious if the agency sets a new course that reverses an earlier determination but does not provide a reasoned explanation for doing so. In those circumstances I agree with the dissenting opinion of Justice Breyer that the agency must explain why "it now reject[s] the considerations that it to adopt that initial policy." . . .

> Where there is a policy change the record may be much more developed because the agency based its prior policy on factual findings. In that instance, an agency's decision to change course may be arbitrary and capricious if the agency ignores or countermands its earlier factual findings without reasoned explanation for doing so. An agency cannot simply disregard contrary or inconvenient factual determinations that it made in the past, any more than it can ignore inconvenient facts when it writes on a blank slate.

Justice Kennedy, however, believed that the FCC, in this case, adequately explained its position. The FCC based its prior position on a Supreme Court decision (*FCC v. Pacifica Foundation*, 438 U.S. 726 (1978)) and then changed its reading of that case.

Questions and Comments

1. Why did the Court rule that the EPA had acted arbitrarily and capriciously in *State Farm*? Was the Court's determination consistent with *Fox Telev.*? With *Chevron*? With *Greater Boston*?

2. Can you explain the meaning of the "hard look" doctrine? How has the meaning of that doctrine changed since the *Fox Telev.* decision?

3. Note that a majority of the Court (the four dissenters in *Fox* plus Justice Kennedy) appears to believe that an agency is required to explain a change of position, especially when its rests on a factual premise. Does Justice Scalia believe that an agency is required to explain its change of position?

B. JUDICIAL REVIEW OF AGENCY REASONING

In the pages above, we examined how the courts, during the 1970s, increasingly demanded that agencies incorporate more procedures into their § 553 rulemaking proceedings. We also saw that the Supreme Court in *Vermont Yankee* ordered a halt to this development. We now consider aspects of judicial approaches to the review of agency reasoning, apart from courts finding that the agency procedures have been procedurally defective. Care and sophistication are required here.

A court which finds that an agency lacks support for its conclusion, either in the rulemaking record or in reasoned argumentation from that record, will not run afoul of the *Vermont Yankee* ruling. *Vermont Yankee* only prevents reviewing courts from ordering the agency to employ some new procedural device or otherwise procedurally expand its rulemaking proceeding.

Since it is but a short step from ruling that the agency rule is not supported by the administrative record to the position that the agency must reopen the record, employing procedures that would develop the kind of evidence which would support the agency rule, the difference between proper judicial review of agency reasoning in the light of the record and improper interference in procedural matters which belong to the agency is a narrow one.

In the cases below, look at the ways in which courts examine agency reasoning, including agency reasoning in technical fields. Assume that you are counsel to a party opposing an agency rule. Consider the kinds of deficiencies in agency reasoning that judges would understand as critical deficiencies. Look for patterns here. You are not concerned here with the merits of particular regulations, but you are concerned with the way judges can be persuaded to act. What patterns of argument were successful in these cases? Unsuccessful? What patterns of agency action (or agency reasoning) were the necessary premises for these arguments of counsel?

Of most interest to us, of course, are the judicial decisions indicating how courts are examining agency decision-making. Several of these decisions are excerpted below, including some decisions that involve quite technical subject-matter. Let's begin with two cases from the 1970s that set the stage for later developments and that may help us to understand contemporary judicial review. Both of these cases involve highly-technical subjects. *International Harvester Co. v. Ruckelshaus*, 478 F.2d 615 *(D.C. Cir. 1973)* reveals particular vulnerabilities of agency rationales to judicial review. By contrast, *Ethyl Corp. v. EPA*, 541 F.2d 1 (D.C. Cir. 1976), cert. denied, 426 U.S. 941 (1976), a case from the same era, reveals the difficulties faced by a party challenging agency rule-making.

International Harvester Co. v. Ruckelshaus, **478 F2d 615 (D.C. Cir. 1973)** In the 1970 Amendments to the Clean Air Act, Congress provided that beginning with the 1975 model year, exhaust emission of hydrocarbons and carbon monoxide from "light duty vehicles" had to be reduced at least 90 per cent from the permissible emission levels in the 1970 model year. Accordingly, the EPA Administrator promulgated regulations limiting hydrocarbon and carbon dioxide emissions from 1975 model light duty vehicles to .41 and 3.4 grams per vehicle mile respectively. Congress provided an "escape hatch" in case the standards turned out to be unachievable despite good faith efforts at compliance. Under section 202(b)(5)(D) of the Act, the Administrator was authorized to grant a one year suspension of the implementation of the 90% reduction requirement if he found, inter alia, that "effective control technology, processes, operating methods, or other alternatives are not available or have not been available for a sufficient period of time to achieve compliance prior to the effective date of such standards. . . ."

In March of 1972 Volvo, Inc. filed an application for suspension of the 90% reduction requirement. The auto companies had run tests on hundreds of vehicles, all but one of which failed to meet the mandated emission standards.

The Administrator, however, took the test data provided by the auto companies and, by reevaluating it, purported to establish that the technology was available to meet the statutory emission standards. The court described the Administrator's determination as follows:

> [T]he Administrator "adjusted" the data of the auto companies by use of several critical assumptions.

> First, he made an adjustment to reflect the assumption that fuel used in 1975 model year cars would either contain an average of .03 grams per gallon or .05 grams per gallon of lead. This usually resulted in an increase of emissions predicted, since many companies had tested their vehicles on lead-free gasoline.

> Second, the Administrator found that the attempt of some companies to reduce emissions of nitrogen oxides below the 1975 Federal standard of 3.0 grams per vehicle mile resulted in increased emissions of hydrocarbons and carbon monoxide. This adjustment resulted in a downward adjustment of observed HC and CO data, by a specified factor.

> Third, the Administrator took into account the effect the "durability" of the preferred systems would have on the emission control obtainable. This required that observed readings at one point of usage be increased by a deterioration factor (DF) to project emissions at a later moment of use. The critical methodological choice was to make this adjustment from a base of emissions observed at 4000 miles. Thus, even if a car had actually been tested over 4000 miles, predicted emissions at 50,000 miles would be

determined by multiplying 4000 mile emissions by the DF factor.

Fourth, the Administrator adjusted for "prototype-to-production slippage." This was an upward adjustment made necessary by the possibility that prototype cars might have features which reduced VIC and CO emissions, but were not capable of being used in actual production vehicles.

Finally, in accord with a regulation assumed, as to substance, in the text of the Decision, but proposed after the suspension hearing, a downward adjustment in the data readings was made on the basis of the manufacturers' ability, in conformance with certification procedures, to replace the catalytic converter "once during 50,000 miles of vehicle operation," a change they had not used in their testing.

With the data submitted and the above assumptions, the Administrator concluded that no showing had been made that requisite technology was not available. . . .

In reviewing the Administrator's determination that the technology to meet the emission standards was available, the court described its approach:

It is with utmost diffidence that we approach our assignment to review the Administrator's decision on "available technology." The legal issues are intermeshed with technical matters, and as yet judges have no scientific aides. Our diffidence is rooted in the underlying technical complexities, and remains even when we take into account that ours is a judicial review, and not a technical or policy redetermination, our review is channeled by a salutary restraint, and deference to the expertise of an agency that provides reasoned analysis. . . .

A. *Requirement of Observed Data From Manufacturers*

Clearly [the statute] . . . requires that the applicants come forward with data which showed that they could not comply with the contemplated standards. The normal rules place such a burden on the party in control of the relevant information. It was the auto companies who were in possession of the data about emission performance of their cars.

The submission of the auto companies unquestionably showed that no car had actually been driven 50,000 miles and achieved conformity of emissions to the 1975 standards. The Administrator's position is that on the basis of the methodology outlined, he can predict that the auto companies can meet the standards, and that the ability to make a prediction saying the companies can comply means that the petitioners have failed to sustain their burden of proof that they cannot comply.

B. *Requisite Reliability of Methodology Relied on by EPA To Predict Feasibility Notwithstanding Lack of Actual Experience*

We agree with the Administrator's proposition in general. Its validity as applied to this case rests on the reliability of his prediction, and the nature of his assumptions. . . . In a matter of this importance, the predictor must make a showing of reliability of the methodology of prediction, when that is being relied on to overcome this "adverse" actual test data of the auto companies. . . .

> The underlying issue is the reasonableness and reliability of the Administrator's methodology, for it alone offsets the data adduced by petitioners in support of suspension. It is the Administrator who must bear the burden on this matter, because the development and use of the methodology are attributable to his knowledge and expertise. . . . In the context of this proceeding, this requires that EPA bear a burden of adducing a reasoned presentation supporting the reliability of its methodology.

The court then examined the Administrator's assumptions and found that the record did not resolve questions crucial to their validity. It then concluded:

V. CONCLUSION AND DISPOSITION

> The number of unexplained assumptions used by the Administrator, the variance in methodology from that of the Report of the National Academy of Sciences, and the absence of an indication of the statistical reliability of the prediction, combine to generate grave doubts as to whether technology is available to meet the 1975 statutory standards. . . . These grave doubts have a legal consequence. This is customarily couched, by legal convention, in terms of "burden of proof." We visualize the problem in less structured terms although the underlying considerations, relating to risk of error, are related. . . . We think the vehicle manufacturers established by a preponderance of the evidence, in the record before us, that technology was not available, within the meaning of the Act, when they adduced the tests on actual vehicles; that the Administrator's reliance on technological methodology to offset the actual tests raised serious doubts and failed to meet the burden of proof which in our view was properly assignable to him, in the light of accepted legal doctrine and the intent of Congress discerned, in part, by taking into account that the risk of an "erroneous" denial of suspension outweighed the risk of an "erroneous" grant of suspension. We do not use the burden of proof in the conventional sense of civil trials, but the Administrator must sustain the burden of adducing a reasoned presentation supporting the reliability of EPA's methodology.

> The case is remanded for further proceedings not inconsistent with this opinion.

Ethyl Corp. v. EPA, 541 F.2d 1 (D.C. Cir. 1976), cert. denied, 426 U.S. 941 (1976). The Administrator of the Environmental Protection Agency issued regulations reducing the lead content of gasoline. In so doing the Administrator acted under section 211(c)(1)(A) *if* the Clean Air Act which authorizes him to regulate gasoline additives whose emission products "will endanger the public health or welfare. . . ." 42 U.S.C. 1857f-6c(c)(1)(A). Consider the following extract from the court's opinion reviewing the EPA's regulations:

> A word about our approach to the evidence may be in order. Contrary to the suggestion of some of the petitioners, we need not seek a single

dispositive study that fully supports the Administrator's determination. Science does not work that way; nor, for that matter, does adjudicatory fact-finding. Rather, the Administrator's decision may be fully supportable if it is based, as it is, on the inconclusive but suggestive results of numerous studies. By its nature, scientific evidence is cumulative: the more supporting, albeit inconclusive, evidence available, the more likely the accuracy of the conclusion. If, as petitioners suggest, one single study or bit of evidence were sufficient independently to mandate a conclusion, there would, of course, be no need for any other studies. Only rarely, however, is such limited study sufficient. Thus, after considering the inferences that can be drawn from the studies supporting the Administrator, and those opposing him, we must decide whether the cumulative effect of all this evidence, and not the effect of any single bit of it, presents a rational basis for the low-lead regulations.

* * * *

The second type of evidence relied upon by the Administrator . . . consisted of epidemiological research. . . . [N]one of the epidemiological studies could control or measure dietary lead intake. This uncertainty in the data severely limited the usefulness of the broadly conceived epidemiological studies and led the Administrator to rely instead on data limited to situations in which dietary exposure could roughly be termed constant.

Following this rationale, the Administrator focused on the consistent relationship found between air and blood lead levels within particular metropolitan areas, rather than on the lack of such a relationship between areas. . . . The Administrator also drew support for his conclusion that lead in the air significantly affects lead in the blood from studies conducted in single neighborhoods. There, too, confounding factors were minimized by proximity, and there, too, a clear direct relationship was found. . . . Thus the epidemiological studies, although perhaps insufficient to justify the Administrator's decision if considered singly or even collectively, were reasonably relied on as part of the basis for the low-lead rules.

While we would have no difficulty in sustaining the low-level regulations solely on the basis of the evidence and conclusions discussed above, the Administrator based his decision to regulate on other evidence as well. He presented a hypothesis, which he found consistent with known information, that urban children are particularly threatened by lead additives in that they are prone to ingest lead emissions that have fallen to the ground and mixed with dust. While the hypothesis is admittedly not proved as fact, we need not decide whether it would be sufficient by itself to support the low-lead regulations, for it is offered only in support of the evidence already presented. . . .

. . . [T]he "will endanger" standard is a precautionary standard that embraces a wide range of permissible proof. It is therefore no objection to the dustfall hypothesis that it is merely a hypothesis. A supportable and reasonable hypothesis may well form the basis for regulations under

Section 211(c)(1)(A). Indeed, the totality of evidence relied upon in the Reserve Mining case [Reserve Mining Co. v. EPA, 514 F.2d 492 (8th Cir. 1975)(en banc)] constituted no more than such a hypothesis. . . .

Affirmed.

Questions and Comments

1. Why was the agency reasoning in *International Harvester* particularly vulnerable? Did the EPA's conclusion in that case depend upon a chain of logical steps? If the reviewing court found any one of the links in such a chain wanting, then the entire chain would be wanting, would it not? Did the EPA reach its result in *International Harvester* in a way that was significantly different from the way it reached its result in *Ethyl?*

2. Consider the following:

> The . . . illustrations suggest two basic modes of drawing conclusions or reaching decisions which agencies employ and which courts tend instinctively to recognize in reviewing agency determinations for rationality. In pure form, these modes represent opposite ends of a spectrum, but in much actual decisionmaking they may coexist in varying proportions.

> The first such mode is linear, in which proposition A is critically dependent upon proposition B which, in turn, is critically dependent upon proposition C and so on. The linear mode resembles classical deductive logic which, indeed, is a form of a linear mode of reaching conclusions, but the linear mode includes a broader class of operations than pure deduction. In this linear mode of reaching conclusions, any weak link destroys the validity of the conclusion.

> The second mode is analogous to the circumstantial evidence method of proof and resembles classical induction, although it may not be coterminus with it. Here, in this second mode, the conclusion is the result of the cumulative effect of several independent premises, no one of which is adequate in itself to compel the conclusion. In this second mode, the demonstration of the invalidity of any one of the supporting props will not necessarily destroy the validity of the conclusion. Because, in the second mode, conclusions are reached by a process of judgment which is not precisely articulable, courts tend to find scope to defer to administrators' judgments. But in the first mode, the scope for deference shrinks. A court tends to find it difficult or impossible to defer to an administrative judgment which depends upon reasoning which is demonstrably wrong. And in a linear mode of reasoning, one invalid link in the chain necessarily invalidates the conclusion; there is no room for a process of judgment; the conclusion either follows from the premises or it does not.

Daniel J. Gifford, *Rulemaking and Rulemaking Review: Struggling Toward a New Paradigm*, 32 Admin. L. Rev. 577, 598–600 (1980).

3. To what extent did the vulnerability of the agency decision in *International Harvester* turn on the court's determination that the agency bore the burden of

establishing the reasonableness and reliability of the methodology used by it to reach its conclusions? If the auto companies had been assigned the burden of disproving the reliability of the agency's methodology, would the agency have won? Does the court's "grave doubt" about the accuracy of the methodology employed invalidate an agency rule when the agency bears the burden of establishing the validity of the methodology?

4. Does the agency normally bear the burden of establishing the reasonableness and reliability of the methodology which it employs? Or do those challenging an agency rule bear the burden of establishing its unreliability? To what extent do the results in these cases turn on the issue of who bears the burden on the issue of the reliability of the agency's methodology?

5. Would a court normally follow the *International Harvester* approach of placing the burden of establishing the reliability of a methodology on the party who employed it? If so, then the agency would generally bear the burden of establishing the reliability of its own methodology, would it not? But are there not circumstances in which it is the private parties who must establish the reliability of their own methodology — as when, for example, they offer an opposing evaluation of data to that employed by the agency?

Note: Judicial review of agency methodology

In *International Harvester*, the court required the EPA to justify its methodology. Sometimes a court, under the guise of requiring an agency to justify its methodology, imposes its own methodology requirements. This was done by the Ninth Circuit in reviewing decisions of the Forset Service, and that Circuit has recently confessed error. See *The Lands Council v. McNair*, 537 F.3d 981 (9th Cir. 2008). An extract from the opinion follows:

> . . . In *Ecology Center* [*Ecology Center, Inc. v. Austin*, 430 F.3d 1057 (9th Cir. 2005, cert. denied, *Mineral County v. Ecology Center, Inc.*, 549 U.S. 1111 (2007)], we rejected reports establishing that soil analysis was conducted in the project area as "too few and of poor quality." . . . We stated, "[t]he record provides little information that enables us to assess the reliability of significance of these reports; for example, we do not know the qualifications of the person conducting the field review, the methodlogy utilized, or whether the field observations confirmed or contradicted the Service's estimates." . . . Esentially, we assessed the quality and detail of on-site analysis and made "fine-grained judgments of its worth." . . . It is not our proper role to conduct such an assessment.
>
> Instead, our proper role is simply to ensure that the Forest Service made no "clear error of judgment" that would render its action "arbitrary and capricious." . . . Thus, as non-scientists, we decline to impose bright-line rules on the Forest Service regarding particular means that it must take in every case to show us that it his met the NFMA's requirements. Rather, we hold that the Forest Service must support its conclusions that a project meets the requirements of the NFMA and relevant Forest Plan with studies that the agency, in its expertise, deems reliable. The Forest

Service must explain the conclusions it has drawn from its chosen methodology, and the reasons it considers the underlying evidence to be reliable. We will conclude that the that the Forest Service acts arbitrarily and capriciously only when the record plainly demonstrates that the Forest Service made a clear error in judgment in concluding that a project meets the requirements of the NFMA and relevant Forest Plan.

Questions and Comments

Is *Lands Council* inconsistent with *International Harvester*? Can you make an argument that it is? that it is not? Under *Lands Council* who bears the burden of proof? What happens if the court is doubtful about aspects of the agency's methodology? What happens if persons opposing the agency's rule bring to the court's attention flaws in the agency's analysis?

Contemporary Approaches to Judicial Review

In *Vermont Yankee*, the Supreme Court stopped the lower courts from imposing additional procedures upon agencies that were not required by the APA. The courts, however, remained free to subject agency rulemaking to careful scrutiny. Below are a few examples of judicial decisions invalidating agency rulemaking decisions. Consider the extent to which these decisions reflect approaches already apparent in *International Harvester* and *Ethyl* above.

C. Hard Look in Action

AMERICAN LUNG ASSOCIATION v. ENVIRONMENTAL PROTECTION AGENCY
134 F.3d 388 (D.C. Cir. 1998)

TATEL, CIRCUIT JUDGE:

On behalf of the nation's nearly nine million asthmatics, the American Lung Association and the Environmental Defense Fund challenge the Environmental Protection Agency's refusal to revise the primary national ambient air quality standards for sulfur dioxide (SO2). Declining to promulgate a more stringent national standard, the EPA Administrator concluded that the substantial physical effects experienced by some asthmatics from exposure to short-term, high-level SO2 bursts do not amount to a public health problem. Because the Administrator failed adequately to explain this conclusion, we remand for further elucidation.

NAAQS for sulfur dioxide

* * * * *need an explanation for the decision*

. . . . [W]e think the Administrator has failed to explain . . . [why] SO2 bursts do not amount to a "public health" problem within the meaning of the Act. The link between this conclusion and the factual record as interpreted by EPA — that "repeated" exposure is "significant" and that thousands of asthmatics are exposed more than once a year — is missing. Why is the fact that thousands of asthmatics can be expected to suffer atypical physical effects from repeated five-minute bursts of high-level sulfur dioxide not a public health problem? Why are from 180,000 to 395,000 annual "exposure events" (the range indicated by the 1994 studies) or some fewer number (as suggested by the industry studies) so "infrequent" as to warrant no regulatory action? Why are disruptions of ongoing activities, use of medication, and hospitalization not "adverse health effects" for asthmatics? Answers to these questions appear nowhere in the administrative record.

In her only statement resembling an explanation for her conclusion that peak SO2 bursts present no public health hazard, the Administrator characterizes the bursts as "localized, infrequent and site-specific." Final Decision at 25,575. But nothing in the Final Decision explains away the possibility that "localized," "site-specific" or even "infrequent" events might nevertheless create a public health problem, particularly since, in some sense, all pollution is local and site-specific, whether spewing from the tailpipes of millions of cars or a few offending smoke stacks. From the record, we know that at least six communities experience "repeated high 5-minute peaks greater than 0.60 ppm SO2," *id.*, and agency counsel told us at oral argument that these so-called "hot spots" are not the only places where repeated exposure occurs. Nowhere, however, does the Administrator explain why these data amount to no more than a "local" problem.

Without answers to these questions, the Administrator cannot fulfill her responsibility under the Clean Air Act to establish NAAQS "requisite to protect the public health," 42 U.S.C. § 7409(b)(1), nor can we review her decision. Judicial deference to decisions of administrative agencies like EPA rests on the fundamental premise that agencies engage in reasoned decision-making. *See Vermont Yankee Nuclear Power Corp. v. Natural Resources Defense Council*, 435 U.S. 519, 524–25, 544–45, 558, 98 S.Ct. 1197, 1202–03, 1211–13, 1219, 55 L.Ed.2d 460 (1978); *SEC v. Chenery Corp.*, 332 U.S. 194, 209, 67 S.Ct. 1575, 1583–84, 91 L.Ed. 1995 (1947) (agency's experience, appreciation of complexities and policies, and responsible treatment of the facts "justify the use of the administrative process"). With its delicate balance of thorough record scrutiny and deference to agency expertise, judicial review can occur only when agencies explain their decisions with precision, for "[i]t will not do for a court to be compelled to guess at the theory underlying the agency's action. . . ." *SEC v. Chenery Corp.*, 332 U.S. at 196–97, 67 S.Ct. at 1577. Where, as here, Congress has delegated to an administrative agency the critical task of assessing the public health and the power to make decisions of national import in which individuals' lives and welfare hang in the balance, that agency has the heaviest of obligations to explain and expose every step of its reasoning. For these compelling reasons, we have always required the Administrator to "cogently explain why [she] has exercised [her] discretion in a given manner." *Motor Vehicle Mfrs. Ass'n v. State Farm Mut. Auto. Ins.*, 463 U.S. 29, 48, 103 S.Ct. 2856, 2869, 77 L.Ed.2d 443 (1983).

In this case, the Administrator may well be within her authority to decide that 41,500 or some smaller number of exposed asthmatics do not amount to a public health problem warranting national protective regulation, or that three or six or twelve annual exposures present no cause for medical concern. But unless she describes the standard under which she has arrived at this conclusion, supported by a "[ ]plausible" explanation, *id.* at 43, 103 S.Ct. at 2866–67, we have no basis for exercising our responsibility to determine whether her decision is "arbitrary, capricious, an abuse of discretion, or otherwise not in accordance with law; . . . [or] in excess of statutory . . . authority, or limitations. . . ." 42 U.S.C. § 7607(d)(9)(A)–(C).

Given the gaps in the Final Decision's reasoning, we must remand this case to permit the Administrator to explain her conclusions more fully.

CANADIAN ASSOCIATION OF PETROLEUM PRODUCERS v. FEDERAL ENERGY REGULATORY COMMISSION
254 F.3d 289 (D.C. Cir. 2001)

[Buyers of natural gas seek review of orders of the Federal Energy Regulatory Commission (FERC) in approving a rate increase to cover costs associated with a previously authorized expansion of its natural gas pipeline facilities. In its decision, the Commission had changed its method of selecting a rate of return appropriate to its equity investors.]

The "just and reasonable" rates calculated by the Commission under 15 U.S.C. § 717c(a) are typically based on a pipeline's costs. Because several of the issues here revolve around one component, the cost of equity capital, we pause briefly to explain it. Each year that a durable utility asset is in use imposes on the utility the annual cost of the capital used for its construction (net of amounts already recovered in depreciation charges). In order to attract capital, a utility must offer a risk-adjusted expected rate of return sufficient to attract investors. This return to investors is the cost to the utility of raising capital. For the portion of capital acquired through bonds, the cost is comparatively easy to compute — the interest the company must pay its bondholders. Common equity is more complicated, for equity investors do not have a legally fixed return. To calculate the rate of return necessary to attract them, the Commission measures the return enjoyed by the company's equity investors by the discounted cash flow ("DCF") model, which assumes that a stock's price is equal to the present value of the infinite stream of expected dividends discounted at a market rate commensurate with the stock's risk. With simplifying assumptions, this can be summarized by the formula

$$P = D/(r\text{-}g)$$

where P is the price of the stock at the relevant time, D is the dividend to be paid at the end of the first year, r is the rate of return and g is the expected growth rate of the firm. See *Illinois Bell Telephone Co. v. FCC*, 988 F.2d 1254, 1259 (D.C. Cir.1993); see also A. LAWRENCE KOLBE ET. AL., THE COST OF CAPITAL: ESTIMATING THE RATE OF RETURN FOR PUBLIC UTILITIES 53-55 (1984). Since r is what the Commission is seeking, the equation is rearranged to the form

$$r = D/P + g$$

Illinois Bell, 988 F.2d at 1259.

For a company that is not publicly traded, market-determined figures for P and D will be missing, and the Commission has recourse to calculating the implicit rate of return on companies that are comparable (or at least companies whose business is predominately the operation of natural gas pipelines) and publicly traded. These companies are called the "proxy group." The Commission then makes adjustments for specific characteristics of the company whose rates are in question. Here, one of the issues involves a contention that Northwest's business risk was comparatively low (so that, petitioners argue, the Commission should have chosen a rate at the low end of those of the proxy group). Another issue involves calculation of the expected growth rates for the proxy group. And a third, assuming that Northwest belongs in the middle of the proxy group, involves how to pick a number best representing the middle.

* * * *

The Commission's orders and brief speak only to the choice between median and midpoint. Its orders pointed to the *Transcontinental* decision, where, besides changing the weighting of short- and long-term growth factors, it also selected the median instead of the midpoint. But it supplied only the most limited reasoning there. See *Transcontinental Gas Pipe Line Corp.*, 84 FERC at 61,427-5. The Commission essentially reiterated its *Transcontinental* reasoning in this case:

> [U]se of the median gives consideration to more of the proxy company numbers. The median is the point at which half of the numbers are higher and half are lower. The midpoint, on the other hand, merely represents an average of the highest and lowest of the numbers and completely disregards the middle three numbers.

Median Rate Order on Rehearing, 92 FERC at 61,095.

To a large extent this "explanation" merely describes the differences in calculating the median and the midpoint. Insofar as it seeks to justify on the basis of the number of numbers considered, it is not wholly accurate. The midpoint doesn't "completely disregard[ ] the middle three numbers"; the highest and lowest numbers achieve their status by reference to all five numbers. But even if acceptable as an explanation for choosing the median over the midpoint, it fails as an explanation for rejecting petitioners' proposal that the Commission use the simple arithmetic mean (either of all five, or of the middle three companies of the proxy group). See No. 99-1488 et al., J.A. at 105, 171, 192–93. The mean of the five, after all, rather directly "uses" all the numbers and weights them all equally, as petitioners pointed out. *Id.* at 192–93.

The Commission simply dismissed the alternative proposal in conclusory terms. See Median Rate Order, 90 FERC at 61,468; Median Rate Order on Rehearing, 92 FERC at 61,094. Counsel for Northwest suggested at oral argument that there was Commission precedent for the view that the median is to be preferred to the average "as a [measure] of central tendency in cases in which the distribution is highly skewed." See No. 99-1488 et al., Oral Arg. Tr. at 22. But the Commission never offered such an explanation, and counsel did not offer an analysis of Commission precedents from which we could infer that the "skewing" here was such that choice of the median was foreordained. See *SEC v. Chenery Corp.*, 332 U.S. 194, 196, 67 S.Ct. 1575, 91 L.Ed. 1995 (1947); cf. *Health & Medicine Policy Research*

Group v. FCC, 807 F.2d 1038, 1045 (D.C.Cir.1986).

The Commission's failure to respond meaningfully to calls for using an average rate of all or of three of the proxy group companies renders its decision to use the median rate arbitrary and capricious. See *City of Brookings Municipal Telephone Co. v. FCC*, 822 F.2d 1153, 1169 (D.C.Cir.1987). Unless the Commission answers objections that on their face seem legitimate, its decision can hardly be classified as reasoned. See *International Harvester Co. v. Ruckelshaus*, 478 F.2d 615, 648 (D.C.Cir.1973); see also *Tesoro Alaska Petroleum Co. v. FERC*, 234 F.3d 1286, 1294 (D.C.Cir.2000). We thus reverse and remand the case to the Commission for reconsideration of its choice of the proxy group's median rate.

[handwritten margin note: — arbitrary + capricious]

In **United States Air Tour Association v. Federal Aviation Agency, 298 F.3d 997 (D.C. Cir. 2002)**, the court reviewed, inter alia, challenges to certain rules of the Federal Aviation Agency (FAA) brought by the Grand Canyon Trust. The FAA rules limited the number of air tours permitted to fly over the Grand Canyon National Park. [These rules were promulgated under the National Parks Over-flights Act in which Congress sought to reduce noise exposure in the Grand Canyon from aircraft overflights. Congress required the Secretary of the Interior to submit to the FAA recommendations that provide "for substantial restoration of the natural quiet and experience of the park" and required the FAA to prepare a plan for managing air traffic in the Grand Canyon that would "implement the recommendations of the Secretary of the Interior without change" except for safety reasons.

The Department of the Interior, through the park Service, then determined that 50% of the Park should experience natural quiet at least 75% of "the day." The FAA then developed rules designed to produce that result for the "average annual day." The Grand Canyon Trust challenged these rules in part on the ground that the Park Service had used the phrase "the day" in the sense of "any given day". The court agreed with the Trust that the FAA had based its overflight rules on a flawed definition of "day:"

> In its 2000 Final Supplemental Environmental Assessment, the FAA stated that it interpreted the phrase "the day" in the Park Service's definition to mean the "average annual day." FSEA at 4–18 to 4–19; *see id.* at 4–12.
>
> The Trust contends that the FAA's interpretation is unlawful because it substitutes a new FAA definition, "the average annual day," for what the Trust believes to be the Park Service's meaning, "any given day." The Trust further contends that the FAA's interpretation results in a definition of the statutory term, "substantial restoration of the natural quiet," that is arbitrary and unreasonable. The FAA replies that because the phrase "the day" is ambiguous, this court should defer to its interpretation.
>
> In *Grand Canyon I* we held that the statutory term was ambiguous, and we therefore deferred to the Park Service's definition. 154 F.3d at 466–67 (citing *Chevron*, 467 U.S. at 841–43, 104 S.Ct. at 2780–82). There is no question that the phrase, "the day," in the Park Service's definition is also ambiguous, and that the Park Service is entitled to deference for its interpretation of its own definition. *See Auer*, 519 U.S. at 461, 117 S.Ct. at

911. The problem for the FAA, however, is that it is not the Park Service, and "deference is inappropriate when [an agency] interprets regulations promulgated by a different agency." *Office of Pers. Mgm't v. FLRA*, 864 F.2d 165, 171 (D.C.Cir.1988); *see Dep't of the Treasury v. FLRA*, 837 F.2d 1163, 1167 (D.C.Cir.1988). Nor is the FAA entitled to deference for its own interpretation of "substantial restoration of the natural quiet," as Congress expressly reserved for the Secretary of the Interior the authority to interpret that statutory term. . . .

As the Trust points out, the use of an annual average does not correspond to the experience of the Park's actual visitors. People do not visit the Park on "average" days, nor do they stay long enough to benefit from averaging noise over an entire year. For the typical visitor, who visits the Grand Canyon for just a few days during the peak summer season, the fact that the Park is quiet "on average" is cold comfort. Indeed, the FAA acknowledges that, "[b]ecause many park visitors typically spend limited time in particular sound environments during specific park visits, the amount of aircraft noise present . . . can have great implications for the visitor's opportunity to experience natural quiet in those particular times and spaces." Limitations Rule, 65 Fed.Reg. at 17,712. The problem with an annual average is that it gives equal weight to summer and winter days, notwithstanding that there are many more visitors during the former than the latter. Thus, theoretically the use of an annual average could permit the statutory standard to be met despite an incessantly noisy summer, assuming that the other seasons were relatively quiet. On the FAA's view, it could then declare that it had achieved substantial restoration of natural quiet and cease any further efforts to restrict aircraft noise.

Questions and Comments

1. Can you find common patterns in the ways that the courts discovered flaws in agency justifications of their rules? Which of these cases involved the most technical issues? The least technical? Did the complexity of the agency decision-making affect its vulnerability to judicial review?

2. In *Air Tour Association* the court was able to reach its result by deferring to the interpretation of the Park Service. It was guided in doing so by *Chevron* and *Auer v. Robbins*, 519 U.S. 452 (1997), the latter holding that an agency's interpretation of its own regulations is entitled to deference. Do you see the relationship between the court's application of *Auer* and the format for judicial review of informal agency action set forth in *Overton Park*? Indeed, the agency action in *Overton* fell when the Court rejected the agency's interpretation of the governing statute, did it not? Generally, however, *Chevron* makes it difficult for a party to invalidate agency action on the ground that the agency rule rested upon an incorrect interpretation of the governing statute.

3. How would you describe the agency's failure in *American Lung*? Was its analysis incorrect? Were the underlying facts found incorrectly? Was there something missing from the agency explanation? Must the agency tell us every step that

it employed in its decision-making? Is this case reminiscent of *International Harvester*?

4. Does *Canadian Association of Petroleum Produc* ers involve the most technical issue in this group of cases? It is, however, an issue that most university students understand, isn't it? Did the court fault the agency for using the median rather than the midpoint? Does this case resemble *International Harvester*? Because the objections to the use of the midpoint appeared legitimate to the court, the court thought that the agency was obliged to respond to them. In *International Harvester*, the court doubted the agency's logic because of several steps that the agency failed to explain satisfactorily. In *Canadian Association*, the failure of the agency to respond to legitimate objections produced the same effect.

Comment: The Ossification of the Rule-Making Process

By the early 1990s, many observers were expressing concern that aggressive judicial review of agency rulemaking was erecting too high a procedural bar to rulemaking; that judicial review was frustrating well-founded agency attempts to regulate; and that many agencies were abandoning rulemaking because of these hurdles. Critics were claiming that the rulemaking process was becoming "ossified." (To be fair to the courts, it was not only aggressive judicial review that was inhibiting agency rulemaking. It was also compliance with a number of forms of review within the executive branch as well. We will examine internal executive-branch review below, in Chapter 11).

The leading exponent of this position that rulemaking has become ossified is University of Texas Law Professor Thomas McGarity, whose 1992 article in the Duke Law Journal sparked widespread discussion of the issue. See Thomas O. McGarity, *Some Thoughts on "Deossifying" the Rulemaking Process*, 41 DUKE L.J. 1385 (1992); Thomas O. McGarity, *The Expanded Debate Over the Future of the Regulatory State*, 63 CHI.L. REV. 1463 (1996); Thomas O. McGarity, *The Courts and the Ossification of Rulemaking: A Response to Professor Seidenfeld*, 75 TEXAS L. REV. 525 (1997).

Consider the following extract from the last cited article by McGarity:

> When federal agencies first began to exercise their rulemaking powers in a serious way in the early 1970s, the District of Columbia Circuit, which heard the bulk of the appeals, crafted the "hard look" metaphor for judicial review of informal rulemaking. Under this approach, the courts must take a hard look at the administrative record and the agency's explanatory material to determine whether the agency used the correct analytical methodology, applied the proper criteria, considered the relevant factors, chose from among the available range of regulatory options, relied upon appropriate policies, and pointed to adequate support in the record for material empirical propositions. The "hard look" metaphor rapidly caught on in the courts of appeals and the legal academy, and the Supreme Court arguably adopted a form of "hard look" review in the seminal *State Farm* case.

By the end of the 1980s, it was becoming increasingly clear that the informal rulemaking model was not faring very well. Its great virtue had been the efficiency with which federal agencies could implement regulatory policy and the degree to which affected members of the public could participate in the policymaking process.[11] Throughout the late 1970s and early 1980s, however, the executive branch and, to a more limited extent, Congress added analytical requirements and review procedures, often at the behest of the regulated industries.[12] These initiatives and the continuing scrutiny of reviewing courts under the hard look doctrine caused the rulemaking process to "ossify" to a disturbing degree.[13] By the mid-1990s, it has become so difficult for agencies to promulgate major rules that some regulatory programs have ground to a halt and others have succeeded only because agencies have resorted to alternative policymaking vehicles.[14] I have joined many observers in concluding that the courts have played a prominent role in the ossification of informal rulemaking and the consequent inability of regulatory agencies to implement their statutory missions. I have suggested that one partial solution to the ossification problem is for the courts to "back off." In an attempt to convey a sense for the reduced judicial scrutiny that I have in mind, I have suggested a "pass-fail professor" test to replace the "hard look" metaphor.

* * * *

. . . [J]udges do not always have a good sense for what matters and what does not in a complex rulemaking initiative. The essence of the blunderbuss

---

[11] See Federal Power Comm'n v. Texaco Inc., 377 U.S. 33, 41–44 (1964) (stressing that the Federal Power Commission could direct its regulatory authority to the point of its greatest efficacy); United States v. Storer Broad. Co., 351 U.S. 192, 205 (1956) (ruling that the Communications Act of 1934 gave the FCC flexibility in determining when to waive its own rules); KENNETH CULP DAVIS, ADMINISTRATIVE LAW TREATISE § 6.15 (1st ed. Supp. 1970) (emphasizing the positive democratic aspects of the administrative rulemaking procedures); Antonin Scalia, *Back to Basics: Making Law Without Making Rules*, REGULATION, July-Aug. 1981, at 25, 25–26 (praising rules as more prospective, more open to diverse interested parties, and more immediately clear than court opinions, while allowing regulatory agencies flexibility in agenda timing).

[12] For example, Congress added criteria for considering standards submitted to the Environmental Protection Agency (EPA) by state governments under the Clean Water Act. See 33 U.S.C. § 1313(c)(2)(A) (1994); see also Thomas O. McGarity, *Some Thoughts on "Deossifying" the Rulemaking Process*, 41 DUKE L.J. 1385, 1403–07 (1992) [hereinafter McGarity, *Thoughts on Deossifying*].

[13] See McGarity, *Thoughts on Deossifying, supra* note 11, at 1385–86 (arguing that the imposition of new analytical procedures and stricter standards of judicial review has led to a more rigid and unresponsive rulemaking process).

[14] See Robert A. Anthony, *Interpretive Rules, Policy Statements, Guidances, Manuals, and the Like — Should Federal Agencies Use Them to Bind the Public?*, 41 DUKE L.J. 1311, 1333–55 (1992) (describing the use of policy documents, statements, and orders to avoid judicial review); Michael Asimow, *Nonlegislative Rulemaking and Regulatory Reform*, 1985 DUKE L.J. 381, 385, 387 (arguing that "countless interpretive rules" and policy statements are adopted by agencies like the IRS, Federal Reserve, and Department of Justice); McGarity, *Thoughts on Deossifying, supra* note 11, at 1393 (noting that agencies "engage in 'nonrule rulemaking' through . . . policy statements, interpretive rules, manuals, and other informal devices"); Peter L. Strauss, *The Rulemaking Continuum*, 41 DUKE L.J. 1463, 1486 (1992) (pointing out that the Wage and Hour Division of the Department of Labor issued more than 750,000 letters interpreting wage and hour laws).

attack on an agency rule is the search for an inconsistency or an instance in which the agency did not analyze a particular matter in sufficient depth. The briefs of the petitioners, which are the primary indicators to the court of the importance of particular issues, therefore tend to elevate trivial issues to whatever level of importance is required to convince the court that the error or failure warrants remand. Not surprisingly, many reviewing judges . . . demonstrate a "remarkable instinct for the capillary" in reviewing agency rules. Not knowing what trivial issue may ultimately doom a rulemaking initiative, the agencies feel compelled to analyze every issue in detail and to waste scarce analytical resources responding to off-the-wall comments. If the reviewing courts subject every issue raised on appeal to a hard look, the blunderbuss attack stands a good chance of producing the desired result — a gumming-up of the regulatory works.

A good example is the Eleventh Circuit's review of OSHA's massive generic air contaminants standard. In that case OSHA promulgated a standard updating the permissible exposure levels (PELs) for 428 workplace air contaminants. OSHA had promulgated "consensus" standards pursuant to congressional direction during the first six months of the agency's existence. These consensus PELs were for the most part based upon recommendations of private standard-setting organizations like the American Council of Governmental Industrial Hygienists (ACGIH) and the American National Standards Institute. Over the years, the private agencies and the newly created National Institute for Occupational Safety and Health (NIOSH) had continued to study the health effects of the contaminants that were the subject of consensus PELs, and the legally enforceable PELs became outdated. OSHA attempted to promulgate a single generic standard updating the PELs based on more recent ACGIH and NIOSH recommendations. OSHA believed that it could accomplish this relatively uncontroversial generic update without making individual findings of significant risk and feasibility for each of the more than 400 contaminants. The Court of Appeals for the Eleventh Circuit thought otherwise. Recognizing that the statute allowed OSHA to engage in generic rulemaking, the court nevertheless held that "the PEL for each substance must be able to stand independently, i.e., that each PEL must be supported by substantial evidence in the record considered as a whole and accompanied by adequate explanation." This meant that OSHA was obliged to support findings that the substances posed a significant risk and that controls sufficient to achieve the PELs were feasible. Although OSHA had taken great pains to summarize the available evidence for all of the 428 substances, it did not undertake individual risk assessments for each of the chemicals, an exercise that would have involved determining the degree of exposure to each of the substances in all (or some representative sample) of the thousands of workplaces in which employees were exposed to those substances. The court held that OSHA's generic determination that the standard overall would prevent 55,000 occupational illnesses and 683 deaths annually was not sufficient. The court apparently thought it appropriate to pick and choose from OSHA's rationales for the 428 substances those explanations that the court found to be the least plausible, even though no one had challenged the PELs for those substances. Since OSHA had understandably put fewer resources into standards that it knew were not likely to be challenged, it was surprised when the court seized on those rationales as examples of poor OSHA reasoning. The court also rejected OSHA's similar generic determination that compliance with the PELs was feasible, noting that "OSHA made no attempt to show the ability of technology to meet specific exposure standards in specific industries." Finally, even though the PELs for the vast majority of the 428 air contaminants were not challenged by any party, the court invalidated the entire standard, thus eliminating the protections afforded by even the uncontroversial PELs.

The Eleventh Circuit's insistence that OSHA build a case for every chemical that it regulates stands as a barrier to future generic rulemaking by that agency. Unless OSHA is prepared to support individualized significant risk and feasibility determinations with a record that can survive judicial review, it may not adopt a generic approach to health or safety risks. Given the resources required to make such individualized determinations, OSHA would be better advised to proceed on a chemical-by-chemical basis.

Questions and Comments

If agencies are deterred from engaging in rulemaking under section 553, what are their alternatives? Will they cease to regulate? Will they regulate through adjudication? Will they issue interpretative rules? What are the advantages and disadvantages of these alternatives?

Chapter 9

THE ADMINISTRATIVE RECORD AND RELATED MATTERS

A. THE NEW PARADIGM OF ADMINISTRATIVE DECISION-MAKING: THE COMMENT RECORD AND INFORMAL RULEMAKING

In the previous section, we have seen how the judicial review of informal rulemaking has evolved over the last several decades. We have seen that, under the new approach to judicial review of informal rulemaking which has evolved since the mid 1960s, judicial review takes place on the comment record. Indeed, a seeming corollary of judicial review on the comment record is that the administrative decision itself must be based on the comment record. Because the comment or administrative record has become so important under the new approach, it is imperative for litigants to get into the comment record all of the data and other material which supports their position, both to secure their position in proceedings at the administrative level and to prepare a base for judicial review.

1. *Getting material into the record; the uses of the Freedom of Information Act in rulemaking litigation.*

a. *The Freedom of Information Act: In general.*

Section 552 of the APA contains the Freedom of Information Act, an elaborate revision of section 3 of the original APA. The FOIA was enacted in 1966 and subsequently modified in minor amendments.

Review the structure of § 552. You have already examined some of the provisions of § 552 in conjunction with the *Morton v. Ruiz* case [supra, Chapter 6]. Note that § 552(a) sets forth material that agencies are required to make available, and procedures for enforcement; while § 552(b) contains a list of exemptions. Note that with respect to the material which is required to be made available, some material (set forth in § 552(a)(1)) is required to be published in the Federal Register, while other material (set forth in § 552(a)(2)) is required only to be made available for public inspection and copying.

Much of the material required to be made available consists of agency rules or material setting forth agency policies. What else does § 552 require to be made available? What material falls within the scope of § 552(a)(3)?

What is the difference between the "statements of general policy or interpretations of general applicability formulated and adopted by the agency" referred to in § 552(a)(1)(D) and the "statements of policy and interpretations which have been adopted by the agency and are not published in the Federal Register" referred to in § 552(a)(2)(B)?

What is the extent of the overlap, if any, between the "administrative staff manuals and instructions to staff that affect a member of the public" referred to in § 552(a)(2)(C) and "inter-agency or intra-agency memorandums or letters which would not be available by law to a party other than an agency in litigation with the agency" referred to in § 552(b)(5)?

b.   *Exemption 5.*

Section 552(b) contains various exemptions from the disclosure requirements mandated by other provisions of the FOIA. The caselaw construing § 552(b)(5) is particularly important to an understanding of the interaction between the FOIA and the administrative decision-making process. To what extent, for example, can a litigant use the FOIA as a basis for discovery against an agency to obtain materials for insertion in the rulemaking record? Before addressing some of the complex issues involving the interaction between the FOIA and rulemaking litigation, we will consider the basic caselaw construing exemption 5.

FEDERAL TRADE COMMISSION v. GROLIER, INC.
462 U.S. 19 (1983)

JUSTICE WHITE delivered the opinion of the Court.

The Freedom of Information Act (FOIA), 5 U.S.C. § 552, mandates that the Government make its records available to the public. Section 552(b)(5) exempts from disclosure "interagency or intra-agency memorandums or letters which would not be available by law to a party . . . in litigation with the agency." It is well established that this exemption was intended to encompass the attorney work-product rule. The question presented in this case is the extent, if any, to which the work-product component of Exemption 5 applies when the litigation for which the requested documents were generated has been terminated.

In 1972, the Federal Trade Commission undertook an investigation of Americana Corp., a subsidiary of respondent Grolier Inc. The investigation was conducted in connection with a civil penalty action filed by the Department of Justice. In 1976, the suit against Americana was dismissed with prejudice when the Government declined to comply with a District Court discovery order. In 1978, respondents filed a request with the Commission for disclosure of documents concerning the investigation of Americana.

. . . . [The Commission refused to release seven documents; and respondent brought suit.] Following in camera inspection, the District Court determined that all the requested documents were exempt from disclosure under § 552(b)(5), either as attorney work product, as confidential attorney-client communications, or as internal predecisional agency material. On appeal, the Court of Appeals held that four documents generated during the Americana litigation could not be withheld on the basis of the work-product rule unless the Commission could show that "litigation related to the terminated action exists or potentially exists." . . .

. . . . The test under Exemption 5 is whether the documents would be "routinely" or "normally" disclosed upon a showing of relevance. . . . At the time this case came to the Court of Appeals, all of the Courts of Appeals that had decided the issue under Rule 26(b)(3) had determined that work-product materials retained their immunity from discovery after termination of the litigation for which the documents were prepared, without regard to whether other related litigation is pending or is contemplated.

Exemption 5 incorporates the privileges which the Government enjoys under the relevant statutory and *caselaw* in the pretrial discovery context." *Renegotiation Board v. Grumman Aircraft Engineering Corp.*, 421 U.S. 168, 184 (1975) (emphasis added). Under this state of the work-product rule it cannot fairly be said that work-product materials are "routinely" available in subsequent litigation.

Under the current state of the law relating to the privilege, work-product materials are immune from discovery unless the one seeking discovery can show substantial need in connection with subsequent litigation. Such materials are thus not "routinely" or "normally" available to parties in litigation and hence are exempt under Exemption 5. This result, by establishing a discrete category of exempt information, implements the congressional intent to provide "workable" rules. . . .

Respondent urges that the meaning of the statutory language is "plain" and that, at least in this case, the requested documents must be disclosed because the same documents were ordered disclosed during discovery in previous litigation. It does not follow, however, from an ordered disclosure based on a showing of need that such documents are routinely available to litigants. The logical result of respondent's position is that whenever work-product documents would be discoverable in any particular litigation, they must be disclosed to anyone under the FOIA. We have previously rejected that line of analysis. In *NLRB v. Sears, Roebuck & Co., supra,* we construed Exemption 5 to "exempt those documents, and only those documents, *normally* privileged in the civil discovery context." . . . It is not difficult to imagine litigation in which one party's need for otherwise privileged documents would be sufficient to override the privilege but that does not remove the documents from the category of the *normally* privileged. . . .

Accordingly, we hold that under Exemption 5, attorney work product is exempt from mandatory disclosure without regard to the status of the litigation for which it was prepared. Only by construing the Exemption to provide a categorical rule can the Act's purpose of expediting disclosure by means of workable rules be furthered. The judgment of the Court of Appeals is reversed.

It is so ordered.

Questions and Comments

1.   The scope of the work product exemption depends upon the need of the party seeking discovery to obtain the materials which he seeks. But the Court has limited the work-product exception incorporated into Exception 5 as coextensive with that "normally privileged". What is the criterion for the "normal" scope of the

work-product exception? Does it follow that other privileges incorporated into Exemption 5 are to be applied in an objective way without regard for the individual circumstances of the party seeking disclosure? Why?

2.   In U.S. *Department of Justice v. Julian*, 486 U.S. 1 (1988), the Government argued that because a pre-sentence report was not routinely discoverable by a third party, Exemption 5 permitted the Government to refuse a request by a prisoner who sought a copy of the pre-sentence report on himself. The Court rejected the Government's position:

> Contrary to the Government's contention . . . nothing in *Grolier*, or in the language of Exemption 5, requires that . . . a privilege must . . . be extended to all requests for these reports, or to none at all. *Grolier* held that the fact that a claim of privilege might be overridden in a particular case by special circumstances did not mean that discovery was "routinely available" within the meaning of Exemption 5. . . . In this case, it seems clear that there is good reason to differentiate between a governmental claim of privilege for presentence reports when a third party is making the request and such a claim when the request is made by the subject of the report. . . . [T]here simply is no privilege preventing disclosure in the latter situation. Even under our ruling in *Grolier*, therefore, discovery of the reports by the defendants themselves can be said to be "routine."

The Court held that the Government could not use Exemption 5 to withhold a pre-sentence report from a prisoner who had requested a copy of the report and who was the subject of that report.

NATIONAL LABOR RELATIONS BOARD v. SEARS, ROEBUCK & CO.
421 U.S. 132 (1975)

Mr. Justice White delivered the opinion of the Court.

The National Labor Relations Board (the Board) and its General Counsel seek to set aside an order of the United States District Court directing disclosure to respondent, Sears, Roebuck & Co. (Sears), pursuant to the Freedom of Information Act, 5 U.S.C. § 552 (Act), of certain memoranda, known as "Advice Memoranda" and "Appeals Memoranda," and related documents generated by the Office of the General Counsel in the course of deciding whether or not to permit the filing with the Board of unfair labor practice complaints.

. . . . Under . . . the National Labor Relations Act, as amended by the Labor Management Relations Act, 1947 . . . the process of adjudicating unfair labor practice cases begins with the filing by a private party of a "charge." . . .

Although Congress has designated the Board as the principal body which adjudicates the unfair labor practice case based on such charge. . . . the Board may adjudicate only upon the filing of a "complaint"; and Congress has delegated to the Office of General Counsel "on behalf of the Board" the unreviewable authority to determine whether a complaint shall be filed. . . . In those cases in which he decides that a complaint shall issue, the General Counsel becomes an advocate before the Board in support of the complaint. In those cases in which he decides not to issue a complaint, no proceeding before the Board occurs at all. The practical effect of this administrative scheme is that a party believing himself the victim of an unfair labor practice can obtain neither adjudication nor remedy under the labor statute without first persuading the Office of General Counsel that his claim is sufficiently meritorious to warrant Board consideration.

In order to structure the considerable power which the administrative scheme gives him, the General Counsel has adopted certain procedures for processing unfair labor practice charges. Charges are filed in the first instance with one of the Board's 31 Regional Directors to whom the General Counsel has delegated the initial power to decide whether or not to issue a complaint. A member of the staff of the Regional Office then conducts an investigation of the charge, which may include interviewing witnesses and reviewing documents. . . . If, on the basis of the investigation, the Regional Director believes the charge has merit, a settlement will be attempted, or a complaint issued. If the charge has no merit in the Regional Director's judgment, the charging party will be so informed by letter with a brief explanation of the reasons. . . . In such a case, the charging party will also be informed of his right to appeal within 10 days to the Office of the General Counsel in Washington, D.C. . . .

[If the charging party appeals the Regional Director's refusal to issue a complaint to the office of the General Counsel, the matter will be considered in that Office and a decision will be embodied in an "Appeals Memorandum".] . . . [T]he Appeals Memorandum is then sent to the Regional Director who follows its instructions. If the appeal is rejected and the Regional Director's decision not to issue a complaint is sustained, a separate document is prepared and sent by the General Counsel in letter form to the charging party, more briefly setting forth the reasons for the denial of his appeal. The Appeals Memoranda, whether sustaining or overruling the Regional Directors, constitute one class of documents at issue in this case.

The appeals process affords the General Counsel's Office in Washington some opportunity to formulate a coherent policy, and to achieve some measure of uniformity, in enforcing the labor laws. The appeals process alone, however, is not wholly adequate for this purpose. . . . Accordingly, to further "fair and uniform administration of the Act," the General Counsel requires the Regional Directors, before reaching an initial decision in connection with charges raising certain issues specified by the General Counsel, to submit the matter to the General Counsel's "Advice Branch," also located in Washington, D.C. In yet other kinds of cases, the Regional Directors are permitted [although not required] to seek the counsel of the Advice Branch.

When a Regional Director seeks "advice" from the Advice Branch, he does so through a memorandum which sets forth the facts of the case, a statement of the issues on which advice is sought, and a recommendation. . . . [T]he General Counsel will decide the issue submitted, and his "final determination" will be communicated to the Regional Director by way of an Advice Memorandum. The memorandum will briefly summarize the facts, against the background of which the legal or policy issue is to be decided, set forth the General Counsel's answer to the legal or policy issue submitted together with a "detailed legal rationale," and contain "instructions for the final processing of the case." . . . Depending upon the conclusion reached in the memorandum, the Regional Director will either file a complaint or send a letter to the complaining party advising him of the Regional Director's decision not to proceed and informing him of his right to appeal. It is these Advice Memoranda which constitute the other class of documents of which Sears seeks disclosure in this case.

II

This case arose in the following context. By letter dated July 14, 1971, Sears requested that the General Counsel disclose to it pursuant to the Act all Advice and Appeals Memoranda issued within the previous five years on the subjects of "the propriety of withdrawals by employers or unions from multi-employer bargaining, disputes as to commencement date of negotiations, or conflicting interpretations in any other context of the Board's *Retail Associates* (120 NLRB 388) rule. . . . By letter dated July 23, 1971, the General Counsel declined Sears' disclosure request in full. . . .

That Congress had the Government's executive privilege specifically in mind in adopting Exemption 5 is clear. . . . The cases uniformly rest the privilege on the policy of protecting the "decision making processes of government agencies The point, plainly made in the Senate Report, is that the "frank discussion of legal or policy matters" in writing might be inhibited if the discussion were made public; and that the "decisions" and "policies formulated" would be the poorer as a result. . . .

Manifestly, the ultimate purpose of this long-recognized privilege is to prevent injury to the quality of agency decisions. The quality of a particular agency decision will clearly be affected by the communications received by the decisionmaker on the subject of the decision prior to the time the decision is made. However, it is difficult to see how the quality of a decision will be affected by communications with respect to the decision occurring after the decision is finally reached; and therefore equally difficult to see how the quality of the decision will be affected by forced disclosure of such communications, as long as prior communications and the ingredients of the decisionmaking process are not disclosed. Accordingly, the lower courts have uniformly drawn a distinction between predecisional communications, which are privileged, . . . and communications made after the decision and designed to explain it, which are not. . . . This distinction is supported not only by the lesser injury to the decisionmaking process flowing from disclosure of post decisional communications, but also, in the case of those communications which explain the decision, by the increased public interest in knowing the basis for agency policy already adopted. The public is only marginally concerned with reasons supporting a policy which an agency has rejected, or with reasons which might have supplied, but did not supply, the basis for a policy which was actually adopted on a different ground. In contrast, the public is vitally concerned with the reasons which did supply the basis for an agency policy actually adopted. These reasons, if expressed within the agency, constitute the "working law" of the agency and have been held by the lower courts to be outside the protection of Exemption 5. . . . Exemption 5, properly construed, calls for "disclosure of all 'opinions and interpretations' which embody the agency's effective law and policy, and the withholding of all papers which reflect the agency's group thinking in the process of working out its policy and determining what its law shall be." Davis, *The Information Act: A Preliminary Analysis*, 34 U. CHI. L. REV. 761, 797 (1967). . . .

This conclusion is powerfully supported by the other provisions of the Act. The affirmative portion of the Act, expressly requiring indexing of "final opinions," "statements of policy and interpretations which have been adopted by the agency," and "instructions to staff that affect a member of the public," 5 U.S.C. § 552(a)(2), represents a strong congressional aversion to "secret [agency] law and represents an affirmative congressional purpose to require disclosure of documents which have the "force and effect of law." . . . We should be reluctant, therefore, to construe Exemption 5 to apply to the documents described in 5 U.S.C. § 552(a)(2); and with respect at least to "final opinions," which not only invariably explain agency action already taken or an agency decision already made, but also constitute "final dispositions" of matters by an agency . . . , we hold that Exemption 5 can never apply.

(ii)

It is equally clear that Congress had the attorney's work-product privilege specifically in mind when it adopted Exemption 5. . . . Whatever the outer boundaries of the attorney's work-product rule are, the rule clearly applies to memoranda prepared by an attorney in contemplation of litigation which set forth the attorney's theory of the case and his litigation strategy. . . .

B

Applying these principles to the memoranda sought by Sears, it becomes clear that Exemption 5 does not apply to those Appeals and Advice Memoranda which conclude that no complaint should be filed and which have the effect of finally denying relief to the charging party; but that Exemption 5 does protect from disclosure those Appeals and Advice Memoranda which direct the filing of a complaint and the commencement of litigation before the Board.

. . . . [These Advice and Appeals Memoranda which direct the dismissal of charges] are "final opinions" made in the "adjudication of cases" which must be indexed pursuant to 5 U.S.C. § 552(a)(2)(A). The decision to dismiss a charge is a decision in a "case" and constitutes an "adjudication": an "adjudication" is defined under the Administrative Procedure Act, of which 5 U.S.C. § 552 is a part, as "agency process for the formulation of an order," 5 U.S.C. § 551(7); an "order" is defined as "the whole or part of a *final disposition*, whether affirmative for] negative . . . of an agency in a matter. . . . 5 U.S.C. § 551(6)(emphasis added); and the dismissal of a charge, as noted above, is a "final disposition." Since an Advice or Appeals Memorandum explains the reasons for the "final disposition" it plainly qualifies as an "opinion"; and falls within 5 U.S.C. § 552(a)(2)(A). . . .

(ii)

Advice and Appeals Memoranda which direct the filing of a complaint, on the other hand, fall within the coverage of Exemption 5. The filing of a complaint does not finally dispose even of the General Counsel's responsibility with respect to the case. The case will be litigated and decided by the Board; and the General Counsel will have the responsibility of advocating the position of the charging party before the Board. The Memoranda will inexorably contain the General Counsel's theory of the case and may communicate to the Regional Director some litigation strategy or settlement advice. Since the Memoranda will also have been prepared in contemplation of the upcoming litigation, they fall squarely within Exemption 5's protection of an attorney's work product. At the same time, the public's interest in disclosure is substantially reduced by the fact . . . that the basis for the General Counsel's legal decision will come out in the course of litigation before the Board; and that the "law" with respect to these cases will ultimately be made not by the General Counsel but by the Board or the courts.

IV

Finally, petitioners argue that the Advice and Appeals Memoranda are exempt, pursuant to 5 U.S.C. §§ 552(b)(2) and (7), and that the documents incorporated therein are protected by Exemption 7. With respect to the Advice and Appeals Memoranda, we decline to reach a decision on these claims for the reasons set forth below, and with respect to the documents incorporated therein, we remand for further proceedings.

In summary, with respect to Advice and Appeals Memoranda which conclude that a complaint should not be filed, we affirm the judgment of the Court of Appeals [requiring disclosure], subject to its decision on remand whether the Government is foreclosed from pursuing its Exemption 7 claim. . . . Insofar as the judgment of the Court of Appeals requires the General Counsel to supply documents not expressly incorporated by reference in these Advice and Appeals Memoranda, or otherwise to explain the circumstances of the case, it is reversed; and with respect to Advice and Appeals Memoranda which conclude that a complaint should be filed, the judgment of the Court of Appeals [requiring disclosure] is likewise reversed.

So ordered.

Renegotiation Board v. Grumman Aircraft Engineering Corp., 421 U.S. 168 (1975), decided the same day as *NLRB v. Sears, Roebuck & Co., supra.* Under the Renegotiation Act of 1951, the Government was entitled to recoup "excessive profits" received by contractors with certain government departments. Recommendations whether to seek recoupment and, if so, how much, were made initially by Regional Boards. Recommendations not to seek recoupment were reviewed by the Renegotiation Board; recommendations to seek recoupment were initially reviewed by a "Division" of the Renegotiation Board which would then make its recommendation in a Division Report to the full Board. The full Board then made its decision. If the Board did not decide to issue a clearance, the contractor was notified of the Board's conclusion and would be given, at its request, a Summary to enable it to decide whether to enter into an agreement with the Board. If an agreement was not reached, the Board would then enter a unilateral order and would issue, at the request of the contractor, a "statement of such determination, of the facts used as a basis therefor, and of its reasons for such determination." In litigation seeking release of certain documents including recommendations made by the Regional Boards and the Divisions of the Renegotiation Board, the Board, in compliance with the ruling of the Court of Appeals, turned over some documents, including Statements and Summaries, but refused to turn over the recommendations of the Regional Boards and the Divisions. On appeal, the Supreme Court ruled that the latter were predecisional documents protected by Exemption 5:

> "Because only the full Board has the power by law to make the decision whether excessive profits exist; because both types of reports involved in this case are prepared prior to that decision and are used by the Board in its deliberations; and because the evidence utterly fails to support the conclusion that the reasoning in the reports is adopted by the Board as its reasoning, even when it agrees with the conclusion of a report, we conclude that the reports are not final opinions and do fall within Exemption 5."

Questions and Comments

1.   Did the Court order the disclosure of all the advice and appeal memoranda sought in the *Sears* case? What memoranda were exempt from disclosure? What was the rationale for the exemption? What was the rationale for the disclosure which was ordered? What provisions of the FOIA did the Court rely upon in ordering disclosure?

2.   Did the Renegotiation Board in *Grumman* adopt a rationale for its decisions? All of its decisions? Some of them? Explain. Was it required to disclose those rationales by the FOIA? Why did the Court not require the disclosure of the recommendations of the Divisions? Did not the recommendations of the Divisions serve as the rationales for the Renegotiation Board determinations which ordered the result recommended by the Divisions?

3.   Can you identify the circumstances in which an agency can be said to have adopted a subordinate's supporting rationale when it follows the subordinate's recommendation as to how it should decide? Is it relevant to know whether the agency is required by statute to supply a rationale for its decision?

Federal Open Market Committee of the Federal Reserve System v. Merrill, **443 U.S. 340 (1979).** The Federal Open Market Committee (FOMC) met monthly to review the overall state of the economy and to consider the appropriate course of monetary and open market policy. The Committee's principal conclusions were embodied in a statement called the Domestic Policy Directive which summarized the economic and monetary policy background of the FOMC's deliberations and indicated in general terms whether the Committee wished to follow an expansionary, deflationary, or unchanged monetary policy in the period ahead. The Committee also attempted to agree on specific tolerance ranges for the growth in the money supply and for the federal funds rate. The practice of the Committee had been to include these tolerance ranges in the Domestic Policy Directive. During the month after each Committee meeting, the Committee's secretariat prepared a "Record of Policy Actions" which contained a general review of economic and monetary conditions at the time of the meeting, the text of the Domestic Policy Directive, any other policy actions taken by the Committee, the votes on these actions, and the dissenting views, if any. A draft of the Record of Policy Actions was distributed to the participants at the next meeting of the Committee for their comments, and was revised and released for publication in the Federal Register a few days later.

Respondent requested certain records of the policy actions taken by the FOMC and was refused, the FMOC explaining that the Records of Policy Actions, including the Domestic Policy Directive, were available only on a delayed basis. Respondent then instituted suit to compel disclosure, which was ordered by the District Court and affirmed by the Court of Appeals for the District of Columbia Circuit. On review by the U.S. Supreme Court, held: Reversed.

There can be little doubt that the FOMC's Domestic Policy Directives constitute "interagency or intra-agency memorandums or letters." FOMC is clearly an "agency" as that term is defined in the Administrative Procedure Act. 5 U.S.C. §§ 551(l), 552(e). And the Domestic Policy Directives are essentially the FOMC's written instructions to the Account Manager, a subordinate official of the agency. These instructions, although possibly of interest to members of the public, are binding only upon the Account Manager. The Directives do not establish rules that govern the adjudication of individual rights, nor do they require particular conduct or forbearance by any other member of the public. They are thus intra-agency memorandums" within the meaning of Exemption 5.

B

Whether the Domestic Policy Directives "would not be available by law to a party . . . in litigation with the agency presents a more difficult question. . . . [The FOMC's] principal argument . . . is that Exemption 5 confers general authority upon an agency to delay disclosure of intra-agency memoranda that would undermine the effectiveness of the agency's policy if released immediately. This general authority exists, according to the FOMC, even if the memoranda in question could be routinely discovered by a party in civil litigation with the agency.

We must reject this analysis. . . .

The FOMC argues, in the alternative, that there are several civil discovery privileges, in addition to the privileges for predecisional communications and an attorney's work product, that would allow a district court to delay discovery of documents such as the Domestic Policy Directives until they are no longer operative. . . .

The federal courts have long recognized a qualified evidentiary privilege for trade secrets and other confidential commercial information. . . .

After examining the legislative history of the FOIA and Exemption 5, the Court concluded that Congress intended to incorporate within Exemption 5 a limited privilege for confidential commercial information generated in the process of awarding government contracts in order not to place the Government in a disadvantageous bargaining position.

The only remaining questions are whether the Domestic Policy Directives constitute confidential commercial information of the sort given qualified protection by Exemption 5, and, if so, whether they would in fact be privileged in civil discovery. Although the analogy is not exact, we think that the Domestic Policy Directives and associated tolerance ranges are substantially similar to confidential commercial information generated in the process of awarding a contract. . . . We are mindful that "the discovery rules can only be applied under Exemption 5 by way of rough analogies" . . . and, in particular, that the individual FOIA applicant's need for information is not to be taken into account in determining whether materials are exempt under Exemption 5. Nevertheless, the sensitivity of the commercial secrets involved, and the harm that would be inflicted upon the Government by premature disclosure, should continue to serve as relevant criteria in determining the applicability of this Exemption 5 privilege. Accordingly, we think that if the Domestic Policy Directives contain sensitive information not otherwise available, and if immediate release of these Directives would significantly harm the Government's monetary functions or commercial interests, then a slight delay in the publication of the Directives . . . would be permitted under Exemption 5.

Questions and Comments

What was the basis for the Court's application of Exemption 5 in *Merrill?* Could you have predicted the *Merrill* result in advance? Why did the lower courts decide as they did? Under what circumstances could the FOMC decide to withhold Domestic Policy Directives for longer periods than one month?

DEPARTMENT OF THE INTERIOR AND BUREAU OF INDIAN AFFAIRS

v.

KLAMATH WATER USERS PROTECTIVE ASSOCIATION
532 U.S. 1 (2001)

JUSTICE SOUTER delivered the opinion of the Court.

Documents in issue here, passing between Indian Tribes and the Department of the Interior, addressed tribal interests subject to state and federal proceedings to determine water allocations. The question is whether the documents are exempt from the disclosure requirements of the Freedom of Information Act, as "intra-agency memorandums or letters" that would normally be privileged in civil discovery. 5 U.S.C. § 552(b)(5). We hold they are not.

I

Two separate proceedings give rise to this case, the first a planning effort within the Department of the Interior's Bureau of Reclamation, and the second a state water rights adjudication in the Oregon courts. Within the Department of the Interior, the Bureau of Reclamation (Reclamation) administers the Klamath Irrigation Project (Klamath Project or Project), which uses water from the Klamath River Basin to irrigate territory in Klamath County, Oregon, and two northern California counties. In 1995, the Department began work to develop a long-term operations plan for the Project, to be known as the Klamath Project Operation Plan (Plan), which would provide for allocation of water among competing uses and competing water users. The Department asked the Klamath as well as the Hoopa Valley, Karuk, and Yurok Tribes (Basin Tribes) to consult with Reclamation on the matter, and a memorandum of understanding between the Department and the Tribes recognized that "[t]he United States Government has a unique legal relationship with Native American tribal governments," and called for "[a]ssessment, in consultation with the Tribes, of the impacts of the [Plan] on Tribal trust resources.

During roughly the same period, the Department's Bureau of Indian Affairs (Bureau) filed claims on behalf of the Klamath Tribe alone in an Oregon state-court adjudication intended to allocate water rights. Since the Bureau is responsible for administering land and water held in trust for Indian tribes, 25 U.S.C. § 1a; 25 CFR subch. H, pts. 150–181 (2000), it consulted with the Klamath Tribe, and the two exchanged written memorandums on the appropriate scope of the claims ultimately submitted by the United States for the benefit of the Klamath Tribe. The Bureau does not, however, act as counsel for the Tribe, which has its own lawyers and has independently submitted claims on its own behalf.[1]

Respondent, the Klamath Water Users Protective Association (Association), is a nonprofit association of water users in the Klamath River Basin, most of whom receive water from the Klamath Project, and whose interests are adverse to the tribal interests owing to scarcity of water. The Association filed a series of requests with the Bureau under the Freedom of Information Act (FOIA), 5 U.S.C. § 552, seeking access to communications between the Bureau and the Basin Tribes during the relevant time period. The Bureau turned over several documents but withheld others as exempt under the attorney work-product and deliberative process privileges. These privileges are said to be incorporated in FOIA Exemption 5, which exempts from disclosure "inter-agency or intra-agency memorandums or letters which would not be available by law to a party other than an agency in litigation with the agency." § 552(b)(5). The Association then sued the Bureau under FOIA to compel release of the documents.

By the time of the District Court ruling, seven documents remained in dispute, three of them addressing the Plan, three concerned with the Oregon adjudication,

---

[1] The Government is "not technically acting as [the Tribes'] attorney. That is, the Tribes have their own attorneys, but the United States acts as trustee." Tr. of Oral Arg. 5. "The United States has also filed claims on behalf of the Project and on behalf of other Federal interests" in the Oregon adjudication. *Id.*, at 6. The Hoopa Valley, Karuk, and Yurok Tribes are not parties to the adjudication. Brief for Respondent 7.

and the seventh relevant to both proceedings. Six of the documents were prepared by the Klamath Tribe or its representative and were submitted at the Government's behest to the Bureau or to the Department's Regional Solicitor; a Bureau official prepared the seventh document and gave it to lawyers for the Klamath and Yurok Tribes.

[The District Court granted the Government's motion for summary judgment, but the Court of Appeals for the Ninth Circuit reversed.] We granted certiorari in view of the decision's significant impact on the relationship between Indian tribes and the Government, and now affirm.

II

Upon request, FOIA mandates disclosure of records held by a federal agency, see 5 U.S.C. § 552, unless the documents fall within enumerated exemptions, see § 552(b). "[T]hese limited exemptions do not obscure the basic policy that disclosure, not secrecy, is the dominant objective of the Act," *Department of Air Force v. Rose*, 425 U.S. 352, 361 (1976); "[c]onsistent with the Act's goal of broad disclosure, these exemptions have been consistently given a narrow compass," *U.S. Department of Justice v. Tax Analysts*, 492 U.S. 136, 151 (1989); see also *FBI v. Abramson*, 456 U.S. 615, 630 (1982) ("FOIA exemptions are to be narrowly construed").

A

Exemption 5 protects from disclosure "inter-agency or intra-agency memorandums or letters which would not be available by law to a party other than an agency in litigation with the agency." 5 U.S.C. § 552(b)(5). To qualify, a document must thus satisfy two conditions: its source must be a Government agency, and it must fall within the ambit of a privilege against discovery under judicial standards that would govern litigation against the agency that holds it.

Our prior cases on Exemption 5 have addressed the second condition, incorporating civil discovery privileges. See, *e.g.*, *United States v. Weber Aircraft Corp.*, 465 U.S. 792, 799-800 (1984); *NLRB v. Sears, Roebuck & Co.*, 421 U.S. 132, 148 (1975) ("Exemption 5 withholds from a member of the public documents which a private party could not discover in litigation with the agency"). So far as they might matter here, those privileges include the privilege for attorney work-product and what is sometimes called the "deliberative process" privilege. Work product protects "mental processes of the attorney," *United States v. Nobles*, 422 U.S. 225, 238 (1975), while deliberative process covers "documents reflecting advisory opinions, recommendations and deliberations comprising part of a process by which governmental decisions and policies are formulated," *Sears, Roebuck & Co.*, 421 U.S., at 150 (internal quotation marks omitted). The deliberative process privilege rests on the obvious realization that officials will not communicate candidly among themselves if each remark is a potential item of discovery and front page news, and its object is to enhance "the quality of agency decisions," *id.*, at 151, by protecting open and frank discussion among those who make them within the Government, see *EPA v. Mink*, 410 U.S. 73, 86-87 (1973); see also *Weber Aircraft Corp., supra*, at 802.

The point is not to protect Government secrecy pure and simple, however, and the first condition of Exemption 5 is no less important than the second; the communication must be "inter-agency or intra-agency." 5 U.S.C. § 552(b)(5). Statutory definitions underscore the apparent plainness of this text. With exceptions not relevant here, "agency" means "each authority of the Government of the United States," § 551(1), and "includes any executive department, military department, Government corporation, Government controlled corporation, or other establishment in the executive branch of the Government . . . , or any independent regulatory agency," § 552(f).

Although neither the terms of the exemption nor the statutory definitions say anything about communications with outsiders, some Courts of Appeals have held that in some circumstances a document prepared outside the Government may nevertheless qualify as an "intra-agency" memorandum under Exemption 5. . . . . In *Department of Justice v. Julian*, 486 U.S. 1 (1988), JUSTICE SCALIA, joined by JUSTICES O'CONNOR and White, explained that "the most natural meaning of the phrase 'intra-agency memorandum' is a memorandum that is addressed both to and from employees of a single agency," *id.*, at 18, n.1 (dissenting opinion). But his opinion also acknowledged the more expansive reading by some Courts of Appeals:

> "It is textually possible and . . . in accord with the purpose of the provision, to regard as an intra-agency memorandum one that has been received by an agency, to assist it in the performance of its own functions, from a person acting in a governmentally conferred capacity other than on behalf of another agency — *e.g.*, in a capacity as employee or consultant to the agency, or as employee or officer of another governmental unit (not an agency) that is authorized or required to provide advice to the agency."

B

The Department purports to rely on this consultant corollary to Exemption 5 in arguing for its application to the Tribe's communications to the Bureau in its capacity of fiduciary for the benefit of the Indian Tribes. The existence of a trust obligation is not, of course, in question, see *United States v. Cherokee Nation of Oklahoma*, 480 U.S. 700, 707 (1987); *United States v. Mitchell*, 463 U.S. 206, 225 (1983); *Seminole Nation v. United States*, 316 U.S. 286, 296–297 (1942). The fiduciary relationship has been described as "one of the primary cornerstones of Indian law," F. COHEN, HANDBOOK OF FEDERAL INDIAN LAW 221 (1982), and has been compared to one existing under a common law trust, with the United States as trustee, the Indian tribes or individuals as beneficiaries, and the property and natural resources managed by the United States as the trust corpus. See, *e.g.*, *Mitchell, supra*, at 225. Nor is there any doubt about the plausibility of the Government's assertion that the candor of tribal communications with the Bureau would be eroded without the protections of the deliberative process privilege recognized under Exemption 5. The Department is surely right in saying that confidentiality in communications with tribes is conducive to a proper discharge of its trust obligation.

From the recognition of this interest in frank communication, which the deliberative process privilege might protect, the Department would have us infer a sufficient justification for applying Exemption 5 to communications with the Tribes, in the same fashion that Courts of Appeals have found sufficient reason to favor a consultant's advice that way. But the Department's argument skips a necessary step, for it ignores the first condition of Exemption 5, that the communication be "intra-agency or inter-agency." The Department seems to be saying that "intra-agency" is a purely conclusory term, just a label to be placed on any document the Government would find it valuable to keep confidential.

There is, however, no textual justification for draining the first condition of independent vitality, and once the intra-agency condition is applied, it rules out any application of Exemption 5 to tribal communications on analogy to consultants' reports (assuming, which we do not decide, that these reports may qualify as intra-agency under Exemption 5). As mentioned already, consultants whose communications have typically been held exempt have not been communicating with the Government in their own interest or on behalf of any person or group whose interests might be affected by the Government action addressed by the consultant. In that regard, consultants may be enough like the agency's own personnel to justify calling their communications "intra-agency." The Tribes, on the contrary, necessarily communicate with the Bureau with their own, albeit entirely legitimate, interests in mind. While this fact alone distinguishes tribal communications from the consultants' examples recognized by several Courts of Appeals, the distinction is even sharper, in that the Tribes are self-advocates at the expense of others seeking benefits inadequate to satisfy everyone.

As to those documents bearing on the Plan, the Tribes are obviously in competition with nontribal claimants, including those irrigators represented by the respondent. The record shows that documents submitted by the Tribes included, among others, "a position paper that discusses water law legal theories" and "addresses issues related to water rights of the tribes," a memorandum "contain-[ing] views on policy the BIA could provide to other governmental agencies," "views concerning trust resources," and a letter "conveying the views of the Klamath Tribes concerning issues involved in the water rights adjudication," While these documents may not take the formally argumentative form of a brief, their function is quite apparently to support the tribal claims. The Tribes are thus urging a position necessarily adverse to the other claimants, the water being inadequate to satisfy the combined demand. As the Court of Appeals said, "[t]he Tribes' demands, if satisfied, would lead to reduced water allocations to members of the Association and have been protested by Association members who fear water shortages and economic injury in dry years."

The Department insists that the Klamath Tribe's consultant-like character is clearer in the circumstances of the Oregon adjudication, since the Department merely represents the interests of the Tribe before a state court that will make any decision about the respective rights of the contenders. But it is not that simple. Even if there were no rival interests at stake in the Oregon litigation, the Klamath Tribe would be pressing its own view of its own interest in its communications with the Bureau. Nor could that interest be ignored as being merged somehow in the fiduciary interest of the Government trustee; the Bureau in its fiduciary capacity would be obliged to adopt the stance it believed to be in the beneficiary's best interest, not necessarily the position espoused by the beneficiary itself. Cf. Restatement (Second) of Trusts § 176, Comment *a* (1957) ("[I]t is the duty of the trustee to exercise such care and skill to preserve the trust property as a man of ordinary prudence would exercise in dealing with his own property . . . ").

But, again, the dispositive point is that the apparent object of the Tribe's communications is a decision by an agency of the Government to support a claim by the Tribe that is necessarily adverse to the interests of competitors. Since there is not enough water to satisfy everyone, the Government's position on behalf of the Tribe is potentially adverse to other users, and it might ask for more or less on behalf of the Tribe depending on how it evaluated the tribal claim compared with the claims of its rivals. The ultimately adversarial character of tribal submissions to the Bureau therefore seems the only fair inference, as confirmed by the Department's acknowledgment that its "obligation to represent the Klamath Tribe necessarily coexists with the duty to protect other federal interests, including in particular its interests with respect to the Klamath Project." . . . The position of the Tribe as beneficiary is thus a far cry from the position of the paid consultant.

Quite apart from its attempt to draw a direct analogy between tribes and conventional consultants, the Department argues that compelled release of the documents would itself impair the Department's performance of a specific fiduciary obligation to protect the confidentiality of communications with tribes. Because, the Department argues, traditional fiduciary standards forbid a trustee to disclose information acquired as a trustee when it should know that disclosure would be against the beneficiary's interests, excluding the Tribes' submissions to the Department from Exemption 5 would handicap the Department in doing what the law requires. And in much the same vein, the Department presses the argument that "FOIA is intended to cast light on existing government practices; it should not be interpreted and applied so as to compel federal agencies to perform their assigned substantive functions in other than the normal manner."

All of this boils down to requesting that we read an "Indian trust" exemption into the statute, a reading that is out of the question for reasons already explored. There is simply no support for the exemption in the statutory text, which we have elsewhere insisted be read strictly in order to serve FOIA's mandate of broad disclosure, which was obviously expected and intended to affect Government operations. In FOIA, after all, a new conception of Government conduct was enacted into law, " 'a general philosophy of full agency disclosure.' " *U.S. Department of Justice v. Tax Analysts*, 492 U.S., at 142 (quoting S.Rep. No. 813, 89th Cong., 1st Sess., 3 (1965)). "Congress believed that this philosophy, put into practice, would help 'ensure an informed citizenry, vital to the functioning of a democratic society.' " 492 U.S., at 142, (quoting *NLRB v. Robbins Tire & Rubber Co.*, 437 U.S. 214, 242 (1978)). Congress had to realize that not every secret under the old law would be secret under the new.

The judgment of the Court of Appeals is affirmed.

It is so ordered.

Questions and Comments

1. Did the Court believe that the Department of the Interior bore a Trust relation to the Tribe? Why did it not follow that communications between the Department and the Tribe should be kept confidential? Was it possible to reach this result under the Freedom of Information Act? Were there other ways of reaching that result?

2. Did fairness require the Department to release the communications from the Tribe to the other parties interested in allocation of water resources?

3. Is there a conflict between the Trust responsibilities of the Bureau of Indian Affairs and the regulatory authority over water uses of the Department of the Interior? Should the Bureau of Indian Affairs be separated from the Department of the Interior? Would such a separation eliminate or mitigate the conflict?

4. In the *Montrose* case, set forth below, the private party contended that it was being treated unfairly when it was not given access to internal agency documents that were used by the agency decision-maker in deciding to revoke the insecticide permit for DDT. How does the claim of the private parties in *Klamath* differ from the claim in *Montrose*? Is *Klamath* a stronger case for disclosure? Why? Is it stronger because the documents from the Tribe are essentially arguments asking the Department to decide water allocation issues adversely to other parties?

c.   *The FOIA, exemption 5, and litigation with an agency in conjunction with rulemaking.*

In ***American Radio Relay League, Inc. v. FCC***, 524 F.3d 227 (D.C. Cir. 2008), the League, acting on behalf of licensed amateur radio operators challenged a rule governing the use of the radio spectrum. In the League's view, the rule afforded insufficient protection for amateur radio operators. The League wanted access to staff reports on which the FCC relied in promulgating its rule, but which the Commission had not made available to the League. The court ruled that the League was entitled to that access under the provisions of § 553 of the APA. In so ruling, the court, drawing from the FOIA jurisprudence, rejected the agency's attempt to justify nondisclosure under a deliberative process rationale:

> The Commission's other bases for redaction and non-publication do not withstand analysis. The FOIA's deliberative process privilege, invoked by the Commission in responding to the League's FOIA request, "does not authorize an agency to throw a protective blanket over all information. . . . Purely factual reports and scientific studies cannot be cloaked in secrecy by an exemption designed to protect only those internal working papers in which opinions are expressed and policies formulated and recommended." *Bristol-Myers Co. v. Fed. Trade Comm'n*, 424 F.2d 935, 939 (D.C. Cir. 1970) (footnote and internal quotation marks omitted). By choosing "to adopt or incorporate by reference" the redacted studies, *NLRB v. Sears, Roebuck & Co.*, 421 U.S. 161, 95 S.Ct.1504, 44 L.Ed.2d 29 (1975), and thereby "us[ing] . . . [them] in its dealings with the public," *Coastal States Gas Corp. v. Dep't of Energy*, 617 F.2d 854, 866 (D.C. Cir. 1980), the Commission ceased treating them as internal working papers.

The Commission's reliance on *Vernal Enterprises, Inc. v. FCC*, 355 F.3d 650, 661 (D.C. Cir. 2004), for the proposition that an agency is not bound by the actions of its staff, is misplaced; unlike the refund rulings in that case, the redacted studies were neither unauthorized staff activities nor binding on the Commission.

MONTROSE CHEMICAL CORPORATION OF CALIFORNIA v. TRAIN
491 F.2d 63 (D.C. Cir. 1974)

WILKEY, CIRCUIT JUDGE:

In an action brought under the Freedom of Information Act [FOIA] Montrose Chemical Corporation is seeking to obtain two summaries of evidence developed at a hearing. . . .

[Hearings were held under the Federal Insecticide, Fungicide, and Rodenticide Act (FIFRA) on the insecticide DDT, the record of which reached 9200 pages. The hearing examiner entered findings and conclusions that all DDT registrations were in compliance with FIFRA. Normally, the case would have been reviewed by the judicial Officer. Because of the importance of the case, the EPA Administrator (William Ruckelshaus) withdrew the case from the Judicial Officer and ordered oral argument before a panel of himself and three other EPA officials (two high-level EPA attorneys and the Judicial Officer). The Administrator then reversed the hearing examiner, and entered an order directing the cancellation of the DDT registrations.]

In the course of his consideration of the case, Ruckelshaus sought the assistance of his staff. Specifically, he requested the three EPA attorneys who were to hear the oral argument with him, and who had not been connected with the EPA position at the hearings, to review the record made at the hearings and to direct the preparation of analyses of the evidence. Two documents which were prepared by the staff are at issue here: one entitled "Analysis of Risks Attributed to DDT," and the other "Summary and Analysis of Evidence of Benefits."

These documents were to be used only to assist Ruckelshaus in his study of the record, and were based wholly on evidence in the record of the hearings.

. . . . It is agreed that the summaries in question are in large part compilations of facts introduced in evidence at the hearings, and on the public record. Montrose contends that such factual materials must be disclosed under the prior decisions discussed above. In contrast, EPA contends that the mere compilation of a summary of the evidence on record, performed by staff members for the use of the Administrator in formulating his decision and final order, is itself a part of the internal deliberative process which should be kept confidential and within the agency. What will be disclosed here if the District Judge's order is upheld, argues the EPA, are not "facts" not yet possessed by Montrose Chemical Corporation, but rather the judgmental evaluation and condensation of the more than 10,000 pages of facts from which the Administrator gained an overview of the record in order to assist his decisionmaking. The only new "information" which disclosure of these summaries would provide Montrose concerns the mental processes of the agency — a process which Montrose is not entitled to probe.

This statement by EPA hits the heart of the issue here: Can Montrose use the FOIA to discover what factual information the Administrator's aides cited, discarded, compared, evaluated, and analyzed to assist the Administrator in formulating his decision? Or would such discovery be an improper probing of the mental processes behind a decision of an agency? These questions must be considered in the light of the statutory provisions of FIFRA, which requires the Administrator's decision cancelling pesticide registrations to be "based only on substantial evidence of record." Of equal importance, it must also be borne in mind that Ruckelshaus did render a 50-page decision, citing voluminous facts and statistics, and explained in detail the rationale of his, the Administrator's final decision. . . . If the exemption is intended to protect only deliberative *materials*, then a factual summary of evidence on the record would not be exempt from disclosure. But if the exemption is to be interpreted to protect the agency's *deliberative process*, then a factual summary prepared to aid an administrator in resolution of a difficult, complex question would be within the scope of the exemption.

The EPA assistants here were exercising their judgment as to what record evidence would be important to the Administrator in making his decision regarding the DDT registrations. Even if they cited portions of the evidence verbatim, the assistants were making an evaluation of the relative significance of the facts recited in the record; separating the pertinent from the impertinent is a judgmental process, sometimes of the highest order. . . .

Ruckelshaus' use of his assistants to winnow down the evidence was similar in many ways to a judge's use of his law clerk to sift through the report of a special master or other lengthy materials in the record. In most situations, when faced with a voluminous record, the decision-maker may wisely utilize his assistants to help him determine what materials will be significant in reaching a proper decision.

To probe the summaries of record evidence would be the same as probing the decision-making process itself. To require disclosure of the summaries would result in publication of the evaluation and analysis of the multitudinous facts made by the Administrator's aides and in turn studied by him in making his decision. Whether he weighed the correct factors, whether his judgmental scales were finely adjusted and delicately operated, disappointed litigants may not probe his deliberative process.

The use of the staff-prepared summaries by the Administrator does not conflict with his duty to decide the case on substantial evidence of record. Ruckelshaus has sworn in his affidavit that the summaries contain only evidence on the public record and analyses thereof. He was not using the summaries to obtain new facts not on the record. Thus the litigants and the public have already had full access to the record on which the decision was made, and what they are now seeking is the analysis of risks and benefits attributed to DDT made by the Administrator's aides to assist him in his ultimate decision. In effect, the litigants seek to know what advice as to importance and unimportance of facts the Administrator received, and how much of it he accepted. Such information is most emphatically *not* part of the public record. To argue, then, that the Administrator has not decided on a public record ignores the real question of what is the public record.

It is possible that the assistants in winnowing down the record may have made errors of inclusion or exclusion, or even gross distortions of fact. But these possibilities reflect human errors and misjudgments which are part of the deliberative process. The fact that errors may creep in and mislead the final decisionmaker merely suggests that there may be errors in the deliberative or adjudicatory process; it does not mean that the preliminary studies by the staff are separate from the adjudicatory process or should be classified as part of the public record. . . .

In reaching the conclusion that the documents here are exempt from disclosure, we do not reject the factual/deliberative test. . . . Instead, we develop that test to recognize that in some cases selection of facts or summaries may reflect a *deliberative process* which exemption 5 was intended to shelter. . . . Here . . . where all facts are already on the record, and where the summaries were used simply as an aid in decision-making, the exemption [5] applies; the order of the District Court requiring disclosure of parts of the summaries is therefore *Reversed.*

Questions and Comments

1. Why do you think the Montrose Chemical Co. wanted the summaries? Would they have used them in further rulemaking proceedings? On judicial review?

2. Did the Administrator's staff perform a function comparable to that performed by the staff of the Ohio Public Utilities Commission in the *Ohio Bell* case [supra, Chapter 4]? Explain.

3. What are the parallels between this case and *Ohio Bell?* With the *Morgan* cases? What are the differences? Why did the Administrator need staff help in sifting through the evidence? Did the staff focus the Administrator's attention on evidence of which Montrose was unaware? Is it an answer to the concerns of Montrose to point out that no evidence was brought to the attention of the Administrator that was not contained in the record? Did the staff focus the Administrator's attention on issues of which Montrose was unaware?

4. Was the DDT proceeding governed by the APA? By APA-like procedures? What procedural provisions worked to narrow the issues for decision? What procedural provisions lessened the analogy between this case and the *Ohio Bell* and *Morgan* cases?

5. Can the FOIA be used to discover studies in the possession of an agency that are relevant to the issues in a rulemaking proceeding? That the agency does not want introduced into the rulemaking record? Can the FOIA be used to discover staff policy recommendations which the agency has rejected? Followed?

6. Does APA § 553 provide a separate basis for obtaining material in the possession of an agency and relevant to issues raised in a rulemaking proceeding?

A Note on Exemption 6 of the FOIA

In Exemption 6, the FOIA exempts from disclosure:

> Personal and medical files and similar files the disclosure of which would constitute a clearly unwarranted invasion of personal privacy.

In ***United States Department of Defense v. Federal Labor Relations Authority***, 510 U.S. 487 (1994), a labor union sought the names and addresses of certain federal agency employees that it was seeking to organize. The agency, viz., the Department of Defense, refused and the Federal Labor Relations Authority that administers the labor law governing federal employees ordered the Department to provide the requested information. Under the governing statute, a federal agency is required to "furnish to the exclusive representative involved, or its authorized representative, upon request and, *to the extent not prohibited by law*, data . . . which is reasonably available and necessary for full and proper discussion, understanding, and negotiation of subjects within the scope of collective bargaining." § 7114(b)(4)(B). The federal Privacy Act (contained in § 552a of the Administrative Procedure Act) provides in part:

> "No agency shall disclose any record which is contained in a system of records by any means of communication to any person, or to another agency, except pursuant to a written request by, or with the prior written consent of, the individual to whom the record pertains, unless disclosure of the record would be . . . (2) required under section 552 of this title [FOIA]." 5 U.S.C. § 552a(b)(2) (1988 ed. and Supp. IV).

The FLRA sought enforcement of its order. In the ensuing litigation, the Supreme Court ruled that because § 7114(b)(4)(B) of the federal labor legislation exempted from disclosure information "prohibited by law," it subjected the labor legislation to the Privacy Act. The Privacy Act, in turn, made the determination of disclosure turn on the provisions of § 552. Thus the issue turned upon whether the disclosure by the Department of Defense to the labor union "would constitute a clearly unwarranted invasion of personal privacy," within the meaning of exemption 6. Whether the invasion of privacy would be "unwarranted" would, the Court thought, depend on a balance of the interest of the employee in privacy and the interest of the public in disclosure. An excerpt from the Court's opinion follows:

> First, in evaluating whether a request for information lies within the scope of a FOIA exemption, such as Exemption 6, that bars disclosure when it would amount to an invasion of privacy that is to some degree "unwarranted," "a court must balance the public interest in disclosure against the interest Congress intended the [e]xemption to protect." *Id.*, at 776. See also *Rose, supra*, 425 U.S., at 372.

> Second, the only relevant "public interest in disclosure" to be weighed in this balance is the extent to which disclosure would serve the "core purpose of the FOIA," which is "contribut[ing] significantly to public understanding *of the operations or activities of the government." Reporters Comm., supra*, 489 U.S., at 775 (internal quotation marks omitted). We elaborated on this point at some length:

"[FOIA's] basic policy of 'full agency disclosure unless information is exempted under clearly delineated statutory language,' indeed focuses on the citizens' right to be informed about what their government is up to. Official information that sheds light on an agency's performance of its statutory duties falls squarely within that statutory purpose. That purpose, however, is not fostered by disclosure of information about private citizens that is accumulated in various governmental files but that reveals little or nothing about an agency's own conduct." 489 U.S., at 773 (quoting *Rose, supra*, 425 U.S., at 360–361) (other internal quotation marks and citations omitted).

See also *Rose, supra*, 425 U.S., at 372 (Exemption 6 cases "require a balancing of the individual's right of privacy against the preservation of the basic purpose of [FOIA] to open agency action to the light of public scrutiny") (internal quotation marks omitted).

Third, "whether an invasion of privacy is *warranted* cannot turn on the purposes for which the request for information is made." *Reporters Comm.*, 489 U.S., at 771. Because "Congress 'clearly intended' the FOIA 'to give any member of the public as much right to disclosure as one with a special interest [in a particular document],' " *ibid.* (quoting *NLRB v. Sears, Roebuck & Co.*, 421 U.S. 132, 149 (1975)), except in certain cases involving claims of privilege, "the identity of the requesting party has no bearing on the merits of his or her FOIA request," 489 U.S., at 771.

The principles that we followed in *Reporters Committee* can be applied easily to this case. We must weigh the privacy interest of bargaining unit employees in nondisclosure of their addresses against the only relevant public interest in the FOIA balancing analysis — the extent to which disclosure of the information sought would "she[d] light on an agency's performance of its statutory duties" or otherwise let citizens know "what their government is up to." *Reporters Comm., supra*, 489 U.S., at 773 (internal quotation marks omitted; emphasis deleted).

The relevant public interest supporting disclosure in this case is negligible, at best. Disclosure of the addresses might allow the unions to communicate more effectively with employees, but it would not appreciably further "the citizens' right to be informed about what their government is up to." 489 U.S., at 773 (internal quotation marks omitted). Indeed, such disclosure would reveal little or nothing about the employing agencies or their activities. Even the Fifth Circuit recognized that "[r]elease of the employees' . . . addresses would not in any meaningful way open agency action to the light of public scrutiny." 975 F.2d, at 1113.

The approach to disclosure taken in the *Department of Defense* case was followed in *Bibles v. Oregon Natural Desert Ass'n*, 519 U.S. 355 (1997). In *Bibles*, the Court ruled that exemption 6 shielded the Bureau of Land Management when it refused to disclose a mailing list to an environmental organization. The court below had ruled in favor of disclosure because there was a "substantial public interest in knowing to whom the government is directing information, or as the ONDA characterizes it, 'propaganda.' so that those persons may receive information from other sources that do not share the BLM's self-interest in presenting government activities in the most favorable light." The Court reversed the decision below on the ground that "the only relevant public interest in the FOIA balancing analysis" is "the extent to which disclosure of the information sought would 'she[d] light on an agency's performance of its statutory duties' or otherwise let citizens know 'what the government is up to.' "

2.   *Advisory committees and other forms of public participation.*

ASSOCIATION OF AMERICAN PHYSICIANS AND SURGEONS, INC. v. HILLARY RODHAM CLINTON
997 F.2d 898 (D.C. Cir. 1993)

SILBERMAN, CIRCUIT JUDGE:

This expedited appeal presents the question whether the President's Task Force on National Health Care Reform ("Task Force") and its working group are advisory committees for purposes of the Federal Advisory Committee Act ("FACA"). If they are, we are asked to decide whether FACA unconstitutionally encroaches on the President's Article II executive powers. We hold that the Task Force is not an advisory group subject to FACA, but remand to the district court for further proceedings to determine the status of the working group.

I

On January 25, 1993, President Clinton established the President's Task Force on National Health Care Reform. The President named his wife, Hillary Rodham Clinton, as the chairman of the Task Force, and appointed as its other members the Secretaries of the Treasury, Defense, Veterans Affairs, Health and Human Services, Labor, and Commerce Departments, the Director of the Office of Management and Budget, the chairman of the Council of Economic Advisers, and three White House advisers. President Clinton charged this body with the task of "listen[ing] to all parties" and then "prepar[ing] health care reform legislation to be submitted to Congress within 100 days of our taking office." . . .

On the same day, the President also announced the formation of an interdepartmental working group. According to the government, the working group was responsible for gathering information and developing various options on health care reform. It was composed of three types of members: (i) approximately 300 permanent federal government employees drawn from the Executive Office of the President, the federal agencies, and Congress; (ii) about 40 "special government employees" hired by the agencies and the Executive Office of the President for a limited duration; and (iii) an unknown number of "consultants" who, it is asserted, "attend working group meetings on an intermittent basis." Ira Magaziner, the senior adviser to the President for Policy Development, headed the working group and was the only member of the Task Force who attended the group's meetings.

*Working group gathered info +
developed policy
for Task Force*
↓
*Task Force proposed
leg. to President*

According to the government, the working group had no contact with the President. In addition to gathering information, the working group developed alternative health care policies for use by the Task Force. But only the Task Force, it was contemplated, would directly advise and present recommendations to the President. On March 29, 1993, the Task Force held one public hearing where interested parties could present comments on health care reform. See 58 Fed.Reg. 16,264 (1993). However, the Task Force met behind closed doors at least 20 times in April and May to "formulate" and "deliberate" on its advice to the President. As the government publicly has announced, in those meetings "the Task Force reviewed materials it received from the interdepartmental working group; formulated proposals and options for health care reform; and presented those proposals and options to the President." Statement of the White House Press Secretary (June 4, 1993). In accordance with its charter, the Task Force then terminated its operations on May 30.[2] All of the working group's meetings remained closed to the public.

*plaintiffs
seek access
to Task Force
meetings*

→ Appellees are the Association of American Physicians and Surgeons, which represents physicians; the American Council for Health Care Reform, which represents health care consumers; and the National Legal & Policy Center, which seeks to promote ethics in government. They sought access to the Task Force's meetings under the Federal Advisory Committee Act. Pub.L. No. 92-463, 86 Stat. 770 (1972) (reproduced at 5 U.S.C.App. 1 (1988)). Their efforts were rebuffed by the Counsel to the President, who informed them that the Task Force was not an advisory committee subject to FACA.

*President says
Task Force
not an
advisory comm*

→ Appellees thereupon brought suit against the Task Force in district court. They claimed that the Task Force was a FACA committee because it was chaired by Mrs. Clinton, a private citizen, and that the Task Force had violated FACA by failing to file an advisory committee charter. They further asserted that FACA permitted them to attend all of the meetings of the Task Force and of any of its subgroups. Appellees sought a temporary restraining order and a preliminary injunction halting the operation of the Task Force until it complied with FACA and allowed the public to attend its meetings. . . .

III

Congress passed FACA in 1972 to control the growth and operation of the "numerous committees, boards, commissions, councils, and similar groups which have been established to advise officers and agencies in the executive branch of the Federal Government." 5 U.S.C. App. 2, § 2(a). As Congress put it, FACA's purpose was: to eliminate unnecessary advisory committees; to limit the formation of new committees to the minimum number necessary; to keep the function of the committees advisory in nature; to hold the committees to uniform standards and procedures; and to keep Congress and the public informed of their activities. *See*

---

[2] The Task Force's "termination" does not render this case moot. As both parties, in anticipation of this event, agreed before oral argument, this case still presents a live controversy concerning the availability of Task Force and working group documents, which the appellees sought below pursuant to FACA.

id. § 2(b)(1)-(6). The statute orders agency heads to promulgate guidelines and regulations to govern the administration and operations of advisory committees. *See id.* § 8.

FACA places a number of restrictions on the advisory committees themselves. Before it can meet or take any action, a committee first must file a detailed charter, *see id.* § 9(c). The committee must give advance notice in the Federal Register of any meetings, see id. § 10(a)(2); and it must hold all meetings in public, *see id.* § 10(a)(1). Under section 10, the committee must keep detailed minutes of each meeting, *see id.* § 10(c), and make the records available — along with any reports, records, or other documents used by the committee — to the public, provided they do not fall within the exemptions of the Freedom of Information Act (FOIA), *see id.* § 10(b). Under section 5, an advisory committee established by the President or by legislation must be "fairly balanced in terms of the points of view represented," *id.* § 5(b)(2).[3] The Act also requires that precautions be taken to ensure that the advice and recommendations of the committee "will not be inappropriately influenced by the appointing authority or by any special interest." *Id.* § 5(b)(3).

The Act's definition of an "advisory" committee is apparently rather sweeping. Section 3 states:

> The term "advisory committee" means any committee, board, commission, council, conference, panel, task force, or other similar group, or any subcommittee or other subgroup thereof (hereinafter in this paragraph referred to as "committee"), which is . . . (B) established or utilized by the President . . . in the interest of obtaining advice or recommendations for the President or one or more agencies or officers of the Federal Government.

Id. § 3(2). The government does not contend that the Task Force was not "established" or "utilized" by the President in the interest of obtaining advice or recommendations. FACA's definition contains one important proviso, however. Section 3(2)(iii) exempts "any committee which is composed wholly of full-time officers or employees of the Federal Government." And, according to the government, the Task Force was not only wholly composed of government officers, it was actually (like the Task Force we encountered in *Meyer v. Bush,* 981 F.2d 1288 (D.C.Cir.1993)) a partial, yet somewhat augmented, cabinet grouping. Thus, subjecting the Task Force to FACA would fall outside Congress' purpose of regulating the growth and use of committees composed of outsiders called in to advise government officials. Appellees would have no quarrel with the government's characterization of the Task Force, except for the description of its chairman, Mrs. Clinton. Appellees contend that she is not an officer or employee of the federal government despite her traditional and ceremonial status as "First Lady." This is not just a technicality according to appellees; she is statutorily barred from appointment as an officer because of the Anti-Nepotism Act. See 5 U.S.C. § 3110(b).

. . . .

---

[3] FACA's "balanced viewpoint" requirement may not be justiciable, however, because it does not provide a standard that is susceptible of judicial application. See Public Citizen v. National Advisory Comm., 886 F.2d 419, 426 (D.C.Cir.1989) (Silberman, J., concurring).

[handwritten margin note: First lady essentially an assistant to the Pres.]

More persuasive, however, is the government's argument that *Congress* itself has recognized that the President's spouse acts as the functional equivalent of an assistant to the President. The legislative authorization to the President to pay his White House aides includes the following provision:

> Assistance and services authorized pursuant to this section to the President are authorized to be provided to *the spouse of the President in connection with assistance provided by such spouse to the President in the discharge of the President's duties and responsibilities.* If the President does not have a spouse, such assistance and services may be provided for such purposes to a member of the President's family whom the President designates.

3 U.S.C. § 105(e) (emphasis added). Of course, even without section 105(e), the President presumably could draw upon his spouse for assistance. The statute's importance, rather, lies in its assistance in helping us interpret the ambiguous terms of FACA *in pari materia.*

. . . .

[handwritten margin note: re: antinepotism act]

The President's implicit authority to enlist his spouse in aid of the discharge of his federal duties also undermines appellees' claim that treating the President's spouse as an officer or employee would violate the anti-nepotism provisions of 5 U.S.C. § 3110. . . . The anti-nepotism statute . . . may well bar appointment only to paid positions in government. See 5 U.S.C. § 3110(c). Thus, even if it would prevent the President from putting his spouse on the federal payroll, it does not preclude his spouse from aiding the President in the performance of his duties.

. . . .

Suffice it to say that the question whether Mrs. Clinton's membership on the Task Force triggers FACA is not an easy one. The government argues, therefore, that we should construe the statute not to apply here, because otherwise we would face a serious constitutional issue. The Supreme Court has noted many times that "where an otherwise acceptable construction of a statute would raise serious constitutional problems, the Court will construe the statute to avoid such problems unless such construction is plainly contrary to the intent of Congress." . . .

We do think that the government's alternative, albeit implicit, argument is more persuasive. Application of FACA to the Task Force clearly would interfere with the President's capacity to solicit direct advice on *any* subject related to his duties from a group of private citizens, separate from or together with his closest governmental associates. That advice might be sought on a broad range of issues in an informal or formal fashion. Presidents have created advisory groups composed of private citizens (sometimes in conjunction with government officials) to meet periodically and advise them (hence the phrase "kitchen cabinets") on matters such as the conduct of a war. Presidents have even created formal "cabinet committees" composed in part of private citizens. This case is no different. Here, the President has formed a committee of his closest advisers — cabinet secretaries, White House advisers, and his wife — to advise him on a domestic issue he considers of the utmost priority.

Applying FACA to the Task Force does not raise constitutional problems simply because the Task Force is involved in proposing legislation. Instead, difficulties arise because of the Task Force's operational proximity to the President himself — that is, because the Task Force provides advice and recommendations directly to the President. The Supreme Court has recognized that a President has a great need to receive advice confidentially:

> [There is a] valid need for protection of communications between high Government officials and those who advise and assist them in the performance of their manifold duties; the importance of this confidentiality is too plain to require further discussion. Human experience teaches that those who expect public dissemination of their remarks may well temper candor with a concern for appearances and for their own interests to the detriment of the decisionmaking process. Whatever the nature of the privilege of confidentiality of Presidential communications in the exercise of Art. II powers, the privilege can be said to derive from the supremacy of each branch within its own assigned area of constitutional duties.

United States v. Nixon, 418 U.S. 683, 705–06, 94 S.Ct. 3090, 3106, 41 L.Ed.2d 1039 (1974) (footnotes omitted). . . .

This Article II right to confidential communications attaches not only to direct communications with the President, but also to discussions between his senior advisers. Certainly Department Secretaries and White House aides must be able to hold confidential meetings to discuss advice they secretly will render to the President. . . .

A statute interfering with a President's ability to seek advice directly from private citizens as a group, intermixed, or not, with government officials, therefore raises Article II concerns. This is all the more so when the sole ground for asserting that the statute applies is that the President's own spouse, a member of the Task Force, is not a government official. For if the President seeks advice from those closest to him, whether in or out of government, the President's spouse, typically, would be regarded as among those closest advisers.

. . . .

We believe it is the Task Force's operational *proximity* to the President, and not its exact function at any given moment, that implicates executive powers and therefore forces consideration of the *Morrison* [*Morrison v. Olson*, 487 U.S. 654 (1988)], test. . . . We follow the Supreme Court's lead, if not its strict precedent, in recognizing that [if the Act] were "[r]ead unqualifiedly, it would extend FACA's requirements to any group of two or more persons, or at least any formal organization, from which the President or an executive agency seeks advice." . . .

We, therefore, read the phrase "full-time officer or employee of the government" in FACA to apply to Mrs. Clinton. In doing so, we express no view as to her status under any other statute.

IV

. . . .

The district court accepted a variation of the government's argument by concluding that the working group was not really a subgroup of the Task Force within the meaning of FACA, but rather only staff to the Task Force. . . .

Our conclusion that the Task Force is a committee wholly composed of government officials makes this case entirely different. In contrast to the situation here, in *Anti-Hunger* [*National Anti-Hunger Coalition v. Executive Committee*, 711 F.2d 1071 (D.C. Cir. 1983)] the top levels of the *outside* advisory groups were covered by FACA — both the executive committee of 150 and the subcommittee of 30. In that scenario, there is less reason to focus on subordinate advisers or consultants who are presumably under the control of the superior groups. It is the superior groups, after all, that will give the advice to the government, and which, in accordance with the statute, must be "reasonably" balanced. But when the Task Force itself is considered part of the government — due to the government officials exemption — we must consider more closely FACA's relevance to the working group. For it is the working group now that is the point of contact between the public and the government. . . .

The point, it seems to us, is that a group is a FACA advisory committee when it is asked to render advice or recommendations, *as a group*, and not as a collection of individuals. The group's activities are expected to, and appear to, benefit from the interaction among the members both internally and externally. Advisory committees not only provide ideas to the government, they also often bestow political legitimacy on that advice. . . .

Finally, the government claims that all of the members of the working groups are full-time officers or employees of the government, and, for that reason alone, the working groups are not FACA advisory committees. The three-hundred members drawn from the agencies, the Executive Office of the President, and from the congressional staffs are concededly within that category. . . .

A third class of persons are described as consultants. According to the government, the consultants attend meetings on an intermittent basis, with or without compensation, and have no "supervisory role or decision-making authority." Drawn from the ranks of the medical profession, the academy, and from business, they only provide information and opinion. These consultants raise a different question from that presented by the other . . . classes of working group employees. The key issue, it seems to us, is not whether these consultants are "full-time" government employees under section 3(2), but whether they can be considered members of the working group at all. When an advisory committee of wholly government officials brings in a "consultant" for a one-time meeting, FACA is not triggered because the consultant is not really a member of the advisory committee. . . .

But a consultant may still be properly described as a member of an advisory committee if his involvement and role are functionally indistinguishable from those of the other members. . . . If a "consultant" regularly attends and fully participates in working group meetings as if he were a "member," he should be regarded as a member. Then his status as a private citizen would disqualify the working group from the section 3(2) exemption for meetings of full-time government officials.

. . . .

We simply have insufficient material in the record to determine the character of the working group and its members. We understand why the district court, believing the Task Force covered by FACA, thought it unnecessary and inappropriate to put the working group under further scrutiny. But, as we have indicated, because we differ with the district court concerning the Task Force, we believe further proceedings, including expedited discovery, are necessary before the district court can confidently decide whether the working group is a FACA committee.

Accordingly, we reverse the district court and lift the preliminary injunction on the operations of the Task Force. The Task Force need not comply with the requirements of FACA because it is a committee composed wholly of full-time government officials. We also reverse the district court's dismissal of appellees' claims as to the working group under Rule 12(b)(6). We remand for further proceedings, including expedited discovery, regarding the working group.

So ordered.

In re Cheney, 406 F.3d 723 (D.C. Cir. 2005). Shortly after taking office, President George W. Bush issued a memorandum establishing the National Energy Policy Development Group (NEPDG) and charged it with developing a national energy policy. The President named Vice President Cheney chairman and assigned cabinet secretaries and other federal officials to serve with the Vice President. The NEPDG issued its final report five months later. It ceased to exist as of September 30, 2001.

Two organizations, Judicial Watch and the Sierra Club filed actions seeking NEPDG documents on the ground that the group was an "advisory committee" within the meaning of the Federal Advisory Committee Act. The only officials the President named to the NEPDG were federal officials. To avoid the exemption in § 3(2) of the FACA, Judicial Watch alleged, on information and belief, that non-federal employees "fully participated in non-public meetings of the NEPDG as if they were members of the NEPDG and, in fact, were members of the NEPDG." Sierra Club claimed that the NEPDG and "Task Force Sub-Groups were not composed wholly of full time officers or employees of the federal government," apparently because "[e]nergy industry executives, including multiple representatives of single energy companies, and other non-federal employees, attended meetings and participated in activities of [the NEPDG] and Task Force Sub-Groups."

Plaintiffs sought broad discovery and the government moved for dismissal. There followed extensive litigation, including review by the Supreme Court. See *Cheney v. U.S. District Court*, 542 U.S. 367 (2004). On remand from the Supreme Court, the D.C. Circuit issued a writ of mandamus to the district court, directing the action be dismissed.

Questions and Comments

1. The Federal Advisory Committee Act is set out in the Appendix. Advisory Committees are frequently used by federal agencies. How did the Task Force on National Health Care Reform differ from typical advisory committees employed by federal agencies?

2. How did the court's determination of the application of the Advisory Committee Act to the Task Force affect the way it approached the working group? When is a government consultant subject to the Act?

3. In addition to the suits brought by Judicial Watch and the Sierra Club, the General Accounting Office (GAO) also brought suit to uncover the documents of the NEPDG. The GAO's suit, however was dismissed for lack of standing in December 2002. Walker v. Cheney, 230 F.Supp.2d 51 (D.D.C. 2002).

4. In the case involving Vice President Cheney, the district court held that the Federal Advisory Committee Act does not create an independent private cause of action. As a result, plaintiffs asserting rights under the FACA were required to assert them under the APA.

5. Observe how the issues differed in the *Cheney* case from those in the *Hillary Clinton* case. But note the sensitivity, in both cases, of issues involving the President's ability to seek advice. How did the issue of the President's right to solicit advice come up in the *Hillary Clinton* case? In that case, the court ruled that the President's spouse was a federal official. In *Cheney* the plaintiffs sought to prove that energy executives were de facto members of the advisory committee, thus making the exemption for committees composed entirely of federal employees inapplicable. The plaintiffs, however, lost because they were unable to conduct the discovery necessary to establish their case.

B. AN ARRAY OF PROCEDURAL PROBLEMS UNDER THE NEW PARADIGM OF ADMINISTRATIVE DECISION-MAKING

Under the model of rulemaking and rulemaking review that developed in the 1970s, the administrative record plays an important role. Since — under *Overton Park* — judicial review takes place on the administrative record, the content of that record is critical for judicial review. For informal rulemaking, the administrative record is the comment record, generated pursuant to § 553. Moreover, this judicial review format effectively controls the structure of decision-making at the agency level. Agencies engaged in informal rulemaking must make their decisions on the comment record and justify those decisions on that record.

This new emphasis on deciding on the comment record in § 553 proceedings introduces a new note of formality into proceedings that are generally described as "informal" rulemaking. Indeed, the question now arises: what distinguishes informal rulemaking under § 553 from "formal" rulemaking under §§ 556 and 557?

1) An Early (1977) Scenario: Home Box Office

An early and famous case to confront that issue was *Home Box Office, Inc. v. Federal Communications Commission,* 567 F.2d 9 (D.C. Cir. 1977), *cert. denied,* 434 U.S. 829 (1977). In that case the Federal Communications Commission was considering rules setting limits on the programming that cable providers might carry. These rules thus would effectively define the scope of competition between broadcast television and cable television. During the rulemaking proceedings representatives of both the cable companies and the network broadcasters had met privately with various Commissioners. When these ex parte meetings came to the attention of the Court of Appeals for the District of Columbia Circuit, the court expressed concern that the content of the FCC rules might be determined by a compromise among the contending cable and broadcast industries that was accepted by the Commission. The court thought that the rules should be determined on the record where the Commission's decision could be reviewed on that record. An excerpt from the court's opinion is set forth below:

> Although it is impossible to draw any firm conclusions about the effect of *ex parte* presentations upon the ultimate shape of the pay cable rules, the evidence is certainly consistent with often-voiced claims of undue industry influence over Commission proceedings, and we are particularly concerned that the final shaping of the rules we are reviewing here may have been by compromise among the contending industry forces, rather than by exercise of the independent discretion in the public interest the Communications Act vests in individual commissioners. . . . Our concern is heightened by the submission of the Commission's Broadcast Bureau to this court which states that in December 1974 broadcast representatives "described the kind of pay cable regulation that, in their view, broadcasters 'could live with.' " If actual positions were not revealed in public comments, as this statement would suggest, and, further, if the Commission relied on these apparently more candid private discussions in framing the final pay cable rules, then the elaborate public discussion in these dockets has been reduced to a sham.

> Even the possibility that there is here one administrative record for the public and this court and another for the Commission and those "in the know" is intolerable. . . . As a practical matter, *Overton Park's* mandate means that the public record must reflect what representations were made to an agency so that relevant information supporting or refuting those representations may be brought to the attention of the reviewing courts by persons participating in the agency proceedings. This course is obviously foreclosed if communications are made to the agency in secret and the agency itself does not disclose the information presented. Moreover, where, as here, an agency justified its actions by reference only to information in the public file while failing to disclose the substance of other relevant information that has been presented to it, a reviewing court cannot presume that the agency has acted property, *Citizens to Preserve Overton Park, Inc. v. Volpe, supra,* 401 U.S. at 415, 91 S.Ct. 814; see K. Davis, Administrative Law of the Seventies § 11-00 at 317 (1976), but must treat the agency's justifications as a fictional account of the actual decisionmak-

ing process and must perforce find its actions arbitrary. . . .

In its decision condemning the ex parte contacts by industry representatives, the court appeared to be especially troubled by the fact that the Commission rules would be "allocating valuable privileges among competing private parties." i.e., between the cable and broadcast industries. In a circumstance in which informal rulemaking allocates valuable economic benefits between contending private parties, there are reasons of fairness why each party should be able to know and to respond to the data, other input and contentions of the other. Although the HBO court treated the informal rulemaking before it as if it were subject to all of the restrictions applicable to formal rulemaking (i.e., rulemaking governed by §§ 556 and 557), that decision probably can be best understood as limited to the context in which opposing private parties contend for a valuable privilege. So understood, it follows an earlier decision that the same court made in a similar context. That earlier decision was:

Sangamon Valley Telev. Corp. v. United States, 294 E2d 742 (D.C. Cir. 1961); 269 F.2d 221 (D.C. Cir. 1959). In its decision of the *Home Box Office* case, the court placed substantial reliance upon an earlier decision of the same Circuit in *Sangamon Valley Telev. Corp. v. United States*. The problem that the FCC was dealing with in Sangamon was how to expand the number of broadcast channels on television. During the 1950s most television broadcasts used the "very high frequency" (or VHF) channels that appear as channels 12 and below on standard television sets. Because reception on the ultra high frequency (or UHF) channels was often of poorer quality than that on the VHF channels, broadcasters were reluctant to broadcast on the UHF channels. In an effort to encourage the use of UHF channels (and thereby to develop a larger number of channels), the Commission adopted a so-called "deintermixture" policy: Under that policy, the Commission was reallocating frequency bands so that UHF and VHF signals would not be broadcast to the same areas. Underlying this policy was the notion that the public would not watch UHF channels if VHF broadcasts were available.

The Commission, acting under § 553, held notice-and-comment proceedings incident to reassigning outstanding frequencies. Signal Hill at that time owned a station in St. Louis and was then broadcasting on UHF channel 36. Tenenbaum, Signal Hill's president wanted the Commission to reallocate VHF channel 2 from Springfield, Illinois to St. Louis, where Signal Hill would have a good chance of getting it. Tenenbaum not only spoke privately with the Commissioners about reallocating Channel 2 to St. Louis, but seven weeks after the end of an extended comment period Tenenbaum wrote each Commissioner a letter in which he contended and tried to prove that "Channel 2, based in St. Louis, would reach 166,700 more homes in the state of Illinois than if it were based in Springfield, Illinois."

The District of Columbia Court of Appeals condemned Tenenbaum's *ex parte* communications with the Commissioners, rejecting the contention of Signal Hill and the Commission that "because the proceeding . . . was 'rulemaking' *ex parte* attempts to influence the Commissioners did not invalidate it." Rather, the Court agreed with the position then taken by the Department of Justice that "whatever the proceeding may be called it involved not only allocation of TV channels among communities but also resolution of conflicting private claims to a valuable privilege, and that basic fairness requires such a proceeding to be carried on in the open."

Because VHF channels were commercially more valuable than UHF channels, broadcast licensees were vitally interested in whether their area would be assigned VHF or UHF channels. Although the proceeding was technically informal rulemaking, it allocated commercially valuable rights to geographic areas with the foreseeable result that the private broadcasters in the benefited areas would succeed to those rights. In these circumstances, Tenenbaum's post-comment period submission about the Illinois coverage of Channel 2 from a St. Louis base prejudiced his rivals, because they had no way of knowing of his submission and hence no way of responding to it. As the Court's opinion suggested, *Sangamon* was contemporaneously understood as an exception to the procedure normally applicable to notice-and-comment rulemaking, an exception applicable to the rare case in which informal rulemaking allocated valuable privileges among contending private interests.

Questions and Comments

1.   Would you say that the court in the *HBO* case imposed an exclusiveness-of-the-record principle upon informal rulemaking? Does not an exclusiveness-of-the-record principle govern formal rulemaking? under what section of the APA? Does that section apply to informal rulemaking?

2.   Does the Supreme Court take the view that informal rulemaking should be reviewed on the administrative record? What cases are you relying upon for your answer to the preceding question? Is the administrative record upon which judicial review is to take place the same as the comment record? Does this approach presuppose that the comment record is the exclusive record for decision?

3.   Does not the *HBO* case merely apply the presupposition underlying some judicial decisions that the comment record in an informal rulemaking proceeding is the exclusive record for decision?

4.   Does the *HBO* case impose constraints upon informal rulemaking which are similar to those which the APA imposes upon formal rulemaking? Has it equated informal and formal rulemaking procedures? To what extent does *HBO* impose constraints upon informal rulemaking which are stricter than an exclusiveness-of-the-record principle would impose? Explain.

5.   Is the *HBO* decision consistent with the Supreme Court's *Vermont Yankee* decision? Does the *HBO* decision impose stricter procedures upon an agency than are required by the APA? Would the last question be answered in the same way by the drafters of the APA and the Justices of the present Court?

6.   Was the *HBO* decision limited to cases like *Sangamon* where private interests were contending for valuable privileges? If so, what constraints imposed on the FCC by the HBO decision would be inapplicable to rulemaking which did not involve such a clash of private interests?

Note: Other Judicial Attempts to Force Agency Decisionmaking Into Formal Structures

In both *HBO* and *Sangamon*, the courts condemned interaction between an agency and interested persons which took place outside of the formal procedures. At the time of the *Sangamon* decision it was generally understood that notice-and-comment procedures were designed primarily to educate an agency about contemplated rulemaking action; and that, accordingly, informal contacts were generally not improper. By reconceptualizing *Sangamon* as a proceeding in which conflicting private interests were vying for valuable privileges, the court reached its conclusion that Tenenbaum's *exparte* contacts were unlawful.

In the *HBO* case the court recognized that informal contacts between the agency and those whom it regulates are the "bread and butter" of the administrative process. Yet it condemned informal contacts during rulemaking. Even though the rulemaking was of the § 553 variety, the court insisted that all input be on the record. The *HBO* opinion can be explained as a replay of *Sangamon*, as the court itself indicated. But the court also expressed concern that the relationship between the FCC and the television industry might be too cozy. Indeed, the court wanted the FCC's decision about restrictions on cable TV to be the result of the FCC's informed discretion as to how the public interest would be best furthered, and not the result of compromise among affected industry segments which the FCC ratified. This unease about the FCC's role was reflected in the court's insistence that the FCC's decision be based exclusively upon the record and not be influenced by any *ex parte* contact.

Other cases also evidence a suspicion that regulatory agencies have become too close to the industry which they are charged with regulating; and have sought to remedy this concern by compelling agencies to abandon negotiation and to substitute formal hearing procedures in their place. In *Moss v. CAB*, **430 F.2d 891 (D.C. Cir. 1970)**, for example, the court disapproved of a procedure employed by the Civil Aeronautics Board to set rates for air carriers. Under the then governing statute, an air carrier could file a rate schedule (tariff) with the Board. On complaint or on its own initiative, the Board could suspend the new rate for 180 days while it investigated the rate. After investigation and hearing the Board could prescribe the lawful rate. The Board could also, on its own motion or on complaint, change an existing rate after notice and hearing. But if a carrier filed a new rate and the Board did not object to it, the rate would go into effect without a hearing. In *Moss*, several major air carriers filed rate increases. Following the filing, the Board conducted private meetings with representatives of the carriers, during which the Board presumably discussed the carriers' rate situation with them. The Board then suspended the filed rates but indicated in its order that if the carriers filed smaller rate increases, the Board would not object and that the rates would go into effect. The carriers took the hint; they refiled with smaller increases; and the Board allowed the new rates to become effective. In a suit brought by Congressman Moss and other congressmen, Judge Wright (writing for the District of Columbia Circuit) ruled that by inducing the carriers to file rates which the Board would not oppose, the Board evaded the statutory requirement that the Board set rates only after a hearing. Judge Wright made it clear that he was concerned that the procedure used by the Board excluded public input and participation; probably he worried that the relationship between the Board and the carriers was too close.

D.C. Federation of Civic Associations v. Volpe, **459 F.2d 1231 (D.C. Cir. 1971),** *cert. denied,* **405 U.S. 1030 (1972)** involved the effect of political pressure on administrative decisionmaking. That case involved a challenge to the approval, by the Secretary of Transportation, of the expenditure of federal funds for the construction of a bridge across the Potomac River. Since the bridge would traverse parkland and affect the Georgetown historic district, the Secretary's approval had to be based, under the governing statute, on a determination that there was "no feasible and prudent alternative" to the use of that land. During the period concerned Congressman Natcher (who was Chairman of the Subcommittee on the District of Columbia) indicated that he would use his position to withhold money for the construction of the District of Columbia's subway system until the bridge plan went forward. Judge Bazelon asserted, in his opinion, that the Secretary's approval would be invalid if based in whole or in part on pressures generated by Congressman Natcher. In Bazelon's view, if the Secretary had been influenced by the congressman's pressure, the Secretary's decision would not have been based solely upon relevant factors and hence would fail the test for nonarbitrary decision-making set out in Supreme Court's *Overton Park* opinion. [supra, Chapter 2].

2) To What Extent is the Comment Record Exclusive?

NATIONAL MINING ASSOCIATION v. CHAO
160 F.Supp.2d 47 (D.D.C. 2001),
affirmed in part and reversed in part,
292 F.3d 849 (D.C. Cir. 2002)

MEMORANDUM OPINION & ORDER

SULLIVAN, District Judge.

INTRODUCTION

Plaintiffs commenced this action for declaratory judgment and injunctive relief and request this Court to enjoin the enforcement of final regulations issued by the defendants on December 20, 2000. The regulations are published at 65 Federal Register 79920-80107 under Title IV of the Federal Coal Mine Health and Safety Act of 1969 as amended, 30 U.S.C. §§ 901-945, also known as the Black Lung Benefits Act("BLBA"). The BLBA provides benefits "to coal miners who are totally disabled due to pneumoconiosis and to the surviving dependents of miners whose death was due to such disease." 30 U.S.C. § 901(a).

[handwritten margin note: seeking inj. to enjoin regulations]

* * * *

THE PARTIES

Plaintiffs are the National Mining Association, the national trade association for the U.S. mining industry, the Old Republic Insurance Company, National Union Fire Insurance Company of Pittsburgh, Pennsylvania, and American Mining Insurance Company, commercial insurance carriers, the Ohio Valley Coal Company, an underground coal operator, and the American Iron & Steel Institute, a trade association whose members have or had financial interests in coal mines.

Defendants are Elaine L. Chao, Secretary of Labor, and the United States Department of Labor ("DOL"). The Secretary of Labor is authorized by the BLBA to issue regulations governing the administration of the BLBA. The DOL has principal responsibility for the implementation and administration of the BLBA.

Intervenors are the United Mine Workers of America, a labor union, the National Black Lung Association, an advocacy group representing current and retired coal miners, Mike South, a former coal miner, a clinic that provides screening, diagnostic and other services to patients with black lung disease, and several current or prospective claimants for benefits.

BACKGROUND

I. Facts Giving Rise to this Litigation

On January 22, 1997, the DOL issued a notice of proposed revisions to the BLBA regulations. 62 Fed.Reg. 3338–3435 (Jan. 22, 1997) (Admin. Record Doc. No. 00001). The DOL allowed interested parties until March 24, 1997 to file comments. That deadline was extended twice. . . .

* * * *

V. Count VII: Inadequacy of the Rulemaking Record

Plaintiffs challenge the adequacy of the DOL's rulemaking proceeding because, plaintiffs allege, the DOL failed to submit the entire record for public comment. More specifically, plaintiffs complain that the consultants hired by the DOL relied on studies that were not part of the public record.

Defendants assert that the complained-of reports (Admin Record Doc. Nos. 01017, 01019, 01025, 01026) were prepared by two physicians to assist the DOL in evaluating medical issues related to the proposed rules. One report (Admin. Record Doc. No. 01016) was prepared by an economist to assist the DOL in preparing the small business impact analysis that it was required to publish with the final regulations pursuant to the Regulatory Flexibility Act, 5 U.S.C. §§ 601-609. Defendants argue that the use of expert consultant reports like these does not violate the rulemaking procedural requirements of either the APA or the

Regulatory Flexibility Act.

The procedural requirements for the promulgation of regulations under the APA are clear.[4] An agency is first required to publish in the Federal Register a "[g]eneral notice of proposed rule making." 5 U.S.C. § 553(b). It is then required to "give interested persons an opportunity to participate in the rule making through the submission of written data, views, or arguments with or without an opportunity for oral presentation." 5 U.S.C. § 553(c). "After consideration of the relevant matter presented," the agency must "incorporate in the rules adopted a concise general statement of their basis and purpose." *Id.* Evidentiary-type hearings are not required for informal rulemaking. *Vermont Yankee Nuclear Power Corp. v. Natural Resources Defense Council*, 435 U.S. 519, 543–48, 98 S.Ct. 1197, 55 L.Ed.2d 460 (1978).

It is well settled that "in the informal rulemaking context private technical consultants may assist the agency in analyzing record data without running afoul" of the APA's procedural requirements. *Nat'l Small Shipments Traffic Conference, Inc. v. ICC*, 725 F.2d 1442, 1449 (D.C.Cir.1984). "Because such consultants operate as the functional equivalent of regular staff, they constitute agency insiders" and therefore "no improper contact between administrative personnel and outside parties ever arises." *Id.*

In *United Steelworkers of America v. Marshall*, 647 F.2d 1189 (D.C.Cir.1980), the D.C. Circuit rejected an objection to the use of consultants' reports similar to the one urged by plaintiffs here. In that case, the plaintiff complained that, "[a]fter closing the record," the DOL "sought help from outside consultants in reviewing the record and preparing the Preamble" for new workplace-safety regulations. *Id.* at 1217. The court held that the plaintiff could not show that it had been "prejudiced" by not having an opportunity to comment on the reports, because the plaintiff failed to establish that (a) the consultants' reports contained "any hard data or new legal arguments" which had not previously been made available for comment in the notice of proposed rulemaking, and (b) the DOL had "demonstrably relied" on this new information "in setting the standard" to which the plaintiff objected. *Id.* at 1218. "[T]he communications between the agency and the consultants were simply part of the deliberative process of drawing conclusions from the public record." *Id.*

The same is true here. The DOL prepared a list of the medical and scientific documents contained in the rulemaking record for its consultants to consider, noting "[o]ur response to comments submitted by parties is limited to these documents or documents . . . referenced in these documents." (Admin. Record Doc. No. 01065). The DOL admits that two reports discuss scientific studies that were not cited or referenced in the rule making record. *See, e.g.,* (Admin. Record Doc. Nos. 01017 and 01019). However, those studies were cumulative in nature, and confirm other studies that were disclosed for public comment, 62 Fed.Reg. 3343–44, 64 Fed.Reg. 54978–79. In the preamble to the final regulations, the DOL relied only on studies disclosed in the rulemaking record. 65 Fed.Reg. 79942–43.

---

[4] The procedural rulemaking requirements of the APA are incorporated in the BLBA by 30 U.S.C. § 936(a).

Plaintiffs were not prejudiced in the manner required by this Circuit to maintain a challenge to the use of non-public consultants' reports. *United Steelworkers*, 647 F.2d at 1218.

Informal rulemaking "does not contemplate a closed record" and "the government is entitled to rely on information not exposed to comment so long as it is supplementary." *Nat'l Mining Ass'n v. Babbitt*, 172 F.3d 906, 912 n.1 (D.C.Cir.1999). *See also Air Transport Ass'n v. FAA*, 169 F.3d 1, 7 (D.C.Cir.1999); *Solite Corp. v. EPA*, 952 F.2d 473, 485 (D.C.Cir.1991); *Building Indus. of Superior California v. Babbitt*, 979 F.Supp. 893, 902–03 (D.D.C.1997). Here, the DOL did not change its position from the notice of proposed rulemaking to the final rulemaking based exclusively on evidence considered by the agency that was not offered for public comment. *Air Transport Ass'n*, 169 F.3d at 7.

Plaintiffs also claim the DOL's use of a report by a consulting economist violated the rulemaking requirements of the Regulatory Flexibility Act. However, any use of consultants that is permissible under the APA is equally permissible under the Regulatory Flexibility Act.

[The Court then denied motions by the plaintiffs and defendants for judgment.]

Questions and Comments

1.   What justification did the court offer for approving administrative rulemaking in a context in which the agency did not include two reports in the administrative record? What did the court mean when it said that rulemaking "does not contemplate a closed record."?

2.   To what extent were the consultants' reports analogous to the staff reports involved in the *Montrose Chemical Corp.* case?

3.   Should the plaintiffs have alleged unlawful ex parte communications? How would the HBO court have treated such claims? If plaintiffs had made such allegations, what provisions of the APA would they rely upon?

SIERRA CLUB v. COSTLE
657 F.2d 298 (D.C. Cir. 1981)

WALD, CIRCUIT JUDGE:

This case concerns the extent to which new coal-fired steam generators that produce electricity must control their emissions of sulfur dioxide and particulate matter into the air. In June of 1979 EPA revised the regulations called "new source performance standards" ("NSPS" or "standards") governing emission control by coal burning power plants. On this appeal we consider challenges to the revised NSPS brought by environmental groups [including the Sierra Club and the Environmental Defense Fund ("EDF")] which contend that the standards are too lax and by electric utilities which contend that the standards are too rigorous . . . For the reasons stated below, we hold that EPA did not exceed its statutory authority under the Clean Air Act in promulgating the NSPS, and we decline to set aside the standards.

V. The 1.2 Lbs./MBTU Emission Ceiling

EPA proposed and ultimately adopted a 1.2 tbs./MBtu ceiling for total sulfur dioxide emissions which is applicable regardless of the percentage of sulfur dioxide reduction attained. . . . EDF challenges this part of the final NSPS on procedural grounds, contending that although there may be evidence supporting the 1. 2 lbs. / MBtu standard, EPA should have and would have adopted a stricter standard if it had not engaged in post-comment period irregularities and succumbed to political pressures. . . .

. . . [T]he 1977 Amendments [to the Clean Air Act] required the agency to establish a "rulemaking docket" for each proposed rule which would form the basis of the record for judicial review. The docket must contain, *inter alia*, (1) "notice of the proposed rulemaking . . . accompanied by a statement of its basis and purpose," and a specification of the public comment period; (2) "all written comments and documentary information on the proposed rule received from any person . . . during the comment period; [t]he transcript of public hearings, if any[;] and [all] documents . . . which become available after the proposed rule has been published and which the Administrator determines are of central relevance to the rulemaking . . . "; (3) drafts of proposed rules submitted for interagency review, and all documents accompanying them and responding to them; and (4) the promulgated rule and the various accompanying agency documents which explain and justify it.

The post-comment period communications about which EDF complains vary widely in their content and mode; some are written documents or letters, others are oral communications and briefings, while still others are meetings where alleged political arm-twisting took place. . . . [N]othing in the statute prohibits EPA from admitting all post-comment communications into the record; nothing expressly requires it, either. Most likely the drafters envisioned promulgation of a rule soon after the close of the public comment period, and did not envision a months-long hiatus where continued outside communications with the agency would continue unabated. We must therefore attempt to glean the law for this case by inference from the procedural framework provided in the statute.

1. Written Comments Submitted During Post-Comment Period

Although no express authority to admit post-comment documents exists, the statute does provide that:

> All documents which become available after the proposed rule has been published and which the Administrator determines are of central relevance to the rulemaking shall be placed in the docket as soon as possible after their availability.

This provision, in contrast to others in the same paragraph, is not limited to the comment period. Apparently it allows EPA not only to put documents into the record after the comment period is over, but also to define which documents are "of central relevance" so as to require that they be placed in the docket. The principal purpose of the drafters was to define in advance, for the benefit of reviewing courts, the record upon which EPA would rely in defending the rule it finally adopted; it was not their purpose to guarantee that every piece of paper or phone call related to the rule which was received by EPA during the post-comment period be included in the docket. EPA thus has authority to place post-comment documents into the docket, but it need not do so in all instances.

Such a reading of the statute accords well with the realities of Washington administrative policymaking, where rumors, leaks, and overreactions by concerned groups abound, particularly as the time for promulgation draws near. In a proceeding such as this, one of vital concern to so many interests — industry, environmental groups, as well as Congress and the Administration — it would be unrealistic to think there would not naturally be attempts on all sides to stay in contact with EPA right up to the moment the final rule is promulgated. The drafters of the 1977 Amendments were practical people, well versed in such activity, and we decline now to infer from their silence that they intended to prohibit the lodging of documents with the agency at any time prior to promulgation. Common sense, after all, must play a part in our interpretation of these statutory procedures.

. . . [U]nder the circumstances of this case, we do not find that it was necessary for EPA to reopen the formal comment period. . . . [T]he comment period lasted over four months, and . . . the statute did put a premium on speedy decisionmaking by setting a one year deadline from the Amendments' enactment to the rules' promulgation. . . . Reopening the formal comment period . . . would . . . have frustrated the Congressional intent that these rules be promulgated expeditiously.

If, however, documents of central importance upon which EPA intended to rely had been entered on the docket too late for any meaningful public comment prior to promulgation, then both the structure and spirit of section 307 would have been violated. The Congressional drafters, after all, intended to provide "thorough and careful procedural safeguards . . . [to] insure an effective opportunity for public participation in the rulemaking process." Indeed the Administrator is obligated by the statute to convene a proceeding to reconsider the rule where an objection of central importance to it is proffered, and the basis of the objection arose after the comment period had closed. . . .

The case before us, however, does not present an instance where documents vital to EPA's support for its rule were submitted so late as to preclude any effective public comment. . . . The decisive point . . . is that EDF itself has failed to show us any particular document or documents to which it lacked an opportunity to respond, and which also were vital to EPA's support for the rule.

EDF makes only one particularized allegation concerning its inability to respond adequately to documents submitted during the post-comment period. It argues that at the April 5 meeting called by EPA, representatives of NCA [the National Coal Association] produced new data purporting to show a significant impact upon available coal reserves of more restrictive emissions ceilings. EDF alleges that additional documents supporting a higher ceiling were thereafter forwarded by NCA to EPA following the April 5 meeting. We find, however, that EDF was not denied an adequate opportunity to respond to this material. EDF was provided with advance notice of the April 5 meeting's time, place, and agenda. At the meeting EDF proceeded to question the assumptions used in the coal industry's studies. After the meeting, on April 19, 1979, it sent a detailed memorandum to EPA asserting that NCA's new claims were "false" and "unsupported by the sheafs of new data the Coal Association has hastened to submit. . . ." Of course EDF would have preferred "additional time" to be able to furnish a "more complete evaluation" of the studies, but we do not find that EDF's preference for more time constitutes substantial evidence of an inability to respond. EDF had many weeks between the meeting and the promulgation of the rule to submit additional material, and its rebuttal material has all been entered on the docket and considered by EPA. The mere wishes of a participant in an informal rulemaking for more time to respond to documents in the record to which it already had opportunity to respond cannot force an agency to delay rulemaking simply because some new rebuttal evidence may be forthcoming; this is particularly so when the statute mandates speedy promulgation of the rule. Were it otherwise, participants could delay promulgation indefinitely since new information continually comes to light on the subject of many proposed rules. Finality, after all, has a place in administrative rulemaking, just as it does in judicial decisionmaking.

2. Meetings Held with Individuals Outside EPA

The statute does not explicitly treat the issue of post-comment period meetings with individuals outside EPA. Oral face-to-face discussions are not prohibited anywhere, anytime, in the Act. . . . Where agency action resembles judicial action, where it involves formal rulemaking, adjudication, or quasi-adjudication among "conflicting private claims to a valuable privilege," the insulation of the decision-maker from ex parte contacts is justified by basic notions of due process to the parties involved. But where agency action involves informal rulemaking of a policyrnaking sort, the concept of ex parte contacts is of more questionable utility.

Under our system of government, the very legitimacy of general policyrnaking performed by unelected administrators depends in no small part upon the openness, accessibility, and amenability of these officials to the needs and ideas of the public from whom their ultimate authority derives, and upon whom their commands must fall. As judges we are insulated from these pressures because of the nature of the judicial process in which we participate; but we must refrain from the easy temptation to look askance at all face-to-face lobbying efforts, regardless of the forum in which they occur, merely because we see them as inappropriate in the judicial context. . . . Informal contacts may enable the agency to win needed support for its program, reduce future enforcement requirements by helping those regulated to anticipate and shape their plans for the future, and spur the provision of information which the agency needs. . . . Under the Clean Air Act procedures, however, "[t]he promulgated rule may not be based (in part or whole) on any information or data which has not been placed in the docket. . . ." Thus EPA must justify its rulemaking solely on the basis of the record it compiles and makes public.

Lacking a statutory basis for its position, EDF would have us extend our decision in *Home Box Office, Inc. v. FCC* to cover all meetings with individuals outside EPA during the post-comment period. Later decisions of this court, however, have declined to apply *Home Box Office* to informal rulemaking of the general policyr-naking sort involved here, and there is no precedent for applying it to the procedures found in the Clean Air Act Amendments of 1977.

It still can be argued, however, that if oral communications are to be freely permitted after the close of the comment period, then at least some adequate summary of them must be made in order to preserve the integrity of the rulemaking docket, which under the statute must be the sole repository of material upon which EPA intends to rely. . . . This is so because unless oral communications of central relevance to the rulemaking are also docketed in some fashion or other, information central to the justification of the rule could be obtained without ever appearing on the docket, simply by communicating it by voice rather than by pen, thereby frustrating the command of section 307 that the final rule not be "based (in part or whole) on any information or data which has not been placed in the docket . . ."

EDF is understandably wary of a rule which permits the agency to decide for itself when oral communications are of such central relevance that a docket entry for them is required. Yet the statute itself vests EPA with discretion to decide whether "documents" are of central relevance and therefore must be placed in the docket; surely EPA can be given no less discretion in docketing oral communications, concerning which the statute has no explicit requirements whatsoever. . . .

(a) Intra-Executive Branch Meetings

We have already held that a blanket prohibition against meetings during the post-comment period with individuals outside EPA is unwarranted, and this perforce applies to meetings with White House officials. We have not yet addressed, however, the issue whether such oral communications with White House staff, or the President himself, must be docketed on the rulemaking record, and we now turn to that issue. The facts . . . present us with a single undocketed meeting held on April 30, 1979, at 10:00 a.m., attended by the President, White House staff, other high ranking members of the Executive Branch, as well as EPA officials, and which concerned the issues and options presented by the rulemaking.

We recognize . . . that there may be instances where the docketing of conversations between the President or his staff and other Executive Branch officers or rulemakers may be necessary to ensure due process. This may be true, for example, where such conversations directly concern the outcome of adjudications or quasi-adjudicatory proceedings; there is no inherent executive power to control the rights of individuals in such settings. Docketing may also be necessary in some circumstances where a statute like this one *specifically requires* that essential "information or data" upon which a rule is based be docketed. But in the absence of any further Congressional requirements, we hold that it was not unlawful in this case for EPA not to docket a face-to-face policy session involving the President and EPA officials during the post-comment period, since EPA makes no effort to base the rule on any "information or data" arising from that meeting. Where the President himself is directly involved in oral communications with Executive Branch officials, Article II considerations — combined with the strictures of *Vermont Yankee* — require that courts tread with extraordinary caution in mandating disclosure beyond that already required by statute.

The purposes of full-record review which underlie the need for disclosing ex parte conversations in some settings do not require that courts know the details of every White House contact, including a Presidential one, in this informal rulemaking setting. After all, any rule issued here with or without White House assistance must have the requisite *factual support* in the rulemaking record, and under this particular statute the Administrator may not base the rule in whole or in part on any *"information or data" which* is not in the record, no matter what the source. The courts will monitor all this, but they need not be omniscient to perform their role effectively. Of course, it is always possible that undisclosed Presidential prodding may direct an outcome that is factually based on the record, but different from the outcome that would have obtained in the absence of Presidential involvement. In such a case, it would be true that the political process did affect the outcome in a way the courts could not police. But we do not believe that Congress intended that the courts convert informal rulemaking into a rarified technocratic process, unaffected by political considerations or the presence of Presidential power. In sum, we find that the existence of intra-Executive Branch meetings during the Post-comment period, and the failure to docket one such meeting involving the President, violated neither the procedures mandated by the Clean Air Act nor due process.

In sum, we conclude that EPA's adoption of the 1.2 Ibs./MBtu emissions ceiling was free from procedural error. . . .

Affirmed

Questions and Comments

1.   Did the *Sierra Club* decision observe the principle of exclusiveness-of-the-record? Can you reconcile *Sierra Club* with *HBO?* Explain.

2.   Is the *Sierra Club* decision consistent with the views of the drafters of the APA on the meaning of the exclusiveness-of-the-record principle? Did the drafters of the APA understand that a decision-maker's consultation outside the record which did not involve the communication of extra-record factual information was permissible? Explain.

3.   Is the result which the court reached in *Sierra Club* necessary for governmental policy coordination? Is the *Sierra Club* result necessary for the executive to perform its constitutional functions? Explain. Would your answer be different if the EPA were a so-called "independent" agency like the FCC or the NLRB?

PORTLAND AUDUBON SOCIETY v. ENDANGERED SPECIES COMMITTEE
984 F.2d 1534 (9th Cir. 1993)

REINHARDT, CIRCUIT JUDGE:

We consider here a motion filed in a most important and controversial case. The motion itself raises a significant issue of first impression. In the underlying proceeding, petitioners Portland Audubon Society et al. (collectively "the environmental groups") challenge the decision of the statutorily-created Endangered Species Committee ("the Committee"), known popularly as "The God Squad", to grant an exemption from the requirements of the Endangered Species Act to the Bureau of Land Management for thirteen timber sales in western Oregon. . . .

I. Background

The Endangered Species Act requires that "[e]ach Federal agency shall . . . insure that any action authorized, funded or carried out by such agency . . . is not likely to jeopardize the continued existence of any endangered species . . . or result in the destruction or adverse modification of [critical] habitat of such species." 16 U.S.C. § 1536(a)(2) (1988). However, if the Secretary of the Interior ("Secretary") finds that a proposed agency action would violate § 1536(a)(2), an agency may apply to the Committee for an exemption from the Endangered Species Act. §§ 1536(a)(2), (g)(1)–(2). The Committee was created by the Endangered Species Act for the sole purpose of making final decisions on applications for exemptions from the Act, § 1536(e), and it is composed of high level officials.[5] Because it is the ultimate arbiter of the fate of an endangered species, the Committee is known as "The God Squad".

The Secretary must initially consider any exemption application, publish a notice and summary of the application in the Federal Register, and determine whether certain threshold requirements have been met. 16 U.S.C. §§ 1536(g)(1)–(3). If so, the Secretary shall, in consultation with the other members of the Committee, hold a hearing on the application (which is conducted by an ALJ), and prepare a written report to the Committee. § 1536(g)(4); 50 C.F.R. § 452.05(a)(2) (Oct. 1, 1991). Within thirty days of receiving the Secretary's report, the Committee shall make a final determination whether or not to grant the exemption from the Endangered Species Act based on the report, the record of the Secretary's hearing, and any additional hearings or written submissions for which the Committee itself may call. § 1536(h)(1)(A); 50 C.F.R. § 453.04. An exemption requires the approval of five of the seven members of the Committee. § 1536(h)(1).

On May 15, 1992, the Committee approved an exemption for the Bureau of Land Management for thirteen of forty-four timber sales. It was only the second exemption ever granted by the Committee. . . .

Both in their petition and in this motion the environmental groups contend that improper ex parte contacts between the White House and members of the Committee tainted the decision-making process. They base their charges on two press reports . . .

II. Ex Parte Communications Between the Committee and the President and

---

[5] The seven-member Committee is composed of: the Secretary of Agriculture, the Secretary of the Army, the Chairman of the Council of Economic Advisors, the Administrator of the Environmental Protection Agency, the Secretary of the Interior, the Administrator of the National Oceanic and Atmospheric Administration, and "one individual from each affected State" appointed by the President. 16 U.S.C. § 1536(e)(3). The Committee members from the affected states have one collective vote. 50 C.F.R. § 453.05(d) (Oct. 1, 1991).

Members of his Staff are Prohibited by Law.

This case raises two important and closely related questions of statutory construction: 1) Are Committee proceedings subject to the ex parte communications ban of 5 U.S.C. § 557(d)(1)? and, 2) are communications from the President and his staff covered by that provision? For the reasons that follow, we answer both questions in the affirmative.

A. The committee's proceedings are subject to the APA's prohibition on ex parte communications.

The environmental groups contend that the Endangered Species Act incorporates by reference the ex parte communications ban of the APA and forbids ex parte contacts with members of the Committee regarding an exemption application. The ex parte prohibition is set forth at 5 U.S.C. § 557(d)(1).[9] Section 557(d)(1) is a broad provision that prohibits any ex parte communications relevant to the merits of an agency proceeding between "any member of the body comprising the agency" or any agency employee who "is or may reasonably be expected to be involved in the decisional process" and any "interested person outside the agency."[10] 5 U.S.C. §§ 557(d)(1)(A)-(B). . . . The purpose of the ex parte communications prohibition is to ensure that " 'agency decisions required to be made on a public record are not influenced by private, off-the-record communications from those personally interested in the outcome.' " *Raz Inland Navigation Co. v. Interstate Commerce Comm'n*, 625 F.2d 258, 260 (9th Cir. 1980) (quoting legislative history).[11]

It is of no consequence that the sections of the Endangered Species Act governing the operations of the Committee fail to mention the APA. The APA itself mandates that its provisions govern certain administrative proceedings. . . . By its terms, section 554 of the APA, which pertains to formal adjudications, applies to "every case of adjudication required by statute to be determined on the record after [the] opportunity for an agency hearing." 5 U.S.C. § 554(a). . . . That section also provides that any hearing conducted and any decision made in connection with such an adjudication shall be "in accordance with sections 556 and 557 of this title." 5 U.S.C. § 554(c)(2).

In other words, by virtue of the terms of APA § 554, sections 556 and 557 are applicable whenever that section applies.[12]. . . . Accordingly, the ex parte communications prohibition applies whenever the three requirements set forth in APA § 554(a) are satisfied: The administrative proceeding must be 1) an adjudication; 2)

---

[9] An "ex parte communication" is defined as: "an oral or written communication not on the public record with respect to which reasonable prior notice is not given, but it shall not include requests for status reports on any matter or proceeding covered by this subchapter." 5 U.S.C. § 551(14).

[10] The government does not dispute that the Committee is an "agency" within the meaning of the APA. See 5 U.S.C. § 551(1).

[11] The APA provides that when such an ex parte contact has occurred, it shall be placed on the public record of the proceeding, and if in the interests of justice, the agency may require the party involved "to show cause why his claim or interest in the proceeding should not be dismissed, denied, disregarded, or otherwise adversely affected on account of such violation." 5 U.S.C. §§ 557(d)(1)(C)–(D).

[12] Section 557 is applicable for another reason as well. By its terms § 557 applies whenever a hearing is required to be conducted in accordance with § 556. 5 U.S.C. § 557(a). Because § 554 is applicable here, § 556 automatically applies as well, and, by virtue of the language of § 556, § 557 applies in turn.

determined on the record; and 3) after the opportunity for an agency hearing.[13] The question is, therefore, are those three conditions met here? We find our answer primarily in the language of section 1536(h)(1)(A) of the Endangered Species Act.[14]

We conclude that the first requirement of APA § 554(a) is satisfied. Certain administrative decisions closely resemble judicial determinations and, in the interests of fairness, require similar procedural protections. . . . Where an agency's task is "to adjudicate disputed facts in particular cases," an administrative determination is quasi-judicial. . . . By contrast, rulemaking concerns policy judgments to be applied generally in cases that may arise in the future; it is *sometimes* guided by more informal procedures. . . .[15] Under the Endangered Species Act the Committee decides whether to grant or deny specific requests for exemptions based upon specific factual showings. Thus, the Committee's determinations are quasi-judicial. Accordingly, they constitute "adjudications" within the meaning of § 554(a).[16]

The legislative history of the Endangered Species Act confirms our conclusion in this respect. The Senate committee report accompanying the 1982 amendments to the Endangered Species Act stated that "the Endangered Species Committee is designed to function as an *administrative court of last resort.*" S.Rep. No. 418, 97th Congress, 2d Sess. 17 (1982) (emphasis added). The Report states that the Committee's decision will be based, in part, upon a "formal adjudicatory hearing." . . . The Report also makes clear that the Committee's duty is to be the ultimate arbiter of conflicts that the parties involved have been unable to resolve. . . .

The language of the Endangered Species Act explicitly meets the second requirement of section 554(a). Section 1536(h)(1)(A) of the Act mandates that the Committee make its final determination of an exemption application "on the record." . . . No further discussion is required on this point.

It is equally clear that the third requirement of APA § 554(a) is satisfied here. Section 1536(h)(1)(A) of the Endangered Species Act also requires that the

---

[13] Section 553(c) of the APA makes the ex parte communications prohibition applicable to formal rulemaking proceedings as well. Under § 553(c), where rules are required by statute to be made on the record after opportunity for agency hearing (formal rulemaking), §§ 556 and 557 apply. In its brief the government contends that Committee decisions are formal rulemaking. While we do not agree, we note that even if the Committee's argument were correct, the ex parte communications prohibition would still apply via § 553(c). . . . Thus, for practical purposes the government all but concedes the applicability of the ex parte communications prohibition to Committee proceedings.

[14] For convenience we refer to the relevant provision as section 1536(h)(1)(A) of the Endangered Species Act. The technically correct designation would be subsection 7(h)(1)(A) of that Act, codified at 16 U.S.C. § 1536(h)(1)(A). The section provides, in relevant part, that Committee determinations shall be "on the record, based on the report of the Secretary, the record of the hearing held under subsection (g)(4) of this section and on such other testimony or evidence as it may receive."

[15] There are two types of rulemaking proceedings — formal . . . and informal. The APA does not bar ex parte communications in informal rulemaking proceedings. Sierra Club v. Costle, 657 F.2d 298 (D.C.Cir.1981).

[16] The APA defines an adjudication as "agency process for the formulation of an order." 5 U.S.C. § 551(7). An order includes all dispositions of an agency in a matter other than rulemaking but including licensing. 5 U.S.C. § 551(6).

Committee's final decision be "*based on* the report of the Secretary, *the hearing* held under (g)(4) of this section [(the Secretary's hearing)] and on such other testimony or evidence as it may receive." 16 U.S.C. § 1536(h)(1)(A) (emphasis added). Wherever the outer bounds of the "after opportunity for an agency hearing" requirement may lie, we hold that where, as here, a statute provides that an adjudication be determined at least in part based on an agency hearing, that requirement is fulfilled.[17]

Because Committee decisions are adjudicatory in nature, are required to be on the record, and are made after an opportunity for an agency hearing, we conclude that the APA's ex parte communication prohibition is applicable. This result is similar to the one we reached in a case involving formal rulemaking, *Central Lincoln Peoples' Util. Dist. v. Johnson*, 735 F.2d 1101, 1119 (9th Cir.1984). There we held that because Congress required rate decisions under the Pacific Northwest Electric Power Conservation Act to be made on the record after a hearing, the procedural protections of the APA were triggered, including the ban on ex parte communications. In that case the applicable provision was APA § 553(c), which, in language almost identical to that contained in § 554(c)(2), provides that "[w]hen rules are required by statute to be made on the record after opportunity for an agency hearing, sections 556 and 557 of this title apply." (emphasis added). Similarly, the pertinent language of the Endangered Species Act, section 1536(h)(1)(A), parallels the language of the statute that we considered in *Central Lincoln*.[18] Thus, the statutory language of the Endangered Species Act, like that of the Pacific Northwest Electric Power Conservation Act, is sufficient to trigger the APA's ex parte communication prohibition.[19]

Neither the government nor the Intervenors Oregon Lands Coalition, *et al.*, ("the lands coalition") has directly responded to the argument that because section 1536(h)(1)(A) provides that Committee determinations are adjudications made on the record and based upon a hearing, APA § 554 applies, and *ipso facto*, so does the ex parte prohibition of § 557(d)(1). Instead, they contend that because one part of the regulations (50 C.F.R. § 452.07(d)) expressly states that "[t]he provisions of 5 U.S.C. § 557(d) apply to the [Secretary's] hearing and preparation of the report," while another part (50 C.F.R. § 453), which relates to the Committee's deliberations,

---

[17] The portion of § 554(a) making that section applicable when a statute provides that an adjudication be determined "after opportunity for an agency hearing" (emphasis added) does not mean that such hearing must be conducted directly by the decision-maker. APA § 556(b) permits "an agency hearing" to be conducted by 1) the agency; 2) one or more members of the agency; or 3) one or more agency ALJs. Here, the Secretary is a member and the chairman of the Committee. 16 U.S.C. §§ 1536(e)(3)(E) & (e)(5)(B). Moreover, the hearing was conducted by an ALJ. We also note that here while the "agency hearing" was conducted by an ALJ on behalf of the Secretary, the Endangered Species Act expressly provides that the Secretary's hearing be held in consultation with the Committee. 16 U.S.C. § 1536(g)(4).

[18] There we construed 16 U.S.C. 839(e)(I)(5), which in relevant part, provides: "The Administrator shall make a final decision establishing a rate or rates based on the record which shall include the hearing transcript, together with exhibits, and such other materials and information as may have been submitted to, or developed by, the Administrator."

[19] Actually, for purposes of § 557(d)(1), it would not matter whether Committee determinations were viewed as formal adjudications or decisions arrived at by means of formal rulemaking proceedings. Either way the APA's ex parte communication prohibition would apply: via section § 554(c)(2) (formal adjudication) or § 553(c) (formal rulemaking).

fails to contain any explicit reference to those provisions, the Committee's deliberative process is exempt from the APA's ban on ex parte contacts. For several reasons we do not agree.

First, the inclusion of a specific reference to the ex parte communications prohibition of 5 U.S.C. § 557(d) in the regulations governing the Secretary's hearing was necessary to clarify an ambiguity in the Endangered Species Act. The Secretary's hearing is governed by 16 U.S.C. § 1536(g)(4), which, in turn, provides that sections 554, 555, and 556 of the APA (except sections 556(b)(1)-(2)) are applicable to such hearings. There is no explicit mention of section 557 in 16 U.S.C. § 1536(g)(4). Although as noted supra, section 557 always applies when sections 554 and 556 do, as a matter of administrative law, the omission of section 557 from 16 U.S.C. § 1536(g)(4) could conceivably lead to considerable confusion. The reference to APA § 557(d) in the part of the regulations implementing subsection (g)(4) serves to eliminate that confusion and remove any doubt as to the applicability of the ex parte communications prohibition to the proceedings before the Secretary.

By contrast, there is no reason to mention section 557(d) in the part of the regulations concerning the Committee's proceedings. The Committee's actions are governed by section 1536(h)(1)(A). No problem comparable to that inherent in 16 U.S.C. § 1536(g)(4) exists with respect to section 1536(h)(1)(A). The text of the latter section, unlike that of the former, does not mention some of the applicable APA provisions but omit section 557; rather, it does not mention any of the applicable APA sections; thus, no ambiguity arises on the face of the part of the statute governing the Committee's proceedings and no curative provision in the corresponding part of the regulations is necessary.

Second, it would make little sense to read the omission of section 557(d) from part of the regulations governing the Committee's proceedings as a license for Committee members to engage in ex parte contacts. The Endangered Species Act as well as the applicable part of its regulations are intended to ensure that all Committee meetings, hearings, and records are open to the public. 16 U.S.C. § 1536(e)(5)(D); 50 C.F.R. §§ 453.04(b)(4), 453.05(e). Notices of all meetings and hearings must be published in the Federal Register. 50 C.F.R. §§ 453.04(b)(3), 453.05(f). If the Committee determines that written submissions are necessary for it to reach a decision, its invitation of such submissions must also be published in the Federal Register. § 453.04(a). The transcribed proceedings of any Committee hearings are to be available for public inspection. § 453.04(b)(5). The Committee's final determination of an exemption application must be documented in a written decision, which itself must be published in the Federal Register. § 453.03(b).

The public's right to attend all Committee meetings, participate in all Committee hearings, and have access to all Committee records would be effectively nullified if the Committee were permitted to base its decisions on the private conversations and secret talking points and arguments to which the public and the participating parties have no access. . . .

For the foregoing reasons we hold the Committee's proceedings are subject to the ex parte communications ban of 5 U.S.C. § 557(d)(1).

B. The president and the white house staff are subject to the APA's prohibition on ex parte communications.

The APA prohibits an "interested person outside the agency" from making, or knowingly causing to be made, an ex parte communication relevant to the merits of the proceeding with a member of the body comprising the agency. 5 U.S.C. § 557(d)(1)(A). Likewise, agency members are prohibited from engaging in such ex parte communication. § 557(d)(1)(B). Although the APA's ban on ex parte communications is absolute and includes no special exemption for White House officials, the government advances three arguments in support of its position that section 557(d)(1) does not apply to the President and his staff.[20]

First, the government argues that because the President is the center of the Executive Branch and does not represent or act on behalf of a particular agency, he does not have an interest in Committee proceedings greater than the interest of the public as a whole. Therefore, the government contends, neither the President nor his staff is an "interested person". Next, the government maintains that the President and his staff do not fall within the terms of section 557(d)(1) because the President's interest as the Chief of the Executive Branch is no different from that of his subordinates on the Committee. Specifically, the government claims that by placing the Chairman of the President's Council of Economic Advisors on the Committee, Congress directly and expressly involved the Executive Office of the President in the decision-making process. In other words, it is the government's position that because the Committee members are Executive Branch officials, communications between them and the White House staff cannot be considered to come from "outside the agency." Finally, the government argues that if the APA's ex parte communications ban encompasses the President and his aides, the provision violates the doctrine of separation of powers. We find all three of the government's arguments to be without merit.

There is little decisional law on the meaning of the term "interested person." Nor is the meaning of the term clear on the face of the statute. . . .

Ultimately, the ex parte communication provision must be interpreted in a common sense fashion. . . . Its purposes are to insure open decision-making and the appearance thereof, to preserve the opportunity for effective response, and to prevent improper influences upon agency decision-makers. . . . To achieve these ends we must give the provision a broad scope rather than a constricted interpretation. The essential purposes of the APA require that all communications that might improperly influence an agency be encompassed within the ex parte contacts prohibition or else the public and the parties will be denied indirectly their guaranteed right to meaningful participation in agency decisional processes.

. . . .

In *PATCO v. FLRA II* [685 F.2d 547 (D.C. Cir. 1982)], the District of Columbia Circuit found that the Secretary of Transportation was an "interested person" within the meaning of APA § 557(d)(1) when he telephoned two members of the Federal Labor Relations Authority regarding an unfair labor practice charge made

---

[20] Neither the affidavit of the environmental groups' counsel nor the newspaper reports state that former President Bush personally met or lobbied Committee members. The government argues, however, that alleged ex parte communications with the Committee should be treated identically whether they are made by the President or by White House staff carrying out his policies.

by the Federal Aviation Association against the air traffic controllers union-
. . . . While the court did not set forth the rationale for its holding, it seems evident
that it reasoned that the Secretary of Transportation has a special interest in a
major transportation dispute which is beyond that of the general public and that he
is, therefore, an interested person.

The government does not contest the validity of *PATCO v. FLRA II* as it applies
to Cabinet level officials and below. However, it argues that the President's broader
policy role places him beyond the reach of the "interested person" language. We
strongly disagree. In fact, we believe the proper argument is quite the opposite
from the one the government advances. We believe the President's position at the
center of the Executive Branch renders him, *ex officio*, an "interested person" for
the purposes of APA § 557(d)(1). As the head of government and chief executive
officer, the President necessarily has an interest in every agency proceeding. No ex
parte communication is more likely to influence an agency than one from the
President or a member of his staff. No communication from any other person is
more likely to deprive the parties and the public of their right to effective
participation in a key governmental decision at a most crucial time. The essential
purposes of the statutory provision compel the conclusion that the President and his
staff are "interested persons" within the meaning of 5 U.S.C. § 557(d)(1).

The government's next argument — that because the President and the
members of the Committee are all members of the executive branch the President
is, for all intents and purposes, a "member" of the Committee and may attempt to
influence its decisions — amounts to a contention that the President is not "outside
the agency" for the purposes of APA § 557(d)(1). The Supreme Court soundly
rejected the basic logic of this argument in *United States ex rel. Accardi v.
Shaughnessy*, 347 U.S. 260, 74 S.Ct. 499, 98 L.Ed. 681 (1954). The Court held that
where legally binding regulations delegated a particular discretionary decision to
the Board of Immigration Appeals, the Attorney General could not dictate a
decision of the Board, even though the Board was appointed by the Attorney
General, its members served at his pleasure, and its decision was subject to his
ultimate review. Here, the Endangered Species Act explicitly vests discretion to
make exemption decisions in the Committee and does not contemplate that the
President or the White House will become involved in Committee deliberations. The
President and his aides are not a part of the Committee decision-making process.
They are "outside the agency" for the purposes of the ex parte communications ban.

The government then argues that *Sierra Club v. Costle* determined that contacts
with the White House do not constitute ex parte communications that would
contaminate the Committee's decision-making process, and that we should follow
that precedent. 657 F.2d 298, 400-10 (D.C.Cir.1981). We disagree. *Costle* is
inapplicable because that case did not consider and, indeed, could not have
considered, whether the APA's definition of ex parte communications includes White
House contacts. The decision in *Costle* that the contacts were not impermissible was
based explicitly on the fact that the proceeding involved was *informal* rulemaking
to which the APA restrictions on ex parte communications are not applicable. . . . In fact, while the *Costle* court recognized that political pressure from the
President may not be inappropriate in *informal* rulemaking proceedings, it
acknowledged that the contrary is true in formal adjudications. . . . Because

Congress has decided that Committee determinations are formal adjudications, *Costle* supports, rather than contradicts, the conclusion that the President and his staff are subject to the APA's ex parte communication ban.

Accordingly, the President and his staff are covered by section 557's prohibition and are not free to attempt to influence the decision-making processes of the Committee through ex parte communications. The APA's ban on such communications is fully applicable to the President and his White House aides, and ex parte contacts by them relevant to the merits of an agency proceeding would be in violation of that Act.

The government next contends that any construction of APA § 557(d)(1) that includes presidential communications within the ban on ex parte contacts would constitute a violation of the separation of powers doctrine. It relies on language in *Myers v. United States* that states that the President has the constitutional authority to "supervise and guide" Executive Branch officials in "their construction of the statutes under which they act." 272 U.S. 52, 135, 47 S.Ct. 21, 31, 71 L.Ed. 160 (1926). The government argues that including the President and his staff within the APA's ex parte communication ban would represent Congressional interference with the President's constitutional duty to provide such supervision and guidance to inferior officials. We reject this argument out of hand.

The Supreme Court established the test for evaluating whether an act of Congress improperly interferes with a presidential prerogative in *Nixon v. Administrator of Gen. Services*, 433 U.S. 425, 97 S.Ct. 2777, 53 L.Ed.2d 867 (1977). First, a court must determine whether the act prevents the executive branch from accomplishing its constitutional functions. . . . If the potential for such disruption exists, the next question is whether the impact is justified by an overriding need to promote objectives within the constitutional authority of Congress. . . . We conclude that Congress in no way invaded any legitimate constitutional power of the President in providing that he may not attempt to influence the outcome of administrative adjudications through ex parte communications and that Congress' important objectives reflected in the enactment of the APA would, in any event, outweigh any *de minimis* impact on presidential power.

While the government's argument to the contrary arises in the context of Committee decisions regarding Endangered Species Act exemption applications, carried to its logical conclusion the government's position would effectively destroy the integrity of all federal agency adjudications. It is a fundamental precept of administrative law that an when an agency performs a quasi-judicial (or a quasi-legislative) function its independence must be protected. There is no presidential prerogative to influence quasi-judicial administrative agency proceedings through behind-the-scenes lobbying. *Myers* itself clearly recognizes that "there may be duties of a quasi-judicial character imposed on executive officers and members of executive tribunals whose decisions after hearing affect interests of individuals, the discharge of which the President can not in a particular case properly influence or control." 272 U.S. at 135, 47 S.Ct. at 31. And in *Humphrey's Executor v. United States* the Court observed that "[t]he authority of Congress, in creating quasi-legislative or quasi-judicial agencies, to require them to act in discharge of their duties independently of executive control cannot well be doubted." 295 U.S. 602, 629, 55 S.Ct. 869, 874, 79 L.Ed. 1611 (1935). The government's position in this case is antithetical to and destructive of these elementary legal precepts, and we unequivocally reject it.

. . . .

Congress might well have established a different procedure for granting exemptions from the Endangered Species Act. However, the language of the Act shows that it intended to create the Committee as a quasi-judicial adjudicatory body subject to the statutory restrictions that the APA imposes on such institutions. Congress clearly has the authority to do so, and thereby to ensure the independence of the agency from presidential control. We conclude that the members of the Committee, despite the Cabinet-level status they otherwise enjoy, are, while serving in their Committee capacities, precisely the kinds of "members of executive tribunals" that *Myers* and *Humphrey's Executor* contemplate are to be free from presidential influence.

In view of the above, we hold that communications between the Committee and the President or his staff are subject to the APA's prohibition on ex parte contacts.

III. The Remedy to Which the Environmental Groups are Entitled

A. Effective Judicial Review Requires Supplementation of the Record if Improper Ex Parte Communications Occurred.

. . . .

. . . . [W]e issue the order filed concurrently herewith directing the Committee to hold, with the aid of a specially appointed administrative law judge, an evidentiary hearing to determine the nature, content, extent, source, and effect of any ex parte communications that may have transpired between any member of the Committee or its staff and the President or any member of his staff regarding the determination of the exemption application at issue. . . .

Following the hearing, the ALJ will request that all interested parties submit proposed findings. When these findings are received, the ALJ will submit the record of the hearing and all proposed findings, as well as the ALJ's own findings and recommendations, to the parties and to the Clerk of the Court. The parties will then advise the court what further proceedings, if any, should, in their opinion, be held, either before the Committee or this court. This panel will retain jurisdiction over this matter pending further order of the court.

. . . .

Questions and Comments

1. Do you agree with the court that the decision of the Committee was "adjudication" under the APA? What is your basis for your conclusion? Is it based upon the language of the APA? Did the court rely upon the APA definitions to reach its conclusion?

2. Does the language of the Senate report referring to the Committee as an "administrative court of last resort" support the court's determination that the proceeding is adjudication? Why or why not?

3. Would the ex parte provisions of § 557 apply if the proceeding were formal rulemaking (i.e., rulemaking governed by §§ 556 and 557)? If so, then why was the court insistent upon labeling the proceeding as adjudication?

4. Did you find the court's analysis of the governing regulations convincing?

5. Do you agree that, for purposes of the § 557 prohibition, the President is an "interested person" outside the agency? The court indicated that the purpose of the provision was to ensure that agency decisions are not influenced by off-the-record communications "from those personally interested in the outcome." Is the President personally interested in the outcome?

6. Was the President's interest different from the interest of the Chairman of the President's Council of Economic Advisors (who was on the Committee)? If their interests were the same, then the President's interest was not "personal", was it?

7. Is this case consistent with *Sierra Club v. Costle* [casebook]? How does the court reconcile its decision with *Sierra Club*? Do you think that the court gave sufficient consideration to the Government's constitutional contentions?

8. The court cites *PATCO v. FLRA II* in support of its decision. Is *PATCO* distinguishable on the basis urged by the Government? Can you think of an additional distinction which the Government could have urged in support of its position?

Chapter 10

PROCEDURAL PROBLEMS INCIDENT TO JUDICIAL REVIEW

A. REVIEWABILITY

Perhaps the most famous of the cases in which the Supreme Court ruled that agency action was not reviewable in the courts was *Switchmen's Union of North America v. National Mediation Board*, 320 U.S. 297 (1943). Acting under the provisions of the Railway Labor Act, the National Mediation Board had investigated a dispute among the yardmen of the New York Central Railroad as to their collective bargaining representative. The Brotherhood of Railroad Trainmen wanted to represent all the yardmen; but the Switchmen's Union contended that yardmen of certain designated parts of the system should be permitted to vote for separate representatives. The Board designated all yardmen as participants in the election; the yardmen selected the Brotherhood as their representative; and the Board duly certified the Brotherhood as the authorized representative of the yardmen.

The Switchmen's Union then brought suit against the Board, the Brotherhood and the carriers to cancel the Board certification and the underlying Board decision designating all yardmen as participants in a single election. The district court upheld the Board and the court of appeals affirmed. On review, the U.S. Supreme Court held that the federal courts lacked jurisdiction to review the action of the Mediation Board. In his opinion for the Court, Justice Douglas took account of the "right" of a majority of any craft or class of employees under the Act to "determine who shall be their [collective bargaining] representative". He stated that "if the absence of jurisdiction of the federal courts meant a sacrifice or obliteration of" that right, then "the inference would be strong" that Congress intended those courts to exercise jurisdiction. Here that "right" was protected by the Mediation Board; and hence "[a] review by the federal district courts of the Board's determination is not necessary to preserve or protect that 'right' ".

The *Switchmen's Union* case is properly understood against the background of labor history, the federal courts, and the philosophy underlying federal labor regulation. In the early part of the twentieth century, workers' attempts to organize were often thwarted by injunctions issued by federal courts responding to employers' claims of unlawful activities by the workers. It was widely believed that injunctions issued during the formative period when workers were organizing — even if later vacated — often destroyed organizing efforts before they could become effective. This belief underlay Congress' enactment of the Norris-LaGuardia Act divesting the federal courts of power to issue injunctions in labor disputes. It also permeated federal labor legislation which — in the Railway Labor Act and later in the National Labor Relations Act — was designed to speed the designation of the bargaining unit and to get the bargaining process underway as quickly as possible. The Court may have believed that its decision in *Switchmen's Union* helped to achieve this goal by preventing dissatisfied litigants from endlessly contesting the decisions of the Mediation Board in the courts.

An interesting comparison with *Switchmen's Union* is***Leedom v. Kyne,* 358 U.S. 184 (1958).** *Leedom* again involved an issue of federal court involvement in the process of designating a bargaining unit, although under a different statute: the National Labor Relations Act. As amended by the Taft-Hartley Act, § 9(b)(1) provides that the National Labor Relations Board shall not designate any unit containing both professional and nonprofessional employees as a bargaining unit unless a majority of the professional employees vote for inclusion in the unit. The Board designated a bargaining unit which contained 233 professional and 9 nonprofessional employees at General Electric's Westinghouse Cheektowaga, N.Y. plant without having first taken a vote among the professional employees to determine whether a majority of them would vote for inclusion in that unit. The professional employees' union then brought suit in district court asserting that the Board had exceeded its jurisdiction in including professional employees, without their consent, in a union with nonprofessional employees. The district court ruled in favor of the professional union and against the Board. The Court of appeals affirmed. On review, the U.S. Supreme Court affirmed: "Here, differently from the Switchmen's case, 'absence of jurisdiction of the federal courts' would mean 'a sacrifice or obliteration of a right which Congress' has given professional employees, for there is no other means, within their control . . . to protect and enforce that right. And 'the inference [is] strong that Congress intended the statutory provisions governing the general jurisdiction of those courts to control.' . . . This Court cannot lightly infer that Congress does not intend judicial protection of rights it confers against agency action taken in excess of delegated powers."

Questions and Comments

1.   Note that the suit in the *Leedom v. Kyne* case was brought in federal district court. Under the National Labor Relations Act, judicial review of actions of the NLRB takes place before the Courts of Appeals. Because in *Leedom v. Kyne* the plaintiff union was asserting that the Board had acted outside of its jurisdiction, it sought relief not under the review provisions of the NLRA, but outside of it. That is why it instituted a proceeding in district court under that court's general federal-question jurisdiction.

2.   To what extent would *Leedom v. Kyne* be likely to engender other suits in which the selection of proper bargaining units would be delayed for long periods by litigation? Was the issue in *Leedom v. Kyne* so clear-cut that the Court's decision would resolve it once and for all? Or would that decision be likely to engender other cases in which challenges would be made to the Board's designation of a bargaining unit? Do you think the Court was influenced by the stronger position in society which unions had generally achieved at the time of *Leedom v. Kyne* (compared to their more precarious position earlier in the century)?

In *McNary v. Haitian Refugee Center,* **498 U.S. 479 (1991),** the Court considered the judicial review provisions of the Immigration Reform and Control Act of 1986. That Act established a "Special Agricultural Workers" (SAW) amnesty program for certain alien farmworkers. Under the SAW program farmworkers illegally present in the United States could regularize their status by proving, *inter alia,* that they had worked 90 days during the 12 month period prior to May 1, 1986. The procedures involved the filing of an application with supporting documentary evidence and an interview before a specially created Legalization Officer (LO). The LO could deny the application at the conclusion of the interview or could recommend positive or negative action. A legalization appeals unit was authorized to make the final decision. Judicial review of a final administrative determination of SAW status was expressly prohibited, except as authorized by § 210(e)(3)(A) [8 U.S.C. § 1160(e)] of the amended Immigration and Nationality Act. That subsection permitted "judicial review of such a denial only in the judicial review of an order of exclusion or deportation."[16]

The case was brought in the U.S. Court for the Southern District of Florida by the Haitian Refugee Center, the Migration and Refugee Services of the Roman Catholic Diocese of Palm Beach and seventeen unsuccessful individual SAW applicants. The complaint alleged that the interview process was conducted in an arbitrary fashion that deprived applicants of the due process guaranteed by the Fifth Amendment. Among other charges, the plaintiffs alleged that Immigration and Naturalization Service (INS) procedures did not allow SAW applicants to be appraised of or to be given opportunity to challenge adverse evidence on which denials were predicated, that applicants were denied the opportunity to present witnesses on their own behalf, that non-English speaking Haitian applicants were unable to communicate effectively with LOs because competent interpreters were not provided, and that no verbatim recording of the interview was made, thus inhibiting even any meaningful administrative review of application denials by LOs or regional processing facilities.

The district court found that a number of INS practices violated the Reform Act and were unconstitutional, and entered an injunction requiring the INS to vacate

---

[16] Section 210(e) of the Immigration and Nationality Act as set forth in 8 U.S.C. § 1160(e) (1988) provides:

(1) Administrative and judicial review

There shall be no administrative or judicial review of a determination respecting an application for adjustment of status under this section except in accordance with this subsection.

. . .

(3) judicial review

(A) Limitation to review of exclusion or deportation

There shall be judicial review of such a denial only in the judicial review of an order of exclusion or deportation under section 1105a of this title.

(B) Standard for judicial review

Such judicial review shall be based solely upon the administrative record established at the time of the review by the appellate authority and the findings of fact and determinations contained in such record shall be conclusive unless the applicant can establish abuse of discretion or that the findings are directly contrary to clear and convincing facts contained in the record considered as a whole.

large categories of denials, and to modify its practices in certain respects. The Court of Appeals affirmed, and was, in turn, affirmed by the Supreme Court.

The Government argued that the judicial review provisions of the Reform Act precluded the plaintiffs from obtaining judicial review of the INS practices, because none of the plaintiffs had yet been ordered excluded or deported. An extract from Justice Stevens opinion for the Court follows:

> Petitioners' entire jurisdictional argument rests on their view that respondents' constitutional challenge is an action seeking "judicial review of a determination respecting an application for adjustment of status" and that district court jurisdiction over the action is therefore barred by the plain language of § 210(e)(1) of the amended INA. See 8 U.S.C. § 1160(e)(1). The critical words in § 210(e)(1), however, describe the provision as referring only to review "of a determination respecting an application" for SAW status (emphasis added). Significantly, the reference to "a determination" describes a single act rather than a group of decisions or a practice or procedure employed in making decisions. . . . This reading of the Reform Act's review provision is supported by the language in § 210(e)(3)(B) of the INA, which provides that judicial review "shall be based solely upon the administrative record established at the time of the review by the appellate authority.

> Because the administrative appeals process does not address the kind of procedural and constitutional claims respondents bring in this action, limiting judicial review of these claims to the procedures set forth in § 210(e) is not contemplated by the language of that provision.

> Given Congress' choice of statutory language, we conclude that challenges to the procedures used by INS do not fall within the scope of § 210(e). Rather, we hold that § 210 applies only to review of denials of individual SAW applications. Because respondents' action does not seek review on the merits of a denial of a particular application, the District Court's general federal question jurisdiction under 28 U.S.C. § 1331 to hear this action remains unimpaired by § 210(e).

Questions and Comments

1.   Can the Court in *McNary* grant review over the procedural issues raised without committing itself to extensive judicial review of SAW proceedings? Does *McNary* therefore involve considerations similar to those of *Leedom v. Kyne?*

2.   Is it helpful to plaintiffs urging broad-based claims like those in *McNary* and *Leedom v. Kyne* that the courts recognize a general presumption in favor of judicial review?

Note: The Judicial Review Provisions of the APA

The judicial review provisions of the APA are contained in Chapter 7 of Title 5 of the U.S. Code. Chapter 7 begins with § 701 which states that:

(a) This chapter applies, according to the provisions thereof, except to the extent that

(1) statutes preclude judicial review; or

(2) agency action is committed to agency discretion by law.

Section 706, which sets forth various standards for review, provides in § 706(2)(A) that:

The reviewing court shall

(2) hold unlawful and set aside agency action, findings, and conclusions found to be

(A) arbitrary, capricious, an abuse of discretion, or otherwise not in accordance with law. . . .

How can a court determine that agency action is "an abuse of discretion" under § 706(2)(A) if action that is "committed to agency discretion" is made unreviewable under § 701 (a)(2)?

When a statute precludes judicial review, must it do so expressly? What is the difference in meaning between the provisions of § 701(a)(1) and § 701(a)(2)? Is agency action always committed to agency discretion expressly or can it be done by implication?

DUNLOP v. BACHOWSKI
421 U.S. 560 (1975)

[In elections held by the United Steelworkers of America (USWA), respondent Bachowski was defeated by the incumbent for district officer in District 20. After exhausting his remedies within USWA, respondent filed a complaint with the Secretary of Labor, alleging violations of § 401 of the Labor Management Reporting and Disclosure Act of 1959 (LMRDA), thus invoking 29 U.S.C. §§ 482(a), (b) which require that the Secretary investigate the complaint and decide whether to bring a civil action to set aside the election. The Secretary advised respondent by letter dated November 7, 1973, that "[biased on the investigative findings [made by the department], it has been determined . . . that civil action to set aside the challenged election is not warranted." Respondent then brought suit in federal district court to compel the Secretary to file suit to set aside the election. The district court dismissed the suit, but the Court of Appeals reversed.]

MR. JUSTICE BRENNAN delivered the opinion of the Court.

We agree that 28 U.S.C. § 1337 confers jurisdiction upon the District Court to entertain respondent's suit, and that the Secretary's decision not to sue is not excepted from judicial review by 5 U.S.C. § 701(a); rather, §§ 702 and 704 subject the Secretary's decision to judicial review under the standard specified in § 706(2)(A). We hold, however, that the Court of Appeals erred insofar as its opinion construes § 706(2)(A) to authorize a trial-type inquiry into the factual bases of the Secretary's conclusion that no violations occurred affecting the outcome of the election. . . . In the absence of an express prohibition in the LMRDA the Secretary . . . bears the heavy burden of overcoming the strong presumption that Congress did not mean to prohibit all judicial review of his decision

[O]nly upon a showing of 'clear and convincing evidence' of a contrary legislative intent should the courts restrict access to judicial review." . . . [The Secretary] has failed to make a showing of "clear and convincing evidence" that Congress meant to prohibit all judicial review of his decision. . . . Our examination of the relevant materials persuades us, however, that although no purpose to prohibit all judicial review is shown, a congressional purpose narrowly to limit the scope of judicial review of the Secretary's decision can, and should, be inferred in order to carry out congressional objectives in enacting the LMRDA.

[Reviewing its prior decisions, the Court indicated that suit by the Secretary was made the exclusive post-election remedy, inter alia, in order to provide a speedy remedy for invalid elections and to preclude suits by private parties which might interfere with the statutory goal of clearing up doubts about the elections as quickly as possible.]

Two conclusions follow from this survey of our decisions: (1) since the statute relies upon the special knowledge and discretion of the Secretary for the determination of both the probable violation and the probable effect, clearly the reviewing court is not authorized to substitute its judgment for the decision of the Secretary not to bring suit; (2) therefore, to enable the reviewing court intelligently to review the Secretary's determination, the Secretary must provide the court and the complaining witness with copies of a statement of reasons supporting his determination. . . .

The necessity that the reviewing court refrain from substitution of its judgment for that of the Secretary thus helps define the permissible scope of review. Except in what must be the rare case, the court's review should be confined to examination of the reasons statement, and the determination whether the statement, without more, evinces that the Secretary's decision is so irrational as to constitute the decision arbitrary and capricious. Thus, review may not extend to cognizance or trial of a complaining member's challenges to the factual bases for the Secretary's conclusion either that no violation occurred or that they did not affect the outcome of the election. The full trappings of adversary trial-type hearings would be defiant of congressional objectives not to permit individuals to block or delay resolution of post-election disputes, but rather "to settle as quickly as practicable the cloud on the incumbents' titles to office"; and "to protect unions from frivolous litigation and unnecessary interference with their elections."

Thus, the Secretary's letter of November 7, 1973, may have sufficed as a "brief statement of the grounds for denial" for the purposes of the Administrative Procedure Act, 5 U.S.C. § 555(e), but plainly it did not suffice as a statement of reasons required by the LMRDA. For a statement of reasons must be adequate to enable the court to determine whether the Secretary's decision was reached for an impermissible reason or for no reason at all. For this essential purpose, although detailed findings of fact are not required, the statement of reasons should inform the court and the complaining member of both the grounds of decision and the essential facts upon which the Secretary's inferences are based.

Questions and Comments

1.   Did the Court rely upon a presumption that judicial review is generally available to reach its result? Was the Court reviewing a decision of the Secretary not to enforce the LMRDA? Was the Court applying § 701(a)(1) or § 701(a)(2)? Did the Court conclude that judicial review of the Secretary's decision was narrowly circumscribed? How did the Court derive its conclusion that the review of the Secretary's decision was narrowly circumscribed? Was this restriction on review derived from the LMRDA? What goals was LMRDA designed to achieve? A speedy resolution of issues surrounding the validity of union elections? How was this goal to be accomplished? Was a restriction on judicial review of the Secretary's decision not to institute a civil action a necessary incident to the effectuation of the goal of resolving disputes about the validity of union elections quickly? Was the LMRDA, then, a statute which partially precluded review?

2.   From what source did the Court extract the Secretary's obligation to provide a statement of reasons for his decision not to institute a complaint? From § 555(e) of the APA? From the Court's conclusion that a statement of reasons is a necessary prerequisite to judicial review? Are you aware of other cases in which the Court insisted that an agency provide an explanation of its actions as an aid to judicial review?

HECKLER v. CHANEY
470 U.S. 821 (1985)

JUSTICE REHNQUIST delivered the opinion of the Court.

This case presents the question of the extent to which a decision of an administrative agency to exercise its "discretion" not to undertake certain enforcement actions is subject to judicial review under the Administrative Procedure Act. . . . Respondents are several inmates convicted of capital offenses and sentenced to death by lethal injection of drugs. They petitioned the Food and Drug Administration (FDA), alleging that under the circumstances the use of these drugs for capital punishment violated the Federal Food, Drug, and Cosmetic Act, 21 U.S.C. § 301 et seq. (FDCA), and requested that the FDA take various enforcement actions to prevent these violations. The FDA refused their request. We review here a decision of the Court of Appeals for the District of Columbia Circuit, which held the FDA's refusal to take enforcement actions both reviewable and an abuse of discretion, and remanded the case with directions that the agency be required "to fulfill its statutory function."

. . . . Respondents first petitioned the FDA, claiming that the drugs used by the States for [the] . . . purpose [of executions], although approved by the FDA for the medical purposes stated on their labels, were not approved for use in human executions. They alleged that the drugs had not been tested for the purpose they were to be used, and that, given that the drugs would likely be administered by untrained personnel, it was also likely that the drugs would not include the quick and painless death intended. They urged that use of these drugs for human execution was the "unapproved use of an approved drug" and constituted a violation of the Act's prohibitions against "misbranding." They also suggested that the FDCA's requirements for approval of "new drugs" applied, since these drugs were now being used for a new purpose. Accordingly, respondents claimed that the FDA was required to approve the drugs as "safe and effective" for human execution before they could be distributed in interstate commerce. See 21 U.S.C. § 355. . . . The FDA Commissioner . . . [refused] to take the requested actions. . . . [He concluded] that FDA jurisdiction in the area was generally unclear but in any event should not be exercised to interfere with this particular aspect of state criminal justice systems. He went on to state:

"Were FDA clearly to have jurisdiction in the area, moreover, we believe we would be authorized to decline to exercise it under our inherent discretion to decline to pursue certain enforcement matters. The unapproved use of approved drugs is an area in which the case law is far from uniform. Generally, enforcement proceedings in this area are initiated only when there is a serious danger to the public health or a blatant scheme to defraud. We cannot conclude that those dangers are present under State lethal injection laws, which are duly authorized statutory enactments in furtherance of proper State functions. . . . "

Respondents then filed the instant suit in the United States District Court for the District of Columbia. . . .

. . . . in reaching our conclusion that the Court of Appeals was wrong . . . we need not and do not address the thorny question of the FDA's jurisdiction. For us, this case turns on the important question of the extent to which determinations by the FDA not to exercise its enforcement authority over the use of drugs in interstate commerce may be judicially reviewed. That decision in turn involves the construction of two separate but necessarily interrelated statutes, the APA and the FDCA.

The APA's comprehensive provisions for judicial review of "agency actions" are contained in 5 U.S.C. §§ 701–706. Any person "adversely affected or aggrieved" by agency action, see § 702, including a "failure to act," is entitled to "judicial review thereof," as long as the action is a "final agency action for which there is no other adequate remedy in a court," see § 704. The standards to be applied on review are governed by the provisions of § 706. But before any review at all may be had, a party must first clear the hurdle of § 701(a). That section provides that the chapter on judicial review "applies, according to the provisions thereof, except to the extent that — (1) statutes preclude judicial review; or (2) agency action is committed to agency discretion by law." Petitioner urges that the decision of the FDA to refuse enforcement is an action "committed to agency discretion by law" under § 701(a)(2).

This Court first discussed § (a)(2) in *Citizens to Preserve Overton Park v. Volpe.* [See casebook, *supra.*]

The relevant federal statute provided that the Secretary "shall not approve" any program or project using public parkland unless the Secretary first determined that no feasible alternatives were available. . . . Interested citizens challenged the Secretary's approval under the APA, arguing that he had not satisfied the substantive statute's requirements. The Court first addressed the "threshold question" of whether the agency's action was at all reviewable. After setting out the language of § 701(a), the Court stated:

"In this case, there is no indication that Congress sought to prohibit judicial review and there is most certainly no 'showing of "clear and convincing evidence" of a . . . legislative intent' to restrict access to judicial review. . . .

"Similarly, the Secretary's decision here does not fall within the exception for action 'committed to agency discretion.' This is a very narrow exception. . . . The legislative history of the Administrative Procedure Act indicates that it is applicable in those rare instances where 'statutes are drawn in such broad terms that in a given case there is no law to apply.' S.Rep. No. 752, 79th Cong., 1st Sess., 26 (1945)." . . .

The above quote answers several of the questions raised by the language of § 701(a), although it raises others. First, it clearly separates the exception provided by § (a)(1) from the § (a)(2) exception. The former applies when Congress has expressed an intent to preclude judicial review. The latter applies in different circumstances; even where Congress has not affirmatively precluded review, review is not to be had if the statute is drawn so that a court would have no meaningful standard against which to judge the agency's exercise of discretion. In such a case, the statute ("law") can be taken to have "committed" the decisionmaking to the agency's judgment absolutely. This construction avoids conflict with the "abuse of discretion" standard of review in § 706 — if no judicially manageable standards are available for judging how and when an agency should exercise its discretion then it is impossible to evaluate agency action for "abuse of discretion." In addition, this construction satisfies the principle of statutory construction mentioned earlier, by identifying a separate class of cases to which § 701(a)(2) applies.

To this point our analysis does not differ significantly from that of the Court of Appeals. That court purported to apply the "no law to apply" standard of *Overton Park.* We disagree, however, with that court's insistence that the "narrow construction" of § (a)(2) required application of a presumption of reviewability even to an agency's decision not to undertake certain enforcement actions. Here we think the Court of Appeals broke with tradition, case law, and sound reasoning.

. . . . This Court has recognized on several occasions over many years that an agency's decision not to prosecute or enforce, whether through civil or criminal process, is a decision generally committed to an agency's absolute discretion . . . This recognition of the existence of discretion is attributable in no small part to the general unsuitability for judicial review of agency decisions to refuse enforcement.

The reasons for this general unsuitability are many. First, an agency decision not to enforce often involves a complicated balancing of a number of factors which are peculiarly within its expertise. Thus, the agency must not only assess whether a violation has occurred, but whether agency resources are best spent on this violation or another, whether the agency is likely to succeed if it acts, whether the particular enforcement action requested best fits the agency's overall policies, and indeed, whether the agency has enough resources to undertake the action at all. . . .

In addition to these administrative concerns, we note that when an agency refuses to act it generally does not exercise its *coercive* power over an individual's liberty or property rights, and thus does not infringe upon areas that courts often are called upon to protect. Similarly, when an agency *does* act to enforce, that action itself provides a focus for judicial review, inasmuch as the agency must have exercised its power in some manner. The action at least can be reviewed to determine whether the agency exceeded its statutory powers. . . . Finally, we recognize that an agency's refusal to institute proceedings shares to some extent the characteristics of the decision of a prosecutor in the Executive Branch, inasmuch as it is the executive who is charged by the Constitution to "take Care that the Laws be faithfully executed." U.S. Const., Art. II, § 3.

We of course only list the above concerns to facilitate understanding of our conclusion that an agency's decision not to take enforcement action should be presumed immune from judicial review under § 701(a)(2). For good reasons, such a decision has traditionally been "committed to agency discretion," and we believe that the Congress enacting the APA did not intend to alter that tradition. . . . In so stating, we emphasize that the decision is only presumptively unreviewable; the presumption may be rebutted where the substantive statute has provided guidelines for an agency to follow in exercising its enforcement powers. . . .

Dunlop v. Bachowski, 421 U.S. 560, 95 S.Ct. 1851, 44 L.Ed.2d 377 (1975) . . . presents an example of statutory language which supplied sufficient standards to rebut the presumption of unreviewability. *Dunlop* involved a suit by a union employee, under the Labor-Management Reporting and Disclosure Act . . . (LMRDA) asking the National Labor Relations Board to investigate and file suit to set aside a union election. Section 482 provided that, upon filing of a complaint by a union member, "[t]he Secretary shall investigate such complaint and, if he finds probable cause to believe that a violation . . . has occurred . . . he shall bring a civil action. . . ." After investigating the plaintiff's claims the Secretary of Labor declined to file suit, and the plaintiff sought judicial review under the APA. This Court held that review was available. . . . Our textual references to the "strong presumption" of reviewability in *Dunlop* were addressed only to the § (a)(1) exception; we were content to rely on the Court of Appeals' opinion that the § (a)(2) exception did not apply. The Court of Appeals, in turn, had found the "principle of absolute prosecutorial discretion" inapplicable, because the language of the LMRDA indicated that the Secretary was required to file suit if certain "clearly defined" factors were present. The decision therefore was not " 'beyond the judicial capacity to supervise.' " . . .

. . . . The danger that agencies may not carry out their delegated powers with sufficient vigor does not necessarily lead to the conclusion that courts are the most appropriate body to police this aspect of their performance. That decision is in the first instance for Congress, and we therefore turn to the FDCA to determine whether in this case Congress has provided us with "law to apply." If it has indicated an intent to circumscribe agency enforcement discretion, and has provided meaningful standards for defining the limits of that discretion, there is "law to apply" under § 701(a)(2), and courts may require the agency follow that law; if it has not, then an agency refusal to institute proceedings is a decision "committed to agency discretion by law" within the meaning of that section.

III

[After examining the provisions of the FDCA, the Court concluded that Act did not circumscribe agency enforcement discretion, at least in circumstances where a violation has not been established to the satisfaction of the FDA.]

IV

We therefore conclude that the presumption that agency decisions not to institute proceedings are unreviewable under § 701(a)(2) of the APA is not overcome by the enforcement provisions of the FDCA. The FDA's decision not to take the enforcement actions requested by respondents is therefore not subject to judicial review under the APA. The general exception to reviewability provided by § 701(a)(2) for action "committed to agency discretion" remains a narrow one, see *Overton Park* . . . but within that exception are included agency refusals to institute investigative or enforcement proceedings, unless Congress has indicated otherwise. In so holding, we essentially leave to Congress, and not to the courts, the decision as to whether an agency's refusal to institute proceedings should be judicially reviewable. . . .

The judgment of the Court of Appeals is *Reversed.*

Questions and Comments

1.   Is there a general presumption of judicial review of agency action? Is there a presumption against judicial review of agency decisions not to take enforcement action?

2.   Did a presumption of judicial review apply to the review of the action of the Secretary of Transportation in the *Overton Park* case?

3.   Did *Dunlop v. Bachowski* hold that the courts could review the decision of the Secretary of Labor not to institute enforcement action under the LMRDA? How was the presumption of unreviewability overcome in that case? Did the Supreme Court address the application of § 701(a)(1) in *Dunlop v. Bachowski?* § 701(a)(2)? Which provision did the Court apply in *Heckler v. Chaney?*

4.   Did the Court contemplate that review in *Dunlop v. Bachowski* would take place on the "abuse of discretion" standard of § 706(2)(A)? How are the provisions of § 701(a)(2) reconciled with the provision of § 706(2)(A) which uses an "abuse of discretion" standard for judicial review?

5.   What considerations underlie the Court's ruling that agency decisions not to enforce should be presumed unreviewable? Did the Court suggest that the courts are ill-equipped to review decisions not to enforce? Why are these decisions more difficult to review than other agency decisions which the courts review routinely? Are agency decisions to enforce generally reviewable? Explain. Does the Court's ruling in *Heckler v. Chaney* partially rest upon a separation-of-powers rationale?

Center for Auto Safety v. Dole, **828 F.2d 799 (D.C. Cir. 1987).** The petitioner requested the National Highway Transportation Safety Administration (NHTSA) to reopen an enforcement investigation against the Ford Motor Company for alleged safety defects in automobiles built between 1966 and 1979. The Secretary of Transportation denied the petitioner's request; and the petitioner challenges the Secretary's denial of its petition to reopen as arbitrary and capricious.

The National Traffic and Motor Vehicle Safety Act of 1966, as amended, states that if the Secretary of Transportation makes a final determination that a safety-related defect exists, the Secretary "shall order the manufacturer [to recall and remedy] such defect. . . ." 15 U.S.C. § 1412(b). The Act also provides that '[a]ny interested person" may petition the Secretary "to commence a proceeding to determine whether to issue a [] [final] order pursuant to section 1412(b)" The NHTSA regulations provide that the agency will grant a petition if the agency finds that there is a "reasonable possibility" of a safety-related defect in the manufacturer's cars. 49 CFR. § 552.8 (1987). NHTSA's regulations also state the decision to grant or deny a petition is to be based on a "technical review" of evidence relevant to the safety issue.

Held: The Secretary's denial of the petition to reopen is reviewable; and review is not confined to the agency's facial rationale as in *Dunlop*, but may extend to the factual record which was before the agency.

> [T]he reasonable possibility standard NHTSA laid down in its own regulations amply rebuts the *Chaney* presumption against reviewability.

> Indeed, if the "reasonable possibility" standard had appeared in the Motor Vehicle Safety Act itself, there could be no doubt that it provided a "judicially manageable" review standard. But the Supreme Court has told us that "[s]o long as [an administrative] regulation is extant it has the force of law. Therefore, NHTSA's own regulation containing the "reasonable possibility" review standard is the legal equivalent of a statutory standard for *Chaney* purposes. . . . In sum, § 552.8 provides a reviewing court with "law to apply" for the purposes of § 701(a)(2).

> In our view, *Dunlop* stands for the . . . principle that courts will not conduct their usual review of the evidence in the administrative record underlying the agency's decision if this kind of review would interfere with *identifiable* congressional objectives of the relevant statute.

> Here, we can identify no congressional objectives of the Motor Vehicle Safety Act with which the normal level of judicial review would interfere. . . .

> The scope of judicial review in this case falls under the "arbitrary" or "capricious" standard of 5 U.S.C. § 706(2)(A), which in this case requires both that the agency's stated reason for denying a citizen petition conform to the rule set forth in its own regulations and that the agency have a sufficient factual basis for its decision.

B. PRIMARY JURISDICTION

Note: The Primary Jurisdiction Doctrine

The primary jurisdiction doctrine originated early in the twentieth century in *Texas & Pacific Ry. v. Abilene Cotton Oil Co.*, 204 U.S. 426 (1907). The doctrine has application when two tribunals — usually an agency and a court — each have jurisdiction over a matter. The doctrine comes into play when a court decides whether another tribunal ought to exercise its jurisdiction first. The doctrine is best understood by considering its derivation in the *Abilene Cotton Oil* case and subsequent development. (a) *The original rationale: Uniformity in rates.* Under the Interstate Commerce Act rail carriers were forbidden to discriminate in their rates among shippers. Carriers were further required to charge reasonable rates; excess charges could be recouped by shippers in reparation actions brought either before the Interstate Commerce Commission or the courts. In its ninth section the Act provided:

> That any person or persons claiming to be damaged by any common carrier subject to the provisions of this act may either make complaint to the Commission, as hereinafter provided for, or may bring suit in his or their own behalf for the recovery of the damages for which such common carrier may be liable under the provisions of this act, in any District or Circuit Court of the United States of competent jurisdiction; but such person or persons shall not have the right to pursue both of said remedies, and must in each case elect which one of the two methods of procedure herein provided for he or they will adopt.

Even prior to the Interstate Commerce Act, a shipper could recoup under the common law the excess paid to a common carrier over a reasonable rate. Section 22 of the Act preserved existing appropriate common law and statutory remedies.

Although the Act thus explicitly allowed shippers which had paid unreasonably high rates to sue for reparations in the amount of the excess paid over the reasonable amounts, the Court held that shippers claiming that they had paid unreasonably high rates had to bring their claims to the Commission for a determination of reasonableness before a court could exercise jurisdiction. The Court imposed this requirement in order that rates should be uniform, and thus prevent the discrimination in rates which the Act sought to prevent.

In the view of the Court rate discrimination would be rampant if each shipper could bring a reparations claim before the courts without going initially to the Commission. Since different courts (and different juries in the same court) might arrive at different determinations of reasonableness in different cases, several shippers which had paid the same rate might receive different recoveries in their respective reparations actions brought before different courts or juries. The result would be that they would have paid different amounts for the same transportation.

To avoid that result, the Court insisted that shippers claiming they had paid amounts in excess of a reasonable rate bring their cases to the Commission for a determination of reasonableness. If all such claims were brought before the same tribunal, according to the Court, all claimants would be treated consistently and each would, in the end, have paid the same amount for the same transportation.

(b) A second rationale: Making use of the regulatory agency's expertise. Later in **Great Northern RR. v. Merchants Elevator Co., 259 U.S. 285 (1922)**, the Court held that the interpretation of a rate schedule (or "tariff") is simply a question of law which can be resolved by the courts without initial resort to the Commission. When the rate schedule (or "tariff") used words in a peculiar or technical sense, however, and where extrinsic evidence was necessary to determine their meaning or proper application, the inquiry was, the Court said, "essentially one of fact and of discretion in technical matters" and the issue must go in the first instance to the Commission. The rationale for the required initial reference to the Commission in this circumstance was that the Commission possessed a superior and specialized competence to resolve these technical issues.

(c) The present state of the primary jurisdiction doctrine. The primary jurisdiction doctrine originated in transportation regulation and grew to maturity there. With the substantial deregulation of transportation rates which has occurred in the last three decades, the importance of the primary-jurisdiction doctrine has declined accordingly. Nonetheless, the doctrine has application in segments of the economy which continue to be subject to regulation. And in those areas its principles continue to be applied. As the *Marquez* case below shows, even though courts and agencies may each be competent to decide an issue, there may well be reasons for requiring that the issue be brought in the first instance to the agency

MARQUEZ v. SCREEN ACTORS GUILD, INC., ET AL.
525 U.S. 33 (1998)

O'CONNOR delivered the opinion of the Court.

Section 8(a)(3) of the National Labor Relations Act (NLRA), 49 Stat. 452, as added, 61 Stat. 140, 29 U.S.C. § 158(a)(3), permits unions and employers to negotiate an agreement that requires union "membership" as a condition of employment for all employees. We have interpreted a proviso to this language to mean that the only "membership" that a union can require is the payment of fees and dues, *NLRB v. General Motors Corp.*, 373 U.S. 734, 742 (1963), and we have held that § 8(a)(3) allows unions to collect and expend funds over the objection of nonmembers only to the extent they are used for collective bargaining, contract administration, and grievance adjustment activities, *Communications Workers v. Beck*, 487 U.S. 735, 745, 762–763 (1988). In this case, we must determine whether a union breaches its duty of fair representation when it negotiates a union security clause that tracks the language of § 8(a)(3) without explaining, in the agreement, this Court's interpretation of that language. We conclude that it does not.

We are also asked to review the Court of Appeals' decision that the District Court did not have jurisdiction to decide a claim that a union breached the duty of fair representation by negotiating a clause that was inconsistent with the statute. We conclude that because this challenge to the union security clause was based purely on an alleged inconsistency with the statute, the Court of Appeals correctly held that this claim was within the primary jurisdiction of the National Labor Relations Board (NLRB or Board).

The language of § 8(a)(3) is at the heart of this case. In pertinent part, it provides as follows:

"It shall be an unfair labor practice for an employer —

"(3) by discrimination in regard to hire or tenure of employment . . . to encourage or discourage membership in any labor organization: *Provided*, That nothing in this subchapter, or in any other statute of the United States, shall preclude an employer from making an agreement with a labor organization . . . to require as a condition of employment membership therein on or after the thirtieth day following the beginning of such employment or the effective date of such agreement, whichever is the later. . . . *Provided further*, That no employer shall justify any discrimination against an employee for nonmembership in a labor organization . . . if he has reasonable grounds for believing that membership was denied or terminated for reasons other than the failure of the employee to tender the periodic dues and the initiation fees uniformly required as a condition of acquiring or retaining membership." 29 U.S.C. § 158(a)(3).

This section is the statutory authorization for "union security clauses," clauses that require employees to become "member[s]" of a union as a condition of employment. . . .

The present dispute arose when petitioner, a part-time actress, successfully auditioned for a one-line role in an episode of the television series, Medicine Ball, which was produced by Lakeside. Petitioner accepted the part, and pursuant to the collective bargaining agreement, Lakeside's casting director called SAG [Screen Actors Guild] to verify that petitioner met the requirements of the union security clause. Because petitioner had previously worked in the motion picture industry for more than 30 days, the union security clause was triggered and petitioner was required to pay the union fees before she could begin working for Lakeside. There is some dispute whether the SAG representative told Lakeside's casting director that petitioner had to "join" or had to "pay" the union; regardless, petitioner understood from the casting director that she had to pay SAG before she could work for Lakeside. Petitioner called SAG's local office and learned that the fees that she would have to pay to join the union would be around $500.

Over the next few days, petitioner attempted to negotiate an agreement with SAG that would allow her to pay the union fees after she was paid for her work by Lakeside. When these negotiations failed to produce an acceptable compromise and petitioner had not paid the required fees by the day before her part was to be filmed, Lakeside hired a different actress to fill the part. At some point after Lakeside hired the new actress, SAG faxed a letter to Lakeside stating that it had no objection to petitioner working in the production. The letter was too late for petitioner; filming proceeded on schedule with the replacement actress.

Petitioner filed suit against Lakeside and SAG alleging, among other things, that SAG had breached the duty of fair representation. According to petitioner, SAG had breached its duty by negotiating and enforcing a union security clause with two basic flaws. First, the union security clause required union "membership" and the payment of full fees and dues when those terms could not be legally enforced under *General Motors* and *Beck*. Petitioner argued that the collective bargaining agreement should have contained language, in addition to the statutory language, informing her of her right not to join the union and of her right, under *Beck*, to pay only for the union's representational activities. Second, the union security clause contained a term that interpreted the 30-day grace period provision to begin running with any employment in the industry. According to petitioner, this interpretation of the grace period provision contravened the express language of § 8(a)(3), which requires that employees be given a 30-day grace period from the beginning of "such employment." She interprets "such employment" to require a new grace period with each employment relationship. Finally, in addition to these claims about the language of the union security clause, petitioner alleged that SAG had violated the duty of fair representation by failing to notify her truthfully about her rights under the NLRA as defined in *Beck* and *General Motors*.

[Petitioner's first claim was that the union breached a duty of fair representation by negotiating a collective bargaining contract with Lakeside that contained a union security provision. According to Petitioner, the collective bargaining agreement should have contained language, in addition to the statutory language that informed her of her right not to join the union and of her right to pay only for the union's representational activities.]. Plaintiff contended that. . . . [T]he union security clause contained a term that interpreted the 30-day grace period provision to begin running with any employment in the industry. According to petitioner, this interpretation of the grace period provision contravened the express language of § 8(a)(3), which requires that employees be given a 30-day grace period from the beginning of "such employment." She interprets "such employment" to require a new grace period with each employment relationship. Finally, in addition to these claims about the language of the union security clause, petitioner alleged that SAG had violated the duty of fair representation by failing to notify her truthfully about her rights under the NLRA as defined in *Beck* and *General Motors*.

The Court of Appeals . . . correctly refused to exercise jurisdiction over petitioner's challenge to the 30-day grace period provision of the union security clause. Petitioner argues that all duty of fair representation claims are cognizable in federal court, and that because she couched her claim as a breach of the duty of fair representation, her claim by definition can be heard in federal court. . . . Petitioner's starting point correctly describes the law. When a plaintiff challenges an action that is "arguably subject to § 7 or § 8 of the [NLRA]," this challenge is within the primary jurisdiction of the NLRB. *San Diego Building Trades Council v. Garmon*, 359 U.S. 236, 245 (1959). These claims are within the primary jurisdiction of the NLRB in part to promote the uniform interpretation of the NLRA. *Id.*, at 242-243. But when a plaintiff alleges a breach of the duty of fair representation, this claim is cognizable in the first instance in federal court. *Vaca v. Sipes*, 386 U.S., at 177–183, *Breininger v. Sheet Metal Workers, supra*, at 73–84. In *Breininger*, we rejected the invitation to create exceptions to this rule based on the expertise of the NLRB, the subject matter of the complaint, or the presence of any other factor. 493 U.S., at 75–77. Thus, petitioner is on solid ground to argue that if her challenge to the grace period provision is a duty of fair representation claim, the lower courts erred in refusing to exercise jurisdiction over that claim.

The qualification — *if* her challenge is a duty of fair representation claim — is important. The ritualistic incantation of the phrase "duty of fair representation" is insufficient to invoke the primary jurisdiction of federal courts. As we noted in *Beck*, "[e]mployees . . . may not circumvent the primary jurisdiction of the NLRB simply by casting statutory claims as violations of the union's duty of fair representation." 487 U.S., at 743. When a plaintiff's only claim is that the union violated the NLRA, the plaintiff cannot avoid the jurisdiction of the NLRB by characterizing this alleged statutory violation as a breach of the duty of fair representation. To invoke federal jurisdiction when the claim is based in part on a violation of the NLRA, there must be something *more* than just a claim that the union violated the statute. The plaintiff must adduce facts suggesting that the union's violation of the statute was arbitrary, discriminatory, or in bad faith.

This does not mean that federal courts cannot resolve statutory issues under the NLRA in the first instance. Although federal district courts cannot resolve pure statutory claims under the NLRA, they can resolve statutory issues to the extent that the resolution of these issues is necessary for a decision on the plaintiff's duty of fair representation claim. *Ibid.* (quoting *Connell Constr. Co. v. Plumbers*, 421 U.S. 616, 626 (1975)). Thus in *Beck*, we resolved the statutory question because it was collateral to the duty of fair representation claim, and that claim was independently within the jurisdiction of the federal courts. 487 U.S., at 743–744. The power of federal courts to resolve statutory issues under the NLRA when they arise as collateral matters in a duty of fair representation suit does not open the door for federal court first instance resolution of all statutory claims. Federal courts can only resolve § 7 and § 8 claims that are collateral to a duty of fair representation claim.

Applying these principles in this case, petitioner's challenge to SAG's grace period provision falls squarely within the primary jurisdiction of the NLRB. Her claim is that SAG employed a term in the collective bargaining agreement that was inconsistent with the NLRA. This allegation, although framed by the recitation that this act breached the duty of fair representation, is at base a claim that SAG's conduct violated § 8(a)(3). This claim is not collateral to any independent basis for federal jurisdiction; there are no facts alleged suggesting that this violation was arbitrary, discriminatory, or in bad faith. Petitioner argues that the term is misleading because it misrepresents the employee's obligations as stated in the NLRA, but this transparent attempt to avoid the jurisdiction of the NLRB is unconvincing. This term is not misleading; the only question is whether the term is consistent with federal law. Because petitioner's only argument is that the term is inconsistent with § 8(a)(3), her claim falls within the primary jurisdiction of the NLRB.

Petitioner attempts to avoid this conclusion by arguing that her challenge to the grace period provision is structurally identical to the duty of fair representation claim considered in *Beck* and to the duty of fair representation claim considered in the first part of this opinion . . . Thus, according to petitioner, because these claims were cognizable in federal trial court, so is her challenge to the grace period provision. But in *Beck* it was the union that relied on § 8(a)(3) as a defense to the plaintiffs' claim that it breached the duty of fair representation. When a claim that a union has breached its duty of fair representation is based in part on an alleged violation of the NLRA, it must be independently supported by some allegations describing arbitrary, discriminatory, or bad faith union conduct. Thus, as we described above, in *Beck*, the duty of fair representation claim was not premised on the mere unlawfulness of the union's conduct. The basis for the fair representation claim was that the union's conduct was arbitrary and possibly in bad faith. Petitioner's challenge to the membership and fees requirements of the union security clause is similarly distinguishable from her challenge to the grace period provision. The claim we considered in the first part of the opinion was that the union's negotiation of the union security clause breached the duty of fair representation because it was arbitrary and in bad faith for the union to negotiate a clause that might mislead employees. This claim, like the claim considered in *Beck*, is not solely about the interpretation of the statute. Petitioner's challenge to the grace period provision, by contrast, is at most an allegation that the union violated the statute. This claim is quintessentially an issue for resolution by the NLRB, and the Court of Appeals correctly refused to uphold District Court jurisdiction over it.

Accordingly, the judgment of the United States Court of Appeals for the Ninth Circuit is affirmed.

It is so ordered.

In an earlier case, ***Ricci v. Chicago Mercantile Exchange***, 409 U.S. 289 (1973), one Ricci, the plaintiff, had brought an antitrust suit against the Chicago Mercantile Exchange, claiming that the Exchange had conspired with others to deny him a seat on the Exchange. Ricci alleged that he:

> had purchased a membership in the Exchange in 1967, using funds borrowed from the Trading Company, and that in February 1969 the Exchange, at the instance of the Trading Company, transferred the membership to another, without notice and hearing, utilizing a blank transfer authorization that had previously been revoked. Allegedly, this course of conduct violated both the rules of the Exchange and the Commodity Exchange Act and was pursuant to an unlawful conspiracy aimed at restraining the conduct of Ricci's business. The result was, the complaint asserted, that Ricci was excluded from trading on the Exchange from February 11, 1969, until March 4, 1969, when he purchased another membership at a considerably higher price than the transferred membership had previously cost.

The Court ruled that:

> given [the Commodity Exchange Commission's] administrative authority to examine the Ricci-Exchange dispute in the light of the regulatory scheme and Exchange rules, the antitrust action should be stayed until the administrative officials have had opportunity to act. This judgment rests on three related premises: (1) that it will be essential for the antitrust court to determine whether the Commodity Exchange Act or any of its provisions are "incompatible with the maintenance of an antitrust action (2) that some facets of the dispute between Ricci and the Exchange are within the statutory jurisdiction of the Commodity Exchange Commission; and (3)

that adjudication of that dispute by the Commission promises to be of material aid in resolving the immunity question. . . .

We . . . think it very likely that a prior agency adjudication of this dispute will be a material aid in ultimately deciding whether the Commodity Exchange Act forecloses this antitrust suit, a matter that seems to depend in the first instance on whether the transfer of Ricci's membership was in violation of the Act for failure to follow Exchange rules. That issue in turn appears to pose issues of fact and questions about the scope, meaning, and significance of Exchange membership rules. These are matters that should be dealt with in the first instance by those especially familiar with the customs and practices of the industry and of the unique marketplace involved in this case. . . . We should recognize "that the courts, while retaining the final authority to expound the statute, should avail themselves of the aid implicit in the agency's superiority in gathering the relevant facts and in marshaling them into a meaningful pattern-." . . . The adjudication of the Commission, if it is forthcoming, will be subject to judicial review and would obviate any necessity for the antitrust court to relitigate the issues actually disposed of by the agency decision. . . . Of course, the question of [antitrust] immunity, as such, will not be before the agency; but if Ricci's complaint is sustained, the immunity issue will dissolve, whereas if it is rejected and the conduct of the Exchange warranted by a valid membership rule, the court will be in a much better position to determine whether the antitrust action should go forward. Affording the opportunity for administrative action will "prepare the way, if the litigation should take its ultimate course, for a more informed and precise determination by the Court of the scope and meaning of the statute as applied to [these] particular circumstances . . .

Questions and Comments

1. Why did the NLRB possess primary jurisdiction over Marquez's claim about the grace period? Which institution (court or agency) possessed primary jurisdiction over a "fair representation" claim? Which institution possessed primary jurisdiction over a claim that a union or employer violated a provision of the labor act? Can you make sense out of the Court's distinction? If a Court possessed primary jurisdiction over violations of the labor act, what would happen to the functioning of the NLRB? Does the integrity of the regulatory scheme established by the National Labor Relations Act demand that the NLRB possess exclusive jurisdiction over violations of the Act? If it possesses exclusive jurisdiction, why did not the Court say that the NLRB possessed exclusive jurisdiction?

2. Is *Ricci* a case in which both the Commodity Exchange Commission and the courts have jurisdiction? Can the Commission rule on Ricci's antitrust claim? Must that claim ultimately be litigated in court if Ricci is to prevail? How then is this a case in which both the Commission and the courts can be said to possess jurisdiction?

3. What rationale underlies the Court's determination that Ricci must first take his complaint to the Commodity Exchange Commission? This is not an application

of the uniformity rationale of the *Abeline* case, is it? Is it an application of the agency expertise rationale of the *Great Northern Ry.* case?

4. Is the Court in effect requiring Ricci to go through two pieces of litigation, one before the Commission and a subsequent one before a court? Will this procedure really assist the court to decide the case better than it otherwise would? Are the costs that this procedure imposes upon litigants worth the supposed improvement in decisional results? Could the Commission assist the court as a party to the court proceedings and thereby obviate the need for two separate pieces of litigation?

5. Has the Court employed some of the rationales for the exhaustion doctrine *[see infra]* as justifications for imposing upon Ricci the obligation to bring his case in the first instance before the Commission?

C.   EXHAUSTION

1.   *The Classic Cases.*

MYERS v. BETHLEHEM SHIPBUILDING CORP.
303 U.S. 41 (1938)

Mr. Justice Brandeis delivered the opinion of the Court.

The question for decision is whether a federal district court has equity jurisdiction to enjoin the National Labor Relations Board from holding a hearing upon a complaint filed by it against an employer alleged to be engaged in unfair labor practices prohibited by the National Labor Relations Act. . . .

We are of opinion that the District Court was without power to enjoin the Board from holding the hearings.

First. There is no claim by the Corporation that the statutory provisions and the rules of procedure prescribed for such hearings are illegal. . . . The claim [of the Corporation] is that the provisions of the Act are not applicable to the Corporation's business at the Fore River Plant, because the operations conducted there are not carried on, and the products manufactured are not sold, in interstate or foreign commerce; that, therefore, the Corporation's relations with its employees at the plant cannot burden or interfere with such commerce; that hearings would, at best, be futile; and that the holding of them would result in irreparable damage to the Corporation, not only by reason of their direct cost and the loss of time of its officials and employees, but also because the hearings would cause serious impairment of the good will and harmonious relations existing between the Corporation and its employees, and thus seriously impair the efficiency of its operations.

Second. The District Court is without jurisdiction to enjoin hearings because the power "to prevent any person from engaging in any unfair practice affecting commerce," has been vested by Congress in the Board. . . . The grant of that exclusive power is constitutional, because the Act provided for appropriate procedure before the Board and in the review by the Circuit Court of Appeals an adequate opportunity to secure judicial protection against possible illegal action on the part of the Board. No power to enforce an order is conferred upon the Board. To secure enforcement, the Board must apply to a Circuit Court of Appeals for its affirmance . . . The Act establishes standards to which the Board must conform. There must be complaint, notice and hearing. The Board must receive evidence and make findings. The findings as to the facts are conclusive, but only if supported by evidence. The order of the Board is subject to review by the designated court, and only when sustained by the court may the order be enforced. Upon that review all questions of the jurisdiction of the Board and the regularity of its proceedings, all questions of constitutional right or statutory authority, are open to examination by the court. We construe the procedural provisions as affording adequate opportunity to secure judicial protection against arbitrary action. . . .

It is true that the Board has jurisdiction only if the complaint concerns interstate or foreign commerce. Unless the Board finds that it does, the complaint must be dismissed. And if it finds that interstate or foreign commerce is involved, but the Circuit Court of Appeals concludes that such finding was without adequate evidence to support it, or otherwise contrary to law, the Board's petition to enforce it will be dismissed, or the employer's petition to have it set aside will be granted. Since the procedure before the Board is adequate, Congress had power to vest exclusive jurisdiction in the Board and the Circuit Court of Appeals. . . .

Third. The Corporation contends that, since it denies that interstate or foreign commerce is involved and claims that a hearing would subject it to irreparable damage, rights guaranteed by the Federal Constitution will be denied unless it be held that the District Court has jurisdiction to enjoin the holding of a hearing by the Board. So to hold would . . . in effect substitute the District Court for the Board as the tribunal to hear and determine what Congress declared the Board exclusively should hear and determine in the first instance. The contention is at war with the long settled rule of judicial administration that no one is entitled to judicial relief for a supposed or threatened injury until the prescribed administrative remedy has been exhausted. That rule has been repeatedly acted on in cases where, as here, the contention is made that the administrative body lacked power over the subject matter.

Obviously, the rule requiring exhaustion of the administrative remedy cannot be circumvented by asserting that the charge on which the complaint rests is groundless and that the mere holding of the prescribed administrative hearing would result in irreparable damage. Lawsuits also often prove to have been groundless; but no way has been discovered of relieving a defendant from the necessity of a trial to establish the fact. . . .

Decrees for preliminary injunction reversed with direction to dismiss the bills.

Questions and Comments

1. In the early twentieth century, manufacturing was considered to be a stationary activity not involving interstate commerce. An appreciation of this older view of manufacturing is necessary in order to make sense of the claims of the Shipbuilding Company.

2. Are the rights of the Shipbuilding Company adequately protected under the procedure ordered by the Court? Does the Company have a right to have its interstate commerce claim considered by a court? Will a court consider that claim? Will a court decide whether the Company's operations take place in interstate commerce? Will a court decide that question *de novo*, or will it merely rule upon whether the Board determination of that question was supported by substantial evidence?

3. What is the significance that the Company claims that the Board is without jurisdiction? If the Board lacks jurisdiction, then the review provisions of the National Labor Relations Act do not apply, do they? Or does the Board have jurisdiction to determine its own jurisdiction? How does this case differ from *Leedom v. Kyne [supra]* where the plaintiff avoided the review provisions of the NLRA because the Board was acting beyond its jurisdiction?

4. Is the claim being made here by the Company a type of claim that many (or even most) companies could make routinely in other cases? Was the Court concerned to prevent employers generally from tying up the Board enforcement proceedings in court litigation? Was the Court trying to force the employers generally to litigate routine issues before the Board? Why?

ALLEN v. GRAND CENTRAL AIRCRAFT CO.
347 U.S. 535 (1954)

[Suit by an employer to enjoin a proceeding against it brought by the Wage Stabilization Board before the National Enforcement Commission. As a result of the outbreak of the Korean War, Congress had enacted the Defense Production Act of 1950 which authorized the establishment of a system of wage and price controls. The administrative machinery for enforcing these controls was established by the President through Executive Order.

Appellee, Grand Central Aircraft Company was engaged in the production and repair of aircraft. The Wage Stabilization Board filed a complaint with the National Enforcement Commission alleging that Grand Central Aircraft had paid wage increases in violation of a wage freeze order. After a hearing was set but before it was held, Appellee Grand Central Aircraft brought suit to enjoin the hearing, contending that the President had no power under the Defense Production Act to establish administrative machinery to enforce wage controls.

Grand Central Aircraft contended that the Defense Production Act of 1950 vested enforcement of the Act in the district courts and left to the President only authority to promulgate general regulations. The district court enjoined the proceedings before the National Enforcement Commission.]

Mr. Justice Burton delivered the opinion of the Court.

The principal question for decision is whether the Defense Production Act of 1950 authorized the President to apply administrative action to the enforcement of its wage stabilization provisions. For the reasons hereafter stated, we decide that it did.

We consider first the claim to injunctive relief which appellee made on the ground that the conduct of the proposed administrative hearings would cause it irreparable damage by weakening its bank credit and depriving it of essential working capital. On that basis, interlocutory relief was granted. . . . That injunction has been made permanent but the Government . . . contends that appellee is acting prematurely in seeking such relief before carrying the prescribed administrative procedure at least to the point where it faces some immediate compulsion and greater probability of damages than it has established.

[handwritten margin note: reason for injunctive relief: irreparable damage by admin hearing]

. . . . Appellee argues that such proceedings [before the National Enforcement Commission] carry the possibility of the disallowance as a business expense, for income-tax purposes, of $750,000, more or less, up to the total wages paid, exceeding $5,500,000. Appellee contends also that the mere threat of such action would jeopardize the bank credit upon which it depends for essential working capital. There is grave doubt of the right of appellee thus to test the validity of administrative procedure before exhausting it or bringing the issues closer to a focus than it has done. However, it is clear that once the right of the Government to hold administrative hearings is established, a litigant cannot enjoin them merely because they might jeopardize his bank credit or otherwise be inconvenient or embarrassing. . . .

It is appellee's principal claim that there is no properly authorized administrative procedure for it to exhaust and that the administrative authorities who seek to determine its case have no lawful right to do so. We, therefore, go directly to the heart of this controversy, which is the question whether the administrative enforcement of the 1950 wage stabilization program has been validly authorized.

[The Court then construed the Defense Production Act of 1950, concluding that it followed closely the Stabilization Act of 1942 under which the President exercised authority similar to that challenged in this case.]. . . . We hold that the specific language of § 405(b) [of the Defense Production Act] should receive the same construction now that was placed on similar language in the Act of 1942. . . .

We have noted the other arguments submitted by appellee concerning the interpretation and constitutionality of the statute but it would be premature action on our part to rule upon these until after the required administrative procedures have been exhausted.

Questions and Comments

1. Why do you think the Court went "directly to the heart of . . . [the] controversy" and dealt with "the question whether the administrative enforcement of the 1950 wage stabilization program has been validly authorized"? Why did the

Court not require the Company to exhaust its administrative remedies before answering that question?

2. What rationale, do you think, explains the Court's failure to apply the exhaustion doctrine to the question of whether the administrative enforcement of the wage stabilization program had been validly authorized? Did it apply the exhaustion doctrine to other issues before it? On what rationale, do you think? Can you reconcile *Allen v. Grand Central Aircraft* with *Myers?*

3. Did *Allen v. Grand Central Aircraft* involve an issue about the jurisdiction of the administrative tribunal? Did *Myers? How* did the jurisdictional issue in *Allen v. Grand Central Aircraft* differ from the jurisdictional issue in *Myers?*

4. Was the jurisdictional issue in *Allen* the kind whose resolution would affect all other cases under the wage stabilization program? Would the determination of the issue as to whether the Bethlehem Shipbuilding Corporation was engaged in interstate commerce resolve interstate commerce issues in other cases? Why not? Was the resolution of the issue in *Myers* dependent upon the facts peculiar to the Bethlehem Shipbuilding Corporation? Was the resolution of the issue in *Allen* dependent upon facts peculiar to the Grand Central Aircraft Company?

2. *The Exhaustion Doctrine in More Modern Dress.*

a. *The Rationale Reconsidered and Articulated.*

MCKART v. UNITED STATES
395 U.S. 185 (1969)

[Petitioner was convicted for failing to report and submit for induction into the armed forces. At trial, petitioner's only defense was that he should have been exempt from military service because he was the "sole surviving son" of a family whose father had been killed in action while in the armed forces. The district court held that he could not raise that defense because he had failed to exhaust the administrative remedies provided by the Selective Service System. He was convicted and sentenced to three years' imprisonment; the court of appeals affirmed. The U.S. Supreme Court then granted certiorari.]

MR. JUSTICE MARSHALL delivered the opinion of the Court.

The Government maintains . . . that petitioner cannot raise the invalidity of his I-A classification and subsequent induction order as a defense to a criminal prosecution for refusal to report for induction. According to the Government, petitioner's failure to appeal his reclassification after the death of his mother constitutes a failure to exhaust available administrative remedies and therefore should bar all judicial review. For the reasons set out below, we cannot agree.

Perhaps the most common application of the exhaustion doctrine is in cases where the relevant statute provides that certain administrative procedures shall be exclusive. . . . The reasons for making such procedures exclusive, and for the judicial application of the exhaustion doctrine in cases where the statutory requirement of exclusivity is not so explicit, are not difficult to understand. A primary purpose is, of course, the avoidance of premature interruption of the administrative process. The agency, like a trial court, is created for the purpose of applying a statute in the first instance. Accordingly, it is normally desirable to let the agency develop the necessary factual background upon which decisions should be based. And since agency decisions are frequently of a discretionary nature or frequently require expertise, the agency should be given the first chance to exercise that discretion or to apply that expertise. And of course it is generally more efficient for the administrative process to go forward without interruption than it is to permit the parties to seek aid from the courts at various intermediate stages. The very same reasons lie behind judicial rules sharply limiting interlocutory appeals.

Closely related to the above reasons is a notion peculiar to administrative law. The administrative agency is created as a separate entity and invested with certain powers and duties. The courts ordinarily should not interfere with an agency until it has completed its action or else has clearly exceeded its jurisdiction. As Professor Jaffe puts it, "[t]he exhaustion doctrine is, therefore, an expression of executive and administrative autonomy." This reason is particularly pertinent where the function of the agency and the particular decision sought to be reviewed involve exercise of discretionary powers granted the agency by Congress, or require application of special expertise.

Some of these reasons apply equally to cases like the present one, where the administrative process is at an end and a party seeks judicial review of a decision that was not appealed through the administrative process. Particularly, judicial review may be hindered by the failure of the litigant to allow the agency to make a factual record, or to exercise its discretion or apply its expertise. In addition, other justifications for requiring exhaustion in cases of this sort have nothing to do with the dangers of interruption of the administrative process. Certain very practical notions of judicial efficiency come into play as well. A complaining party may be successful in vindicating his rights in the administrative process. If he is required to pursue his administrative remedies, the courts may never have to intervene. And notions of administrative autonomy require that the agency be given a chance to discover and correct its own errors. Finally, it is possible that frequent and deliberate flouting of administrative processes could weaken the effectiveness of an agency by encouraging people to ignore its procedures.

. . . . We are not here faced with a premature resort to the courts — all administrative remedies are now closed to petitioner. We are asked instead to hold that petitioner's failure to utilize a particular administrative process — an appeal — bars him from defending a criminal prosecution on grounds which could have been raised on that appeal. We cannot agree that application of the exhaustion doctrine would be proper in the circumstances of the present case.

First of all, it is well to remember that use of the exhaustion doctrine in criminal cases can be exceedingly harsh. The defendant is often stripped of his only defense; he must go to jail without having any judicial review of an assertedly invalid order. This deprivation of judicial review occurs not when the affected person is affirmatively asking for assistance from the courts but when the Government is attempting to impose criminal sanctions on him. Such a result should not be tolerated unless the interests underlying the exhaustion rule clearly outweigh the severe burden imposed upon the registrant if he is denied judicial review. . . .

The question of whether petitioner is entitled to exemption as a sole surviving son is . . . solely one of statutory interpretation. The resolution of that issue does not require any particular expertise on the part of the appeal board; the proper interpretation is certainly not a matter of discretion. In this sense, the issue is different from many Selective Service classification questions which do involve expertise or the exercise of discretion, both by the local boards and the appeal boards. Petitioner's failure to take his claim through all available administrative appeals only deprived the Selective Service System of the opportunity of having its appellate boards resolve a question of statutory interpretation. Since judicial review would not be significantly aided by an additional administrative decision of this sort, we cannot see any compelling reason why petitioner's failure to appeal should bar his only defense to a criminal prosecution. . . .

We hold that petitioner's failure to appeal his classification and failure to report for his pre-induction physical do not bar a challenge to the validity of his classification as a defense to his criminal prosecution for refusal to submit to induction. We also hold that petitioner was entitled to exemption from military service as a sole surviving son. Accordingly, we reverse the judgment of the court below and remand the case for entry of a judgment of acquittal.

It is so ordered.

Questions and Comments

1. In *McKart* the Court considers in detail the rationales underlying the exhaustion doctrine. Do these rationales fit the other cases which you have read? It will aid your grasp of the exhaustion doctrine to review these cases in the light of the discussion in *McKart*.

2. Does the parallel between the exhaustion doctrine of administrative law and the rule in the federal court system against interlocutory appeals help you to predict when a court will insist upon exhaustion of administrative remedies and when it will not?

3. Are you helped in applying the exhaustion doctrine by inquiring whether the issue being litigated is a general one which is likely to arise in many cases, or whether the issue is a highly particularistic one whose resolution will affect only the parties to the case at hand?

4. What would be the policy arguments for imposing a requirement of exhaustion in a case like *McKart?* for not applying such a requirement? Besides the harsh effect that the application of an exhaustion requirement would have had in *McKart*, were there other reasons for not applying it?

5. Do you see any parallels between *McKart* and *Grand Central Aircraft?* Do both cases involve issues which are general ones? whose resolution applies to other cases as well as the one being decided? are these issues of "law"? in what sense? Explain.

DARBY v. CISNEROS
509 U.S. 137 (1993)

[Petitioner R. Gordon Darby was a real estate developer who obtained mortgage insurance from the Department of Housing and Urban Development (HUD) under circumstances which the Department later viewed as improper. As a result HUD instituted proceedings to debar Darby from further participation in all HUD procurement contracts and in any nonprocurement transaction with any federal agency. A hearing was conducted before an ALJ who ruled that Darby had employed a "sham" financing method which improperly circumvented HUD rules. Because of the presence of mitigating factors, however, the ALJ concluded that Darby's period of debarment should be limited to 18 months. Rather than seeking review from the Secretary, Darby brought suit in federal district court for an injunction against the implementation of the debarment order.]

JUSTICE BLACKMUN delivered the opinion of the Court.

This case presents the question whether federal courts have the authority to require that a plaintiff exhaust available administrative remedies before seeking judicial review under the Administrative Procedure Act (APA), 5 U.S.C. § 701 et seq., where neither the statute nor agency rules specifically mandate exhaustion as a prerequisite to judicial review. At issue is the relationship between the judicially created doctrine of exhaustion of administrative remedies and the statutory requirements of § 10(c) of the APA.[1]

. . . .

Under HUD regulations,

"[t]he hearing officer's determination shall be final unless, pursuant to 24 CFR part 26, the Secretary or the Secretary's designee, within 30 days of receipt of a request decides as a matter of discretion to review the finding of the hearing officer. The 30 day period for deciding whether to review a determination may be extended upon written notice of such extension by the Secretary or his designee. Any party may request such a review in writing within 15 days of receipt of the hearing officer's determination." 24 CFR § 24.314(C) (1992).

---

[1] Section 10(c), 5 U.S.C. § 704, provides: "Agency action made reviewable by statute and final agency action for which there is no other adequate remedy in a court are subject to judicial review. A preliminary, procedural, or intermediate agency action or ruling not directly reviewable is subject to review on the review of the final agency action. Except as otherwise expressly required by statute, agency action otherwise final is final for the purposes of this section whether or not there has been presented or determined an application for a declaratory order, for any form of reconsideration, or, unless the agency otherwise requires by rule and provides that the action meanwhile is inoperative, for an appeal to superior agency authority."

We note that the statute as codified in the United States Code refers to "any form of reconsiderations," with the last word being in the plural. The version of § 10(c) as enacted, however, uses the singular "reconsideration." See ch. 404, § 10(c), 79th Cong., 2d Sess., 60 Stat. 243 (1946). We quote the text as enacted in the Statutes at Large. See Stephan v. United States 319 U.S. 423, 426 (1943) ("[T]he Code cannot prevail over the Statutes at Large when the two are inconsistent").

Neither petitioners nor respondents sought further administrative review of the ALJ's "Initial Decision and Order."

On May 31, 1990, petitioners filed suit in the United States District Court for the District of South Carolina. They sought an injunction and a declaration that the administrative sanctions were imposed for purposes of punishment, in violation of HUD's own debarment regulations, and therefore were "not in accordance with law" within the meaning of § 10(e)(B)(1) of the APA, 5 U.S.C. § 706(2)(A).

Respondents moved to dismiss the complaint on the ground that petitioners, by forgoing the option to seek review by the Secretary, had failed to exhaust administrative remedies. The District Court denied respondents' motion to dismiss, reasoning that the administrative remedy was inadequate and that resort to that remedy would have been futile. . . . [but the Court of Appeals for the Seventh Circuit reversed]. . . .

II

Section 10(c) of the APA bears the caption "Actions reviewable." It provides in its first two sentences that judicial review is available for "final agency action for which there is no other adequate remedy in a court," and that "preliminary, procedural, or intermediate agency action . . . is subject to review on the review of the final agency action." The last sentence of § 10(c) reads:

> "Except as otherwise expressly required by statute, agency action otherwise final is final for the purposes of this section whether or not there has been presented or determined an application for a declaratory order, for any form of reconsideration . . . or, unless the agency otherwise requires by rule and provides that the action meanwhile is inoperative, for an appeal to superior agency authority." 5 U.S.C. § 704.

Petitioners argue that this provision means that a litigant seeking judicial review of a final agency action under the APA need not exhaust available administrative remedies unless such exhaustion is expressly required by statute or agency rule. According to petitioners, since § 10(c) contains an explicit exhaustion provision, federal courts are not free to require further exhaustion as a matter of judicial discretion.

. . . . the text of the APA leaves little doubt that petitioners are correct. Under § 10(a) of the APA, "[a] person suffering legal wrong because of agency action, or adversely affected or aggrieved by agency action within the meaning of a relevant statute, *is entitled to judicial review thereof.*" 5 U.S.C. § 702 (emphasis added). Although § 10(a) provides the general right to judicial review of agency actions under the APA, § 10(c) establishes when such review is available. When an aggrieved party has exhausted all administrative remedies expressly prescribed by statute or agency rule, the agency action is "final for the purposes of this section" and therefore "subject to judicial review" under the first sentence. While federal courts may be free to apply, where appropriate, other prudential doctrines of judicial administration to limit the scope and timing of judicial review, § 10(c), by its very terms, has limited the availability of the doctrine of exhaustion of administrative remedies to that which the statute or rule clearly mandates.

The last sentence of § 10(c) refers explicitly to "any form of reconsideration" and "an appeal to superior agency authority." Congress clearly was concerned with making the exhaustion requirement unambiguous so that aggrieved parties would know precisely what administrative steps were required before judicial review would be available. If courts were able to impose additional exhaustion requirements beyond those provided by Congress or the agency, the last sentence of § 10(c) would make no sense. To adopt respondents' reading would transform § 10(c) from a provision designed to " 'remove obstacles to judicial review of agency action,' " . . . into a trap for unwary litigants. Section 10(c) explicitly requires exhaustion of all intra-agency appeals mandated either by statute or by agency rule; it would be inconsistent with the plain language of § 10(c) for courts to require litigants to exhaust optional appeals as well.

. . . . [T]his case requires the recognition that, with respect to actions brought under the APA, Congress effectively codified the doctrine of exhaustion of administrative remedies in § 10(c). Of course, the exhaustion doctrine continues to apply as a matter of judicial discretion in cases not governed by the APA. But where the APA applies, an appeal to "superior agency authority" is a prerequisite to judicial review only when expressly required by statute or when an agency rule requires appeal before review and the administrative action is made inoperative pending that review. Courts are not free to impose an exhaustion requirement as a rule of judicial administration where the agency action has already become "final" under § 10(c).

The judgment of the Court of Appeals is reversed, and the case is remanded for further proceedings consistent with this opinion.

It is so ordered.

Questions and Comments

1. The Court had earlier ruled in *McCarthy v. Madigan*, 503 U.S. 140 (1992) that a federal prisoner seeking money damages against prison officials for denial of medical care was not subject to a requirement that he first exhaust the Federal Bureau of Prisons administrative remedy procedure. In so ruling the Court weighed the individual interests of the prisoner against the institutional interests favoring an exhaustion requirement, concluding that the individual interests were more weighty in the circumstances.

In deciding *McCarthy v. Madigan*, the Court noted that the limited exhaustion requirement imposed in the Civil Rights of Institutionalized Persons Act [discussed in *Patsy v. Board of Regents*, 457 U.S. 496 (1982), casebook, *infra*] applied only to state prisoners.

2. Would the ruling in *Darby* change the result in circumstances replicating the facts in any of the exhaustion cases with which you are familiar?

THUNDER BASIN COAL CO. v. REICH
510 U.S. 200 (1994)

JUSTICE BLACKMUN delivered the opinion of the Court.

In this case, we address the question whether the statutory-review scheme in the Federal Mine Safety and Health Amendments Act of 1977, 91 Stat. 1292, as amended, 30 U.S.C. §§ 801 et seq. (1988 ed. and Supp. IV) (Mine Act or Act), prevents a district court from exercising subject-matter jurisdiction over a pre-enforcement challenge to the Act. We hold that it does.

I

Congress adopted the Mine Act "to protect the health and safety of the nation's coal or other miners." 30 U.S.C. § 801(g). The Act requires the Secretary of Labor or his representative to conduct periodic, unannounced health and safety inspections of the Nation's mines. Section § 813(f) provides:

> "A representative of the operator and a representative authorized by his miners shall be given an opportunity to accompany the Secretary or his authorized representative during the physical inspection of any coal or other mine . . . for the purpose of aiding such inspection and to participate in pre- or post-inspection conferences held at the mine."

Regulations promulgated under this section define a miners' representative as "[a]ny person or organization which represents two or more miners at a coal or other mine for purposes of the Act." 30 CFR § 40.1(b)(1) (1993).

In addition to exercising these "walk-around" inspection rights under § 813(f), persons designated as representatives of the miners may obtain certain health and safety information and promote health and safety enforcement. Once the mine employees designate one or more persons as their representatives, the employer must post at the mine information regarding these designees. 30 CFR § 40.4.

The Secretary has broad authority to compel immediate compliance with Mine Act provisions through the use of mandatory civil penalties, discretionary daily civil penalties, and other sanctions. Challenges to enforcement are reviewed by the Federal Mine Safety and Health Review Commission, 30 U.S.C. §§ 815 and 823, which is independent of the Department of Labor, and by the appropriate United States Court of Appeals, § 816.

II

Petitioner Thunder Basin Coal Company operates a surface coal mine in Wyoming with approximately 500 nonunion employees. In 1990, petitioner's employees selected two employees of the United Mine Workers of America (UMWA), who were not employees of the mine, to serve as their miners' representatives pursuant to § 813(f). Petitioner did not post the information regarding the miners' representatives as required by 30 CFR § 40.4, but complained to the Mine Safety and Health Administration (MSHA) that the designation compromised its rights under the National Labor Relations Act. . . . The MSHA District Manager responded with a letter instructing petitioner to post the miners' representative designations. . . .

Rather than post the designations and before receiving the MSHA letter, petitioner filed suit in the United States District Court for the District of Wyoming for pre-enforcement injunctive relief. . . . Petitioner contended that the designation of non-employee UMWA "representatives" violated the principles of collective-bargaining representation under the NLRA as well as the company's NLRA rights to exclude union organizers from its property. . . . Petitioner argued then, as it does here, that deprivation of these rights would harm the company irreparably by "giv[ing] the union organizing advantages in terms of access, personal contact and knowledge that would not be available under the labor laws, as well as enhanced credibility flowing from the appearance of government imprimatur." . . .

Petitioner additionally alleged that requiring it to challenge the MSHA's interpretation of 30 U.S.C. § 813(f) and 30 CFR pt. 40 through the statutory-review process would violate the Due Process Clause of the Fifth Amendment, since the company would be forced to choose between violating the Act and incurring possible escalating daily penalties, or, on the other hand, complying with the designations and suffering irreparable harm. The District Court enjoined respondents from enforcing 30 CFR pt. 40, finding that petitioner had raised serious questions going to the merits and that it might face irreparable harm. . . .

III

In cases involving delayed judicial review of final agency actions, we shall find that Congress has allocated initial review to an administrative body where such intent is "fairly discernible in the statutory scheme." *Block v. Community Nutrition Institute*, 467 U.S. 340, 351 (1984), quoting *Data Processing Service v. Camp*, 397 U.S. 150, 157 (1970). Whether a statute is intended to preclude initial judicial review is determined from the statute's language, structure, and purpose, its legislative history, *Block*, 467 U.S., at 345, and whether the claims can be afforded meaningful review. . . .

A

Applying this analysis to the review scheme before us, we conclude that the Mine Act precludes district court jurisdiction over the pre-enforcement challenge made here. The Act establishes a detailed structure for reviewing violations of "any mandatory health or safety standard, rule, order, or regulation promulgated" under the Act. § 814(a). A mine operator has 30 days to challenge before the Commission any citation issued under the Act, after which time an uncontested order becomes "final" and "not subject to review by any court or agency." §§ 815(a) and (d). Timely challenges are heard before an administrative law judge (ALJ), § 823(d)(1), with possible Commission review. Only the Commission has authority actually to impose civil penalties proposed by the Secretary, § 820(I), and the Commission reviews all proposed civil penalties de novo according to six criteria. The Commission may grant temporary relief pending review of most orders, § 815(b)(2), and must expedite review where necessary, § 815(d).

Mine operators may challenge adverse Commission decisions in the appropriate Court of Appeals, § 816(a)(1), whose jurisdiction "shall be exclusive and its judgment and decree shall be final" except for possible Supreme Court review. . . . The Court of Appeals must uphold findings of the Commission that are substantially supported by the record, *ibid.*, but may grant temporary relief pending final determination of most proceedings, § 816(a)(2).

Although the statute establishes that the Commission and the courts of appeals have exclusive jurisdiction over challenges to agency enforcement proceedings, the Act is facially silent with respect to pre-enforcement claims. The structure of the Mine Act, however, demonstrates that Congress intended to preclude challenges such as the present one. The Act's comprehensive review process does not distinguish between pre- and post-enforcement challenges, but applies to all violations of the Act and its regulations. § 814(a). Contrary to petitioner's suggestion . . . , actions before the Commission are initiated not by the Secretary but by a mine operator who claims to be aggrieved. See § 815(a). The Act expressly authorizes district court jurisdiction in only two provisions, §§ 818(a) and 820(j), which respectively empower the Secretary to enjoin habitual violations of health and safety standards and to coerce payment of civil penalties. Mine operators enjoy no corresponding right but are to complain to the Commission and then to the Court of Appeals.

B

The legislative history of the Mine Act confirms this interpretation. . . . We consider the legislative history and these amendments to be persuasive evidence that Congress intended to direct ordinary challenges under the Mine Act to a single review process.

Abbott Laboratories v. Gardner, 387 U.S. 136 (1967), is not to the contrary. In that case, this Court held that statutory review of certain provisions of the Federal Food, Drug, and Cosmetic Act, 52 Stat. 1040, as amended by the Drug Amendments of 1962, 76 Stat. 780, 21 U.S.C. § 301 *et seq.*, did not preclude district court jurisdiction over a pre-enforcement challenge to regulations promulgated under separate provisions of that Act. In so holding, the Court found that the presence of a statutory saving clause, see 387 U.S., at 144, and the statute's legislative history demonstrated "rather conclusively that the specific review provisions were designed to give an additional remedy and not to cut down more traditional channels of review." *Id.*, at 142. It concluded that Congress' primary concern in adopting the administrative-review procedures was to supplement review of specific agency determinations over which traditional forms of review might be inadequate. *Id.*, at 142–144. Contrary to petitioner's contentions, no comparable statutory language or legislative intent is present here. Indeed, as discussed above, the Mine Act's text and legislative history suggest precisely the opposite. The prospect that federal jurisdiction might thwart effective enforcement of the statute also was less immediate in *Abbott Laboratories,* since the *Abbott* petitioners did not attempt to stay enforcement of the challenged regulation pending judicial review, as petitioner did here. *Id.*, at 155–156.

C

We turn to the question whether petitioner's claims are of the type Congress intended to be reviewed within this statutory structure. This Court previously has upheld district court jurisdiction over claims considered "wholly 'collateral'" to a statute's review provisions and outside the agency's expertise . . . particularly where a finding of preclusion could foreclose all meaningful judicial review. . . . The Commission, which was established as an independent-review body to "develop a uniform and comprehensive interpretation" of the Mine Act . . . has extensive experience interpreting the walk-around rights and recently addressed the precise NLRA claims presented here. Although the Commission has no particular expertise in construing statutes other than the Mine Act, we conclude that exclusive review before the Commission is appropriate since "agency expertise [could] be brought to bear on" the statutory questions presented here. . . .

As for petitioner's constitutional claim, we agree that "[a]djudication of the constitutionality of congressional enactments has generally been thought beyond the jurisdiction of administrative agencies". . . . This rule is not mandatory, however, and is perhaps of less consequence where, as here, the reviewing body is not the agency itself but an independent commission established exclusively to adjudicate Mine Act disputes. . . . The Commission has addressed constitutional questions in previous enforcement proceedings. Even if this were not the case, however, petitioner's statutory and constitutional claims here can be meaningfully addressed in the court of appeals.

We conclude that the Mine Act's comprehensive enforcement structure, combined with the legislative history's clear concern with channeling and streamlining the enforcement process, establishes a "fairly discernible" intent to preclude district court review in the present case. See *Block v. Community Nutrition Institute*, 467 U.S., at 351. Petitioner's claims are "pre-enforcement" only because the company sued before a citation was issued, and its claims turn on a question of statutory interpretation that can be meaningfully reviewed under the Mine Act. . . .

IV

Petitioner finally contends, in the alternative, that due process requires district court review because the absence of pre-enforcement declaratory relief before the Commission will subject petitioner to serious and irreparable harm. We need not consider this claim, however, because neither compliance with, nor continued violation of, the statute will subject petitioner to a serious prehearing deprivation.

The record before us contains no evidence that petitioner will be subject to serious harm if it complies with 30 U.S.C. § 813(f) and 30 CFR pt. 40 by posting the designations, and the potential for abuse of the miners' representative position appears limited. . . .

Nor will petitioner face any serious prehearing deprivation if it refuses to post the designation while challenging the Secretary's interpretation. Although the Act's civil penalties unquestionably may become onerous if petitioner chooses not to comply, the Secretary's penalty assessments become final and payable only after full review by both the Commission and the appropriate Court of Appeals. 30 U.S.C. §§ 820(I) and 816. A mine operator may request that the Commission expedite its proceedings, § 815(d), and temporary relief of certain orders is available from the Commission and the Court of Appeals. §§ 815(b)(2) and 816(a)(2). Thus, this case does not present the situation confronted in *Ex Parte Young*, 209 U.S. 123, 148 (1908), in which the practical effect of coercive penalties for non-compliance was to foreclose all access to the courts. Nor does this approach a situation in which compliance is sufficiently onerous and coercive penalties sufficiently potent that a constitutionally intolerable choice might be presented.

V

We conclude that the Mine Act's administrative structure was intended to preclude district court jurisdiction over petitioner's claims and that those claims can be meaningfully reviewed through that structure consistent with due process.[23] The judgment of the Court of Appeals is affirmed.

It is so ordered.

JUSTICE SCALIA, with whom JUSTICE THOMAS joins, concurring in part, and concurring in the judgment.

I join all except Parts III-B, IV, and V of the Court's opinion. The first of these consists of a discussion of the legislative history of the Federal Mine Safety and Health Amendments Act of 1977, 30 U.S.C. § 801 et seq. (1988 ed. and Supp. IV), which is found to "confir[m]" . . . the Court's interpretation of the statute. I find that discussion unnecessary to the decision. It serves to maintain the illusion that legislative history is an important factor in this Court's deciding of cases, as opposed to an omnipresent make-weight for decisions arrived at on other grounds. See Wisconsin Public Intervenor v. Mortier, 501 U.S. 597, 517, (1991) (SCALIA, J., concurring in judgment).

. . . .

And finally, as to Part IV: The Court holds that the preclusion of review is constitutional "because neither compliance with, nor continued violation of, the statute will subject petitioner to a serious prehearing deprivation." . . . I presume this means that any such deprivation will be de minimis (since I know of no doctrine which lets stand unconstitutional injury that is more than de minimis but short of some other criterion of gravity). It seems to me, however, that compliance with the inspection regulations will cause petitioner more than de minimis harm (assuming, as we must in evaluating the harm resulting from compliance, that petitioner is correct on the merits of his claims). . . .

In my view, however, the preclusion of pre-enforcement judicial review is constitutional *whether or not* compliance produces irreparable harm — at least if a summary penalty does not cause irreparable harm (*e.g.*, if it is a recoverable

---

[23] Because we have resolved this dispute on statutory preclusion grounds, we do not reach the parties' arguments concerning final agency action, a cause of action, ripeness, and exhaustion.

summary fine) or if judicial review is provided before a penalty for *non*-compliance can be imposed. (The latter condition exists here, as it does in most cases, because the penalty for noncompliance can only be imposed in court.) Were it otherwise, the availability of pre-enforcement challenges would have to be the rule rather than the exception, since complying with a regulation later held invalid almost always produces the irreparable harm of nonrecoverable compliance costs. Petitioner's claim is that the imposition of a choice between (1) complying with what the government says to be the law, and (2) risking potential penalties (without a prior opportunity to challenge the law in district court) denies due process. This is similar to the constitutional challenge brought in the line of cases beginning with *Ex parte Young*, 209 U.S. 123 (1908), but with one crucial difference. As the Court notes . . . petitioner, unlike the plaintiff in *Young*, had the option of complying and then bringing a judicial challenge. The constitutional defect in *Young* was that the dilemma of either obeying the law and thereby forgoing any possibility of judicial review, or risking "enormous" and "severe" penalties, effectively cut off all access to the courts. . . . That constitutional problem does not exist here, nor does any other of which I am aware. . . . I would decide the second constitutional challenge (Part IV) on the simple grounds that the company can obtain judicial review if it complies with the agency's request, and can obtain presanction judicial review if it does not.

Questions and Comments

1. Administration of the Federal Mine Safety Act follows the route of the alternative model of administration considered in Chapter 5. Under the Act the Secretary of Labor issues regulations and brings enforcement proceedings. Adjudications, however, fall within the authority of the Federal Mine Safety and Health Review Commission. Generally an ALJ presides at an adjudicatory hearing and the ALJ's decision is subject to review by the Commission. This format resembles that of the administration of OSHA where the Secretary also acts as the enforcement body and the independent Occupational Safety and Health Review Commission adjudicates.

2. Do you think that the special role played by the Federal Mine Safety and Health Review Commission made it especially difficult to obtain pre-enforcement review?

3. Did the facts of this case reveal any special reason why the exhaustion doctrine should not be applied? Should *Darby* have affected the application of the exhaustion doctrine here? Why did the Company not wait for a proceeding to be brought by the Secretary and then defend before the Commission?

4. Is the Court majority weakening the force of *Abbott Laboratories* [casebook, *infra*, as a precedent for granting pre-enforcement review?

5. Did Justice Scalia say anything new about what a plaintiff must establish to justify exemption from the exhaustion requirement? Is Justice Scalia asserting that there is no showing of irreparable injury which would be relevant to allowing a pre-enforcement action to go forward? How does he reconcile his position with *Ex parte Young*? Would Justice Scalia grant pre-enforcement judicial review in a case like *Abbott Laboratories*?

Note: The Exhaustion Doctrine in the Context of a Criminal Prosecution

In *Yakus v. United States*, 321 U.S. 414 (1944) the Court affirmed the petitioners' conviction for selling beef at prices above the maximum prices prescribed by the Office of Price Administration under the Emergency Price Control Act. The petitioners had not availed themselves of the statutory procedure by which any person subject to a maximum price regulation could test its validity by protest to and hearing before the Administrator within 60 days of its issuance. The trial court refused to let the petitioners establish the invalidity of the regulation as a defense in the criminal action. When the case reached the U.S. Supreme Court, that Court held, *inter alia*, that "petitioners have failed to seek the administrative remedy and the statutory review which were open to them. . . . And we are pointed to no principle of law or provision of the Constitution which precludes Congress from making criminal the violation of an administrative regulation, by one who has failed to avail himself of an adequate separate procedure for the adjudication of its validity, or which precludes the practice in many ways desirable, of splitting the trial for violations of an administrative regulation by committing the determination of the issue of its validity to the agency which created it, and the issue of violation to a court which is given jurisdiction to punish violations."

In *McKart*, of course, the Court took a less harsh stance, permitting the defendant to raise the lawfulness of his classification as a defense to his criminal prosecution for failing to report for induction under the Selective Service Act. More recently, in *Adamo Wrecking Co. v. United States*, 434 U.S. 275, 282 (1978) the petitioner was indicted for violating an "emission standard" promulgated by the Administrator of the Environmental Protection Agency under the Clean Air Act. The indictment alleged that the petitioner had violated the emission standard for asbestos while demolishing a building. The statute provided (in § 307(b)(1) that judicial review of an emission standard may be filed only in the U.S. Court of Appeals for the District of Columbia Circuit within 30 days from the promulgation of the standard. The statute further explicitly provided (in § 307(b)(2)) that Action of the Administrator with respect to which review could have been obtained under paragraph (1) shall not be subject to judicial review in civil or criminal proceedings for enforcement.

The Supreme Court observed that the Administrator was authorized to promulgate several kinds of regulations besides "emission standards", and that the harshest penalties were reserved for violation of the latter: "All of this leads us to conclude that Congress intended, within broad limits, that 'emission standards' be regulations of a certain type and that it did not empower the Administrator, after the manner of Humpty Dumpty in Through the Looking Glass, to make a regulation an 'emission standard' by his mere designation. . . . We conclude, therefore, that a federal court in which a criminal prosecution under § 113(c)(1)(C) of the Clean Air Act is brought may determine whether or not the regulation which the defendant is alleged to have violated is an 'emission standard' within the meaning of the Act."

In *United States v. Goodner Bros. Aircraft, Inc.*, 966 F.2d 380 (8th Cir. 1992), *cert. denied*, 506 U.S. 1049 (1993), defendants were convicted of violating a provision of the Resource Conservation and Recovery Act (RCRA) which provides criminal penalties for "[a]ny person who . . . knowingly treats, stores, or disposes of any hazardous waste identified or listed under this subchapter . . . without a permit . . ." 42 U.S.C. § 6928(d)(2)(A) (1988). The jury was instructed that one of the elements necessary for conviction was that the wastes were listed by the EPA as hazardous pursuant to the RCRA. The jury was also instructed that (under the EPA's "mixture regulation") when a listed waste was mixed with a solid, liquid, or semisolid material, the resulting mixture was also a hazardous waste. In another case, the mixture regulation was set aside because of the failure of the EPA to follow notice-and-comment procedures under § 553. Since the jury verdict could have been dependent upon the mixture regulation, the court set aside the conviction. Note that the court assumed that if the regulation was invalid, a jury conviction based upon it was defective. The issue of exhaustion was not mentioned. The defendants' failure to challenge the regulation at the time of its promulgation did not act as a bar to their raising the defect in the regulation in the judicial proceedings.

b.   *Exhaustion in Section 1983 Claims.*

PATSY v. BOARD OF REGENTS OF THE STATE OF FLORIDA
457 U.S. 496 (1982)

Justice Marshall delivered the opinion of the Court.

This case presents the question whether exhaustion of state administrative remedies is a prerequisite to an action under 42 U.S.C. § 1983. . . .

Petitioner alleges that even though she is well qualified and has received uniformly excellent performance evaluations from her superiors, she has been rejected for more than 13 positions at FIU [Florida International University]. She further claims that FIU has unlawfully filled positions through intentional discrimination on the basis of race and sex. She seeks declaratory and injunctive relief or, in the alternative, damages.

The United States District Court for the Southern District of Florida granted respondent Board of Regents' motion to dismiss because petitioner had not exhausted available administrative remedies. On appeal, a panel of the Court of Appeals reversed, and remanded the case for further proceedings. . . . The full court then granted respondent's petition for rehearing and vacated the panel decision.

The Court of Appeals reviewed numerous opinions of this Court holding that exhaustion of administrative remedies was not required, and concluded that these cases did not preclude the application of a "flexible" exhaustion rule. . . . After canvassing the policy arguments in favor of an exhaustion requirement, the Court of Appeals decided that a § 1983 plaintiff could be required to exhaust administrative remedies if the following minimum conditions are met: (1) an orderly system of review or appeal is provided by statute or agency rule; (2) the agency can grant relief more or less commensurate with the claim; (3) relief is available within a reasonable period of time; (4) the procedures are fair, are not unduly burdensome, and are not used to harass or discourage those with legitimate claims; and (5) interim relief is available, in appropriate cases, to prevent irreparable injury and to preserve the plaintiff's rights during the administrative process. . . .

The question whether exhaustion of administrative remedies should ever be required in a § 1983 action has prompted vigorous debate and disagreement. . . . Our resolution of this issue, however, is made much easier because we are not writing on a clean slate. . . . Beginning with *McNeese v. Board of Education*, 373 U.S. 668, 671-673 (1963), we have on numerous occasions rejected the argument that a § 1983 action should be dismissed where the plaintiff has not exhausted state administrative remedies. . . .

A

In determining whether our prior decisions misconstrued the meaning of § 1983, we begin with a review of the legislative history to § 1 of the Civil Rights Act of 1871. . . . Although we recognize that the 1871 Congress did not expressly contemplate the exhaustion question, we believe that the tenor of the debates over § 1 supports our conclusion that exhaustion of administrative remedies in § 1983 actions should not be judicially imposed. . . .

[The Court then reviewed the Civil Rights of Institutionalized Persons Act, 42 U.S.C. § 1997 *et seq.*] In § 1997e, Congress . . . created a specific, limited exhaustion requirement for adult prisoners bringing actions pursuant to § 1983. Section 1997e and its legislative history demonstrate that Congress understood that exhaustion is not generally required in § 1983 actions, and that it decided to carve out only a narrow exception to this rule. A judicially imposed exhaustion requirement would be inconsistent with Congress' decision to adopt § 1997e and would usurp policy judgments that Congress has reserved for itself.

C

Respondent and the Court of Appeals argue that exhaustion of administrative remedies should be required because it would further various policies. They argue that an exhaustion requirement would lessen the perceived burden that § 1983 actions impose on federal courts; would further the goal of comity and improve federal-state relations by postponing federal court review until after the state administrative agency had passed on the issue; and would enable the agency, which presumably has expertise in the area at issue, to enlighten the federal court's ultimate decision.

As we noted earlier, policy considerations alone cannot justify judicially imposed exhaustion unless exhaustion is consistent with congressional intent. . . . Furthermore, as the debates over incorporating the exhaustion requirement in § 1997e demonstrate, the relevant policy considerations do not invariably point in one direction, and there is vehement disagreement over the validity of the assumptions underlying many of them. The very difficulty of these policy considerations, and Congress' superior institutional competence to pursue this debate, suggest that legislative not judicial solutions are preferable.

Beyond the policy issues that must be resolved in deciding *whether* to require exhaustion, there are equally difficult questions concerning the design and scope of an exhaustion requirement. These questions include how to define those categories of § 1983 claims in which exhaustion might be desirable; how to unify and centralize the standards for judging the kinds of administrative procedures that should be exhausted; what tolling requirements and time limitations should be adopted; what is the res judicata and collateral estoppel effect of particular administrative determinations; what consequences should attach to the failure to comply with procedural requirements of administrative proceedings; and whether federal courts could grant necessary interim injunctive relief and hold the action pending exhaustion, or proceed to judgment without requiring exhaustion even though exhaustion might otherwise be required, where the relevant administrative agency is either powerless or not inclined to grant such interim relief. These and similar questions might be answered swiftly and surely by legislation, but would create costly, remedy-delaying, and court-burdening litigation if answered incrementally by the judiciary in the context of diverse constitutional claims relating to thousands of different state agencies.

IV

Based on the legislative histories of both § 1983 and § 1997e, we conclude that exhaustion of state administrative remedies should not be required as a prerequisite to bringing an action pursuant to § 1983. We decline to overturn our prior decisions holding that such exhaustion is not required. The decision of the Court of Appeals is reversed, and the case is remanded for proceedings consistent with this opinion.

It is so ordered.

Justice O'Connor, with whom Justice Rehnquist joins, concurring.

As discussed in Justice Powell's dissenting opinion, as well in the opinion of the court below, considerations of sound policy suggest that a § 1983 plaintiff should be required to exhaust adequate state administrative remedies before filing his complaint. At the very least, prior state administrative proceedings would resolve many claims, thereby decreasing the number of § 1983 actions filed in the federal courts, which are now straining under excessive caseloads. However, for the reasons set forth in the Court's opinion, this Court already has ruled that, in the absence of additional congressional legislation, exhaustion of administrative remedies is not required in § 1983 actions. Perhaps Congress' enactment of the Civil Rights of Institutionalized Persons Act . . . which creates a limited exhaustion requirement for prisoners bringing § 1983 suits, will prompt it to reconsider the possibility of requiring exhaustion in the remainder of § 1983 cases. Reluctantly, I concur.

Questions and Comments

1. Section 1983 is derived from a statute enacted during the Reconstruction period. At that time the Congress was concerned with protecting blacks newly freed from slavery from hostile governments in the South. To what extent should the views of that Congress affect the application of § 1983 which now covers a broad range of claims, many of which have nothing to do with racial discrimination?

2. Are you aware of instances in which the Court had required § 1983 claimants to seek redress through their state remedies before asserting claims in federal court? Are you aware of instances in which § 1983 claimants have been told that if adequate state remedies are available, then no § 1983 claim exists? Did the court say that in *Ingraham v. Wright* [*supra*, Chapter 3]? in *Parratt v. Taylor*[1] [*supra*, Chapter 3]? Consider, in this regard, Justice Stevens proposed revisionist interpretation of *Paul v. Davis* [*supra*, Chapter 3] in his concurring opinion in *Ingraham v. Wright*.

3. The state remedies to which claimants were referred in the cases last cited were state judicial remedies. What is the significance of the fact that the state remedies from which the claimant was excused from making recourse in *Patsy* were state administrative remedies? Are the policy arguments in favor of exhausting state remedies the same whether the remedies in question are judicial or administrative?

4. Does *Patsy* mean that a welfare recipient (under a state general assistance program) who receives a notice of termination is entitled to assert a § 1983 claim of property deprivation directly in federal court without first contesting the termination in a state administrative proceeding? Would not such a person be unable to assert that he/she had been denied "due" procedures? In the circumstances described, the deprivation would not occur until the person had exercised his/her rights in the state administrative proceedings, would it? And then the deprivation, if it occurred, would have been effected with "due process", would it not? Does this hypothetical case resemble *Ingraham*? *Parratt*? *Paul*?

5. ***Wilder v. Virginia Hospital Assn*, 496 U.S. 498 (1990).** Under the Boren Amendment to the Medicaid Act, a state plan for medical assistance must provide for payment of hospital services:

> which the State finds, and makes assurances satisfactory to the Secretary, are reasonable and adequate to meet the costs which must be incurred by efficiently and economically operated facilities. . . .

42 U.S.C. § 1396a(a)(13)(A) (1988).

In *Wilder*, the Supreme Court held that a hospital's claim that a state had failed to adopt rates providing adequate compensation under the Boren Amendment could be asserted under § 1983 as a civil rights claim. Following *Patsy*, the Court:

> reject[ed] petitioner's argument that the existence of administrative procedures whereby health care providers can obtain review of individual

---

[1] Overruled in Daniels v. Williams, 474 U.S. 327 (1986) [*supra*].

claims for payment evidences an intent to foreclose a private remedy in the federal courts. The availability of state administrative remedies ordinarily does not foreclose resort to § 1983.

496 U.S. at 523.

c.   *Statutory Exhaustion Requirements.*

HECKLER v. RINGER
466 U.S. 602 (1984)

[The Medicare Act establishes a federally subsidized health insurance program to be administered by the Secretary of Health and Human Services. Part A of the Act provides insurance for the cost of hospital and related posthospital services, but the Act precludes reimbursement for any "items or services . . . which are not reasonably necessary for the diagnosis or treatment of illness or injury." The Medicare Act authorizes the Secretary to determine what claims are covered by the Act "in accordance with the regulations prescribed by him." Judicial review of claims arising under the Medicare Act is available only after the Secretary renders a "final decision" on the claim, in the same manner as is provided in 42 U.S.C. § 405(g)[17] for old age and disability claims arising under Title I1 of the Social Security Act. 42 U.S.C. § 1395ff(b)(1)(C).

[Pursuant to her rulemaking authority, the Secretary has provided that a "final decision" is rendered on a Medicare claim only after the individual claimant has pressed his claim through all designated levels of administrative review. First, the Medicare Act authorizes the Secretary to enter into contracts with fiscal intermediaries providing that the latter will determine whether a particular medical service is covered by Part A, and if so, the amount of the reimbursable expense for that service. If the intermediary determines that a particular service is not covered under Part A, the claimant can seek reconsideration by the Health Care Financing Administration (HCFA) in the Department of Health and Human Services. If the denial of the claim is affirmed after reconsideration and if the claim exceeds $100, the claimant is entitled to a hearing before an administrative law judge (ALJ). If the claim is again denied, the claimant may seek review in the Appeals Council. If the Appeals Council also denies the claim and if the claim exceeds $ 1,000, only then may the claimant seek judicial review in federal district court of the "Secretary's final decision."

[In January 1979, the Secretary through the HCEA issued an administrative instruction to all fiscal intermediaries, instructing them that no payment is to be made for Medicare claims arising out of bilateral carotid body resection (BCBR) surgical procedure when performed to relieve respiratory distress. Relying on information from the National Heart, Lung and Blood Institute of the National

---

[17] Title 42 U.S.C. § 405(g) provides in part as follows:

"Any individual, after any final decision of the Secretary made after a hearing to which he was a party, irrespective of the amount in controversy, may obtain a review of such decision by a civil action commenced within sixty days after the mailing to him of notice of such decision or within such further time as the Secretary may allow. . . . The findings of the Secretary as to any fact, if supported by substantial evidence, shall be conclusive. . . ."

Institutes of Health, the HCFA explained that BCBR has been "shown to lack [the] general acceptance of the professional medical community" and that "controlled clinical studies establishing the safety and effectiveness of this procedure are needed."

[In response to rulings of the ALJs and the Appeals Council in favor of BCBR claims, on October 28, 1980, the Secretary through the HCFA issued a formal administrative ruling prohibiting ALJs and the Appeals Council from ordering Medicare payments for BCBR operations occurring after that date.

[Respondents challenged the Secretary's instructions and her administrative ruling in an action brought in the U.S. District Court for the Central District of California. The District Court dismissed their complaint, but the Court of Appeals for the Ninth Circuit reversed. The Supreme Court then granted certiorari.]

Justice Rehnquist delivered the opinion of the Court.

Preliminarily, we must point out that, although the Court of Appeals seemed not to have distinguished them, there are in fact two groups of respondents in this case. Respondents Holmes, Vescio, and Webster-Zieber constitute one group of respondents, those who have had BCBR surgery before October 28, 1980, and who have requested reimbursement at some, but not all, levels of the administrative process. Although the Court of Appeals did not seem to realize it, there is no dispute that the Secretary's formal administrative ruling simply does not apply to those three respondents' claims for reimbursement for their BCBR surgery. Their claims only make sense then if they are understood as challenges to the Secretary's instructions to her intermediaries, instructions which resulted in those respondents' having to pursue administrative remedies in order to get payment. They have standing to challenge the formal ruling as well only because, construing their complaint liberally, they argue that the existence of the formal rule creates a presumption against payment of their claims in the administrative process, even though the rule does not directly apply to bar their claims. The relief respondents request is that the Secretary change her policy so as to allow payment for BCBR surgery so that respondents simply will not have to resort to the administrative process.

. . . . Arguably respondents do assert objections to the Secretary's "procedure" for reaching her decision — for example, they challenge her decision to issue a generally applicable rule rather than to allow individual adjudication, and they challenge her alleged failure to comply with the rulemaking requirements of the APA in issuing the instructions and the rule. We agree with the District Court, however, that those claims are "inextricably intertwined" with respondents' claims for benefits. . . .

The third sentence of 42 U.S.C. § 405(h)[18] made applicable to the Medicare Act

---

[18] That provision reads as follows:

"The findings and decisions of the Secretary after a hearing shall be binding upon all individuals who were parties to the hearing. No findings of fact or decision of the Secretary shall be reviewed by any person, tribunal, or governmental agency except as herein provided.

by 42 U.S.C. § 1395ii, provides that § 405(g), to the exclusion of 28 U.S.C. § 1331, is the sole avenue for judicial review for all "claim[s] arising under" the Medicare Act . . . Thus, to be true to the language of the statute, the inquiry in determining whether § 405(h) bars federal-question jurisdiction must be whether the claim "arises under" the Act, not whether it lends itself to a "substantive" rather than a "procedural" label. . . .

In *Weinberger v. Salfi* [422 U.S. 749 (1975)] . . . we construed the "claim arising under" language quite broadly to include any claims in which "both the standing and the substantive basis for the presentation" of the claims is the Social Security Act. . . .

Under that broad test, we have no trouble concluding that all aspects of respondents Holmes, Vescio's, and Webster-Zieber's challenge to the Secretary's BCBR payment policy "aris[e] under" the Medicare Act.

The Court of Appeals also relied on the mandamus statute as a basis for finding jurisdiction over a portion of those three respondents' claims. . . . Assuming without deciding that the third sentence of § 405(h) does not foreclose mandamus jurisdiction in all Social Security cases . . . the District Court did not err in dismissing respondents' complaint here because it is clear that no writ of mandamus could properly issue in this case. The common-law writ of mandamus, as codified in 28 U.S.C. § 1361, is intended to provide a remedy for a plaintiff only if he has exhausted all other avenues of relief and only if the defendant owes him a clear nondiscretionary duty. . . .

Here respondents clearly have an adequate remedy in § 405(g) for challenging all aspects of the Secretary's denial of their claims for payment for the BCBR surgery, including any objections they have to the instructions or to the ruling if either ultimately should play a part in the Secretary's denial of their claims. The Secretary's decision as to whether a particular medical service is "reasonable and necessary" and the means by which she implements her decision, whether by promulgating a generally applicable rule or by allowing individual adjudication, are clearly discretionary decisions. . . .

Thus § 405(g) is the only avenue for judicial review of respondents' Holmes', Vescio's, and Webster-Zieber's claims for benefits, and, when their complaint was filed in District Court, each had failed to satisfy the exhaustion requirement that is a prerequisite to jurisdiction under that provision. We have previously explained that the exhaustion requirement of § 405(g) consists of a nonwaivable requirement that a "claim for benefits shall have been presented to the Secretary," . . . and a waivable requirement that the administrative remedies prescribed by the Secretary be pursued fully by the claimant. All three respondents satisfied the nonwaivable requirement by presenting a claim for reimbursement for the expenses of their BCBR surgery, but none satisfied the waivable requirement.

. . . . [R]espondents do not raise a claim that is wholly "collateral" to their claim for benefits under the Act, and . . . they have no colorable claim that an

No action against the United States, the Secretary, or any officer or employee thereof shall be brought under section 1331 or 1346 of title 28 to recover on any claim arising under this subchapter." 42 U.S.C. § 405(h).

erroneous denial of BCBR benefits in the early stages of the administrative process will injure them in a way that cannot be remedied by the later payment of benefits. And here, it cannot be said that the Secretary has in any sense waived further exhaustion. In the face of the Secretary's vigorous disagreement, the Court of Appeals concluded that the Secretary's formal ruling denying payment for BCBR claims rendered further exhaustion futile. But as we have pointed out above, the administrative ruling is not even applicable to respondents' claims because they had their surgery before October 28, 1980. We therefore agree with the Secretary that exhaustion is in no sense futile for these three respondents and that the Court of Appeals erred in second-guessing the Secretary's judgment.

Respondents also argue that there would be a presumption against them as they pursue their administrative appeals because of the very existence of the Secretary's instructions and her formal ruling and thus that exhaustion would not fully vindicate their claims. The history of this litigation as recited to us by respondents belies that conclusion. Indeed, according to respondents themselves, in every one of 170 claims filed with ALJs between the time of the Secretary's instructions to her intermediaries and the filing of this lawsuit, before the formal ruling became effective, ALJs allowed recovery for BCBR claims. . . . In promulgating the formal ruling, the Secretary took pains to exempt from the scope of the ruling individuals in respondents' position who may have had the surgery relying on the favorable ALJ rulings. . . . Although respondents would clearly prefer an immediate appeal to the District Court rather than the often lengthy administrative review process, exhaustion of administrative remedies is in no sense futile for these respondents, and they, therefore, must adhere to the administrative procedure which Congress has established for adjudicating their Medicare claims.

III

Respondent Ringer is in a separate group from the other three respondents in this case. He raises the same challenges to the instructions and to the formal ruling as are raised by the other respondents. His position is different from theirs, however, because he wishes to have the operation and claims that the Secretary's refusal to allow payment for it precludes him from doing so. Because Ringer's surgery, if he ultimately chooses to have it, would occur after the effective date of the formal ruling, Ringer's claim for reimbursement, unlike that of the others, would be covered by the formal ruling. Ringer insists that . . . the only relief that will vindicate his claim is a declaration that the formal ruling, and presumably the instructions as well, are invalid and an injunction compelling the Secretary to conclude that BCBR surgery is "reasonable and necessary". . . . It is only after that declaration and injunction, Ringer insists, that he will be assured of payment and thus only then that he will be able to have the operation.

. . . [W]e see Ringer's claim as essentially one requesting the payment of benefits for BCBR surgery, a claim cognizable only under § 405(g). Our discussion of the unavailability of mandamus jurisdiction over the claims of the other three respondents is equally applicable to Ringer. As to § 1331 jurisdiction, as with the other three respondents, all aspects of Ringer's claim "aris[e] under" the Medicare Act in that the Medicare Act provides both the substance and the standing for

Ringer's claim. . . . Thus, consistent with our decision with respect to the other three respondents, we hold that §§ 1331 and 1361 are not available as jurisdictional bases for vindicating Ringer's claim.

Ringer's situation does differ from that of the other three respondents in one arguably significant way. Because he has not yet had the operation and thus no reimbursable expenses, it can be argued that Ringer does not yet have a "claim" to present to the Secretary and thus that he does not have a "claim arising under" the Medicare Act so as to be subject to § 405(h)'s bar to federal-question jurisdiction. The argument is that Ringer's claim . . . has not yet blossomed into a "claim" cognizable under § 405(g). We find that argument superficially appealing but ultimately unavailing.

Although it is true that Ringer is not seeking the immediate payment of benefits, he is clearly seeking to establish a right to future payments should he ultimately decide to proceed with BCBR surgery. . . . The claim for future benefits must be construed as a "claim arising under" the Medicare Act because any other construction would allow claimants substantially to undercut Congress' carefully crafted scheme for administering the Medicare Act.

If we allow claimants in Ringer's position to challenge in federal court the Secretary's determination, embodied in her rule, that BCBR surgery is not a covered service, we would be inviting them to bypass the exhaustion requirements of the Medicare Act by simply bringing declaratory judgment actions in federal court before they undergo the medical procedure in question. . . . Congress clearly foreclosed the possibility of obtaining such advisory opinions from the Secretary herself, requiring instead that a claim could be filed for her scrutiny only after the medical service for which payment is sought has been furnished. . . . Under the guise of interpreting the language of § 405(h), we refuse to undercut that choice by allowing federal judges to issue such advisory opinions. Thus it is not the case that Ringer has no "claim" cognizable under § 405(g); it is that he must pursue his claim under that section in the manner which Congress has provided. Because Ringer has not given the Secretary an opportunity to rule on a concrete claim for reimbursement, he has not satisfied the nonwaivable exhaustion requirement of § 405(g). The District Court, therefore, had no jurisdiction as to respondent Ringer.

JUSTICE STEVENS, with whom JUSTICE BRENNAN and JUSTICE MARSHALL join, concurring in the judgment in part and dissenting in part.

Ringer is not seeking to "bypass the exhaustion requirement of the Medicare Act but rather to be *able* to exhaust something he can only do if the rule is enjoined so that he and his surgeon can seek reimbursement through the administrative process. Ringer's challenge to the operation of a rule that prevents him from having a "claim" he can pursue under § 205 is therefore not a claim covered by § 205(h) — it is a challenge to a procedural rule that could prove meritorious even if Ringer is ultimately not entitled to reimbursement. Hence it can be asserted under § 1331.

. . . . Requiring the administrative process to be invoked so it can be determined whether applications such as Ringer's could also be denied on some other ground would simply be "a commitment of administrative resources unsupported by any administrative or judicial interest," especially since Ringer is not seeking the payment of benefits at this juncture. When a case is ripe for summary judgment because of a dispositive legal question, we do not require district courts to hold a trial anyway to determine if the complaint might be meritless on some other ground. . . .

Questions and Comments

1.   Did the Court, in your opinion, reach the result which Congress intended? What objective did Congress seek in imposing an exhaustion requirement? Should the normal exceptions to the exhaustion doctrine apply here?

2.   Do you understand the difference between the "waivable" and "nonwaivable" exhaustion requirements applicable to Medicare reimbursement claims? Why should not Ringer be excused from the "waivable" exhaustion requirements on the ground that exhaustion of administrative remedies would be futile? But if Ringer were excused from the waivable exhaustion requirements, his claim would nonetheless fail to meet a nonwaivable exhaustion requirement (presentation to the Secretary), would it not?

3.   Does not this case waste administrative resources by forcing Ringer through procedures whose outcome is known in advance? Will not the Secretary's position on the BCBR procedure have to be addressed by the courts at some time? Would it not save time and resources for everyone concerned for the courts to address that question now?

4.   Justice Stevens in dissent argued that it would be a waste of resources to require Ringer to pursue his claim administratively. Suppose Ringer later decides against the surgery. Would resources still have been saved? How would you answer the contention that, because Ringer might change his mind, judicial review of the Secretary's ruling at this stage would be tantamount to the rendering of an advisory opinion by the Court?

5.   The dissent also argued that because Ringer merely sought a declaratory ruling and not a present payment reimbursing him for medical expenses, his claim was more entitled to judicial review.

6.   Is the result in *Ringer* consistent with *McNary v. Haitian Refugee Center, Inc., supra*?

Note: Judicial Review of Rules Under State Administrative Procedcure Acts and the Exhaustion Doctrine

1.   The 1946 model act provides for judicial review of rules in a declaratory judgment proceeding. In such a proceeding the court is authorized to declare the rule invalid if it violates constitutional provisions, exceeds the agency's authority or was adopted without compliance with statutory rulemaking procedures. 1946 Model Act § 6. The act expressly excuses the petitioner from exhausting available

administrative remedies.

2.   The 1961 model act also provides for judicial review of rules in a declaratory judgment proceeding. In addition to permitting the court to declare the rule invalid, the 1961 act also permits the court to determine the applicability of the rule. 1961 Model Act § 7. Like its 1946 predecessor, the 1961 act also dispenses with the need to exhaust administrative remedies before bringing the declaratory judgment. The 1961 act, however, requires that the agency be made a party to the declaratory judgment proceedings.

What do you think that the drafters of the 1961 act had in mind when they required that the agency be a party to the declaratory judgment proceedings? To what extent does this requirement complement the dispensation of the exhaustion requirement?

3.   Does the 1961 act's authorization to the reviewing court to pass upon the "applicability" of agency rules create an allocation of power between courts and agencies which is different from the allocation in the federal system? Can you identify any particular problems which are likely to arise from this different allocation? Are these problems exacerbated by the elimination of the exhaustion requirement? Why do you think that the 1961 act expressly requires persons to exhaust their administrative remedies before seeking judicial review of a contested case? 1961 Model Act § 15.

4.   The 1981 model act provides for judicial review of rules, but contrary to its predecessors, imposes an exhaustion requirement. 1981 Model Act § 5-107.

D.   RIPENESS AND FINALITY

1.   *Note: The Evolution of the Ripeness Doctrine.*

Standard Computing Scale Co. v. Farrell, 249 U.S. 571 (1919). Under the statutes of New York State, a sealer of weights and measures was appointed in every county and city by the local authorities. New York also had a state official, the State Superintendent of weights and measures who was given general supervision of weights, and measuring and weighing devices in the state. The Superintendent also published a bulletin of instruction and information to dealers, and weights and measures officials. In his bulletin for August, 1914, the following appeared:

Specifications.
Automatic Computing Scales.

All combination spring and level computing scales must be equipped with a device which will automatically compensate for changes of temperature at zero balance and throughout the whole range of weight graduations.

Plaintiff manufactured a combination spring and lever computing scale which was equipped with a compensating device which was not automatic. Because of the "specifications" published in the Superintendent's bulletin, some county and city sealers of weights and measures neglected to seal scales of plaintiff's make and warned scale users to discontinue the use of plaintiff's make of scales. As a result, plaintiff's sales in New York diminished.

Plaintiff brought suit against the Superintendent, asking that the specifications, which it termed a "rule", be declared an invalid exercise of the police power and their enforcement enjoined. The district court dismissed the suit and the U.S. Supreme Court affirmed on the ground that the specifications did not require any one to do anything and hence had no legal effect: ". . . the function of the 'specifications' is educational and, at most, advisory. . . . [S]ince the 'specifications' are not in the nature of a law or regulation, the prohibitions of the Federal Constitution cannot apply." Thus, despite the substantial injury to the plaintiff's business, it could not challenge the Superintendent's specifications in court; those specifications were at most advice which the county and city sealers followed but were not obliged to follow.

Columbia Broadcasting System, Inc. v. United States, 316 U.S. 407 (1942). The Federal Communications Commission issued regulations under which the Commission will refuse to grant licenses (including renewal licenses) to radio stations which enter or maintain contracts with broadcast networks containing specified provisions, including provisions by which a station options for network broadcasting more than three hours within each of four specified segments of the broadcast day. Because the regulations were interfering with the relations between the Columbia Broadcasting System (CBS) and its network affiliates, CBS sued to enjoin their implementation. In its suit, CBS alleged that as a result of the regulations, many broadcasting stations affiliated with it would be afraid to renew their contracts and many affiliated stations were threatening to repudiate their contracts with CBS. Although the Government argued that the Commission's regulations did not require CBS to do anything, the Court ruled that CBS could challenge the validity of the regulations in court. CBS could obtain review because it "alleged without contradiction that numerous affiliated stations have conformed to the regulations to avoid loss of their licenses with consequent injury to" CBS. Responding to the Government's contention above, the Court stated:

> It is no answer to say that the regulations are addressed only to the Commission and merely prohibit it from granting-and authorizing it to cancel-licenses in the case of all stations entering into such contracts, and that accordingly all stations are left free to enter into contracts or not, as they choose. They are free only in the sense that all those who do not choose to conform to regulations which may be determined to be lawful are free by their choice to accept the legal consequences of their acts. Failure to comply with the regulations entails such consequences to the station owner and to appellant. These are the loss of the affiliated stations' licenses if they adhere to their contracts, and disruption of appellant's network through the declared unlawfulness of the contracts, if the regulations are valid.

Questions and Comments

1. In neither of the above cases had a government official or agency taken enforcement action. The Superintendent had not tried to enforce his specifications by bringing an action against those who sold or used scales without automatic

compensating devices. At the time of the CBS case, the FCC had not taken action to revoke (or to refuse to renew) the license of any radio station because it had not repudiated the contracts which the FCC had identified in its rule.

2. In *Standard Computing* Scale the Court held that the Superintendent's "specifications" were not judicially reviewable because they did not have any legal effect. At most, they were advice to the local sealers of weights and measures which the latter were free to reject.

3. Why did not the Court accept the Government's contention in the CBS case that the FCC's regulations did not require anyone to do anything, and therefore had no legal effect? It is true that the regulations had a major damaging effect on CBS' business, but how was that different from the major damaging effect that the Superintendent's "specifications" had upon the business of the Standard Computing Scale Company? What kind of legal effect, if any, did the FCC regulations have?

4. Is it relevant that the FCC regulations coerced the stations to repudiate their contracts with CBS? whereas the Superintendent's specifications did not coerce the local sealers of weights and measures? Would it be easier to distinguish the cases if it had been the stations who had brought suit to enjoin the enforcement of the FCC regulations?

5. Do you agree with the assertion above that the radio stations were coerced by the regulations to repudiate their contracts with CBS? How were they coerced? They were faced with a choice of either repudiating the contracts or losing their licenses, were they not? Without their licenses, they could not continue to operate. Their choice was: comply or go out of business.

6. The Court would always allow judicial review of a statute or administrative regulation whose violation carried criminal sanctions. In many such circumstances, judicial review would have to be allowed before the statute was actually enforced in a criminal action against a violator if it was to be had at all. Because most people would not be willing to risk criminal sanctions, they would obey the statute or regulation. And the lawfulness of the statute or regulation would not be tested in court. Sometimes statutes or regulations whose violation carried criminal sanctions would be referred to as "self-executing," because the criminal sanctions compelled compliance.

7. The FCC regulations in the CBS case were in effect "self-executing" because most radio stations would not risk their licenses in order to challenge them. In theory, the stations could challenge the validity of those regulations by violating them and then contest their validity in a subsequent proceeding brought by the FCC to revoke their licenses; or they could challenge the validity of the regulations when, after they had violated them, the FCC used the regulations as a basis for denying the stations renewals of their licenses. But, as a practical matter, most stations would not be willing to risk the licenses in order to test the validity of the regulations. The stations would be coerced into complying with the FCC's wishes, just as others would be coerced into complying with a possibly invalid statute or regulation whose violation carried criminal sanctions.

2. *The Ripeness Doctrine Today.*

OHIO FORESTRY ASSOCIATION, INC. v. SIERRA CLUB
523 U.S. 726 (1998)

JUSTICE BREYER delivered the opinion of the Court.

The Sierra Club challenges the lawfulness of a federal land and resource management plan adopted by the United States Forest Service for Ohio's Wayne National Forest on the ground that the plan permits too much logging and too much clearcutting. We conclude that the controversy is not yet ripe for judicial review.

I

The National Forest Management Act of 1976 (NFMA) requires the Secretary of Agriculture to "develop, maintain, and, as appropriate, revise land and resource management plans for units of the National Forest System." 90 Stat. 2949, as renumbered and amended, 16 U.S.C. § 1604(a). . . .

This case focuses upon a plan that the Forest Service has developed for the Wayne National Forest located in southern Ohio. When the Service wrote the plan, the forest consisted of 178,000 federally owned acres (278 sq. mi.) in three forest units that are interspersed among privately owned lands, some of which the Forest Service plans to acquire over time. . . . . The Plan permits logging to take place on 126,000 (197 sq. mi.) of the federally owned acres. . . . At the same time, it sets a ceiling on the total amount of wood that can be cut — a ceiling that amounts to about 75 million board feet over 10 years, and which, the Plan projects, would lead to logging on about 8,000 acres (12.5 sq. mi.) during that decade. . . . According to the Plan, logging on about 5,000 (7.8 sq. mi.) of those 8,000 acres would involve clearcutting, or other forms of what the Forest Service calls "even-aged" tree harvesting. . . .

Although the Plan sets logging goals, selects the areas of the forest that are suited to timber production, and determines which "probable methods of timber harvest" are appropriate, it does not itself authorize the cutting of any trees. Before the Forest Service can permit the logging, it must: (a) propose a specific area in which logging will take place and the harvesting methods to be used; (b) ensure that the project is consistent with the Plan; (c) provide those affected by proposed logging notice and an opportunity to be heard; (d) conduct an environmental analysis pursuant to the National Environmental Policy Act of 1969 (NEPA), to evaluate the effects of the specific project and to contemplate alternatives; and (e) subsequently make a final decision to permit logging, which affected persons may challenge in an administrative appeals process and in court. (citations omitted) Furthermore, the statute requires the Forest Service to "revise" the Plan "as appropriate." 16 U.S.C. § 1604(a). Despite the considerable legal distance between the adoption of the Plan and the moment when a tree is cut, the Plan's promulgation nonetheless makes logging more likely in that it is a logging precondition; in its absence logging could not take place. See *ibid.*

(requiring promulgation of forest plans); § 1604(i) (requiring all later forest uses to conform to forest plans).

When the Forest Service first proposed its Plan, the Sierra Club and the Citizens Council on Conservation and Environmental Control each objected. In an effort to bring about the Plan's modification, they (collectively Sierra Club), pursued various administrative remedies. See Administrative Decision of the Chief of the Forest Service (Nov. 14, 1990), Pet. for Cert. 66a; Appeal Decision, Wayne National Forest Land and Resource Management Plan (Jan. 14, 1992), *id.*, at 78a. The Sierra Club then brought this lawsuit in federal court, initially against the Chief of the Forest Service, the Secretary of Agriculture, the Regional Forester, and the Forest Supervisor. The Ohio Forestry Association, some of whose members harvest timber from the Wayne National Forest or process wood products obtained from the forest, later intervened as a defendant.

The Sierra Club's second amended complaint sets forth its legal claims. That complaint initially states facts that describe the Plan in detail and allege that erroneous analysis leads the Plan wrongly to favor logging and clearcutting. The complaint then sets forth three claims for relief.

The first claim for relief says that the "defendants in approving the plan for the Wayne [National Forest] and in directing or permitting below-cost timber sales accomplished by means of clearcutting" violated various laws including the NFMA, the NEPA, and the Administrative Procedure Act

The second claim says that the "defendants' actions in directing or permitting below-cost timber sales in the Wayne [National Forest] under the plan violate [their] duties as public trustees."

The third claim says that, in selecting the amount of the forest suitable for timber production, the defendants followed regulations that failed properly to identify "economically unsuitable lands." It adds that, because the Forest Service's regulations thereby permitted the Service to place "economically unsuitable lands" in the category of land where logging could take place, the regulations violated their authorizing statute, NFMA, 16 U.S.C. § 1600 *et seq.*, and were "arbitrary, capricious, an abuse of discretion, and not in accordance with law," pursuant to the Administrative Procedure Act, 5 U.S.C. § 701 *et seq.* The Complaint finally requests as relief: (a) a declaration that the Plan "is unlawful as are the below-cost timber sales and timbering, including clearcutting, authorized by the plan," (b) an "injunction prohibiting the defendants from permitting or directing further timber harvest and/or below-cost timber sales" pending plan revision, (c) costs and attorney's fees, and (d) "such other further relief as may be appropriate."

The District Court reviewed the Plan, decided that the Forest Service had acted lawfully in making the various determinations that the Sierra Club had challenged, and granted summary judgment for the Forest Service. The Sierra Club appealed. The Court of Appeals for the Sixth Circuit held that the dispute was justiciable, finding both that the Sierra Club had standing to bring suit, and that since the suit was "ripe for review," there was no need to wait "until a site-specific action occurs." The Court of Appeals disagreed with the District Court about the merits. It held that the Plan improperly favored clearcutting and therefore violated NFMA. We granted certiorari to determine whether the dispute about the Plan presents a controversy that is justiciable now, and if so, whether the Plan conforms to the statutory and regulatory requirements for a forest plan.

II

Petitioner alleges that this suit is nonjusticiable both because the Sierra Club lacks standing to bring this case and because the issues before us — over the Plan's specifications for logging and clearcutting — are not yet ripe for adjudication. We find that the dispute is not justiciable, because it is not ripe for court review. Cf. *Steel Co.* v. *Citizens For Better Environment,* 523 U.S., at 100–101, n.3 (1998).

> As this Court has previously pointed out, the ripeness requirement is designed "to prevent the courts, through avoidance of premature adjudication, from entangling themselves in abstract disagreements over administrative policies, and also to protect the agencies from judicial interference until an administrative decision has been formalized and its effects felt in a concrete way by the challenging parties." *Abbott Laboratories v. Gardner,* 387 U.S. 136, 148–149 (1967).

In deciding whether an agency's decision is, or is not, ripe for judicial review, the Court has examined both the "fitness of the issues for judicial decision" and the "hardship to the parties of withholding court consideration." *Id.*, at 149. To do so in this case, we must consider: (1) whether delayed review would cause hardship to the plaintiffs; (2) whether judicial intervention would inappropriately interfere with further administrative action; and (3) whether the courts would benefit from further factual development of the issues presented. These considerations, taken together, foreclose review in the present case.

First, to "withhol[d] court consideration" at present will not cause the parties significant "hardship" as this Court has come to use that term. *Ibid.* For one thing, the provisions of the Plan that the Sierra Club challenges do not create adverse effects of a strictly legal kind, that is, effects of a sort that traditionally would have qualified as harm. To paraphrase this Court's language in *United States v. Los Angeles & Salt Lake R. Co.*, 273 U.S. 299, 309–310 (1927) (opinion of Brandeis, J.), they do not command anyone to do anything or to refrain from doing anything; they do not grant, withhold, or modify any formal legal license, power, or authority; they do not subject anyone to any civil or criminal liability; they create no legal rights or obligations. Thus, for example, the Plan does not give anyone a legal right to cut trees, nor does it abolish anyone's legal authority to object to trees being cut.

Nor have we found that the Plan now inflicts significant practical harm upon the interests that the Sierra Club advances — an important consideration in light of this Court's modern ripeness cases. See, *e.g.*, *Abbott Laboratories, supra,* at 152–154. As we have pointed out, before the Forest Service can permit logging, it must focus upon a particular site, propose a specific harvesting method, prepare an environmental review, permit the public an opportunity to be heard, and (if challenged) justify the proposal in court. The Sierra Club thus will have ample opportunity later to bring its legal challenge at a time when harm is more imminent and more certain. Any such later challenge might also include a challenge to the lawfulness of the present Plan if (but only if) the present Plan then matters, *i.e.*, if the Plan plays a causal role with respect to the future, then-imminent, harm from logging. Hence we do not find a strong reason why the Sierra Club must bring its challenge now in order to get relief. Cf. *Abbott Laboratories, supra*, at 152.

Nor has the Sierra Club pointed to any other way in which the Plan could now force it to modify its behavior in order to avoid future adverse consequences, as, for example, agency regulations can sometimes force immediate compliance through fear of future sanctions. Cf. *Abbott Laboratories, supra*, at 152–153 (finding challenge ripe where plaintiffs must comply with Federal Drug Administration labeling rule at once and incur substantial economic costs or risk later serious criminal and civil penalties for unlawful drug distribution); *Columbia Broadcasting System, Inc. v. United States*, 316 U.S. 407, 417–419 (1942) (finding challenge ripe where plaintiffs must comply with burdensome Federal Communications Commission rule at once or risk later loss of license and consequent serious harm).

The Sierra Club does say that it will be easier, and certainly cheaper, to mount one legal challenge against the Plan now, than to pursue many challenges to each site-specific logging decision to which the Plan might eventually lead. It does not explain, however, why one initial site-specific victory (if based on the Plan's unlawfulness) could not, through preclusion principles, effectively carry the day. See *Lujan v. National Wildlife Federation*, 497 U.S. 871, 894 (1990). And, in any event, the Court has not considered this kind of litigation cost saving sufficient by itself to justify review in a case that would otherwise be unripe. The ripeness doctrine reflects a judgment that the disadvantages of a premature review that may prove too abstract or unnecessary ordinarily outweigh the additional costs of — even repetitive — postimplementation litigation. See, *e.g., ibid.* ("The case-by-case approach . . . is understandably frustrating to an organization such as respondent, which has as its objective across-the-board protection of our Nation's . . . forests- . . . . But this is the traditional, and remains the normal, mode of operation of the courts"); *FTC* v. *Standard Oil Co. of Cal.*, 449 U.S. 232, 244 (1980); *Renegotiation Bd. v. Bannercraft Clothing Co.*, 415 U.S. 1, 24 (1974); *Petroleum Exploration, Inc. v. Public Serv. Comm'n*, 304 U.S. 209, 222 (1938).

Second, from the agency's perspective, immediate judicial review directed at the lawfulness of logging and clearcutting could hinder agency efforts to refine its policies: (a) through revision of the Plan, *e.g.*, in response to an appropriate proposed site-specific action that is inconsistent with the Plan, or (b) through application of the Plan in practice, *e.g.*, in the form of site-specific proposals, which are subject to review by a court applying purely legal criteria. Cf. *Abbott Laboratories, supra*, at 149; *Pacific Gas & Elec. Co.* v. *State Energy Resources Conservation and Development Comm'n*, 461 U.S. 190, 201 (1983). Cf. *Standard Oil Co., supra*, at 242 (premature review "denies the agency an opportunity to correct its own mistakes and to apply its expertise"). And, here, the possibility that further consideration will actually occur before the Plan is implemented is not theoretical, but real. See, *e.g.*, 60 Fed.Reg. 18886, 18901 (1995) (forest plans often not fully implemented), *id.*, at 18905–18907 (discussing process for amending forest plans); 58 Fed.Reg. 19369, 19370–19371 1993) (citing administrative appeals indicating that plans are merely programmatic in nature and that plan cannot foresee all effects on forest); Appeal Nos. 92-09-11-0008, 92-09-11-0009 (Lodging II) (successful Sierra

Club administrative appeals against Wayne timber harvesting site-specific projects). Hearing the Sierra Club's challenge now could thus interfere with the system that Congress specified for the agency to reach forest logging decisions.

Third, from the courts' perspective, review of the Sierra Club's claims regarding logging and clearcutting now would require time-consuming judicial consideration of the details of an elaborate, technically based plan, which predicts consequences that may affect many different parcels of land in a variety of ways, and which effects themselves may change over time. That review would have to take place without benefit of the focus that a particular logging proposal could provide. Thus, for example, the court below in evaluating the Sierra Club's claims had to focus upon whether the Plan as a whole was "improperly skewed," rather than focus upon whether the decision to allow clearcutting on a particular site was improper, say, because the site was better suited to another use or logging there would cumulatively result in too many trees being cut. See 105 F.3d, at 250-251. And, of course, depending upon the agency's future actions to revise the Plan or modify the expected methods of implementation, review now may turn out to have been unnecessary. See *Standard Oil Co., supra*, at 242.

This type of review threatens the kind of "abstract disagreements over administrative policies," *Abbott Laboratories*, 387 U.S., at 148, that the ripeness doctrine seeks to avoid. In this case, for example, the Court of Appeals panel disagreed about whether or not the Forest Service suffered from a kind of general "bias" in favor of timber production and clearcutting. Review where the consequences had been "reduced to more manageable proportions," and where the "factual components [were] fleshed out, by some concrete action" might have led the panel majority either to demonstrate that bias and its consequences through record citation (which it did not do) or to abandon the claim. *National Wildlife Federation, supra*, at 891. All this is to say that further factual development would "significantly advance our ability to deal with the legal issues presented" and would "aid us in their resolution." *Duke Power Co. v. Carolina Environmental Study Group, Inc.*, 438 U.S. 59, 82 (1978).

Finally, Congress has not provided for preimplementation judicial review of forest plans. Those plans are tools for agency planning and management. The Plan is consequently unlike agency rules that Congress has specifically instructed the courts to review "preenforcement." Cf. *National Wildlife Federation, supra*, at 891; 15 U.S.C. § 2618 (Toxic Substances Control Act) (providing pre-enforcement review of agency action); 30 U.S.C. § 1276(a) (Surface Mining Control and Reclamation Act of 1977) (same); 42 U.S.C. § 6976 (Resource Conservation and Recovery Act of 1976) (same); § 7607(b) (Clean Air Act) (same); 43 U.S.C. § 1349(c)(3) (Outer Continental Shelf Lands Act); *Harrison v. PPG Industries, Inc.*, 446 U.S. 578, 592–593 (1980). Nor does the Plan, which through standards guides future use of forests, resemble an environmental impact statement prepared pursuant to NEPA. That is because in this respect NEPA, unlike the NFMA, simply guarantees a particular procedure, not a particular result. Compare 16 U.S.C. § 1604(e) (requiring that forest plans provide for multiple coordinated *use* of forests, including timber and wilderness) with 42 U.S.C. § 4332 (requiring that agencies prepare environmental impact statements where major agency action would significantly affect the environment). Hence a person with standing who is injured by a failure to comply with the NEPA procedure may complain of that failure at the time the failure takes place, for the claim can never get riper.

III

The Sierra Club makes one further important contrary argument. It says that the Plan will hurt it in many ways that we have not yet mentioned. Specifically, the Sierra Club says that the Plan will permit "many intrusive activities, such as opening trails to motorcycles or using heavy machinery," which "will go forward without any additional consideration of their impact on wilderness recreation." Brief for Respondents 34. At the same time, in areas designated for logging, "affirmative measures to promote undisturbed backcountry recreation, such as closing roads and building additional hiking trails," will not take place. *Ibid.* These are harms, says the Sierra Club, that will not take place at a distant future time. Rather, they will take place now.

This argument suffers from the legally fatal problem that it makes its first appearance here in this Court in the briefs on the merits. The Complaint, fairly read, does not include such claims. Instead, it focuses on the amount and method of timber harvesting. The Sierra Club has not referred us to any other court documents in which it protests the Plan's approval of motorcycles or machinery, the Plan's failure to close roads or to provide for the building of trails, or other disruptions that the Plan might cause those who use the forest for hiking. As far as we can tell, prior to the argument on the merits here, the harm to which the Sierra Club objected consisted of too much, and the wrong kind of, logging.

The matter is significant because the Government concedes that if the Sierra Club had previously raised these other kinds of harm, the ripeness analysis in this case with respect to those provisions of the Plan that produce the harm would be significantly different. The Government's brief in the Court of Appeals said:

> "If, for example, a plan incorporated a final decision to close a specific area to off-road vehicles, the plan itself could result in imminent concrete injury to a party with an interest in the use of off-road vehicles in that area." Brief for Federal Appellees in No. 94-3407(CA6), p. 20.

And, at oral argument, the Solicitor General agreed that if the Sierra Club's claim was "that [the] plan was allowing motorcycles into a bird-watching area or something that like, that would be immediately justiciable." Tr. of Oral Arg. 5. Thus, we believe these other claims that the Sierra Club now raises are not fairly presented here, and we cannot consider them.

IV

For these reasons, we find the respondents' suit not ripe for review. We vacate the judgment of the Court of Appeals, and we remand this case with instructions to dismiss.

It is so ordered.

Note: The Case Law Background to *Ohio Forestry Association, Inc. v. Sierra Club.*

In 1967, the Supreme Court decided a triplet of cases that have constituted the core of the ripeness doctrine since that time. These are: *Abbott Laboratories v. Gardner,* 387 U.S. 136 (1967); *Gardner v. Toilet Goods Association,* 387 U.S. 167 (1967); and *Toilet Goods Association, Inc. v. Gardner,* 387 U.S. 158 (1967).

Abbott Laboratories v. Gardner, Secretary of Health, Education, and Welfare, 387 U.S. 136 (1967). A then-recent amendment to the Federal Food, Drug, and Cosmetic Act required manufacturers of prescription drugs to print the "established name" of the drug "prominently and in type at least half as large as that used thereon for any proprietary name or designation for such drug," on labels and other printed material. The "established name" is one designated by the Secretary of Health, Education, and Welfare pursuant under the Act while the "proprietary name" is usually a trade name under which a particular drug is marketed. The underlying purpose of the 1962 amendment was to bring to the attention of doctors and patients the fact that many of the drugs sold under familiar trade names are actually identical to drugs sold under their "established" or less familiar trade names at significantly lower prices. The Commissioner of Food and Drugs, exercising authority delegated to him by the Secretary promulgated the following regulation

> "If the label or labeling of a prescription drug bears a proprietary name or designation for the drug or any ingredient thereof, the established name, if such there be, corresponding to such proprietary name or designation, shall accompany each appearance of such proprietary name or designation."

A group of 37 individual drug manufacturers and the Pharmaceutical Manufacturers Association then brought suit to declare the regulations invalid and to enjoin their implementation, on the ground that the Commissioner exceeded his authority by promulgating an order requiring labels, advertisements, and other printed matter relating to prescription drugs to designate the established name of the particular drug involved every time its trade name is used anywhere in such material. The district court granted the injunctive and declaratory relief requested, but the court of appeals reversed, ruling that no "actual case or controversy" existed and therefore no relief was available. The Supreme Court (through Justice Harlan) characterized the issue as one of ripeness:

> Without undertaking to survey the intricacies of the ripeness doctrine it is fair to say that its basic rationale is to prevent the courts, through avoidance of premature adjudication, from entangling themselves in abstract disagreements over administrative policies, and also to protect the agencies from judicial interference until an administrative decision has been formalized and its effects felt in a concrete way by the challenging parties. The problem is best seen in a twofold aspect, requiring us to evaluate both the fitness of the issues for judicial decision and the hardship to the parties of withholding court consideration.

As to the former factor, we believe the issues presented are appropriate for judicial resolution at this time. First, all parties agree that the issue tendered is a purely legal one: whether the statute was properly construed by the Commissioner to require the established name of the drug to be used *every time* the proprietary name is employed. . . . It is suggested that the justification for this rule might vary with different circumstances, and that the expertise of the Commissioner is relevant to passing upon the validity of the regulation. This of course is true, but the suggestion overlooks the fact that both sides have approached this case as one purely of congressional intent, and that the Government made no effort to justify the regulation in factual terms.

Second, the regulations in issue we find to be "final agency action" within the meaning of § 10 of the Administrative Procedure Act, 5 U.S.C. § 704, as construed in judicial decisions. An "agency action" includes any "rule," defined by the Act as "an agency statement of general or particular applicability and future effect designed to implement, interpret, or prescribe law or policy," §§ 2 (c), 2 (g), 5 U.S.C. §§ 551 (4), 551 (13). The cases dealing with judicial review of administrative actions have interpreted the "finality" element in a pragmatic way. . . .

We find decision in the present case following *a fortiori* from these precedents. The regulation challenged here, promulgated in a formal manner after announcement in the Federal Register and consideration of comments by interested parties is quite clearly definitive. There is no hint that this regulation is informal . . . or only the ruling of a subordinate official . . . or tentative. It was made effective upon publication, and the Assistant General Counsel for Food and Drugs stated in the District Court that compliance was expected.

This is also a case in which the impact of the regulations upon the petitioners is sufficiently direct and immediate as to render the issue appropriate for judicial review at this stage. These regulations purport to give an authoritative interpretation of a statutory provision that has a direct effect on the day-to-day business of all prescription drug companies; its promulgation puts petitioners in a dilemma that it was the very purpose of the Declaratory judgment Act to ameliorate. As the District Court found on the basis of uncontested allegations, "Either they must comply with the every time requirement and incur the costs of changing over their promotional material and labeling or they must follow their present course and risk prosecution." . . . The regulations are clear-cut, and were made effective immediately upon publication; as noted earlier the agency's counsel represented to the District Court that immediate compliance was expected. If petitioners wish to comply they must change all their labels, advertisements, and promotional materials; they must destroy stocks of printed matter; and they must invest heavily in new printing type and new supplies. The alternative to compliance — continued use of material which they believe in good faith meets the statutory requirements, but which clearly does not meet the regulation of the Commissioner — may be even more costly. That course would risk serious criminal and civil penalties for the unlawful distribution of "misbranded" drugs.

It is relevant at this juncture to recognize that petitioners deal in a sensitive industry, in which public confidence in their drug products is especially important. To require them to challenge these regulations only as a defense to an action brought by the Government might harm them severely and unnecessarily. Where the legal issue presented is fit for judicial resolution, and where a regulation requires an immediate and significant change in the plaintiffs' conduct of their affairs with serious penalties attached to noncompliance, access to the courts under the Administrative Procedure Act and the Declaratory Judgment Act must be permitted, absent a statutory bar or some other unusual circumstance, neither of which appears here.

Gardner v. Toilet Goods Assn, 387 U.S. 167 (1967). Under the Federal Food, Drug, and Cosmetic Act as amended by the Color Additive Amendments of 1960, the use of color additives is strictly regulated. The Act requires clearance of every color additive in the form of a regulation prescribing conditions for use of that particular additive, and also certification of each "batch" unless exempted by regulation. The Act defines a color additive as "a dye, pigment, or other substance . . . [which] when added or applied to a food, drug, cosmetic, or to the human body or any part thereof, is capable (alone or through reaction with other substance) of imparting color thereto. . . ." Acting under his general rulemaking power, the Commissioner amplified the statutory definition in three ways: First, the Commissioner included as color additives all diluents, that is, "any component of a color additive mixture that is not of itself a color additive and has been intentionally mixed therein to facilitate the use of the mixture in coloring foods, drugs, or cosmetics or in coloring the human body." Second, the Commissioner included as a color additive any "substance that, when applied to the human body results in coloring . . . unless the function of coloring is purely incidental to its intended use, such as in the case of deodorants. Lipstick, rouge, eye makeup colors, and related cosmetics intended for coloring the human body are 'color additives.' " Third, the Commissioner issued a regulation concerning a statutory exemption for hair dyes. Under the statute hair dyes are totally exempt from coverage of the statute if they display a certain cautionary notice on their labels prescribing a "patch test" to determine whether the dye will cause skin irritation on the particular user. The Commissioner's regulation recognized the exemption, but went on to declare: "If the poisonous or deleterious substance in the 'hair dye' is one to which the caution is inapplicable and for which patch-testing provides no safeguard, the exemption does not apply; nor does the exemption extend to the poisonous or deleterious diluents that may be introduced as wetting agents, hair conditioners, emulsifiers, or other components in a color shampoo, rinse, tint, or similar dual-purpose cosmetics that alter the color of the hair."

In an action by cosmetics manufacturers, the Supreme Court (again through Justice Harlan) ruled that pre-enforcement review of these regulations was proper:

The issue as framed by the parties is a straightforward legal one: what general classifications of ingredients fall within the coverage of the Color Additive Amendments?. . . . We agree . . . that this is not a situation in which consideration of the underlying legal issues would necessarily be facilitated if they were raised in the context of a specific attempt to enforce the regulations. . . .

This result is supported as well by the fact that these regulations are self-executing, and have an immediate and substantial impact upon the respondents. . . . The Act . . . prescribes penalties for the distribution of goods containing color additives unless they have been cleared both by listing in a regulation and by certification of the particular batch. Faced with these regulations the respondents are placed in a quandary. . . .

Questions and Comments

1. What are the two aspects of the ripeness question which a court must evaluate in order to apply that doctrine? Do you see a relationship, in the *Abbott Laboratories* case, between the question of whether the "every time" regulation was fit for judicial review and the question of hardship to the parties of withholding review?

2. What are the standards for determining when issues presented by agency action are fit for review? Whether they are "legal" issues? Whether the agency action is "final"? What are the criteria for determining finality? Can agency action be "final" for purposes of the APA and not final for purposes of the ripeness doctrine? Explain. What is the relevance of whether the agency action is "informal"? The ruling of a subordinate? Tentative?

3. What are the standards for evaluating the hardship to the parties of withholding review? The Court referred to the impact of the regulations upon the petitioners as being "direct and immediate"? What are the standards for determining when the impact of regulations can be said to be "direct and immediate"? In what way did the regulation have a "direct effect on the day-to-day business" of all prescription drug companies?

4. What was the dilemma in which the petitioners in *Abbott Laboratories* were placed? How hard would it have been for the petitioners to comply with the regulation? Must they show that compliance will be very costly? Is the dilemma (i) comply or risk the penalties for violation; or (ii) incur the costs of compliance or risk the penalties for violation? Do you understand the difference? If the costs of compliance were minimal, would the regulation ever be reviewed? Were the companies in *Gardner v. Toilet Goods Ass'n, supra*, placed in a dilemma comparable to the one in *Abbott Laboratories?*

5. When the Court referred to the petitioners being placed in a dilemma, was it describing the effect of a "self-executing" regulation from the viewpoint of those subject to it? Did the Court in *Gardner v. Toilet Goods Ass'n, supra*, describe what it meant by "self-executing" regulations? Were the radio stations in the *CBS* case subject to a dilemma similar to the one in which the *Abbott Laboratories* petitioners found themselves? CBS itself was not subject to a dilemma, though, was it? There was no dilemma involved in the *Standard Computing Scale* case, was there?

6. What is the relationship between the dilemma in which a party is placed by the regulation and the fitness of the agency policy for review? Note that in *Toilet Goods Ass'n v. Gardner*, 367 U.S. 167 (1967), *infra*, the Court found both that the issues were not fit for judicial review and that the parties were not subject to a dilemma similar to the one in *Abbott Laboratories.*

7. Are the standards which the Court set forth in *Abbott Laboratories* consistent with those which were applied in the *CBS* case?

Toilet Goods Association, Inc. v. Gardner, Secretary of Health, Education, and Welfare, 387 U.S. 158 (1967). In this case the Court ruled that preenforcement review of another set of regulations issued under the Food, Drug and Cosmetic Act was improper, because the issue was not yet ripe for review. These regulations, applying to color additives, provided:

"(a) When it appears to the Commissioner that a person has:

"(4) Refused to permit duly authorized employees of the Food and Drug Administration free access to all manufacturing facilities, processes, and formulae involved in the manufacture of color additives and intermediates from which such color additives are derived;

"he may immediately suspend certification service to such person and may continue such suspension until adequate corrective action has been taken." . . .

Unlike the regulations in the two companion cases, this regulation was not ripe for review. An extract from Justice Harlan's opinion for the Court, explaining that conclusion, follows:

In determining whether a challenge to an administrative regulation is ripe for review a two fold inquiry must be made: first to determine whether the issues tendered are appropriate for judicial resolution, and second to assess the hardship to the parties if judicial relief is denied at that stage.

As to the first of these factors, we agree with the Court of Appeals that the legal issue as presently framed is not appropriate for judicial resolution. This is not because the regulation is not the agency's considered and formalized determination, for we are in agreement with petitioners that . . . there can be no question that this regulation — promulgated in a formal manner after notice and evaluation of submitted comments — is a "final agency action" under § 10 of the Administrative Procedure Act, 5 U.S.C. § 704. . . . Also, we recognize the force of petitioners' contention that the issue as they have framed it presents a purely legal question: whether the regulation is totally beyond the agency's power under the statute, the type of legal issue that courts have occasionally dealt with without requiring a specific attempt at enforcement . . . or exhaustion of administrative remedies. . . .

These points which support the appropriateness of judicial resolution are, however, outweighed by other considerations. The regulation serves notice only that the Commissioner may under certain circumstances order inspection of certain facilities and data, and that further certification of additives may be refused to those who decline to permit a duly authorized inspection until they have complied in that regard. At this juncture we have no idea whether or when such an inspection will be ordered and what reasons the Commissioner will give to justify his order. The statutory authority asserted for the regulation is the power to promulgate regulations "for the efficient enforcement" of the Act, § 701(a). Whether the regulation is justified thus depends not only, as petitioners appear to suggest, on whether Congress refused to include a specific section of the Act authorizing such inspections, although this factor is to be sure a highly relevant one, but also on whether the statutory scheme as a whole justified promulgation of the regulation. . . . This will depend not merely on an inquiry into statutory purpose, but concurrently on an understanding of what types of enforcement problems are encountered by the FDA, the need for various sorts of supervision in order to effectuate the goals of the Act, and the safeguards devised to protect legitimate trade secrets. . . . We believe that judicial appraisal of these factors is likely to stand on a much surer footing in the context of a specific application of this regulation than could be the case in the framework of the generalized challenge made here.

We are also led to this result by consideration of the effect on the petitioners of the regulation. . . . The regulation challenged here is not analogous to those . . . where the impact of the administrative action could be said to be felt immediately by those subject to it in conducting their day-to-day affairs. . . .

This is not a situation in which primary conduct is affected — when contracts must be negotiated, ingredients tested or substituted, or special records compiled. This regulation merely states that the Commissioner may authorize inspectors to examine certain processes or formulae; no advance action is required of cosmetics manufacturers, who since the enactment of the 1938 Act have been under a statutory duty to permit reasonable inspection of a "factory, warehouse, establishment, or vehicle and all pertinent equipment, finished and unfinished materials; containers, and labeling therein." § 704 (a). Moreover, no irremediable adverse consequences flow from requiring a later challenge to this regulation by a manufacturer who refuses to allow this type of inspection. Unlike the other regulations challenged in this action, in which seizure of goods, heavy fines, adverse publicity for distributing "adulterated" goods, and possible criminal liability might penalize failure to comply, see *Gardner v. Toilet Goods Assn.* . . . a refusal to admit an inspector here would at most lead only to a suspension of certification services to the particular party, a determination that can then be promptly challenged through an administrative procedure,[19] which in turn is reviewable by a court. Such review will

---

[19] See 21 CFR §§ 8.28(b), 130.14–130.26. We recognize that a denial of certification might under certain circumstances cause inconvenience and possibly hardship, depending upon such factors as how large a supply of certified additives the particular manufacturer may have, how rapidly the administrative hearing and judicial review are conducted, and what temporary remedial or protective provisions, such as compliance with a reservation pending litigation, might be available to a manufacturer testing the regulation. In the context of the present case we need only say that such inconvenience is speculative and

provide an adequate forum for testing the regulation in a concrete situation.

. . . . [G]iven the fact that only minimal, if any, adverse consequences will face petitioners if they challenge the regulation in this manner, we think it wiser to require them to exhaust this administrative process through which the factual basis of the inspection order will certainly be aired and where more light may be thrown on the Commissioner's statutory and practical justifications for the regulation. . . .

For these reasons the judgment of the Court of Appeals is *Affirmed.*

Questions and Comments

1.   Can you explain why the issues were less fit for judicial resolution here than in *Abbott Laboratories* and in *Gardner v. Toilet Goods Ass'n?* Do you know whether the agency had fully developed its inspection policy at this time? Did the regulation embody a complete development of that agency policy? Did the regulation in *Abbott Laboratories?* in *Gardner v. Toilet Goods Ass'n?*

2.   Why was the situation here not one "in which primary conduct *is* affected"? What did the Court mean by "primary conduct"? Were the companies put in a dilemma by the inspection regulation comparable to the dilemma in which they were placed by the "every time" regulation in *Abbott Laboratories?* What would be the costs which the companies would incur by violating regulation and then challenging its validity when the agency sought to enforce it?

3.   Do you see a relationship between the fitness of the issues for judicial review and the impact of the regulation upon the parties? If the parties are placed in a dilemma comparable to the ones involved in *Abbott Laboratories* and in *Gardner v. Toilet Goods Ass'n*, will the agency *policy* necessarily have been more fully developed than it was in this case?

4.   Are the policies which underlie the ripeness doctrine related to the policies underlying the exhaustion doctrine? Explain. If administrative remedies have not been exhausted, would a case ever be ripe for judicial review? Explain.

3.   Finality.

Finality, as we have observed, is a component of the ripeness doctrine. Finality sometimes, however, can be an exclusive focus of judicial attention. For example, finality is a requirement under section 704 of the APA for judicial review.

---

we have been provided with no information that would support an assumption that much weight should be attached to this possibility.

FRANKLIN, SECRETARY OF COMMERCE v. MASSACHUSETTS
505 U.S. 788 (1992)

JUSTICE O'CONNOR delivered the opinion of the Court, except as to Part III.

[Under the automatic reapportionment statute, after each decennial census the Secretary of Commerce transmits the census count, tabulated by state, to the President who then transmits to the Congress "a statement showing the whole number of persons in each State . . . as ascertained under the . . . decennial census of the population, and the number of Representatives to which each State would be entitled under an apportionment of the then existing number of Representatives by the method known as the method of equal proportions. . . ." The statute provides that each state is entitled to the number of Representatives shown in the President's statement and requires the Clerk of the House of Representatives to send to the executive of each state a certificate of the number of representatives to which such state is entitled.

Massachusetts is challenging the census count on the ground, inter alia, that military personnel stationed abroad were assigned to their home states under the census count. Massachusetts asserts that such assignment was unlawful and that if no such assignment occurred, Massachusetts would have one additional representative in the Congress.]

. . . .

II

Appellees raise claims under both the APA and the Constitution. We address first the statutory basis for our jurisdiction under the APA. . . .

The APA sets forth the procedures by which federal agencies are accountable to the public and their actions subject to review by the courts. The Secretary's report to the President is an unusual candidate for "agency action" within the meaning of the APA, because it is not promulgated to the public in the Federal Register, no official administrative record is generated, and its effect on reapportionment is felt only after the President makes the necessary calculations and reports the result to the Congress. . . .

The APA provides for judicial review of "final agency action for which there is no other adequate remedy in a court." 5 U.S.C. § 704. At issue in this case is whether the "final" action that appellees have challenged is that of an "agency" such that the federal courts may exercise their powers of review under the APA. We hold that the final action complained of is that of the President, and the President is not an agency within the meaning of the Act. Accordingly, there is no final agency action that may be reviewed under the APA standards.

To determine when an agency action is final, we have looked to, among other things, whether its impact "is sufficiently direct and immediate" and has a "direct effect on . . . day-to-day business." *Abbott Laboratories v. Gardner*, 387 U.S. 136,

152 (1967). An agency action is not final if it is only "the ruling of a subordinate official," or "tentative." . . . The core question is whether the agency has completed its decision-making process, and whether the result of that process is one that will directly affect the parties. In this case, the action that creates an entitlement to a particular number of Representatives and has a direct effect on the reapportionment is the President's statement to Congress, not the Secretary's report to the President.

Unlike other statutes that expressly require the President to transmit an agency's report directly to Congress, § 2a does not. . . . After receiving the Secretary's report, the President is to "transmit to the Congress a statement showing the whole number of persons in each State . . . as ascertained under the . . . decennial census of the population." 2 U.S.C. § 2a. Section 2a does not expressly require the President to use the data in the Secretary's report, but, rather, the data from the "decennial census." There is no statute forbidding amendment of the "decennial census" itself after the Secretary submits the report to the President. For potential litigants, therefore, the "decennial census" still presents a moving target, even after the Secretary reports to the President. In this case, the Department of Commerce, in its press release issued the day the Secretary submitted the report to the President, was explicit that the data presented to the President was still subject to correction. . . . Moreover, there is no statute that rules out an instruction by the President to the Secretary to reform the census, even after the data is submitted to him. It is not until the President submits the information to Congress that the target stops moving, because only then are the States entitled by § 2a to a particular number of Representatives. Because the Secretary's report to the President carries no direct consequences for the reapportionment, it serves more like a tentative recommendation than a final and binding determination. It is, like "the ruling of a subordinate official," *Abbott Laboratories v. Gardner, supra,* at 151, not final and therefore not subject to review. . . .

The statutory structure in this case differs from that at issue in *Japan Whaling Assn. v. American Cetacean Soc.,* 478 U.S. 221 (1986), in which we held that the Secretary of Commerce's certification to the President that another country was endangering fisheries was "final agency action." . . . In that case, the Secretary's certification to the President under 22 U.S.C. § 1978(a)(1) automatically triggered sanctions by the Secretary of State under 16 U.S.C. § 1821(e)(2)(B), regardless of any discretionary action the President himself decided to take. . . . Under 13 U.S.C. § 141(a), by contrast, the Secretary's report to the President has no direct effect on reapportionment until the President takes affirmative steps to calculate and transmit the apportionment to Congress.

   . . . .

As enacted, 2 U.S.C. § 2a provides that the Secretary cannot act alone; she must send her results to the President, who makes the calculations and sends the final apportionment to Congress. That the final act is that of the President is important to the integrity of the process and bolsters our conclusion that his duties are not merely ceremonial or ministerial. Thus, we can only review the APA claims here if the President, not the Secretary of Commerce, is an "agency" within the meaning of the Act.

The APA defines "agency" as "each authority of the Government of the United States, whether or not it is within or subject to review by another agency, but does not include — (A) the Congress; (B) the courts of the United States; (C) the governments of the territories or possessions of the United States; (D) the government of the District of Columbia." 5 U.S.C. §§ 701(b)(1), 551(1). The President is not explicitly excluded from the APA's purview, but he is not explicitly included, either. Out of respect for the separation of powers and the unique constitutional position of the President, we find that textual silence is not enough to subject the President to the provisions of the APA. We would require an express statement by Congress before assuming it intended the President's performance of his statutory duties to be reviewed for abuse of discretion. . . . As the APA does not expressly allow review of the President's actions, we must presume that his actions are not subject to its requirements. Although the President's actions may still be reviewed for constitutionality, see *Youngstown Sheet & Tube Co. v. Sawyer*, 343 U.S. 579 (1952), *Panama Refining Co. v. Ryan*, 293 U.S. 388 (1935), we hold that they are not reviewable for abuse of discretion under the APA. . . . The District Court erred in proceeding to determine the merits of the APA claims.

[After holding that the President's action was not reviewable for abuse of discretion nder the APA, the Court dealt with the Constitutional issue of equal representation. The court concluded that it was not necessary to consider injunctive relief against the President, because it could proceed by declaratory relief against the Secretary of Commerce alone. On the merits, the Court ruled that Massachusetts had failed on the merits to make out a case of disparate representation.]

Questions and Comments

1. *Franklin* is a recent example of a type of case in which a final decision is made by the President. What comes to the President as a recommendation is not "final", and therefore fails to meet the finality requirements of the ripeness doctrine. When the President acts, the matter is "final" but courts do not like to subject Presidential decision-making to judicial review. How did the Court decide in this case that the President's decision was not subject to judicial review?

2. Was the Court correct in deciding that the President was not an "agency" within the meaning of the APA? What provisions in the APA support your conclusion?

3. The Court distinguished *Japan Whaling Ass'n v. American Cetacean Soc'y*, 478 U.S. 221 (1986). Can you employ this distinction to assist in predicting the outcome of other cases?

PUBLIC CITIZEN v. UNITED STATES TRADE REPRESENTATIVE

5 F.3d 549 (D.C. Cir. 1993), *cert. denied*, 510 U.S. 1041 (1994)

MIKVA, CHIEF JUDGE:

Appellees Public Citizen, Friends of the Earth, Inc., and the Sierra Club (collectively "Public Citizen") sued the Office of the United States Trade Representative, claiming that an environmental impact statement was required for the North American Free Trade Agreement ("NAFTA"). The district court granted Public Citizen's motion for summary judgment and ordered that an impact statement be prepared "forthwith." In its appeal of that ruling, the government contends that the Trade Representative's preparation of NAFTA without an impact statement is not "final agency action" under the Administrative Procedure Act ("APA") and therefore is not reviewable by this court. Because we conclude that NAFTA is not "final agency action" under the APA, we reverse the decision of the district court and express no view on the government's other contentions.

I. BACKGROUND

In 1990, the United States, Mexico, and Canada initiated negotiations on the North American Free Trade Agreement. NAFTA creates a "free trade zone" encompassing the three countries by eliminating or reducing tariffs and "non-tariff" barriers to trade on thousands of items of commerce. After two years of negotiations, the leaders of the three countries signed the agreement on December 17, 1992. NAFTA has not yet been transmitted to Congress. If approved by Congress, NAFTA is scheduled to take effect on January 1, 1994.

. . . .

II. DISCUSSION

The National Environmental Policy Act ("NEPA") requires federal agencies to include an EIS "in every recommendation or report on proposals for legislation and other major Federal actions significantly affecting the quality of the human environment. . . ." 42 U.S.C. § 4332(2)(C). In drafting NEPA, however, Congress did not create a private right of action. Accordingly, Public Citizen must rest its claim for judicial review on the Administrative Procedure Act. Section 702 of the APA confers an action for injunctive relief on persons "adversely affected or aggrieved by agency action within the meaning of a relevant statute." 5 U.S.C. § 702; see *Public Citizen I*, 970 F.2d at 918. Section 704, however, allows review only of "*final* agency action." 5 U.S.C. § 704 (emphasis added); see *Lujan v. National Wildlife Fed'n*, 497 U.S. 871, 882, 110 S.Ct. 3177, 3185, 111 L.Ed.2d 695 (1990). The central question in this appeal then is whether Public Citizen has identified some agency action that is final upon which to base APA review.

In support of its argument that NAFTA does not constitute "final agency action" within the meaning of the APA, the government relies heavily on *Franklin v. Massachusetts*, 505 U.S. 788, 112 S.Ct. 2767, 120 L.Ed.2d 636 (1992). *Franklin* involved a challenge to the method used by the Secretary of Commerce to calculate the 1990 census. The Secretary acted pursuant to a reapportionment statute requiring that she report the "tabulation of total population by States . . . to the President." 13 U.S.C. § 141(b). After receiving the Secretary's report, the President must transmit to Congress the number of Representatives to which each state is entitled under the method of equal proportions. 2 U.S.C. § 2a(a). The Supreme Court held that APA review was unavailable because the final action under the reapportionment statute (transmittal of the apportionment to Congress) was that of the President, and the President is not an agency. . . .

To determine whether an agency action is final, "[t]he core question is whether the agency has completed its decisionmaking process, *and* whether the result of that process is one that will directly affect the parties." *Franklin*, 505 U.S. at __, 112 S.Ct. at 2773 (emphasis added). The *Franklin* Court found that although the Secretary had completed her decisionmaking process, the action that would directly affect the plaintiffs was the President's calculation and transmittal of the apportionment to Congress, not the Secretary's report to the President. *Id.*

This logic applies with equal force to NAFTA. Even though the OTR has completed negotiations on NAFTA, the agreement will have no effect on Public Citizen's members unless and until the President submits it to Congress. Like the reapportionment statute in *Franklin*, the Trade Acts involve the President at the final stage of the process by providing for him to submit to Congress the final legal text of the agreement, a draft of the implementing legislation, and supporting information. 19 U.S.C. § 2903(a)(1)(B). The President is not obligated to submit any agreement to Congress, and until he does there is no final action. If and when the agreement is submitted to Congress, it will be the result of action by the President, action clearly not reviewable under the APA.

The district court attempts to distinguish *Franklin* by noting that unlike the census report (which the President was authorized to amend before submitting to Congress), NAFTA is no longer a "moving target" because the "final product . . . will not be changed before submission to Congress." 822 F. Supp. at 26. The district court goes on to say that NAFTA "shall" be submitted to Congress. *Id.* This distinction is unpersuasive. NAFTA is just as much a "moving target" as the census report in *Franklin* because in both cases the President has statutory discretion to exercise supervisory power over the agency's action. It is completely within the President's discretion, for example, to renegotiate portions of NAFTA before submitting it to Congress or to refuse to submit the agreement at all. In fact, President Clinton has conditioned the submission of NAFTA on the successful negotiation of side agreements on the environment, labor, and import surges. . . .

Public Citizen seeks to distinguish *Franklin* by arguing that the EIS requirement is an independent statutory obligation for the OTR and thus the agency's failure to prepare an EIS is reviewable final agency action. But the preparation of the census report in *Franklin* was also an "independent statutory obligation" for the Secretary of Commerce. The Court held nonetheless that because the report would have no effect on the plaintiffs without the President's subsequent involvement, the agency's action would not have the "direct effect" necessary for "final agency actions." Furthermore, although the argument that the absence of an EIS "directly affects" Public Citizen's ability to lobby Congress and disseminate information seems persuasive on its face, this court has stated that an agency's failure to prepare an EIS, by itself, is not sufficient to trigger APA review in the absence of identifiable substantive agency action putting the parties at risk. *Foundation on Economic Trends v. Lyng*, 943 F.2d 79, 85 (D.C.Cir.1991).

Finally, Public Citizen argues that applying *Franklin* in this case would effectively nullify NEPA's EIS requirement because often "some other step must be taken before" otherwise final agency actions will result in environmental harm. . . . In support of this position, it catalogs a number of cases in which courts have reviewed NEPA challenges to agency actions that require the involvement of some other governmental or private entity before becoming final. . . . Although we acknowledge the stringency of *Franklin*'s "direct effect" requirement, we disagree that it represents the death knell of the legislative EIS. *Franklin* is limited to those cases in which the President has final constitutional or statutory responsibility for the final step necessary for the agency action directly to affect the parties. Moreover, *Franklin* notes explicitly the importance of the President's role in the "integrity of the process" at issue. . . . [T]he requirement that the President, and not OTR, initiate trade negotiations and submit trade agreements and their implementing legislation to Congress indicates that Congress deemed the President's involvement essential to the integrity of international trade negotiations. When the President's role is not essential to the integrity of the process, however, APA review of otherwise final agency actions may well be available.

The government advances many other arguments opposing the preparation of an EIS, including weighty constitutional positions on the separation of powers and Public Citizen's lack of standing, as well as the inapplicability of NEPA to agreements executed pursuant to the Trade Acts in general, and NAFTA in particular. It also suggests that the judicial branch should avoid any conflict with the President's power by exercising the "equitable discretion" given it by § 702 of the APA. We need not and do not consider such arguments in light of the clear applicability of the *Franklin* precedent.

The ultimate destiny of NAFTA has yet to be determined. Recently negotiated side agreements may well change the dimensions of the conflict that Public Citizen sought to have resolved by the courts. More importantly, the political debate over NAFTA in Congress has yet to play out. Whatever the ultimate result, however, NAFTA's fate now rests in the hands of the political branches. The judiciary has no role to play.

In sum, under the reasoning and language of *Franklin v. Massachusetts*, the "final agency action" challenged in this case is the submission of NAFTA to Congress by the President. Because the Trade Acts vest in the President the discretion to renegotiate NAFTA before submitting it to Congress or to refuse to submit it at all, his action, and not that of the OTR, will directly affect Public Citizen's members. The President's actions are not "agency action" and thus cannot be reviewed under the APA. The district court's grant of summary judgment in favor of Public Citizen is, therefore, *Reversed.*

Randolph, Circuit Judge, concurring:

I agree with my colleagues that the injunction against the United States Trade Representative must be set aside. . . ."

. . . . I get a bit concerned when the opinion announces that it is too early to toll the bell for judicial review in a "legislative EIS" case and then starts trying to limit *Franklin*. . . . The idea behind this is that proposing legislation to Congress can constitute "final . . . action," and that when an "agency" rather than the President does the proposing, § 704 of the APA will be satisfied. . . . I am not so sure. *Franklin* held not only that the President is outside the APA's definition of "agency," but also that "action" cannot be considered "final" under the APA unless it "will directly affect the parties." . . . When the alleged "action" consists of a proposal for legislation, how can this condition for judicial review be satisfied? In *Franklin*, the President's submission to Congress directly affected the parties because, under the "automatic reapportionment statute," congressional action was not required. . . . In general, however, it is difficult to see how the act of proposing legislation could generate direct effects on parties, or anyone else for that matter. . . .

Questions and Comments

1. Does *Public Citizen* follow from *Franklin*? In *Franklin* the Court majority ruled that the President's decision was not subject to judicial review, but nonetheless allowed judicial review of action by the Secretary of Commerce. Why was some version of the *Franklin* technique not available here to permit the court to order compliance with NEPA's requirement for an environmental impact statement? Was the court correct in concluding that it could not order the preparation of an EIS?

2. Did Congress intend NEPA's requirement for environmental impact statements to apply to circumstances like the proposed legislation implementing NAFTA? Why or why not? Should the court have addressed this issue on the merits?

3. Judge Randolph, concurring, suggested that proposed legislation will rarely be "final" under the criteria of *Franklin*. Was he thus suggesting that compliance with NEPA's mandate of an environmental impact statement on proposed legislation will rarely be judicially reviewable?

BENNETT v. SPEAR
520 U.S. 154 (1997)

[In this case ranch operators and irrigation districts brought suit alleging violations of the Endangered Species Act concerning proposed use of reservoir water to protect certain fish. Plaintiffs directed their challenge at a Biological Opinion issued by the Fish and Wildlife Service which they contended was flawed. The Biological Opinion guides the future action of the federal agency concerned, here the Bureau of Reclamation overseeing the Klamath Irrigation Project. That part of the opinion which deals with finality is reproduced below.]

B

The Government contends that petitioners theory that the Biological Opinion does not constitute "final agency action," 5 U.S.C. § 704, because it does not conclusively determine the manner in which Klamath Project water will be allocated:

> "Whatever the practical likelihood that the [Bureau] would adopt the reasonable and prudent alternatives (including the higher lake levels) identified by the Service, the Bureau was not legally obligated to do so. Even if the Bureau decided to adopt the higher lake levels, moreover, nothing in the biological opinion would constrain the [Bureau's] discretion as to how the available water should be allocated among potential users." Brief for Respondents 33.

This confuses the question whether the Secretary's action is final with the separate question whether petitioners' harm is "fairly traceable" to the Secretary's action (a question we have already resolved against the Government, see Part III-A, *supra*). As a general matter, two conditions must be satisfied for agency action to be "final": First, the action must mark the "consummation" of the agency's decision-making process, *Chicago & Southern Air Lines, Inc. v. Waterman S.S. Corp.*, 333 U.S. 103 (1948) — it must not be of a merely tentative or interlocutory nature. And second, the action must be one by which "rights or obligations have been determined," or from which "legal consequences will flow," *Port of Boston Marine Terminal Ass'n v. Rederiaktiebolaget Translantic*, 400 U.S. 62, 71 (1970). It is uncontested that the first requirement is met here; and the second is met because, as we have discussed above, the Biological Opinion and accompanying Incidental Take Statement alter the legal regime to which the action agency is subject, authorizing it to take the endangered species if (but only if) it complies with the prescribed conditions. In this crucial respect the present case is different from the cases upon which the Government relies, *Franklin v. Massachusetts*, 505 U.S. 788 (1992), and *Dalton v. Specter*, 511 U.S. 462 (1994). In the former case, the agency action in question was the Secretary of Commerce's presentation to the President of a report tabulating the results of the decennial census; our holding that this did not constitute "final agency action" was premised on the observation that the report carried "no direct consequences" and served "more like a tentative recommendation than a final and binding determination." 505 U.S., at 798. And in the latter case, the agency action in question was submission to the President of base closure recommendations by the Secretary of Defense and the Defense Base Closure and Realignment Commission; our holding that this was not "final agency action" followed from the fact that the recommendations were in no way binding on the President, who had absolute discretion to accept or reject them. 511 U.S., at 469–471. Unlike the reports in *Franklin* and *Dalton*, which were purely advisory and in no way affected the legal rights of the relevant actors, the Biological Opinion at issue here has direct and appreciable legal consequences.

* * * *

The judgment of the Court of Appeals is reversed, and the case is remanded for further proceedings consistent with this opinion.

It is so ordered.

Questions and Comments

1. The finality requirements of *Franklin* and of *Bennett v. Spear* both derive from APA § 704. Are they the same? How do they differ?

2. How, if at all, does the finality issue under APA § 704 discussed in *Bennett v. Spear, supra*, differ from the fitness issue that is a part of the ripeness doctrine? Do you recall cases in which the issues were final but not yet ripe? Would *Toilet Goods Ass'n v. Gardner, supra*, be such a case? Would *Weight Watchers International, Inc. v. FTC, infra*?

3. To what extent does the *Bennett v. Spear* requirement that the the action must be one by which "rights or obligations have been determined," or from which "legal consequences will flow" overlap the "hardship" element of the ripeness analysis of *Abbott Laboratories*?

4. On the relation of finality under *Bennett v. Spear* and the ripeness doctrine, see Gwendolyn McKee, *Judicial Review of Agency Guidance Documents: Rethinking the Finality Doctrine*, 60 ADMIN. L. REV. 371 (2008).

4.   The Interplay of Section 704 Finality and Ripeness.

WEIGHT WATCHERS INTERNATIONAL, INC. v. FEDERAL TRADE COMMISSION
47 F.3d 990 (9th Cir. 1995)

T.G. NELSON, CIRCUIT JUDGE:

Weight Watchers International and Weight Watchers of Greater Washington State ("WW") appeal the district court's dismissal of their claim that the Federal Trade Commission ("FTC" or "Commission") violated statutory requirements for rulemaking by impermissibly altering the existing legal guidelines regulating the weight loss industry on an adjudicatory case-by-case basis. The district court, holding that the action was premature and therefore not justiciable, dismissed for lack of jurisdiction. . . . We affirm in part, reverse in part, and remand.

II

The underlying dispute between Weight Watchers and the Federal Trade Commission ("FTC") concerns Weight Watchers' allegation that the FTC is making new rules to regulate the weight loss industry without following the procedures laid out in the FTC rulemaking statute, 15 U.S.C. § 57a(b).[1] Weight Watchers

---

[1] Title 15 U.S.C. § 57a(a)(1) provides that the FTC may prescribe:

(A) interpretive rules and general statements of policy with respect to unfair or deceptive acts or practices in or affecting commerce [under 15 U.S.C. § 45(a)(1)], and (B) rules which define with specificity acts or practices which are unfair or deceptive acts or practices in or affecting commerce. . . .

contends that the agency is circumventing the rulemaking statute by proceeding improperly to effect regulatory changes through adjudication. The FTC denies that it is engaged in rulemaking.[2]

III

The Administrative Procedure Act ("APA") provides that:

> Agency action made reviewable by statute and final agency action for which there is no other adequate remedy in a court are subject to judicial review. . . . Except as otherwise expressly required by statute, agency action otherwise final is final for the purposes of this section whether or not there has been presented or determined an application for a declaratory order. 5 U.S.C. § 704.

It further provides that the reviewing court shall:

> (1) compel agency action unlawfully withheld or unreasonably delayed; and (2) hold unlawful and set aside agency action, findings, and conclusions found to be —

> (A) arbitrary, capricious, an abuse of discretion, or otherwise not in accordance with law; (B) contrary to constitutional right, power, privilege, or immunity; (C) in excess of statutory jurisdiction, authority, or limitation, or short of statutory right; (D) without observance of procedure required by law; (E) unsupported by substantial evidence . . . ; or (F) unwarranted by the facts. . . . 5 U.S.C. § 706.

"An agency's denial of a petition for rulemaking constitutes final, reviewable agency action, except where there is evidence of a clear and convincing legislative intent to negate review." . . .

While it is true that most of the cases cited deal with the parties' efforts to initiate agency action . . . rather than with "spurious" rulemaking, or the anticipated effects thereof, it is by no means clear that Weight Watchers' allegation of injuries caused by adjudicatory activities renders the denial of its rulemaking petition anything other than a final action. . . .

Because there does not appear to be any legislative intent to preclude review of

---

When prescribing a rule under subsection (B), the Commission is required to proceed in accordance with section 553 of Title 5, U.S.C., and:

(A) publish a notice of proposed rulemaking stating with particularity the text of the rule, including any alternatives, which the Commission proposes to promulgate, and the reason for the proposed rule; (B) allow interested persons to submit written data, views, and arguments, and make all such submissions publicly available; (C) provide an opportunity for an informal hearing . . . ; and (D) promulgate, if appropriate, a final rule . . . together with a statement of basis and purpose. 15 U.S.C. § 57a(b)(1).

[2] A rulemaking document which cannot be characterized as interpreting existing legislation, and which has legal effect, is subject to comment and notice procedures. See R. Anthony, " 'Interpretative' Rules, 'Legislative' Rules and 'Spurious' Rules: Lifting the Smog, 8 Admin. L.J. Am. U. 1 (1994); American Mining Congress v. Mine Safety and Health Admin., 995 F.2d 1106, 1112 (D.C. Cir. 1993) (discussing "legal effect").

FTC denial of rulemaking petitions, and because such denials appear to be final orders as a matter of law, we hold that the district court has jurisdiction to review the FTC's denial of the rulemaking petition under the APA and 28 U.S.C. § 1331. Where an agency's refusal to institute a rulemaking is held to be final agency action subject to judicial review, it is reviewed under the arbitrary and capricious standard of 5 U.S.C. § 706(2)(A). . . . Therefore, the district court erred when it held that this portion of Weight Watchers' claim was nonjusticable.

refusal to review rulemaking petition denials

IV

. . . . Taking all allegations of material fact as true, and construing them in the light most favorable to Weight Watchers, . . . we nevertheless hold that the dismissed complaint pertains to issues which are not yet ripe for review. . . . While the district court must accept for review the FTC's denial of the rulemaking petition, it may neither enjoin the agency's ongoing investigation of the weight loss industry, nor require the FTC to proceed by rule-making rather than adjudication, until the FTC has issued a final order against the moving party. Cease-and-desist orders issued by the FTC are appealed directly to the court of appeals. 15 U.S.C. § 45(d).

— not yet — ripeness

— need a final order

V

For the foregoing reasons, we. . . . REVERSE on the question of jurisdiction or justiciability of the FTC's denial of Weight Watchers' rulemaking petition, and REMAND to the district court for review of the order denying the petition under the arbitrary and capricious standard. 5 U.S.C. § 706(2)(A).

AFFIRMED in part, REVERSED in part, and REMANDED. No costs allowed.

Questions and Comments

1. In this case the plaintiff Weight Watchers was complaining that the Federal Trade Commission was failing to engage in rulemaking in violation of a statutory command. When will this issue be ripe for judicial review?

2. The court is treating Weight Watchers' complaint as unripe. Could the complaint be dismissed on the grounds that Weight Watchers failed to exhaust its administrative remedies? Why or why not?

3. The court remanded the case back to the district court for review of the FTC's denial of Weight Watchers' petition for rulemaking. Will Weight Watchers obtain effective review of its complaint about the FTC's substitution of adjudication for rulemaking in the proceeding on remand?

4. What are Weight Watchers' chances for prevailing on the merits of its complaint about the FTC's failure to use rulemaking?

5.   Ripeness, State Administrative Procedures, and Civil Rights Litigation.

WILLIAMSON COUNTY REGIONAL PLANNING COMMISSION v. HAMILTON BANK OF JOHNSON CITY
473 U.S. 172 (1985)

JUSTICE BLACKMUN delivered the opinion of the Court.

A

Under Tennessee law, responsibility for land-use planning is divided between the legislative body of each State's counties and regional and municipal "planning commissions." . . .

The developer submitted a preliminary plat for the cluster development of its tract, the Temple Hills Country Club Estates (Temple Hills), to the Williamson County Regional Planning Commission for approval. Once approved the preliminary plat served as a basis for the preparation of a final plat. The final plat was required to conform substantially to the preliminary plat, and, in addition, to include such details as the lines of all streets, lots, boundaries, and building setbacks.

On May 23, 1973, the Commission approved the developer's preliminary plat for Temple Hills. The plat indicated that the development was to include 676 acres, of which 260 acres would be open space, primarily in the form of a golf course. A notation on the plat indicated that the number of allowable dwelling units for total development was 736, but lot lines were drawn in for only 469 units. . . . The density of 736 allowable dwelling units was calculated by multiplying the number of acres (676) by the number of units allowed per acre (1.089). Although the zoning regulations in effect in 1973 required that density be calculated "on the basis of total acreage less fifty percent (50%) of the land lying in the flood plain . . . and less fifty percent (50%) of all land lying on a slope with a grade in excess of twenty-five percent (25%)," no deduction was made from the 676 acres for such land.

In 1977, the county changed its zoning ordinance to require that calculations of allowable density exclude 10% of the total acreage to account for roads and utilities. In addition, the number of allowable units was changed to one per acre from the 1.089 per acre allowed in 1973. The Commission continued to apply the zoning ordinance and subdivision regulations in effect in 1973 to Temple Hills, however, and reapproved the preliminary plat in 1978. In August 1979, however, the Commission reversed its position and decided that plats submitted for renewal should be evaluated under the zoning and subdivision regulations in effect when the renewal was sought. The Commission then renewed the Temple Hills plat under the ordinances and regulations in effect at that time.

In January 1980, the Commission asked the developer to submit a revised preliminary plat before it sought final approval for the remaining sections of the subdivision. . . . The developer submitted a revised preliminary plat for approval in October 1980. [At that time a special committee (Temple Hills Committee) was appointed to work with the developer on the revision of the preliminary plat.] Upon review, the Commission's staff and the Temple Hills Committee noted several problems with the revised plat. First, the allowable density under the zoning ordinance and subdivision regulations then in effect was 548 units, rather than the 736 units claimed under the preliminary plat approved in 1973. The difference reflected a decrease in 18.5 acres for the parkway, a decrease of 66 acres for the 10% deduction for roads, and an exclusion of 44 acres for 50% of the land lying on slopes exceeding a 25% grade. Second, two cul-de-sac roads that had become necessary because of the land taken for the parkway exceeded the maximum length allowed for such roads under the subdivision regulations in effect in both 1980 and 1973. Third, approximately 2000 feet of road would have grades in excess of the maximum allowed by county road regulations. Fourth, the preliminary plat placed units on land that had grades in excess of 25% and thus was considered undevelopable under the zoning and subdivision regulations. Fifth, the developer had not fulfilled its obligations regarding the construction and maintenance of the main access road. Sixth, there were inadequate fire protection services for the area, as well as inadequate open space for children's recreational activities. Finally, the lots proposed in the preliminary plat had a road frontage that was below the minimum required by the subdivision regulations in effect in 1980.

The Temple Hills Committee recommended that the Commission grant a waiver of the regulations regarding the length of the cul-de-sacs, the maximum grade of the roads, and the minimum frontage requirement. . . . Without addressing the suggestion that those three requirements be waived, the Commission disapproved the plat on two other grounds: first, the plat did not comply with the density requirements of the zoning ordinance or subdivision regulations, because no deduction had been made for the land taken for the parkway, and because there had been no deduction for 10% of the acreage attributable to roads or for 50% of the land having a slope of more than 25%; and second, lots were placed on slopes with a grade greater than 25%. . . .

The developer then appealed to the County Board of Zoning Appeals. . . . On November 11, 1980, the Board determined that the Commission should apply the zoning ordinance and subdivision regulations that were in effect in 1973 in evaluating the density of Temple Hills. . . . It also decided that in measuring which lots had excessive grades, the Commission should define the slope in a manner more favorable to the developer.

 . . . . In June 1981, respondent [Hamilton Bank of Johnson City which had acquired the undeveloped property in Temple Hills through foreclosure] submitted two preliminary plats to the Commission — the plat that had been approved in 1973 and subsequently reapproved several times, and a plat indicating respondent's plans for the undeveloped areas, which was similar to the plat submitted by the developer in 1980. The new plat proposed the development of 688 units; the reduction from 736 units represented respondent's concession that 18.5 acres should be removed from the acreage because that land had been taken for the parkway. . . .

On June 18, the Commission disapproved the plat for eight reasons, including the density and grade problems cited in the October 1980 denial, as well as the objection the Temple Hills Committee had raised in 1980 to the length of two cul-de-sacs, the grade of various roads, the lack of fire protection, the disrepair of the main-access road, and the minimum frontage. . . . The Commission declined to follow the decision of the Board of Zoning Appeals that the plat should be evaluated by the 1973 zoning ordinance and subdivision regulations, stating that the Board lacked jurisdiction to hear appeals from the Commission. . . .

B

Respondent then filed this suit in the United States District Court for the Middle District of Tennessee, pursuant to 42 U.S.C. § 1983, alleging that the Commission had taken its property without just compensation. . . . Respondent's expert witnesses testified that the design that would meet each of the Commission's eight objections would allow respondent to build only 67 units, 409 fewer than respondent claims it is entitled to build, and that the development of only 67 sites would result in a net loss of over $1 million. . . .

[After a jury verdict in favor of the respondent in the amount of $350,000] the court . . . granted judgment notwithstanding the verdict in favor of the Commission on the taking claim, reasoning in part that respondent was unable to derive economic benefit from its property on a temporary basis only, and that such a temporary deprivation, as a matter of law, cannot constitute a taking. . . . In addition, the court modified its permanent injunction to require the Commission merely to apply the zoning ordinance and subdivision regulations in effect in 1973 to the project, rather than requiring approval of the plat, in order to allow the parties to resolve "legitimate technical questions of whether plaintiff meets the requirements of the 1973 regulations," . . . through the applicable state and local appeals procedures.

A divided panel of the United States Court of Appeals for the Sixth Circuit reversed. . . . The court held that application of government regulations affecting an owner's use of property may constitute a taking if the regulation denies the owner all "economically viable" use of the land, and that the evidence supported the jury's finding that the property had no economically feasible use during the time between the Commission's refusal to approve the preliminary plat and the jury's verdict. . . .

II

We granted certiorari to address the question whether federal, state, and local governments must pay money damages to a landowner whose property allegedly has been "taken" temporarily by the application of government regulations. . . . Petitioners and their *amici* contend that we should answer the question in the negative by ruling that government regulation can never effect a "taking" within the meaning of the Fifth Amendment. They recognize that government regulation may be so restrictive that it denies a property owner all reasonable beneficial use of its property, and thus has the same effect as an appropriation of the property for public use, which concededly would be a taking under the Fifth Amendment. Instead, such regulation should be viewed as a violation of the Fourteenth Amendment's Due Process Clause, because it is an attempt by government to use its police power to effect a result that is so unduly oppressive to the property owner that it constitutionally can be effected only through the power of eminent domain. Violation of the Due Process Clause, petitioners' argument concludes, need not be remedied by "just compensation."

The Court twice has left this issue undecided. . . . Once again, we find that the question is not property presented, and must be left for another day. For whether we examine the Planning Commission's application of its regulations under Fifth Amendment "taking" jurisprudence, or under the precept of due process, we conclude that respondent's claim is premature.

III

We examine the posture of respondent's cause of action first by viewing it as stating a claim under the just Compensation Clause. . . .

A

As the Court had made clear in several recent decisions, a claim that the application of government regulations effects a taking of a property interest is not ripe until the government entity charged with implementing the regulations has reached a final decision regarding the application of the regulations to the property in issue. . . . Respondent has submitted a plan for developing its property. . . . [but] respondent did not then seek variances that would have allowed it to develop the property according to its proposed plat, notwithstanding the Commission's finding that the plat did not comply with the zoning ordinance and subdivision regulations. It appears that variances could have been granted to resolve at least five of the Commission's eight objections to the plat. The Board of Zoning Appeals had the power to grant certain variances from the zoning ordinance, including the ordinance's density requirements and its restriction on placing units on land with slopes having a grade in excess of 25%. . . . The Commission had the power to grant variances from the subdivision regulations, including the cul-de-sac, road grade, and frontage requirements. Indeed, the Temple Hills Committee had recommended that the Commission grant variances from those regulations. Nevertheless, respondent did not seek variances from either the Board or the Commission.

Indeed, in a letter to the Commission written shortly before its June 18, 1981, meeting to consider the preliminary sketch, respondent took the position that it would not request variances from the Commission until *after* the Commission approved the proposed plat:

"[Respondent] stands ready to work with the Planning Commission concerning the necessary variances. Until the initial sketch is renewed, however, and the developer has an opportunity to do detailed engineering work it is impossible to determine the exact nature of any variances that may be needed." . . .

The Commission's regulations clearly indicated that unless a developer applied for a variance in writing and upon notice to other property owners, "any condition shown on the plat which would require a variance will constitute grounds for disapproval of the plat Thus, in the face of respondent's refusal to follow the procedures for requesting a variance, and its refusal to provide specific information about the variances it would require, respondent hardly can maintain that the Commission's disapproval of the preliminary plat was equivalent to a final decision that no variances would be granted.

. . . . Our reluctance to examine taking claims until . . . a final decision has been made is compelled by the very nature of the inquiry required by the just Compensation Clause. . . . [T]his Court consistently has indicated that among the factors of particular significance in the inquiry are the economic impact of the challenged action and the extent to which it interferes with reasonable investment-backed expectations. . . . Those factors simply cannot be evaluated until the administrative agency has arrived at a final, definitive position regarding how it will apply the regulations at issue to the particular land in question.

Respondent asserts that it should not be required to seek variances from the regulations because its suit is predicated upon 42 U.S.C. § 1983, and there is no requirement that a plaintiff exhaust administrative *remedies before* bringing a § 1983 action. *Patsy v. Florida Board of Regents*, 457 U.S. 496 (1982). The question whether administrative remedies must be exhausted is conceptually distinct, however, from the question whether an administrative action must be final before it is judicially reviewable. . . . While the policies underlying the two concepts often overlap, the finality requirement is concerned with whether the initial decision-maker has arrived at a definitive position on the issue that inflicts an actual, concrete injury; the exhaustion requirement generally refers to administrative and judicial procedures by which an injured party may seek review of an adverse decision and obtain a remedy if the decision is found to be unlawful or otherwise inappropriate. *Patsy* concerned the latter, not the former.

The difference is best illustrated by comparing the procedure for seeking a variance with the procedures that, under *Patsy*, respondent would not be required to exhaust. While it appears that the State provides procedures by which an aggrieved property owner may seek a declaratory judgment regarding the validity of zoning and planning actions taken by county authorities . . . respondent would not be required to resort to those procedures before bringing its § 1983 action, because those procedures clearly are remedial. Similarly, respondent would not be required to appeal the Commission's rejection of the preliminary plat to the Board of Zoning Appeals, because the Board was empowered, at most, to review that rejection, not to participate in the Commission's decision-making.

Resort to those procedures would result in a judgment whether the Commission's actions violated any of respondent's rights. In contrast, resort to the procedure for obtaining variances would result in a conclusive determination by the Commission whether it would allow respondent to develop the subdivision in the manner respondent proposed. The Commission's refusal to approve the preliminary plat does not determine that issue; it prevents respondent from developing its subdivision without obtaining the necessary variances, but leaves open the possibility that respondent may develop the subdivision according to its plat after obtaining the variances. In short, the commission's denial of approval does not conclusively determine whether respondent will be denied all reasonable beneficial use of its property, and therefore is not a final, reviewable decision.

B

A second reason the taking claim is not yet ripe is that respondent did not seek compensation through the procedures the State has provided for doing so. The Fifth Amendment does not proscribe the taking of property; it proscribes taking without just compensation. . . .

The recognition that a property owner has not suffered a violation of the just Compensation Clause until the owner has unsuccessfully attempted to obtain just compensation through the procedures provided by the State for obtaining such compensation is analogous to the Court's holding in *Parratt v. Taylor*, 451 U.S. 527 (1981). There, the Court ruled that a person deprived of property through a random and unauthorized act by a state employee does not state a claim under the Due Process Clause merely by alleging the deprivation of property. In such a situation, the Constitution does not require predeprivation process because it would be impossible or impracticable to provide a meaningful hearing before the deprivation. Instead, the Constitution is satisfied by the provision of meaningful postdeprivation. process. Thus, the State's action is not "complete" in the sense of causing a constitutional injury "unless or until the State fails to provide an adequate postdeprivation remedy for the property loss." *Hudson v. Palmer*, 468 U.S. 517, 532, n.12 (1984). Likewise, because the Constitution does not require pretaking compensation, and is instead satisfied by a reasonable and adequate provision for obtaining compensation after the taking, the State's action here is not "complete" until the State fails to provide adequate compensation for the taking.

Under Tennessee law, a property owner may bring an inverse condemnation action to obtain just compensation for an alleged taking of property under certain circumstances. Tenn. Code Ann. § 29-16-123 (1980). . . . The Tennessee state courts have interpreted § 29-16123 to allow recovery through inverse condemnation where the "taking" is effected by restrictive zoning laws or development regulations. . . . Respondent has not shown that the inverse condemnation procedure is unavailable or inadequate, and until it has utilized that procedure, its taking claim is premature.

IV

We turn to an analysis of respondent's claim under the due process theory that petitioners espouse. As noted, under that theory government regulation does not effect a taking for which the Fifth Amendment requires just compensation; instead, regulation that goes so far that it has the same effect as a taking by eminent domain is an invalid exercise of the police power, violative of the Due Process Clause of the Fourteenth Amendment. Should the Government wish to accomplish the goals of such regulation, it must proceed through the exercise of its eminent domain power, and, of course, pay just compensation for any property taken. The remedy for a regulation that goes too far, under the due process theory, is not "just compensation," but invalidation of the regulation, and if authorized and appropriate, actual damages.

. . . .

We need not pass upon the merits of petitioners' arguments, for even if viewed as a question of due process, respondent's claim is premature. Viewing a regulation that "goes too far" as an invalid exercise of the police power, rather than as a "taking" for which just compensation must be paid, does not resolve the difficult problem of how to distinguish the point at which regulation becomes so onerous that it has the same effect as an appropriation of the property through eminent domain or physical possession. . . . [R]esolution of that question depends, in significant part, upon an analysis of the effect the Commission's application of the zoning ordinance and subdivision regulations had on the value of respondent's property and investment-backed profit expectations. That effect cannot be measured until a final decision is made as to how the regulations will be applied to respondent's property. No such decision had been made at the time respondent filed its § 1983 action, because respondent failed to apply for variances from the regulations.

V

In sum, respondent's claim is premature, whether it is analyzed as a deprivation of property without due process under the Fourteenth Amendment, or as a taking under the just Compensation Clause of the Fifth Amendment. We therefore reverse the judgment of the Court of Appeals and remand the case for further proceedings consistent with this opinion.

It is so ordered.[20]

Questions and Comments

1.   What did you learn from the Court's discussion of *Patsy v. Board of Regents?* After having read *Williamson*, are you better able to distinguish issues of exhaustion of administrative remedies from issues of ripeness?

2.   What were the procedures for obtaining variances? Could the Planning Commission grant variances? Could the Board of Zoning Appeals grant variances? Was the developer required to seek variances from the Planning Commission before bringing its § 1983 action? Was it required to seek variances from the Board of Zoning Appeals before bringing its § 1983 action?

3.   Would your answers to any of the above questions be affected by the standard of review applied by the Board of Zoning Appeals to the decisions of the Planning Commission? Suppose the Board of Zoning Appeals reviewed decisions of the Planning Commission *de novo*. Would such *de novo* review mean that the real decisionmaker was the Board rather than the Commission? Would it mean that the Board was "participating" in the decisionmaking rather than merely reviewing it?

---

[20] Citations to the record omitted.

How would this procedural variation affect the point at which a developer could seek relief in court on a taking claim? Suppose that the Planning Commission itself acted after the issues had been sorted out in a report filed by a hearing officer and who made an initial decision which was routinely reviewed *de novo* by the Commission at the request of any interested person. Or suppose that the hearing officer's report contained a recommendation rather than an initial decision. How would these variations affect the point at which a developer could seek relief in a § 1983 action?

4.   When the Court indicated that final action by the Planning Commission would be required before the issues would be ripe but that appeals to the Board of Zoning Appeals would be unnecessary, was it not necessarily saying that an issue can be ripe even though administrative remedies have not been exhausted?

5.   Did not the Court indicate in *Abbott Laboratories* that an issue was not ripe if it was only the decision of a subordinate? Does not this mean that a subordinate's determination must be appealed administratively before the issue will be ripe? Why was the decision of the Planning Commission in *Williamson* not the decision of a body subordinate to the Board of Zoning Appeals? If the Planning Commission was a subordinate body, then an appeal to the Board would be necessary before the issue would be ripe, would it not?

6.   The Court later reached the issue as to whether compensation is required for a temporary taking. In *First English Evangelical Lutheran Church of Glendale v. County of Los Angeles*, 482 U.S. 304 (1987), the Court ruled that a landowner is entitled to compensation for deprivation of the use of its land by legislation during the period of deprivation preceding a judicial ruling that the legislation is invalid. (In that case, the church owned riverfront property the buildings on which were destroyed by a flood. The county then enacted an ordinance prohibiting construction or reconstruction in a newly created flood protection area which included the church's property. The California courts had held that the church was not entitled to compensation for any period prior to the time when the ordinance was ruled invalid.)

The Court, however, avoided addressing the question as to the extent, if any, to which a landowner is entitled to compensation for being denied use of its property during the time consumed by normal administrative proceedings incident to obtaining a variance from zoning restrictions. ("We . . . do not deal with the quite different questions that would arise in the case of normal delays in obtaining building permits, changes in zoning ordinances, variances, and the like which are not before us." 482 U.S. at 321).

E.   STANDING

1.   *Note: Standing Concepts Before 1970.*

The traditional approach to standing. Traditionally, standing to challenge governmental action was governed by the so-called "legal interest" test. That test is relatively easy to understand, although it takes two sentences or so to state it. First, pretend that the adverse impact upon the plaintiff was caused by a private party rather than the government. If the plaintiff would have a cause of action against a private party, then the plaintiff has standing to complain of the government's action in court.

Thus in the *CBS* case, *supra*, for example, the FCC was threatening to revoke the licenses of radio stations who failed to repudiate their contracts with the CBS network. Had a private party coerced the stations to repudiate their contracts with CBS, the latter would have had a cause of action for interference with contractual relations. Therefore, CBS had standing to challenge the lawfulness of the government action interfering with those contracts.

Standing developments under special review statutes. Many regulatory statutes contain provisions specifically dealing with judicial review. The Communications Act, for example, provides that decisions of the Federal Communications Commission can be appealed to the Court of Appeals of the District of Columbia (1) by an applicant for a license or permit, or (2) "by any other person aggrieved or whose interests are adversely affected by any decision of the Commission granting or refusing any such application [for a license or permit]." That provision was construed in *FCC v. Sanders Brothers Radio Station*, 309 U.S. 470 (1940).

In *Sanders*, the Telegraph Herald applied for a permit to erect a broadcasting station in Dubuque, Iowa. Sanders, which had operated a station in East Dubuque, Ill., opposed the application on the ground that there was insufficient advertising revenue in the area to support two stations. The Commission nonetheless approved the Telegraph Herald's application. Sanders sought judicial review of the Commission's decision; and when the case reached the Supreme Court, that Court ruled upon the question of whether Sanders could properly seek judicial review.

The problem arose from the statutory standard under which the Commission acted. The Commission was required to decide in a way which furthered the public interest, convenience or necessity. Under such a standard, the private economic interest suffered by Sanders as a result of increased competition from a rival station would be irrelevant.

The Court ruled, however, that while the Communications Act did not protect one station from economic injury caused by competition with rival stations, nonetheless economic injury furnished a motive for a station to call to the attention of the courts errors of law made by the Commission. The Court concluded that the review provisions of the Communications Act gave a station suffering economic injury as a result of Commission action standing to challenge the Commission action in court. Otherwise, Commission errors would go unchallenged and the public — which was the intended beneficiary of Commission regulation — would be the loser. Sanders (which was threatened by such economic injury) therefore was a person "aggrieved" or "adversely affected" within the meaning of the judicial review provisions of the Communications Act:

> . . . . It does not follow that, because the licensee of a station cannot resist the grant of a license to another, on the ground that the resulting competition may work economic injury to him, he has no standing to appeal from an order of the Commission granting the application.
>
> Section 402(b) of the Act provides for an appeal to the Court of Appeals of the District of Columbia (1) by an applicant for a license or permit, or (2)

"by any other person aggrieved or whose interests are adversely affected by any decision of the Commission granting or refusing any such application."

The petitioner insists that as economic injury to the respondent was not a proper issue before the Commission it is impossible that § 402(b) was intended to give the respondent standing to appeal, since absence of right implies absence of remedy. This view would deprive subsection (2) of any substantial effect.

Congress had some purpose in enacting § 402(b)(2). It may have been of opinion that one likely to be financially injured by the issue of a license would be the only person having a sufficient interest to bring to the attention of the appellate courts errors of law in the action of the Commission in granting the license. It is within the power of Congress to confer such standing to prosecute an appeal.

We hold, therefore, that the respondent had the requisite standing to appeal and to raise, in the court below, any relevant question of law in respect of the order of the Commission.

Prior to the *Sanders* decision,[21] the meaning of the term "aggrieved" was unclear. After that decision the term "aggrieved" in the Communications Act was understood to confer standing upon existing radio stations to challenge license grants to rivals which would adversely affect their economic interests. Since the standard under which license decisions were made was the furtherance of the public interest, the "aggrieved" station was required to bring to the attention of the reviewing court errors of law by the Commission which impinged upon rights, not of itself, but of the public. The Court reiterated this view in *Scripps-Howard Radio, Inc. v. FCC*, 316 U.S. 4, 14 (1942) ("These private litigants have standing only as representatives of the public interest.") The implications of *Sanders*, however, ran deeper. The term "aggrieved" was contained in the judicial review provisions of many other statutes. The implication of *Sanders* was that these judicial review provisions should be construed like § 402(b)(2) of the Communications Act.

In ***Associated Industries of N. Y State, Inc. v. Ickes*, 134 F.2d 694, 705 (2d Cir. 1943), *vacated on grounds of mootness*, 320 U.S. 707 (1943),** Judge Frank articulated a "private attorney general" rationale for the standing analysis developed in *Sanders*. In that case an association of manufacturers challenged a decision of the Department of the Interior's Bituminous Coal Division raising coal prices. Although the manufacturers had no legal right to any particular level of coal prices, they were held to be "aggrieved" persons within the meaning of the judicial review provisions of the Bituminous Coal Act. Using the *Sanders* rationale, the court ruled that the manufacturers' economic injury (resulting from higher prices which they would pay for coal) gave them the motivation to bring to the reviewing court's attention errors of law committed by the Bituminous Coal Division.

---

[21] *See* Daniel J. Gifford, *Decisions, Decisional Referents, and Administrative Justice*, 37 Law & Contemp. Prob. 3, 34–35 (1972).

The "Private attorney general" rationale which Judge Frank developed in support of his decision can be summarized as follows: Since Congress could authorize the Attorney General to seek judicial relief against Commission action extending beyond its statutory mandate, it could as easily confer standing on others to challenge such action by, in effect, creating private or *ad hoc* attorneys general to vindicate the public interest in lawful agency action in particular cases. Judge Frank held that Congress conferred standing upon private persons to enforce the public interest when it authorized persons "aggrieved" to seek judicial review of decisions of the Bituminous Coal Division. Persons aggrieved were, under the *Sanders* rationale, those whose economic injury gave them a strong motive for pointing out to the reviewing court, the agency's errors of law. This strong motive ensured that the case would be presented in an adversary way. *Associated Industries* not only furnished a widely accepted rationale for the standing which *Sanders* conferred upon persons "aggrieved", it also recognized that economic injury to a consumer interest was sufficient to confer standing under a special review statute. Later cases recognized consumer interests as a basis for challenging agency action increasing prices under a number of price or rate-regulating statutes.

In 1965, the Second Circuit decided ***Scenic Hudson Preservation Committee v. FPC*, 354 F.2d 608 (2d Cir. 1965), *cert. denied*, 384 U.S. 941 (1966).** In that case the court extended the private attorney general doctrine to embrace those whose motives for seeking judicial review of agency action were based upon their ideological or philosophical orientation. The Federal Power Commission had licensed the construction of a pumped storage hydroelectric project on the Hudson River. After the Commission's decision, an association of neighboring landowners which had been a party to the administrative licensing proceedings asked the court of appeals to invalidate the Commission's license grant. The court did so largely because the Commission had made its licensing decision primarily on engineering grounds and had failed adequately to consider aesthetic and environmental factors in its decision. In order for the case to have been brought before the court, however, the appealing landowners had to establish standing. The Federal Power Act conferred standing upon "aggrieved" parties, and the court found standing in the association under the *Sanders* and *Associated Industries* rationales. The court found that the association possessed the motivation to bring Commission errors to the attention of the reviewing court, not so much because it suffered economic injury at the hands of the Commission, but because the association was composed of "those who by their activities and conduct have exhibited a special interest" in the "aesthetic, conservational, and recreational aspects of power development". This "special interest" served the same function as economic injury served in *Sanders* and *Associated Industries:* it was the motivating factor for the appealing parties to bring agency errors of law to the attention of the reviewing court and thereby further the public's interest in lawful Commission decisionmaking.

2. *The APA provisions.*

Section 702 provides that:

A person suffering legal wrong because of agency action, or adversely affected or aggrieved by agency action within the meaning of a relevant statute, is entitled to judicial review thereof.

The common understanding at the time that the APA was enacted was that this provision merely codified existing law. A person "suffering legal wrong" was a person who had standing under the traditional "legal interest" test described above. A person "adversely affected or aggrieved by agency action within the meaning of a relevant statute" was a person who had standing under a special statutory review provision contained in the regulatory statute conferring power on the agency from whose decision an appeal is being taken.

Such a person was thus one — like Sanders or Associated Industries — who was given standing by the judicial review provision of a particular regulatory statute conferring standing upon an "aggrieved" person. Thus the phrase "adversely affected or aggrieved" used in § 702 is substantially identical to the language of § 402(b)(2) of the Communications Act construed and applied in the *Sanders* case. And the phrase "within the meaning of a relevant statute" referred to the particular statute (such as § 402(b)(2) of the Communications Act, for example) granting review.

In short, § 702 was understood as merely a restatement or codification of existing law. It said, in effect, that there are two sources of standing: the legal interest doctrine; and special review statutes conferring standing upon "aggrieved" parties.

3. *Taxpayer and Citizen Standing: Background to the Standing of an Injured Person to Seek Judicial Relief From Agency Action.*

In *Frothingham v. Mellon*, 262 U.S. 447 (1923), a taxpayer attacked the Maternity Act of 1921 which had established a federal program of grants to those states which undertook programs to reduce maternal and infant mortality. The taxpayer alleged that Congress lacked power to enact the Maternity Act and that her taxes would be increased as a result of this allegedly unconstitutional legislation. The Court ruled that because a federal taxpayer's "interest in the moneys of the Treasury . . . is comparatively minute and indeterminable" that "the effect upon future taxation, of any payment out of the [Treasury's] funds . . . [is] remote, fluctuating and uncertain." Under this analysis, the taxpayer had failed to allege the type of "direct injury" necessary to confer standing[22]

Except as modified by the Court's 1968 decision in *Flast v. Cohen, infra*, *Frothingham* has retained its vitality. *Frothingham* continues to bar standing to taxpayers who seek to challenge the legal validity of statutes or government programs and whose only asserted injury is the impact of the challenged program upon their tax liability.

In 1968 the Supreme Court decided *Flast v. Cohen*, 392 U.S. 83 (1968) which created a limited place for taxpayer standing. In *Flast* the plaintiff taxpayers

---

[22] *See* discussion of *Frothingham* in Flast v. Cohen, 392 U.S. 83 (1968).

challenged the validity of expenditures under Titles I and II of the Elementary and Secondary Education Act of 1965 to purchase textbooks used in religious schools. The Court created a limited exception to *Frothingham's* bar to taxpayer standing:

> The nexus demanded of federal taxpayers has two aspects to it. First, the taxpayer must establish a logical link between that status and the type of legislative enactment attacked. Thus, a taxpayer will be a proper party to allege the unconstitutionality only of exercises of congressional power under the taxing and spending clause of Art. I, § 8, of the Constitution. It will not be sufficient to allege an incidental expenditure of tax funds in the administration of an essentially regulatory statute. . . . Secondly, the taxpayer must establish a nexus between that status and the precise nature of the constitutional infringement alleged. Under this requirement, the taxpayer must show that the challenged enactment exceeds specific constitutional limitations imposed upon the exercise of the congressional taxing and spending power and not simply that the enactment is generally beyond the powers delegated to Congress by Art. I, § 8. When both nexuses are established, the litigant will have shown a taxpayer's stake in the outcome of the controversy and will be a proper and appropriate party to invoke a federal court's jurisdiction.

> We have noted that the Establishment Clause of the First Amendment does specifically limit the taxing and spending power conferred by Art. I, § 8. Whether the Constitution contains other specific limitations can be determined only in the context of future cases. However, whenever such specific limitations are found, we believe a taxpayer will have a clear stake as a taxpayer in assuring that they are not breached by Congress. Consequently, we hold that a taxpayer will have standing consistent with Article III to invoke federal judicial power when he alleges that congressional action under the taxing and spending clause is in derogation of those constitutional provisions which operate to restrict the exercise of the taxing and spending power. The taxpayer's allegation in such cases would be that his tax money is being extracted and spent in violation of specific constitutional protections against such abuses of legislative power. Such an injury is appropriate for judicial redress, and the taxpayer has established the necessary nexus between his status and the nature of the allegedly unconstitutional action to support his claim of standing to secure judicial review.

More recently, the Court reaffirmed and reapplied *Flast* in *Bowen v. Kendrick*, 487 U.S. 589 (1988) to permit taxpayer standing to challenge the administration of the Adolescent Family Life Act as a violation of the establishment clause. The Act provided for federal grants to public or nonprofit organizations or agencies "for services and research in the area of premarital adolescent sexual relations." The plaintiffs challenged both the validity of the Act on its face and the validity of the Act "as applied." In making the latter challenge, the plaintiffs contended that the Secretary of Health and Human Services who administered the Act had funded premarital sex counseling by religious organizations, and, according to the plaintiffs, such counseling could not be carried out by religious organizations without at the same time promoting religious doctrine. Against the contention that taxpayer standing did not extend to the administration of the Act because the funding decisions under challenge were made by the executive rather than by Congress, the Court held that the taxpayer plaintiffs were nonetheless challenging the exercise of the congressional and spending power even though the actual funding decisions were routed through the Secretary of Health and Human Services:

> . . . [I]n this case there is no dispute that appellees have standing to raise their challenge to the AFLA on its face. What is disputed, however, is whether appellees have standing to challenge the statute as applied. The answer to this question turns on our decision in *Valley Forge Christian College v. Americans United for Separation of Church and State, Inc.*, 454 U.S. 464 (1982). In *Valley Forge*, we ruled that taxpayers did not have standing to challenge a decision by the Secretary of Health, Education, and Welfare (HEW) to dispose of certain property pursuant to the Federal Property and Administrative Services Act of 1949. . . . We rejected the taxpayers claim of standing for two reasons: first, because "the source of their complaint is not a congressional action, but a decision by HEW to transfer a parcel of federal property and second, because "the property transfer about which [the taxpayers] complain was not an exercise of authority conferred by the Taxing and Spending Clause of Art. 1, § 8". . . . Appellants now contend that appellees' standing in this case is deficient for the former reason; they argue that a challenge to the AFLA "as applied" is really a challenge to executive action, not to an exercise of congressional authority under the Taxing and Spending Clause. We do not think, however, that appellees' claim that AFLA funds are being used improperly by individual grantees is any less a challenge to congressional taxing and spending power simply because the funding authorized by Congress has flowed through and been administered by the Secretary. Indeed, *Flast* itself was a suit against the Secretary of HEW, who had been given the authority under the challenged statute to administer the spending program that Congress had created. In subsequent cases . . . we have not questioned the standing of taxpayer plaintiffs to raise Establishment Clause challenges, even when their claims raised questions about the administratively made grants. . . . The AFLA is at heart a program of disbursement of funds pursuant to Congress' taxing and spending powers, and appellees' claims call into question how the funds authorized by Congress are being disbursed pursuant to the AFLA's statutory mandate. In this case there is thus a sufficient nexus between the taxpayer's standing as a taxpayer and the congressional exercise of taxing and spending power, notwithstanding the role the Secretary plays in administering the statute.

4. *The Post-Flast Landscape.*

50 U.S.C. § 403j(b) provides that the Central Intelligence Agency (CIA) may account for its expenditures "solely on the certificate of the Director." In *United States v. Richardson*, 418 U.S. 166 (1974), the respondent sought to obtain from the Government information concerning detailed expenditures of the CIA. In response to his inquiries, he received from the Treasury a document known as the Combined Statement of Receipts, Expenditures, and Balances of the United States

Government, but which did not show detailed CIA expenditures. Relying upon the Constitutional provision set forth below, respondent then brought suit to enjoin the publication of the Combined Statement and to obtain a ruling that 50 U.S.C. § 403j(b) was unconstitutional. Article 1, § 9, cl. 7 of the U.S. Constitution provides:

> No Money shall be drawn from the Treasury, but in Consequence of Appropriations made by Law; and a regular Statement and Account of the Receipts and Expenditures of all public Money shall be published from time to time.

The Supreme Court ruled that the respondent lacked standing to assert his claim in court. Referring back to its decision in *Flast* which had created a limited scope for taxpayer standing, the Court held that the respondent had not brought himself within the criteria governing taxpayer standing set forth in *Flast:*

> The Court [in *Flast*] . . . announced a two-pronged standing test which requires allegations: (a) challenging an enactment under the Taxing and Spending Clause of Art. 1, § 8, of the Constitution; and (b) claiming that the challenged enactment exceeds specific constitutional limitations imposed on the taxing and spending power. . . . The mere recital of the respondent's claims and an examination of the statute under attack demonstrate how far he falls short of the standing criteria of *Flast* and how neatly he falls within the *Frothingham* holding left undisturbed. Although the status he rests on is that he is a taxpayer, his challenge is not addressed to the taxing or spending power, but to the statutes regulating the CIA, specifically 50 U.S.C. § 403j(b). That section provides different accounting and reporting requirements and procedures for the CIA, as is also done with respect to other governmental agencies dealing in confidential areas.

> Respondent makes no claim that appropriated funds are being spent in violation of a "specific constitutional limitation upon the . . . taxing and spending power. . . ." Rather, he asks the courts to compel the Government to give him information on precisely how the CIA spends its funds. Thus there is no "logical nexus" between the asserted status of taxpayer and the claimed failure of the Congress to require the Executive to supply a more detailed report of the expenditures of that agency.

> The question presented thus is simply and narrowly whether these claims meet the standards of taxpayer standing set forth in *Flast;* we hold they do not. Respondent is seeking "to employ a federal court as a forum in which to air his generalized grievances about the conduct of government." Both *Frotbingham* and *Flast* . . . reject that basis for standing.

At the end of its opinion, the Court spoke broadly about standing and the role of the courts. As you read standing cases arising in other contexts, you may wish to consider whether the views expressed by the Court in the *Richardson* case help to explain its actions elsewhere. The Court's opinion continued:

> It can be argued that if respondent is not permitted to litigate this issue, no one can do so. In a very real sense, the absence of any particular individual or class to litigate these claims gives support to the argument that the subject matter is committed to the surveillance of Congress, and

ultimately to the political process. Any other conclusion would mean that the Founding Fathers intended to set up something in the nature of an Athenian democracy or a New England town meeting to oversee the conduct of the National Government by means of lawsuits in federal courts. The Constitution created a *representative* Government with the representatives directly responsible to their constituents at stated periods of two, four, and six years; that the Constitution does not afford a judicial remedy does not, of course, completely disable the citizen who is not satisfied with the "ground rules" established by the Congress for reporting expenditures of the Executive Branch. Lack of standing within the narrow confines of Art. III jurisdiction does not impair the right to assert his views in the political forum or at the polls. Slow, cumbersome, and unresponsive though the traditional electoral process may be thought at times, our system provides for changing members of the political branches when dissatisfied citizens convince a sufficient number of their fellow electors that elected representatives are delinquent in performing duties committed to them.

In *Schlesinger v. Reservists Committee to Stop the War*, 418 U.S. 208 (1974) respondents sought declaratory and injunctive relief against members of Congress holding offices in the armed forces reserves. Respondents based their suit upon Art. I, § 6, cl. 2 of the U.S. Constitution, which provides:

> No Senator or Representative shall, during the Time for which he was elected, be appointed to any civil Office under the Authority of the United States, which shall have been created, or the Emoluments whereof shall have been encreased during such time; and no Person holding any Office under the United States, shall be a Member of either House during his Continuance in Office.

The Court denied respondents' standing to maintain their suit, both as citizens and as taxpayers:

> As relevant here, citizens and taxpayers were alleged in respondents' complaint to have suffered injury because Members of Congress holding a Reserve position in the Executive Branch were said to be subject to the possibility of undue influence by the Executive Branch, in violation of the concept of the independence of Congress implicit in Art. I of the Constitution. Reserve membership was also said to place upon Members of Congress possible inconsistent obligations which might cause them to violate their duty faithfully to perform as reservists or as Members of Congress. . . .

Citizen Standing

> To have standing to sue as a class representative it is essential that a plaintiff must be a part of that class, that is, he must possess the same interest and suffer the same injury shared by all members of the class he represents. . . .

> The only interest all citizens share in the claim advanced by respondents is one which presents injury in the abstract. Respondents seek to have the

judicial Branch compel the Executive Branch to act in conformity with the Incompatibility Clause, an interest shared by all citizens. The very language of respondents' complaint . . . reveals that it is nothing more than a matter of speculation whether the claimed nonobservance of that Clause deprives citizens of the faithful discharge of the legislative duties of reservist Members of Congress. And that claimed nonobservance, standing alone, would adversely affect only the generalized interest of all citizens in constitutional governance, and that is an abstract injury.

The Court reaffirmed *Ex Parte Levitt*, 302 U.S. 633 (1937) holding that citizenship alone did not confer standing to attack (as contrary to U.S. Const., Art. 1, § 6, cl. 2) an appointment to the Supreme Court of a senator who had held office when the retirement benefits of Supreme Court Justices had been increased:

> We reaffirm *Levitt* in holding that standing to sue may not be predicated upon an interest of the kind alleged here which is held in common by all members of the public, because of the necessarily abstract nature of the injury all citizens share. . . .

> . . . . [The District Court observed] that if respondents could not obtain judicial review of petitioners' action, "then as a practical matter no one can." Our system of government leaves many crucial decisions to the political processes. The assumption that if respondents have no standing to sue, no one would have standing is not a reason to find standing. . . .

The Court then summarily ruled that the respondents lacked standing as taxpayers, on the ground that they had not raised a claim under Art. I, § 8, and accordingly had not brought themselves within the criteria for taxpayer standing set forth in *Flast*.

5.   *Towards a New Standing Paradigm.*

a.   *Data Processing and the Redefinition of Standing in 1970.*

ASSOCIATION OF DATA PROCESSING SERVICE ORGANIZATIONS, INC. v. CAMP, COMPTROLLER OF THE CURRENCY
397 U.S. 150 (1970)

Mr. Justice Douglas delivered the opinion of the Court.

Petitioners sell data processing services to businesses generally. In this suit they seek to challenge a ruling by respondent Comptroller of the Currency that, as an incident to their banking services, national banks, including respondent American National Bank & Trust Company, may make data processing services available to other banks and to bank customers. The District Court dismissed the complaint for lack of standing of petitioners to bring suit. . . . The Court of Appeals affirmed. . . . The case is here on a petition for writ of certiorari which we granted. . . .

Generalizations about standing to sue are largely worthless as such. One generalization is, however, necessary and that is that the question of standing in the federal courts is to be considered in the framework of Article III which restricts judicial power to "cases" and "controversies

The first question is whether the plaintiff alleges that the challenged action has caused him injury in fact, economic or otherwise. There can be no doubt but that petitioners have satisfied this test. The petitioners not only allege that competition by national banks in the business of providing data processing services might entail some future loss of profits for the petitioners, they also allege that respondent American National Bank & Trust Company was performing or preparing to perform such services for two customers for whom petitioner Data Systems, Inc., had previously agreed or negotiated to perform such services. The petitioners' suit was brought not only against the American National Bank & Trust Company, but also against the Comptroller of the Currency. The Comptroller was alleged to have caused petitioners injury in fact by his 1966 ruling which states:

> "Incidental to its banking services, a national bank may make available its data processing equipment or perform data processing services on such equipment for other banks and bank customers." . . .

The Court of Appeals viewed the matter differently. . . . [It denied standing, relying upon] . . . prior decisions of this Court, such as *Tennessee Power Co. v. TVA*, 306 U.S. 118, where private power companies sought to enjoin TVA from operating, claiming that the statutory plan under which it was created was unconstitutional. The Court denied the competitors' standing, holding that they did not have that status "unless the right invaded is a legal right,—one of property, one arising out of contract, one protected against tortious invasion, or one founded on a statute which confers a privilege." . . .

The "legal interest" test goes to the merits. The question of standing is different. It concerns, apart from the "case" or "controversy" test, the question whether the interest sought to be protected by the complainant is arguably within the zone of interests to be protected or regulated by the statute or constitutional guarantee in question. Thus the Administrative Procedure Act grants standing to a person "aggrieved by agency action within the meaning of a relevant statute." 5 U.S.C. § 702. . . .

That interest, at times, may reflect "aesthetic, conservational, and recreational" as well as economic values. *Scenic Hudson Preservation Conf. v. FPC*, 354 F.2d 608, 616; *Office of Communication of United Church of Christ v. FCC*, 359 F2d 994, 1000–1006, 123 U.S. App. D.C. 328, 334–340. . . .

Where statutes are concerned, the trend is toward enlargement of the class of people who may protest administrative action. The whole drive for enlarging the category of aggrieved "persons" is symptomatic of that trend. In a closely analogous case we held that an existing entrepreneur had standing to challenge the legality of the entrance of a newcomer into the business, because the established business was allegedly protected by a valid city ordinance that protected it from unlawful competition. *Chicago v. Atchison, T & S.ER. Co.*, 357 U.S. 77, 83–84. In that tradition was *Hardin v. Kentucky Utilities Co.*, 390 U.S. 2, which involved a section of the TVA Act designed primarily to protect, through area limitations, private utilities against TVA competition. We held that no explicit statutory provision was necessary to confer standing, since the private utility bringing suit was within the class of persons that the statutory provision was designed to protect.

It is argued here that the *Chicago* case and the *Hardin* case are relevant here because of § 4 of the Bank Service Corporation Act of 1962 . . . which provides:

> "No bank service corporation may engage in any activity other than the performance of bank services for banks."

. . . . We . . . think . . . that § 4 arguably brings a competitor within the zone of interests protected by it.

[The Court then held that judicial review of the Comptroller's action had not been precluded.]

Whether anything in the Bank Service Corporation Act or the National Bank Act gives petitioners a "legal interest" that protects them against violations of those Acts, and whether the actions of respondents did in fact violate either of those Acts, are questions which go to the merits and remain to be decided below.

We hold that petitioners have standing to sue and that the case should be remanded for a hearing on the merits.

Reversed and remanded.

Barlow v. Collins, **397 U.S. 159 (1970).** The petitioners were tenant farmers eligible for payments under the upland cotton program enacted as part of the Food and Agricultural Act of 1965. They sought to challenge a regulation issued by the Secretary of Agriculture which would have made their payments under the program assignable to secure rent for a farm. The petitioners alleged that under the new regulation they would be forced to assign their upland cotton program benefits in advance to their landlords and as a result would be made totally dependent upon their landlords for other necessary financing. Following *Data Processing,* the Supreme Court held that the tenant farmers had standing to challenge the regulation:

> First, there is no doubt that in the context of this litigation the tenant farmers, petitioners here, have the personal stake and interest that impart the concrete adverseness required by Article III. Second, the tenant farmers are clearly within the zone of interests protected by the Act. Implicit in the statutory provisions and their legislative history is a congressional intent that the Secretary protect the interests of tenant farmers. . . .

Questions and Comments

1. Did the Supreme Court rely upon the Administrative Procedure Act when it ruled that the plaintiffs in *Data Processing* and *Barlow* had standing?

2. How did the Supreme Court reinterpret the meaning of § 702 of the APA in these two cases?

3. Would the Association of Data Processing Organizations have had standing under the legal interest test? Would the tenant farmers have had standing under the legal interest test?

4. Did the Bank Service Corporation Act contain a special review provision like § 402(b)(2) of the Communications Act? Did the Food and Agricultural Act of 1965? Did the Court point to any such special review statute?

5. Did the Court give a new meaning to the phrase in § 702 that judicial review may be had at the instance of a person "adversely affected or aggrieved within the meaning of a relevant statute"?

6. Were the data processing organizations "aggrieved" within the meaning of the Bank Service Corporation Act, even though that Act contained no special review provision? Were they "arguably" aggrieved?

7. Was the APA necessary for the standing of the data processing organizations and of the tenant farmers? Explain. Or were the provisions of § 702 merely restatements of a new understanding of existing law?

8. From where did the Court derive the "zone of interests" component of the standing test which it announced? Is the zone of interests criterion related to any of the provisions of § 702? Explain.

9. What is the relation between the injury in fact requirement and the zone of interests test? Must the injury be to an interest which the statute relied upon is designed to protect or to regulate? Is there a "nexus" connecting the two requirements similar to the nexus between the elements of taxpayer standing set forth in *Flast?* Compare *Duke Power Co. v. Carolina Environmental Study Group, Inc.,* 438 U.S. 59 (1978), *infra.*

b.   *Standing to Vindicate Noneconomic Values: The Transformation of the* Scenic Hudson *Approach.*

Sierra Club v. Morton, **405 U.S. 727 (1972).** The Sierra Club, a membership corporation with a special interest in conservation sought a declaratory judgment that a proposed development of a wilderness area into a ski resort contravened federal laws and regulations and that the actions of the Forest Service approving the development were illegal. Although the Court reaffirmed the broad reading of the standing provisions contained in APA § 702 set forth in its *Data Processing* decision, it nonetheless ruled that the Sierra Club lacked standing to bring its suit:

The injury alleged by the Sierra Club will be incurred entirely by reason of the change in the uses to which Mineral King will be put, and the attendant change in the aesthetics and ecology of the area. Thus, in referring to the road to be built through Sequoia National Park, the complaint alleged that the development "would destroy or otherwise adversely affect the scenery, natural and historic objects and wildlife of the park and would impair the enjoyment of the park for future generations." We do not question that this type of harm may amount to an "injury in fact" sufficient to lay the basis for standing under § 10 of the APA. Aesthetic and environmental well-being, like economic well-being, are important ingredients of the quality of life in our society, and the fact that particular environmental interests are shared by the many rather than the few does not make them less deserving of legal protection through the judicial process. But the "injury in fact" test requires more than an injury to a cognizable interest. It requires that the party seeking review be himself among the injured. . . . The alleged injury will be felt directly only by those who use Mineral King and Sequoia National Park, and for whom the aesthetic and recreational values of the area will be lessened by the highway and ski resort. The Sierra Club failed to allege that it or its members would be affected in any of their activities or pastimes by the Disney development. Nowhere in the pleadings or affidavits did the Club state that its members use Mineral King for any purpose, much less that they use it in any way that would be significantly affected by the proposed actions of the respondents.

The Club apparently regarded any allegations of individualized injury as superfluous, on the theory that this was a "public" action involving questions as to the use of natural resources, and that the Club's longstanding concern with and expertise in such matters were sufficient to give it standing as a "representative of the public." This theory reflects a misunderstanding of our cases involving so-called "public actions" in the area of administrative law.

[The Court then discussed *Scripps-Howard Radio v. FCC*, 316 U.S. 4 and FCC v. *Sanders Bros. Radio Station*, 309 U.S. 470, 477.]

Taken together, *Sanders* and *Scripps-Howard* thus established a dual proposition: the fact of economic injury is what gives a person standing to seek judicial review under the statute, but once review is properly invoked, that person may argue the public interest in support of his claim that the agency has failed to comply with its statutory mandate. It was in the latter sense that the "standing" of the appellant in *Scripps-Howard* existed only as a "representative of the public interest." It is in a similar sense that we have used the phrase "private attorney general" to describe the function performed by persons upon whom Congress has conferred the right to seek judicial review of agency action. . . .

The trend of cases arising under the APA and other statutes authorizing judicial review of federal agency action has been toward recognizing that injuries other than economic harm are sufficient to bring a person within the meaning of the statutory language, and toward discarding the notion that an injury that is widely shared is ipso facto not an injury sufficient to provide the basis for judicial review. . . . But broadening the categories of injury that may be alleged in support of standing is a different matter from abandoning the requirement that the party seeking review must himself have suffered an injury.

. . . It is clear that an organization whose members are injured may represent those members in a proceeding for judicial review. . . . But a mere "interest in a problem," no matter how longstanding the interest and no matter how qualified the organization is in evaluating the problem, is not sufficient by itself to render the organization "adversely affected" or "aggrieved" within the meaning of the APA. . . .

Questions and Comments

1. In a passage not quoted above, the Court indicated that *Data Processing* and *Barlow v. Collins* were decided under the review provisions of § 702 of the APA. Do you agree?

2. In rejecting the concept of an ideologically-motivated plaintiff, did the Court include ideologically-motivated plaintiffs claiming standing under special review statutes? How do you know? Does *Scenic Hudson [supra]* retain any significance at all?

3. Explain how non-economic injury can give rise to standing if ideology cannot provide the basis for plaintiffs' motivation to seek judicial review.

4. What is the status of the private attorney general doctrine after *Data Processing, Barlow,* and *Sierra Club?* Do special review statutes provide standing to plaintiffs who would lack standing without them?

United States v. Students Challenging Regulatory Agency Procedures **(SCRAP), 412 U.S. 669 (1973).** In this case a group of five law students tested the limits of the Court's *Sierra Club* decision. The Interstate Commerce Commission had declined to suspend a 2.5% surcharge on nearly all freight rates filed by substantially all of the railroads in the United States. SCRAP, the students' organization, brought suit challenging the ICC's action on the ground that the surcharge discouraged recycling and that the ICC had failed to include a detailed environmental impact statement as required by § 102(2)(C) of the National Environmental Policy Act. SCRAP claimed that each of its members "suffered economic, recreational and aesthetic harm directly as a result of the adverse environmental impact of the railroad freight structure as that structure resulted from the ICC's actions. SCRAP alleged that each of its members was forced to pay more for finished products, that each of its members "[u]ses the forests, rivers, streams, mountains, and other natural resources surrounding the Washington Metropolitan area and at his legal residence, for camping, hiking, fishing, sightseeing, and other recreational [and] aesthetic purposes and that these uses have been adversely affected by the increased freight rates, that each of its members breathes the air within the Washington metropolitan area and the area of his legal residence and that this air has suffered increased pollution caused by the modified rate structure, and that each member has been forced to pay increased taxes because of the sums which must be expended to dispose of otherwise reusable waste materials.

The Court upheld the students' standing: "[N]either the fact that the appellees here claimed only a harm to their use and enjoyment of the natural resources of the Washington area, nor the fact that all those who use those resources suffered the same harm, deprives them of standing. . . . Of course, pleadings must be something more than an ingenious academic exercise in the conceivable. A plaintiff must allege that he has been or will in fact be perceptibly harmed by the challenged agency action, not that he can imagine circumstances in which he could be affected by the agency's action. And it is equally clear that the allegations must be true and capable of proof at trial. . . . We cannot say on these pleadings that the appellees could not prove their allegations which, if proved, would place them squarely among those persons injured in fact by the Commission's action, and entitled under the clear import of *Sierra Club* to seek review. . . .

Questions and Comments

1. The Court ruled in favor of the plaintiffs' standing because they brought themselves within the criteria which the Court had set forth in *Sierra Club*. The Court then ruled against them on the merits.

2. What was the injury which the plaintiffs claimed to have sustained as a result of the Commission's action? Were the plaintiffs injured more than anyone else by that action?

3. Did not the members of the Sierra Club share, with all the citizens of the United States, the loss of Mineral King Valley's unspoiled wilderness? But that loss was insufficient to constitute the "injury in fact" which was a prerequisite for standing. How did the loss claimed to be suffered by SCRAP members differ from the loss claimed to be suffered by Sierra Club members?

4. When the Court ruled in *Sierra Club* that only those whose uses of Mineral King Valley would be interfered with would have standing to challenge the Forest Service's action in approving the development, was the Court not granting standing to a class smaller than the public in general?

5. Was not the plaintiffs' claim in SCRAP merely "an ingenious academic exercise in the conceivable"? How attenuated can the causal connection be between the challenged agency action and the alleged injury?

DIRECTOR, OFFICE OF WORKERS' COMPENSATION PROGRAMS, DEPARTMENT OF LABOR v. NEWPORT NEWS
SHIPBUILDING AND DRY DOCK CO.
514 U.S. 122 (1995)

[The Longshore and Harbor Workers' Compensation Act (LHWCA) establishes a system for compensating workers injured or killed while employed on the navigable waters or adjoining, shipping-related land areas of the United States and vests administration of the Act in the Department of Labor. The Secretary of Labor has delegated most of the administration of the LHWCA to the Director of the Office of Workers' Compensation Programs (OWCP).

A worker seeking compensation under the Act must file a claim with an OWCP district director. If the district director cannot resolve the claim informally, the claim is referred for decision to an ALJ. The ALJ's decision is reviewable by the Benefits Review Board, whose members are appointed by the Secretary. The Board's decision is in turn appealable to a United States court of appeals, at the instance of "[a]ny person adversely affected or aggrieved by" the Board's order. § 921(c).]

JUSTICE SCALIA delivered the opinion of the Court.

The question before us in this case is whether the Director of the Office of Workers' Compensation Programs in the United States Department of Labor has standing under § 921(c) of the Longshore and Harbor Workers' Compensation Act (LHWCA), 44 Stat. 1424, as amended, 33 U.S.C. § 901 et seq., to seek judicial review of decisions by the Benefits Review Board that in the Director's view deny claimants compensation to which they are entitled.

[In this case, one Jackie Harcum sustained an injury to his lower back when he was struck by a piece of metal while working for his employer, the respondent Newport News Shipbuilding and Dry Dock Co. He was paid benefits until he returned to light-duty work. When he was unable thereafter to perform his regular duties, his employment was terminated.] . . .

Harcum filed a claim for further benefits under the LHWCA. Respondent contested the claim, and the dispute was referred to an Administrative Law Judge (ALJ). One of the issues was whether Harcum was entitled to benefits for total disability, or instead only for partial disability, from the date he stopped work for respondent until he began his new job. "Disability" under the LHWCA means "incapacity because of injury to earn the wages which the employee was receiving at the time of injury in the same or any other employment." 33 U.S.C. § 902(10).

After a hearing on October 20, 1989, the ALJ determined that Harcum was partially, rather than totally, disabled when he left respondent's employ, and that he was therefore owed only partial-disability benefits for the interval of his unemployment. On appeal, the Benefits Review Board affirmed the ALJ's judgment, and also ruled that under 33 U.S.C. § 908(f), the company was entitled to cease payments to Harcum after 104 weeks, after which time the LHWCA special fund would be liable for disbursements pursuant to § 944.

The Director petitioned the United States Court of Appeals for the Fourth Circuit for review of both aspects of the Board's ruling. Harcum did not seek review and, while not opposing the Director's pursuit of the action, expressly declined to intervene on his own behalf in response to an inquiry by the Court of Appeals. The Court of Appeals *sua sponte* raised the question whether the Director had standing to appeal the Board's order. . . . It concluded that she did not have standing with regard to that aspect of the order denying Harcum's claim for full-disability compensation, since she was not "adversely affected or aggrieved" by that decision within the meaning of § 921(C) of the Act, 33 U.S.C. § 921(c).[23] We granted the Director's petition for certiorari. 512 U.S. 1287 (1994).

II

. . . .

With regard to claims that proceed to ALJ hearings, the Act does not by its

---

[23] The court found that, as administrator of the § 944 special fund, the Director did have standing to appeal the Board's decision to grant respondent relief under § 908(f). That ruling is not before us and we express no view upon it.

terms make the Director a party to the proceedings, or grant her authority to prosecute appeals to the Board, or thence to the federal court of appeals. The Director argues that she nonetheless had standing to petition the Fourth Circuit for review of the Board's order, because she is "a person adversely affected or aggrieved" under § 921(c). Specifically, she contends the Board's decision injures her because it impairs her ability to achieve the Act's purposes and to perform the administrative duties the Act prescribes.

The phrase "person adversely affected or aggrieved" is a term of art used in many statutes to designate those who have standing to challenge or appeal an agency decision, within the agency or before the courts. See, e.g., Federal Communications Act of 1934, 47 U.S.C. § 402(b)(6); Occupational Safety and Health Act of 1970, 29 U.S.C. § 660(a); Federal Mine Safety and Health Act of 1977, 30 U.S.C. § 816. The terms "adversely affected" and "aggrieved," alone or in combination, have a long history in federal administrative law, dating back at least to the Federal Communications Act of 1934, § 402(b)(2) (codified, as amended, 47 U.S.C. § 402(b)(6)). They were already familiar terms in 1946, when they were embodied within the judicial review provision of the Administrative Procedure Act (APA), 5 U.S.C. § 702, which entitles "[a] person . . . adversely affected or aggrieved by agency action within the meaning of a relevant statute" to judicial review. In that provision, the qualification "within the meaning of a relevant statute" is not an addition to what "adversely affected or aggrieved" alone conveys; but is rather an acknowledgment of the fact that what *constitutes* adverse effect or aggrievement varies from statute to statute. As the U.S. Dept. of Justice, Attorney General's Manual on the Administrative Procedure Act (1947) put it, "The determination of . . . who is 'adversely affected or aggrieved . . . within the meaning of any relevant statute' has 'been marked out largely by the gradual judicial process of inclusion and exclusion, aided at times by the courts' judgment as to the probable legislative intent derived from the spirit of the statutory scheme.' " *Id.*, at 96 (citation omitted). We have thus interpreted § 702 as requiring a litigant to show, at the outset of the case, that he is injured in fact by agency action and that the interest he seeks to vindicate is arguably within the "zone of interests to be protected or regulated by the statute" in question. *Association of Data Processing Service Organizations, Inc. v. Camp*, 397 U.S. 150, 153 (1970); see also *Clarke v. Securities Industry Assn.*, 479 U.S. 388, 395–396 (1987).

Given the long lineage of the text in question, it is significant that counsel have cited to us no case, neither in this Court nor in the courts of appeals, neither under the APA nor under individual statutory-review provisions such as the present one, which holds that, without benefit of specific authorization to appeal, an agency, in its regulatory or policy-making capacity, is "adversely affected" or "aggrieved." . . .

That an agency in its governmental capacity is not "adversely affected or aggrieved" is strongly suggested, as well, by two aspects of the United States Code: First, the fact that the Code's general judicial review provision, contained in the APA, does not include agencies within the category of "person adversely affected or aggrieved." See 5 U.S.C. § 551(2) (excepting agencies from the definition of "person"). Since, as we suggested in *United States v. ICC*, the APA provision reflects "the general legislative pattern of administrative and judicial relationships," 337 U.S., at 433-434, it indicates that even under specific "adversely affected or aggrieved" statutes (there were a number extant when the APA was adopted) agencies as such normally do not have standing. And second, the United States Code displays throughout that when an agency in its governmental capacity is meant to have standing, Congress says so. The LHWCA's silence regarding the Secretary's ability to take an appeal is significant when laid beside other provisions of law. . . . It is particularly illuminating to compare the LHWCA with the Occupational Safety and Health Act of 1970 (OSHA), 29 U.S.C. § 651 et seq. Section 660(a) of OSHA is virtually identical to § 921(c): it allows "[a]ny person adversely affected or aggrieved" by an order of the Occupational Safety and Health Review Commission (a body distinct from the Secretary, as the Benefits Review Board is) to petition for review in the courts of appeals. OSHA, however, further contains a § 660(b), which expressly grants such petitioning authority to the Secretary — suggesting, of course, that the Secretary would not be considered "adversely affected or aggrieved" under § 660(a), and should not be considered so under § 921(c).

All of the foregoing indicates that the phrase "person adversely affected or aggrieved" does not refer to an agency acting in its governmental capacity. Of course the text of a particular statute could make clear that the phrase is being used in a peculiar sense. But the Director points to no such text in the LHWCA, and relies solely upon the mere existence and impairment of her governmental interest. If that alone could ever suffice to contradict the normal meaning of the phrase (which is doubtful), it would have to be an interest of an extraordinary nature, extraordinarily impaired. As we proceed to discuss, that is not present here.

III

The LHWCA assigns four broad areas of responsibility to the Director: (1) supervising, administering, and making rules and regulations for calculation of benefits and processing of claims, 33 U.S.C. §§ 906, 908–910, 914, 919, 930, and 939 (2) supervising, administering, and making rules and regulations for provision of medical care to covered workers, § 907; (3) assisting claimants with processing claims and receiving medical and vocational rehabilitation, § 939(c); and (4) enforcing compensation orders and administering payments to and disbursements from the special fund established by the Act for the payment of certain benefits, §§ 921(d) and 944. The Director does not assert that the Board's decision hampers her performance of these express statutory responsibilities. She claims only two categories of interest that are affected, neither of which remotely suggests that she has authority to appeal Board determinations.

. . . .

If the correctness of adjudications were essential to the Director's performance of her assigned duties, Congress would presumably have done what it has done with many other agencies: made adjudication *her* responsibility. In fact, however, it has taken pains to *remove* adjudication from her realm. The LHWCA Amendments of 1972, 86 Stat. 1251, assigned administration to the Director, 33 U.S.C. § 939(a); assigned initial adjudication to ALJ's, § 919(d); and created the Board to consider appeals from ALJ's, § 921. The assertion that proper adjudication is essential to proper performance of the Director's functions is quite simply contrary to the whole structure of the Act. To make an implausible argument even worse, the Director must acknowledge that her lack of control over the adjudicative process does not even deprive her of the power to resolve legal ambiguities in the statute. She retains the rulemaking power, see § 939(a), which means that if her problem with the present decision of the Board is that it has established an erroneous rule of law, see *Chevron U.S.A. Inc. v. Natural Resources Defense Council, Inc.*, 467 U.S. 837 (1984), she has full power to alter that rule. . . .

The Director seeks to derive support for her position from Congress' later enactment of the BLBA [Black Lung Benefits Act] in 1978, but it seems to us that the BLBA militates precisely *against* her position. The BLBA expressly provides that "[t]he Secretary shall be a party in any proceeding relative to a claim for benefits under this part." 30 U.S.C. § 932(k). The Director argues that since the Secretary is explicitly made a party under the BLBA, she must be meant to be a party under the LHWCA as well. That is not a form of reasoning we are familiar with. The normal conclusion one would derive from putting these statutes side by side is this: when, in a legislative scheme of this sort, Congress wants the Secretary to have standing, it says so.

. . . .

For these reasons, the judgment of the United States Court of Appeals for the Fourth Circuit is affirmed.

So ordered.

Questions and Comments

1.   Administration of the Longshore and Harbors Workers' Compensation Act (LHWCA) takes place under the alternative model of administration considered in Chapter 5. We have considered other systems of administration falling within the alternative model: The Occupational Health and Safety Act (OSHA) was the setting for *Martin v. Occupational Safety and Health Review Commission* [casebook, *supra*] and *Reich v. Occupational Safety and Health Review Commission, supra.*. The Federal Mine Safety and Health Act (FMSHA) was the setting for *Thunder Basin Coal Co. v. Reich, supra*. The structure of the LHWCA resembles that of OSHA and the FMSHA; under the latter two statutes adjudication takes place initially before an ALJ whose decisions are subject to review by a fully independent adjudicatory body whose members are appointed by the President and confirmed by the Senate. Under the LHWCA, the Secretary of Labor (or the Director of the Office of Workers' Compensation Programs to whom he has delegated his powers) administers the benefits provided for under the act and when a dispute arises requiring adjudication, that adjudication takes place initially before an ALJ whose decisions are subject to review by a Benefits Review Board whose members are appointed by the Secretary.

2.   In *Newport News*, the Court used the bifurcated structure of the adminis-tration as a basis for concluding that the Director lacked any inherent power to seek

judicial review of a determination of the Benefits Review Board. Do you agree with the Court's reasoning?

c.   *Causation and Redressability as Elements of Standing.*

LUJAN v. DEFENDERS OF WILDLIFE
504 U.S. 555 (1992)

Justice SCALIA delivered the opinion of the Court with respect to Parts I, II, III A, and IV, and an opinion with respect to Part III B in which the Chief Justice, Justice WHITE, and Justice THOMAS join.

This case involves a challenge to a rule promulgated by the Secretary of the Interior interpreting § 7 of the Endangered Species Act of 1973 (ESA), 87 Stat. 884, 892, as amended, 16 U.S.C. § 1536, in such fashion as to render it applicable only to actions within the United States or on the high seas. The preliminary issue, and the only one we reach, is whether the respondents here, plaintiffs below, have standing to seek judicial review of the rule. In this case we must decide whether respondent, the National Wildlife Federation (hereinafter respondent), is a proper party to challenge actions of the Federal Government relating to certain public lands.

I

The ESA, 87 Stat. 884, as amended, 16 U.S.C. § 1531 et seq., seeks to protect species of animals against threats to their continuing existence caused by man. . . . The ESA instructs the Secretary of the Interior to promulgate by regulation a list of those species which are either endangered or threatened under enumerated criteria, and to define the critical habitat of these species. 16 U.S.C. §§ 1533, 1536. Section 7(a)(2) of the Act then provides, in pertinent part:

> "Each Federal agency shall, in consultation with and with the assistance of the Secretary [of the Interior], insure that any action authorized, funded, or carried out by such agency . . . is not likely to jeopardize the continued existence of any endangered species or threatened species or result in the destruction or adverse modification of habitat of such species which is determined by the Secretary, after consultation as appropriate with affected States, to be critical." 16 U.S.C. § 1536(a)(2).

In 1978, the Fish and Wildlife Service (FWS) and the National Marine Fisheries Service (NMFS), on behalf of the Secretary of the Interior and the Secretary of Commerce respectively, promulgated a joint regulation stating that the obligations imposed by § 7(a)(2) extend to actions taken in foreign nations. 43 Fed. Reg. 874 (1978). The next year, however, the Interior Department began to reexamine its position. . . . A revised joint regulation, reinterpreting § 7(a)(2) to require consultation only for actions taken in the United States or on the high seas, was proposed in 1983 . . . and promulgated in 1986 . . . .

Shortly thereafter, respondents, organizations dedicated to wildlife conservation and other environmental causes, filed this action against the Secretary of the

Interior, seeking a declaratory judgment that the new regulation is in error as to the geographic scope of § 7(a)(2), and an injunction requiring the Secretary to promulgate a new regulation restoring the initial interpretation. . . .

II

. . . .

Over the years, our cases have established that the irreducible constitutional minimum of standing contains three elements: First, the plaintiff must have suffered an "injury in fact" an invasion of a legally protected interest which is (a) concrete and particularized . . . and (b) "actual or imminent, not 'conjectural' or 'hypothetical'". . . . Second, there must be a causal connection between the injury and the conduct complained of—the injury has to be "fairly . . . trace[able] to the challenged action of the defendant, and not . . . th[e] result [of] the independent action of some third party not before the court.". . . Third, it must be "likely," as opposed to merely "speculative," that the injury will be "redressed by a favorable decision.". . . .

III

We think the Court of Appeals failed to apply the foregoing principles in denying the Secretary's motion for summary judgment. Respondents had not made the requisite demonstration of (at least) injury and redressability.

A.

Respondents' claim to injury is that the lack of consultation with respect to certain funded activities abroad "increas[es] the rate of extinction of endangered and threatened species.". . . Of course, the desire to use or observe an animal species, even for purely aesthetic purposes, is undeniably a cognizable interest for purpose of standing. See, e.g., *Sierra Club v. Morton*, 405 U.S., at 734. "But the 'injury in fact' test requires more than an injury to a cognizable interest. It requires that the party seeking review be himself among the injured.". . . To survive the Secretary's summary judgment motion, respondents had to submit affidavits or other evidence showing, through specific facts, not only that listed species were in fact being threatened by funded activities abroad, but also that one or more of respondents' members would thereby be "directly" affected apart from their "'special interest' in th[e] subject." *Id.*, at 735, 739. See generally *Hunt v. Washington State Apple Advertising Comm'n*, 432 U.S. 333, 343 (1977).

With respect to this aspect of the case, the Court of Appeals focused on the affidavits of two Defenders' members Joyce Kelly and Amy Skilbred. Ms. Kelly stated that she traveled to Egypt in 1986 and "observed the traditional habitat of the endangered Nile crocodile there and intend[s] to do so again, and hope[s] to observe the crocodile directly," and that she "will suffer harm in fact as a result of [the] American . . . role . . . in overseeing the rehabilitation of the Aswan High Dam on the Nile . . . and [in] develop[ing] . . . Egypt's . . . Master Water Plan.". . . Ms. Skilbred averred that she traveled to Sri Lanka in 1981 and "observed th[e] habitat" of "endangered species such as the Asian elephant and the leopard" at what is now the site of the Mahaweli Project funded by the Agency for International Development (AID), although she "was unable to see any of the endangered species;" "this development project," she continued, "will seriously reduce endangered, threatened, and endemic species habitat including areas that I visited . . . [, which] may severely shorten the future of these species;" that threat, she concluded, harmed her because she "intend[s] to return to Sri Lanka in the future and hope[s] to be more fortunate in spotting at least the endangered elephant and leopard.". . . When Ms. Skilbred was asked at a subsequent deposition if and when she had any plans to return to Sri Lanka, she reiterated that "I intend to go back to Sri Lanka," but confessed that she had no current plans: "I don't know [when]. There is a civil war going on right now. I don't know. Not next year, I will say. In the future.". . .

We shall assume for the sake of argument that these affidavits contain facts showing that certain agency funded projects threaten listed species—though that is questionable. They plainly contain no facts, however, showing how damage to the species will produce "imminent" injury to Mss. Kelly and Skilbred. That the women "had visited" the areas of the projects before the projects commenced proves nothing. . . . And the affiants' profession of an "inten[t]" to return to the places they had visited before—where they will presumably, this time, be deprived of the opportunity to observe animals of the endangered species—is simply not enough. Such "some day" intentions—without any description of concrete plans, or indeed even any specification of when the some day will be—do not support a finding of the "actual or imminent" injury that our cases require. . . .

Besides relying upon the Kelly and Skilbred affidavits, respondents propose a series of novel standing theories. The first, inelegantly styled "ecosystem nexus," proposes that any person who uses any part of a "contiguous ecosystem" adversely affected by a funded activity has standing even if the activity is located a great distance away. This approach, as the Court of Appeals correctly observed, is inconsistent with our opinion in *National Wildlife Federation*, which held that a plaintiff claiming injury from environmental damage must use the area affected by the challenged activity and not an area roughly "in the vicinity" of it. . . . It makes no difference that the general purpose section of the ESA states that the Act was intended in part "to provide a means whereby the ecosystems upon which endangered species and threatened species depend may be conserved," 16 U.S.C. § 1531(b). To say that the Act protects ecosystems is not to say that the Act creates (if it were possible) rights of action in persons who have not been injured in fact, that is, persons who use portions of an ecosystem not perceptibly affected by the unlawful action in question.

Respondents' other theories are called, alas, the "animal nexus" approach, whereby anyone who has an interest in studying or seeing the endangered animals anywhere on the globe has standing; and the "vocational nexus" approach, under which anyone with a professional interest in such animals can sue. Under these theories, anyone who goes to see Asian elephants in the Bronx Zoo, and anyone who is a keeper of Asian elephants in the Bronx Zoo, has standing to sue because the Director of AID did not consult with the Secretary regarding the AID funded project in Sri Lanka. This is beyond all reason. Standing is not "an ingenious academic exercise in the conceivable," *United States v. Students Challenging*

Regulatory Agency Procedures (SCRAP), 412 U.S. 669, 688 (1973), but as we have said requires, at the summary judgment stage, a factual showing of perceptible harm. It is clear that the person who observes or works with a particular animal threatened by a federal decision is facing perceptible harm, since the very subject of his interest will no longer exist. It is even plausible though it goes to the outermost limit of plausibility to think that a person who observes or works with animals of a particular species in the very area of the world where that species is threatened by a federal decision is facing such harm, since some animals that might have been the subject of his interest will no longer exist, see *Japan Whaling Assn. v. American Cetacean Soc.*, 478 U.S. 221, 231, n. 4 (1986). It goes beyond the limit, however, and into pure speculation and fantasy, to say that anyone who observes or works with an endangered species, anywhere in the world, is appreciably harmed by a single project affecting some portion of that species with which he has no more specific connection.

B.

Besides failing to show injury, respondents failed to demonstrate redressability. Instead of attacking the separate decisions to fund particular projects allegedly causing them harm, the respondents chose to challenge a more generalized level of government action (rules regarding consultation), the invalidation of which would affect all overseas projects. This programmatic approach has obvious practical advantages, but also obvious difficulties insofar as proof of causation or redressability is concerned. As we have said in another context, "suits challenging, not specifically identifiable Government violations of law, but the particular programs agencies establish to carry out their legal obligations . . . [are], even when premised on allegations of several instances of violations of law, . . . rarely if ever appropriate for federal court adjudication." *Allen*, 468 U.S., at 759 760.

The most obvious problem in the present case is redressability. Since the agencies funding the projects were not parties to the case, the District Court could accord relief only against the Secretary: He could be ordered to revise his regulation to require consultation for foreign projects. But this would not remedy respondents' alleged injury unless the funding agencies were bound by the Secretary's regulation, which is very much an open question. Whereas in other contexts the ESA is quite explicit as to the Secretary's controlling authority, see, *e.g.*, 16 U.S.C. § 1533(a)(1) ("The Secretary shall" promulgate regulations determining endangered species); § 1535(d)(1) ("The Secretary is authorized to provide financial assistance to any State"), with respect to consultation the initiative, and hence arguably the initial responsibility for determining statutory necessity, lies with the agencies, see § 1536(a)(2) (*"Each Federal agency shall*, in consultation with and with the assistance of the Secretary, insure that any" funded action is not likely to jeopardize endangered or threatened species) (emphasis added)). When the Secretary promulgated the regulation at issue here, he thought it was binding on the agencies . . . . The Solicitor General, however, has repudiated that position here, and the agencies themselves apparently deny the Secretary's authority. . . .

Respondents assert that this legal uncertainty did not affect redressability (and hence standing) because the District Court itself could resolve the issue of the

Secretary's authority as a necessary part of its standing inquiry. Assuming that it is appropriate to resolve an issue of law such as this in connection with a threshold standing inquiry, resolution by the District Court would not have remedied respondents' alleged injury anyway, because it would not have been binding upon the agencies. They were not parties to the suit, and there is no reason they should be obliged to honor an incidental legal determination the suit produced. The Court of Appeals tried to finesse this problem by simply proclaiming that "[w]e are satisfied that an injunction requiring the Secretary to publish [respondents' desired] regulatio[n] . . . would result in consultation.". . . We do not know what would justify that confidence, particularly when the Justice Department (presumably after consultation with the agencies) has taken the position that the regulation is not binding. The short of the matter is that redress of the only injury in fact respondents complain of requires action (termination of funding until consultation) by the individual funding agencies; and any relief the District Court could have provided in this suit against the Secretary was not likely to produce that action.

A further impediment to redressability is the fact that the agencies generally supply only a fraction of the funding for a foreign project. AID, for example, has provided less than 10% of the funding for the Mahaweli Project. Respondents have produced nothing to indicate that the projects they have named will either be suspended, or do less harm to listed species, if that fraction is eliminated. As in *Simon*, . . . it is entirely conjectural whether the nonagency activity that affects respondents will be altered or affected by the agency activity they seek to achieve. There is no standing.

IV

The Court of Appeals found that respondents had standing for an additional reason: because they had suffered a "procedural injury." The so called "citizen suit" provision of the ESA provides, in pertinent part, that "any person may commence a civil suit on his own behalf (A) to enjoin any person, including the United States and any other governmental instrumentality or agency . . . who is alleged to be in violation of any provision of this chapter." 16 U.S.C. § 1540(g). The court held that, because § 7(a)(2) requires interagency consultation, the citizen suit provision creates a "procedural righ[t]" to consultation in all "persons" so that anyone can file suit in federal court to challenge the Secretary's (or presumably any other official's) failure to follow the assertedly correct consultative procedure, notwithstanding their inability to allege any discrete injury flowing from that failure. . . . To understand the remarkable nature of this holding one must be clear about what it does not rest upon: This is not a case where plaintiffs are seeking to enforce a procedural requirement the disregard of which could impair a separate concrete interest of theirs (e.g., the procedural requirement for a hearing prior to denial of their license application, or the procedural requirement for an environmental impact statement before a federal facility is constructed next door to them).[7] Nor is

---

[7] There is this much truth to the assertion that "procedural rights" are special: The person who has been accorded a procedural right to protect his concrete interests can assert that right without meeting all the normal standards for redressability and immediacy. Thus, under our case law, one living adjacent to the site for proposed construction of a federally licensed dam has standing to challenge the licensing

it simply a case where concrete injury has been suffered by many persons, as in mass fraud or mass tort situations. Nor, finally, is it the unusual case in which Congress has created a concrete private interest in the outcome of a suit against a private party for the government's benefit, by providing a cash bounty for the victorious plaintiff. Rather, the court held that the injury in fact requirement had been satisfied by congressional conferral upon all persons of an abstract, self contained, noninstrumental "right" to have the Executive observe the procedures required by law. We reject this view.

We have consistently held that a plaintiff raising only a generally available grievance about government—claiming only harm to his and every citizen's interest in proper application of the Constitution and laws, and seeking relief that no more directly and tangibly benefits him than it does the public at large—does not state an Article III case or controversy. . . .

To be sure, our generalized grievance cases have typically involved Government violation of procedures assertedly ordained by the Constitution rather than the Congress. But there is absolutely no basis for making the Article III inquiry turn on the source of the asserted right. Whether the courts were to act on their own, or at the invitation of Congress, in ignoring the concrete injury requirement described in our cases, they would be discarding a principle fundamental to the separate and distinct constitutional role of the Third Branch—one of the essential elements that identifies those "Cases" and "Controversies" that are the business of the courts rather than of the political branches. "The province of the court," as Chief Justice Marshall said in *Marbury v. Madison*, 5 U.S. (1 Cranch) 137, 170 (1803) "is, solely, to decide on the rights of individuals." Vindicating the *public* interest (including the public interest in government observance of the Constitution and laws) is the function of Congress and the Chief Executive. The question presented here is whether the public interest in proper administration of the laws (specifically, in agencies' observance of a particular, statutorily prescribed procedure) can be converted into an individual right by a statute that denominates it as such, and that permits all citizens (or, for that matter, a subclass of citizens who suffer no distinctive concrete harm) to sue. If the concrete injury requirement has the separation of powers significance we have always said, the answer must be obvious: To permit Congress to convert the undifferentiated public interest in executive officers' compliance with the law into an "individual right" vindicable in the courts is to permit Congress to transfer from the President to the courts the Chief Executive's most important constitutional duty, to "take Care that the Laws be faithfully executed," Art. II, § 3. It would enable the courts, with the permission of Congress, "to assume a position of authority over the governmental acts of another and co equal department". . . and to become "'virtually continuing monitors of the

---

agency's failure to prepare an Environmental Impact Statement, even though he cannot establish with any certainty that the Statement will cause the license to be withheld or altered, and even though the dam will not be completed for many years. (That is why we do not rely, in the present case, upon the Government's argument that, even if the other agencies were obliged to consult with the Secretary, they might not have followed his advice.) What respondents' "procedural rights" argument seeks, however, is quite different from this: standing for persons who have no concrete interests affected persons who live (and propose to live) at the other end of the country from the dam.

wisdom and soundness of Executive action.'"... We have always rejected that vision of our role . . .

Nothing in this contradicts the principle that "[t]he. . . injury required by Art. III may exist solely by virtue of 'statutes creating legal rights, the invasion of which creates standing.'" *Warth*, 422 U.S., at 500 (quoting *Linda R. S. v. Richard D.*, 410 U.S. 614, 617, n. 3 (1973)). Both of the cases used by *Linda R. S.* as an illustration of that principle involved Congress's elevating to the status of legally cognizable injuries concrete, *de facto* injuries that were previously inadequate in law (namely, injury to an individual's personal interest in living in a racially integrated community, see *Trafficante v. Metropolitan Life Ins. Co.*, 409 U.S. 205, 208 212 (1972), and injury to a company's interest in marketing its product free from competition, see *Hardin v. Kentucky Utilities Co.*, 390 U.S. 1, 6 (1968)). As we said in Sierra Club, "[Statutory] broadening [of] the categories of injury that may be alleged in support of standing is a different matter from abandoning the requirement that the party seeking review must himself have suffered an injury.". . . Whether or not the principle set forth in *Warth* can be extended beyond that distinction, it is clear that in suits against the government, at least, the concrete injury requirement must remain.

****

We hold that respondents lack standing to bring this action and that the Court of Appeals erred in denying the summary judgment motion filed by the United States. The opinion of the Court of Appeals is hereby reversed, and the cause remanded for proceedings consistent with this opinion.

It is so ordered.

Justice KENNEDY, with whom Justice SOUTER joins, concurring in part and concurring in the judgment.

. . . .

In light of the conclusion that respondents have not demonstrated a concrete injury here sufficient to support standing under our precedents, I would not reach the issue of redressability that is discussed by the plurality in Part III B.

. . . .

Justice STEVENS, concurring in the judgment.

. . . .

The plurality also concludes that respondents' injuries are not redressable in this litigation for two reasons. First, respondents have sought only a declaratory judgment that the Secretary of the Interior's regulation interpreting § 7(a)(2) to require consultation only for agency actions in the United States or on the high seas is invalid and an injunction requiring him to promulgate a new regulation requiring consultation for agency actions abroad as well. But, the plurality opines, even if respondents succeed and a new regulation is promulgated, there is no guarantee that federal agencies that are not parties to this case will actually consult with the Secretary. . . . Furthermore, the plurality continues, respondents have not demonstrated that federal agencies can influence the behavior of the foreign governments where the affected projects are located. Thus, even if the agencies consult with the Secretary and terminate funding for foreign projects, the foreign governments might nonetheless pursue the projects and jeopardize the endangered species. . . . Neither of these reasons is persuasive.

We must presume that if this Court holds that § 7(a)(2) requires consultation, all affected agencies would abide by that interpretation and engage in the requisite consultations. Certainly the Executive Branch cannot be heard to argue that an authoritative construction of the governing statute by this Court may simply be ignored by any agency head. Moreover, if Congress has required consultation between agencies, we must presume that such consultation will have a serious purpose that is likely to produce tangible results. As JUSTICE BLACKMUN explains . . . it is not mere speculation to think that foreign governments, when faced with the threatened withdrawal of United States assistance, will modify their projects to mitigate the harm to endangered species.

II

Although I believe that respondents have standing, I nevertheless concur in the judgment of reversal because I am persuaded that the Government is correct in its submission that § 7(a)(2) does not apply to activities in foreign countries. . . .

Justice BLACKMUN, with whom Justice O'CONNOR joins, dissenting.

I part company with the Court in this case in two respects. First, I believe that respondents have raised genuine issues of fact sufficient to survive summary judgment both as to injury and as to redressability. Second, I question the Court's breadth of language in rejecting standing for "procedural" injuries. I fear the Court seeks to impose fresh limitations on the constitutional authority of Congress to allow citizen suits in the federal courts for injuries deemed "procedural" in nature. I dissent.

B.

A plurality of the Court suggests that respondents have not demonstrated redressability: a likelihood that a court ruling in their favor would remedy their injury. . . . The plurality identifies two obstacles. The first is that the "action agencies" (e.g., the Agency for International Development) cannot be required to undertake consultation with petitioner Secretary, because they are not directly bound as parties to the suit and are otherwise not indirectly bound by being subject to petitioner Secretary's regulation. Petitioner, however, officially and publicly has taken the position that his regulations regarding consultation under § 7 of the Act are binding on action agencies. 50 CFR § 402.14(a) (1991). And he has previously taken the same position in this very litigation, having stated in his answer to the complaint that petitioner "admits the Fish and Wildlife Service (FWS) was designated the lead agency for the formulation of regulations concerning section 7 of the ESA.". . . I cannot agree with the plurality that the Secretary (or the Solicitor General) is now free, for the convenience of this appeal, to disavow his prior public and litigation positions. More generally, I cannot agree that the Government is free to play "Three Card Monte" with its description of agencies' authority to defeat standing against the agency given the lead in administering a statutory scheme.

Emphasizing that none of the action agencies are parties to this suit (and having rejected the possibility of their being indirectly bound by petitioner's regulation), the plurality concludes that "there is no reason they should be obliged to honor an incidental legal determination the suit produced.". . . I am not as willing as the plurality is to assume that agencies at least will not try to follow the law. Moreover, I wonder if the plurality has not overlooked the extensive involvement from the inception of this litigation by the Department of State and the Agency for International Development. Under principles of collateral estoppel, these agencies are precluded from subsequently relitigating the issues decided in this suit.

> "[O]ne who prosecutes or defends a suit in the name of another to establish and protect his own right, or who assists in the prosecution or defense of an action in aid of some interest of his own, and who does this openly to the knowledge of the opposing party, is as much bound by the judgment and as fully entitled to avail himself of it as an estoppel against an adverse party, as he would be if he had been a party to the record." *Souffront v. Compagnie des Sucreries*, 217 U.S. 475, 487 (1910).

This principle applies even to the Federal Government. In *Montana v. United States*, 440 U.S. 147 (1979), this Court held that the Government was estopped from relitigating in federal court the constitutionality of Montana's gross receipts tax, because that issue previously had been litigated in state court by an individual contractor whose litigation had been financed and controlled by the Federal Government. "Thus, although not a party, the United States plainly had a sufficient 'laboring oar' in the conduct of the state court litigation to actuate principles of estoppel.". . . In my view, the action agencies have had sufficient "laboring oars" in this litigation since its inception to be bound from subsequent relitigation of the extraterritorial scope of the § 7 consultation requirement. As a result, I believe respondents' injury would likely be redressed by a favorable decision.

The second redressability obstacle relied on by the plurality is that "the [action] agencies generally supply only a fraction of the funding for a foreign project.". . . What this Court might "generally" take to be true does not eliminate the existence of a genuine issue of fact to withstand summary judgment. Even if the action agencies supply only a fraction of the funding for a particular foreign project, it remains at least a question for the finder of fact whether threatened withdrawal of that fraction would affect foreign government conduct sufficiently to avoid harm to listed species.

The plurality states that "AID, for example, has provided less than 10% of the funding for the Mahaweli project.". . . The plurality neglects to mention that this "fraction" amounts to $170 million, . . . not so paltry a sum for a country of only 16 million people with a gross national product of less than $6 billion in 1986 when respondents filed the complaint in this action. . . .

The plurality flatly states: "Respondents have produced nothing to indicate that the projects they have named will . . . do less harm to listed species, if that fraction is eliminated.". . . As an initial matter, the relevant inquiry is not, as the plurality suggests, what will happen if AID or other agencies stop funding projects, but what will happen if AID or other agencies comply with the consultation requirement for projects abroad. Respondents filed suit to require consultation, not a termination of funding. Respondents have raised at least a genuine issue of fact that the projects harm endangered species and that the actions of AID and other U.S. agencies can mitigate that harm.

The plurality overlooks an Interior Department memorandum listing eight endangered or threatened species in the Mahaweli project area and recounting that "[t]he Sri Lankan government has requested the assistance of AID in mitigating the negative impacts to the wildlife involved.". . . Further, a letter from the Director of the Fish and Wildlife Service to AID states:

> "The Sri Lanka government lacks the necessary finances to undertake any long term management programs to avoid the negative impacts to the wildlife. The donor nations and agencies that are financing the [Mahaweli project] will be the key as to how successfully the wildlife is preserved. If wildlife problems receive the same level of attention as the engineering project, then the negative impacts to the environment can be alleviated. This means that there has to be long term funding in sufficient amounts to stem the negative impacts of this project.". . .

I do not share the plurality's astonishing confidence that, on the record here, a factfinder could only conclude that AID was powerless to ensure the protection of listed species at the Mahaweli project.

As for the Aswan project, the record again rebuts the plurality's assumption that donor agencies are without any authority to protect listed species. Kelly asserted in her affidavit and it has not been disputed that the Bureau of Reclamation was "overseeing" the rehabilitation of the Aswan project. . . . See also *id.*, at 65 (Bureau of Reclamation publication stating: "In 1982, the Egyptian government . . . requested that Reclamation serve as its engineering advisor for the nine year [Aswan] rehabilitation project").

I find myself unable to agree with the plurality's analysis of redressability, based as it is on its invitation of executive lawlessness, ignorance of principles of collateral estoppel, unfounded assumptions about causation, and erroneous conclusions about what the record does not say. In my view, respondents have satisfactorily shown a genuine issue of fact as to whether their injury would likely be redressed by a decision in their favor.

. . . .

Note: The Case Law Background to *Lujan v. Defenders of Wildlife*

Results similar to those in *Lujan v. Defenders of Wildlife* were reached in *Lujan v. National Wildlife Federation*, 497 U.S. 871 (1990). In *National Wildlife*, the Federation attempted to show injury to two of its members from the opening up of certain federal lands to mining. The area which was newly opened to mining involved a tract of 4500 acres within a 2,000,000 acre area. When the government moved for summary judgment, the Federation submitted affidavits from two of its members asserting injury. Neither of the two affidavits, however, recited facts from which it could be determined that the land used by the affiants would be affected by mining on the 4500 acres. At best, the affidavits were ambiguous on this point.

The Court of Appeals had ruled that on motion for summary judgment ambiguities in the affidavits submitted in opposition to the motion should be resolved in favor of the nonmoving party. Justice Scalia pointed out that while ambiguities in pleadings should be resolved in favor of the nonmoving party on a motion for dismissal on the pleadings, Rule 56 of the Federal Rules of Civil Procedure (governing summary judgment) requires the nonmoving party to show specific facts, establishing that there is a factual dispute. Because the nonmoving party failed to produce those specific facts showing injury, summary judgment was proper. Justice Scalia then added the following remarks, by way of further explanation:

> Respondent placed great reliance, as did the Court of Appeals, upon our decision in *United States v. Students Challenging Regulatory Agency Procedures* (SCRAP), 412 U.S. 669. The SCRAP opinion, whose expansive expression of what would suffice for § 702 review under its particular facts has never since been emulated by this Court, is of no relevance there, since it involved not a Rule 56 motion for summary judgment but a Rule 12(b) motion to dismiss on the pleadings. The latter, unlike the former, presumes that general allegations embrace those specific facts that are necessary to support the claim. . . .

In **Warth v. Seldin, 422 U.S. 490 (1975)**, the plaintiffs claimed that actions by the town of Penfield, NY and its zoning, planning and town boards excluded persons of low and moderate income from the town in violation of various statutory and Constitutional provisions. The Court ruled that the plaintiffs lacked standing to assert their claims because they had not alleged that the defendants' unlawful actions had caused them injury:

> Petitioners must allege facts from which it reasonably could be inferred that, absent the respondents' restrictive zoning practices, there is a substantial probability that they would have been able to purchase or lease in Penfield and that, if the court affords the relief requested, the asserted inability of the petitioners will be removed. .

The Court stated that the petitioners' ability to live in Penfield depended upon the action of third parties, building contractors, who might decide to build low or moderate income housing units which would satisfy their needs at prices which they could afford. The record, however, showed no proposals by building contractors to provide such housing which had been frustrated by the defendants' exclusionary behavior:

> Indeed, petitioners' descriptions of their individual financial situations and housing needs suggests precisely the contrary — that their inability to reside in Penfield is the consequence of the economics of the area housing market, rather than of respondents' assertedly illegal acts.

In *Simon v. Eastern Kentucky Welfare Rights Organization*, 426 U.S. 26 (1976), several indigents and organizations composed of indigents sued the Secretary of the Treasury and the Commissioner of Internal Revenue asserting that the Internal Revenue Service violated the Internal Revenue Code and the Administrative Procedure Act by issuing Revenue Ruling 69-545 under which a nonprofit hospital that offered only emergency-room treatment to indigents would be treated as a "charitable" organization under IRC § 501(c)(3) with consequent exemption of its income from tax and deductibility, by contributors, of their contributions to such organizations under §§ 170(a), (c)(2). Under a prior Ruling hospitals were required to accept patients who could not pay for services in order to qualify as charitable organizations for purposes of § 501(c)(3). The Court ruled that the respondents lacked standing because the injury incurred by respondents — denial of hospital services to them because of their indigency — could not be traced to the challenged ruling.

> . . . It does not follow from the allegation [that the challenged IRS ruling "encouraged" hospitals to deny services to indigents] . . . that the denial of access to hospital services in fact results from petitioners' new Ruling, or that a court-ordered return by petitioners to their previous policy would result in these respondents' receiving the hospital services they desire. It is purely speculative whether the denials of service specified in the complaint fairly can be traced to petitioners' "encouragement" or instead result from decisions made by the hospitals without regard to the tax implications.

> It is equally speculative whether the desired exercise of the court's remedial powers in this suit would result in the availability to respondents of such services. So far as the complaint sheds light, it is just as plausible that the hospitals to which respondents may apply for service would elect to forgo favorable tax treatment to avoid the undetermined financial drain of an increase in the level of uncompensated services. . . .

In *Allen v. Wright*, 468 U.S. 737 (1984), the parents of black public school children alleged in a nationwide class action that the Internal Revenue Service (IRS) had not adopted sufficient standards and procedures to fulfill its obligation to deny tax-exempt status to racially discriminatory private schools. In denying standing the Court held that the plaintiffs had not incurred the injury requisite for standing and brought up separation of powers considerations that it subsequently revived in *Defenders of Wildlife*:

> Respondents allege two injuries in their complaint. . . . First, they say that they are harmed directly by the mere fact of Government financial aid to discriminatory private schools. Second, they say that the federal tax exemptions to racially discriminatory private schools in their communities impair their ability to have their public schools desegregated. . . .

> 1

> Respondents' first claim of injury can be interpreted in two ways. It might be a claim simply to have the Government avoid the violation of law alleged in respondents' complaint. Alternatively, it might be a claim of

stigmatic injury, or denigration, suffered by all members of a racial group when the Government discriminates on the basis of race. . . .

[Respondents] here have no standing to complain simply that their Government is violating the law.

Neither do they have standing to litigate their claims based on the stigmatizing injury often caused by racial discrimination. There can be no doubt that this sort of noneconomic injury is one of the most serious consequences of discriminatory government action and is sufficient in some circumstances to support standing. . . . Our cases make clear, however, that such injury accords a basis for standing only to "those persons who are personally denied equal treatment" by the challenged discriminatory conduct. . . .

The consequences of recognizing respondents' standing on the basis of their first claim of injury illustrate why our cases plainly hold that such injury is not judicially cognizable. If the abstract stigmatic injury were cognizable, standing would extend nationwide to all members of the particular racial groups against which the Government was alleged to be discriminating by its grant of a tax exemption to a racially discriminatory school, regardless of the location of that school. All such persons could claim the same sort of abstract stigmatic injury respondents assert in their first claim of injury. A black person in Hawaii could challenge the grant of a tax exemption to a racially discriminatory school in Maine. Recognition of standing in such circumstances would transform the federal courts into "no more than a vehicle for the vindication of the value interests of concerned bystanders." . . . Constitutional limits on the role of the federal courts preclude such a transformation.

2

It is in their complaint's second claim of injury that respondents allege harm to a concrete, personal interest that can support standing in some circumstances. The injury they identify — their children's diminished ability to receive an education in a racially integrated school — is, beyond any doubt, not only judicially cognizable but . . . one of the most serious injuries recognized in our legal system. Despite the constitutional importance of curing the injury alleged by respondents, however, the federal judiciary may not redress it unless standing requirements are met. In this case, respondents' second claim of injury cannot support standing because the injury alleged is not fairly traceable to the Government conduct respondents challenge as unlawful.

The illegal conduct challenged by respondents is the IRS' grant of tax exemptions to some racially discriminatory schools. The line of causation between that conduct and desegregation of respondents' schools is attenuated at best. From the perspective of the IRS, the injury to respondents is highly indirect and "results from the independent action of some third party not before the court," *Simon v. Eastern Kentucky Welfare Rights Org.*, 426 U.S., at 42. . . .

The diminished ability of respondents' children to receive a desegregated education would be fairly traceable to unlawful IRS grants of tax exemptions only if there were enough racially discriminatory private schools receiving tax exemptions in respondents' communities for withdrawal of those exemptions to make an appreciable difference in public-school integration. Respondents have made no such allegation. It is, first, uncertain how many racially discriminatory private schools are in fact receiving tax exemptions. Moreover, it is entirely speculative . . . whether withdrawal of a tax exemption from any particular school would lead the school to change its policies. . . . It is just as speculative whether any given parent of a child attending such a private school would decide to transfer the child to public school as a result of any changes in educational or financial policy made by the private school once it was threatened with loss of tax-exempt status. It is also pure speculation whether, in a particular community, a large enough number of the numerous relevant school officials and parents would reach decisions that collectively would have a significant impact on the racial composition of the public schools.

The links in the chain of causation between the challenged Government conduct and the asserted injury are far too weak for the chain as a whole to sustain respondents' standing. . . .

The idea of separation of powers that underlies standing doctrine explains why our cases preclude the conclusion that respondents' alleged injury "fairly can be traced to the challenged action" of the IRS. . . . That conclusion would pave the way generally for suits challenging, not specifically identifiable Government violations of law, but the particular programs agencies establish to carry out their legal obligations. . . . When transported into the Art. III context, that principle [that the Government has traditionally been granted the widest latitude in the "dispatch of its own internal affairs"], grounded as it is in the idea of separation of powers, counsels against recognizing standing in a case brought, not to enforce specific legal obligations whose violation works a direct harm, but to seek a restructuring of the apparatus established by the Executive Branch to fulfill its legal duties. The Constitution, after all, assigns to the Executive Branch, and not to the judicial Branch, the duty to "take Care that the Laws be faithfully executed." U.S. Const., Art. 11, § 3. We could not recognize respondents' standing in this case without running afoul of that structural principle.

Questions and Comments

1. Did the Court impose additional standing requirements in *Lujan v. Defenders of Wildlife, Lujan v. National Wildlife Federation, Allen v. Wright, Warth v. Seldin,* and *Simon v. Eastern Kentucky Welfare Rights Organization* which were absent from *Data Processing* and the earlier standing cases? Were the standing requirements of *Defenders of Wildlife* present, at least by implication, in the earlier cases? What does *Defenders of Wildlife* add to the standing analysis developed in *National Wildlife Federation* and earlier cases?

2. Do you agree that Ms. Kelly and Ms. Skilbred were not injured? Were you surprised that the Court did not think that they could establish injury? Who had the more attenuated case of injury, Ms. Kelly or Ms. Skilbred? What would the women have to allege (and be prepared to prove) to establish standing?

3. What standards govern determination of causation? Were the plaintiffs injured in *Defenders of Wildlife*? in *National Wildlife Federation*? in *Allen*? in *Warth*? in *Simon*? Would a favorable ruling on the merits have remedied the injuries of which the plaintiffs complained in *Defenders of Wildlife*? in *National Wildlife Federation*? in *Allen*? in *Warth*? in *Simon*?

4. Did the result in *Defenders of Wildlife* follow from *National Wildlife Federation*? Did the result in *Allen v. Wright* follow from *Simon v. Eastern Kentucky Welfare Rights Organization*?

5. Is injury in fact a constitutionally-required element in standing? Is causation? Explain. Do you understand that the tests for causation are the same when standing is asserted under the APA as for when it is asserted outside the APA?

6. Were the plaintiffs' injuries in *Defenders of Wildlife* and *National Wildlife Federation* similar to the injuries suffered by the plaintiffs in *SCRAP*? Were the plaintiffs' injuries in *Allen v. Wright* similar or different from the injuries suffered by the plaintiffs in *SCRAP*? in *Sierra Club*? Is *SCRAP* a relevant precedent? Is *Sierra Club*? Did *SCRAP* or *Sierra Club* deal with the causation issue? Explain.

What do you make of the somewhat derogatory way Justice Scalia referred to SCRAP in his *National Wildlife Federation* opinion? Is SCRAP still a viable precedent? How would you identify the particular aspect of SCRAP on which Justice Scalia has cast aspersions? Is it the question of whether the ICC action has "caused" increased environmental harm to which the plaintiffs were exposed? Or is it the fact that the injury to which the plaintiffs were exposed was shared by everyone else? Or a combination of the two?

7. Can you explain how the separation-of-powers rationale underlies the Court's standing determinations in *Allen v. Wright*? Do you see similar issues involved in *Defenders of Wildlife*?

8. In *Defenders of Wildlife*, Justice Scalia's views on redressability were challenged by Justices Stevens, Blackmun and O'Connor. Justice Scalia does not think that the funding agencies would be bound by a judicial interpretation in this action because they are not parties. Do you agree? On what basis do the other Justices conclude that the funding agencies would follow the legal interpretation of the district court? Do agencies always follow judicial interpretations of statutes, even when they are not parties to the case in which the interpretation was made? Do agencies always follow judicial interpretations of statutes, even when they are parties to the case in which the interpretation was made? What does "nonacquiescence" mean?

9. What position do Justices Blackmun and O'Connor take on the question of whether cessation of funding by the United States would halt the foreign development projects? Would the effects of a termination of U.S. aid be a question of fact for proof at trial? Would the litigation of such a major and complex question

frustrate any of the purposes of the standing doctrine?

10. To what extent does the Court's split on the redressability issue indicate a possible revision of standing doctrine?

11. Can you describe the "ecosystem nexus", the "animal nexus" and "vocational nexus" theories asserted by the plaintiffs? Has the Court dealt with similar standing theories previously? Are these theories reminiscent of the plaintiff's approach to standing in *Sierra Club*? Why or why not? in *Allen v. Wright*? in *National Wildlife Federation*?

12. To what extent can a person assert standing for violation of a "procedural right"? To what extent can Congress confer procedural rights on citizens?

13. In *National Wildlife Federation*, the Supreme Court reversed the Court of Appeals' application of Rule 56 of the Federal Rules of Civil Procedure. You probably read Rule 56 in your first year course in civil procedure. You should now reread Rule 56 to appreciate its finer points. Note that *SCRAP* was distinguished on the grounds that the motion there was a motion to dismiss on the pleadings where the Court reads the pleadings on the assumption that the facts alleged by the nonmoving party are true. By contrast, under Rule 56 governing motions for summary judgment, the defendant can force the plaintiff to identify evidence supporting its complaint and thereby to show the existence of a triable issue of fact. If the plaintiff has insufficient evidence to go to trial, then the court can dismiss the action. In this way, Rule 56 helps courts to clear nonmeritorious actions from their calendars without the necessity of trial. The Supreme Court endorsed this use of Rule 56 as a docket clearing device in a series of three cases in the mid-1980s: *Celotex Corp. v. Catrett*, 477 U.S. 317 (1986); *Anderson v. Liberty Lobby, Inc.*, 477 U.S. 242 (1986) and *Matsushita Elec. Indus. Corp. v. Zenith Radio Corp.*, 475 U.S. 574 (1986).

It is important to appreciate the procedural dimensions of the causation issue raised in *National Wildlife Federation*. A plaintiff must muster evidence that it will suffer injury as a result of the government action challenged. As that case shows, it is inadequate to produce an affidavit in which the plaintiff fails to connect its injury with the particular government action challenged. Other cases, especially *Defenders of Wildlife*, *Warth*, and *Simon v. Eastern Kentucky Welfare Rights Organization* show that general assertions of injury are insufficient. *National Wildlife Federation*, however, shows the power of Rule 56(e)'s requirement that the nonmoving party show evidence of "specific facts".

d. *Procedrual Rights and the Standing of States*

In ***Massachusetts v. Environmental Protection Agency***, **549 U.S. 497 (2007)** the Court dealt with the refusal of the EPA to regulate greenhouse gas omissions under the Clean Air Act. A group of private organizations had petitioned the EPA to regulate greenhouse gas omissions from new motor vehicles under that Act. The EPA denied the rulemaking petition on the grounds (1) that "the Clean Air Act does not authorize the EPA to issue mandatory regulations to address general climate change"; and (2) "that even if the agency had the authority to set greenhouse emission standards, it would be unwise to do so at this time."

On review, Massachusetts intervened in support of the petitioners. When the case reached the Supreme Court, the Court upheld the standing of Massachusetts. An excerpt from Justice Stevens majority opinion follows:

> To ensure the proper adversarial presentation, *Lujan* holds that a litigant must demonstrate that it has suffered a concrete and particularized injury that is either actual or imminent, that the injury is fairly traceable to the defendant, and that it is likely that a favorable decision will redress that injury [citing *Lujan v. Defenders of Wildlife*, 504 U.S. 555, 560-561 (1992)]. However, a litigant to whom congress has "accorded a procedural right to protect his concrete interests," *Id.*, at 572 n.7—here the right to challenge agency action unlawfully withheld, . . ."can assert that right without meeting all the normal standards for redressability and immediacy.". . . When a litigant is vested with a procedural right, that litigant has standing if there is some possibility that the requested relief will prompt the injury-causing party to reconsider the decision that allegedly harmed the litigant. *Ibid.*; see also *Sugar Cane Growers Cooperative of Fla. v. Veneman*, 289 F.3d 89, 94-95 (C.A.D.C. 2002) ("A [litigant] who alleges a deprivation of a procedural protection to which he is entitled never has to prove that if he had received the procedure the substantive result would have been altered. All that is necessary is to show that the procedural step was connected to the substantive result").

> Only one of the petitioners needs to have standing to permit us to consider the petition for review. . . . We stress here . . . the special position and interest of Massachusetts. It is of considerable relevance that the party seeking review is a sovereign state and not, as it was in *Lujan*, a private individual.

> Well before the creation of the modern administrative state, we recognized that States are not normal litigants for purpose of invoking federal jurisdiction. As Justice Holmes explained in *Georgia v. Tennessee Copper Co.*, 206 U.S. 230, 237 (1907), a case in which Georgia sought to protect its citizens from air pollution originating outside its borders:

>> "The case has been argued largely as it it were one between private parties; but it is not. The very elements that would be relied upon in a suit between fellow-citizens as a ground for equitable relief are wanting here. The State owns very little of the territory alleged to be affected, and the damage to it capable of estimate in money, possibly, at least, is small. This is a suit by a State in its capacity of *quasi*-Sovereign. In that capacity the State has an interest independent of and behind the titles of its citizens, in all earth and air within its domain. It has the last word as to whether its mountains shall be stripped of their forests and its inhabitants shall breathe pure air."

> When a State enters the Union, it surrenders certain sovereign prerogatives. . . . These sovereign prerogatives are now lodged in the Federal Government, and Congress has ordered EPA to protect Massachusetts (among others) by prescribing standards applicable to the "emission of any air pollutant from any class or classes of new motor vehicle engines, which

in [the Administrator's] judgment cause, or contribute to, air pollution which may reasonably be anticipated to endanger public health or welfare." 42 U.S.C. § 752(a)(1). Congress has moreover recognized a concomitant procedural right to challenge the rejection of its rulemaking petition as arbitrary and capricious. § 7607(b)(1). Given that procedural right and Massachusetts stake in protecting its quasi-sovereign interests, the Commonwealth is entitled to special solicitude in our standing analysis.

With that in mind, it is clear that petitioners' submissions as they pertain to Massachusetts have satisfied the most demanding standards of the adversarial process. EPA's steadfast refusal to regulate greenhouse gas emissions presents a risk of harm to Massachusetts that is both "actual" and "imminent." *Lujan*, 504 U.S. at 560. . . . There is, moreover, a "substantial likelihood that the judicial relief requested" will prompt EPA to take steps to reduce that risk. *Duke Power Co. v. Carolina Environmental Study Group, Inc.*, 438 U.S. 59, 79 (1978).

Questions and Comments

1.   What is a procedural right? Why is standing to seek a procedural right different from other standing? When a plaintiff is asking a court to require an agency to issue a an environmental impact statement, is his standing governed by the less demanding standards applicable to the assertion of procedural rights?

2.   Reread Part IV of Justice Scalia's opinion in *Defenders of Wildlife*. What does Justice Scalia say about standing to enforce a procedural right? Look especially at his footnote 7.

3.   What is the procedural right in *Massachusetts v. EPA*? Do you understand that the procedural right involved is a right to challenge the denial of a rulemaking petition in court? Who has a right to challenge the denial of a rulemaking petition in court? The Court recognized standing only in Massachusetts and did not pass on the standing of the other rulemaking petitioners. Do you think that only a state would have standing to obtain judicial review of the denial of a rulemaking petition involving climate change?

4.   The Court said that the combination of a procedural right and Massachusetts' "quasi-sovereign" interest entitled Massachusetts to "special solicitude in our standing analysis." Would anyone who was injured by agency action and who was denied a procedural right have standing to challenge that denial? If so, was the "quasi-sovereign" interest of the state irrelevant to its standing?

e.   *Citizen Suits*

In a number of regulatory statutes, Congress has authorized so-called "citizen suits" — lawsuits brought by citizens as means for enforcing the obligations imposed upon regulated subjects. These citizen suits, however, must comply with the standing requirements of Article III. We here look at a sample of citizen suit cases.

STEEL CO. v. CITIZENS FOR BETTER ENVIRONMENT
523 U.S. 83 (1998)

JUSTICE SCALIA delivered the opinion of the Court.

This is a private enforcement action under the citizen-suit provision of the Emergency Planning and Community Right-To-Know Act of 1986 (EPCRA). . . .

I

Respondent, an association of individuals interested in environmental protection, sued petitioner, a small manufacturing company in Chicago, for past violations of EPCRA. EPCRA establishes a framework of state, regional, and local agencies designed to inform the public about the presence of hazardous and toxic chemicals, and to provide for emergency response in the event of health-threatening release. Central to its operation are reporting requirements compelling users of specified toxic and hazardous chemicals to file annual "emergency and hazardous chemical inventory forms" and "toxic chemical release forms," which contain, inter alia, the name and location of the facility, the name and quantity of the chemical on hand, and, in the case of toxic chemicals, the waste-disposal method employed and the annual quantity released into each environmental medium. . . .

Enforcement of EPCR can take place on many fronts. The Environmental Protection Agency (EPA) has the most powerful enforcement arsenal: it may seek criminal, civil, or administrative penalties. . . . State and local governments can also seek civil penalties, as well as injunctive relief. . . . For purposes of this case, however, the crucial enforcement mechanism is the citizen-suit provision. . . .

[As a prerequisite to bringing a citizen suit, the complainant must give notice to the Administrator of the EPA, the State in which the alleged violation occurred, and the alleged violator. The citizen suit may not go forward if the Administrator has "commenced and is diligently pursuing an administrative order or civil action" against the alleged violator.

In this case, the EPA chose not to bring suit. Respondent filed suit in federal court. Petitioner then moved to dismiss on the ground that its filings had been brought up to date and because EPCRA does not allow suit for a purely historical violation.]

. . . [R]espondent asserts petitioner's failure to provide EPCRA information in a timely fashion, and the lingering effects of that failure, as injury in fact to itself and its members. We have not had occasion to decide whether being deprived of information that is supposed to be disclosed under EPRCA — or at least being deprived of it when one has a particular plan for its use — is a concrete injury in fact that satisfies Article III. Cf. *Lujan v. Defenders of Wildlife*, 504 U.S., at 578. And we neet not reach that question in the present case because, assuming injury in fact, the complaint fails the third test of standing, redressability.

The complaint asks for (1) a declaratory judgment that petitioner violated

EPCRA; (2) authorization to inspect periodically petitioner's facility and records (with costs borne by petitioner); (3) an order requiring petitioner to provide respondent copies of all compliance reports submitted to the EPA; (4) an order requiring petitioner to pay civil penalties of $25,000 per day for each violation of §§ 11022 and 11023; (5) an award of all respondent's "costs, in connection with the investigation and prosecution of this matter, including reasonable attorney and expert witness fees, as authorized by Section 326(f) of [EPCRA]"; and (6) such further relief as the court deems appropriate. . . .

The first item, the request for a declaratory judgment that petitioner violated EPCRA, can be disposed of summarily. There being no controversy over whether petitioner failed to file reports, or whether such a failure constitutes a violation, the declaratory judgment is not only worthless to respondent, it is seemingly worthless to all the world. . . .

Item (4), the civil penalties authorized by the statute . . . might be viewed as a sort of compensation or redress to respondent if they were payable to respondent. But they are not. These penalties — the only damages authorized by EPCRA — are payable to the United States Treasury. In requesting them, therefore, respondent seeks not remediation of its own injury — reimbursement for the costs it incurred as a result of the late filing — but vindication of the rule of law — the "undifferentiated public interest" in faithful execution of the EPCRA. . . . This does not suffice. . . . But although a suitor may derive great comfort and joy from the fact that the United States Treasury is not cheated, that a wrongdoer gets his just deserts, or that the Nation's laws are faithfully enforced, that psychic satisfaction is not an acceptable Article III remedy because it does not redress a cognizable Article III injury. . . .

Item (5),the "investigation and prosecution" costs . . . would assuredly benefit respondent as opposed to the citizenry at large. Obviously, however, a plaintiff cannot achieve standing to litigate a substantive issue by bringing suit for the cost of bringing suit. The litigation must give the plaintiff some other benefit besides reimbursement of costs that are a byproduct of the litigation itself. . . .

The remaining relief respondent seeks (item (2), giving respondent authority to inspect petitioner's facility and records, and item (3), compelling petitioner to provide respondent copies of EPA compliance reports) is injunctive in nature. It cannot conceivably remedy any past wrong but is aimed at deterring petitioner from violating EPCRA in the future. . . . The latter objective can of course be "remedial" for Article III purposes, when threatened injury is one of the gravamens of the complaint. If respondent had alleged a continuing violation, the injunctive relief requested would remedy that alleged harm. But there is no such allegation here — and on the facts of the case, there seems no basis for it. Nothing supports the requested injunctive relief except respondent's generalized interest in deterrence, which is insufficient for purposes of Article III.

Questions and Comments

Steel Co. shows dramatically how the citizen-suit provisions of a regulatory statute are confined by the Article III cases and controversies requirements of the Constitution. Justice Scalia identifies each item of relief sought by the plaintiff and shows that the plaintiff fails to establish the necessary injury for each. Why did the plaintiff not allege continuing or threatened future injury? Was this a failure on the part of the plaintiff's lawyers? Or did the defendant's action in bringing its filings up to date preclude an allegation of threatened future injury?

In *Friends of the Earth, Inc. v. Laidlaw Environmental Services,* 528 U.S. 167 (2000), environmental groups brought an action under the Clean Water Act's citizen-suit provisions. The defendant company, had been discharging various pollutants into a nearby river in amounts continuously exceeding the limits contained in its permit. After the commencement of suit, the defendant brought itself into compliance. The lower court then dismissed the action as moot. In the Supreme Court, Justice Ginsburg dealt with a number of contentions, including the meaning of injury and standing to seek civil penalties:

> Laidlaw contends first that FOE [Friends of the Earth] lacked standing from the outset even to seek injunctive relief, because the plaintiff organizations failed to show that any of their members had sustained or faced the threat of any "injury in fact" from Laidlaw's activities. In support of this contention Laidlaw points to the District Court's finding . . . that there had been "no demonstrated proof of harm to the environment" from Laidlaw's mercury discharge violations. . . .

> The relevant showing for purposes of Article III standing, however, is not injury to the environment but injury to the plaintiff. To insist upon the former rather than the latter as part of the standing inquiry . . . is to raise the standing hurdle higher than the necessary showing for success on the merits in an action alleging noncompliance with an NPDES permit. Focusing properly on injury to the plaintiff, the District Court found that FOE had demonstrated sufficient injury to establish standing. . . . For example, FOE member Kenneth Lee Curtis averred in affidavits that he lived a half-mile from Laidlaw's factory; that he occasionally drove over the North Tyger River, and that it looked and smelled polluted; and that he would like to fish, camp, swim, and picnic in and near the river between 3 and 15 miles downstream from the facility, as he did when he was a teenager, but would not do so because he was concerned that the water was polluted by Laidlaw's discharges. . . .

> Laidlaw argues next that even if FOE had standing to seek injunctive relief, it lacked standing to seek civil penalties. Here the asserted defect is not injury but redressability. Civil penalties offer no redress to private plaintiffs, Laidlaw argues, because they are paid to the Government, and therefore a citizen plaintiff can never have standing to seek them.

> Laidlaw is right to insist that a plaintiff must demonstrate standing separately for each form of relief sought. . . .

It can scarcely be doubted that, for a plaintiff who is injured or faces the threat of future injury due to illegal conduct ongoing at the time of suit, a sanction that effectively abates that conduct and prevents its recurrence provides a form of redress. Civil penalties can fit that description. To the extent that they encourage defendants to discontinue current violations and deter them from committing future ones, they afford redress to citizen plaintiffs who are injured or threatened with injury as a consequence of ongoing unlawful conduct.

* * * *

We recognize that there may be a point at which the deterrent effect of a claim for civil penalties becomes so insubstantial or so remote that it cannot support citizen standing. The fact that this vanishing point is not easy to ascertain does not detract from the deterrent power of such penalties in the ordinary case. . . .

Laidlaw contends that the reasoning of our decision in *Steel Co.* directs the conclusion that citizen plaintiffs have no standing to seek civil penalties under the Act. We disagree. *Steel Co.* established that citizen suitors lack standing to seek civil penalties for violations that have abated by the time of suit. . . . We specifically noted in that case that there was no allegation in the complaint of any continuing or imminent violation, and that no basis for such an allegation appeared to exist. . . . In short, *Steel Co.*, held that private plaintiffs, unlike the Federal Government, may not sue to assess penalties for wholly past violations, but our decision in the case did not reach the issue of standing to seek penalties for violations that are ongoing at the time of the complaint and that could continue into the future if undeterred.

Questions and Comments

In her opinion, Justice Ginsburg was able to justify the plaintiff's standing in circumstances remarkably similar to those in which Justice Scalia had denied standing in *Steel Co.* Is the difference between *Laindlaw* and *Steel Co.* that *Steel Co.* remedied its violation after notice of an intended suit but before that suit was commenced? Was it easier for Steel Co. to cure its violations that it would have been for Laidlaw?

In ***Vermont Agency of Natural Resources v. United States ex rel. Stevens***, **529 U.S.765 (2000),** the Court upheld the standing of a private individual to bring a qui tam action under the False Claims Act.

The False Claims Act imposes civil liability upon "[a]ny person" who, inter alia, "knowingly presents, or causes to be presented, to an officer or employee of the United States Government . . . a false or fraudulent claim for payment or approval. The defendant is liable for up to treble damages and a civil penalty of up to $10,000 per claim. The Government itself may bring a civil action against the false claimant. Or, a private person (the relator) may bring a qui tam action "for the person and for the United States Government" against the false claimant, "in the name of the Government."

If the relator initiates the FCA action, he must deliver a copy of the complaint and any supporting evidence to the Government, which has 60 days to intervene in the action. If the Government does so, it assumes primary responsibility for prosecuting the action, although the relator may continue to participate in the litigation and is entitled to a hearing before voluntary dismissal and to a court determination of reasonableness before settlement. If the Government doesn't intervene within the 60-day period, the relator has the exclusive right to conduct the action. The relator receives a share of any proceeds from the action — generally ranging from 15 to 25 percent if the Government intervenes and from 25 to 30 percent if it does not — plus attorney fees and costs.

In the case, the relator brought this action against the Vermont Agency of Natural Resources, his former employer, alleging that it had submitted false claims to the Environmental Protection Agency in connection with various grant programs administered by it. The United States declined to intervene.

In the Supreme Court, Justice Scalia struggled with the relator's standing:

> Respondent Stevens contends that he is suing to remedy an injury in fact suffered by the United States. It is beyond doubt that the complaint asserts an injury to the United States — both the injury to its sovereignty arising from violation of its laws (which suffices to support a criminal lawsuit by the Government) and the proprietary injury resulting from the alleged fraud. But "[t]he Art. III judicial power exists only to redress or otherwise to protect against injury *to the complaining party.*" *Warth v. Seldin,* 422 U.S. 490, 499 (1975) (emphasis added); see also *Sierra Club v. Morton,* 405 U.S. 727, 734-735 (1972). It would perhaps suffice to say that the relator here is simply the statutorily designated agent of the United States, *in whose name* (as the statute provides, see 31 U.S.C. § 3730(b)) the suit is brought and — that the relator's bounty is simply the fee he receives *out of the United States' recovery* for filing and/or prosecuting a successful action on behalf of the Government. This analysis is precluded, however, by the fact that the statute gives the relator himself an interest *in the lawsuit,* and not merely the right to retain a fee out of the recovery. Thus, it provides that "[a] person may bring a civil action for a violation of section 3729 *for the person and for the United States Government,*" § 3730(b) (emphasis added); gives the relator "the right to continue as a party to the action" even when the Government itself has assumed "primary responsibility" for prosecuting it, § 3730(c)(1); entitles the relator to a hearing before the Government's voluntary dismissal of the suit, § 3730(c)(2)(A); and prohibits the Government from settling the suit over the relator's objection without a judicial determination of "fair[ness], adequa[cy] and reasonable[ness]," § 3730(c)(2)(B). For the portion of the recovery retained by the relator, therefore, some explanation of standing other than agency for the Government must be identified.
>
> There is no doubt, of course, that as to this portion of the recovery — the bounty he will receive if the suit is successful — a *qui tam* relator has a

"concrete private interest in the outcome of [the] suit." *Lujan, supra,* at 573. But the same might be said of someone who has placed a wager upon the outcome. An interest unrelated to injury in fact is insufficient to give a plaintiff standing. See *Valley Forge Christian College v. Americans United for Separation of Church and State, Inc.,* 454 U.S. 464, 486 (1982); *Sierra Club, supra,* at 734-735. The interest must consist of obtaining compensation for, or preventing, the violation of a legally protected right. See *Lujan, supra,* at 560-561. A *qui tam* relator has suffered no such invasion — indeed, the "right" he seeks to vindicate does not even fully materialize until the litigation is completed and the relator prevails.[1] This is not to suggest that Congress cannot define new legal rights, which in turn will confer standing to vindicate an injury caused to the claimant. See *Warth, supra,* at 500. As we have held in another context, however, an interest that is merely a "byproduct" of the suit itself cannot give rise to a cognizable injury in fact for Article III standing purposes. See *Steel Co.,* 523 U.S., at 107 ("[A] plaintiff cannot achieve standing to litigate a substantive issue by bringing suit for the cost of bringing suit"); see also *Diamond v. Charles,* 476 U.S. 54, 69-71 (1986) (holding that assessment of attorney's fees against a party does not confer standing to pursue the action on appeal).

We believe, however, that adequate basis for the relator's suit for his bounty is to be found in the doctrine that the assignee of a claim has standing to assert the injury in fact suffered by the assignor. The FCA can reasonably be regarded as effecting a partial assignment of the Government's damages claim. Although we have never expressly recognized "representational standing" on the part of assignees, we have routinely entertained their suits, see, *e.g., Poller v. Columbia Broadcasting System, Inc.,* 368 U.S. 464, 465 (1962); *Automatic Radio Mfg. Co. v. Hazeltine Research, Inc.,* 339 U.S. 827, 829 (1950); *Hubbard v. Tod,* 171 U.S. 474, 475 (1898) — and also suits by subrogees, who have been described as "equitable assign[ees]," L. Simpson, Law of Suretyship 205 (1950); see, *e.g., Vimar Seguros y Reaseguros, S.A. v. M/V Sky Reefer,* 515 U.S. 528, 531 (1995); *Musick, Peeler & Garrett v. Employers Ins. of Wausau,* 508 U.S. 286, 288 (1993). We conclude, therefore, that the United States' injury in fact suffices to confer standing on respondent Stevens.

We are confirmed in this conclusion by the long tradition of *qui tam* actions in England and the American Colonies. That history is particularly relevant to the constitutional standing inquiry since, as we have said elsewhere, Article III's restriction of the judicial power to "Cases" and "Controversies" is properly understood to mean "cases and controversies of the sort traditionally amenable to, and resolved by, the judicial process." *Steel Co., supra,* at 102; see also *Coleman v. Miller,* 307 U.S. 433, 460 (1939) (opinion of Frankfurter, J.) (the Constitution established that "[j]udicial power could come into play only in matters that were the traditional

---

[1] Blackstone noted, with regard to English *qui tam* actions, that "no particular person, A or B, has any right, claim or demand, in or upon [the bounty], till after action brought," and that the bounty constituted an "inchoate imperfect degree of property . . . [which] is not consummated till judgment." 2 W. Blackstone, Commentaries *437.

concern of the courts at Westminster and only if they arose in ways that to the expert feel of lawyers constituted 'Cases' or 'Controversies' ").

[The Court then discussed the history of *qui tam* actions, pointing out that they were familiar to the residents of the American colonies at the time of the adoption of the United States Constitution.]'

We think this history well nigh conclusive with respect to the question before us here: whether *qui tam* actions were "cases and controversies of the sort traditionally amenable to, and resolved by, the judicial process." *Steel Co.*, 523 U.S., at 102. When combined with the theoretical justification for relator standing discussed earlier, it leaves no room for doubt that a *qui tam* relator under the FCA has Article III standing.[1]

Questions and Comments

Qui tam actions involve a form of citizen standing that has presented a puzzle under prevailing standing doctrine. In his *Vermont Agency* opinion, Justice Scalia has provided a workable solution that not only grounded his conclusion in history, but identified a injury in fact to the relator that accords with current standing doctrine.

f. The "zone of interest" revisited.

CLARKE v. SECURITIES INDUSTRIES ASSOCIATION
479 U.S. 388 (1987)

JUSTICE WHITE delivered the opinion of the Court.

In these cases, we review an application of the so-called "zone of interest" standing test that was first articulated in *Association of Data Processing Service Organizations, Inc. v. Camp*, 397 U.S. 150 (1970). Concluding that respondent [Securities Industry Ass'n] is a proper litigant, we also review, and reverse, a judgment that the Comptroller of the Currency exceeded his authority in approving the applications of two national banks for the establishment or purchase of discount brokerage subsidiaries.

[The respondent Securities Industry Ass'n contended that bank discount brokerage offices are branches within the meaning of § 36(f) of the McFadden Act

---

[1] In so concluding, we express no view on the question whether *qui tam* suits violate Article II, in particular the Appointments Clause of § 2 and the "take Care" Clause of § 3. Petitioner does not challenge the *qui tam* mechanism under either of those provisions, nor is the validity of *qui tam* suits under those provisions a jurisdictional issue that we must resolve here. See *Steel Co. v. Citizens for a Better Environment*, 523 U.S. 83, 102, n. 4 (1998) ("[O]ur standing jurisprudence, . . . though it may sometimes have an impact on Presidential powers, derives from Article III and not Article II"); see also *Lujan v. Defenders of Wildlife*, 504 U.S. 555, 576-578 (1992).

The dissent implicitly attacks us for "introduc[ing] [this question] *sua sponte." Post*, at 1878. We raise the question, however, only to make clear that it is not at issue in this case. It is only the dissent that proceeds to volunteer an answer.

and thus are subject to the geographical limitations imposed by § 36(c). Section 36(c) provides that a national bank is permitted to branch only in its home state and only to the extent that state law permits a state bank to branch. The Comptroller disputed this position on the merits and also argued that the respondent lacks standing because it is not within the zone of interests protected by the McFadden Act. The Comptroller contended that Congress passed the McFadden Act not to protect securities dealers but to establish competitive equality between state and national banks.]

The "zone of interest" formula in *Data Processing* has not proved self-explanatory, but significant guidance can nonetheless be drawn from that opinion. *First.* The Court interpreted the phrase "a relevant statute" in § 702 broadly; the data processors were alleging violations of 12 U.S.C. § 24 Seventh, see 397 U.S., at 157, n. 2, yet the Court relied on the legislative history of a much later statute, § 4 of the Bank Service Corporation Act of 1962, in holding that the data processors satisfied the zone of interest test. *Second.* The Court approved the "trend . . . toward [the] enlargement of the class of people who may protest administrative action." At the same time, the Court implicitly recognized the potential for disruption inherent in allowing every party adversely affected by agency action to seek judicial review. The Court struck the balance in a manner favoring review, but excluding those would-be plaintiffs not even "arguably within the zone of interests to be protected or regulated by the statute . . . *Id.*, at 153.

The reach of the "zone of interest" test, insofar as the class of potential plaintiffs is concerned, is demonstrated by the subsequent decision in *Investment Company Institute v. Camp*, 401 U.S. 617 (1971). There, an association of open-end investment companies sought . . . review of a Comptroller's regulation that authorized banks to operate collective investment funds. The companies alleged that the regulation violated the Glass-Stegal Banking Act of 1933, which prohibits banks from underwriting or issuing securities. . . . [The Court ruled] that the plaintiffs not only suffered actual injury but, as in *Data Processing*, suffered injury from the competition that Congress had arguably legislated against by limiting the activities available to national banks.

Justice Harlan, in dissent, complained that there was no evidence that Congress had intended to benefit the plaintiff's class when it limited the activities permitted national banks. The Court did not take issue with this observation; it was enough to provide standing that Congress, for its own reasons, primarily its concern for the soundness of the banking system, had forbidden banks to compete with plaintiffs by entering the investment company business.

Our decision in *Block v. Community Nutrition Institute*, 467 U.S. 340 (1984), provides a useful reference point for understanding the zone of interest test. There, we held that while milk handlers have the right to seek judicial review of pricing orders issued by the Secretary of Agriculture under the Agricultural Marketing Agreement Act of 1937, consumers have no such right, because "[a]llowing consumers to sue the Secretary would severely disrupt [the] complex and delicate administrative scheme." 467 U.S., at 348. We recognized the presumption in favor of judicial review of agency action, but held that this presumption is "overcome whenever the congressional intent to preclude judicial review is 'fairly discernable in the statutory scheme.'" Id., at 351. . . . The essential inquiry is whether Congress "intended for [a particular] class [of plaintiffs] to be relied upon to challenge agency disregard of the law." 467 U.S., at 347 (citing *Barlow v. Collins* . . .)

The zone of interest test is a guide for deciding whether, in view of Congress' evident intent to make agency action presumptively reviewable, a particular plaintiff should be heard to complain of a particular agency decision. In cases where the plaintiff is not itself the subject of the contested regulatory action, the test denies a right of review if the plaintiffs interests are so marginally related to or inconsistent with the purposes implicit in the statute that it cannot reasonably be assumed that Congress intended to permit the suit. The test is not meant to be especially demanding; in particular, there need be no indication of congressional purpose to benefit any would-be plaintiff. *Investment Company Institute*, supra.

The inquiry into reviewability does not end with the zone of interest test. In *Community Nutrition Institute*, the interests of consumers were arguably within the zone of interests meant to be protected by the Act, see 467 U.S., at 347, but the Court found that point not dispositive, because at bottom the reviewability question turns on congressional intent, and all indicators helpful in discerning that intent must be weighed.[16]

---

[16] The principal cases in which the zone of interest test has been applied are those involving claims under the APA, and the test is most usefully understood as a gloss on the meaning of § 702. While inquiries into reviewability or prudential standing in other contexts may bear some resemblance to a zone of interest inquiry under the APA, it is not a test of universal application. *Data Processing* speaks of claims "arguably within the zone of interests to be protected or regulated by the statute *or constitutional guarantee* in question." 397 U.S., at 153, (emphasis added). We doubt, however, that it is possible to formulate a single inquiry that governs all statutory and constitutional claims. As the Court commented in *Data Processing:* "Generalizations about standing to sue are largely worthless as such." *Id.*, at 151. We have occasionally listed the zone of interest inquiry among general prudential considerations bearing on standing, see, *e.g., Valley Forge Christian College v. Americans United for Separation of Church and State, Inc.*, 454 U.S. 464, 475 (1982), and have on one occasion conducted a zone of interests inquiry in a case brought under the Commerce Clause, see *Boston Stock Exchange v. State Tax Comm'n*, 429 U.S. 318, 320-321, n.3 (1977). While the decision that there was standing in Boston Stock Exchange was undoubtedly correct, the invocation of the zone of interest test there should not be taken to mean that the standing inquiry under whatever constitutional or statutory provision a plaintiff asserts is the same as it would be if the "generous review provisions" of the APA apply, *Data Processing,* supra, 397 U.S., at 156.

The difference made by the APA can be readily seen by comparing the "zone of interest" cases in which a private right of action under a statute is asserted in conditions that make the APA inapplicable. See, *e.g., Cort v. Ash*, 422 U.S. 66 (1975); *Cannon v. University of Chicago*, 441 U.S. 677 (1979). In *Cort*, corporate shareholders sought recovery of funds that a corporate official had expended in alleged violation of 18 U.S.C. § 610, the then-current version of the Corrupt Practices Act, which prohibits corporate expenditures and contributions from influencing federal elections. The Court gave the would-be plaintiffs the threshold burden of showing that they were "one of the class for whose *especial* benefit the statute was enacted," 422 U.S., at 78 (internal quotation omitted; emphasis in original). The shareholders argued that § 610 was motivated in part by Congress' conviction that corporate officials have no moral right to use corporate assets for political purposes. The Court, in holding that this was not enough to give the shareholders an implied right of action under § 610, observed that "the protection of ordinary stockholders was at best a secondary concern [underlying § 610]." *Id.*, at 81. Clearly, the Court was requiring more from the would be plaintiffs in *Cort* than a showing that their interests were arguably within the zone protected or regulated by § 610.

In considering whether the zone of interest test provides or denies standing in this case, we first observe that the Comptroller's argument focuses too narrowly on 12 U.S.C. § 36 in the overall context of the National Bank Act. As *Data Processing* demonstrates, we are not limited to considering the statute under which respondents sued, but may consider any provision that helps us to understand Congress' overall purposes in the National Bank Act. . . .

Section 36 is a limited exception to the otherwise applicable requirement of § 81 that "the general business of each national banking association shall be transacted in the place specified in its organization certificate. . . ." Prior to the enactment of § 36, § 81 had been construed to prevent branching by national banks. . . . It is significant for our present inquiry that Congress rejected attempts to allow national banks to branch without regard to state law. . . .

The interest respondent asserts has a plausible relationship to the policies underlying §§ 36 and 81 of the National Bank Act. Congress has shown a concern to keep national banks from gaining a monopoly control over credit and money through unlimited branching. Respondent's members compete with banks in providing discount brokerage services — activities which give banks access to more money, in the form of credit balances, and enhanced opportunities to lend money, viz., for margin purchases. . . .

These cases can be analogized to *Data Processing* and *Investment Company Institute.* In those cases the question was what activities banks could engage in at all; here, the question is what activities banks can engage in without regard to the limitations imposed by state branching law. In both cases, competitors who allege an injury that implicates the policies of the National Bank Act are very reasonable candidates to seek review of the Comptroller's rulings. There is sound reason to infer that Congress "intended [petitioner's] class [of plaintiffs] to be relied upon to challenge agency disregard of the law." *Community Nutrition Institute*, 467 U.S. at 347. And we see no indications of the kind presented in *Community Nutrition Institute* that make "fairly discernible" a congressional intent to preclude review at respondent's behest. We conclude, therefore, that respondent was a proper party to bring this lawsuit, and we now turn to the merits.

[The Court then ruled that the Comptroller properly ruled that Congress did not intend to subject a bank's conduct of a securities business to the branching restrictions imposed by 12 U.S.C. § 36(f).]

JUSTICE STEVENS, with whom the CHIEF JUSTICE and JUSTICE O'CONNOR join, concurring in part, and concurring in the judgment.

Analysis of the purposes of the branching limitations on national banks demonstrates that respondent is well within the "zone of interest" as that test has been applied in our prior decisions. Because I believe that these cases call for no more than a straightforward application of those prior precedents, I do not join Part II of the Court's opinion, which, in my view, engages in a wholly unnecessary exegesis on the "zone of interest" test. . . . There will be time enough to deal with the broad issues surrounding that [zone of interest] test when a case requires us to do so.

Questions and Comments

1. Has the zone of interest test been modified? How would you describe the zone of interest test as it exists today? What parts of the opinion in *Clarke v. Securities Industry Ass'n* would require you to state that test in terms different from the test as it emerged from *Association of Data Processing Service Organizations v. Camp?*

2. Is standing easier or more difficult when sought under the APA than otherwise? Do you understand the zone of interest test to apply to non-APA standing?

3. Before you draw your final conclusions about the meaning of *Clarke,* consider the Supreme Court's application of the zone-of-interests test in the decision below:

Air Courier Conference of America v. American Postal Workers Union, AFL-CIO, **498 U.S. 517 (1991).** The U.S. Postal Service is given a monopoly over the carriage of letters in and from the United States under a group of statutes known as the Private Express Statutes (PES). 18 U.S.C. §§ 1693-99; 39 U.S.C. §§ 601-06 (1988). The Postal Service, however, is authorized by statute to "suspend [the postal monopoly] upon any mail route where the public interest requires the suspension." International remailing is a practice under which private courier systems deposit with foreign postal systems letters destined for foreign addresses. In 1986 the Postal Service, after notice-and-comment procedures, issued a rule suspending the postal monopoly with respect to foreign remailing.

The American Postal Workers Union, AFL-CIO and the National Association of Letter Carriers then sought judicial review of the rule, claiming that the rulemaking record was inadequate to support the suspension. The Unions' suit was dismissed in district court but reinstated by the Court of Appeals for the District of Columbia Circuit. The U.S. Supreme Court held that the Unions lacked standing to challenge the rule:

> The Unions' claim on the merits is that the Postal Service has failed to comply with the mandate of 39 U.S.C. § 601(b) that the PES be suspended only if the public interest requires. . . . [It has been] demonstrated that the PES were not designed to protect postal employment or further postal job opportunities, but the Unions argue that the courts should look beyond the PES to the entire 1970 Postal Reorganization Act [PRA] in applying the zone-of-interests test. The Unions argue that because one of the purposes of the labor-management provisions of the PRA was to stablize labor-management relations within the Postal Service, and because the PES is the "linchpin" of the Postal Service, employment opportunities of postal workers are arguably within the zone of interests covered by the PES. The Unions rely upon our opinion in *Clarke v. Securities Industry Assn.,* 479 U.S. 388 (1987), to support this contention.
>
> . . . . In *Clarke,* we said that "we are not limited to considering the statute under which respondents sued, but may consider any provision that helps us to understand Congress' overall purposes in the National Bank Act." 479 U.S., at 401. This statement, like all others in our opinions, must be taken in the context in which it was made. In the next paragraph of the

opinion, the Court pointed out that 12 U.S.C. § 36, which the plaintiffs in that case claimed had been misinterpreted by the Comptroller, was itself "a limited exception to the otherwise applicable requirement of [12 U. S. C.] § 81," limiting the places at which a national bank could transact business to its headquarters and any "branches" permitted by § 36. Thus the zone-of-interests test was to be applied not merely in the light of § 36, which was the basis of the plaintiffs' claim on the merits, but also in the light of § 81, to which § 36 was an exception.

The situation in the present case is quite different. The only relationship between the PES, upon which the Unions rely for their claim on the merits, and the labor-management provisions of the PRA, upon which the Unions rely for their standing, is that both were included in the general codification of postal statutes embraced in the PRA. The statutory provisions enacted and re-enacted in the PRA are spread over some 65 pages in the United States Code, and take up an entire title of that volume. We said in *Lujan*, that "the relevant statute [under the APA] of course, is the statute whose violation is the gravamen of the complaint." 497 U.S., at 886. To adopt petitioners' contention would require us to hold that the "relevant statute" in this case is the PRA, with all of its various provisions united only by the fact that they deal with the Postal Service. But to accept this level of generality in defining the "relevant statute" could deprive the zone-of-interests test of virtually all meaning.

Unlike the two sections of the National Bank Act discussed in *Clarke, supra*, none of the provisions of the PES has any integral relationship with the labor-management provisions of the PRA. . . .

None of the documents constituting the PRA legislative history suggests that those concerned with postal reforms saw any connection between the PES and the provisions of the PRA dealing with labor-management relations. The Senate and House Reports simply note that the proposed bills continue existing law without change and require the Postal Service to conduct a study of the PES. The Court of Appeals referred to the PES as the "linchpin" of the Postal Service, which it may well be; but it stretches the zone-of-interests test too far to say that because of that fact those whom a different part of the PRA was designed to benefit may challenge a violation of the PES.

It would be a substantial extension of our holdings in *Clarke, supra*, *Data Processing, supra*, and *Investment Co. Institute, supra*, to allow the Unions in this case to leapfrog from their asserted protection under the labor-management provisions of the PRA to their claim on the merits under the PES. We decline to make that extension, and hold that the Unions do not have standing to challenge the Postal Service's suspension of the PES to permit private couriers to engage in international remailing. We therefore do not reach the merits of the Unions' claim that the suspension was not in the public interest. The judgment of the Court of Appeals is

Reversed.

National Credit Union Administration v. First National Bank & Trust Co.,
522 U.S. 479 (1998). Section 109 of the Federal Credit Union Act, 12 U.S.C. § 1219, provides that "[f]ederal credit union membership shall be limited to groups having a common bond of occupation or association, or to groups within a well-defined neighbourhood, community, or rural district." Since 1982, the National Credit Union Administration (NCUA), the agency charged with administering the FCUA, has interpreted § 109 to permit federal credit unions to be composed of multiple unrelated employer groups, each having its own common bond of occupation. In this action, respondents, five banks and the American Bankers Association, challenged this interpretation on the ground that § 109 unambiguously requires that the *same* common bond of occupation unite every member of an occupationally defined federal credit union. When the issue reached the Supreme Court, the Court initially had to determine whether the plaintiffs had standing to challenge the NCUA interpretation in court, and more particularly, whether the interests which they were asserting fell within the zone of interests sought to be protected or regulated by the statute. An excerpt from Justice Thomas' opinion for the Court follows:

> Summarizing our prior holdings, we stated [in *Clarke*] that although the "zone of interests" test "denies a right of review if the plaintiff's interests are . . . marginally related to or inconsistent with the purposes implicit in the statute," [479 U.S.] at 399, "there need be no indication of congressional purpose to benefit the would-be plaintiff," *id.*, at 399-400 (citing *ICI*). We then determined that by limiting the ability of national banks to do business outside their home States, "Congress ha[d] shown a concern to keep national banks from gaining a monopoly control over credit and money." 479 U.S., at 403. The interest of the securities dealers in preventing national banks from expanding into the securities markets directly implicated this concern because offering discount brokerage services would allow national banks "access to more money, in the form of credit balances, and enhanced opportunities to lend money, viz., for margin purchases." *Ibid.* The case was thus analogous to *Data Processing* and *ICI:* "In those cases the question was what activities banks could engage in at all; here, the question is what activities banks can engage in without regard to the limitations imposed by state branching law." 479 U.S., at 403.

> Our prior cases, therefore, have consistently held that for a plaintiff's interests to be arguably within the "zone of interests" to be protected by a statute, there does not have to be an "indication of congressional purpose to benefit the would-be plaintiff." *Id.*, at 399-400 (citing *ICI*); see also *Arnold Tours*, 400 U.S., at 46 (citing *Data Processing*). The proper inquiry is simply "whether the interest sought to be protected by the complainant is arguably within the zone of interests to be protected . . . by the statute." *Data Processing*, 397 U.S., at 153 (emphasis added). Hence in applying the "zone of interests" test, we do not ask whether, in enacting the statutory provision at issue, Congress specifically intended to benefit the plaintiff. Instead, we first discern the interests "arguably . . . to be protected" by the statutory provision at issue; we then inquire whether the plaintiff's interests affected by the agency action in question are among them.

Section 109 provides that "[f]ederal credit union membership shall be limited to groups having a common bond of occupation or association, or to groups within a well-defined neighborhood, community, or rural district." 12 U.S.C. § 1759. By its express terms, § 109 limits membership in every federal credit union to members of definable "groups." Because federal credit unions may, as a general matter, offer banking services only to members, see, e.g., 12 U.S.C. §§ 1757(5)-(6), § 109 also restricts the markets that every federal credit union can serve. Although these markets need not be small, they unquestionably are limited. The link between § 109's regulation of federal credit union membership and its limitation on the markets that federal credit unions can serve is unmistakable. Thus, even if it cannot be said that Congress had the specific purpose of benefiting commercial banks, one of the interests "arguably . . . to be protected" by § 109 is an interest in limiting the markets that federal credit unions can serve. This interest is precisely the interest of respondents affected by the NCUA's interpretation of § 109. As competitors of federal credit unions, respondents certainly have an interest in limiting the markets that federal credit unions can serve, and the NCUA's interpretation has affected that interest by allowing federal credit unions to increase their customer base.

Questions and Comments

1.   How does *Air Courier Conference* modify *Clarke? Clarke* indicated that the zone-of-interest test would deny standing to a plaintiff who sought to vindicate an interest only marginally related to the statute sued upon. The opinion in *Air Courier Conference* can be understood as saying that the Unions' interest in employment was at best no more than marginally related to the Private Express Statutes.

Does *Air Courier Conference* provide tools for determining when an interest is so distantly related to the statute sued upon as to fall outside of the zone-of-interests which that statute protects or regulates? *Air Courier* makes clear that the "relevant statute" for zone-of-interest purposes must be narrowly construed, does it not?

2.   *Data Processing* and *Barlow v. Collins* asserted that a plaintiff passed the zone-of-interest test, if "the interest sought to be protected . . . is *arguably* within the zone of interests to be protected or regulated by the statute or constitutional guarantee in question." (emphasis supplied). To apply that test, it is necessary to make an initial estimate of the scope of interests to be protected or regulated by the provision in question, in order to determine whether the interest which the plaintiff seeks to protect falls "arguably" within the protected zone. Under *Clarke* and *Air Courier Conference*, an interest is not arguably within the zone if it is no more than marginally connected with the concerns of the statute under which suit is brought.

3.   Does *National Credit Union* help to supply a needed balance to the opinions in *Clarke* and *Air Courier?* Are all of these cases properly understood against the background of *Block v. Community Nutrition Institute*, discussed in *Air Courier?*

An interplay between citizen standing and the zone of inerests

BENNETT v. SPEAR
520 U.S. 154 (1997)

[Suit brought by ranch operators and irrigation districts under citizen-suit provisions of Endangered Species Act (ESA). In the suit, the plaintiffs challenged a biological opinion issued by the Fish and Wildlife Service which would cause water, otherwise available for plaintiffs' uses, to be used to protect certain endangered species of fish. The Court of Appeals had held that the "zone of interests" test limits the class of persons who may obtain judicial review not only under the APA, but also under the citizen-suit provision of the ESA, and that "only plaintiffs who allege an interest in the *preservation* of endangered species fall within the zone of interests protected by the ESA."]

Justice Scalia delivered the opinion of the Court.

* * * *

The zone of interests formulation was first employed in *Association of Data Processing Service Organizations, Inc. v. Camp*, 397 U.S. 150 (1970). There, certain data processors sought to invalidate a ruling by the Comptroller of the Currency authorizing national banks to sell data processing services on the ground that it violated, inter alia, § 4 of the Bank Service Corporation Act of 1962 . . . which prohibited bank service corporations from engaging in "any activity other than the performance of bank services for banks." The Court of Appeals had held that the banks' data-processing competitors were without standing to challenge the alleged violations of § 4. In reversing, we stated the applicable prudential standing requirement to be "whether the interest sought to be protected by the complainant is arguably within the zone of interests be protected or regulated by the statute or constitutional guarantee in question." *Data Processing, supra*, at 153. *Data Processing* and its companion case, *Barlow v. Collins*, 397 U.S. 159 (1970), applied the zone-of-interests test to suits under the APA, but later cases have applied it also to suits not involving review of federal administrative action, see *Dennis v. Higgins*, 498 U.S. 439, 449 (1991): *Boston Stock Exchange v. State Tax Comm'n*, 429 U.S. 318, 320-321, n.3 (1977); see also Note, A Defense of the "Zone of Interests" Standing Test, 1983 Duke L.J. 447, 455-456, and nn. 40-49 (1983) (cataloging lower court decisions), and have specifically listed it among other prudential standing requirements of general application, see, e.g., *Allen, supra*, at 751; *Valley Forge, supra*, at 474-475. We have made clear, however, that the breadth of the zone of interests varies according to the provisions of the law at issue, so that what comes within the zone of interests of a statute for purposes of obtaining judicial review of administrative action under the " 'generous review provisions' " of the APA may not do so for other purposes, *Clarke v. Securities Industry Assn.*, 479 U.S. 388, 400, n. 16 (1987) (quoting *Data Processing, supra*, at 156).

Congress legislates against the background of our prudential standing doctrine, which applies unless it is expressly negated. See *Block v. Community Nutrition Institute*, 467 U.S. 340, 345-348 (1984). Cf. *Associated Gen. Contractors of Cal.*,

Inc. v. Carpenters, 459 U.S. 519, 532-533, and n.28 (1978). The first question in the present case is whether the ESA's citizen-suit provision . . . negates the zone-of-interest test (or, perhaps more accurately, expands the zone of interests). We think it does. The first operative provision says that "any person may commence a civil suit" — an authorization of remarkable breadth when compared with language Congress ordinarily uses. Even in some other environmental statutes, Congress has used more restrictive formulations, such as "[any person] having an interest which is or may be adversely affected," 33 U.S.C. § 1365(g) (Clean Water Act). . . .

Our readiness to take "any person" at face value is greatly augmented by two interrelated considerations: that the overall subject matter of this legislation is the environment (a matter in which it is common to think all persons have an interest) and the obvious purpose of the particular provision in question is to encourage enforcement by so-called "private attorneys general" — evidenced by its elimination of the usual amount-in-controversy and diversity-of-citizenship requirements, its provision for recovery of the costs of litigation (including even expert witness fees), and its reservation to the Government of a right of first refusal to pursue the action initially and a right to intervene later. Given these factors, we think the conclusion of expanded standing follows *a fortiori* from our decision in *Trafficante v. Metropolitan Life Ins. Co.*, 409 U.S. 205 (1972), which held that standing was expanded to the full extend permitted under Article III by § 810(a) of the Civil Rights Act of 1966 . . . that authorized "[a]ny person who claims to have been injured by a discriminatory housing practice" to sue for violations of the Act. There also we relied on textual evidence of a statutory scheme to rely on private litigation to ensure compliance with the Act. . . . The statutory language here is even clearer, and the subject of the legislation makes the intent to permit enforcement by everyman even more plausible.

It is true that the plaintiffs here are seeking to prevent application of environmental restrictions rather than to apply them. But the "any person" formulation applies to all the causes of action authorized by § 1540(g) — not only to actions against private violators of environmental restrictions, and not only to actions against the Secretary asserting underenforcement under § 1533, but also to actions against the Secretary asserting overenforcement under § 1533. . . . [T]he citizen-suit provision does favor environmentalists in that it covers all private violations of the ESA but not all failures of the Secretary to meet his administrative responsibilities; but there is no textual basis for saying that its expansion of standing requirements applies to environmentalists alone. The Court of Appeals therefore erred in concluding that the petitioners lacked standing under the zone-of-interests test to bring their claims under the ESA's citizen-suit provision.

Questions and Comments

1. In *Bennett v. Spear*, the Court relied on the citizen suit provisions of the Endangered Species Act to justify its expansion of the relevant zone of interests. Assuming contra-factually that the ESA had no citizen suit provision, how would a plaintiff's standing under that Act be analyzed? Was it necessary for the Court to rely on the citizen-suit provisions to uphold the plaintiff's standing? Can we

generalize *Bennett v. Spear* to find an expansion of the zone of interests whenever we find a citizen-suit provision in the governing statute?

2.   Recall that the zone of interests test originated in *Data Processing* and *Barlow v. Collins* as part of an analysis keyed to the expansion of standing. Yet the zone of interests test is a prudential limitation of the scope of standing that would be constitutionally permissible. The origin of that test nonetheless shows that it is intimately connected with a broad expansion of standing.

Note: Standing under the State Administrative Procedure Acts

1.   Several state administrative procedure acts grant standing to "aggrieved" persons to seek judicial review of agency trial-type proceedings. 1946 Model Act § 12(l); 1961 Model Act § 15. See also 1981 Model Act § 5-106(5). Consider the extent to which this wording is likely to facilitate the incorporation of caselaw developed in the federal system governing standing of persons to challenge agency action.

2.   Read the provisions of the 1946 and 1961 model acts governing judicial review of rules in declaratory judgment proceedings. 1946 Model Act § 6; 1961 Model Act § 7. What is the test for standing under these provisions? Do they adopt a "legal interest" test of standing?

3.   The 1981 model act incorporates more detailed standing provisions than either of its predecessors. See 1981 Model Act § 5-106.

4.   Does the 1981 model act incorporate federal case law on standing in § 5-106(5)? Does this provision incorporate the causation requirements developed in the federal cases? The injury-in-fact requirement? The zone-of-interests test?

Chapter 11

CONSTITUTIONAL DIMENSIONS OF ADMINISTRATIVE REGULATION

A. THE (LIMITED) ROLE OF THE COURTS

1. *Legislative Courts and Agency Adjudication: Constitutional Underpinnings.*

a. *Article III and the Federal Judicial Power.*

Article III of the U.S. Constitution provides in part that:

> The judicial Power of the United States, shall be vested in one supreme Court, and in such inferior Courts as the Congress may from time to time ordain and establish. The judges, both of the supreme and inferior Courts, shall hold their Offices during good Behavior, and shall, at stated Times, receive for their Services a Compensation which shall not be diminished during their Continuance in Office.

Despite the provisions of Article III, Congress has often vested administrative tribunals with the task of adjudicating disputes, most frequently between the Government and private parties, but sometimes between contending private parties. In so doing, why is not the Congress bestowing upon these administrative tribunals "judicial power" which properly belongs to the federal courts?

b. *The Matter of Legislative Courts.*

Acting under the powers bestowed upon it under Article I, Congress has at times established non-Article III courts, frequently referred to as "legislative courts". The courts established by Congress for the Territories are examples of non-Article III or "legislative" courts. So are the local courts for the District of Columbia as well as military tribunals. The judges of these courts do not hold constitutionally protected life tenure nor are they guaranteed by the Constitution that their salaries will not be reduced.

If Congress may, in carrying out its Article I functions, establish legislative courts without restraint, then Congress could confer unrestricted adjudicating powers upon administrative tribunals. These tribunals would merely be another species of legislative Courts.

The problem is, however, that Congress cannot create non-Article III or legislative courts without restraint. If Congress could do so, the provisions in Article III, designed to ensure the independence of the judiciary, could be easily evaded. The most recent Supreme Court case restricting the congressional power to establish non-Article III courts *is Northern Pipeline Constr. Co. v. Marathon Pipe Line Co., 458 U.S. 50 (1982).*

c. *Northern Pipeline.*

When Congress enacted the Bankruptcy Act of 1978, it established bankruptcy courts whose judges, *inter* alia, were appointed to office for 14 year terms and whose salaries were set by statute and are subject to adjustment under the Federal Salary Act. Bankruptcy courts were given jurisdiction over all "civil proceedings arising under title II [the Bankruptcy title] or arising in or related to cases under title II." Among the matters falling under the bankruptcy courts' jurisdiction were causes of action owned by the bankrupt at the time of the petition for bankruptcy. After Northern filed a petition for bankruptcy, it filed, in bankruptcy court, an action against Marathon Pipe Line Co. for breach of contract and warranty, alleged misrepresentation, coercion, and duress. Marathon moved for dismissal on the ground that the Bankruptcy Act unconstitutionally conferred Article III jurisdiction upon judges who lacked life tenure and protection against salary diminution. The Bankruptcy Court denied the motion, but on appeal, the District Court reversed. The Supreme Court affirmed.

In holding the bankruptcy courts constitutionally invalid, the Court held that Congress' power to establish legislative courts was limited to three situations: the establishment of territorial courts and courts for the District of Columbia; the establishment of courts martial for the military; and the establishment of legislative courts and administrative agencies to adjudicate cases involving "public rights", i.e., certain congressionally created rights arising between the government and others.

Finally, the Court rejected a contention that the bankruptcy court could be upheld as merely an adjunct to the District Court. Although the Court recognized that Congress could assign certain fact-finding functions to administrative tribunals under such a rationale, the Court held that such a role is easier to accept when the rights involved are "public rights":

> . . . the cases before us, which center upon appellant Northern's claim for damages for breach of contract and misrepresentation, involve a right created by state law, a right independent of and antecedent to the reorganization petition that conferred jurisdiction upon the Bankruptcy Court. Accordingly, Congress' authority to control the manner in which that right is adjudicated, through assignment of historically judicial functions to a non-Art. III "adjunct," plainly must be deemed at a minimum.

The Court also ruled that the functions of the adjunct must be limited in such a way that the "essential attributes" of judicial power are retained in the Article III court. In *Northern,* the Court found these limitations missing. Comparing the bankruptcy court involved in *Northern* with the agency whose fact-finding functions had been reviewed in *Crowell v. Benson,* 285 U.S. 22 (1932) [*infra*] the Court pointed to a number of significant places at which Congress neglected to limit the functions of the bankruptcy courts:

First, the agency in *Crowell* made only specialized, narrowly confined factual determinations regarding a particularized area of law. In contrast, the subject-matter jurisdiction of the bankruptcy courts encompasses not only traditional matters of bankruptcy, but also "all civil proceedings arising under title 11 or arising in or *related* to cases under title 11. . . . Second, while the agency in *Crowell* engaged in statutorily channeled fact-finding functions, the bankruptcy courts exercise " *all* of the jurisdiction" conferred by the Act on the district courts. . . . Third, the agency in *Crowell* possessed only a limited power to issue compensation orders pursuant to specialized procedures, and its orders could be enforced only by order of the district court. By contrast, the bankruptcy courts exercise all ordinary powers of district courts, including the power to preside over jury trials. . . . the power to issue writs of habeas corpus. . . . and the power to issue any order, process, or judgment appropriate for the enforcement of the provisions of Title 11. . . . Fourth, while orders issued by the agency in *Crowell* were to be set aside if "not supported by the evidence," the judgments of the bankruptcy courts are apparently subject to review only under the more deferential "clearly erroneous" standard. . . . Finally, the agency in *Crowell* was required by law to seek enforcement of its compensation orders in the district court. In contrast, the bankruptcy courts issue final judgments, which are binding and enforceable even in the absence of an appeal.

d.   *Other Relevant Supreme Court Decisions.*

Thomas v. Union Carbide Agricultural Prods. Co., 473 U.S. 568 (1985). Under the 1978 amendments to the Federal Insecticide, Fungicide, and Rodenticide Act (FIFRA) Congress provided that an applicant for the registration of a pesticide could make use of certain data submitted earlier by another so long as the person who submitted the data was compensated. In the event that the applicant and the person who had submitted the data could not reach agreement on the amount of compensation, the amount was to be determined by binding arbitration.

In *Thomas*, the appellees (the original data submitters) contended that their right to compensation was a matter of state law and thus, under *Northern Pipeline*, they could not be compelled to have recourse to a non-Article III federal tribunal for the determination of that issue. The Supreme Court (through Justice O'Connor) disagreed. The right to compensation forming the subject of the arbitration was provided by FIFRA rather than state law. The Court also rejected an argument that FIFRA had created a "private right" to compensation which, under *Northern Pipeline*, could not be adjudicated in a non-Article III tribunal; and it rejected a contention that a right to an adjudication by an Article III tribunal is absolute unless the Government is a party of record.

. . . we note several aspects of FIFRA that persuades us the arbitration scheme adopted by Congress does not contravene Article III. First, the right created by FIFRA is not a purely "private" right, but bears many of the characteristics of a "public" right. Use of a registrant's data to support a follow-on registration serves a public purpose as an integral part of a program safeguarding the public health. Congress has the power, under

Article I, to authorize an agency administering a complex regulatory scheme to allocate costs and benefits among voluntary participants in the program without providing an Article III adjudication.

The Court also drew from the history of the FIFRA amendments. Registration was being impeded by litigation over data compensation and trade secret protection. Congress decided to use arbitration to speed compensation decisions and so to break the logjam on registration. Article III, the Court ruled, did not prohibit Congress from employing a speedy and efficient decisional process to remedy these problems.

The Court also ruled that because the arbitration scheme embodied its own system of internal enforcement and relied "tangentially, if at all," upon judicial enforcement, it was easier to uphold: "The danger of Congress or the Executive encroaching on the Article III judicial powers is at a minimum when no unwilling defendant is subjected to judicial enforcement power as a result of the agency 'adjudication.' . . . [and] [i]n any event, under FIFRA, the only potential object of judicial enforcement power is the follow-on registrant who explicitly consents to have his rights determined by arbitration." Finally, the Court observed that the arbitration decision was subject to limited judicial review for "fraud, misconduct, or misrepresentation", review for constitutional error, "including whatever review is independently required by due process limitations." This limited review by Article III courts again supported the Court's ruling that the binding arbitration provisions of the FIFRA amendments did not contravene Article III.

Commodity Futures Trading Comm'n v. Schor, 478 U.S. 833 (1986). Under the Commodities Exchange Act, disgruntled customers of professional commodity brokers may seek redress before the Commodities Futures Trading Commission (CFTC) for their brokers' violations of the Act or the CFTC regulations, including an order to pay reparations to the complainant. CFTC orders are enforceable in federal district court. Congress intended this administrative procedure to be an "inexpensive and expeditious" alternative to the courts and arbitration, where such disputes could also be resolved. In conformance with the congressional goal of promoting efficient dispute resolution, the CFTC promulgated a regulation allowing it to adjudicate counterclaims "aris[ing] out of the transaction or occurrence or series of transactions or occurrences set forth in the complaint." This permissive counterclaim rule leaves the respondent in a reparations proceeding free to seek relief against the reparations complainant in other fora.

Schor brought a reparations proceeding before the CFTC against ContiCommodity Services, Inc. (Conti) a commodities futures broker and Conti then asserted a counterclaim against Schor to recover a debit balance on Schor's account. Conti had previously brought suit against Schor in federal court. During the pendency of the federal court litigation, Schor had argued to the federal court that it should dismiss Conti's suit because it could better be handled in the CFTC proceeding. Although the district court declined to stay or dismiss Conti's suit, Conti voluntarily dismissed the court action and presented his claim to the CFTC as a counterclaim in Schor's proceeding. After the Administrative Law Judge ruled in favor of Conti on both the claim and counterclaim, Schor contended that the CFTC lacked statutory jurisdiction over Conti's counterclaim. The CFTC denied review. On review by the Court of Appeals for the District of Columbia, that court, sua sponte, raised the issue of whether Article III permitted the CFTC to adjudicate Conti's counterclaim. It then decided that issue adversely to Conti, ordering the dismissal of Conti's counterclaim.

On review, the Supreme Court reversed. Schor waived any right he might have possessed to trial by an Article III court by demanding that the federal court dismiss Conti's claim in favor of CFTC adjudication. Further, by bringing his own action before the CFTC, Schor also effectively agreed to an adjudication by the CFTC of the entire controversy.

The Court stated, however, that Article III bars "congressional attempts 'to transfer jurisdiction [to non-Article III tribunals] for the purpose of emasculating' constitutional courts" and that, when this structural principle is implicated in a case, the parties cannot by consent cure the constitutional difficulty because the constitutional "limitations serve institutional interests that the parties cannot be expected to protect."

The Court nonetheless upheld the CFTC's jurisdiction over the counterclaim:

> . . . the congressional scheme does not impermissibly intrude on the province of the judiciary. The CFTC's adjudicatory powers depart from the traditional agency model in just one respect: the CFTC's jurisdiction over common law counterclaims. While wholesale importation of concepts of pendent or ancillary jurisdiction into the agency context may create greater constitutional difficulties, we decline to endorse an absolute prohibition on such jurisdiction out of fear of where some hypothetical "slippery slope" may deposit us. . . . Aside from its authorization of counterclaim jurisdiction, the CEA leaves far more of the "essential attributes of judicial power" to Article III courts than did that portion of the Bankruptcy Act found unconstitutional in *Northern Pipeline.*

The Court explained that the CFTC deals only with a "particularized area of law"; that its orders are enforceable only by federal district courts; that its orders are reviewable "under the same 'weight of the evidence' standard sustained in *Crowell,* rather than the more deferential standard found lacking in *Northern Pipeline*"; that the legal rulings of the CFTC are subject to *de novo* judicial review; and that the CFTC does not exercise all of the ordinary powers of district courts, such as presiding over jury trials or issuing writs of habeas corpus.

Although the Court stated that "where private, common law rights are at stake, our examination of the congressional attempt to control the manner in which those rights are adjudicated has been searching", no substantial threat to the separation of powers principle arose from the CFTC's counterclaim jurisdiction:

> . . . it seems self evident that just as Congress may encourage parties to settle a dispute out of court or resort to arbitration without impermissible incursions on the separation of powers, Congress may make available a quasijudicial mechanism through which willing parties may, at their option, elect to resolve their differences. . . .

It also bears emphasis that the CFTC's assertion of counterclaim jurisdiction is limited to that which is necessary to make the reparations procedure workable. . . . The CFTC adjudication of common law counterclaims is incidental to, and completely dependent upon, adjudication of reparations claims created by federal law, and in actual fact is limited to claims arising out of the same transaction or occurrence as the reparations claim.

In such circumstances, the magnitude of any intrusion on the Judicial Branch can only be termed *de minimis*. . . .

***Freytag v. Commissioner of Internal Revenue*, 501 U.S. 868 (1991).** This case involved a dispute over the power of the chief judge of the Tax Court to appoint a special trial judge to perform functions in connection with a case before the Tax Court. In the course of upholding the chief judge's power, Justice Blackmun (for the majority) and Justice Scalia (for the minority) expressed their views on the place of the Tax and other legislative courts in the constitutional scheme.

In this case the chief judge of the Tax Court assigned a special trial judge (Carleton D. Powell) to preside over the trial of petitioners' case and to prepare written findings and an opinion which was subsequently adopted by the chief judge as that of the Tax Court. Both majority and minority agreed that a special trial judge was an "inferior Officer". Under the Appointments Clause (Art. II, § 2) Congress can vest the power to appoint an inferior Officer "in the President alone, in the Courts of Law, or in the Heads of Departments."

Justice Blackmun took the view that the Tax Court was a "Court of Law" for purposes of the Appointments Clause, even though it was not an Article III tribunal. He contended that legislative courts like the Tax Court exercised "the judicial power of the United States" and therefore were "Courts of Law" within the meaning of the Appointments Clause. Blackmun rejected the Government's contention that the Tax Court was a "Department" in the Executive Branch and that the chief judge of the Tax Court was therefore a "Head of Department" as that term is used in the Appointments Clause. The meaning of the latter phrase must be confined, Blackmun argued, to "executive divisions like the Cabinet-level departments" in order to constrain the distribution of the appointment power.

Justice Scalia agreed with the Government's contention that the Tax Court is properly conceived as a "Department" within the Executive Branch. The fact that the Tax Court adjudicates cases is not inconsistent with this position, since adjudication is a function performed by many officials within the Executive:

It is no doubt true that all such bodies "adjudicate," i.e., they determine facts, apply a rule of law to those facts, and thus arrive at a decision. But there is nothing "inherently judicial" about "adjudication." To be a federal officer and to adjudicate are necessary but not sufficient conditions for the exercise of federal judicial power, as we recognized almost a century and a half ago.

According to Justice Scalia, the Appointments Clause is designed to ensure accountability to the President. Thus each major component of the Executive Branch is a Department within the meaning of the Appointments Clause. The

Heads of Departments are referred to as "Officers of the United States" who must be appointed by the President with the concurrence of the Senate. Their subordinates, however, may be appointed by the President alone or by the Head of the Department whom they serve.

Under Justice Scalia's analysis, legislative courts — like administrative agencies — would be understood as part of the national Executive. His analysis has the appeal of providing a coherent conceptual framework for many institutions in modern government which were not anticipated by the Framers. The Appointments Clause rationale employed in his analysis — accountability to the President — fits the regulatory agencies well. Their job is to develop and apply policy, a task for which they should be accountable to the President. It fits less well with legislative courts whose task is not often seen as involving major policy responsibility.

2.   Article III Courts and the Decision of "Jurisdictional" Facts.

Crowell v. Benson, 285 U.S. 22 (1922). *Crowell's significance* — *Crowell* reviewed the procedure governing the administration of the Longshoremen's and Harbor Workers' Compensation Act, a federal act modeled upon state workers' compensation statutes. Because (as shown below) *Crowell* had upheld the validity of administrative fact-finding against a contention that the facts had to be determined in an Article III court, it was extensively cited, discussed, and distinguished in *Northern Pipeline.* In addition to upholding the use generally of administrative fact-finding under the Longshoremen's and Harbor Workers' Act, however, *Crowell* imposed a substantial limitation upon administrative fact-finding: it required Article III courts to make their own determinations of certain kinds of factual issues — those whose determinations are "fundamental" or "jurisdictional".

The Longshoremen's and Harbor Workers' Compensation Act. — That Act provided compensation for accidental injuries incurred by workers engaged in maritime employment upon the navigable waters. Employers were made liable for the prescribed compensation regardless of fault. In *Crowell*, a deputy commissioner of the United States Employees' Compensation Commission had found that one Knudsen was injured while in the employ of Benson and performing service upon the navigable waters of the United States.

Administrative fact-finding. — In response to a challenge to the procedure based upon Article III, the Court first observed that because the courts retained the authority to decide all questions of law, the challenge to the Act's procedure related only to determinations of fact. The Court then adverted to a distinction which it found in the preexisting case-law between cases of "private right" and cases involving "public rights.". The Court stated that Congress possessed broad power to provide for the means of determining matters of public right: "Congress may reserve to itself the power to decide, may delegate that power to executive officers, or may commit it to judicial tribunals."

The case before it, however, the Court held involved a matter of private right, "that is, of the liability of one individual to another under the law as defined." Even so, the Court ruled that "there is no requirement that, in order to maintain the essential attributes of the judicial power, all determinations of fact in constitutional courts shall be made by judges." The Court analogized the factual determinations made by the deputy commissioner to those made by masters or assessors whose findings in practice had usually been followed by the courts which they had advised. Because the factual issues were limited ones and because the procedure employed relieved the federal courts of a serious burden, the Court ruled that Article III was not infringed when deputy commissioners made the requisite factual determinations under the Act.

Jurisdictional facts. — The Court distinguished "jurisdictional" from other facts, imposing different procedural requirements for their determination:

> What has been said thus far relates to the determination of claims of employees within the purview of the Act. A different question is presented where the determinations of fact are fundamental or "jurisdictional," in the sense that their existence is a condition precedent to the operation of the statutory scheme. These fundamental requirements are that the injury occur upon the navigable waters of the United States and that the relation of master and servant exist. These conditions are indispensable to the application of the statute, not only because the Congress has so provided explicitly . . . but also because the power of the Congress to enact the legislation turns upon the existence of these conditions.

The Court then ruled that the federal court must determine for itself the existence of these fundamental or jurisdictional facts; and it further held that in ruling upon those factual issues the Court could accept evidence in addition to that which was introduced before the deputy commissioner.

St. Joseph Stock Yards Co. v. United States, 298 U.S. 38 (1936). In this case, involving ratemaking under the Packers and Stockyards Act, the Court held that the courts are required by the due process clause to make an independent judgment upon the facts pertinent to confiscation and to other constitutional issues. But the Court also ruled that the courts should exercise that independent judgment in the light of the administrative proceedings already conducted; and that "the complaining party carries the burden of making a convincing showing. . . ."

Analogous obligations imposed upon state courts. ***Ohio Valley Water Co. v. Ben Avon Borough,*** 253 U.S. 287 (1920). The Court ruled that when a utility challenges as confiscatory the rates set for it by a governmental body, the utility is entitled to have its claim determined by a court exercising its own "independent judgment". The opinion thus requires states to provide a special type of judicial review on the issue of confiscation: review must be conducted by courts exercising judgment independent from that of the rate-setting agency.

Interestingly enough, the *Ben Avon* opinion failed to provide any guidance as to how to distinguish which state tribunals are, and are not, "courts" within the meaning of its ruling. (Article III helps to define constitutional courts within the federal system by setting forth the requirements of life tenure and no salary reduction. But there are no federal criteria governing the characteristics of state courts.) Since the ultimate source of this obligation of the states to provide this review is the due process clause of the Fourteenth Amendment, the Court must have taken the view that the Fourteenth Amendment due process clause imposes some form of a separation of powers principle upon the states.

Questions and Comments

1. Under what circumstances may Congress entrust the determination of factual issues to an administrative body? To what extent must that body's determinations be subject to review by an Article III court?

2. What is the difference between a matter of public right and a matter of private right? How does this distinction impinge upon your answers to the questions in paragraph I above? Were matters of private right involved in *Northern Pipeline?* in *Crowell?* What saved the procedure in *Crowell?* What significant differences from *Crowell* accounted for the invalidity of the procedure in *Northern Pipeline?*

3. Do you understand the concept of jurisdictional facts which the Court employed in *Crowell?* Which issues were jurisdictional ones? Why? Was the issue of causation (between the accident and the injury) a jurisdictional one? Explain.

4. For a particularly insightful discussion of the legislative court problem, *see* Richard H. Fallon, Jr., *Of Legislative Courts, Administrative Agencies, and Article III*, 101 Harv. L. Rev. 915 (1988).

3. *Delegation to the "Judicial Branch": The Case of the Sentencing Guidelines.*

MISTRETTA v. UNITED STATES
488 U.S. 361 (1989)

Justice Blackmun delivered the opinion of the Court.

In this litigation, we granted certiorari before judgment in the United States Court of Appeals for the Eighth Circuit in order to consider the constitutionality of the Sentencing Guidelines promulgated by the United States Sentencing Commission. The Commission is a body created under the Sentencing Reform Act of 1984. . . .

B
The Act

The Act . . . revises the old sentencing process in several ways:

1. It rejects imprisonment as a means of promoting rehabilitation . . . and it states that punishment should serve retributive, educational, deterrent, and incapacitative goals. . . .

2. It consolidates the power that had been exercised by the sentencing judge and the Parole Commission to decide what punishment an offender should suffer. This is done by creating the United States Sentencing Commission, directing that

Commission to devise guidelines to be used for sentencing, and prospectively abolishing the Parole Commission. . . .

. . . .

4. It makes the Sentencing Commission's guidelines binding on the courts, although it preserves for the judge the discretion to depart from the guideline applicable to a particular case if the judge finds an aggravating or mitigating factor present that the Commission did not adequately consider when formulating guidelines. . . . The Act also requires the court to state its reasons for the sentence imposed and to give "the specific reason" for imposing a sentence different from that described in the guideline.

5. It authorizes limited appellate review of the sentence. . . .

Thus, guidelines were meant to establish a range of determinate sentences for categories of offenses and defendants according to various specific factors, "among others." . . . The maximum of the range ordinarily may not exceed the minimum by more than the greater of 25% or six months, and each sentence is to be within the limit provided by existing law. . . .

C
The Sentencing Commission

The Commission is established "as an independent commission in the judicial branch of the United States." § 991(a). It has seven voting members (one of whom is the Chairman) appointed by the President "by and with the advice and consent of the Senate." "At least three of the members shall be Federal judges selected after considering a list of six judges recommended to the President by the Judicial Conference of the United States." *Ibid.* No more than four members of the Commission shall be members of the same political party. The Attorney General, or his designee, is an ex officio non-voting member. The Chairman and other members of the Commission are subject to removal by the President "only for neglect of duty or malfeasance in office or for other good cause shown." § 991(a) Except for initial staggering of terms, a voting member serves for six years and may not serve more than two full terms. . . .

IV
Separation of Powers

A
Location of the Commission

The Sentencing Commission unquestionably is a peculiar institution within the framework of our Government. Although placed by the Act in the Judicial Branch, it is not a court and does not exercise judicial power. . . .

First, although the Commission is located in the Judicial Branch, its powers are not united with the powers of the judiciary in a way that has meaning for separation-of-powers analysis. Whatever constitutional problems might arise if the powers of the Commission were vested in a court, the Commission is not a court, does not exercise judicial power, and is not controlled by or accountable to members of the Judicial Branch. The Commission, on which members of the judiciary may be a minority, is an independent agency in every relevant sense. In contrast to a court's exercising judicial power, the Commission is fully accountable to Congress, which can revoke or amend any or all of the Guidelines as it sees fit either within the 180-day waiting period, see § 235(a)(1)(B)(ii)(III) of the Act, 98 Stat. 2031, or at any time. In contrast to a court, the Commission's members are subject to the President's limited powers of removal. In contrast to a court, its rule-making is subject to the notice and comment requirements of the Administrative Procedure Act. . . . While we recognize the continuing vitality of Montesquieu's admonition: " 'Were the power of judging joined with the legislative, the life and liberty of the subject would be exposed to arbitrary controul,' " The Federalist No. 47, p. 236 (J.Cooke ed.1961) (Madison), quoting Montesquieu, because Congress vested the power to promulgate sentencing guidelines in an independent agency, not a court, there can be no serious argument that Congress combined legislative and judicial power within the Judicial Branch.

C
Presidential Control

. . . . [W]e do not believe that the President's appointment and removal powers over the Commission afford him influence over the functions of the Judicial Branch or undue sway over its members.

The notion that the President's power to appoint federal judges to the Commission somehow gives him influence over the Judicial Branch or prevents, even potentially, the Judicial Branch from performing its constitutionally assigned functions is fanciful. . . .

The President's removal power over the Commission members poses a similarly negligible threat to judicial independence. The Act does not, and could not under the Constitution, authorize the President to remove, or in any way diminish the status of Article III judges, as judges. Even if removed from the Commission, a federal judge appointed to the Commission would continue, absent impeachment, to enjoy tenure "during good Behavior" and a full judicial salary. U.S.Const., Art. III § 1. Also, the President's removal power under the Act is limited. In order to safeguard the independence of the Commission from executive control, Congress specified in the Act that the President may remove the Commission members only for good cause. Such congressional limitations on the President's removal power, like the removal provisions upheld in *Morrison v. Olson*, . . . *and Humphrey's Executor v. United States*, . . . are specifically crafted to prevent the President from exercising "coercive influence" over independent agencies. . . . Under these circumstances, we see no risk that the President's limited removal power will compromise the impartiality of Article III judges serving on the Commission and, consequently, no risk that the Act's removal provision will prevent the judicial Branch from performing its constitutionally assigned function of fairly adjudicating cases and controversies.

V

We conclude that in creating the Sentencing Commission — an unusual hybrid in structure and authority — Congress neither delegated excessive legislative power nor upset the constitutionally mandated balance of powers among the coordinate Branches. The Constitution's structural protections do not prohibit Congress from delegating to an expert body located within the Judicial Branch the intricate task of formulating sentencing guidelines consistent with such significant statutory direction as is present here. Nor does our system of checked and balanced authority prohibit Congress from calling upon the accumulated wisdom and experience of the Judicial Branch in creating policy on a matter uniquely within the ken of judges. Accordingly, we hold that the Act is constitutional. . . .

JUSTICE SCALIA, dissenting.

The lawmaking function of the Sentencing Commission is completely divorced from any responsibility for execution of the law or adjudication of private rights under the law. It is divorced from responsibility for execution of the law not only because the Commission is not said to be "located in the Executive Branch" (as I shall discuss presently, I doubt whether Congress can "locate" an entity within one Branch or another for constitutional purposes by merely saying so); but more importantly, because the Commission neither exercises any executive power on its own, nor is subject to the control of the President who does. . . . And the Commission's lawmaking is completely divorced from the exercise of judicial powers since, not being a court, it has no judicial powers itself, nor is it subject to the control of any other body with judicial powers. The power to make law at issue here, in other words, is not ancillary but quite naked. The situation is no different in principle from what would exist if Congress gave the same power of writing sentencing laws to a congressional agency such as the General Accounting Office, or to members of its staff.

The delegation of lawmaking authority to the Commission is, in short, unsupported by any legitimate theory to explain why it is not a delegation of legislative power. To disregard structural legitimacy is wrong in itself — but since structure has purpose, the disregard also has adverse practical consequences. In this case, as suggested earlier, the consequence is to facilitate and encourage judicially uncontrollable delegation. . . .

By reason of today's decision, I anticipate that Congress will find delegation of its lawmaking powers much more attractive in the future. If rulemaking can be entirely unrelated to the exercise of judicial powers, I foresee all manner of "expert" bodies, insulated from the political process, to which Congress will delegate various portions of its responsibility. How tempting to create an expert Medical Commission (mostly MDs, with perhaps a few PhDs in moral philosophy) to dispose of such thorny, "no-win" political issues as the withholding of life-support systems in federally funded hospitals, or the use of fetal tissue for research. This is an undemocratic precedent that we set not because of the scope of the delegated power, but because its recipient is not one of the three Branches of Government. The only governmental power the Commission possesses is the power to make law; and it is not the Congress.

****

Today's decision may aptly be described as the *Humphrey's Executor* of the Judicial Branch, and I think we will live to regret it. Henceforth there may be agencies "within the Judicial Branch" (whatever that means), exercising governmental powers, that are neither courts nor controlled by courts, nor even controlled by judges. . . .

Today's decision follows the regrettable tendency of our recent separation-of-powers jurisprudence . . . to treat the Constitution as though it were no more than a generalized prescription that the functions of the Branches should not be commingled too much — how much is too much to be determined, case-by-case, by this Court. The Constitution is not that. Rather, as its name suggests, it is a prescribed structure, a framework, for the conduct of government. In designing that structure, the framers *themselves* considered how much commingling was, in the generality of things, acceptable, and set forth their conclusions in the document. That is the meaning of the statements concerning acceptable commingling made by Madison in defense of the proposed Constitution, and now routinely used as an excuse for disregarding it. When he said, as the Court correctly quotes, that separation of powers "d[oes] not mean that these [three] departments ought to have no *partial agency* in, or no *controul* over the acts of each other," . . . quoting from The Federalist No. 47, pp. 325–326 U.Cooke ed.1961), his point was that the commingling specifically provided for in the structure that he and his colleagues had designed — the presidential veto over legislation, the Senate's confirmation of executive and judicial officers, the Senate's ratification of treaties, the Congress' power to impeach and remove executive and judicial officers — did not violate a proper understanding of separation of powers. He would be aghast, I think, to hear these words used as justification for ignoring that carefully designed structure so long as, in the changing view of the Supreme Court from time to time, "too much commingling" does not occur. . . .

I think the Court errs, in other words, not so much because it mistakes the degree of commingling, but because it fails to recognize that this case is not about commingling, but about the creation of a new branch altogether, a sort of junior-varsity Congress. It may well be that in some circumstances such a branch would be desirable; perhaps the agency before us here will prove to be so. But there are many desirable dispositions that do not accord with the constitutional structure we live under. And in the long run the improvisation of a constitutional structure on the basis of currently perceived utility will be disastrous.

Questions and Comments

1. Why did Congress choose to locate the Sentencing Commission "in the Judicial Branch"? What does it mean to say that the Commission is "in the Judicial Branch"? Does the U.S. Constitution refer to a "Judicial Branch"? If not, how can we understand that reference?

2. Does Congress have the power to veto the action of the Sentencing Commission? Does the Congressional veto power require Presidential assent? If not, do you see any Constitutional problem? If the Congressional veto does require

Presidential assent, what problems would that entail? Explain. Reconsider this question after you have read INS v. *Chadha, infra.*

3. What underlies Justice Scalia's objection to the Sentencing Commission? Would a more extensive Presidential removal power lessen his objections? Would Scalia object to the Sentencing Commission if it were placed "in the Executive Branch"? Explain.

4. Could the work of the Sentencing Commission have been entrusted to the U.S. Supreme Court? Is the Court's responsibility for the Federal Rules of Civil Procedure different from the responsibility that it would exercise if it promulgated sentencing guidelines?

5. Is Justice Scalia's complaint primarily that the Court has not developed predictable standards for applying the separation-of-powers doctrine? Is he correct? Does it matter? Explain.

B.   THE (LIMITED) ROLE OF THE LEGISLATURE

1.   Bowsher v. Synar

BOWSHER v. SYNAR
478 U.S. 714 (1986)

CHIEF JUSTICE BURGER delivered the opinion of the Court.

The question presented by these appeals is whether the assignment by Congress to the Comptroller General of the United States of certain functions under the Balanced Budget and Emergency Deficit Control Act of 1985 violates the doctrine of separation of powers.

[The Balanced Budget and Emergency Deficit Control Act of 1985 (or Gramm-Rudman-Hollings Act) sets a maximum deficit amount for federal spending for each of fiscal years 1986 through 1991. If the deficit exceeds the maximum permitted deficit for that year by more than a specified sum, the Act requires across-the-board cuts in federal spending to reach the targeted deficit level. To accomplish this result, the Directors of the Office of Management and Budget (OMB) and the Congressional Budget Office (CBO) independently estimate the amount of the federal budget deficit each year for the forthcoming fiscal year. If the deficit exceeds the maximum permitted, the Directors of the OMB and CBO calculate the necessary reductions. The Act then requires that the Directors report jointly their deficit estimates and budget reduction calculations to the Comptroller General. The Comptroller General, after reviewing these reports, then reports his conclusions to the President. The President in turn must issue a "sequestration" order mandating the spending reductions specified by the Comptroller General. If Congress does not act to reduce spending in the necessary amount within a specified period, the sequestration order becomes effective and the spending reductions included in that order are made.

In the event that the above procedures are ruled constitutionally invalid, the Act provides that the Directors of OMB and CBO report to a Temporary Joint Committee on Deficit Reduction which must report a joint resolution to both Houses setting forth the content of the Directors' reports. Congress then votes on the resolution and, if passed and signed by the President, it serves as the basis for a Presidential sequestration order.]

. . . [T]he District Court . . . held that the role of the Comptroller General in the deficit reduction process violated the constitutionally imposed separation of powers. The court first explained that the Comptroller General exercises executive functions under the Act. However, the Comptroller General, while appointed by the President with the advice and consent of the Senate, is removable not by the President but only by a joint resolution of Congress or by impeachment. The District Court reasoned that this arrangement could not be sustained under this Court's decisions in *Myers v. United States*, 272 U.S. 52 (1926) and *Humphrey's Executor v. United States*, 295 U.S. 602 (1935). Under the separation of powers established by the Framers of the Constitution, the court concluded, Congress may not retain the power of removal over an officer performing executive functions. The congressional removal power created a "here-and-now subservience" of the Comptroller General to Congress. . . .

Appeals were taken directly to this Court pursuant to § 274(b) of the Act. We noted probable jurisdiction and expedited consideration of the appeals. . . . We affirm.

The Constitution does not contemplate an active role for Congress in the supervision of officers charged with the execution of the laws it enacts. The President appoints "Officers of the United States" with the "Advice and Consent of the Senate. . . ." Article II, § 2. Once the appointment has been made and confirmed, however, the Constitution explicitly provides for removal of Officers of the United States by Congress only upon impeachment by the House of Representatives and conviction by the Senate. An impeachment by the House and trial by the Senate can rest only on "Treason, Bribery or other high Crimes and Misdemeanors." Article II, § 4. A direct congressional role in the removal of officers charged with the execution of the laws beyond this limited one is inconsistent with separation of powers.

. . . . [W]e conclude that Congress cannot reserve for itself the power of removal of an officer charged with the execution of the laws except by impeachment. To permit the execution of the laws to be vested in an officer answerable only to Congress would, in practical terms, reserve in Congress control over the execution of the laws. As the District Court observed, "Once an officer is appointed, it is only the authority that can remove him, and not the authority that appointed him, that he must fear and, in the performance of his functions, obey." . . . The structure of the Constitution does not permit Congress to execute the laws; it follows that Congress cannot grant to an officer under its control what it does not possess.

Appellants suggest that the duties assigned to the Comptroller General in the Act are essentially ministerial and mechanical so that their performance does not constitute "execution of the law" in a meaningful sense. On the contrary, we view these functions as plainly entailing execution of the law in constitutional terms. Interpreting a law enacted by Congress to implement the legislative mandate is the very essence of "execution" of the law. Under § 251, the Comptroller General must exercise judgment concerning facts that affect the application of the Act. He must also interpret the provisions of the Act to determine precisely what budgetary calculations are required. Decisions of that kind are typically made by officers charged with executing a statute.

The executive nature of the Comptroller General's functions under the Act is revealed in § 252(a)(3) which gives the Comptroller General the ultimate authority to determine the budget cuts to be made. Indeed, the Comptroller General commands the President himself to carry out, without the slightest variation . . . the directive of the Comptroller General as to the budget reductions: [quoting the statute].

Congress of course initially determined the content of the Balanced Budget and Emergency Deficit Control Act; and undoubtedly the content of the Act determines the nature of the executive duty. However, as *Chadha* makes clear, once congress makes its choice in enacting legislation, its participation ends. Congress can thereafter control the execution of its enactment only indirectly — by passing new legislation. . . . By placing the responsibility for execution of the Balanced Budget and Emergency Deficit Control Act in the hands of an officer who is subject to removal only by itself, Congress in effect has retained control over the execution of the Act and has intruded into the executive function. The Constitution does not permit such intrusion.

No one can doubt that Congress and the President are confronted with fiscal and economic problems of unprecedented magnitude, but "the fact that a given law or procedure is efficient, convenient, and useful in facilitating functions of government, standing alone, will not save it if it is contrary to the Constitution. Convenience and efficiency are not the primary objectives — or the hallmarks — of democratic government . . .

We conclude the District Court correctly held that the powers vested in the Comptroller General under § 251 violate the command of the Constitution that the Congress play no direct role in the execution of the laws. Accordingly, the judgment and order of the District Court are affirmed.

Questions and Comments

1.   The premise of Chief Justice Burger's opinion is that the power to remove an official is the power to control that official, is it not? Do you agree that the power to remove is tantamount to the power to control? What are the difficulties in equating Congress' power to remove the Comptroller General with Congressional control over his behavior? Is it easy for Congress to exercise its removal power? Is it easier or harder for Congress to exercise its removal powers than for the President to exercise the removal powers which he possesses over various officials in the executive branch? Explain.

2.   Do you understand Burger's conception of the separation of powers principle? Does he mean that the legislative, executive and judicial powers cannot be

blended? That some instruments of government cannot act in ways that are partly executive and partly legislative?

3. Chief Justice Burger appears to have a very definite view as to what constitutes "executive" action in the constitutional sense, does he not? Can you describe Burger's understanding of "executive" action? Of "legislative" action? What are the boundaries of "legislative" action? Do the meanings of these terms vary, depending upon whether they are used descriptively (to describe the kind of action an official is performing) or in their constitutional sense (to refer to one of the three constitutional branches)?

4. We know, do we not, that many officials in the executive branch act in ways that are analogous to the ways legislators and judges act? The Administrator of the Environmental Protection Agency (an executive branch official), for example, issues "legislative" rules and thus acts in a way analogous to the way Congress acts. Many other executive branch agencies do the same thing. Many agencies conduct adjudications and therefore act in ways analogous to the way judges act.

Whatever may be Burger's conception of the separation of powers principle, he surely did not mean to undercut the legitimacy of such normal everyday government action. Indeed, without the tools of adjudication and legislative rulemaking, the executive branch would be unable to enforce and administer the laws; and the President, accordingly, would be unable to carry out his constitutional duty (in Article II, § 3) to "take Care that the Laws be faithfully executed. . . ."

5. One major impediment to the discussion of the separation of powers principle is the vocabulary in which the principle has often been discussed. As pointed out in paragraph 4 above, executive branch officials routinely act in ways that resemble the action of a legislature or the action of the courts. Yet, the actions of these officials nonetheless fall within the constitutional responsibilities of the executive branch. Thus, although the core function of the executive branch is the administration and enforcement of the laws, the exercise of that constitutional function entails behavior which resembles the core functions of the other two constitutional branches, viz., the issuance of legislative rules and the adjudication of cases.

When a judge, lawyer, or scholar uses the term "executive" (or "legislative" or "judicial") it is necessary to inquire whether he is using the term to describe the work of a government official or whether he is making a reference to a constitutionally designated power allocated to one of the three government branches. The meanings of these terms differ substantially according to which usage is being employed.

6. Does *Bowsher* suggest that all government behavior must be performed by one of the three constitutional branches? Explain. In what branch is the Federal Trade Commission, for example? Does *Bowsher* cast doubt upon the legitimacy of the so-called "independent agencies"? Explain.

7. In a footnote in his *Bowsher* opinion, Chief Justice Burger wrote:

Appellants . . . are wide of the mark in arguing that an affirmance in this case requires casting doubt on the status of "independent" agencies because no issues involving such agencies are presented here. The statutes establishing independent agencies typically specify either that the agency members are removable by the President for specified causes . . . or else do not specify a removal procedure. . . . This case involves nothing like these statutes, but rather a statute that provides for direct Congressional involvement over the decision to remove the Comptroller General. Appellants have referred us to no independent agency whose members are removable by the Congress for certain causes short of impeachable offenses, as is the Comptroller General . . .

Is this footnote consistent with the rest of his opinion? Explain.

8. The removal cases provide significant background to the *Bowsher* decision. The leading removal cases are set forth below.

Note: The Removal Cases

The Appointments Clause and the Presidential removal power.

Article II, § 2 provides, *inter alia*, that the President:

> . . . shall nominate, and by and with the Advice and Consent of the Senate, shall appoint Ambassadors, other public Ministers and Consuls, Judges of the supreme Court, and all other Officers of the United States, whose Appointments are not herein otherwise provided for, and which shall be established by Law; but the Congress may by Law vest the Appointment of such inferior Officers, as they think proper, in the President alone, in the Courts of Law, or in the Heads of Departments.

In the decision of 1789 referred to in *Myers* case below, the First Congress rejected the contention that because the Senate had the constitutional power to consent to a Presidential appointment, it also possessed the power to consent to (or to withhold consent from) a removal.

Myers v. United States, 272 U.S. 52 (1926). Myers had been appointed by the President and, pursuant to statute, confirmed by the Senate to the office of postmaster first class at Portland, Oregon for a term of four years. Subsequently the President removed Myers from office. The statute provided that persons holding offices such as the one held by Myers could be removed by the President only with the consent of the Senate.

The Supreme Court held that the President possessed plenary power to remove officers in the Executive Branch appointed by him with the consent of the Senate and that the provision of the statute requiring Senate consent to the removal from office of such persons unconstitutionally interfered with the President's responsibility as Chief Executive. The Court conceded that Congress by legislation could vest the appointment of inferior officers, *inter alia*, in cabinet officials, and that the Congress might impose restrictions upon the removal of such officers. Even here, however, Congress itself could not participate in the removal decision.

(In its opinion the Court relied heavily upon the so-called decision of 1789, a determination by the first Congress not to include in a bill establishing a Department of Foreign Affairs a reference to the power of the President to remove the officer in charge. The Congress eliminated the reference because it recognized the President's removal power was a constitutionally conferred power, and it wished to avoid any implication that the removal power was conferred by legislative grace.)

Questions and Comments

To what extent did the Court in *Myers* incorporate an analysis of the Appointments Clause into its opinion? Did *Myers follow* the decision of 1789? Did the decision of 1789 construe the Appointments Clause? Did the Court in *Myers* distinguish the President's power to remove superior officers from his power to remove inferior officers? According to *Myers*, does the President possess plenary power to remove superior officers? in the absence of Congressional action, what is his power over inferior officers? May Congress restrict his power to remove inferior officers? Why was Myers not an inferior officer?

Humphrey's Executor v. United States, **295 U.S. 602 (1935).** Nine years after its decision in *Myers*, the Supreme Court drastically restricted its scope. Humphrey had been appointed by President Hoover to a seven year term as a Commissioner of the Federal Trade Commission and was confirmed by the Senate. President Roosevelt, however, requested Humphrey's resignation, and, when Humphrey refused to resign, removed him from office.

The Court ruled that Humphrey's removal was unlawful. *Myers* was distinguished on the ground that it involved the President's power over an executive officer. An extract from the Court's opinion follows:

> The Federal Trade Commission is an administrative body created by Congress to carry into effect legislative policies embodied in the statute in accordance with the legislative standard therein prescribed, and to perform other specified duties as a legislative or as a judicial aid. Such a body cannot in any proper sense be characterized as an arm or an eye of the executive. Its duties are performed without executive leave and, in the contemplation of the statute, must be free from executive control. In administering the provisions of the statute in respect of "unfair methods of competition" —that is to say in filling in and administering the details embodied by that general standard — the commission acts in part quasi-legislatively and in part quasi-judicially. . . .

> We think it plain under the Constitution that illimitable power of removal is not possessed by the President in respect of officers of the character of [Commissioners of the Interstate Commerce Commission and judges of the Court of Claims]. . . . The authority of Congress, in creating quasi-legislative or quasi-judicial agencies, to require them to act in discharge of their duties independently of executive control cannot well be doubted; and that authority includes, as an appropriate incident, power to fix the period during which they shall continue in office, and to forbid their removal except for cause in the meantime. For it is quite evident that one who holds his office only during the pleasure of another, cannot be depended upon to maintain an attitude of independence against the latter's will.

Questions and Comments

1. One of the tenets of the so-called progressive movement in the early twentieth century was the removal of various tasks of governmental administration from politics. In the view of the progressives, much government administration involves tasks which are primarily technical and can best be performed by nonpolitical experts. The city manager form of government, for example, originated in the progressive movement. There the day-to-day tasks of government were removed from the political arena and assigned to a nonpolitical technician.

The Federal Trade Commission Act was enacted in 1914 at the height of the progressive movement. The Commissioners were to be from different political parties and were to be appointed by the President and confirmed by the Senate for fixed terms. This arrangement was to guarantee their independence from the President and from party control.

The primary task assigned to the Commission was to enforce section 5 of the Federal Trade Commission Act which prohibited "unfair methods of competition." This task was conceived as a technical one, which would be facilitated by experience devoted to studying business methods and adjudicating cases applying that broad standard.

The Commission thus could be conceived as a governmental agency which was to perform its regulatory task through the use of technical skill, unhampered by irrelevant intrusions from the political sectors of government.

2. From a slightly different perspective, the institutional arrangements which freed the Commission from Presidential control were frequently pointed to as indicating that the Commission was in effect an instrumentality of the Congress. Congress legislated in broad and imprecise terms in section 5, employing the Commission to complete its task of defining unfair methods of competition as the Commission learned more about the subject through the adjudication of cases.

3. In *Humphrey's Executor*, the Court indicated that the Commission was not part of the executive branch. Of what branch or branches was it a part? Must a government agency belong to one of the three government branches established by the Constitution?

The opinion in *Humphrey's Executor is* particularly misleading. The Court held that the Commission could not be part of the executive branch because it performs tasks in aid of the legislature and the judiciary. The legislative tasks referred to are certain investigatory tasks which the Commission performs for Congress in connection with the consideration of new legislation. The judicial tasks consist in advice rendered to a court shaping a decree in an antitrust case. Yet the core task of the Commission is the enforcement of the prohibition against unfair methods of competition. When the Court referred to the latter task it conspicuously employed the prefix "quasi" before its references to legislative and judicial roles, thus indicating that the Court was aware that these functions of the Commission were not part of the constitutional work of the Congress and the courts.

Humphrey's Executor is often cited for the proposition that the Commission is an agency of the Congress. What does such a statement mean? Can the Commission be an instrumentality of the Congress when it enforces § 5 of the Federal Trade Commission Act? Explain.

What kind of supervision, if any, ought the President to exercise over the Federal Trade Commission? Should the President be able to exert influence over the Commission's determinations of adjudicative fact? Who normally determines adjudicative fact issues in cases coming before the Commission? What role does the Commission normally play in connection with adjudicative fact issues?

Should the President be able to remove Commissioners who persist in applying policies with which he disagrees? Explain.

Weiner v. United States, 357 U.S. 349 (1958). The petitioner was appointed to the War Claims Commission by President Truman and confirmed by the Senate. The statute provided tenure for the Commissioners for the life of the Commission which was limited to three years after the expiration of the period for filing claims. President Eisenhower removed the petitioner from membership in the War Claims Commission. Alleging his removal was illegal, the petitioner brought suit for back pay. The Supreme Court upheld the statutory tenure provisions against the defense that the President possessed an inherent power of removal under the Constitution:

> Judging the matter in all the nakedness in which it is presented, namely, the claim that the President could remove a member of an adjudicatory body like the War Claims Commission merely because he wanted his own appointees on such a Commission, we are compelled to conclude that no such power is given to the President directly by the Constitution, and none is impliedly conferred upon him by statute simply because Congress said nothing about it. The philosophy of *Humphrey's Executor*, in its explicit language as well as its implications, precludes such a claim.

Questions and Comments

In *Weiner* the Court protected the integrity of the judging process by insulating the members of the War Claims Commission from Presidential threats of removal. Why could not the Court develop an approach which would restrict the President's removal power over officials charged with adjudicating cases on the basis of record evidence and preexisting legal standards, even if those officials technically belonged to the executive branch? Such an approach would achieve the objective of protecting the integrity of individual decisions, but it would avoid the sweeping ramifications of *Humphrey's Executor* under which the President's supervisory power over the independent agencies may be unduly limited.

Note: The Solicitor General's Brief and the Independent Agencies

Consider the following extracts from the brief of the Solicitor General to the Supreme Court in *Bowsher v. Synar:*

> There is no occasion here to consider the current soundness of the premises underlying *Humphrey's Executor.* As the district court concluded

. . . developments since *Humphrey's Executor* do, however, appear to have cast a shadow upon those premises. For example, the Court explained in *Chadha* that the fact that Executive Branch officers perform what might be characterized as 'quasi-legislative' or 'quasi-judicial' functions does not mean that they are exercising something other than executive power within the meaning of Article II. . . . This Court also affirmed the decision in *Consumers Union v. FTC*, 691 F.2d 575 (D.C. Cir. 1982) (en banc), aff'd, 463 U.S. 1216 (1983), which invalidated a legislative veto provision applicable to the FTC, thereby establishing that at least for that aspect of the doctrine of separation of powers, the FTC is not to be distinguished from other agencies in the Executive Branch.

Brief for the United States, p. 46 n.32, Bowsher v. Synar, 478 U.S. 714 (1986).

Questions and Comments

1.   How did the Court deal with the question of the constitutional validity of the independence of the independent agencies in *Bowsher?* Did the Court deal forthrightly with the matter in the footnote [quoted in text in paragraph 7 of the Questions and Comments following the *Bowsher* opinion]?

2.   If Congress' constitutional role is exhausted by the enactment of legislation, the Federal Trade Commission is not performing an Article I role when it elaborates the Federal Trade Commission Act in issuing legislative rules, is it? Is it performing an Article II role? Explain.

3.   Do you find anything in Justice Scalia's analysis in *Freytag (supra)* which is helpful in answering these questions?

2.   The Appointments Clause as an Instrument for Constraining Congressional Control Over Administration.

BUCKLEY v. VALEO
424 U.S. 1 (1976)

Per Curiam:

IV. THE FEDERAL ELECTION COMMISSION

The 1974 amendments to the Act create an eight-member Federal Election Commission (Commission) and vest in it primary and substantial responsibility for administering and enforcing the Act. . . . [T]he Commission is given extensive rulemaking and adjudicative powers. . . . [T]he Commission is empowered to make such rules "as are necessary to carry out the provisions of this Act." . . .

The Commission's enforcement power is both direct and wide ranging. It may institute a civil action for (i) injunctive or other relief against "any acts or practices which constitute or will constitute a violation of this Act, . . . (ii) declaratory or injunctive relief "as may be appropriate to implement or con[s]true any provisions"

. . . governing administration of funds for Presidential election campaigns and national party conventions. . . . and (iii) "such injunctive relief as is appropriate to implement any provision" . . . governing the payment of matching funds for Presidential primary campaigns. . . . If . . . it finds an overpayment, it is empowered to seek repayment of all funds due the Secretary of the Treasury. . . .

The body in which this authority is reposed consists of eight members. The Secretary of the Senate and the Clerk of the House of Representatives are ex officio members of the Commission without the right to vote. Two members are appointed by the President pro tempore of the Senate "upon the recommendations of the majority leader of the Senate and the minority leader of the Senate." Two more are to be appointed by the Speaker of the House of Representatives, likewise upon the recommendations of its respective majority and minority leaders. The remaining two members are appointed by the President. Each of the six voting members of the Commission must be confirmed by the majority of both Houses of Congress, and each of the three appointing authorities is forbidden to choose both of their appointees from the same political party.

B. The Merits

Appellants urge that since Congress has given the Commission wide-ranging rulemaking and enforcement powers with respect to the substantive provisions of the Act, Congress is precluded under the principle of separation of powers from vesting in itself the authority to appoint those who will exercise such authority. Their argument is based on the language of Art. II, § 2, cl.2, of the Constitution, which provides in pertinent part as follows:

> [The President] shall nominate, and by and with the Advice and Consent of the Senate, shall appoint . . . all other Officers of the United States, whose Appointments are not herein otherwise provided for, and which shall be established by Law: but the Congress may by Law vest the Appointment of such inferior Officers, as they think proper, in the President alone, in the Courts of Law, or in the Heads of Departments."

. . . .

We think that the term "Officers of the United States" as used in Art. II . . . is a term intended to have substantive meaning. We think its fair import is that any appointee exercising significant authority pursuant to the laws of the United States is an "Officer of the United States," and must, therefore, be appointed in the manner prescribed by § 2, cl.2, of that Article.

Although two members of the Commission are initially selected by the President, his nominations are subject to confirmation not merely by the Senate, but by the House of Representatives as well. The remaining four voting members of the Commission are appointed by the President pro tempore of the Senate and by the Speaker of the House. While the second part of the Clause authorizes Congress to vest the appointment of the officers described in that part in "the Courts of Law, or in the Heads of Departments," neither the Speaker of the House nor the President pro tempore of the Senate comes within this language.

The phrase "Heads of Departments," used as it is in conjunction with the phrase "Courts of Law," suggests that the Departments referred to are themselves in the Executive Branch or at least have some connection with that branch. While the Clause expressly authorizes Congress to vest the appointment of certain officers in the "Courts of Law," the absence of similar language to include Congress must mean that neither Congress nor its officers were included within the language "Heads of Departments" in this part of cl.2.

Thus with respect to four of the six voting members of the Commission, neither the President, the head of any department, nor the Judiciary has any voice in their selection.

. . . . Appellee Commission has argued, and the Court of Appeals agreed, that the Appointments Clause of Art. II should not be read to exclude the "inherent power of Congress" to appoint its own officers to perform functions necessary to that body as an institution. But there is no need to read the Appointments Clause contrary to its plain language in order to reach the result sought by the Court of Appeals. Article 1, § 3, cl.5, expressly authorizes the selection of the President pro tempore of the Senate, and § 2, cl.5, of that Article provides for the selection of the Speaker of the House. Ranking nonmembers, such as the Clerk of the House of Representatives, are elected under the internal rules of each House and are designated by statute as "officers of the Congress." There is no occasion for us to decide whether any of these member officers are "Officers of the United States" whose "appointment" is otherwise provided for within the meaning of the Appointments Clause, since even if they were such officers their appointees would not be. Contrary to the fears expressed by the majority of the Court of Appeals, nothing in our holding with respect to Art. II, § 2, cl.2, will deny to Congress "all power to appoint its own inferior officers to carry out appropriate legislative functions."

Insofar as the powers confided in the Commission are essentially of an investigative and informative nature, falling in the same general category as those powers which Congress might delegate to one of its own committees, there can be no question that the Commission as presently constituted may exercise them. . . .

But when we go beyond this type of authority to the more substantial powers exercised by the Commission, we reach a different result. The Commission's enforcement power, exemplified by its discretionary power to seek judicial relief, is authority that cannot possibly be regarded as merely in aid of the legislative function of Congress. A lawsuit is the ultimate remedy for a breach of the law, and it is to the President, and not to the Congress, that the Constitution entrusts the responsibility to "take Care that the Laws be faithfully executed." Art. II, § 3.

We hold that these provisions of the Act, vesting in the Commission primary responsibility for conducting civil litigation in the courts of the United States for vindicating public rights, violate Art. II, § 2, cl.2, of the Constitution. Such functions may be discharged only by persons who are "Officers of the United States" within the language of that section.

Questions and Comments

1. Does *Buckley v. Valeo* tell you anything about Congress' power to control the administration and enforcement of the laws? How is the Appointments Clause involved with Congress' ability or inability to control administration and enforcement? just through Congress' inability to control the appointments? Does the application of the Appointments Clause in *Buckley* suggest the result in *Bowsher?* How?

2. The rationale for the Court's result in *Bowsher* was based upon the impropriety of Congressional control over an officer exercising Article II powers, was it not? Was the Court's application of the Appointments Clause in *Buckley* based upon the same rationale? Explain. Is the decision of 1789 about the Appointments Clause corroborative of this rationale? Explain.

3. Subsequent to the Supreme Court's decision in *Buckley v. Valeo*, Congress restructured the Federal Election Commission in attempt to avoid constitutional problems. The reconstituted Commission nevertheless contained the Secretary of the Senate and the Clerk of the House of Representatives as non-voting ex officio members. In *Federal Election Commission v. NRA Political Victory Fund*, **6 F.3d 821 (D.C. Cir. 1993),** *petition for cert. dismissed,* **513 U.S. 88 (1994),** the U.S. Court of Appeals for the District of Columbia Circuit ruled that the composition of the reconstituted Federal Election Commission violated the separation-of-powers principle. Even though the ex-officio members did not vote, Congress, by establishing the ex-officio members, must have intended their presence to exert a significant influence upon the work of the Commission. The Secretary of the Senate and the Clerk of the House of Representatives are agents of the Congress and "the mere presence of agents of Congress on an entity with executive powers offends the Constitution." Subsequently, the U.S. Supreme Court dismissed the Commission's petition for certiorari on the ground that the governing statute did not confer authority on the Commission to petition for certiorari. *Federal Election Commission v. NRA Political Victory Fund*, 513 U.S. 88 (1994).

4. Does the Composition of the Endangered Species Committee — described in *Portland Audubon Society v. Endangered Species Committee*, 984 F.2d 1534 (9th Cir. 1993), *supra,* — comport with Constitutional requirements? Why or why not?

3.   *The Legislative Veto.*

IMMIGRATION AND NATURALIZATION SERVICE v. CHADHA
462 U.S. 919 (1983)

[Chadha, an East Indian who was born in Kenya and held a British passport, overstayed a student visa. At a deportation hearing, Chadha conceded that he was deportable but filed a request for suspension of deportation under § 244(a)(1) of the Immigration and Nationality Act, 8 U.S.C. § 1254(a)(1) which provides:

(a) . . . [T]he Attorney General may, in his discretion, suspend deportation and adjust the status to that of an alien lawfully admitted for permanent residence, in the case of an alien who applies to the Attorney General for suspension of deportation and

(1) is deportable under any law of the United States except the provisions specified in paragraph (2) of this subsection; has been physically present in the United States for a continuous period of not less than seven years immediately preceding the date of such application, and proves that during all of such period he was and is a person of good moral character; and is a person whose deportation would, in the opinion of the Attorney General, result in extreme hardship to the alien or to his spouse, parent or child, who is a citizen of the United States or an alien lawfully admitted for permanent residence.

Acting for the Attorney General, the immigration judge ruled in Chadha's favor, ordering that his deportation be suspended. Pursuant to § 244(c)(1) of the Act, a report of the suspension was transmitted to Congress. Section 244(c)(2) of the Act provides:

(2) In case of an alien specified in paragraph (1) of subsection (a) of this subsection if during the session of the Congress at which a case is reported, or prior to the close of the session of the Congress next following the session at which a case is reported, either the Senate or the House of Representatives passes a resolution stating in substance that it does not favor the suspension of such deportation, the Attorney General shall thereupon deport such alien. . . .

The House of Representatives passed a resolution disapproving the suspension of Chadha's deportation. The immigration judge then reopened the proceedings to order Chadha deported. Chadha contended that § 244(c)(2) was unconstitutional, but the INS [the Immigration and Naturalization Service] declined to rule on that claim. Chadha then sought review of his deportation order in the U.S. Court of Appeals for the Ninth Circuit which ruled in his favor. The Supreme Court then granted *certiorari*.]

CHIEF JUSTICE BURGER delivered the opinion of the Court.

. . . . [T]he Framers were acutely conscious that the bicameral requirement and the Presentment Clauses would serve essential constitutional functions. The President's participation in the legislative process was to protect the Executive Branch from Congress and to protect the whole people from improvident laws. The division of the Congress into two distinctive bodies assures that the legislative power would be exercised only after opportunity for full study and debate in separate settings. The President's unilateral veto power, in turn, was limited by the power of two thirds of both Houses of Congress to overrule a veto thereby precluding final arbitrary action of one person. . . . It emerges clearly that the prescription for legislative action in Art. 1, §§ 1, 7, represents the Framers' decision that the legislative power of the Federal government be exercised in accord with a single, finely wrought and exhaustively considered, procedure.

The legislative character of the one-House veto in this case is confirmed by the character of the Congressional action it supplants. Neither the House of Representatives nor the Senate contends that, absent the veto provision in § 244(c)(2), either of them, or both of them acting together, could effectively require the Attorney General to deport an alien once the Attorney General, in the exercise of legislatively delegated authority, had determined the alien should remain in the United States. Without the challenged provision in § 244(c)(2), this could have been achieved, if at all, only by legislation requiring deportation. Similarly, a veto by one House of Congress under § 244(c)(2) cannot be justified as an attempt at amending the standards set out in § 244(a)(1), or as a repeal of § 244 as applied to Chadha. Amendment and repeal of statutes, no less than enactment, must conform with Art. I.

The nature of the decision implemented by the one-House veto in this case further manifests its legislative character. After long experience with the clumsy, time consuming private bill procedure, Congress made a deliberate choice to delegate to the Executive Branch, and specially to the Attorney General, the authority to allow deportable aliens to remain in this country in certain specified circumstances. It is not disputed that this choice to delegate authority is precisely the kind of decision that can be implemented only in accordance with the procedures set out in Art. I. Disagreement with the Attorney General's decision on Chadha's deportation — that is, Congress' decision to deport Chadha — no less than Congress' original choice to delegate to the Attorney General the authority to make that decision, involves determinations of policy that Congress can implement in only one way: bicameral passage followed by presentment to the President. Congress must abide by its delegation of authority until that delegation is legislatively altered or revoked.

We hold that the Congressional veto provision in § 244(c)(2) is severable from the Act and that it is unconstitutional. Accordingly, the judgment of the Court of Appeals is

Affirmed.

Metropolitan Washington Airports Authority v. Citizens for the Abatement of Aircraft Noise, Inc., **501 U.S. 252 (1991).** *By* legislation, Congress transferred operating control of two major airports from the Federal Government to the Metropolitan Washington Airport Authority (MWAA), a body created pursuant to legislation of Virginia and Maryland. The Congressional legislation authorizing the transfer, however, required that MWAA must establish a board of review holding a veto power over its action, and it provided that members of the board of review would be taken from membership of Congressional committees concerned with transportation and not residing in either Virginia or Maryland.

Relying on *Chadha*, the Court (speaking through Justice Stevens) invalidated the review board provisions, holding:

> that the Board of Review's power is constitutionally impermissible. If the power is executive, the Constitution does not permit an agent of Congress to exercise it. If the power is legislative, Congress must exercise it in conformity with the bicameralism and presentment requirements of Art. I, § 7. In short, when Congress "[takes] action that ha[s] the purpose and effect of altering the legal rights, duties, and relations of persons . . .

outside the Legislative Branch," it must take that action by the procedures authorized in the Constitution. . . .

One might argue that the provision for a Board of Review is the kind of practical accommodation between the Legislature and the Executive that should be permitted in a "workable government." Admittedly, Congress imposed its will on the regional authority created by the District of Columbia and the Commonwealth of Virginia by means that are unique and that might prove to be innocuous. However, the statutory scheme challenged today provides a blueprint for extensive expansion of the legislative power beyond its constitutionally-confined role. Given the scope of the federal power to dispense benefits to the States in a variety of forms and subject to a host of statutory conditions, Congress could, if this Board of Review were valid, use similar expedients to enable its Members or its agents to retain control, outside the ordinary legislative process, of the activities of state grant recipients charged with executing virtually every aspect of national policy. . . .

Questions and Comments

Some observers have argued that the legislative veto encourages bad legislation, because it encourages Congress to delegate power on a broad scale with inadequate standards.

1. Instead of facing the hard policy questions and developing criteria for dealing with them, the Congress grants broad powers to the executive branch and reserves power to itself to reject the executive branch decisions on an *ad hoc* basis. Thus in *Chadha*, for example, the Congress granted broad authority to the Attorney General to suspend the deportation of otherwise deportable aliens, but reserved the power to reverse any of the Attorney General's decisions. Without that reservation of power, the Congress might have been unwilling to grant to the Attorney General the broad power which he was given.

2. To what extent does *Chadha* proceed from the same conceptual premise about the limits on the constitutional role of Congress which underlay the *Bowsher* and *Buckley* opinions? Under that premise Congress completes its constitutional role when it enacts legislation and must leave the administration and enforcement of that legislation to the executive branch. Are there good reasons behind such a premise?

3. Is the premise that Congress exhausts its formal role with the enactment of legislation based upon the view that such a role definition is best designed to encourage Congress to shape up to its constitutional responsibilities by enacting precisely drawn and well-considered legislation?

4. Do you agree with Justice Stevens that the practical accommodation which Congress had worked out with Virginia and Maryland was unacceptable because it "provides a blueprint for extensive expansion of the legislative power beyond its constitutionally-confined role"? Why was any such encroachment by Congress upon the states a matter for separation-of-powers analysis?

5. Would Congress be encroaching on the autonomy of the states by conditioning, say, a grant of highway funds upon the State's imposition of a minimum drinking age? In his opinion in *Metropolitan Washington Airports Authority*, Justice Stevens distinguished *South Dakota v. Dole*, 483 U.S. 203 (1987) where that issue arose. There the Court had held that such a conditioned grant was lawful even assuming that Congress might lack the power to impose a national minimum drinking age directly.

The Legislative Veto

The Court has had occasion to consider other legislation that avoids the bicameral and presentment clauses. In another such case, the Court invalidated the Line Item Veto Act, which gave the President power to reject particular spending items contained in a law enacted by Congress. *Clinton v. City of New York*, 524 U.S. 417 (1998). The Court deemed the Act to permit the President unilaterally to amend an Act of Congress and thus to conflict with Article I, § 7 of the Constitution.

4.   *Constitutional Issues Involving Inferior Officers*

How does the Court's disposition of *Morrison v. Olson* add to your appreciation of *Bowsher* and the removal cases?

MORRISON v. OLSON
487 U.S. 654 (1988)

[The Ethics in Government Act established a procedure for the appointment of an independent counsel to investigate and to prosecute, if warranted, crimes committed by certain high-ranking federal officials. The Attorney General initially determined whether the appointment of an independent counsel is warranted. If the Attorney General concluded such an appointment was warranted, he requested such an appointment from the Special Division, a panel of three judges appointed by the Chief Judge of the U.S. Court of Appeals for the District of Columbia.

The appellant independent counsel caused a grand jury to serve subpoenas upon respondents, who then moved to quash the subpoenas upon the ground that the independent counsel provisions of the Act were unconstitutional. The District Court upheld the subpoenas and denied the motions to quash. The Court of Appeals for the District of Columbia reversed. The Supreme Court then granted *certiorari*.].

CHIEF JUSTICE REHNQUIST delivered the opinion of the Court.

This case presents us with a challenge to the independent counsel provisions of the Ethics in Government Act of 1978. . . . We hold today that these provisions of the Act do not violate the Appointments Clause of the Constitution, Art. II § 2, cl. 2, or the limitations of Article III, nor do they impermissibly interfere with the President's authority under Article II in violation of the constitutional principle of separation of powers.

The Appointments Clause of Article II reads as follows:

"[T]he President shall nominate, and by and with the Advice and Consent of the Senate, shall appoint Ambassadors, other public Ministers and Consuls, judges of the supreme Court, and all other Officers of the United States, whose Appointments are not herein otherwise provided for, and which shall be established by Law: but the Congress may by Law vest the Appointment of such inferior officers, as they think proper, in the President alone, in the Courts of Law, or in the Heads of Departments." U.S Const., Art. II, § 2, cl. 2.

The parties do not dispute that "[t1he Constitution for purposes of appointment . . . divides all its officers into two classes." . . . As we stated in *Buckley v. Valeo* . . . "[p]rincipal* officers are selected by the President with the advice and consent of the Senate. Inferior officers Congress may allow to be appointed by the President alone, by the heads of departments, or by the judiciary. The initial question is, accordingly, whether appellant is an "inferior" or a "principal" officer. If she is the latter, as the Court of Appeals concluded, then the Act is in violation of the Appointments Clause.

The line between "inferior" and "principal" officers is one that is far from clear, and the Framers provided little guidance into where it should be drawn. . . . We need not attempt here to decide exactly where the line falls between the two types of officers, because in our view appellant clearly falls on the "inferior officer" side of that line. Several factors lead to this conclusion.

First, appellant is subject to removal by a higher Executive Branch official. Although appellant may not be "subordinate" to the Attorney General (and the President) insofar as she possesses a degree of independent discretion to exercise the powers delegated to her under the Act, the fact that she can be removed by the Attorney General indicates that she is to some degree "inferior" in rank and authority. Second, appellant is empowered by the Act to perform only certain, limited duties. An independent counsel's role is restricted primarily to investigation and, if appropriate, prosecution for certain federal crimes. Admittedly, the Act delegates to appellant "full power and independent authority to exercise all investigative and prosecutorial functions and powers of the Department of Justice," § 594(a), but this grant of authority does not include any authority to formulate policy for the Government or the Executive Branch, nor does it give appellant any administrative duties outside of those necessary to operate her office. The Act specifically provides that in policy matters appellant is to comply to the extent possible with the policies of the Department. § 594(f).

Third, appellant's office is limited in jurisdiction. Not only is the Act itself restricted in applicability to certain federal officials suspected of certain serious federal crimes, but an independent counsel can only act within the scope of the jurisdiction that has been granted by the Special Division pursuant to a request by the Attorney General. Finally, appellant's office is limited in tenure. There is concededly no time limit on the appointment of a particular counsel. Nonetheless, the office of independent counsel is "temporary" in the sense that an independent counsel is appointed essentially to accomplish a single task, and when that task is over the office is terminated, either by the counsel herself or by action of the Special Division. Unlike other prosecutors, appellant has no ongoing responsibilities that extend beyond the accomplishment of the mission that she was appointed for and authorized by the Special Division to undertake. In our view, these factors relating to the "ideas of tenure, duration . . . and duties" of the independent counsel . . . are sufficient to establish that appellant is an "inferior" officer in the constitutional sense.

[The Court then considered whether the Appointments Clause contemplated "interbranch appointments" in which an officer of one branch is appointed by officers of another branch. The Court held that the Appointments Clause does not prohibit Congress from authorizing interbranch appointments unless the provisions for appointment had the potential to impair the constitutional functions assigned to one of the branches. Such appointments, the Court referred to as "incongruous" interbranch appointments.] In this case . . . we do not think it impermissible for Congress to vest the power to appoint independent counsels in a specially created federal court. We thus disagree with the Court of Appeals' conclusion that there is an inherent incongruity about a court having the power to appoint prosecutorial officers. We have recognized that courts may appoint private attorneys to act as prosecutor for judicial contempt judgments. . . . In the light of the Act's provision making the judges of the Special Division ineligible to participate in any matters relating to an independent counsel they have appointed, 28 U.S.C. § 49(f), we do not think that appointment of the independent counsels by the court runs afoul of the constitutional limitation on "incongruous" interbranch appointments.

We now turn to consider whether the Act is invalid under the constitutional principle of separation of powers. Two related issues must be addressed: The first is whether the provision of the Act restricting the Attorney General's power to remove the independent counsel to only those instances in which he can show "good cause," taken by itself, impermissibly interferes with the President's exercise of his constitutionally appointed functions. The second is whether, taken as a whole, the Act violates the separation of powers by reducing the President's ability to control the prosecutorial powers wielded by the independent counsel.

A

. . . . [O]ur present considered view is that the determination of whether the Constitution allows Congress to impose a "good cause,"-type restriction on the President's power to remove an official cannot be made to turn on whether or not that official is classified as "purely executive." The analysis contained in our removal cases is designed not to define rigid categories of those officials who may or may not be removed at will by the President, but to ensure that Congress does not interfere with the President's exercise of the "executive power" and his constitutionally appointed duty to "take care that the laws be faithfully executed" under Article II. . . .

Considering for the moment the "good cause" removal provision in isolation from the other parts of the Act at issue in this case, we cannot say that the imposition of a "good cause" standard for removal by itself unduly trammels on executive authority. . . . [T]he independent counsel is an inferior officer under the Appointments Clause, with limited jurisdiction and tenure and lacking policymaking or significant administrative authority. Although the counsel exercises no small amount of discretion and judgment in deciding how to carry out her duties under the Act, we simply do not see how the President's need to control the exercise of that discretion is so central to the functioning of the Executive Branch as to require as a matter of constitutional law that the counsel be terminable at will by the President.

Nor do we think that the "good cause" removal provision at issue here impermissibly burdens the President's power to control or supervise the independent counsel as an executive official, in the execution of her duties under the Act. This is not a case in which the power to remove an executive official has been completely stripped from the president, thus providing no means for the President to ensure the "faithful execution" of the laws. Rather, because the independent counsel may be terminated for "good cause," the Executive, through the Attorney General, retains ample authority to assure that the counsel is competently performing her statutory responsibilities in a manner that comports with the provisions of the Act. Although we need not decide in this case exactly what is encompassed within the term "good cause" under the Act, the legislative history of the removal provision also makes clear that the Attorney General may remove an independent counsel for "misconduct." . . . Here . . . the congressional determination to limit the removal power of the Attorney General was essential, in the view of Congress, to establish the necessary independence of the office. We do not think that this limitation as it presently stands sufficiently deprives the President of control over the independent counsel to interfere impermissibly with his constitutional obligation to ensure the faithful execution of the laws.

B

The final question to be addressed is whether the Act, taken as a whole, violates the principle of separation of powers by unduly interfering with the role of the Executive Branch. . . .

We observe first that this case does not involve an attempt by Congress to increase its own powers at the expense of the Executive Branch. . . . The Act does empower certain members of Congress to request the Attorney General to apply for the appointment of an independent counsel, but the Attorney General has no duty to comply with the request, although he must respond within a certain time limit. § 529(g). Other than that, Congress' role under the Act is limited to receiving reports or other information and oversight of the independent counsel's activities, § 595(a), functions that we have recognized generally as being incidental to the legislative functions of Congress. . . .

Finally, we do not think that the Act "impermissibly undermine[s]" the powers of the Executive Branch [citing *Schor*] or "disrupts the proper balance between the coordinate branches [by] prevent[ing] the Executive Branch from accomplishing its constitutionally assigned functions," *Nixon v. Administrator of General Services, supra*, 433 U.S., at 443. It is undeniable that the Act reduces the amount of control or supervision that the Attorney General and, through him, the President exercises over the investigation and prosecution of a certain class of alleged criminal activity. The Attorney General is not allowed to appoint the individual of his choice; he does not determine the counsel's jurisdiction; and his power to remove a counsel is limited. Nonetheless, the Act does give the Attorney General several means of supervising or controlling the prosecutorial powers that may be wielded by an independent counsel. Most importantly, the Attorney General retains the power to remove the counsel for "good cause," a power that we have already concluded provides the Executive with substantial ability to ensure that the laws are "faithfully executed" by an independent counsel. No independent counsel may be appointed without a specific request by the Attorney General, and the Attorney General's decision not to request appointment if he finds "no reasonable grounds to believe that further investigation is warranted" is committed to his unreviewable discretion. The Act thus gives the Executive a degree of control over the power to initiate an investigation by independent counsel. In addition, the jurisdiction of the independent counsel is defined with reference to the facts submitted by the Attorney General, and once a counsel is appointed, the Act requires that the counsel abide by Justice Department policy unless it is not "possible" to do so. Notwithstanding the fact that the counsel is to some degree "independent" and free from Executive supervision to a greater degree than other federal prosecutors, in our view these features of the Act give the Executive Branch sufficient control over the independent counsel to ensure that the President is able to perform his constitutionally assigned duties.

VI

In sum, we conclude today that it does not violate the Appointments Clause for Congress to vest the appointment of independent counsels in the Special Division; that the powers exercised by the Special Division under the Act do not violate Article III; and that the Act does not violate the separation of powers principle by impermissibly interfering with the functions of the Executive Branch. The decision of the Court of Appeals is therefore

Reversed.

Justice Kennedy took no part in the consideration or decision of this case.

JUSTICE SCALIA, dissenting.

. . . . I cannot avoid commenting . . . about the essence of what the Court has done to our removal jurisprudence today.

Since our 1935 decision in *Humphrey's Executor v. United States*, 295 U.S. 602 — which was considered by many at the time the product of an activist, anti-New Deal court bent on reducing the power of President Franklin Roosevelt — it has been established that the line of permissible restriction upon removal of principal officers lies at the point at which the powers exercised by those officers are no longer purely executive. . . . What *Humphrey's Executor* (and presumably Myers [*Myers v.* United States, 272 U.S. 52 (1927)]) really means, we are now told, is not that there are any "rigid categories of those officials who may or may not be removed at will by the President," but simply that Congress cannot "interfere with the President's exercise of the 'executive power' and his constitutionally appointed duty to 'take care that the laws be faithfully executed' ". . . .

One can hardly grieve for the shoddy treatment given today to *Humphrey's Executor*, which, after all, accorded the same indignity (with much less justification) to Chief Justice Taft's opinion 10 years earlier in *Myers v. United States, supra* — gutting, in six quick pages devoid of textual or historical precedent for the novel principle it set forth, a carefully researched and reasoned 70-page opinion. It is in fact comforting to witness the reality that he who lives by the *ipse dixit* dies by the *ipse dixit*. But one must grieve for the Constitution. *Humphrey's Executor* at least had the decency formally to observe the constitutional principle that the President had to be the repository of all executive power . . . which, as *Myers* carefully explained, necessarily means that he must be able to discharge those who do not perform executive functions according to his liking. As we noted in *Bowsher*, once an officer is appointed " 'it is only the authority that can remove him, and not the authority that appointed him, that he must fear and, in the performance of his functions, obey.' " . . . By contrast, "our present considered view" is simply that any Executive officer's removal can be restricted, so long as the President remains "able to accomplish his constitutional role." . . . There are now no lines. If the removal of a prosecutor, the virtual embodiment of the power to "take care that the laws be faithfully executed," can be restricted, what officer's removal cannot? This is an open invitation for Congress to experiment. What about a special Assistant Secretary of State, with responsibility for one very narrow area of foreign policy, who would not only have to be confirmed by the Senate but could also be removed only pursuant to certain carefully designed restrictions? Could this possibly render the President "[un]able to accomplish his constitutional role"? Or a special Assistant Secretary of Defense for Procurement? The possibilities are endless, and the Court does not understand what the separation of powers, what '[a]mbition . . . counteract[ing] ambition," Federalist No. 51, P. 322 (Madison), is all about, if it does not expect Congress to try them. As far as I can discern from the Court's opinion, it is now open season upon the President's removal power for all executive officers, with not even the superficially principled restriction of *Humphrey's Executor* as cover. The Court essentially says to the President. "Trust us. We will make sure that you are able to accomplish your constitutional role." I think the Constitution gives the President — and the people — more protection than that.

. . . . A government of laws means a government of rules. Today's decision on the basic issue of fragmentation of executive power is ungoverned by rule, and hence ungoverned by law. It extends into the very heart of our most significant constitutional function the "totality of the circumstances" mode of analysis that this Court has in recent years become fond of. Taking all things into account, we conclude that the power taken away from the President here is not really too much. The next time executive power is assigned to someone other than the President we may conclude, taking all things into account, that it is too much. That opinion, like this one, will not be confined by any rule. We will describe, as we have today (though I hope more accurately) the effects of the provision in question, and will authoritatively announce: "The President's need to control the exercise of the [subject officer's] discretion is so central to the functioning of the Executive Branch as to require complete control." This is not analysis; it is ad hoc judgment. . . .

Questions and Comments

What troubles Justice Scalia about the majority's approach? Is Justice Scalia's approach here similar to the one he took in *Freytag? Do you* agree with him that the majority has made separation of powers decisions unpredictable and ungoverned by rules or principles or standards? Do you think that Justice Scalia's approach is too rigid or inflexible?

The seminal work in this area is Peter L. Strauss, *The Place of Agencies in Government: Separation of Powers and the Fourth Branch*, 84 Colum. L. Rev. 573 (1984). *See also* Peter L. Strauss, *Forinal and Functional Approaches to Separation of Powers Questions — A Foolish Inconsistency?* 72 Cornell L. Rev. 488 (1987); Daniel J. Gifford, *The Separation of Powers Doctrine and the Regulatory Agencies After Bowsher v. Synar*, 55 Geo. Wash. L. Rev. 441 (1987).

FREE ENTERPRISE FUND v. PUBLIC COMPANY ACCOUNTING OVERSIGHT BOARD
U.S. Supreme Court
June 28, 2010

CHIEF JUSTICE ROBERTS delivered the opinion of the Court.

* * * *

I

A

After a series of celebrated accounting debacles, Congress enacted the Sarbanes-Oxley Act of 2002 (or Act), 116 Stat. 745. Among other measures, the Act introduced tighter regulation of the accounting industry under a new Public Company Accounting Oversight Board. The Board is composed of five members, appointed to staggered 5-year terms by the Securities and Exchange Commission. It was modeled on private self-regulatory organizations in the securities industry — such as the New York Stock Exchange — that investigate and discipline their own members subject to Commission oversight. Congress created the Board as a private "nonprofit corporation," and Board members and employees are not considered Government "officer[s] or employee[s]" for statutory purposes. 15 U.S.C. §§ 7211(a), (b). The Board can thus recruit its members and employees from the private sector by paying salaries far above the standard Government pay scale. See §§ 7211(f)(4), 7219.

Unlike the self-regulatory organizations, however, the Board is a Government-created, Government-appointed entity, with expansive powers to govern an entire industry. Every accounting firm — both foreign and domestic — that participates in auditing public companies under the securities laws must register with the Board, pay it an annual fee, and comply with its rules and oversight. §§ 7211(a),

7212(a), (f), 7213, 7216(a)(1). The Board is charged with enforcing the Sarbanes-Oxley Act, the securities laws, the Commission's rules, its own rules, and professional accounting standards. §§ 7215(b)(1), (c)(4). To this end, the Board may regulate every detail of an accounting firm's practice, including hiring and professional development, promotion, supervision of audit work, the acceptance of new business and the continuation of old, internal inspection procedures, professional ethics rules, and "such other requirements as the Board may prescribe." § 7213(a)(2)(B).

The Board promulgates auditing and ethics standards, performs routine inspections of all accounting firms, demands documents and testimony, and initiates formal investigations and disciplinary proceedings. §§ 7213–7215 (2006 ed. and Supp. II). The willful violation of any Board rule is treated as a willful violation of the Securities Exchange Act of 1934, 48 Stat. 881, 15 U. S. C. § 78a *et seq.* — a federal crime punishable by up to 20 years' imprisonment or $25 million in fines ($5 million for a natural person). §§ 78ff(a), 7202(b)(1) (2006 ed.). And the Board itself can issue severe sanctions in its disciplinary proceedings, up to and including the permanent revocation of a firm's registration, a permanent ban on a person's associating with any registered firm, and money penalties of $15 million ($750,000 for a natural person). § 7215(c)(4). Despite the provisions specifying that Board members are not Government officials for statutory purposes, the parties agree that the Board is "part of the Government" for constitutional purposes, *Lebron* v. *National Railroad Passenger Corporation*, 513 U. S. 374, 397 (1995), and that its members are " 'Officers of the United States' " who "exercis[e] significant authority pursuant to the laws of the United States," *Buckley* v. *Valeo*, 424 U. S. 1, 125–126 (1976) (*per curiam*) (quoting Art. II, § 2, cl. 2). . . .

The Act places the Board under the SEC's oversight, particularly with respect to the issuance of rules or the imposition of sanctions (both of which are subject to Commission approval and alteration). §§ 7217(b)–(c). But the individual members of the Board — like the officers and directors of the self-regulatory organizations — are substantially insulated from the Commission's control. The Commission cannot remove Board members at will, but only "for good cause shown," "in accordance with" certain procedures. § 7211(e)(6).

Those procedures require a Commission finding, "on the record" and "after notice and opportunity for a hearing," that the Board member

"(A) has willfully violated any provision of th[e] Act, the rules of the Board, or the securities laws;

"(B) has willfully abused the authority of that member; or

"(C) without reasonable justification or excuse, has failed to enforce compliance with any such provision or rule, or any professional standard by any registered public accounting firm or any associated person thereof." § 7217(d)(3).

Removal of a Board member requires a formal Commission order and is subject to judicial review. See 5 U. S. C. §§ 554(a), 556(a), 557(a), (c)(B); 15 U. S. C. § 78y(a)(1). Similar procedures govern the Commission's removal of officers and directors of the private self-regulatory organizations. See § 78s(h)(4). The parties agree that the Commissioners cannot themselves be removed by the President except under the *Humphrey's Executor* standard of "inefficiency, neglect of duty, or malfeasance in office," 295 U. S., at 620 (internal quotation marks omitted) . . . and we decide the case with that understanding.

B

Beckstead and Watts, LLP, is a Nevada accounting firm registered with the Board. The Board inspected the firm, released a report critical of its auditing procedures, and began a formal investigation. Beckstead and Watts and the Free Enterprise Fund, a nonprofit organization of which the firm is a member, then sued the Board and its members, seeking (among other things) a declaratory judgment that the Board is unconstitutional and an injunction preventing the Board from exercising its powers. . . . .

III

We hold that the dual for-cause limitations on the removal of Board members contravene the Constitution's separation of powers.

A

The Constitution provides that "[t]he executive Power shall be vested in a President of the United States of America." Art. II, § 1, cl. 1. As Madison stated on the floor of the First Congress, "if any power whatsoever is in its nature Executive, it is the power of appointing, overseeing, and controlling those who execute the laws." 1 Annals of Cong. 463 (1789).

* * * *

The landmark case of *Myers* v. *United States* reaffirmed the principle that Article II confers on the President "the general administrative control of those executing the laws." 272 U. S., at 164. It is *his* responsibility to take care that the laws be faithfully executed. The buck stops with the President, in Harry Truman's famous phrase. As we explained in *Myers*, the President therefore must have some "power of removing those for whom he can not continue to be responsible." *Id.*, at 117.

Nearly a decade later in *Humphrey's Executor*, this Court held that *Myers* did not prevent Congress from conferring good-cause tenure on the principal officers of certain independent agencies. That case concerned the members of the Federal Trade Commission, who held 7-year terms and could not be removed by the President except for " 'inefficiency, neglect of duty, or malfeasance in office.' " 295 U. S., at 620 (quoting 15 U. S. C. § 41). The Court distinguished *Myers* on the ground that *Myers* concerned "an officer [who] is merely one of the units in the executive department and, hence, inherently subject to the exclusive and illimitable power of removal by the Chief Executive, whose subordinate and aid he is." 295 U. S., at 627. By contrast, the Court characterized the FTC as "quasi-legislative and quasi-judicial" rather than "purely executive," and held that Congress could require it "to act . . . independently of executive control." *Id.*, at 627–629. Because "one who holds his office only during the pleasure of another, cannot be depended upon to maintain an attitude of independence against the latter's will," the Court held that Congress had power to "fix the period during which [the Commissioners] shall continue in office, and to forbid their removal except for cause in the meantime." *Id.*, at 629.

Humphrey's Executor did not address the removal of inferior officers, whose appointment Congress may vest in heads of departments. If Congress does so, it is ordinarily the department head, rather than the President, who enjoys the power of removal. See *Myers, supra*, at 119, 127; *Hennen, supra*, at 259–260. This Court has upheld for-cause limitations on that power as well.

* * * *

We again considered the status of inferior officers in *Morrison*. That case concerned the Ethics in Government Act, which provided for an independent counsel to investigate allegations of crime by high executive officers. The counsel was appointed by a special court, wielded the full powers of a prosecutor, and was removable by the Attorney General only " 'for good cause.' " 487 U. S., at 663 (quoting 28 U. S. C. § 596(a)(1)). We recognized that the independent counsel was undoubtedly an executive officer, rather than " 'quasi-legislative' " or " 'quasi-judicial,' " but we stated as "our present considered view" that Congress had power to impose good-cause restrictions on her removal. 487 U. S., at 689–691. The Court noted that the statute "g[a]ve the Attorney General," an officer directly responsible to the President and "through [whom]" the President could act, "several means of supervising or controlling" the independent counsel — "[m]ost importantly . . . the power to remove the counsel for good cause." *Id.*, at 695–696 (internal quotation marks omitted). Under those circumstances, the Court sustained the statute. *Morrison* did not, however, address the consequences of more than one level of good-cause tenure — leaving the issue, as both the court and dissent below recognized, "a question of first impression" in this Court. 537 F. 3d, at 679; see *id.*, at 698 (dissenting opinion).

B

As explained, we have previously upheld limited restrictions on the President's removal power. In those cases, however, only one level of protected tenure separated the President from an officer exercising executive power. It was the President — or a subordinate he could remove at will — who decided whether the officer's conduct merited removal under the good-cause standard.

The Act before us does something quite different. It not only protects Board members from removal except for good cause, but withdraws from the President any decision on whether that good cause exists. That decision is vested instead in other tenured officers — the Commissioners — none of whom is subject to the President's direct control. The result is a Board that is not accountable to the President, and a President who is not responsible for the Board.

The added layer of tenure protection makes a difference. Without a layer of insulation between the Commission and the Board, the Commission could remove a

Board member at any time, and therefore would be fully responsible for what the Board does. The President could then hold the Commission to account for its supervision of the Board, to the same extent that he may hold the Commission to account for everything else it does.

A second level of tenure protection changes the nature of the President's review. Now the Commission cannot remove a Board member at will. The President therefore cannot hold the Commission fully accountable for the Board's conduct, to the same extent that he may hold the Commission accountable for everything else that it does. The Commissioners are not responsible for the Board's actions. They are only responsible for their own determination of whether the Act's rigorous good-cause standard is met. And even if the President disagrees with their determination, he is powerless to intervene — unless that determination is so unreasonable as to constitute "inefficiency, neglect of duty, or malfeasance in office." *Humphrey's Executor*, 295 U. S., at 620 (internal quotation marks omitted).

This novel structure does not merely add to the Board's independence, but transforms it. Neither the President, nor anyone directly responsible to him, nor even an officer whose conduct he may review only for good cause, has full control over the Board. The President is stripped of the power our precedents have preserved, and his ability to execute the laws — by holding his subordinates accountable for their conduct — is impaired.

That arrangement is contrary to Article II's vesting of the executive power in the President. Without the ability to oversee the Board, or to attribute the Board's failings to those whom he *can* oversee, the President is no longer the judge of the Board's conduct. He is not the one who decides whether Board members are abusing their offices or neglecting their duties. He can neither ensure that the laws are faithfully executed, nor be held responsible for a Board member's breach of faith. This violates the basic principle that the President "cannot delegate ultimate responsibility or the active obligation to supervise that goes with it," because Article II "makes a single President responsible for the actions of the Executive Branch." *Clinton* v. *Jones*, 520 U.S. 681, 712–713 (1997) (BREYER, J., concurring in judgment).

Indeed, if allowed to stand, this dispersion of responsibility could be multiplied. If Congress can shelter the bureaucracy behind two layers of good-cause tenure, why not a third? At oral argument, the Government was unwilling to concede that even *five* layers between the President and the Board would be too many. Tr. of Oral Arg. 47–48. The officers of such an agency — safely encased within a Matryoshka doll of tenure protections — would be immune from Presidential oversight, even as they exercised power in the people's name.

* * * *

The diffusion of power carries with it a diffusion of accountability. The people do not vote for the "Officers of the United States." Art. II, § 2, cl. 2. They instead look to the President to guide the "assistants or deputies . . . subject to his superintendence." The Federalist No. 72, p. 487 (J. Cooke ed. 1961) (A. Hamilton). Without a clear and effective chain of command, the public cannot "determine on whom the blame or the punishment of a pernicious measure, or series of pernicious measures ought really to fall." *Id.*, No. 70, at 476 (same). That is why the Framers sought to ensure that "those who are employed in the execution of the law will be in their proper situation, and the chain of dependence be preserved; the lowest officers, the middle grade, and the highest, will depend, as they ought, on the President, and the President on the community." 1 Annals of Cong., at 499 (J. Madison).

By granting the Board executive power without the Executive's oversight, this Act subverts the President's ability to ensure that the laws are faithfully executed — as well as the public's ability to pass judgment on his efforts. The Act's restrictions are incompatible with the Constitution's separation of powers.

* * * *

The Constitution that makes the President accountable to the people for executing the laws also gives him the power to do so. That power includes, as a general matter, the authority to remove those who assist him in carrying out his duties. Without such power, the President could not be held fully accountable for discharging his own responsibilities; the buck would stop somewhere else. Such diffusion of authority "would greatly diminish the intended and necessary responsibility of the chief magistrate himself." The Federalist No. 70, at 478.

While we have sustained in certain cases limits on the President's removal power, the Act before us imposes a new type of restriction — two levels of protection from removal for those who nonetheless exercise significant executive power. Congress cannot limit the President's authority in this way.

The judgment of the United States Court of Appeals for the District of Columbia Circuit is affirmed in part and reversed in part, and the case is remanded for further proceedings consistent with this opinion.

It is so ordered.

Questions and Comments

1. The Court acknowledges that it had upheld a restriction on the President's removal power in *Humphrey's Executor*. Yet the Court finds that the tenure in office accorded to the members of the Accounting Board are unconstitutional. Can you explain the difference?

2. In *Free Enterprise Fund*, the members of the Accounting Board are appointed by the Securities Exchange Commission. The Commission may remove members of the Accounting Board, but only for cause established in an evidentiary hearing. Similar tenure in office was upheld in *Morrison v. Olson*. But in *Morrison*, the removing agency was the Attorney General, who is removable at will by the President. What the Court objects to in *Free Enterprise Fund* is the second layer of protection against removal. Why should one layer of protection be permissible, but a second layer impermissible? Is not the President's removal power constrained in both situations?

3. Chief Justice Roberts, in discussing *Humphrey's Executor,* said that: "Because 'one who holds his office only during the pleasure of another, cannot be depended upon to maintain an attitude of independence against the latter's will,' the Court held that Congress had power to 'fix the period during which [the Commissioners] shall continue in office, and to forbid their removal except for cause in the meantime." This is an accurate description of *Humphrey's Executor,* but can that description be reconciled with the enforcement responsibilities of the Federal Trade Commission?

4. Is the Court laying the ground for an eventual overruling of *Humphrey's Executor?*

5.   *The Anti-Delegation Doctrine.*

AMERICAN TRUCKING ASSOCIATIONS, INC. v. UNITED STATES ENVIRONMENTAL PROTECTION AGENCY
175 F.3d 1027 (D.C. Cir. 1999)

PER CURIAM:

Introduction

The Clean Air Act requires EPA to promulgate and periodically revise national ambient air quality standards ("NAAQS") for each air pollutant identified by the agency as meeting certain statutory criteria. See Clean Air Act §§ 108-09, 42 U.S.C. §§ 7408–09. For each pollutant, EPA sets a "primary standard" — a concentration level "requisite to protect the public health" with an "adequate margin of safety" — and "secondary standard" — a level "requisite to protect the public welfare." Id. § 7409(b).

In July 1997 EPA issued final rules revising the primary and secondary NAAQS for particulate matter ("PM") and ozone. See National Ambient Air Quality Standards for Particulate Matter, 62 Fed.Reg. 38,652 (1997) ("PM Final Rule"); National Ambient Air Quality Standards for Ozone, 62 Fed.Reg. 38,856 (1997) ("Ozone Final Rule"). Numerous petitions for review have been filed for each rule.

In Part I we find that the construction of the Clean Air Act on which EPA relied in promulgating the NAAQS at issue here effects an unconstitutional delegation of legislative power. See U.S. Const. art. I, § 1 ("All legislative powers herein granted shall be vested in a Congress of the United States."). We remand the cases for EPA to develop a construction of the act that satisfies this constitutional requirement.

* * * *

I. Delegation

Certain "Small Business Petitioners" argue in each case that EPA has construed §§ 108 & 109 of the Clean Air Act so loosely as to render them unconstitutional delegations of legislative power. We agree. Although the factors EPA uses in determining the degree of public health concern associated with different levels of ozone and PM are reasonable, EPA appears to have articulated no "intelligible principle" to channel its application of these factors; nor is one apparent from the statute. The nondelegation doctrine requires such a principle. See J.W. Hampton, Jr. & Co. v. United States, 276 U.S. 394, 409, 48 S.Ct. 348, 72 L.Ed. 624, Treas. Dec. 42706 (1928). Here it is as though Congress commanded EPA to select "big guys," and EPA announced that it would evaluate candidates based on height and weight, but revealed no cut-off point. The announcement, though sensible in what it does say, is fatally incomplete. The reasonable person responds, "How tall? How heavy?"

EPA regards ozone definitely, and PM likely, as non-threshold pollutants, i.e., ones that have some possibility of some adverse health impact (however slight) at any exposure level above zero. See Ozone Final Rule, 62 Fed.Reg. at 38,863/3 ("Nor does it seem possible, in the Administrator's judgment, to identify [an ozone concentration] level at which it can be concluded with confidence that no 'adverse' effects are likely to occur."); National Ambient Air Quality Standards for Ozone and Particulate Matter, 61 Fed.Reg. 65,637, 65,651/3 (1996) (proposed rule) ("[T]he single most important factor influencing the uncertainty associated with the risk estimates is whether or not a threshold concentration exists below which PM-associated health risks are not likely to occur."). For convenience, we refer to both as non-threshold pollutants; the indeterminacy of PM's status does not affect EPA's analysis, or ours.

Thus the only concentration for ozone and PM that is utterly risk-free, in the sense of direct health impacts, is zero. Section 109(b)(1) says that EPA must set each standard at the level "requisite to protect the public health" with an "adequate margin of safety." 42 U.S.C. § 7409(b)(1). These are also the criteria by which EPA must determine whether a revision to existing NAAQS is appropriate. See 42 U.S.C. § 7409(d)(1) (EPA shall "promulgate such new standards as may be appropriate in accordance with . . . [§ 7409(b)]"); see also infra Part II.A. For EPA to pick any non-zero level it must explain the degree of imperfection permitted. The factors that EPA has elected to examine for this purpose in themselves pose no inherent nondelegation problem. But what EPA lacks is any determinate criterion for drawing lines. It has failed to state intelligibly how much is too much.

We begin with the criteria EPA has announced for assessing health effects in setting the NAAQS for non-threshold pollutants.[1] They are "the nature and severity of the health effects involved, the size of the sensitive population(s) at risk, the types of health information available, and the kind and degree of uncertainties that must be addressed." Ozone Final Rule, 62 Fed.Reg. at 38,883/2; EPA, "Review of the National Ambient Air Quality Standards for Particulate Matter: Policy Assessment of Scientific and Technical Information: OAQPS Staff Paper," at II-2 (July 1996) ("PM Staff Paper") (listing same factors). Although these criteria, so stated, are a bit vague, they do focus the inquiry on pollution's effects on public

---

[1] Technically, EPA describes the criteria as used only for setting the "adequate margin of safety." There might be thought to be a separate step in which EPA determines what standard would protect public health without any margin of safety, and that step might be governed by different criteria. But EPA did not use such a process, and it need not. See NRDC v. EPA, 902 F.2d 962, 973 (D.C.Cir.1990). Thus, the criteria mentioned in the text govern the whole standard-setting process.

health. And most of the vagueness in the abstract formulation melts away as EPA applies the criteria: EPA basically considers severity of effect, certainty of effect, and size of population affected. These criteria, long ago approved by the judiciary, see Lead Industries Ass'n v. EPA, 647 F.2d 1130, 1161 (D.C.Cir.1980) ("Lead Industries"), do not themselves speak to the issue of degree.

Read in light of these factors, EPA's explanations for its decisions amount to assertions that a less stringent standard would allow the relevant pollutant to inflict a greater quantum of harm on public health, and that a more stringent standard would result in less harm. Such arguments only support the intuitive proposition that more pollution will not benefit public health, not that keeping pollution at or below any particular level is "requisite" or not requisite to "protect the public health" with an "adequate margin of safety," the formula set out by § 109(b)(1).

Consider EPA's defense of the 0.08 ppm level of the ozone NAAQS. EPA explains that its choice is superior to retaining the existing level, 0.09 ppm, because more people are exposed to more serious effects at 0.09 than at 0.08. See Ozone Final Rule, 62 Fed.Reg. at 38,868/1. In defending the decision not to go down to 0.07, EPA never contradicts the intuitive proposition, confirmed by data in its Staff Paper, that reducing the standard to that level would bring about comparable changes. See EPA, "Review of National Ambient Air Quality Standards for Ozone: Assessment of Scientific and Technical Information: OAQPS Staff Paper," at 156 (June 1996) ("Ozone Staff Paper"). Instead, it gives three other reasons. The principal substantive one is based on the criteria just discussed:

> The most certain O_3-related effects, while judged to be adverse, are transient and reversible (particularly at O_3 exposures below 0.08 ppm), and the more serious effects with greater immediate and potential long-term impacts on health are less certain, both as to the percentage of individuals exposed to various concentrations who are likely to experience such effects and as to the long-term medical significance of these effects.

Ozone Final Rule, 62 Fed.Reg. at 38,868/2.

In other words, effects are less certain and less severe at lower levels of exposure. This seems to be nothing more than a statement that lower exposure levels are associated with lower risk to public health. The dissent argues that in setting the standard at 0.08, EPA relied on evidence that health effects occurring below that level are "transient and reversible," Dissent at 1059, evidently assuming that those at higher levels are not. But the EPA language quoted above does not make the categorical distinction the dissent says it does, and it is far from apparent that any health effects existing above the level are permanent or irreversible.

In addition to the assertion quoted above, EPA cited the consensus of the Clean Air Scientific Advisory Committee ("CASAC") that the standard should not be set below 0.08. That body gave no specific reasons for its recommendations, so the appeal to its authority, also made in defense of other standards in the PM Final Rule, see PM Final Rule, 62 Fed.Reg. at 38,677/2 (daily fine PM standard); id. at 38,678/3 (annual coarse PM standard); id. at 38,679/1 (daily coarse PM standard), adds no enlightenment. The dissent stresses the undisputed eminence of CASAC's members, Dissent at 1059, but the question whether EPA acted pursuant to lawfully delegated authority is not a scientific one. Nothing in what CASAC says helps us discern an intelligible principle derived by EPA from the Clean Air Act.

Finally, EPA argued that a 0.07 standard would be "closer to peak background levels that infrequently occur in some areas due to nonanthropogenic sources of O_3 precursors, and thus more likely to be inappropriately targeted in some areas on such sources." Ozone Final Rule, 62 Fed.Reg. at 38,868/3. But a 0.08 level, of course, is also closer to these peak levels than 0.09. The dissent notes that a single background observation fell between 0.07 and 0.08, and says that EPA's decision "ensured that if a region surpasses the ozone standard, it will do so because of controllable human activity, not uncontrollable natural levels of ozone." Dissent at 1060. EPA's language, coupled with the data on background ozone levels, may add up to a backhanded way of saying that, given the national character of the NAAQS, it is inappropriate to set a standard below a level that can be achieved throughout the country without action affirmatively extracting chemicals from nature. That may well be a sound reading of the statute, but EPA has not explicitly adopted it.

EPA frequently defends a decision not to set a standard at a lower level on the basis that there is greater uncertainty that health effects exist at lower levels than the level of the standard. See Ozone Final Rule, 62 Fed.Reg. at 38,868/2; PM Final Rule, 62 Fed.Reg. at 38,676/3 (annual fine PM standard); id. at 38,677/2 (daily fine PM standard). And such an argument is likely implicit in its defense of the coarse PM standards. See PM Final Rule, 62 Fed.Reg. at 38,678/3-79/1. The dissent's defense of the fine particulate matter standard cites exactly such a justification. See Dissent at 1060 ("The Agency explained that 'there is generally greatest statistical confidence in observed associations . . . for levels at and above the mean concentration [in certain studies]' ") (emphasis added in dissent). But the increasing-uncertainty argument is helpful only if some principle reveals how much uncertainty is too much. None does.

The arguments EPA offers here show only that EPA is applying the stated factors and that larger public health harms (including increased probability of such harms) are, as expected, associated with higher pollutant concentrations. The principle EPA invokes for each increment in stringency (such as for adopting the annual coarse particulate matter standard that it chose here) — that it is "possible, but not certain" that health effects exist at that level, see PM Final Rule, 62 Fed.Reg. at 38,678/3[2] — could as easily, for any nonthreshold pollutant, justify a standard of zero. The same indeterminacy prevails in EPA's decisions not to pick a still more stringent level. For example, EPA's reasons for not lowering the ozone standard from 0.08 to 0.07 ppm — that "the more serious effects . . . are less certain" at the lower levels and that the lower levels are "closer to peak background levels," see Ozone Final Rule, 62 Fed.Reg. at 38,868/2 — could also be employed to justify a refusal to reduce levels below those associated with London's "Killer Fog"

---

[2] EPA did cite qualitative evidence for further support for its annual standard, and argued that the evidence "does not provide evidence of effects below the range of 40–50 μ g/m^3," the standard level. PM Final Rule, 62 Fed.Reg. at 38,678/3. The referenced document, however, bears no indication that the qualitative evidence demonstrates effects *at* the level of the standard, either. See EPA, "Air Quality Criteria for Particulate Matter," at 13–79 (April 1996).

of 1952. In that calamity, very high PM levels (up to 2,500 μ g/m^3) are believed to have led to 4,000 excess deaths in a week.[3] Thus, the agency rightly recognizes that the question is one of degree, but offers no intelligible principle by which to identify a stopping point.

The latitude EPA claims here seems even broader than that OSHA asserted in *International Union, UAW v. OSHA* (" *Lockout/Tagout I*"), 938 F.2d 1310, 1317 (D.C.Cir.1991), which was to set a standard that would reduce a substantial risk and that was not infeasible. In that case, OSHA thought itself free either to "do nothing at all" or to "require precautions that take the industry to the brink of ruin," with "all positions in between . . . evidently equally valid." *Id*. Here, EPA's freedom of movement between the poles is equally unconstrained, but the poles are even farther apart — the maximum stringency would send industry not just to the brink of ruin but hurtling over it, while the minimum stringency may be close to doing nothing at all.

In *Lockout/Tagout I* certain special conditions that have justified an exceptionally relaxed application of the nondelegation doctrine were absent, *id*. at 1317-18, and they are equally absent here. The standards in question affect the whole economy, requiring a "more precise" delegation than would otherwise be the case, see *A.L.A. Schechter Poultry Corp. v. United States*, 295 U.S. 495, 553, 55 S.Ct. 837, 79 L.Ed. 1570 (1935). No "special theories" justifying vague delegation such as the war powers of the President or the sovereign attributes of the delegatee have been or could be asserted. Nor is there some inherent characteristic of the field that bars development of a far more determinate basis for decision. (This is not to deny that there are difficulties; we consider some below.)

EPA cites prior decisions of this Court holding that when there is uncertainty about the health effects of concentrations of a particular pollutant within a particular range, EPA may use its discretion to make the "policy judgment" to set the standards at one point within the relevant range rather than another. *NRDC v. EPA*, 902 F.2d 962, 969 (D.C.Cir.1990); *American Petroleum Inst. v. Costle*, 665 F.2d 1176, 1185 (D.C.Cir.1981); *Lead Industries*, 647 F.2d at 1161 (D.C.Cir.1980). We agree. But none of those panels addressed the claim of undue delegation that we face here, and accordingly had no occasion to ask EPA for coherence (for a "principle," to use the classic term) in making its "policy judgment." The latter phrase is not, after all, a self-sufficient justification for every refusal to define limits.

It was suggested at oral argument that EPA's vision of its discretion in application of § 109(b)(1) is no broader than that asserted by OSHA after a remand by this court and upheld by this court in *International Union, UAW v. OSHA* (" *Lockout/Tagout II*"), 37 F.3d 665 (D.C.Cir.1994). But there, in fact, OSHA allowed itself to set only standards falling somewhere between maximum feasible stringency and some "moderate" departure from that level. Id. at 669. As our prior discussion should have indicated, here EPA's formulation of its policy judgment leaves it free to pick any point between zero and a hair below the concentrations yielding London's Killer Fog.

---

[3] See W.P.D. Logan, "Mortality in the London Fog Incident, 1952," The Lancet, Feb. 4, 1953, at 336–38.

The dissent argues that a nondelegation challenge similar to this one was rejected in *South Terminal Corp. v. EPA*, 504 F.2d 646 (1st Cir.1974), and cites that case's language that "the rationality of the means can be tested against goals capable of fairly precise definition in the language of science," *id.* at 677. See Dissent at 1058. But the action challenged in *South Terminal* was EPA's adoption of a plan for ending or preventing violations in Boston of already-established NAAQS, not its promulgation of the NAAQS themselves. Thus, it seems likely that the "means" were the plan's provisions — e.g., a prohibition on most new parking in the city, see 504 F.2d at 671, and the "fairly precise[ly] defin[ed]" goals were the NAAQS themselves.

Where (as here) statutory language and an existing agency interpretation involve an unconstitutional delegation of power, but an interpretation without the constitutional weakness is or may be available, our response is not to strike down the statute but to give the agency an opportunity to extract a determinate standard on its own. *Lockout/Tagout I*, 938 F.2d at 1313. Doing so serves at least two of three basic rationales for the nondelegation doctrine. If the agency develops determinate, binding standards for itself, it is less likely to exercise the delegated authority arbitrarily. See *Amalgamated Meat Cutters v. Connally*, 337 F.Supp. 737, 758–59 (D.D.C.1971) (Leventhal, J., for three-judge panel). And such standards enhance the likelihood that meaningful judicial review will prove feasible. See id. at 759. A remand of this sort of course does not serve the third key function of non-delegation doctrine, to "ensure[ ] to the extent consistent with orderly governmental administration that important choices of social policy are made by Congress, the branch of our Government most responsive to the popular will," *Industrial Union Dep't, AFL-CIO v. American Petroleum Inst.*, 448 U.S. 607, 685, 100 S.Ct. 2844, 65 L.Ed.2d 1010 (1980) ("*Benzene*") (Rehnquist, J., concurring). The agency will make the fundamental policy choices. But the remand does ensure that the courts not hold unconstitutional a statute that an agency, with the application of its special expertise, could salvage. In any event, we do not read current Supreme Court cases as applying the strong form of the nondelegation doctrine voiced in Justice Rehnquist's concurrence. See *Mistretta v. United States*, 488 U.S. 361, 377–79, 109 S.Ct. 647, 102 L.Ed.2d 714 (1989).

What sorts of "intelligible principles" might EPA adopt? Cost-benefit analysis, mentioned as a possibility in *Lockout/Tagout I*, 938 F.2d at 1319- 21, is not available under decisions of this court. Our cases read § 109(b)(1) as barring EPA from considering any factor other than "health effects relating to pollutants in the air." *NRDC*, 902 F.2d at 973; see also *Lead Industries*, 647 F.2d at 1148; *American Lung Ass'n v. EPA*, 134 F.3d 388, 389 (D.C.Cir.1998); *American Petroleum Inst.*, 665 F.2d at 1185 (echoing the same themes).

In theory, EPA could make its criterion the eradication of any hint of direct health risk. This approach is certainly determinate enough, but it appears that it would require the agency to set the permissible levels of both pollutants here at zero. No party here appears to advocate this solution, and EPA appears to show no inclination to adopt it.[4]

---

[4] A zero-risk policy might seem to imply de-industrialization, but in fact even that seems inadequate

EPA's past behavior suggests some readiness to adopt standards that leave non-zero residual risk. For example, it has employed commonly used clinical criteria to determine what qualifies as an adverse health effect. See Ozone Staff Paper at 59-60 (using American Thoracic Society standards to determine threshold for "adverse health effect" from ozone). On the issue of likelihood, for some purposes it might be appropriate to use standards drawn from other areas of the law, such as the familiar "more probable than not" criterion.

Of course a one-size-fits-all criterion of probability would make little sense. There is no reason why the same probability should govern assessments of a risk of thousands of deaths as against risks of a handful of people suffering momentary shortness of breath. More generally, all the relevant variables seem to range continuously from high to low: the possible effects of pollutants vary from death to trivialities, and the size of the affected population, the probability of an effect, and the associated uncertainty range from "large" numbers of persons with point estimates of high probability, to small numbers and vague ranges of probability. This does not seem insurmountable. Everyday life compels us all to make decisions balancing remote but severe harms against a probability distribution of benefits; people decide whether to proceed with an operation that carries a 1/1000 possibility of death, and (simplifying) a 90% chance of cure and a 10% chance of no effect, and a certainty of some short-term pain and nuisance. To be sure, all that requires is a go/no-go decision, while a serious effort at coherence under § 109(b)(1) would need to be more comprehensive. For example, a range of ailments short of death might need to be assigned weights. Nonetheless, an agency wielding the power over American life possessed by EPA should be capable of developing the rough equivalent of a generic unit of harm that takes into account population affected, severity and probability. Possible building blocks for such a principled structure might be found in the approach Oregon used in devising its health plan for the poor. In determining what conditions would be eligible for treatment under its version of Medicaid, Oregon ranked treatments by the amount of improvement in "Quality-Adjusted Life Years" provided by each treatment, divided by the cost of the treatment.[5] Here, of course, EPA may not consider cost, and indeed may well find

---

to the task (and even if the calculus is confined to direct risks from pollutants, as opposed to risks from the concomitant poverty). First, PM (at least) results from almost all combustion, so only total prohibition of fire or universal application of some heretofore unknown control technology would reduce manmade emissions to zero. See PM Staff Paper at IV-1. Second, the combustion associated with pastoral life appears to be rather deadly. See World Bank, World Development Report 1992: Development and the Environment 52 (1992) (noting that "biomass" fuels (i.e., wood, straw, or dung) are often the only fuels that "poor households, mostly in rural areas" can obtain or afford, and that indoor smoke from biomass burning "contributes to acute respiratory infections that cause an estimated 4 million deaths annually among infants and children.").

[5] The "quality" of various health states was determined by poll, and medical professionals determined the probabilities and durations of various health states with and without the treatment in question. Oregon was twice forced to revise its system because the United States Department of Health & Human Services determined that the original proposal and a revision violated the Americans with Disabilities Act, 42 U.S.C. §§ 12101-12213. The reason given for this determination was that both versions undervalued the lives of persons with disabilities: The original plan measured quality of life according to the attitudes of the general population rather than the attitudes of persons with disabilities. See HHS, "Analysis Under the Americans with Disabilities Act ('ADA') of the Oregon Reform Demonstration" (Aug. 3, 1992), reprinted in 9 Issues in L. & Med. 397, 410, 410 (1994). The revised plan ranked

a completely different method for securing reasonable coherence. Alternatively, if EPA concludes that there is no principle available, it can so report to the Congress, along with such rationales as it has for the levels it chose, and seek legislation ratifying its choice.

We have discussed only the primary standards. Because the secondary standards are at least in part based on those, see Ozone Final Rule, 62 Fed.Reg. at 38,875/3-76/1; PM Final Rule, 62 Fed.Reg. at 38,680/3, we also remand the cases to the agency with regard to the secondary standards as well, for further consideration in light of this opinion.

WHITMAN v. AMERICAN TRUCKING ASSOCIATIONS, INC.
531 U.S. 457 (2001)

JUSTICE SCALIA delivered the opinion of the Court.

These cases present the following questions: (1) Whether § 109(b)(1) of the Clean Air Act (CAA) delegates legislative power to the Administrator of the Environmental Protection Agency (EPA). (2) Whether the Administrator may consider the costs of implementation in setting national ambient air quality standards (NAAQS) under § 109(b)(1). (3) Whether the Court of Appeals had jurisdiction to review the EPA's interpretation of Part D of Title I of the CAA, 42 U.S.C. §§ 7501-7515, with respect to implementing the revised ozone NAAQS. (4) If so, whether the EPA's interpretation of that part was permissible.

I

Section 109(a) of the CAA, as added, 84 Stat. 1679, and amended, 42 U.S.C. § 7409(a), requires the Administrator of the EPA to promulgate NAAQS for each air pollutant for which "air quality criteria" have been issued under § 108, 42 U.S.C. § 7408. Once a NAAQS has been promulgated, the Administrator must review the standard (and the criteria on which it is based) "at five-year intervals"

---

treatments leaving the patient in a "symptomatic" state lower than those leaving the patient asymptomatic, and certain disabling conditions were considered "symptoms." See Letter from Timothy B. Flanagan, Assistant Attorney General, to Susan K. Zagame, Acting General Counsel, HHS (Jan. 19, 1993), reprinted in 9 Issues in L. & Med. 397, 418, 421 (1994). The Department's determination was extensively criticized when issued. See Maxwell J. Mehlman et al., "When Do Health Care Decisions Discriminate Against Persons with Disabilities?" 22 J. Of Health Politics, Policy & L. 1385, 1390 (1997) (HHS's "decision provoked a storm of disbelief and denunciation"). We take no position on whether HHS's view was correct, or if the underlying norm also governs EPA's decisions under § 109(b)(1). An affirmative answer, however, would not seem to preclude use of some of Oregon's approach. The first step would be giving appropriate weight to the views of persons with disabilities. The second might be measuring the seriousness of a pollution-induced health effect by the absolute level of well-being that the effect brings about, not by the decrease in level that the effect causes. In other words, if the maximum well-being level is 100 and the average asthmatic whose asthma constitutes a disability has a well-being of 80 in the absence of air pollution (according to a measure that appropriately considers asthmatics' own assessments of their condition), then a response to air pollution that reduces the asthmatics' well-being to 70 could be counted as an effect of magnitude 30 (the difference from full health), rather than 10 (the difference from the level without the pollution). That approach would ensure that effects on persons with disabilities were not underestimated, even in the broad sense of that term apparently adopted by HHS.

and make "such revisions . . . as may be appropriate." CAA § 109(d)(1), 42 U.S.C. § 7409(d)(1). These cases arose when, on July 18, 1997, the Administrator revised the NAAQS for particulate matter (PM) and ozone. . . . American Trucking Associations, Inc . . . challenged the new standards in the Court of Appeals for the District of Columbia Circuit. . . .

The District of Columbia Circuit accepted some of the challenges and rejected others. It agreed with the . . . respondents . . . that § 109(b)(1) delegated legislative power to the Administrator in contravention of the United States Constitution, Art. I, § 1, because it found that the EPA had interpreted the statute to provide no "intelligible principle" to guide the agency's exercise of authority. *American Trucking Assns., Inc. v. EPA*, 175 F.3d 1027, 1034 (C.A.D.C.1999). The court thought, however, that the EPA could perhaps avoid the unconstitutional delegation by adopting a restrictive construction of § 109(b)(1), so instead of declaring the section unconstitutional the court remanded the NAAQS to the agency. . . . (On this delegation point, Judge Tatel dissented, finding the statute constitutional as written. *Id.*, at 1057.) On the second issue that the Court of Appeals addressed, it unanimously rejected respondents' argument that the court should depart from the rule of *Lead Industries Assn., Inc. v. EPA*, 647 F.2d 1130, 1148 (C.A.D.C.1980), that the EPA may not consider the cost of implementing a NAAQS in setting the initial standard. . . .

The Administrator and the EPA petitioned this Court for review. . . . Respondents conditionally cross-petitioned for review. . . . We granted certiorari on both petitions.

II

In *Lead Industries Assn., Inc. v. EPA*, supra, at 1148, the District of Columbia Circuit held that "economic considerations [may] play no part in the promulgation of ambient air quality standards under Section 109" of the CAA. In the present cases, the court adhered to that holding, 175 F.3d, at 1040–1041, as it had done on many other occasions. . . . Respondents argue that these decisions are incorrect. We disagree . . .

III

Section 109(b)(1) of the CAA instructs the EPA to set "ambient air quality standards the attainment and maintenance of which in the judgment of the Administrator, based on [the] criteria [documents of § 108] and allowing an adequate margin of safety, are requisite to protect the public health." 42 U.S.C. § 7409(b)(1). The Court of Appeals held that this section as interpreted by the Administrator did not provide an "intelligible principle" to guide the EPA's exercise of authority in setting NAAQS. "[The] EPA," it said, "lack[ed] any determinate criteria for drawing lines. It has failed to state intelligibly how much is too much." 175 F.3d, at 1034. The court hence found that the EPA's interpretation (but not the statute itself) violated the nondelegation doctrine. . . . We disagree.

In a delegation challenge, the constitutional question is whether the statute has delegated legislative power to the agency. Article I, § 1, of the Constitution vests

"[a]ll legislative Powers herein granted . . . in a Congress of the United States."
This text permits no delegation of those powers, *Loving v. United States*, 517 U.S.
748 (1996); see *id.*, at 776–777 (SCALIA, J., concurring in part and concurring in
judgment), and so we repeatedly have said that when Congress confers
decisionmaking authority upon agencies *Congress* must "lay down by legislative act
an intelligible principle to which the person or body authorized to [act] is directed
to conform." *J.W. Hampton, Jr., & Co. v. United States*, 276 U.S. 394, 409, Treas.
Dec. 42706 (1928). We have never suggested that an agency can cure an unlawful
delegation of legislative power by adopting in its discretion a limiting construction
of the statute. Both *Fahey v. Mallonee*, 332 U.S. 245, 252–253 (1947), and *Lichter v.
United States*, 334 U.S. 742 (1948), mention agency regulations in the course of
their nondelegation discussions, but *Lichter* did so because a subsequent Congress
had incorporated the regulations into a revised version of the statute, . . . and
Fahey because the customary practices in the area, implicitly incorporated into the
statute, were reflected in the regulations. . . . The idea that an agency can cure
an unconstitutionally standardless delegation of power by declining to exercise
some of that power seems to us internally contradictory. The very choice of which
portion of the power to exercise — that is to say, the prescription of the standard
that Congress had omitted — would *itself* be an exercise of the forbidden
legislative authority. Whether the statute delegates legislative power is a question
for the courts, and an agency's voluntary self-denial has no bearing upon the
answer.

We agree with the Solicitor General that the text of § 109(b)(1) of the CAA at a
minimum requires that "[f]or a discrete set of pollutants and based on published
air quality criteria that reflect the latest scientific knowledge, [the] EPA must
establish uniform national standards at a level that is requisite to protect public
health from the adverse effects of the pollutant in the ambient air." . . . Requisite,
in turn, "mean[s] sufficient, but not more than necessary." . . . These limits on the
EPA's discretion are strikingly similar to the ones we approved in *Touby v. United
States*, 500 U.S. 160 (1991), which permitted the Attorney General to designate a
drug as a controlled substance for purposes of criminal drug enforcement if doing
so was " 'necessary to avoid an imminent hazard to the public safety.' " . . . They
also resemble the Occupational Safety and Health Act provision requiring the
agency to " 'set the standard which most adequately assures, to the extent feasible,
on the basis of the best available evidence, that no employee will suffer any
impairment of health' " — which the Court upheld in *Industrial Union Dept.,
AFL-CIO v. American Petroleum Institute*, 448 U.S. 607, 646 (1980), and which
even then — JUSTICE REHNQUIST, who alone in that case thought the statute violated
the nondelegation doctrine, see *id.*, at 671 (opinion concurring in judgment), would
have upheld if, like the statute here, it did not permit economic costs to be
considered. See *American Textile Mfrs. Institute, Inc. v. Donovan*, 452 U.S. 490,
545 (1981) (REHNQUIST, J., dissenting).

The scope of discretion § 109(b)(1) allows is in fact well within the outer limits of
our nondelegation precedents. In the history of the Court we have found the
requisite "intelligible principle" lacking in only two statutes, one of which provided
literally no guidance for the exercise of discretion, and the other of which conferred
authority to regulate the entire economy on the basis of no more precise a standard

than stimulating the economy by assuring "fair competition." See *Panama Refining Co. v. Ryan*, 293 U.S. 388 (1935); *A.L.A. Schechter Poultry Corp. v. United States*, 295 U.S. 495 (1935). We have, on the other hand, upheld the validity of § 11(b)(2) of the Public Utility Holding Company Act of 1935, 49 Stat. 821, which gave the Securities and Exchange Commission authority to modify the structure of holding company systems so as to ensure that they are not "unduly or unnecessarily complicate[d]" and do not "unfairly or inequitably distribute voting power among security holders." *American Power & Light Co. v. SEC*, 329 U.S. 90 (1946). We have approved the wartime conferral of agency power to fix the prices of commodities at a level that " 'will be generally fair and equitable and will effectuate the [in some respects conflicting] purposes of th[e] Act.' " *Yakus v. United States*, 321 U.S. 414, 420, 423–426 (1944). And we have found an "intelligible principle" in various statutes authorizing regulation in the "public interest." See, *e.g.*, *National Broadcasting Co. v. United States*, 319 U.S. 190, 225–226 (1943) (FCC's power to regulate airwaves); *New York Central Securities Corp. v. United States*, 287 U.S. 12, 24–25 (1932) (ICC's power to approve railroad consolidations). In short, we have "almost never felt qualified to second-guess Congress regarding the permissible degree of policy judgment that can be left to those executing or applying the law." *Mistretta v. United States*, 488 U.S. 361, 416 (1989) (SCALIA, J., dissenting); see id., at 373 (majority opinion).

It is true enough that the degree of agency discretion that is acceptable varies according to the scope of the power congressionally conferred. See *Loving v. United States, supra,* at 772–773; *United States v. Mazurie*, 419 U.S. 544, 556–557 (1975). While Congress need not provide any direction to the EPA regarding the manner in which it is to define "country elevators," which are to be exempt from new-stationary-source regulations governing grain elevators, see § 7411(i), it must provide substantial guidance on setting air standards that affect the entire national economy. But even in sweeping regulatory schemes we have never demanded, as the Court of Appeals did here, that statutes provide a "determinate criterion" for saying "how much [of the regulated harm] is too much." 175 F.3d, at 1034. In *Touby*, for example, we did not require the statute to decree how "imminent" was too imminent, or how "necessary" was necessary enough, or even — most relevant here — how "hazardous" was too hazardous. 500 U.S., at 165–167. Similarly, the statute at issue in *Lichter* authorized agencies to recoup "excess profits" paid under wartime Government contracts, yet we did not insist that Congress specify how much profit was too much. 334 U.S., at 783–786. It is therefore not conclusive for delegation purposes that, as respondents argue, ozone and particulate matter are "nonthreshold" pollutants that inflict a continuum of adverse health effects at any airborne concentration greater than zero, and hence require the EPA to make judgments of degree. "[A] certain degree of discretion, and thus of lawmaking, inheres in most executive or judicial action." *Mistretta v. United States, supra,* at 417 (SCALIA, J., dissenting) (emphasis deleted); see 488 U.S., at 378–379 (majority opinion). Section 109(b)(1) of the CAA, which to repeat we interpret as requiring the EPA to set air quality standards at the level that is "requisite" — that is, not lower or higher than is necessary — to protect the public health with an adequate margin of safety, fits comfortably within the scope of discretion permitted by our precedent.

We therefore reverse the judgment of the Court of Appeals remanding for reinterpretation that would avoid a supposed delegation of legislative power. It will remain for the Court of Appeals — on the remand that we direct for other reasons — to dispose of any other preserved challenge to the NAAQS under the judicial-review provisions contained in 42 U.S.C. § 7607(d)(9).

* * * *

To summarize our holdings in these unusually complex cases: (1) The EPA may not consider implementation costs in setting primary and secondary NAAQS under § 109(b) of the CAA. (2) Section 109(b)(1) does not delegate legislative power to the EPA in contravention of Art. I, § 1, of the Constitution. . . .

The judgment of the Court of Appeals is affirmed in part and reversed in part, and the cases are remanded for proceedings consistent with this opinion.

It is so ordered.

JUSTICE THOMAS, concurring.

I agree with the majority that § 109's directive to the agency is no less an "intelligible principle" than a host of other directives that we have approved. . . . I also agree that the Court of Appeals' remand to the agency to make its own corrective interpretation does not accord with our understanding of the delegation issue. . . . I write separately, however, to express my concern that there may nevertheless be a genuine constitutional problem with § 109, a problem which the parties did not address.

The parties to this case who briefed the constitutional issue wrangled over constitutional doctrine with barely a nod to the text of the Constitution. Although this Court since 1928 has treated the "intelligible principle" requirement as the only constitutional limit on congressional grants of power to administrative agencies, see *J.W. Hampton, Jr., & Co. v. United States*, 276 U.S. 394, 409, Treas. Dec. 42706 (1928), the Constitution does not speak of "intelligible principles." Rather, it speaks in much simpler terms: " *All* legislative Powers herein granted shall be vested in a Congress." U.S. Const., Art. 1, § 1 (emphasis added). I am not convinced that the intelligible principle doctrine serves to prevent all cessions of legislative power. I believe that there are cases in which the principle is intelligible and yet the significance of the delegated decision is simply too great for the decision to be called anything other than "legislative."

As it is, none of the parties to this case has examined the text of the Constitution or asked us to reconsider our precedents on cessions of legislative power. On a future day, however, I would be willing to address the question whether our delegation jurisprudence has strayed too far from our Founders' understanding of separation of powers.

JUSTICE STEVENS, with whom JUSTICE SOUTER joins, concurring in part and concurring in the judgment.

Section 109(b)(1) delegates to the Administrator of the Environmental Protection Agency (EPA) the authority to promulgate national ambient air quality standards (NAAQS). In Part III of its opinion, . . . the Court convincingly explains why the Court of Appeals erred when it concluded that § 109 effected "an unconstitutional delegation of legislative power." *American Trucking Assns., Inc. v. EPA*, 175 F.3d 1027, 1033 (C.A.D.C.1999) (per curiam). I wholeheartedly endorse the Court's result and endorse its explanation of its reasons, albeit with the following caveat.

The Court has two choices. We could choose to articulate our ultimate disposition of this issue by frankly acknowledging that the power delegated to the EPA is "legislative" but nevertheless conclude that the delegation is constitutional because adequately limited by the terms of the authorizing statute. Alternatively, we could pretend, as the Court does, that the authority delegated to the EPA is somehow not "legislative power." Despite the fact that there is language in our opinions that supports the Court's articulation of our holding, I am persuaded that it would be both wiser and more faithful to what we have actually done in delegation cases to admit that agency rulemaking authority is "legislative power."

* * * *

My view is not only more faithful to normal English usage, but is also fully consistent with the text of the Constitution. In Article I, the Framers vested "All legislative Powers" in the Congress, Art. I., § 1, just as in Article II they vested the "executive Power" in the President, Art. II, § 1. Those provisions do not purport to limit the authority of either recipient of power to delegate authority to others. . . .

It seems clear that an executive agency's exercise of rulemaking authority pursuant to a valid delegation from Congress is "legislative." As long as the delegation provides a sufficiently intelligible principle, there is nothing inherently unconstitutional about it. Accordingly, while I join Parts I, II, and IV of the Court's opinion, and agree with almost everything said in Part III, I would hold that when Congress enacted § 109, it effected a constitutional delegation of legislative power to the EPA.

JUSTICE BREYER, concurring in part and concurring in the judgment.

I join Parts I, III, and IV of the Court's opinion. I also agree with the Court's determination in Part II that the Clean Air Act does not permit the Environmental Protection Agency to consider the economic costs of implementation when setting national ambient air quality standards under § 109(b)(1) of the Act. But I would not rest this conclusion solely upon § 109's language or upon a presumption, such as the Court's presumption that any authority the Act grants the EPA to consider costs must flow from a "textual commitment" that is "clear." *Ante*, at 909–910. In order better to achieve regulatory goals — for example, to allocate resources so that they save more lives or produce a cleaner environment — regulators must often take account of all of a proposed regulation's adverse effects, at least where those adverse effects clearly threaten serious and disproportionate public harm. Hence, I believe that, other things being equal, we should read silences or ambiguities in the language of regulatory statutes as permitting, not forbidding, this type of rational regulation.

In this case, however, other things are not equal. Here, legislative history, along with the statute's structure, indicates that § 109's language reflects a congressional decision not to delegate to the agency the legal authority to consider economic costs of compliance.

* * * *

To read this legislative history as meaning what it says does not impute to Congress an irrational intent. Technology-forcing hopes can prove realistic. . . .

Moreover, the Act does not, on this reading, wholly ignore cost and feasibility. As the majority points out . . . , the Act allows regulators to take those concerns into account when they determine how to implement ambient air quality standards. Thus, States may consider economic costs when they select the particular control devices used to meet the standards, and industries experiencing difficulty in reducing their emissions can seek an exemption or variance from the state implementation plan. See *Union Elec.*, *supra*, at 266 ("[T]he most important forum for consideration of claims of economic and technological infeasibility is before the state agency formulating the implementation plan").

The Act also permits the EPA, within certain limits, to consider costs when it sets deadlines by which areas must attain the ambient air quality standards. 42 U.S.C. § 7502(a)(2)(A) (providing that "the Administrator may extend the attainment date . . . for a period no greater than 10 years from the date of designation as nonattainment, considering the severity of nonattainment and the availability and feasibility of pollution control measures"); § 7502(a)(2)(C) (permitting the Administrator to grant up to two additional 1-year extensions); cf. §§ 7511(a)(1), (5) (setting more rigid attainment deadlines for areas in nonattainment of the ozone standard, but permitting the Administrator to grant up to two 1-year extensions). And Congress can change those statutory limits if necessary. Given the ambient air quality standards' substantial effects on States, cities, industries, and their suppliers and customers, Congress will hear from those whom compliance deadlines affect adversely, and Congress can consider whether legislative change is warranted. See, *e.g.*, Steel Industry Compliance Extension Act of 1981, 95 Stat. 139 (codified at 42 U.S.C. § 7413(e) (1988 ed.)) (repealed 1990) (granting the Administrator discretion to extend the ambient air quality standard attainment date set in the 1977 Act by up to three years for steelmaking facilities).

Finally, contrary to the suggestion of the Court of Appeals and of some parties, this interpretation of § 109 does not require the EPA to eliminate every health risk, however slight, at any economic cost, however great, to the point of "hurtling" industry over "the brink of ruin," or even forcing "deindustrialization." *American Trucking Assns., Inc. v. EPA*, 175 F.3d 1027, 1037, 1038, n. 4 (C.A.D.C.1999); see also Brief for Cross-Petitioners in No. 99-1426, p. 25. The statute, by its express terms, does not compel the elimination of *all* risk; and it grants the Administrator sufficient flexibility to avoid setting ambient air quality standards ruinous to industry.

Section 109(b)(1) directs the Administrator to set standards that are "requisite to protect the public health" with "an adequate margin of safety." But these words do not describe a world that is free of all risk — an impossible and undesirable objective. See *Industrial Union Dept., AFL-CIO v. American Petroleum Institute*, 448 U.S. 607, 642 (1980) (plurality opinion) (the word "safe" does not mean "risk-free"). Nor are the words "requisite" and "public health" to be understood independent of context. We consider football equipment "safe" even if its use entails a level of risk that would make drinking water "unsafe" for consumption. And what counts as "requisite" to protecting the public health will similarly vary with background circumstances, such as the public's ordinary tolerance of the particular health risk in the particular context at issue. The Administrator can consider such background circumstances when "decid[ing] what risks are acceptable in the world in which we live." *Natural Resources Defense Council, Inc. v. EPA*, 824 F.2d 1146, 1165 (C.A.D.C.1987).

The statute also permits the Administrator to take account of comparative health risks. That is to say, she may consider whether a proposed rule promotes safety overall. A rule likely to cause more harm to health than it prevents is not a rule that is "requisite to protect the public health." For example, as the Court of Appeals held and the parties do not contest, the Administrator has the authority to determine to what extent possible health risks stemming from reductions in tropospheric ozone (which, it is claimed, helps prevent cataracts and skin cancer) should be taken into account in setting the ambient air quality standard for ozone. See 175 F.3d, at 1050–1053 (remanding for the Administrator to make that determination).

The statute ultimately specifies that the standard set must be "requisite to protect the public health" " *in the judgment of the Administrator*," § 109(b)(1), 84 Stat. 1680 (emphasis added), a phrase that grants the Administrator considerable discretionary standard-setting authority.

The statute's words, then, authorize the Administrator to consider the severity of a pollutant's potential adverse health effects, the number of those likely to be affected, the distribution of the adverse effects, and the uncertainties surrounding each estimate. Cf. Sunstein, *Is the Clean Air Act Unconstitutional?*, 98 MICH. L.REV. 303, 364 (1999). They permit the Administrator to take account of comparative health consequences. They allow her to take account of context when determining the acceptability of small risks to health. And they give her considerable discretion when she does so.

This discretion would seem sufficient to avoid the extreme results that some of the industry parties fear. After all, the EPA, in setting standards that "protect the public health" with "an adequate margin of safety," retains discretionary authority to avoid regulating risks that it reasonably concludes are trivial in context. Nor need regulation lead to deindustrialization. Preindustrial society was not a very healthy society; hence a standard demanding the return of the Stone Age would not prove "requisite to protect the public health."

Although I rely more heavily than does the Court upon legislative history and alternative sources of statutory flexibility, I reach the same ultimate conclusion. Section 109 does not delegate to the EPA authority to base the national ambient air quality standards, in whole or in part, upon the economic costs of compliance.

A.L.A. SCHECHTER POULTRY CORP. v. UNITED STATES
295 U.S. 495 (1935)

[Petitioners, slaughterhouse operators, were convicted on an indictment charging violations of the "Live Poultry Code". The particular violations involved, inter alia, breach of the minimum wage and maximum hour provisions of the code and of code provisions requiring purchasers for resale to accept the run of any coop and denying to them the privilege of selecting individual chickens.]

The Live Poultry Code was promulgated under § 3 of the National Industrial Recovery Act. That section . . . authorizes the President to approve "codes of fair competition." Such a code may be approved for a trade or industry, upon application by one or more trade or industrial associations or groups, if the President finds (1) that such associations or groups "impose no inequitable restrictions on admission to membership therein and are truly representative," and (2) that such codes are not designed "to promote monopolies or to eliminate or oppress small enterprises and will not operate to discriminate against them, and will tend to effectuate the policy" of Title I of the Act. . . . As a condition of his approval, the President may "impose such conditions (including requirements for the making of reports and the keeping of accounts) for the protection of consumers, competitors, employees, and others, and in furtherance of the public interest, and may provide such exceptions to and exemptions from the provisions of such code as the President in his discretion deems necessary to effectuate the policy herein declared." . . . The Recovery Act provides that . . . when a code is approved, its provisions are to be the "standards of fair competition" for the trade or industry concerned, and any violation of such standards in any transaction in or affecting interstate or foreign commerce is deemed "an unfair method of competition" within the meaning of the Federal Trade Commission Act. . . . [T]he approval of a code by the President is conditioned on his finding that it "will tend to effectuate the policy of this title." . . . The "policy herein declared" is manifestly that set forth in section one. That declaration embraces a broad range of objectives. . . . It is there declared to be "the policy of Congress" —

> "to remove obstructions to the free flow of interstate and foreign commerce which tend to diminish the amount thereof; and to provide for the general welfare by promoting the organization of industry for the purpose of cooperative action among trade groups, to induce and maintain united action of labor and management under adequate governmental sanctions and supervision, to eliminate unfair competitive practices, to promote the fullest possible utilization of the present productive capacity of industries, to avoid undue restriction of production (except as may be temporarily required), to increase the consumption of industrial and agricultural products by increasing purchasing power, to reduce and relieve unemployment, to improve standards of labor, and otherwise to rehabilitate industry and to conserve natural resources."

Under § 3, whatever "may tend to effectuate" these general purposes may be included in the "codes of fair competition." . . . [T]he purpose is clearly disclosed to authorize new and controlling prohibitions through codes of laws which would embrace what the formulators would propose, and what the President would approve, or prescribe, as wise and beneficent measures of the government of trades and industries in order to bring about their rehabilitation, correction and development, according to the general declaration of policy in section one. . . .

The question, then, turns upon the authority which § 3 of the Recovery Act vests in the President to approve or prescribe. If the codes have standing as penal statutes, this must be due to the effect of the executive action. But Congress cannot delegate legislative power to the President to exercise an unfettered discretion to make whatever laws he thinks may be needed or advisable for the rehabilitation and expansion of trade or industry. . . .

. . . . Section 3 of the Recovery Act is without precedent. It supplies no standards for any trade, industry or activity. It does not undertake to prescribe rules of conduct to be applied to particular states of fact determined by appropriate administrative procedure. Instead of prescribing rules of conduct, it authorizes the making of codes to prescribe them. For that legislative undertaking, § 3 sets up no standards, aside from the statement of the general aims of rehabilitation, correction and expansion described in section one. In view of the scope of that broad declaration, and of the nature of the few restrictions that are imposed, the discretion of the President in approving or prescribing codes, and thus enacting laws for the government of trade and industry throughout the country, is virtually unfettered. We think that the code-making authority thus conferred is an unconstitutional delegation of legislative power.

. . . . [W]e hold the code provisions here in question to be invalid and that the judgment of conviction must be reversed.

In other decisions of the New Deal era the Court also found regulatory statutes constitutionally defective on delegation grounds. *Panama Refining Co. v. Ryan*, 293 U.S. 388 (1935); *Carter v. Carter Coal Co.*, 298 U.S. 238, 311 (1936). (In *Panama Refining*, the Congress empowered the President to ban the interstate shipment of oil and gasoline that had been produced in violation of state proration laws, but failed to provide the President with standards for exercising that power. In the *Carter Coal Co.* case, the Court held that delegation to a majority of producers the power to fix maximum hours of work was the worst kind of delegation because powers were delegated to private persons who may have interests opposed to those subject to their power.)

Under the delegation doctrine (or, as it is sometimes called, the anti-delegation doctrine), Congress must provide a minimal degree of guidance to those officials charged with administering its statutes. Since apparently valid statutes have employed exceedingly broad and imprecise standards, very little guidance seems actually to be required, however. Consider, for example, the provision in the Interstate Commerce Act which charged the Interstate Commerce Commission with enforcing an obligation of rail and motor carriers not to charge unreasonably high rates and the provision in the Communications Act which charged the Federal Communications Commission with issuing radio and television broadcasting licenses under a standard of furthering the public interest, convenience and necessity.

Modern critics have charged that Congress has often evaded the responsibilities which the Framers of the Constitution intended to place upon it by delegating hard policy decisions to administrative officials. Thus Congress may, by employing vague and imprecise terms in the legislation which it enacts avoid facing important policy issues which thus are effectively delegated to the decision, in the first instance, of unelected administrative officials. Then, when those officials make a decision which is unpopular with the constituents of a particular congressman, he is free to curry favor with those constituents by criticizing it. Yet because the Congressman avoided voting on the policy issue involved, he also avoided offending those of his constituents which approved of that administrative decision.

Consider, for example, the many regulatory issues which Congress delegated away to the Federal Trade Commission when it cast its prohibition in the language of "unfair methods of competition". (In the highly imprecise language of the Sherman Act, Congress effectively delegated away the resolution of many regulatory issues to the courts.) Some critics have urged the Supreme Court to reinvigorate the delegation doctrine as a means of forcing Congress to face the hard policy choices; and then to account for their policy decisions to the electorate. See, e.g., Peter H. Aranson, Ernest Gellhorn & Glen O. Robinson, *A Theory of Legislative Delegation*, 68 Cornell L. Rev. 1 (1983). Compare Jerry L. Mashaw, *Prodelegation: Why Administrators Should Make Political Decisions*, I J. Law, Econ. & Organ. 81 (1985).

6.   *Justice Rehnquist and the Delegation Doctrine.*

In two cases from the 1980s Justice Rehnquist claimed that the delegation doctrine should have invalidated certain provisions of § 6(b)(5) of the Occupational Safety and Health Act of 1970. Under that Act, the Secretary of Labor is authorized to issue "occupational safety and health standards", setting forth controls "reasonably necessary or appropriate to provide safe or healthful employment and places of employment." Where toxic materials or harmful physical agents are concerned, an occupational safety and health standard must comply with § 6(b) (5) which provides:

> The Secretary, in promulgating standards dealing with toxic materials or harmful physical agents under this subsection, shall set the standard which most adequately assures, to the extent feasible, on the basis of the best available evidence, that no employee will suffer material impairment of health or functional capacity even if such employee has regular exposure to the hazard dealt with by such standard for the period of his working life. Development of standards under this subsection shall be based upon research, demonstrations, experiments, and such other information as may be appropriate. In addition to the attainment of the highest degree of health and safety protection for the employee, other considerations shall be the latest available scientific data in the field, the feasibility of the standards, and experience gained under this and other health and safety laws.

In *Industrial Union Dept., AFL-CIO v. American Petroleum Institute*, 448 U.S. 607 (1980), the Court struck down an OSHA regulation limiting exposure to airborne concentrations of benzene to one part per million on the ground that there was no evidence that such exposures created a significant health risk. In its decision, the Court observed that relatively few workers would be protected by the standard, that the workers most exposed to benzene, gas station attendants, were expressly excluded from the standard's coverage, and that the implementation of the standard would impose very large costs upon industry.

In *American Textile Manufacturers Institute, Inc. v. Donovan*, 452 U.S. 490 (1981), where the Court upheld an OSHA occupational safety and health standard limiting the exposure of textile workers to cotton dust, the Court ruled that the Secretary of Labor was not required under the Act to employ cost-benefit analysis by demonstrating that the anticipated health benefits were significant in relation to their costs.

Dissenting in *American Textile Manufacturers*, Justice Rehnquist had this to say:

> Throughout its opinion, the Court refers to § 6(b)(5) as adopting a "feasibility standard" or a "feasibility requirement." . . . But as I attempted to point out last Term in *Industrial Union Dept. v. American Petroleum Institute* . . . the "feasibility standard" is no standard at all. Quite the contrary, I argued that the insertion into § 6(b)(5) of the words "to the extent feasible" rendered what had been a clear, if somewhat unrealistic, statute into one so vague and precatory as to be an unconstitutional delegation of legislative authority to the Executive Branch. Prior to the inclusion of the "feasibility" language, § 6(b)(5) simply required the Secretary to "set the standard which most adequately assures, on the basis of the best available professional evidence, that no employee will suffer any impairment of health. . . ". . . . Had that statute been enacted, it would undoubtedly support the result the Court reaches in these cases, and it would not have created an excessive delegation problem. . . .

> But Congress did not enact that statute. The legislative history of the Act reveals a number of Members of Congress . . . engaged Congress in a lengthy debate about the extent to which the Secretary should be authorized to create a risk-free work environment. Congress had at least three choices. It could have required the Secretary to engage in a cost-benefit analysis prior to the setting of exposure levels, it could have prohibited cost-benefit analysis, or it could have permitted the use of such an analysis. Rather than make that choice and resolve that difficult policy issue, however, Congress passed. Congress simply said that the Secretary should set standards "to the extent feasible." . . . I am convinced that the reason that Congress did not speak with greater "clarity" was because it could not. The words "to the extent feasible" were used to mask a fundamental policy disagreement in Congress. I have no doubt that if Congress had been required to choose whether to mandate, permit, or prohibit the Secretary from engaging in a cost-benefit analysis, there would have been no bill for the President to sign.

The Court seems to argue that Congress *did* make a policy choice when it enacted the "feasibility" language. Its view is that Congress required the Secretary to engage in something called "feasibility analysis." . . . But those words mean nothing at all. They are a "legislative mirage, appearing to some Members [of Congress] but not to others, and assuming any form desired by the beholder." *American Petroleum Institute, supra*, at 681. Even the Court does not settle on a meaning. It first suggests that the language requires the Secretary to do what is "capable of being done." . . . But, if that is all the language means, it is merely precatory and "no more than an admonition to the Secretary to do his duty. . . . The Court then seems to adopt the Secretary's view that feasibility means "technological and economic feasibility." But there is nothing in the words of § 6(b)(5), or their legislative history, to suggest why they should be so limited. One wonders why the "requirement" of § 6(b)(5).could not include considerations of administrative or even political feasibility. As even the Court recognizes, when Congress has wanted to limit the concept of feasibility to technological and economic feasibility, it has said so. . . . Thus the words "to the extent feasible" provide no meaningful guidance to those who will administer the law.

In believing that § 6(b)(5) amounts to an unconstitutional delegation of legislative authority to the Executive Branch, I do not mean to suggest that Congress, in enacting a statute, must resolve all ambiguities or must "fill in all of the blanks." . . . It is not unusual for the various factions supporting or opposing a proposal to accept some departure from the language they would prefer and to adopt substitute language agreeable to all. But that sort of compromise is a far cry from this case, where Congress simply abdicated its responsibility for the making of a fundamental and most difficult policy choice — whether and to what extent "the statistical possibility of future deaths should . . . be disregarded in light of the economic costs of preventing those deaths." . . . That is a "quintessential legislative" choice and must be made by the elected representatives of the people, not by nonelected officials in the Executive Branch. . . .

Compare with Justice Rehnquist's views, the Court's longstanding approach recently exemplified in *Mistretta v. United States*, 488 U.S. 361 (1989) [supral and *Skinner v. Mid-America Pipeline Co.*, 490 U.S. 212 (1989) where the Court reaffirmed [490 U.S. at 218] its "longstanding principle that so long as Congress provides an administrative agency with standards guiding its actions such that a court could 'ascertain whether the will of Congress has been obeyed,' no delegation of legislative authority trenching on the principle of separation of powers has occurred." In the latter case, the Court (through Justice O'Connor) held that Congress could validly direct the Secretary of Transportation to establish a system of user fees to cover the costs of administering certain federal pipeline safety programs:

Mid-America contends . . . that notwithstanding the constitutional soundness of § 7005 under ordinary nondelegation analysis, the assessment of these pipeline safety user fees must be scrutinized under a more exacting nondelegation lens. When so scrutinized, Mid-America argues, § 7005 is revealed to be constitutionally inadequate. In Mid-America's view, the assessments permitted by § 7005, although labeled "user fees," are actually tax assessments levied by the Secretary on [regulated] firms. . . . Congress' taxing power, Mid-American further contends, unlike any of Congress' other enumerated powers, if delegable at all, must be delegated with much stricter guidelines than is required for other congressional delegations of authority. . . .

We find no support . . . for Mid-America's contention that the text of the Constitution or the practices of Congress require the amplification of a different and stricter nondelegation doctrine in cases where Congress delegates discretionary authority to the Executive under its taxing power. . . .

C. THE (LIMITED) ROLE OF THE EXECUTIVE

1. *Unilateral Actions by the President.*

Youngstown Sheet & Tube Co. v. Sawyer, 343 U.S. 579 (1952). To advert a nation-wide strike of steel workers during the Korean War, President Truman issued an order directing the Secretary of Commerce to take possession of and to operate most of the Nation's steel mills. Claiming that the President acted unconstitutionally, the mill owners sought injunctive and declaratory relief in court. Affirming the district court's grant of a preliminary injunction, the Supreme Court held that the President had no statutory authorization to seize the mills and that his claims that he possessed inherent power under the Constitution to order the seizure were unfounded:

> Nor can the seizure order be sustained because of the several constitutional provisions that grant executive power to the President. In the framework of our Constitution, the President's power to see that the laws are faithfully executed refutes the idea that he is to be a lawmaker. The Constitution limits his functions in the lawmaking process to the recommending of laws he thinks wise and the vetoing of laws he thinks bad. And the Constitution is neither silent nor equivocal about who shall make laws which the President is to execute. The first section of the first article says that "All legislative Powers herein granted shall be vested in a Congress of the United States. . . ."

Questions and Comments

When the Court invalidated the Presidential seizures in the *Youngstown* case, it equated his actions with legislation, which requires Congressional action. In *Schechter* the Court had ruled that Congress could not delegate its responsibilities to the President; and in *Youngstown* the Court ruled that the President could not assume those responsibilities himself. Underlying these decisions is the Court's conception of the lawmaking role assigned to Congress, is it not? Can you describe that conception? Can you set forth the reasons behind it? Do these reasons underlie the structure which the Framers incorporated into the federal government? Explain the extent to which the constitutional framework supports the Court's decisions in *Schechter* and *Youngstown*. Can you explain how an opposite answer could also be justified?

2.   *Executive Policy and Agency Rulemaking.*

Policy Coordination and the Lack of It

Although the Constitution (in Article II, § 3) charges the President to "take Care that the Laws be faithfully executed", and authorizes him (in Article II, § 2) to "require the Opinion, in writing, of the principal Officer in each of the executive Departments, upon any subject relating to the Duties of their respective Offices," the vast size of the federal government makes it exceedingly difficult for the President to gain effective control over all of its operations.

This difficulty has been compounded by the independent status of many of the regulatory agencies. Indeed, observers have long criticized the lack of effective policy coordination in the federal bureaucracy, especially as this lack of coordination involves the independent agencies. *See, e.g.*, Louis J. Hector, *Problems of the CAB and the Independent Regulatory Commissions*, 69 Yale LJ. 930, 949–953 (1960); Harold H. Bruff, *Presidential Power and Administrative Rulemaking*, 88 Yale LJ. 451 (1979).

Presidential Initiatives

Recent Presidents have increasingly sought to expand their control over the activities of the various government agencies through the issuance of Executive Orders imposing various reporting and other requirements upon them in connection with rulemaking.

In Executive Order No. 11,821, issued in 1974, President Ford required an inflation impact statement to accompany all major legislative proposals, regulations, and rules emanating from the executive branch of the Government. The Director of the Office of Management and Budget was designated to develop criteria for the identification of such major executive branch actions "which may have a significant impact upon inflation, and to prescribe procedures for their evaluation."

In an attempt to improve the regulatory process, President Carter issued Executive Order No. 12,044 in 1978. Executive Order No. 12,044 required executive agencies to publish semiannually an agenda of significant regulations under development or review. In determining which of their regulations were "significant" for purposes of the Executive Order, that Order required agencies to consider among other things: "(1) the type and number of individuals, businesses, organizations, State and local governments affected; (2) the compliance and reporting requirements likely to be involved; (3) direct and indirect effects of the regulation including the effect on competition; and (4) the relationship of the regulations to those of other programs and agencies." In the case of regulations deemed "significant", the Order also required agencies to prepare a regulatory analysis early in the decision-making process.

President Reagan sought to exert further control over agency rulemaking. In February 1981, he issued Executive Order No. 12,291. Section 2 of the Order required agencies engage in cost-benefit analyses and to set regulatory priorities. Executive Order no. 12,291 conferred substantial supervisory authority over agency rulemaking upon the Office of Management and Budget. It required executive branch agencies to determine, under the supervision of the OMB Director which of their rules are "major" rules, and in connection with the issuance of such rules these agencies were required to prepare a Regulatory Impact Analysis (which could be combined with any Regulatory Flexibility Analyses performed under 5 U.S.C. §§ 603 and 604). A preliminary Regulatory Impact Analysis was required to be transmitted to the Director prior to the publication of notice of proposed rulemaking and a final Regulatory Impact Analysis was required to be transmitted to the Director prior to the publication of the rule as a final rule. The Regulatory Impact Analysis was required to contain a cost-benefit analysis and a description of alternative approaches as well as an explanation why the regulation was chosen over alternative approaches. Executive Order No. 12,291 also required each agency to publish twice each year agendas of proposed regulations that the agency had issued or expected to issue and currently effective rules that were under agency review.

Executive Order No. 12,498, promulgated in January 1985, expanded the scope of OMB review of agency rulemaking actions. The Order required each agency subject to Executive Order No. 12,291 to submit to the OMB Director, each year, a statement of its regulatory program for the forthcoming year which was to include a statement of its regulatory policies, goals, and objectives for the year and information concerning all significant regulatory actions underway or planned. The submission was first to be in draft form which would be reviewed by the Director, *inter alia*, for "consistency . . . with the Administration's policies and priorities". In the event of disagreement between the Director and the agency head, either could "raise issues for further review by the President or by such appropriate Cabinet Council or other forum as the President may designate." The agency's final regulatory plan was to be used by the OMB Director in the publication of the Administration's Regulatory Program for the year.

President Clinton, on September 30, 1993, issued Executive Order No. 12,866, revoking Executive Order No. 12,498, but continuing its approach towards supervision of agency rulemaking, especially of "significant" rulemaking having substantial economic or budgetary impact. Executive Order 12,866 brought the independent agencies within the scope of Presidential regulatory planning. It also explicitly conferred on the Office of Information and Regulatory Affairs (within the Office of Management and Budget) supervisory authority over rulemaking and establishes rules governing communications between OIRA personnel and persons not employed by the executive branch. OIRA was also required to provide public access to all documents exchanged between OIRA and the relevant agency after that agency had adopted a regulatory action or decided against doing so.

President George W. Bush retained Executive Order No. 12,866, but in January 18, 2007, amended it with Executive Order No. 13,422. This Order's major change was to include "guidance documents" within the scope of the Order's concern. A "Guidance Document" is defined as "an agency statement of general applicability and future effect, other than a regulatory action, that sets forth a policy on a statutory, regulatory, or technical issue." Executive Order No. 13,422 also appears designed to require a specific market failure (to be identified by an agency) as a prerequisite to regulatory action.

Appendix A

SELECTED PROVISIONS FROM TITLE 5 OF THE U.S. CODE GOVERNING ADMINISTRATIVE PROCEDURE AND JUDICIAL REVIEW

Chapter 5   Administrative Procedure Act and related legislation

Subchapter II.   Administrative Procedure

§ 551.   Definitions

For the purpose of this subchapter [5 USCS §§ 551 et seq.] —

(1) "agency" means each authority of the Government of the United States, whether or not it is within or subject to review by another agency, but does not include —

(A) the Congress;

(B) the courts of the United States;

(C) the governments of the territories or possessions of the United States;

(D) the government of the District of Columbia;

or except as to the requirements of section 552 of this title [5 USCS § 552] —

(E) agencies composed of representatives of the parties or of representatives of organizations of the parties to the disputes determined by them;

(F) courts martial and military commissions;

(G) military authority exercised in the field in time of war or in occupied territory; or

(H) functions conferred by sections 1738, 1739, 1743, and 1744 of title 12; chapter 2 of title 41 [41 USCS §§ 101 et seq.]; subchapter II of chapter 471 of title 49 [49 USCS §§ 47151 et seq.]; or sections 1884, 1891–1902, and former section 1641(b)(2), of title 50, appendix;

(2) "person" includes an individual, partnership, corporation, association, or public or private organization other than an agency;

(3) "party" includes a person or agency named or admitted as a party, or properly seeking and entitled as of right to be admitted as a party, in an agency proceeding, and a person or agency admitted by an agency as a party for limited purposes;

(4) "rule" means the whole or a part of an agency statement of general or particular applicability and future effect designed to implement, interpret, or prescribe law or policy or describing the organization, procedure, or practice requirements of an agency and includes the approval or prescription for the

future of rates, wages, corporate or financial structures or reorganizations thereof, prices, facilities, appliances, services or allowances therefor or of valuations, costs, or accounting, or practices bearing on any of the foregoing;

(5) "rule making" means agency process for formulating, amending, or repealing a rule;

(6) "order" means the whole or a part of a final disposition, whether affirmative, negative, injunctive, or declaratory in form, of an agency in a matter other than rule making but including licensing;

(7) "adjudication" means agency process for the formulation of an order;

(8) "license" includes the whole or a part of an agency permit, certificate, approval, registration, charter, membership, statutory exemption or other form of permission;

(9) "licensing" includes agency process respecting the grant, renewal, denial, revocation, suspension, annulment, withdrawal, limitation, amendment, modification, or conditioning of a license;

(10) "sanction" includes the whole or a part of an agency —

(A) prohibition, requirement, limitation, or other condition affecting the freedom of a person;

(B) withholding of relief;

(C) imposition of penalty or fine;

(D) destruction, taking, seizure, or withholding of property;

(E) assessment of damages, reimbursement, restitution, compensation, costs, charges, or fees;

(F) requirement, revocation, or suspension of a license; or

(G) taking other compulsory or restrictive action;

(11) "relief" includes the whole or a part of an agency —

(A) grant of money, assistance, license, authority, exemption, exception, privilege, or remedy;

(B) recognition of a claim, right, immunity, privilege, exemption, or exception; or

(C) taking of other action on the application or petition of, and beneficial to, a person;

(12) "agency proceeding" means an agency process as defined by paragraphs (5), (7), and (9) of this section;

(13) "agency action" includes the whole or a part of an agency rule, order, license, sanction, relief, or the equivalent or denial thereof, or failure to act; and

(14) "ex parte communication" means an oral or written communication not on the public record with respect to which reasonable prior notice to all parties is not

given, but it shall not include requests for status reports on any matter or proceeding covered by this subchapter [5 USCS §§ 551 etc.].

§ 552. Public information; agency rules, opinions, orders, records, and proceedings

(a) Each agency shall make available to the public information as follows:

(1) Each agency shall separately state and currently publish in the Federal Register for the guidance of the public —

(A) descriptions of its central and field organization and the established places at which, the employees (and in the case of a uniformed service, the members) from whom, and the methods whereby, the public may obtain information, make submittals or requests, or obtain decisions;

(B) statements of the general course and method by which its functions are channeled and determined, including the nature and requirements of all formal and informal procedures available;

(C) rules of procedure, descriptions of forms available or the places at which forms may be obtained, and instructions as to the scope and contents of all papers, reports, or examinations;

(D) substantive rules of general applicability adopted as authorized by law, and statements of general policy or interpretations of general applicability formulated and adopted by the agency; and

(E) each amendment, revision, or repeal of the foregoing.

Except to the extent that a person has actual and timely notice of the terms thereof, a person may not in any manner be required to resort to, or be adversely affected by, a matter required to be published in the Federal Register and not so published. For the purpose of this paragraph, matter reasonably available to the class of persons affected thereby is deemed published in the Federal Register when incorporated by reference therein with the approval of the Director of the Federal Register.

(2) Each agency, in accordance with published rules, shall make available for public inspection and copying —

(A) final opinions, including concurring and dissenting opinions, as well as orders, made in the adjudication of cases;

(B) those statements of policy and interpretations which have been adopted by the agency and are not published in the Federal Register;

(C) administrative staff manuals and instructions to staff that affect a member of the public;

(D) copies of all records, regardless of form or format, which have been released to any person under paragraph (3) and which, because of the nature of their subject matter, the agency determines have become or are likely to become the subject of subsequent requests for substantially the same records; and

(E) a general index of the records referred to under subparagraph (D); unless the materials are promptly published and copies offered for sale. . . .

*   *   *

A final order, opinion, statement of policy, interpretation, or staff manual or instruction that affects a member of the public may be relied on, used, or cited as precedent by an agency against a party other than an agency only if —

(i) it has been indexed and either made available or published as provided by this paragraph; or

(ii) the party has actual and timely notice of the terms thereof.

(3) (A) Except with respect to the records made available under paragraphs (1) and (2) of this subsection, and except as provided in subparagraph (E), each agency, upon any request for records which (i) reasonably describes such records and (ii) is made in accordance with published rules stating the time, place, fees (if any), and procedures to be followed, shall make the records promptly available to any person.

*   *   *

(b) This section does not apply to matters that are —

(1) (A) specifically authorized under criteria established by an Executive order to be kept secret in the interest of national defense or foreign policy and (B) are in fact properly classified pursuant to such Executive order;

(2) related solely to the internal personnel rules and practices of an agency;

(3) specifically exempted from disclosure by statute (other than section 552b of this title [5 USCS § 552b]), if that statute —

(A) (i) requires that the matters be withheld from the public in such a manner as to leave no discretion on the issue; or

(ii) establishes particular criteria for withholding or refers to particular types of matters to be withheld; and

(B) if enacted after the date of enactment of the OPEN FOIA Act of 2009 [enacted Oct. 28, 2009], specifically cites to this paragraph.

(4) trade secrets and commercial or financial information obtained from a person and privileged or confidential;

(5) inter-agency or intra-agency memorandums or letters which would not be available by law to a party other than an agency in litigation with the agency;

(6) personnel and medical files and similar files the disclosure of which would constitute a clearly unwarranted invasion of personal privacy;

(7) records or information compiled for law enforcement purposes, but only to the extent that the production of such law enforcement records or information (A) could reasonably be expected to interfere with enforcement proceedings, (B) would deprive a person of a right to a fair trial or an impartial adjudication, (C)

could reasonably be expected to constitute an unwarranted invasion of personal privacy, (D) could reasonably be expected to disclose the identity of a confidential source, including a State, local, or foreign agency or authority or any private institution which furnished information on a confidential basis, and, in the case of a record or information compiled by criminal law enforcement authority in the course of a criminal investigation or by an agency conducting a lawful national security intelligence investigation, information furnished by a confidential source, (E) would disclose techniques and procedures for law enforcement investigations or prosecutions, or would disclose guidelines for law enforcement investigations or prosecutions if such disclosure could reasonably be expected to risk circumvention of the law, or (F) could reasonably be expected to endanger the life or physical safety of any individual;

(8) contained in or related to examination, operating, or condition reports prepared by, on behalf of, or for the use of an agency responsible for the regulation or supervision of financial institutions; or

(9) geological or geophysical information and data, including maps, concerning wells.

Any reasonably segregable portion of a record shall be provided to any person requesting such record after deletion of the portions which are exempt under this subsection. The amount of information deleted, and the exemption under which the deletion is made, shall be indicated on the released portion of the record, unless including that indication would harm an interest protected by the exemption in this subsection under which the deletion is made. If technically feasible, the amount of the information deleted, and the exemption under which the deletion is made, shall be indicated at the place in the record where such deletion is made.

* * *

(f) For purposes of this section, the term —

(1) "agency" as defined in section 551(1) of this title [5 USCS § 551(1)] includes any executive department, military department, Government corporation, Government controlled corporation, or other establishment in the executive branch of the Government (including the Executive Office of the President), or any independent regulatory agency; and

(2) "record" and any other term used in this section in reference to information includes —

(A) any information that would be an agency record subject to the requirements of this section when maintained by an agency in any format, including an electronic format; and

(B) any information described under subparagraph (A) that is maintained for an agency by an entity under Government contract, for the purposes of records management.

(g) The head of each agency shall prepare and make publicly available upon request, reference material or a guide for requesting records or information from the agency, subject to the exemptions in subsection (b), including —

(1) an index of all major information systems of the agency;

(2) a description of major information and record locator systems maintained by the agency; and

(3) a handbook for obtaining various types and categories of public information from the agency pursuant to chapter 35 of title 44 [44 USCS §§ 3501 et seq.], and under this section.

*   *   *

§ 552a. Records maintained on individuals

(a)   Definitions. For purposes of this section —

(1) the term "agency" means agency as defined in section 552[(f)](e) of this title;

(2) the term "individual" means a citizen of the United States or an alien lawfully admitted for permanent residence;

(3) the term "maintain" includes maintain, collect, use, or disseminate;

(4) the term "record" means any item, collection, or grouping of information about an individual that is maintained by an agency, including, but not limited to, his education, financial transactions, medical history, and criminal or employment history and that contains his name, or the identifying number, symbol, or other identifying particular assigned to the individual, such as a finger or voice print or a photograph;

(5) the term "system of records" means a group of any records under the control of any agency from which information is retrieved by the name of the individual or by some identifying number, symbol, or other identifying particular assigned to the individual;

(6) the term "statistical record" means a record in a system of records maintained for statistical research or reporting purposes only and not used in whole or in part in making any determination about an identifiable individual, except as provided by section 8 of title 13;

(7) the term "routine use" means, with respect to the disclosure of a record, the use of such record for a purpose which is compatible with the purpose for which it was collected; and

(8) the term "matching program". . . .

*   *   *

(b)   Conditions of disclosure. No agency shall disclose any record which is contained in a system of records by any means of communication to any person, or to another agency, except pursuant to a written request by, or with the prior written consent of, the individual to whom the record pertains, unless disclosure of the record would be —

(1) to those officers and employees of the agency which maintains the record who have a need for the record in the performance of their duties;

(2) required under section 552 of this title [5 USCS § 552];

(3) for a routine use as defined in subsection (a)(7) of this section and described under subsection (e)(4)(D) of this section;

(4) to the Bureau of the Census for purposes of planning or carrying out a census or survey or related activity pursuant to the provisions of title 13;

(5) to a recipient who has provided the agency with advance adequate written assurance that the record will be used solely as a statistical research or reporting record, and the record is to be transferred in a form that is not individually identifiable;

(6) to the National Archives and Records Administration as a record which has sufficient historical or other value to warrant its continued preservation by the United States Government, or for evaluation by the Archivist of the United States or the designee of the Archivist to determine whether the record has such value;

(7) to another agency or to an instrumentality of any governmental jurisdiction within or under the control of the United States for a civil or criminal law enforcement activity if the activity is authorized by law, and if the head of the agency or instrumentality has made a written request to the agency which maintains the record specifying the particular portion desired and the law enforcement activity for which the record is sought;

(8) to a person pursuant to a showing of compelling circumstances affecting the health or safety of an individual if upon such disclosure notification is transmitted to the last known address of such individual;

(9) to either House of Congress, or, to the extent of matter within its jurisdiction, any committee or subcommittee thereof, any joint committee of Congress or subcommittee of any such joint committee;

(10) to the Comptroller General, or any of his authorized representatives, in the course of the performance of the duties of the General Accounting Office [Government Accountability Office];

(11) pursuant to the order of a court of competent jurisdiction; or

(12) to a consumer reporting agency in accordance with section 3711(e) of title 31.

*   *   *

§ 552b.   Open meetings

(a) For purposes of this section —

(1) the term "agency" means any agency, as defined in section 552(e) of this title [5 USCS § 552(e)], headed by a collegial body composed of two or more individual members, a majority of whom are appointed to such position by the

President with the advice and consent of the Senate, and any subdivision thereof authorized to act on behalf of the agency;

(2) the term "meeting" means the deliberations of at least the number of individual agency members required to take action on behalf of the agency where such deliberations determine or result in the joint conduct or disposition of official agency business, but does not include deliberations required or permitted by subsection (d) or (e); and

(3) the term "member" means an individual who belongs to a collegial body heading an agency.

(b) Members shall not jointly conduct or dispose of agency business other than in accordance with this section. Except as provided in subsection (c), every portion of every meeting of an agency shall be open to public observation.

(c) Except in a case where the agency finds that the public interest requires otherwise, the second sentence of subsection (b) shall not apply to any portion of an agency meeting, and the requirements of subsections (d) and (e) shall not apply to any information pertaining to such meeting otherwise required by this section to be disclosed to the public, where the agency properly determines that such portion or portions of its meeting or the disclosure of such information is likely to —

(1) disclose matters that are (A) specifically authorized under criteria established by an Executive order to be kept secret in the interests of national defense or foreign policy and (B) in fact properly classified pursuant to such Executive order;

(2) relate solely to the internal personnel rules and practices of an agency;

(3) disclose matters specifically exempted from disclosure by statute (other than section 552 of this title [5 USCS § 552]), provided that such statute (A) requires that the matters be withheld from the public in such a manner as to leave no discretion on the issue, or (B) establishes particular criteria for withholding or refers to particular types of matters to be withheld;

(4) disclose trade secrets and commercial or financial information obtained from a person and privileged or confidential;

(5) involve accusing any person of a crime, or formally censuring any person;

(6) disclose information of a personal nature where disclosure would constitute a clearly unwarranted invasion of personal privacy;

(7) disclose investigatory records compiled for law enforcement purposes, or information which if written would be contained in such records, but only to the extent that the production of such records or information would (A) interfere with enforcement proceedings, (B) deprive a person of a right to a fair trial or an impartial adjudication, (C) constitute an unwarranted invasion of personal privacy, (D) disclose the identity of a confidential source and, in the case of a record compiled by a criminal law enforcement authority in the course of a criminal investigation, or by an agency conducting a lawful national security intelligence investigation, confidential information furnished only by the confi-

dential source, (E) disclose investigative techniques and procedures, or (F) endanger the life or physical safety of law enforcement personnel;

(8) disclose information contained in or related to examination, operating, or condition reports prepared by, on behalf of, or for the use of an agency responsible for the regulation or supervision of financial institutions;

(9) disclose information the premature disclosure of which would —

(A) in the case of an agency which regulates currencies, securities, commodities, or financial institutions, be likely to (i) lead to significant financial speculation in currencies, securities, or commodities, or (ii) significantly endanger the stability of any financial institution; or

(B) in the case of any agency, be likely to significantly frustrate implementation of a proposed agency action, except that subparagraph (B) shall not apply in any instance where the agency has already disclosed to the public the content or nature of its proposed action, or where the agency is required by law to make such disclosure on its own initiative prior to taking final agency action on such proposal; or

(10) specifically concern the agency's issuance of a subpoena, or the agency's participation in a civil action or proceeding, an action in a foreign court or international tribunal, or an arbitration, or the initiation, conduct, or disposition by the agency of a particular case of formal agency adjudication pursuant to the procedures in section 554 of this title [5 USCS § 554] or otherwise involving a determination on the record after opportunity for a hearing.

(d) (1) Action under subsection (c) shall be taken only when a majority of the entire membership of the agency (as defined in subsection (a)(1)) votes to take such action. A separate vote of the agency members shall be taken with respect to each agency meeting a portion or portions of which are proposed to be closed to the public pursuant to subsection (c), or with respect to any information which is proposed to be withheld under subsection (c). A single vote may be taken with respect to a series of meetings, a portion or portions of which are proposed to be closed to the public, or with respect to any information concerning such series of meetings, so long as each meeting in such series involves the same particular matters and is scheduled to be held no more than thirty days after the initial meeting in such series. The vote of each agency member participating in such vote shall be recorded and no proxies shall be allowed.

(2) Whenever any person whose interests may be directly affected by a portion of a meeting requests that the agency close such portion to the public for any of the reasons referred to in paragraph (5), (6), or (7) of subsection (c), the agency, upon request of any one of its members, shall vote by recorded vote whether to close such meeting.

(3) Within one day of any vote taken pursuant to paragraph (1) or (2), the agency shall make publicly available a written copy of such vote reflecting the vote of each member on the question. If a portion of a meeting is to be closed to the public, the agency shall, within one day of the vote taken pursuant to paragraph (1) or (2) of this subsection, make publicly available a full written

explanation of its action closing the portion together with a list of all persons expected to attend the meeting and their affiliation.

(4) Any agency, a majority of whose meetings may properly be closed to the public pursuant to paragraph (4), (8), (9)(A), or (10) of subsection (c), or any combination thereof, may provide by regulation for the closing of such meetings or portions thereof in the event that a majority of the members of the agency votes by recorded vote at the beginning of such meeting, or portion thereof, to close the exempt portion or portions of the meeting, and a copy of such vote, reflecting the vote of each member on the question, is made available to the public. The provisions of paragraphs (1), (2), and (3) of this subsection and subsection (c) shall not apply to any portion of a meeting to which such regulations apply: Provided, That the agency shall, except to the extent that such information is exempt from disclosure under the provisions of subsection (c), provide the public with public announcement of the time, place, and subject matter of the meeting and of each portion thereof at the earliest practicable time.

(e) (1) In the case of each meeting, the agency shall make public announcement, at least one week before the meeting, of the time, place, and subject matter of the meeting, whether it is to be open or closed to the public, and the name and phone number of the official designated by the agency to respond to requests for information about the meeting. Such announcement shall be made unless a majority of the members of the agency determines by a recorded vote that agency business requires that such meeting be called at an earlier date, in which case the agency shall make public announcement of the time, place, and subject matter of such meeting, and whether open or closed to the public, at the earliest practicable time.

(2) The time or place of a meeting may be changed following the public announcement required by paragraph (1) only if the agency publicly announces such change at the earliest practicable time. The subject matter of a meeting, or the determination of the agency to open or close a meeting, or portion of a meeting, to the public, may be changed following the public announcement required by this subsection only if (A) a majority of the entire membership of the agency determines by a recorded vote that agency business so requires and that no earlier announcement of the change was possible, and (B) the agency publicly announces such change and the vote of each member upon such change at the earliest practicable time.

(3) Immediately following each public announcement required by this subsection, notice of the time, place, and subject matter of a meeting, whether the meeting is open or closed, any change in one of the preceding, and the name and phone number of the official designated by the agency to respond to requests for information about the meeting, shall also be submitted for publication in the Federal Register.

(f) (1) For every meeting closed pursuant to paragraphs (1) through (10) of subsection (c), the General Counsel or chief legal officer of the agency shall publicly certify that, in his or her opinion, the meeting may be closed to the public and shall state each relevant exemptive provision. A copy of such certification, together with a statement from the presiding officer of the meeting setting forth the time and place of the meeting, and the persons present, shall be retained by the agency. The agency shall maintain a complete transcript or electronic recording adequate to record fully the proceedings of each meeting, or portion of a meeting, closed to the public, except that in the case of a meeting, or portion of a meeting, closed to the public pursuant to paragraph (8), (9)(A), or (10) of subsection (c), the agency shall maintain either such a transcript or recording, or a set of minutes. Such minutes shall fully and clearly describe all matters discussed and shall provide a full and accurate summary of any actions taken, and the reasons therefor, including a description of each of the views expressed on any item and the record of any rollcall vote (reflecting the vote of each member on the question). All documents considered in connection with any action shall be identified in such minutes.

(2) The agency shall make promptly available to the public, in a place easily accessible to the public, the transcript, electronic recording, or minutes (as required by paragraph (1)) of the discussion of any item on the agenda, or of any item of the testimony of any witness received at the meeting, except for such item or items of such discussion or testimony as the agency determines to contain information which may be withheld under subsection (c). Copies of such transcript, or minutes, or a transcription of such recording disclosing the identity of each speaker, shall be furnished to any person at the actual cost of duplication or transcription. The agency shall maintain a complete verbatim copy of the transcript, a complete copy of the minutes, or a complete electronic recording of each meeting, or portion of a meeting, closed to the public, for a period of at least two years after such meeting, or until one year after the conclusion of any agency proceeding with respect to which the meeting or portion was held, whichever occurs later.

(g) Each agency subject to the requirements of this section shall, within 180 days after the date of enactment of this section [enacted Sept. 13, 1976], following consultation with the Office of the Chairman of the Administrative Conference of the United States and published notice in the Federal Register of at least thirty days and opportunity for written comment by any person, promulgate regulations to implement the requirements of subsections (b) through (f) of this section. Any person may bring a proceeding in the United States District Court for the District of Columbia to require an agency to promulgate such regulations if such agency has not promulgated such regulations within the time period specified herein. Subject to any limitations of time provided by law, any person may bring a proceeding in the United States Court of Appeals for the District of Columbia to set aside agency regulations issued pursuant to this subsection that are not in accord with the requirements of subsections (b) through (f) of this section and to require the promulgation of regulations that are in accord with such subsections.

(h) (1) The district courts of the United States shall have jurisdiction to enforce the requirements of subsections (b) through (f) of this section by declaratory judgment, injunctive relief, or other relief as may be appropriate. Such actions may be brought by any person against an agency prior to, or within sixty days after, the meeting out of which the violation of this section arises, except that if public announcement of such meeting is not initially provided by the agency in accordance with the requirements of this section, such action may be instituted pursuant to this section at any time prior to sixty days after any public announcement of such meeting. Such actions may be brought in the district court of the United States for the district in which the agency meeting is held or in which the agency in question has its headquarters, or in the District Court for the District of Columbia. In such actions a defendant shall serve his answer within thirty days after the service of the complaint. The burden is on the defendant to sustain his action. In deciding such cases the court may examine in camera any portion of the transcript, electronic recording, or minutes of a meeting closed to the public, and may take such additional evidence as it deems necessary. The court, having due regard for orderly administration and the public interest, as well as the interests of the parties, may grant such equitable relief as it deems appropriate, including granting an injunction against future violations of this section or ordering the agency to make available to the public such portion of the transcript, recording, or minutes of a meeting as is not authorized to be withheld under subsection (c) of this section.

(2) Any Federal court otherwise authorized by law to review agency action may, at the application of any person properly participating in the proceeding pursuant to other applicable law, inquire into violations by the agency of the requirements of this section and afford such relief as it deems appropriate. Nothing in this section authorizes any Federal court having jurisdiction solely on the basis of paragraph (1) to set aside, enjoin, or invalidate any agency action (other than an action to close a meeting or to withhold information under this section) taken or discussed at any agency meeting out of which the violation of this section arose.

(i) The court may assess against any party reasonable attorney fees and other litigation costs reasonably incurred by any other party who substantially prevails in any action brought in accordance with the provisions of subsection (g) or (h) of this section, except that costs may be assessed against the plaintiff only where the court finds that the suit was initiated by the plaintiff primarily for frivolous or dilatory purposes. In the case of assessment of costs against an agency, the costs may be assessed by the court against the United States.

(j) Each agency subject to the requirements of this section shall annually report to the Congress regarding the following:

(1) The changes in the policies and procedures of the agency under this section that have occurred during the preceding 1-year period.

(2) A tabulation of the number of meetings held, the exemptions applied to close meetings, and the days of public notice provided to close meetings.

(3) A brief description of litigation or formal complaints concerning the implementation of this section by the agency.

(4) A brief explanation of any changes in law that have affected the responsibilities of the agency under this section.

(k) Nothing herein expands or limits the present rights of any person under section 552 of this title [5 USCS § 552], except that the exemptions set forth in subsection (c) of this section shall govern in the case of any request made pursuant to section 552 [5 USCS § 552] to copy or inspect the transcripts, recordings, or minutes described in subsection (f) of this section. The requirements of chapter 33 of title 44, United States Code [44 USCS §§ 3301 et seq.], shall not apply to the transcripts, recordings, and minutes described in subsection (f) of this section.

(l) This section does not constitute authority to withhold any information from Congress, and does not authorize the closing of any agency meeting or portion thereof required by any other provision of law to be open.

(m) Nothing in this section authorizes any agency to withhold from any individual any record, including transcripts, recordings, or minutes required by this section, which is otherwise accessible to such individual under section 552a of this title [5 USCS § 552a].

§ 553. Rule making

(a) This section applies, according to the provisions thereof, except to the extent that there is involved —

(1) a military or foreign affairs function of the United States; or

(2) a matter relating to agency management or personnel or to public property, loans, grants, benefits, or contracts.

(b) General notice of proposed rule making shall be published in the Federal Register, unless persons subject thereto are named and either personally served or otherwise have actual notice thereof in accordance with law. The notice shall include —

(1) a statement of the time, place, and nature of public rule making proceedings;

(2) reference to the legal authority under which the rule is proposed; and

(3) either the terms or substance of the proposed rule or a description of the subjects and issues involved.

Except when notice or hearing is required by statute, this subsection does not apply —

(A) to interpretative rules, general statements of policy, or rules of agency organization, procedure, or practice; or

(B) when the agency for good cause finds (and incorporates the finding and a brief statement of reasons therefor in the rules issued) that notice and public procedure thereon are impracticable, unnecessary, or contrary to the public interest.

(c) After notice required by this section, the agency shall give interested persons an opportunity to participate in the rule making through submission of written data, views, or arguments with or without opportunity for oral presentation. After consideration of the relevant matter presented, the agency shall incorporate in the rules adopted a concise general statement of their basis and purpose. When rules are required by statute to be made on the record after opportunity for an agency hearing, sections 556 and 557 of this title [5 USCS §§ 556 and 557] apply instead of this subsection.

(d) The required publication or service of a substantive rule shall be made not less than 30 days before its effective date, except —

(1) a substantive rule which grants or recognizes an exemption or relieves a restriction;

(2) interpretative rules and statements of policy; or

(3) as otherwise provided by the agency for good cause found and published with the rule.

(e) Each agency shall give an interested person the right to petition for the issuance, amendment, or repeal of a rule.

§ 554. Adjudications

(a) This section applies, according to the provisions thereof, in every case of adjudication required by statute to be determined on the record after opportunity for an agency hearing, except to the extent that there is involved —

(1) a matter subject to a subsequent trial of the law and the facts de novo in a court;

(2) the selection or tenure of an employee, except a [an] administrative law judge appointed under section 3105 of this title [5 USCS § 3105];

(3) proceedings in which decisions rest solely on inspections, tests, or elections;

(4) the conduct of military or foreign affairs functions;

(5) cases in which an agency is acting as an agent for a court; or

(6) the certification of worker representatives.

(b) Persons entitled to notice of an agency hearing shall be timely informed of —

(1) the time, place, and nature of the hearing;

(2) the legal authority and jurisdiction under which the hearing is to be held; and

(3) the matters of fact and law asserted.

When private persons are the moving parties, other parties to the proceeding shall give prompt notice of issues controverted in fact or law; and in other instances agencies may by rule require responsive pleading. In fixing the time and place for hearings, due regard shall be had for the convenience and necessity of the parties or their representatives.

(c) The agency shall give all interested parties opportunity for —

(1) the submission and consideration of facts, arguments, offers of settlement, or proposals of adjustment when time, the nature of the proceeding, and the public interest permit; and

(2) to the extent that the parties are unable so to determine a controversy by

consent, hearing and decision on notice and in accordance with sections 556 and 557 of this title [5 USCS §§ 556 and 557].

(d) The employee who presides at the reception of evidence pursuant to section 556 of this title [5 USCS § 556] shall make the recommended decision or initial decision required by section 557 of this title [5 USCS § 557], unless he becomes unavailable to the agency. Except to the extent required for the disposition of ex parte matters as authorized by law, such an employee may not —

(1) consult a person or party on a fact in issue, unless on notice and opportunity for all parties to participate; or

(2) be responsible to or subject to the supervision or direction of an employee or agent engaged in the performance of investigative or prosecuting functions for an agency.

An employee or agent engaged in the performance of investigative or prosecuting functions for an agency in a case may not, in that or a factually related case, participate or advise in the decision, recommended decision, or agency review pursuant to section 557 of this title [5 USCS § 557], except as witness or counsel in public proceedings. This subsection does not apply —

(A) in determining applications for initial licenses;

(B) to proceedings involving the validity or application of rates, facilities, or practices of public utilities or carriers; or

(C) to the agency or a member or members of the body comprising the agency.

(e) The agency, with like effect as in the case of other orders, and in its sound discretion, may issue a declaratory order to terminate a controversy or remove uncertainty.

§ 555. Ancillary matters

(a) This section applies, according to the provisions thereof, except as otherwise provided by this subchapter [5 USCS §§ 551 et seq.].

(b) A person compelled to appear in person before an agency or representative thereof is entitled to be accompanied, represented, and advised by counsel or, if permitted by the agency, by other qualified representative. A party is entitled to appear in person or by or with counsel or other duly qualified representative in an agency proceeding. So far as the orderly conduct of public business permits, an interested person may appear before an agency or its responsible employees for the presentation, adjustment, or determination of an issue, request, or controversy in a proceeding, whether interlocutory, summary, or otherwise, or in connection with an agency function. With due regard for the convenience and necessity of the parties or their representatives and within a reasonable time, each agency shall proceed to conclude a matter presented to it. This subsection does not grant or deny a person who is not a lawyer the right to appear for or represent others before an agency or in an agency proceeding.

(c) Process, requirement of a report, inspection, or other investigative act or demand may not be issued, made, or enforced except as authorized by law. A person compelled to submit data or evidence is entitled to retain or, on payment of lawfully prescribed costs, procure a copy or transcript thereof, except that in a nonpublic investigatory proceeding the witness may for good cause be limited to inspection of the official transcript of his testimony.

(d) Agency subpoenas authorized by law shall be issued to a party on request and, when required by rules of procedure, on a statement or showing of general relevance and reasonable scope of the evidence sought. On contest, the court shall sustain the subpoena or similar process or demand to the extent that it is found to be in accordance with law. In a proceeding for enforcement, the court shall issue an order requiring the appearance of the witness or the production of the evidence or data within a reasonable time under penalty of punishment for contempt in case of contumacious failure to comply.

(e) Prompt notice shall be given of the denial in whole or in part of a written application, petition, or other request of an interested person made in connection with any agency proceeding. Except in affirming a prior denial or when the denial is self-explanatory, the notice shall be accompanied by a brief statement of the grounds for denial.

§ 556. Hearings; presiding employees; powers and duties; burden of proof; evidence; record as basis of decision

(a) This section applies, according to the provisions thereof, to hearings required by section 553 or 554 of this title [5 USCS § 553 or 554] to be conducted in accordance with this section.

(b) There shall preside at the taking of evidence —

(1) the agency;

(2) one or more members of the body which comprises the agency; or

(3) one or more administrative law judges appointed under section 3105 of this title [5 USCS § 3105].

This subchapter [5 USCS §§ 551 et seq.] does not supersede the conduct of specified classes of proceedings, in whole or in part, by or before boards or other employees specially provided for by or designated under statute. The functions of presiding employees and of employees participating in decisions in accordance with section 557 of this title [5 USCS § 557] shall be conducted in an impartial manner. A presiding or participating employee may at any time disqualify himself. On the filing in good faith of a timely and sufficient affidavit of personal bias or other disqualification of a presiding or participating employee, the agency shall determine the matter as a part of the record and decision in the case.

(c) Subject to published rules of the agency and within its powers, employees presiding at hearings may —

(1) administer oaths and affirmations;

(2) issue subpoenas authorized by law;

(3) rule on offers of proof and receive relevant evidence;

(4) take depositions or have depositions taken when the ends of justice would be served;

(5) regulate the course of the hearing;

(6) hold conferences for the settlement or simplification of the issues by consent of the parties or by the use of alternative means of dispute resolution as provided in subchapter IV of this chapter [5 USCS §§ 581 et seq.];

(7) inform the parties as to the availability of one or more alternative means of dispute resolution, and encourage use of such methods;

(8) require the attendance at any conference held pursuant to paragraph (6) of at least one representative of each party who has authority to negotiate concerning resolution of issues in controversy;

(9) dispose of procedural requests or similar matters;

(10) make or recommend decisions in accordance with section 557 of this title [5 USCS § 557]; and

(11) take other action authorized by agency rule consistent with this subchapter [5 USCS §§ 551 et seq.].

(d) Except as otherwise provided by statute, the proponent of a rule or order has the burden of proof. Any oral or documentary evidence may be received, but the agency as a matter of policy shall provide for the exclusion of irrelevant, immaterial, or unduly repetitious evidence. A sanction may not be imposed or rule or order issued except on consideration of the whole record or those parts thereof cited by a party and supported by and in accordance with the reliable, probative, and substantial evidence. The agency may, to the extent consistent with the interests of justice and the policy of the underlying statutes administered by the agency, consider a violation of section 557(d) of this title [5 USCS § 557(d)] sufficient grounds for a decision adverse to a party who has knowingly committed such violation or knowingly caused such violation to occur. A party is entitled to present his case or defense by oral or documentary evidence, to submit rebuttal evidence, and to conduct such cross- examination as may be required for a full and true disclosure of the facts. In rule making or determining claims for money or benefits or applications for initial licenses an agency may, when a party will not be prejudiced thereby, adopt procedures for the submission of all or part of the evidence in written form.

(e) The transcript of testimony and exhibits, together with all papers and requests filed in the proceeding, constitutes the exclusive record for decision in accordance with section 557 of this title [5 USCS § 557] and, on payment of lawfully prescribed costs, shall be made available to the parties. When an agency decision rests on official notice of a material fact not appearing in the evidence in the record, a party is entitled, on timely request, to an opportunity to show the contrary.

§ 557.   Initial decisions; conclusiveness; review by agency; submissions by parties; contents of decisions; record

(a) This section applies, according to the provisions thereof, when a hearing is required to be conducted in accordance with section 556 of this title [5 USCS § 556].

(b) When the agency did not preside at the reception of the evidence, the presiding employee or, in cases not subject to section 554(d) of this title [5 USCS § 554(d)], an employee qualified to preside at hearings pursuant to section 556 of this title [5 USCS § 556], shall initially decide the case unless the agency requires, either in specific cases or by general rule, the entire record to be certified to it for decision. When the presiding employee makes an initial decision, that decision then becomes the decision of the agency without further proceedings unless there is an appeal to, or review on motion of, the agency within time provided by rule. On appeal from or review of the initial decision, the agency has all the powers which it would have in making the initial decision except as it may limit the issues on notice or by rule. When the agency makes the decision without having presided at the reception of the evidence, the presiding employee or an employee qualified to preside at hearings pursuant to section 556 of this title [5 USCS § 556] shall first recommend a decision, except that in rule making or determining applications for initial licenses —

(1) instead thereof the agency may issue a tentative decision or one of its responsible employees may recommend a decision; or

(2) this procedure may be omitted in a case in which the agency finds on the record that due and timely execution of its functions imperatively and unavoidably so requires.

(c) Before a recommended, initial, or tentative decision, or a decision on agency review of the decision of subordinate employees, the parties are entitled to a reasonable opportunity to submit for the consideration of the employees participating in the decisions —

(1) proposed findings and conclusions; or

(2) exceptions to the decisions or recommended decisions of subordinate employees or to tentative agency decisions; and

(3) supporting reasons for the exceptions or proposed findings or conclusions.

The record shall show the ruling on each finding, conclusion, or exception presented. All decisions, including initial, recommended, and tentative decisions, are a part of the record and shall include a statement of —

(A) findings and conclusions, and the reasons or basis therefor, on all the material issues of fact, law, or discretion presented on the record; and

(B) the appropriate rule, order, sanction, relief, or denial thereof.

(d) (1) In any agency proceeding which is subject to subsection (a) of this section, except to the extent required for the disposition of ex parte matters as authorized by law —

(A) no interested person outside the agency shall make or knowingly cause to be made to any member of the body comprising the agency, administrative law judge, or other employee who is or may reasonably be expected to be involved in the decisional process of the proceeding, an ex parte communication relevant to the merits of the proceeding;

(B) no member of the body comprising the agency, administrative law judge, or other employee who is or may reasonably be expected to be involved in the decisional process of the proceeding, shall make or knowingly cause to be made to any interested person outside the agency an ex parte communication relevant to the merits of the proceeding;

(C) a member of the body comprising the agency, administrative law judge, or other employee who is or may reasonably be expected to be involved in the decisional process of such proceeding who receives, or who makes or knowingly causes to be made, a communication prohibited by this subsection shall place on the public record of the proceeding:

(i) all such written communications;

(ii) memoranda stating the substance of all such oral communications; and

(iii) all written responses, and memoranda stating the substance of all oral responses, to the materials described in clauses (i) and (ii) of this subparagraph;

(D) upon receipt of a communication knowingly made or knowingly caused to be made by a party in violation of this subsection, the agency, administrative law judge, or other employee presiding at the hearing may, to the extent consistent with the interests of justice and the policy of the underlying statutes, require the party to show cause why his claim or interest in the proceeding should not be dismissed, denied, disregarded, or otherwise adversely affected on account of such violation; and

(E) the prohibitions of this subsection shall apply beginning at such time as the agency may designate, but in no case shall they begin to apply later than the time at which a proceeding is noticed for hearing unless the person responsible for the communication has knowledge that it will be noticed, in which case the prohibitions shall apply beginning at the time of his acquisition of such knowledge.

(2) This subsection does not constitute authority to withhold information from Congress.

§ 558.   Imposition of sanctions; determination of applications for licenses; suspension, revocation, and expiration of licenses

(a) This section applies, according to the provisions thereof, to the exercise of a power or authority.

(b) A sanction may not be imposed or a substantive rule or order issued except within jurisdiction delegated to the agency and as authorized by law.

(c) When application is made for a license required by law, the agency, with due regard for the rights and privileges of all the interested parties or adversely affected persons and within a reasonable time, shall set and complete proceedings required to be conducted in accordance with sections 556 and 557 of this title [5 USCS §§ 556 and 557] or other proceedings required by law and shall make its decision. Except in cases of willfulness or those in which public health, interest, or safety requires otherwise, the withdrawal, suspension, revocation, or annulment of a license is lawful only if, before the institution of agency proceedings therefor, the licensee has been given —

(1) notice by the agency in writing of the facts or conduct which may warrant the action; and

(2) opportunity to demonstrate or achieve compliance with all lawful requirements.

When the licensee has made timely and sufficient application for a renewal or a new license in accordance with agency rules, a license with reference to an activity of a continuing nature does not expire until the application has been finally determined by the agency.

Chapter 7. Judicial Review

§ 701. Application; definitions

(a) This chapter [5 USCS §§ 701 et seq.] applies, according to the provisions thereof, except to the extent that —

(1) statutes preclude judicial review; or

(2) agency action is committed to agency discretion by law.

(b) For the purpose of this chapter [5 USCS §§ 701 et seq.] —

(1) "agency" means each authority of the Government of the United States, whether or not it is within or subject to review by another agency, but does not include —

(A) the Congress;

(B) the courts of the United States;

(C) the governments of the territories or possessions of the United States;

(D) the government of the District of Columbia;

(E) agencies composed of representatives of the parties or of representatives of organizations of the parties to the disputes determined by them;

(F) courts martial and military commissions;

(G) military authority exercised in the field in time of war or in occupied territory; or

(H) functions conferred by sections 1738, 1739, 1743, and 1744 of title 12; chapter 2 of title 41 [41 USCS §§ 101 et seq.]; subchapter II of chapter 471 of title 49 [49 USCS §§ 47151 et seq.]; or sections 1884, 1891–1902, and former section 1641(b)(2), of title 50, appendix, and

(2) "person," "rule," "order," "license," "sanction," "relief," and "agency action" have the meanings given them by section 551 of this title [5 USCS § 551].

§ 702. Right of review

A person suffering legal wrong because of agency action, or adversely affected or aggrieved by agency action within the meaning of a relevant statute, is entitled to judicial review thereof. An action in a court of the United States seeking relief other than money damages and stating a claim that an agency or an officer or employee thereof acted or failed to act in an official capacity or under color of legal authority shall not be dismissed nor relief therein be denied on the ground that it is against the United States or that the United States is an indispensable party. The United States may be named as a defendant in any such action, and a judgment or decree may be entered against the United States: *Provided*, That any mandatory or injunctive decree shall specify the Federal officer or officers (by name or by title), and their successors in office, personally responsible for compliance. Nothing herein (1) affects other limitations on judicial review or the power or duty of the court to dismiss any action or deny relief on any other appropriate legal or equitable ground; or (2) confers authority to grant relief if any other statute that grants consent to suit expressly or impliedly forbids the relief which is sought.

§ 703. Form and venue of proceeding

The form of proceeding for judicial review is the special statutory review proceeding relevant to the subject matter in a court specified by statute or, in the absence or inadequacy thereof, any applicable form of legal action, including actions for declaratory judgments or writs of prohibitory or mandatory injunction or habeas corpus, in a court of competent jurisdiction. If no special statutory review proceeding is applicable, the action for judicial review may be brought against the United States, the agency by its official title, or the appropriate officer. Except to the extent that prior, adequate, and exclusive opportunity for judicial review is provided by law, agency action is subject to judicial review in civil or criminal proceedings for judicial enforcement.

§ 704. Actions reviewable

Agency action made reviewable by statute and final agency action for which there is no other adequate remedy in a court are subject to judicial review. A preliminary, procedural, or intermediate agency action or ruling not directly reviewable is subject to review on the review of the final agency action. Except as otherwise expressly required by statute, agency action otherwise final is final for the purposes of this section whether or not there has been presented or determined an application for a declaratory order, for any form of reconsideration, or, unless the agency otherwise requires by rule and provides that the action meanwhile is inoperative, for an appeal to superior agency authority.

§ 705. Relief pending review

When an agency finds that justice so requires, it may postpone the effective date of action taken by it, pending judicial review. On such conditions as may be required and to the extent necessary to prevent irreparable injury, the reviewing court, including the court to which a case may be taken on appeal from or on application for certiorari or other writ to a reviewing court, may issue all necessary and appropriate process to postpone the effective date of an agency action or to preserve status or rights pending conclusion of the review proceedings.

§ 706. Scope of review

To the extent necessary to decision and when presented, the reviewing court shall decide all relevant questions of law, interpret constitutional and statutory provisions, and determine the meaning or applicability of the terms of an agency action. The reviewing court shall —

(1) compel agency action unlawfully withheld or unreasonably delayed; and

(2) hold unlawful and set aside agency action, findings, and conclusions found to be —

(A) arbitrary, capricious, an abuse of discretion, or otherwise not in accordance with law;

(B) contrary to constitutional right, power, privilege, or immunity;

(C) in excess of statutory jurisdiction, authority, or limitations, or short of statutory right;

(D) without observance of procedure required by law;

(E) unsupported by substantial evidence in a case subject to sections 556 and 557 of this title [5 USCS §§ 556 and 557] or otherwise reviewed on the record of an agency hearing provided by statute; or

(F) unwarranted by the facts to the extent that the facts are subject to trial de novo by the reviewing court.

In making the foregoing determinations, the court shall review the whole record or those parts of it cited by a party, and due account shall be taken of the rule of prejudicial error.

Appendix B

REGULATORY FLEXIBILITY ACT

Title 5 of the U.S. Code:

Chapter 6. The Analysis of Regulatory Functions

§ 601. Definitions

For purposes of this chapter [5 USCS §§ 601 et seq.] —

(1) the term "agency" means an agency as defined in section 551(1) of this title [5 USCS § 551(1)];

(2) the term "rule" means any rule for which the agency publishes a general notice of proposed rulemaking pursuant to section 553(b) of this title [5 USCS § 553(b)], or any other law, including any rule of general applicability governing Federal grants to State and local governments for which the agency provides an opportunity for notice and public comment, except that the term "rule" does not include a rule of particular applicability relating to rates, wages, corporate or financial structures or reorganizations thereof, prices, facilities, appliances, services, or allowances therefor or to valuations, costs or accounting, or practices relating to such rates, wages, structures, prices, appliances, services, or allowances;

(3) the term "small business" has the same meaning as the term "small business concern" under section 3 of the Small Business Act [15 USCS § 632], unless an agency, after consultation with the Office of Advocacy of the Small Business Administration and after opportunity for public comment, establishes one or more definitions of such term which are appropriate to the activities of the agency and publishes such definition(s) in the Federal Register;

(4) the term "small organization" means any not-for-profit enterprise which is independently owned and operated and is not dominant in its field, unless an agency establishes, after opportunity for public comment, one or more definitions of such term which are appropriate to the activities of the agency and publishes such definition(s) in the Federal Register;

(5) the term "small governmental jurisdiction" means governments of cities, counties, towns, townships, villages, school districts, or special districts, with a population of less than fifty thousand, unless an agency establishes, after opportunity for public comment, one or more definitions of such term which are appropriate to the activities of the agency and which are based on such factors as location in rural or sparsely populated areas or limited revenues due to the population of such jurisdiction, and publishes such definition(s) in the Federal Register;

(6) the term "small entity" shall have the same meaning as the terms "small

business", "small organization" and "small governmental jurisdiction" defined in paragraphs (3), (4) and (5) of this section; [and]

(7) the term "collection of information" —

(A) means the obtaining, causing to be obtained, soliciting, or requiring the disclosure to third parties or the public, of facts or opinions by or for an agency, regardless of form or format, calling for either —

(i) answers to identical questions posed to, or identical reporting or recordkeeping requirements imposed on, 10 or more persons, other than agencies, instrumentalities, or employees of the United States; or

(ii) answers to questions posed to agencies, instrumentalities, or employees of the United States which are to be used for general statistical purposes; and

(B) shall not include a collection of information described under section 3518(c)(1) of title 44, United States Code. [; and]

(8) Recordkeeping requirement. The term "recordkeeping requirement" means a requirement imposed by an agency on persons to maintain specified records.

§ 602. Regulatory agenda

(a) During the months of October and April of each year, each agency shall publish in the Federal Register a regulatory flexibility agenda which shall contain —

(1) a brief description of the subject area of any rule which the agency expects to propose or promulgate which is likely to have a significant economic impact on a substantial number of small entities;

(2) a summary of the nature of any such rule under consideration for each subject area listed in the agenda pursuant to paragraph (1), the objectives and legal basis for the issuance of the rule, and an approximate schedule for completing action on any rule for which the agency has issued a general notice of proposed rulemaking,[;] and

(3) the name and telephone number of an agency official knowledgeable concerning the items listed in paragraph (1).

(b) Each regulatory flexibility agenda shall be transmitted to the Chief Counsel for Advocacy of the Small Business Administration for comment, if any.

(c) Each agency shall endeavor to provide notice of each regulatory flexibility agenda to small entities or their representatives through direct notification or publication of the agenda in publications likely to be obtained by such small entities and shall invite comments upon each subject area on the agenda.

(d) Nothing in this section precludes an agency from considering or acting on any matter not included in a regulatory flexibility agenda, or requires an agency to consider or act on any matter listed in such agenda.

§ 603. Initial regulatory flexibility analysis

(a) Whenever an agency is required by section 553 of this title [5 USCS § 553], or any other law, to publish general notice of proposed rulemaking for any proposed rule, or publishes a notice of proposed rulemaking for an interpretative rule involving the internal revenue laws of the United States, the agency shall prepare and make available for public comment an initial regulatory flexibility analysis. Such analysis shall describe the impact of the proposed rule on small entities. The initial regulatory flexibility analysis or a summary shall be published in the Federal Register at the time of the publication of general notice of proposed rulemaking for the rule. The agency shall transmit a copy of the initial regulatory flexibility analysis to the Chief Counsel for Advocacy of the Small Business Administration. In the case of an interpretative rule involving the internal revenue laws of the United States, this chapter [5 USCS §§ 601 et seq.] applies to interpretative rules published in the Federal Register for codification in the Code of Federal Regulations, but only to the extent that such interpretative rules impose on small entities a collection of information requirement.

(b) Each initial regulatory flexibility analysis required under this section shall contain —

(1) a description of the reasons why action by the agency is being considered;

(2) a succinct statement of the objectives of, and legal basis for, the proposed rule;

(3) a description of and, where feasible, an estimate of the number of small entities to which the proposed rule will apply;

(4) a description of the projected reporting, recordkeeping, and other compliance requirements of the proposed rule, including an estimate of the classes of small entities which will be subject to the requirement and the type of professional skills necessary for preparation of the report or record;

(5) an identification, to the extent practicable, of all relevant Federal rules which may duplicate, overlap or conflict with the proposed rule.

(c) Each initial regulatory flexibility analysis shall also contain a description of any significant alternatives to the proposed rule which accomplish the stated objectives of applicable statutes and which minimize any significant economic impact of the proposed rule on small entities. Consistent with the stated objectives of applicable statutes, the analysis shall discuss significant alternatives such as —

(1) the establishment of differing compliance or reporting requirements or timetables that take into account the resources available to small entities;

(2) the clarification, consolidation, or simplification of compliance and reporting requirements under the rule for such small entities;

(3) the use of performance rather than design standards; and

(4) an exemption from coverage of the rule, or any part thereof, for such small entities.

§ 604. Final regulatory flexibility analysis

(a) When an agency promulgates a final rule under section 553 of this title [5 USCS § 553], after being required by that section or any other law to publish a general notice of proposed rulemaking, or promulgates a final interpretative rule involving the internal revenue laws of the United States as described in section 603(a) [5 USCS § 603(a)], the agency shall prepare a final regulatory flexibility analysis. Each final regulatory flexibility analysis shall contain —

(1) a succinct statement of the need for, and objectives of, the rule;

(2) a summary of the significant issues raised by the public comments in response to the initial regulatory flexibility analysis, a summary of the assessment of the agency of such issues, and a statement of any changes made in the proposed rule as a result of such comments;

(3) a description of and an estimate of the number of small entities to which the rule will apply or an explanation of why no such estimate is available;

(4) a description of the projected reporting, recordkeeping and other compliance requirements of the rule, including an estimate of the classes of small entities which will be subject to the requirement and the type of professional skills necessary for preparation of the report or record; and

(5) a description of the steps the agency has taken to minimize the significant economic impact on small entities consistent with the stated objectives of applicable statutes, including a statement of the factual, policy, and legal reasons for selecting the alternative adopted in the final rule and why each one of the other significant alternatives to the rule considered by the agency which affect the impact on small entities was rejected.

(b) The agency shall make copies of the final regulatory flexibility analysis available to members of the public and shall publish in the Federal Register such analysis or a summary thereof.

§ 605. Avoidance of duplicative or unnecessary analyses

(a) Any Federal agency may perform the analyses required by sections 602, 603, and 604 of this title [5 USCS §§ 602, 603, and 604] in conjunction with or as a part of any other agenda or analysis required by any other law if such other analysis satisfies the provisions of such sections.

(b) Sections 603 and 604 of this title [5 USCS §§ 603 and 604] shall not apply to any proposed or final rule if the head of the agency certifies that the rule will not, if promulgated, have a significant economic impact on a substantial number of small entities. If the head of the agency makes a certification under the preceding sentence, the agency shall publish such certification in the Federal Register at the time of publication of general notice of proposed rulemaking for the rule or at the time of publication of the final rule, along with a statement providing the factual basis for such certification. The agency shall provide such certification and statement to the Chief Counsel for Advocacy of the Small Business Administration.

(c) In order to avoid duplicative action, an agency may consider a series of closely related rules as one rule for the purposes of sections 602, 603, 604 and 610 of this title [5 USCS §§ 602, 603, 604, and 610].

§ 606. Effect on other law

The requirements of sections 603 and 604 of this title [5 USCS §§ 603 and 604] do not alter in any manner standards otherwise applicable by law to agency action.

§ 607. Preparation of analyses

In complying with the provisions of sections 603 and 604 of this title [5 USCS §§ 603 and 604], an agency may provide either a quantifiable or numerical description of the effects of a proposed rule or alternatives to the proposed rule, or more general descriptive statements if quantification is not practicable or reliable.

§ 608. Procedure for waiver or delay of completion

(a) An agency head may waive or delay the completion of some or all of the requirements of section 603 of this title [5 USCS § 603] by publishing in the Federal Register, not later than the date of publication of the final rule, a written finding, with reasons therefor, that the final rule is being promulgated in response to an emergency that makes compliance or timely compliance with the provisions of section 603 of this title [5 USCS § 603] impracticable.

(b) Except as provided in section 605(b) [5 USCS § 605(b)], an agency head may not waive the requirements of section 604 of this title [5 USCS § 604]. An agency head may delay the completion of the requirements of section 604 of this title [5 USCS § 604] for a period of not more than one hundred and eighty days after the date of publication in the Federal Register of a final rule by publishing in the Federal Register, not later than such date of publication, a written finding, with reasons therefor, that the final rule is being promulgated in response to an emergency that makes timely compliance with the provisions of section 604 of this title [5 USCS § 604] impracticable. If the agency has not prepared a final regulatory analysis pursuant to section 604 of this title [5 USCS § 604] within one hundred and eighty days from the date of publication of the final rule, such rule shall lapse and have no effect. Such rule shall not be repromulgated until a final regulatory flexibility analysis has been completed by the agency.

§ 609. Procedures for gathering comments

(a) When any rule is promulgated which will have a significant economic impact on a substantial number of small entities, the head of the agency promulgating the rule or the official of the agency with statutory responsibility for the promulgation of the rule shall assure that small entities have been given an opportunity to participate in the rulemaking for the rule through the reasonable use of techniques such as —

(1) the inclusion in an advanced notice of proposed rulemaking, if issued, of a statement that the proposed rule may have a significant economic effect on a substantial number of small entities;

(2) the publication of general notice of proposed rulemaking in publications likely to be obtained by small entities;

(3) the direct notification of interested small entities;

(4) the conduct of open conferences or public hearings concerning the rule of small entities including soliciting and receiving comments over computer networks; and

(5) the adoption or modification of agency procedural rules to reduce the cost or complexity of participation in the rulemaking by small entities.

(b) Prior to publication of an initial regulatory flexibility analysis which a covered agency is required to conduct by this chapter [5 USCS §§ 601 et seq.] —

(1) a covered agency shall notify the Chief Counsel for Advocacy of the Small Business Administration and provide the Chief Counsel with information on the potential impacts of the proposed rule on small entities and the type of small entities that might be affected;

(2) not later than 15 days after the date of receipt of the materials described in paragraph (1), the Chief Counsel shall identify individuals representative of affected small entities for the purpose of obtaining advice and recommendations from those individuals about the potential impacts of the proposed rule;

(3) the agency shall convene a review panel for such rule consisting wholly of full time Federal employees of the office within the agency responsible for carrying out the proposed rule, the Office of Information and Regulatory Affairs within the Office of Management and Budget, and the Chief Counsel;

(4) the panel shall review any material the agency has prepared in connection with this chapter, including any draft proposed rule, collect advice and recommendations of each individual small entity representative identified by the agency after consultation with the Chief Counsel, on issues related to subsections 603(b), paragraphs (3), (4) and (5) and 603(c) [5 USCS § 603];

(5) not later than 60 days after the date a covered agency convenes a review panel pursuant to paragraph (3), the review panel shall report on the comments of the small entity representatives and its findings as to issues related to subsections 603(b), paragraphs (3), (4) and (5) and 603(c) [5 USCS § 603], provided that such report shall be made public as part of the rulemaking record; and

(6) where appropriate, the agency shall modify the proposed rule, the initial regulatory flexibility analysis or the decision on whether an initial regulatory flexibility analysis is required.

(c) An agency may in its discretion apply subsection (b) to rules that the agency intends to certify under subsection 605(b) [5 USCS § 605(b)], but the agency believes may have a greater than de minimis impact on a substantial number of small entities.

(d) For purposes of this section, the term "covered agency" means the Environmental Protection Agency and the Occupational Safety and Health Administration of the Department of Labor.

(e) The Chief Counsel for Advocacy, in consultation with the individuals identified in subsection (b)(2), and with the Administrator of the Office of Information and Regulatory Affairs within the Office of Management and Budget, may waive the requirements of subsections (b)(3), (b)(4), and (b)(5) by including in the rulemaking record a written finding, with reasons therefor, that those requirements would not advance the effective participation of small entities in the rulemaking process. For purposes of this subsection, the factors to be considered in making such a finding are as follows:

(1) In developing a proposed rule, the extent to which the covered agency consulted with individuals representative of affected small entities with respect to the potential impacts of the rule and took such concerns into consideration.

(2) Special circumstances requiring prompt issuance of the rule.

(3) Whether the requirements of subsection (b) would provide the individuals identified in subsection (b)(2) with a competitive advantage relative to other small entities.

§ 610. Periodic review of rules

(a) Within one hundred and eighty days after the effective date of this chapter, each agency shall publish in the Federal Register a plan for the periodic review of the rules issued by the agency which have or will have a significant economic impact upon a substantial number of small entities. Such plan may be amended by the agency at any time by publishing the revision in the Federal Register. The purpose of the review shall be to determine whether such rules should be continued without change, or should be amended or rescinded, consistent with the stated objectives of applicable statutes, to minimize any significant economic impact of the rules upon a substantial number of such small entities. The plan shall provide for the review of all such agency rules existing on the effective date of this chapter, within ten years of that date and for the review of such rules adopted after the effective date of this chapter within ten years of the publication of such rules as the final rule. If the head of the agency determines that completion of the review of existing rules is not feasible by the established date, he shall so certify in a statement published in the Federal Register and may extend the completion date by one year at a time for a total of not more than five years.

(b) In reviewing rules to minimize any significant economic impact of the rule on a substantial number of small entities in a manner consistent with the stated objectives of applicable statutes, the agency shall consider the following factors —

(1) the continued need for the rule;

(2) the nature of complaints or comments received concerning the rule from the public;

(3) the complexity of the rule;

(4) the extent to which the rule overlaps, duplicates or conflicts with other Federal rules, and, to the extent feasible, with State and local governmental rules; and

(5) the length of time since the rule has been evaluated or the degree to which

technology, economic conditions, or other factors have changed in the area affected by the rule.

(c) Each year, each agency shall publish in the Federal Register a list of the rules which have a significant economic impact on a substantial number of small entities, which are to be reviewed pursuant to this section during the succeeding twelve months. The list shall include a brief description of each rule and the need for and legal basis of such rule and shall invite public comment upon the rule.

§ 611. Judicial review

(a) (1) For any rule subject to this chapter [5 USCS §§ 601 et seq.], a small entity that is adversely affected or aggrieved by final agency action is entitled to judicial review of agency compliance with the requirements of sections 601, 604, 605(b), 608(b), and 610 [5 USCS §§ 601, a604, 605(b), 608(b), and 610] in accordance with chapter 7 [5 USCS §§ 701 et seq.]. Agency compliance with sections 607 and 609(a) [5 USCS §§ 607 and 609(a)] shall be judicially reviewable in connection with judicial review of section 604 [5 USCS § 604].

(2) Each court having jurisdiction to review such rule for compliance with section 553 [5 USCS § 553], or under any other provision of law, shall have jurisdiction to review any claims of noncompliance with sections 601, 604, 605(b), 608(b), and 610 [5 USCS §§ 601, 604, 605(b), 608(b) and 610] in accordance with chapter 7 [5 USCS §§ 701 et seq.]. Agency compliance with sections 607 and 609(a) [5 USCS §§ 607 and 609(a)] shall be judicially reviewable in connection with judicial review of section 604 [5 USCS § 604].

(3) (A) A small entity may seek such review during the period beginning on the date of final agency action and ending one year later, except that where a provision of law requires that an action challenging a final agency action be commenced before the expiration of one year, such lesser period shall apply to an action for judicial review under this section.

(B) In the case where an agency delays the issuance of a final regulatory flexibility analysis pursuant to section 608(b) of this chapter [5 USCS § 608(b)], an action for judicial review under this section shall be filed not later than —

(i) one year after the date the analysis is made available to the public, or

(ii) where a provision of law requires that an action challenging a final agency regulation be commenced before the expiration of the 1-year period, the number of days specified in such provision of law that is after the date the analysis is made available to the public.

(4) In granting any relief in an action under this section, the court shall order the agency to take corrective action consistent with this chapter and chapter 7 [5 USCS §§ 601 et seq., 701 et seq.], including, but not limited to —

(A) remanding the rule to the agency, and

(B) deferring the enforcement of the rule against small entities unless the court finds that continued enforcement of the rule is in the public interest.

(5) Nothing in this subsection shall be construed to limit the authority of any

court to stay the effective date of any rule or provision thereof under any other provision of law or to grant any other relief in addition to the requirements of this section.

(b) In an action for the judicial review of a rule, the regulatory flexibility analysis for such rule, including an analysis prepared or corrected pursuant to paragraph (a)(4), shall constitute part of the entire record of agency action in connection with such review.

(c) Compliance or noncompliance by an agency with the provisions of this chapter [5 USCS §§ 601 et seq.] shall be subject to judicial review only in accordance with this section.

(d) Nothing in this section bars judicial review of any other impact statement or similar analysis required by any other law if judicial review of such statement or analysis is otherwise permitted by law.

§ 612.　Reports and intervention rights

(a) The Chief Counsel for Advocacy of the Small Business Administration shall monitor agency compliance with this chapter [5 USCS §§ 601 et seq.] and shall report at least annually thereon to the President and to the Committees on the Judiciary and Small Business of the Senate and House of Representatives.

(b) The Chief Counsel for Advocacy of the Small Business Administration is authorized to appear as amicus curiae in any action brought in a court of the United States to review a rule. In any such action, the Chief Counsel is authorized to present his or her views with respect to compliance with this chapter [5 USCS §§ 601 et seq.], the adequacy of the rulemaking record with respect to small entities and the effect of the rule on small entities.

(c) A court of the United States shall grant the application of the Chief Counsel for Advocacy of the Small Business Administration to appear in any such action for the purposes described in subsection (b).

Appendix C

FEDERAL ADVISORY COMMITTEE ACT

5 U.S.C. app.
As Amended

§ 1. Short title

This Act may be cited as the "Amendments."

§ 2. Findings and purpose

(a) The Congress finds that there are numerous committees, boards, commissions, councils, and similar groups which have been established to advise officers and agencies in the executive branch of the Federal Government and that they are frequently a useful and beneficial means of furnishing expert advice, ideas, and diverse opinions to the Federal Government.

(b) The Congress further finds and declares that —

(1) the need for many existing advisory committees has not been adequately reviewed;

(2) new advisory committees should be established only when they are determined to be essential and their number should be kept to the minimum necessary;

(3) advisory committees should be terminated when they are no longer carrying out the purposes for which they were established;

(4) standards and uniform procedures should govern the establishment, operation, administration, and duration of advisory committees;

(5) the Congress and the public should be kept informed with respect to the number, purpose, membership, activities, and cost of advisory committees; and

(6) the function of advisory committees should be advisory only, and that all matters under their consideration should be determined, in accordance with law, by the official, agency, or officer involved.

§ 3. Definitions

For the purpose of this Act —

(1) The term "Administrator" means the Administrator of General Services.

(2) The term "advisory committee" means any committee, board, commission, council, conference, panel, task force, or other similar group, or any subcommittee or other subgroup thereof (hereafter in this paragraph referred to as "committee"), which is —

(A) established by statute or reorganization plan, or

(B) established or utilized by the President, or

(C) established or utilized by one or more agencies, in the interest of obtaining advice or recommendations for the President or one or more agencies or officers of the Federal Government, except that such term excludes (i) any committee that is composed wholly of full-time, or permanent part-time, officers or employees of the Federal Government, and (ii) any committee that is created by the National Academy of Sciences or the National Academy of Public Administration.

(3) The term "agency" has the same meaning as in section 551(1) of Title 5, United States Code.

(4) The term "Presidential advisory committee" means an advisory committee which advises the President.

§ 4. Applicability; restrictions

(a) The provisions of this Act or of any rule, order, or regulation promulgated under this Act shall apply to each advisory committee except to the extent that any Act of Congress establishing any such advisory committee specifically provides otherwise.

(b) Nothing in this Act shall be construed to apply to any advisory committee established or utilized by —

(1) the Central Intelligence Agency; or

(2) the Federal Reserve System.

(c) Nothing in this Act shall be construed to apply to any local civic group whose primary function is that of rendering a public service with respect to a Federal program, or any State or local committee, council, board, commission, or similar group established to advise or make recommendations to State or local officials or agencies.

§ 5. Responsibilities of Congressional committees; review; guidelines

(a) In the exercise of its legislative review function, each standing committee of the Senate and the House of Representatives shall make a continuing review of the activities of each advisory committee under its jurisdiction to determine whether such advisory committee should be abolished or merged with any other advisory committee, whether the responsibilities of such advisory committee should be revised, and whether such advisory committee performs a necessary function not already being performed. Each such standing committee shall take appropriate action to obtain the enactment of legislation necessary to carry out the purpose of this subsection.

(b) In considering legislation establishing, or authorizing the establishment of any advisory committee, each standing committee of the Senate and of the House of Representatives shall determine, and report such determination to the Senate or to the House of Representatives, as the case may be, whether the functions of the proposed advisory committee are being or could be performed by one or more agencies or by an advisory committee already in existence, or by enlarging the mandate of an existing advisory committee. Any such legislation shall —

(1) contain a clearly defined purpose for the advisory committee;

(2) require the membership of the advisory committee to be fairly balanced in terms of the points of view represented and the functions to be performed by the advisory committee;

(3) contain appropriate provisions to assure that the advice and recommendations of the advisory committee will not be inappropriately influenced by the appointing authority or by any special interest, but will instead be the result of the advisory committee's independent judgment;

(4) contain provisions dealing with authorization of appropriations, the date for submission of reports (if any), the duration of the advisory committee, and the publication of reports and other materials, to the extent that the standing committee determines the provisions of section 10 of this Act to be inadequate; and

(5) contain provisions which will assure that the advisory committee will have adequate staff (either supplied by an agency or employed by it), will be provided adequate quarters, and will have funds available to meet its other necessary expenses.

(c) To the extent they are applicable, the guidelines set out in subsection (b) of this section shall be followed by the President, agency heads, or other Federal officials in creating an advisory committee.

§ 6. Responsibilities of the President; report to Congress; annual report to Congress; exclusion

(a) The President may delegate responsibility for evaluating and taking action, where appropriate, with respect to all public recommendations made to him by Presidential advisory committees.

(b) Within one year after a Presidential advisory committee has submitted a public report to the President, the President or his delegate shall make a report to the Congress stating either his proposals for action or his reasons for inaction, with respect to the recommendations contained in the public report.

(c) [Annual report] Repealed by the Federal Reports Elimination and Sunset Act of 1995, Pub. L. No. 104-66, § 3003, 109 Stat. 707, 734-36 (1995), amended by Pub. L. No. 106-113, § 236, 113 Stat. 1501, 1501A-302 (1999) (changing effective date to May 15, 2000).

§ 7. Responsibilities of the Administrator of General Services; Committee Management Secretariat, establishment; review; recommendations to President and Congress; agency cooperation; performance guidelines; uniform pay guidelines; travel expenses; expense recommendations

(a) The Administrator shall establish and maintain within the General Services Administration a Committee Management Secretariat, which shall be responsible for all matters relating to advisory committees.

(b) The Administrator shall, immediately after October 6, 1972, institute a comprehensive review of the activities and responsibilities of each advisory committee to determine —

(1) whether such committee is carrying out its purpose;

(2) whether, consistent with the provisions of applicable statutes, the responsibilities assigned to it should be revised;

(3) whether it should be merged with other advisory committees; or

(4) whether it should be abolished.

The Administrator may from time to time request such information as he deems necessary to carry out his functions under this subsection. Upon the completion of the Administrator's review he shall make recommendations to the President and to either the agency head or the Congress with respect to action he believes should be taken. Thereafter, the Administrator shall carry out a similar review annually. Agency heads shall cooperate with the Administrator in making the reviews required by this subsection.

(c) The Administrator shall prescribe administrative guidelines and management controls applicable to advisory committees, and, to the maximum extent feasible, provide advice, assistance, and guidance to advisory committees to improve their performance. In carrying out his functions under this subsection, the Administrator shall consider the recommendations of each agency head with respect to means of improving the performance of advisory committees whose duties are related to such agency.

(d) (1) The Administrator, after study and consultation with the Director of the Office of Personnel Management, shall establish guidelines with respect to uniform fair rates of pay for comparable services of members, staffs, and consultants of advisory committees in a manner which gives appropriate recognition to the responsibilities and qualifications required and other relevant factors. Such regulations shall provide that —

(A) no member of any advisory committee or of the staff of any advisory committee shall receive compensation at a rate in excess of the rate specified for GS-18 of the General Schedule under section 5332 of Title 5, United States Code;

(B) such members, while engaged in the performance of their duties away from their homes or regular places of business, may be allowed travel expenses, including per diem in lieu of subsistence, as authorized by section

5703 of Title 5, United States Code, for persons employed intermittently in the Government service; and

(C) such members —

(i) who are blind or deaf or who otherwise qualify as handicapped individuals (within the meaning of section 501 of the Rehabilitation Act of 1973 (29 U.S.C. § 794)), and

(ii) who do not otherwise qualify for assistance under section 3102 of Title 5, United States Code, by reason of being an employee of an agency (within the meaning of section 3102(a)(1) of such Title 5),

may be provided services pursuant to section 3102 of such Title 5 while in performance of their advisory committee duties.

(2) Nothing in this subsection shall prevent —

(A) an individual who (without regard to his service with an advisory committee) is a full-time employee of the United States, or

(B) an individual who immediately before his service with an advisory committee was such an employee, from receiving compensation at the rate at which he otherwise would be compensated (or was compensated) as a full-time employee of the United States.

(e) The Administrator shall include in budget recommendations a summary of the amounts he deems necessary for the expenses of advisory committees, including the expenses for publication of reports where appropriate.

§ 8. Responsibilities of agency heads; Advisory Committee Management Officer, designation

(a) Each agency head shall establish uniform administrative guidelines and management controls for advisory committees established by that agency, which shall be consistent with directives of the Administrator under section 7 and section 10. Each agency shall maintain systematic information on the nature, functions, and operations of each advisory committee within its jurisdiction.

(b) The head of each agency which has an advisory committee shall designate an Advisory Committee Management Officer who shall —

(1) exercise control and supervision over the establishment, procedures, and accomplishments of advisory committees established by that agency;

(2) assemble and maintain the reports, records, and other papers of any such committee during its existence; and

(3) carry out, on behalf of that agency, the provisions of section 552 of Title 5, United States Code, with respect to such reports, records, and other papers.

§ 9. Establishment and purpose of advisory committees; publication in Federal Register; charter: filing, contents, copy

(a) No advisory committee shall be established unless such establishment is —

(1) specifically authorized by statute or by the President; or

(2) determined as a matter of formal record, by the head of the agency involved after consultation with the Administrator, with timely notice published in the Federal Register, to be in the public interest in connection with the performance of duties imposed on that agency by law.

(b) Unless otherwise specifically provided by statute or Presidential directive, advisory committees shall be utilized solely for advisory functions. Determinations of action to be taken and policy to be expressed with respect to matters upon which an advisory committee reports or makes recommendations shall be made solely by the President or an officer of the Federal Government.

(c) No advisory committee shall meet or take any action until an advisory committee charter has been filed with (1) the Administrator, in the case of Presidential advisory committees, or (2) with the head of the agency to whom any advisory committee reports and with the standing committees of the Senate and of the House of Representatives having legislative jurisdiction of such agency. Such charter shall contain the following information:

(A) the committee's official designation;

(B) the committee's objectives and the scope of its activity;

(C) the period of time necessary for the committee to carry out its purposes;

(D) the agency or official to whom the committee reports;

(E) the agency responsible for providing the necessary support for the committee;

(F) a description of the duties for which the committee is responsible, and, if such duties are not solely advisory, a specification of the authority for such functions;

(G) the estimated annual operating costs in dollars and man-years for such committee;

(H) the estimated number and frequency of committee meetings;

(I) the committee's termination date, if less than two years from the date of the committee's establishment; and

(J) the date the charter is filed.

A copy of any such charter shall also be furnished to the Library of Congress.

§ 10. Advisory committee procedures; meetings; notice, publication in Federal Register; regulations; minutes; certification; annual report; Federal officer or employee, attendance

(a) (1) Each advisory committee meeting shall be open to the public.

(2) Except when the President determines otherwise for reasons of national security, timely notice of each such meeting shall be published in the Federal Register, and the Administrator shall prescribe regulations to provide for other types of public notice to insure that all interested persons are notified of such meeting prior thereto.

(3) Interested persons shall be permitted to attend, appear before, or file statements with any advisory committee, subject to such reasonable rules or regulations as the Administrator may prescribe.

(b) Subject to section 552 of Title 5, United States Code, the records, reports, transcripts, minutes, appendixes, working papers, drafts, studies, agenda, or other documents which were made available to or prepared for or by each advisory committee shall be available for public inspection and copying at a single location in the offices of the advisory committee or the agency to which the advisory committee reports until the advisory committee ceases to exist.

(c) Detailed minutes of each meeting of each advisory committee shall be kept and shall contain a record of the persons present, a complete and accurate description of matters discussed and conclusions reached, and copies of all reports received, issued, or approved by the advisory committee. The accuracy of all minutes shall be certified to by the chairman of the advisory committee.

(d) Subsections (a)(1) and (a)(3) of this section shall not apply to any portion of an advisory committee meeting where the President, or the head of the agency to which the advisory committee reports, determines that such portion of such meeting may be closed to the public in accordance with subsection (c) of section 552b of Title 5, United States Code. Any such determination shall be in writing and shall contain the reasons for such determination. If such a determination is made, the advisory committee shall issue a report at least annually setting forth a summary of its activities and such related matters as would be informative to the public consistent with the policy of section 552(b) of Title 5, United States Code.

(e) There shall be designated an officer or employee of the Federal Government to chair or attend each meeting of each advisory committee. The officer or employee so designated is authorized, whenever he determines it to be in the public interest, to adjourn any such meeting. No advisory committee shall conduct any meeting in the absence of that officer or employee.

(f) Advisory committees shall not hold any meetings except at the call of, or with the advance approval of, a designated officer or employee of the Federal Government, and in the case of advisory committees (other than Presidential advisory committees), with an agenda approved by such officer or employee.

§ 11. Availability of transcripts; "agency proceeding"

(a) Except where prohibited by contractual agreements entered into prior to the effective date of this Act, agencies and advisory committees shall make available to any person, at actual cost of duplication, copies of transcripts of agency proceedings or advisory committee meetings.

(b) As used in this section "agency proceeding" means any proceeding as defined in section 551 (12) of Title 5, United States Code.

§ 12. Fiscal and administrative provisions; record-keeping; audit; agency support services

(a) Each agency shall keep records as will fully disclose the disposition of any funds which may be at the disposal of its advisory committees and the nature and extent of their activities. The General Services Administration, or such other agency as the President may designate, shall maintain financial records with respect to Presidential advisory committees. The Comptroller General of the United States, or any of his authorized representatives, shall have access, for the purpose of audit and examination, to any such records.

(b) Each agency shall be responsible for providing support services for each advisory committee established by or reporting to it unless the establishing authority provides otherwise. Where any such advisory committee reports to more than one agency, only one agency shall be responsible for support services at any one time. In the case of Presidential advisory committees, such services may be provided by the General Services Administration.

§ 13. Responsibilities of Library of Congress; reports and background papers; depository

Subject to section 552 of Title 5, United States Code, the Administrator shall provide for the filing with the Library of Congress of at least eight copies of each report made by every advisory committee and, where appropriate, background papers prepared by consultants. The Librarian of Congress shall establish a depository for such reports and papers where they shall be available to public inspection and use.

§ 14. Termination of advisory committees; renewal; continuation

(a) (1) Each advisory committee which is in existence on the effective date of this Act shall terminate not later than the expiration of the two-year period following such effective date unless —

(A) in the case of an advisory committee established by the President or an officer of the Federal Government, such advisory committee is renewed by the President or that officer by appropriate action prior to the expiration of such two-year period; or

(B) in the case of an advisory committee established by an Act of Congress, its duration is otherwise provided for by law.

(2) Each advisory committee established after such effective date shall termi-

nate not later than the expiration of the two-year period beginning on the date of its establishment unless —

(A) in the case of an advisory committee established by the President or an officer of the Federal Government such advisory committee is renewed by the President or such officer by appropriate action prior to the end of such period; or

(B) in the case of an advisory committee established by an Act of Congress, its duration is otherwise provided for by law.

(b) (1) Upon the renewal of any advisory committee, such advisory committee shall file a charter in accordance with section 9(c).

(2) Any advisory committee established by an Act of Congress shall file a charter in accordance with such section upon the expiration of each successive two-year period following the date of enactment of the Act establishing such advisory committee.

(3) No advisory committee required under this subsection to file a charter shall take any action (other than preparation and filing of such charter) prior to the date on which such charter is filed.

(c) Any advisory committee which is renewed by the President or any officer of the Federal Government may be continued only for successive two-year periods by appropriate action taken by the President or such officer prior to the date on which such advisory committee would otherwise terminate.

§ 15. Requirements relating to the National Academy of Sciences and the National Academy of Public Administration

(a) In General- An agency may not use any advice or recommendation provided by the National Academy of Sciences or National Academy of Public Administration that was developed by use of a committee created by that academy under an agreement with an agency, unless —

(1) the committee was not subject to any actual management or control by an agency or an officer of the Federal Government;

(2) in the case of a committee created after the date of the enactment of the Federal Advisory Committee Act Amendments of 1997, the membership of the committee was appointed in accordance with the requirements described in subsection (b)(1); and

(3) in developing the advice or recommendations, the academy compiled with —

(A) subsection (b)(2) through (6), in the case of any advice or recommendation provided by the National Academy of Sciences; or

(B) subsection (b)(2) and (5), in the case of any advice or recommendation provided by the National Academy of Public Administration.

(b) Requirements- The requirements referred to in subsection (a) are as follows:

(1) The Academy shall determine and provide public notice of the names and brief biographies of individuals that the Academy appoints or intends to appoint to serve on the committee. The Academy shall determine and provide a reasonable opportunity for the public to comment on such appointments before they are made or, if the Academy determines such prior comment is not practicable, in the period immediately following the appointments. The Academy shall make its best efforts to ensure that (A) no individual appointed to serve on the committee has a conflict of interest that is relevant to the functions to be performed, unless such conflict is promptly and publicly disclosed and the Academy determines that the conflict is unavoidable, (B) the committee membership is fairly balanced as determined by the Academy to be appropriate for the functions to be performed, and (C) the final report of the Academy will be the result of the Academy's independent judgment. The Academy shall require that individuals that the Academy appoints or intends to appoint to serve on the committee inform the Academy of the individual's conflicts of interest that are relevant to the functions to be performed.

(2) The Academy shall determine and provide public notice of committee meetings that will be open to the public.

(3) The Academy shall ensure that meetings of the committee to gather data from individuals who are not officials, agents, or employees of the Academy are open to the public, unless the Academy determines that a meeting would disclose matters described in section 552(b) of Title 5, United States Code. The Academy shall make available to the public, at reasonable charge if appropriate, written materials presented to the committee by individuals who are not officials, agents, or employees of the Academy, unless the Academy determines that making material available would disclose matters described in that section.

(4) The Academy shall make available to the public as soon as practicable, at reasonable charge if appropriate, a brief summary of any committee meeting that is not a data gathering meeting, unless the Academy determines that the summary would disclose matters described in section 552(b) Title 5, United States Code. The summary shall identify the committee members present, the topics discussed, materials made available to the committee, and such other matters that the Academy determines should be included.

(5) The Academy shall make available to the public its final report, at reasonable charge if appropriate, unless the Academy determines that the report would disclose matters described in section 552(b) of Title 5, United States Code. If the Academy determines that the report would disclose matters described in that section, the Academy shall make public an abbreviated version of the report that does not disclose those matters.

(6) After publication of the final report, the Academy shall make publicly available the names of the principal reviewers who reviewed the report in draft form and who are not officials, agents, or employees of the Academy.

(c) Regulations- The Administrator of General Services may issue regulations implementing this section.

§ 16. Effective Date

Except as provided in section 7(b), this Act shall become effective upon the expiration of ninety days following October 6, 1972.

Appendix D

Executive Order 12866

Executive Order 12866

Regulatory Planning and Review

September 30, 1993

The American people deserve a regulatory system that works for them, not against them: a regulatory system that protects and improves their health, safety, environment, and well-being and improves the performance of the economy without imposing unacceptable or unreasonable costs on society; regulatory policies that recognize that the private sector and private markets are the best engine for economic growth; regulatory approaches that respect the role of State, local, and tribal governments; and regulations that are effective, consistent, sensible, and understandable. We do not have such a regulatory system today.

With this Executive order, the Federal Government begins a program to reform and make more efficient the regulatory process. The objectives of this Executive order are to enhance planning and coordination with respect to both new and existing regulations; to reaffirm the primacy of Federal agencies in the regulatory decision-making process; to restore the integrity and legitimacy of regulatory review and oversight; and to make the process more accessible and open to the public. In pursuing these objectives, the regulatory process shall be conducted so as to meet applicable statutory requirements and with due regard to the discretion that has been entrusted to the Federal agencies.

Accordingly, by the authority vested in me as President by the Constitution and the laws of the United States of America, it is hereby ordered as follows:

Sec. 1. Statement of Regulatory Philosophy and Principles.

(a) The Regulatory Philosophy. Federal agencies should promulgate only such regulations as are required by law, are necessary to interpret the law, or are made necessary by compelling public need, such as material failures of private markets to protect or improve the health and safety of the public, the environment, or the well-being of the American people. In deciding whether and how to regulate, agencies should assess all costs and benefits of available regulatory alternatives, including the alternative of not regulating. Costs and benefits shall be understood to include both quantifiable measures (to the fullest extent that these can be usefully estimated) and qualitative measures of costs and benefits that are difficult to quantify, but nevertheless essential to consider. Further, in choosing among alternative regulatory approaches, agencies should select those approaches that maximize net benefits (including potential economic, environmental, public health and safety, and other advantages; distributive impacts; and equity), unless a statute requires another regulatory approach.

(b) The Principles of Regulation. To ensure that the agencies' regulatory programs are consistent with the philosophy set forth above, agencies should adhere to the following principles, to the extent permitted by law and where applicable:

(1) Each agency shall identify the problem that it intends to address (including, where applicable, the failures of private markets or public institutions that warrant new agency action) as well as assess the significance of that problem.

(2) Each agency shall examine whether existing regulations (or other law) have created, or contributed to, the problem that a new regulation is intended to correct and whether those regulations (or other law) should be modified to achieve the intended goal of regulation more effectively.

(3) Each agency shall identify and assess available alternatives to direct regulation, including providing economic incentives to encourage the desired behavior, such as user fees or marketable permits, or providing information upon which choices can be made by the public.

(4) In setting regulatory priorities, each agency shall consider, to the extent reasonable, the degree and nature of the risks posed by various substances or activities within its jurisdiction.

(5) When an agency determines that a regulation is the best available method of achieving the regulatory objective, it shall design its regulations in the most cost-effective manner to achieve the regulatory objective. In doing so, each agency shall consider incentives for innovation, consistency, predictability, the costs of enforcement and compliance (to the government, regulated entities, and the public), flexibility, distributive impacts, and equity.

(6) Each agency shall assess both the costs and the benefits of the intended regulation and, recognizing that some costs and benefits are difficult to quantify, propose or adopt a regulation only upon a reasoned determination that the benefits of the intended regulation justify its costs.

(7) Each agency shall base its decisions on the best reasonably obtainable scientific, technical, economic, and other information concerning the need for, and consequences of, the intended regulation.

(8) Each agency shall identify and assess alternative forms of regulation and shall, to the extent feasible, specify performance objectives, rather than specifying the behavior or manner of compliance that regulated entities must adopt.

(9) Wherever feasible, agencies shall seek views of appropriate State, local, and tribal officials before imposing regulatory requirements that might significantly or uniquely affect those governmental entities. Each agency shall assess the effects of Federal regulations on State, local, and tribal governments, including specifically the availability of resources to carry out those mandates, and seek to minimize those burdens that uniquely or significantly affect such

governmental entities, consistent with achieving regulatory objectives. In addition, as appropriate, agencies shall seek to harmonize Federal regulatory actions with related State, local, and tribal regulatory and other governmental functions.

(10) Each agency shall avoid regulations that are inconsistent, incompatible, or duplicative with its other regulations or those of other Federal agencies.

(11) Each agency shall tailor its regulations to impose the least burden on society, including individuals, businesses of differing sizes, and other entities (including small communities and governmental entities), consistent with obtaining the regulatory objectives, taking into account, among other things, and to the extent practicable, the costs of cumulative regulations.

(12) Each agency shall draft its regulations to be simple and easy to understand, with the goal of minimizing the potential for uncertainty and litigation arising from such uncertainty.

Sec. 2. Organization.

An efficient regulatory planning and review process is vital to ensure that the Federal Government's regulatory system best serves the American people.

(a) The Agencies. Because Federal agencies are the repositories of significant substantive expertise and experience, they are responsible for developing regulations and assuring that the regulations are consistent with applicable law, the President's priorities, and the principles set forth in this Executive order.

(b) The Office of Management and Budget. Coordinated review of agency rulemaking is necessary to ensure that regulations are consistent with applicable law, the President's priorities, and the principles set forth in this Executive order, and that decisions made by one agency do not conflict with the policies or actions taken or planned by another agency. The Office of Management and Budget (OMB) shall carry out that review function. Within OMB, the Office of Information and Regulatory Affairs (OIRA) is the repository of expertise concerning regulatory issues, including methodologies and procedures that affect more than one agency, this Executive order, and the President's regulatory policies. To the extent permitted by law, OMB shall provide guidance to agencies and assist the President, the Vice President, and other regulatory policy advisors to the President in regulatory planning and shall be the entity that reviews individual regulations, as provided by this Executive order.

(c) The Vice President. The Vice President is the principal advisor to the President on, and shall coordinate the development and presentation of recommendations concerning, regulatory policy, planning, and review, as set forth in this Executive order. In fulfilling their responsibilities under this Executive order, the President and the Vice President shall be assisted by the regulatory policy advisors within the Executive Office of the President and by such agency officials and personnel as the President and the Vice President may, from time to time, consult.

Sec. 3. Definitions.

For purposes of this Executive order:

(a) "Advisors" refers to such regulatory policy advisors to the President as the President and Vice President may from time to time consult, including, among others: (1) the Director of OMB; (2) the Chair (or another member) of the Council of Economic Advisers; (3) the Assistant to the President for Economic Policy; (4) the Assistant to the President for Domestic Policy; (5) the Assistant to the President for National Security Affairs; (6) the Assistant to the President for Science and Technology; (7) the Assistant to the President for Intergovernmental Affairs; (8) the Assistant to the President and Staff Secretary; (9) the Assistant to the President and Chief of Staff to the Vice President; (10) the Assistant to the President and Counsel to the President; (11) the Deputy Assistant to the President and Director of the White House Office on Environmental Policy; and (12) the Administrator of OIRA, who also shall coordinate communications relating to this Executive order among the agencies, OMB, the other Advisors, and the Office of the Vice President.

(b) "Agency," unless otherwise indicated, means any authority of the United States that is an "agency" under 44 U.S.C. 3502(1), other than those considered to be independent regulatory agencies, as defined in 44 U.S.C. 3502(10).

(c) "Director" means the Director of OMB.

(d) "Regulation" or "rule" means an agency statement of general applicability and future effect, which the agency intends to have the force and effect of law, that is designed to implement, interpret, or prescribe law or policy or to describe the procedure or practice requirements of an agency. It does not, however, include:

(1) Regulations or rules issued in accordance with the formal rulemaking provisions of 5 U.S.C. 556, 557;

(2) Regulations or rules that pertain to a military or foreign affairs function of the United States, other than procurement regulations and regulations involving the import or export of non-defense articles and services;

(3) Regulations or rules that are limited to agency organization, management, or personnel matters; or

(4) Any other category of regulations exempted by the Administrator of OIRA.

(e) "Regulatory action" means any substantive action by an agency (normally published in the Federal Register) that promulgates or is expected to lead to the promulgation of a final rule or regulation, including notices of inquiry, advance notices of proposed rulemaking, and notices of proposed rulemaking.

(f) "Significant regulatory action" means any regulatory action that is likely to result in a rule that may:

(1) Have an annual effect on the economy of $100 million or more or adversely affect in a material way the economy, a sector of the economy,

productivity, competition, jobs, the environment, public health or safety, or State, local, or tribal governments or communities;

(2) Create a serious inconsistency or otherwise interfere with an action taken or planned by another agency;

(3) Materially alter the budgetary impact of entitlements, grants, user fees, or loan programs or the rights and obligations of recipients thereof; or

(4) Raise novel legal or policy issues arising out of legal mandates, the President's priorities, or the principles set forth in this Executive order.

Sec. 4. Planning Mechanism.

In order to have an effective regulatory program, to provide for coordination of regulations, to maximize consultation and the resolution of potential conflicts at an early stage, to involve the public and its State, local, and tribal officials in regulatory planning, and to ensure that new or revised regulations promote the President's priorities and the principles set forth in this Executive order, these procedures shall be followed, to the extent permitted by law:

(a) Agencies' Policy Meeting. Early in each year's planning cycle, the Vice President shall convene a meeting of the Advisors and the heads of agencies to seek a common understanding of priorities and to coordinate regulatory efforts to be accomplished in the upcoming year.

(b) Unified Regulatory Agenda. For purposes of this subsection, the term "agency" or "agencies" shall also include those considered to be independent regulatory agencies, as defined in 44 U.S.C. 3502(10). Each agency shall prepare an agenda of all regulations under development or review, at a time and in a manner specified by the Administrator of OIRA. The description of each regulatory action shall contain, at a minimum, a regulation identifier number, a brief summary of the action, the legal authority for the action, any legal deadline for the action, and the name and telephone number of a knowledgeable agency official. Agencies may incorporate the information required under 5 U.S.C. 602 and 41 U.S.C. 402 into these agendas.

(c) The Regulatory Plan. For purposes of this subsection, the term "agency" or "agencies" shall also include those considered to be independent regulatory agencies, as defined in 44 U.S.C. 3502(10).

(1) As part of the Unified Regulatory Agenda, beginning in 1994, each agency shall prepare a Regulatory Plan (Plan) of the most important significant regulatory actions that the agency reasonably expects to issue in proposed or final form in that fiscal year or thereafter. The Plan shall be approved personally by the agency head and shall contain at a minimum:

(A) A statement of the agency's regulatory objectives and priorities and how they relate to the President's priorities;

(B) A summary of each planned significant regulatory action including, to the extent possible, alternatives to be considered and preliminary estimates of the anticipated costs and benefits;

(C) A summary of the legal basis for each such action, including whether any aspect of the action is required by statute or court order;

(D) A statement of the need for each such action and, if applicable, how the action will reduce risks to public health, safety, or the environment, as well as how the magnitude of the risk addressed by the action relates to other risks within the jurisdiction of the agency;

(E) The agency's schedule for action, including a statement of any applicable statutory (F) The name, address, and telephone number of a person the public may contact for additional information about the planned regulatory action.

(2) Each agency shall forward its Plan to OIRA by June 1st of each year.

(3) Within 10 calendar days after OIRA has received an agency's Plan, OIRA shall circulate it to other affected agencies, the Advisors, and the Vice President.

(4) An agency head who believes that a planned regulatory action of another agency may conflict with its own policy or action taken or planned shall promptly notify, in writing, the Administrator of OIRA, who shall forward that communication to the issuing agency, the Advisors, and the Vice President.

(5) If the Administrator of OIRA believes that a planned regulatory action of an agency may be inconsistent with the President's priorities or the principles set forth in this Executive order or may be in conflict with any policy or action taken or planned by another agency, the Administrator of OIRA shall promptly notify, in writing, the affected agencies, the Advisors, and the Vice President.

(6) The Vice President, with the Advisors' assistance, may consult with the heads of agencies with respect to their Plans and, in appropriate instances, request further consideration or inter-agency coordination.

(7) The Plans developed by the issuing agency shall be published annually in the October publication of the Unified Regulatory Agenda. This publication shall be made available to the Congress; State, local, and tribal governments; and the public. Any views on any aspect of any agency Plan, including whether any planned regulatory action might conflict with any other planned or existing regulation, impose any unintended consequences on the public, or confer any unclaimed benefits on the public, should be directed to the issuing agency, with a copy to OIRA.

(d)   Regulatory Working Group. Within 30 days of the date of this Executive order, the Administrator of OIRA shall convene a Regulatory Working Group ("Working Group"), which shall consist of representatives of the heads of each agency that the Administrator determines to have significant domestic regulatory responsibility, the Advisors, and the Vice President. The Administrator of OIRA shall chair the Working Group and shall periodically advise the Vice President on the activities of the Working Group. The Working Group shall serve as a forum to assist agencies in identifying and analyzing important regulatory issues (including, among others (1) the development of innovative regulatory techniques, (2) the methods, efficacy, and utility of comparative risk assessment in regulatory decision-making, and (3) the development of short forms and other streamlined regulatory approaches for small businesses and other entities). The Working Group shall meet at least quarterly and may meet as a whole or in subgroups of agencies with an interest in particular issues or subject areas. To inform its discussions, the Working Group may commission analytical studies and reports by OIRA, the Administrative Conference of the United States, or any other agency.

(e) Conferences. The Administrator of OIRA shall meet quarterly with representatives of State, local, and tribal governments to identify both existing and proposed regulations that may uniquely or significantly affect those governmental entities. The Administrator of OIRA shall also convene, from time to time, conferences with representatives of businesses, nongovernmental organizations, and the public to discuss regulatory issues of common concern.

Sec. 5. Existing Regulations.

In order to reduce the regulatory burden on the American people, their families, their communities, their State, local, and tribal governments, and their industries; to determine whether regulations promulgated by the executive branch of the Federal Government have become unjustified or unnecessary as a result of changed circumstances; to confirm that regulations are both compatible with each other and not duplicative or inappropriately burdensome in the aggregate; to ensure that all regulations are consistent with the President's priorities and the principles set forth in this Executive order, within applicable law; and to otherwise improve the effectiveness of existing regulations:

(a) Within 90 days of the date of this Executive order, each agency shall submit to OIRA a program, consistent with its resources and regulatory priorities, under which the agency will periodically review its existing significant regulations to determine whether any such regulations should be modified or eliminated so as to make the agency's regulatory program more effective in achieving the regulatory objectives, less burdensome, or in greater alignment with the President's priorities and the principles set forth in this Executive order. Any significant regulations selected for review shall be included in the agency's annual Plan. The agency shall also identify any legislative mandates that require the agency to promulgate or continue to impose regulations that the agency believes are unnecessary or outdated by reason of changed circumstances.

(b) The Administrator of OIRA shall work with the Regulatory Working Group and other interested entities to pursue the objectives of this section. State, local, and tribal governments are specifically encouraged to assist in the identification of regulations that impose significant or unique burdens on those governmental entities and that appear to have outlived their justification or be otherwise inconsistent with the public interest.

(c) The Vice President, in consultation with the Advisors, may identify for review by the appropriate agency or agencies other existing regulations of an agency or groups of regulations of more than one agency that affect a particular group, industry, or sector of the economy, or may identify legislative mandates that may be appropriate for reconsideration by the Congress.

Sec. 6.   Centralized Review of Regulations.

The guidelines set forth below shall apply to all regulatory actions, for both new and existing regulations, by agencies other than those agencies specifically exempted by the Administrator of OIRA:

(a)   Agency Responsibilities. (1) Each agency shall (consistent with its own rules, regulations, or procedures) provide the public with meaningful participation in the regulatory process. In particular, before issuing a notice of proposed rulemaking, each agency should, where appropriate, seek the involvement of those who are intended to benefit from and those expected to be burdened by any regulation (including, specifically, State, local, and tribal officials). In addition, each agency should afford the public a meaningful opportunity to comment on any proposed regulation, which in most cases should include a comment period of not less than 60 days. Each agency also is directed to explore and, where appropriate, use consensual mechanisms for developing regulations, including negotiated rulemaking.

(2) Within 60 days of the date of this Executive order, each agency head shall designate a Regulatory Policy Officer who shall report to the agency head. The Regulatory Policy Officer shall be involved at each stage of the regulatory process to foster the development of effective, innovative, and least burdensome regulations and to further the principles set forth in this Executive order.

(3) In addition to adhering to its own rules and procedures and to the requirements of the Administrative Procedure Act, the Regulatory Flexibility Act, the Paperwork Reduction Act, and other applicable law, each agency shall develop its regulatory actions in a timely fashion and adhere to the following procedures with respect to a regulatory action:

(A) Each agency shall provide OIRA, at such times and in the manner specified by the Administrator of OIRA, with a list of its planned regulatory actions, indicating those which the agency believes are significant regulatory actions within the meaning of this Executive order. Absent a material change in the development of the planned regulatory action, those not designated as significant will not be subject to review under this section unless, within 10 working days of receipt of the list, the Administrator of OIRA notifies the agency that OIRA has determined that a planned regulation is a significant regulatory action within the meaning of this Executive order. The Administrator of OIRA may waive review of any planned regulatory action designated by the agency as significant, in which case the agency need not further comply with subsection (a)(3)(B) or subsection (a)(3)(C) of this section.

(B) For each matter identified as, or determined by the Administrator of OIRA to be, a significant regulatory action, the issuing agency shall provide to OIRA:

(i) The text of the draft regulatory action, together with a reasonably detailed description of the need for the regulatory action and an explanation of how the regulatory action will meet that need; and

(ii) An assessment of the potential costs and benefits of the regulatory action, including an explanation of the manner in which the regulatory action is consistent with a statutory mandate and, to the extent permitted by law, promotes the President's priorities and avoids undue interference with State, local, and tribal governments in the exercise of their governmental functions.

(C) For those matters identified as, or determined by the Administrator of OIRA to be, a significant regulatory action within the scope of section 3(f)(1), the agency shall also provide to OIRA the following additional information developed as part of the agency's decision-making process (unless prohibited by law):

(i) An assessment, including the underlying analysis, of benefits anticipated from the regulatory action (such as, but not limited to, the promotion of the efficient functioning of the economy and private markets, the enhancement of health and safety, the protection of the natural environment, and the elimination or reduction of discrimination or bias) together with, to the extent feasible, a quantification of those benefits;

(ii) An assessment, including the underlying analysis, of costs anticipated from the regulatory action (such as, but not limited to, the direct cost both to the government in administering the regulation and to businesses and others in complying with the regulation, and any adverse effects on the efficient functioning of the economy, private markets (including productivity, employment, and competitiveness), health, safety, and the natural environment), together with, to the extent feasible, a quantification of those costs; and

(iii) An assessment, including the underlying analysis, of costs and benefits of potentially effective and reasonably feasible alternatives to the planned regulation, identified by the agencies or the public (including improving the current regulation and reasonably viable nonregulatory actions), and an explanation why the planned regulatory action is preferable to the identified potential alternatives.

(D) In emergency situations or when an agency is obligated by law to act more quickly than normal review procedures allow, the agency shall notify OIRA as soon as possible and, to the extent practicable, comply with subsections (a)(3)(B) and (C) of this section. For those regulatory actions that are governed by a statutory or court-imposed deadline, the agency shall, to the extent practicable, schedule rulemaking proceedings so as to permit sufficient time for OIRA to conduct its review, as set forth below in subsection (b)(2) through (4) of this section.

(E) After the regulatory action has been published in the Federal Register or otherwise issued to the public, the agency shall:

(i) Make available to the public the information set forth in subsections (a)(3)(B) and (C);

(ii) Identify for the public, in a complete, clear, and simple manner, the substantive changes between the draft submitted to OIRA for review and the action subsequently announced; and

(iii) Identify for the public those changes in the regulatory action that were made at the suggestion or recommendation of OIRA.

(F) All information provided to the public by the agency shall be in plain, understandable language.

(b) OIRA Responsibilities. The Administrator of OIRA shall provide meaningful guidance and oversight so that each agency's regulatory actions are consistent with applicable law, the President's priorities, and the principles set forth in this Executive order and do not conflict with the policies or actions of another agency. OIRA shall, to the extent permitted by law, adhere to the following guidelines:

(1) OIRA may review only actions identified by the agency or by OIRA as significant regulatory actions under subsection (a)(3)(A) of this section.

(2) OIRA shall waive review or notify the agency in writing of the results of its review within the following time periods:

(A) For any notices of inquiry, advance notices of proposed rulemaking, or other preliminary regulatory actions prior to a Notice of Proposed Rulemaking, within 10 working days after the date of submission of the draft action to OIRA;

(B) For all other regulatory actions, within 90 calendar days after the date of submission of the information set forth in subsections (a)(3)(B) and (C) of this section, unless OIRA has previously reviewed this information and, since that review, there has been no material change in the facts and circumstances upon which the regulatory action is based, in which case, OIRA shall complete its review within 45 days; and

(C) The review process may be extended (1) once by no more than 30 calendar days upon the written approval of the Director and (2) at the request of the agency head.

(3) For each regulatory action that the Administrator of OIRA returns to an agency for further consideration of some or all of its provisions, the Administrator of OIRA shall provide the issuing agency a written explanation for such return, setting forth the pertinent provision of this Executive order on which OIRA is relying. If the agency head disagrees with some or all of the bases for the return, the agency head shall so inform the Administrator of OIRA in writing.

(4) Except as otherwise provided by law or required by a Court, in order to ensure greater openness, accessibility, and accountability in the regulatory review process, OIRA shall be governed by the following disclosure requirements:

(A) Only the Administrator of OIRA (or a particular designee) shall receive oral communications initiated by persons not employed by the executive branch of the Federal Government regarding the substance of a regulatory action under OIRA review;

(B) All substantive communications between OIRA personnel and persons not employed by the executive branch of the Federal Government regarding a regulatory action under review shall be governed by the following guidelines:

(i) A representative from the issuing agency shall be invited to any meeting between OIRA personnel and such person(s);

(ii) OIRA shall forward to the issuing agency, within 10 working days of receipt of the communication(s), all written communications, regardless of format, between OIRA personnel and any person who is not employed by the executive branch of the Federal Government, and the dates and names of individuals involved in all substantive oral communications (including meetings to which an agency representative was invited, but did not attend, and telephone conversations between OIRA personnel and any such persons); and

(iii) OIRA shall publicly disclose relevant information about such communication(s), as set forth below in subsection (b)(4)(C) of this section.

(C) OIRA shall maintain a publicly available log that shall contain, at a minimum, the following information pertinent to regulatory actions under review:

(i) The status of all regulatory actions, including if (and if so, when and by whom) Vice Presidential and Presidential consideration was requested;

(ii) A notation of all written communications forwarded to an issuing agency under subsection (b)(4)(B)(ii) of this section; and

(iii) The dates and names of individuals involved in all substantive oral communications, including meetings and telephone conversations, between OIRA personnel and any person not employed by the executive branch of the Federal Government, and the subject matter discussed during such communications.

(D) After the regulatory action has been published in the Federal Register or otherwise issued to the public, or after the agency has announced its decision not to publish or issue the regulatory action, OIRA shall make available to the public all documents exchanged between OIRA and the agency during the review by OIRA under this section.

(5) All information provided to the public by OIRA shall be in plain, understandable language.

Sec. 7. Resolution of Conflicts.

To the extent permitted by law, disagreements or conflicts between or among agency heads or between OMB and any agency that cannot be resolved by the Administrator of OIRA shall be resolved by the President, or by the Vice President acting at the request of the President, with the relevant agency head (and, as appropriate, other interested government officials). Vice Presidential and Presidential consideration of such disagreements may be initiated only by the Director, by the head of the issuing agency, or by the head of an agency that has a significant interest in the regulatory action at issue. Such review will not be undertaken at the request of other persons, entities, or their agents.

Resolution of such conflicts shall be informed by recommendations developed by the Vice President, after consultation with the Advisors (and other executive branch officials or personnel whose responsibilities to the President include the subject matter at issue). The development of these recommendations shall be concluded within 60 days after review has been requested.

During the Vice Presidential and Presidential review period, communications with any person not employed by the Federal Government relating to the substance of the regulatory action under review and directed to the Advisors or their staffs or to the staff of the Vice President shall be in writing and shall be forwarded by the recipient to the affected agency(ies) for inclusion in the public docket(s). When the communication is not in writing, such Advisors or staff members shall inform the outside party that the matter is under review and that any comments should be submitted in writing.

At the end of this review process, the President, or the Vice President acting at the request of the President, shall notify the affected agency and the Administrator of OIRA of the President's decision with respect to the matter.

Sec. 8. Publication.

Except to the extent required by law, an agency shall not publish in the Federal Register or otherwise issue to the public any regulatory action that is subject to review under section 6 of this Executive order until (1) the Administrator of OIRA notifies the agency that OIRA has waived its review of the action or has completed its review without any requests for further consideration, or (2) the applicable time period in section 6(b)(2) expires without OIRA having notified the agency that it is returning the regulatory action for further consideration under section 6(b)(3), whichever occurs first. If the terms of the preceding sentence have not been satisfied and an agency wants to publish or otherwise issue a regulatory action, the head of that agency may request Presidential consideration through the Vice President, as provided under section 7 of this order. Upon receipt of this request, the Vice President shall notify OIRA and the Advisors. The guidelines and time period set forth in section 7 shall apply to the publication of regulatory actions for which Presidential consideration has been sought.

Sec. 9. Agency Authority.

Nothing in this order shall be construed as displacing the agencies' authority or responsibilities, as authorized by law.

Sec. 10. Judicial Review.

Nothing in this Executive order shall affect any otherwise available judicial review of agency action. This Executive order is intended only to improve the internal management of the Federal Government and does not create any right or benefit, substantive or procedural, enforceable at law or equity by a party against the United States, its agencies or instrumentalities, its officers or employees, or any other person.

Sec. 11. Revocations.

Executive Orders Nos. 12291 and 12498; all amendments to those Executive orders; all guidelines issued under those orders; and any exemptions from those orders heretofore granted for any category of rule are revoked.

WILLIAM CLINTON
THE WHITE HOUSE,
September 30, 1993.

Appendix E

Executive Order 13422

Executive Order 13422

Further Amendment to Executive Order 12866 on Regulatory Planning and
Review
January 18, 2007

By the authority vested in me as President by the Constitution and laws of the
United States of America, it is hereby ordered that Executive Order 12866 of
September 30, 1993, as amended, is further amended as follows:

Sec. 1.

Section 1 is amended as follows:

(a) Section 1(b)(1) is amended to read as follows:

"(1) Each agency shall identify in writing the specific market failure (such as
externalities, market power, lack of information) or other specific problem that it
intends to address (including, where applicable, the failures of public institutions)
that warrant new agency action, as well as assess the significance of that problem,
to enable assessment of whether any new regulation is warranted."

(b) by inserting in section 1(b)(7) after "regulation" the words "or guidance
document".

(c) by inserting in section 1(b)(10) in both places after "regulations" the words
"and guidance documents".

(d) by inserting in section 1(b)(11) after "its regulations" the words "and
guidance documents".

(e) by inserting in section 1(b)(12) after "regulations" the words "and guidance
documents".

Sec. 2.

Section 2 is amended as follows:

(a) by inserting in section 2(a) in both places after "regulations" the words
"and guidance documents".

(b) by inserting in section 2(b) in both places after "regulations" the words
"and guidance documents".

Sec. 3.

Section 3 is amended as follows:

(a) by striking in section 3(d) "or 'rule' " after " 'Regulation' ";

(b) by striking in section 3(d)(1) "or rules" after "Regulations";

(c) by striking in section 3(d)(2) "or rules" after "Regulations";

(d) by striking in section 3(d)(3) "or rules" after "Regulations";

(e) by striking in section 3(e) "rule or" from "final rule or regulation";

(f) by striking in section 3(f) "rule or" from "rule or regulation";

(g) by inserting after section 3(f) the following:

"(g) "Guidance document" means an agency statement of general applicability and future effect, other than a regulatory action, that sets forth a policy on a statutory, regulatory, or technical issue or an interpretation of a statutory or regulatory issue.

(h) "Significant guidance document" —

(1) Means a guidance document disseminated to regulated entities or the general public that, for purposes of this order, may reasonably be anticipated to:

(A) Lead to an annual effect of $100 million or more or adversely affect in a material way the economy, a sector of the economy, productivity, competition, jobs, the environment, public health or safety, or State, local, or tribal governments or communities;

(B) Create a serious inconsistency or otherwise interfere with an action taken or planned by another agency;

(C) Materially alter the budgetary impact of entitlements, grants, user fees, or loan programs or the rights or obligations of recipients thereof; or

(D) Raise novel legal or policy issues arising out of legal mandates, the President's priorities, or the principles set forth in this Executive order; and

(2) Does not include:

(A) Guidance documents on regulations issued in accordance with the formal rulemaking provisions of 5 U.S.C. 556, 557;

(B) Guidance documents that pertain to a military or foreign affairs function of the United States, other than procurement regulations and regulations involving the import or export of non-defense articles and services;

(C) Guidance documents on regulations that are limited to agency organization, management, or personnel matters; or

(D) Any other category of guidance documents exempted by the Administrator of OIRA."

Sec. 4.

Section 4 is amended as follows:

(a) Section 4(a) is amended to read as follows: "The Director may convene a meeting of agency heads and other government personnel as appropriate to seek a common understanding of priorities and to coordinate regulatory efforts to be accomplished in the upcoming year."

(b) The last sentence of section 4(c)(1) is amended to read as follows: "Unless specifically authorized by the head of the agency, no rulemaking shall commence nor be included on the Plan without the approval of the agency's Regulatory Policy Office, and the Plan shall contain at a minimum:".

(c) Section 4(c)(1)(B) is amended by inserting "of each rule as well as the agency's best estimate of the combined aggregate costs and benefits of all its regulations planned for that calendar year to assist with the identification of priorities" after "of the anticipated costs and benefits".

(d) Section 4(c)(1)(C) is amended by inserting ", and specific citation to such statute, order, or other legal authority" after "court order".

Sec. 5.

Section 6 is amended as follows:

(a) by inserting in section 6(a)(1) "In consultation with OIRA, each agency may also consider whether to utilize formal rulemaking procedures under 5 U.S.C. 556 and 557 for the resolution of complex determinations" after "comment period of not less than 60 days."

(b) by amending the first sentence of section 6(a)(2) to read as follows: "Within 60 days of the date of this Executive order, each agency head shall designate one of the agency's Presidential Appointees to be its Regulatory Policy Officer, advise OMB of such designation, and annually update OMB on the status of this designation."

Sec. 6.

Sections 9-11 are redesignated respectively as sections 10-12.

Sec. 7.

After section 8, a new section 9 is inserted as follows:

"Sec. 9. Significant Guidance Documents. Each agency shall provide OIRA, at such times and in the manner specified by the Administrator of OIRA, with advance notification of any significant guidance documents. Each agency shall take such steps as are necessary for its Regulatory Policy Officer to ensure the agency's compliance with the requirements of this section. Upon the request of the Administrator, for each matter identified as, or determined by the Administrator to be, a significant guidance document, the issuing agency shall provide to OIRA the content of the draft guidance document, together with a brief explanation of the need for the guidance document and how it will meet that need. The OIRA

Administrator shall notify the agency when additional consultation will be required before the issuance of the significant guidance document."

Sec. 8.

Newly designated section 10 is amended to read as follows:

"Sec. 10.1 Preservation of Agency Authority. Nothing in this order shall be construed to impair or otherwise affect the authority vested by law in an agency or the head thereof, including the authority of the Attorney General relating to litigation."

GEORGE W. BUSH
THE WHITE HOUSE,
January 18, 2007.
Exec. Order No. 13,422, 2007 WL 142760 (Pres.Exec.Order), 72 FR 2703

Appendix F*

UNIFORM LAW COMMISSIONERS' MODEL STATE ADMINISTRATIVE PROCEDURE ACT (1961)

§ 1. [Definitions].

As used in this Act:

(1) "agency" means each state [board, commission, department, or officer], other than the legislature or the courts, authorized by law to make rules or to determine contested cases;

(2) "contested case" means a proceeding, including but not restricted to ratemaking, [price fixing], and licensing, in which the legal rights, duties, or privileges of a party are required by law to be determined by an agency after an opportunity for hearing;

(3) "license" includes the whole or part of any agency permit, certificate, approval, registration, charter, or similar form of permission required by law, but it does not include a license required solely for revenue purposes;

(4) "licensing" includes the agency process respecting the grant, denial, renewal, revocation, suspension, annulment, withdrawal, or amendment of a license;

(5) "party" means each person or agency named or admitted as a party, or properly seeking and entitled as of right to be admitted as a party;

(6) "persons" means any individual, partnership, corporation, association, governmental subdivision, or public or private organization of any character other than an agency;

(7) "rule" means each agency statement of general applicability that implements, interprets, or prescribes law or policy, or describes the organization, procedure, or practice requirements of any agency. The term includes the amendment or repeal of a prior rule, but does not include (A) statements concerning only the internal management of an agency and not affecting private rights or procedures available to the public, or (B) declaratory rulings issued pursuant to Section 8, or (C) intra-agency memoranda.

---

* The 1961 model state administrative procedure act was a revision of a 1946 version. The Commissioners later promulgated a further and thoroughly revised version in 1981. See Appendix G. As this casebook goes to press, the Commissioners are about to consider a new model state administrative procedure act. In mid-July 2010, the Commissioners will be considering a proposal for an updated model act which draws from both the 1961 and 1981 versions

§ 2. [Public Information; Adoption of Rules; Availability of Rules and Orders].

(a) In addition to other rule-making requirements imposed by law, each agency shall:

(1) adopt as a rule a description of its organization, stating the general course and method of its operations and the methods whereby the public may obtain information or make submissions or requests;

(2) adopt rules of practice setting forth the nature and requirements of all formal and informal procedures available, including a description of all forms and instructions used by the agency;

(3) make available for public inspection all rules and all other written statements of policy or interpretations formulated, adopted, or used by the agency in the discharge of its functions;

(4) make available for public inspection all final orders, decisions, and opinions.

(b) No agency rule, order, or decision is valid or effective against any person or party, nor may it be invoked by the agency for any purpose, until it has been made available for public inspection as herein required. This provision is not applicable in favor of any person or party who has actual knowledge thereof.

§ 3. [Procedure for Adoption of Rules].

(a) Prior to the adoption, amendment, or repeal of any rule, the agency shall:

(1) give at least 20 days' notice of its intended action. The notice shall include a statement of either the terms or substance of the intended action or a description of the subjects and issues involved, and the time when, the place where, and the manner in which interested persons may present their views thereon. The notice shall be mailed to all persons who have made timely request of the agency for advance notice of its rule-making proceedings and shall be published in [here insert the medium of publication appropriate for the adopting state];

(2) afford all interested persons reasonable opportunity to submit data, views, or arguments, orally or in writing. In case of substantive rules, opportunity for oral hearing must be granted if requested by 25 persons, by a governmental subdivision or agency, or by an association having not less than 25 members. The agency shall consider fully all written and oral submissions respecting the proposed rule. Upon adoption of a rule, the agency, if requested to do so by an interested person either prior to adoption or within 30 days thereafter, shall issue a concise statement of the principal reasons for and against its adoption, incorporating therein its reasons for overruling the considerations urged against its adoption.

(b) If an agency finds that an imminent peril to the public health, safety, or welfare requires adoption of a rule upon fewer than 20 days' notice and states in writing its reasons for that finding, it may proceed without prior notice or hearing or upon any abbreviated notice and hearing that it finds practicable, to adopt an emergency rule. The rule may be effective for a period of not longer than 120 days [renewable once for a period not exceeding (4) days], but the adoption of an identical rule under subsections (a)(1) and (a)(2) of this Section is not precluded.

(c) No rule hereafter adopted is valid unless adopted in substantial compliance with this Section.

A proceeding to contest any rule on the ground of non-compliance with the procedural requirements of this Section must be commenced within 2 years from the effective date of the rule.

§ 4.　[Filing and Taking Effect of Rules].

(a) Each agency shall file in the office of the [Secretary of State] a certified copy of each rule adopted by it, including all rules existing on the effective date of this Act. The [Secretary of State] shall keep a permanent register of the rules open to public inspection.

(b) Each rule hereafter adopted is effective 20 days after filing, except that:

(1) if a later date is required by statute or specified in the rule, the later date is the effective date;

(2) subject to applicable constitutional or statutory provisions, an emergency rule becomes effective immediately upon filing with the [Secretary of State], or at a stated date less than 20 days thereafter, if the agency finds that this effective date is necessary because of imminent peril to the public health, safety, or welfare. The agency's finding and a brief statement of the reasons therefor shall be filed with the rule. The agency shall take appropriate measures to make emergency rules known to the persons who may be affected by them.

§ 5.　[Publication of Rules].

(a) The [Secretary of State] shall compile, index, and publish all effective rules adopted by each agency. Compilations shall be supplemented or revised as often as necessary [and at least once every 2 years].

(b) The [Secretary of State] shall publish a [monthly] bulletin setting forth the text of all rules filed during the preceding [month] excluding rules in effect upon the adoption of this Act.

(c) The [Secretary of State] may omit from the bulletin or compilation any rule the publication of which would be unduly cumbersome, expensive, or otherwise inexpedient, if the rule in printed or processed form is made available on application to the adopting agency, and if the bulletin or compilation contains a notice stating the general subject matter of the omitted rule and stating how a copy thereof may be obtained.

(d) Bulletins and compilations shall be made available upon request to [agencies and officials of this State] free of charge and to other persons at prices fixed by the [Secretary of State] to cover mailing and publication costs.

§ 6.　[Petition for Adoption of Rules].

An interested person may petition an agency requesting the promulgation, amendment, or repeal of a rule. Each agency shall prescribe by rule the form for petitions and the procedure for their submission, consideration, and disposition. Within 30 days after submission of a petition, the agency either shall deny the petition in writing (stating its reasons for the denials) or shall initiate rule-making proceedings in accordance with Section 3.

§ 7. [Declaratory Judgment on Validity or Applicability of Rules].

The validity or applicability of a rule may be determined in an action for declaratory judgment in the [District Court of . . . County], if it is alleged that the rule, or its threatened application, interferes with or impairs, or threatens to interfere with or impair, the legal rights or privileges of the plaintiff. The agency shall be made a party to the action. A declaratory judgment may be rendered whether or not the plaintiff has requested the agency to pass upon the validity or applicability of the rule in question.

§ 8. [Declaratory Rulings by Agencies].

Each agency shall provide by rule for the filing and prompt disposition of petitions for declaratory rulings as to the applicability of any statutory provision or of any rule or order of the agency. Rulings disposing of petitions have the same status as agency decisions or orders in contested cases.

§ 9. [Contested Cases; Notice; Hearing; Records].

(a) In a contested case, all parties shall be afforded an opportunity for hearing after reasonable notice.

(b) The notice shall include:

(1) a statement of the time, place, and nature of the hearing;

(2) a statement of the legal authority and jurisdiction under which the hearing is to be held;

(3) a reference to the particular sections of the statutes and rules involved;

(4) a short and plain statement of the matters asserted. If the agency or other party is unable to state the matters in detail at the time the notice is served, the initial notice may be limited to a statement of the issues involved. Thereafter upon application a more definite and detailed statement shall be furnished.

(c) Opportunity shall be afforded all parties to respond and present evidence and argument on all issues involved.

(d) Unless precluded by law, informal disposition may be made of any contested case by stipulation, agreed settlement, consent order, or default.

(e) The record in a contested case shall include:

(1) all pleadings, motions, intermediate rulings;

(2) evidence received or considered;

(3) a statement of matters officially noticed;

(4) questions and offers of proof, objections, and rulings thereon;

(5) proposed findings and exceptions;

(6) any decision, opinion, or report by the officer presiding at the hearing;

(7) all staff memoranda or data submitted to the hearing officer or members of the agency in connection with their consideration of the case.

(f) Oral proceedings or any part thereof shall be transcribed on request of any party.

(g) Findings of fact shall be based exclusively on the evidence and on matters officially noticed.

§ 10.   [Rules of Evidence; Official Notice].

In contested cases:

(1) irrelevant, immaterial, or unduly repetitious evidence shall be excluded. The rules of evidence as applied in [non-jury] civil cases in the [District Courts of this State] shall be followed. When necessary to ascertain facts not reasonably susceptible of proof under those rules, evidence not admissible thereunder may be admitted (except where precluded by statute) if it is of a type commonly relied upon by reasonably prudent men in the conduct of their affairs. Agencies shall give effect to the rules of privilege recognized by law. Objections to evidentiary offers may be made and shall be noted in the record. Subject to these requirements, when a hearing will be expedited and the interests of the parties will not be prejudiced substantially, any part of the evidence may be received in written form;

[(2) documentary evidence may be received in the form of copies or excerpts, if the original is not readily available. Upon request, parties shall be given an opportunity to compare the copy with the original;]

(3) a party may conduct cross-examinations required for a full and true disclosure of the facts;

(4) notice may be taken of judicially cognizable facts. In addition, notice may be taken of generally recognized technical or scientific facts within the agency's specialized knowledge. Parties shall be notified either before or during the hearing, or by reference in preliminary reports or otherwise, of the material noticed, including any staff memoranda or data, and they shall be afforded an opportunity to contest the material so noticed. The agency's experience, technical competence, and specialized knowledge may be utilized in the evaluation of the evidence.

§ 11.   [Examination of Evidence by Agency].

When in a contested case a majority of the officials of the agency who are to render the final decision have not heard the case or read the record, the decision, if adverse to a party to the proceeding other than the agency itself, shall not be made until a proposal for decision is served upon the parties, and an opportunity is afforded to each party adversely affected to file exceptions and present briefs and oral argument to the officials who are to render the decision.

The proposal for decision shall contain a statement of the reasons therefor and of each issue of fact or law necessary to the proposed decision, prepared by the person who conducted the hearing or one who has read the record. The parties by written stipulation may waive compliance with this section.

§ 12.   [Decisions and Orders].

A final decision or order adverse to a party in a contested case shall be in writing or stated in the record. A final decision shall include findings of fact and conclusions of law, separately stated. Findings of fact, if set forth in statutory language, shall be accompanied by a concise and explicit statement of the underlying facts supporting the findings. If, in accordance with agency rules, a party submitted proposed findings of fact, the decision shall include a ruling upon each proposed finding. Parties shall be notified either personally or by mail of any decision or order. Upon request a copy of the decision or order shall be delivered or mailed forthwith to each party and to his attorney of record.

§ 13.   [Ex Parte Consultations].

Unless required for the disposition of ex parte matters authorized by law, members or employees of an agency assigned to render a decision or to make findings of fact and conclusions of law in a contested case shall not communicate, directly or indirectly, in connection with any issue of fact, with any person or party, nor, in connection with any issue of law, with any party or his representative, except upon notice and opportunity for all parties to participate. An agency member

(1) may communicate with other members of the agency, and

(2) may have the aid and advice of one or more personal assistants.

§ 14.   [Licenses].

(a) When the grant, denial, or renewal of a license is required to be preceded by notice and opportunity for hearing, the provisions of this Act concerning contested cases apply.

(b) When a licensee has made timely and sufficient application for the renewal of a license or a new license with reference to any activity of a continuing nature, the existing license does not expire until the application has been finally determined by the agency, and, in case the application is denied or the terms of the new license limited, until the last day for seeking review of the agency order or a later date fixed by order of the reviewing court.

(c) No revocation, suspension, annulment, or withdrawal of any license is lawful unless, prior to the institution of agency proceedings, the agency gave notice by mail to the licensee of facts or conduct which warrant the intended action, and the licensee was given an opportunity to show compliance with all lawful requirements for the retention of the license. If the agency finds that public health, safety, or welfare imperatively requires emergency action, and incorporates a finding to that effect in its order, summary suspension of a license may be ordered pending proceedings for revocation or other action. These proceedings shall be promptly instituted and determined.

§ 15.   [Judicial Review of Contested Cases].

(a) A person who has exhausted all administrative remedies available within the agency and who is aggrieved by a final decision in a contested case is entitled to judicial review under this Act. This Section does not limit utilization of or the scope of judicial review available under other means of review, redress, relief, or trial de novo provided by law. A preliminary, procedural, or intermediate agency action or ruling is immediately reviewable if review of the final agency decision would not provide an adequate remedy.

(b) Proceedings for review are instituted by filing a petition in the [District Court of the _____ County] within [30] days after [mailing notice of] the final decision of the agency or, if a rehearing is requested, within [30] days after the decision thereon. Copies of the petition shall be served upon the agency and all parties of record.

(c) The filing of the petition does not itself stay enforcement of the agency decision. The agency may grant, or the reviewing court may order, a stay upon appropriate terms.

(d) Within [30] days after the service of the petition, or within further time allowed by the court, the agency shall transmit to the reviewing court the original or a certified copy of the entire record of the proceeding under review. By stipulation of all parties to the review proceedings, the record may be shortened. A party unreasonably refusing to stipulate to limit the record may be taxed by the court for the additional costs. The court may require or permit subsequent corrections or additions to the record.

(e) If, before the date set for hearing, application is made to the court for leave to present additional evidence, and it is shown to the satisfaction of the court that the additional evidence is material and that there were good reasons for failure to present it in the proceeding before the agency, the court may order that the additional evidence be taken before the agency upon conditions determined by the court. The agency may modify its findings and decision by reason of the additional evidence and shall file that evidence and any modifications, new findings, or decisions with the reviewing court.

(f) The review shall be conducted by the court without a jury and shall be confined to the record.

In cases of alleged irregularities in procedure before the agency, not shown in the record, proof thereon may be taken in the court. The court, upon request, shall hear oral argument and receive written briefs.

(g) The court shall not substitute its judgment for that of the agency as to the weight of the evidence on questions of fact. The court may affirm the decision of the agency or remand the case for further proceedings. The court may reverse or modify the decision if substantial rights of the appellant have been prejudiced because the administrative findings, inferences, conclusions, or decisions are:

(1) in violation of constitutional or statutory provisions;

(2) in excess of the statutory authority of the agency;

(3) made upon unlawful procedure;

(4) affected by other error of law;

(5) clearly erroneous in view of the reliable, probative, and substantial evidence on the whole record; or

(6) arbitrary or capricious or characterized by abuse of discretion or clearly unwarranted exercise of discretion.

§ 16. [Appeals].

An aggrieved party may obtain a review of any final judgment of the [District Court] under this Act by appeal to the [Supreme Court]. The appeal shall be taken as in other civil cases.

§ 17. [Severability].

If any provision of this Act or the application thereof to any person or circumstance is held invalid, the invalidity does not affect other provisions or applications of the Act which can be given effect without the invalid provision or application, and for this purpose the provisions of this Act are severable.

§ 18. [Repeal].

The following acts and parts of acts are repealed:

(1) _____;

(2) _____;

(3) _____.

§ 19. [Time of Taking Effect and Scope of Application].

This Act takes effect . . . . and (except as to proceedings then pending) applies to all agencies and agency proceedings not expressly exempted.

Appendix G

UNIFORM LAW COMMISSIONERS' MODEL STATE ADMINISTRATIVE PROCEDURE ACT (1981)

§ 1-101. [Short Title].

This Act may be cited as the [state] Administrative Procedure Act.

§ 1-102. [Definitions].

As used in this Act:

(1) "Agency" means a board, commission, department, officer, or other administrative unit of this State, including the agency head, and one or more members of the agency head or agency employees or other persons directly or indirectly purporting to act on behalf or under the authority of the agency head. The term does not include the [legislature] or the courts [, or the governor] [, or the governor in the exercise of powers derived directly and exclusively from the constitution of this State]. The term does not include a political subdivision of the state or any of the administrative units of a political subdivision, but it does include a board, commission, department, officer, or other administrative unit created or appointed by joint or concerted action of an agency and one or more political subdivisions of the state or any of their units. To the extent it purports to exercise authority subject to any provision of this Act, an administrative unit otherwise qualifying as an "agency" must be treated as a separate agency even if the unit is located within or subordinate to another agency.

(2) "Agency action" means:

(i) the whole or a part of a rule or an order;

(ii) the failure to issue a rule or an order; or

(iii) an agency's performance of, or failure to perform, any other duty, function, or activity, discretionary or otherwise.

(3) "Agency head" means an individual or body of individuals in whom the ultimate legal authority of the agency is vested by any provision of law.

(4) "License" means a franchise, permit, certification, approval, registration, charter, or similar form of authorization required by law.

(5) "Order" means an agency action of particular applicability that determines the legal rights, duties, privileges, immunities, or other legal interests of one or more specific persons. [The term does not include an "executive order" issued by the governor pursuant to Section 1-104 or 3-202.]

(6) "Party to agency proceedings," or "party" in context so indicating, means:

(i) a person to whom the agency action is specifically directed; or

(ii) a person named as a party to an agency proceeding or allowed to intervene or participate as a party in the proceeding.

(7) "Party to judicial review or civil enforcement proceedings," or "party" in context so indicating, means:

(i) a person who files a petition for judicial review or civil enforcement or

(ii) a person named as a party in a proceeding for judicial review or civil enforcement or allowed to participate as a party in the proceeding.

(8) "Person" means an individual, partnership, corporation, association, governmental subdivision or unit thereof, or public or private organization or entity of any character, and includes another agency.

(9) "Provision of law" means the whole or a part of the federal or state constitution, or of any federal or state (i) statute, (ii) rule of court, (iii) executive order, or (iv) rule of an administrative agency.

(10) "Rule" means the whole or a part of an agency statement of general applicability that implements, interprets, or prescribes (i) law or policy, or (ii) the organization, procedure, or practice requirements of an agency. The term includes the amendment, repeal, or suspension of an existing rule.

(11) "Rule making" means the process for formulation and adoption of a rule.

§ 1-103. [Applicability and Relation to Other Law].

(a) This Act applies to all agencies and all proceedings not expressly exempted.

(b) This Act creates only procedural rights and imposes only procedural duties. They are in addition to those created and imposed by other statutes. To the extent that any other statute would diminish a right created or duty imposed by this Act, the other statute is superseded by this Act, unless the other statute expressly provides otherwise.

(c) An agency may grant procedural rights to persons in addition to those conferred by this Act so long as rights conferred upon other persons by any provision of law are not substantially prejudiced.

§ 1-104. [Suspension of Act's Provisions When Necessary to Avoid Loss of Federal Funds or Services].

(a) To the extent necessary to avoid a denial of funds or services from the United States which would otherwise be available to the state, the [governor by executive order] [attorney general by rule] [may] [shall] suspend, in whole or in part, one or more provisions of this Act. The [governor by executive order] [attorney general by rule] shall declare the termination of a suspension as soon as it is no longer necessary to prevent the loss of funds or services from the United States.

[(b) An executive order issued under subsection (a) is subject to the requirements applicable to the adoption and effectiveness of a rule.]

(c) If any provision of this Act is suspended pursuant to this section, the [governor] [attorney general] shall promptly report the suspension to the [legislature]. The report must include recommendations concerning any desirable legislation that may be necessary to conform this Act to federal law.]

§ 1-105. [Waiver].

Except to the extent precluded by another provision of law, a person may waive any right conferred upon that person by this Act.

§ 1-106. [Informal Settlements].

Except to the extent precluded by another provision of law, informal settlement of matters that may make unnecessary more elaborate proceedings under this Act is encouraged. Agencies shall establish by rule specific procedures to facilitate informal settlement of matters. This section does not require any party or other person to settle a matter pursuant to informal procedures.

§ 1-107. [Conversion of Proceedings].

(a) At any point in an agency proceeding the presiding officer or other agency official responsible for the proceeding:

(1) may convert the proceeding to another type of agency proceeding provided for by this Act if the conversion is appropriate, is in the public interest, and does not substantially prejudice the rights of any party; and

(2) if required by any provision of law, shall convert the proceeding to another type of agency proceeding provided for by this Act.

(b) A conversion of a proceeding of one type to a proceeding of another type may be effected only upon notice to all parties to the original proceeding.

(c) If the presiding officer or other agency official responsible for the original proceeding would not have authority over the new proceeding to which it is to be converted, that officer or official, in accordance with agency rules, shall secure the appointment of a successor to preside over or be responsible for the new proceeding.

(d) To the extent feasible and consistent with the rights of parties and the requirements of this Act pertaining to the new proceeding, the record of the original agency proceeding must be used in the new agency proceeding.

(e) After a proceeding is converted from one type to another, the presiding officer or other agency official responsible for the new proceeding shall:

(1) give such additional notice to parties or other persons as is necessary to satisfy the requirements of this Act pertaining to those proceedings;

(2) dispose of the matters involved without further proceedings if sufficient proceedings have already been held to satisfy the requirements of this Act pertaining to the new proceedings; and

(3) conduct or cause to be conducted any additional proceedings necessary to satisfy the requirements of this Act pertaining to those proceedings.

(f) Each agency shall adopt rules to govern the conversion of one type of proceeding to another. Those rules must include an enumeration of the factors to be considered in determining whether and under what circumstances one type of proceeding will be converted to another.

§ 1-108.   [Effective Date].

This Act takes effect on [date] and does not govern proceedings pending on that date. This Act governs all agency proceedings, and all proceedings for judicial review or civil enforcement of agency action, commenced after that date. This Act also governs agency proceedings conducted on a remand from a court or another agency after the effective date of this Act.

§ 1-109.   [Severability].

If any provision of this Act or the application thereof to any person or circumstance is held invalid, the invalidity does not affect other provisions or applications of the Act which can be given effect without the invalid provision or application, and for this purpose the provisions of this Act are severable.

§ 2-101.   [Administrative Rules Editor; Publication, Compilation, Indexing, and Public Inspection of Rules].

(a) There is created, within the executive branch, an [administrative rules editor]. The governor shall appoint the [administrative rules editor] who shall serve at the pleasure of the governor.

(b) Subject to the provisions of this Act, the [administrative rules editor] shall prescribe a uniform numbering system, form, and style for all proposed and adopted rules caused to be published by that office [, and shall have the same editing authority with respect to the publication of rules as the [reviser of statutes] has with respect to the publication of statutes].

(c) The [administrative rules editor] shall cause the [administrative bulletin] to be published in pamphlet form [once each week]. For purposes of calculating adherence to time requirements imposed by this Act, an issue of the [administrative bulletin] is deemed published on the later of the date indicated in that issue or the date of its mailing. The [administrative bulletin] must contain:

(1) notices of proposed rule adoption prepared so that the text of the proposed rule shows the text of any existing rule proposed to be changed and the change proposed;

(2) newly filed adopted rules prepared so that the text of the newly filed adopted rule shows the text of any existing rule being changed and the change being made;

(3) any other notices and materials designated by [law] [the administrative rules editor] for publication therein; and

(4) an index to its contents by subject.

(d) The [administrative rules editor] shall cause the [administrative code] to be compiled, indexed by subject, and published [in loose-leaf form]. All of the effective rules of each agency must be published and indexed in that publication. The [administrative rules editor] shall also cause [loose-leaf] supplements to the [administrative code] to be published at least every [3 months]. [The loose-leaf supplements must be in a form suitable for insertion in the appropriate places in the permanent [administrative code] compilation.]

(e) The [administrative rules editor] may omit from the [administrative bulletin or code] any proposed or filed adopted rule the publication of which would be unduly cumbersome, expensive, or otherwise inexpedient, if:

(1) knowledge of the rule is likely to be important to only a small class of persons;

(2) on application to the issuing agency, the proposed or adopted rule in printed or processed form is made available at no more than its cost of reproduction; and

(3) the [administrative bulletin or code] contains a notice stating in detail the specific subject matter of the omitted proposed or adopted rule and how a copy of the omitted material may be obtained.

(f) The [administrative bulletin and administrative code] must be furnished to [designated officials] without charge and to all subscribers at a cost to be determined by the [administrative rules editor]. Each agency shall also make available for public inspection and copying those portions of the [administrative bulletin and administrative code] containing all rules adopted or used by the agency in the discharge of its functions, and the index to those rules.

(g) Except as otherwise required by a provision of law, subsections (c) through (f) do not apply to rules governed by Section 3-116, and the following provisions apply instead:

(1) Each agency shall maintain an official, current, and dated compilation that is indexed by subject, containing all of its rules within the scope of Section 3-116. Each addition to, change in, or deletion from the official compilation must also be dated, indexed, and a record thereof kept. Except for those portions containing rules governed by Section 3-116(2), the compilation must be made available for public inspection and copying. Certified copies of the full compilation must also be furnished to the [secretary of state, the administrative rules counsel, and members of the administrative rules review committee], and be kept current by the agency at least every [30] days.

(2) A rule subject to the requirements of this subsection may not be relied on by an agency to the detriment of any person who does not have actual, timely knowledge of the contents of the rule until the requirements of paragraph (1) are satisfied. The burden of proving that knowledge is on the agency. This provision is also inapplicable to the extent necessary to avoid imminent peril to the public health, safety, or welfare.

§ 2-102. [Public Inspection and Indexing of Agency Orders].

(a) In addition to other requirements imposed by any provision of law, each agency shall make all written final orders available for public inspection and copying and index them by name and subject. An agency shall delete from those orders identifying details to the extent required by any provision of law [or necessary to prevent a clearly unwarranted invasion of privacy or release of trade secrets]. In each case the justification for the deletion must be explained in writing and attached to the order.

(b) A written final order may not be relied on as precedent by an agency to the detriment of any person until it has been made available for public inspection and indexed in the manner described in subsection (a). This provision is inapplicable to any person who has actual timely knowledge of the order. The burden of proving that knowledge is on the agency.

§ 2-103. [Declaratory Orders].

(a) Any person may petition an agency for a declaratory order as to the applicability to specified circumstances of a statute, rule, or order within the primary jurisdiction of the agency. An agency shall issue a declaratory order in response to a petition for that order unless the agency determines that issuance of the order under the circumstances would be contrary to a rule adopted in accordance with subsection (b). However, an agency may not issue a declaratory order that would substantially prejudice the rights of a person who would be a necessary party and who does not consent in writing to the determination of the matter by a declaratory order proceeding.

(b) Each agency shall issue rules that provide for: (i) the form, contents, and filing of petitions for declaratory orders; (ii) the procedural rights of persons in relation to the petitions and (iii) the disposition of the petitions. Those rules must describe the classes of circumstances in which the agency will not issue a declaratory order and must be consistent with the public interest and with the general policy of this Act to facilitate and encourage agency issuance of reliable advice.

(c) Within [15] days after receipt of a petition for a declaratory order, an agency shall give notice of the petition to all persons to whom notice is required by any provision of law and may give notice to any other persons.

(d) Persons who qualify under Section 4-209(a)(2) and (3) and file timely petitions for intervention according to agency rules may intervene in proceedings for declaratory orders. Other provisions of Article IV apply to agency proceedings for declaratory orders only to the extent an agency so provides by rule or order.

(e) Within [30] days after receipt of a petition for a declaratory order an agency, in writing, shall:

(1) issue an order declaring the applicability of the statute, rule, or order in question to the specified circumstances;

(2) set the matter for specified proceedings;

(3) agree to issue a declaratory order by a specified time; or

(4) decline to issue a declaratory order, stating the reasons for its action.

(f) A copy of all orders issued in response to a petition for a declaratory order must be mailed promptly to petitioner and any other parties.

(g) A declaratory order has the same status and binding effect as any other order issued in an agency adjudicative proceeding. A declaratory order must contain the names of all parties to the proceeding on which it is based, the particular facts on which it is based, and the reasons for its conclusion.

(h) If an agency has not issued a declaratory order within [60] days after receipt of a petition therefor, the petition is deemed to have been denied.

§ 2-104.   [Required Rule Making].

In addition to other rule-making requirements imposed by law, each agency shall:

(1) adopt as a rule a description of the organization of the agency which states the general course and method of its operations and where and how the public may obtain information or make submissions or requests;

(2) adopt rules of practice setting forth the nature and requirements of all formal and informal procedures available to the public, including a description of all forms and instructions that are to be used by the public in dealing with the agency; [and]

(3) as soon as feasible and to the extent practicable, adopt rules, in addition to those otherwise required by this Act, embodying appropriate standards, principles, and procedural safeguards that the agency will apply to the law it administers [; and] [.]

[(4) as soon as feasible and to the extent practicable, adopt rules to supersede principles of law or policy lawfully declared by the agency as the basis for its decisions in particular cases.]

§ 2-105.   [Model Rules of Procedure].

In accordance with the rule-making requirements of this Act, the [attorney general] shall adopt model rules of procedure appropriate for use by as many agencies as possible. The model rules must deal with all general functions and duties performed in common by several agencies. Each agency shall adopt as much of the model rules as is practicable under its circumstances. To the extent an agency adopts the model rules, it shall do so in accordance with the rule-making requirements of this Act. Any agency adopting a rule of procedure that differs from the model rules shall include in the rule a finding stating the reasons why the relevant portions of the model rules were impracticable under the circumstances.

§ 3-101.   [Advice on Possible Rules before Notice of Proposed Rule Adoption].

(a) In addition to seeking information by other methods, an agency, before publication of a notice of proposed rule adoption under Section 3-103, may solicit comments from the public on a subject matter of possible rule making under active consideration within the agency by causing notice to be published in the [administrative bulletin] of the subject matter and indicating where, when, and how persons may comment.

(b) Each agency may also appoint committees to comment, before publication of a notice of proposed rule adoption under Section 3-103, on the subject matter of a possible rule making under active consideration within the agency. The membership of those committees must be published at least [annually] in the [administrative bulletin].

§ 3-102. [Public Rule-making Docket].

(a) Each agency shall maintain a current, public rule-making docket.

(b) The rule-making docket [must] [may] contain a listing of the precise subject matter of each possible rule currently under active consideration within the agency for proposal under Section 3-103, the name and address of agency personnel with whom persons may communicate with respect to the matter, and an indication of the present status within the agency of that possible rule.

(c) The rule-making docket must list each pending rule-making proceeding. A rule-making proceeding is pending from the time it is commenced, by publication of a notice of proposed rule adoption, to the time it is terminated, by publication of a notice of termination or the rule becoming effective. For each rule-making proceeding, the docket must indicate:

(1) the subject matter of the proposed rule;

(2) a citation to all published notices relating to the proceeding;

(3) where written submissions on the proposed rule may be inspected;

(4) the time during which written submissions may be made;

(5) the names of persons who have made written requests for an opportunity to make oral presentations on the proposed rule, where those requests may be inspected, and where and when oral presentations may be made;

(6) whether a written request for the issuance of a regulatory analysis of the proposed rule has been filed, whether that analysis has been issued, and where the written request and analysis may be inspected;

(7) the current status of the proposed rule and any agency determinations with respect thereto;

(8) any known timetable for agency decisions or other action in the proceeding;

(9) the date of the rule's adoption;

(10) the date of the rule's filing, indexing, and publication; and

(11) when the rule will become effective.

§ 3-103. [Notice of Proposed Rule Adoption].

(a) At least [30] days before the adoption of a rule an agency shall cause notice of its contemplated action to be published in the [administrative bulletin]. The notice of proposed rule adoption must include:

(1) a short explanation of the purpose of the proposed rule;

(2) the specific legal authority authorizing the proposed rule;

(3) subject to Section 2-101(e), the text of the proposed rule;

(4) where, when, and how persons may present their views on the proposed rule; and

(5) where, when, and how persons may demand an oral proceeding on the proposed rule if the notice does not already provide for one.

(b) Within [3] days after its publication in the [administrative bulletin], the agency shall cause a copy of the notice of proposed rule adoption to be mailed to each person who has made a timely request to the agency for a mailed copy of the notice. An agency may charge persons for the actual cost of providing them with mailed copies.

§ 3-104. [Public Participation].

(a) For at least [30] days after publication of the notice of proposed rule adoption, an agency shall afford persons the opportunity to submit in writing, argument, data, and views on the proposed rule.

(b) (1) An agency shall schedule an oral proceeding on a proposed rule if, within [20] days after the published notice of proposed rule adoption, a written request for an oral proceeding is submitted by [the administrative rules review committee,] [the administrative rules counsel,] a political subdivision, an agency, or [25] persons. At that proceeding, persons may present oral argument, data, and views on the proposed rule.

(2) An oral proceeding on a proposed rule, if required, may not be held earlier than [20] days after notice of its location and time is published in the [administrative bulletin].

(3) The agency, a member of the agency, or another presiding officer designated by the agency, shall preside at a required oral proceeding on a proposed rule. If the agency does not preside, the presiding official shall prepare a memorandum for consideration by the agency summarizing the contents of the presentations made at the oral proceeding. Oral proceedings must be open to the public and be recorded by stenographic or other means.

(4) Each agency shall issue rules for the conduct of oral rule-making proceedings. Those rules may include provisions calculated to prevent undue repetition in the oral proceedings.

§ 3-105. [Regulatory Analysis].

(a) An agency shall issue a regulatory analysis of a proposed rule if, within [20] days after the published notice of proposed rule adoption, a written request for the analysis is filed in the office of the [secretary of state] by [the administrative rules review committee, the governor, a political subdivision, an agency, or [300] persons signing the request]. The [secretary of state] shall immediately forward to the agency a certified copy of the filed request.

(b) Except to the extent that the written request expressly waives one or more of the following, the regulatory analysis must contain:

(1) a description of the classes of persons who probably will be affected by the proposed rule, including classes that will bear the costs of the proposed rule and classes that will benefit from the proposed rule;

(2) a description of the probable quantitative and qualitative impact of the proposed rule, economic or otherwise, upon affected classes of persons;

(3) the probable costs to the agency and to any other agency of the implementation and enforcement of the proposed rule and any anticipated effect on state revenues;

(4) a comparison of the probable costs and benefits of the proposed rule to the probable costs and benefits of inaction;

(5) a determination of whether there are less costly methods or less intrusive methods for achieving the purpose of the proposed rule; and

(6) a description of any alternative methods for achieving the purpose of the proposed rule that were seriously considered by the agency and the reasons why they were rejected in favor of the proposed rule.

(c) Each regulatory analysis must include quantification of the data to the extent practicable and must take account of both short-term and long-term consequences.

(d) A concise summary of the regulatory analysis must be published in the [administrative bulletin] at least [10] days before the earliest of:

(1) the end of the period during which persons may make written submissions on the proposed rule;

(2) the end of the period during which an oral proceeding may be requested; or

(3) the date of any required oral proceeding on the proposed rule.

(e) The published summary of the regulatory analysis must also indicate where persons may obtain copies of the full text of the regulatory analysis and where, when, and how persons may present their views on the proposed rule and demand an oral proceeding thereon if one is not already provided.

(f) If the agency has made a good faith effort to comply with the requirements of subsections (a) through (c), the rule may not be invalidated on the ground that the contends of the regulatory analysis are insufficient or inaccurate.

§ 3-106.   [Time and Manner of Rule Adoption].

(a) An agency may not adopt a rule until the period for making written submissions and oral presentations has expired.

(b) Within [180] days after the later of (i) the publication of the notice of proposed rule adoption, or (ii) the end of oral proceedings thereon, an agency shall adopt a rule pursuant to the rule-making proceeding or terminate the proceeding by publication of a notice to that effect in the [administrative bulletin].

(c) Before the adoption of a rule, an agency shall consider the written submissions, oral submissions or any memorandum summarizing oral submissions, and any regulatory analysis, provided for by this Chapter.

(d) Within the scope of its delegated authority, an agency may use its own experience, technical competence, specialized knowledge, and judgment in the adoption of a rule.

§ 3-107. [Variance between Adopted Rule and Published Notice of Proposed Rule Adoption].

(a) An agency may not adopt a rule that is substantially different from the proposed rule contained in the published notice of proposed rule adoption. However, an agency may terminate a rule-making proceeding and commence a new rule-making proceeding for the purpose of adopting a substantially different rule.

(b) In determining whether an adopted rule is substantially different from the published proposed rule upon which it is required to be based, the following must be considered:

(1) the extent to which all persons affected by the adopted rule should have understood that the published proposed rule would affect their interests;

(2) the extent to which the subject matter of the adopted rule or the issues determined by that rule are different from the subject matter or issues involved in the published proposed rule; and

(3) the extent to which the effects of the adopted rule differ from the effects of the published proposed rule had it been adopted instead.

§ 3-108. [General Exemption from Public Rule-making Procedures].

(a) To the extent an agency for good cause finds that any requirements of Sections 3-103 through 3-107 are unnecessary, impracticable, or contrary to the public interest in the process of adopting a particular rule, those requirements do not apply. The agency shall incorporate the required finding and a brief statement of its supporting reasons in each rule adopted in reliance upon this subsection.

(b) In an action contesting a rule adopted under subsection (a), the burden is upon the agency to demonstrate that any omitted requirements of Sections 3- 103 through 3-107 were impracticable, unnecessary, or contrary to the public interest in the particular circumstances involved.

(c) Within [2] years after the effective date of a rule adopted under subsection (a), the [administrative rules review committee or the governor] may request the agency to hold a rule-making proceeding thereon according to the requirements of Sections 3-103 through 3-107. The request must be in writing and filed in the office of the [secretary of state]. The [secretary of state] shall immediately forward to the agency and to the [administrative rules editor] a certified copy of the request. Notice of the filing of the request must be published in the next issue of the [administrative bulletin]. The rule in question ceases to be effective [180] days after the request is filed. However, an agency, after the filing of the request, may subsequently adopt an identical rule in a rule-making proceeding conducted pursuant to the requirements of Sections 3-103 through 3-107.

§ 3-109.   [Exemption for Certain Rules].

(a) An agency need not follow the provisions of Sections 3-103 through 3-108 in the adoption of a rule that only defines the meaning of a statute or other provision of law or precedent if the agency does not possess delegated authority to bind the courts to any extent with its definition. A rule adopted under this subsection must include a statement that it was adopted under this subsection when it is published in the [administrative bulletin], and there must be an indication to that effect adjacent to the rule when it is published in the [administrative code].

(b) A reviewing court shall determine wholly de novo the validity of a rule within the scope of subsection (a) that is adopted without complying with the provisions of Sections 3-103 through 3-108.

§ 3-110.   [Concise Explanatory Statement].

(a) At the time it adopts a rule, an agency shall issue a concise explanatory statement containing:

(1) its reasons for adopting the rule; and

(2) an indication of any change between the text of the proposed rule contained in the published notice of proposed rule adoption and the text of the rule as finally adopted, with the reasons for any change.

(b) Only the reasons contained in the concise explanatory statement may be used by any party as justifications for the adoption of the rule in any proceeding in which its validity is at issue.

§ 3-111.   [Contents, Style, and Form of Rule].

(a) Each rule adopted by an agency must contain the text of the rule and:

(1) the date the agency adopted the rule;

(2) a concise statement of the purpose of the rule;

(3) a reference to all rules repealed, amended, or suspended by the rule;

(4) a reference to the specific statutory or other authority authorizing adoption of the rule;

(5) any findings required by any provision of law as a prerequisite to adoption or effectiveness of the rule; and

(6) the effective date of the rule if other than that specified in Section 3-115(a).

[(b) To the extent feasible, each rule should be written in clear and concise language understandable to persons who may be affected by it.]

(c) An agency may incorporate, by reference in its rules and without publishing the incorporated matter in full, all or any part of a code, standard, rule, or regulation that has been adopted by an agency of the United States or of this state, another state, or by a nationally recognized organization or association, if incorporation of its text in agency rules would be unduly cumbersome, expensive, or otherwise inexpedient. The reference in the agency rules must fully identify the incorporated matter by location, date, and otherwise, [and must state that the rule does not include any later amendments or editions of the incorporated matter]. An agency may incorporate by reference such matter in its rules only if the agency, organization, or association originally issuing that matter makes copies of it readily available to the public. The rules must state where copies of the incorporated matter are available at cost from the agency issuing the rule, and where copies are available from the agency of the United States, this State, another state, or the organization or association originally issuing that matter.

(d) In preparing its rules pursuant to this Chapter, each agency shall follow the uniform numbering system, form, and style prescribed by the [administrative rules editor].

§ 3-112.   [Agency Rule-making Record].

(a) An agency shall maintain an official rule-making record for each rule it (i) proposes by publication in the [administrative bulletin] of a notice of proposed rule adoption, or (ii) adopts. The record and materials incorporated by reference must be available for public inspection.

(b) The agency rule-making record must contain:

(1) copies of all publications in the [administrative bulletin] with respect to the rule or the proceeding upon which the rule is based;

(2) copies of any portions of the agency's public rule-making docket containing entries relating to the rule or the proceeding upon which the rule is based;

(3) all written petitions, requests, submissions, and comments received by the agency and all other written materials considered by the agency in connection with the formulation, proposal, or adoption of the rule or the proceeding upon which the rule is based;

(4) any official transcript of oral presentations made in the proceeding upon which the rule is based or, if not transcribed, any tape recording or stenographic record of those presentations, and any memorandum prepared by a presiding official summarizing the contents of those presentations;

(5) a copy of any regulatory analysis prepared for the proceeding upon which the rule is based;

(6) a copy of the rule and explanatory statement filed in the office of the [secretary of state];

(7) all petitions for exceptions to, amendments of, or repeal or suspension of, the rule;

(8) a copy of any request filed pursuant to Section 3-108(c);

[(9) a copy of any objection to the rule filed by the [administrative rules review committee] pursuant to Section 3-204(d) and the agency's response;] and

(10) a copy of any filed executive order with respect to the rule.

(c) Upon judicial review, the record required by this section constitutes the official agency rule-making record with respect to a rule. Except as provided in Section 3-110(b) or otherwise required by a provision of law, the agency rule-making record need not constitute the exclusive basis for agency action on that rule or for judicial review thereof.

§ 3-113. [Invalidity of Rules Not Adopted According to Chapter; Time Limitation].

(a) A rule adopted after [date] is invalid unless adopted in substantial compliance with the provisions of Sections 3-102 through 3-108 and Sections 3-110 through 3-112. However, inadvertent failure to mail a notice of proposed rule adoption to any person as required by Section 3- 103(b) does not invalidate a rule.

(b) An action to contest the validity of a rule on the grounds of its noncompliance with any provision of Sections 3-102 through 3-108 or Sections 3-110 through 3-112 must be commenced within [2] years after the effective date of the rule.

§ 3-114. [Filing of Rules].

(a) An agency shall file in the office of the [secretary of state] each rule it adopts and all rules existing on the effective date of this Act that have not previously been filed. The filing must be done as soon after adoption of the rule as is practicable. At the time of filing, each rule adopted after the effective date of this Act must have attached to it the explanatory statement required by Section 3-110. The [secretary of state] shall affix to each rule and statement a certification of the time and date of filing and keep a permanent register open to public inspection of all filed rules and attached explanatory statements. In filing a rule, each agency shall use a standard form prescribed by the [secretary of state].

(b) The [secretary of state] shall transmit to the [administrative rules editor], [administrative rules counsel], and to the members of the [administrative rules review committee] a certified copy of each filed rule as soon after its filing as is practicable.

§ 3-115. [Effective Date of Rules].

(a) Except to the extent subsection (b) or (c) provides otherwise, each rule adopted after the effective date of this Act becomes effective [30] days after the later of (i) its filing in the office of the [secretary of state] or (ii) its publication and indexing in the [administrative bulletin].

(b) (1) A rule becomes effective on a date later than that established by subsection (a) if a later date is required by another statute or specified in the rule.

(2) A rule may become effective immediately upon its filing or on any subsequent date earlier than that established by subsection (a) if the agency establishes such an effective date and finds that:

(i) it is required by constitution, statute, or court order;

(ii) the rule only confers a benefit or removes a restriction on the public or some segment thereof;

(iii) the rule only delays the effective date of another rule that is not yet effective; or

(iv) the earlier effective date is necessary because of imminent peril to the public health, safety, or welfare.

(3) The finding and a brief statement of the reasons therefor required by paragraph (2) must be made a part of the rule. In any action contesting the effective date of a rule made effective under paragraph (2), the burden is on the agency to justify its finding.

(4) Each agency shall make a reasonable effort to make known to persons who may be affected by it a rule made effective before publication and indexing under this subsection.

(c) This section does not relieve an agency from compliance with any provision of law requiring that some or all of its rules be approved by other

§ 3-116. [Special Provision for Certain Classes of Rules].

Except to the extent otherwise provided by any provision of law, Sections 3- 102 through 3-115 are inapplicable to:

(1) a rule concerning only the internal management of an agency which does not directly and substantially affect the procedural or substantive rights or duties of any segment of the public;

(2) a rule that establishes criteria or guidelines to be used by the staff of an agency in performing audits, investigations, or inspections, settling commercial disputes, negotiating commercial arrangements, or in the defense, prosecution, or settlement of cases, if disclosure of the criteria or guidelines would:

(i) enable law violators to avoid detection;

(ii) facilitate disregard of requirements imposed by law; or

(iii) give a clearly improper advantage to persons who are in an adverse position to the state;

(3) a rule that only establishes specific prices to be charged for particular goods or services sold by an agency;

(4) a rule concerning only the physical servicing, maintenance, or care of agency owned or operated facilities or property;

(5) a rule relating only to the use of a particular facility or property owned, operated, or maintained by the state or any of its subdivisions, if the substance of the rule is adequately indicated by means of signs or signals to persons who use the facility or property;

(6) a rule concerning only inmates of a correctional or detention facility, students enrolled in an educational institution, or patients admitted to a hospital, if adopted by that facility, institution, or hospital;

(7) a form whose contents or substantive requirements are prescribed by rule or statute, and instructions for the execution or use of the form;

(8) an agency budget; [or]

(9) an opinion of the attorney general [; or] [.]

(10) [the terms of a collective bargaining agreement.]

§ 3-117. [Petition For Adoption of Rule].

Any person may petition an agency requesting the adoption of a rule. Each agency shall prescribe by rule the form of the petition and the procedure for its submission, consideration, and disposition. Within [60] days after submission of a petition, the agency shall either (i) deny the petition in writing, stating its reasons therefor, (ii) initiate rule-making proceedings in accordance with this Chapter, or (iii) if otherwise lawful, adopt a rule.

§ 3-201. [Review by Agency].

At least [annually], each agency shall review all of its rules to determine whether any new rule should be adopted. In conducting that review, each agency shall prepare a written report summarizing its findings, its supporting reasons, and any proposed course of action. For each rule, the [annual] report must include, at least once every [7] years, a concise statement of:

(1) the rule's effectiveness in achieving its objectives, including a summary of any available data supporting the conclusions reached;

(2) criticisms of the rule received during the previous [7] years, including a summary of any petitions for waiver of the rule tendered to the agency or granted by it; and

(3) alternative solutions to the criticisms and the reasons they were rejected or the changes made in the rule in response to those criticisms and the reasons for the changes. A copy of the [annual] report must be sent to the [administrative rules review committee and the administrative rules counsel] and be available for public inspection.

§ 3-202. [Review by Governor; Administrative Rules Counsel].

(a) To the extent the agency itself would have authority, the governor may rescind or suspend all or a severable portion of a rule of an agency. In exercising this authority, the governor shall act by an executive order that is subject to the provisions of this Act applicable to the adoption and effectiveness of a rule.

(b) The governor may summarily terminate any pending rule-making proceeding by an executive order to that effect, stating therein the reasons for the action. The executive order must be filed in the office of the [secretary of state], which shall promptly forward a certified copy to the agency and the [administrative rules editor]. An executive order terminating a rule-making proceeding becomes effective on [the date it is filed] and must be published in the next issue of the [administrative bulletin].

(c) There is created, within the office of the governor, an [administrative rules counsel] to advise the governor in the execution of the authority vested under this

Article. The governor shall appoint the [administrative rules counsel] who shall serve at the pleasure of the governor.

§ 3-203. [Administrative Rules Review Committee].

There is created the ["administrative rules review committee"] of the [legislature]. The committee must be [bipartisan] and composed of [3] senators appointed by the [president of the senate] and [3] representatives appointed by the [speaker of the house]. Committee members must be appointed within [30] days after the convening of a regular legislative session. The term of office is [2] years while a member of the [legislature] and begins on the date of appointment to the committee. While a member of the [legislature], a member of the committee whose term has expired shall serve until a successor is appointed. A vacancy on the committee may be filled at any time by the original appointing authority for the remainder of the term. The committee shall choose a chairman from its membership for a [2]-year term and may employ staff it considers advisable.

§ 3-204. [Review by Administrative Rules Review Committee].

(a) The [administrative rules review committee] shall selectively review possible, proposed, or adopted rules and prescribe appropriate committee procedures for that purpose. The committee may receive and investigate complaints from members of the public with respect to possible, proposed, or adopted rules and hold public proceedings on those complaints.

(b) Committee meetings must be open to the public. Subject to procedures established by the committee, persons may present oral argument, data, or views at those meetings. The committee may require a representative of an agency whose possible, proposed, or adopted rule is under examination to attend a committee meeting and answer relevant questions. The committee may also communicate to the agency its comments on any possible, proposed, or adopted rule and require the agency to respond to them in writing. Unless impracticable, in advance of each committee meeting notice of the time and place of the meeting and the specific subject matter to be considered must be published in the [administrative bulletin].

(c) The committee may recommend enactment of a statute to improve the operation of an agency. The committee may also recommend that a particular rule be superseded in whole or in part by statute. The [speaker of the house and the president of the senate] shall refer those recommendations to the appropriate standing committees. This subsection does not preclude any committee of the legislature from reviewing a rule on its own motion or recommending that it be superseded in whole or in part by statute.

[(d) (1) If the committee objects to all or some portion of a rule because the committee considers it to be beyond the procedural or substantive authority delegated to the adopting agency, the committee may file that objection in the office of the [secretary of state]. The filed objection must contain a concise statement of the committee's reasons for its action.]

(2) The [secretary of state] shall affix to each objection a certification of the date and time of its filing and as soon thereafter as practicable shall transmit a certified copy thereof to the agency issuing the rule in question, the [adminis-

trative rules editor, and the administrative rules counsel]. The [secretary of state] shall also maintain a permanent register open to public inspection of all objections by the committee.

(3) The [administrative rules editor] shall publish and index an objection filed pursuant to this subsection in the next issue of the [administrative bulletin] and indicate its existence adjacent to the rule in question when that rule is published in the [administrative code]. In case of a filed objection by the committee to a rule that is subject to the requirements of Section 2-101(g), the agency shall indicate the existence of that objection adjacent to the rule in the official compilation referred to in that subsection.

(4) Within [14] days after the filing of an objection by the committee to a rule, the issuing agency shall respond in writing to the committee. After receipt of the response, the committee may withdraw or modify its objection.

[(5) After the filing of an objection by the committee that is not subsequently withdrawn, the burden is upon the agency in any proceeding for judicial review or for enforcement of the rule to establish that the whole or portion of the rule objected to is within the procedural and substantive authority delegated to the agency.]

(6) The failure of the [administrative rules review committee] to object to a rule is not an implied legislative authorization of its procedural or substantive validity.]

(e) The committee may recommend to an agency that it adopt a rule. [The committee may also require an agency to publish notice of the committee's recommendation as a proposed rule of the agency and to allow public participation thereon, according to the provisions of Sections 3-103 through 3-104. An agency is not required to adopt the proposed rule.]

(f) The committee shall file an annual report with the [presiding officer] of each house and the governor.

§ 4-101. [Adjudicative Proceedings; When Required; Exceptions].

(a) An agency shall conduct an adjudicative proceeding as the process for formulating and issuing an order, unless the order is a decision:

(1) to issue or not to issue a complaint, summons, or similar accusation;

(2) to initiate or not to initiate an investigation, prosecution, or other proceeding before the agency, another agency, or a court; or

(3) under Section 4-103, not to conduct an adjudicative proceeding.

(b) This Article applies to rule-making proceedings only to the extent that another statute expressly so requires.

§ 4-102. [Adjudicative Proceedings; Commencement].

(a) An agency may commence an adjudicative proceeding at any time with respect to a matter within the agency's jurisdiction.

(b) An agency shall commence an adjudicative proceeding upon the application of any person, unless:

(1) the agency lacks jurisdiction of the subject matter;

(2) resolution of the matter requires the agency to exercise discretion within the scope of Section 4-101(a);

(3) a statute vests the agency with discretion to conduct or not to conduct an adjudicative proceeding before issuing an order to resolve the matter and, in the exercise of that discretion, the agency has determined not to conduct an adjudicative proceeding;

(4) resolution of the matter does not require the agency to issue an order that determines the applicant's legal rights, duties, privileges, immunities, or other legal interests;

(5) the matter was not timely submitted to the agency; or

(6) the matter was not submitted in a form substantially complying with any applicable provision of law.

(c) An application for an agency to issue an order includes an application for the agency to conduct appropriate adjudicative proceedings, whether or not the applicant expressly requests those proceedings.

(d) An adjudicative proceeding commences when the agency or a presiding officer:

(1) notifies a party that a pre-hearing conference, hearing, or other stage of an adjudicative proceeding will be conducted; or

(2) begins to take action on a matter that appropriately may be determined by an adjudicative proceeding, unless this action is:

(i) an investigation for the purpose of determining whether an adjudicative proceeding should be conducted; or

(ii) a decision which, under Section 4-101(a), the agency may make without conducting an adjudicative proceeding.

§ 4-103.   [Decision Not to Conduct Adjudicative Proceeding].

If an agency decides not to conduct an adjudicative proceeding in response to an application, the agency shall furnish the applicant a copy of its decision in writing, with a brief statement of the agency's reasons and of any administrative review available to the applicant.

§ 4-104.   [Agency Action on Applications].

(a) Except to the extent that the time limits in this subsection are inconsistent with limits established by another statute for any stage of the proceedings, an agency shall process an application for an order, other than a declaratory order, as follows:

(1) Within [30] days after receipt of the application, the agency shall examine

the application, notify the applicant of any apparent errors or omissions, request any additional information the agency wishes to obtain and is permitted by law to require, and notify the applicant of the name, official title, mailing address and telephone number of an agency member or employee who may be contacted regarding the application.

(2) Except in situations governed by paragraph (3), within [90] days after receipt of the application or of the response to a timely request made by the agency pursuant to paragraph (1), the agency shall:

(i) approve or deny the application, in whole or in part, on the basis of emergency or summary adjudicative proceedings, if those proceedings are available under this Act for disposition of the matter;

(ii) commence a formal adjudicative hearing or a conference adjudicative hearing in accordance with this Act; or

(iii) dispose of the application in accordance with Section 4-103.

(3) If the application pertains to subject matter that is not available when the application is filed but may be available in the future, including an application for housing or employment at a time no vacancy exists, the agency may proceed to make a determination of eligibility within the time provided in paragraph (2). If the agency determines that the applicant is eligible, the agency shall maintain the application on the agency's list of eligible applicants as provided by law and, upon request, shall notify the applicant of the status of the application.

(b) If a timely and sufficient application has been made for renewal of a license with reference to any activity of a continuing nature, the existing license does not expire until the agency has taken final action upon the application for renewal or, if the agency's action is unfavorable, until the last day for seeking judicial review of the agency's action or a later date fixed by the reviewing court.

§ 4-105. [Agency Action Against Licensees].

An agency may not revoke, suspend, modify, annul, withdraw, or amend a license unless the agency first gives notice and an opportunity for an appropriate adjudicative proceeding in accordance with this Act or other statute. This section does not preclude an agency from (i) taking immediate action to protect the public interest in accordance with Section 4-501 or (ii) adopting rules, otherwise within the scope of its authority, pertaining to a class of licensees, including rules affecting the existing licenses of a class of licensees.

§ 4-201. [Applicability].

An adjudicative proceeding is governed by this chapter, except as otherwise provided by:

(1) a statute other than this Act;

(2) a rule that adopts the procedures for the conference adjudicative hearing or summary adjudicative proceeding in accordance with the standards provided in this Act for those proceedings;

(3) Section 4-501 pertaining to emergency adjudicative proceedings; or

(4) Section 2-103 pertaining to declaratory proceedings.

§ 4-202. [Presiding Officer, Disqualification, Substitution].

(a) The agency head, one or more members of the agency head, one or more administrative law judges assigned by the office of administrative hearings in accordance with Section 4-301 [, or, unless prohibited by law, one or more other persons designated by the agency head], in the discretion of the agency head, may be the presiding officer.

(b) Any person serving or designated to serve alone or with others as presiding officer is subject to disqualification for bias, prejudice, interest, or any other cause provided in this Act or for which a judge is or may be disqualified.

(c) Any party may petition for the disqualification of a person promptly after receipt of notice indicating that the person will preside or promptly upon discovering facts establishing grounds for disqualification, whichever is later.

(d) A person whose disqualification is requested shall determine whether to grant the petition, stating facts and reasons for the determination.

(e) If a substitute is required for a person who is disqualified or becomes unavailable for any other reason, the substitute must be appointed by:

(1) the governor, if the disqualified or unavailable person is an elected official; or

(2) the appointing authority, if the disqualified or unavailable person is an appointed official.

(f) Any action taken by a duly-appointed substitute for a disqualified or unavailable person is as effective as if taken by the latter.

§ 4-203. [Representation].

(a) Any party may participate in the hearing in person or, if the party is a corporation or other artificial person, by a duly authorized representative.

(b) Whether or not participating in person, any party may be advised and represented at the party's own expense by counsel or, if permitted by law, other representative.

§ 4-204. [Pre-hearing Conference — Availability, Notice].

The presiding officer designated to conduct the hearing may determine, subject to the agency's rules, whether a pre-hearing conference will be conducted. If the conference is conducted:

(1) The presiding officer shall promptly notify the agency of the determination that a pre-hearing conference will be conducted. The agency shall assign or request the office of administrative hearings to assign a presiding officer for the pre-hearing conference, exercising the same discretion as is provided by Section 4-202 concerning the selection of a presiding officer for a hearing.

(2) The presiding officer for the pre-hearing conference shall set the time and

place of the conference and give reasonable written notice to all parties and to all persons who have filed written petitions to intervene in the matter. The agency shall give notice to other persons entitled to notice under any provision of law.

(3) The notice must include:

(i) the names and mailing addresses of all parties and other persons to whom notice is being given by the presiding officer;

(ii) the name, official title, mailing address, and telephone number of any counsel or employee who has been designated to appear for the agency;

(iii) the official file or other reference number, the name of the proceeding, and a general description of the subject matter;

(iv) a statement of the time, place, and nature of the pre-hearing conference;

(v) a statement of the legal authority and jurisdiction under which the pre-hearing conference and the hearing are to be held;

(vi) the name, official title, mailing address and telephone number of the presiding officer for the pre-hearing conference;

(vii) a statement that at the pre-hearing conference the proceeding, without further notice, may be converted into a conference adjudicative hearing or a summary adjudicative proceeding for disposition of the matter as provided by this Act; and

(viii) a statement that a party who fails to attend or participate in a pre-hearing conference, hearing, or other state of an adjudicative proceeding may be held in default under this Act.

(4) The notice may include any other matter that the presiding officer considers desirable to expedite the proceedings.

§ 4-205. [Pre-hearing Conference — Procedure and Pre-hearing Order].

(a) The presiding officer may conduct all or part of the pre-hearing conference by telephone, television, or other electronic means if each participant in the conference has an opportunity to participate in, to hear, and, if technically feasible, to see the entire proceeding while it is taking place.

(b) The presiding officer shall conduct the pre-hearing conference, as may be appropriate, to deal with such matters as conversion of the proceeding to another type, exploration of settlement possibilities, preparation of stipulations, clarification of issues, rulings on identity and limitation of the number of witnesses, objections to proffers of evidence, determination of the extent to which direct evidence, rebuttal evidence, or cross-examination will be presented in written form, and the extent to which telephone, television, or other electronic means will be used as a substitute for proceedings in person, order of presentation of evidence and cross-examination, rulings regarding issuance of subpoenas, discovery orders and protective orders, and such other matters as will promote the orderly and prompt conduct of the hearing. The presiding officer shall issue a pre-hearing order incorporating the matters determined at the pre-hearing conference.

(c) If a pre-hearing conference is not held, the presiding officer for the hearing may issue a pre-hearing order, based on the pleadings, to regulate the conduct of the proceedings.

§ 4-206. [Notice of Hearing].

(a) The presiding officer for the hearing shall set the time and place of the hearing and give reasonable written notice to all parties and to all persons who have filed written petitions to intervene in the matter.

(b) The notice must include a copy of any pre-hearing order rendered in the matter.

(c) To the extent not included in a pre-hearing order accompanying it, the notice must include:

(1) the names and mailing addresses of all parties and other persons to whom notice is being given by the presiding officer;

(2) the name, official title, mailing address and telephone number of any counsel or employee who has been designated to appear for the agency;

(3) the official file or other reference number, the name of the proceeding, and a general description of the subject matter;

(4) a statement of the time, place, and nature of the hearing;

(5) a statement of the legal authority and jurisdiction under which the hearing is to be held;

(6) the name, official title, mailing address, and telephone number of the presiding officer;

(7) a statement of the issues involved and, to the extent known to the presiding officer, of the matters asserted by the parties; and

(8) a statement that a party who fails to attend or participate in a pre- hearing conference, hearing, or other stage of an adjudicative proceeding may be held in default under this Act.

(d) The notice may include any other matters the presiding officer considers desirable to expedite the proceedings.

(e) The agency shall give notice to persons entitled to notice under any provision of law who have not been given notice by the presiding officer. Notice under this subsection may include all types of information provided in subsections (a) through (d) or may consist of a brief statement indicating the subject matter, parties, time, place, and nature of the hearing, manner in which copies of the notice to the parties may be inspected and copied, and name and telephone number of the presiding officer.

§ 4-207. [Pleadings, Briefs, Motions, Service].

(a) The presiding officer, at appropriate stages of the proceedings, shall give all parties full opportunity to file pleadings, motions, objections and offers of settlement.

(b) The presiding officer, at appropriate stages of the proceedings, may give all parties full opportunity to file briefs, proposed findings of fact and conclusions of law, and proposed initial or final orders.

(c) A party shall serve copies of any filed item on all parties, by mail or any other means prescribed by agency rule.

§ 4-208.   [Default].

(a) If a party fails to attend or participate in a pre-hearing conference, hearing, or other stage of an adjudicative proceeding, the presiding officer may serve upon all parties written notice of a proposed default order, including a statement of the grounds.

(b) Within [7] days after service of a proposed default order, the party against whom it was issued may file a written motion requesting that the proposed default order be vacated and stating the grounds relied upon. During the time within which a party may file a written motion under this subsection, the presiding officer may adjourn the proceedings or conduct them without the participation of the party against whom a proposed default order was issued, having due regard for the interests of justice and the orderly and prompt conduct of the proceedings.

(c) The presiding officer shall either issue or vacate the default order promptly after expiration of the time within which the party may file a written motion under subsection (b).

(d) After issuing a default order, the presiding officer shall conduct any further proceedings necessary to complete the adjudication without the participation of the party in default and shall determine all issues in the adjudication, including those affecting the defaulting party.

§ 4-209.   [Intervention].

(a) The presiding officer shall grant a petition for intervention if:

(1) the petition is submitted in writing to the presiding officer, with copies mailed to all parties named in the presiding officer's notice of the hearing, at least [3] days before the hearing;

(2) the petition states facts demonstrating that the petitioner's legal rights, duties, privileges, immunities, or other legal interests may be substantially affected by the proceeding or that the petitioner qualifies as an intervener under any provision of law; and

(3) the presiding officer determines that the interests of justice and the orderly and prompt conduct of the proceedings will not be impaired by allowing the intervention.

(b) The presiding officer may grant a petition for intervention at any time, upon determining that the intervention sought is in the interests of justice and will not impair the orderly and prompt conduct of the proceedings.

(c) If a petitioner qualifies for intervention, the presiding officer may impose conditions upon the intervener's participation in the proceedings, either at the time that intervention is granted or at any subsequent time. Conditions may include:

(1) limiting the intervener's participation to designated issues in which the intervener has a particular interest demonstrated by the petition;

(2) limiting the intervener's use of discovery, cross-examination, and other procedures so as to promote the orderly and prompt conduct of the proceedings; and

(3) requiring 2 or more interveners to combine their presentations of evidence and argument, cross-examination, discovery, and other participation in the proceedings.

(d) The presiding officer, at least [24 hours] before the hearing, shall issue an order granting or denying each pending petition for intervention, specifying any conditions, and briefly stating the reasons for the order. The presiding officer may modify the order at any time, stating the reasons for the modification. The presiding officer shall promptly give notice of an order granting, denying, or modifying intervention to the petitioner for intervention and to all parties.

§ 4-210. [Subpoenas, Discovery and Protective Orders].

(a) The presiding officer [at the request of any party shall, and upon the presiding officer's own motion,] may issue subpoenas, discovery orders and protective orders, in accordance with the rules of civil procedure.

(b) Subpoenas and orders issued under this section may be enforced pursuant to the provisions of this Act on civil enforcement of agency action.

§ 4-211. [Procedure at Hearing].

At a hearing:

(1) The presiding officer shall regulate the course of the proceedings in conformity with any pre-hearing order.

(2) To the extent necessary for full disclosure of all relevant facts and issues, the presiding officer shall afford to all parties the opportunity to respond, present evidence and argument, conduct cross-examination, and submit rebuttal evidence, except as restricted by a limited grant of intervention or by the pre-hearing order.

(3) The presiding officer may give nonparties an opportunity to present oral or written statements. If the presiding officer proposes to consider a statement by a nonparty, the presiding officer shall give all parties an opportunity to challenge or rebut it and, on motion of any party, the presiding officer shall require the statement to be given under oath or affirmation.

(4) The presiding officer may conduct all or part of the hearing by telephone, television, or other electronic means, if each participant in the hearing has an opportunity to participate in, to hear, and, if technically feasible, to see the entire proceeding while it is taking place.

(5) The presiding officer shall cause the hearing to be recorded at the agency's

expense. The agency is not required, at its expense, to prepare a transcript, unless required to do so by a provision of law. Any party, at the party's expense, may cause a reporter approved by the agency to prepare a transcript from the agency's record, or cause additional recordings to be made during the hearing if the making of the additional recordings does not cause distraction or disruption.

(6) The hearing is open to public observation, except for the parts that the presiding officer states to be closed pursuant to a provision of law expressly authorizing closure. To the extent that a hearing is conducted by telephone, television, or other electronic means, and is not closed, the availability of public observation is satisfied by giving members of the public an opportunity, at reasonable times, to hear or inspect the agency's record, and to inspect any transcript obtained by the agency.

§ 4-212.   [Evidence, Official Notice].

(a) Upon proper objection, the presiding officer shall exclude evidence that is irrelevant, immaterial, unduly repetitious, or excludable on constitutional or statutory grounds or on the basis of evidentiary privilege recognized in the courts of this state. In the absence of proper objection, the presiding officer may exclude objectionable evidence. Evidence may not be excluded solely because it is hearsay.

(b) All testimony of parties and witnesses must be made under oath or affirmation.

(c) Statements presented by nonparties in accordance with Section 4-211(3) may be received as evidence.

(d) Any part of the evidence may be received in written form if doing so will expedite the hearing without substantial prejudice to the interests of any party.

(e) Documentary evidence may be received in the form of a copy or excerpt. Upon request, parties must be given an opportunity to compare the copy with the original if available.

(f) Official notice may be taken of (i) any fact that could be judicially noticed in the courts of this State, (ii) the record of other proceedings before the agency, (iii) technical or scientific matters within the agency's specialized knowledge, and (iv) codes or standards that have been adopted by an agency of the United States, of this State or of another state, or by a nationally recognized organization or association. Parties must be notified before or during the hearing, or before the issuance of any initial or final order that is based in whole or in part on facts or material noticed, of the specific facts or material noticed and the source thereof, including any staff memoranda and data, and be afforded an opportunity to contest and rebut the facts or material so noticed.

§ 4-213.   [Ex parte Communications].

(a) Except as provided in subsection (b) or unless required for the disposition of ex parte matters specifically authorized by statute, a presiding officer serving in an adjudicative proceeding may not communicate, directly or indirectly, regarding any issue in the proceeding, while the proceeding is pending, with any party, with any person who has a direct or indirect interest in the outcome of the proceeding, or with any person who presided at a previous stage of the proceeding, without notice and opportunity for all parties to participate in the communication.

(b) A member of a multi-member panel of presiding officers may communicate with other members of the panel regarding a matter pending before the panel, and any presiding officer may receive aid from staff assistants if the assistants do not (i) receive ex parte communications of a type that the presiding officer would be prohibited from receiving or (ii) furnish, augment, diminish, or modify the evidence in the record.

(c) Unless required for the disposition of ex parte matters specifically authorized by statute, no party to an adjudicative proceeding, and no person who has a direct or indirect interest in the outcome of the proceeding or who presided at a previous stage of the proceeding, may communicate, directly or indirectly, in connection with any issue in that proceeding, while the proceeding is pending, with any person serving as presiding officer, without notice and opportunity for all parties to participate in the communication.

(d) If, before serving as presiding officer in an adjudicative proceeding, a person receives an ex parte communication of a type that could not properly be received while serving, the person, promptly after starting to serve, shall disclose the communication in the manner prescribed in subsection (e).

(e) A presiding officer who receives an ex parte communication in violation of this section shall place on the record of the pending matter all written communications received, all written responses to the communications, and a memorandum stating the substance of all oral communications received, all responses made, and the identity of each person from whom the presiding officer received an ex parte communication, and shall advise all parties that these matters have been placed on the record. Any party desiring to rebut the ex parte communication must be allowed to do so, upon requesting the opportunity for rebuttal within [10] days after notice of the communication.

(f) If necessary to eliminate the effect of an ex parte communication received in violation of this section, a presiding officer who receives the communication may be disqualified and the portions of the record pertaining to the communication may be sealed by protective order.

(g) The agency shall, and any party may, report any willful violation of this section to appropriate authorities for any disciplinary proceedings provided by law. In addition, each agency by rule may provide for appropriate sanctions, including default, for any violations of this section.

§ 4-214. [Separation of Functions].

(a) A person who has served as investigator, prosecutor or advocate in an adjudicative proceeding or in its pre-adjudicative stage may not serve as presiding officer or assist or advise a presiding officer in the same proceeding.

(b) A person who is subject to the authority, direction, or discretion of one who has served as investigator, prosecutor, or advocate in an adjudicative proceeding or in its pre-adjudicative stage may not serve as presiding officer or assist or advise a presiding officer in the same proceeding.

(c) A person who has participated in a determination of probable cause or other equivalent preliminary determination in an adjudicative proceeding may serve as presiding officer or assist or advise a presiding officer in the same proceeding, unless a party demonstrates grounds for disqualification in accordance with Section 4-202.

(d) A person may serve as presiding officer at successive stages of the same adjudicative proceeding, unless a party demonstrates grounds for disqualification in accordance with Section 4-202.

§ 4-215. [Final Order, Initial Order].

(a) If the presiding officer is the agency head, the presiding officer shall render a final order.

(b) If the presiding officer is not the agency head, the presiding officer shall render an initial order, which becomes a final order unless reviewed in accordance with Section 4-216.

(c) A final order or initial order must include, separately stated, findings of fact, conclusions of law, and policy reasons for the decision if it is an exercise of the agency's discretion, for all aspects of the order, including the remedy prescribed and, if applicable, the action taken on a petition for stay of effectiveness. Findings of fact, if set forth in language that is no more than mere repetition or paraphrase of the relevant provision of law, must be accompanied by a concise and explicit statement of the underlying facts of record to support the findings. If a party has submitted proposed findings of fact, the order must include a ruling on the proposed findings. The order must also include a statement of the available procedures and time limits for seeking reconsideration or other administrative relief. An initial order must include a statement of any circumstances under which the initial order, without further notice, may become a final order.

(d) Findings of fact must be based exclusively upon the evidence of record in the adjudicative proceeding and on matters officially noticed in that proceeding. Findings must be based upon the kind of evidence on which reasonably prudent persons are accustomed to rely in the conduct of their serious affairs and may be based upon such evidence even if it would be inadmissible in a civil trial. The presiding officer's experience, technical competence, and specialized knowledge may be utilized in evaluating evidence.

(e) If a person serving or designated to serve as presiding officer becomes unavailable, for any reason, before rendition of the final order or initial order, a substitute presiding officer must be appointed as provided in Section 4-202. The substitute presiding officer shall use any existing record and may conduct any further proceedings appropriate in the interests of justice.

(f) The presiding officer may allow the parties a designated amount of time after conclusion of the hearing for the submission of proposed findings.

(g) A final order or initial order pursuant to this section must be rendered in writing within [90] days after conclusion of the hearing or after submission of proposed findings in accordance with subsection (f) unless this period is waived or extended with the written consent of all parties or for good cause shown.

(h) The presiding officer shall cause copies of the final order or initial order to be delivered to each party and to the agency head.

§ 4-216. [Review of Initial Order; Exceptions to Reviewability].

(a) The agency head, upon its own motion may, and upon appeal by any party shall, review an initial order, except to the extent that:

(1) a provision of law precludes or limits agency review of the initial order; or

(2) the agency head, in the exercise of discretion conferred by a provision of law,

(i) determines to review some but not all issues, or not to exercise any review,

(ii) delegates its authority to review the initial order to one or more persons, or

(iii) authorizes one or more persons to review the initial order, subject to further review by the agency head.

(b) A petition for appeal from an initial order must be filed with the agency head, or with any person designated for this purpose by rule of the agency, within [10] days after rendition of the initial order. If the agency head on its own motion decides to review an initial order, the agency head shall give written notice of its intention to review the initial order within [10] days after its rendition. The [10]-day period for a party to file a petition for appeal or for the agency head to give notice of its intention to review an initial order on the agency head's own motion is tolled by the submission of a timely petition for reconsideration of the initial order pursuant to Section 4-218, and a new [10]-day period starts to run upon disposition of the petition for reconsideration. If an initial order is subject both to a timely petition for reconsideration and to a petition for appeal or to review by the agency head on its own motion, the petition for reconsideration must be disposed of first, unless the agency head determines that action on the petition for reconsideration has been unreasonably delayed.

(c) The petition for appeal must state its basis. If the agency head on its own motion gives notice of its intent to review an initial order, the agency head shall identity the issues that it intends to review.

(d) The presiding officer for the review of an initial order shall exercise all the decision-making power that the presiding officer would have had to render a final order had the presiding officer presided over the hearing, except to the extent that the issues subject to review are limited by a provision of law or by the presiding officer upon notice to all parties.

(e) The presiding officer shall afford each party an opportunity to present briefs and may afford each party an opportunity to present oral argument.

(f) Before rendering a final order, the presiding officer may cause a transcript to be prepared, at the agency's expense, of such portions of the proceeding under review as the presiding officer considers necessary.

(g) The presiding officer may render a final order disposing of the proceeding or may remand the matter for further proceedings with instructions to the person who rendered the initial order. Upon remanding a matter, the presiding officer may order such temporary relief as is authorized and appropriate.

(h) A final order or an order remanding the matter for further proceedings must be rendered in writing within [60] days after receipt of briefs and oral argument unless that period is waived or extended with the written consent of all parties or for good cause shown.

(i) A final order or an order remanding the matter for further proceedings under this section must identify any difference between this order and the initial order and must include, or incorporate by express reference to the initial order, all the matters required by Section 4-215(c).

(j) The presiding officer shall cause copies of the final order or order remanding the matter for further proceedings to be delivered to each party and to the agency head.

§ 4-217.   [Stay].

A party may submit to the presiding officer a petition for stay of effectiveness of an initial or final order within [7] days after its rendition unless otherwise provided by statute or stated in the initial or final order. The presiding officer may take action on the petition for stay, either before or after the effective date of the initial or final order.

§ 4-218.   [Reconsideration].

Unless otherwise provided by statute or rule:

(1) Any party, within [10] days after rendition of an initial or final order, may file a petition for reconsideration, stating the specific grounds upon which relief is requested. The filing of the petition is not a prerequisite for seeking administrative or judicial review.

(2) The petition must be disposed of by the same person or persons who rendered the initial or final order, if available.

(3) The presiding officer shall render a written order denying the petition, granting the petition and dissolving or modifying the initial or final order, or granting the petition and setting the matter for further proceedings. The petition may be granted, in whole or in part, only if the presiding officer states, in the written order, findings of fact, conclusions of law, and policy reasons for the decision if it is an exercise of the agency's discretion, to justify the order. The petition is deemed to have been denied if the presiding officer does not dispose of it within [20] days after the filing of the petition.

§ 4-219.   [Review by Superior Agency].

If, pursuant to statute, an agency may review the final order of another agency, the review is deemed to be a continuous proceeding as if before a single agency. The final order of the first agency is treated as an initial order and the second agency functions as though it were reviewing an initial order in accordance with Section 4-216.

§ 4-220. [Effectiveness of Orders].

(a) Unless a later date is stated in a final order or a stay is granted, a final order is effective [10] days after rendition, but:

(1) a party may not be required to comply with a final order unless the party has been served with or has actual knowledge of the final order;

(2) a nonparty may not be required to comply with a final order unless the agency has made the final order available for public inspection and copying or the nonparty has actual knowledge of the final order.

(b) Unless a later date is stated in an initial order or a stay is granted, the time when an initial order becomes a final order in accordance with Section 4-215 is determined as follows:

(1) when the initial order is rendered, if administrative review is unavailable;

(2) when the agency head renders an order stating, after a petition for appeal has been filed, that review will not be exercised, if discretion is available to make a determination to this effect; or

(3) [10] days after rendition of the initial order, if no party has filed a petition for appeal and the agency head has not given written notice of its intention to exercise review.

(c) Unless a later date is stated in an initial order or a stay is granted, an initial order that becomes a final order in accordance with subsection (b) and Section 4-215 is effective [10] days after becoming a final order, but:

(1) a party may not be required to comply with the final order unless the party has been served with or has actual knowledge of the initial order or of an order stating that review will not be exercised; and

(2) a nonparty may not be required to comply with the final order unless the agency has made the initial order available for public inspection and copying or the nonparty has actual knowledge of the initial order or of an order stating that review will not be exercised.

(d) This section does not preclude an agency from taking immediate action to protect the public interest in accordance with Section 4-501.

§ 4-221. [Agency Record].

(a) An agency shall maintain an official record of each adjudicative proceeding under this Chapter.

(b) The agency record consists only of:

(1) notices of all proceedings;

(2) any pre-hearing order;

(3) any motions, pleadings, briefs, petitions, requests, and intermediate rulings;

(4) evidence received or considered;

(5) a statement of matters officially noticed;

(6) proffers of proof and objections and rulings thereon;

(7) proposed findings, requested orders, and exceptions;

(8) the record prepared for the presiding officer at the hearing, together with any transcript of all or part of the hearing considered before final disposition of the proceeding;

(9) any final order, initial order, or order on reconsideration;

(10) staff memoranda or data submitted to the presiding officer, unless prepared and submitted by personal assistants and not inconsistent with Section 4-213(b); and

(11) matters placed on the record after an ex parte communication.

(c) Except to the extent that this Act or another statute provides otherwise, the agency record constitutes the exclusive basis for agency action in adjudicative proceedings under this Chapter and for judicial review thereof.

§ 4-301.   [Office of Administrative Hearings — Creation, Powers, Duties].

(a) There is created the office of administrative hearings within the [Department of _____], to be headed by a director appointed by the governor [and confirmed by the senate].

(b) The office shall employ administrative law judges as necessary to conduct proceedings required by this Act or other provision of law. [Only a person admitted to practice law in [this State] [a jurisdiction in the United States] may be employed as an administrative law judge.]

(c) If the office cannot furnish one of its administrative law judges in response to an agency request, the director shall designate in writing a full- time employee of an agency other than the requesting agency to serve as administrative law judge for the proceeding, but only with the consent of the employing agency. The designee must possess the same qualifications required of administrative law judges employed by the office.

(d) The director may furnish administrative law judges on a contract basis to any governmental entity to conduct any proceeding not subject to this Act.

(e) The office may adopt rules:

(1) to establish further qualifications for administrative law judges, procedures by which candidates will be considered for employment, and the manner in which public notice of vacancies in the staff of the office will be given;

(2) to establish procedures for agencies to request and for the director to assign administrative law judges; however, an agency may neither select nor reject any individual administrative law judge for any proceeding except in accordance with this Act;

(3) to establish procedures and adopt forms, consistent with this Act, the model rules of procedure, and other provisions of law, to govern administrative law judges;

(4) to establish standards and procedures for the evaluation, training, promotion, and discipline of administrative law judges; and

(5) to facilitate the performance of the responsibilities conferred upon the office by this Act.

(f) The director may:

(1) maintain a staff of reporters and other personnel; and

(2) implement the provisions of this section and rules adopted under its authority.

§ 4-401. [Conference Adjudicative Hearing — Applicability].

A conference adjudicative hearing may be used if its use in the circumstances does not violate any provision of law and the matter is entirely within one or more categories for which the agency by rule had adopted this chapter [; however, those categories may include only the following:

(1) a matter in which there is no disputed issue of material fact; or

(2) a matter in which there is a disputed issue of material fact, if the matter involves only:

(i) a monetary amount of not more than [$1,000];

(ii) a disciplinary sanction against a prisoner;

(iii) a disciplinary sanction against a student which does not involve expulsion from an academic institution or suspension for more than [10] days;

(iv) a disciplinary sanction against a public employee which does not involve discharge from employment or suspension for more than [10] days;

(v) a disciplinary sanction against a licensee which does not involve revocation, suspension, annulment, withdrawal, or amendment of a license; or

(vi) . . . .]

§ 4-402. [Conference Adjudicative Hearing — Procedures].

The procedures of this Act pertaining to formal adjudicative hearings apply to a conference adjudicative hearing, except to the following extent:

(1) If a matter is initiated as a conference adjudicative hearing, no pre-hearing conference may be held.

(2) The provisions of Section 4-210 do not apply to conference adjudicative hearings insofar as those provisions authorize the issuance and enforcement of subpoenas and discovery orders, but do apply to conference adjudicative hearings insofar as those provisions authorize the presiding officer to issue protective orders at the request of any party or upon the presiding officer's motion.

(3) Paragraphs (1), (2) and (3) of Section 4-211 do not apply; but,

(i) the presiding officer shall regulate the course of the proceedings,

(ii) only the parties may testify and present written exhibits, and

(iii) the parties may offer comments on the issues.

§ 4-403.   [Conference Adjudicative Hearing — Proposed Proof].

(a) If the presiding officer has reason to believe that material facts are in dispute, the presiding officer may require any party to state the identity of the witnesses or other sources through whom the party would propose to present proof if the proceeding were converted to a formal adjudicative hearing, but if disclosure of any fact, allegation, or source is privileged or expressly prohibited by any provision of law, the presiding officer may require the party to indicate that confidential facts, allegations, or sources are involved, but not to disclose the confidential facts, allegations, or sources.

(b) If a party has reason to believe that essential facts must be obtained in order to permit an adequate presentation of the case, the party may inform the presiding officer regarding the general nature of the facts and the sources from whom the party would propose to obtain those facts if the proceeding were converted to a formal adjudicative hearing.

§ 4-501.   [Emergency Adjudicative Proceedings].

(a) An agency may use emergency adjudicative proceedings in a situation involving an immediate danger to the public health, safety, or welfare requiring immediate agency action.

(b) The agency may take only such action as is necessary to prevent or avoid the immediate danger to the public health, safety, or welfare that justifies use of emergency adjudication.

(c) The agency shall render an order, including a brief statement of findings of fact, conclusions of law, and policy reasons for the decision if it is an exercise of the agency's discretion, to justify the determination of an immediate danger and the agency's decision to take the specific action.

(d) The agency shall give such notice as is practicable to persons who are required to comply with the order. The order is effective when rendered.

(e) After issuing an order pursuant to this section, the agency shall proceed as quickly as feasible to complete any proceedings that would be required if the matter did not involve an immediate danger.

(f) The agency record consists of any documents regarding the matter that were considered or prepared by the agency. The agency shall maintain these documents as its official record.

(g) Unless otherwise required by a provision of law, the agency record need not constitute the exclusive basis for agency action in emergency adjudicative proceedings or for judicial review thereof.

§ 4-502. [Summary Adjudicative Proceedings — Applicability].

An agency may use summary adjudicative proceedings if:

(1) the use of those proceedings in the circumstances does not violate any provision of law;

(2) the protection of the public interest does not require the agency to give notice and an opportunity to participate to persons other than the parties; and

(3) the matter is entirely within one or more categories for which the agency by rule has adopted this section and Sections 4-503 to 4-506 [; however, those categories may include only the following:

(i) a monetary amount of not more than [$100];

(ii) a reprimand, warning, disciplinary report, or other purely verbal sanction without continuing impact against a prisoner, student, public employee, or licensee;

(iii) the denial of an application after the applicant has abandoned the application;

(iv) the denial of an application for admission to an educational institution or for employment by an agency;

(v) the denial, in whole or in part, of an application if the applicant has an opportunity for administrative review in accordance with Section 4-504;

(vi) a matter that is resolved on the sole basis of inspections, examinations, or tests;

(vii) the acquisition, leasing, or disposal of property or the procurement of goods or services by contract;

(viii) any matter having only trivial potential impact upon the affected parties; and

(ix) . . . .]

§ 4-503. [Summary Adjudicative Proceedings — Procedures].

(a) The agency head, one or more members of the agency head, one or more administrative law judges assigned by the office of administrative hearings in accordance with Section 4-301 [, or, unless prohibited by law, one or more other persons designated by the agency head], in the discretion of the agency head, may be the presiding officer. Unless prohibited by law, a person exercising authority over the matter is the presiding officer.

(b) If the proceeding involves a monetary matter or a reprimand, warning, disciplinary report, or other sanction:

(1) the presiding officer, before taking action, shall give each party an opportunity to be informed of the agency's view of the matter and to explain the party's view of the matter; and

(2) the presiding officer, at the time any unfavorable action is taken, shall give each party a brief statement of findings of fact, conclusions of law, and policy reasons for the decision if it is an exercise of the agency's discretion, to justify the action, and a notice of any available administrative review.

(c) An order rendered in a proceeding that involves a monetary matter must be in writing. An order in any other summary adjudicative proceeding may be oral or written.

(d) The agency, by reasonable means, shall furnish to each party notification of the order in a summary adjudicative proceeding. Notification must include at least a statement of the agency's action and a notice of any available administrative review.

§ 4-504.   [Administrative Review of Summary Adjudicative Proceedings — Applicability].

Unless prohibited by any provision of law, an agency, on its own motion, may conduct administrative review of an order resulting from summary adjudicative proceedings, and shall conduct this review upon the written or oral request of a party if the agency receives the request within [10] days after furnishing notification under Section 4-503(d).

§ 4-505.   [Administrative Review of Summary Adjudicative Proceedings — Procedures].

Unless otherwise provided by statute [or rule]:

(1) An agency need not furnish notification of the pendency of administrative review to any person who did not request the review, but the agency may not take any action on review less favorable to any party than the original order without giving that party notice and an opportunity to explain that party's view of the matter.

(2) The reviewing officer, in the discretion of the agency head, may be any person who could have presided at the summary adjudicative proceeding, but the reviewing officer must be one who is authorized to grant appropriate relief upon review.

(3) The reviewing officer shall give each party an opportunity to explain the party's view of the matter unless the party's view is apparent from the written materials in the file submitted to the reviewing officer. The reviewing officer shall make any inquiries necessary to ascertain whether the proceeding must be converted to a conference adjudicative hearing or a formal adjudicative hearing.

(4) The reviewing officer may render an order disposing of the proceeding in any manner that was available to the presiding officer at the summary adjudicative proceeding or the reviewing officer may remand the matter for further proceedings, with or without conversion to a conference adjudicative hearing or a formal adjudicative hearing.

(5) If the order under review is or should have been in writing, the order on review must be in writing, including a brief statement of findings of fact,

conclusions of law, and policy reasons for the decision if it is an exercise of the agency's discretion, to justify the order, and a notice of any further available administrative review.

(6) A request for administrative review is deemed to have been denied if the reviewing officer does not dispose of the matter or remand it for further proceedings within [20] days after the request is submitted.

§ 4-506. [Agency Record of Summary Adjudicative Proceedings and Administrative Review].

(a) The agency record consists of any documents regarding the matter that were considered or prepared by the presiding officer for the summary adjudicative proceeding or by the reviewing officer for any review. The agency shall maintain these documents as its official record.

(b) Unless otherwise required by a provision of law, the agency record need not constitute the exclusive basis for agency action in summary adjudicative proceedings or for judicial review thereof.

§ 5-101. [Relationship Between this Act and Other Law on Judicial Review and Other Judicial Remedies].

This Act establishes the exclusive means of judicial review of agency action, but:

(1) The provisions of this Act for judicial review do not apply to litigation in which the sole issue is a claim for money damages or compensation and the agency whose action is at issue does not have statutory authority to determine the claim.

(2) Ancillary procedural matters, including intervention, class actions, consolidation, joinder, severance, transfer, protective orders, and other relief from disclosure of privileged or confidential material, are governed, to the extent not inconsistent with this Act, by other applicable law.

(3) If the relief available under other sections of this Act is not equal or substantially equivalent to the relief otherwise available under law, the relief otherwise available and the related procedures supersede and supplement this Act to the extent necessary for their effectuation. The applicable provisions of this Act and other law must be combined to govern a single proceeding or, if the court orders, 2 or more separate proceedings, with or without transfer to other courts, but no type of relief may be sought in a combined proceeding after expiration of the time limit for doing so.

§ 5-102. [Final Agency Action Reviewable].

(a) A person who qualifies under this Act regarding (i) standing (Section 5-106), (ii) exhaustion of administrative remedies (Section 5-107), and (iii) time for filing the petition for review (Section 5-108), and other applicable provisions of law regarding bond, compliance, and other pre- conditions is entitled to judicial review of final agency action, whether or not the person has sought judicial review of any related non-final agency action.

(b) For purposes of this section and Section 5-103:

(1) "Final agency action" means the whole or a part of any agency action other than non-final agency action;

(2) "Non-final agency action" means the whole or a part of an agency determination, investigation, proceeding, hearing, conference, or other process that the agency intends or is reasonably believed to intend to be preliminary, preparatory, procedural, or intermediate with regard to subsequent agency action of that agency or another agency.

§ 5-103. [Non-final Agency Action Reviewable].

A person is entitled to judicial review of non-final agency action only if:

(1) it appears likely that the person will qualify under Section 5-102 for judicial review of the related final agency action; and

(2) postponement of judicial review would result in an inadequate remedy or irreparable harm disproportionate to the public benefit derived from postponement.

§ 5-104. [Jurisdiction, Venue]. [ALTERNATIVE A].

(a) The [trial court of general jurisdiction] shall conduct judicial review.

(b) Venue is in the [district] [that includes the state capital] [where the petitioner resides or maintains a principal place of business] unless otherwise provided by law.

§ 5-104. [Jurisdiction, Venue]. [ALTERNATIVE B].

(a) The [appellate court] shall conduct judicial review.

(b) Venue is in the [district] [that includes the state capital] [where the petitioner resides or maintains a principal place of business] unless otherwise provided by law.

(c) If evidence is to be adduced in the reviewing court in accordance with Section 5-114(a), the court shall appoint a [referee, master, trial court judge] for this purpose, having due regard for the convenience of the parties.

§ 5-105. [Form of Action].

Judicial review is initiated by filing a petition for review in [the appropriate] court. A petition may seek any type of relief available under Sections 5-101(3) and 5-117.

§ 5-106. [Standing].

(a) The following persons have standing to obtain judicial review of final or non-final agency action:

(1) a person to whom the agency action is specifically directed;

(2) a person who was a party to the agency proceedings that led to the agency action;

(3) if the challenged agency action is a rule, a person subject to that rule;

(4) a person eligible for standing under another provision of law; or

(5) a person otherwise aggrieved or adversely affected by the agency action. For purposes of this paragraph, no person has standing as one otherwise aggrieved or adversely affected unless:

(i) the agency action has prejudiced or is likely to prejudice that person;

(ii) that person's asserted interests are among those that the agency was required to consider when it engaged in the agency action challenged; and

(iii) a judgment in favor of that person would substantially eliminate or redress the prejudice to that person caused or likely to be caused by the agency action.

[(b) A standing committee of the legislature which is required to exercise general and continuing oversight over administrative agencies and procedures may petition for judicial review of any rule or intervene in any litigation arising from agency action.]

§ 5-107. [Exhaustion of Administrative Remedies].

A person may file a petition for judicial review under this Act only after exhausting all administrative remedies available within the agency whose action is being challenged and within any other agency authorized to exercise administrative review, but:

(1) a petitioner for judicial review of a rule need not have participated in the rule-making proceeding upon which that rule is based, or have petitioned for its amendment or repeal;

(2) a petitioner for judicial review need not exhaust administrative remedies to the extent that this Act or any other statute states that exhaustion is not required; or

(3) the court may relieve a petitioner of the requirement to exhaust any or all administrative remedies, to the extent that the administrative remedies are inadequate, or requiring their exhaustion would result in irreparable harm disproportionate to the public benefit derived from requiring exhaustion.

§ 5-108. [Time for Filing Petition for Review].

Subject to other requirements of this Act or of another statute:

(1) A petition for judicial review of a rule may be filed at any time, except as limited by Section 3-113(b).

(2) A petition for judicial review of an order is not timely unless filed within [30] days after rendition of the order, but the time is extended during the pendency of the petitioner's timely attempts to exhaust administrative remedies, if the attempts are not clearly frivolous or repetitious.

(3) A petition for judicial review of agency action other than a rule or order is not timely unless filed within [30] days after the agency action, but the time is extended:

(i) during the pendency of the petitioner's timely attempts to exhaust administrative remedies, if the attempts are not clearly frivolous or repetitious; and

(ii) during any period that the petitioner did not know and was under no duty to discover, or did not know and was under a duty to discover but could not reasonably have discovered, that the agency had taken the action or that the agency action had a sufficient effect to confer standing upon the petitioner to obtain judicial review under this Act.

§ 5-109.   [Petition for Review — Filing and Contents].

(a) A petition for review must be filed with the clerk of the court.

(b) A petition for review must set forth:

(1) the name and mailing address of the petitioner;

(2) the name and mailing address of the agency whose action is at issue;

(3) identification of the agency action at issue, together with a duplicate copy, summary, or brief description of the agency action;

(4) identification of persons who were parties in any adjudicative proceedings that led to the agency action;

(5) facts to demonstrate that the petitioner is entitled to obtain judicial review;

(6) the petitioner's reasons for believing that relief should be granted; and

(7) a request for relief, specifying the type and extent of relief requested.

§ 5-110.   [Petition for Review — Service and Notification].

(a) A petitioner for judicial review shall serve a copy of the petition upon the agency in the manner provided by [statute] [the rules of civil procedure].

(b) The petitioner shall use means provided by [statute] [the rules of civil procedure] to give notice of the petition for review to all other parties in any adjudicative proceedings that led to the agency action.

§ 5-111.   [Stay and Other Temporary Remedies Pending Final Disposition].

(a) Unless precluded by law, the agency may grant a stay on appropriate terms or other temporary remedies during the pendency of judicial review.

(b) A party may file a motion in the reviewing court, during the pendency of judicial review, seeking interlocutory review of the agency's action on an application for stay or other temporary remedies.

(c) If the agency has found that its action on an application for stay or other temporary remedies is justified to protect against a substantial threat to the public health, safety, or welfare, the court may not grant relief unless it finds that:

(1) the applicant is likely to prevail when the court finally disposes of the matter;

(2) without relief the applicant will suffer irreparable injury;

(3) the grant of relief to the applicant will not substantially harm other parties to the proceedings; and

(4) the threat to the public health, safety, or welfare relied on by the agency is not sufficiently serious to justify the agency's action in the circumstances.

(d) If subsection (c) does not apply, the court shall grant relief if it finds, in its independent judgment, that the agency's action on the application for stay or other temporary remedies was unreasonable in the circumstances.

(e) If the court determines that relief should be granted from the agency's action on an application for stay or other temporary remedies, the court may remand the matter to the agency with directions to deny a stay, to grant a stay on appropriate terms, or to grant other temporary remedies, or the court may issue an order denying a stay, granting a stay on appropriate terms, or granting other temporary remedies.

§ 5-112. [Limitation on New Issues].

A person may obtain judicial review of an issue that was not raised before the agency, only to the extent that:

(1) the agency did not have jurisdiction to grant an adequate remedy based on a determination of the issue;

(2) the person did not know and was under no duty to discover, or did not know and was under a duty to discover but could not reasonably have discovered, facts giving rise to the issue;

(3) the agency action subject to judicial review is a rule and the person has not been a party in adjudicative proceedings which provided an adequate opportunity to raise the issue;

(4) the agency action subject to judicial review is an order and the person was not notified of the adjudicative proceeding in substantial compliance with this Act; or

(5) the interests of justice would be served by judicial resolution of an issue arising from:

(i) a change in controlling law occurring after the agency action; or

(ii) agency action occurring after the person exhausted the last feasible opportunity for seeking relief from the agency.

§ 5-113. [Judicial Review of Facts Confined to Record for Judicial Review and Additional Evidence Taken Pursuant to Act].

Judicial review of disputed issues of fact must be confined to the agency record for judicial review as defined in this Act, supplemented by additional evidence taken pursuant to this Act.

§ 5-114.   [New Evidence Taken by Court or Agency Before Final Disposition].

(a) The court [(if Alternative B of Section 5-104 is adopted), assisted by a referee, master, trial court judge as provided in Section 5-104(c),] may receive evidence, in addition to that contained in the agency record for judicial review, only if it relates to the validity of the agency action at the time it was taken and is needed to decide disputed issues regarding:

(1) improper constitution as a decision-making body, or improper motive or grounds for disqualification, of those taking the agency action;

(2) unlawfulness of procedure or of decision-making process; or

(3) any material fact that was not required by any provision of law to be determined exclusively on an agency record of a type reasonably suitable for judicial review.

(b) The court may remand a matter to the agency, before final disposition of a petition for review, with directions that the agency conduct fact-finding and other proceedings the court considers necessary and that the agency take such further action on the basis thereof as the court directs, if:

(1) the agency was required by this Act or any other provision of law to base its action exclusively on a record of a type reasonably suitable for judicial review, but the agency failed to prepare or preserve an adequate record;

(2) the court finds that (i) new evidence has become available that relates to the validity of the agency action at the time it was taken, that one or more of the parties did not know and was under no duty to discover, or did not know and was under a duty to discover but could not reasonably have discovered, until after the agency action, and (ii) the interests of justice would be served by remand to the agency;

(3) the agency improperly excluded or omitted evidence from the record; or

(4) a relevant provision of law changed after the agency action and the court determines that the new provision may control the outcome.

§ 5-115.   [Agency Record for Judicial Review — Contents, Preparation, Transmittal, Cost].

(a) Within [_____] days after service of the petition, or within further time allowed by the court or by other provision of law, the agency shall transmit to the court the original or a certified copy of the agency record for judicial review of the agency action, consisting of any agency documents expressing the agency action, other documents identified by the agency as having been considered by it before its action and used as a basis for its action, and any other material described in this Act as the agency record for the type of agency action at issue, subject to the provisions of this section.

(b) If part of the record has been preserved without a transcript, the agency shall prepare a transcript for inclusion in the record transmitted to the court, except for portions that the parties stipulate to omit in accordance with subsection (d).

(c) The agency shall charge the petitioner with the reasonable cost of preparing any necessary copies and transcripts for transmittal to the court. [A failure by the petitioner to pay any of this cost to the agency does not relieve the agency from the responsibility for timely preparation of the record and transmittal to the court.]

(d) By stipulation of all parties to the review proceedings, the record may be shortened, summarized, or organized.

(e) The court may tax the cost of preparing transcripts and copies for the record:

(1) against a party who unreasonably refuses to stipulate to shorten, summarize, or organize the record;

(2) as provided by Section 5-117; or

(3) in accordance with any other provision of law.

(f) Additions to the record pursuant to Section 5-114 must be made as ordered by the court.

(g) The court may require or permit subsequent corrections or additions to the record.

§ 5-116. [Scope of Review; Grounds for Invalidity].

(a) Except to the extent that this Act or another statute provides otherwise:

(1) The burden of demonstrating the invalidity of agency action is on the party asserting invalidity; and

(2) The validity of agency action must be determined in accordance with the standards of review provided in this section, as applied to the agency action at the time it was taken.

(b) The court shall make a separate and distinct ruling on each material issue on which the court's decision is based.

(c) The court shall grant relief only if it determines that a person seeking judicial relief has been substantially prejudiced by any one or more of the following:

(1) The agency action, or the statute or rule on which the agency action is based, is unconstitutional on its face or as applied.

(2) The agency has acted beyond the jurisdiction conferred by any provision of law.

(3) The agency has not decided all issues requiring resolution.

(4) The agency has erroneously interpreted or applied the law.

(5) The agency has engaged in an unlawful procedure or decision-making process, or has failed to follow prescribed procedure.

(6) The persons taking the agency action were improperly constituted as a decision-making body, motivated by an improper purpose, or subject to disqualification.

(7) The agency action is based on a determination of fact, made or implied by

the agency, that is not supported by evidence that is substantial when viewed in light of the whole record before the court, which includes the agency record for judicial review, supplemented by any additional evidence received by the court under this Act.

(8) The agency action is:

(i) outside the range of discretion delegated to the agency by any provision of law;

(ii) agency action, other than a rule, that is inconsistent with a rule of the agency; [or]

(iii) agency action, other than a rule, that is inconsistent with the agency's prior practice unless the agency justifies the inconsistency by stating facts and reasons to demonstrate a fair and rational basis for the inconsistency. [; or] [.]

(iv) [otherwise unreasonable, arbitrary or capricious.]

§ 5-117.   [Type of Relief].

(a) The court may award damages or compensation only to the extent expressly authorized by another provision of law.

(b) The court may grant other appropriate relief, whether mandatory, injunctive, or declaratory; preliminary or final; temporary or permanent; equitable or legal. In granting relief, the court may order agency action required by law, order agency exercise of discretion required by law, set aside or modify agency action, enjoin or stay the effectiveness of agency action, remand the matter for further proceedings, render a declaratory judgment, or take any other action that is authorized and appropriate.

(c) The court may also grant necessary ancillary relief to redress the effects of official action wrongfully taken or withheld, but the court may award attorney's fees or witness fees only to the extent expressly authorized by other law.

(d) If the court sets aside or modifies agency action or remands the matter to the agency for further proceedings, the court may make any interlocutory order it finds necessary to preserve the interests of the parties and the public pending further proceedings or agency action.

§ 5-118.   [Review by Higher Court].

Decisions on petitions for review of agency action are reviewable by the [appellate court] as in other civil cases.

§ 5-201.   [Petition by Agency for Civil Enforcement of Rule or Order].

(a) In addition to other remedies provided by law, an agency may seek enforcement of its rule or order by filing a petition for civil enforcement in the [trial court of general jurisdiction.]

(b) The petition must name, as defendants, each alleged violator against whom the agency seeks to obtain civil enforcement.

(c) Venue is determined as in other civil cases.

(d) A petition for civil enforcement filed by an agency may request, and the court may grant, declaratory relief, temporary or permanent injunctive relief, any other civil remedy provided by law, or any combination of the foregoing.

§ 5-202. [Petition by Qualified Person for Civil Enforcement of Agency's Order].

(a) Any person who would qualify under this Act as having standing to obtain judicial review of an agency's failure to enforce its order may file a petition for civil enforcement of that order, but the action may not be commenced:

(1) until at least [60] days after the petitioner has given notice of the alleged violation and of the petitioner's intent to seek civil enforcement to the head of the agency concerned, to the attorney general, and to each alleged violator against whom the petitioner seeks civil enforcement;

(2) if the agency has filed and is diligently prosecuting a petition for civil enforcement of the same order against the same defendant; or

(3) if a petition for review of the same order has been filed and is pending in court.

(b) The petition must name, as defendants, the agency whose order is sought to be enforced and each alleged violator against whom the petitioner seeks civil enforcement.

(c) The agency whose order is sought to be enforced may move to dismiss on the grounds that the petition fails to qualify under this section or that enforcement would be contrary to the policy of the agency. The court shall grant the motion to dismiss unless the petitioner demonstrates that (i) the petition qualifies under this section and (ii) the agency's failure to enforce its order is based on an exercise of discretion that is improper on one or more of the grounds provided in Section 5-116(c)(8).

(d) Except to the extent expressly authorized by law, a petition for civil enforcement filed under this section may not request, and the court may not grant any monetary payment apart from taxable costs.

§ 5-203. [Defenses; Limitation on New Issues and New Evidence].

A defendant may assert, in a proceeding for civil enforcement:

(1) that the rule or order sought to be enforced is invalid on any of the grounds stated in Section 5-116. If that defense is raised, the court may consider issues and receive evidence only within the limitations provided by Sections 5-112, 5-113, and 5-114; and

(2) any of the following defenses on which the court, to the extent necessary for the determination of the matter, may consider new issues or take new evidence:

(i) the rule or order does not apply to the party;

(ii) the party has not violated the rule or order;

(iii) the party has violated the rule or order but has subsequently complied, but a party who establishes this defense is not necessarily relieved from any sanction provided by law for past violations; or

(iv) any other defense allowed by law.

§ 5-204. [Incorporation of Certain Provisions on Judicial Review].

Proceedings for civil enforcement are governed by the following provisions of this Act on judicial review, as modified where necessary to adapt them to those proceedings:

(1) Section 5-101(2) (ancillary procedural matters); and

(2) Section 5-115 (agency record for judicial review — contents, preparation, transmittal, cost.)

§ 5-205. [Review by Higher Court].

Decisions on petitions for civil enforcement are reviewable by the [appellate court] as in other civil cases.

TABLE OF CASES

[References are to pages]

[References are to pages]

D

E

F

[References are to pages]

[References are to pages]

INDEX

[References are to page numbers.]

[References are to page numbers.]

[References are to page numbers.]